MILTON STUDIES

IX

MILTON STUDIES

IX *Edited by*

James D. Simmonds

UNIVERSITY OF PITTSBURGH PRESS

MILTON STUDIES

is published annually by the University of Pittsburgh Press as a forum for Milton scholarship and criticism. Articles submitted for publication may be biographical; they may interpret some aspect of Milton's writings; or they may define literary, intellectual, or historical contexts—by studying the work of his contemporaries, the traditions which affected his thought and art, contemporary political and religious movements, his influence on other writers, or the history of critical response to his work.

Manuscripts should be upwards of 3,000 words in length and should conform to the *MLA Style Sheet*. Manuscripts and editorial correspondence should be addressed to James D. Simmonds, Department of English, University of Pittsburgh, Pittsburgh, Pa. 15260.

Milton Studies does not review books.

Within the United States, *Milton Studies* may be ordered from the University of Pittsburgh Press, Pittsburgh, Pa. 15260.

Overseas orders should be addressed to Feffer and Simons, Inc., 100 Park Avenue, New York, N.Y. 10017, U.S.A.

Library of Congress Catalog Card Number 69-12335

ISBN 0-8229-3174-5 (Volume I) (out of print)

ISBN 0-8229-3194-x (Volume II)

ISBN 0-8229-3218-0 (Volume III)

ISBN 0-8229-3244-x (Volume IV)

ISBN 0-8229-3272-5 (Volume V)

ISBN 0-8229-3288-1 (Volume VI)

ISBN 0-8229-3305-5 (Volume VII)

ISBN 0-8229-3310-1 (Volume VIII)

ISBN 0-8229-3329-2 (Volume IX)

US ISSN 0076-8820

MILTON STUDIES

IX *Edited by*

James D. Simmonds

UNIVERSITY OF PITTSBURGH PRESS

MILTON STUDIES

is published annually by the University of Pittsburgh Press as a forum for Milton scholarship and criticism. Articles submitted for publication may be biographical; they may interpret some aspect of Milton's writings; or they may define literary, intellectual, or historical contexts—by studying the work of his contemporaries, the traditions which affected his thought and art, contemporary political and religious movements, his influence on other writers, or the history of critical response to his work.

Manuscripts should be upwards of 3,000 words in length and should conform to the *MLA Style Sheet*. Manuscripts and editorial correspondence should be addressed to James D. Simmonds, Department of English, University of Pittsburgh, Pittsburgh, Pa. 15260.

Milton Studies does not review books.

Within the United States, *Milton Studies* may be ordered from the University of Pittsburgh Press, Pittsburgh, Pa. 15260.

Overseas orders should be addressed to Feffer and Simons, Inc., 100 Park Avenue, New York, N.Y. 10017, U.S.A.

Library of Congress Catalog Card Number 69-12335

ISBN 0-8229-3174-5 (Volume I) (out of print)

ISBN 0-8229-3194-x (Volume II)

ISBN 0-8229-3218-0 (Volume III)

ISBN 0-8229-3244-x (Volume IV)

ISBN 0-8229-3272-5 (Volume V)

ISBN 0-8229-3288-1 (Volume VI)

ISBN 0-8229-3305-5 (Volume VII)

ISBN 0-8229-3310-1 (Volume VIII)

ISBN 0-8229-3329-2 (Volume IX)

US ISSN 0076-8820

Copyright © 1976, University of Pittsburgh Press

Feffer & Simons, Inc., London

Manufactured in the United States of America

CONTENTS

MILTON STUDIES

IX

"A FREE AND OPEN ENCOUNTER": MILTON AND THE MODERN READER

Marcia Landy

Literature embodies not universal or essential truths, but ideas and values which, like the reader's own, are conditioned and limited by history. Thus, Milton's views of authority relations, power, marriage, kinship relations, dominance and subordination, and his use of typification to define normative and deviant behavior, are subject to evaluation, rejection, or acceptance in the light of modern conceptions, drawn partly from anthropological and sociological research. In Satan and his women characters, Milton struggles to reconcile mutuality, hierarchy, and individual action. Eve's relation to Satanic deviancy, her learning of prescribed roles, and her acceptance of familial and domestic responsibilities define the woman's sphere in *Paradise Lost*. Similarly circumscribed, the Lady in *Comus* affirms community, sociability, and culture. The portrait of Dalila defines proper conjugal relations in terms of female subordination and service. Besides illuminating historical attitudes toward women, these characterizations compel the reader to question the presence of "universal truths" in Milton or any literature.

RECENTLY, IN an article critical of feminist criticism of Milton and particularly critical of my discussion of the role of women in *Paradise Lost*, Barbara K. Lewalski affirmed the "capacity of great art to transcend these lesser categories of human experience and speak to our common humanity." She further asserted that "great writers" are "gloriously and supremely right about the most essential things." The *Iliad*, for example, "should perhaps be made required reading for presidents and Pentagon officials."[1] My essay will explore the implications of these critical assumptions, particu-

3

larly as they relate to Milton's presentations of women. Lewalski's critical position raises fundamental questions for the contemporary literary critic, questions like: For whom do writers write? Why do they write? Are there essential truths identifiable with all people in a culture and cross-culturally? If there are essential truths, what are they? And who conveys these truths—the writer, the critic, or both? What is the role of the critic in contemporary society?[2]

An artist writes to feel human, to make contact with others even if the other is a reconstitution of the self. Milton himself was aware of the socializing dimension of art. Language was his vehicle for mitigating solitude and for envisioning a "new heaven and new earth." In his elevation of reciprocity and mutuality, he saw language as the means of creating and enhancing social solidarity. He saw language when abused and perverted as a means of isolating individuals; disregard for "fit conversation" was, for him, akin to psychic death and a sign of destructive social relations. In all of his works, both prose and poetry, he explored the importance of communication. Yet the language Milton used is now accessible to only a few. Even in the universities, reading Milton makes teachers and students aware of his remoteness in time. The extensive footnotes necessary to read a Milton work and the care required to construct the meaning of the text attest to the necessity of contending with Milton in order to understand him. Many undergraduates will not take the time and trouble to read Milton. Even more significant than the linguistic problems, which can be surmounted by careful study, are the challenges he poses in his Christian heroism, his theology, his stringent morality, his presentations of satanism, and his portrayal of women. Reading Milton is thus not a passive act, but rather a contentious one, something he was well aware of himself, but for different reasons perhaps. His presentations create immediate disjunctions between the world in which we live and the world he envisioned and portrayed.

If we allow that the writer creates to feel human through making contact with another, we might also allow that the reader undertakes reading for a similar reason. In sentiments which might not have been unwelcome to Milton, Jean-Paul Sartre identifies the relationship between writer and reader thus: "Reading is a pact of generosity between author and reader. Each one trusts the other; each one counts on the other, demands of the other as much as he demands of himself. For this confidence is itself generosity. Nothing can force the author to believe that his reader will use his freedom; nothing can force the reader to believe that the author has used his. Both of them make a free decision."[3] Reading is a process of grappling with another human being. The interaction between writer and reader is dialectical. The writer puts himself into his work; but, by referring to the writer's identity, I am not referring to the private thoughts and fantasies of a single individual. I am referring rather to the complex set of attitudes, values, and behavior which constitute the individual and are the result of historical circumstances—familial attitudes, education, class, politics, and, in Milton's case, religion. Sartre comments further:

Authors too are historical. And that is precisely the reason that some of them want to escape from history by a leap into eternity. The book, serving as a go-between, establishes a historical contact among the men who are steeped in the same history and likewise contribute to its making. Writing and reading are two facets of the same historical fact, and the freedom to which the writer invites us is not a pure abstract consciousness of being free. Strictly speaking, it is *not;* it wins itself in a historical situation; each book proposes a concrete liberation on the basis of a particular alienation. Hence, in each one there is an implicit recourse to institutions, customs, certain forms of oppression and conflict, to the wisdom and folly of the day, to lasting passions and passing stubbornness, to superstitions and recent victories of common sense, to evidence and ignorance, to particular modes of reasoning.[4]

The reader, too, brings himself into the creative act of reading. How one sees the world, how one sees oneself, enter into the reading of the text. In the act of contending with the writer, the reader attempts to engage the text in a dialogue.[5] As with all ideas and all human interactions, the reader will actively accept or reject some, if not all, of what a writer has to say.

Few modern readers can wholeheartedly affirm the presence of essential truths in Milton; many of his attitudes are alien to the modern world. Some critics may legitimately regret that Milton's ideas are not our own, seeing in them a possible alternative to the political and social struggles in contemporary society. Their hope is that if we could endorse and internalize his vision of reality, we might become more humane and better able to cope with the modern world. Those who believe that literature conveys transcendent truths hold up earlier writers as a model for civilizing and educating today's citizens. It is important, however, to question our relationship to these earlier writers, even more to examine the idea of literature as a civilizing agent.

In *Areopagitica,* Milton argues for the vitality of books, but he does not argue that the book is in itself either the civilizing or corrupting agent. Nor does he argue for the intactness of truth. His metaphor of the dismembered body of Truth, the pieces of which are as yet undiscovered and will not be fully recovered until the Second Coming, underscores his sense of the necessity of destroying and reconstituting ideas.[6] The "essential" element in Milton resides in the flexibility of his commitment to the quest for truth. History and historical change play an important part in Milton's poetry and prose. While books can reinforce, while education can guide, all of Milton's writings reveal his interest in relating behavior to concepts of community and social reality. He therefore did not find it demeaning to explore questions of politics, government, education, marriage, divorce, individual "psychology," the behavior of the sexes toward each other, sex roles, or public and domestic roles and attitudes. His poetic creations, as so many critics have noted, are not restatements of classical truths or re-creations of classical forms but are rooted in his character, in the exciting conflicts of his time, and in the many changes that were taking place in the world about him which he, in part, helped to realize.[7] In this practice, he is consistent with his admonitions to others to examine ideas, to cull, to exercise choice. It is not the universal truths in Milton which compel, but rather his own creative identity which compels, as he seeks to order and assign meaning to external reality, to differentiate among ideas and among actions, and to speak out: "Give me the liberty to know, to utter, and to argue freely, according to conscience, above all liberties."[8]

Milton's unceasing quest for knowledge and meaningful communication is not his only interesting and engaging quality. He communicates, not absolute truths, but his need to confront mortality, his desire for self-esteem, and his need to order his world as a resistance to physical and psychic death, the loss of contact with others, and the loss of the sense of self. He explores the evolution of self and the relations between the self and others, either in the form of a single companion or in the form of a creative group—the "fit sociability" he so often describes and dramatizes, particularly in *Paradise Lost*. These are not truths to be taught; these are not moral qualities so much as revelations of the human enterprise of creating a meaningful reality. Works of literature do not teach; they illuminate. But Milton desired, as other writers before and after him have desired, to teach others and to alter society. His conjunction of poet and orator, poet and instructor, testifies to the social engagement of his work, but his works are subject to the passage of time and historical change. Milton now stands before us unsupported by his intentions, read only in terms of his imaginative vision, and sustained by the same choices he exalted. The modern reader engages with Milton authentically only when the reader exercises his fullest freedom in questioning, accepting, or denying the human contact Milton offers.

Who are Milton's modern readers? They are found mainly in the universities: serious-minded individuals who have been trained in the arts of reading and of literary criticism. Milton has always had a limited audience, unlike the novelist and unlike Shakespeare, who have a broad audience inside and outside the university. Milton's critics have puzzled seriously over his relationship to tradition, his use of poetic forms, his language, his rhetoric, his sources, his religion, his politics, his style, his use of myth, his relationship to the other arts, and his relationship to other poets. But many of the critics have seemed defensive, particularly on the subject of Milton's Satan and his portrait of God the Father. Another area of defensiveness has centered on Milton's presentations of women. Why are these topics controversial? Why are Milton's religious and social views a subject of continuing debate? We cannot attribute the difficulty merely to bad readers; although, in part, some of the difficulty may have been caused by critics' desires to defend or debunk Milton. Milton *is* controversial. He belongs and does not belong to our world. He could foresee many of the problems of the modern world—competing ideas, relativistic ideas of morality, the importance of self-validation and individual judgment against ideas of tradition and conformity, conflicts over power and authority—but his solutions were designed to mitigate conflict by the institution of "absolute" ideas of morality which he legitimated through religion. While he does not solve, any more than we do, the struggle between notions of equality and of individual merit, he does seek recourse to hierarchical ideas and to ideas of dominance and subordination to minimize competition, conflict, and aggression. In questioning these ideas, he reveals his modernity; in solving them, he often reveals his historical limitations.[9]

The fact of Satan's evil is problematic to the modern reader for several reasons. Satan was certainly the embodiment of evil to Milton, so that elevating him to the status of the hero in *Paradise Lost* is an irrelevant enterprise. But the appeal of Satan cannot be attributed solely to misreading on the part of the modern audience. There is in the portrait of Satan an energy and a subversiveness which attract, but also repel. No amount of moralizing or referring to Milton's text can remove the response Satan elicits from certain readers. Referring to this response as wrong does not go very far in helping to understand why it exists.

Satan is the remnant of a heroic tradition which still attracts, even though Milton presents it in debased terms;[10] Satan is also the embodiment of modern Faustianism. He is the rebel against ideas of hierarchical order and the status quo, although Milton was quick to differentiate legitimate and illegitimate forms of rebellion and resistance to conformity. Satan differs from his moral counterpart, Christ, the true exemplar of nonconformity, in his undifferentiated conflict against all morality and tradition. The moral hero acknowledges an authority and order which he accepts as benevolent, and he continuously seeks to differentiate between appropriate and inappropriate resistance. Milton did not believe in unlimited change or in ideas of equality of ability and opportunity. He was not a collectivist or a thoroughgoing revolutionary. He did not extend an equal voice to all in his vision of the ideal community, in his vision of familial relations, or in his vision of authority relations. Although his sense of personal relations was mutual, his sense of authority relations was hierarchical. Abdiel, in explaining to Satan why he cannot join him and why he has made his choice for God, is quite clear on the meaning of equality. God's love is equally dispensed throughout creation, but his power is not:

> shalt thou dispute
> With him the points of liberty, who made
> Thee what thou art, and form'd the Pow'rs of Heav'n
> Such as he pleas'd, and circumscrib'd thir being?
> Yet by experience taught we know how good,
> And of our good, and of our dignity
> How provident he is, how far from thought
> To make us less, bent rather to exalt
> Our happy state under one Head more near
> United. But to grant it thee unjust,
> That equal over equals Monarch Reign:
> Thyself though great and glorious dost thou count,
> Or all Angelic Nature join'd in one,
> Equal to him begotten Son, by whom
> As by his Word the mighty Father made
> All things, ev'n thee, and all the Spirits of Heav'n
> By him created in thir bright degrees.   (*PL* V, 822–38)

Abdiel takes pains to indicate God's benevolence, but he does not obfuscate the fact that God's benevolence operates within the spirit of "bright degrees."

Milton distinguishes also between divine and human authority. Human authority relations are not subject to "Dominion absolute." Of Nimrod, Adam says:

> O execrable Son so to aspire
> Above his Brethren, to himself assuming
> Authority usurpt, from God not giv'n:
> He gave us only over Beast, Fish, Fowl
> Dominion absolute; that right we hold
> By his donation; but Man over men
> He made not Lord, such title to himself
> Reserving, human left from human free.   (*PL* XII, 64–71)

This passage might seem to argue for egalitarianism. It certainly argues against externally imposed dominion by king or overlord. Yet the equality of fraternity is qualified throughout *Paradise Lost* by the idea of merit, as in the case of the Son's superiority over Satan and of Adam's superiority over Eve; and distinguishing boundaries between meritorious and irresponsible action is a problem, not only for Milton, but for the contemporary world. Milton attributes the confusion between affections and degree to bad faith and ill will. The

denial of differences in talent, intent, and commitment is subversive
of order and communal relations. Satan represents confusion and
subversion of boundaries and is thus appropriately styled the father
of death and social disorder. But in our contemporary concern to
understand the nature of merit and limits, to understand the reason
for the boundaries, the very principles Satan represents are more,
rather than less, a matter of social and aesthetic concern.

Milton's angels are a projection of his ideal human society,
which was reflected to some extent in the seventeenth-century Puritan community. His view of primitive human groups prior to the rise
of Nimrod also reflects a saintly community whose members "Shall
spend thir days in joy unblam'd, and dwell / Long time in peace by
Families and Tribes / Under paternal rule" (PL XII, 22–24). In such
a society, without immutable class divisions and without external
and clear-cut role designations, there is inevitably ambiguity about
ideas of merit and about ways of distinguishing acceptable from
unacceptable roles, behavior, and attitudes.[11] To facilitate social
objectives, such a society will rely heavily on the deviant to carry the
message of desirable and undesirable behavior. Unattractive qualities and negative behavior will be stigmatized through typifications.
Individuals and groups who do not possess the necessary prerequisites for entry into the dominant group will be associated with
nonhuman qualities and will take on the attributes of the bestial, the
unclean, or the demonic and thus will be distanced from others.[12]

The phenomenon of satanism in Milton is interesting in this
context. Milton does not construct his saintly community in terms of
external rituals, prescriptions, class identifications, and roles. Rather, his society depends heavily on internalized notions of merit,
behavior, and values. While he can understand the changing nature
of institutions and social responsibility, he does not subject moral
values to the same process of historical change. In order to insure the
continuity, incorruptibility, and universality of these moral qualities, he creates powerful typifications of positive and negative behavior and attitudes. The satanic thus typifies the qualities Milton
considers detrimental to the well-being of the group. Human actions
are defined against two typifications, the divine and the demonic.[13]
In this way, Milton can remove certain actions from the realm of
temporality and give them permanent legitimation. Satanism as a

phenomenon is essential to Milton's poetic world, where internal controls must take the place of external rituals, performances, and roles. The fascination of the reader with the figure of Satan may derive from our continuing attraction and repulsion for the deviant. We fear the deviant; we are also curious about him, but we do not want to share in his isolation from the group. If, however, we feel like deviants ourselves, we may identify with those stigmatized. We may, in fact, rebel against notions of exclusion and typification.

Milton's presentation of Satan as a deviant challenges, too, the modern identification with oppressed groups who have been typified, labeled, deprived of their rights, and excluded from the benefits of society. While Milton does, in fact, dramatize that Satan has excluded himself from participation in the heavenly community, the modern reader might question this form of rationalization and might resist the very notion of typification as a mode of creating social and artistic order. A contemporary reader of *Paradise Lost* who does not take into account the appeal of the satanic and the complexities of Satan's role may be seduced into a one-dimensional view of that role, thus limiting the possibilities for understanding contemporary responses to artistic representations. A theological reading cannot penetrate the subtleties of human creativity; a moral interpretation cannot account for the psychological and social complexities of poetic creation. The reconstruction of an ideal correct reading falsifies the dialectic between poet and reader. The reader actively engages with the poet, bringing to the dialogue his own reality, which enlarges and transforms the poem. A more integrated and helpful critical approach lies in identifying Milton's modern readers and understanding their responses in terms of contemporary psychological, sociological, and historical reality. Much in Milton has relevance still, but much also must be subjected to critical inquiry.

In the case of Milton's treatment of women, the other highly controversial area of Milton criticism, new evaluations are in order. It is unreasonable to argue that Milton was a misogynist, that because of his personal situation he was ill equipped to present women empathically in his poetry. I agree with Lewalski that Milton attempted to present in positive and human terms Adam and Eve's mutual dependency and that he attempted to give a human portrait of the role of woman.[14]

I agree, moreover, that in spite of his historical circumstances he attempted to transcend certain stereotypic presentations of women and to elevate women as thinking and attractive human beings. In general, Protestantism did advance in a more humane direction the treatment of women.[15] But in our contemporary thinking about the roles and social status of women, we have gone much beyond Milton's advanced thinking on marriage, divorce, and domestic relations. Surely we bring this knowledge to bear when we interact with Milton's presentations of female characters. Surely Milton's portraits of women can tolerate examination from a feminist perspective. As with examination of modern responses to satanism, we can learn more about ourselves and about Milton.

Lewalski finds that feminist criticism suffers from being sociological rather than literary in its treatment of literary works. She echoes here other literary critics like Northrop Frye, René Wellek, and Austin Warren in excluding from literary analysis theories from the social sciences as extrinsic to aesthetic concerns.[16] While the language and theoretical constructs of the social sciences may appear alien to aesthetic considerations, the truths they uncover are about human behavior and are part of our general responses to social phenomena. Interacting with a work of art engages the same human responses we bring to other human encounters. When we respond to a work of literature, we do not respond with a merely formal set of demands. Personal response and formal concerns are interrelated, just as intellectual and emotional responses are intertwined. We respond to a work with as full a knowledge of ourselves, our world, and the world inhering in the literary text as is possible. We bring formal or intuitive knowledge of sociology, social roles, anthropology, and psychology into our reading just as much as we bring whatever knowledge we have, and continue to acquire, about the historical and formal characteristics pertaining to Milton's writing. While it is reasonable to allow for Milton's historical limitations in his treatment of women, we cannot ignore the differences between his world and ours. It is helpful to see Eve, in *Paradise Lost*, as a poet in her own right and as growing into a maturity which the poet promises; but it is also helpful to see how her identity is prescribed, how contradictions make the fullest realization of her character portrayal improbable, given the difficulty that Mary Wollstonecraft exposed long ago of reconciling hierarchical relations and the desire for companionship.[17] We know from his prose that Milton was devoted to the idea that men and women who were incompatible should not be forced to remain yoked to each other through civil law. Milton also could envision polygamy. He could even envision that rare situation wherein a woman would be exceptional in intelligence, and in such a case he allowed that the woman's judgment should hold sway. Within her domain, the woman is allowed latitude and may exceed the man in the exercise of intuition. In his portrait of Eve, Milton also reveals himself to be an admirer of female beauty, and his sonnets hardly suggest an antipathy toward women.

We can say all of these things and more, and yet the poetic representations of women in Milton reveal how carefully he circumscribes their roles by dichotomizing their behavior in terms of virtue and deviancy. When women rebel, they typify a negative reality akin to Satan and Sin. Furthermore, his selection of the figure of Eve and even more that of Dalila is problematic, since neither of these characters exemplifies that "virtuous" woman, rarely found. (I will examine, later in the essay, Milton's treatment of the Lady in *Comus*.) His presentations of women reveal a great deal about his views of creativity, sociability, order, and social discourse.

I am aware that a discussion of the uses of myth in poetry and of the relationship between a poetic work and its historical circumstances must be handled carefully. A work of poetry does not mirror directly the social reality of its time, nor does it necessarily reflect the "true" circumstances of its creator and his milieu. But, in a very special way, myth is a true account of existing social relations.[18] It reveals, indirectly, social and historical phenomena. Poetry, too, most often does not reflect historical events directly. In discussing the functions of myth, history, and poetry, the critic must find ways of translating social history into poetic functions.[19] In *Paradise Lost*, myth legitimates Milton's views of roles, character relations, and situations. In discussing the role of women, the critic must have recourse to the context for the characters' behavior and actions. The characters must be seen as emerging through the familial roles and relations which Milton carefully develops, and the presentation of these roles and relations will provide the reader with information about Milton's deviation from the cultural norms, his accommo-

dations to existing attitudes, and his attempts to alter in a new
direction the thinking of his time. Because of the tendency of poetry
and myth to transcend time and space, the circumstances they portray will appear mystifying and elusive, with a quality of inaccessibility. In attempting to translate and demystify, the critic must
locate the underlying structures which reveal actual social relations.
The myth of the Fall and the woman's role in the myth cannot, of
course, be substantiated in historical fact. And yet the recurrence of
the myth and the psychological and social truths it reveals are a
challenge to the critic in understanding not only the prevalence of
the myth, but its appeal, its impact on the actual relations between
men and women, particularly the relations between individuals and
ideas of authority. The myth challenges us, too, to understand the
role that religious superstructures play in managing social reality, in
overcoming the fear of mortality, and in providing a means for minimizing discontinuity and affirming culture over the claims of
nature.[20]

Throughout Milton's work one finds a central concern for overcoming the reality of loss and of physical and psychic death. The
myth of the Fall dramatizes the first Adam's succumbing to the
"Bond of nature" (IX, 956). Adam's choice to remain with Eve results
in his loss of paradise. By identifying his needs in terms of nature, he
forgets Raphael's reminders to him of the relationship between
mind and body' and the necessary subordination of the body to
reason: "Love . . . hath his seat in Reason" (VIII, 589–90). Adam
thus loses intimate contact with God and his heavenly messengers
and brings death into the world. Most particularly, Adam's loss
involves the temporary loss of connection to others, the experience
of isolation, the confrontation of boundaries and limits which suggest mortality and the constrictions of temporality. The treacherous-
ness of reliance on the "Bond of nature" is brought home fully to
Adam and Eve after the Fall. Although Adam has been advised of his
superiority to his physical environment and had been told by
Raphael that he was to exercise dominance over the other animals, in
succumbing to Eve's invitation to eat the fruit out of fear of losing the
pleasures of her company, he obliterated the special relationship he
had to nature (VIII, 561–94). He thus revealed his difficulty in
maintaining the delicate relationship he was to observe between his

humanity and the demands of the flesh and of the spirit. The myth of the Fall is only a partial myth for Milton: The myth of the second Adam must be grafted onto it in order to dramatize the necessity of transcendence over life in nature.[21] The pattern of Christ thus becomes the fullest expression of the human entry into culture. It is culture, the symbolic expression of the human mind, which defeats death and biology. Through the creation of culture, man is able to differentiate himself from the other animals, assert the continuity of the group, and insure that his creations endure even if individuals are subject to death.[22] Furthermore, on a personal level, the individual can be assured that his own actions are not meaningless but can be placed against the larger principle of human continuity. Although Milton portrays how mankind might have resisted the temptation to experience mortality, he also reveals how the seduction could be foreseen. He does not question the occurrence of the Fall but believes that it did indeed take place as God foresaw that it would. The more significant question for Milton is how humanity copes with the knowledge of death and discontinuity.

The divine world, the Creation, and the behavior of the Son represent specific ways in which Milton affirms performance and meaningful personal and group relations. Milton is consistent in seeing creation as a defense against loss. The original Creation entails the institution of boundaries, the circumscribing and differentiation of forms, ideas, roles, and attitudes, and the belief that communication is meaningful and efficacious to action. Human creativity entails also a sense of self-esteem and a commitment to the idea that assigning meaning is a worthwhile enterprise.[23] Milton's concern for order manifests itself in many ways. It can be seen in his recurrent presentations of the concept of hierarchy, the observance of degree in relations. Most particularly, the kinship relations in *Paradise Lost* are Milton's means of dramatizing degree and the proper observance of hierarchy as opposed to authoritarianism. He presents filial, sibling, and conjugal relationships in terms of positive and negative typifications, and he extends his typifications beyond character portrayal to landscape. The regions of the universe enhance Milton's project of differentiating positive and negative behavior. The major distinction resides in the contrast between clear-cut and visible order and boundaries, in opposition to amorphous, undifferentiated, shapeless reality. Through the process of circumscribing and bounding, much as the Son circumscribes and bounds, Milton conveys the nature of creative action. Creativity thus becomes the means of transcending the oppressiveness of the self, the sense of isolation, and the loss of belief and trust in another.

The role of the woman in *Paradise Lost* seems problematic when set into this context. While she is an important actor in the pre-lapsarian world, she is most important as the vehicle for causing the man to succumb to the "Bond of Nature." Adam's motives for eating the fruit differ from Eve's. She is lured by Satan's appeal to her narcissism, his promises to her of equality, perhaps superiority, and she is easily deceived by his gorgeous show of rhetoric. Adam eats because he cannot bear to be deprived of Eve's companionship. He is most vulnerable to the fear of isolation, while Eve is vulnerable in her self-image. She must be moved away from herself and toward Adam:

> What thou seest,
> What there thou seest fair Creature is thyself,
> With thee it came and goes: but follow me,
> And I will bring thee where no shadow stays
> Thy coming, and thy soft imbraces, hee
> Whose image thou art, him thou shalt enjoy
> Inseparably thine, to him shalt bear
> Multitudes like thyself, and thence be call'd
> Mother of human Race.   (IV, 467–75)

Milton's presentation of the dangers of narcissism and of the need to be aware of another person is certainly psychologically sound. In order to live in the world with others, individuals must abandon primary narcissism and see their reflection in another human being.[24] The difficulty resides in the nature of the reflection. There is some question about whether the reflection Eve sees in Adam is of her own needs and desires or of Adam's needs and desires. She sees in Adam a superior intelligence, a master over nature, and a person to whom she can turn for guidance, education, and affection—if she observes the idea of male dominance and female subordination. Her choices to act must exist within the context of Adam's guiding intelligence. She can exercise power only within her own limited sphere. In this principle of subordination, she is not alone, but is subject, as Adam is, to the Miltonic ideas of respect for limits. She is able to question; she is able to share information with Adam, but her information is subject to the pedagogical supervision of her "instructor." A contradiction is thus set up between Adam's larger domain and Eve's more circumscribed one, and an even greater contradiction between the Miltonic desire for order and his insistence on mutuality. It is hard not to identify with Eve's struggle to assert herself, even though we know that within the Miltonic world such behavior can only be associated with the demonic actions of Satan. By bounding spheres of relations and separating authority relations and personal relations, Milton created a situation which could function only if the individual could accept both the specific need for the boundaries and the belief that reciprocal relations could function best within the confines of hierarchy. While in the larger psychological sense the necessity of boundaries is inescapable, the nature of the boundaries and the need for hierarchical boundaries are subject to question.

We are told by the narrator, lest we misunderstand, that Adam and Eve are "not equal, as thir sex not equal seem'd" (IV, 296). Eve's appearance is meant to imply "subjection," but a gentle subjection. The presentation of Adam and Eve before the Fall reveals their happy relations. In their first conversations with each other, they share their perceptions of their environment. Adam instructs Eve in the conditions for the maintenance of pleasure in paradise, indicating that the proper response to the gift of creation is gratitude and obedience. Eve's recounting of her creation follows appropriately. God has offered creation to mankind for use and for pleasure, and Eve is designed for pleasure with Adam and for procreation. It is true that her role is more than maternal; she is considered an "individual solace dear." Milton does not consider a purely physical function as sufficient in itself when describing human behavior. Eve's function as "Mother of human Race" is asymmetrical from Adam's in several ways. While he has a divine model of paternity in heaven, no such model exists for the maternal role. When Adam is designated as "our general ancestor," as "our Father," we are aware of the differences in attitudes and values associated with the roles of father and mother. Their roles are further asymmetrical in that Eve seems closer to the natural function in her procreative role. She seems to be a necessary intermediary in the dialectic between nature and culture.[25] It is appropriate that Eve should be the primary agent in succumbing to the serpent. Even Satan recognizes her vulnerability, which resides in her closer affinity with nature and in the more tenuous character of her direct links to heaven.

Both Adam and Eve are educated as fully as possible in the meaning of their roles. Eve's designation as the mother of the human race is no empty title, nor does it mean the same thing as Adam's education in the responsibilities of his own paternity and the nature of divine paternity. Different moral and psychological qualities are associated with the role assignments. It is also important to note that the designation gives prior information about the roles so that the individual can base his or her action on this knowledge. Lewalski has objected to my discussion of the prescription of roles. She finds that the "text of the poem does not sustain an assertion that the recognition of Eve as mother is prior to and sanction for her role as lover and spouse."[26] The literal following of the text shows Eve as on her honeymoon and, further, as growing into the role of mother in the future. But the information that Eve first receives about herself concerns both procreation and pleasure. When we first meet her, she already has been apprised of this important facet of her responsibility. In *Comus*, too, Milton conjoins the observance of chastity and virginity with the appropriate familial (and, thus, cultural) responsibilities.[27] Future action will be based on an understanding of the relationship between familial roles and the pursuit of proper pleasure. Prior knowledge is common in Milton, and actions are dependent on an assimilation of this knowledge into the behavior choices of the characters. Adam is given knowledge about the injunction not to eat the forbidden fruit. The reader is given knowledge about the predictable outcome of events. Raphael provides information to Adam which, it is hoped, will determine Adam's behavior in the future. The sacrifice of the Son, prefigured in Book III of the epic, will determine the course of events. Roles determine actions; the information is meant to be taken seriously and incorporated into choice and action. The kinship designations, while not fully realized, should determine the actions of the character. Eve's role as the mother of the human race should be a self-fulfilling prophecy. Prior to the connubial bliss in the bower, Adam and Eve are conscious of their roles in relation to each other.

Arguing for the symmetrical dimensions of the roles of Adam and Eve does not present the fullest picture of the complexity of their relationship, nor does it help us to understand the problematic nature of aspects of Milton's poetic vision. The case for Eve's poetic nature, her collective sharing in the work with Adam, and her presence as a listener at Raphael's discourse expands our awareness and appreciation of her. There is no doubt that, prior to the Fall, she is a good companion, a fine conversationalist with Adam, a good listener, a gracious hostess, and a poet of sorts. She is an interested and respectful student with her instructor, Adam. Balance all of these qualities against the facts that she is restricted to a more confined role, that heaven is unpopulated by women, that she is the bringer of sin and death into the world, that she shares qualities in common with Sin and Death after the Fall, that she is the object of Adam's antifeminist attacks, and that her self-image must be censored through the masculine image. The poetic world which Milton creates in his own image, as God creates the world in his own image, determines the role of the woman.

What can be said of Eve's susceptibility to deviance? How can the modern reader, particularly the feminist reader, ignore the stereotypic treatment of that woman? Eve's situation contains certain contradictions. She is allowed freedom within the familial and social context, but this freedom must be circumscribed by existing hierarchical structures of power and authority. The demarcation between acceptable and unacceptable behavior is unambiguous. By violating boundaries and moving to adopt more power through Satan's offers of equality, power, and authority, Eve identifies herself as a deviant. In other words, her resistance to subordination is invalidated and stigmatized through its association with the archetypal subverter, Satan. Are we to consider Eve's rebellion and the rebellion of all women against subordination as evil? And how do we account for Eve's susceptibility to vanity and flattery, classical charges against woman's character? Her motives for eating are much more self-centered than Adam's; he, at least, eats out of fondness and interest in another human being:

> However I with thee have fixt my Lot,
> Certain to undergo like doom; if Death
> Consort with thee, Death is to mee as Life;
> So forcible within my heart I feel
> The Bond of Nature draw me to my own,
> My own in thee, for what thou art is mine;
> Our State cannot be sever'd, we are one,
> One Flesh; to lose thee were to lose myself.   (IX, 952–59)

He is unwilling to lose her company, even if this means death and the loss of paradise. Satan, too, stresses the asymmetry in Adam's and Eve's roles, acknowledging Adam's "higher intellectual" powers, his "strength" and "courage haughty." Eve is much easier prey for him. Her inexperience with his style of language makes her vulnerable, too, unaccustomed as she is to such a display of rhetoric. Adam's intelligence could have discerned the spuriousness of Satan's language. Knowledge lures Eve; equality lures her. She is attracted by power. Most specifically, she is vulnerable in her weaker capacity to discern boundaries. When Satan informs her that there are no consequences for actions, that God does not mean what he says, he alludes to the arbitrariness of boundaries, and Eve does not challenge this:

> do not believe
> Those rigid threats of Death, ye shall not Die:
> How should ye? by the Fruit? it gives you Life
> To Knowledge: By the Threat'ner? look on mee,
> Mee who have touch'd and tasted, yet both live,
> And life more perfet have attain'd than Fate
> Meant mee, by vent'ring higher than my Lot.
> Shall that be shut to Man, which to the Beast
> Is open? or will God incense his ire
> For such a petty Trespass?   (IX, 684–93)

Eve's acquiescence in Satan's appeal to the flexibility of boundaries and to the inconsequence of rules fills out the picture of a character who is indeed appealing and attractive, but who does not seem able to function autonomously or maturely. Perhaps Lewalski is correct; perhaps we cannot expect a fully mature picture of Eve since she must grow into a deeper sense of herself. But the presentation of Eve during and after the Fall does not offer much evidence of the potential for later maturity.

The scenes immediately following the Fall depend, too, on archetypal qualities associated with the woman. Eve contemplates secrecy and dissembling. She chooses to brazen it out with the truth and put the best possible construction on her actions:

> But to *Adam* in what sort
> Shall I appear? shall I to him make known
> As yet my change, and give him to partake
> Full happiness with mee, or rather not,
> But keep the odds of Knowledge in my power
> Without Copartner? so to add what wants
> In Female Sex, the more to draw his Love,
> And render me more equal, and perhaps,
> A thing not undesirable, sometime
> Superior: for inferior who is free? (IX, 816–25)

The speech portrays the idea of equality as confused in Eve's mind with dominance. She errs, like Satan, in confusing hierarchy and equality of affection. The question, "for inferior who is free?" is an indictment of Eve rather than an expression of a realistic sentiment, since she reveals a deep misunderstanding of the delicate balance between power and love.

After Adam's decision to eat the fruit and remain with Eve, the two "disport" themselves like the animals through their experience of lust, and Adam rises from his sexual pleasures, like Samson, "shorn of his strength." Now he reproaches Eve. Now he desires to live in solitude and hide himself in his shame. His reproaches to her are in language reminiscent of *Samson Agonistes:*

> Thus it shall befall
> Him who to worth in Woman overtrusting
> Lets her Will rule; restraint she will not brook,
> And left to herself, if evil thence ensue,
> Shee first his weak indulgence will accuse. (IX, 1182–86)

The amicable relationship has been transformed into conflict and "vain contest." Adam's anger continues unabated for a while as he struggles to restore his sense of self-worth and to come to terms with his new knowledge of sin and mortality. Interspersed with his lamentations are further accusations to Eve: "But for thee I had persisted happy" (X, 873–74). He questions the creation of woman, why God did not rather have Earth "peopl'd . . . With Spirits Masculine" (X, 889–90). Woman becomes the familiar confounder of "household peace."

Eve's earlier bravado has now totally vanished; she becomes a petitioner, a suppliant, begging Adam to put aside his anger. She asks to assume the guilt and to become the sole object of God's wrath; and the vision of Eve "at his feet submissive in distress" (X, 942) causes Adam to abandon his anger:

> But rise, let us no more contend, nor blame
> Each other, blam'd enough elsewhere, but strive
> In offices of Love, how we may light'n
> Each other's burden in our share of woe.   (X, 958–61)

Furthermore, Eve attempts to express her remorse for her actions by contemplating race suicide, abstention from propagating the species, as an alternative to their condition of death and woe. She also contemplates actual suicide:

> Let us seek Death, or he not found, supply
> With our own hands his Office on ourselves;
> Why stand we longer shivering under fears,
> That show no end but Death, and have the power,
> Of many ways to die the shortest choosing,
> Destruction with destruction to destroy.   (X, 1001–06)

It seems appropriate that Eve should be the one to utter these sentiments. The ambivalent association of the woman with both life and death seems to be common to many myths. While, as mother of the human race, she is to populate the species, her role is also associated with that of the destroyer. This ambivalent role is not unique to Milton's presentations. Eve's portrait also seems to echo the satanic insistence on getting the feared event over with; despair leads Satan, in *Paradise Lost* and *Paradise Regained,* to court his own destruction. The creative impulse is toward life, toward proper conceptions of time, and toward the recognition of boundaries. Adam exerts his dominant role by reminding Eve of the future prophecy. It is he who dissuades her and introduces an appropriate temporal perspective on events. She has in common with Satan, too, her preoccupation with the present, but Adam tells her, "Remember with what mild / And gracious temper he both heard and judg'd / Without wrath or reviling" (X, 1046–48). Adam takes the lead in executing the course of action they must now follow in mitigating their lot.

Eve's later speeches are brief, emphasizing mainly her acknowledgment of her transgression, her readiness now to remain by Adam's side (XI, 162–80; XII, 610–23). Lewalski has also pointed out that though Eve sleeps when the angel reveals the future to Adam, she, too, is in contact with God, for "God is also in sleep" (XII, 611). Yet again Eve does not play an active role: Perhaps she plays an even lesser role than before the Fall as a result of her transgression. That God has not deserted her, and that she is privy to certain information and to restored contact with the divine, does not alter the reinstitution of even more stringent boundaries than before her transgression. Authority relations are once more made firm, and domestic relations are restored within those confines.

The verbal conflict between Adam and Eve can be seen as a satiric commentary on marital discord. Neither party is free from using strategies to control the other. Adam displaces his anger with himself onto Eve; Eve plays the role of penitent in order to appease Adam's anger. Both partners are complicit. In this respect, it would be unfair to see Milton as totally unreflexive in this presentation of Adam and Eve. Yet, in spite of his psychological insight into the ways in which mental conflict is acted out, he does not see their struggle as arising from the stringent boundaries of hierarchy, with male dominance and female subordination, which make conflict inevitable.

It is significant in Milton's poetry that he always subordinated political, monarchical, and military designations to kinship relations. God is, for the most part, not the king; the Son is not the prince. The ideal relations are reflected through the father-son role, through the respect that brothers have for each other, and through the proper observance of the roles of husband and wife. These charities are preferable to external and political social roles. In all of his poems, he focuses on the primacy of domestic relations, elevating them to principles of heroic proportion. And it is in this context that the woman's role must be set. The infernal trinity—Satan, Sin, and Death, portrayed in Book II, in particular—is the negative paradigm of family relations. What Milton dramatizes is the violation of the incest taboo. He portrays the confusion of the roles of father and son, brother and brother, and "husband" and "wife." No boundaries are clear; roles are intermixed, and the belligerent and subversive behavior displayed is the concomitant of the confused roles. Unlike heaven and earth before the Fall, among these typifications there exists no respect for the difference between hierarchical relations and affectional attitudes, no regard for companionship, and no respect for social solidarity. The respect for the incest taboo insures the perpetuation of the holy family and insures the continuity of culture.[28] The institution of culture demarcates the human family from the bestial family, and the incestuous coupling of Satan and Sin allies them with nature rather than culture.[29] Eve's league with Satan thus associates her with this destructive state of affairs. She, too, brings discord and sin into the world; she, too, is party to domestic discord and the confusion of just relations. Only through restitution of proper relations can the discord of the infernal trinity be delimited.

Eve's remorse, contrition, and humility after the Fall restore her subordinate relationship to Adam. The dual image of woman as creator and as destroyer is thus part of the mythology of *Paradise Lost,* as it is part of other mythologies which portray the necessity for women to be constrained and educated. The portrait of Eve restored to herself by acceptance of the destructive aspects of her behavior is construed in Milton to be a positive portrayal. One does not question the engaging qualities of Eve as companion and solace in *Paradise Lost;* what one questions is the painful vision of woman controlled by external demands which she must accept and internalize. Adam, too, labors under stringent restrictions, but his portrayal does not suffer from the taint of demonic associations. He is neither as suggestible as Eve nor directly in league with Satan. One questions both the prescriptions which make rebellion possible and Milton's negation of the legitimacy of Eve's demand for equality of relations. Even the presentation of Satan is more acceptable in this vein, because the reader recognizes and accepts the symbolic qualities which Milton unloads on him as the archetypal deviant. He is removed from the human, but the human characters, even though idealized and typified to a degree, are closer to the reader, functioning in both symbolic and realistic terms. Yet Eve's presentation veers more toward the symbolic in both idyllic and deviant terms than Adam's. For some readers, the traditional images associated with the woman create obstacles to empathizing with her human situation as Milton presents it.

One final point about *Paradise Lost* is worth mentioning in behalf of the many modern women poets who are finding a voice. Lewalski has objected to my association of Milton with the masculine tradition of poetry. The woman is not seen as poet but rather as the muse who inspires the poet. Her access to language is through the man. While the muse inspires, the man articulates. It is not only the fact that Adam names the animals that reveals woman's subordinate relationship to language. Milton identifies his poetic craft with the male poets of the past, "Blind *Thamyris* and blind *Maeonides* / And *Tiresias* and *Phineas* Prophets old" (III, 35–36). Both the heroic tradition and the biblical tradition that Milton chooses to engraft on the classical present the male hero or the patriarchal ethos as dominant. In his selections from the Bible and in his descriptions of future history in Books XI and XII, he chooses to single out for praise the heroic behavior of men. When the woman is praised it is for her capacity to serve and for the right relations she bears to the man. The vision of Mary, the second Eve, is of one who will be the instrument of salvation:

> Of *David* (so I name this King) shall rise
> A Son, the Woman's Seed to thee foretold,
> Foretold to *Abraham*, as in whom shall trust
> All Nations, and to Kings foretold, of Kings
> The last, for of his Reign shall be no end.   (XII, 326–30)

Not only do traditional identifications mark Milton's identification with the male heroic image and with the male poet, but the actions of the poem indicate the woman's secondary role in relation to authority and to language. Lewalski may indeed see Eve as a poet of sorts, and Eve's speeches may indeed indicate a capacity for poetic sentiment and language, but the evidence points again to the limitations of Eve's linguistic creativity. The larger portion of speeches given to Adam, the questioning, submissive quality of Eve's prelapsarian speeches, the greater ignorance she displays in language usage evidenced in her susceptibility to Satan's rhetoric, and her increasing silence after the restoration of amicable and submissive relations to Adam—all these factors make her a questionable poet. In defending Milton, we must assert that his presentations of women are determined by his historical circumstances, his predilection for classical and biblical forms, his attraction to a heroic vision, his essentially patriarchal Protestantism, and his personal circumstances. Yet we can also explore his limitations and contradictions without the necessity of apology. This is the only way to appreciate "fit conversation" with his poetry.

If we turn from *Paradise Lost* to *Comus*, we find certain basic similarities, except that the Lady does not fall. She is an exemplification of virtue, and uncloistered virtue at that. Her trials on her journey through the dark wood are not only for herself but are in the interests of the court and the familial and social relations of an orderly society. An interesting dimension of this positive portrait of a woman in Milton is that the Lady, unlike Eve, could also be a young man. The descriptions of the Lady are far less sensual, and physical description is held to a minimum. The sensuality in the masque is more characteristic of Comus, the son of Circe. The advantage of a female figure at the center of the masque relates to the importance of the themes of chastity and virginity. In presenting the relationship between sexuality and just familial and social relations, the woman becomes the appropriate vehicle. She does, indeed, occupy the "seat at the center."[30] The maintenance of civilized society hinges on the control of bodily desires, which must be transformed in the interests of culture and continuity. The struggle between Comus and the Lady is basically over due regard for nature and for the proper uses of time, and over the question of respect for the trustworthiness of language. Comus lives in the present, sees nature as abundant and the demands of hunger and sexuality as needing immediate gratification:

> Beauty is nature's coin, must not be hoarded,
> But must be current, and the good thereof
> Consists in mutual and partak'n bliss,
> Unsavory in th' enjoyment of itself.
> If you let slip time, like a neglected rose
> It withers on the stalk with languish't head.   (739–44)

The Lady virtuously responds:

> Impostor, do not charge most innocent nature,
> As if she would her children should be riotous
> With her abundance; she, good cateress,
> Means her provision only to the good

> That live according to her sober laws
> And holy dictate of spare Temperance.   (762–67)

While there is no doubt that Milton is capable of creating a positive image of woman, as Lewalski has noted, one must also question the nature of the affirmative representation. Why is the woman here the bridge, the intermediary between nature and culture? Why would a weakness on her part unhinge civilized order and creativity? Milton reinforces the traditional image, from the affirmative side, of woman's role as being closer to nature, and the crucial importance, therefore, of her self-control in the transformation of that nature in the interests of social harmony.

The Lady is capable of choice, and her choices reinforce her strength in resisting the attractive arguments of Comus. Her speeches are respectful and discerning. She is able to distinguish the motives and strategies of the tempter. She is capable of righteous indignation at Comus' perversion of language, a point Milton dramatizes quite carefully. There is not a hint that she is vulnerable to the tempter's attractive rhetoric. Her role in the work is far more important than that of her brothers, who are also seeking their way through the dark wood and are attempting to understand the nature of evil and subversion. One must also note that the Lady is assisted in her virtuous actions by another female figure, Sabrina. The Lady's salvation is, in part, effected by Sabrina and the power of song. But one remembers also that the overall actions in the masque are directed by the Attendant Spirit, and that the point of all the action is the celebration of the power, wisdom, and authority of the "Noble Peer":

> A noble Peer of mickle trust and power
> Has in his charge, with temper'd awe to guide
> An old and haughty Nation proud in Arms;
> Where his fair offspring nurs't in Princely lore,
> Are coming to attend their Father's state
> And new-entrusted Scepter.   (31–36)

The Lady's actions may be at the center of the masque, but her actions are an important support for the communal vision which revolves around the father's role.

It is important to note that Milton does not consider the woman's role unimportant. Quite the contrary, in all of his works and in his emphasis on the importance of marriage, he takes particular care to describe the positive and negative dimensions of that role in portraying the important ideas of sociability, creativity, and the nature of culture. Even in his presentations of the power of poetry and of the poet, he seems to indicate the value of his feminine muse. In *Ad Patrem*, for example, where he seeks to convince his father of the greatness of poetry and of its sister art music, he aligns himself and, he hopes, his father with the muse. But the end of poetry and the object of the gift is the father, just as the Lady's actions are in the interests of the court, where her father's state is the important issue. Not only is the woman the helpmeet to the man, a figure of service and altruism, but the male hero, like Christ in *Paradise Regained*, has this same important quality of service. What is at issue in a feminist reading of Milton's poems is the circumscribed image of the woman, not whether Milton's attitude toward that image is positive or negative.

Dalila in *Samson Agonistes* represents the woman on the other side of the divide from the Lady. It is difficult to ignore or to rationalize Milton's powerful statements on hierarchy and woman's role articulated by the Chorus in the poem:

> Favor'd of Heav'n who finds
> One virtuous, rarely found,
> That in domestic good combines:
> Happy that house! his way to peace is smooth:
> But virtue which breaks through all opposition,
> And all temptation can remove,
> Most shines and most is acceptable above.
>   Therefore God's universal Law
> Gave to the man despotic power
> Over his female in due awe,
> Nor from that right to part an hour,
> Smile she or lour:
> So shall he least confusion draw
> On his whole life, not sway'd
> By female usurpation, nor dismay'd.   (1046–60)

In fairness to Milton, one should explore the possibility that the Chorus's sentiments are unreliable. Samson's vision is larger than theirs, and Milton's is larger yet. However, no tension seems to exist between the Chorus's viewpoint and Samson's on the subject of women's virtue and their potential for treachery. The context of the drama reaffirms Milton's ideas of hierarchy and the necessity of circumscribing roles, though the role models have shifted from the human to the transcendent sphere. During the course of the drama, Samson relinquishes all human relationships and comes to depend solely on God.

The poem explores familial relations between father and son, husband and wife. There is also the comparison between the human father and the divine Father.[31] Samson's movement through the work is seen in his sloughing off the past and the human ties that bind him to his prison, the double prison of body and mind.[32] The conjugal relations between Samson and Dalila are part of a larger social fabric. Role patterns, notions of hierarchy, of dominance and subordination, positive attitudes and values—all emanate from the divine paradigm. The relation of the heavenly Father to his creations is both model and sanction for human patterns of authority relations. Dalila's behavior can in no way be considered apart from these ideas. Her role, whether regarded from a sympathetic or unsympathetic point of view, must be discussed in the context of Milton's expectations concerning conjugal responsibility. William Empson's "Defense of Delilah" falters because he attempts to humanize the situation, trying to see her claims to public issues as having equal validity with Samson's.[33] We know that Milton's morality does not operate in a realm beyond good and evil; his views of hierarchy enforce the supremacy of one term of a moral dialectic over the other term.[34] There is no question about the supremacy of the Israelite cause and the superiority of Samson's claim to championship of this righteous people and of their God. Dalila must thus be made a double traitor, to the cause of truth ("God's universal Law") and to "domestic good."

Milton's need for an artistic vehicle to explore the nature of heroic behavior, self-transcendence, and the affirmation of a religious vision precluded, as did his use of the myth of the Fall and of the second Adam, the choice of a story which portrays the complexity of women, of seeing them in tragic and empathic terms. The portrait of Dalila, like his divine and demonic characters, is subject to the demands of typification. When women err, they belong to the camp

of the deviants, like Dalila and like Eve after the Fall and before she
is restored to her human potential. When women persevere, like
the Lady in *Comus*, they assume the qualities of the ideal. Milton's
epics preclude the possibility of presenting women as independently heroic or seeing them in terms of the human conflicts,
contradictions, and loyalties they might potentially experience. His
ideas of community, of necessary and fit discourse, of divorce, of the
necessity of contending in order to discover the truth about the self
and others, are not lessened because of his presentations of women;
but his portraits of women do present stumbling blocks on the way to
affirming certain "essential truths" in his poetry.

Dalila's role is restrictive and stereotypical. In the angry encounters between Samson and Dalila, Milton presents her as using
typical female wiles to confound Samson. The scenes are filled with
threats of physical abuse by Samson, verbal abuse by both, and
inflexibility on the part of both. Dalila's appearance, billowing,
sailing like a ship, bedecked, ornamented, gay, in contrast to
Samson's pitiable condition, and her perfumed, amber scent mark
her as a seductress attempting to overwhelm Samson sensually. But
she is presented as a typical female, not only in her appearance, but
also in her rhetorical strategies and in her general demeanor. She
lies. While the reader knows from the Chorus's report that she is
sailing in with "streamers waving," she describes herself as coming
with "doubtful feet and wavering resolution" (732). The Chorus
describes how she has adopted a penitent stance, declining her head
and dissolving into tears. She presents herself as coming in Samson's
behalf. Yet the reader knows her already as the agent of Samson's
plight and knows also that Samson's interests do not lie in living out a
life of ease until he dies. His rejection of Manoa's offers has already
indicated that Samson has a much larger sense of the means to
restoration of his self-esteem and his contact with God. Samson thus
rejects her, tells her to leave, and exposes her "wonted arts, / And
arts of every woman false like thee" (748–49). In response to him, she
acknowledges her feminine frailty, her curiosity, and her inability to
keep a secret. Furthermore, she reproaches him, as Eve had reproached Adam after the Fall, for not having exercised more control
himself. She legitimates her actions on the basis of her feminine
desire to hold on to him, her fear of losing him, "lest one day thou

wouldst leave me" (794). She wants him all to herself. She asks him to consider the possibility that what she did was done for love. Milton has Samson reject these claims, exposing the fallacy of regarding people as possessions, demystifying the notion that love conquers all, and obliterating other considerations of self-esteem and responsibility. He also presents a convincing portrayal of domestic wrangling, the way in which relationships can turn into a struggle for power without regard for human considerations of affection and communication. But he does not explore the deeper implications of the origin of the conflict and the behavior, since his critique of Dalila grows from a solid base of familial and domestic loyalties and from the assumption of Samson's dominance.

As the dialogues between Samson and Dalila continue, the level of affect is intensified. Samson validates Dalila's weaknesses but finds them inexcusable. He accuses her of "furious rage / To satisfy thy lust" (836–37). He tells her that succumbing to the entreaties of the Philistine lords shows her lack of faith and trust in him and reveals her lack of loyalty and trust in the marriage bond. In effect, he accuses her of conformity in a situation where nonconformity should have prevailed in the name of truth and love. Actually, she should have conformed to the higher loyalty of the conjugal relationship.

Samson exposes Dalila's spurious sentiments. Dalila is guilty of articulating the age-old reproach of women: "In argument with men a woman ever / Goes by the worse, whatever be her cause." (*SA*, 903–04). Undaunted by his rejection of her, Dalila offers Samson domestic ease, pleasures of the senses, and care in his old age. Samson rejects this Circe's "fair enchanted cup, and warbling charms" (934). To relent and accept her offer would be another form of imprisonment to him. It is not the fact of Samson's rejection of Dalila that troubles us. Given the situation Milton has created, the reader assents to Samson's righteous indignation, even manages to affirm Milton's realistic portrait of hostile domestic interactions. What is absent in Milton is recognition of the possibility (which a modern reader could affirm) that the hostile interaction might arise inevitably from a vision of the world which produces contradictions between public and domestic loyalties. This, I think, is the point that Empson was trying to expose in his essay on Dalila. Milton's heroic vision and his ideas of hierarchy produce the contradiction, as do his idealized expectations of the marriage state.[35] While he criticizes a bad marriage and can envision divorce, he does not criticize his expectations of marriage, particularly the prescriptions he sets for the woman's role.

The contact between Samson and Dalila escalates to the level of open rage and verbal violence, with one threat of physical violence. To Dalila's request to touch him (a picture of the woman who tries to solve marital discord by physical contact), Samson responds with vehemence; he threatens her that his memory of the past might be aroused, might "wake / My sudden rage to tear thee joint by joint" (952–53). In order to get her to leave, he tells her that he has forgiven her, "go with that" (954). He also tells her that she should suffer from the fact that she will be excluded from the roll call of "illustrious women, faithful wives" (957). Her ultimate punishment—since the work stresses the importance of memory, history, and recorded events—is to be negatively immortalized. She becomes part of the historical record of faithless and deceitful women. Dalila reveals too that she is aware of the importance of remembrance, stating that she will rather be recorded as "the famousest / of Women, sung at solemn Festivals, / Living and dead recorded" (982–84), because of her efforts "to save / My country from a fierce destroyer" (984–85). Milton contrasts her sense of time with Samson's, much as he contrasts Satan's and Christ's in *Paradise Regained*. Dalila seems preoccupied with the present and present rewards. She thinks, not of the future, but of enjoying honor in her lifetime. Throughout his poetry, Milton distinguishes between appropriate and inappropriate conceptions of fame and immortality. Dalila has shortsighted views about immediate gratification and the judgments of history.

When Dalila leaves, the Chorus describes her as "a manifest Serpent by her sting" (997), and Samson describes her as a "viper" sent to debase him. She is a source of conflict, "a thorn / Intestine" (1037–38). Then follows the long speech quoted earlier on the proper role and behavior of women in relation to God's universal law. Given the context of Milton's views of matrimony, Dalila's character portrayal is consistent. She has few redeeming qualities. She is associated with the archetypal serpent, and her characteristics inherit the demonic qualities of the satanic figure. Her behavior not only typifies the unexemplary woman but also enforces, by comparison, the norm for acceptable female behavior. Milton has indeed "recorded" another example of female treachery.

Milton's presentations of Eve, Dalila, and the Lady reveal his continuing concern to explore domestic relations in his poetry. They say much about the importance of marriage, marital discord, kinship relations, proper notions of dominance and subordination, and reciprocity in Milton's exploration of community and sociability. One cannot deny the importance of women in Milton's poetry or the fact that he captures traditional mythic qualities associated with women. He also conveys realistically the effects of conflict and the necessity of positive affectional relations. But his mythology creates inflexible alternatives for roles, thus making his presentations of women liable to criticism.

The "truths" Milton records about women are subject to historical change. Milton's work belongs in history and so is governed by that very sense of time he sought to transcend. We do not read Milton for the same reasons or with the same mind as the seventeenth-century reader. Constructing an ideal sympathetic reader has its value. Constructing a realistic and empathic reader is much kinder to the enterprise of literary criticism and to the cause of truth. Essential truths about human beings are inseparable from the historical circumstances and particular forms in which they are expressed. Some truths may still be valid; all truths deserve questioning and examination. We read Milton, or any writer for that matter, to understand ourselves and our world. Much that he has to say speaks to us now. Some of what he portrays is transformed by the modern reader's sense of psychic and social reality.

University of Pittsburgh

NOTES

1. Marcia Landy, "Kinship and the Role of Women in *Paradise Lost*," in *Milton Studies*, IV, ed. James D. Simmonds (Pittsburgh, 1972), pp. 3–18; Barbara K. Lewalski, "Milton on Women—Yet Once More," in *Milton Studies*, VI, ed. James D. Simmonds (Pittsburgh, 1974), pp. 4–5.
2. Contemporary critical theory has been struggling with all of these questions. For example, Jean-Paul Sartre, *What Is Literature* (New York, 1965); Georg Lukacs,

History and Class Consciousness (Cambridge, Mass., 1971) and his studies of the novel; Ernst Fischer, *The Necessity of Art* (Harmondsworth, Middlesex, 1963); Lucien Goldmann, *The Hidden God* (London, 1964) and *Pour une sociologie du roman* (Paris, 1964); Roland Barthes, *Writing Degree Zero* (New York, 1968); Frederick Jameson, *Marxism and Form* (Princeton, 1974); Walter Benjamin, *Illuminations* (New York, 1969); Theodor Adorno, *Prisms* (London, 1967) and *The Dialectic of Enlightenment* (Seabury, N.Y., 1972) have examined inevitable connections between the artist and his society, the artist and contemporary society, the artist and his audience, the nature and function of art, and the historical circumstances from which no writer escapes. Feminist criticism, too, has explored these issues, particularly as they affect the creativity of women artists, literary critics, and social critics. Writers like Kate Millett, *Sexual Politics* (Garden City, N.Y., 1970); Sheila Rowbotham, *Woman's Consciousness/Man's World* (Harmondsworth, Middlesex, 1973); Eva Figes, *Patriarchal Attitudes* (Greenwich, Conn., 1970); Juliet Mitchell, *Psychoanalysis and Feminism* (New York, 1974); Simone de Beauvoir, *The Second Sex* (New York, 1974); Shulamith Firestone, *The Dialectic of Sex* (New York, 1971); and many other feminist literary critics are seriously examining the role of women in the context of historical and social change.

3. Sartre, *What Is Literature*, pp. 49–50:

Ainsi la lecture est un pacte de générosité entre l'auteur et le lecteur; chacun fait confiance à l'autre, chacun compte sur l'autre, exige de l'autre autant qu'il exige de lui-même. Car cette confiance est elle-même générosité: nul ne peut obliger l'auteur à croire que son lecteur usera de sa liberté; nul ne peut obliger le lecteur à croire que l'auteur a usé de la sienne. C'est une décision libre qu'ils prennent l'un et l'autre. ("Qu'est-ce que la littérature," *Situations, II* [Paris, 1948], p. 105)

4. Ibid., p. 64:

Les auteurs aussi sont historiques; et c'est précisément pour cela que certains d'entre eux souhaitent échapper à l'histoire par un saut dans l'éternité. Entre ces hommes qui sont plongés dans une même histoire et qui contribuent pareillement à la faire, un contact historique s'établit par le truchement du livre. Ecriture et lecture sont les deux faces d'un même fait d'histoire et la liberté à laquelle l'écrivain nous convie, ce n'est pas une pure conscience abstraite d'être libre. Elle n'*est pas,* à proprement parler, elle se conquiert dans une situation historique; chaque livre propose une libération concrète à partir d'une aliénation particulière. Aussi y a-t-il en chacun un recours implicite à des institutions, à des moeurs, à certaines formes d'oppression et de conflit, à la sagesse et à la folie du jour, à des passions durables et à des obstinations passagères, à des superstitions et à des conquêtes récentes du bon sens, à des évidences et à des ignorances, a des façons particulières de raisonner. ("Qu'est-ce que la littérature," pp. 118–19)

5. See Joseph H. Summers, "The Embarrassments of *Paradise Lost,*" in *Approaches to "Paradise Lost": The York Tercentenary Lectures,* ed. C. A. Patrides (Toronto, 1968), pp. 65–80.

6. John F. Huntley, "The Images of Poet and Poetry in Milton's *The Reason of Church Government,*" in *Achievements of the Left Hand: Essays on the Prose of John*

Milton, ed. Michael Lieb and John Shawcross (Amherst, 1974), pp. 83–120; see also Harry Smallenburg, "Government of the Spirit: Style, Structure, and Theme in *Treatise of Civil Power*," ibid., pp. 219–38.

7. See Christopher Hill, *Reformation to Industrial Revolution* (Harmondsworth, Middlesex, 1970).

8. "Areopagitica," in *John Milton: Complete Poems and Major Prose,* ed. Merritt Y. Hughes (New York, 1957), p. 746. All quotations are from this edition.

9. For a discussion of Milton and modern political issues, see John Shawcross, "The Higher Wisdom of *The Tenure of Kings and Magistrates*," in *Achievements of the Left Hand,* pp. 142–59.

10. Father Walter J. Ong, S.J., "Logic and the Epic Muse: Reflections on Noetic Structures in Milton's Milieu," in *Achievements of the Left Hand,* p. 261; John M. Steadman, *Milton and the Renaissance Hero* (Oxford, 1967).

11. Peter Berger and Thomas Luckman, *The Social Construction of Reality: A Treatise on the Sociology of Knowledge* (Garden City, N.Y., 1969).

12. Paul Rock, *Deviant Behaviour* (London, 1973).

13. See Edmund Leach, "Anthropological Aspects of Language: Animal Categories and Verbal Abuse," in *Mythology,* ed. Pierce Miranda (Harmondsworth, Middlesex, 1972), p. 50.

14. "Milton on Women—Yet Once More," pp. 5–7.

15. Figes, *Patriarchal Attitudes,* pp. 66–80.

16. Northrop Frye, "Polemical Introduction" to his *Anatomy of Criticism: Four Essays* (New York, 1967), pp. 3–29; René Wellek and Austin Warren, *Theory of Literature* (New York, 1956).

17. Mary Wollstonecraft, *A Vindication of the Rights of Woman with Strictures on Political and Moral Subjects* (New York, 1967).

18. Claude Lévi-Strauss, "Overture," in his *The Raw and the Cooked: An Introduction to the Science of Mythology* (New York, 1969), pp. 1–32.

19. See, for example, Joan Bamberger, "The Myth of Matriarchy," in *Women, Culture, and Society,* ed. Michelle Zimbalist Rosaldo and Louise Lamphere (Stanford, Calif., 1974), pp. 263–79.

20. George Balandier, *Political Anthropology* (New York, 1972); Peter Berger, *The Sacred Canopy: Elements of a Sociological Theory of Religion* (Garden City, N.Y., 1969); Bronislaw Malinowski, *Magic, Science and Religion and Other Essays* (Garden City, N.Y., 1948).

21. Paul Ricoeur, *The Symbolism of Evil* (Boston, 1967).

22. Herman Feifel, ed., *The Meaning of Death* (New York, 1959).

23. William Philips, ed., *Art and Psychoanalysis* (Cleveland, 1957).

24. Juliet Mitchell, "Narcissism," in her *Psychoanalysis and Feminism,* pp. 30–41. See also Heinz Kohut, *The Analysis of the Self: A Schematic Approach to the Psychoanalytic Treatment of Personality Disorders* (New York, 1971); Jacques Lacan, *The Language of the Self: The Function of Language in Psychoanalysis,* ed. Anthony Wilden (Baltimore, 1968), pp. 9–12.

25. Sherry B. Ortner, "Is Female to Male as Nature Is to Culture?" in *Woman, Culture, and Society,* pp. 64–88.

26. "Milton on Women—Yet Once More," p. 9.

27. Angus Fletcher, *The Transcendental Masque* (Ithaca, 1973).

28. Claude Lévi-Strauss, *The Elementary Structures of Kinship* (Boston, 1969), pp. 12–68.

29. Juliet Mitchell, "The Holy Family," in her *Psychoanalysis and Feminism*, pp. 361–416.

30. Roger G. Wilkenfeld, "*Comus:* The Seat at the Center," in *Critical Essays from ELH* (Baltimore, 1969), p. 140.

31. Nancy Y. Hoffman, "Samson's Other Father: The Character of Manoa in *Samson Agonistes*," in *Milton Studies*, II, ed. James D. Simmonds (Pittsburgh, 1970), pp. 195–210.

32. Anthony Low, *The Blaze of Noon: A Reading of Samson Agonistes* (New York, 1974), pp. 139–41.

33. "A Defense of Delilah," *Sewanee Review*, LXVIII (Winter 1960), 240–55.

34. On the subject of dialectical and hierarchical relations, see Kenneth Burke, *A Rhetoric of Motives* (Berkeley, 1969).

35. For a discussion of Milton's views on marriage, see John Halkett, *Milton and the Idea of Matrimony* (New Haven, 1970).

THE SACRED HEAD:
MILTON'S SOLAR MYSTICISM

Don Parry Norford

Milton aspires to light, to free himself from the body. A celebrant of the solar Logos, he is preoccupied with the conflict between spirit and nature and the frightening possibility of the dissolution of consciousness. The central figures in Milton's poems are associated with the death and rebirth of the sun. In his early poems the figure of Orpheus, whose Apollonian song tamed Dionysian nature, inspires the triumph of the Christ-child over the pagan deities, the death and rebirth of Lycidas, the mystique of the Lady's "sun-clad power of chastity." In the later poems solar power tends to become apocalyptically destructive: Samson annihilates the Philistines, and the Son overwhelms the rebel angels in his solar chariot. Milton's ideal, symbolized by the chariot of Deity, is to harness physical energies in service of the Logos. This ideal of sublimation, which has alchemical affinities, is displayed in *A Mask*. Ideally, sublimation should lead to integration and higher wholeness. Yet in Milton, transcendence seems ultimately based upon dismemberment—the mortification of nature in the interests of spirit.

A C C O R D I N G   T O   Plato, the eye is the most sunlike of all the sense organs, and the power of vision is "dispensed by the Sun, like a stream flooding the eye."[1] As the sun is the source of vision, so is the Good the source of intelligence. Ficino, in his *De sole*, neatly epitomizes the Platonist analogy:

The Sun creates both the eyes and their colors; and gives to the former the ability to see and to the latter the capability of being seen. It joins both by means of light. God also acts thus in respect to all intellects and to all intelligible beings. In fact, God creates the intelligible species of things, and also the intellects, giving them the rational power which is proper to them.[2]

37

Thus, the divine intellect is an incorporeal sun, the cause of knowledge and truth, yet beyond them, as the sun transcends the light and vision it imparts to the world. The sun, says Plato, causes genesis —the world of becoming—but is not itself genesis. Or as Nicholas of Cusa puts it, God is an eye whose angle of vision is not limited, but infinite: "Thy sight is an eye of sphericity and of infinite perfection. Wherefore it seeth at one and the same time all things around and above and below."[3] The marvelous power of light, "not encompassed within any definite quantity or figure; extended in infinite space, while yet filling the macrocosm with its omnipresence" (Ficino, p. 130), is a visible approximation to the power of divine sphericity. And the human soul partakes of the solar power of God's all-seeing eye:

> I was an Inward *Sphere of Light*,
> Or an Interminable Orb of *Sight*,
> An Endless and a Living Day,
> A *vital Sun* that round about did *ray*
> All Life and Sence,
> A Naked Simple Pure *Intelligence*.[4]

The sun, the eye, the mind, and God—the essence of each is light. "God is light, and in him is no darkness at all" (1 John i, 5). Philo of Alexandria says that the human mind is akin to the divine Logos, being a fragment or light ray of the Blessed Nature. And Plotinus uses the figure of sun and ray to explain the relation between the world and the ineffable One: "The Soul can never cease to abide in the *Nous*, being attached to *nous* by a connexion far firmer than that by which the light surrounding the sun is attached to the sun" (III. v. 2).[5] Light is the divine Logos or *Nous*, the intelligible and eternal order upon which the sensible world is modeled and to which man aspires. For Plotinus, "intelligence denotes a step in the spiritual life, a stage in the upward journey of the soul toward its final goal."[6]

Though most eloquently expressed by philosophers and mystics, this solar aspiration is universal. In his profound study of the origins and history of consciousness, Erich Neumann shows that the ego consciousness, as it develops, tends to make itself independent of the body, thereby creating a tension between conscious and unconscious minds. The goal of all initiation, from the rites of puberty to the religious mysteries, is the transformation of consciousness

—the begetting of a higher spiritual man who can experience his kinship with a spiritual and heavenly world. The hero of mythology, a symbol of progressing consciousness, "enters into an alliance with heaven, with light and wind, cosmic symbols of the spirit that is not of this earth, bodiless and an enemy of the body":

Heaven is the dwelling place of gods and genii, symbolizing the world of light and consciousness as contrasted with the earthy, body-bound world of the unconscious. Seeing and knowing are the distinctive functions of consciousness, light and sun the transpersonal heavenly factors that are its higher condition, and eye and head the physical organs that are correlated with conscious discrimination. Hence in the psychology of symbols the spiritual soul descends from heaven and in the psychic body scheme is apportioned to the head, just as the loss of this soul is mythologically represented as a blinding, as the death of the sun-horse, or as a plunge into the sea—in other words, the overthrow of masculinity always follows the path of regression. It entails the dissolution of the higher masculinity in its lower phallic form and therefore loss of consciousness, of the light of knowledge, of the eye, and a relapse into the body-bound chthonic world of animality.[7]

As Logos symbols, sun, eye, and head are distinctively masculine: "The sun as masculine principle is ruler of the day, of consciousness, of work and achievement and of conscious understanding and discrimination, the Logos." In contrast, the moon, the feminine principle, "is ruler of the night, of the unconscious. She is the goddess of love, controller of those mysterious forces beyond human understanding, which attract certain human beings irresistibly to each other, or as unaccountably force them apart. She is the Eros, powerful and fateful, and incomprehensible."[8] The path of regression, the "relapse into the body-bound chthonic world of animality," is thus the dissolution of the masculine in the feminine, the triumph of Eros over Logos: It is the extinction of consciousness. Neumann remarks that "for the ego and the male, the female is synonymous with the unconscious and the nonego, hence with darkness, nothingness, the void, the bottomless pit":

Mother, womb, the pit, and hell are all identical. The womb of the female is the place of origin from whence one came, and so every female is, as a womb, the primordial womb of the Great Mother of all origination, the womb of the unconscious. She threatens the ego with the danger of self-noughting, of self-loss—in other words, with death and castration.[9]

Neumann's account of the development of consciousness, the detachment of the ego from the unconscious and its heroic struggle for individuation, utilizes the insights of the nineteenth-century Swiss historian J. J. Bachofen, best known for his theory of social development which maintains that the first period in human history was matriarchal. Although this theory has generally been found unacceptable, it holds true at least for the development of the psyche, for as Neumann says, "the world experienced by the waking ego of humanity is the world of J. J. Bachofen's matriarchate with its goddesses of motherhood and destiny."[10] According to Bachofen, there are three religious stages in the development of society: "First the tellurian, in which there is motherhood without marriage, no agriculture, and apparently nothing resembling a state; then the lunar, in which there is conjugal motherhood and authentic or legitimate birth and in which agriculture is practiced in settled communities; and lastly the solar period, in which there is conjugal father right, a division of labor, and individual ownership."[11]

The lowest stage of religion, "pure tellurism," gives primacy to the maternal womb. "It situates the seat of virility in the tellurian waters and in the winds, which belong to the earth's atmosphere and hence to the chthonian system." The male principle is subordinated to the female; the night is identified with the earth and interpreted as a maternal-chthonian power: "Here the night is the oldest of deities and stands in a special relation to woman."

When men begin to turn their eyes from night to the sun, the gradual ascendance of the patriarchate begins, a development which itself has three stages. The symbol of the first is the sunrise, which is associated with triumph over the maternal darkness. But in this early phase the radiant son is still wholly governed by his mother, the mythological son-lover of the Great Mother Goddess (see Neumann, chap. 2, "The Great Mother"). "Total liberation from the maternal bond occurs only when the sun achieves the full unfolding of its luminous power." At its noon "it is triumphant paternity, sub-jugating the mother with its radiance." Bachofen calls this second stage Dionysian, "the stage of the god who is celebrated both as the fully developed solar power and as the founder of paternity." "Like the sun in its fullest virility, Dionysian paternity is the phallic fecundator; like Sol, the Dionysian father forever seeks receptive

matter in order to arouse it to life." The third stage of solar development is the Apollonian, transcending the Dionysian:

The phallic sun, forever fluctuating between rising and setting, coming into
being and passing away, is transformed into the immutable source of light. It
enters the realm of solar being, leaving behind it all idea of fecundation, all
yearning for mixture with feminine matter. Dionysus merely raised paternity over the mother; Apollo frees himself entirely from any bond with
woman. His paternity is motherless and spiritual . . . hence immortal,
immune to the night of death which forever confronts Dionysus because he
is phallic.[12]

Whatever the historical accuracy of Bachofen's analysis, his essential insight that the development of civilization and culture is masculine and solar is supported by the explorations of analytical psychology. Neumann relates man to culture, woman to nature: "The man's
world, representing 'heaven,' stands for law and tradition, for the
gods of aforetime, so far as they were masculine gods. It is no
accident that all human culture, and not Western civilization alone,
is masculine in character, from Greece and the Judaeo-Christian
sphere of culture to Islam and India" (p. 143).

This aspiration to light, the "begetting of a higher spiritual man
who may experience his kinship with a spiritual and heavenly
world"; the consequent tension between conscious and unconscious, masculine and feminine, Logos and Eros; the preoccupation
with regression, the "relapse into the body-bound chthonic world of
animality"—all this may be found preeminently in the poetry of.
Milton, the celebrant of the solar Logos. Milton is the poet of light,
order, harmony—and patriarchal domination. One of the central
symbols in his work is Orpheus, the archetypal poet-priest whose
songs charmed and tamed the brute, irrational forces of earth, yet
who ultimately was dismembered by savage women, the Bacchae.
In one version the Bacchae, worshipers of Dionysus, murdered
Orpheus because he slighted their god: "Every morning he would
rise to greet the dawn on the summit of Mount Pangaeum, preaching
that Helius, whom he named Apollo, was the greatest of all gods."[13]
As a sun-worshiper, Orpheus was also a culture hero, in the Renaissance commonly typifying the power of learning and civility:

Therefore well may these drunken *Bacchides* be taken for the heady rage of
mutiny and Sedition, which silence the authority of the law, and infringe

that concord (the musicke of *Orpheus*) which had reduced wild people to civility; returning now to their former pravity and naturall fiercenesse: himselfe, the life of philosophy, torne in peeces by their fury. . . . *Orpheus* his head and Harp being throwne into *Hebrus;* are borne away by the murmuring current. So the scattered reliques of learning, expulsed from one country, are transported to another.[14]

The symbol of Orpheus' civilizing power is the lyre, which from quite early times was associated with the harmony of the universe and of the well-tuned soul. Apollo is said to have been the teacher of Orpheus; the god gave him lessons on the lyre which Hermes had given him and which he presented to Orpheus. A later legend of Hermes relates that after he invented the lyre he went up into the heavens, "and passing the planets, he marvelled aloud that from the swing of the planets through their orbits came forth a harmony similar to that of the lyre which he himself had constructed." Aristides Quintilianus, a musical theorist of the fourth century, says that instruments made of tuned strings resemble the ethereal, dry, and simple part of the cosmos, as well as its microcosm, the soul. The lyre, therefore, is "an enemy of the lower realms of earth and water, where humidity would cause its strings to lose their tension, just as material concerns would weight the soul and impede its journey to the One." The power of the lyre thus symbolizes the power of the rational soul over the passions. In this way the lyre "connected Orpheus with a body of Neoplatonic ideas about the harmony of the universe and the return of the soul to its celestial home, while his power over wild beasts as well as over the gods of Hades caused him frequently to be compared with Christ and sometimes conflated with him." In Christian art the Orpheus-Christus shepherd figure in a paradise surrounded by animals "demonstrated the power of the Logos over wild nature."[15]

This tension between the Logos and wild nature is movingly presented in *Lycidas,* in which death by water is associated with the dismemberment of Orpheus: The brute—and implicitly female—irrationality of nature is represented by the "blind Fury," the "Blind mouths" of the bishops, the extinction of sight, the eclipse of consciousness:

> It was that fatal and perfidious bark
> Built in the eclipse, and rigged with curses dark,
> That sunk so low that sacred head of thine.[16]

The haunting image of a head sinking beneath the waves and weltering at the "bottom of the monstrous world" (158) shows that the
"enchanting son" (59) of Calliope has no charm to enchant the forces
of chaos: "His gory visage down the stream was sent, / Down the
swift Hebrus to the Lesbian shore" (62–63). Ultimately, however, by
a change in perspective, Lycidas becomes associated with the sun
and Christ. Christ is the true Orpheus who brought his bride out of
hell, as the sun rises out of the ocean:

> So sinks the day-star in the ocean bed,
> And yet anon repairs his drooping head,
> And tricks his beams, and with new spangled ore,
> Flames in the forehead of the morning sky.   (168–71)

Here the rising sun is both head and eye: as irrational death was
associated with blindness and dismemberment, so rebirth is at the
same time the regaining of sight and reparation of physical and
psychic integrity. From his sleep on the ocean floor, Lycidas ascends
to the realm of eternal wakefulness, where the "pure eyes, / And
perfect witness of all-judging Jove" (81–82) never slumber.[17] And
Lycidas also becomes "the genius of the shore" (183), a force for
order, a rational limit to the occult power of the "remorseless deep."

The supernatural power of the poet-priest over the remorseless
deep is particularly important in Milton's early poems. In *Ad Patrem*
the young Milton writes that nothing shows man's divinity more
than poetry, which "still retains some blessed trace of the Promethean fire. The gods love poetry: poetry has power to stir the quiver-
ing depths of Tartarus and to bind the deities of hell" (20–22). The
Attendant Spirit in *A Mask* is an Orpheus figure, "Who with his soft
pipe, and smooth-dittied song, / Well knows to still the wild winds
when they roar, / And hush the waving woods" (86–88). And the
Lady claims to share these powers of her daemon:

> Yet should I try, the uncontrolled worth
> Of this pure cause would kindle my rapt spirits
> To such a flame of sacred vehemence,
> That dumb things would be moved to sympathize,
> And the brute Earth would lend her nerves, and shake. (792–96)

Here the power of the Logos, associated with the "sun-clad power of
chastity" (781), verges upon the destructive: The devouring flame of
"sacred vehemence" (cf. the Promethean fire of *Ad Patrem*) brings to

mind the purifying holocaust of the Last Judgment, in which the voice of the trumpet replaces the lyre. In Milton, solar power often has apocalyptic overtones, as when in *Lycidas* the clear spirit, refusing "To sport with Amaryllis in the shade, / Or with the tangles of Neaera's hair" (68–69), hopes "to burst out into sudden blaze" (74) or, more important, in the Nativity ode, when the rising Son of God awes the earthly sun into stopping his wonted course, frightens nature into thinking that the world has come to an end (stanza X), and drives the pagan shades back to "the infernal jail."

Rosemond Tuve, trying to rationalize Milton's depiction of nature in the ode as leprous and deformed, distinguishes between the effect of the Incarnation upon nature and upon the pagan deities, finding in nature a humble, obedient, shamefast acknowledgment of her deformities; though nature does not fully understand the Incarnation, she is reassured by Peace and glorifies God, hoping for her last fulfillment. The false gods, on the other hand, withdraw with sullen regret, hostile to the *concordia* between heaven and earth.[18]

There is some truth to this distinction; yet J. B. Broadbent, in a brilliant critique of the ode and Tuve's essay on it, emphasizes that not only does Milton present the effect of the Nativity on paganism as ruin, not enlightenment, but also, "though dealing with the occasion on which spirit became flesh, he is indifferent to most of the traditions that expressed joy in the perfecting of nature. He concentrates on those elements—peace, light, harmony—which lie at the non-human end of the spectrum."[19] The line between nature and pagan evil is very thin indeed, especially when Milton goes out of his way to bring in the "horrid clang" from Mt. Sinai, the terror of Old Testament justice: "The aged earth aghast / With terror of that blast, / Shall from the surface to the centre shake" (160–62). Moses almost supplants Jesus. I think Broadbent is correct in saying that the direction Milton takes in his poem "is away from the incarnate towards the ideate" (p. 23), that "the peace and harmony and light realize, with typically Miltonic solidity and force, what is an ideate condition: an architectural world founded in chaos, harmony metallically rung out of discord, the gleaming angels vertical against a globe of light in the midst of uncomprehending darkness" (p. 27).

G. Wilson Knight has also commented upon Milton's love for the formed, the architectural, the metallic, even the mechanical, concluding that Milton thinks less in terms of ideas than of energies, that his poetry is characterized preeminently by power: "Power surges in Milton. His encased, metallic cast of thought, the ironside battalions of his imagery, are the measure of the tumultuous energies to be controlled."[20] At first glance, Broadbent's "ideate condition" seems to contradict Knight's belief that Milton thinks in terms of energies rather than ideas, until one realizes that for Milton ideas *are* energies that must be embodied in order to become effective; and matter —the chaos of unactualized potency, nonbeing, the turbid, unconscious realm of the Mother—resists the solar imprint of form. One thinks of the hostility of Night and Chaos ("this wild abyss, / The womb of nature and perhaps her grave" [*PL* II, 910–11]) to God in *Paradise Lost*. Though we are told that matter is essentially good, it seems peculiarly liable to depravation.[21] Everywhere in Milton the fluid, confused, and mysterious must be purified and irradiated by *Nous:* "Dark illusions are defeated in *Comus*, the same weltering waves and tangled hair of nymphs are transcended in 'Lycidas', the same mystical rays of solid light dazzle error in the prose and *Paradise Lost*, the same gigantic force ruins idolatry in *Samson*."[22]

It is thus no accident that the central image of the ode concerns the triumph of architectural form over chaotic matter:

> While the creator great
> His constellations set,
>   And the well-balanced world on hinges hung,
> And cast the dark foundations deep,
> And bid the welt'ring waves their oozy channel keep.   (120–24)

The "welt'ring waves" recall the fate of Lycidas. Here oozy impurities are channeled, just as Lycidas washes his disordered hair: "with nectar pure his oozy locks he laves" (175). The ode really celebrates the creative and purifying power of God, and more covertly of the poet himself. As Broadbent says, the technical care Milton lavishes upon the flight of the pagan gods suggests "that they are being defeated by this art rather than by Christ," so that "the ultimate sanction of the poem's action is not divine power but Miltonic art and intellect" (pp. 28–29). The central concern of the ode, then, is the "conquest by hard-edged right reason of the soft dim liquid allures of passion" (p. 28). Milton is exorcising his recent sensuous elegies, particularly the pagan Elegy 5 ("On the Coming of Spring"), which relates poetic inspiration to the fertilizing intercourse between sun and earth and concludes, "Long may each grove have its own particular deities."[23] The ode cannot "admit 'The uncontrollable mystery on the bestial floor': partly because Milton associated the animal with sin, and mystery with chaos; but also because he was a magus determined to control the mystery" (Broadbent, p. 31). There is indeed a Faustian element in the young Milton who, in his seventh Prolusion, believes that knowledge can make man divine: "He [the man of universal learning] will indeed seem to be one whose rule and dominion the stars obey, to whose command earth and sea hearken, and whom winds and tempests serve; to whom, lastly, Mother Nature herself has surrendered, as if indeed some god had abdicated the throne of the world and entrusted its rights, laws, and administration to him as governor."[24] One is reminded of Prospero and his books, and his repression of Caliban. Prospero, however, renounces magic and accepts the Caliban in himself: "this thing of darkness I / Acknowledge mine" (V, i, 275–76). Milton, though he ultimately renounced knowledge in *Paradise Lost* and *Paradise Regained,* never lost his almost gnostic hostility to the world, his desire to transcend the boundaries of human existence.

Broadbent uses the phrase "mystical rays of solid light" to describe Milton's solar mystique. In *A Mask,* the Elder Brother invokes the "long levelled rule of streaming light" (339) to "disinherit Chaos, that reign's here / In double night of darkness, and of shades" (333–34). The pun on "rule" (the straight, the rigid, ruled line or ruler; mathematical measure or order, the axiom; code of behavior, law, kingship) blends the concrete or physical and the abstract or mental. In *Paradise Lost* the sun is "of this great world both eye and soul" (V, 171), yet its "magnetic beam" is at the same time phallic: "that gently warms / The universe, and to each inward part / With gentle penetration, though unseen, / Shoots invisible virtue even to the deep" (III, 583–86).[25] The power of eye and phallus, spiritual and sexual power, are identified.

This intimate relation between spiritual and physical strength is the subject of *Samson Agonistes,* in which the loss of spiritual vision, "impotence of mind" (52), leads to the loss of hair and eyes and to bondage at the mill of the Philistines, worshipers of the bestial chthonic deity Dagon ("Dagon his name, sea monster, upward man /

And downward fish" [*PL* I, 462–63]). Samson's unshorn hair, the sign of his covenant with God, is the source of his strength, so that hair is the link between spiritual and physical: Of the head, it is mental, yet also has obvious physical and sexual overtones. It used to be thought that Samson was a solar hero, his name being derived from *shemesh*, "of the sun." Samson's career could be seen as a sun myth in which the hero is swallowed every evening by a nocturnal sea monster dwelling in the west, but who hacks his way out of the monster to be reborn in the east as the *sol invictus*. In accordance with this line of thought, "Manoah," Samson's father, could mean "rest," out of which the sun is born; and "Dalila" could mean "weakness," "exhaustion," or "night." The sun sinks into the lap of night, which puts out its eye. Samson at the mill might represent the monotonous daily round of the sun.[26] Modern authorities generally reject the solar interpretation of Samson in reaction against the solar enthusiasm of folklorists around the turn of the century.[27]

Milton's conception of Samson, however, tends to bear out the older view: In the *Reason of Church-Government*, for example, Milton speaks of Samson's "illustrious and sunny locks the laws waving and curling about his god like shoulders" (YP, I, 859). For Milton, Samson is a solar hero who, like Lycidas, is associated with the death and rebirth of the sun. Samson too has, as it were, plunged into the ocean, suffering "total eclipse": "O dark, dark, dark, amid the blaze of noon" (80). Dagon, it seems, was a corn god, a vegetation deity, the father of Baal, whose territories were subject to the Great Mother of the Canaanites. "Samson's captivity is therefore an expression of the servitude of the conquered male under the Great Mother, just as were the labors of Herakles under Omphale, when he wore women's clothes—another well-known symbol of enslavement to the Great Mother, to whom we must also attribute the mill as a symbol of fertility."[28] Samson has been "Effeminately vanquished" (562) and obsessively berates himself for his mental impotence ("O impotence of mind, in body strong!" [52]) and lack of manhood ("But foul effeminacy held me yoked / Her bond-slave" [410–11]). His fault is female, as Dalila cruelly reminds him, and he is therefore appropriately punished by symbolic castration, shaved of his "precious fleece" like a "tame wether" (538) or castrated ram. He is a "burdenous drone" (567), a male worker bee without a sting, subservient to

the queen bee. Perhaps in Samson's precious fleece there is an echo
of the golden fleece sought by Jason, which was kept by Aeetes,
whose name was derived from his land of Aea, sacred to Helius.
"Aea" seems to mean "Land of Morning" and was the place where
the sun rested at night. Aeetes' palace was thus the House of the Sun,
and the golden fleece had a solar significance.[29] It hung in a tree
guarded by an unsleeping dragon, a mythologem analogous to the
golden apples on the tree of the Hesperides, which were also
guarded by a vigilant dragon. In A Mask, the Second Brother compares his sister's chastity to these golden apples:

> But Beauty like the fair Hesperian tree
> Laden with blooming gold, had need the guard
> Of dragon-watch with unenchanted eye,
> To save her blossoms, and defend her fruit
> From the rash hand of bold Incontinence.   (392–96)

Here the dragon is the guardian of the "sun-clad power of chastity,"
an image that finds its correspondence in the comparison of Samson
to an "evening dragon" (1692) when he pulls down the theater upon
the Philistines.

This notorious comparison of Samson to a dragon or snake rifling
a hen house has been examined by Lee Sheridan Cox, who has
compiled some interesting material.[30] According to Philostratus, in
his Life of Apollonius of Tyana, there are red dragons of the plains
and golden dragons of the mountains, near the Red Sea, which are
hunted for the precious jewels, the fiery stones, that they have for
eyes. These precious stones possess a mystical power. The hunters
charm the dragon to sleep, cut off its head, and steal the jewels
(eyes). Thus the "golden dragon loses his mystical power which is
his vision; Samson loses his mystical power, a loss related to loss of
both physical and spiritual vision" (p. 582). Cox, citing Bruno Snell's
Discovery of the Mind, points out that "dragon" means "the seeing
one" but that the verb $\delta\acute{\epsilon}\rho\kappa\epsilon\sigma\theta\alpha\iota$, from which $\delta\rho\acute{\alpha}\kappa\omega\nu$ is derived, did
not mean "to see" in the sense of getting knowledge or an impres-
sion through the eyes, but rather "to have a particular look in one's
eyes, referring not so much to the function of the eye as to its
uncanny glint as noticed by someone else." The verb is used of the
Gorgon, whose glance incites terror. Cox thus defends the decorum
of Milton's dragon image, concluding that "Milton is evoking the

image of fowls transfixed into attention at the sight of the great serpent . . . with the uncanny fire radiating from his eyes. He is showing the terribly blind Samson commanding the fascinated attention of the onlookers" (p. 583).

The "unenchanted eye" of the dragon therefore seems analogous to the transfixing stare of the Gorgon, who in *A Mask* also appears as the guardian of chastity. The Elder Brother compares the Lady's sun-clad power of chastity to the Gorgon's head as depicted on Athene's shield:

> What was that snaky-headed Gorgon shield
> That wise Minerva wore, unconquered virgin,
> Wherewith she freezed her foes to congealed stone?
> But rigid looks of chaste austerity,
> And noble grace that dashed brute violence
> With sudden adoration, and blank awe.[31]   (446–51)

John Carey notes that Conti allegorizes the Gorgon's head as the sun "because no one can turn his eyes against the light of the sun or against wisdom and remain unharmed" (*Poems*, p. 198). Here the Orphean power over nature is heightened to the apocalyptic note we saw in connection with the Lady's "flame of sacred vehemence." A fiery—or freezing—apocalyptic consummation often attaches to solar power in Milton: the Gorgon's eye of the spirit darts forth a supernatural power that stuns, petrifies, shatters, or consumes the earthly. And as the Gorgon's power is associated with her snaky hair, so too is Samson's:

Methinks I see in my mind a noble and puissant Nation rousing herself like a strong man after sleep, and shaking her invincible locks: Methinks I see her as an Eagle muing her mighty youth, and kindling her undazl'd eyes at the full midday beam; purging and unscaling her long abused sight at the fountain it self of heav'nly radiance; while the whole noise of timorous and flocking birds, with those also that love the twilight, flutter about, amaz'd at what she means. (*Areopagitica*, YP, II, pp. 557–58)

The function of the Gorgon image in *A Mask* must be examined more closely later. Here the association of the dragon or snake with hair and the sun calls for comment. If the name of the snake, "dragon," means "the seeing one" or "to see," its association with the sun is not hard to understand. Snakes were thought in ancient times to have particularly sharp eyesight; and the snake sheds its skin and becomes young again, just as the sun sets and rises with new youth. Philo of Byblos writes that the serpent "is the most pneumatic [πνευματικώτατον] of all beasts and of a fiery nature [πυρῶδες]." Hans Leisegang, from whom I draw these observations, comments that "Fire and the pneuma as wind, life breath, or spirit make the snake the beast of Helios." And he relates the serpent's power of rejuvenation to the "Heraclitean-Stoic doctrine of the development of the world from an original element, fire, to which the cosmos returns after the cosmic year has run its course."[32] As the symbol of the rejuvenating power from which the cosmos originates, and to which it returns, the serpent might signify the life force, which would account for its association with hair, also a sign of fertility and reproductive power. Samson's long hair, in fact, can be related to the phallic beams of the sun, which night shears off. In *Paradise Lost*, for example, Satan's obscured glory seems "as when the sun new risen / Looks through the horizontal misty air / Shorn of his beams" (I, 594–96). And when Adam awakes after his lustful intercourse with Eve, he is compared to Samson:

> so rose the Danite strong
> Herculean Samson from the harlot-lap
> Of Philistean Dalilah, and waked
> Shorn of his strength.   (IX, 1059–62)

As with Samson, spiritual and physical strength are identified here: Adam has lost virtue with this fall into lust.

Samson's blinding and loss of hair seem therefore symbolically equivalent: Both are symbolized by the extinction of the sun. Samson has succumbed to a spiritual castration, a loss of the masculine or mental strength that opposes the bodily or female portion of his being. In Bachofen's terms, his chthonic or phallic masculinity has caused the loss of solar masculinity. Yet as the day-star in *Lycidas* ultimately "Flames in the forehead of the morning sky," and as the eagle mews or renews her youth and fading sight, according to the old bestiaries, at the fountain of the sun, so also Samson ends his enslavement to Dagon with the resurgence of his Apollonian solar power:

> But he though blind of sight,
> Despised and thought extinguished quite,
> With inward eyes illuminated

His fiery virtue roused
From under ashes into sudden flame,
And as an evening dragon came,
Assailant on the perched roosts.   (1687–93)

In the major reversal of the play, the Philistines have been "with blindness internal struck" (1686) while Samson has become "the seeing one," not only because of his Gorgonian stare, but also because he has been granted insight, spiritual vision. A twelfth-century bestiary says of serpents:

When they are getting old their eyes grow blind, and if they want to renovate themselves, they go away somewhere and fast for a long time until their skins are loose. Then they look for a tight crack in the rocks, and go in, and lay aside the old skin by scraping it off. Thus we, through much tribulation and abstinence for the sake of Christ, put off the old man and his garment. In this way we may seek the spiritual Rock, Jesus, and the tight crack, i.e. the Strait Gate.[33]

Just so, adversity enlightens Samson. The idea of rebirth implicit in the serpent image is made explicit by the reference to the Arabian sun-bird, the phoenix, who "Revives, reflourishes, then vigorous most / When most unactive deemed" (1704–05). Samson finally unites wisdom and strength, the serpent and the phoenix: Vision nourishes power.[34]

It is unfortunate that Samson's integration should culminate in a cataclysmic act of destruction. Like a meteor Samson flares briefly and goes out; in destroying the Philistines he consumes himself. Solar power here does not shine, but burns or negates. The paradox of fire, which Shakespeare handles beautifully in Sonnet 73, is that its life is its death, "consumed with that which it was nourished by." In Samson's climactic act we can see a death wish, despite Milton's attempt to mitigate it ("And Samson said, Let me die with the Philistines" [Judges xvi, 30]). Samson's phoenix fame (and flame) can live on only if he dies.

Gaston Bachelard has coined a term, the Empedocles complex, to characterize the desire for death by fire. Fire, he says, "suggests the desire to change, to speed up the passage of time, to bring all of life to its conclusion, to its hereafter. . . . The fascinated individual hears *the call of the funeral pyre.* For him destruction is more than a change, it is a renewal. . . . This total death which leaves no trace is the guarantee that our whole person has departed for the beyond."[35] Iamblichus says that the daemons approve sacrifices through fire because fire annihilates and assimilates the matter of the sacrifice to itself.

They [the daemons] likewise assimilate whatever is in us to the Gods, in the same manner as fire assimilates all solid and resisting substances to luminous and attenuated bodies. And they elevate us through sacrifices and the sacrifice fire to the fire of the Gods, in the same manner as fire elevates to fire, and draws upward gravitating and resisting substances to divine and celestial natures.[36]

Fire thus can symbolize transcendence through destruction. Bachelard quotes D'Annunzio: "After having gained all through skill, through love or through violence you must give up all, you must annihilate yourself." And he cites Giono's observation that it is the highly intellectual urge in the old races, for whom "the head has become merely a globe of pure intelligence," that leads to the sacrificial pyre: only these intellectual people "can force the door of the furnace and enter into the mystery of the fire" (pp. 17–18). Milton was one who could enter into the mystery.

A constellation of solar images akin to those of *Samson Agonistes* may be found in Milton's depiction of the chariot of paternal deity in *Paradise Lost*. The Son, "all armed / Of radiant urim" (VI, 760–61), rides forth in a throne-chariot "convoyed / By four cherubic shapes," each having four faces, their bodies and wings all "set with eyes, with eyes the wheels / Of beryl, and careering fires between" (VI, 752–56). Ezekiel's imagery, and Milton's adaptation of it, is richly solar. The word "urim" seems to mean light; and, according to Gunnar Qvarnström, the seventeenth-century biblical scholar John Spencer argued that it stands for the fiery light of the angels. Qvarnström also points out that in alchemical thought the urim was associated with the philosopher's stone: "*Urim* signified not only this 'heaven-endowed stone' believed capable of giving to the Sun its supernatural light and power, but also divine Grace or Christ, and hence also the Sun itself."[37] The high priest's breastplate, with which the *urim* and *thummim* were associated, significantly appears in the magnificent description of the sun as a heavenly philosopher's stone in Book III, 593 ff. In *Paradise Lost* the sun is associated with precious stones (the jeweled eyes of the dragon) and with alchemical transmutation; the sun itself, fed by exhalations from earth and the lower spheres, constantly undergoes a process of transmutation of humid materials into its own substance: "What wonder then if fields and regions here / Breathe forth elixir pure, and rivers run / Potable gold" (III, 606–08). The light generated by this transmutation provides the life-giving energy that supports creation.[38]

The Son, therefore, as Qvarnström says, "is dressed in the substance of the Sun, the fiery metal of light." The "Messiah represents *the divine Sun on the Throne of omnipotence.*" And the structure of *Paradise Lost* reflects this Christocentric point of view, for the point in Book VI at which the Son ascends the chariot of deity to drive out the rebel angels is the center (by line count of the first edition) of the physical body of the epic, as well as of the temporal scheme: "The Sun, the symbol of Christ among the celestial bodies, is created on the Day which forms the mid-point of the epic chronology—the seventeenth Day in a scheme which comprises thirty-three Days."[39] The Son in his triumph ascends to noon.

Aside from the *urim,* the eyes, faces, fire, and wheels of the chariot itself are solar. J. H. Adamson holds that "the vision of the Chariot must have been, in its earliest beginning, an imaginative symbolizing of the sun chariot upon whose daily and seasonal victories over the powers of darkness and chaos the life of the world depends."[40] According to the *Interpreter's Bible,* Ezekiel's throne-chariot is a symbolic representation of the temple at Jerusalem, which was so oriented that at the equinoxes the rays of the rising sun could shine directly across from the Mount of Olives, through the east gate of the temple area, and into the temple to illuminate the holy of holies, which contained the ark.[41] The ark was guarded by cherubs, in Hebrew tradition winged lions with human heads which, as Adamson says, symbolize the power and creative energy of God (*Bright Essence,* p. 103.). In Christian tradition, cherubim were commonly depicted as winged heads; John of Damascus, in his *Exposition of the Orthodox Faith,* speaks of cherubim as "many-eyed."[42] The eyes of the chariot symbolize the all-seeing Godhead; and the "fourfold-visaged four" (*PL* VI, 845) might, as Alastair Fowler notes (*Poems,* p. 754), symbolize the realm of nature, which is the vehicle for divinity. Adamson, after examining Cabbalistic speculation on the chariot, concludes that "the rider of the Divine Chariot is the Son, the Logos, wholly obedient to the will of God, and the Chariot itself . . . is a representation of the . . . world of creation wholly obedient to the will of the Son."[43]

In his later article Adamson interestingly traces the development of the conception of the Logos among the pre-Socratic philosophers, a development which, by way of Philo and Jewish mysticism, influenced interpretation of Ezekiel's chariot. At first the Logos was thought to be a material substratum out of which the cosmos arose (for example, Thales' water), a substratum that had mysterious spiritual qualities, for it shaped and directed creation. Heraclitus then identified the Logos with fire, a divine, self-moving substance that penetrated, irradiated, and directed the cosmos. After Heraclitus, Anaxagoras said that the Logos of the universe was Mind, which was independent of matter. Thus, mind rather than substance gradually became the basic reality. This development seems to have influenced Philo Judaeus, who interprets the charioteer as the Logos steering the chariot of the universe (the substratum).[44] This development, by the way, is an excellent example of the evolution of consciousness among the ancient Greeks.

The emphasis upon quaternities in Ezekiel's vision bears out the idea of the chariot as the world of nature, for four in traditional number symbolism was the number of earth or matter. Philo Judaeus says that four is the first number to display the nature of the solid cube, one being associated with the point, two with the line, three with the plane. Four adds depth. And since four is the first number which is a square, it is the number of justice and equality. Philo concludes: "At present it is sufficient to add this that it was the foundation of the creation of the whole heaven and the whole world. For the four elements, out of which this universe was made, flowed from the number four as from a fountain. And in addition to the four elements the seasons of the year are also four, which are the causes of the generation of animals and plants."[45]

Four also signifies strength and wholeness. In the war in heaven the good angels fight "In cubic phalanx" and are therefore "invulnerable, impenetrably armed" (VI, 399–400). The *Interpreter's Bible* (vol. 6, pp. 71–74) remarks that Ezekiel's fourfold chariot is reflected in Blake's four Zoas—Urizen, Luvah, Los, and Tharmas

—the four eternal senses in man, which are equivalent to Jung's four functions of consciousness—thought, feeling, intuition, and sensation. In Jungian psychology the quaternity symbolizes psychic wholeness, the raising of the dark side of man to consciousness and the realization of the self.[46] Chariot and rider thus symbolize the divinely possessed, integrated soul. One recalls Plato's version (*Phaedrus* 246a–254e) of the soul as a chariot drawn by two winged horses, one black, one white; the charioteer, or reason, must govern and integrate the passionate and appetitive parts of the soul. In Ezekiel's vision the "four living creatures"—Milton's "four cherubic shapes"—have "the likeness of a man," yet each has four faces: of man, lion, ox, and eagle (Ezekiel i, 5–10). The foursquare world of created nature is embodied in man, who in turn is assimilated to the angels and to God.

Jung, in his *Symbols of Transformation*, quotes a passage from the Shvetashvatara Upanishad describing the Indian creator-god Rudra: "He has eyes on all sides, faces on all sides, arms on all sides, feet on all sides. He is the one God who created heaven and earth, forging all things together with his hands and wings."[47] The resemblance to Ezekiel's chariot is striking. Jung sees in Rudra "the All-Creator, and behind him the sun, who is winged and scans the world with a thousand eyes." The fourfold, many-eyed god symbolizes, according to Jung, "the creative power of our own soul" (p. 121), solar or psychic energy, for just as the sun is a source of energy, so our "physiological life, regarded as an energy process, is entirely solar" (p. 122; cf. the solar serpent as the life force). This, I believe, is the essence of Ezekiel's vision as well, and even more so of Milton's adaptation of Ezekiel. There is in Milton a will to know more than others, to annihilate all things to thought, to plumb the secrets of heaven and earth—a will to power, to crush all resistance to his ideals—an aspiration which Gaston Bachelard has called the Prometheus complex, the desire to steal fire from, to rival, Zeus: "The Prometheus complex is the Oedipus complex of the life of the intellect."[48] The Son of God is a successful Phaeton. In the fiery chariot we may see the omnipotent creative power of the integrated soul triumphing over hostile unconscious forces, as Samson's integration of mind and body annihilates the worshipers of Dagon.

As Samson pulled down the theater "with burst of thunder"

(1651), so in the chariot of paternal deity "every eye / Glared lightning, and shot forth pernicious fire" (VI, 848–49). Milton consistently associates eyes and fire, mind and energy. Satan arises from the burning lake with "eyes / That sparkling blazed" (I, 193–94). After the Fall, Adam and Eve feel that their eyes have been opened with new knowledge, yet they confuse knowledge with lust, glancing at each other with "amorous intent," Eve's eyes darting "contagious fire" (IX, 1036). And in Michael's vision of history, God's eye is associated with the fire of Abel's sacrifice: "His offering soon propitious fire from heaven / Consumed with nimble glance" (XI, 441–42). We have seen that the sun in *Paradise Lost* is both eye and phallus, that Samson's solar power is both mental and physical. In connection with his discussion of Rudra, Jung includes an illustration of the Egyptian god Bes, who became associated with the young sun god Horus; Bes is winged, and there are Horus-eyes on his wings and all over his body. But most significantly, the god is shown with an erect phallus.[49] We should therefore not be surprised when Broadbent finds phallic associations in the chariot of deity, which emerges spontaneously from between two brazen mountains (*PL* VII, 201 ff.): "This version reveals it as a phallic chariot, omnipotent genitalia with which the Son is 'girt.'"[50] Though the textual evidence is slight, his intuition seems valid. After all, we are told that the Logos "Dove-like sat'st brooding on the vast abyss / And madest it pregnant" (*PL* I, 21–22); and so also the poet prays for the fertilizing influence of the Spirit of God: "what in me is dark / Illumine, what is low raise and support" (I, 22–23).[51] The Logos "broods," which can mean to breed or to hatch—and to think or ponder. Milton seems to agree with Plotinus, who says that, according to the "mystical wisdom of the ancient sages, the phallic symbols on terminal statues of Hermes suggest that all generation derives from the mind" (*Enneads*, III, vi, 19).[52]

The ancient Greeks, it seems, believed that the head was the source of the human seed, as demonstrated by its fertility in growing hair: the head is the life or the seat of life. Thus when Odysseus must confront Circe's drugs and magic, Hermes gives him moly: "Go with this goodly herb to Kirkē's halls that it may ward off from your head the evil day" (*Odyssey*, X, 286 ff.).[53] Hermes, the messenger of Zeus, the guide of souls, the mediator between heaven and earth, was for the Greeks, "the λόγιος, the personification of all that is bright and clear in thought, he is, one might say, the logos in its articulate utterances. . . . He is by no means only a heavenly being, he is also of the earth, and for that very reason, since he knows them, able to combat the chthonic powers."[54] Hermes thus represents both mind and phallus. And moly, the gift of Hermes, has the same significance. Its black root and bright blossom suggested the dual nature of man and his ability to heal this spiritual division by "tearing his own roots out of the dark and lifting them up to the light, for only thus do the roots become capable of making him whole."[55] For neo-Platonists, moly "stood for παιδεία, the spiritual education of man that would enable him to raise the power of the light within him and so dispel the darkness of his earthly and sensual being" (Rahner, p. 198). For alchemists, moly represented the philosopher's stone, which made possible the transmutation of base metals to gold (p. 219). The association of head and phallus thus seems intimately associated with hermetic transmutation or the transformation of consciousness. Erich Neumann observes that the close symbolic connection between head and phallus is "of the utmost significance in the mythological stages of conscious development," for the power of the head arises from the ascendance of psychic energy; the head is the higher phallus or higher masculinity, in Bachofen's terms the Apollonian rather than Dionysian or phallic sun.[56]

Here, however, we have run into a contradiction. Does all generation, as Plotinus says, derive from the mind, or does the power of mind derive from the generative powers? A consideration of the historical development of the *herm,* the stone pillar from which Hermes developed, suggests the latter, for the aniconic form of the god was a phallic *herm;* gradually the god became more anthropomorphic in conception. "He was given a phallus to promote fertility, and finally emerged as a fully human figure."[57] The head thus arises from the phallus. As Blake says, the Devil's version of the Fall is that the Messiah fell and formed a heaven of what he stole from the abyss. The development of Hermes parallels that of Osiris, who was first associated with the phallus and fertility and represented by the *djed* pillar, a phallic symbol. Gradually the *djed* became humanized, the lower part of it being associated with the backbone of the dismembered Osiris and the upper part with his head. Thus the symbol of Osiris' immortality finally becomes the head; the lower principle of immortality, the phallus, is raised up: "I am Osiris, the Lord of the heads that live, mighty of breast and powerful of back, with a phallus which goeth to the remotest men and women. . . . I have become a spirit." The dismembered god has been reunited: "I have made myself whole and complete." This self-transformation, resurrection, and sublimation, Neumann points out, "is described in Egyptian texts as the union of Osiris, God of the Underworld, with the Sun-God, Ra."[58] Like Jesus, Osiris proves that "I and the Father are one."

The Son mounted on the omnipotent paternal chariot in *Paradise Lost* seems to express the same idea: solar or psychic energy raised to a higher power, the energies of the body harnessed in service of the Logos. The emphasis on wholeness in the depiction of the chariot and in the related mythological material suggests that this sort of sublimation is compatible, or more precisely, synonymous, with wholeness, with the integration of the psyche. Ungoverned instincts are chaotic and divisive. Man is made whole, not by the elimination or suppression of these instincts, but by transforming them: "Rather must all these mobile or static forces, seized by the soul's rapture, plunge of their own accord, as it were, into the mightiness of decision and dissolve within it. Until the soul as form has such great power over the soul as matter, until chaos is subdued and shaped into cosmos, what an immense resistance!"[59]

Our consideration of solar symbolism in Milton thus leads to the problem of sublimation, a word that has alchemical overtones. The essence of Milton's vision, the transmutation of physical energies to spiritual, might be called alchemical. Michael Lieb has shown how important alchemical concepts are to Milton's handling of creation in *Paradise Lost*.[60] According to Jung the aim of alchemy was "to produce a *corpus subtile*, a transfigured and resurrected body, i.e., a body that was at the same time spirit."[61] Milton was fascinated by this possibility, as we see in *A Mask* (460 ff.) and *Paradise Lost* (V, 469 ff.). The "Chemical Marriage" between spirit and body took place in the hermetic vessel or egg—the *rotundum*—whose spherical shape signified wholeness, the regaining of man's integral nature. The *rotundum* was also transparent, which indicated its connection with the soul: "It is none other than consciousness deflected from the outer world and turned inwards, thus constituting, so to say,

an isolated sphere."[62] The *rotundum* thus naturally became associated with the head, which is round, and "the abode of the divine
part, namely the soul." The head or brain participates in the alchemical process, a fact which led Albertus Magnus to believe that gold is
formed in the head.[63] Jung says that "as far back as Zosimos [a Greek
neo-Platonic philosopher of the third century] we find the philosophers described as 'children of the golden head.'"[64] A Hermetic
treatise entitled ὁ κραγήρ ("the crater" or "cup") says:

After the creation of the world, God filled this vessel [the divine vessel of
transmutation, that is, the human body, particularly the head] with nous
(νοῦς =pneuma) and sent it down to earth as a kind of baptismal font. By
doing so God gave man, who wished to free himself from his natural,
imperfect, sleeping state of ἄνοια (or, as we should say, insufficient consciousness) an opportunity to dip himself in the nous and thus partake of the
higher state of ἔννοια, i.e., enlightenment or higher consciousness. . . . The
nous is thus a kind of βαφεῖον, dyestuff or tincture, that ennobles base
substances. Its function is the exact equivalent of the tincturing stone-
extract, which is also a pneuma.[65]

The *rotundum* is thus the head or sun, the container of *nous*, the
active, masculine, generative side of the psyche; yet as such it is also
the *sol niger* or "black sun," sunk in the darkness of the unconscious.
The ambivalent *rotundum*, as its name suggests, stands at the beginning as well as at the end of the great work.[66] Sol is the *prima materia*
as well as the resulting gold tincture, or in other words both phallus
and head. It is for this reason that the alchemical athanor or oven,
which contains the egg-shaped glass vessel or *rotundum*, has a
phallic shape. The fire of transmutation corresponds to the "generative power, which is first aroused and then tamed in order to serve
inward contemplation."[67] Thomas Vaughan, in his *Euphrates*,
speaks eloquently of this inward or original fire, "which Paracelsus
calls the Archaeus and Sendivogius the Central Sun," and which lies
imprisoned and unseen in the earth, yet which gives rise to sun and
stars in the world and to the brightness of the human countenance:
"All the brightness of man is in his face, for there he sheds his light at
the eyes; but the first source of it, namely, that fire which is at the
heart, is no more seen than that which is in the earth." And in *Magia
Adamica* he expounds on the correspondences between above and
below in terms very like those of Raphael in *Paradise Lost*, who says

mysteriously, "though what if earth / Be but the shadow of heaven, and things therein / Each to other like, more than on earth is thought?" (V, 574–76):

To speak plainly [says Vaughan], heaven itself was originally extracted from inferiors, yet not so entirely but some portion of the heavenly natures remained here below and are the very same in essence and substance with the separated stars and skies. Heaven here below differs not from that above but in her capacity and that above differs not from this below but in her liberty. The one is imprisoned in the matter, the other is freed from the grossness and impurities of it; but they are both of one and the same nature, so that they easily unite.[68]

Jung interprets the *sol niger* as the "provisional extinction of the conscious standpoint owing to an invasion from the unconscious." The alchemist Ripley says that "You must go through the gate of blackness if you would gain the light of Paradise in the whiteness."[69] Jung concludes: "The sun is evidently an instrument in the physiological and psychological drama of return to the prima materia, the death that must be undergone if man is to get back to the original condition of the simple elements and attain the incorrupt nature of the pre-worldly paradise."[70] The *sol niger* thus coincides with the *nigredo* and *putrefactio,* the stage of death. In terms of the mythological stages of evolving consciousness described by Neumann, the *sol niger* seems analogous to the dragon fight, in which the "successful masculinization of the ego finds expression in its combativeness and readiness to expose itself to the danger which the dragon [the unconscious] symbolizes":

This struggle is variously represented as the entry into the cave, the descent to the underworld, or as being swallowed—i.e., incest with the mother. This is shown most clearly in the hero myths which take the form of sun myths; here the swallowing of the hero by the dragon—night, sea, underworld —corresponds to the sun's nocturnal journey, from which it emerges victoriously after having conquered the darkness.[71]

The *sol niger* is thus the "night-sea journey" of the sun hero, the active exposure of the hero "to the dangerous influence of the female, and the overcoming of man's immemorial fear of woman" (Neumann, p. 156), a consciously willed descent into hell or the womb in order to kill the terrible female aspect of the Great Mother and "to liberate the fruitful and bountiful aspect" (p. 163). In this way the hero is reborn by descending again into the womb, bravely undertaking what Neumann calls "regenerative incest"; the hero wins his *anima*, his other feminine half, his creative soul, freeing the princess from the dragon, an act analogous to the alchemical liberation of the soul from matter: "Gold comes into being only through the liberation of the divine soul or pneuma from the chains of the flesh."[72]

The night-sea journey, or something akin to it, is central in Milton's poetry. The Lady in *A Mask* descends into the forest of the unconscious, undergoes a deathlike trance in Comus' enchanted chair, then rises to a higher life. Lycidas and Samson plunge violently from noon to midnight, and each is reborn, in a way, as the *sol invictus*. In *Paradise Lost*, the Fall of Man leads to death, yet also is a *felix culpa* that brings about a happier paradise within. Adamson comments that the "pattern of harmonious creation, rebellion with attendant chaos, and re-creation through the Logos becomes one of the basic patterns of all of Milton's poetry."[73] Destruction, it seems, is an essential part of the process of creation. One thinks of Hegel's moving tribute to the negative in the development of the world spirit: "But not the life that shrinks from death and keeps itself undefiled by devastation, but the life that endures, and preserves itself through, death is the life of the spirit. Spirit gains its truth only by finding itself in absolute dismemberment." Spirit looks the negative in the face and abides with it: "This abiding is the magic force which converts the negative into being."[74] Kaufmann notes that Hegel is alluding to Dionysus Zagreus, who was dismembered but who was ever reborn. For Hegel, consciousness, self-consciousness, or reason is the negative since it can become conscious of itself only by dividing itself into subject and object. Spirit produces its own double, becomes an other to itself—rends itself—but then mediates or sublimates[75] this otherness by taking the object back into consciousness, into the subject, into a higher unity which preserves otherness. Yet it transcends this division by recognizing that subject and object, spirit and matter, are mutually dependent (as are subject and predicate) and that as such the object is not "outside" the subject, an activity directed against it, but rather part of its own self-movement. The negative, the division between ego and object, is the soul or moving power of spirit since it gives rise to the world process which we call experience or life. Being is the whole that perfects itself through self-division (that is, becoming): "The true is its own becoming, the circle that presupposes its end as its aim and thus has it for its beginning—that which is actual only through its execution and end" (p. 30). In short, becoming is an essential part of the realization of Being. The self returns to itself, regaining the wholeness it had at the beginning, for "the self is the identity and simplicity that relates itself to itself" (p. 34).

Hegel's account of the triadic development of consciousness (wholeness, division, higher wholeness) finds an interesting parallel in Neumann's account of the evolution of consciousness. According to Neumann, consciousness evolves from the primal matrix, the undifferentiated ocean of the unconscious, symbolized by the Uroboros, the circular snake biting its own tail. In its prenatal stage the undeveloped germ of ego consciousness sleeps in the ocean of the All; in the succeeding divisive stage the waking ego struggles for independence against the unconscious realm of the Great Mother; and finally, if all goes well, the mature individual attains individuation or centroversion, a stage in which the primal unity is regained in higher form through the conscious realization of the essential unity of the psyche.[76]

Neumann points out that this development resembles the Hermetic process in alchemy. In Hermetic tradition, universal nature in its latent condition is represented as a coiled-up serpent, the "dragon Uroboros." Nature in its dynamic or awakened phase, on the other hand, is represented by two serpents wound around an axis in opposing directions—the caduceus of Hermes. In alchemy the two serpents symbolize the opposing forces of sulphur and quicksilver, activity and passivity, masculine and feminine, form and matter, spirit and soul. These forces war against each other savagely so long as nature remains untamed; but the struggle is necessary, for they must "kill" each other (cf. the dragon fight) and dissolve in order to be reborn in a "nobler and better form":

This fable supplements the Hermetic myth of the Staff of Hermes. Hermes or Mercury struck with his staff a pair of serpents in combat with one another. The blow tamed the serpents, which wound themselves round his staff and conferred on him the theurgic power of "binding" and "loosing." This means the transmutation of chaos into cosmos, of conflict into order, through the power of a spiritual act, which both discriminates and unites.[77]

This discrimination or dismemberment resembles Hegel's power of the negative. The blow must be struck, the serpents severed, before they can join fruitfully: Discrimination is essential to unity.

So also, in Spenser's "An Hymne in Honour of Love," Eros creates the world by rising out of chaos, "Whose sundrie parts he from them selves did sever, / The which before had lyen confused ever" (76–77). This separation causes the now distinct elements to war against each other: "Ayre hated earth, and water hated fyre, / Til Love relented their rebellious yre" (83–84) by "tempering goodly well / Their contrary dislikes with loved meanes" (85–86). Order is a *concordia discors;* and only with this order comes the possibility of transmutation. Since each element has a quality in common with its neighbor ("loved meanes"), the elements do not only coexist but also may be transformed into one another through an exchange of qualities, a view of the old physics that is the basis of alchemical speculation. A way is provided, therefore, for matter to work its way up to spirit: A higher unity arises out of division, creation out of destruction. As Milton says in the *Reason of Church-Government*, "if we look but on the nature of elementall and mixt things, we know they cannot suffer any change of one kind, or quality into another without the struggl of contrarieties."[78]

The descent of the sun to the underworld, the "struggl of contrarieties" or death that must be undergone in order to achieve transcendence, may best be illustrated by what seems to be the most Hermetic of Milton's works, *A Mask*. We have seen that the "sun-clad power of chastity" is symbolized by the "snaky-headed Gorgon shield / That wise Minerva wore" (446–47), and that Conti allegorized the Gorgon's head as the sun. We have also seen that the serpent is the beast of Helios, a symbol of the rejuvenating power or life force. We should distinguish, however, between the Gorgon *per se* and as it appears on Athene's shield. Of itself the Gorgon seems to represent solar power in its chthonic form, the *sol niger* or nocturnal sun, sunk in the darkness of the unconscious.[79] The Gorgon also seems to have been associated with the ugly, Erinys side of the Great Mother Goddess who rules over wild animals: The Great Mother, with uncouth, grimacing face, appears in early Asiatic and Ionian works of art surrounded by birds, lions, or snakes.[80] In *A Mask* this

frightening, Gorgonic power of the Great Mother is embodied in
Circe, also a mistress of wild beasts and the "daughter of the Sun"
(51), whom Conti allegorized as the generative principle in nature.[81]
Comus, or intemperance, is thus the offspring of libido, which is in
turn the product of the sun.

In *A Mask*, then, both the Lady and Circe are associated with the
sun: We have a conflict between two views of solar power, one
associating it with the body, the other with chastity. More precisely,
the Lady and Comus struggle for the possession of psychic energy; if
the Lady should win, she would appropriate the power of the Gorgon as did the wise Athene, "unconquered virgin, / Wherewith she
freezed her foes to congealed stone" (447–48). The real subject of *A
Mask* is what Jung calls the transformation of libido, a transformation
signified by the Gorgon on Athene's aegis. According to Neumann,
the fact that Athene wears the Gorgon's head on her shield signifies
her victory over the Great Mother of the unconscious. Athene, born
from the head of Zeus, is motherless; as she says in the *Oresteia*, she
upholds the father's claim and male supremacy in all things. Thus,
Perseus is able to kill the Gorgon with her shield, which he uses as a
mirror to see the Gorgon's head reflected. The reflecting shield here
becomes a symbol of consciousness: "The power of the Great
Mother is too overwhelming for any consciousness to tackle direct.
Only by indirect means, when reflected in Athene's mirror, can the
Gorgon be destroyed—in other words, only with the help of the
patron goddess of consciousness, who, as the daughter of Zeus,
stands for 'heaven.'"[82] Unconscious forces can be tamed by being
raised to reflective consciousness. With the help of Athene libido is
freed from the Great Mother and spiritualized, a process symbolized, according to Neumann, by Perseus' winged horse Pegasus:
The chthonic-phallic is given wings. So also in *A Mask*—if Circe can
reduce one to the level of a beast, the mastery of Circe reveals a
world of "clear dream, and solemn vision" (456), commerce with
which will

> Begin to cast a beam on the outward shape,
> The unpolluted temple of the mind,
> And turns it by degrees to the soul's essence,
> Till all be made immortal.   (459–62)

The Lady, therefore, like Lycidas and Samson, descends into and rises out of the unconscious realm. We have not space for a detailed analysis of *A Mask*. I should like merely to comment upon the Lady's paralysis in Comus' enchanted chair. When the Attendant Spirit and the brothers rout Comus, they forget to steal his wand: "without his rod reversed, / And backward mutters of dissevering power, / We cannot free the Lady that sits here / In stony fetters fixed, and motionless" (815–18). The "rod reversed" may signify, as Wilson Knight says, the reversal and redirection of instinct: "But the rod is lost, instinct sunk in repression."[83] This insight is supported by Sears Jayne's observation that it is the Lady's *rejection* of Comus that results in her being paralyzed.[84] Instead of being redirected, instinct has been rejected or repressed. It appears that the introduction of haemony, like its prototype moly a symbol of reason, philosophical knowledge, or the Logos, causes a self-division leading to a stalemate, a kind of death to both mind and body: The Lady can neither speak nor move. That Comus is driven away suggests a complete disjunction between spirit and nature: They have killed each other. But this symbolic death is necessary, it seems, so that mind and body may be reborn in a higher unity.

The Lady finally must be freed from her paralysis by Sabrina, and it is significant that she must be "right invoked in warbled song" (853). The Attendant Spirit has come down from heaven to help the innocent Lady, but her liberation cannot be effected by him alone, which suggests, as Richard Neuse says, the limitations of pure spirit.[85] The liberating power ultimately comes, not from above, but from below—from the bottom of the river. I believe Neuse is correct in interpreting Sabrina, the river goddess, as the lower, unconscious life of nature (p. 94). Yet since the Attendant Spirit has the magical power of song with which to induce Sabrina to "unlock / The clasping charm, and thaw the numbing spell" (851–52), it is, perhaps, not so much a matter of the limitation of spirit as of its operation. As we have seen, haemony and the power of Orpheus' song are both associated with the Logos, the rational soul that controls the lower instincts. Yet while haemony causes sharp division and repression, Orpheus' song brings about sublimation: Orpheus charms nature into doing his bidding by the beauty of his song. In *A Mask*, Milton carefully distinguishes between the powers and effects of haemony and of song, haemony signifying the power to know and to resist Comus ("for by this means / I knew the foul enchanter though disguised" [643–44]), and song the power to transform and reorder the forces that Comus has debased. Haemony therefore precedes song in a two-stage operation of the Logos: Discrimination or division precedes unifying transmutation. Sabrina, then, who was drowned but "underwent a quick immortal change" (840), can represent man's lower nature "transformed . . . no longer in conflict with spirit and reason, but . . . harmoniously responsive to them."[86] The Lady can be freed only when water, the realm of the unconscious, no longer is an enemy to the lyrelike soul but acquires baptismal powers of regeneration. As Sabrina's death by water brought about "a quick immortal change," so that she "with moist curb sways the smooth Severn stream" (824)—cf. Lycidas as "genius of the shore"—so her baptism of the Lady suggests that the Lady, by dying to the old self and putting on the new, now controls and is sustained by the very powers that before threatened to destroy her. Now she can follow her daemon and climb "Higher than the sphery chime" (1020). The dragon has been tamed and now protects and nourishes the tree of life, from which bloom the golden apples of chastity.

    This analysis of Milton's solar mysticism supports the remark of Michael Lieb that the central pattern in *Paradise Lost*—and indeed, we might add, in nearly all of Milton's poetry—"is one in which union proceeds through destruction to reunion. Destruction thereby becomes the vehicle by which the ultimate state is attained."[87] The Hermetic process certainly helps one to understand better the role of conflict and destruction in Milton's works.

    Yet when all is said and done, Milton's idea of transformation may ultimately differ from that of alchemy. Broadbent finds sadistic elements in the triumph of the Son, mounted in the omnipotent paternal chariot, over the rebel angels in *Paradise Lost*. He objects that the phallic associations of the chariot show a confusion between spiritual power and "a masculine eroto-motive force that is naturally as blindly destructive as creative," between the Logos, symbolized by the chariot's multitude of eyes, and the "careening spermatazoa," the sheer potency, of the Son's triumph, and concludes that the chariot, for all its eyes, symbolizes destructive rather than creative power.[88]

Part of this criticism might be answered by remarking that the chariot is the higher phallus or head, so that its destructiveness is not simply sexual. Furthermore, this destructiveness might be seen as part of an alchemical process. Lieb relates the chariot to the alchemical *rotundum* and interprets the Son's triumph as the "transmutation of corrupt matter [the rebel angels] to its *nigredo* state as a prelude to regeneration." The rebel angels are returned to the chaos of *prima materia* as part of a process by which the universe will be purged of impurity and God will become All in All.[89]

The difficulty here is that the rebels themselves are not regenerated. At the end of the world God will not quite be All in All since Hell will still exist: "hell her numbers full, / Thenceforth shall be for ever shut" (*PL* III, 332–33). Corrupt matter has not entirely been transmuted to spirit. This ultimate dualism seems related to Milton's enthusiastic emphasis upon destruction in his depiction of the chariot, which in Book VII has nowhere near as important a role in the process of creation. So also in the Nativity ode the evil powers of nature are not assimilated but expelled. Though one might argue that nature is redeemed, the redemption seems to involve the emasculation of nature, the overthrow of the "scaly horror" of the dragon's "folded tail." Broadbent, in his essay on the ode, argues that Milton betrays "incest anxiety" in his hysterical repudiation of the intercourse between sky and earth.[90] Here there is no regenerative incest: The sun has banished its shadow.

Samson shows the same hysteria in his rejection of Dalila ("My wife, my traitress, let her not come near me" [725]); and he too emasculates the worshipers of the fish-tailed Dagon, in a way, by pulling down the theater upon their heads. Recalling the phallic associations of the head, it is significant that the Son, "Girt with omnipotence" (*PL* VII, 194), rides over the "helmed heads" (*PL* VI, 840) of the prostrate rebels. An echo of this emasculation or dismemberment of nature finds its way even into *A Mask* when the Lady warns Comus that, if she wished, she could kindle her sun-clad power of chastity "To such a flame of sacred vehemence" that "the brute Earth would lend her nerves and shake, / Till all thy magic structures reared so high, / Were shattered into heaps o'er thy false head" (792–98). Just as the Bacchae dismembered Orpheus, tearing his head from his body, so the Lady, like Samson, threatens to "pay my underminers in their coin" (*SA*, 1204).

In short, the threat of one kind of dismemberment is countered by another. For the most part, the Miltonic solar hero can attain transcendence only through destruction, through what Neumann calls "patriarchal castration," the mortification of the lower masculinity in the interests of the higher, through the enfeebling of the feminine side of the psyche, to which the lower masculinity belongs. Fearful of being submerged, striving for the heights, the sun hero tries to sever himself from the mother.[91] In alchemy, it is true, gold comes into being through the liberation of the divine soul from the chains of the flesh, yet in this liberation the awakening antagonism between Sol and Luna involves their mutual transformation and interpenetration, so that ultimately they are united, like man and woman, in the "Chemical Marriage." The imperfect coagulations of the soul are dissolved, the soul reduced to its *materia* and then crystallized anew in a nobler form. Matter is thus redeemed because it is latently divine, an aspect of God. And the alchemical work, we are told, can be accomplished, not through the violation of nature, but only in unison with it: "The progress of the work pleases nature greatly."[92] Though in Milton, particularly *Paradise Lost*, we can find the idea that matter is divine, one does not often feel that the transformation of the psyche which is Milton's major concern "pleases nature greatly." These matters are, of course, highly obscure and deserve further study.

We may conclude, then, that in Milton there is for the most part no "Chemical Marriage," because spirit can thrive only at the expense of matter. An illuminating statement in this regard may be found in the *Second Defence*. In answering an attack upon his blindness as a judgment of God, Milton argues that, far from being a curse, his blindness is a blessing, a sign of election that makes him godlike, almost too sacred to attack:

There is a certain road which leads through weakness, as the apostle teaches, to the greatest strength. May I be entirely helpless, provided that in my weakness there may arise all the more powerfully this immortal and more perfect strength; provided that in my shadows the light of the divine countenance may shine forth all the more clearly. For then I shall be at once the weakest and the strongest, at the same time blind and most keen in vision. By this infirmity may I be perfected, by this completed. So in this darkness, may I be clothed in light. (YP, IV, pt. 1, pp. 589–90)

Bodily infirmity invigorates the energies of his rational and immortal spirit: Completion ("by this completed") or integration paradoxically comes from dismemberment. This is the power of the negative with a vengeance.

In an important article, Ernest Sirluck has conjectured that around 1637 Milton took upon himself a vow of chastity in order to hasten the flowering of his inward ripeness, and that after the failure of his first marriage Milton lost his poetic inspiration for twenty years, only regaining it after he was blind. Blindness then replaced chastity as the symbol of poetic creativity.[93] It thus appears that for Milton creativity is inseparable from asceticism, from symbolic castration or dismemberment.

One feels in Milton what Edmund Wilson feels in Sophocles' *Philoctetes:* "the conception of superior strength as inseparable from disability." Wilson concludes from his study of Philoctetes' wound that "genius and disease, like strength and mutilation, may be inextricably bound up together."[94] The strength of Philoctetes' invincible bow was proportional to the gravity of his incurable wound, which occurred when he was bitten in the foot by a snake while offering a sacrifice to the nymph Chryse. The foot, as Jung notes, has a chthonic and phallic significance, since it is in contact with mother earth ("Oedipus"="Swell-foot"); and he interprets Philoctetes' wound as being caused by the rejection of the unconscious: According to a scholiast, Chryse cursed Philoctetes when he rejected her love.[95]

In connection with the wound of Philoctetes, it is interesting to note that in mythology fire gods and sun heroes often are deformed, lame, or missing a limb.[96] Hephaestus and Ptah are crippled, Polyphemus has his eye gouged out, Prometheus is tortured by an eagle that gnaws his liver by day. According to a talmudic tradition, Samson was lame in both feet.[97] In an African tale, a boy steals fire from heaven and is made lame by the vengeful sky god. Culture has its price. Unconsciousness may be, as Teilhard de Chardin says, echoing Hegel, "a sort of ontological inferiority or evil, since the world can only fulfill itself in so far as it expresses itself in a systematic and reflective perception."[98] Yet the birth of consciousness, though it is a triumph, is also a fall from primordial unity—a destructive act of dismemberment: consciousness is dis-ease. As Freud observed, the development of civilization inevitably involves a certain amount of neurosis. Whether or not psychic wholeness can be regained at a higher level by means of sublimation remains an open question. The work of Milton, at any rate, is an awesome exemplification of Bachelard's remark that "man is perhaps the first natural object in which nature has tried to contradict itself."[99]

Geneseo, New York

NOTES

1. *Republic*, VI. 508b, trans. Francis MacDonald Cornford (New York and London, 1961), p. 219.

2. Chap. 9, trans. Arturo B. Fallico and Herman Shapiro, in *Renaissance Philosophy*, vol. 1, *The Italian Philosophers* (New York, 1967), p. 130.

3. *The Vision of God*, trans. Emma Gurney Salter (New York, 1960), p. 38. On Nicholas and the Renaissance hieroglyph of the winged eye of God see Edgar Wind's *Pagan Mysteries in the Renaissance*, rev. and enl. ed. (Harmondsworth, Middlesex, 1967), pp. 230 ff. and passim. The sun is naturally associated with the head as well as the eye: Ficino says that the "sign in which the sun reigns, Aries, becomes for this reason the prince of constellations, and represents the head in all living creatures" (*De sole*, p. 121).

4. Thomas Traherne, "The Preparative," in *Centuries, Poems, and Thanksgivings*, ed. H. M. Margoliouth, 2 vols. (Oxford, 1958), vol. II, p. 20, ll. 15–20.

5. From Edwyn Bevan, *Symbolism and Belief* (1938; reprint ed., Boston, 1957), pp. 135, 138.

6. Emile Bréhier, *The Philosophy of Plotinus*, trans. Joseph Thomas (Chicago, 1958), p. 83.

7. *The Origins and History of Consciousness*, trans. R. F. C. Hull (Princeton, 1954), p. 311.

8. M. Esther Harding, *Woman's Mysteries: Ancient and Modern* (1935; rev. ed., New York, 1973), p. 42.

9. Neumann, *Origins and History*, pp. 157–58.

10. Ibid., p. 39.

11. This summary by George Boas comes from the preface to *Myth, Religion, and Mother Right: Selected Writings of J. J. Bachofen*, trans. Ralph Manheim (Princeton, 1967), p. xix.

12. Ibid., pp. 114–15.

13. Robert Graves, *The Greek Myths*, 2 vols. (Baltimore, 1960), vol. I, p. 112.

14. George Sandys, *Ovid's Metamorphosis Englished, Mythologized, and Represented in Figures* (1632), ed. Karl K. Hulley and Stanley T. Vandersall (Lincoln, Nebr., 1970), p. 519. For more background on Orpheus see Caroline W. Mayerson, "The Orpheus Image in *Lycidas*," *PMLA*, LXIV (March 1949), 189–207; Michael

Fixler, "The Orphic Technique of 'L'Allegro' and 'Il Penseroso,'" *ELR*, I, no. 2 (Spring 1971), 165–77; and the illuminating study by John Block Friedman, *Orpheus in the Middle Ages* (Cambridge, Mass., 1970).

15. Friedman, *Orpheus*, pp. 45, 76, 80–83.

16. *Lycidas, The Poems of John Milton*, ed. John Carey and Alastair Fowler (London, 1968), ll. 100–02. All subsequent references to Milton's poetry are to this edition.

17. Other references to eyes in the poem: "opening eye-lids of the morn" (26); flowers as "quaint enamelled eyes, / That on the green turf suck the honied showers" (139–40); and finally the angels in heaven "wipe the tears for ever from his eyes" (181).

18. *Images and Themes in Five Poems by Milton* (Cambridge, Mass., 1962), pp. 50–52.

19. "The Nativity Ode," in *The Living Milton*, ed. Frank Kermode (London, 1960), p. 17.

20. *Poets of Action* (London, 1967), p. 131. Chap. 3 is an abridged version of his *Chariot of Wrath* (London, 1942).

21. See A. B. Chambers, "Chaos in *Paradise Lost*," *JHI*, XXIV (1963), 55–84.

22. Broadbent, "The Nativity Ode," p. 28.

23. See ibid., p. 21; and cf. A. S. P. Woodhouse, who sees the ode as a kind of conversion experience in which Milton repudiates his sensuous elegies to dedicate his talents henceforth to God ("Notes on Milton's Early Development," *UTO*, XIII [1943], 66–101).

24. *Complete Prose Works*, ed. Don M. Wolfe et al. (New Haven, 1953–), vol. I, p. 296. Henceforth cited as YP.

25. Cf. V, 300–02: "while now the mounted sun / Shot down direct his fervid rays to warm / Earth's inmost womb." W. B. C. Watkins has remarked on the "curious phallic symbolism of the eye" in *An Anatomy of Milton's Verse* (1955; reprint ed., Hamden, Conn., 1965), p. 37. Watkins observes that "the sun rarely 'shines' in Milton. He 'impresses his beams' or 'smites' or 'gently penetrates'" (p. 57).

26. For the solar background see Kenneth Fell, "From Myth to Martyrdom: Towards a View of Milton's *Samson Agonistes*," *ES*, XXXIV (1953), 145–55; Neumann, *Origins and History*, pp. 154–60; and Northrop Frye, who has commented on the solar myth in *Samson* in "Agon and Logos: Revolution and Revelation," in *The Prison and the Pinnacle: Papers to Commemorate the Tercentenary of "Paradise Regained" and "Samson Agonistes*," ed. Balachandra Rajan (London, 1973), p. 145.

27. For example, Theodor H. Gaster, *Myth, Legend, and Custom in the Old Testament* (New York, 1969), p. 434.

28. Neumann, *Origins and History*, p. 160. Further light is thrown on the significance of the mill by a statement from *The Doctrine and Discipline of Divorce*, where Milton protests against the rigidity of divorce laws that would force a man "to grind in the mill of an undelighted and servil copulation" (YP, vol. II, p. 258).

29. See C. Kerényi, *The Heroes of the Greeks*, trans. H. J. Rose (London, 1959), pp. 250–51.

30. "The 'Ev'ning Dragon' in *Samson Agonistes*: A Reappraisal," *MLN*, LXXVI (1961), 577–84.

31. Cf. Milton's retraction of his sensuous elegies, where he says that the discovery of Plato enabled him to quench the flames of passion: "My heart is frozen solid, packed around with thick ice; so that even the boy himself is afraid to let the frost get at

his arrows, and Venus fears the strength of a Diomedes" (*Poems*, pp. 231–32).

32. "The Mystery of the Serpent" (an essay on a Gnostic mystery cup), in *The Mysteries: Papers from the Eranos Yearbooks*, vol. 2 (New York, 1955), pp. 194–260, 221.

33. *The Bestiary: A Book of Beasts*, trans. T. H. White (New York, 1960), p. 187. In confrontation with Dalila, Samson compares himself with a serpent: "So much of adder's wisdom I have learnt / To fence my ear against thy sorceries" (936–37).

34. Cf. Roger B. Wilkenfeld, who says the phoenix emblem represents the conjoining of knowledge and power ("Act and Emblem: The Conclusion of *Samson Agonistes*," *ELH*, XXXII [1965], 160–68).

35. *The Psychoanalysis of Fire*, trans. Alan C. M. Ross (Boston, 1968), pp. 16–17.

36. *Iamblichus on the Mysteries of the Egyptians, Chaldeans, and Assyrians*, trans. Thomas Taylor, 3d ed. (London, 1968), pp. 245–46.

37. *The Enchanted Palace: Some Structural Aspects of "Paradise Lost"* (Stockholm, 1967), p. 63.

38. See Walter Clyde Curry, *Milton's Ontology, Cosmogony, and Physics* (Lexington, Ky., 1957), p. 124; and William B. Hunter, "Milton's Materialistic Life Principle," *JEGP*, XLV (1946), 68–76.

39. Qvarnström, *Enchanted Palace*, p. 64.

40. "The War in Heaven: The *Merkabah*," in *Bright Essence: Studies in Milton's Theology*, ed. W. B. Hunter, C. A. Patrides, and J. H. Adamson (Salt Lake City, 1971), pp. 103–14. See also Adamson's earlier, more detailed article, "The War in Heaven: Milton's Version of the *Merkabah*," *JEGP*, LVII (1958), 690–703.

41. *Interpreter's Bible*, vol. 6 (New York and Nashville, 1956), 69–73.

42. Gustav Davidson, *A Dictionary of Angels* (New York, 1967), p. 86.

43. "War in Heaven," *JEGP*, 697.

44. *Bright Essence*, pp. 105–06.

45. "On the Creation of the World," in *The Essential Philo*, ed. Nahum N. Glatzer (New York, 1971), pp. 13–14. On the quaternity, see Michael Lieb, *The Dialectics of Creation: Patterns of Birth and Regeneration in "Paradise Lost"* (Amherst, Mass., 1970), pp. 108–10, n. 1, and p. 232, n. 6; and Maren-Sofie Røstvig, "Structure as Prophecy: the Influence of Biblical Exegesis Upon Theories of Literary Structure," in *Silent Poetry: Essays in Numerological Analysis*, ed. Alastair Fowler (London, 1970), pp. 32–64, esp. pp. 57 ff.

46. C. G. Jung, *Mysterium Coniunctionis: An Inquiry Into the Separation and Synthesis of Psychic Opposites in Alchemy*, trans. R. F. C. Hull (New York, 1963): "Psychologically the vision of Ezekiel is a symbol of the self consisting of four individual creatures and wheels, i.e., of different functions" (pp. 206–07); "The quaternity of the self appears in Ezekiel's vision as the true psychological foundation of the God-concept. God uses it as his vehicle" (p. 208).

47. Second ed., trans. R. F. C. Hull (Princeton, 1967), p. 122.

48. *Psychoanalysis of Fire*, p. 12.

49. *Symbols of Transformation*, p. 123.

50. *Some Graver Subject: An Essay on Paradise Lost* (London, 1960), p. 232.

51. John T. Shawcross, in "The Metaphor of Inspiration in *Paradise Lost*," traces the metaphor of impregnation in the relation between the poet and his muse, the spirit of God (*Th' Upright Heart and Pure*, ed. Amadeus P. Fiore [Pittsburgh, 1967], pp. 75–85).

52. Quoted in Wind, *Pagan Mysteries*, p. 27. There seems to be an etymological

relation between the Indo-European roots for "to know" (GEN[KEN]; also gnā, gnō. L. *gnō-scere;* AS. *cnā-wan.* Ex. gnostic, ignorant, can, ken, know, etc.) and "to beget" (GEN [KEN]; Skt. *jan,* to beget; L. *gi-gn-ere.* Ex. genesis, cosmogony, genus, kin, kind, etc.). See Henry Alden Bunker and Bertram D. Lewin, "A Psychoanalytic Notation on the Root GN, KN, CN," in *Psychoanalysis and Culture: Essays in Honor of Géza Róheim* (New York, 1951), pp. 363–67. Cf. the biblical use of "know" meaning sexual relations.

53. Richard Broxton Onians, *The Origins of European Thought* (Cambridge, 1951), p. 96. See also pp. 108 ff. and 231 ff. The connection between Samson's long hair and physical strength suggests that belief in the fertility of the head was not exclusively Greek.

54. Hugo Rahner, *Greek Myths and Christian Mystery,* trans. Brian Battershaw (1963; reprint ed., New York, 1971), pp. 190–91. Cf. Wind, *Pagan Mysteries:* "To humanists Mercury was above all the 'ingenious' god of the probing intellect, sacred to grammarians and metaphysicians. . . . the revealer of secret or 'Hermetic' knowledge, of which his magical staff became a symbol" (p. 122). According to A. M. Hocart, Hermes, who invented fire and fire-sticks and held the first burnt sacrifice, is analogous to the Vedic solar god Agni (="fire") (*Kings and Councillors: An Essay in the Comparative Anatomy of Human Society,* ed. Rodney Needham [1936; reprint ed., Chicago, 1970], pp. 17–20). Cf. pp. 51–52 in this article and Heraclitus' notion of fire as the Logos.

55. Rahner, *Greek Myths,* p. 180.

56. *Origins and History,* pp. 77, 158 ff. And see Bachofen on the duality of the male generative power, both tellurian and solar, in *Myth, Religion, and Mother Right,* pp. 35–36.

57. W. K. C. Guthrie, *The Greeks and Their Gods* (Boston, 1955), p. 89.

58. Neumann, *Origins and History,* pp. 231, 232, 234.

59. Martin Buber, *Good and Evil* (New York, 1952), p. 129.

60. *The Dialectics of Creation,* appendix, pp. 229–44.

61. C. G. Jung, *Psychology and Alchemy,* 2d ed., trans. R. F. C. Hull (Princeton, 1968), pp. 427–28. Cf. Titus Burckhardt, *Alchemy: Science of the Cosmos, Science of the Soul,* trans. William Stoddart (Baltimore, 1971), p. 83.

62. Burckhardt, *Alchemy,* p. 164.

63. Jung, *Psychology and Alchemy,* pp. 87–88, and *Mysterium Coniunctionis,* pp. 436, 514.

64. "Transformation Symbolism in the Mass," in *Psychology and Religion: West and East,* 2d ed., trans. R. F. C. Hull (Princeton, 1969), p. 240.

65. Jung, *Psychology and Alchemy,* p. 299.

66. See Jung, *Psychology and Alchemy,* p. 88 and fig. 34; see also *Mysterium Coniunctionis,* pp. 92 ff.

67. Burckhardt, *Alchemy,* p. 162. See the athanor illustrated on p. 163.

68. *The Works of Thomas Vaughan,* ed. Arthur Edward Waite (1919; reprint ed., New York, 1968). For the passage from Euphrates see pp. 403–04; for *Magia Adamica,* p. 182. Cf. *PL* V, 469 ff., where we find that spirit and matter differ "but in degree, of kind the same."

69. Jung, *Mysterium Coniunctionis,* p. 98, n. 40.

70. Ibid., p. 99.

71. Neumann, *Origins and History,* pp. 154–55. See also Jung, *Symbols of Transformation,* pp. 210 ff. and 355 ff.

72. Jung, *Mysterium Coniunctionis*, p. 262.

73. "The War in Heaven," *JEGP*, 698.

74. From the preface to *The Phenomenology of the Spirit*, trans. Walter Kaufmann, in *Hegel: Texts and Commentary* (New York, 1966), p. 50.

75. Kaufmann translates Hegel's *aufheben*, which can mean "to cancel, preserve, or lift up," as "sublimate." In sublimation an impulse is also paradoxically preserved, canceled, and lifted up. For discussion see Kaufmann's *Nietzsche: Philosopher, Psychologist, Antichrist*, 3d ed., rev. and enl. (New York, 1968), pp. 263 ff. His whole discussion of Nietzsche's concept of sublimation is illuminating.

76. For a summary see Neumann, *Origins and History*, pp. 409–12.

77. Burckhardt, *Alchemy*, pp. 131–35. A similar story about Tiresias is told by Ovid in Book III of the *Metamorphoses*.

78. YP, vol. I, p. 795. Lieb quotes this passage as central to an understanding of Milton and comments: "The point is that Milton views the world as process: the 'work' . . . is always 'in doing,' forever undergoing constructive 'change' through the 'struggl of contrarieties'" (*Dialectics of Creation*, p. 5, n. 4). Cf. Milton's famous statement in *Areopagitica*: "that which purifies us is triall, and triall is by what is contrary" (YP, vol. II, p. 515).

79. Cf. Hans Leisegang, who cites the *Studien zur Gorgo* (Berlin, 1936) of Kaiser Wilhelm II ("The Mystery of the Serpent," in *The Mysteries*, p. 246).

80. Neumann, *Origins and History*, p. 215, and Jane Harrison, *Prolegomena to the Study of Greek Religion* (3d ed., 1922; reprint ed., New York, 1957), p. 194.

81. Tuve, *Images and Themes*, p. 131.

82. Neumann, *Origins and History*, p. 216.

83. *Poets of Action*, p. 26.

84. "The Subject of Milton's Ludlow *Mask*," reprinted in *Milton: Modern Essays in Criticism*, ed. Arthur E. Barker (New York, 1965), pp. 88–111, 97.

85. "Metamorphosis and Symbolic Action in *Comus*," in *Critical Essays on Milton from ELH* (Baltimore, 1969), pp. 87–102, 93.

86. Ibid., p. 96.

87. *Dialectics of Creation*, p. 85.

88. *Some Graver Subject*, p. 232.

89. *Dialectics of Creation*, p. 233.

90. *Living Milton*, p. 21.

91. Neumann, *Origins and History*, pp. 187–90, 253–54, 385–86. See also R. J. Zwi Werblowsky, *Lucifer and Prometheus: A Study of Milton's Satan* (London, 1952), pp. 31–33.

92. Burckhardt, *Alchemy*, p. 123.

93. "Milton's Idle Right Hand," *JEGP*, LX (1961), 749–85.

94. *The Wound and the Bow: Seven Studies in Literature* (New York, 1959), pp. 287 ff. Years ago my attention was first called to the problem of dismemberment in Milton and to Wilson's essay by the Milton lectures of Professor Edward W. Tayler of Columbia University.

95. Jung, *Symbols of Transformation*, pp. 295, 315.

96. Ibid., p. 239, n. 50.

97. Gerald Massey, "Luniolatry, Ancient and Modern," in *Gerald Massey's Lectures* (1900; reprint ed., New York, 1974), p. 177. Perhaps Satan can be included as a fire god and culture hero: in medieval morality plays Satan could always be recognized by the limp that his portrayer affected—a result (as with Hephaestus) of his fall

from heaven. See the *New Catholic Encyclopedia* (New York, 1967), vol. 12, p. 1094. On the lame sacred king, see Robert Graves, *The White Goddess* (New York, 1958), pp. 355 ff.: "The lame King is almost always associated with the mysteries of smith-craft" (p. 361).

98. *The Phenomenon of Man*, trans. Bernard Wall (New York, 1965), p. 249.

99. *Psychoanalysis of Fire*, p. 76.

THE NON-NARRATIVE APPROACHES TO *PARADISE LOST:* A GENTLE REMONSTRANCE

Burton J. Weber

The critics who have attacked the traditional narrative approach to *Paradise Lost* have not provided satisfactory accounts of the poem. The mythic critics have argued that recurrent symbols provide the poem's structure, and Stanley Fish, the primary exponent of the rhetorical approach, has claimed that the poem is a Platonic dialogue in which the poet deliberately misleads and then corrects the reader. The strained readings and arbitrary assertions of these critics render the hypotheses unlikely. Furthermore, the structures proposed by the mythic critics are loose ones, and the poetic strategy outlined by Fish produces an emotionally arid reading; the mythic critics distort the poem's outline and Fish misrepresents its emotive effects. The non-narrative critics offer structural and thematic objections to the narrative view; but Milton's handling of his materials accords with Aristotelian principles, and Milton *can* achieve his stated didactic ends by narrative means.

P ARADISE LOST is like a picture of leviathan. While a few old men stand in front of it, puzzling it out—"It's backed like a camel"—in walk a confident crew, armed with templates. Placing these over the picture, they say, "See, it's a hawk." While they call in the crowds, one of the old men peeks under the template. Sure enough, the shape of the hawk doesn't fit the picture. And what those youngsters call a claw is really a fin, or flipper. He steps back a moment. Those hawks are badly drawn, too; you can hardly tell them from handsaws. But the crowds have come; the confident men begin their demonstration. The audience nods and beams; the hawkers have their day.

77

I

The gentlemen with the templates are the critics who claim that
Paradise Lost is not a narrative. There are two main groups. The first,
the mythic critics, argue that the poem's structure is provided by
symbolic leitmotifs. I have chosen as their representatives Isabel
MacCaffrey, the founder of the school, and Jackson Cope, its sys-
tematizer. Asserting that the subject of *Paradise Lost* is the "mono-
myth" of separation, initiation, and return, MacCaffrey argues that
mythic thought is spatial rather than temporal. Accordingly,
Paradise Lost is organized not temporally but spatially, its means of
organization being, she says, the "accumulation of meaning in words
that shoot invisible virtue through the poem, parallel actions, similes
of a heightened relevance, symmetrical architectonic structure,"
and, "most important of all," the "creation of definite physical areas
whose relation to one another and to the actors conveys an implicit
'moral' meaning": The poem's structure is provided by symbolic
words, images, incidents, and settings. Cope uses the same basic
ideas in a more concentrated way. Asserting that *Paradise Lost* has
an "atemporal, nonsequential" structure, he argues that the poem is
organized around recurrent symbols, the most important of which
are the archetypal images of rising and falling, and of light and
darkness.[1]

No one would deny that Milton sometimes makes use of symbols; but is his symbolism so prominent and so consistent as to
warrant the claim that it provides the organizational basis of *Paradise
Lost?* Sometimes the claimants force symbolic readings on literal
passages. Identifying the motif of the journey with the second stage
of the mythic pattern, the stage of initiation, MacCaffrey asserts that
"wander" is a "key word" in *Paradise Lost,* "summarizing the theme
of the erring, bewildered human pilgrimage." She draws attention to
the presence of the word in a passage she terms "suggestive," Eve's
lament for the loss of Eden (II, 268–85). Eve asks, "whither" she will
"wander down / into a lower world" a world "obscure / And wild,"
and she asks how she and Adam can "breathe in other air less pure,
accustomed to immortal fruits." Arguing that the description of the
"lower world" relies on the poem's archetypal light imagery,
MacCaffrey glosses the passage thus: "*Obscure* because farther removed from the fountain of light, and because the planets that

illuminate it have been turned oblique; *wild* because nature is now hostile; its air *less pure* than the clear brilliance of Paradise." The word "wander," MacCaffrey explains, represents Eve's "recognition of her loss." She fails to notice, however, that viewed in their context, Eve's words have less remote, less symbolic senses. She does not quote, or consider, the opening of Eve's sentence. Eve, turning from her flowers, says, "Thee lastly, nuptial bower, by me adorned / With what to sight or smell was sweet; from thee / How shall I part, and whither wander down?" Eve is contrasting the "lower world" with the nuptial bower. That world is "obscure" because it lacks the bright flowers, its air "less pure" because it lacks the sweet spices with which she adorned the bower. It is "wild" because it has no place consecrated to man's use. Eve is lamenting the loss of her home, and in the word "wander" she complains that in the new world she will have no home toward which to direct her steps.[2]

The dramatic context, furthermore—Michael's reply (XI, 287–92) and Eve's later reference to her plaint (XII, 614–19)—suggests that the passage is ethical rather than mythic. In her opening outcry, "O unexpected stroke, worse than of Death!" Eve protests God's order. Later, imagining compliance, she thinks only of an unwilling departure. Michael gently explains the meaning of these choices. To set her heart on Eden, to think of staying in defiance of God's order, is to repeat the Fall: "nor set thy heart . . . on that which is not thine" delicately reminds Eve of her theft of the forbidden fruit. Going unwillingly, Michael continues, would be a violation of Eve's role as helpmeet. Cautioning Eve, "Thy going is not lonely; with thee goes / Thy husband, him to follow thou art bound," Michael warns her that she is overvaluing the comforts of her garden and her home and failing to honor the husband whose presence will keep her steps from being aimless. Thus, Michael opens a third alternative, that of willing departure, and after the dream, which strengthens and instructs Eve as Adam is strengthened and instructed during Michael's prophecy, Eve accepts this alternative. The propitious dream reconciles her to God's ways, and Eve next rights her relationship to her husband. Telling Adam, "Thou to me / Art all things under heaven, all places / Thou," Eve refers to the "thing" she has lamented, her flowers, and to the "place," the nuptial bower. She sets the love of Adam above her sensory pleasures. In the words, "With thee to go, / Is to stay here," she repudiates her apostrophe to the bower, "from thee / How shall I part?" If Milton had been concerned with the three-stage mythic pattern, he would have needed only a mention of the exile from Eden, and a reference to the symbolic act of wandering. Instead, he distinguishes two kinds of exile, willing and unwilling, and he interferes with the symbolic meaning of "wander" by attributing more "err[or]" to staying, refusing to wander, than to wandering. What concerned him, it would seem, was not so much the rendering of a mythic pattern as the discrimination of various moral conditions.

The lines MacCaffrey remarks for their "suggestive[ness]" are literal rather than symbolic, then. Similarly, at what he calls a "signal point in the epic," Cope imposes a symbolic scheme on literal lines. Noting that without scriptural warrant Milton sets Eve's temptation at noon, Cope argues that Milton is seeking a paradoxical elaboration of his light imagery. He is drawing, Cope says, on the exegetical tradition surrounding Psalm xci, whose Vulgate translation speaks of a *daemonio meridiano*, a midday devil. Interestingly, one passage that Cope cites casts doubt on the compatibility of this tradition with the traditions surrounding the Fall. Augustine, glossing David's contrast of the nighttime terrors and pestilence with the daytime arrow and the devil at noon, connects the day with conscious sin, and the night with unconscious sinning. Milton orthodoxly distinguishes between the fall of Eve, who fell "unhappily deceived" (X, 916–17), and that of Adam, who fell "not deceived" (IX, 997–99). To use Augustine's equations, Milton would have had to have contrasted a midnight fall with the noonday one; and in fact he does not mention noon in connection with Adam, the conscious sinner, and does mention it in describing the "unweeting" Eve.[3]

Even if the tradition could have been useful to Milton, the question remains as to whether he used it. He could have chosen noon for literal reasons. As Maurice Kelley long ago observed, there is a tradition that the Fall included all human sins, and if there is traditionally a rational sin associated with Eve, credulity, there is also traditionally a passional sin, gluttony. With respect to that sin, a temptation at ten o'clock or at three in the afternoon would have presented Milton with difficulties. Either Eve's eating would have

implied that God had made the fruit irresistibly tempting, so tempting as to arouse hunger even at an odd hour (Dennis Burden explores
the implications of this at length), or it would have implied that Eve's
primary sin was appetitive. Neither of these implications would
have suited Milton's purposes. A noontime temptation would raise
the subject of appetite quite naturally; it would place no undue
stress on Eve's appetitiveness (Eve would be bound to be hungry at
dinnertime); and it would not give undue emphasis to the attrac-
tiveness of the fruit (food would naturally look good at noon).[4]

If Milton were interested in the symbolic properties of noon, on
the other hand, he would have to call attention to these at what Cope
calls a "signal point in the epic." The description of how the serpent
led Eve to the forbidden tree (IX, 631–45) is a sample of the kind of
formal treatment the occasion demands. In that passage, Milton
chooses two literal details as his points of departure, the speed and
the brightness of the serpent. He then attaches morally suggestive
images to these descriptive pegs: The swift snake "made intricate
seem straight," he glowed like the "delusive light" that "misleads
th' amazed night-wanderer." Milton ends with explicit moralizing or
application: The snake was "To mischief swift," he "glistered" and
"into fraud / Led Eve our credulous mother." Here is Milton's
description of the temptation at noon (IX, 739–43): "Meanwhile the
hour of noon drew on, and waked / An eager appetite, raised by the
smell / So savory of that fruit, which . . . solicited her longing eye."
The passage is a description of Eve's hunger. The senses involved in
that hunger, smell and sight, are described through the stimuli
which act upon them, the scent and color of the fruit. The time of day
is the least prominent element in the description; it provides a
preliminary explanation for the hunger. This is hardly the sort of
explicit emblematic treatment needed to evoke the tradition of the
daemonio meridiano; in fact, it is not even a description of the time
of day. It is, however, the sort of passage one would expect if Milton
had literal reasons for selecting noon as the time of Eve's temptation.

Sometimes the belief that *Paradise Lost* has a consistent symbolic system causes the mythic critics to accept impossible readings.
Satan's voyage from hell to paradise is important to MacCaffrey's
symbolic scheme. It is the main representation of the second stage of
the mythic pattern, the analogue toward which all the imagery of

journeys points. According to MacCaffrey's symbols of light and
space, a journey upward toward the light should image virtue. But
Satan's interviews with Sin and Chaos clearly prove the voyage evil.
Instead of questioning her symbol system, MacCaffrey affirms the
reading. "In the nature of Satan's journey," she says, "we can find,
perhaps, one of the sources of our sympathy, or empathy, with him."
Borrowing the technique of the subjective critics—of whom more
later—MacCaffrey explains the discrepancy between the reading
and the text by appealing to Milton's subconscious intentions:
"Some of Milton's most intimate feelings were certainly involved in
his portrait of Satan. . . . Satan's pilgrimage through the dark toward
Paradise re-traces the necessity that life imposes on us all."[5]

MacCaffrey's book looks back to the age of impressionism, but
Cope, writing from a different and New Critical perspective, appeals
in such cases to ambiguity and paradox. Finding noon symbolism in
the description of the fall of Mulciber (I, 742–46)—"from Morn / To
Noon he fell, from Noon to dewy Eve, / A summer's day"—Cope sets
out to connect this passage with the noonday Fall of Man. Since, in
his symbolic scheme, rising is associated with light, and falling with
darkness, Cope needs a spatial reference to go with the references to
light. This he supplies with an ambiguity in the word "noon," which
had a spatial sense in the Renaissance, he says: It meant "a zenith."
This meaning creates difficulties with the sense, but Cope resolves
the difficulties with a paradox: "One rises to fall . . . and falls to rise."
A second problem Cope himself raises: In this passage, falling is
associated with light rather than with darkness. This problem, too,
Cope solves with an ambiguity: "Noon" also meant "midnight" in
the Renaissance. Here there is also a difficulty with the sense, but
here too paradox can resolve it, the paradox of darkness at noon.
Cope attaches his two paradoxes to the Fall of Man with a third
ambiguity, the "ambiguous promise of a later fall in that description
of how the demon fell 'from Noon to dewy Eve.' " In sum, then,
Mulciber fell on Lemnos like a falling star by falling upward to the
zenith. He fell for a summer's day—a day which ran from morn to
midnight and from midnight to sunset. "From Noon" (perhaps the
phrase meant "at noon" in the Renaissance) the demon fell on the
mother of mankind, whom Milton (do I detect a note of disrespect?)
calls "dewy" Eve. In this passage Cope sees "the whole pattern of

Milton's symbolism overlaid on the apparent idyllic naturalism of the genre miniature of a classical Mulciber." Surely there *is* a discrepancy between the miniature and the overlay. Some dealers, though, think the miniature authentic, and as for the overlay, "Well," they say, "a good restorer. . ."[6]

II

Even if the examples of symbolism proposed by these critics were persuasive, how well would their structural schemes account for the structure of *Paradise Lost?* For MacCaffrey, the main structural divisions of the poem occur at the opening, the beginning of Raphael's narration in Book V, and the invocation to Book VII. These major divisions are supplemented with five subunits which are parallel to one another. These are the interlude in heaven in Book III, Eve's dream, Adam's ascent of the hill of vision in Book XI, the Creation episode, and the building of the bridge of Sin and Death in Book X. The last pair of subunits are related by way of inversion. Cope sets out no such all-over pattern but argues that, of the recurrent images which, he says, unite the poem, one subclass interlinks the following passages: the description of the building of Pandaemonium, the introduction to Beelzebub's speech in the infernal council, the description of the sun when Satan lands there, Uriel's directions to Gabriel, the morning prayer of Adam and Eve, and the introduction to Eve's speech before the Fall. These are puzzling lists of structurally significant points. In the prologue to Book IX, Milton announces a marked change in the direction of his poem. A reader might wonder why this point is not as structurally significant as the opening of Raphael's narration. He might also wonder why, of all the events in the life of Adam and Eve, only Eve's dream and Adam's ascent of the hill of vision were worth singling out. Cope's list sounds like the inventory of a virtuoso: the prayer which resolves a stressful situation, but not the situation; a speech in a transitional episode which prepares for a later scene, but not that scene; two settings without the events that take place there; two introductions without the speeches they introduce.[7]

The critics provide elaborate justifications for their structural accounts. MacCaffrey's three major divisions represent the low, high, and middle points in the poem's spatial organization. The five subunits have a common panoramic vision from a high spot and are related to the three major divisions because the panoramic views suggest the view downward from a mountaintop, while the "great inverted V" formed by the three places of the setting suggests a mountain. In the creation episode there is a voyage down and up, while in the incident of the building of the bridge of Sin and Death there is a voyage up and down. The two complementary voyages repeat the great V of the central pattern. MacCaffrey justifies this structural account by appealing to Milton's description of God's vision: Milton, she says, "transposed the intuitive single glance of God into the poem's mythical structure. Our vision of history becomes, for the time being, that of the Creator, 'whose eye Views all things at one view' (ii.189–90); like him we are stationed on a 'prospect high Wherein past, present, future he beholds' (iii.77–78)." Cope's list is of references to noon, references which build toward the noonday temptation of Eve. Cope associates the noon references with both the imagery of rising and falling and the imagery of light and darkness, the two great sets of recurrent symbols which, he says, provide the poem its "atemporal, nonsequential structure." He defends this structure by comparing *Paradise Lost* to a painting: The poem, he says, is "meticulously structured, as a painting is quite naturally constructed, utilizing spatial line (the basic movement upward and downward within a given area) and the interplay of light and dark tones as both the formal and the meaning pattern"; the poem is a "world of emanating light, 'Light from above, from the fountain of light,' which trickles away into the palpable darkness of hell."[8]

Objections could be raised to the critics' use of metaphor. It might be noted that the metaphors conceal the looseness of the structural schemes. What relation is there between the fact that five scenes in a poem involve a vision downward from above, and the fact that the poem moves from a low setting to a high setting to a middle setting? Only if the changes of place are compared to a "great inverted V" and the V itself is "seen in three dimensions," as a mountain, can the changes of place be united with the five scenes, and then only when those scenes are compared to views from a mountain peak. The scheme is held together only by the critic's metaphor. There is much less patterning in a series of recurrent symbols than in

a painting's balanced set of shapes and colors. The presence or
absence of a shape or color in a painting would make a visible
difference, but references to noon could be removed from the poem
at will. Would there be a noticeable gap if the word "noon" did not
appear in the introduction to Beelzebub's speech? Can the ordinary
reader even remember how the word is introduced? And references
to noon could be displaced at will. "Noon" could be lifted from
Uriel's report to Gabriel and dropped into Uriel's encounter with the
disguised Satan; in fact, speaking of the hypocrisy at the height of
noon, Cope treats the word as if it were present in the earlier scene.[9]
It might also be noted that the critics' metaphors suggest, invalidly,
that their particular structural accounts are as inherently related to
Paradise Lost as a Coleridgean symbol is to its referent. To compare
the poem's structure to God's vision of the universe or to God's
creative effluence is to suggest that the interpretive schemes will of
necessity assert eternal providence or justify the ways of God. In
fact, there is no inherent relationship between the poem and a "great
inverted V" or a series of references to noon. Cope and MacCaffrey
assert by metaphor what they could not prove logically, and when
their metaphors are discounted, their interpretations lose much of
their neatness and much of their apparent applicability.

But even if the accounts are granted this neatness, and granted
an abstract symbolic appropriateness to the subject, they are still
open to the objection that, like Aristotle's circular orbits, they do not
fit the facts. The interpretations attribute importance to insignificant
details and pass over spots of greater prominence. The lists of structurally significant points create a puzzlement which increases when
the schemes are explained. For if the transition from the high to the
middle point of the poem's setting is announced by the poet's request that the heavenly muse, having led him up "Into the heav'n of
heav'ns," guide him "down" to his "native element" (VII, 12–16),
why is there no transition from the low to the high point at the earlier
parallel description of the poet's flight (III, 13–21)—the passage in
which the poet asserts that, having "Escaped the Stygian pool," he
has been "Taught by the Heavenly Muse to venture down / The dark
descent, and up to reascend"? If Milton is carefully building toward
a "signal point in the epic," the temptation at noon, why does he
include among his references to noon an incident which apparently

has no symbolic significance worth mentioning, the noontime visit
of Raphael to Adam and Eve (V, 310–11)? All in all, the poem seems
to have been constructed along lines other than those suggested by
the mythic critics. . .[10]

Perhaps along temporal, sequential lines. The mythic critics of
course deny this, offering two structural arguments. The first stems
from Dr. Johnson's famous comment on the plan of *Paradise Lost,*
that "What is not unexpected cannot surprise." MacCaffrey uses the
passage to argue that Milton is a mythic rather than a narrative writer.
Her argument is restated more bluntly and succinctly by Michael
Wilding: "The poem could hardly succeed if it were organized
primarily on a narrative principle, on the principle of asking 'What
happens next?' We know what happens next, except with minor
unbiblical features such as the Sin and Death allegory. Instead of a
linear narrative, Milton has built a structure of cross-reference,
parallelism, echo, parody, ironic prolepsis; the questions we ask are
'What will be compared to what next, what will presage or re-enact
what next?' "[11]

It does not follow from the fact that Milton chose a historical or
legendary subject that he could not choose to treat that subject
narratively. It is clear what such a choice would entail. The writer
would have to show that what actually took place conformed to the
laws of the probable and possible. Milton does this with ingenuity
and care. Satan must have imbruted himself in the serpent, since
snakes have been punished for his crime; but Milton takes care to
explain why Satan chose this cumbersome mode of disguise when
he had available the easier mode of shape-shifting. Eve must have
been alone when Satan tempted her; but, as Burden has shown,
Milton is much more careful than other writers in explaining how
she came to be alone.[12] A narrative writer treating historical characters would have to show that what they actually did and said
corresponded to what persons of their type would have been likely
to do and say under the circumstances, if not according to the law of
necessity, then according to the law of probability. This Milton does.
Adam and Eve fell in particular ways; but, inventing the incidents of
Eve's gazing at the pool and her question about the stars, Adam's
confession of passion and his question about the stars, Milton shows

that the ways in which each fell were appropriate to their characters, and he treats these characters in terms of the types they represent, the types of Man and Woman. Milton does what a neoclassical poet would be expected to do with a historical subject; and if that subject precluded his supplying surprising answers to the question "What happens next?" it did not preclude his providing interesting answers to the questions "How did these events come about?" "What do these words and deeds reveal about human nature?"

The second argument advanced by the mythic critics is that the dislocations of time in *Paradise Lost* prove that Milton is organizing his poem spatially rather than temporally. MacCaffrey says that Milton substitutes for the *"ab ovo* birth of the story" a "spatially coherent" plan. Cope, borrowing the metaphor that is central to MacCaffrey's structural account, elaborates it thus: "The stage of heaven-earth-hell is set in motion by the circle in which eternity encompasses history, all things happening at once as God looks upon time as a place, which the poet describes as God himself might, nonsequentially narrating the swing from the beginning of history at the first fall to the end of history at the last resurrection." But it does not follow, from the fact that Milton does not tell the history of the world from its beginning to its end in chronological order, that he is not telling a story. There is an obvious alternative explanation for his displacements of time, and this explanation fits the facts. Milton's action is the fall of Adam and Eve. He begins that action at the point at which the pair inadvertently reveal to their enemy the information needed for their overthrow. He ends the story at the point at which the consequences of the Fall are revealed. The events in the lives of Adam and Eve prior to the arrival of Satan he makes relevant to his account of the Fall, narrating them in such a way as to avoid the *Herakliad*'s *ab ovo* chronicle. Avoiding the *Herakliad*'s *ad mortem* chronicle, he omits the later events in the lives of Adam and Eve, events like the births of Cain and Abel. The second action, the fall of Satan, has causal, formal, and thematic relations to the first. Milton narrates this action in such a way as to subordinate it to the main one. He tells directly only that half of the story which is causally relevant to the fall of Adam and Eve, beginning at the point where Satan becomes their potential enemy. He ends abruptly after the completion of Satan's attack; and by inventing for the ending a metamorphosis which reenacts the Fall, Milton ties to the main action the only scene causally unconnected to it.[13]

The half of Satan's story which has no direct causal bearing on the Fall of Man Milton narrates indirectly and out of order. Converting it into an informative exemplum for Adam and Eve, he includes it within the main action. The two episodes of angelic instruction have much history in them, but that history is not presented to the reader by a verse historian in a divinely disordered way. It is presented by characters to characters for reasons necessary to the action. Adam and Eve had to be provided with doctrinal knowledge and with tests of faith if Milton was to portray the final stage in their spiritual evolution as he imagined it, the stage of salvation. It was necessary that Adam be told God's plan for saving mankind, and the first half of Michael's prophecy, his account of the two evils of Satan's bringing, death and sin, not only shows the necessity for God's plan, but provides Adam with moral trials.

Lawrence A. Sasek has shown how conscientiously Milton labored to turn an episode of prophecy into a drama of education. Milton could not have made the Fall morally significant if Adam and Eve were either unaware of their danger or ignorant of the consequences of evil. It was necessary that Adam and Eve be informed about Satan and shown the nature and wages of sin. The function of the second half of Raphael's narration is suggested by an observation of Burden's: "The account of the creation . . . though relying on the Bible for its facts, nevertheless so manipulates those facts that they manifest much more emphatically than they do in Genesis the power and the munificence of God." God's greatness and goodness are the reasons that Adam and Eve should obey and love him, and though Rajan's theory of the alternation of destructive and creative phases does not describe *Paradise Lost* as a whole, it does describe the structure of the angelic narratives: A positive exhortation to goodness follows the negative warning against evil in Raphael's cautionary, as in Michael's curative, instructions. Were it not a pleasure to speak of Milton's narrative skill, it would embarrass me to be the bringer of such old news, the bearer of such stale truths: Surely Milton disorders time not in the interest of a spatial organization, but, like a good neoclassicist, in the interest of an Aristotelian unity of action.[14]

III

Leaving the claim that the poem is a compound of many symbols, I will turn to the view that *Paradise Lost* is, metaphorically speaking, a Platonic dialogue between the writer and the reader. This is the rhetorical view of Stanley Fish. Asserting that the reader is the poem's "centre of reference" and its "subject," Fish argues that Milton's aim is to "educate the reader to an awareness of his position and responsibilities as a fallen man, and to a sense of the distance which separates him from the innocence once his." In order to make the reader aware of his own spiritual imperfections, Milton tempts him to misjudge the poem's situations and characters; he makes the reader "fall again," Fish says, "exactly as Adam did and with Adam's troubled clarity, that is to say, 'not deceived.' "[15] How plausible is this view of Milton's poetic strategy?

First, Fish claims that Milton intends certain misreadings of his poem. The misreadings he designates are mostly those of the subjective critics, the descendants, though sometimes distant descendants, of William Blake. Imposing on Milton's God and Satan his own dichotomy of reason and passion, Blake evaluated the characters in a clearly un-Miltonic way. The subjective critics similarly refuse to grant Milton his premises—sometimes explicitly. A. J. A. Waldock, for instance, says that when a reader's feelings clash with the values of a work, the reader cannot be expected to "anesthetize" temporarily his "emotional nature"—cannot be expected, in other words, to suspend his disbelief. Sometimes the refusal to grant premises is implicit, as when Millicent Bell, failing to ask what Milton means by innocence, supplies her own, non-Miltonic criterion, "liability to temptation." Blake distinguished between Milton's conscious and unconscious allegiances, correlating these with variations in the poem's dramatic effectiveness. The subjective critics have followed his lead, distinguishing conscious and unconscious meanings, contrasting what is intended with what is rendered, arguing from what they consider the dramatically vivid, and disregarding what they think of as the merely stated. I refer, of course, to the well-known procedures of Waldock and E. M. W. Tillyard. The methods of the subjective critics could result in an infinite number of misreadings: A reader could start from any premise and disregard any passage which interfered with his conclusions.

It is hard to see, therefore, how Milton could have planned that readers propose definition A and disregard passage B, when they could have proposed definition B and disregarded passage C.[16]

Fish's answer is that Milton sets up a series of situations which demand a choice between two, and only two, opposed alternatives. Building on Waldock's contention that the reader of Milton often feels a tension between what he has "really read" in a passage and what he knows "Milton is wishing [him] to read into it," Fish asserts that Milton continually forces choices between a wrong and a right interpretation. He argues, for example, that by alluding to the myth of Narcissus in his description of the newly awakened Eve, Milton forces the reader to choose between a wrong view of that allusion— the view that Eve is like Narcissus, and therefore imperfect and doomed to fall—and a right view of the allusion—that Eve is unlike Narcissus, and therefore innocent and free to stand. By tempting the reader to a wrong interpretation, Fish explains, Milton makes him aware of his own spiritual limitations, his tendency to forget or to question God.[17]

Two objections may be made to this view. First, it is doubtful that the poem's materials elicit choices between black-and-white alternatives. If the allusion to Narcissus, for example, were a heterogeneous yoking—a comparison of the aspiring soul to Nimrod's tower, say—then the shock might force the sort of choice Fish outlines. But the scene of Eve's gazing in the pool is not reducible to this kind of juxtaposition of opposites. A passage from Ovid is worked into a new and original action, an action whose closing episodes—God's intervention and Eve's first encounter with Adam—are related to the opening episode, but not to Ovid's tale: It would be unwise, for example, to deduce Milton's Turkish contempt for females from the fact that while Narcissus eventually realizes that he is viewing his own image, Eve requires a nudge from her (heavenly) Father. The action has its parallel elsewhere in the poem. Adam's account of his awakening parallels Eve's gazing in the pool; God's testing of his newly created man parallels his instruction of Eve; and Adam's description of how Eve affects him parallels Eve's description of her feelings about Adam. The structural characteristics of the scene do not pose the question, "Is Eve like or unlike Narcissus?" but ask, rather, for the careful analysis of an action and of its relation to parallel incidents within the poem.

Furthermore, when this analysis is performed, the question, "Is Eve like or unlike Narcissus?" proves only intermittently and obliquely relevant. The action as a whole proves that Eve is capable of errors of feeling—errors which could jeopardize her proper relationship to God and to Adam—but that she has the power to overcome and reject these errors. The parallel shows, first of all, that Eve differs from Adam in ways which accord with Milton's initial description of the two sexes (IV, 290–308), and second, that Eve's emotional limitation differs from Adam's in a way which accords with Milton's depiction of the Fall. To one of these points, Eve's emotional limitation, the question of her relation to Narcissus is relevant; but even here no choice between alternatives is demanded. Eve is like Narcissus in her attraction to beauty (Narcissus is the victim, Ovid says, of the features which made him loved), and love of beauty poses a danger to Eve as it does to Narcissus, for it figures in Eve's later attraction to the forbidden fruit and in her unwillingness to leave the flowers of Eden and her nuptial bower. (The scene at the pool is usually interpreted as evidence of Eve's vanity, but Eve believes that she is admiring not her reflection but some beautiful creature, and Milton does not paraphrase the passage in Ovid in which Narcissus comes to realize that he is admiring his own image and resolves to persist in his hopeless love.) On the other hand, Eve's likeness to Narcissus is carefully qualified. Her capacity for error cannot be thought of as a flaw, for when God inspects his handiwork, he shows no more displeasure with his newly created woman than he showed for the newly awakened Adam.

For a second point, the contrast of the natures of man and woman, Milton makes use of the incident in Ovid but does not allude to Narcissus. As Burden has observed, the longing for companionship that Eve displays at the pool parallels Adam's desire for a mate. But Eve's first act is to seek companionship, while Adam first seeks to know his God: He was created "for God only," she "for God in him." Eve at the pool sees her own beauty and sweetness. These are her proper attributes: She was made for "softness" and "sweet attractive grace." Adam, on the other hand, logically examines his nature and source: He was made for "contemplation." For the other points of the incident, reference to Ovid is irrelevant. Eve learns that spiritual beauty is higher than sensory beauty, and by learning this she honors both God and Adam. In correcting her emotional error,

Eve contrasts with Adam, whose tendency to error requires a stern rebuke from Raphael. As Burden has observed, Milton's portrayal of the Fall relies on 1 Timothy: "Adam was not deceived, but the woman being deceived was in the transgression."[18] Eve's fall is primarily a rational sin, Adam's an emotional sin: He falls "fondly overcome with female charm." Hence, in the anticipatory scenes Eve's emotional limitation is minimized, while Adam's is stressed. The allusion to Narcissus, then, does not have so central a place as Fish assigns it, nor is it of the kind he describes. The pattern of black-and-white alternatives misrepresents the scene, and the misrepresentation casts doubt as well on the account of Milton's strategy.

In the second place, Fish's description of Milton's tactic requires that the choice between alternative interpretations of a scene correlate with a choice between the affirmation and the doubt of God; but even if the existence of alternatives is granted, it is doubtful that these can be correlated with antithetical moral conclusions. If, for example, it is granted that the reader must choose between finding Eve like Narcissus or finding her unlike Narcissus, it does not follow that the reader who finds her like Narcissus must end by doubting God, as Fish contends. Here, as elsewhere, Fish bases his case on the assertions of particular subjective critics. He is thinking of Bell's account of how an Eve vain from the moment of her creation comes step by step to an inevitable doom.[19] But even if a reader believes that Eve has a predilection to vanity, or, preferably, a tendency to put a lower, sensory beauty in the place of the higher love that God has ordained for her, he need not conclude that God has worked shoddily and thereby made Eve's fall inevitable. He may note that it is as much a condition of man's freedom that he be "free to fall" as that he be "Sufficient to have stood." As God says, man's loyalty would have no meaning if he were not free to be disloyal (III, 98–106). Eve's inclination to vanity, or her tendency to overvalue sensory beauty, would merely prove that God had made, not an artificial Eve, but a free moral agent; and since Eve's sufficiency to stand is demonstrated by her final decision to honor the claims of Adam and the ordinances of God, the reader can easily incorporate her likeness to Narcissus within an orthodox reading of the scene. If

what Fish calls the wrong interpretive choice can lead to what he
calls the right moral conclusion as well as to what he calls the wrong
one—and that is true not only with regard to the scene at the pool but
with regard to many of the other scenes he cites—then it may be
doubted that Milton can foresee, control, and utilize the misreadings
of his poem in the way that Fish describes.

Fish's second claim is that Milton rebukes and thereby educates
the readers whose errors he anticipates and intends. Even with
regard to the simplest examples, however, Fish's explanations are
strained. For example, Fish says that the errant reader admires the
rhetoric of Satan's first speech and is rebuked by the commentary
which Milton appends to that speech: "So spake th' apostate
Angel ... Vaunting aloud, but racked with deep despair" (I,
125–26). In that commentary Fish hears an "imperious voice" which
"taunt[s]" the reader thus: " 'I know you *have been* carried away by
what you have just heard; you should not have been; you have made
a mistake, just as I knew you would.' " The simplest explanation for
Milton's commentary is provided by Arnold Stein: that the comment
places Satan's speech in a "larger context"—the context temporarily
obscured by the *medias res* opening. To Fish's alternative reading it
may be objected, first, that Milton's commentary contains no direct
address to the reader and, second, that it is too flat a comment to be
described as an imperious rebuke. In fact, so distant is the paraphrase from the text that the reading would puzzle anyone un-
familiar with Waldock's gloss, which provides Fish his point of
departure. Milton, Waldock says, "will put some glorious thing in
Satan's mouth, then, anxious about the effect of it, will pull us gently
by the sleeve, saying (for this is what it amounts to): 'Do not be
carried away by this fellow: he *sounds* splendid, but take my word
for it.' " Waldock compares Milton's commentary to a direct address
to the reader, and Fish turns Waldock's tentative analogy into a
literal description. Waldock says that the passage contains a gentle
warning, and Fish blows the warning into an imperious rebuke. The
persuasiveness of the argument lies not in the accuracy and justice of
the reading, but in the rhetorical skill with which Fish builds his
unlikely case.[20]

Fish's explanations for his more complicated examples are even more strained. Interpreting the Fall of Man as an uncaused lapse of faith, Fish argues that rational error has nothing to do with Eve's fall. Eve falls, not because she fails to detect Satan's sophistries, but because she consents to reason about matters which she should take on faith. The reader who makes the wrong interpretive choice attempts to understand Eve's fall, and ends by forgiving it. Tempted by the sophistries of Satan's speech to find rational errors in Eve's response, the reader is led to view the antecedent events as a "succession of smaller and understandable failures." Inventing explanations, the errant reader forgets Eve's heinous breach of faith, and, distracted by reason from faith, he falls like Eve. Herein lies his rebuke. The reader who makes the right interpretive choice, on the other hand, hears in Satan's seduction speech (IX, 679–732) unintentional double meanings which, according to Fish, warn against the misapplication of reason and the neglect of faith. Comparing the technique in the passage to that in a "medieval punctuation poem," Fish claims that Satan gives two unintentional warnings to Eve: "Queen of this universe do not believe," and "That ye should be as gods . . . is but proportion meet, I of brute-human, ye of human-gods." The first, Fish explains, tells Eve not to think of herself as the queen of the universe—that is, not to think that her reason makes her its fit judge. The second, Fish paraphrases thus: "If [Satan] is human, he is brutishly human, sub-human, less than human, and as is meet, [Adam and Eve] will become human Gods, humans posing as Gods, not Gods at all." The reader who hears these warnings avoids the sin of heedless Eve.[21]

The same objections may be made to Fish's reading of this scene as to his reading of the incident of Eve's gazing in the pool. It is doubtful that the scene forces the alternatives of either understanding Eve or condemning her, nor must the reader who chooses to understand Eve end by joining her in her defection. As with the scene at the pool, Fish generalizes from the conclusions of a subjective critic. This time the critic is John Peter, whom Fish quotes thus: " 'To brand her [Eve] as infamous requires an effort, and one which the reader is encouraged to neglect.' Merely to analyze the process by which she arrives at her decision, he continues, 'is to go part of the way towards excusing her . . . *tout comprendre, c'est tout pardonner.*' " Burden, however, who finds a rational lapse in Eve's fall, and who traces the antecedent events, does not end by excusing Eve. He shows, rather, how her fall and the events support Milton's thesis and bear on his defense of God.[22]

A more important objection is the arbitrariness of Fish's account. If Milton had wished to indicate that Eve's fall was a lapse of faith—of faith as opposed to reason—then he would have provided Satan a set of arguments as rationally unanswerable as possible, making faith Eve's *only* recourse. Instead he provides him a set of arguments that are not only, as Fish concedes, fallacious—they would have to be fallacious, of course—but, as Waldock has observed, mutually contradictory. The open sophistry of the speech suggests that reason could have saved Eve, and therefore that her fall is a rational sin. But the reader who reaches this reasonable conclusion is, Fish asserts, rebuked. On the other hand, the double meanings Fish proposes are quite unlikely. First of all, the glosses are too strained. "Queen of this universe" has to be glossed as "judge of this universe," and that must be given a particular meaning relating to rational overreaching. "Human Gods" must be glossed not as "superhuman beings" but as "humans posing as Gods." Furthermore, the sentences which result from Fish's repunctuation are ungrammatical. "Queen of this universe do not believe" is a sentence with an omitted word: it must be changed to "do not believe *yourself* queen of this universe" or "do not believe *the* queen of this universe." The sentence which begins "That ye should be as gods" would make sense only if the word "of" were twice omitted: "That ye should be as gods . . . is but proportion meet I [ ] brute-human, ye [ ] human-gods." Yet the reader who, repunctuating Satan's speech in the search for double meanings, finds himself balked by recalcitrant words and uncooperative sentence structures is not rebuked thereby, but rewarded for his "attentive[ness]."[23] Surely justice to Milton requires a protest against the ascription to him of such a procedure.

IV

Supposing, with Burden, that as a neoclassicist Milton believed in the "reasonable disposition of the episodes within a poem" and in the "self-consistency of a poem," and supposing that Milton expected a critic to "systematize a poem in the same way that a com-

mentator will systematize the Bible," a narrative critic might arrive
at a more plausible interpretation of *Paradise Lost*. He would only
have to account for the episodes of the work, not for the misinter-
pretations of those episodes or for the clashes of the misreadings
with the facts of the text. The attempt to systematize these extraneous materials produces Fish's Procrustean lops and stretches.
But Fish rejects a narrative reading, using a thematic argument. He
claims that Milton could not have intended any straightforward
empathetic involvement with the characters of his poem, for an
empathetic response to Satan or to Adam and Eve would cause the
reader to forget or to doubt God—an effect incompatible with
Milton's didactic aims. In order to achieve those aims, Milton turns
the episodes of the story into a series of moral tests for the reader:
The reader's responses rather than the characters or the action are
the center of the poem. The poem's structure is that of trial and
reward. In the first ten books of *Paradise Lost*, Milton tries the
reader. Tempting him to side with God's creatures and to neglect or
spurn the Creator, he rebukes the lapses. In Book XII, Milton rewards the morally purified, providing the now fit reader with a
mystical exaltation, an exaltation which he experiences during the
announcement of the Incarnation of the Son.[24]

This argument may be challenged on grounds of evidence.
First, there is no warrant for the devotional rapture that Fish substitutes for the empathetic feelings aroused by a tragic narrative. Fish
offers doctrinal, structural, and rhetorical proofs for his reading, but
it will suffice to examine his dramatic proof: The other proofs are no
more convincing. Arguing that the reader's exaltation is guided by
Adam's, Fish asserts that during Michael's narration, Adam ceases to
be a pupil and becomes an antiphonal voice in a "ritual dialogue";
and he claims that at the announcement of the Incarnation of the Son,
Adam is lifted "out of himself and out of time into union with the
divine." But if Milton had been rendering a ritual dialogue, he
would not have assigned Adam the pupil's ignorance about the way
in which the Son is to defeat Satan: Adam does not ask a ritual
question, he guesses wrongly. And if Milton were portraying a
mystical union, he would have allowed Adam a speech more lofty
than that which begins, "O goodness infinite, goodness immense!"
(XII, 469–84). Even mystics must descend, says Fish, but Adam's

mundane question suggests the pilgrim rather than the returning flier: "What will betide the few / [Christ's] faithful, left among th' unfaithful herd?" Furthermore, it might be argued that the Incarnation does not have the prominence Fish assigns it, that in his doctrinal summing up—the passage beginning "to obey is best" (XII, 561–73)—Adam places no more stress on Christ than on the redeemed who figure in the other stages of God's redemptive plan. "To obey" may be seen as a reference to the patriarchs (XII, 244–48), the men "obedient to his will" with whom God deigns "To dwell." "To walk as in [God's] presence" would refer, then, to the just (XII, 537–43), the men who have nothing to fear from Christ's Second Coming, their day "of respiration." The apostles and their converts (XII, 485–537) may plausibly be identified with the "good" who triumph, the "weak" and "meek" who overcome the "worldly strong" and "worldly wise"; Adam in promising "ever to observe / [God's] providence, and on him sole depend" would be following *their* example. In this reading, the break in parallelism which occurs at the clause "That suffering for truth's sake / Is fortitude to highest victory" would mark the shift to the example of Christ. But even if the phrase, "Taught this by his [Christ's] example" is taken as referring to the entire list of virtues, and if therefore the references to the patriarchs, the apostles, and the just are seen as references to Christ's analogues, analogues summed up in their original, the speech still tells against Fish's portrait of a mystical Adam; for Adam does not refer to the Son as an object of mystical devotion, but to Christ as an "example" of earthly virtue. Moreover, the virtues Adam names—obedience, justice, openness to grace, and faithful fortitude—do not evoke the *ecstasis* of the mystic.[25]

There is little evidence, then, that Milton rewards his readers with a devotional exaltation, but he does elicit empathy from them, leading them with expressions of his own empathetic concern for the characters of his story: "O for that warning voice" (IV, 1–8), "O much deceived, much failing, hapless Eve." Characteristically, Fish argues that the passages do not incite empathy but, on the contrary, urge the self-control needed to conquer a tendency to excessive— doctrinally unwarranted—sympathy. Reading the second passage (IX, 404–11), for instance, in terms of his theory of black-and-white alternatives, Fish says that the wrong interpretive choice is to view

Eve as already fallen. He cites the interpretation of Christopher Ricks, who argues that at first the reader takes "deceived" and "failing" as absolute. Then he finds that the words are particular in their reference: They refer only to Eve's "presumed return." But in the end, says Ricks, the reader realizes that the two meanings are one: "For Eve to be wrong about anything . . . is for her to be wrong about everything." The right interpretive choice is to take Eve's failing as an innocent error, like that of Uriel, and to see Eve as sinless up to the moment of her decision to pluck the forbidden fruit. Certain words in Milton's exclamation suggest the inevitability of Eve's fall, Fish argues: "much deceived, much failing," "Thou never from that hour in Paradise," "Despoiled of innocence, of faith, of bliss." But in each case there is a drawing back: Eve is "deceived" only about her return; what she will never more experience is merely "sweet repast," not innocence; her "Despoil[ment]" is contingent; the word "or" in the phrases describing Satan's intentions—"to intercept [Eve's] way, or send [her] back / Despoiled"—shows that the despoilment is still only one possibility among several. At this crucial time, Fish says, the narrator himself is tempted by his empathy to rush ahead to Eve's fall as if that fall were inevitable. But remembering in time the doctrine of free will, he draws back, presenting the reader with a model for the control of rebellious sympathy.[26]

There are two weak points in this analysis. The first is Fish's account of the rhetorical structure. Though his readings here are not as arbitrary as his repunctuation of Satan's seduction speech, nevertheless it is not obvious that the lines, "Thou never from that hour in Paradise / Found'st either sweet repast or sound repose" are "dramatically disappointing," or that the reader expects instead "never from that hour . . . knew innocence." A second weak point is the fallibility and moral conflict attributed to the narrator. Though Fish believes that Milton is an innovator in this respect, he admits that in the classical epic the narrator's voice is authoritative. A reading which avoids these weaknesses would be preferable, and the key to one such reading lies in the inadequacy of Fish's black-and-white alternatives. It is true that at this point in the action Eve cannot be "wrong about everything," as Ricks claims; Fish rightly notes that when she stands before the forbidden tree, Eve is "yet sinless" (IX,

659). But it is not true that Eve's error in parting from Adam is simply a mistake, as Fish contends. For when the fallen Eve refuses blame, she defends not only her conduct at the tree, but this decision as well: "Was I to have never parted from thy side?" (IX, 1153); and when the contrite Eve takes blame, she is penitent not only for her seduction of Adam after her fall, but for her decision to part from him: "let us forth, / I never from thy side henceforth to stray" (XI, 175–76). Eve's decision is not a sin against God, but it *is* a sin against Adam, a "want of proper regard for her husband," just as Adam, yielding to Eve's persistence, is guilty of "uxoriousness." In *De Doctrina Christiana* Milton, listing the sins included in the Fall, lumps with the sins against God these two sins against man, but in *Paradise Lost* he separates the two moral spheres, treating the Fall in human relationships in a separate scene, the scene of the morning quarrel.[27]

Milton's exclamation, then, is not a lament for the religious fall, which has not yet taken place, but a lament for the domestic fall, which has already occurred. If "deceived" and "failing" suggest sin, they do so because in the human sphere Eve is already a sinner. Eve is "hapless" because she is also a victim of sin: She has been deserted by her husband at a time of danger. In the words, "of thy presumed return," the narrator does not retreat from a premature lament for the fall of Eve. He accurately identifies the sphere in which the pair have already lapsed. Eve's "return" represents the continuance of the domestic relationship of Adam and Eve, the relationship which has just been broken. There is no anticlimax in the assertion that Eve will nevermore find "sweet repast or sound repose." The pair dine and rest in their bower in the heat of the day, and these activities in the one private place in Eden stand for the companionate aspect of their married life. The narrator does not draw back from blaming Eve for the loss of her religious innocence, nor does the reader expect to hear this blame. Rather, Milton laments the loss of the remedy for loneliness provided for Adam and Eve, and the reader shares his feelings. Even Satan is viewed in this passage as a disrupter of the relationship of husband and wife. He intends to "intercept [Eve's] way" (to prevent her return to her husband) "or send [her] back / Despoiled of innocence, of faith, of bliss" (to corrupt her). He is a would-be rapist or would-be seducer. The word "or," which separates these two alternatives, does not refer to the contingency of Eve's fate, but to the alternative tactics open to Satan, the tactics of force or fraud. The narrator is not restraining an excess of empathy, then, but reacting in a balanced way to a complex situation. Eve has sinned against her husband and is about to reap the rewards of that sin; but she is also the victim of Adam's sin, and about to suffer the consequences of his neglect. Furthermore, what the pair have done to their own relationship is about to be aggravated by the intervention of an enemy, and an enemy of a particularly terrible sort. Milton elicits not self-control but the tragic emotions of fear and pity, and Fish's intricate arguments are directed at denying the most prominent quality of the passage, what Burden calls its "warmth and tenderness of tone."[28]

If Fish is wrong about the emotive qualities of *Paradise Lost*, then he must be wrong in his rejection of a narrative reading. For if Milton asks empathy for his characters, and if he has didactic aims, as Fish rightly asserts, then empathy must not be the moral snare that Fish alleges. In support of the contention, Fish again draws on the subjective critics. Waldock, as he notes, credits Satan with "fortitude in adversity, enormous endurance, a certain splendid recklessness, remarkable powers of rising to an occasion," and "extraordinary qualities of leadership (shown not least in his salutary taunts)." John Peter does not feel inclined to blame Eve, and he says that we can "begin to reproach" Adam only "by inverting our own natures and values." But these critics refuse to grant the poem's premises (Peter is quite explicit about that here), and they attempt no comprehensive reading, responding to selected details and disregarding others which interfere with their impressions (in "salutary taunts," for instance, Waldock dismisses Milton's "Vaunting aloud").[29]

A narrative critic, systematizing the episodes of the poem, would view the characters very differently, but he would feel empathy nonetheless. He would respond to Satan as one responds to Macbeth, sharing a progressively restricted consciousness, feeling the narrowing of options and the inevitability of retribution. He would respond to Adam and Eve as one responds to Othello, suffering in the eclipse of a noble nature, feeling the beauty and pathos of the not-unaltered reemergence of that nature. These responses would relate to the didactic ends of *Paradise Lost*. Fish supposes that Milton achieves those ends directly, by presenting the reader with a series of moral tests. But Milton could, of course, use his actions to "assert Eternal Providence" and "justify the ways of God." Attributing absolute power and perfect goodness to God, Milton could show what happens to creatures who deny those attributes and the consequences of acknowledging them. The reader's empathetic reactions to the changing fortunes and natures of the characters would be the means by which he would learn the barrenness of sin and the preciousness of grace. Fish's argument against the narrative approach is invalid, then, and though a narrative reading may seem homey and plain, it may nevertheless fit the poem better than does Fish's rhetorical account, which is ingenious but, alas, misshapen, like a Laputan suit.

The mythic and the rhetorical critics, those who have argued that *Paradise Lost* is not a narrative, have been careful to suggest that their new approaches are really old approaches, that the techniques they ascribe to Milton have their roots in Renaissance logic or religion. But the techniques they describe were made familiar by Eliot and Joyce and Beckett; and at least Cope, who compares *Paradise Lost* to *Finnegans Wake,* is explicitly accommodating Milton to modern tastes.[30]

No good, I fear, can come of this. It is unwise to attribute to a writer qualities he does not have, even if those qualities are fashionable ones. Readers excited by the thought that Milton copied from the moderns will eventually discover that he copied them badly, and scorn him for it. And it is unwise to deny a writer his virtues even when those virtues are out of fashion. A few fit readers might treasure Milton's qualities, if only they knew what qualities he had. And so, I think, it is time to call the critics back from their exciting prospects, from the bull of novelty. The common field waits, and cushy cow bonnie the cow of truth, who will still let down her milk to anyone willing to whisper the familiar words.

University of Regina

102 MILTON STUDIES

NOTES

I am now as blind as Milton, but alas, I have no daughters. A colleague, Joan Givner, has spent many hours reading into a tape recorder the materials cited in this paper. I am deeply indebted to her for her kindness.

1. Isabel Gamble MacCaffrey, *"Paradise Lost" as "Myth"* (Cambridge, Mass., 1959), pp. 23–25, 53–54; quotation from p. 54. Jackson I. Cope, *The Metaphoric Structure of "Paradise Lost"* (Baltimore, 1962), p. 79; quotation from p. 75. To avoid the proliferation of notes, I have, wherever possible, gathered a paragraph's documentation into a single note.

2. MacCaffrey's thesis, *"Paradise Lost" as "Myth,"* p. 188; her example, p. 191. All my quotations of *Paradise Lost* are taken from the modernized text edited by Douglas Bush in *The Complete Poetical Works of John Milton* (Boston, 1965).

3. Cope, *Metaphoric Structure*, pp. 130–34; phrase quoted from p. 134. On p. 132, Cope quotes in Latin from St. Augustine's *Enarrationes in Psalmos*.

4. Maurice Kelley, *This Great Argument: A Study of Milton's "De Doctrina Christiana" as a Gloss Upon "Paradise Lost"* (Princeton, 1941), p. 148. The tradition stemming from 1 Timothy implies a dichotomy between reason and passion, while an alternative tradition, the tradition of the triple equation—discussed extensively by Elizabeth Marie Pope in *"Paradise Regained": The Tradition and the Poem* (Baltimore, 1947), pp. 51–69—entails a tripartite division of the soul. I believe that Milton used the latter in *Paradise Regained*, but the former in *Paradise Lost*. Dennis H. Burden, *The Logical Epic: A Study of the Argument of "Paradise Lost"* (London, 1967), pp. 125–28.

5. MacCaffrey's symbols, *"Paradise Lost" as "Myth,"* p. 59; Satan's voyage, pp. 179, 191; quotations from p. 191.

6. Cope, *Metaphoric Structure*, pp. 134–36; quotation from pp. 135–36.

7. MacCaffrey, *"Paradise Lost" as "Myth,"* pp. 54–62. Cope, *Metaphoric Structure*, p. 136.

8. MacCaffrey's central metaphor, *"Paradise Lost" as "Myth,"* p. 53; its applications, pp. 56, 61. Cope's symbolic links, *Metaphoric Structure*, pp. 135–36; his central metaphor, pp. 75–76.

9. See Cope, *Metaphoric Structure*, p. 136: "Satan's first betrayal of Uriel upon that flaming orb takes place 'at highth of Noon' (IV, 564). The hypocrisy which 'neither Man nor Angel can discern' is unrevealed even in light upon light."

10. On p. 58, MacCaffrey notes the parallel between the prologues to Books III and VII, but she does not see the structural problem the parallel presents.

Albert R. Cirillo does find symbolic significance in the noontime visit of Raphael ("Noon-Midnight and the Temporal Structure of *Paradise Lost*," *ELH*, XXIX [1962], 372–95), but I have the same doubts about his cautious and scholarly case for noon symbolism that I have about the case of the more flamboyant Cope.

11. MacCaffrey, *"Paradise Lost" as "Myth,"* pp. 44–45. Michael Wilding, *Milton's "Paradise Lost": An Approach to the Poem* (Sydney, Australia, 1969), p. 10.

12. Burden, *Logical Epic*, pp. 81–82.

13. MacCaffrey, *"Paradise Lost" as "Myth,"* p. 54. Cope, *Metaphoric Structure*, pp. 76–77.

14. Lawrence A. Sasek, "The Drama of *Paradise Lost*, Books XI and XII," in *Studies in English Renaissance Literature*, ed. Waldo F. McNeir, Louisiana State

University Studies, Humanities Series, no. 12 (Baton Rouge, 1962), pp. 181–96. Though Sasek rather overestimates Milton's success, he is clearly right about Milton's intentions. Burden, *Logical Epic*, p. 25. Balachandra Rajan, *Paradise Lost and The Seventeenth Century Reader* (London, 1947), p. 44. See also *The Lofty Rhyme* (London, 1970), p. 58.

15. The metaphor is Fish's own: Stanley E. Fish, *Surprised by Sin: The Reader in "Paradise Lost"* (London, 1967), p. 49. Milton's strategy is described on pp. 39–40; the summaries are quoted from p. 1.

16. A. J. A. Waldock, *"Paradise Lost" and Its Critics* (Cambridge, 1947); on premises, pp. 53–54, quotation from p. 54; on unconscious, pp. 15, 77–78. Millicent Bell, "The Fallacy of the Fall in *Paradise Lost*," *PMLA*, LXVIII (1953), 863–83. E. M. W. Tillyard, *Milton* (London, 1930), pp. 276–88.

17. Fish's thesis, *Surprised by Sin*, p. 214, where he quotes Waldock, *"Paradise Lost" and Its Critics*, p. 26. Fish's example, pp. 216–19.

18. Burden, *Logical Epic*, p. 84; his citation of 1 Timothy ii, 14, p. 89.

19. On p. 225, *Surprised by Sin*, Fish cites Bell's reading and on p. 218, the similar, if less extreme, reading of Waldock, *"Paradise Lost" and Its Critics*, p. 61.

20. Fish's thesis, *Surprised by Sin*, pp. 214–15; his example, pp. 4–9. On p. 5, Fish quotes Waldock, *"Paradise Lost" and Its Critics*, pp. 77–78. Arnold Stein, *Answerable Style: Essays on "Paradise Lost"* (Minneapolis, 1953), p. 124.

21. Fish, *Surprised by Sin*, pp. 241–45, 252–57; phrase quoted from p. 256, sentence from p. 253. I have repunctuated Milton's text in accordance with Fish's reading.

22. Fish, *Surprised by Sin*, p. 256, quotes John Peter, *A Critique of "Paradise Lost"* (London, 1960), pp. 128–29. Burden, *Logical Epic*, pp. 76–102.

23. Fish on sophistry, *Surprised by Sin*, p. 255; on "attentive reader," p. 253. Waldock, *"Paradise Lost" and Its Critics*, p. 37 n.

24. Burden, *Logical Epic*, pp. 9, 12. Fish on empathy, *Surprised by Sin*, pp. 42–44, 239; on reader's reward, pp. 327–31.

25. Fish's proofs, *Surprised by Sin*, pp. 300 ff.; Adam's rapture, pp. 322–24; quotations from pp. 323, 324.

26. Fish, *Surprised by Sin*, pp. 234–36. On p. 235, Fish quotes Christopher Ricks, *Milton's Grand Style* (Oxford, 1964), p. 97.

27. Fish on epic voice, *Surprised by Sin*, pp. 46–47; phrases quoted from p. 236. John Milton, *De Doctrina Christiana*, Bk. I, chap. 11.

28. Burden, *Logical Epic*, p. 95.

29. On p. 4, *Surprised by Sin*, Fish quotes Waldock, *"Paradise Lost" and Its Critics*, p. 77; on p. 271, he quotes Peter, *A Critique*, p. 131.

30. Cope's historical argument, *Metaphoric Structure*, pp. 27–49; his references to *Finnegans Wake*, pp. 75–77. Fish, *Surprised by Sin*, pp. 50–53. MacCaffrey, *"Paradise Lost" as "Myth,"* p. 53.

MILTON'S HOUSEHOLD EPIC

Harold E. Toliver

Formal epic is both consummated and altered by Milton in
Paradise Lost and *Paradise Regained,* which absorb much of
the tradition but recast it. The focus in *Paradise Lost* on Adam
and Eve is part of Milton's conscious resistance to chivalric epic
on behalf of Puritan and domestic values. In contrast to the
royalist apologetic still active in his day, Milton subordinated
civil to religious institutions. The sublime domesticity of Adam
and Eve is expressed by the meet conversations of Book IV,
where Milton defines a new love language and combines
pastoral and heroic virtues. The Fall adds the moral values of
redemption in a chastened Adam and Eve and in Christ, who
completes the heroic paradigm. This notion of the heroic is not
new, but reformative; it goes back to scriptural precedents. But
it is also provoked by the times, and Milton invents a new style
to handle the scriptural materials.

THE DEVELOPMENT of genres and styles sometimes takes
unpredictable turns. This is especially true of epic, which is
influenced by comparatively few poets, each of whom has a disproportionate effect. It is one of the ironies of epic, for instance, that
its major English example, *Paradise Lost,* is so full of its predecessors and so indebted to them, yet so ambivalent toward them; so
read and imitated by later poets, yet so clearly the last of its kind. No
text could demonstrate more decisively how subject the epic is to
willed, individual change—to repudiation, or to admiration deflected into the byways of unique sensibilities. (In the lyric, by
contrast, the controlling norms are well diffused and less vulnerable
to either selective expropriation or idiosyncratic recasting.)

In any event, Milton's personality and intellect were scarcely a
neutral prism through which epic light was distributed to the future:
Everything about his career when he came to *Paradise Lost* and

105

Paradise Regained predicted the great personal impact on the form
that we finally see in the poems. On the one hand, as *Lycidas*
indicates, he was an almost incredible assimilator of tradition; yet on
the other, he managed his echoic and allusive distances skillfully.
He also did so consciously, as is demonstrated by his reflections on
the nature of each poetic remaking he was in the midst of performing. Thus, the writing of *Lycidas* became one of the subjects of the
poem; the nature of poetry, both in Eden and in the epic narrator,
became one of the subjects of *Paradise Lost;* the nature of song, a
concern of *Comus;* the development of the poet, a concern of
L'Allegro and *Il Penseroso.* Milton's main poetic works, in fact, are
some of the leading critical documents of the seventeenth century.
As such, the epics help to explain some of the stages along the
remarkable path from *The Faerie Queene* through *Pilgrim's Progress*
to *Robinson Crusoe*—in some ways a direct route from feudal to
bourgeois narrative, in other ways one of the notable cases of how
literary influences work from poet to poet.

I

However, I want to set aside the larger question of Milton's
place in the greater evolution of narrative forms and isolate, if I can, a
single factor in the literary, personal, and social influences that he
brought to bear on epic form. My focus is largely on a climate change
that contributed to Milton's shaping of an alternative, household
notion of the heroic. No description of *Paradise Lost* as a domestic
epic should, of course, be taken to imply a definitive genre for it—as
a new heroic mode equatable to *Pilgrim's Progress* or akin to the
novel (that ultimate instrument for the exploration of bourgeois
family relations). Nonetheless, at the heart of Milton's epic, with its
focus on a married couple who become archetypal parents, is a
concern sufficiently different from that of other epics to provoke our
asking whether or not Milton purposely set about constructing heroic models for the same civil, domestic, and religious reforms on
behalf of which he labored so long.

In this regard, several preliminary historical matters should be
noted concerning the lingering taste for chivalric epic in Milton's
formative and mature years and the Puritan reaction to it. As Ruth

Nevo suggests in *The Dial of Virtue*, though royalist apologetic changed significantly from early to mid-century, it held fast for some time to the advisability of reserving heroic poetry for upper-class bearing and values: "Never had that conception of the heroic which has its roots in court culture and the politics of monarchy been affirmed in more grandiose, superhuman, and absolute a fashion. When these affirmations conflicted with the realities of impoverished exchequers, inconclusive trade wars, and the chicaneries of international diplomacy, the heroic image became the subject of revengeful mockery and derision."[1] Sir William D'Avenant, in the Preface to *Gondibert* (1650), for instance, proposed a tactical association of religious myth and social theory. In linking ancient heroes to current princes and choosing for his own epic a "story of such persons as profess'd Christian religion," he found religious matters a stimulus to chivalric honor, conducive "more to explicable virtue, to plain demonstrative justice and even to honor" than any other set of values.[2] One of the poet's functions is clearly to construct models of social order. D'Avenant admonished his readers to remember what former epic poets had done for their princes: "To leaders of armies . . . whose office requires the uttermost aids of art and nature, and rescues the sword of justice when 'tis wrested from supreme power by commotion, I am now addressed, and must put them in mind, though not upbraidingly, how much their mighty predecessors were anciently obliged to poets, whose songs, recording the praises of conduct and valor, were esteemed the chiefest rewards of victory" (p. 36). Thus, as Homer offered models to Alexander, the elder Scipio to Ennius, Virgil to Augustus, and Tasso to Italy, a modern epic should seek to instruct princes (pp. 31–32). Given that aim, the sacred element of heroic poetry might be used to reinforce civil authority, drawing together in a single action the army, polity, law, and religion, and directing all of these to the control of those "beasts whose appetite is liberty, and their liberty a license of lust."

With some of these opinions, Thomas Hobbes concurred in his "Answer to Davenant's Preface to Gondibert" (1650): "For there is in Princes and men of conspicuous power, anciently called Heroes, a lustre and influence upon the rest of men resembling that of the heavens; and an insincereness, inconstancy, and troublesome hu-

mor of those that dwell in populous cities like the mobility, blus-
tering, and impurity of the air; and a plainness, and though dull, yet
nutritive faculty in rural people, that endures a comparison with the
earth they labor."[3] It was on these grounds that Hobbes divided
poetry into heroic, satiric, and pastoral kinds, each with an appropriate scene and purpose: inconstant cities and dull earth for the
lower ranks, appropriately treated in satire and pastoral, and heaven
for heroic actions whose appropriate style is the elevated decorum of
princes. This alliance of divine and royal modes is poetry's equivalent to the joining of church and state on the state's terms. Its pyra-
midal concept of style serves a social hierarchy whose apex displays
the ornaments of princely splendor and the equipage of conspicuous
power. Given the presuppositions of that alliance, royalist apologists
could be expected to take a dim view of any rival alliance that
considered lesser men models of heroic *virtu* and propriety. This is,
of course, only one of the several concerns that Hobbes, D'Avenant,
and Abraham Cowley had in defining the heroic, and we should not
make it more central to criticism of the epic than it is. But it focuses
on an issue that has a place, alongside the removal of the fantastic
and the concept of epic action, as one of the sensitive matters of
continued serious debate.

   On the street level, too, satiric broadsides of the day were filled
with jibes at the noisy impropriety of uniting divine and domestic
affairs—especially by "rhapsodists" whose aim was to overthrow
traditional civility:

> Lest the Elect should go astray,
> Let coblers teach you the right way
>   To Heavens door.[4]

A flood of mock remonstrances, mock humble petitions, mock
parliamentary pedigrees, mad songs, riddles, odes, alarms, characters of mad zealots, hues and cries after sanctity, madrigals, and
ditties attested to a sensibility, in at least one portion of Milton's
potential audience, that even long after the civil strife was over had
much to put behind it before it could respond without misgiving to
Paradise Lost. Although it would have been unlike Milton to pay
much attention to that particular audience—secure as he was in high
poetry's superiority to popular art—the issues it raised were

symptomatic of a social problem which was by no means settled, and may even have been intensified for Milton personally in his post-Restoration period. Once he abandoned his youthful idea for an Arthurian poem, he was naturally not enamored of any association of social elevation and high style; and as an outcast in proximity to the noisy decadence of the restored court, his distaste would have been redoubled. The Christian wayfarer, after all, sought fulfillment in an inner vision that replaced and transcended the imaginal grandeur of heroic exploits.

Implicit in Milton's opinion of classical and Renaissance epics on that score is a proposition that he entertained throughout his prose as well as his poetic career: Civil power ought to remain a branch of spiritual reform and be its executive arm. And if, indeed, reformation and a return to heroic dignity are to go hand in hand, might not *Paradise Lost* and *Paradise Regained* become thrusts on behalf of a moral revolution as significant as the revolution that had slipped away? If they did their job, the reform that had failed in public ways might still have success in the inner worlds of a fit few. The two kinds of panegyric—one associating the majesty of secular princes with the power of the gods and the other severing all such connections between spiritual authority and splendor—might be made to wage a kind of stylistic battle as polar tensions, thrusting up between them in their collision a dramatic epic structure. More particularly, by forging a continuous chain from the first man and wife to heaven, the epic poet might find real power in the weakness of a Puritan household.

II

Whatever Milton's speculations in this regard, in the epics themselves he justified an overturning of certain expectations on the grounds that an original cosmic upset long ago distorted our concepts of the heroic and planted seeds of ambition and vanity that flower as strongly in contemporary society as ever. Heroic fictions of a rival sort were born precisely when Satan and Eve began to imagine grander roles for themselves than their stations sanctioned. As Michael tells Adam after the Fall, even the simple teachings of the apostles will fall into the hands of wolves capable of exploiting holy truths for class advantage:

> but in thir room, as they forewarn,
> Wolves shall succeed for teachers, grievous Wolves,
> Who all the sacred mysteries of Heav'n
> To thir own vile advantages shall turn
> Of lucre and ambition, and the truth
> With superstitions and traditions taint,
> Left only in those written Records pure,
> Though not but by the Spirit understood.
> Then shall they seek to avail themselves of names,
> Places and titles, and with these to join
> Secular power, though feigning still to act
> By spiritual.   (XII, 507–18)

But the initial existence of Adam and Eve is equally good evidence against a concept of heroic propriety that associates "Places and titles" and "Secular Power" with spiritual authority. Though technically they never encounter each other, Satan and Adam stage the central examples of the contest, one surrounded with princely majesty in war and statesmanship, the other requiring no symbols or icons, only the image of the maker shining in mind and act:

> Two of far nobler shape erect and tall,
> Godlike erect, with native Honor clad
> In naked Majesty seem'd Lords of all,
> And worthy seem'd, for in thir looks Divine
> The image of thir glorious Maker shone,
> Truth, Wisdom, Sanctitude severe and pure,
> Severe, but in true filial freedom plac't.   (IV, 288–94)

In bodies made from clay and in the conversation of the first parents, celestial dignity bends to its human variation. The portrait of the first parents thus offers both an idyllic dream of masculine and feminine dignity and a model for restoring honor to contemporary households. It is significantly interwoven with reactions from Satan, who promises a different kind of entertainment for them; from the narrator, who blesses wedded love and laments its debasement in his own times in "Court amours, / Mixed Dance, or wanton Mask, or Midnight Ball, / Or Serenate, which the starv'd Lover sings" (IV, 767–69); and from "Celestial voices" adding heaven's blessings to earth's.

The main demonstrations of sublime domesticity are this consummation of the marriage rites and the meet conversation that precedes it. In this central display of Milton's concept of the domestic model, Adam (in two long speeches of twenty-four and twenty-nine lines) and Eve (in one speech of twenty-four lines) illustrate in their different ways both the reciprocity of man and woman and the most sacred and responsive language of their ritualized dignity. Adam's first speech, though concerned with work, is well armed against the contemporary scorn of middle-class knights and cobbler heroes:

> *Adam* thus to *Eve*: Fair Consort, th' hour
> Of night, and all things now retir'd to rest
> Mind us of like repose, since God hath set
> Labor and rest, as day and night to men
> Successive, and the timely dew of sleep
> Now falling with soft slumbrous weight inclines
> Our eye-lids; other Creatures all day long
> Rove idle unimploy'd, and less need rest;
> Man hath his daily work of body or mind
> Appointed, which declares his Dignity,
> And the regard of Heav'n on all his ways;
> While other Animals unactive range,
> And of thir doings God takes no account.
> Tomorrow ere fresh Morning streak the East
> With first approach of light, we must be ris'n,
> And at our pleasant labor, to reform
> Yon flow'ry Arbors, yonder Alleys green,
> Our walk at noon, with branches overgrown,
> That mock our scant manuring, and require
> More hands than ours to lop thir wanton growth:
> Those Blossoms also, and those dropping Gums,
> That lie bestrown unsightly and unsmooth,
> Ask riddance, if we mean to tread with ease;
> Meanwhile, as Nature wills, Night bids us rest.   (IV, 610–33)

Though they are not responsible for nature's original creation, their daily task is to put each thing in an assigned place. Nature in turn requires them to adhere closely to it in their formal cycles of work, hunger, and repose. Labor and rest are part of Eden's gentle dialectic of opposites—not as London's cobblers and butchers illustrate them, but as part of a presiding order: Labor is their "doing" and they are sure God takes account of it, since it declares them and gives them something to preside over in addition to the larger purpose of their own increase and the founding of a human kingdom. Milton lays

Adam's muscular weariness on the limbs in the ponderousness of "slumbrous weight," in the falling rhythm of the first sentence, in the pauses after "repose" and "successive," and the gentleness of the sibilants. But that weariness is not slovenly: Adam renews the energy of his speech and the purpose of their work with thoughts of the morrow.

Adam's speech balances the several currents of daily living and concludes with a brief falling rhythm that sums up the argument, postpones the next expenditure of labor, and poses the first parents on the verge of their next moment. The rhetoric is practiced and dignified enough to suggest a speaker higher than rustic, and the reiteration of sound and image manifests an orderly as well as a masculine sensibility seeking to improve upon an already orderly nature; yet at no point is Adam in danger of becoming merely a gentleman gardener set apart from the basic earth and its vegetation. The order of his discourse is neither too strict nor too highly ornamented. The line "Yon flow'ry Arbors, yonder Alleys green," for instance, has enough balance between the two halves to suggest orderly rows of things, not regimented but repeated, beautiful but not effeminate. The shift of the second adjective behind the noun varies the rhythm and stays distant enough from common idiom to maintain an elevated decorum. The style plays with the workingman's idiom (as in "lop," which sets a strong hand against the weak riot of "wanton growth"), but its blossoms, its pervasive reason, and its Latinate diction prevent it from falling merely to that. (Milton's wisdom in deciding not to rhyme *Paradise Lost* is perhaps nowhere so evident as in the slow, cumulative dignity of Adam's speeches; rhyme, an "invention of a barbarous Age, to set off wretched matter and lame meter," as a preliminary note to the poem remarks, would have hindered the natural cadences and paragraph movement that Adam requires.)

Eve's answer is equally effective in setting humble circumstances to a dignified music. Although it suggests at points the style of love sonnets, it avoids excessive paint and powder:

> To whom thus *Eve* with perfect beauty adorn'd.
> My Author and Disposer, what thou bidd'st
> Unargu'd I obey; so God ordains,
> God is thy Law, thou mine: to know no more

Is woman's happiest knowledge and her praise.
With thee conversing I forget all time,
All seasons and thir change, all please alike.
Sweet is the breath of morn, her rising sweet,
With charm of earliest Birds; pleasant the Sun
When first on this delightful Land he spreads
His orient Beams, on herb, tree, fruit, and flow'r,
Glist'ring with dew; fragrant the fertile earth
After soft showers; and sweet the coming on
Of grateful Ev'ning mild, then silent Night
With this her solemn Bird and this fair Moon,
And these the Gems of Heav'n, her starry train:
But neither breath of Morn when she ascends
With charm of earliest Birds, nor rising Sun
On this delightful land, nor herb, fruit, flow'r,
Glist'ring with dew, nor fragrance after showers,
Nor grateful Ev'ning mild, nor silent Night
With this her solemn Bird, nor walk by Moon,
Or glittering Star-light without thee is sweet.
But wherefore all night long shine these, for whom
This glorious sight, when asleep hath shut all eyes?

                                        (IV, 634–58)

Eve reiterates the sweetness of their life much more often and more
prettily than Adam. Eden for her is more repeated pleasure than
work. The inverted syntax stresses the adjectives ("sweet," "pleasant," "fragrant," and "sweet" again) and at the same time suggests
the formality of a pastoral more gently dignified by the inversions
than Adam's. The length of the clauses lends grace to the catalogue
as Eve gathers the devices of Petrarchan poetic and lays them at the
feet of her Puritan marriage—purifying, by the moral purpose of the
speech, the reiteration, excessive symmetry, and imagery of the
paradisal *topos* and its ceremonial games. Past and future dissolve in
the parade of the present, but not less into its sensuousness than into
its daily signs and objects, whose recurrence provides the pattern for
Eve's own leisurely doubling back and twofold savoring of phrases.
Except for certain wholesome physical experiences, Eve is more
interested in the things themselves than how they feel, and if she
drifts from them at all it is upward to their purposes rather than
downward to their separate properties. She is not at this point disposed to ask what romantic wonders they may conceal, merely, in a
lover's leading curiosity, what function they serve when she and

Adam are asleep and cannot appreciate them. Even these legitimate
pleasures of Eden, however, take second place in her catalogue to
Adam's enlightening conversation. Though she places her experiences in a simple inventory that seems barely to carry her imprint,
her mind and will are nonetheless there, and their fullest dedication
is to matrimonial love. As a final proof of that, she ends tactfully with
a question that allows Adam to resume her education—as she knows
he wants to. If we are not entirely convinced that she really absorbs
all the facts he gives her, we see clearly that at least for the moment
she craves being told.

Altogether, the speech is a magnificent recasting of love dialogue on a plane far removed from medieval *Frauendienst,* Spenser,
Ariosto, or the classical tradition. By degrees in the two speeches,
Adam and Eve transpose divine harmony into their key, reaching
successfully for a style of natural elevation that does not depend
upon exploits. Pastoral is epic's strongest ally here. For Milton, the
two simple "rustics" are obviously a mirror of the best possible
human dignity and conjugal love, an archetype of what men and
women could have been had they remained free of self-delusions
and ambition. Accordingly, although the question of family authority
and the place of the sexes will intrude later, at this juncture he is
careful to keep the two portraits free of all details that would disturb
the fusion of the divine and the domestic. If it is true that Adam
sometimes approaches the gregarious vegetarian that Hippolyte
Taine found him to be (as in the lines "with branches
overgrown / That mock our scant *manuring*"—whatever intent Milton may have had to avoid English "compost" on the way to Latin
"hand work"), Milton nonetheless protects Adam from most of the
household debasements that the broadsides of the day associated
with Puritan households: Eve is generally manageable before the
Fall and soon becomes so afterwards; all finagling and bickering
have dropped out of sight on the long trip through time to Eden.
Liberated from skepticism, the first marriage can thus be the foundation of spiritual life—not only the last barrier against solitude but the
single institutional mirror of God's bounty in which Milton invested.
Thus, domestic awakening is the time for hymns; going to bed for
reverence and ceremony; eating lunch for true conversation and
catechism. All learning, verse, reception of visions, and expressions

of praise Milton associates with the daily routines of the two first people. (It is not surprising that he should conclude from the nature of marriage that domestic failure undermines the relations between man and God, "crushing the very foundation" of man's "inmost nature." "Doubtless his whole duty of serving God," Milton said of the man ready for divorce, "must need be blurred and tainted with a sad unpreparedness and dejection of spirit, wherein God has no delight" and the husband no "solace.")[5]

III

As Milton prepares for the Fall and the final stages of his image of Christian heroism, he appeals to the "Celestial Patroness" to bring him a style answerable to a version of epic that he contrasts more directly than ever with highly ornamented grandeur:

> Not sedulous by Nature to indite
> Wars, hitherto the only Argument
> Heroic deem'd, chief maistry to dissect
> With long and tedious havoc fabl'd Knights
> In Battles feign'd; the better fortitude
> Of Patience and Heroic Martyrdom
> Unsung; or to describe Races and Games,
> Or tilting Furniture, emblazon'd Shields,
> Impreses quaint, Caparisons and Steeds;
> Bases and tinsel Trappings, gorgeous Knights
> At Joust and Tournament.   (IX, 27–37)

Later, when Adam and Eve actually go forth to labor in the fields under the weight of the judgment against them, Milton can assign them deeds to go with their inherent dignity. In the interim, he finds a number of ways of intensifying the heroic image. Actually, even before the Fall, the idea of an initiation or test is never far off. The tree of science, for instance, provides an occasion for the exercise of moral will and self-control decidedly beyond that afforded by non-Christian pastoral. As Milton indicated in *Areopagitica*, the tree is intended by God as a *provoking* object:

Many there be that complain of divine providence for suffering Adam to transgress, foolish tongues! When God gave him reason, he gave him freedom to choose, for reason is but choosing; he had been else a mere artificial Adam, such an Adam as he is in the motions [marionette shows]. We ourselves esteem not of that obedience, or love, or gift, which is of force: God therefore left him free, set before him a provoking object, ever almost in his eyes; herein consisted his merit, herein the right of his reward, the praise of his abstinence. Wherefore did he create passions within us, pleasures round about us, but that these rightly tempered are the very ingredients of virtue? (YP, II, p. 527)

In effect, the tree's fruit represents a reminder of another range of glory that Eve mistakenly thinks obtainable—despite Adam's warning that it is "The only sign of our obedience left / Among so many signs of power and rule / Conferr'd upon us" (IV, 428–30). Hence the tree makes it possible for them to affirm the dignity of moral will without exercising hard choices.

Milton faced quite different problems in other aspects of his domestic-heroic combination, especially in the crisis of the Fall and its immediate aftermath. Caught between a happy period of obedience and the working out of redemption, Adam and Eve falter in meeting their first real test. Milton had to search inwardly to discover grounds for the heroic in Adam, and unfortunately Adam gives little immediate hope of his finding it there, either in his first soliloquy or later. Adam's decisive speech in accepting the fruit weaves divinity and royalty into a new decorum, both romantic and chivalric in its exaggerations of love's power:

> if Death
> Consort with thee, Death is to mee as Life;
> So forcible within my heart I feel
> The Bond of Nature draw me to my own,
> My own in thee, for what thou art is mine;
> Our State cannot be sever'd, we are one,
> One Flesh; to lose thee were to lose myself.   (IX, 953–59)

The new manner of courtship uses despair over the loss of the lady for gains in rhetorical persuasion. Its overtones compose an ironic combination of domestic and cosmic interests that *transfers* one to the other rather than expounding clearly what is inherent in them. It is slightly bogus in comparison to the earlier love talk. Death, Adam says melodramatically, is to be life, life death, which is too reminiscent of Satan's definition of evil as good to satisfy us. Domestic dialogue begins to look sophistic, though no doubt Adam feels the pinch of his dilemma sufficiently to give his words some urgency.

Despite these difficulties in a fallen household, Milton ex-

ploited even the failings of Adam and Eve to establish a postlapsarian version of the heroic. Indeed, he staked everything on it in
refuting the chivalric tradition—falling back in the process on another well-used but recast Christian paradox: One must be cast down
in humility, confessing that no one has dignity in himself, in order to
be raised up; the humbler one is and the more one abandons all
innate claims to glory, the more boldly the maker's image shines
forth in one's redemption. Growing out of the destruction of Adam's
native majesty in Books IX and X, the last two books of *Paradise Lost*
locate in Old Testament history the saving image of a god who also
humbles himself, who comes forward in a confusion of false idols,
towers of Babel, and human vanity—all of which spring from Satan's
desire to be a god and Eve's to be a goddess. He thereby demonstrates that true godliness grows in the manger and the household
and tests itself not in military or civil deeds but in the desert, far from
the visible battles of empire. The contest of epic styles is thus
revealed to be merely one aspect of the necessary historic strengthening of good by evil and the discovery, first through dim types and
symbols and then, in the Incarnation itself, of the grace and mercy
attendant upon the loss of self-possessed dignity.

The ultimate place of domesticity in the restored image of God
that Christ brings to the desert and in Milton's view of paradise
restored is problematic in some respects, although the foreground of
both epics is clear: In *Paradise Regained* Christ returns to his
mother's house and begins his submission to the circumstances that
will bring the Crucifixion; in *Paradise Lost,* Adam and Eve go forth
in the wilderness as helpmates, their tasks well defined for them by
the judgment, the enemies they have to fight, and the prophetic
vision of Michael. There is also Raphael's promise of a purified love
in heaven, which we are undoubtedly meant to take as definitive in
its way. Even so, the exact place of domestic relations is not completely definable. On the one hand, the domestic would seem to
dissolve in the soul's union with Christ; on the other, paradise may
allow a kind of lingering proximity to one's earthly spouse—as in the
twenty-third sonnet: "yet once more I trust to have / Full sight of her
in Heaven without restraint." If, as Milton wrote, "our happiness
may orb itself into a thousand vagancies of glory and delight, and
with a kind of eccentrical equation be as it were an invariable Planet

of joy and felicity,"[6] Adam, too, may be reunited with his consort. Perhaps the domestic and divine orders find a higher perfection under the new dispensation despite the fact that the Son's "eternal inheritance" of love commands all saints to observe the one King foremost: "Christian liberty is that whereby we are loosed as it were by enfranchisement, through Christ our deliverer, from the bondage of sin, and consequently from the rule of the law and of man; to the extent that being made sons instead of servants, and perfect men instead of children, we may serve God in love through the guidance of the Spirit of Truth."[7] But saints who circle the divine center may also have their own adventurous, eccentric motions, dancing *before* the high throne but *next to* others—presumably fusing the uniquely human and the highest dimensions of bliss.

IV

But this is a purely speculative matter that violates the focus of the epic on vistas well short of the apocalyptic. The marriage of the sacred and humble ultimately depends upon the paradoxes of the earthly incarnation and points up a strong element of continuity in what I have portrayed perhaps too exclusively as a distinctly new heroic mode. Milton's emphasis upon the dignity of labor, the grand humbleness of the household, and above all the worth of the inner man united to Christ is "medieval" as well as "Puritan"; indeed, as Auerbach's analysis of Old Testament prose suggests in *Mimesis*,[8] it is even older than that. In every literary rebellion one finds beneath the surface violence certain continuities, recurrent styles, and neglected traditions. We cannot avoid hearing in Milton's epic voice at times not only the same scornful class feeling that tossed up the medieval couplet "When Adam delv'd and Eve span / Who was then the gentleman," but also the original voices of scriptural narration. Paradoxically, from Milton's viewpoint, only by being revolutionary could one return to the ideals of Hebraic and Christian poetic forms.

However, these are merely hints of a usable style until they are actually fitted into place in Milton's version of epic. In *Paradise Lost* they become parts of a structure quite different in total from anything preceding, even Old Testament narrative—which suggests that it is in the recasting of poetic forms, in the accommodation of values misplaced or inarticulate in other forms, that a large poetic talent finds its independence. The inclusive, encyclopedic narrative of *Paradise Lost* was both the discipline to which Milton submitted and the liberation from tradition he required: It gave him timely rules for reformulating those parts of his supreme fiction that the imagination could seize upon. Indeed, when we back away from the balanced mixture of the humble and the grand in the Eden portraits before and after the Fall, we can only speculate that it was too sensitive a product of its times to be perpetuated or imitated—that it was too much the product of a single brilliant imagination to have raised poetic echoes except of a distant kind. Its main elements proved to be as remote from Augustan and romantic poets as they were from feudal narrative. The novel picks up daily life as one of its subjects, but on a different scale and in a totally different tone. In conventional eighteenth-century shepherd idylls, pastoral moves backward, toward formulaic artifices or toward parodies of these. Milton's blank verse is itself frequently used, of course, but for subjects quite removed from the sacred-domestic union of Eden. (The personal matters of *The Prelude,* for instance, are as far from the intimacies of both Milton's confessional passages and domestic dialogues as *Paradise Lost* is from the chivalric epic.) The portraits of Adam and Eve required a timely confluence of the religious and mythic systems brought together by Christian thought, the rising concept of inner vision and worth, the provocative need to recoil from a social and cultural situation of great distaste, and a personal career shaped to its task by a poet always keenly aware of the tradition he inherited and the formal task he was undertaking.

University of California, Irvine

NOTES

1. (Princeton, 1963), p. 15.
2. In *Critical Essays of the Seventeenth Century,* vol. 2, ed. J. E. Spingarn (Oxford, 1908), p. 9.
3. "Answer to Davenant's Preface to Gondibert," ibid., p. 55.
4. See *Rump: or an Exact Collection of the Choycest Poems and Songs, 1639–1661* (London, 1662).

5. *Doctrine and Discipline of Divorce*, Bk. I, chap. 7, in *Complete Prose Works of John Milton*, gen. ed. Don M. Wolfe (New Haven, 1953–), vol. II, p. 259, hereafter cited as YP. I have modernized the spelling of prose quotations.

6. "Reason of Church-Government," YP, I, p. 752.

7. "Christian Doctrine," in *Complete Poems and Major Prose*, ed. Merritt Y. Hughes (New York, 1957), p. 1012. Quotations from the poems are from this edition.

8. Erich Auerbach, *Mimesis: The Representation of Reality in Western Literature* (Princeton, 1953), pp. 22–23: "Domestic realism, the representation of daily life, remains in Homer in the peaceful realm of the idyllic, whereas, from the very first, in the Old Testament stories, the sublime, tragic, and problematic take shape precisely in the domestic and commonplace. . . . The sublime influence of God here reaches so deeply into the everyday that the two realms of the sublime and the everyday are not only actually unseparated but basically inseparable."

"HEE FOR GOD ONLY, SHEE FOR GOD IN HIM": STRUCTURAL PARALLELISM IN *PARADISE LOST*

Kathleen M. Swaim

Three sections of *Paradise Lost*—Eve's love song and astronomical query in Book IV and Adam's parallel dealings with Raphael in Book VIII, Adam and Eve's fateful parting and their fallen evaluations of it in Book IX, and the reconciliation and reunion through prayer in Book X—illuminate the thematic relationship of the epistemologies of experience and faith in the poem. Eve's relationship with Adam parallels Adam's with divine agency. The Eve-Adam data provide experiential guidelines for more fully presenting the abstract analogues of Adam's intercourse with a divinity that must remain essentially mysterious. Adam's justification of himself, "I warned thee, I admonish'd thee . . . force upon Free Will hath here no place," gives dramatic human narrative form to the divine theory of Book III and to Raphael's lessoning in Books V–VIII, as in Book X Eve's prostration to Adam and redemptive model provide a human equivalent for the mystery of the need, gift, and reception of grace. The Adam-Eve data mirror the God-man relationship in Milton's representation of difficult theological issues for inescapable human comprehension.

PARALLELISM, WHETHER of diction, action, or character, is one of Milton's major means of tightening the poetry and structure of *Paradise Lost*. It is safe to say that criticism with a textual foundation has difficulty avoiding some inclusion of relevant commentary on what I am calling parallelism, but is also called comparison/contrast, structural symmetry, repetition/recurrence, or "retrospection and anticipation."[1] In its largest units it is essential to the coherence of the poem; these units consist most obviously of the parallel falling of Eve and Adam and of humans and angels, the parallel recitals of Eve's and Adam's creation stories, the parallel temptations of the toad-inspired dream in Books IV–V and the serpentine reality of Book IX, and the parallel councils, trinities, volunteers, and even gates of heaven and parodic hell. The list could be easily multiplied to include most of the text of *Paradise Lost*. Criticism that concentrates on illuminating the designed patterning of parallels as an artistic and thematic principle and that pursues less obvious data is rare and elusive. It is this that I will concentrate on in this essay.

Joseph Summers has observed that the single action which is the subject of *Paradise Lost* is "the patterned relationship between God and man throughout time and eternity" (p. 177). Adam's relationship with divine agency changes and deepens in the course of the poem. The chief proposition of this essay is that Eve's relationship with Adam parallels Adam's relationship with such agency, with Raphael, God, and God through Christ, and that the Eve-Adam data provide explicit experiential guidelines for more fully comprehending the abstract analogues of Adam's intercourse with a divinity that must remain essentially mysterious. Thematically, the pattern of parallels adumbrates the relationship between experience and faith. My examples are of action, character, diction, and even grammar, and deal not with the negative act of falling or the negative stylistics of parody, but with hierarchical aspiration and the insight, open-endedness, and affirmation of faith. After introducing the design, I shall focus on the three textual units which serve as its principal exposition: Eve's love song in Book IV and Adam's parallel account to Raphael in Book VIII; Adam and Eve's fateful parting and their fallen evaluations of it in Book IX; and the reconciliation and reunion through prayer in Book X.

Generally speaking, an epic undertakes to encompass all the knowledge of the culture it celebrates. One of Milton's problems, inherent in any Christian epic, was that his culture included much that is and must remain to a large extent mysterious. Although the experiential must be the stuff of his imagery and conception, the Christian poet celebrates faith rather than experience. I am using *experience* in its dictionary senses of "proof by actual trial," "the events that have taken place within the knowledge of an individual," "knowledge resulting from actual observation or from what one has undergone" (*OED*). What matters here is that the epistemology of experience looks to the past and to what has been as its standard of measurement. Experience thus contrasts with faith, which looks to the future and is, to put the matter in familiar biblical terms, "the substance of things hoped for, the evidence of things not seen" (Hebrews xi, 1).[2] One way of interpreting the meaning of the Fall is that Adam and Eve accept experience as their prime guide at the expense of faith. Experience is based on things, facts, and reason; its mindset is literal; its extreme is despair. Faith eludes the rational as the sensory; its mindset is creative and imaginative; its culmination is the mystery of grace. Spiritually as poetically the former killeth, the latter quickeneth. In the postlapsarian world faith has this chronological complexity, that although its realization is a future category, its basis is in the past. It is a question of *promise,* but that promise is *remembered.* The Hebrew word for *faith* also means *memory* (see *PL* X, 12–13). In Christian eras there is the further complication that for Milton Christ gives form to God, and that form penetrates the world of experience with the light of faith. For Christian believers Christ is, again, both memory and anticipation. In the poem Christ is the focus of paradox, through whom Milton justifies the contradictory complexity of life in the world to his fit audience. Milton provides guidelines, but truth is dizzying, even as faith and this account of faith with its opening layers of meaning must be. Unless the Christian poem and the reading of it acknowledge apprehension through faith and keep its meanings ever open and opening, the author betrays his subject (also a theological fault) as well as his audience.

One of the ways Milton solves this problem of reconciling poetic data with Christian themes without debasing the mystery of faith is through the hierarchy of characters in *Paradise Lost.* The lines describing the relationship of Adam and Eve, based on 1 Corinthians xi, 2–16, are familiar:

> For contemplation hee and valor form'd,
> For softness shee and sweet attractive Grace,
> Hee for God only, shee for God in him. (IV, 297–99)[3]

Or in Eve's words to Adam, "God is thy Law, thou mine" (IV, 637). A verbal category will amplify the point and outline the hierarchy. The Son is "the radiant image" of God's glory (III, 63) and "Image of thee [God] in all things" (VI, 736), "Divine Similitude" giving available form to the "Bright effluence of bright essence increate" that is God (III, 384, 6). In Adam and Eve, "God's latest Image" (IV, 567), "the image of thir glorious Maker shone" (IV, 292), and in Book VII we read that God made man in his image: "in his own Image hee / Created thee, in the Image of God / Express" (VII, 526–28; and similarly VII, 519, 627; VIII, 221, 441; and XI, 508, 514, 515, 525). But what is not directly available from Genesis, here echoed, is the Miltonic pattern at issue, that is, that Eve is designed as Adam's image: "Best Image of myself and dearer half" in Adam's words (V, 95), "hee / Whose image thou art" (IV, 472) in God's words. There is a layering at work here, as we see in Adam's statement to Raphael that Eve is his inferior, "resembling less / His Image who made both" (VIII, 543–44). Man is to propagate by number and multiply his Image (VIII, 424). Similar evidence, though not invoking the word *image*, occurs in Eve's first words of the epic:

> O thou for whom
> And from whom I was form'd flesh of thy flesh,
> And without whom am to no end, my Guide
> And Head, what thou hast said is just and right. (IV, 440–43)

—words which, with some metaphorical qualification for *flesh*, Adam might well address to the Deity. In the argument that follows we will see more of such metaphorical qualification. Throughout the poem Adam and Eve sometimes combine to provide one rung of the hierarchical ladder; at other times they are carefully distinguished. I am concerned with their distinct roles rather than their conflation.

In sum, Eve is made in Adam's image as Adam is made in the divine image. Hierarchically, since Christ is closest to the Father, a rephrasing of the human formula is called for: Christ for God, man for God in Him. As we move down the chain of being, the lower unit "images" its superior. As Raphael clarifies the design:

> O *Adam*, one Almighty is, from whom
> All things proceed, and up to him return,

> If not deprav'd from good, created all
> Such to perfection, one first matter all,
> Indu'd with various forms, various degrees
> Of substance, and in things that live, of life;
> But more refin'd, more spiritous, and pure,
> As nearer to him plac't or nearer tending
> Each in thir several active Spheres assign'd,
> Till body up to spirit work, in bounds
> Proportion'd to each kind.   (V, 469–79)

The scale is set, the thrust is upward. "The hierarchy of being," in Barbara Lewalski's words, depends "not only upon rank at creation but also upon the dynamics of self-development."[4] The means is clarified a few lines later by Adam:

> the scale of Nature set
> From centre to circumference, whereon
> In contemplation of created things
> By steps we may ascend to God.   (509–12)

"Created things" supply experience; "contemplation"—for which Adam was formed in IV, 297—transmutes to faith. The materials of theology and faith that surmount the reach of human sense (V, 571–72) are available (are only available) to humans through imaginatively likening spiritual to corporal forms (573). Eve's experiential feminine loveliness, seemingly so absolute (VIII, 547), "is excelled by manly grace / And wisdom, which alone is truly fair" (IV, 490–91) in the pattern of contemplation that encourages ascent to God. The threat to wisdom lies in "attributing overmuch to *things* / Less excellent" (VIII, 565–66, emphasis added).

Another example, this one from action and setting rather than diction, will outline the pattern in question. In dismissing Adam and Eve from paradise, Michael advises Eve thus:

> Thy going is not lonely, with thee goes
> Thy Husband, him to follow thou art bound;
> Where he abides, think there thy native soil.   (XI, 290–92)

Eve's prospective loneliness is dealt with as narrative social fact, but Adam's "higher intellectual" is assuaged metaphorically with the assurance of God's omnipresence:[5]

> Surmise not then
> His presence to these narrow bounds confin'd
> Of Paradise or *Eden* . . .
>
> .   .   .   .
>
> Yet doubt not but in Valley and in Plain
> God is as here, and will be found alike
> Present, and of his presence many a sign
> Still following thee, still compassing thee round
> With goodness and paternal Love, his Face
> Express, and of his steps the track Divine.
>
> (XI, 340–42, 349–54)

Socially Adam has Eve's company; spiritually he has "many a sign." The image of himself (Eve) he apprehends through experience; what he is the image of (God) must be apprehended through faith and creative imagination. In the finale of Book XII, Eve says explicitly to Adam what Adam feels and would say to the deity:

> But now lead on;
> In mee is no delay; with thee to go,
> Is to stay here; without thee here to stay,
> Is to go hence unwilling; thou to mee
> Art all things under Heav'n, all places thou.   (XII, 614–18)

"All things" are now qualified by moral placement as "under Heav'n"; the "things" now valued lose their materiality, are those—recalling Guido del Duca in *Purgatorio* XIV—that are multiplied rather than diminished by sharing. Comparably, for Adam to travel with God is to maintain the Edenic; Eden without God ceases to be Eden. Contemplation transmutes places as well as things; the removal of Eden by the Flood teaches "that God attributes to place / No sanctity, if none be thither brought" (XI, 836–37). Internal paradise is non- or anticorporal, free, and faith-generated. It is a lesson made clear narratively and socially to Adam and the reader through Eve. The same lesson has been offered historically and typologically in the faithful Abraham who, when called by God's vision from his father's house, "straight obeys, / Not knowing to what Land, yet firm believes / . . . Not wand'ring poor, but trusting all his wealth / With God, who call'd him, in a land unknown" (XII, 120–34).[6] Through this example, a shadowy type, Adam is lessoned to see and respond rightly to the challenge of his own call to faith. It

is the third-person version of Eve's first-person "But now lead on."
The world, choice, their guiding providence, and wandering steps
are all before Adam and Eve, but also the removal of the old Eden (a
fact of experience) and the goal of the paradise within (the reward of
faith). For my present purposes the point is this: Eve's relationship
(and frequently vocabulary) to Adam parallels Adam's to the deity.
For Adam and the reader, Eve presents explicit and experiential
forms of ideas and action which guide us to perceptions of divine
equivalents that are elusive and provocative of faith.

I

Prominent among instances of parallelism earlier in the poem is
the alignment of Eve's expressions of love for Adam with Adam's for
Raphael and the divinity he makes sociable. The parallelism is
primarily of diction; the evidence has the special advantage of
measurement against an explicit satanic parody. The initial passage
illustrates the prelapsarian standard by which the postlapsarian attitudes toward place we have just glimpsed are to be measured; it
shows, in Isabel MacCaffrey's words, that "Adam *is* Eden, in a very
real sense, for Eve; he is what gives Paradise its special splendor" (p.
77). The passage is Eve's majestic and passionate love lyric in Book
IV, 641–56; for reasons that will become clear I cite also the two lines
preceding and the two following the song itself:

> With thee conversing I forget all time,
> All seasons and thir change, all please alike.
> Sweet is the breath of morn, her rising sweet,
> With charm of earliest Birds; pleasant the Sun
> When first on this delightful Land he spreads
> His orient Beams, on herb, tree, fruit, and flow'r,
> Glist'ring with dew; fragrant the fertile earth
> After soft showers; and sweet the coming on
> Of grateful Ev'ning mild, then silent Night
> With this her solemn Bird and this fair Moon,
> And these the Gems of Heav'n, her starry train:
> But neither breath of Morn when she ascends
> With charm of earliest Birds, nor rising Sun
> On this delightful land, nor herb, fruit, flow'r,
> Glist'ring with dew, nor fragrance after showers,
> Nor grateful Ev'ning mild, nor silent Night
> With this her solemn Bird, nor walk by Moon,

Or glittering Star-light without thee is sweet.
But wherefore all night long shine these, for whom
This glorious sight, when sleep hath shut all eyes?

The speech—which echoes Adam's assessment of Edenic labor
"which were it toilsome, yet with thee were sweet" two hundred
lines earlier (IV, 439)—is regularly acknowledged to be one of the
poetic highlights of the epic; in the words of Addison, it is "infinitely
pleasing" and "cannot be sufficiently admired."[7] Several critics
have called attention to the circularity of its artistry and themes as
mirroring the Edenic situation.[8] The pleasing, sensuous sweetness
of nature and the diurnal cycle emerge from the rich variations of
ameliorative adjectives and descriptive nouns: *sweet, charm, earliest* (significantly the only instance of the comparative or superlative in the lyric), *pleasant, delightful, fragrant, fertile, soft, grateful, mild, silent, solemn, fair,* and *glittering.* Most of these terms,
sometimes via *traductio,* are twice repeated; the four instances of
sweet emphatically define the picture and mood. The love song,
with opening and closing invocations of *sweet,* folds back upon itself
and divides into two repeating stanzas. Its division into a nine-line
and a seven-line unit invites comparison with the sonnet's characteristic octave and sestet; as the hinge word of the second stanza, *but*
(650) makes a similar invitation.[9] Against this lyricism, the question
in the last two lines cited comes as a shock,[10] but within that juxtaposition may be seen the largest themes of the epic: the loss of
exquisite Eden through the questioning of the divine order, and the
misjudgment of man's and the earth's positions in the total scheme.
It is the problem of knowledge, the conflict of experience and faith,
the capacity to reason at odds with the incapacity of innocence to
judge rightly. Such questioning, as we shall see, is a more prominent
feature of Adam's equivalent intercourse with Raphael in Book VIII,
where it is given full moral review and assessment.

As noted earlier, a major instance of the parallelism in the poem
occurs in Eve's taking occasion to recount to Adam the moments of
her first awakening (IV, 440–90) and Adam's making occasion to
recount his initial history to Raphael (VIII, 204–06, 253 ff.). What is
perhaps not at first apparent are the echoes of Eve's love lyric in
Adam's introduction to his narration, induced as Adam says by "Desire with thee [Raphael] still longer to converse" (252 and cf. IX,

909). "Converse" is the verbal key, and "with thee" is also repeated. Conversing with Adam, the sensuous Eve forgets all time; the more intellectually aware Adam sees the human involvement in time's patterns and the need to make time serve the great task-master's ends. His sense of time persists in a longer passage that again echoes Eve's lyric and that shifts to a placement of sensuousness within a larger more-than-earthly and diurnal context:

> Now hear mee relate
> My Story, which perhaps thou hast not heard;
> And Day is yet not spent; till then thou seest
> How subtly to detain thee I devise,
> Inviting thee to hear while I relate,
> Fond, were it not in hope of thy reply:[11]
> For while I sit with thee, I seem in Heav'n,
> And sweeter thy discourse is to my ear
> Than Fruits of Palm-tree pleasantest to thirst
> And hunger both, from labor, at the hour
> Of sweet repast; they satiate, and soon fill,
> Though pleasant, but thy words with Grace Divine
> Imbu'd, bring to thir sweetness no satiety.   (VIII, 204–16)

Sweeter, pleasantest, sweet, pleasant, and *sweetness* recall the sensuous Eve's descriptive terminology, but the sweet and pleasant of Edenic satiating earth are judged and placed by Adam's use of comparative and superlative adjectives. These embody the use of judgment, the faculty that measures occasions against each other and chooses, and thus distinguish the characterization of Adam from that of Eve. Ever more delicious, divinely imbued discourse outclasses the things of Eden, an invitation to the timeless. Eve is more closely tied to the earth, the phenomenal, as her first gestures of life were looking downward and experiencing beautiful things, whereas Adam rose erect in thought and praise of the Creator. To draw the contrast otherwise, Adam recognizes that intercourse with the heavenly is open-ended and freeing, that no satiety is possible with divine sweetness; Eve does not distance herself from the sweetness through intellection. Adam is likewise cognizant of detaining Raphael with his talk; Eve detains, but without the consciousness of intention or time. The indisputable emphases on *sweetness* here insist on comparative alignment with the earlier analogue; the emergent differences show succinctly what we learn more largely throughout the poem of the characters and psychologies of Adam and Eve and of the rewards of sense and mind and aspiration.

Eve's love lyric is recalled also in Satan's first temptation of her through the toad-inspired dream in Book V. As with the temptation in the garden later, Satan builds his case upon data which the first couple unknowingly supply him. Initially these are Eve's data, though the mode of discourse is so much Adam's that Eve can say "I thought it [the voice] thine"—"But with addition strange" (V, 37, 116), Adam adds. Eve recounts to Adam Satan's speech thus:

> Why sleep'st thou *Eve?* now is the pleasant time,
> The cool, the silent, save where silence yields
> To the night-warbling Bird, that now awake
> Tunes sweetest his love-labor'd song; now reigns
> Full Orb'd the Moon, and with more pleasing light
> Shadowy sets off the face of things; in vain,
> If none regard; Heav'n wakes with all his eyes,
> Whom to behold but thee, Nature's desire,
> In whose sight all things joy, with ravishment
> Attracted by thy beauty still to gaze.   (V, 38–47)[12]

Satan here recalls Eve's love passage on the things of earth and the ways of the heavens. His "night-warbling Bird" with its "love-labored song" echoes but distorts Eve's "solemn Bird" of "silent Night." Her "fair Moon" becomes regnant and "full Orb'd," and "its shadowy light" is misleadingly judged "more pleasing." Eve's "gems of Heav'n, her starry train" and "glittering starlight" are satanically rendered as "Heav'n wakes with all his eyes." Eve's lyric is echoed in satanic adjectives, *pleasant, silent, sweetest, more pleasing,* but what stands out in a comparison of this speech with hers is less what he takes from Eve or the shift toward comparative and superlative in the final two terms here, and more the terms Satan proceeds to add: the desire, joy, and ravishment, dangerous excesses subtly introduced, especially along with "love-labored" sexual excesses. Satan invokes the word *sweet* to exploit what he apprehends of Eve's values three times on this occasion, most prominently in "O Fruit Divine, / Sweet of thyself, but much more sweet thus cropt" (V, 67–68 and 59). What Satan can and does make most of is the question that concludes Eve's love lyric; "But wherefore all night long shine these?" is judged as settled in Satan's "in vain, / If none

regard." Again Satan's "Heav'n wakes with all his eyes" is in contrast to Eve's "when sleep hath shut all eyes." Satan imposes for
good and ill a moral dimension on Eve's sensuously apprehended
cosmos—intentionally for ill, potentially for greater fallen good. As
elsewhere in the poem, the questioning of the operation and power
of the night is metaphorically a question of the nature of evil, but
Eve's concern is with closed human eyes, not alert and constant
divine vision and vigilance. Eve's vocabulary and awareness are
limited to the earthly. Her innocence cannot comprehend night
without ceasing to be innocence. Thus, the attempted judgment in
her query is clumsy and dissonant, Satan's insinuations and re-
shaping, characteristically and dangerously smooth. Again the
echoes are indisputable evidence of intended comparison; again the
poem's largest issues are succinctly posed.

As Eve's lyric had ended in a dangerous questioning of the
heavens, so in Adam's conversation with Raphael we find a similar
doubt posed:

> When I behold this goodly Frame, this World
> Of Heav'n and Earth consisting, and compute
> Thir magnitudes, this Earth a spot, a grain,
> An Atom, with the Firmament compar'd
> And all her number'd Stars, that seem to roll
> Spaces incomprehensible (for such
> Thir distance argues and thir swift return
> Diurnal) merely to officiate light
> Round this opacous Earth, this punctual spot,
> One day and night; in all thir vast survey
> Useless besides; reasoning I oft admire,
> How Nature wise and frugal could commit
> Such disproportions, with superfluous hand
> So many nobler Bodies to create,
> Greater so manifold to this one use,
> For aught appears, and on thir Orbs impose
> Such restless revolution day by day
> Repeated, while the sedentary Earth,
> That better might with far less compass move,
> Serv'd by more noble than herself, attains
> Her end without least motion, and receives
> As Tribute such a sumless journey brought
> Of incorporeal speed, her warmth and light;
> Speed, to describe whose swiftness Number fails.

(VIII, 15–38)

As Eve's query is narrow, selfish, earthbound, practical, innocent, and brief, so Adam's questioning is larger, more philosophical, more cognizant, and more dangerous. It is to be noted that Eve asks a direct question of Adam but that Adam describes to Raphael the process of his own questioning within himself. This has the effect of a direct question and Raphael treats it as such, but in fact Adam is playing mental games with himself—"Fond, were it not in hope of thy reply," indeed. Both Adam and Eve offer human focus on the diurnal pattern. We might align Eve with L'Allegro's vision and Adam with Il Penseroso's. Eve scans one sensuous day; Adam abstracts the design of "day by day / Repeated." Adam's diction turns regularly to mathematics, measurement, and thought processes (*compute, magnitudes, compar'd, number'd, argues, reasoning, describe, admire*) and to comparatives and superlatives (*nobler, greater, better, least*). Indeed the whole argument is an extended comparison between earth (*spot, grain, atom, punctual, sedentary, one*) and the encompassing cosmos (*incomprehensible, vast, so manifold, sumless,* where speed is incorporeal and number fails). He offers qualifications of his perspective (*seem to, for aught appears*) but discounts them in proceeding to pass dangerous judgments on the designs beyond his ken (*useless besides, such disproportions, superfluous, restless, that better might, far less compass*). "Served by more noble than herself" illustrates both his judging and his use of the values he has been provided. Joseph Summers, one of the few critics to cite the parallel of Eve's and Adam's curiosity about the heavens, describes Eve's question as "cruder and more naive than Adam's."[13] That is true, but it is not the whole issue. To put it simply, Eve asks, Why? and Adam asks, Why not? In thus finding fault, Adam imposes his own human standard of measurement on the cosmos and the divine.

In answering Eve's question Adam was confident, even complacent, condescending to share with her weaker reason the perceptions available to his higher perspective. The confident answer he supplied her testified to God's plan within the natural order and the constancy of divine beneficence. God does not need or lack; the stars "shine not in vain" (refuting Satan's V, 43–44); and the whole natural and supernatural order engages in "ceaseless praise" of the Creator. To her Adam affirmed God's order, the incomprehensibility of the operations of light to human understanding, and the proper human attitudes of wonder and gratitude. Summers observes, "Adam had answered her question, resolved her doubt, with reason and eloquence which assured her that their central position in the universe was not quite so simple as she had imagined" (p. 156). Adam's answer to Eve recurs to higher data and to faith; he seeks to expand her perception and multiply her awe.

Raphael's response to Adam opens up the problem of knowledge and touches also the issue of faith. Like Adam's to Eve, it is a lesson in awe. His reply is very much open-ended; he answers curiosity with more questions: *What if* (122, 128, 140), *whether . . . or whether not* (159), and *whether . . . or* (160, 163).[14] "*Adam . . .* is doubtfully answer'd, and exhorted to search rather things more worthy of knowledge," in the words of the Argument to Book VIII. Since Adam's question was negatively posed, Raphael's answer must encompass some severity to point out and relieve the greater threat to their perfection. The "prime Wisdom" Raphael offers—misleadingly in some critics' views—is to "be lowly wise" (173) and "solicit not thy thoughts with matters hid" (167). At first glance Raphael's response seems contradictory: On the one hand, condescending, teasing questions that if taken seriously are provocative of further inquiry, and on the other hand aphoristic moralizing that seeks to close off inquiry. But Raphael's chief point is his opening one, not his conclusion. He begins, not by condemning questioning, but by teaching the right way to ask questions.

>   the rest
> From Man or Angel the great Architect
> Did wisely to conceal, and not divulge
> His secrets to be scann'd by them who ought
> Rather admire.   (VIII, 71–75)

The two definitions of the verb *to wonder* demonstrate the problem.[15] In one we find, to question idly; in the other, to admit one's lack of knowledge in awe. The former closes productive inquiry and feeling, the latter is open to faith. Raphael guides Adam away from the former and to the latter. Right questioning turns to the unknown with affirmation and faith; it moves from and toward praise of the Creator. Earlier the dissembling Satan evaded Uriel's identification at the end of Book III by apparently right questioning and motives in his "unspeakable desire to see" the "wondrous works" of "The Universal Maker" in order to praise them and him (662–76). Uriel found praiseworthy the "desire which tends to know / The works of God, thereby to glorify / The great Work-Master" (694–98). The key phrase is *to glorify.* Wrong questioning, Adam's fault in Book VIII and our all too frequent legacy, in turning to the unknown, insists on imposing its old closed experiential structures and judgments on whatever it may find. Its base is critical arrogance, not wondering praise; its guide is insistently experience at the expense of faith.

Adam's answer and tone are appropriate to solace Eve's weaker understanding, if not to contain his own energies. His persistent curiosity, pushing beyond the boundaries of his own best understanding, provokes Raphael's check. The seeds of ambition and curiosity are not, as some aver, all in Eve's half of the fateful apple. Adam has not yet achieved what we shall see as a turning point in the poem in Book X (section III of this essay): He must learn to learn from Eve and his experience with her, he must draw lessons from the experiential below him in the hierarchy without sacrificing his faith above. Thus Raphael's "Be lowly wise" must be placed in hierarchical perspective. For our present structural purposes, however, clearly Adam reshapes to Raphael the matter and thrust of Eve's query to himself about the heavens. Once set, the comparative base holds, the contrasts provoke questions, questions about questions, and some suggestive answers. Some later observations recur to this incident.

II

Further evidence of parallelism with resonant implications grows out of the conversation between Adam and Eve about working separately in Book IX of *Paradise Lost.* This preamble to the Fall brings into focus Raphael's mission to Adam and God's discourse on free will in Book III. The evidence relies on matter and structure more than diction, though verbal echoes occur. Adam begins to answer Eve's suggestion by applauding her study of household good (233)—an application of "be lowly wise." Before proceeding to warn her against separation,[16] he invokes the verbal pattern we have seen above in "converse" with expansive alliteration targeted on *sweet:*

> But if much converse perhaps
> Thee satiate, to short absence I could yield.
> For solitude sometimes is best society,
> And short retirement urges sweet return.   (IX, 247–50)

He knows and has judged the potential satiety of sweetness and the senses, and he credits Eve with his own enlarged perspective.

Adam proceeds to translate and focus the evidence of Raphael's visit upon the immediate human situation, the question of separation. These extended data (Books V–VIII) are summarized in God's outline of Raphael's assignment to the first couple:

> Such discourse bring on,
> As may advise him of his happy state,
> Happiness in his power left free to will,
> Left to his own free Will, his Will though free,
> Yet mutable; whence warn him to beware
> He swerve not too secure: tell him withal
> His danger, and from whom, what enemy
> Late fall'n himself from Heaven, is plotting now
> The fall of others from like state of bliss;
> By violence, no, for that shall be withstood,
> But by deceit and lies; this let him know,
> Lest wilfully transgressing he pretend
> Surprisal, unadmonisht, unforewarn'd.   (V, 233–45)

The warning calls attention to the essentials of the trial: human sufficiency, the enemy, the deceitful means. A selection of passages from Adam's replies to Eve's new working plan will make the point of equivalence:

> For thou know'st
> What hath been warn'd us, what malicious Foe
> Envying our happiness, and of his own
> Despairing, seeks to work us woe and shame
> By sly assault; and somewhere nigh at hand
> Watches, no doubt, with greedy hope to find
> His wish and best advantage, us asunder.   (IX, 252–58)

> Subtle he needs must be, who could seduce
> Angels.   (307–08)

> Within himself
> The danger lies, yet lies within his power:
> Against his will he can receive no harm.
> But God left free the Will, for what obeys

> Reason, is free, and Reason he made right,
> But bid her well beware, and still erect,
> Lest by some fair appearing good surpris'd
> She dictate false, and misinform the Will
> To do what God expressly hath forbid.   (348–56)

> Firm we subsist, yet possible to swerve,
> Since Reason not impossibly may meet
> Some specious object by the Foe suborn'd,
> And fall into deception unaware,
> Not keeping strictest watch, as she was warn'd.   (359–63)

We see Adam as teacher again, lessoning Eve soundly, lessons he again forgets or sets aside when his own occasion of temptation occurs. Like Raphael to himself, Adam focuses on the sly, envious, eager foe, the sufficient human defenses, and the imminent deception. He sees with perfect clarity the situation before them and its abstract moral pattern and possible manifestations. When his temptation occurs, its form is nonexperiential, an abstract principle, or love, or whatever; Eve is tempted by a designedly experiential serpent.

Raphael has fulfilled his assignment point by point in Books V–VIII, but one portion of the lesson does not penetrate Adam's thinking, or later Eve's: the warning "to beware / He swerve not too secure." The condition of innocence makes this security inevitable; the analogues are, however, nonetheless painful. In Adam's case:

> But say,
> What meant that caution join'd, *if ye be found*
> *Obedient?* can we want obedience then
> To him, or possibly his love desert
> Who form'd us from the dust, and plac'd us here
> Full to the utmost measure of what bliss
> Human desires can seek or apprehend?   (V, 512–18)

And later:

> Nor knew I not
> To be both will and deed created free;
> Yet that we never shall forget to love
> Our maker, and obey him whose command
> Single, is yet so just, my constant thoughts
> Assur'd me and still assure.   (V, 548–53)

"Sufficient to have stood" enters human thinking as "though free to fall" does not and cannot. In Arnold Stein's words, Adam "is over-estimating the power within himself by underestimating the danger within."[17] Eve, like Adam, 'assumes too complacently her security and capacity, and her homey equivalent response borders on petulance:

> But that thou shouldst my firmness therefore doubt
> To God or thee, because we have a foe
> May tempt it, I expected not to hear.
> . . . .
>
> His fraud is then thy fear, which plain infers
> Thy equal fear that my firm Faith and Love
> Can by his fraud be shak'n or seduc't;
> Thoughts, which how found they harbor in thy breast,
> *Adam*, misthought of her to thee so dear? (IX, 279–81, 285–89)

The wonderful syntactic distortion of the final two lines mirrors Eve's awkward psychological state. Despite the clarity of his vision and the soundness of his judgment and fears, Adam accedes to Eve's request in lines that recall Raphael's reply to Adam's comparable query (V, 514, 520–23):

> But if thou think, trial unsought may find
> Us both securer than thus warn'd thou seem'st,
> Go; for thy stay not free, absents thee more;
> Go in thy native innocence, rely
> On what thou hast of virtue, summon all,
> For God towards thee hath done his part, do thine.
> (IX, 370–75)

Several critics—most prominently Joseph Summers and Arnold Stein[18]—view Adam's giving in as an anticipation of his fall, his fond submission to his weaker part, the faltering of judgment before loved beauty. The alternative view is that force upon free will can have no place in Eden. God loves his beautiful images, too, but cannot force their actions without distorting, embruting, destroying their freedom, reason, and creativity, the ways in which they are made in and manifest his image. Adam's final admonition of Eve echoes Raphael's final warning to himself at the end of Book VIII:

> Be strong, live happy, and love, but first of all
> Him whom to love is to obey, and keep
> His great command; take heed lest Passion sway

Thy Judgment to do aught, which else free Will
Would not admit; thine and of all thy Sons
The weal or woe in thee is plac't; beware.
I in thy persevering shall rejoice,
And all the Blest: Stand fast; to stand or fall
Free in thine own Arbitrement it lies.
Perfet within, no outward aid require;
And all temptation to transgress repel.   (633–43)

E. M. W. Tillyard is surely right in observing that Adam's speech to
Eve (IX, 343–75) "echoes God's discourse on Free Will uttered in
Heaven (Book Three, lines 80–134)" and that "Adam is here the
mouthpiece of Heaven for the benefit of Eve" (p. 254). The same
terms recur in Books III and IX—the distinction between force and
false perverting guile, the roles of will and reason, with a continuing
emphasis upon human energy, responsibility, and self-definition—
but in Book III the ideas are surrounded by an aura of the elusive
mystery of faith and doctrine in the abstract. A verbal pattern will
illuminate the point. Key words are often repeated in divine discourse: "Freely they stood who stood, and fell who fell" (III, 102);
"I form'd them free, and free they must remain, / Till they enthrall
themselves" (III, 124–25); and later Raphael's "freely we
serve, / Because we freely love, as in our will / To love or not" (V,
538–40). The dilated terms are *free* and *will* chiefly, but also *reason*,
love, and *obey* and references to standing and falling, warning and
temptation. Through such dilation the words themselves become
ritualized and magnified. These, like other divine mysteries, elude
human categories of utterance as of mind. The reading of divine
discourse in Book III calls for openness of mind, for the application
of faith more than experience. Book IX grounds comparable ideas in
human intercourse for the first couple; for Milton's fit reading audience it is doctrine by narrative example rather than mere precept.

As this selection of evidence suggests, it would be possible to
cite a much fuller array of parallel passages. The pattern of evidence
comes fully into focus, however, with the "mutual accusation" of the
final lines of Book IX. When Eve asks in complaint:

Was I to have never parted from thy side?
As good have grown there still a lifeless Rib.
Being as I am, why didst not thou the Head
Command me absolutely not to go,
Going into such danger as thou said'st?   (1153–57)

she is posing in human terms the abstract theory of the heavenly conversation on free will and predestination in Book III. For her it is hindsight and recrimination, to be sure, but she is asking the crucial question of all novice readers of *Paradise Lost* and the Genesis myth, of all of us who suffer the painful effects of lost innocence and perfection, who seek to lay blame and wish fleetingly or lingeringly that our personal and cosmic contexts might have been ordered otherwise. She is asking one of the all-encompassing questions of the epic, as does Adam in Book X: "Ah, why should all mankind / For one man's fault thus guiltless be condemn'd, / If guiltless?" (822–24). Eve here, in brief, asks mankind's enduring query of her head Adam, and Adam in replying to her voices what God might well reply to us:

> And am I now upbraided, as the cause
> Of thy transgressing? not enough severe,
> It seems, in thy restraint: What could I more?
> I warn'd thee, I admonish'd thee, foretold
> The danger, and the lurking Enemy
> That lay in wait; beyond this had been force,
> And force upon free Will hath here no place.   (IX, 1168–74)

Adam summarizes Raphael's lengthy dealings with himself and his own right action and advice to Eve before their parting, an occasion recalled early in Book X when the angelic guards present themselves before the throne of God to account their vigilance and be approved by his justice. Book IX thus offers a dramatic adumbration of doctrine via human intercourse as it brings Raphael's Books V–VIII into focus and makes human and reader-involving the abstract, difficult, distancing theory of Book III. That early theory seemed disjointed and resistant because we readers, who are "surprised by sin" through the epic's processes, were recalcitrant and out of focus. The movement is toward our coherence and grasp and the epic's wholeness. Through the parallels, responsibility and context are securely placed; the Christian prospect, the *felix culpa*, will emerge in the poem's conclusion. For the present, the parallels might be extended to interpret Adam's pronouncement that he "might have liv'd and joy'd immortal bliss, / Yet willingly chose rather Death with thee" (IX, 1166–67) as a perspective on the mystery of Christ's role and mission, another of the resounding, abstract, and difficult issues of the Book III conversation. Adam's relationship and presentation to Eve mirror God's relationship to us and Milton's representation of theological issues for our comprehension.

III

The last major body of evidence I wish to explore opens out, like Eve's lyric, from contiguous repeating stanzas (the only two occasions of this rhetorical strategem in the poem); the final lines of Book X draw us and the Edenic pair above Book X's adumbration of despair toward the prayerful energies of Book XI. With some qualification, Rajan has noted that in this instance too the dogma of Book III is translated into drama. His qualification invites our notice as relating to the thrust of the present essay: "But as the poem puts each disclosure in its place and expounds its potencies and limitations, the final understanding takes shape as the knowledge that there is always more to be understood. The paraphrase is not the poem and while the poem through the wise use of its resources can move closer to what is seen from the highest of heights, the poem in its turn is not the vision."[19] The passage at issue is this:

> What better can we do, than to the place
> Repairing where he judg'd us, prostrate fall
> Before him reverent, and there confess
> Humbly our faults, and pardon beg, with tears
> Watering the ground, and with our sighs the Air
> Frequenting, sent from hearts contrite, in sign
> Of sorrow unfeign'd, and humiliation meek.
>
> . . . .
>
> So spake our Father penitent, nor *Eve*
> Felt less remorse: they forthwith to the place
> Repairing where he judg'd them prostrate fell
> Before him reverent, and both confess'd
> Humbly thir faults, and pardon begg'd, with tears
> Watering the ground, and with thir sighs the Air
> Frequenting, sent from hearts contrite, in sign
> Of sorrow unfeign'd, and humiliation meek.
>
> (X, 1086–92, 1097–1104)

Except for *there/both*, the only changes in language and line/word placement are of mood, tense (present to past), and person (first plural to third plural). The mood and tense changes emphasize possibility actualized. The person or point-of-view changes demonstrate distancing toward the divine perspective of the early lines of Book XI. That the earlier two-stanza structure compressed nine lines into seven with vocabulary shifts but without loss of content and ended where it began with *sweet* may be seen to realize the confined and confining Edenic context; the later two-stanza structure renders in form as in content the widening prospect of the fallen condition, possibility actualized and perspective distanced, the openness of faith rather than the closedness of sensory or merely experiential knowledge within the innocent paradise.[20]

What I wish to stress at present, however, is not so much the verbal texture as the structural shaping. Approximately the first 160 lines of Book XI render explicit and implicit definitions of prayer, its processes, pattern, and effects—a prayer offered together by a reunited Adam and Eve. That reunion or fallen union is significant, for Book X has shown us Adam and Eve at their most separate. Adam's despair, isolation, and awful loss realize the mutual accusation, fruitless hours, and vain contest of Book IX's ending, with Adam lamenting loud in Book X through the "damps and dreadful gloom" of night's "black Air" and his own "evil Conscience" (X, 845–49). When a contrite Eve appears, Adam dismisses and damns her as a false and hateful serpent, full of inward fraud and hellish falsehood and of overweening and wandering vanity, a show, a sinister rib, crooked by nature, and a fair defect of nature (X, 867–92). Adam imposes on her the damnation—the Old Testament justice—he expects and projects from heaven on himself. In her response, Eve shows Adam the way to heavenly reconcilement. In Joseph Summers' words: "Eve offers herself as a redeemer, and however inadequate she is to fulfill that role, her attempt mirrors the redemptive actions of the Son, both in His first moment of undertaking and throughout the poem."[21]

> but *Eve*
> Not so repulst, with Tears that ceas'd not flowing,
> And tresses all disorder'd, at his feet
> Fell humble, and imbracing them, besought
> His peace.   (X, 909–13)

Eve's action and attitude and the poetic texture anticipate Book X's finale. Here and in her prayer to Adam are all the terms of the double stanzas: the penitence, remorse, prostration, reverence, confession, pardon begg'd, tears, sighs, contrite heart, unfeign'd sorrow, and meek humiliation.[22] Summers again supplies a valuable formulation of the point. For him Eve provides untheoretical comfort as opposed to Adam's despairing theorizing; her speech (X, 914–36) offers "the fullest human expression of the will to redemptive love"; and "Eve's speech is the turning point, for it is here that one of the guilty pair first attempts to take upon herself the burden of guilt, shows love and asks for love. The direction once taken, Adam is moved to similar affection, and the resulting reconciliation between man and woman is the inevitable prologue and type of the ensuing reconciliation between man and God" (pp. 182–83, 176). In a nice formulation of the distinction between Old and New Dispensations, Arnold Stein observes: "Unfallen creatures love God through obeying, the fallen obey through loving."[23] That loving is both of God directly and of God through each other.

In reading Eve's prayer to Adam we are invited—indeed correct reading requires us—to supply the divine dimension and translate character designations. For "Forsake me [Eve] not thus, *Adam*," we must concurrently note "Forsake me [Adam] not thus, God." Happily, in Book XI *me* becomes *us*, and union and reunion have human and divine arenas. Eve's prayer and the necessity for reading it in just this way proceed:

> Witness Heav'n
> What love sincere, and reverence in my heart
> I bear thee, and unweeting have offended,
> Unhappily deceiv'd; thy suppliant
> I beg, and clasp thy knees; bereave me not,
> Whereon I live, thy gentle looks, thy aid,
> Thy counsel in this uttermost distress,
> My only strength and stay: forlorn of thee,
> Whither shall I betake me, where subsist?
> While yet we live, scarce one short hour perhaps,
> Between us two let there be peace, both joining,
> As join'd in injuries, one enmity
> Against a Foe by doom express assign'd us,
> That cruel Serpent.   (914–27)

Eve is referring to a real deception and to palpable knees, but no great imaginative stretch is needed to conjure up the more contemplative Adam's heavenly strength and stay, the gentle looks, aid, and counsel available to faith rather than experience. That God's encompassing plan calls for cooperative human warfare against the cosmic foe—for him a metaphorically understood Bruiser of Heels, not a beast with hairy mane terrific—is too complex an issue to be more than mentioned at present. But multidimensional reading is clearly called for in the context, a new deployment with a radically different tone and purpose of the rhetorical device of Sin's reigning at Satan's "right hand voluptuous" late in Book II.

Adam's and Eve's double-stanza prayer succeeds in evoking the descent of prevenient grace (XI, 3). Here in Book X Eve succeeds in drawing from Adam an earthly human equivalent of that ultimate mystery:

> She ended weeping, and her lowly plight,
> Immovable till peace obtain'd from fault
> Acknowledg'd and deplor'd, in *Adam* wrought
> Commiseration; soon his heart relented
> Towards her, his life so late and sole delight,
> Now at his feet submissive in distress,
> Creature so fair his reconcilement seeking,
> His counsel whom she had displeas'd, his aid;
> As one disarm'd, his anger all he lost,
> And thus with peaceful words uprais'd her soon.   (937–46)[24]

In the foreground kneels the penitent narrative Eve. In the background lie the "Forgive us our trespasses as we forgive those who trespass against us" of the Lord's Prayer and the anticipation of the New Dispensation to be actualized in the remaining two books of *Paradise Lost*, the theory of grace and prayer as well as the facts of Old Testament history to be read typologically. The typological emerges explicitly in Michael's explanation of the origins of the rainbow to the questioning Adam at the end of Book XI, a passage that again invites and rewards close comparison with the spiritual processes and the relationship to divinity we have been examining:

> So willingly doth God remit his Ire,
> Though late repenting him of Man deprav'd,
> Griev'd at his heart, when looking down he saw

The whole Earth fill'd with violence, and all flesh
Corrupting each thir way; yet those remov'd,
Such grace shall one just Man find in his sight,
That he relents, not to blot out mankind,
And makes a Cov'nant never to destroy
The Earth again by flood, nor let the Sea
Surpass his bounds, nor Rain to drown the World
With Man therein or Beast; but when he brings
Over the Earth a Cloud, will therein set
His triple-color'd Bow, whereon to look
And call to mind his Cov'nant: Day and Night,
Seed-time and Harvest, Heat and hoary Frost
Shall hold thir course, till fire purge all things new,
Both Heav'n and Earth, wherein the just shall dwell.

(XI, 885–901)

The context is now the fallen world; macrocosm mirrors the microcosm of the stormy relationship of Adam and Eve in the latter part of Book IX, for example, 1121–26, and throughout Book X, a storm now calmed and reconciled. The final books of *Paradise Lost* demonstrate Adam's control over the methods of right reading of experience and typology and parallels, of his own image within a hierarchy of images of fact and faith, and of his own place within a scheme of geography, history, ontology, eschatology, and anagogy.

A final verbal pattern will characterize a number of lesser instances of similar evidence. In X, 941, we hear Adam's view of Eve as "his life so late and sole delight." Earlier Adam called her "My fairest, my espous'd, my latest found, / Heav'n's last best gift, my ever new delight" (V, 18–19); and for Milton and Satan and one who has been long in populous city pent, in simile and by analogy, Eve "in her look sums all delight" (IX, 454). When hoodwinking Uriel, Satan calls man God's "chief delight and favor" (III, 664) and later cites God's "new delight" (IV, 106). In IX, 242–43, Adam explains to Eve that man was made for delight and—the supplementation in Adam's repetition is crucial—for "delight to Reason join'd." To carry the design to a final and its highest stage, Christ praises the Father for always glorifying his Son and sons, and considers his glory, exaltation, and "whole delight" to be pleasing God and fulfilling his will (IV, 724–29). *Delight* may be a personification, a principle, or a spiritual passion, but it reflects an aspect of God and, like questioning, is part of human communication and interrelationship with him.

The structural pattern is a continuing and vital and poetic one: Woman is to man as man (and mankind) is to God.

In the background of the psychological and social action in Book X lies evidence for complementing a design earlier noted, that Adam can answer Eve's questioning of the heavens to her but poses his own similar questioning in conversation with Raphael. Adam can work his way through despair in soliloquy only to negative propositions and clarification of the distance between himself and God. Even when with imaginative effort Adam draws an analogy between his relationship to a son and God's relationship to him (X, 760–65)—turning as it does to experience rather than faith—Adam attains only the vague relief of submission to "Natural necessity." But after their reconciliation and under the influence of exampled redemptive love, facing in conversation Eve's desperate measures that echo his own earlier ones, he can move, verbally must move, out of the static dungeon of his own despair. She provides the experiential agency that allows him to make the leap of faith. Whether in the need for articulation, or in his recognition of the mirroring she offers him, or under the influence of the dawning New Dispensation, he comes to exercise his right reason. His masculine characteristics are tempered by feminine submission, his reason by a pattern of redemptive love, in confirmation of their new relationship, wholeness, and future mission.

With this evidence in view we can summarize the present findings. Adam and Eve are both distinct characterizations and a composite of one psychology and mankind. The design coincides with the traditional levels of allegory and their definitive time schemes. As distinct narrative characters, they present the literal and typological levels; we read them in terms of the past. When we see Adam and Eve as a composite psychology of reason and fancy (or other preferred categories) we are in the realm of moral allegory and the present time. When we see in them all mankind, the prospect of the encompassing divine plan, anagogical allegory, and the future open before us. The time scheme and complete and correct reading reconcile and synthesize experience and faith.

Adam is dominant and our chief focus. With him we see the self and the world with double vision, both downward via Eve to the mixed realm of earth, the senses, the concrete, the experiential, the securely graspable, and upward via the layered divine agencies to the mysterious realm of the heavenly and of faith, the abstract, the spiritually provocative. Those layered agencies include Raphael, Christ, and God, but include also the individual's capacities for creative thought, imagination, leaps of faith. Eve's relationship to Adam and Adam's to Eve make available, to minds grounded in the experiential, patterns that guide the energies of faith and imagination toward the incomprehensible, toward what is beyond our control and perilous judgment, thus allowing us to grow toward fullest humanity, which is fuller divinity. It is no casual gesture that Eve should turn from her idolatry of the tree to a worship of experience (wrongly judged as "Best Guide" and opener of "wisdom's way," IX, 807–09). Experience by definition looks to the past and locks itself to what has been. It coincides with despair. Adam's parallel gesture emerges in his closed question, "But past who can recall, or done undo?" (IX, 926)—described by the narrator as "Submitting to what seem'd remediless" (919) and judged by God as "believing lies / Against his Maker" (X, 42–43). The other way of knowing, by faith, looks to and grows toward what will be. It coincides with the capacity to receive the operations of Grace. Mankind with its postlapsarian double nature lives at the meeting point of past and future, the present time, and at the meeting point of downward and upward, the present place, whether a wide wilderness, a happy garden, or a far happier paradise within. When Milton speaks of justifying the ways of God to men, we must take into account the open-endedness of such justification through faith.

Grammatically we have worked our way through the declarative, the imperative, and the interrogative, to find ourselves and the poem's culmination in the exclamatory, the sense of wonder and the affirmation of the wonderful that define innocence and that silence falling human experiential judgment in the presence and awareness of glory—"O goodness infinite, goodness immense!" (XII, 470 ff.). The grammar is a lesson in faith and marks a shift from Old Testament to New Testament epistemology. Adam must and does learn to read Eve's actions, expressions, and nature in the light of the encompassing divine plan for himself and history; through her corporal form and Michael's lessoning he comes to terms with the right relationship of experience and faith. Essentially this structural design demonstrates Milton doing for us what Raphael has done for Adam: likening spiritual matters to the corporal forms that best express them in order to relate to human sense invisible exploits and explanations that otherwise surmount the reach of our minds (V, 564–74). The parallelism I have been examining here aids us in knowing and placing characters hierarchically and in variously apprehended contexts; it assists us also in defining and fully realizing some of the most abstract, complex, and elusive concepts of the poem; it calls attention to yet another way to see the wonderful artistry of *Paradise Lost*, the intricate resonant interaction of form, fact, feeling, and faith.

University of Massachusetts, Amherst

NOTES

1. The phrase in quotation marks is Isabel G. MacCaffrey's in *"Paradise Lost" as "Myth"* (Cambridge, Mass., 1959), of which the third chapter, "Structural Patterns in *Paradise Lost*," pp. 44–91, is among the best comments on parallelism. Also valuable are Joseph H. Summers, *The Muse's Method: An Introduction to Paradise Lost* (New York, 1962), passim, esp. pp. 61–70, 98, and 177–78; and Stanley E. Fish, *Surprised by Sin: The Reader in Paradise Lost* (Berkeley, 1971), passim, esp. pp. 216–32, 296–305.

2. And see Hebrews xi, 3, and vi, 12 (which speaks of "them who through faith and patience inherit the promises"), and Romans xiv, 23 ("whatsoever is not of faith is sin").

3. The text for the present study is *John Milton: Complete Poems and Major Prose*, ed. Merritt Y. Hughes (New York, 1957).

4. "Innocence and Experience in Milton's Eden," in *New Essays on Paradise Lost*, ed. Thomas Kranidas (Berkeley, 1971), pp. 103–04.

5. In *Paradise Lost: A Poem in Twelve Books* (London, 1757), vol. II, pp. 340–41, Thomas Newton cites Pope: "When the Angel is driving them both out of Paradise, Adam grieves that he must leave a place where he had conversed with God and his Angels; but Eve laments that she shall never more behold the fine flowers of Eden: Here Adam mourns like a man, and Eve like a woman."

6. See Hebrews xi, 8–10 and 13–16, and Fish, *Surprised by Sin*, pp. 141, 200–01.

7. Quoted in Newton, *Poem in Twelve Books*, vol. I, pp. 309–10.

8. See MacCaffrey, *"Paradise Lost" as "Myth,"* p. 77; John R. Knott, Jr., *Milton's Pastoral Vision: An Approach to "Paradise Lost"* (Chicago, 1971), p. 8; Anne Davidson Ferry, *Milton's Epic Voice: The Narrator in "Paradise Lost"* (Cambridge, Mass.,

1963), pp. 161, 163–64; *The Poems of John Milton*, ed. John Carey and Alastair Fowler (London, 1968), p. 650; and Arnold Stein, *Answerable Style: Essays on Paradise Lost* (Minneapolis, 1953), p. 86. Stein cites the parallel passage (IV, 610–16) and calls Eve's lyric "a prettier poem than Adam's"; he observes also that Adam praises "not the things, but their relationship to the Creator."

9. Ferry reads the evidence differently but makes a comparable point; for her the stanzas have eleven and seven lines, and the lyric begins and ends with "thee" (639, 656) (*Milton's Epic Voice*, p. 162). Carey and Fowler (*Poems of John Milton*, p. 650) remind us to "note that the 9-line spiritual portion refers to Paradise with Adam, the mutable 7-line portion to Paradise without Adam. In the latter portion each item in the former suffers alteration; though this alteration is as yet hypothetical and held in check by negation."

10. Lewalski provides an excellent commentary on this question, noting how it arises from Eve's lyric, especially line 656, and calling attention to its faulty moral assumptions ("Innocence and Experience," pp. 101–02). See also Carey and Fowler, *Poems of John Milton*, p. 651, and Stein, *Answerable Style*, p. 86.

11. Cf. IV, 449, for Eve's introduction to her account; the reply she receives—"fond"?—is loving smiles and "kisses pure" (502).

12. Stein hears the speaker's voice here as a projection of Eve's own mind (*Answerable Style*, pp. 84–88).

13. Summers, *Muse's Method*, p. 155, see also 153–60; Ferry, *Milton's Epic Voice*, p. 158; and Russell E. Smith, Jr., "Adam's Fall," in *Critical Essays on Milton from ELH* (Baltimore, 1969), pp. 184–90. Smith goes so far as to assert that Adam's sudden recognition that "he is to Raphael what Eve has been to him—inferior" disturbs "Adam's sense of equilibrium" and makes Adam reach for "a confirmation of his own worth" in questioning Raphael about angels (p. 186). Lewalski ("Innocence and Experience," pp. 106–08) calls attention to a cosmic discrepancy in Raphael's account in Book VII which provokes Adam to speculate beyond the earlier discussion with Eve on astronomy. In her view, the astronomical query in Book VIII is less presumptuous, less a venture toward forbidden knowledge, than that at VII, 90–93. Contrarily, Newton cites Richardson to describe the occasion as "most proper" and Adam's proposals as "very judicious" (*Poem in Twelve Books*, vol. II, p. 68).

14. See Fish, *Surprised by Sin*, pp. 28–29, and Lewalski, "Innocence and Experience," pp. 110–11. Northrop Frye supports the view "that the question is unanswerable within the framework of *Paradise Lost*" with the observation that "Adam is asking a question about nature, and the nature of nature . . . depends on Adam's behaviour" (*The Return of Eden: Five Essays on Milton's Epics* [Toronto, 1965], p. 42 and similarly pp. 55–57).

15. Summers (*Muse's Method*, p. 157) makes a comparable point about the two senses of *admire* in VIII, 26.

16. For a very careful and carefully reasoned review of Adam and Eve's separation, see Dennis H. Burden, *The Logical Epic: A Study of the Argument of "Paradise Lost"* (Cambridge, Mass., 1967), pp. 81–82 and esp. 85–93.

17. *Answerable Style*, pp. 99–100. See also Fish, *Surprised by Sin*, pp. 229–30 and 238–39. In another connection earlier (pp. 13–14), Fish cites William Haller to make the point that "nothing is more indicative of a graceless state than a sense of security."

18. Summers, *Muse's Method*, pp. 63 and 174; Stein, *Answerable Style*, pp. 99–100 and 113. Carey and Fowler say: "Adam, the image of God, here experiences

the same kind of dilemma as God himself in iii 100ff. He sees the risk of letting Eve go perfectly well, as 1.361 shows; so that his judgment does not fail. But to keep Eve in passive obedience would be to lose her (with 1.372 cp. iii 110). Eve, already in the grip of temptation, has put Adam in an impossible position, transmitting to him the pressure, the excessive motion, put on her by Satan" (*Poems of John Milton*, pp. 876–77).

19. " 'To Which Is Added *Samson Agonistes*—'," in *The Prison and the Pinnacle* (Toronto, 1973), pp. 90–91. Other links with Book III are discussed on pp. 84–86; on pp. 84–85 Rajan describes the repeating stanzas at the end of Book X as "curiously stilted to the modern reader," but cf. Newton, quoting Bentley (*Poem in Twelve Books*, vol. II, p. 310). Knott (*Milton's Pastoral Vision*, p. 25) and Fish (*Surprised by Sin*, pp. 145–46) compare the ending of Book X with the morning hymn in Book V.

20. Rajan makes the point that the unit of Adam and Eve's prayer is spread over two books of *Paradise Lost* to allow readers two perspectives: "First the existential progress from recognition to the amending response and then the cosmic perspective which enables us to esteem the fruit of responsibility rightly exercised" (*Prison and the Pinnacle*, p. 83). Lawrence A. Sasek finds Adam and Eve's joy upon their repentance at the opening of Book XI "a sign of instability" ("The Drama of *Paradise Lost*, Books XI and XII," in *Milton: Modern Essays in Criticism*, ed. Arthur E. Barker [New York, 1965], p. 347).

21. Summers, *Muse's Method*, pp. 177–78. For other comments relating this occasion to redemption and seeing Eve as a redeemer, parallel with Christ, see ibid., pp. 183, 185; Fish, *Surprised by Sin*, pp. 133, 285; Stein, *Answerable Style*, pp. 128–29; Rajan, *Prison and the Pinnacle*, p. 86; and Lawrence W. Hyman, *The Quarrel Within: Art and Morality in Milton's Poetry* (Port Washington, N.Y., 1972), p. 65 (where Helen Gardner is also cited). For Adam's redemptive love for Eve as typologically Christic, see Frank L. Huntley, "Before and After the Fall: Some Miltonic Patterns of Systasis," in *Approaches to "Paradise Lost": The York Tercentenary Lectures*, ed. C. A. Patrides (London, 1968), p. 5. For Frye, "this is the point at which the human race becomes, from God's point of view, something worth redeeming" (*Return of Eden*, p. 81).

22. Compare with the four steps to regeneration in Milton's *Christian Doctrine*, Bk. I, chap. xix. Summers echoes Tillyard in finding X, 910–12, anticipated in V, 129–36, where Eve's being comforted after the bad dream "is a gracious foreshadowing of the human motions of sin, repentance, forgiveness, reconciliation in love, and continued life" (*Muse's Method*, p. 74).

23. Stein, *Answerable Style*, p. 118. See also Hyman, *Quarrel Within*, p. 72; Fish, *Surprised by Sin*, pp. 273–76; and Rajan, *Prison and the Pinnacle*, p. 88. The latter states: "Though Adam must make the decision it is Eve who by casting her contribution in the hierarchic mould (X, 930–1), restores the rightness of her relationship with Adam and so enables Adam to find his relationship with God."

24. Newton, quoting Thyer, offers the following on this passage, especially X, 940: "This picture of Eve's distress, her submissive tender address to her husband, and his generous reconcilement to her are extremely beautiful, I had almost said beyond anything in the whole poem" (*Poem in Twelve Books*, vol. II, p. 301).

MILTON'S MOON

Dustin Griffin

In discussing the sublimity of *Paradise Lost*, Addison distinguished between the turbulence of the War in Heaven and the
"composed and sedate majesty" of the Creation. The moonlit
evening in Eden (*PL* IV, 598–609) is a supreme instance of that
milder sublime and one of the great moments of the poem. At the
climax of Milton's description of the arrival of evening, the moon
"unveil'd her peerless Light, / And o'er the dark her silver
mantle threw." This startling moment is an emblem of divine
presence and protectiveness in unfallen Eden. Familiar with
moon lore and with poetic descriptions of the moon, Milton
shunned allegorical links to the Virgin and the historical church
and seemed to associate this unveiling-investing gesture with
Christ, the "unclouded deity," with the Creator who invests
the world "as with a mantle," and with the process of poetic
creation in a poet, his eyes "veiled," who prays that mists might
be purged and that he himself might be "clothed in light." But
after the Fall, the benign and creative moon is simply "blank."

WHEN JOHNSON noted that Milton's "peculiar power is to
astonish," he was saying nothing new.[1] Eighteenth-century
critics regularly praised Milton for his "sublimity," by which they
meant in part a capacity to elevate and at once to fill the mind of the
reader with wonder or, as Johnson says, to display the vast and
illuminate the splendid. Although we may find the term "sublime"
imprecise and may now choose as critics to emphasize Milton's
defter, subtler effects, we should not forget what his first century of
readers found so powerfully moving. No reader, of course, is in
danger of underestimating the sublimity of Milton's hell, or of the
awesome "chariot of paternal deity" from which the Son strikes
terror into the falling angelic legions, or of the creation by fiat:

151

"Silence, ye troubled waves, and thou deep, peace" (VII, 216).[2] But the power to astonish is not displayed only in scenes of supernatural grandeur. Milton has also a milder, more reticent sublime, in which the astonishing beauty and harmony of God's created world is brought home to the reader. Addison recognized this "composed and sedate majesty" in comparing the sublimity of Book VI with that of Book VII:

The Seventh Book, which we are now entering upon, is an Instance of that Sublime, which is not mixt and work'd up with Passion. The Author appears in a kind of composed and sedate Majesty; and tho' the Sentiments do not give so great an Emotion as those in the former Book, they abound with as magnificent Ideas. The Sixth Book, like a troubled Ocean, represents Greatness in Confusion; the Seventh affects the Imagination like the Ocean in a Calm, and fills the Mind of the Reader without producing in it any thing like tumult or Agitation.[3]

Addison finds this sublime particularly in the seventh book, but it can be found occasionally in the earlier descriptions of Creation, in the fourth book. It is on one of those sublime Edenic moments that I wish to concentrate.

As the first evening in Eden comes gradually on, Hesperus appears, forerunning night and the moon:

>Now came still evening on, and twilight grey
>Had in her sober livery all things clad;
>Silence accompanied, for beast and bird,
>They to their grassy couch, these to their nests
>Were slunk, all but the wakeful nightingale;
>She all night long her amorous descant sung;
>Silence was pleased: now glowed the firmament
>With living sapphires: Hesperus that led
>The starry host, rode brightest, till the moon
>Rising in clouded majesty, at length
>Apparent queen unveiled her peerless light,
>And o'er the dark her silver mantle threw.   (IV, 598–609)[4]

The moon removes her veils to reveal, like Ovid's Vertumnus, her nakedness. The effect is sublime—startling and awesome: a sudden view of purity, as Calidore had in coming upon the hundred naked maidens on Mt. Acidale.[5] But Milton goes further. The moon, though naked, is still clothed,[6] for she then removes her "silver mantle," removes, as it were, her very self, though she still retains it. Surely, this is one of the great moments of the poem. We are moved because we sense in this scene, as elsewhere in *Paradise Lost*, that the natural world immediately figures forth God's goodness. But why this moment is so extraordinarily moving is a question worth trying to answer. What are the sources of its power?

The passage was praised by eighteenth-century critics for its descriptive power: "Surely here is the most enchanting Description of the Ev'ning that ever was made."[7] Mere natural description, however, seems only a part of what is going on. The brief scene is subtly moralized. The sapphirelike stars recall the "living sapphire" of heaven's battlements (II, 1050). "Living," a jeweler's term meaning "native" or "unshaped, uncut," makes the sapphire stars *naturally* artful, or rather divinely artful, like the altar of unhewn stones in Exodus xx, 25. More important, "living sapphires," like "vegetable gold" (IV, 220), are not mere drossy decorative riches, but signs and witnesses of God's living art. Hesperus, the evening star, leads his "starry host" in the service of a greater light. Satan, the "Morning Star," by contrast misguides *his* "starry flock." He "allured them, and with lies / Drew after him the third part of Heaven's host" (V, 708–10), leading them in the service, not of God, but of himself. The moon, too, bears moral meaning. Though much of its presentation here and elsewhere can be seen in the context of accumulated moon lore, mythological, folkloric, scientific, or poetic, it is probably Milton who sensed, in the moon's modest regal gesture, both self-effacing and protective—unveiling her light and throwing that light (in the form of a mantle) over the world—a moment instinct with divinity.

Milton was far from the first to describe a moonlit night. Eighteenth-century editors compared the simile in the *Iliad*, where the Trojans' thousand fires before Troy are compared to the stars shining around the gleaming moon on a clear night (VIII, 555–59), and the brief description of a moonlit sea in the *Aeneid* (VII, 8–9).[8] Neither Homer nor Virgil in any sense provided a source for Milton, but he no doubt knew the passages, as he must have known Renaissance descriptions such as those in Drayton's *Endimion and Phoebe*. Milton's contemporaries and immediate predecessors commonly spoke of the moon being veiled or clothed with clouds and, in that aspect, often described her either as a queen of night or a pale watery star.[9] Milton may well have remembered one such regal description. The moon

> from the wave-embatteled shrowds,
> Opening the west, comes streaming through the clouds.
> With shining troops of silver tressed stars
> Attending on her, as her torch-bearers,
> And all the lesser lights about her throne,
> With admiration stand as lookers on,
> Whilst she alone, in height of all her pride,
> The queen of light along her sphere doth glide.[10]

As in *Paradise Lost,* the moon, described as a queen, breaks through the clouds, attended by hosts of stars. But unlike Milton's moon, this one is proud; instead of *acting* (throwing her mantle), she simply glides along her sphere receiving admiration. But neither is the Edenic moon a pale and demure night wanderer, as she is, for example, in *Il Penseroso:*

> The wandering moon
> Riding near her highest noon,
> Like one that had been led astray
> Through the heaven's wide pathless way;
> And oft, as if her head she bowed,
> Stooping through a fleecy cloud.   (67–72)[11]

The moon in paradise is a figure neither of pride nor of pathos; she is regal but mild, queen and yet a servant.

The moon has a long history in myth and folklore, as well as in poetry. As he so often does, Milton seems to have sought to gather within *Paradise Lost* various speculations on a subject without necessarily unifying them into a single conception. Thus, the moon appears as the *dea triformis* (III, 730), "triform" because of her three phases and because in classical myth she rules in heaven, earth, and hell, where she is known as Cynthia, Diana, and Hecate. The moon appears also as Astarte, the Phoenician moon goddess (I, 439), and as the queen of faery (I, 784–86), "arbitress" (witness) of their revels.[12] He alludes also to the superstition that witches and magicians had the power to attract the moon down to earth and that the moon in eclipse was thought to be laboring.[13] As Fowler notes, in populating the moon with "translated saints, or middle spirits . . . Betwixt the angelical and human kind" (*PL* III, 460–62), Milton joins a series of speculators who had done the same.

The moon had likewise long been the subject of scientific speculation which reached a climax in the seventeenth century after Galileo's *Siderius Nuncius* (1610) and John Wilkins' *The Discovery of a World in the Moone* (1638).[14] Milton recognizes this interest by including diverse speculation on lunar spots (I, 287–91; V, 419–20), on the possibility that the moon is itself another world like the earth, with its own inhabitants (VII, 621; VIII, 140), and on the moon's borrowed light (III, 730; VII, 375–79).

Finally, of course, the moon is part of God's Creation, as described in Genesis. Milton reiterates the fact that the moon, whatever else it may be or seem, was made by God (IV, 723), resounds his praise (V, 175), and was designed by him to reign over the dark, illuminating the earth and checking the powers of night (VII, 346–86; III, 726–32). It is this function, perhaps above all others, that most interests Milton in the poem, a protective function first hinted at in a simile at the end of Book I, where the "belated peasant" sees midnight faery revels, "while overhead the moon / Sits arbitress, and nearer to the earth wheels her pale course" (I, 984–86). The peasant's heart rebounds with "joy and fear," perhaps in part because he is uncertain whether the moon draws near as alien queen of faery (or even is herself *drawn* by faery magic) or as a protective presence for him. In the evening scene in Book IV these uncertainties vanish. There the moon is clearly revealed, acting under her own power, as a heavenly protector.

One body of moon lore that Milton appears to have deliberately excluded, however, is allegorical interpretation, largely perhaps because those interpretations were chiefly based on the unstable moon's waxing and waning: The moon in Eden is always at the full. The medieval encyclopaedist Rabanus Maurus sees the waxing and waning of the moon sometimes as a figure for mortal life, perpetually unstable and liable to eclipse, sometimes as a figure for the state of the church, likewise variable in its earthly fortunes.[15] This allegorical tradition persisted well into Milton's time, when Protestants like David Pareus saw the moon as a figure for the church:

For the Church (saith Ambrose) hath her own defects and risings like the moon: having not her own brightness, but borrowes her light from Christ, as the moon doth from the sun. So Austin: the Church is sometimes darkened, and as it were clothed with the multitude of scandals: sometimes she ap-

peares quiet and free by the tranquillity of the time: otherwhile she is
covered and troubled with the floods of tribulations and temptations. And
againe: the moon increasing and decreasing signifies the Church: because
so far as the Church is spirituall she shineth: but so far as she is carnal, she is
obscure.[16]

Though, as his introductory note to *Samson Agonistes* indicates,
Milton knew Pareus' work, it is unlikely that the moon in *Paradise
Lost*, now veiled by clouds, now clearly shining, is meant to signify
the "Churches condition diverse in this life: sometimes shining in
ful light; other while . . . scarcely to be seen, and sometimes not at
all, untill again her light break forth as out of darknes." Milton's
concern in the poem, and especially in the middle books, is not with
the historical church, but with individual man's relation to God.
Furthermore, on the level of imagery, Pareus' moon is variable and
passive, not in control of its fortunes. Milton's is constant and active,
choosing to unveil her light and to *throw* it, in the form of a silver
mantle, over the dark. Even the fact of the moon's borrowed light, a
prominent feature of Pareus' account (and most others), is played
down. The idea of borrowed light is admitted (III, 730), but in the
long account of the moon's creation Milton follows Genesis in making the moon an independent luminary:

> First in his east the glorious lamp was seen,
> Regent of day
>
>   .   .   .   .
>
>   Less bright the moon,
> But opposite in levelled west was set
> His mirror, with full face borrowing her light
> From him, *for other light she needed none
> In that aspect,* and still that distance keeps
> Till night, then in the east her turn she shines,
> Revolved on heaven's great axle, and her reign
> With thousand lesser lights dividual holds,
> With thousand thousand stars, that then appeared
> Spangling the hemisphere: then first adorned
> With their bright luminaries that set and rose,
> Glad evening and glad morn crowned the fourth day.
>   (VII, 370–71, 375–86, italics added)

The moon's light during the day is borrowed while the moon is *in
that aspect,* that is, in the west, opposite the sun.[17] Milton says here,

not that the moon is not self-luminous, but that in this one aspect of opposition the moon's own light (the passage clearly implies that the moon has "other light") is not needed. Fowler's note (p. 797) alerts us to the astronomical context: "The point of the passage lies in an allusion to a theory of Anastasius Synaita's, that 'when God made these two luminaries, the greater—namely the sun—he placed immediately at the east of the firmament; but the moon at the west' . . . Hence it was full moon at creation, and the sun and the moon were in an aspect of opposition (180° apart)."[18] At night the moon shines by her own power.

The notion that the moon has its own "proper light" is not only biblical. It persisted in popular science well into the seventeenth century. Swan's *Speculum Mundi* (1635) reported that the moon has its own "native light":

For although she shineth to us with a borrowed light, yet it is no consequence to say, she hath therefore no own proper light. There is . . . a double light of the moon; Proper and Strange. The Proper is that which is Homogeneall to it self, or *lux congenita*, a light begotten together with the moon, and essential to it, although it be but weak. The other is that which it borroweth from the sunne.[19]

With the authority of the Bible and contemporary belief for the idea that the moon has its own proper light, Milton elsewhere in the poem hints at such power. Raphael speculates that there may be other suns and moons "communicating male and female light . . . stored in each orb" (VIII, 150)—that is, each has its own kind of light. Earlier he links the moon into a universal alimentary chain—a popular conception in Milton's time:

> The grosser feeds the purer, the earth the sea,
> Earth and the sea feed air, the air those fires
> Ethereal, and as lowest first the moon
>
> . . . .
>
> Nor doth the moon no nourishment exhale
> From her moist continent to higher orbs.
> The sun that light imparts to all, receives
> From all his alimental recompense.   (V, 416–18, 21–24)

The culmination of these hints at proper light and power is, of course, the description of the moon's own "peerless light" and the "silver mantle" which she casts over the dark.

If Milton's moon has figurative value, something richer than the historical church or the Virgin (another symbolic identification he would have eschewed)[20] may be involved. Indeed, as I wish to show, the moon in *Paradise Lost* is in curious ways associated with Christ, with the Creator, and with the process of poetic creation.

In associating the moon with Christ, Milton would go against much inherited tradition. The moon had already acquired figurative meanings (its gender, in tradition and in the poem, is feminine), while Christ himself was often linked with the sun (Son of God, Sun of Righteousness, the day-star of *Lycidas*) or with the evening star.[21] Another problem is that a Christ-moon might seem to strong Trinitarians subversively subordinate to a God-sun. But Milton was no strong Trinitarian[22] and in any case takes pains to give the moon independent status. Finally, as Albert Cirillo has recently noted, the moon is occasionally associated in the poem with Satan.[23] Satan's shield hangs on his shoulders "like the moon" (I, 287); the devilish Ashtoreth is a moon goddess (I, 439); and Satan first tempts Eve by praising the moon's shadowy light ("Now reigns full orb'd the moon," V, 41). In fact, however, these associations are not conclusive. Linked with Satan's shield by simile only, the moon quickly becomes part of the creative achievement of the Tuscan artist. Ashtoreth is given crescent horns but is not in fact identified with the moon. Milton carefully says only that her "image" is worshiped "nightly by the moon." The report of Satan's temptation by moonlight comes *after* the narrator's description of the same moonlit night. Satanic associations, it is clear, are only in Satan's mind. In any case, as with Ashtoreth, good things may always be put to bad ends. The moon is not corrupted by such association with Satan. Furthermore, Satan is linked with other heavenly bodies fully as much as with the moon. His banner is likened to a meteor (I, 537) and he himself, to a comet (II, 708), the morning star (V, 708), and the sun (II, 488). At one point, in fact, he is like the sun eclipsed by the *moon*:

> his form had yet not lost
> All her original brightness, nor appeared
> Less than archangel ruined, and the excess
> Of glory obscured: as when the sun new risen
> Looks through the horizontal misty air
> Shorn of his beams, or from behind the moon
> In dim eclipse disastrous twilight sheds.   (I, 591–97)

If the moon, as I argue, has Christlike associations, then this passage, usually taken as a foreshadowing of the Fall, can refer both backward, to the defeat of Satan by the Son in the War in Heaven, and forward, to Christ's final triumph. The moon's femininity, furthermore, is not a problem. Milton's divinities are all functionally bisexual. Urania and "Eternal Wisdom" are feminine aspects of God the Father (VII, 9–11). The feminine Urania, as Fowler notes, has herself been identified with God the Father, the Holy Spirit, and with Christ. Angels "can either sex assume or both" (I, 424). Milton makes it clear that "two great sexes animate the world" (VIII, 155). Light is both "Male and Female." It may well be that the male sun is a manifestation of the masculine aspect of God (the strong light of procreation and judgment), and the female Moon, a manifestation of the feminine aspect (the softer light of protection and mercy). But Milton explicitly avoids restricting God the Father to sun-creator-judge and the Son to moon-redeemer-forgiver. The Son is both agent of creation (Bk. VII) and judge (Bk. XII); the Father is both just and merciful (III, 132–34).

Finally, allegorical tradition was sufficiently unrigorous and inclusive that Milton could have found warrant in it for seeing the moon as a figure for Christ. Rabanus Maurus, for example, says the moon can stand for human life, for the church, or for Christ.[24] For neo-Platonists too the moon, as Diana *triformis*, was only one of many pagan triadic gods interpreted as figures of the Trinity.[25] Even typologists, who seek out specific prefigurations, seem to have allowed much liberty in interpretation. The moon, usually a type of the historical church,[26] can also be a type for the regeneration of baptism, the three hypostases of the Trinity, Eve, God's "renovation of the Creatures in the course of Providence," and the Incarnation of Christ.[27]

Obstacles to an association between Christ and the moon, then, do not appear to be insuperable. Just such an association, furthermore, seems hinted at in the most remarkable aspects of Milton's description. The moon, in "clouded majesty," unveils her light to become visible or "apparent" and then casts a mantle of light on the world.[28] "Clouded majesty" is the first phrase to draw our attention, for it recalls Milton's descriptions of God the Father, particularly in his relation to the Son.

> How oft amidst
> Thick *clouds* and dark doth heaven's all-ruling sire
> Choose to reside, his glory unobscured,
> And with the *majesty* of darkness round
> Covers his throne.   (II, 263–67; italics added)

With numerous biblical texts as his authority,[29] Milton describes God's light as invisible because too bright, and therefore hidden in clouds:

> Fountain of light, thy self invisible
> Amidst the glorious brightness where thou sit'st
> Throned inaccessible, but when thou shadest
> The full blaze of thy beams, and through a cloud
> Drawn round about thee like a radiant shrine,
> Dark with excessive bright thy skirts appear.   (III, 375–80)

God is never described directly. His light is too bright for either human or angelic eyes.[30] Only to the Son does God reveal himself "without cloud" (XI, 45; see also VI, 719–20).

The Son, on the other hand, is the "unclouded deity" (X, 65), who manifests and makes visible all his Father's glory:

> Beyond compare the Son of God was seen
> Most glorious, in him all his Father shone
> Substantially expressed, and in his face
> Divine compassion visibly appeared.   (III, 138–41)

The Son's light is milder; in a sense it is mediated, or reflected, though no less divine. He is God made visible to man:

> Begotten Son, divine similitude,
> In whose conspicuous countenance, without cloud
> Made visible, the almighty Father shines,
> Whom else no creature can behold; on thee
> Impressed the effulgence of his glory abides,
> Transfused on thee his ample Spirit rests.   (III, 384–89)

Hume's comment (p. 113) brings out the biblical background and emphasizes the cloud imagery: "The Law, at its Promulgation by Moses, was delivered with Thunders and Lightenings, great Earthquakes and Terrors, and Mt. Sinai was covered with a Cloud [he quotes from Exodus, chap. xix]. But when our Saviour appeared, the Cloud was removed [he quotes from 2 Corinthians, chap. iv]." Milton's moon in "clouded majesty," then, seems to hint at God the

Father. The cloudless moon, in turn, seems to hint at the invisible godhead choosing to unveil itself in Christ. The moon (Christ), however, is not a mere reflection of the sun's (Father's) glory; rather, Christ shines with both his Father's and his own light. Perhaps, finally, in revealing the moon to us "without cloud," Milton intends to create for his reader the effect of seeing God as only Christ was able to see him.

"Apparent queen" might seem at first to be Milton's plain sign that such suspicions of divine presence are mistaken. But the term may have been carefully chosen to confirm and to limit our sense of present divinity. As Fowler notes, "apparent queen" means manifest or visible queen, but also plays on "heir-apparent" (often shortened to "apparent"). Christ, as we have seen, makes God's glory visible or apparent to men. He is likewise called God's resplendent "heir" (V, 720; VI, 887). Indeed, God permits the War in Heaven in order "To manifest thee worthiest to be heir / Of all things, to be heir and to be king" (VI, 707–08). "Apparent" may, however, have another sense. It may signal, indeed, that we should sense an affinity between moon and Christ, yet stop short of complete identification. Wary of deifying what is astronomically but not theologically a heavenly body, Milton may have thought "queen of heaven" too like Mariolatry or pagan worship (see Jeremiah xliv, 18–23, condemning worshipers of the "queen of heaven"). "Apparent" hedges the divinity.[31]

Most suggestive of divinity in Milton's description of the moon is not its appearance or its title but its activity. "In her pale dominion," says Uriel, the moon "checks the night" (III, 732). Christ's office, too, is to check the night, or the powers of night. He fulfills that office by defeating Satan in the War in Heaven and will fulfill it again at the Last Judgment. Though Hume thought (p. 130) "pale dominion" emphasized the moon's feebleness, the phrase may be a Christian oxymoron—strength in meekness, triumph through lowliness, life through death—especially if we think of the derivation of "dominion" from *dominus*, "lord," and "pale" as the pallor of death. Like Christ too, the moon, in a supreme gesture of humility and self-sacrifice, removes her silver mantle of light and throws it over the world. The parallel might be general—Christ's self-sacrifice in becoming mortal in order that man become immortal—or specific—

the moon's silver mantle may be like the light with which the Lord covers himself "as with a garment" (Psalm civ, 2) and the "robe of righteousness" which Isaiah (lxi, 10) prophesies will be given to man by the Messiah. The "type" of this event figures centrally in Christ's visit to the garden after the Fall. Like the moon, he appears after sunset and the arrival of evening (X, 92–99):

> pitying how they stood
> Before him naked to the air, that now
> Must suffer change, [he] disdained not to begin
> Thence forth the form of servant to assume,
> As when he washed his servants' feet, so now
> As father of his Family he clad
> Their nakedness. . . .
>
> . . . .
>
> Nor hee thir outward only with the skins
> Of beasts, but inward nakedness, much more
> Opprobrious, with his robe of righteousness,
> Arraying covered from his Father's sight. (X, 211–17, 20–23)

Milton here combines Genesis with New Testament accounts of Christ washing his disciples' feet to make Christ, like the moon, both master ("Father of his Family") and "servant."

Equally significant in this context is the Son's role in the Creation, for the moon casting a mantle of light on the dark is an emblem of the Son's original creative act. Milton makes clear that the Son is the agent of Creation ("and thou my Word, begotten Son, by thee / This I perform, speak thou, and be it done," VII, 163–64) and that the act consists in bringing order out of chaos and lighting the dark. That light Milton praises:

> Before the heavens thou wert, and at the voice
> Of God, as with a *mantle* didst invest
> The rising world of waters dark and deep,
> Won from the void and formless infinite.
> (III, 9–12; italics added)

By casting a silver *mantle,* the moon does again—or does in effect—what the Son did. Other minor details contribute to the parallel. The Son's first creating words are "Silence, ye troubl'd waves, and thou Deep, peace" (VII, 216). "Silence" accompanies evening and, pleased with the nightingale's song, offers a kind of prelude to the moon's rising (IV, 600–04). At the divine fiat the sun sojourned "in a cloudy tabernacle" (VII, 248). So too, at the sunset prior to moonrise, the sun arrayed "with reflected purple and gold / the clouds that on his western throne attend" (IV, 596–97). The moon's action is in fact not only an emblem of the original creative act, but a mysterious yet perfectly quotidian reenactment of the Creation.

In describing the relationship between moon and Christ, I have used the terms "emblem" and "association" with deliberate imprecision. It would perhaps be inadvisable (and even impossible) to characterize any more precisely the relationship between physical and spiritual worlds that Milton implies. His century habitually read the natural world (the Book of God's Works) for signs of the Creator's glory. The proliferation of terms for these signs—ranging from analogy and similitude, through emblem, hieroglyph, figure, image, and metaphor, to shadow and type—suggests that several kinds of relationship were thought possible, ranging from logical similarity between two distinct realms ("lik'ning spiritual to corporal forms," *PL* V, 273), through what we would call symbol (a concrete manifestation of another world), to the specific relationship intended by the strict use of typology ("Earth . . . the shadow of Heav'n," *PL* V, 574). But in actual practice (with the exception of type), most of these relational terms seem to have been used interchangeably. What the proliferation of terms suggests more than anything else is the "emblematic habit of mind."[32]

In any case, Milton, who makes use of typology elsewhere in *Paradise Lost*, does not seem to draw on it here in his description of the moon. He shows little interest in determining the precise nature and degree of the presence of the spiritual in its natural emblem. In general, despite his "rationalistic approach to metaphor" in *Christian Doctrine*,[33] he shuns in *Paradise Lost* the kind of symbol, like Pareus' waxing and waning moon, that is understood through a process of abstraction from the concrete, in favor of the sensuous awareness that poetry can create. We will come closer to the sources of the power of Milton's moon piece if we think of him, not as scholastic theologian, but as poet, less concerned with the "subtle and fine" distinctions than with the "simple, sensuous, and passionate" mode of poetry. In *Paradise Lost*, the moon's function in the created world sensuously bespeaks Christ's function in the redemptive world. But Milton makes it clear that, especially before the Fall, the "created world" and the "redemptive world" are not distinct. His description evokes a sense that God and the Son are immanent in creation, that the moon (and everything else) participates in the unity and divinity of the cosmos. Above all, Milton (I think) succeeds in making a reader feel himself, as Adam and Eve once did, in the immediate presence of divinity.

Divine associations, however, do not detract from the scene's natural beauty. The appearance of the moon from behind clouds is benign and beautiful in itself and also as an expression of God's original benignity. All the universe declares the glory of God, either literally or figuratively. Nor do such different (if related) meanings exhaust the passage. One of the reasons the appearance of the un-veiled moon is so dramatic and moving is that the reader has heard, in the proem to the previous book, Milton's moving complaint of the pain that *veilings* have caused him.[34] In that context the description of a moonlit night becomes a kind of answer to Milton's prayer for vision.

In the Hymn to Light, Milton says that his eyes have been "veiled" by "dim suffusion" (III, 26), that he himself is surrounded by "cloud . . . and ever-during dark" (III, 45). Whether or not his physical vision in fact seemed to him veiled or clouded,[35] he chose to describe it in terms that connect that blinded vision and his prayer for illumination to the clouded and unclouded moon. He asks that celestial light

> Shine inward, and the mind through all her powers
> Irradiate, there plant eyes, all mist from thence
> Purge and disperse, that I may see and tell
> Of things invisible to mortal sight.   (III, 52–55)

Significantly, one of the natural beauties the blind Milton can no longer see is "the sweet approach of ev'n or morn" (III, 42); he compares himself, in his darkness, to the nightingale, "the wakeful bird" who "Sings darkling, and in shadiest covert hid / Tunes her nocturnal note." It is appropriate, then, that the nightingale sing her amorous descant as evening comes on in Eden, and as the moon rises to reveal her peerless light. Even the moon's mantle of light seems connected in Milton's mind with his blindness. In the autobiograph-ical digression in the *Second Defence,* he finds a strength in weakness: "May I be entirely helpless . . . provided that in my shadows the light of the divine countenance may shine forth all the more clearly. For then I shall be at once the weakest and the strongest, at the same time blind and most keen in vision. . . . So in this darkness, may I be clothed in light."[36] Milton's own poetic vision and inspired creation thus become associated with the moonlit scene (both the unveiling and the clothing), with the origins of all creativeness, and with the original creative act.

After the Fall, all is changed. When God lets the dogs of hell havoc and lay waste the world, he orders also that the heavenly bodies be altered. The moon, once queen of heaven, is now simply "the blank moon." She is not only empty; her "office" is not even specified. Our final baleful glimpse of the moon is in the cave of death, where Adam sees a very catalogue of maladies:

> Demoniac frency, moping melancholy
> And moon-struck madness, pining atrophy,
> Marasmus, and wide-wasting pestilence.   (XI, 485–87)

Just as evening, once grateful and mild, becomes after the Fall a time of dangerous mists, so the moon, once benign and creative, now strikes fallen man with lunacy. He can no longer—after the Fall— participate in a harmonious, sympathetic universe in which, as we have seen, the very fabric of the evening and night is woven through with calm, peace, and divinity.

New York University

NOTES

1. *Life of Milton*, in *Lives of the Poets*, ed. G. B. Hill (Oxford, 1905), vol. I, p. 177.

2. All quotations from *Paradise Lost* are taken from the *Poems of John Milton*, ed. A. Fowler and J. Carey (London, 1968).

3. *The Spectator*, ed. D. F. Bond (Oxford, 1965), vol. III, p. 255.

4. I have discussed the first part of this passage in "Milton's Evening," *Milton Studies*, VI, ed. James D. Simmonds (Pittsburgh, 1974), pp. 259–76.

5. Startling too, as Fowler well notes, because of the "elaborate images of cloth- ing" in 596–99 (*Poems of Milton*, p. 648).

6. "Naked yet veiled" is a motif central to Eden. Compare Adam and Eve, "with native honor clad / In naked majesty" (IV, 289–90); and "Innocence, that as a veil / Had shadowed them from knowing ill, was gone, / Just confidence and native

righteousness / And honor from about them, naked left / To guilty shame he covered, but his robe / Uncovered more" (IX, 1054–59). Compare also the biblical robes of righteousness and salvation in Psalm cxxxii, 9, 16; 2 Chronicles vi, 41; Isaiah lxi, 10.

7. Jonathan Richardson and Jonathan Richardson, Jr., *Explanatory Notes on Paradise Lost* (1734), p. 73.

8. Thomas Newton, ed., *Paradise Lost*, 9th ed. (1740), vol. I, pp. 306–07; Patrick Hume, *Annotations on Milton's Paradise Lost* (1695; reprint ed., Folcroft, Pa., 1971), p. 154.

9. For example, Spenser, *Faerie Queene*, II.7.29.

10. Joshua Poole, *The English Parnassus* (London, 1677 [first published 1657]), p. 438. See another passage quoted in Poole, p. 438: "crown'd with blazing light and majesty / She proudly sits." Du Bartas calls the moon "Queene of Night" and "Chaste Emperesse" (*Divine Weeks and Works* [1605], I. 4 [p. 129], I. 7 [p. 247]).

11. See also "sad Cynthia . . . Night-wandring, and pale watry star," quoted in Poole, *English Parnassus*, p. 438.

12. See Fowler's note to I, 781–87. Hume (*Annotations*, p. 51) notes that Selden in *De Diis Syriis* calls the moon "Noctis Arbitram."

13. *PL* II, 662–66. Richardson's note (*Explanatory Notes*, p. 73) summarizes the superstitions.

14. See M. H. Nicolson, *A World in the Moon*, Smith College Studies in Modern Languages, XVII, no. 2 (1935–36).

15. *De Universo*, bk. IX, chap. 10, and "De Luna," in *Opera* (Cologne, 1626), vol. I, p. 148.

16. *A Commentary Upon the Divine Revelation of the Apostle and Evangelist John*, trans. Elias Arnold (Amsterdam, 1644), pp. 258–59.

17. See Hume, *Annotations*, p. 221.

18. See Anastasius Synaita, *In hexaemeron*, bk. IV, in *Patrologia Graeca*, ed. Migne, vol. 89 (Fowler incorrectly has 79), cols. 902–04.

19. P. 330. Milton speaks of the stars' and planets' "small peculiar" (*PL* VII, 368).

20. According to the medieval encyclopaedist Berchorius, the moon's phases correspond to the phases of Mary—conception, visitation, incarnation, assumption (*Dictionarium Reportorium Morale* [Cologne, 1712], pp. 565–67). The tradition continued well into the eighteenth century. See Frances Peck, *New Memoirs of the Life and Poetical Works of Milton* (London, 1740), p. 133.

21. *Malachi* iv, 2; see *Animadversions*, in *Works of John Milton*, ed. Frank Allen Paterson et al. (New York, 1931–38), vol. III, p. 163. See Fowler's note to V, 166–70, and *PR* I, 294, based on Revelation ii, 28; xxii, 16.

22. See W. B. Hunter, "Milton's Arianism Reconsidered," *Harvard Theological Review*, LII (1959), 9–35, arguing that Milton's view is Subordinationist.

23. "Noon-Midnight and the Temporal Structure of *Paradise Lost*," *ELH*, XXIX (1962), 372–95.

24. *De Universo*, bk. IX, chap. 10, p. 148.

25. Edgar Wind, *Pagan Mysteries in the Renaissance* (New Haven, 1967), p. 249, quoting Natalis Comes, bk. III, chaps. 17, 18 ("De Luna," "De Diana").

26. Despite W. G. Madsen's claim that in strict usage "a recurrent event, such as the rising and setting of the sun," is not a type (*From Shadowy Types to Truth: Studies in Milton's Symbolism* [New Haven, 1968], p. 4), the term was sometimes used, more loosely, for natural objects such as the moon, for example, by Rabanus Maurus, *De Universo*, bk. IX, chap. 10, and others. See note 27.

27. Anastasius Synaita, *In hexaemeron*, bk. IV, in *Patrologia Graeca*, ed. Migne, vol. 89, cols. 891–907; Samuel Mather, *The Figures or Types of the Old Testament*, 2d ed. (London, 1705 [1st ed., 1683]), pp. 442–44. For William Guild, *Moses Unvailed* (London, 1620), sig. A4, types of Christ are to Christ as the moon and stars are to the sun.

28. On the related ideas of the heavens as mantle or tent, see Robert Eisler, *Weltenmantel und Himmelszelt*, 2 vols. (Munich, 1910), a study in comparative mythology. Milton's image of light as mantle probably derives, however, from the Bible. See pp. 161–63 of this essay.

29. Numbers xi, 25; 2 Chronicles v, 13–vi, 1; Psalms xviii, xcvii; Mark ix, 7; Timothy vi, 16; Exodus xxiv, 16–18, xxxiii, 20–24.

30. *PL* III, 381–82, and Isaiah vi, 2.

31. Compare Ficino, *De Sole*, chap. 13, warning against excessive adoration of the sun, moon, and stars, or venerating them as Author and as Father of intellectual gifts.

32. See Brendan O Hehir, *Expans'd Hieroglyphicks*, (Berkeley, 1969) pp. 17–21, and Madsen, *From Shadowy Types to Truth*, p. 5.

33. Madsen, *From Shadowy Types to Truth*, p. 70.

34. Unveilings are generally important in *Paradise Lost* (as in the *Aeneid*). Compare Satan's revelation of his true self at IV, 810, Christ's revelation of his true power in the War (VI), the appearance of Venus as Goddess when her robes fall (*Aeneid* I), the appearance of Aeneas out of a cloudy mist (I). Both Raphael (V, 276) and Michael (XI, 203) descend veiled to earth before appearing in their proper shape.

35. On the continuing debate over the nature of Milton's blindness, see W. R. Parker, *Milton: A Biography* (Oxford, 1968), vol. II, p. 988.

36. *Complete Prose Works of John Milton*, ed. Don M. Wolfe et al, 6 vols. (New Haven, 1953–73), vol. IV, p. 590.

CONTIGUITIES AND MOVING LIMBS: STYLE AS ARGUMENT IN *AREOPAGITICA*

Harry R. Smallenburg

Milton presents his forceful argument against censorship in a form that dramatizes the nature of the truth humans must not attempt to suppress. Sentences in the introduction have "broken" syntactical patterns; the explicit order of arguments becomes confused and the divisions are blurred as reasons overlap from section to section; flights of "inspired" rhetoric seem to appear randomly; finally, the imagery toward the end of the tract represents truth as fragmented and incomplete. Although critics have seen a disparity between the intuitive, imaginative persuasiveness of the tract and a logical, discursive weakness, both kinds of argumentation are actually integrated and suggest that truth, which has a divine life of its own, must be allowed to appear freely, unconstrained by the necessarily limited forms and perceptions of human beings.

ALAN F. PRICE, in "Incidental Imagery in *Areopagitica*," argues that "the reader's mind is colored against licensing more by vivid imaginative impressions [created by the imagery] than by the underlying rational argument." "Milton's argument," he says, "is usually more persuasive when it is intuitive rather than discursive."[1] John X. Evans, in a later article, argues for a closer relationship between the imagery and the argument than Price had considered: He regards the patterns of metaphor as "parathematic statements, which not only add dramatic emphasis to a context, but conceptualize it in different terms, and thereby help compensate for the absence of the argument for separation of church and state, which Milton did not use for fear of antagonizing the Erastians."[2] Although major image patterns in *Areopagitica* have thus been analyzed, both Price and Evans separate imagery from nonimagistic language. We have yet to understand the text as an integrated whole. Evans goes on to say, "Certainly after a close examination of *Areopagitica* one can construct a very convincing argument by ignoring everything but the imagery" (p. 191). But images are combined with other elements for an affective purpose that reinforces Milton's logical argument. In the moment-to-moment process of encountering disjunctive sentences and a formal arrangement apparently subject to momentary whim and spontaneity, the reader is made to feel the essential nature of truth: Its energetic and exhilarating life cannot be confined by the limited measures of fallen humans. Rather, it must be allowed a free and open hand to appear as it will, without the censorship of the licensing act.

The disjointed first sentence of *Areopagitica* implicitly introduces this theme and prefigures the mode of presentation that will demonstrate vividly the wisdom of granting toleration to unorthodox opinions.

They who to States and Governours of the Commonwealth direct their Speech, High Court of Parlament, or wanting such accesse in a private condition, write that which they foresee may advance the publick good; I suppose them as at the beginning of no meane endeavour, not a little alter'd and mov'd inwardly in their mindes: Some with doubt of what will be the successe, others with feare of what will be the censure; some with hope, others with confidence of what they have to speake. (p. 486)[3]

The nominative plural pronoun "they" implicitly begins a main clause which is immediately displaced by the subordinate clause beginning with "who." At the point where we would expect the original sentence to continue (after "may advance the publick good"), the nominative reference becomes the objective pronoun in a new construction ("I suppose *them*"). This develops into two nicely balanced sets of clauses—"some with doubt," etc. The sentence begins in one way but is completed in another. The reader is required to readjust himself midway, to abandon or detach himself from one set of syntactical expectations for a slightly different set by which he moves to the end. There his satisfaction is fully assured and symbolized by the rhetorically familiar isocolon, alliteration, and ellipsis. A similar pattern occurs three sentences later:

For this is not the liberty which wee can hope, that no grievance ever should arise in the Commonwealth, that let no man in this World expect; but when complaints are freely heard, deeply consider'd, and speedily reform'd, then is the utmost bound of civil liberty attain'd, that wise men looke for. (p. 487)

The implicit "not this . . . but this" formula is displaced by the syntactical coordinates "then . . . when." As with the previous sentence analyzed, the logical promise of the first half of the sentence is fulfilled, though the syntax has been altered. These "broken" patterns, along with the syntactical twists and turns of other sentences in the exordium, look forward to discontinuities and disruptions in larger features of the tract.[4]

With his argument implicit in the syntactical dislocations of the opening sentences of the introduction, Milton proceeds to a more overt stylistic demonstration with the *partitio* which concludes the introduction. According to Quintilian, this may or may not be used to give a definite sense of order and clarity to the orator's subsequent speech.[5] Milton employs it exactly to give the reader a sense of order that turns out to be misleading.

I shall now attend with such a Homily, as shall lay before ye, first the inventors of it to bee those whom ye will be loath to own; next what is to be thought in generall of reading, what ever sort the Books be; and that this Order avails nothing to the suppressing of scandalous, seditious, and libellous Books, which were mainly intended to be supprest. Last, that it will be primely to the discouragement of all learning, and the stop of Truth, not only by disexercising and blunting our abilities in what we know already, but by hindring and cropping the discovery that might bee yet further made both in religious and civill Wisdome. (pp. 491–92)

The parts in this well-organized tract, a *partitio* suggests (though the development within the *partitio* shows disjunctions similar to those earlier in the exordium), will be distinct in themselves and clearly marked off from each other. Moreover, there will be a progressive ascent (*gradatio*) to the organization of the topics—from the inventors of this particular act, to reading and the efficacy of the act, and finally to civil and religious wisdom in general. However, instead of talking about the inventors of the licensing act—explicitly the first topic—Milton introduces a digression on the nature of books.[6] The appearance of a digression here instead of in its traditional place later in the argument reinforces the sense that the unorthodox and unexpected must not be condemned. As the first disruption of his explicit plan, and a rhetorically and stylistically spectacular tour de force, it almost forcibly "opens" the reader to a felt understanding of the broadest implications of unrestricted publication. By contrast, the licensing act is revealed to be short-sighted, defensive, and self-defeating.

Having been presented this intensified but generalized summary of the issues, the reader is ready to encounter a formal design that continuously and in detailed arguments extends and reinforces his understanding. He experiences concomitantly the progressive breakdown of the organization he has been led to expect and the inspired truths and insights that leave human expectations far behind.[7] The passage on the nature of books is eminently out of an explicitly established order. The digression brings us ultimately around, however, to a point that differs only slightly from what we originally anticipated. In the outline, Milton announced that he would "now attend with such a Homily, as shall lay before ye, first the inventors of it to bee those whom ye will be loath to own" (p. 491). By the time we have come through the digression, the immediate, explicit reason for the historical survey is not to show the origins of licensing, but to give examples of ancient practice and how it developed into modern practice: "I refuse not the paines to be so much Historicall, as will serve to shew what hath been done by ancient and famous Commonwealths, against this disorder, till the very time that this project of licencing crept out of the Inquisition, was catcht up by our Prelates, and hath caught some of our Presbyters" (p. 493). One set of expectations is dismissed but then satisfied after all. We seem at first to miss out on truth because form and order have been disrupted; but we can look for eventual fulfillment, even in the guise of a new form. The pattern is that established by the first sentence of the tract. Although the speaker in both instances does not adhere strictly to the formal pattern, or the "letter" of his statement, yet the "spirit" of what he says perfectly fulfills the requirements he established for himself at the outset. The implication is never that such "external," "logical," traditional human creations as transitions, topic statements, even the oration, should be violated, destroyed, or utterly disregarded. Rather, they are to be treated loosely and never slavishly adhered to at the expense of that freedom which can develop into a general truth. To confine truth to forms, again, is to place human devices, limited and discursive modes of thought and communication, above the inspired and intuitive processes that, as Raphael says in *Paradise Lost* (V, 486–89), approach more nearly the divine. Indeed, the richly imagistic visionary passages have just this implication: They stand as "proofs" of the human potential for divine insight under the auspices of freedom and truth. Their recurrent and seemingly "independent" appearance demonstrates and verifies the immediate "logical" point: Do not create instruments of censorship; do not try to regulate religious belief. Truth must appear freely to be recognized and separated from untruth.

The historical survey of licensing appears in its new due order (after the digression), beginning with Athens. Although clear and straightforward in its chronological development, this discussion nonetheless prefigures more conspicuous divergencies in later "sections." Milton follows the history he sets out to follow, but he moves the reader from an informative and objective account of Athens to an increasingly scornful and severely judgmental account of the councils. The language at the beginning of the survey, concerning Protagoras, is typically straightforward and historical:

Thus the Books of *Protagoras* were by the Judges of *Areopagus* commanded to be burnt, and himselfe banisht the territory for a discourse begun with his confessing not to know *whether there were gods, or whether not:* And against defaming, it was decreed that none should be traduc'd by name, as was the manner of *Vetus Comoedia*, whereby we may guesse how they censur'd libelling: And this course was quick enough, as *Cicero* writes, to quell both the desperate wits of other Atheists, and the open way of defaming, as the event shew'd. (p. 494)

It is apparent, on the other hand, that Milton feels no impulse to be objective toward the church censors; rather than praise and satisfaction, which predominated earlier, outright contempt, scorn, and sarcasm ensure that the reader will not mistake the nature of prohibiting:

These are the prety responsories, these are the deare Antiphonies that so bewitcht of late our Prelats, and their Chaplaines with the goodly Eccho they made; and besotted us to the gay imitation of a lordly *Imprimatur,* one

from Lambeth house, another from the West end of *Pauls;* so apishly
Romanizing, that the word of command still was set downe in Latine; as if
the learned Gramaticall pen that wrote it, would cast no ink without Latine:
or perhaps, as they thought, because no vulgar tongue was worthy to ex-
presse the pure conceit of an *Imprimatur;* but rather, as I hope, for that our
English, the language of men ever famous, and formost in the atchievements
of liberty, will not easily finde servile letters anow to spell such a dictatorie
presumption English. (pp. 504–05)

The final sentence of this section follows a metaphorical summary of
the survey. Although it clearly ends the first topic and recalls the
phrasing of the *partitio* ("first the inventors of [licensing] to bee
those whom ye will be loath to own"), its logic makes demands
similar to those the reader has encountered before: "That ye like not
now these most certain Authors of this licencing order, and that all
sinister intention was farre distant from your thoughts, when ye were
importun'd the passing it, all men who know the integrity of your
actions, and how ye honour Truth, will clear ye readily" (p. 507). The
sentence is syntactically inverted, beginning with two parallel noun
clauses which depend logically on the independent clause "all
men . . . will clear ye readily." If we read strictly according to the
syntax, however, the sentence makes no logical sense, for Milton
certainly did not mean to clear his audience of not liking the "most
certain Authors of this licensing order." They are, rather, clear only
of "all sinister intention." Yet the parallel dependent clauses and the
coordinating conjunction create this misleading logical connection.
The reader must revise his understanding of the initial clause
according to data he encounters later in the sentence. The pieces do
not coalesce into a coherent whole; instead, they are left behind as
the progressive activity of reading may require. The reader as member of the commonwealth thus learns from unsatisfactory (because
incomplete) articulations of truth to value that freedom of expression
which makes for a perhaps fluctuating but vital, continually growing
and expanding, and corrective understanding.

   If the survey of licensing deviates slightly but meaningfully
from its explicit preface, other sections of the tract exhibit similarly
important but unobtrusive devices. Though apparently insignificant, they create temporary disruptions of the reading, making it
difficult to keep one's place in the argument. Yet Milton's points *do*
get made. *Areopagitica* continually validates its own argument as

local disruptions give way in the reader's mind to a completed work. Immediately following the survey, for example, Milton inserts a short paragraph that sets out to be a response to the possible objection that licensing might be beneficial notwithstanding its origin. The actual effect of the paragraph and the material following, however, is to disrupt the orderly, explicitly stated organization once again. For the reader familiar with traditional oratorical form, the response to objections appears out of its usual place. In Aristotle, Cicero, and the *Rhetorica Ad Herrenium,* the *refutatio* or *reprehensio* appears after the amplifications and proofs.[8] But the paragraph is even more immediately confusing, for it both does and does not do what it initially proposes. Milton disables the objection with a general observation and insists again on the argument against licensing that he has just given, reinforcing his point with a metaphor:

yet if that thing be no such deep invention, but obvious, and easie for any man to light on, and yet best and wisest Commonwealths through all ages, and occasions have forborne to use it, and falsest seducers, and oppressors of men were the first who tooke it up, and to no other purpose but to obstruct and hinder the first approach of Reformation; I am of those who beleeve, it will be a harder alchymy then *Lullius* ever knew, to sublimat any good use out of such an invention. (p. 507)

In the sentence following, Milton effectively alters the apparent and original purpose of the paragraph, at the same time seeming to establish the next set of topics: "Yet this only is what I request to gain from this reason, that it may be held a dangerous and suspicious fruit, as certainly it deserves, for the tree that bore it, untill I can dissect one by one the properties it has" (p. 507). Yet this new order is set aside to continue with the original discussion, which has not yet been completed. The reader follows one course ("I will not answer an objection . . ."), only to be told that it was not really what the writer intended ("Yet this only is what I request to gain from this reason . . ."); he is asked to suspend one train of thought until the completion of another (dissection of the properties); finally, he is told that this course must be set temporarily aside for the original course ("What is to be thought in general of reading books"), which by this time comes as a surprise, although consistent with the order of the *partitio*. The experience of reading the paragraph is somewhat jarring. What is happening? Where are we going? the reader asks. Yet the emergence at what may seem the new topic is really, after several intervening fits and starts, an arrival at the true order established at the beginning. The style, which brings the reader through local confusions and uncertainties to a solid and established order, implies again that one can trustingly allow a variety of possibilities without ultimate jeopardy to truth. As we learn repeatedly, "so Truth be in the field, we do injuriously by licencing and prohibiting to misdoubt her strength" (p. 561).

The larger faith on which Milton's affirmation rests derives from the spiritual history fundamental to himself and his audience and dramatized in *Paradise Lost*. The divine order and tranquility broken by human disobedience eventuated in a long series of breaks and divergences, leavings-off, and takings-up again: As Michael says to Adam in the middle of the visions on the mountain, "Thus thou hast seen one World begin and end; / And Man as from a second stock proceed" (*PL* XII, 5–6). Only at the end of human history will the order toward which the world is proceeding be realized. God will "raise / From the conflagrant mass, purg'd and refin'd, / New Heav'ns, new Earth, Ages of endless date / Founded in righteousness and peace and love, / To bring forth fruits Joy and eternal Bliss" (*PL* XII, 547–51). In the meantime we are left with the vagaries and discontinuities of human experience symbolized by the interrupted developments of the tract. The human condition is made a part of the reader's experience.

Toward the middle of *Areopagitica*, Milton proceeds again to an apparent *refutatio*, establishing yet another suborganization. This section develops into the narrator's own explicit realization of a prevailing decorum that can only be out of his human control: "See the ingenuity of Truth, who when she gets a free and willing hand, opens her self faster, then the pace of method and discours can overtake her" (p. 521). Further complication drives this home. Milton's exhortation to "See the ingenuity of Truth" interposes itself between what he "promis'd to deliver next" and what we believe will be the fulfillment of the expectation thus set up, a discussion of why the licensing act cannot be effective. Instead, however, Milton takes us again completely off the track and back to the first section of his argument to rebut a possible objection: "It was the task which I began with, To shew that no Nation, or well instituted State, if they valu'd books at all, did ever use this way of licencing; and it might be answer'd, that this is a piece of prudence lately discover'd" (521–22). As in the case of the digression on the nature of books, however, further reading brings us to the fulfillment, but again in a way that is slightly unexpected. The fulfillment comes as an elaboration of the impossibility in Plato's republic of regulating all things that might "corrupt the mind." The allusion to Plato, in turn, comes as the exception to Milton's assertion that among the ancients "it was not the not knowing, but the not approving, which was the cause" of not using licensing. Milton leads us around to the national corruptions of England and to the justification of man's being able to choose between good and evil before stating drily what we had already become aware of: "it appears that this order hitherto is far insufficient to the end which it intends" (p. 528). We are then taken through a whole series of impossible necessities to show explicitly (and redundantly) why the act is futile.

The final twist in this process comes as the reader recalls that from pages 507 to 530 in the Yale edition, which reproduces faithfully the 1644 text, he has seen no paragraph indentations. If we can be sure that the original text reproduces, in this respect at least, Milton's intentions, the experience intended is not orderly, easily distinguishable movements to the argument (as texts like Hughes' suggest by frequent paragraphing),[9] but a sense of formal, outward unity to everything between "Not to insist upon the examples of *Moses, Daniel & Paul,* who were skilful in all learning" (p. 507) and "Another reason, whereby to make it plain that this order will miss the end it seeks" (p. 530). Of course, the rhetoric and our responses themselves belie, and move in spite of, the typographically suggested unity. We find very much the rushing, continuous subordinations, qualifications, amplifications, and lack of "proper" sequence that K. G. Hamilton describes as part of the typically Miltonic sentence.[10] Both he and Gilman would see these features as weaknesses; however, they constitute part of the experience necessary to understand the nature of truth.

Finally, even this large "paragraph" is given in an interrupted order. Milton has been replying to the objection: "What though the Inventors were bad, the thing [licensing] for all that may be good?"

(p. 507). For the reply itself, however, he asks merely that people see fit to hold licensing "as a dangerous and suspicious fruit . . . until I can dissect one by one the properties it has," implying that he is dropping the reply for the time being to discuss in detail the nature of the act. Instead even of *that*, however, he reminds us that the original plan has been disrupted and claims that he must return to it: "But I have first to finish, as was propounded, what is to be thought in general of reading books, whatever sort they be, and whether be more the benefit, or the harm that thence proceeds?" Of course, during this forward, backward, to-both-sidesward discussion, he does talk about the nature of the act; but he does that also in later sections. He does not try to press truth into forms, but rather lets it take its way.

The largest symbol of the freedom to speak is, most appropriately, the formal oration into which Milton casts his argument. The *partitio*, to repeat, "prepares" us at the outset for what is to come. As with the history of licensing, where the initial objectivity does not control the whole discussion, however, the *partitio* does not control the entire tract. Milton virtually builds his point into the oratorical form by using the final exhortations as an extension beyond the reader's original expectations, which have been fulfilled by the time he reaches the image of England "as an Eagle muing her mighty youth, and kindling her undazl'd eyes at the full midday beam; purging and unscaling her long abused sight at the fountain it self of heav'nly radiance" (p. 558).

The order of topics at this point soon begins to reduce to irrelevance (significantly) logical analysis and organized description. Milton shows that Parliament virtually suppresses itself if it suppresses "all this flowry crop of knowledge and new light sprung up and yet springing daily in this city" (p. 558). This argument comes in response to the rhetorical question, "What should ye do then?" (p. 558). The beginning of the next paragraph poses the same question in a slightly altered form, but with the kind of reverse that the reader experienced in the paragraph (discussed earlier) which responded but did not respond to objections. The sentence on page 560 begins like a rhetorical question that might preface a solution: "What would be best advis'd then, if it be found so hurtfull and so unequall to suppresse opinions for the newnes, or the unsutablenes to a customary acceptance" The sentence momentarily withdraws its apparent initial proposal—"will not be my task to say"—but then immediately goes on to present the solution offered by Lord Brooke: "He . . . exhorts us to hear with patience and humility those, however they be miscall'd, that desire to live purely, in such a use of Gods Ordinances, as the best guidance of their conscience gives them, and to tolerat them, though in some disconformity to our selves" (p. 561). From the end of this paragraph, Milton continues with expatiations on the immediate necessity and benefit of allowing all divergent opinions (except Catholic) to be promulgated. The final, astructural sequence of statements continually affirms and reaffirms the implications of the argument that has been carried on throughout the tract: "Yet if all cannot be of one mind, as who looks they should be? this doubtles is more wholesome, more prudent, and more Christian that many be tolerated, rather then all compell'd" (p. 565). The assertions appear in an order that is set up and realized from moment to moment, as though the state of having discarded "the letter of human trust" (as symbolized by the supposedly controlling *partitio*) to "walk in the Spirit" frees man from the need to impose structural controls at all. In fact, as Milton warns, "while we still affect by all means a rigid externall formality, we may as soon fall again into a grosse conforming stupidity" (p. 564).

Inevitably, major images which toward the end of *Areopagitica* bring together the stylistic-argumentative points of the tract are images of things not yet completed. The moving fable of Truth, adapted from the Osiris myth, has several immediately apparent functions in addition to its reference to incompleteness and dispersion. First, it occurs within the intentionally misorganized development as part of that which "is yet behind of what I purpos'd to lay open, the incredible losse, and detriment that this plot of licencing puts us to, more then if som enemy at sea should stop up all our hav'ns and ports, and creeks, it hinders and retards the importation of our richest Marchandize, Truth" (p. 548). Second, it retroactively pervades the tract with a metaphoric significance not yet realized, and in so doing reinforces once again earlier implications that meaning and understanding cannot be considered complete at any one time. They must be continually seen in the perspective of what succeeds. The tract itself becomes an image of the scattered limbs. Finally, a fable, by its very nature, exemplifies the diversity of modes by which truth may be made manifest; like the other rhetorical and stylistic devices of *Areopagitica*, it symbolizes the enormous diversity of reality.

Truth once appeared with her divine master, Milton says, "and was a perfect Shape most glorious to look on." When the master ascended, a race of deceivers arose who "hewd her lovely form into a thousand peeces, and scatter'd them to the four winds" (p. 549). Since then the friends of Truth have gone about searching for her limbs and gathering them up, though they know they will be unable to find them all until her master's "second coming." In the meantime, there are, Milton says, "the dividers of unity,"

who neglect and permit not others to unite those dissever'd peeces which are yet wanting to the body of Truth. To be still searching what we know not, by what we know, still closing up truth to truth as we find it (for all her body is *homogeneal*, and proportionall) this is the golden rule in *Theology* as well as in Arithmetick, and makes up the best harmony in a Church; not the forc't and outward union of cold, and neutrall, and inwardly divided minds. (pp. 550–51)

The experience of the tract is designed to make its readers such searchers and promoters of unity. We must first be opened and receptive to truth. We then become conscious of its intrinsic nature. Truth anticipates human structures at some points, joins them at others, and may also ignore them. Forms such as the typographical and organizational ones we have seen, as well as the large and traditional oratorical form, manifest truth best by existing for it to depart from. In this way they show its vital and exuberant willfulness and become metaphors for humans with *their* limitations. Truth needs the "free and willing hand" Milton allows it exactly because, as we have seen, it cannot be confined. Truth "opens herself faster than the pace of method and discourse can overtake her."

The licensing act, thus, cannot possibly protect or promote truth. It would deprive us of such experience as we have had throughout the tract, where truth has been allowed to unfold itself freely, even when it carries us away from the forms we would recognize and expect. Indeed, the licensing act, like Cadmus' attack on Echion (alluded to in the digression), interferes with our progress toward the realization of God's purpose, Christian unity on earth, and thus defeats our own best intentions: "We stumble and are impatient at the least dividing of one visible congregation from another, though it be not in fundamentalls; and through our forwardnes to suppresse, and our backwardnes to recover any enthrall'd peece of truth out of the gripe of custom, we care not to keep truth separated from truth, which is the fiercest rent and disunion of all" (p. 564).

The images of Truth's scattered limbs and the building of the Lord's temple (begun in the Cadmus allusion in the digression) are implicitly related in the admonition that there are men in England who desire "to advance truth in others" (p. 539), "sitting by their studious lamps, musing, searching, revolving new notions and idea's wherewith to present, as with their homage and their fealty the approaching Reformation: others as fast reading, trying all things, assenting to the force of reason and convincement" (p. 554). The energetic, restless, forward-moving rhythms recall the movements of the whole treatise. These are the men seeking to reunite the limbs of Truth. They search for "what we know not, by what we know, still closing up truth to truth as we find it." Neither they nor their readers should be hindered, for when "the people, or the greater part . . . wholly tak'n up with the study of highest and most important matters to be reformed, should be disputing, reasoning, inventing, discoursing, ev'n to a rarity, and admiration" (p. 557), then the temple of the Lord can be forwarded in the true Reformation. Like Truth, whose parts must be yoked together but cannot be made completely whole, "when every stone is laid artfully together" by the reasoners, discoursers, readers, and searchers, the building "cannot be united into a continuity, it can but be contiguous in this world; neither can every peece of the building be of one form; nay, rather the perfection consists in this, that out of many moderat varieties and brotherly dissimilitudes that are not vastly disproportionall arises the goodly and graceful symmetry that commends the whole pile and structure" (p. 555). The image aptly describes *Areopagitica* itself. Each word, phrase, clause, sentence, and so on upward constitutes one of the limbs of Truth, one of the artfully hewn blocks in the building, all reflecting the nature of truth and God's temple in their movement (we are made to feel the limbs drawn together, put into motion as living entities) and in their

"brotherly dissimilitudes" and "not vastly disproportionall" structure. This literally makes the reader as well as Milton one of those
"closing up truth to truth" as he finds it.

   Areopagitica, then, is not just an argument for freedom of the
press, but an affecting experience of what it as a construct of attitudes
and ideas actually is and what any such construct might be: truth
alive and busy, manifesting itself in the world as it should be allowed
to, unlicensed (literally so, for Milton did not have the tract licensed
for publication), unregistered, left as unencumbered as possible by
the forms we create for it, though absolute freedom and wholeness
must await Christ's Second Coming.

   Although Gilman is being critical when he observes that the
reader occasionally must reorient himself in the discussion and is
therefore imposed upon, this is exactly what Milton wants.[11] The
reader is a normal, weak human being, trying to return to the familiar
and comfortable, but under the pressure of a force that constantly
sweeps him into new and totally engaging experiences to which he
must give himself up, whatever the uncertainty. As the digression
makes the reader break out of a narrow and constricting consciousness, makes him receptive to the small and partial but elevating
illuminations of truth in the remainder of the tract, so the tract itself
should be an "opening"; the treatment of syntactical, logical, and
oratorical forms in conjunction with—not apart from—the imagery
should move readers (the real "pathetic" force of the tract) not only
to repeal the licensing act, but to release their dependence on all
mere human devices, especially those of religion, the realm of ultimate truth: "[Christ's] doctrine is, that he who eats or eats not, regards a day or regards it not, may doe either to the Lord. How many
other things might be tolerated in peace, and left to conscience, had
we but charity, and were it not the chief strong hold of our hypocrisie
to be ever judging one another" (p. 563). Only then, when spiritual
brothers do not incite civil war by fear, distrust, and failure to act on
the word of God, can the nation achieve the apocalyptic triumph
toward which the tract (and human history) has been moving:

Methinks I see in my mind a noble and puissant Nation rousing herself like a
strong man after sleep, and shaking her invincible locks: Methinks I see her
as an Eagle muing her mighty youth, and kindling her undazl'd eyes at the
full midday beam; purging and unscaling her long abused sight at the

fountain itself of heavenly radiance; while the whole noise of timorous and flocking birds, with those also that love the twilight, flutter about, amaz'd at what she means, and in their envious gabble would prognosticate a year of sects and schisms. (pp. 557–58)

But, as in actuality this cannot be the final vision, so it cannot complete the structure of the tract. There is, as with Adam, a return from the mount to the world, where men, now regenerated and reformed, are exhorted outright to extend the necessary "free and willing hand" to truth. The tract, in imitation of the way truth must continue to appear in the world, itself continues in the same vigorous prose we have seen all along, the pieces moving and contiguities being built up in our own individual minds. Milton ends with a final—and not the strongest (truth continues to ignore our expectations)—exhortation to repeal the act that essentially cuts minds off from each other, from building into further contiguities and unifications the partial wholes at which each can arrive.

Wayne State University

NOTES

1. *MP*, XLIX (1952), 218, 214.
2. "Imagery as Argument in Milton's *Areopagitica*," *Texas Studies in Literature and Language*, VIII (1966–67), 190.
3. References are to *Areopagitica* in *The Complete Prose Works of John Milton*, vol. II, ed. Don M. Wolfe et al. (New Haven, 1953–), cited in the text by page number only.
4. What I have thus analyzed is the "style" (at least one aspect of it)—the articulation or formulation of the statement as it occurs in time and creates a basic "response" in the reader. Such responses, directed by style and created continuously during the process of reading, are what I refer to by the word "experience." They take place whether the reader is Presbyterian, Catholic, or twentieth-century agnostic, because they are responses to the basic mechanics of the formulation. On the basis of the general bearing of Milton's argument, one can then go on to suggest that the reader feels the validity and safety of allowing new forms to replace accustomed ones. The reader who is able to posit this interpretation of the reading experience is the same reader every critic posits when interpreting a text. Stanley Fish, from whose work with stylistics my own clearly derives, describes him as "the *informed* reader," one who is "sufficiently experienced as a reader to have internalized the properties of

literary discourses, including everything from the most local of devices (figures of speech, etc.) to whole genres" ("Literature in the Reader: Affective Stylistics," *New Literary History*, II [1970], 145). Fish's books, *Surprised by Sin: The Reader in Paradise Lost* (New York, 1967) and *Self-Consuming Artifacts. The Experience of Seventeenth-Century Literature* (Berkeley, 1973) are major examples of affective stylistics in practice. I define the term "experience" explicitly to avoid confusion with a different level of responses on the part of *partisan* readers, responses discussed by Evans (see note 2); Ernest Sirluck, *Complete Prose Works*, vol. II, p. 177; and Joseph Anthony Wittreich, "Milton's *Areopagitica*: Its Isocratic and Ironic Contexts," *Milton Studies*, IV, ed. James D. Simmonds (Pittsburgh, 1972), pp. 101–15.

5. *Institutio Oratoria*, trans. H. E. Butler, Loeb Classical Library ed. (London and New York, 1920–22), vol. IV, pp. 147–49, 151.

6. Sirluck (*Complete Prose Works*, vol. II, pp. 170–71) designates the parts of the introduction somewhat differently, including the separate paragraph that begins "I deny not" in the partition. This does not seem possible, for it clearly comes between the actual partition and the beginning of the arguments outlined there. G. K. Hunter ("The Structure of Milton's *Areopagitica*," *English Studies*, XXXIX (1958), 117–19) finds difficulty fitting Milton's "justa oratio" to the classical divisions of oratory, and even after revising Jebb's divisions finds one passage out of place. His conclusions correspond to my own independently originated and pursued argument: "Milton makes a point of this transition not so much because it is important in the structure but because he wishes to emphasize the 'ingenuity of truth' breaking through the formal divisions of argument" (p. 118).

7. The structure of *Areopagitica* has been considered detrimental rather than helpful to the argument by Wilbur Gilman (*Milton's Rhetoric: Studies in the Defense of Liberty* [Columbia, Mo., 1939], p. 15). More recently, K. G. Hamilton finds that individual sentences carry the burden of argument generally in Milton's tracts, while the overall structures tend not to cohere logically as they should. Hamilton's description of the "typically Miltonic" sentence suggests as well the complex development of larger units of a tract: see "The Structure of Milton's Prose," in *Language and Style in Milton*, ed. Ronald Emma and John Shawcross (New York, 1967), pp. 312–13.

8. For a brief summary of handbook statements of parts of an oration, see Richard Lanham's *Handlist of Rhetorical Terms* (Berkeley and Los Angeles, 1968), pp. 112–13.

9. *Areopagitica*, in *John Milton: Complete Poems and Major Prose*, ed. Merritt Y. Hughes (New York, 1957), pp. 717–49.

10. See note 7.

11. *Milton's Rhetoric*, p. 15.

"THE WARS OF TRUTH": WISDOM AND STRENGTH IN *AREOPAGITICA*

Juanita Whitaker

Milton's epistemology, embodied in the image of the warfaring Christian who dialectically struggles with truth and error alike, informs all arguments in *Areopagitica*. The wisdom-and-strength *topos* provides a model for understanding a range of images which support this theme. For Milton, complete wisdom and strength is man's dedicated struggle to know God's truth, and the occasion of the treatise clearly manifests the *topos:* Books (wisdom) are fighting (strength) to exist in England. The book metaphor admits the full epistemological scope of a free press: Society has all options for positive or perverted wisdom and strength. Censorship, however, is both a violent act (perverted strength) and a fear of ideas (intellectual weakness). His own heroic wisdom and strength is revealed in Milton's courage in voicing *Areopagitica,* which itself affirms the wisdom and strength of language and celebrates the power of the word.

THIS ESSAY finds its context in Milton criticism which is attentive to the intrinsic literary achievement of *Areopagitica,* especially as this achievement is manifest in Milton's imagery and metaphor. The earliest studies of language in the tract, Theodore Banks' *Milton's Imagery* (New York, 1950) and Alan F. Price's "Incidental Imagery in the *Areopagitica*" (*MP,* XLIX [1952], 217–22), while valuable in their classifications of image patterns, did not attempt to demonstrate the thematic content or structural function of the imagery. Not until John X. Evans' "Imagery as Argument in Milton's *Areopagitica*" (*TSLL,* VIII [1966], 189–205), written as a corrective to Price, was imagery seen as organic. Finding two themes, freedom of the press and religious liberty, Evans dichotomized the tract when he said, "There is a point in the essay

185

... where Milton's interest shifts to the second issue, religious liberty. Coincident with this transition is the appearance of new figures—commercial, military, and light-darkness images—which form clusters Milton plainly reserved for this part of the argument" (p. 197). My own reading of *Areopagitica*, which seeks to provide a new perspective for Milton's imagery, begins with the conviction that Milton's attention does not shift from freedom of the press to religious liberty; rather, freedom of the press is an issue which allows him to speculate broadly upon liberty, power, wisdom, and truth. Like the Lycidas-poet, the orator seizes upon the occasion, transcends it, and articulates perennial themes which many Englishmen may not have seen as resident in the occasion. Nor do I believe it is properly emphatic to speak of a shift in image clusters, for those new figures which appear later in the tract are implicit in the earliest tropes and fulfill a larger thematic pattern that has not been recognized in previous work on *Areopagitica*.

Underlying all *Areopagitica*'s arguments and finally emerging as a major theme is an epistemological concern: How can man know truth, and knowing it, how should he act in the world? To express this theme, Milton employs a range of images which cohere and assume structural authority when seen under the rubric of wisdom and strength as an ideal of human endeavor. Possessed of an ancient classical and biblical tradition, the theme of wisdom and strength has manifested itself as the formula for heroic action, *sapientia et fortitudo*.[1] Both A. B. Chambers, in his analysis of *Samson Agonistes*, and John Steadman, in his study of *Paradise Lost*, have found Milton to be writing within this tradition of heroism.[2] While my intent is not to demonstrate Milton's conscious employment of this *topos* in *Areopagitica*, I do submit that the ideal is inherent in his epistemology. The theme of wisdom and strength is eminently suited to an argument for human endeavor and also subtly corroborates Milton's own wisdom and courage in penning the tract. As a guide to analysis, this *topos*, I believe, will provide an illuminating framework for study of a language and imagery which always capably and often brilliantly advance the themes of the tract. Milton's achievement is to surpass conventional handlings of the oratorical form with an intrinsic literary structure as crucial to the argument as the five-part division which is its external form.

The ideal of wisdom and strength that one encounters in Milton, quite unlike that found in his classical models, follows Christian tradition and attaches special importance to *sapientia* while it redefines *fortitudo* altogether. *Sapientia,* or human wisdom, is gained from education, reason, revelation; it is man's perception of truth in whatever form is available to him. *Fortitudo,* no longer strictly physical strength or courage in battle, embraces those Christian virtues of patience, faith, steadfastness, that "Heroic magnitude of mind" (*SA,* 1279) which Samson attains.[3] A strength of mind rather than of body, *fortitudo* is a moral force, an intellectual courage "Not less but more Heroic than the wrath / Of stern *Achilles*" (*PL* IX, 14–15). Complete wisdom and strength, in Milton, is man's dedicated struggle to know God's truth.

Because this human ideal exists in a fallen world, the manifestation of wisdom and strength is imperfectly realized. Rhetorical tradition, for example, gives us the ancient disputation of the pen versus the sword,[4] a debate which dichotomizes experience (as experience in a fallen world will necessarily be fragmented) and prompts effort toward the unattainable goal of fusing the two activities in one accomplished individual. History and literature alike provide few heroes of this sort. Elizabethan England pointed to that brilliantly skilled man, Sir Philip Sidney, but John Milton was to celebrate the only truly perfect man in Jesus Christ. A harmonious balance of *fortitudo* and *sapientia* is rare among humankind. One is more apt to encounter unwise courage or weak wisdom. Often the ideal is found in some perverted state: Too much *fortitudo,* or excessive power, may destroy wisdom; while wisdom itself may become corrupted by *malitia,* the desire to do evil ("out of good still to find means of evil," *PL* I, 165).[5] Despite rhetorical tradition, Milton's philosophy of action in *Areopagitica* clearly implies that Englishmen might realize the ideal.

The argument for intellectual and religious liberty in the treatise is advanced by a presiding Miltonic theme, the belief that for man the championship of truth is a struggle, the Pauline conviction that every Christian is a warrior in God's army—a theme which clearly partakes of the wisdom-and-strength formula. The occasion of the treatise reinforces this idea. Figuratively, books (wisdom) are fighting (strength) for the freedom to exist in England. Literally, with the aid of these books, every Christian is fighting to know and to articulate truth—to realize, in fact, God's kingdom on earth.

The English perversion of the ideal, in the licensing act that inspired *Areopagitica*, is further evidenced by Milton's oblique handling of the model after which the treatise is patterned. Isocrates advocated a form of *sapientia* in opting for the reinstatement and supremacy of a former governing body, the Council of Areopagus. Behind his desire that this assembly of wise lawgivers be invested with complete authority over the citizens of Athens and that it be given the power to enforce its laws resides the concept of *fortitudo*. As Milton constructs his treatise, the compatibility with his model is destroyed and the formula is reversed.[6] Parliament (Isocrates' Council of Areopagus), which represents the wisdom of England, has actually ceased to attain *sapientia* because it is using law as a perverted force (*fortitudo*) to suppress books, or the availability of *sapientia*. Isocrates recommends that the few control a nation's wisdom and that these few use force to assure control. Milton argues that the wisdom of the few (Parliament) is no longer true wisdom because it has perverted the power of law in denying the availability of wisdom to the majority. Such an inversion of Isocrates suggests that Milton's title is ironic, that his posture of latter-day Isocrates is imposture, and that the orator-audience rapport is false.

Despite Parliament's perversion of wisdom and strength with its licensing act, Milton's rhetorical strategy is to assume that Parliament believes in the true ideal and that wisdom and learning are cherished values in England. Stated in its syllogistic form, the reasoning of *Areopagitica* begins in the opening argument of the confirmation with the assumption that learned nations are superior to warlike societies (a proof drawn from history). Athens, "where Books and Wits were ever busier then in any other part of *Greece*" (*YP*, vol. II, p. 494), is contrasted with "That other leading City of *Greece, Lacedaemon*," of which Milton says, "it is to be wonder'd how muselesse and unbookish they [the Lacedaemonians] were, minding nought but the feats of Warre" (p. 496). Similarly, "The Romans also for many ages train'd up only to a military roughnes, resembling most the *Lacedaemonion* guise, knew of learning little" (p. 497). Despite his ostensible comparison between England and Athens, Milton ironically implies that England is worse off than

Lacedaemon, for a Parliament bent on licensing is obviously not to be compared to the wise lawgiver, Lycurgus, who "was so addicted to elegant learning, as to have been the first that brought out of *Ionia* the scatter'd works of Homer, and sent the Poet *Thales* from *Creet* to prepare and mollifie the Spartan surlinesse with his smooth songs and odes, the better to plant among them law and civility" (p. 496).

The minor premise of Milton's argument maintains that England belongs with those nations in history who have been considered learned and wise. His insistence upon English wisdom accounts for much of the nationalistic fervor of *Areopagitica*. As licensing, he writes, "is a particular disesteem of every knowing person alive, and most injurious to the writt'n labours and monuments of the dead, so to me it seems an undervaluing and vilifying of the whole Nation. I cannot set so light by all the invention, the art, the wit, the grave and solid judgement which is in England" (p. 535). In the so-called national digression, he exhorts, "Lords and Commons of England, consider what Nation it is wherof ye are, and wherof ye are the governours: a Nation not slow and dull, but of a quick, ingenious, and piercing spirit, acute to invent, suttle and sinewy to discours, not beneath the reach of any point the highest that human capacity can soar to" (p. 551). Innately endowed with superior mental capacities, England is both the father of European learning and the "Nation chos'n before any other, that out of her as out of *Sion* should be proclam'd and sounded forth the first tidings and trumpet of Reformation to all *Europ*" (pp. 551–52). The final claim makes prophets and visionaries of Englishmen, "a knowing people, a Nation of Prophets, of Sages, and of Worthies" (p. 554).

The corollary argument to national learning and wisdom maintains that Parliament, too, is wise. The exordium voices a criterion for measuring England's freedoms which conforms completely to the *sapientia et fortitudo topos:* "it ['the utmost bound of civill liberty attain'd, that wise men looke for'] will bee attributed first, as is most due, to the strong assistance of God our deliverer, next to your faithfull guidance and undaunted Wisdome, Lords and Commons of *England*" (p. 487). Having established that the nation must be led by God's strength and Parliament's wisdom, Milton rhetorically assumes that Parliament also honors wisdom and learning and that it believes a nation of letters is superior to a nation of arms: "how much better I find ye esteem it to imitate the old and elegant humanity of Greece, then the barbarick pride of a *Hunnish* and *Norwegian* statelines" (p. 489). And he praises "those ages, to whose polite wisdom and letters we ow that we are not yet *Gothes* and *Jutlanders*" (p. 489). The duty of this contemporary Parliament, therefore, is to act wisely. The rhetorical and thematic climax to the various proofs which constitute the division is the goal of "religious and civill Wisdome" (p. 492)—a goal toward which the nation, Parliament, and *Areopagitica* are striving. "To ordain wisely as in this world of evill, in the midd'st whereof God hath plac't us unavoidably" (p. 526) is the only means of combating evil, but of Popish licensing, Milton declares, "Wisdom we cannot call it" (p. 537). Thus, while he begins with an assumption of Parliament's wise ruling, Milton reverses that judgment midway in the treatise—a reversal which he, in turn, expects of Parliament, as *Areopagitica*'s final statement to Parliament makes clear: "to redresse willingly and speedily what hath bin err'd, and in highest autority to esteem a plain advertisement more then others have done a sumptuous bribe, is a vertue (honour'd Lords and Commons) answerable to Your highest actions, and whereof none can participat but greatest and wisest men" (p. 570).

Wisdom (*sapientia*), an ideal which receives strategic structural emphasis in the exordium, the division, the opening argument of the confirmation, and the concluding sentence of the treatise, is the highest human goal toward which man strives. It is so that one may achieve wisdom, Milton believes, that he is allowed intellectual and religious freedom. Not only an ideal which gives meaning to the immediate political issue, the wisdom-and-strength theme informs the language of *Areopagitica* as well, providing a structure for understanding a diversity of metaphoric patterns in the prose.

The legislation of censorship, a legal mandate concerning the dispensation of human thought, is inherently related to human wisdom and strength. Nor, for obvious reasons, is one surprised to find that the book metaphor is a dominant vehicle for analysis of England's attainment of the ideal. In *Paradise Lost* Milton was to lament, in equating books and wisdom, that "the Book of knowledge fair / [Is] presented with a Universal blanc / . . . [And] Nature's works to me [are] expung'd and ras'd, / And wisdom at one entrance [is] quite shut out" (III, 47–50). Written in 1644, some years prior to his blindness and before the Book of Creatures was closed to him, *Areopagitica* asserts that all experience is our book: "what ever thing we hear or see, sitting, walking, travelling, or conversing may be fitly call'd our book" (YP, vol. II, p. 528). Because human knowledge is partial, however, reality constantly qualifies the ideality with which we have invested the book. Paradoxically, the totality of experience which Milton sees as "our book" may be repressive, as the occasion that calls forth *Areopagitica* is, so that one must "read" and learn from the very attempt to limit knowledge.

The book metaphor in *Areopagitica* is by theological necessity ambiguous. In the first extended metaphor of the treatise, an image against which later book tropes should be measured, the ideal of human wisdom, though flawed, is celebrated:

For Books are not absolutely dead things, but doe contain a potencie of life in them to be as active as that soule was whose progeny they are; nay they do preserve as in a violl the purest efficacie and extraction of that living intellect that bred them. I know they are as lively, and as vigorously productive, as those fabulous Dragons teeth; and being sown up and down, may chance to spring up armed men. And yet on the other hand unlesse warinesse be us'd, as good almost kill a Man as kill a good Book; who kills a Man kills a reasonable creature, Gods Image; but hee who destroyes a good Booke, kills reason it selfe, kills the Image of God, as it were in the eye. (p. 492)

Though his position on censorship is here directly stated for the first time in the treatise, the complexity of Milton's epistemology invades the rhetoric, making the statement itself indirect. The ambiguity is immediate: "Books are not absolutely dead things." Are we to interpret "not absolutely dead" to mean "nearly dead," "partially alive," or "almost totally alive"—the opposite of the surface meaning of the statement? The transitional "but" would indicate that books are quite alive, although "*a* potencie of life" (italics added) again qualifies the meaning: Can there be partial potency? The strategy of the rhetoric calls for a gradual revelation of meaning and intention. The movement of the passage proceeds from "dead things" to "a potencie of life," in fact, to "active . . . soule" and "purest efficacie and extraction of that living intellect." The initial contrast between books metaphorically dead and alive is abandoned as the rhetoric forces us, and books, toward greater vitality. In the opening sentence books are equated with the wisdom burden of the formulaic ideal. As the passage continues, Milton crosses from the mental and spiritual quality of books to their physical reality, to the force and strength, the *fortitudo* of which books are possessed. Not simply "dead things" nor merely unembodied spiritual forces, books in fact are active physical agents, "armed men." Though a regressive movement, cosmologically, in the sequence from spiritual essence to mortal being, the rhetoric has a progressive psychological effect: Far from being almost dead, books have a real, tangible, and visible force operative in this world. Not merely "dead," not simply of another spiritual world, books are regenerative and may chance "to spring up" as seeds and add to the cycle of life. However, the impact of the image is upon the destructive potential in books, an admission designed to retain the sympathies of his audience.

Despite the rhetorical strategy, the confusion and ambiguity of the language, the passage does clarify Milton's position. While the potential for destruction is resident in intellectual freedom, just as Adam was "Sufficient to have stood, though free to fall" (*PL* III, 99), the Miltonic vision requires a delicate balance between wisdom and strength. Ideally, books admit both positive wisdom ("the purest efficacie and extraction of that living intellect," that is, "reason") and positive strength ("active" and "vigorously productive"). Falling short of this ideal, books may not always be "good" but may be harmful and destructive. However, Milton asserts, greater destructive potential rests in the censorship of books than in the destructive power potential in books ("may chance to spring up armed men"). As the argument of *Areopagitica* unfolds, wisdom-and-strength images formulate the full range of epistemological possibility—positive or perverted wisdom, positive or perverted strength.

A basic assumption of *Areopagitica* is that censorship, deriving from faulty thinking, results in a perverted strength. The paradox of a fallacious law (law should be an ordering force in society, but unwise laws may be socially disruptive) gives rise to the theme of censorship as violent act. Attempting to define Parliament's legislation, Milton ironically notes, "Wisdom we cannot call it" (YP, vol. II, p. 537), thus providing the transition from idea (wisdom) to act (force) that allows him to term censorship "this obstructing violence" (p. 542) and permits him to speak of "this violence" (p. 534) done to the helpless

author. The paradox of censorship as violence provides the metaphorical basis for Milton's initial book trope, where he speaks of
licensing as a potential "killing" of books: "We should be wary
therefore what persecution we raise against the living labours of
publick men, how we spill that season'd life of man preserv'd and
stor'd up in Books; since we see a kinde of homicide may be thus
committed, sometimes a martyrdome, and if it extend to the whole
impression, a kinde of massacre, whereof the execution ends not in
the slaying of an elementall life, but strikes at that ethereall and fift
essence, the breath of reason it selfe, slaies an immortality rather
then a life" (p. 493). While the paradox of the metaphor causes it to
turn upon itself to reveal the absurdity of licensing (the immortal
cannot be slain), history reveals nations that have nonetheless enforced such absurd laws. Censorship as violent act has historical
precedent in the Inquisition, which Milton refers to in an extended
book trope: "Which cours [censorship] *Leo* the 10, and his successors
follow'd, untill the Councell of Trent, and the Spanish Inquisition
engendring together brought forth, or perfeted those Catalogues,
and expurging Indexes that rake through the entralls of many an old
good Author, with a violation wors then any could be offer'd to his
tomb. Nor did they stay in matters Hereticall, but any subject that
was not to their palat, they either condemn'd in a prohibition, or had
it strait into the new Purgatory of an Index" (pp. 502–03). In another
personification of the book structure, Milton further dramatizes the
violent power of the licensing act by emphasizing the passive help-
lessness of the author: "Sometimes 5 *Imprimaturs* are seen together
dialogue-wise in the Piatza of one Title page, complementing and
ducking each to other with their shav'n reverences, whether the
Author, who stands by in perplexity at the foot of his Epistle, shall to
the Presse or to the spunge" (p. 504). Extending this thought, Milton
continues, "What advantage is it to be a man over it is to be a boy at
school, if we have only scapt the ferular, to come under the fescu of
an *Imprimatur*?" (p. 531). For the boy in school (seeking wisdom)
the ferula, the rod used to beat him, represents a perverted physical
strength which distorts the learning process. The mature man, under
the control of censorship laws (perverted intellectual strength), is
dominated by the fescue, a pointer used in teaching, which metaphorically wielded by the Imprimatur distorts the intellectual proc-

ess by pointing to what may be read, what not. The identification of unnatural mental experiences with violent controls is nicely balanced in the parallelism of ferula and fescue as the man, and sentence, move from schoolmaster to Imprimatur, both authoritarians who are inimical to learning and threaten meaningful autonomy. The confusion of the ideal is further explored, and more directly, in Milton's outburst: "I hate a pupil teacher, I endure not an instructor that comes to me under the wardship of an overseeing fist" (p. 533). The emphasis at this point in the treatise has moved from the destructiveness of books, when Milton is discussing the impact of a free press upon the ignorant, to the destructiveness of censorship, when he is discussing the impact of censorship upon the educated.

As *Areopagitica* develops the theme of censorship as perverted wisdom and misdirected strength, the focus shifts from censorship as active force to censorship as defensive impulse. Analyzing the causes of the licensing act, Milton contends that censorship derives from fear and intellectual laziness—that is, from a lack of strength of mind. Again relying upon extended book tropes, he traces the intellectual timidity of English clergymen, who ought to be the intellectual stalwarts of the nation by virtue of their educational advantages:

It is no new thing never heard of before, for a *parochiall* Minister, who has his reward, and is at his *Hercules* pillars in a warm benefice, to be easily inclinable, if he have nothing else that may rouse up his studies, to finish his circuit in an English concordance and a *topic folio*, the gatherings and savings of a sober graduatship, a *Harmony* and a *Catena*, treading the constant round of certain common doctrinall heads, attended with their uses, motives, marks and means, out of which as out of an alphabet or sol fa by forming and transforming, joyning and dis-joyning variously a little book-craft, and two hours meditation might furnish him unspeakably to the performance of more then a weekly charge of sermoning: not to reck'n up the infinit helps of interlinearies, breviaries, *synopses*, and other loitering gear. (p. 546)

In ironic reference to Hercules, "symbol of heroic physical and moral force,"[7] the passage describes intellectual laziness (that is, no *fortitudo*) as the perverted wisdom that is only capable of cataloguing and classifying and copying. Such weak-mindedness obliges one to erect some kind of defense—defenses that appear in the prose as ironic siege metaphors. Armed not with strong minds and meaningful ideas, the minister "never need fear of Pulpit provision, having where so plenteously to refresh his magazin. But if his rear and flanks be not impal'd, if his back dore be not secur'd by the rigid licencer, but that a bold book may now and then issue forth, and give the assault to some of his old collections in their trenches, it will concern him then to keep waking, to stand in watch, to set good guards and sentinells about his receiv'd opinions" (p. 547). The impulse toward censorship is a product of a similar ironic, or misdirected, *fortitudo:* "There is yet behind of what I purpos'd to lay open, the incredible losse, and detriment that this plot of licencing puts us to, more then if som enemy at sea should stop up all our hav'ns and ports, and creeks, it hinders and retards the importation of our richest Marchandize, Truth" (p. 548). In both instances, the siege images suggest an ironic protectiveness born of a weak-minded fear of ideas. With clergymen the defense mechanism of "magazin" (the lazy intellectual pursuits of topic folios and so forth) keeps out the foe (the free exchange of ideas, such as is found in *Areopagitica* that revitalizes the stale ideas of topic folios).[8] The effort is meaningless, however, because the clergymen have no vital thought to protect. In the political instance, the siege image reverses the irony. While there is much of value within the defensive line, that is, truth, there is no foe without, or rather, the threat without is self-made, that is, the restriction in licensing.

Subsequent siege images invert the wisdom-and-strength theme to describe freedom of the press and of speech. In an early passage, writing of the need to study learning and philosophy outside one's culture, Milton favorably contrasts "the examples of *Moses, Daniel & Paul,* who were skilfull in all the learning of the Aegyptians, Caldeans, and Greeks" with "*Julian* the Apostat, and suttlest enemy to our faith, [who] made a decree forbidding Christians the study of heathen learning: for, said he, they wound us with our own weapons, and with our owne arts and sciences they overcome us" (pp. 507–08). Such reasoning produces the doctrine that learning is a weapon, its own best defense, and provides, in turn, the basis for the concluding siege images of the treatise. The tenor of the metaphor is appropriately enlarged from the clergy to the entire populace of London:

Behold now this vast City; a City of refuge, the mansion house of liberty, encompast and surrounded with his protection; the shop of warre hath not there more anvils and hammers waking, to fashion out the plates and instruments of armed Justice in defence of beleaguer'd Truth, then there be pens and heads there, sitting by their studious lamps, musing, searching, revolving new notions and idea's wherewith to present, as with their homage and their fealty the approaching Reformation: others as fast reading, trying all things, assenting to the force of reason and convincement. (pp. 553–54)

London, under siege, is ironically the city of liberty, but she can claim this title only because of her intellectual freedoms. (Milton continues to assume the proposition he wishes to argue, that London *does* have intellectual freedom.) In so arguing, Milton's metaphoric structure moves from an ironic *fortitudo* to a positive *sapientia*, fighting with pens, as Milton is doing in the act of writing *Areopagitica,* rather than with swords, in defense of truth. And, in a similar passage, Milton declares that "when a City shall be as it were besieg'd and blockt about, her navigable river infested, inrodes and incursions round, defiance and battell oft rumor'd to be marching up ev'n to her walls, and suburb trenches, . . . then the people, or the greater part, more then at other times, wholly tak'n up with the study of highest and most important matters to be reform'd, should be disputing, reasoning, reading, inventing, discoursing, ev'n to a rarity, and admiration, things not before discourst or writt'n of" (pp. 556–57). The metaphoric structure, seen in the light of wisdom-and-strength images, gives full support to the thematic thrust of the argument—positive, meaningful strength derives from intellectual freedom.

Viewed from its broadest perspective in the treatise, the wisdom-and-strength theme is a vehicle for epistemological analysis. In a fable explicitly compared to the Osiris myth, Milton argues that our perception of reality and truth is distorted because the perfect shape of truth (or the wholeness of our vision) has been lost: "a wicked race of deceivers . . . took the virgin Truth, hewd her lovely form into a thousand peeces, and scatter'd them to the four winds" (p. 549). Consequently, truth having been fragmented, man's quest must be to reunite the pieces. The central conflict of our social condition is that of the "dividers" (p. 550) versus the re-formers. True to the inquiring and independent spirit of the Reformation, Milton's epistemology submits that, truth having been destroyed by false minds and perverted strength, we are now required "To be still searching what we know not, by what we know" (p. 551).

In another significant passage, Milton gives additional clarification to his vision of good and evil, which "we know in the field of this World grow up together almost inseparably" (p. 514). The allegory in this case reverses the *fortitudo* of the image of truth from helpless virgin to vigorous warrior: "And though all the windes of doctrin were let loose to play upon the earth, so Truth be in the field, we do injuriously by a licencing and prohibiting to misdoubt her strength. Let her and Falsehood grapple; who ever knew Truth put to the wors, in a free and open encounter?" (p. 561). We should note that the principle is twofold: The epistemology not only asserts the ascendance of truth over error, and thus of man's ability to achieve higher knowledge, but argues also for the primacy of the struggle itself to know truth. Active confrontation (note the word choice of "grapple" and "encounter"), whenever Milton speaks of human knowledge, is a central tenet. "La vertue est toute dans l'effort," as William Carlos Williams was to write in *Paterson*.[9]

So it is, in one of the most justifiably famous passages in the prose writings, that Milton provides the central heroic image of human endeavor:

He that can apprehend and consider vice with all her baits and seeming pleasures, and yet abstain, and yet distinguish, and yet prefer that which is truly better, he is the true warfaring Christian. I cannot praise a fugitive and cloister'd vertue, unexercis'd & unbreath'd, that never sallies out and sees her adversary, but slinks out of the race, where that immortall garland is to be run for, not without dust and heat. Assuredly we bring not innocence into the world, we bring impurity much rather: that which purifies us is triall, and triall is by what is contrary. (pp. 514–15)

Inconclusive textual evidence regarding the "warfaring" and "wayfaring" controversy forces us to the context of the image for clarity.[10] Two actions are suggested. The first image is that of the medieval knight ("I cannot praise a fugitive and cloister'd vertue, unexercis'd & unbreath'd, that never sallies out and sees her adversary") and is reinforced by an adjacent image of Spenser's Sir Guyon (Temperance, who "can apprehend and consider vice with all her baits and seeming pleasures, and yet abstain, and yet distinguish, and yet prefer that which is truly better"). The second image is one of the ancient athlete ("but slinks out of the race, where that immortall garland is to be run for, not without dust and heat"). Both images, of soldier ("warfaring") and athlete ("wayfaring"), are perhaps indebted to St. Paul, who in his epistles frequently compared the Christian endeavor to that of the soldier and the athlete, and was to say of himself, "I have fought the good fight, I have finished the course, I have kept the faith" (2 Timothy iv, 7).[11] The "true warfaring Christian," therefore, embraces both virtues of the heroic ideal: The wisdom is tried and proven by active competition and confrontation. A similar fusion of wisdom and strength concludes the section when Milton writes that his audience, implicitly compared to Sir Guyon and St. Paul, must "scout" out the enemy by reading and reasoning.

Out of this epistemological construct, Milton fashions the transcendent, apocalyptic image of the treatise, producing a climax to the many images of prophecy, vision, rejuvenation, and rebirth that have contrapuntally offset the demonic effect of perverted wisdom-and-strength *topoi*. In this apocalyptic vision of England reborn, Milton transcends all that is demonic in England's false political and social condition. Beginning, "it betok'ns us not degenerated, nor drooping to a fatall decay, but casting off the old and wrincl'd skin of corruption to outlive these pangs and wax young again, entring the glorious waies of Truth and prosperous vertue destin'd to become great and honourable in these latter ages" (p. 557), Milton borrows from two ancient commonplaces, "idleness is to be shunned" and the youth–old-age paradox. Arguing for a reformation, he does so in terms of the wisdom-and-strength formula: Physical decline should lead to a new birth, a concept suggestive of the phoenix's miraculous self-renewal. Paradoxically, the physical image "betok'ns" a rebirth of the mind. From possibility Milton next moves to prophetic realization: "Methinks I see in my mind a noble and puissant Nation rousing herself like a strong man after sleep, and shaking her invincible locks" (pp. 557–58). The comparison of England to Samson is fraught with wisdom-and-strength *topoi*, an image of the biblical hero as both wise and strong that has been fully explored by A. B. Chambers.[12] The interplay of the terms of the formula, from Milton's prophetic "methinks" to the "puissant Nation" he envisions, parallels the previous sentence, where another miraculous regeneration and rebirth of great wisdom and strength is occurring. The final sentence of the prophecy, in a rhetorical climax to the imagery of birth, youth–old age, and sight-light, envisions England's destiny in the figure of the eagle. "Methinks I see her as an Eagle muing her mighty youth, and kindling her undazl'd eyes at the full midday beam; purging and unscaling her long abused sight at the fountain it self of heav'nly radiance; while the whole noise of timorous and flocking birds, with those also that love the twilight, flutter about, amaz'd at what she means, and in their envious gabble would prognosticat a year of sects and schisms" (p. 558). Symbol of renewal in the medieval bestiaries,[13] the eagle image is both transcendent wisdom ("purging and unscaling her long abused sight at the fountain it self of heav'nly radiance") and transcendent strength ("mighty youth"). The paradox of renewed strength, anticipated in the previous Samson image, where the main emphasis is upon *fortitudo*, is further suggested in the New Testament parallel of St. Paul's conversion, where the main emphasis is upon *sapientia*. St. Paul's conversion was also accompanied by a brilliant heavenly vision, which, though initially physically debilitating, resulted ultimately in his renewed strength. Such renewal, the symbol suggests, is possible for England as well.

If the eagle is England, it is also the poet, and the passage reveals an epistemology of aesthetics that has been implicit throughout Milton's previous discussion of human knowledge. Not only does the eagle (England) experience a renewed vision, but the poet-orator also undergoes a transcendent imaginative experience ("Methinks I see"): What the eagle sees, the poet also witnesses. Against this higher knowledge of the poet, we should measure the perverted wisdom of "timorous and flocking" birds (note, too, Milton's independence and courage of mind and vision in contrast to the dependence and fear of his "flocking" detractors). Against this transcendent prophecy of Milton the poet-orator, we should measure the "envious gabble . . . [which] prognosticat[s] a year of sects and schisms." Against the single-minded unity of Milton's vision, we should measure the division of Parliament and England's sects and schisms. In this final unifying prophecy of *Areopagitica*, Milton re-forms the fragmented truth that Parliament by its licensing act would further destroy.

"While Isocrates regarded rhetoric as a purely verbal art not fundamentally related to knowledge," Milton, according to Joseph Wittreich, embraced the concept of symbolic style.[14] The theory of language that espouses symbolic style, when applied to *Areopagitica*, means that in creating images of wisdom and strength, Milton gains not simply ornament and analogue but argument as well. The rhetorical *topos*, according to such an aesthetic, becomes theme. Building upon wisdom-and-strength images which enrich textual detail, *Areopagitica*, in its prophetic authority, affirms the wisdom and strength of language itself: It celebrates the power of the word. Certainly the occasion of *Areopagitica*, like that of *Lycidas*, provided Milton the opportunity to demonstrate the way language, in the hands of a prophetic artist, can transform reality by changing our perception of the possible.

Newport News, Virginia

NOTES

1. This *topos* is amply discussed in Ernst Robert Curtius' mammoth *European Literature and the Latin Middle Ages,* trans. Willard R. Trask (New York, 1953).

2. "Wisdom and Fortitude in *Samson Agonistes*," *PMLA*, LXXVIII (1963), 315–20; *Milton and the Renaissance Hero* (Oxford, 1967).

3. The text of Milton's poetry cited throughout is *John Milton: Complete Poems and Major Prose,* ed. Merritt Y. Hughes (New York, 1957). Following the Christian elevation of *sapientia*, Milton writes, in the *Second Defense*, of his own attainment of the ideal: "Having from early youth been especially devoted to the liberal arts, with greater strength of mind than of body, I exchanged the toils of war, in which any stout trooper might outdo me, for those labors which I better understood, that with such wisdom as I owned I might add as much weight as possible to the counsels of my country and to this excellent cause, using not my lower but my higher and stronger powers" (*Complete Prose Works of John Milton*, ed. Don M. Wolfe et al. [New Haven, 1953–], vol. IV, p. 553, hereafter cited as YP).

4. Cf. Milton's use of the *topos* in the *Second Defense*, when, referring to his *First Defense* against Salmasius' attack, he recalls, "I met him in single combat and plunged into his reviling throat this pen, the weapon of his own choice" (YP, vol. IV, p. 556).

5. A similar and helpful analysis of *sapientia et fortitudo* perverted by the patristic *malitia* is provided by R. E. Kaske, "*Sapientia et Fortitudo* as the Controlling Theme of *Beowulf*," *SP*, LV (1958), 423–57.

6. See Joseph Antony Wittreich, Jr., "Milton's *Areopagitica*: Its Isocratic and Ironic Contexts," *Milton Studies*, IV, ed. James D. Simmonds (Pittsburgh, 1972), p.

109, for a convincing demonstration of Milton's ironic treatment of the Isocrates parallel.

7. *The Prose of John Milton*, ed. J. Max Patrick (Garden City, N.Y., 1967), p. 313, n. 303.

8. Milton's revitalization of rhetorical *topoi* is dramatically demonstrated by a comparison of his Commonplace Book with the poetry, where *topoi* are reborn as theme and image. Extremely useful in this regard is Ruth Mohl's *John Milton and His Commonplace Book* (New York, 1969).

9. (New York, 1946), bk. IV, iii.

10. In the Columbia edition, William Haller follows the printed text with "wayfaring"; see *The Works of John Milton*, ed. Frank A. Patterson et al. (New York, 1931), vol. IV, p. 311. Subsequent editors have generally emended to "warfaring," reflecting the four hand-corrected presentational copies and at least five other copies in the first edition. See Ernest Sirluck in YP, vol. II, p. 515; Hughes, *Complete Poems*, p. 728; and Patrick, *Prose of John Milton*, p. 287. A case against "warfaring" is made by Ruth M. Kivette in "The Ways and Wars of Truth," *Milton Quarterly*, VI (1972), 81–86.

11. King James Version. Cf. Hebrews xii, 1; 1 Corinthians ix, 24–25; Philippians ii, 16, iii, 13–14; and 1 Timothy vi, 12.

12. In "Wisdom and Fortitude in *Samson Agonistes*."

13. Most editors remark upon the similarity of Milton's imagery to that of medieval bestiaries. See T. H. White's translation of a twelfth-century bestiary in *A Book of Beasts* (New York, 1954), pp. 105–08.

14. Wittreich, "Milton's *Areopagitica*," pp. 108–09. Ruth Wallerstein's discussion of symbolic style is an appropriate context for the study of Milton's theory of language; see *Studies in Seventeenth-Century Poetic* (Madison, Wis., 1950), pp. 11–58.

L'ALLEGRO, IL PENSEROSO, AND "THE CYCLE OF UNIVERSAL KNOWLEDGE"

Norman B. Council

The subject of *L'Allegro* and *Il Penseroso* is the experience of education as Milton conceived it. All his statements on education assume the ideal expressed in the Seventh Prolusion: to aspire to a time "when the cycle of universal knowledge has been completed." This idealization of the humanist educational tradition leads Milton to reject as partial any education fettered by vocational goals. The apparent anomaly in the tradition, that a few "good writers" were thought to provide the total experience necessary to moral insight, anticipates Milton's representative and emblematic technique in the poems. Active Mirth and contemplative Melancholy divide experience between them. Within this frame, Milton identifies the educational experience that L'Allegro and Il Penseroso acquire as archetypal and ubiquitous. The temporal patterns, the natural images, and the cultural tradition which each observes provide the total experience and "immortality in the past" that Milton's educational theory promised. The particular experience of each figure emblematically represents all experience. The consequence for both is the harmonious poetic vision that Milton's ideal education constantly sought. One vision neither excludes nor includes the other. Two leaves of a diptych, *L'Allegro* and *Il Penseroso* together provide the picture of Milton's "cycle of universal knowledge."

MERRITT HUGHES has wisely remarked that *L'Allegro* and *Il Penseroso* "still resist criticism's best efforts to appraise their wealth."[1] The consequence is that most people who are concerned about such matters adopt an uneasy, though pedagogically profitable, variety of critical judgments about the poems. Day and night, mirth and melancholy, and a neo-Platonic ascent to intuitive knowledge are certainly among the major concerns of the poems; but since each of these major concerns and a host of minor concerns are quite distinct from one another, a vexing question has remained: In what context, if any, do these various themes of the poems cohere? I should like to propose that Milton's concept of education, of which his education tract is a convenient if anachronistic summary, provides that context. The poems are an emblematic description—a sort of humanist *speculum*—of the ideal of education that Milton continually championed.

In the Seventh Prolusion Milton suggests that education can aspire to a time "when the cycle of universal knowledge has been completed" (p. 625). This hyperbole is, of course, part of a display of wit and rhetoric, but it nevertheless expresses the basic assumption on which Milton's various statements about education rest. From the early prolusions and *Ad Patrem* to the 1644 education tractate, Milton's defense of humanist educational principles assumes one basic idea: Education, unfettered by vocational, rhetorical, or other limiting concerns, should ideally provide access to universal experience. Unlike the vocational and factual focus of the Comenian reforms that Samuel Hartlib was advocating, and unlike the scholasticism of Cambridge and the exaggerated rhetorical focus of what J. W. Adamson has called a "new scholasticism" in seventeenth-century grammar schools, again with a vocational focus, the tradition Milton espoused continued to assert the values Erasmus and John Colet and the other humanist reformers of Henry VIII's time had helped to establish—although for their own vocational, or at least political, purposes.[2] In practical fact Milton's educational ideals suffered from political ironies as frustrating as those More had Hythloday complain of, but the same ideal of the broadest possible education as the avenue to moral perfectibility lay behind both.

The anomaly in the tradition is, of course, that a very few "good writers" were thought to provide this universal insight. Sir Thomas Elyot, for instance, having recommended his wide variety of Greek and Latin writers to the student of grammar and rhetoric, suggests for moral philosophy the first two books of "the work of Aristotle called *Ethicae*," *De Officiis*, and Plato. "Those three books," he concluded, "be almost sufficient to make a perfect and excellent governor."[3] But it is only an apparent anomaly, and indeed the selective nature of the experience thought capable of providing insight into a universal ideal may help explain the emblematic technique of the companion poems. Milton's "cycle of universal knowledge" is neither repetitive nor merely symbolic; like the curriculum Elyot proposes, it is representative. "Ascend Mount Aetna in eruption," Milton urges his fellow students. "Cross the surging Adriatic unhurt" (p. 606). By study or experience of the typical instances, one acquires the total experience they represent, just as L'Allegro and Il Penseroso acquire typical experience representative of the whole.

Gabriel Harvey provides further evidence of this aspect of the tradition, for he recommends the same sort of education for poets that Milton will later propose. His marginal comments on Dionysius Periegetes' *De Situ Orbis*, for instance, assert the customary humanist values but emphasize the breadth of knowledge and experience to be acquired:

Others commend Chawcer & Lidgate for their witt, pleasant veine, varietie of poetical discourse, and all humanities: I specially note their astronomie, philosophie, & other parts of profound or cunning art. Wherein few of their time were more exactly learned. It is not sufficient for poets, to be superficial humanists: but they must be exquisite artists, curious vniuersal schollers.[4]

The Milton of the third and seventh prolusions, of *Ad Patrem*, and of the 1644 tractate emphasizes this capacity of humanistic education to aspire to universal knowledge. Thus, as Milton argues in *Of Education*, languages are principally to be learned not for argumentative or rhetorical purposes, but to provide access to the experience of other cultures than one's own: "And seeing every nation affords not experience and tradition enough for all kind of learning, therefore we are chiefly taught the languages of those people who have at any time been most industrious after wisdom" (p. 631).

In the Third Prolusion, Milton proposes to his fellow students a grand, humanist alternative to the "warty disputes of the sophists" (p. 605) and clearly asserts that a proper education will break down chronological and spatial barriers to provide access to universal experience. This may be the statement of a young idealist practicing his rhetorical skills, but it is nevertheless the statement of a young idealist who was shortly to write *L'Allegro* and *Il Penseroso*. Indeed,

Milton recommends to his fellow students the sort of experience he later provides in the companion poems. "Look at the places where the heroes walked of old," Milton suggests. "Explore the regions made glorious by wars, triumphs, and the tales of famous poets." Each experience he recommends is either the most typical of its kind—"ascend Mount Aetna in eruption"—or ubiquitous—"You must follow the sun on his journey—be his companions and call time itself to a reckoning, and demand an account of its eternal flight" (pp. 606–07). He concludes with a suggestion that Don Cameron Allen sees as evidence of the Hermetic qualities of Milton's thought. Milton proposes that the mind "reach the summit of knowledge and learn to know itself and at the same time to know those blessed minds and intelligences with whom hereafter it will enter into eternal fellowship" (p. 607). Allen thinks that Milton's "procedure [in the Third Prolusion] has a certain likeness to that of the hermetic thinker," and that "this procedure explains the total structure of the two poems."[5]

The context of Milton's advice to his fellow students is, however, clear, and it is not as Hermetic apologist that he is speaking; he is opposing what he sees as the clerkly exercises imposed by the Cambridge curriculum and proposing his humanist ideal. That includes, by definition, Hermetic and Platonic elements, but to identify the pattern of either the Third Prolusion or the companion poems as Hermetic is to mistake the part for the whole. The idea that students should progress from the sensible to the abstract and from the simpler to the more complicated is not, after all, uniquely Hermetic or Platonic. The idea formed part, for instance, of the Comenian reforms that Hartlib was introducing into England, and Ernest Sirluck has argued that this similarity in technique may have misled Milton to believe that he shared the Comenian goals, which were in fact much more limited than his own.[6] And the fact is that Milton does not propose any particular pattern of educational experience in the Third Prolusion. The ideal is ubiquity, and Milton details all of the areas to which education provides access. The Seventh Prolusion, which echoes the third in this regard, identifies all the aspects of the natural and supernatural world that may be experienced. "How much it means to grasp all the principles of the heavens and their stars. . . . How much it means to get an insight into the fluctuating winds and the exhalations and gases which the earth and sea emit, and—if it be possible—into the nature and the sensory experience of every living creature" (p. 625). "If it be possible" is not quite so plaintive or hypothetical an aside as it sounds. The consequence of this experience—or, again as Milton puts it, "when the cycle of universal knowledge has been completed"—is that "the man who is in possession of the stronghold of wisdom . . . will seem to have the stars under his control. . . . It is as if some god had abdicated the government of the world and committed its justice, laws, and administration to him as ruler" (p. 625).

Large as this experience is, it is only half the experience Milton sees as the goal of an ideal education, for it is not experience of the past or of the future. Accordingly, Milton next affirms that ubiquity in time is also among the pleasures that learning affords. "This is the way to live in all the epochs of history, Gentlemen, and to be a contemporary of time itself. And while we are looking forward to the future glory of our name, this will also . . . extend life backward from the womb to extort from unwilling Fate a kind of immortality in the past" (p. 625). *Ad Patrem* and *Of Education* share this vision. In the former, Milton defends the ideal education of the poet against the narrower experience available in a political or legal education. He has, at his father's urging and expense, acquired the languages (including "the eloquence which the modern Italian pours from his degenerate mouth") necessary to total experience, an experience he describes in grand but specific terms. "And finally, all that heaven contains and earth . . . and the air that flows between earth and heaven, and whatever the waters and the trembling surface of the sea cover, your kindness gives me the means to know" (p. 85). *Of Education* suggests a scheme through which the ideal Milton had consistently held might be achieved and brings the humanist concept of education to its moral apotheosis: "to repair the ruins of our first parents." This is but the logical conclusion of Milton's statements on education, for the assumption behind his early "when the cycle of universal knowledge has been completed" remained with him throughout.

Another aspect of Milton's ideas of education should be examined before turning to the poems. The quest for universal experience does not, of course, result in moral relativism, and the humanist theoretic quest for universal experience was highly selective. As in didactic, so in moral terms, this is only an apparent paradox. Experience, from this point of view, can be rightly or wrongly apprehended. Moral responsibility resides in rightly apprehending it so as to choose the right path from among the deceptive variety available. The humanist revival embraced this ancient and commonplace idea. It lies behind Elyot's choosing the portions of classical authors which should and should not be read by the young student. "It were better that a child should never read any part of Lucian than all Lucian" (I.x). It lies behind Sidney's defense of poets as those who "most properly imitate to teach & delight: and to imitate, borrow nothing of what is, hath bin, or shall be, but range onely reined with learned discretion, into the divine consideration of what may be and should be."[7] It is, in a moral and political sense, the great subject of *The Faerie Queene*. Each knight threads his way among the instructive and deceitful details of his allegorical world until accumulated experience—and grace—perfect his particular virtue; the way of each knight is strewn with those who misconceive or pervert their experience. In *Paradise Lost*, the vision Milton provides for Adam after his fall is moral education of precisely this kind. In Books XI and XII Adam experiences the laborious and agonized process of properly understanding—that is, of understanding the divine plan in—the brutal history Michael unfolds before him; that history, too, is strewn with those who misconceive or pervert their experience.

The difference between all of these and a minor book that Milton suggests in *Of Education* is immense, but the same idea of universal education with a moral goal accounts for his suggestion, and it can turn our attention back to the companion poems. Milton proposes that "to make them [young students] expert in the usefullest points of grammar, and withal to season them and win them early to the love of virtue and true labor . . . some easy and delightful book of education would be read to them, whereof the Greeks have store; as Cebes, Plutarch, and other Socratic discourses" (p. 633). Milton obviously thought of these only as primers, but the reason that the technique and moral content of *The Table of Cebes*, for instance, should seem to him appropriate at this stage of the student's career is clear. In it, the narrator is walking in a temple in a strange land, where he sees a picture of a grave man giving directions to a multitude. He discovers that followers of Pythagoras and Parmenides had dedicated the temple and picture to Saturn and is given an explanation of the scene:

If a man conceive not this [picture] aright . . . it will infect his whole life with a continual corrosion. . . . But contrarywise, if one apprehend it with a true conceit, Ignorance breaketh his own necke, and the whole course of his life that understandeth it aright, shall be replenished with perfect beatitude.[8]

The "enclosure . . . is called LIFE," and the multitude are about to enter it, directed by the old man, who is "Life's GENIVS" (F8). The narrator then shifts to a chronological description of the experience the "picture" relates. There are a number of experiences to choose among. Some are false enticements, while some are true steps to knowledge, which permits the few who gain it to achieve "Beatitude." "Virtues" then lead the beatified man back through earlier stages of experience so he can rightly understand them all. An elementary and insignificant book, Cebes' *Table* provides us with only a skeletal outline of humanist educational ideas, but most of the important bones are there. In an ancient book with, therefore, classic authority, a picture labeled "LIFE" delights while instructing its observer. It allegorically figures the acquisition through total experience of the self-knowledge which grants wisdom and virtue, and describes that acquisition as a series of choices between rightly conceiving and wrongly conceiving experience.

L'Allegro and *Il Penseroso* have basic affinities with this tradition. To see them as the emblematic expression of the kind of experience which Milton conceived ideal education to be is to synthesize many of the revealing explanations of the details of that experience which recent criticism has provided. Active Mirth and contemplative Melancholy divide experience between them. It is a binary perception of experience; a third companion poem is inconceivable. It is also, of course, a commonplace distinction, although not one usually associated with educational theory. In Lodowick Bryskett's *A Discourse of Civill Life,* however, the association is made when, during a discussion of proper education, the speaker is challenged because he claims his goal to be "humane felicitie." His challenger asserts that that is only to be found in heaven; the speaker answers that he means the two kinds Plato mentions: "the one a contemplative felicitie . . . the other an active or practicke felicitie."9

These two modes, in any event, provide Milton with the context in which the total experience of the poems can be acquired. The contrary modes, "loathed melancholy" and "vain deluding joys," which are banished at the beginning of each poem, have of course been the object of much debate, but that is moot here. Whether, as I think, Milton had the Galenic sort of melancholy in mind when he banished "loathed melancholy" and had "vain" joys quite unlike the real delights of *L'Allegro* in mind when he banished them from *Il Penseroso* is a pertinent question. But there seems no question at all of why he banished them or of the symbolic appropriateness of the places to which they are exiled. Each otherwise would prevent or pervert the experience of the poems. The "loathed" and "deluding" paths which would prevent both forms of experience are assigned to their appropriate places. The daughter of the hellish monster and "blackest midnight," an obvious foe, takes her place in the Cimmerian desert, where, in the traditional Homeric description to which Milton is alluding, "Never does the bright sun look down on them with his rays . . . but baneful night is spread over wretched mortals" (*Odyssey*, bk. 11, ll. 15–19). To accompany this guide would be to abandon all the experience of life. In the other poem, "The brood of folly without father bred" is deluding rather than loathed, so a more dangerous foe, but properly understood her gaudy shapes can likewise be seen to prevent the educative experience necessary to moral understanding. Her identification with Morpheus is illumined by a similar moment in *The Faerie Queene*, when Archimago's messenger has to struggle to awaken Morpheus so the benumbed god will loose one of his dreams to delude Red Cross. Il Penseroso, unlike Red Cross, is made to recognize the "fickle Pensioners of *Morpheus'* train," to banish them, and—with L'Allegro—to beckon the appropriate goddess to direct his acquisition of universal experience.

A. S. P. Woodhouse has clarified our understanding of the focus each goddess provides. "They are not," he responded to Tillyard's idea that the poems praised an ideal day and night, "poems in praise respectively of day and night, but poems setting forth rival conceptions of a life of pleasure, the one active and social, the other contemplative and solitary."10 The active and contemplative life, or, analogously, the social and solitary life, are the two available modes of perceiving and acquiring experience. To acquire the experience of both modes is, emblematically, to acquire all experience. Mirth, like her companion goddess, is ubiquitous. "In Heav'n yclep'd Euphrosyne, / And by men, heart-easing Mirth," her mythic parentage provided both by the classical and Olympian Venus and Bacchus and by the natural and sensuous Zephyr and Aurora, Mirth offers to her votary all the attributes of the active life, properly conceived. Likewise, the lineage Milton invents for Melancholy establishes her domain as ancient and universal. Her "Saintly visage . . . / O'erlaid with black," compared with "Memnon's sister" and Cassiopeia, yet "higher far descended," she springs from the Golden Age, daughter of Saturn and Vesta, "While yet there was no fear of Jove." The identity of each goddess is thus distinct, but each is similarly defined as having ubiquitous dominion over the mode of experience she governs.[11]

By having the action each goddess governs occur in a series of different time frames, Milton further provides first L'Allegro and then Il Penseroso with the ubiquity in time and space that the Seventh Prolusion had promised the followers of humanistic studies. For the first poem, after the invocation of the goddess, has L'Allegro perceive a series of events remote from one another in time but conceived of as a single experience of an ideal day. The season of the year is idealized in the same way, as it appears now in its springtime then its autumn garb, moving from ploughing to harvest to binding the sheaves to "The upland Hamlets" where "young and old come forth to play / On a Sunshine Holiday." Likewise, what might be called the cultural history that L'Allegro perceives transcends the normal limits of chronology to contribute to his ubiquitous experience. The classical pastoral names assigned to the previously native English milkmaids and ploughmen make them residents of both worlds, an emblematic technique quite unlike, for instance, Spenser's inclusion of homely details in the *Epithalamion*. Likewise, the aural, country folk tales of Faery Mab and the Lubber Fiend begin L'Allegro's cultural experience at an appropriately primitive level.

When these "Tales are done," he enlarges his experience to include the sophisticated and urban forms of triumph and masque.

Both of these are particularly appropriate choices in a poem designed to emblematize universal experience, for they allow reference to a wide variety of cultural and artistic traditions. The neo-chivalric triumphs popularized in England, particularly during the reigns of Henry VIII and Elizabeth, and retained in a vestigial way in the Stuarts' time—though increasingly replaced by the masque—took many allegorical forms. As deliberate anachronisms, however, they generally shared the intention of bringing classical and Christian attributes, as adopted by medieval chivalry, to bear on the affairs and persons of sixteenth- and seventeenth-century England.[12] To do so they employed a wide variety of the arts, including painting, poetry, emblematic and often classically allusive costuming, song, and even rudimentary dramatic arts. A triumph thus serves as reference to a wide variety of cultural, artistic, and social traditions. If Todd was right in suggesting that Milton's reference to the knights' and barons' tilting "In weeds of peace" is a deliberate echo of *Troilus and Cressida*,[13] then it may well be that Milton by referring through Shakespeare to the Trojan legend intends to encapsulate an entire cultural tradition in his triumph, even as actual triumphs had often done. Indeed, the echoes of Shakespeare, Spenser, and various classical writers that Milton includes in the poems may be seen as expanding L'Allegro's experience into the cultural past to which the poem thus alludes.[14]

This effect is comparable to the effect of the much-debated generalness of the natural images. As Rosemond Tuve has pointed out, the images create a sense of "particularity" without limiting themselves to "individual-ity." As a consequence, she suggests, "We have a sense that Milton has covered his subject."[15] These much-debated lines, for instance, are so metaphorically rich that they have prompted widely divergent readings: "Mountains on whose barren breast / The labouring clouds do often rest." But there seems little doubt that the word *often* opens a window on the total experience, as it forever repeats itself. L'Allegro, here as elsewhere, participates in an instance of a total experience. In the same way, the descriptions of triumphs and masques include or imply the whole cultural and artistic tradition of which they are a part. The "Ladies, whose bright eyes / Rain influence, and judge the prize / Of Wit, or Arms," like the participants and spectators of the wedding masque, provide the living context in which the experience celebrated by "antique Pageantry" can prosper.

Milton's distinction, too, between Shakespeare and Jonson— which was to help create that critical cliché—might be seen rather as part of the effort to encapsulate an entire tradition in a single allusion than as an intrusive bit of dramatic criticism. For *L'Allegro* moves from triumph and masque to "the well-trod stage" to encounter the two extremes of the comic experience, "Jonson's learned Sock" or "sweetest *Shakespeare*, fancy's child." Jonson had himself made the commonplace identification of these attributes as the polar complements of the complete dramatic poet. Whatever his private opinions of Shakespeare's artful learning, Jonson in his public praise has Shakespeare the beneficiary both of that and of imagination or fancy. "Yet must I not give Nature all: Thy Art / My gentle Shakespeare, must enjoy a part."[16] In his "On Shakespeare," Milton echoed this commonplace idea that art and fancy are the two sources available to the poet: "To the shame of slow-endeavoring art, / Thy easy numbers flow." (9–10). But in *L'Allegro*, one is not praised at the expense of the other; by identifying Shakespeare and Jonson as the polar complements of the comic mode, Milton once again opens a window on the whole tradition of which they are a part.

As the banishment of the debilitating modes and the invocation of the appropriate goddesses are parallel in the two poems, so this acquisition of experience in the central movement of *L'Allegro* is paralleled in *Il Penseroso*. By identifying two modes of life which divide experience between them, Milton provides himself a context which can be emblematically filled with the universal experience theoretically offered by a humanist education. The two poems make, as it were, a diptych of Cebes' *Table;* and though, as in Cebes, "Life" would be an accurate and more pithy title on the frame, "The Cycle of Universal Knowledge" is more Miltonic and more descriptive of the companion poems. *Il Penseroso*, as the other panel of this diptych, displays the contemplative experience Melancholy provides.

Milton's effort to universalize this experience has been more clearly recognized than has the similar effort in *L'Allegro*. Woodhouse's important identification of the Platonic and Christian implications of the "Cherub Contemplation" who accompanies

Melancholy has clarified Il Penseroso's educative and Platonic ascent through all the levels of human experience.[17] But it is not quite
true that the poem moves systematically from the study of nature
through a hierarchy of intellectual experiences to contemplation of
the ideal. As late as line 139, for one instance, after the series of intellectual and artistic experiences, Il Penseroso observes "the Bee with
Honied thigh, / That at her flow'ry work doth sing." So Allen's
commonly accepted notion that "a continued mounting of the slopes
of the intellect from common experience, to intellectual experience,
to religious inspiration" leads to "something like Prophetic strain"
does not describe the poem quite accurately.[18] The emphasis is,
again, on the ubiquity of the experience Il Penseroso enjoys. Milton
first frees him from chronological bounds to provide him with experience representative of all the experience of evening:

> I walk unseen
> On the dry smooth-shaven green,
> To behold the wand'ring Moon.
>   .   .   .   .
> I hear the far-off *Curfew* sound,
> Over some wide-water'd shore
>   .   .   .   .
> Or if the Air will not permit,
> Some still removed place will fit
> Where glowing Embers through the room
> Teach light to counterfeit a gloom
>   .   .   .   .
> Or let my Lamp at midnight hour
> Be seen in some high lonely tow'r.

In this wide chronological context, Il Penseroso, like L'Allegro, is
given emblematic cultural and artistic experiences so that he may,
again in the words of the Seventh Prolusion, gain "a kind of immortality in the past." He "may oft outwatch the *Bear*, / With thrice great
Hermes, or unsphere / The spirit of Plato to unfold / What Worlds, or
what vast Regions hold / The immortal mind." To suggest, as has
been recently done, that the structure of the poem systematically
reflects the Hermetic ascent of the mind of Il Penseroso is to reduce
the poem to one of its parts.[19] Hermes and Plato provide the philo-
sophic experience. Il Penseroso requires that experience of Melan-

choly just as he requires the experience of tragedy, of lyric, and of allegoric verse. It is notable that the various forms he requires are defined in ways that can fairly be called archetypal. "Gorgeous Tragedy" presents "what (though rare) of later age, / Ennobled hath the Buskin'd stage." Orpheus, nearly always for Milton the archetypal poet, whose harp Milton compared with true education in *Of Education,* and Musaeus, the servant of the muses, provide the lyric verse.[20] If Osgood and Hughes are right in suggesting that Milton is referring to the appearance of Musaeus in the *Aeneid,* and that Milton's "bower" echoes the grove in which Aeneas discovers Musaeus in Elysium,[21] then what we once again have is Milton capturing a large cultural tradition with a single allusion.

Milton's treatment of "The story of Cambuscan bold," which provides the next part of Il Penseroso's experience, displays a similar technique and intent:

> Or call up him that left half told
> The story of Cambuscan bold
> Of *Camball,* and of *Algarsife*
> And who had Canace to Wife,
> That own'd the virtuous Ring and Glass.
> .   .   .   .
>
> And if aught else great Bards beside
> In sage and solemn tunes have sung
> .   .   .   .
>
> Where more is meant than meets the ear.

Woodhouse suggested that the *Squire's Tale* is here rather than in the seemingly more appropriate *L'Allegro* because Spenser "had deliberately turned the tale to allegorical purpose—a type of reading consonant with Il Penseroso's interests."[22] But, questions of "type" aside, it is clear that Spenser's retelling of Chaucer's tale provided Milton with the perfect image of the timelessness of the cultural tradition. Spenser had himself introduced the tale with a brief discourse on the nature of time and art, and imagining the conclusion of Chaucer's tale to be lost, he described himself as restoring to posterity the image of the heroic ideal the tale represents:

> Though now their acts be no where to be found,
> As that renowned Poet them complyed,
> With Warlike numbers and Heroicke sound,

Dan Chaucer, well of English vndefyled,
On Fames eternall beadroll worthie to be fyled.

But wicked Time that all good thoughts doth waste,
And workes of noblest wits to nought out weare,
That famous moniment hath quite defaste,
And robd the world of treasure endlesse deare
The which mote haue enriched all vs heare.

(Faerie Queene, IV.ii.32–33)

Begging pardon of Chaucer, "O most sacred happie spirit," Spenser justifies his boldness by claiming that Chaucer's spirit is alive in him:

Ne dare I like, but through infusion sweete
Of thine owne spirit, which doth in me surviue,
I follow here the footing of thy feete,
That with thy meaning so I may the rather meete.   (IV.ii.34)

By having Melancholy call up the Chaucer of the *Squire's Tale,* Milton can provide for the reappearance of the bardic voice in Spenser and for "aught else great Bards beside / In sage and solemn tunes have sung . . . / Where more is meant than meets the ear." Just as the actual enactment of the neochivalric allegory of the tournament allows L'Allegro access to the medieval and Trojan tradition behind the allegory and to the various artistic forms it employs, so Il Penseroso's contemplation of Chaucer and Spenser provides him access to the whole tradition of heroic romance.

Morning, "Not trickt and frounc't as she was wont / With the Attic Boy to hunt, / But kerchieft in a comely Cloud, / While rocking Winds are Piping loud, / Or usher'd with a shower still"—and thus an indefinite several mornings or all mornings—interrupts these cultural delights, and Melancholy leads Il Penseroso to the traditional, even clichéd, melancholiac's pose in the isolation of a wood, "in close covert by some Brook."[23] He thus takes on archetypal qualities himself, and as the type of contemplative melancholiac he is granted his final vision.

The consequences of these universalized experiences are similar in the two poems, though the contemplative vision transcends the vision acquired through the experience of Mirth. L'Allegro and Il Penseroso give artful form and harmony to the total experience they have acquired. They become archetypal poets, the ideal that education as Milton defined it constantly sought. Like Spenser invoking Chaucer's spirit to speak through him to the present age, L'Allegro and Il Penseroso give present form to the ancient and universal truths they have experienced. "Orpheus' self" recognizes the perfection to which experience has brought the song L'Allegro hears. The marriage of "*Lydian* Airs" and "immortal verse" is an inclusive symbol of the poetic strain stemming from Orpheus. Lydian is the appropriate mode, for, as Harris Fletcher has demonstrated, Milton followed Charles Butler in believing that the Lydian is the mode in which one can "attain grave sublimity."[24] And "immortal verse" is of course the necessary complement. In *Ad Patrem* Milton refers to the blend of music and verse in Orphic song with much the same intent as here. Music without verse is incomplete. "Such music is good enough for the forest choirs, but not for Orpheus, who by his song— not by his cithara—restrained rivers and gave ears to the oaks, and by his singing stirred the ghosts of the dead to tears. That fame he owes to his song." Again, as his father is a musician and he a poet, Milton in *Ad Patrem* claims that "Phoebus himself, wishing to part himself between us two, gave some gifts to me and others to my father; and, father and son, we share the possession of the divided god" (p. 84). The "melting voice" L'Allegro hears "Untwisting all the chains that tie / The hidden soul of harmony" is the cumulative and revealing stage of his acquisition of the experience of mirth.

The relationship between the Christian Platonism of the cumulative vision Il Penseroso attains and the one L'Allegro attains has remained perplexing. David Miller's rewarding study of the poems leads him to conclude that "the delights of L'Allegro are real and valued, but like the glories of Greece they cannot stand against the ecstasy of Christian contemplation."[25] He is led to this because he believes that the two poems are organized in a continuous, vertical structure; the "humor therapy" of *L'Allegro* produces the balanced mental state of the beginning of *Il Penseroso*, a state which "is one that can be improved by education. And the therapy for 'vain deluding joys' is just that."[26] This is an expansion of the view popularized by Allen and shares with such views the problem that no schematic, patterned ascent of this kind accounts for all the multitudinous details of the poems. *L'Allegro* and *Il Penseroso* break down normal temporal and spatial order to capture in their complementary visions the total experience that Milton's idea of education theoretically embraced. The contemplative mode, by definition, can achieve a transcendent vision unavailable to the active mode, but they are complementary, not adversary or progressive modes. There is no sense that Il Penseroso includes L'Allegro in his experience, just as, for instance, Red Cross's beatific and transcendent vision does not include the triumph of Guyon's temperance. Both knights combine with the others to form the "noble person in virtuous and gentle discipline." There is no Arthur, however, in the scheme of *L'Allegro* and *Il Penseroso*. Two leaves of a diptych, they together provide the picture of Milton's "cycle of universal knowledge."

University of California, Santa Barbara

NOTES

1. *John Milton, Complete Poems and Major Prose*, ed. Merritt Y. Hughes (New York, 1957), p. 67. All references in the text to the poetry and prose of Milton are to this edition. The publication of vol. II of *A Variorum Commentary on The Poems of John Milton*, ed. A. S. P. Woodhouse and Douglas Bush (New York, 1972), has provided convenient access to the various critical judgments of the poems. Subsequent critical arguments are cited below.

2. J. W. Adamson, *A Short History of Education* (Cambridge, 1919), p. 129. Ernest Sirluck and Donald Dorian have provided a persuasive account of Milton's role in the continuing educational controversy of the 1630s and 1640s. See Ernest Sirluck, ed., *Complete Prose Works of John Milton*, vol. II (New Haven, 1959), pp. 184–216, 351–60, and nn. 362–415. Hereafter cited as YP. See also Harris Francis Fletcher, *The Intellectual Development of John Milton* (Urbana, Ill., 1956).

3. *The Book Named The Governor*, ed. S. E. Lehmberg (London, 1962), p. 39.

4. *Gabriel Harvey's Marginalia*, ed. G. C. Moore Smith (Stratford-Upon-Avon, 1913), pp. 160–61.

5. *The Harmonious Vision*, enlarged ed. (Baltimore, 1970), p. 16.

6. YP, vol. II, pp. 196–97, 204–05.

7. Sir Philip Sidney, *Complete Works*, ed. Albert Feuillerat (Cambridge, 1923), vol. III, p. 10.

8. J. Healey, trans., *The Table of Cebes, The Theban Philosopher* . . . (London, 1610), F7–8.

9. *A Discourse of Civill Life* (London, 1606), pp. 22–23.

10. "Notes on Milton's Early Development," *UTQ*, XIII (1942–43), 85. E. M. W. Tillyard, *Milton: "L'Allegro" and "Il Penseroso"* (The English Association, 1932).

11. Rosemond Tuve, *Images and Themes in Five Poems by Milton* (Cambridge, Mass., 1957), has demonstrated that each poem begins as an encomium. She does not, however, explain the fact that the poems do not maintain this rhetorical scheme throughout. The encomiastic pattern is complete, or at least abandoned, by line 40 of the first and line 63 of the second poem.

12. See Frances Yates, "Queen Elizabeth as Astraea," *JWCI*, X (1947), 27–82, and "Elizabethan Chivalry: The Romance of the Accession Day Tilts," *JWCI*, XX (1957), 4–25.

13. Cited in *Variorum*, p. 300.

14. John Carey and Alastair Fowler, eds., *The Poems of John Milton* (London, 1968), p. 131 and nn., provide a useful survey of the allusions.

15. *Images and Themes*, p. 22.

16. "On Shakespeare," 55–56.

17. "Notes on Milton's Early Development," pp. 86–88.

18. *Harmonious Vision*, p. 17.

19. The *Variorum* provides a useful summary.

20. See K. R. R. Gros Louis, "The Triumph and Death of Orpheus in the English Renaissance," *SEL*, IX (1969), 63–80.

21. *Variorum*, p. 327, and Hughes, *Complete Poems and Major Prose*, p. 74, n. 104.

22. *Variorum*, p. 328, and "Notes on Milton's Early Development," p. 88, n. 34.

23. The cult of Melancholy is a familiar enough topic, but one might note its appearance in portrait painting, where the scene Milton describes is often duplicated. See Roy Strong, "The Elizabethan Malady: Melancholy in Elizabethan and Jacobean Painting," *Apollo*, LXXIX (1964), 264–69.

24. *Intellectual Development*, p. 351.

25. David Miller, "From Delusion to Illumination: A Larger Structure for *L'Allegro—Il Penseroso*," *PMLA*, LXXXVI (1971), 37.

26. Ibid., p. 35.

THE DREAD VOICE IN *LYCIDAS*

Mother M. Christopher Pecheux

Preoccupation with the two-handed engine in *Lycidas* has obscured a question raised by the lines which follow: Why is the "dread voice" which has just uttered the denunciation of the clergy said to shrink the streams? Examination of the biblical context of the lines indicates that the shrinking of the streams may be related to the drying up of the Red Sea at the Exodus; this possibility in turn reinforces the suggestion made some years ago that the speaker described as "the Pilot of the Galilean lake" is not necessarily St. Peter. Exegetical tradition, literary precedents, and Milton's other works support the theory that the figure is a composite of Moses, Peter, and Christ. Such an interpretation is in harmony with the allusive ambivalence so markedly present elsewhere in *Lycidas*. Moreover, the biblical overtones of the dread voice help to define the structure of the poem as a progression from pagan consolation through the partial enlightenment given by the Old Law to the final revelation of the New, a movement reflected in the echoes throughout the poem of its opening phrase, "yet once more."

I

IN THE voluminous literature which has gathered around the two-handed engine in *Lycidas*, surprisingly little attention has been given to the immediate context of the provocative lines which form the famous crux: "But that two-handed engine at the door / Stands ready to smite once, and smite no more" (130–31).[1] They have been commented on, certainly, as the climax of the passage which precedes them but have not usually been seen as integrally related to the lines which immediately follow. An exploration of this relationship can shed light, I think, not (alas!) on the two-handed engine, but on some other matters no less crucial to the poem.

221

From the variety of explanations offered there seems to have
emerged a consensus that the engine is probably to be understood in
a biblical context and that the lines refer in some way to a judgment
on the corrupt clergy.[2] But preoccupation with the exact meaning of
the engine has tended to obscure the fact that the lines in question,
which conclude St. Peter's speech, are succeeded by two others in
which Milton thought it worthwhile to characterize the speaker's
voice and recall its effects: "Return *Alpheus*, the dread voice is
past / That shrunk thy streams" (132–33). The speech is thus firmly
anchored in the structure of the poem. Line 131 ends one movement,
but it is not dissociated from the first line of the following movement.
The technique of thus simultaneously establishing and bridging a
gap resembles the treatment in many of Milton's sonnets, where the
break of thought in the sestet does not coincide exactly with the
formal break in rhyme.

The diatribe against the unworthy clergy concludes with the
threat of the engine which "stands ready to smite once, and smite no
more." Several years ago John Reesing pointed out that the phrase
"once . . . more" echoes the first line of *Lycidas*, "Yet once more, O
ye Laurels, and once more,"[3] and he developed a suggestion made
previously by David S. Berkeley that this first line draws on the
diction of Hebrews xii, 26, and Haggai ii, 6–7.[4] Stuart Baker, in a
different context, has noted and developed the parallelism in lines 1
and 131;[5] and Edward R. Weismiller has mentioned the auditory
effect of the echoing "no more" both here and in lines 165 and 182.[6]

The twelfth chapter of Hebrews, upon which Berkeley and
Reesing build their explications, describes the manifestation of God
on Mt. Sinai. It then continues:

See that ye refuse not him that speaketh: for if they escaped not who refused
him that spake on earth, much more shall not we escape, if we turn away
from him that speaketh from heaven: whose voice then shook the earth: but
now he hath promised, saying, *Yet once more* I shake not the earth only, but
also heaven. And this word, *Yet once more*, signifieth the removing of those
things that are shaken, as of things that are made, that those things which
cannot be shaken may remain. (Hebrews xii, 25–27; italics added)

Both the King James and the Geneva Bibles give a cross-
reference to Haggai ii, 6–7: "For thus saith the Lord of hosts; *Yet*

once, it is a little while, and I will shake the heavens, and the earth, and the sea, and the dry land; and I will shake all nations, and the Desire of all nations shall come: and I will fill this house with glory, saith the Lord of hosts" (italics added).

The direct quotation from Haggai is supplemented by the preceding allusion to the appearance of God on Mt. Sinai. Exodus describes the "voice of the trumpet exceeding loud; so that all the people that was in the camp trembled" (xix, 16). Moses is then called to the top of the mount; "and when the voice of the trumpet sounded long, and waxed louder and louder, Moses spake, and God answered him by a voice" (xix, 19). The following chapter continues the narration, stressing the effect of the apparition on the people: "And all the people saw the thunderings, and the lightnings, and the noise of the trumpet, and the mountain smoking: and when the people saw it, they removed, and stood afar off. And they said unto Moses, Speak thou with us, and we will hear: but let not God speak with us, lest we die" (xx, 18–19).

These three related scriptural passages, which seem to be evoked by the echoing "once more," add resonance to the tone of mysterious vengeance appropriate at this point in *Lycidas*. They provide background for consideration of the "dread voice" which now ceases to speak: "Return *Alpheus*, the dread voice is past / That shrunk thy streams." These lines raise two questions which have never been satisfactorily answered: Whose voice has been heard? Why should a voice be said to shrink streams?

To the first question, the almost unanimous answer is "St. Peter's," and to many readers it may seem satisfactory. As far as I know, Ralph Hone was for a long time the only critic to have strongly supported a different answer, one which I accept in part and which I hope to develop. Briefly, Hone argued that the development of Milton's antiprelatical thought in the late 1630s; the antiprelatical viewpoint that Christ is the Shepherd and Bishop under whom all mortal pastors serve, and Milton's specific statement that Christ is the supreme Bishop; the relevance to *Lycidas* of the keys of Revelation, chapter i, where Christ is said to hold the keys of death and hell; and the greater unity of the poem when the image of Christ walking the waves (173) is related to a previous appearance as the Pilot of the

Galilean lake—all call for an identification of the Pilot, not with
Peter, but with Christ. More recently, Berkeley has cogently supported such an identification.[7]

Even if the Pilot is not Christ (and the possibility cannot be
dismissed), at least he has some very close relationship with Christ.
There has been a tendency in recent years to emphasize a fluidity in
the characters who appear in the poem, a tendency that converges
from several different directions. From the point of view of myth
criticism, Northrop Frye, speaking of Edward King, remarks that "as
priest, his archetype is Peter, who would have drowned in the
'Galilean lake' without the help of Christ. . . . Christ does not enter
the poem as a character, but he pervades every line of it so completely that the poem, so to speak, enters him."[8] Roy Daniells,
linking Milton with mannerism and the baroque, says: "Phoebus, St.
Peter, Edward King all become something other than their normal
selves in obedience to Milton's needs."[9] John C. Ulreich, Jr., approaches the poem typologically: "Because the old letter prefigures
its fulfillment by the new spirit," he explains, "typological allusions
invariably require double vision." In *Lycidas*, images that are initially classical are redefined, through allusions, as Christian: Orpheus and Phoebus become Peter and Christ; "the pagan type is
reintegrated into a Christian context."[10] Kathleen Swaim fuses Peter
with Atropos and Atropos with the Furies.[11]

I think it is time to reexamine the Pilot in a way that moves from
a one-dimensional equivalence with Peter to something more consonant with the extraordinary richness and ambivalence that are
clearly present in other parts of the poem.

The second question has also been answered with some unanimity: The dread voice shrinks the streams because the invective
and satire of the passage just ended are not compatible with the
mood of pastoral poetry represented by Alpheus. There are variations on this answer, many of them helpful as far as they go. It is said,
for example, that water and fright have been associated before in the
poem (although the same critic notes the anomaly that now the water
is frightened by the man); that the time of the Last Judgment, when
the sword smites no more, will indeed shrink even Alpheus' innocent stream; that the landscape answers the voice as it has done
elsewhere in the poem.[12] Possible allegorical interpretation has

been suggested, particularly by Don Cameron Allen, who alludes to the Renaissance representation of Alpheus as truth and Arethusa as nobility, now united.[13]

It seems to me, however, that all these observations leave the metaphor hanging in midair, as it were; they explain what it means, but there is no grounding in reality. Daffadillies do, as a matter of fact, fill their cups with dew, if not with tears; shears do slit cloth, if not life; fingers do pluck berries; and so on. But voices do not shrink streams.

Or do they? I have asked the next question of several colleagues and students: "Has anyone's voice ever dried a stream?" Hesitantly they answer: "Yes—in the story of the crossing of the Red Sea." Their perception is not quite accurate, as we shall see, but the associations which give rise to it are justified.

What I wish to explore in the rest of this essay is the possibility that the figure of Moses may give a clue to an answer to both questions I have raised: the identity of the speaker behind the dread voice and the effect of his words. If Moses can plausibly be shown to have some connection with the speech traditionally ascribed to Peter, and if the consequent associations indicate that the crossing of the Red Sea may lie behind the shrinking of Alpheus, then we may have deeper appreciation of two lines in *Lycidas* and further insight into its structure. The importance of Moses in *Paradise Lost* has been recognized recently by several scholars;[14] it would be interesting to find the same figure functioning in the earlier poem. What I propose is a hypothesis, but not an idle one. To test it, I shall examine its background in scripture, in exegesis, in literary tradition, and in Milton's other works. These different threads do seem to converge, and the resulting pattern, if not too thin-spun, may be seen as one more element in the richly allusive perfection of the poem.

II

Following the critics cited above, it can be taken as fairly well established that the echo of "yet once more" in line 131 is designed to send us to the verses cited from Hebrews and Haggai, as well as to the passages in Exodus to which the author of Hebrews is evidently referring. But these passages already tend to amalgamate Moses, Christ, and God. Commenting on Hebrews xii, 25, Calvin remarks "that God or Moses spoke then on earth, but that the same God or Christ speaks now from heaven. At the same time I prefer regarding God in both instances as the speaker. And he is said to have spoken on earth, because he spoke in a lower strain."[15]

The close association between Moses and Christ has its primary source in Deuteronomy xviii, 15: "The Lord thy God will raise up unto thee a Prophet from the midst of thee, of thy brethren, like unto me; unto him ye shall hearken." The identification of the prophet like Moses as Christ is recorded explicitly in the New Testament. Such scriptural sanction would weigh heavily with Milton, who later incorporated the typology into his *Christian Doctrine*.[16] Eusebius insists that the statement can refer only to Christ; after elaborating a series of parallels—including Moses' drying up of the sea and Christ's walking on the waters—he concludes that there is no need to go on, since the resemblance is so clear.[17] And the admonitory voice in *Lycidas* is appropriate to Moses, whose role as judge and accuser has a sanction in Christ's words in John v, 45–46: "Do not think that I will accuse you to the Father: there is one that accuseth you, even Moses, in whom ye trust. For had ye believed Moses, ye would have believed me: for he wrote of me."

In the life of Moses the most striking event was the crossing of the Red Sea. Though neither the beginning nor the end, this was the triumphant turning point of the Exodus, so that in Israel one could speak of the God who led his people from Egypt merely by referring to the miracle.[18] The prodigy occurred when Moses stretched out his hand over the sea (Exodus xiv, 21), but it was, of course, the power of the Lord which performed it. Later books of the Bible can therefore refer to the event in a way which amalgamates the two, the Lord's hand, not that of Moses, being outstretched. "And the Lord shall utterly destroy the tongue of the Egyptian sea; and with his mighty wind shall he shake his hand over the river, and shall smite it in the seven streams" (Isaiah xi, 15). "And he . . . shall smite the waves in the sea, and all the deeps of the river shall dry up" (Zechariah x, 11). Commenting on Psalm lxxiv, 13 ("Thou didst divide the sea by thy strength"), Calvin writes: "The prophet does not here recount all the miracles which God had wrought at the departure of the people from the land of Egypt; but in adverting to some of them, he comprehends by the figure synechdoche, all that Moses had narrated concerning them at greater length."[19]

As the poets and prophets recalled the event, they joined with it the circumstances surrounding the theophany on Sinai, so that, especially in the Psalms, God's power was symbolized at times by his arm, at times by his voice:

At thy rebuke, O God of Jacob, both the chariot and horse are cast into a dead sleep.

Thou, even thou, art to be feared: and who may stand in thy sight when once thou art angry?

Thou didst cause judgments to be heard from heaven; the earth feared, and was still. (Psalm lxxvi, 6–8)

Psalm cxiv, "When Israel went out of Egypt," mentions also the later crossing of the Jordan: "The sea saw it, and fled: Jordan was driven back" (verse 3). Psalm lxxvii brings together several motifs:

Thou hast with thine arm redeemed thy people, the sons of Jacob and Joseph.

The waters saw thee, O God, the waters saw thee; they were afraid: the depths also were troubled.

The clouds poured out water: the skies sent out a sound: thine arrows also went abroad.

The voice of thy thunder was in the heaven: the lightnings lightened the world: the earth trembled and shook.

Thy way is in the sea, and thy path in the great waters, and thy footsteps are not known.

Thou leddest thy people like a flock by the hand of Moses and Aaron. (verses 15–20)

All these poetic juxtapositions lie behind the verse in Haggai quoted in Hebrews ("Yet once, it is a little while, and I will shake the heavens, and the earth, and the sea, and the dry land"). St. Jerome, in his comment on the verse, makes an explicit connection: He asks, "When did the Lord do this?" and the Lord answers, "I moved the heaven, when from heaven my voice was heard. . . . I moved the Red Sea, when I showed the way for the people to cross over."[20] Calvin, commenting this time on Psalm cxiv, observes that the psalmist does not list all the miracles of the Exodus "but briefly alludes to the sea, which, though a lifeless and senseless element, is yet struck with terror at the power of God. Jordan did the same, and the very mountains shook."[21] The "lifeless and senseless element [which] is . . . struck with terror" may well be an analogue for the shrinking of the streams in *Lycidas*.

The exegetical tradition which tended to fuse on the one hand the theophany on Sinai with the crossing of the Red Sea and on the other the figure of Christ with that of Moses had many facets. The Reformation might be expected to emphasize the preaching of the word of God, Christ being seen less as the high priest than as the prophet-preacher. The mitered speaker in *Lycidas* does not contradict such an emphasis, for a bishop is among other things the chief preacher of his diocese, and the content of the speech draws heavily on the familiar analogy between the word of God and food. The miter certainly signifies in the poem the role of the bishop (and therefore at least in part that of the first bishop, St. Peter), but this significance is not necessarily "prelatical" in the sense conveyed in seventeenth-century polemics. The miter was originally a garment worn by the high priest of the Old Testament and perhaps by lesser priests; it is therefore a liturgical garment of the Old Covenant as well as the New and in the former had the sanction of—and indeed was worn at the command of—Moses himself.[22]

All these traditions help to identify the last mourner in *Lycidas*, not as Moses, not as Peter, not as Christ, but as a composite of the three, an ideal figure who speaks in the name of God. Commenting on the "blind mouths" of line 119, G. B. Christopher quotes Calvin's dictum that the preacher is the mouth of God (*Inst.* II.1018); God "deigns to consecrate to himself the tongues of men that his voice may resound in them" (ibid.). Elsewhere Calvin recalls that "the first thing in faith is to know that it is Christ who speaks by his ministers."[23] The tones of Edward King, of Moses, of Peter, of Christ himself can inspire fear only because a mightier voice speaks through them.

Ruth Ames has demonstrated the continuity in medieval literature of Moses' typological role. For example, she cites Grosseteste, who, when he wanted to prove the right of visitation in his diocese, explained that Moses is the type of the Christian prelate; Moses and the prophets had made it clear that the sins of the assistants and the people would be held against neglectful prelates.[24] Three sources she mentions are particularly interesting in connection with *Lycidas;* I shall deal with them only briefly, since Milton is not likely to have known—or been impressed by—them, although in each case it would not be impossible for him to have known them.

The first of these is the fourth-century apocryphal "Vision of Paul." One of its modern editors remarks that it had an immense vogue in the Middle Ages and that Dante refers to it in *Inferno* ii.28,[25] while another editor notes that one of its versions was popular in England.[26] In the course of his adventures in the other world Paul meets Moses, who is weeping; Paul asks him why, and Moses answers: "I weep for them whom I planted with much labour, for they have borne no fruit, neither doth any of them do well. And I have seen all the sheep whom I fed that they are scattered and become as having no shepherd, and that all the labours which I have endured for the children of Israel are come to nought, and however great wonders I did in their midst they understood not."[27]

Grosseteste, writing in the thirteenth century, declared in Letter 127 that Moses typifies prelates appointed by God to lead the people from sin and ignorance through baptism and penance to the heavenly Jerusalem. Because the work was heavy, he had subordinate ministers but kept the supreme power himself; similarly, Christ gave power to his apostles but kept his own.[28] Milton might have been interested in Grosseteste as an early opponent of the power of Rome, and there was a manuscript of the letter in the library of Trinity College, Cambridge.[29] In Lydgate's fifteenth-century *Pilgrimage of the Life of Man*, Moses is both a Hebrew prophet and a Christian bishop who confirms the pilgrim and who evinces great zeal against the enemies of God, asking when he may use his horns to punish them.[30] These traditions may have been strong enough to survive the reaction against medievalism which characterized the sixteenth and seventeenth centuries. At any rate, with Lydgate we move from a theological to a professedly literary tradition and, in the sixteenth century, to authors certainly known by Milton.

A generation earlier, Milton's acknowledged guide and teacher, Edmund Spenser, had in *The Shepheardes Calender* produced the outstanding predecessor to *Lycidas*. The November eclogue, in the genre of pastoral elegy, and the May eclogue, as an example of ecclesiastical satire, are commonly cited by editors of *Lycidas*, as is the July eclogue, which is more striking than either of the others in its resemblance to this section of the poem. The headnote declares: "This Aeglogue is made in the honour and commendation of good shepeheardes, and to the shame and disprayse of proude and ambitious Pastours."[31] Abel and the twelve sons of Jacob are described as good shepherds; then the poem continues:

> Sike one (sayd Algrin) *Moses* was,
>   that sawe hys makers face,
> His face more cleare, then Christall glasse,
>   and spake to him in place.   (157–60)

Aaron is next singled out for praise but declared not to be the equal of Moses: "A shepheard trewe, yet not so true, / as he that earst I hote" (163–64).

To these good shepherds are contrasted the wicked ones who live in Rome like lords:

> Theyr sheepe han crustes, and they the bread:
>   the chippes, and they the chere:
> They han the fleece, and eke the flesh,
>   (O seely sheepe the while)
> The corne is theyrs, let other thresh,
>   their hands they may not file.
> They han great stores, and thriftye stockes,
>   great freendes and feeble foes:
> What neede hem caren for their flocks?
>   theyr boyes can looke to those.   (187–96)

Even when allowance is made for general similarities in pastoral satire, the tone and diction here (especially in lines 187, 190, and 195) are remarkably close to Milton's; and it is Moses who is the good shepherd par excellence.

Spenser's contemporary, Michael Drayton, undertook a lengthy poem on "Moses His Birth and Miracles." The crossing of the Red Sea is accomplished expeditiously, the refugees feeling the power of God, who

> sends the windes as Currers forth before
> To make them way from *Pharaohs* power to flie,
> And to convay them to a safer shore,
> Such is his might that can make *Oceans* drie.[32]

The "safer shore" forecasts the famous simile in *Paradise Lost*, where the "Sojourners of *Goshen* . . . beheld / From the safe shore thir floating Carcasses" (I, 309–10), but it is the drying up of the ocean that interests me here.

Another work certainly known to Milton was Sylvester's translation of Du Bartas' *Devine Weekes and Workes.* Its influence on *Paradise Lost* has long been recognized, but it has not been examined in connection with *Lycidas,* although it had appeared in several editions before 1637. Du Bartas refers more than once to the crossing of the Red Sea. Thus, in the Second Day of the First Week he cites the miracle as a proof of the power of God, "whose powerfull hand / Bay'd-up the *Red-Sea* with a double Wall, / That *Israels* Hoast might scape *Egyptian* thrall."[33] Similarly, in the Third Day:

> For what could not, that great, High-Admirall
> Worke in the Waues, sith at his servants call,
> His dreadfull voice (to save his ancient Sheepe)
> Did cleave the bottome of th'*Erithrean* Deepe?
> And toward the Cristall of his double source
> Compelled *Iordan* to retreat his course?   (p. 77)

The dreadful voice and the ancient sheep have their counterparts in *Lycidas;* and if God can be a High Admiral to Du Bartas, we may allow him to be a Pilot to Milton—a term which as a matter of fact Du Bartas also uses:

> Lord, I acknowledge and confesse before,
> This Ocean hath no bottome, nor no shoare;
> But (sacred Pilot) thou canst safely steere
> My vent'rous Pinnasse to her wished Peere.
>   (p. 272; Second Week, First Day)

God is the "Steers-man" of the Ark (First Week, Second Day; p. 74) and is addressed by the same epithet in the story of Arion and the Dolphin:

> O be my Steeres-man, and vouchsafe to guide
> The stern-lesse Boat, and bit-lesse Horse I ride.
>   (p. 170; First Week, Fifth Day)

The dolphins are invited to waft King's body in *Lycidas,* and Du Bartas makes the dolphin a symbol of Moses:

> Where-to the *Dolphin,* but to that meeke Man
> Who dry-shod guides through Seas *Erythrean*
> Old *Iacobs* Frye: and *Iordans* liqquid Glasse,
> Makes all his Hoast dry (without Boat) to passe?
>   (p. 486; The Columns)

In the light of all these allusions, it is not preposterous to see in the shrinking of the streams in *Lycidas* the work of a composite figure, an ideal shepherd and bishop, approximated most closely in the Old Testament by Moses and by Peter in the New—both, however, serving only as delegates of the supreme bishop, Christ, who embodies the mighty power of God.

In Milton's own poetry, the well-known simile in Book I of *Paradise Lost* on the crossing of the Red Sea has already been referred to. This is not the only place, however, where he made poetic use of the episode. What seems to be his earliest poem, written at the age of fifteen, was a paraphrase of Psalm cxiv, one of the best-known songs of the Exodus. Where the original says simply that the sea fled, Milton personifies it in a way which may hint at the legend of Alpheus and Arethusa:

> That saw the troubl'd Sea, and shivering fled,
> And sought to hide his froth-becurled head
> Low in the earth; Jordan's clear streams recoil.   (7–9)

Alpheus too hid his head, disappearing and flowing under the sea until he rose again in Sicily. Even at the age of fifteen, Milton would have read the story in Ovid, and he may have been familiar with the account of the legend in Pausanias, who says that the river Alpheus really does pass through the sea and mingle with the fountain. "And in the land of the Hebrews," he adds, "as I can myself bear witness, the river Jordan passes through a lake called Tiberias, and then, entering another lake called the Dead Sea, it disappears in it."[34] (The Lake of Tiberias is another name for the Sea of Galilee.) Milton's first poem, therefore, may contain an example of his lifelong penchant for fusing the classical and the Christian.

Some years later he made another paraphrase of the same psalm, this time in Greek. The poem was evidently written between November 23 and 29, 1634; Parker speculates that November 23 may have been his father's birthday and notes that Psalm cxiv was prescribed for Evening Prayer on that date.[35] In the Trinity MS, *Lycidas* is headed "November 1637";[36] possibly the same recurrence brought the psalm again to his special consciousness.

The most interesting line, from the present perspective, is the nineteenth: "Σ είεο, γαῖα, τρέουσα Θεὸν μεγάλ᾽ ἐκτυπέοντα," rendered by Hughes as "Shake, O earth, and fear the Lord who does mighty things." The Greek word σείεο, meaning "shake," is the verb used both in Hebrews xii, 26, and in Haggai ii, 6–7, but not in Psalm cxiv. The fact that Milton used the term in his paraphrase indicates a strong connection in his own mind between the passages. His 1624 English paraphrase had translated the same line as "Shake earth, and at the presence be aghast," although contemporary versions were content with saying that the earth trembled and the sea fled.[37]

Allusions in *Paradise Lost* to the crossing of the Red Sea are too well known to need quotation, and they are, of course, considerably later than *Lycidas*. For someone with the prodigious memory and the lifelong consistency of Milton, however, one passage is worth citing:

> But the voice of God
> To mortal ear is dreadful; they beseech
> That *Moses* might report to them his will,
> And terror cease; he grants what they besought,
> Instructed that to God is no access
> Without Mediator, whose high Office now
> *Moses* in figure bears, to introduce
> One greater, of whose day he shall foretell,
> And all the Prophets in thir Age the times
> Of great *Messiah* shall sing.   (XII, 235–44)

Here again is a dread voice, mediated through Moses, the figure of Christ.

Of more significance because of its close chronological proximity is the draft for a drama on the Fall which appears in the Trinity College MS on the page following *Lycidas* and may therefore be presumed to be close to it in time.[38] In the third draft it is Moses who speaks the prologue, explaining that his body "corrupts not because of his [being] with god in the mount." The mount could be Sinai, or the Mount of the Transfiguration, or both. At any rate, Moses' presence here may indicate that he loomed large in Milton's poetic consciousness at the time. Another minor point may have some relevance. After Moses has spoken his prologue, the synopsis continues "whence he hasts." James Holly Hanford maintained that the reading should be "whence he exhorts" (the prefix "ex" is now missing in the MS because of damage to the margin but was in a

facsimile made by Sotheby in 1661).[39] "Exhorts" reinforces the
traditional role of Moses as a figure of authority, shepherd and guide
of his people.

Also fairly close in time to *Lycidas* was *The Doctrine and Discipline of Divorce* (1643). Here Milton accuses his opponents of
trying to "reverse the infallible judgment of *Moses* and his great
director" (chap. 22; CM, vol. III, p. 506) and, more strongly still, of
using evasions "to reconcile those contradictions which they make
between Christ and *Moses*, between Christ and Christ" (chap. 9;
CM, vol. III, p. 462). It is clear that both Milton's poetry and his
theology made Moses not only a forerunner but even a representative of Christ.

What, then, becomes of St. Peter? I have concentrated on the
figure of Moses, since for three centuries Peter has evidently been
able to fend for himself, but I do not wish to banish him from the
poem. There is the miter (which is also associated with the Old Law
and with bishops in general); there is the Galilean Lake (upon which
Christ also walked, as line 173 of *Lycidas* explicitly states); there are
the massy keys (which may stem from Matthew xvi, 19, but may also,
as Hone and others have suggested, be an echo of Revelation i, 18: "I
am he that liveth, and was dead; and, behold, I am alive for ever-
more, Amen; and have the keys of hell and death"). Perhaps *Lycidas*
could subsist without Peter. Nevertheless, I believe that he is present: The most common use of the miter is on the head of the bishop;
Peter is closely associated with the Sea of Galilee; and on the whole
the two keys, one of which opens and the other closes, suggest
Matthew before they lead to Revelation. But in the procession of
mourners St. Peter does not walk alone. As prophet, apostle, and
high priest he brings with him the memories of the great prophet and
lawgiver of the older covenant, as he humbly imitates the inaugu-
rator of the new. Both Moses and Peter are fulfilled in Christ.
"Wherefore, holy brethren, partakers of the heavenly calling," exhorts the author of Hebrews, "consider the Apostle and High Priest
of our profession, Christ Jesus; who was faithful to him that appointed him, as also Moses was faithful in all his house" (iii, 1–2).
The collocation of these three figures occurs again in what is surely a
significant position, at the beginning of the *Christian Doctrine*. The
opening definition, which undergirds the whole treatise, might

stand in itself as an apologia for seeing the Pilot in *Lycidas* as a composite figure: "The Christian Doctrine is that divine revelation disclosed in various ages by Christ (though he was not known under that name in the beginning). . . . Under the name of Christ are also comprehended Moses and the Prophets, who were his forerunners, and the Apostles whom he sent" (bk. I, chap. 1; CM, vol. XIV, pp. 17, 19). Such a view enlarges the figure of the Pilot to a greater stature, gives a commensurate universality to his utterance, and above all explains how his voice can be said to have shrunk the streams.

III

Whatever the identity of the speaker, the dread voice is one of the most important structural links in the poem. Through each of God's spokesmen, in differing ways, the divine voice of retribution is heard, threatening imminent destruction; but each transmits also the message of consolation. The striking of the two-handed engine, like the miracle at the Red Sea, is terrible only to those who, like the Egyptians, attempt to bind the word of God and hold the faithful captive. Finally, therefore, the message even of the dread voice is one of peace.

Because the voice "is past,"[40] there is a promise of renewal after the engine has done its work; the action has a positive and hopeful meaning as well as a negative and threatening one. The purpose of the "shaking" is "that those things which cannot be shaken may remain." The fact that the engine will strike once means it is so powerful that no second stroke will be needed; but the fact that it will strike no more marks the inauguration of a new era in history as well as the beginning of the final phase of the poem. Alpheus can return, and the flowers can bloom, because the stroke of justice which purifies the church gives stability and security to that which remains. When the day of retribution is past, there will be need for neither a dread voice nor a shaking of the earth.

Turning again to the passage from Hebrews which speaks of the shaking of the earth, we find that its context, too, is one of consolation. The preceding verses draw a contrast between the past and the future:

For ye are not come unto the mount that might be touched, and that burned with fire, nor unto blackness, and darkness, and tempest, and the sound of a trumpet, and the voice of words; . . . But ye are come unto mount Zion, and unto the city of the living God, the heavenly Jerusalem, and to an innumerable company of angels, to the general assembly and church of the firstborn, which are written in heaven, and to God the Judge of all, and to the spirits of just men made perfect. (xii, 18–19, 22–23)

It is this culmination to which *Lycidas* looks forward and with the description of which it concludes.

The transition effected in lines 132–33 is dramatic but carefully modulated: There is a quick alternation of phrases which look both backward and forward. A more conventional transition would have been written: "The dread voice that shrunk thy streams is past; return Alpheus," in a straight pattern which might be described as A followed by B, the past by the future. Instead the syntax is wrenched to produce an undulating pattern: B ("Return Alpheus,"), A ("the dread voice"), B ("is past"), A ("that shrunk thy streams"). There follow the return of the Sicilian Muse, the flower passage, and the vision of the guarded Mount.

Then, finally, the "no more" of line 131 can be picked up at the beginning of the penultimate section in a line whose rhythm echoes syllable for syllable the opening line of the poem. A schematization of the parallels observed by Weismiller[41] helps to reveal the importance to the poem of its opening phrase:

Yet once more, / O ye Laurels, / and once more	(1)
Weep no more, / woeful Shepherds / weep no more,	(165)

Between them has intervened line 131:

Stands ready / to smite once, / and smite no more.

Here the pattern is varied, the repetitions occurring at the main caesura and the end. What this line does is to form a perfect transition—rhythmically, verbally, and thematically—between the sadness of the beginning and the joy of the end of the poem, relating "yet once more," with its richly allusive overtones, to the total meaning.

. . . once more . . . once more	(1)
. . . once . . . no more	(131)
. . . no more . . . no more	(165)

The middle line modifies the pathos of the first by inserting the negative; the final stroke of God's wrath will put an end to the empty repetitions of pagan cyclical time and will introduce the eternity which ends all weeping, as "once" is replaced by "no more . . . no more." The perfect balancing and progression of the phrases in these three lines mirrors the movement of the poem and helps to define its structure.

The divisions of *Lycidas* have been explained and justified on many grounds. There is general recognition that a partial answer to the problem raised by King's early death is given by Phoebus, another by the dread voice, and a final one in the apotheosis at the end. A typical recent explanation suggests that the progression is from the less final to the more final, the lower to the higher: Phoebus represents a barely Christianized stoicism, Peter the church militant, the ending the church triumphant; Phoebus is a pagan god, Peter an active Christian saint and martyr, Lycidas a type of the resurrected Christ.[42] To such a pattern (the general lines of which would be accepted by most critics) the allusions to Moses make a contribution. They complete the pattern by including the Old Law, in keeping with the full weight of the tradition which sees the providential preparation for Christianity remotely in the pagan religions, proximately in the Old Law, which is the pedagogue leading to Christ.

The unfolding consolation in *Lycidas* moves from the pagan answer (not false but radically incomplete) through the partial answer given by the Old Law to the full consolation of the heavenly Jerusalem, which subsumes its predecessors without destroying them. The conclusion of *Lycidas* is an epitome of these three elements:

> So *Lycidas*, sunk low, but mounted high,
> Through the dear might of him that walk'd the waves,
> Where other groves, and other streams along,
> With *Nectar* pure his oozy Locks he laves,
> And hears the unexpressive nuptial Song,
> In the blest Kingdoms meek of joy and love.
> There entertain him all the Saints above,
> In solemn troops, and sweet Societies
> That sing, and singing in their glory move,
> And wipe the tears for ever from his eyes.   (172–81)

The lovely lines, after invoking the classical allusions to groves and nectar, weave together imagery from different parts of the Bible, notably the book of Revelation but with echoes too of Hebrews and of the prophetical books of the Old Testament. Prominent among these is Isaiah, chapter li:

Awake, awake, put on strength, O arm of the Lord; awake, as in the ancient days, in the generations of old. . . . Art thou not it which hath dried the sea, the waters of the great deep; that hath made the depths of the sea a way for the ransomed to pass over? Therefore the redeemed of the Lord shall return, and come with singing unto Zion; and everlasting joy shall be upon their head: they shall obtain gladness and joy; and sorrow and mourning shall flee away. (verses 9–11)

And in Revelation xv, 3, these redeemed are singing "the song of Moses the servant of God, and the song of the Lamb."

A final detail reinforces the structural importance of the dread voice as it relates to the earlier part of the poem. After Phoebus' intervention on fame the speaker in the poem returns to his lament:

> O Fountain *Arethuse*, and thou honor'd flood,
> Smooth-sliding *Mincius;* crown'd with vocal reeds,
> That strain I heard was of a higher mood. (85–87)

The "higher mood" is undoubtedly, as editors point out, a musical term: the motif which has sounded faintly is now submerged, to reappear in later movements. But the "higher" mood may also refer to the foreshadowing of the Christian consolation which is to emerge at the end of the poem. Virgil had begun his Fourth Eclogue with the words, "Sicilian Muses, let us sing a somewhat loftier strain."[43] Milton recalls these muses to his poem at the beginning of its end: "Return *Alpheus*, the dread voice is past / That shrunk thy streams; Return *Sicilian* Muse"—the muse who at the beginning of the poem had swept the string "somewhat" loudly. As is well known, Virgil's eclogue, which predicts the birth of a child and the return of a golden age, was for centuries taken as a prophecy of the birth of Christ. In the context of *Lycidas*, the speech of Phoebus represents an advance on the rebellious questioning which has preceded it and is therefore of a higher mood. Calvin, it will be remembered, describes pre-Christian revelation as a "lower strain" when compared with the Christian; and the Geneva Bible, glossing Hebrews xii, 25, observes that the voice which formerly shook the earth "spake but rudely in comparison with Christ, who preached not the Lawe but the Gospel." The words of Phoebus foreshadow the final revelation, as Phoebus himself foreshadows Christ, the true Sun, even in the messianic reading of the Eclogue: "Thine own Apollo now is King!" (10). Fittingly, then, Virgil's Sicilian Muse may return now that the final revelation has clarified its meaning.

As the intricate rhyme scheme of *Lycidas* quiets into the ottava rima of the coda, so do the images and symbols of the poem fuse into a whole which is greater than the sum of its parts. The reader finishes with a sense of having heard a multitude of overtones difficult to disentangle one from the other, at times even seeming to clash, but all in the end resolved. "The crowning achievement of *Lycidas*," says Roy Daniells, "lies in the enormously ramified complex of reactions, conscious and unconscious, which it provokes. These are not in the nature of sequences of ideas merely or numbers of identifiable references or rows of problems solved. They are rather in the nature of innumerable conflicting forces."[44] Perhaps we shall never solve its problems, but with each fresh insight into its possibilities we may hear with a more sensitive ear the nuances which underlie its ultimate harmony.

College of New Rochelle

NOTES

1. Citations from Milton's poetry are to *John Milton: Complete Poetry and Major Prose*, ed. Merritt Y. Hughes (New York, 1957).
2. Helpful summaries and bibliographies of comments on the lines may be found, inter alia, in *Milton's Lycidas*, ed. Scott Elledge (New York, 1966), pp. 293–97, and in *A Variorum Commentary on the Poems of John Milton*, ed. A. S. P. Woodhouse and Douglas Bush (New York, 1972), vol. II, pt. 2, pp. 686–706.
3. *Milton's Poetic Art* (Cambridge, Mass., 1968), pp. 47–48.
4. "A Possible Biblical Allusion in 'Lycidas,' 1," *N&Q*, n.s. VIII (1961), 178. In a later study, *Inwrought with Figures Dim* (The Hague, 1974), Berkeley enlarges on the typological aspects of *Lycidas*. His book is a very rich, penetrating, and wide-

ranging exposition of several themes: the sea, the ship, eclipses, the sun, sea monsters, baptism. He touches briefly on some of the particular points in which I also am interested (see pp. 74, 130, 194), but from different perspectives.

5. "Milton's Uncouth Swain," *Milton Studies*, III, ed. James D. Simmonds (Pittsburgh, 1971), pp. 47–48.

6. "Studies of Verse Forms in the Minor English Poems," *Variorum Commentary*, vol. II, pt. 3, p. 1066.

7. Ralph Hone, " 'The Pilot of the *Galilean* Lake,' " *SP*, LVI (1959), 55–61; Berkeley, *Inwrought with Figures Dim*, passim, esp. pp. 75–77, 197.

8. *Anatomy of Criticism* (Princeton, 1957), pp. 121–22.

9. *Milton, Mannerism and Baroque* (Toronto, 1963; reprint ed., 1964), p. 48.

10. "The Typological Structure of Milton's Imagery," *Milton Studies*, V, ed. James D. Simmonds (Pittsburgh, 1973), pp. 75–77.

11. "Lycidas and the Dolphins of Apollo," *JEGP*, LXXII (1973), 343.

12. Wayne Shumaker, "Flowerets and Sounding Seas: A Study in the Affective Structure of *Lycidas*," *PMLA*, LXVI (1951), 490; Rosemond Tuve, *Images and Themes in Five Poems by Milton* (Cambridge, Mass., 1957), p. 78; Christopher Grose, "Lucky Words: Process of Speech in 'Lycidas,' " *JEGP*, LXX (1971), 396.

13. "Milton's 'Alpheus,' " *MLN*, LXXI (1956), 172–73.

14. Harold Fisch has observed that the entire account of the defeat of the rebel angels in Book VI of *Paradise Lost* suggests the situation at the Red Sea ("Hebraic Style and Motifs in *Paradise Lost*," in *Language and Style in Milton*, ed. Ronald Emma and John T. Shawcross [New York, 1967], p. 48). John T. Shawcross, in "*Paradise Lost* and the Theme of Exodus," *Milton Studies*, II, ed. James D. Simmonds (Pittsburgh, 1970), pp. 3–26, examines the typological role of Moses. Jason P. Rosenblatt, in "Structural Unity and Temporal Concordance: The War in Heaven in *Paradise Lost*," *PMLA*, LXXXVII (1972), 31–42, sees the typology of the Exodus as an important feature in the poem. At the MLA meeting of 1973, in a paper on "The Mosaic Voice in *Paradise Lost*," he dealt with the figure of Moses from neo-Platonic and typological viewpoints.

15. John Calvin, *Commentaries on the Epistle of Paul the Apostle to the Hebrews*, trans. John Owen (Grand Rapids, 1949), p. 336.

16. Citations from Milton's prose are to *The Works of John Milton*, ed. Frank A. Patterson et al., 18 vols. (New York, 1931–40), hereafter cited as CM. Milton quotes Deuteronomy xviii, 15, in *CD* I, 5, and I, 14 (CM, vol. XIV, p. 291, and vol. XV, p. 259). In Acts it is recorded once by Peter (iii, 22) and once by Stephen (vii, 37); Hebrews iii, 2, makes a similar comparison.

17. "Demonstratio evangelica," III.ii, *Patrologiae, Series Graeca*, ed. J. P. Migne, 22 (1857), 171–74.

18. Martin Noth, *Exodus, A Commentary* (Philadelphia, 1962), p. 104.

19. *Commentaries on the Book of Psalms*, trans. James Andersen, 5 vols. (Grand Rapids, 1949), vol. III, p. 176.

20. "In Aggaeum Prophetam," *Patrologiae, Series Latina*, ed. J. P. Migne, 25 (Paris, 1884), 1403.

21. *Commentaries on the Book of Psalms*, vol. IV, p. 338.

22. The miter is mentioned in Exodus xxviii, 4; xxxix, 28, 31; Leviticus xvi, 4; and Zechariah iii, 5. See also the examples and definitions in *OED*.

23. "A Note on the 'Blind Mouths' of 'Lycidas,' " *N&Q*, n.s. XX (1973), 380.

24. *The Fulfillment of the Scriptures: Abraham, Moses, and Piers* (Evanston, Ill., 1970), p. 38.

25. "The Apocalypse of Paul," in *The Aprocryphal New Testament*, trans. Montague Rhodes James (Oxford, 1924), p. 525.

26. *Visio Sancti Pauli*, ed. Theodore Silverstein (London, 1935), p. 10.

27. Chap. 48 (p. 551 in James ed.)

28. Roberti Grosseteste, *Epistolae*, ed. Henry R. Luard (London, 1861), pp. 357–58, 411, 418.

29. Ibid., p. xcl.

30. Ames, *Fulfillment of the Scriptures*, p. 158.

31. *The Poetical Works of Edmund Spenser*, ed. J. C. Smith and E. de Selincourt (London, 1926).

32. *The Works of Michael Drayton*, ed. J. William Hebel, vol. III (Oxford, 1961), p. 397 (bk. III, 17–20).

33. *Bartas: His Devine Weekes and Workes*, trans. Joshua Sylvester (London, 1605; reprint ed., Gainesville, Fla., 1965), p. 71.

34. *Descriptio Graecae*, bk. V (Elis I. vii.4-5), trans. W. H. S. Jones and H. A. Ormerod, Loeb Classical Library ed. (Cambridge, Mass., 1960).

35. William Riley Parker, *Milton: A Biography*, 2 vols. (Oxford, 1968), vol. II, p. 795. The *Variorum Commentary* agrees with Parker and most others that Psalm cxiv is the Greek poem referred to in a letter of December 4, 1634 (*The Latin and Greek Poems*, ed. Douglas Bush, *Variorum Commentary*, I [New York, 1970], p. 257).

36. *Facsimile of the Manuscript of Milton's Minor Poems Preserved in the Library of Trinity College, Cambridge*, ed. W. Aldis Wright (Cambridge, 1899).

37. Harris Fletcher cites the translations in the Great Bible of 1539, King James, and Douay, as well as the Vulgate and Tremellius-Junius versions; I have checked also the Geneva and Septuagint texts. See *The Intellectual Development of John Milton*, (Urbana, Ill., 1956), vol. I, pp. 189–91.

38. *Lycidas* is completed on p. 32 of the Wright *Facsimile*; the draft is on p. 33. See also the text of the draft in CM, vol. XVIII, p. 229.

39. "That Shepherd, Who First Taught the Chosen Seed: A Note on Milton's Mosaic Inspiration," *UTQ*, VIII (1939), 403.

40. There is a comma at the end of line 132, after "is past," in the Trinity MS; it is omitted in 1638 but restored in the editions of 1645 and 1673 (CM, vol. I, p. 469). The slight end-stopping of the line when the comma is there, as Milton seems to have wanted it, adds emphasis.

41. See note 6; see also Edgar F. Daniels, "Climactic Rhythms in 'Lycidas,'" *AN&Q*, VI (1968), 100–01, for another set of parallels.

42. George W. Nitchie, "*Lycidas*: A Footnote," *N&Q*, n.s. XIII (1966), 377. Many other readings affirm a similar movement from classical to Christian, and J. E. Hardy sees lines 132–33 as crucial in the union of the two elements ("*Lycidas*," *Kenyon Review*, VII [1945], 102).

43. *Eclogues*, trans. H. Rushton Fairclough, Loeb Classical Library ed. (Cambridge, Mass., 1960). For another viewpoint on the levels of style, see Baker, "Milton's Uncouth Swain."

44. *Milton, Mannerism and Baroque*, p. 49.

DE DOCTRINA CHRISTIANA: ITS STRUCTURAL PRINCIPLES AND ITS UNFINISHED STATE

Gordon Campbell

Milton's *De Doctrina Christiana* was conceived as a systematic exposition of Christian teaching. The method according to which Milton systematized his theology was that outlined in his *Artis Logicae*. Milton begins with a definition, then distributes this definition into its integral parts, and continues with this procedure until he arrives at the indivisible elements of theology. The parts of the treatise are joined together by formal transitions, as recommended in the *Artis Logicae*. The last five chapters of Book I of *De Doctrina* are internally confused, not connected to the preceding chapters with an adequate transition, and not integrated into the structure of the rest of the treatise. A series of deleted notes in the manuscript shows that the treatise once stood in ten parts. Milton had apparently completed the reorganization of everything except the sixth part. *De Doctrina Christiana* must accordingly be seen as unfinished.

IN THE preface to *De Doctrina Christiana*, Milton acknowledges that he had long desired "to possess a systematic exposition of Christian teaching, or at any rate a written investigation of it." I should like to argue that *De Doctrina* represents Milton's attempt to construct such a treatise, that the method according to which he systematized his theology was that promulgated in his *Artis Logicae*, and that he did not complete this process of systematization.

The stated purpose of the treatise was to "assist my faith or my memory or both." The suggestion that the treatise could somehow act as a mnemonic aid is expanded in the chapter on the definition of Christian doctrine, in which Milton explains that he intends "to assist the reader's memory by collecting together, as it were, into a single book texts which are scattered here and there throughout the Bible, and by systematizing them under definite headings." Milton explains that this method could be defended on grounds of Christian prudence, but he prefers to rest the case on Paul's command to "hold fast the pattern." Paul, Milton observes, had provided the Ephesians with "a complete corpus of doctrine, conceived in terms of a definite course of instruction," although the slimness of the evidence forces Milton to concede that this corpus was probably "of no great length."[1] The idea of organizing or systematizing knowledge for the sake of memory was a prominent feature of books written in the Ramist tradition. When Ramus redistributed Cicero's five parts of rhetoric, memory found no explicit place in the new scheme. The reason, as scholars of the Ramist movement have pointed out, is that Ramus' entire schema of the arts, based as it was on a topically conceived logic, was a system of local memory.[2] Milton's method of organizing knowledge evidently helped his own memory, for as Aubrey notes of Milton, "he had a very good memory: but I believe yᵗ his excellent method of thinking & disposing did much to helpe his memorie."[3]

Throughout *De Doctrina,* Milton remains conscious of the methodical nature of his work. He interrupts his discussion of the providence of God, for example, "to anticipate a later stage" of his argument. This suggestion of a carefully arranged argument would seem to be related to the "reform" mentioned by Milton when he argued that religion "needed to be measured with greater strictness against the yardstick of the Bible, and reformed with greater care."[4] Milton's source was to be the Bible; the careful reform to which he alludes was to be an organization of his argument on the principles advocated in his *Artis Logicae.* The evidence for this contention may be found in the structure of Milton's systematic theology.

The primary division of *De Doctrina* is into two books: faith, or the knowledge of God, and worship, or the love of God. The basis of this division is explained in the *Artis Logicae.* In the preface to his logic book, Milton explains that the study of knowledge "is properly known as doctrine or science: doctrine when it teaches the precepts of the arts; science, when the art, which is a sort of habit of the mind, is learned from those precepts, and as it were possessed." When the word "art" refers to doctrine, Milton continues, "it is the orderly body or scheme of precepts and examples, by which something useful is taught." In another section of *Artis Logicae,* Milton returns to this distinction but deploys a different vocabulary: "Doctrine" and "science" are replaced by "matter" and "form." The members of an integer, he explains, "are symbols of the essential causes, of matter and form, in which consists the whole essence of the integer." Matter and form are inclusive in two senses: In the first, the single members are taken to constitute the matter, while the form refers to the members taken together. The second sense is illustrated by reference to dialectic, which is made up of "the matter, that is, precepts, and the form also, which is the methodical disposition of those precepts."[5] It is the second sense which will concern us as we examine Milton's theological treatise.

In the closing paragraph of the first chapter of *De Doctrina,* Milton introduces a distinction articulated by Augustine to explain the subject of Book I: "faith, however, in this section, does not mean the habit of believing, but the things which must habitually be believed."[6] Milton's choice of words is very precise: Book I is going to examine faith in the doctrinal sense, that is, the precepts of faith, rather than in the scientific sense, the habit of mind. Book II is concerned with worship, which, as Milton explains, is primarily "eagerness to do good works." The word "faith" as used in the second book is explained in language which alludes to specifically logical terminology: "that is, faith, as form, gives form to the works, so that they can be good." As Milton continues, we recognize the essential Protestantism of his statement:

So it is conformity with faith, not with the ten commandments, which must be considered as the form of good works. . . . It is faith that justifies, not compliance with the commandments; and only that which justifies can make any work good. It follows that no work of ours can be good except through faith. Faith, then, is the form of good works, because the definition of *form* is *that through which a thing is what it is.*[7]

The definition of "form" in the last line is an exact quotation from Milton's *Artis Logicae.*[8] With the aid of precise logical terminology Milton is explaining that in Book II of *De Doctrina* he will be using the word "faith" in the "scientific" sense, meaning "the habit of believing," the "methodical disposition of precepts." Milton does not regard faith and works as two separate phenomena. Rather, his treatise—his entire treatise—is about faith. Faith in Book I is a doctrinal concept: the precepts, or "matter" of Christianity; in Book II faith is a "scientific" idea: the habit, or "form," which is worship, as manifested in works.

Having established this basic distinction, Milton begins to subdivide the subjects of *De Doctrina* into their constituent parts. This process of continuous subdivision is outlined in the *Artis Logicae*, where Milton explains that in discussing an art one must begin with a definition, because it contains the causes, and then distribute this definition into its integral parts, subjoining consectaries in the process, and continuing with this procedure until the smallest particles of the art are discovered.[9] This is the organizing principle of *De Doctrina Christiana*. The government of the universe, for example, is defined in the context of the previous division (as "the last kind of external divine efficiency"), then distributed into general and special government. General government, which may be ordinary or extraordinary, is defined and distributed in Book I, chapter 8. Special government, which may refer to angels or to men, is then considered: Chapter 9 deals with the special government of the universe as it pertains to angels, who are either good or evil, while chapter 10 begins the discussion of special government as it relates to man, who is either prelapsarian or postlapsarian.[10] This process of definition and distribution enables Milton to isolate and discuss the individual points of Christian doctrine.

These individual points of doctrine had doubtless been established and documented by Milton long before he began to organize his treatise according to the method of the *Artis Logicae*. In the preface to *De Doctrina*, Milton explains that as a boy he started "to list under general headings all passages from the scriptures which suggested themselves for quotation, so that I might have them ready at hand when necessary."[11] I shall contend below that the process of organizing these headings was never completed. But the dichotomous structure of Milton's treatise may conveniently be seen in figures 1.a–c, which plot the first twenty-eight chapters of Book I of *De Doctrina*. Similar charts may be found in earlier theological treatises organized according to the method of Ramus.[12]

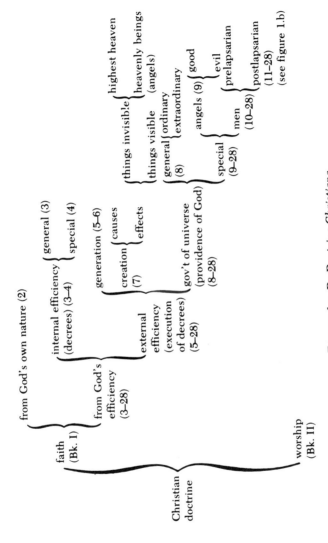

FIGURE 1.a. *De Doctrina Christiana*

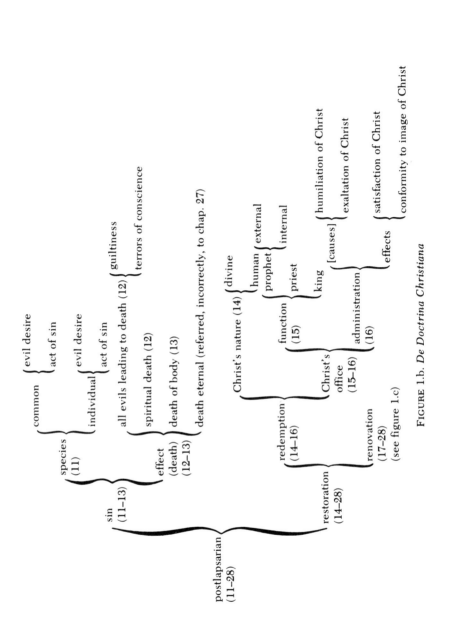

FIGURE 1.b. *De Doctrina Christiana*

postlapsarian (11–28)

sin (11–13)
- species (11)
  - common
    - evil desire
    - act of sin
  - individual
    - evil desire
    - act of sin
- effect (death) (12–13)
  - all evils leading to death (12)
    - guiltiness
    - terrors of conscience
  - spiritual death (12)
  - death of body (13)
  - death eternal (referred, incorrectly, to chap. 27)

restoration (14–28)
- redemption (14–16)
  - Christ's nature (14)
    - divine
    - human
  - Christ's office (15–16)
    - function (15)
      - prophet
        - external
        - internal
      - priest
      - king
    - administration (16)
      - [causes]
        - humiliation of Christ
        - exaltation of Christ
      - effects
        - satisfaction of Christ
        - conformity to image of Christ
- renovation (17–28) (see figure 1.c)

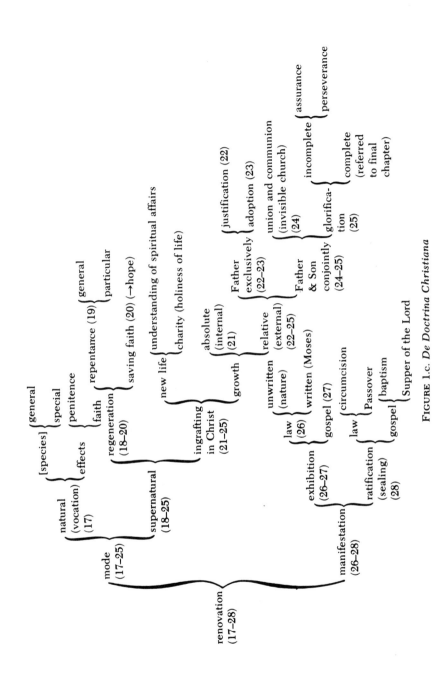

FIGURE 1.c. *De Doctrina Christiana*

Another characteristic of the method of the *Artis Logicae* which may be found in the organization of *De Doctrina* is the use of formal transitions. In the logic book Milton explains that if long passages intervene between the delineations of the parts of the subject, then these *"are to be joined together by bands of transition, for this restores and refreshes the hearer."* As always, there is a subdivision: "a transition is either perfect or imperfect." A perfect transition is one "which briefly shows both what has been said and what follows." As an example Milton gives the beginning of the second book of *Artis Logicae:* "UP to this point has been treated the first part of the art of logic, which deals with the invention of arguments; the second part which now follows deals with their disposition." Perfect transitions are common in *De Doctrina.* At the outset of Book I, chapter 22, for example, Milton says "SO much for the absolute or internal growth of the regenerate man: now follows my discussion of his relative or external growth."[13] An imperfect transition, on the other hand, "is that which shows in some other way merely what has been said or what follows." Milton's example is the beginning of Book I, chapter 18 of *Artis Logicae:* "*SIMPLE arguments, both consentany and dissentany, are as I have said.*" *De Doctrina* has many imperfect transitions, such as the opening of Book I, chapter 15: "I HAVE described the nature, human as well as divine, of Christ as mediator."[14]

One transition in *De Doctrina* is so imperfect as to be impenetrable, and the hints afforded by this flaw impel one toward the conclusion that Milton never completed the organization of his treatise. Such a conclusion is by no means wholly acceptable to many Milton scholars. "The treatise," we are assured, "is in no sense an unfinished document."[15] When mollified by observations of the mixed calligraphy of the manuscript, this idea is phrased in terms of the treatise standing "essentially complete" in 1660, "at least in first draft."[16] The calligraphic qualification is occasioned by the fact that the second draft, that written in the hand of Daniel Skinner, is complete only to page 196 of the manuscript. After that point, the handwriting is mostly that of Jeremie Picard, the amanuensis of the "essentially complete" draft.[17] The idea that the treatise is a finished work draws support from the words of the anonymous biographer who said that Milton's *"Body of Divinity"* was "finish'd after the

Restoration." This opinion was accepted by Anthony à Wood, who noted that the *"Body of Divinity* . . . [was] finished after his Majesty's Restauration."[18] The abortive efforts made to publish the treatise after Milton's death would also seem to suggest a completed treatise.[19]

Other scholars argue that *De Doctrina* is in some sense unfinished. Originally this thesis was argued on the grounds that the abrupt ending of the treatise indicates an incomplete work.[20] It must be granted that the treatise has no concluding chapter, but this does not prove that the work is unfinished. A treatise organized according to the principles of Ramist logic was deemed to be finished when all the indivisible components of the art had been established and discussed. This idea of completion accounts for the fact that Milton's systematic theology, in common with all other Ramist treatises, concludes with a discussion of the final point in the analysis rather than with a summary of the conclusions which could have been drawn from that which had gone before.

In recent years, two critics have argued in a more qualified way that the treatise is incomplete. One argues that it is unfinished in the sense that it was "never conceived as a whole" and because it contains contradictions. The other argues that it "is unfinished in the sense that, Milton's expectations notwithstanding, it is a singularly gross expedition into theology."[21] Although I would dispute the notion that the treatise was never conceived as a whole, I would agree that it contains some contradictions and that its theology is unworthy of Milton. I would also argue that its unfinished state can be demonstrated by reference to a group of five unorganized chapters at the end of Book I.

As I suggested earlier, the treatise is constructed as a series of dichotomies, beginning with the definition of Christian doctrine, and subdividing until the smallest points of theology are established. Each discussion is connected by a transition which summarizes what has gone before and introduces what is to follow. At the end of Book I, chapter 28, however, the procedure falters; it is more than coincidence that the two critics who have tried to diagram *De Doctrina* have both truncated their charts of Book I at this point.[22] Although neither mentions the fact, it is impossible to continue the charts beyond chapter 28 to the end of Book I.

Chapter 28 is a discussion of the ratification, or external sealing, of the covenant of grace, both under the law, in which the seal is manifested in circumcision and Passover, and under the gospel, in which the seal is represented by baptism and the Supper of the Lord. Chapter 29 ("Of the Visible Church") begins, as expected, with a transition summarizing that which has gone before:

SO far I have dealt with vocation and its consequences, whether these constitute mere alteration [chapter 17], or whether they are regeneration and the growth of the regenerate man [chapters 18–25]. I have also discussed the various manifestations of the covenant which is offered to those who are called [chapters 26–27], and its sealing [chapter 28]. (I, 29; YP, vol. VI, p. 563; CM, vol. XVI, p. 218)

These summaries are usually followed by a transitional phrase which indicates the next subject to be considered, but in this instance there is no such phrase. Milton's next words are "THE ASSEMBLY OF THOSE WHO ARE CALLED is THE VISIBLE CHURCH." Although a verbal link exists between "VOCATIONE" and "VOCATORUM," there is not the slightest logical link between the introduction to the chapter and the matter it contains, nor, more importantly, is there any explanation earlier in the treatise of how this section is a logical continuation of the process of division and distribution.

This break, the first in twenty-eight chapters, is only the beginning of a series of unexplained transitions. The visible church is inexorably split into its constituent parts: the universal church and the particular church. The former is treated in chapter 29, the latter in chapters 31 and 32. This return to order, however, is disturbed by the presence of chapter 30 ("Of the Holy Scripture") and chapter 33 ("Of Complete Glorification"). The discussion of sacred writ contains a few references to the visible church, but Milton offers no reason for its inclusion at this point. The chapter on complete glorification seems utterly disconnected, despite the fact that eight chapters earlier Milton had promised to "deal with [complete glorification] in the last chapter of the present book." Chapter 33 also contains a discussion of eternal death, an anomaly given that Milton had assured his readers earlier that "chapter xxvii deals with this."[23]

De Doctrina runs a smooth and ordered course for twenty-eight chapters of its first book, and for all of its second.[24] But the concluding five chapters of the first book are chaotic. The only plausible explanation for this disruption would seem to be that the work, as it survives, has not been completely transformed into a "systematic exposition." The work was unfinished. That Milton at some point intended to publish the book is demonstrated by the existence and content of the preface. It may be that the book was left unfinished because of Milton's death, but this theory is complicated by the testimony of the seventeenth-century writers who stated that the work was finished shortly after 1660;[25] their remarks may, however, have sprung from the observation that Milton stopped working on the treatise about that time. If Milton did abandon the work, he might have done so because the theological idiosyncrasies of the text made it inexpedient to publish. Such was the view of the anonymous biographer, who opined that the "Body of Divinity" contained judgments "differing perhaps from that commonly receivd, (and which is thought to bee the reason that never was printed)."[26] However, Milton's earlier defense of unacceptable views on divorce and his defiant apology for republicanism weeks before the Restoration militate against the hypothesis that Milton was afraid to publish that which he considered to be the truth. The only tenable explanation of why *De Doctrina* was not published is that the work was not yet ready for publication, and that Milton never completed it. The treatise as it now stands is almost complete: All that remained was the working out of an arrangement for the final chapters of Book I and a final revision to eliminate the theological discrepancies inevitably present in a work written "from time to time"[27] over the course of many years. But for reasons that will probably never be known, Milton did not complete that final arrangement and revision.

Although it is impossible to reconstruct the organization that Milton's discussion of the precepts of faith might have taken in its closing chapters, the surviving evidence would seem to justify a conjecture about how the chapter on the Holy Scriptures might have been integrated into the final chapters. Other evidence would seem to point toward a reasonable explanation of why the organization of the treatise crumbles at the particular place that it does.

The chapter on Holy Scripture was probably intended as an extension of an earlier part of the treatise. Such a connection may initially be argued by analogy with Ames' *Medvlla S.S. Theologiae*, which is, of course, complete.[28] Discussing the church, Ames distinguishes between those ministers of the church who are extraordinary (chapter 33) and those who are ordinary (chapter 35). Chapter 34 of Ames' treatise, a discussion of the Holy Scriptures, is an extension of the discussion of extraordinary ministers, a term which had been defined in the previous chapter: "extraordinarij ministri fuerunt Prophetae, Apostoli, & Evangelistae."[29] Milton's work also devotes a chapter (29) to the ministers of the church (the universal visible church), whom Milton divides into ordinary and extraordinary ministers, following Ames' definitions as well as his dichotomy.[30] Thus, when Milton's chapter on Holy Scripture opens with a definition of Scripture as "SCRIPTA prophetarum, apostolorum, evangelistarum," we realize that Milton had intended to take up the thread of his discussion of extraordinary ministers of the visible church. The suggestion that the chapter on the Holy Scriptures is part of the discussion of the universal visible church is reinforced by the transition at the outset of chapter 31: "SO far I have spoken of THE UNIVERSAL VISIBLE CHURCH."[31] Milton clearly planned to relate his discussion of the Holy Scriptures in chapter 30 to the ministry of the universal visible church.

Even with this link established, the problem of the internal order of the last five chapters is not solved, although one senses that other connections are just beyond our reach. If we examine other systematic theologies organized according to the method of Ramus to discover how Milton might have joined his final chapter, on the Final Judgment and complete glorification, to the rest of Book I, we immediately notice that this subject was always treated in the same place. But the connecting structure is never exactly the same as Milton's: Ames' discussion of perfect glorification is the third variation of the manner by which the application of redemption by the New Covenant is administered; Wolleb's analysis of glorification is the fourth part of that portion of the special providence of God which is applicable to man; Cartwright's exposition is the last part of that portion of the Office of Christ which pertains to his kingdom; and in Dudley Fenner's *Sacra Theologica* (Geneva, 1586), the Last Judgment is the second part of Christ's office.[32] All of these schemes are similar to Milton's, but none is close enough to allow an inference of what Milton conceived to be the connection, if indeed he had established the connection in his own mind. In all probability he only knew that in keeping with the mimetic pattern of the treatise, and in fulfillment of the promise made several chapters earlier, he would be treating the Final Judgment and perfect glorification at the end of the first book.

When we confront the question of why the organizational scheme collapses at the particular point that it does, no clear answer presents itself. But one possibility exists: It may be that the conclusion of chapter 28 was a natural breaking point, at the end of part five of a ten-part treatise. The idea of a ten-part systematic theology within the Ramist tradition was not unprecedented: The treatises of Fenner and Polanus, both of which Milton had read, are cast in this form.[33] The evidence that Milton's theology once stood in ten parts consists of a series of deleted notes in the manuscript of *De Doctrina*. The notes always follow completed chapters and read as follows: after Book I, chapter 4, "Primae partis finis"; after Book I, chapter 6, "Finis partis secundae"; after Book I, chapter 13, "Finis Tertiae Partis"; after Book I, chapter 25, "Quartae partis Finis"; after Book I, chapter 28, "Quintae Partis finis"; after Book I, chapter 33, "Finis Libri Primi" (not deleted) followed by "et sextae partis" (deleted); after Book II, chapter 4, "Septimae partis finis"; after Book II, chapter 7, "Finis Octavae partis"; and after Book II, chapter 14, "Nonae Partis finis." Kelley has identified the handwriting in these notes as Daniel Skinner's.[34] Thus, they may have been added at a later date (Skinner had the manuscript after Milton's death) or may have been entered at the command of Milton.[35] But even in this ten-part scheme an anomaly exists. As noted above, the words "Quartae partis Finis" following chapter 25 have been deleted. However, the words "Finis Quartae Partis" appear, and have been deleted, after Book I, chapter 22.[36] Kelley thinks the hand is not Skinner's, noting that the phrase "suggests that Milton dictated the division before Skinner worked on the manuscript and that other evidence of this fact has been lost."[37] Even if the "surviving" ten-part scheme were Skinner's, an earlier ten-part plan may have been devised by Milton himself. In either case, the five unorganized chapters at the end of Book I are coterminous with section six in the earlier version. If

Milton was revising one section at a time, then he had completed revising, or systematizing, nine of the original ten sections. All that remained was the organization of section six, and a final revision to eliminate the theological inconsistencies, before the treatise could be published.

That Milton felt completion to be imminent is indicated by a passage in his *Treatise of Civil Power* (1659), which seems to have been designed as a plea for public toleration of his forthcoming treatise on Christian doctrine.[38] In *A Treatise of Civil Power*, Milton explains that "what euangelic religion is, is told in two words, faith and charitie; or beleef and practise." The exposition of "practise" confirms the connection with the divisions and thought of *De Doctrina:* "our whole practical dutie in religion is containd in charitie, or the love of God and our neighbour."[39] Book II of *De Doctrina* also divides worship (charity) into the love of God and the love of man.[40] The attack on forced religion in the tract on *Civil Power* is of course an argument for a general principle, but it seems likely that Milton had in mind a specific example, his treatise on the "beleef" and "practise" of the Christian faith.

Milton almost finished reorganizing and revising his treatise. But what was he reorganizing? Not, I think, an earlier treatise based on those of Ames and Wolleb,[41] nor a treatise based on the *Index Theologicus,*[42] but rather a treatise written "from time to time" over the course of many years, a treatise which was called a "System of Divinity" in the 1640s, and "Body of Divinity" or "Idea Theologiae" in the 1650s.[43] The title *De Doctrina Christiana* may well have been Daniel Skinner's contribution to the confusion, for it first appears in his handwriting; alternatively, it may have been the final title on which Milton settled. The "system" of the 1640s, in all probability a presentation in ten parts of Milton's own ideas on theological matters, doubtless became too restricted a venture in Milton's mind: His censure in 1643 of those who would not go beyond "the easie creek of a System or a Medulla"[44] clearly reflects discomfiture about his own efforts. In the 1650s Milton probably superseded the mere "medulla" by fleshing out his points with copious documentation from the Scriptures. Finally, as the treatise grew into the *De Doctrina Christiana* of the 1660s, Milton began the task of systematizing his treatise according to the method described in his *Artis Logicae*. Section six of the earlier ten-part version was never reorganized; so as it stands, *De Doctrina Christiana* is unfinished.

The University of Liverpool

NOTES

1. *De Doctrina Christiana* (*DDC*), trans. John Carey, in *Complete Prose Works of John Milton*, ed. D. M. Wolfe (New Haven, 1953–), vol. VI, pp. 120, 127, 128. This edition will be cited as YP. The Latin text may be found in *The Works of John Milton*, ed. F. A. Patterson, 18 vols. (New York, 1931–1938), vol. XIV, pp. 6, 20, 22. References to *DDC* in this latter edition, abbreviated as CM, are to the Latin text.

2. W. J. Ong, *Ramus: Method, and the Decay of Dialogue* (Cambridge, Mass., 1958), p. 280; F. Yates, *The Art of Memory* (London, 1966), pp. 231–42.

3. *The Early Lives of Milton*, ed. H. Darbishire (London, 1932), p. 4. Cf. Carlo Dati, who addressed Milton as the man in whose memory lives the whole world (*"in Memoria totus Orbis"; CM*, vol. I, p. 166), and Antonio Francini, who announced that all good poetry and history were present in Milton's memory (*"Che s'opre degne di Poema e storia / Furon gia, l'hai presenti alla memoria"*; ibid., p. 162).

4. I, 8 (YP, vol. VI, p. 331; CM, vol. XV, p. 68); preface (YP, vol. VI, p. 120; CM, vol. XIV, p. 8).

5. *Artis Logicae* (*AL*), preface and I, 26 (CM, vol. XI, pp. 9, 233). References to *AL* are to the translation by A. H. Gilbert; the Latin text is printed on the facing verso pages.

6. I, 1 (YP, vol. VI, p. 129; CM, vol. XIV, p. 24). Kelley, the annotator of the Yale edition of *DDC*, notes a similar passage in Polanus' *Syntagma Theologiae* (YP, vol. VI, p. 129, n. 12), to which might be added George Downham's distinction in *A Treatise of Iustification* (London, 1639), preface (unnumbered page). The distinction may be found in Augustine, *De Trinitate*, XIII, 2 (see *Corpvs Christianorvm*, Series Latina, 50 (A), 386).

7. II, 1 (YP, vol. VI, pp. 637, 639; CM, vol. XIV, pp. 2, 6, 8).

8. The Latin text of *DDC* is "sic enim forma definitur, per quam res est id quod est" (CM, vol. XVII, p. 8). In *AL* I, 7, Milton says *"forma est causa per quam res est id quod est"* and adds the source of his definition: It "joins those of Plato and Aristotle. For Plato defines form as the cause through which, Aristotle as that which is" (CM, vol. XI, pp. 58, 59). The definition of "form" in *AL* and *DDC* also appears in *Tetrachordon:* "the *Form* by which the thing is what it is" (YP, vol. II, p. 608).

9. II, 17 (CM, vol. XI, p. 477).

10. I, 8, 9, 10 (YP, vol. VI, pp. 326, 340, 343, 351; CM, vol. XV, pp. 54, 92, 96, 112).

11. (YP, vol. VI, p. 119; CM, vol. XIV, p. 4).

12. Ames, *The Marrow of Sacred Divinity*, trans. anon. (London, 1642) is prefaced with twenty-five pages of charts; Wolleb's *The Abridgment of Christian Divin-*

itie, trans. A. Ross (London, 1650) includes nine pages of charts "for the help of weak Memories"; each chapter in Thomas Cartwright's *A Treatise of Christian Religion* (London, 1616) begins with an explanatory chart; each of the six books of Johann-Heinrich Alsted's *Methodus SS Theologiae* (Offenbach, 1611) begins with a diagrammatic summary of its contents. These detailed tables of dichotomies were so typical of Ramist treatises that Fuller could remark, without being esoteric, that "all I will adde of *Carps* is this, that *Ramus* himself doth not so much redound in *Dichotomies* as they do. Seeing no one bone is to be found in their body, which is not *forked* or divided into two parts at the end thereof" (*The History of the Worthies of England* [London, 1662], 3d pagination ser., p. 98).

13. *AL* II, 17 (CM, vol. XI, p. 477); *AL* II, 1 (CM, vol. XI, p. 295); *DDC* I, 22 (YP, vol. VI, p. 485). Carey's colloquial translation of the opening phrase rather obscures the parallel between the "fuit . . . sequitur" formulae which govern both the example taken from the logic (*AL* II, 1 [CM, vol. XI, p. 294]) and the theology (CM, vol. XVI, p. 24).

14. *AL* II, 17 (CM, vol. XI, p. 477); *AL* I, 8 (CM, vol. XI, p. 151); *DDC* I, 15 (YP, vol. VI, p. 430; CM, vol. XV, p. 284).

15. M. Kelley, *This Great Argument: A Study of Milton's "De Doctrina Christiana" as a Gloss Upon "Paradise Lost"* (Gloucester, Mass., 1941), p. 22, n. 27. Kelley has elaborated this conclusion in YP, vol. VI, pp. 103–04.

16. W. R. Parker, *Milton: A Biography,* 2 vols. (Oxford, 1968), p. 1056.

17. See Kelley's detailed introduction to the manuscript in YP, vol. VI, pp. 11–35.

18. Darbishire, *Early Lives,* pp. 29, 46.

19. See Kelley's discussion in YP, vol. VI, pp. 36–40.

20. H. J. Todd, *Some Account of the Life and Writings of John Milton* (London, 1826), p. 345, and *Monthly Review,* CVII (1825), 293, cited in Kelley, *Great Argument,* p. 21, n. 27.

21. Arthur Sewell, *A Study in Milton's Christian Doctrine* (London, 1939), pp. x, 11; and C. A. Patrides, "*Paradise Lost* and the Language of Theology," in *Language and Style in Milton,* ed. R. D. Emma and J. T. Shawcross (New York, 1967), p. 105.

22. A. J. Th. Eisenring, *Milton's "De Doctrina Christiana"* (Fribourg, 1946), pp. 108–09; and H. F. Irwin, Jr., "Ramistic Logic in Milton's Prose Works" (Ph.D. thesis, Princeton, 1941), between pp. 68 and 69. Irwin's study is the first to note the Ramist principles of organization in *DDC.* Kelley, *This Great Argument,* p. 195, observes that *DDC* is organized on the principles detailed in Milton's *Artis Logicae* but does not elaborate.

23. *DDC* I, 25 (YP, vol. VI, p. 514; CM, vol. XVI, p. 96); *DDC* I, 13 (YP, vol. VI, p. 414; CM, vol. XV, p. 250). Kelley (YP, vol. VI, p. 414, n. 39) acknowledges that "*The Eclectic Review* (n.s. XXV [1826], 131) notes that the chapter actually referred to is xxxiii and suggests that six chapters must have been afterwards added or an alteration made in the arrangement," but argues that "the Picard draft fails to indicate any such addition or alteration, and the error may be either a fossil from 'A perfect System' or a Skinner mistake in copying."

24. In YP, vol. VI, p. 103, Kelley notes that some referents are lacking in Book I, chapters 8 and 11, and that some proof texts are given contradictory interpretations. But his further claims—that there are two discussions of the sabbath, and that the second part of one basis of division is not discussed—are unjustified.

25. See the statements documented in note 18.

26. Darbishire, *Early Lives,* p. 31.

27. The phrase is Edward Phillips'. Phillips says that in the early 1640s Milton was occupied with "the writing from his own dictation, some part, from time to time, of a Tractate which he thought fit to collect from the ablest of Divines, who had written of the subject; *Amesius, Wollebius,* &c. *viz.* A perfect System of Divinity" (ibid., p. 61).

28. Ames' treatise was originally published in Amsterdam in 1623. That Milton knew Ames' systematic theology is evident from Phillips' remark, cited in note 27. On the influence of the *Medvlla* on *DDC* see Kelley's remarks in YP, vol. VI, pp. 18–21, and the index entries s.v. "Amesius, Gulielmus" in YP, vol. VI, p. 851.

29. Ames, *Medvlla S.S. Theologiae* (Londini, 1630) I. 33, p. 177, item 37.

30. "Tales fuere prophetae, apostoli, evangelistae, et similes" (*DDC* I, 29 [CM, vol. XVI, p. 238; YP, vol. VI, p. 570]). Kelley (YP, vol. VI, p. 570, n. 9) records the parallel and adds another from Wolleb.

31. *DDC* I, 30 (CM, vol. XVI, p. 248; YP, vol. VI, p. 574); *DDC* I, 31 (YP, vol. VI, p. 593; CM, vol. XVI, p. 284).

32. Although no English translation of Fenner's treatise has ever been published, MS translations may be found in the British Museum (Harleian 6879), in the Lambeth Library, and in Dr. William's Library.

33. Fenner is not mentioned in *DDC*, but he and Cartwright were once described by Milton as "two of the Lernedest" of English divines (*The Tenure of Kings and Magistrates*, YP, vol. III, p. 248), and Milton quotes from *Sacra Theologica* in *Tenure* (p. 249). Milton cites Polanus' *Syntagma* (in order to disagree) in *DDC* I, 27 (YP, vol. VI, p. 535; CM, vol. XVI, pp. 148, 150).

34. Kelley, *Great Argument*, p. 56, n. 197, and YP, vol. VI, pp. 36–37, n. 4. The divisions in Book I occur at natural breaking points in the treatise. But in Book II only the break after chapter 7 corresponds to a major division in the text.

35. Aubrey records "Idea Theologiae in MS. in yᵉ hands of Mʳ Skinner a merchant's sonne in Marke Lane" (Darbishire, *Early Lives*, pp. 9–10).

36. YP, vol. VI, p. 821, s.v. MS page 282; CM, vol. XVII, p. 449, s.v. page 48. An examination of the MS in the P.R.O. (SP 9/61) shows that Kelley's note in *Great Argument* (p. 57, n. 197) that the phrase appears "at the end of chapter xvii (p. 235)" is incorrect, though the three illegible deleted words found at the end of chapter 17 are written in the same hand and in the same ink, as noted by Kelley in YP, vol. VI, p. 818, s.v. MS page 235, and pp. 33, 37, n. 4. I am grateful to Mary Hamilton of the P.R.O. staff for confirming these points.

37. YP, vol. VI, p. 37, n. 4, a restatement of *Great Argument*, p. 57, n. 197.

38. See Parker, *Milton: A Biography*, pp. 518–24.

39. *A Treatise of Civil Power* (YP, vol. VII, p. 257).

40. Cf. the concluding sentence of *Doctrine and Discipline of Divorce*, where Milton notes that God the Son has subsumed all his commandments "under the feet of charity" (YP, vol. II, p. 356).

41. The existence of an earlier treatise based on those of Ames and Wolleb, suggested by the passage in Phillips cited in note 27, is assumed by Parker (*Milton: A Biography*, p. 1056) and Kelley (*Great Argument*, p. 27).

42. See Kelley's argument that the *Index Theologicus* "contributed little, if anything, to the completed *Christian Doctrine*" (YP, vol. VI, p. 20).

43. On the title "System of Divinity" see Phillips' remark cited in note 27 and Toland's comment that Milton "wrote likewise a *System of Divinity*" (Darbishire, *Early Lives*, p. 192). On the title "Body of Divinity" see Wood, who records Milton's

"framing a *Body of Divinity* out of the Bible" before the publication of *Pro Se Defensio* in 1655 (ibid., p. 46). Wood was drawing on the comments of the anonymous biographer, who says that after Milton's blindness (1651?) he began "the framing a *Body of Divinity* out of the Bible" (ibid., p. 29) and comments upon Milton's "Judgment in his Body of Divinity concerning some speculative points" (ibid., p. 31). On the title "Idea Theologiae," note Wood's remark about "*The body of Divinity*, which my friend calls Idea *Theologiae*" (ibid., p. 47). His "friend" was John Aubrey, who had recorded among Milton's works the "Idea Theologiae in MS" (ibid., p. 9).

44. *Doctrine and Discipline of Divorce*, YP, vol. II, p. 232.

PARADISE REGAINED AND
THE SECOND ADAM

Richard Douglas Jordan

While some modern critics have tried to read *Paradise Regained* as a psychologically realistic dramatic presentation, the text itself does not support such a reading. The poem is rather an exploration of Christ's role as the second Adam, and it is meant to be read as a sequel to *Paradise Lost* offering certain typological contrasts between Adam and Christ. The major contrasts are Adam's fallibility as contrasted with Christ's infallibility, the contrasting types of knowledge available to the two heroes, and the differences shown between man under the law and under grace. This last contrast is supported by the numerological structure of *Paradise Regained*. Thus, the work is not realism, but ritual drama; and the audience identifies with the main character, not as with a limited mortal, but as with a culture hero.

MODERN CRITICISM of *Paradise Regained* could be described as an attempt to rescue the poem from the relative disfavor into which it had fallen by reading it as a neo-Shakespearean drama with a psychological conflict between two realistic characters, Satan and Christ, in which the first is defeated and the second gains knowledge through the experience and is confirmed in his vocation.[1] Some objections have recently been made to this view, but the alternative readings proposed (for instance, *Paradise Regained* as pure ritual or as Platonic dialogue),[2] while containing their measure of truth, do not seem to explain satisfactorily much of what happens in this rather unusual poem. I should like in this article, then, to approach the problems of Milton's brief epic through a consideration of Milton's Christ in terms of his role as the second

Adam, a reading that offers an alternative to some current conceptions of what happens in the poem.

That the Christ of *Paradise Regained* is to be viewed as the
second Adam is the main thrust of Milton's induction:

> I who erewhile the happy garden sung,
> By one man's disobedience lost, now sing
> Recovered Paradise to all mankind,
> By one man's firm obedience fully tried
> Through all temptation, and the Tempter foiled
> In all his wiles, defeated and repulsed,
> And Eden raised in the waste wilderness.[3]

During the poem Milton extends his typology to include many other
figures who were types of Christ, making particularly important
parallels with Job (as has been admirably demonstrated by Barbara
Lewalski).[4] But the primary comparison, even though not always
stressed directly, remains throughout that between Adam and
Christ. Milton, after pointing out the parallel at the beginning of the
poem, could have assumed that his readers would make the necessary connections elsewhere, not only because the Adam-Christ figure was the most commonly used typology in seventeenth-century
literature and theology, but also because he had titled his poem
Paradise Regained, which seems to invite a direct comparison between the main characters of the two Miltonic epics.

But more than that, Milton's title invites a contrast, for it is a
reversal of the name of the earlier epic. Appreciating the real importance of the Adam-Christ link in *Paradise Regained* requires a
recognition of the fact that theologically this typology was far more
important as an antithesis than as a parallel. As Martin Luther
phrased it: "Therefore Adam is an image of Christ, as Paul says in
Rom. 5:14 where he enlarges on both. However, the latter is far
better and different, indeed, it effects the direct opposite of what its
antitype, Adam, effected."[5] It is oppositions that Milton stresses in
his title and induction: oppositions between the old and the new
Eden, between the first and the second Adam. Even the rhetoric of
the induction uses antithetical structure along with parallels to
emphasize this point. The origin of the typological contrasts between Adam and Christ is in the origin of the typology itself. In 1
Corinthians, chapter xv, for instance, Adam is described as "natural"

man and Christ as "spiritual," Adam as "of the earth," Christ as "the Lord from heaven." In Romans v, 14, Paul says that Adam brought death into the world, but Christ came to remove it. In all of these biblical ways the Christ of *Paradise Regained* is set against the first Adam, and he is in other ways as well dramatically opposed to the Adam of *Paradise Lost.*

Several contrasts might be made, such as that between Adam's culpability in his passion for his wife in *Paradise Lost* and even Satan's recognition that Christ could not be tempted by these means in *Paradise Regained;* but one major contrast, highly important in the interpretation of *Paradise Regained* and functioning both theologically and dramatically in the poem, is that between Adam's fallibility and the infallibility of Christ. The point needs to be stressed because much recent criticism seems to have adopted, though sometimes in modified or implied ways, Barbara Lewalski's argument that "for the encounter between Christ and Satan to constitute a genuine dramatic action and a real conflict, Christ's character must be conceived in such a way that the test or temptation is real: he must be able to fall, must be capable of growth, and must be genuinely (not just apparently) uncertain of himself" (p. 135). Lewalski goes on to argue that Milton's Christ does indeed meet these criteria for dramatic action.

Two of the eighteenth-century editors of *Paradise Regained* made the same reading of Christ's character and suspected Milton of being a Socinian or, to quote Warton, "at least an Arian."[6] However, theologically and dramatically the Christ of Milton's poem is incapable of falling, nor does he ever suspect it possible that he might. Milton's Christ cannot fail because his success has been divinely predestined. This is quite different from the temptations of Adam and Eve, whose fall was only foreknown, not predestined by God. Milton's Christ had, of course, free will, since all creatures in Milton's theology (and Christ was for him a creature) had such freedom; but freedom of the will is not important to *Paradise Regained* as it was to *Paradise Lost.* Indeed, freedom of the will is never directly mentioned in the second epic; it is God's will that gets the emphasis.

Milton himself, in his role of narrator, tells the reader early on in the first book of *Paradise Regained* that Christ's success is predestined. In describing Satan's journey to the Jordan to subvert "this man of men, attested Son of God" (I, 122), Milton comments, "But contrary unweeting he fulfilled / The purposed counsel *preordained and fixed* / Of the Most High" (I, 126–28, italics added). God himself then informs the angels of the certain outcome of the event. He describes it, not as a test, but as an "exercise" in which Christ "shall first lay down the rudiments / Of his great warfare, ere I send him forth / To conquer Sin and Death" (I, 156–59). The frame of reference is military; but it is a war game, not a real battle, that is anticipated, a preparation for the real thing which will come later. The angels listening have no doubt of the outcome: "The Father knows the Son; therefore secure / Ventures his filial virtue, though untried, / Against whate'er may tempt" (I, 176–78). It was even before the Fall in *Paradise Lost* that God willed the eventual salvation of man ("and," as he says elsewhere, "what I will is fate" [*PL* VII, 173]). Nor is it a contradiction in Milton's theology that he presents Christ's victory as predestined; in both Book III of *Paradise Lost* and in *Christian Doctrine* Milton had stressed the ability of God to destine events so that they will produce good, and to select some individuals "of peculiar grace / Elect above the rest" (*PL* III, 183–84).

All of this, given to the reader prior to the temptations, makes a dramatic interest in whether or not Christ will succeed rather difficult to maintain. It would be hard to argue that the reader is expected to suspend suddenly his knowledge of the preordained outcome at line 182 of Book I and observe Christ simply as a man facing a trial. We know throughout that he is more than just a man, and he knows it as well. He has had a heavenly announcement that he was God's "belovèd Son" (I, 32) or, as he remembers it later, "his belovèd Son, in whom alone / He was well pleased" (I, 285–86); and his reading of Scripture has told him something of this even before. He does not put off his divinity to behave solely as a man. Though there was, as Elizabeth Pope has pointed out, a tradition for regarding Christ in this episode of his life as acting only as a man, there were as well traditions opposed to such a view (also acknowledged by Pope).[7] That Milton believed Christ acted solely *quasi homo* during the temptations is a modern critical assumption that cannot be demonstrated from the poem or from Milton's other works. Milton answers for himself in *Christian Doctrine:*

Once his two natures have coalesced hypostatically into a single person, whatever Christ says of himself he must say it (unless he makes a distinction himself) not as if he possessed one nature or the other, but as a whole person speaking about a whole person. Those who take it upon themselves to tear apart this hypostatical union, as it is called, rob Christ's speeches and replies of all sincerity. They substitute for Christ an unknown quantity, now one person, now another, and everything it says is ambiguous and uncertain, true and false at the same time. When dealing with such opponents, one may aptly ask Horace's question: With what knot shall I hold this face-changing Proteus?[8]

There is nothing the Christ of *Paradise Regained* does as a man that he could not also have done as a member of the Godhead. Some things he says and does indicate that he is at least no ordinary man. That he goes without food for forty days and does not hunger shows him as neither God nor man, since divine intervention applies. As John Calvin said, "God worked a great miracle when he released His Son from the necessity of eating."[9] That he finally does hunger makes it no more certain that he is behaving as a man, for, as Milton went to great lengths to explain in *Paradise Lost*, eating and hunger are characteristic of heavenly creatures as well as earthly. "And food alike those pure / Intelligential substances require / As doth your rational," says Raphael (V, 407–09), and then falls to "with keen dispatch / Of real hunger" (436–37). Christ's words to Satan during the banquet temptation ("I can at will, doubt not, as soon as thou, / Command a table in this wilderness, / And call swift flights of angels ministrant, / Arrayed in glory, on my cup to attend" [II, 383–86]) demonstrate conclusively that the Christ of *Paradise Regained* sees himself and presents himself to Satan as something more than a higher form of Adamic man. It is the power of Christ's *will* to perform miracles that is being asserted at this point. He does not distinguish between his two natures even in his words from the top of the pinnacle (an argument that I shall take up again later).

Another important way in which the Christ of *Paradise Regained* is a reversal of at least the fallen Adam of *Paradise Lost* is in the type of knowledge that is available to him. One of the main purposes of Michael's narration to Adam in the last books of *Paradise Lost* is to supply historical knowledge as a substitute for the great intuitive knowledge Adam had, according to Milton and rabbinic tradition, before the Fall. *Paradise Regained* reverses the learning process of *Paradise Lost*. The growth of Christ's knowledge began with the study of the law and especially of those typological parallels with Christ that Adam saw as future events but Christ studied in the past. However, the Christ we meet in *Paradise Regained* has already augmented that historical knowledge with divine intuition. There is little he has left to learn when he goes into the wilderness.

The soliloquy in the desert (I, 196–294) deals with Christ's growth of knowledge; it is all in the past tense. Christ tells the reader that some time ago (it is mentioned just after the visit to the temple "ere yet my age / Had measured twice six years" [209–10]) he had thought about "victorious deeds" (215):

> To rescue Israel from the Roman yoke,
> Then to subdue and quell o'er all the earth
> Brute violence and proud tyrannic pow'r,
> Till truth were freed, and equity restored;
> Yet held it more humane, more heavenly, first
> By winning words to conquer willing hearts,
> And make persuasion do the work of fear.   (217–23)

Having made this decision already, he cannot be said to make it subsequently when tempted by Satan with military power. Christ knows that he is the fulfillment of all the prophecies concerning the Messiah that he has read (I, 262). He knows that he alone is the chosen Son of God (284–87) and that it is now time for his ministry to begin. What, then, can Satan really offer or Christ learn except minor things? All Christ is unsure about is why he is drawn into the wilderness, but the answer to this he trusts to revealed knowledge: "For what concerns my knowledge God reveals" (293). All of this is at the beginning of the forty days in the wilderness, and Satan does not appear until after those days are over. His thoughts during these forty days, we are told, are all along the same lines as those in the soliloquy (299–302).

Toward the end of Book I, Christ informs Satan that "God hath now sent his living Oracle / Into the world, to teach his *final will*" (460–61, italics added), which would also indicate that he has knowledge of his mission already. After the first temptation Christ again

> Into himself descended, and at once
> All his great work to come before him set:
> How to begin, how to accomplish best
> His end of being on earth, and mission high.   (II, 111–14)

This is not in question form, and it is presented as an instantaneous event rather than as part of a reasoning process. Christ is by this point fully aware of his vocation and knows that it will be a spiritual, not a material, victory he will seek. Critics seem sometimes to forget that the narrative portions of *Paradise Regained* present *two* events in the life of Christ, the baptism as well as the temptation. It was traditionally the baptism, not the temptation, that was regarded as the beginning of Christ's public mission, though the temptation could be seen as a secondary confirmation of it. As Thomas Becon glossed it in the sixteenth century: "Christ, although sent down for that purpose, took not on him the office of preaching till he was openly called of his heavenly Father, having his vocation confirmed by a visible sign of the Holy Ghost, which came down from heaven upon him in the likeness of a dove."[10]

That Milton accepted this view of the baptism is confirmed by a major change he makes in the Bible story. Where all the scriptural accounts have Christ going directly from the baptism to the wilderness, Milton has his Christ remain "some days" (I, 183) in Bethabara where he spends the time, not only in meditation, but also in talking and lodging with Andrew and Simon (II, 6–7), who were by this convinced that Christ was the Messiah, that God had "sent his Anointed, and to us revealed him, / By his great Prophet, pointed at and shown, / In public, and with him we have conversed" (II, 50–52).[11] They do not yet know the spiritual emphasis of Christ's mission; but Milton's Christ does and has already publicly begun it. Milton links the baptism with the temptation for the same reasons that they were often linked in commentary, because both were regarded as fulfillments of the law and as examples to be followed by every man.

Christ's knowledge is, as I have said, largely revealed knowledge. Such knowledge has two forms: scriptural revelation and direct revelation from on high. Milton calls attention to both. That many of Christ's responses are divine revelations is evident not only from his direct claim to such revelation, quoted earlier, but also from the form some of his speeches take: questions that he answers himself within the same speech.[12] Christ also is able, through this kind of intuitive knowledge, to penetrate the disguise of Satan.[13] But more important for the ordinary man and for the poem is revealed knowledge communicated by way of the Scriptures. Milton, like some of the earlier commentators, takes the fact that the Christ of the Bible answers Satan with scriptural quotation and expands this to a presentation of this type of knowledge as an adequate defense against the devil and superior to all other forms of knowledge short of direct revelation.

The importance of this shield provided by Scripture is part of the reason for the emphasis Milton places on Christ's early studies. It is also why the highest dramatic moment in the poem is reached in a scriptural quotation. Those readers who suggest that Christ reveals himself as a member of the Godhead in his answer from the pinnacle often leave out the first four words of Christ's speech: "*Also it is written,* / 'Tempt not the Lord thy God' " (IV, 560–61). Christ is asserting nothing about himself;[14] he is quoting. There is thus little ambiguity in the reply; at least Satan does not seem to have much time to work out any ambiguities before his fall. Though Milton chose to follow the order of the temptations in Luke, he makes this speech a modified version of that in Matthew: "It is written again, Thou shalt not tempt the Lord thy God" (iv, 6). The version in Luke was much more direct: "It is said *etc.*" (iv, 12). Milton's "also" delays the dramatic effect and calls attention to the fact that this is a quotation and related to the other quotations.[15] Satan's fall, then, is not the result of any direct announcement by Christ that he is the second member of the Trinity; it is rather the symbolic and type-fulfilling antithesis of Christ's miraculous stand.

As Adam's fall had raised Satan and his crew from hell to reside in middle air, so Christ's triumph dislodges him from that position. It is a foreshadowing of Satan's final fall, which will come after Christ's last victory; and it is also the lessening, the binding of Satan's powers that Christ's appearance in the world brought about. Satan's fall is as inevitable as Christ's triumph over the temptations. Both were predestined, and predestined so that they might serve as examples of what was to come and of how man should behave until the Second Coming.

The temptation has traditionally been regarded as an exemplum for every man. That is why biblical commentary stressed so heavily the nature of Christ as the second Adam in this episode, for as all men were involved in the sin of the first Adam, so all men are involved in the triumph of the last. It is not Christ who is really being attacked by

Satan in the temptation; it is, as Calvin said, "our salvation that he attacked in the Person of Christ."

I have no doubt that God displayed in the Person of His Son, as on a brilliant screen, how hostile and persistent an adversary Satan is against the salvation of man. . . . So as often as Satan attacks us, let us remember that we can in no other way sustain and repulse his assaults than by the protection of that shield.[16]

This aspect of the temptation meant little, however, until after the Crucifixion. It was only then that by Christ's imputed righteousness man could be saved. Thus, for the time being, the deed remained "in secret done" (I, 15), example only to the angels of what would later be an example to all men (I, 163–67). The way this event would become known to all men was, of course, through the Scriptures.

One other major contrast between the first Adam and the second which should be noticed is that contained in the contrast between man under the law and man under grace. The Christ of *Paradise Regained* is involved in both, for, as Milton emphasized in *Paradise Lost*, mercy does not eliminate justice. Adam fell under the law but had the promise of grace; Christ brought grace but also fulfilled the law—and fulfilling the law was an impossible task for anyone except Christ.

The superimposition of law and grace is pointed up in one way by the numerical structure of the epic. The four-book structure was chosen for the brief biblical epic, as Barbara Lewalski has noted, because of the parallel with the four gospels. Four, then, is a number representing the New Law, the covenant of grace. Within this four-book structure Milton has set ten linked temptations arranged in the following order:

Book I: Stones-to-bread temptation
Book II: Banquet temptation
          Riches temptation
Book III: Glory temptation
          Throne-of-Israel temptation
          Parthia temptation
Book IV: Rome temptation
          Learning-of-Greece temptation
          Storm temptation
          Pinnacle-of-temple temptation[17]

The number of temptations in each book appears to be equal to the number of that book, thus providing one kind of dramatic build-up in the accelerating imposition of temptations. All of these are temptations under the law, and ten is of course the number of the Decalogue, the "ten words" of Moses, here set against the divine Word. There is a precedent for this numerological interpretation of the temptation in Ludolphus de Saxonia's *Vita Jesu Christi:*

> Quadraginta autem diebus et quadraginta noctibus Dominus jejunavit; quia quadragenarius numerus ex quatuor constat et decem: quater enim decem vel decies quatuor, faciunt quadraginta. Per quatuor autem Novum Testamentum, quod in quatuor Evangelistis consistit, significatur; per decem vero Vetus, quia in mandatis Legis continetur. Quadraginta ergo diebus jejunare, est utriusque Testamenti praecepta servare.

> [So the Lord was fasting for forty days and forty nights; because the number forty is made up of four and ten: for four times ten, or ten times four, makes forty. Now by four is signified the New Testament, which is based upon the four Evangelists; and by ten is signified the Old Testament, because within it is contained the commandments of the Law. Therefore, to fast for forty days is to obey the precepts of each Testament.][18]

A new edition of Ludolphus had been published in Lyons in 1642.

The numbers four and ten are emphasized by Milton in other ways as well; for instance, in the forty days' wandering in the wilderness, which Christ rather awkwardly refers to as "four times ten days" (II, 245). There seems also to be an attempt to call attention to the number ten in the rhetoric of Book IV. Satan in his speeches tends to catalogue things in rather cumbersome groups of ten:

> Since neither *wealth*, nor *honor, arms* nor *arts*,
> *Kingdom* nor *empire* pleases thee, nor aught
> By me proposed in *life contemplative*,
> Or *active*, tended on by *glory*, or *fame*,
> What dost thou in this world?
>
> · · · · · · · ·
>
> *Sorrows*, and *labors, opposition, hate*,
> Attends thee, *scorns, reproaches, injuries*,
> *Violence* and *stripes*, and lastly cruel *death*.
>   (IV, 368–72, 386–88, italics added)

And Christ lays down the law to Satan in his last speech from the pinnacle in ten words. Thus, in the events, structure, and rhetoric of *Paradise Regained*, the life of Christ encompasses grace and the law.

As Adam is visited by angels before his fall, so Christ is visited by the angels following his triumph. Their songs again point up the Adam-Christ antithesis:

> Now thou hast avenged
> Supplanted Adam, and by vanquishing
> Temptation hast regained lost Paradise,
> And frustrated the conquest fraudulent.
> He never more henceforth will dare set foot
> In Paradise to tempt; his snares are broke.
> For though that seat of earthly bliss be failed,
> A fairer Paradise is founded now
> For Adam and his chosen sons, whom thou
> A Saviour art come down to reinstall;
> Where they shall dwell secure, when time shall be
> Of tempter and temptation without fear.   (IV, 606–17)

The angels go on to interpret this event as a foreshadowing of the future victories of Christ over Satan. The "fairer Paradise . . . founded now" will not be fully realized until "time shall be / Of tempter and temptation without fear." It is not the paradise within that has been established here so much as the paradise beyond, which will come to fulfillment in its proper time. This has been the first step in that establishment, not an interval after the baptism. The foundations have been laid, not for Christ, but for man: "Now enter, and begin to save mankind" (IV, 635).

Milton's seventeenth-century readers would have needed no more than the initial emphasis on the Adam-Christ typology in order for them to identify with Christ. They knew that as all men were involved in Adam, so all were involved in Christ. Christ went through the temptations in the wilderness to give an example to every man of how temptations should be met; but more important than that, he went through them so that men would not have to meet the Devil's tempting power in such direct confrontations. Because Christ bore for us the brunt of Satan's assault, Satan was forever thereafter restrained in his dealings with men. It is this surrogate action by Christ that linked the temptation to the Crucifixion for Milton and his contemporaries. As Jeremy Taylor said of the temptation:

As soon as it was permitted to the devil to tempt our Lord, he, like fire, had no power to suspend his act, but was entirely determined by the fulness of his malice as a natural agent by the appetites of nature; that we may know to whom we owe the happiness of all those hours and days of peace in which we sit under the trees of paradise, and see no serpent encircling the branches and presenting us with fair fruits to ruin us. It is the mercy of God we have the quietness of a minute; for if the devil's chain were taken off, he would make our very beds a torment, our tables to be a snare, our sleeps fantastic, lustful, and illusive, and every sense should have an object of delight and danger, a hyena to kiss, and to perish in its embraces. But the holy Jesus having been assaulted by the devil and felt his malice by the experiments of humanity, is become so merciful a High priest, and so sensible of our sufferings and danger by the apprehensions of compassion, that He hath put a hook in the nostrils of Leviathan.[19]

It is this aspect of Christ's life that makes possible George Herbert's response to his temptations:

> Yet when the houre of thy designe
> To answer these fine things shall come;
> Speak not at large; say, I am thine:
> And then they have their answer home.[20]

I doubt that Milton even questioned whether his readers could identify imaginatively with Christ, though modern critics have found this one of the main problems of the epic. Such identification, however, was one of the "givens" of the tradition in which Milton was working. Of course, no man is as good as Christ, but the imitation of Christ was always understood to have limits, for Christ is always more than just an example. Christ in *Paradise Regained* is teaching us to use Scripture against temptation; but even more important, he is using it for us. The point lies in the concept of imputed righteousness. We watch a defeat of the devil in what is ultimately, to cite Calvin again, an attack on our salvation. Because Christ is victorious in this second of his three battles with Satan, we know he will win the last as well, for that is the way typology works. Because Christ takes on our sins and meets the devil for us, we can be saved. Christ is not regaining paradise for himself in this poem; he is regaining salvation for the reader and doing so both under the law and through grace. Thus, we identify with Christ as we do with any dramatic hero who embodies the ideal virtues of a people and who uses those virtues in their defense.

Even though the work is an epic poem, it deserves to be treated as a drama. Indeed, aside from a few descriptive and narrative passages, the epic is nearly all in dialogue. But it must be recognized what sort of drama this is. It is not a realistic drama of psychologically complex characters engaged in an intellectual struggle for an uncertain victory. It is a biblical drama, a ritual drama, which is also (it should be added) something more than simply a ritual. Because we as readers are expected to be totally familiar with the main events and characters and even some of the speeches, their appearance in *Paradise Regained* is ritual. But because Milton has changed the story, has added some things and has been very specific about others, we are constantly being dramatically surprised. In fact, not only are the changes and additions thrown into relief by their appearance within a ritual performance, but they emphasize the author's interpretation of the story and force us to meet it in terms of these glosses and not with the soothing effects of ritual.

I think most readers of the seventeenth century would have been pleased with what they saw (even though they might have liked *Paradise Lost* better). Compared with other treatments of the story, *Paradise Regained* is dramatically forceful while remaining doctrinally moderate. Where John Bale, in his play on the temptation, went to great lengths to show that Christ's long fast was not one of the things in the story to be imitated, a very Protestant view of the matter, Milton has one short speech:

> That fast
> To virtue I impute not, or count part
> Of what I suffer here; if nature need not,
> Or God support nature without repast
> Though needing, what praise is it to endure?   (II, 247–51)

Where the pseudo-Bonaventura's *Life of Christ* stressed heavily the Savior's return home to his mother after the temptation, even to the point of claiming that the food the angels brought Jesus came from Mary, Milton has only those moving last two lines of the poem: "He unobserved / Home to his mother's house private returned," lines which call attention to the as yet private nature of this act of his public mission, an act that combined the aspects of his active and contemplative life and would be recorded in Scripture for the benefit of all men.

The University of Western Australia

NOTES

1. For a summary of current opinion on *Paradise Regained,* see Arthur E. Barker, "Calm Regained Through Passion Spent: The Conclusions of the Miltonic Effort," in *The Prison and the Pinnacle: Papers to Commemorate the Tercentenary of "Paradise Regained" and "Samson Agonistes" 1671–1971,* ed. Balachandra Rajan (London, 1973), pp. 3–48.

Walter MacKellar's *Variorum Commentary on the Poems of John Milton,* vol. 4, *Paradise Regained* (New York and London, 1975) was not available to me until this article was in press. I wish to note, however, that MacKellar also, in his introduction, points out passages in *Paradise Regained* that show Christ to have knowledge of his own divinity (see pp. 36–37). MacKellar maintains, nonetheless, that in spite of these repeated assertions of divinity, "Christ in his divine nature cannot be tempted" and thus "it is Christ the *man,* meeting trials on a strictly human level, whom we are to witness" (p. 35). MacKellar does not resolve this apparent contradiction.

2. Jackson I. Cope, "*Paradise Regained*: Inner Ritual," in *Milton Studies,* I, ed. James D. Simmonds (Pittsburgh, 1969), pp. 51–65; Irene Samuel, "The Regaining of Paradise," in *Prison and the Pinnacle,* pp. 111–34.

3. *PR* I, 1–7, *The Complete Poetical Works of John Milton,* ed. Douglas Bush (Boston, 1965). All citations of Milton's poetry refer to this edition.

4. The classic article on the typology of *Paradise Regained* is that of Northrop Frye ("The Typology of *Paradise Regained*," *MP,* LIII [1956], 227–38). Because his purposes are different from mine, he refers only briefly to the Adam-Christ relationship. Barbara Kiefer Lewalski discusses the typology in *Milton's Brief Epic: The Genre, Meaning, and Art of "Paradise Regained"* (Providence, 1966), pp. 164–82 *et passim.* She feels, however, that emphasis is drawn away from the Adam-Christ figure to point up the Job-Christ typology. But since Job, like Christ, was seen as a reversal of Adam, the references to Job could be taken as a means to reinforce the importance of the original typology.

5. *Luther's Works,* ed. Hilton C. Oswald (St. Louis, 1973), XXVIII, 113.

6. The other commentator was Calton. Both base their judgments on Book I, lines 163–67. They are cited in Henry J. Todd's edition of *The Poetical Works of John Milton* (London, 1809; reprint ed., New York, 1970), vol. 5, pp. 26–27.

7. *"Paradise Regained": The Tradition and the Poem* (1947; reprint ed., New York, 1962).

8. *Complete Prose Works of John Milton,* ed. Don M. Wolfe et al. (New Haven, 1953–), vol. VI, p. 228.

9. *A Harmony of the Gospels Matthew, Mark and Luke,* trans. A. W. Morrison (Edinburgh, 1972), vol. I, p. 135.

10. *Prayers and Other Pieces of Thomas Becon,* ed. Rev. John Ayre (Cambridge, 1844), p. 505. The baptism would also have been important for Milton's poem because baptism was a type of the entrance into paradise.

11. This change was probably based, as Dr. Newton pointed out in the eighteenth century, on John, chapter 1.

12. See, for example, II, 245–59 or III, 188–97. The thoughts of the disciples and Mary sometimes follow this same pattern also.

13. The reader should perhaps assume that Christ also penetrates the falseness of the visions Satan presents; for, unlike what Michael shows to Adam in *Paradise Lost,*

Satan's visions are unreal. When Satan leaves for the second temptation, he takes with him

> a chosen band
> Of Spirits likest to himself in guile
> To be at hand, and at his beck appear,
> If cause were to unfold some active scene
> Of various persons, each to know his part.   (II, 236–40)

The scenes Satan presents are, then, like the shades of Alexander and Helen in Marlowe's *Faustus*, devils in disguise, which surely Christ recognizes, though for the sake of argument he does not question their reality. Such unreal things could hardly be tempting to Christ.

14. In this I am in agreement with Irene Samuel, "Regaining of Paradise."

15. For a view that this "also" makes the lines *more* effective dramatically, see Lee Sheridan Cox, "Food-Word Imagery in Paradise Regained," *ELH*, XXVIII (1961), 225–43.

16. *Harmony of the Gospels*, vol. I, p. 135.

17. I am aware of the effort that has been made to group the events of this poem under the "triple equation" of biblical temptations. While Milton may have intended such a grouping to be made, it is more important to observe that he, like some of the Church Fathers, did not feel confined to the belief that Satan offered only those three temptations given in the Bible. Noting each of Satan's attempts separately produces the list I give here.

18. Ed. L. M. Rigollot (Paris and Brussels, 1878), pt. 1, vol. I, pp. 195–96.

19. *The Great Exempler*, in *The Whole Works of the Right Rev. Jeremy Taylor*, ed. Rev. Charles Page Eden (London, 1856), vol. II, p. 198.

20. "The Quip," in *The Works of George Herbert*, ed. F. E. Hutchinson (Oxford, 1941), p. 111.

6038021

D1715279

WITHDRAWN

Moral Animals

Moral Animals

Ideals and Constraints in Moral Theory

CATHERINE WILSON

CLARENDON PRESS · OXFORD

OXFORD

UNIVERSITY PRESS

Great Clarendon Street, Oxford OX2 6DP

Oxford University Press is a department of the University of Oxford.
It furthers the University's objective of excellence in research, scholarship,
and education by publishing worldwide in

Oxford   New York

Auckland Bangkok Buenos Aires Cape Town Chennai
Dar es Salaam Delhi Hong Kong Istanbul Karachi Kolkata
Kuala Lumpur Madrid Melbourne Mexico City Mumbai Nairobi
São Paulo Shanghai Taipei Tokyo Toronto

Oxford is a registered trade mark of Oxford University Press
in the UK and in certain other countries

Published in the United States
by Oxford University Press Inc., New York

British Library Cataloguing in Publication Data
Data available

Library of Congress Cataloging in Publication Data
Data available

ISBN 0-19-926767-7

1 3 5 7 9 10 8 6 4 2

Typeset by Kolam Information Services Pvt. Ltd, Pondicherry, India
Printed in Great Britain
on acid-free paper by
Biddles Ltd., King's Lynn, Norfolk

To my maternal grandparents,
Harry Helson (1898–1977) and Lida G. Helson (1900–1979)
in memoriam

Preface

The aims of this book are first, to furnish a foundation for moral theory that is independent of any particular set of moral commitments and second, to defend a particular version of egalitarianism on that foundation. Though meta-ethics and political philosophy can be and are often treated independently, there is a reason for offering a content-neutral theory of moral judgement and moral practice along with a defence of particular normative claims. The most powerful arguments against egalitarianism in contemporary moral theory gain much of their force from the ostensibly non-normative theories of the place of the self in the world and the allied accounts of the nature of moral judgement that frame them.

Moral judgements, according to the descriptive theory advanced here, form a subset of normative judgements. Unlike aesthetic and non-moral practical judgements regarding what ought to be done, they reflect the endorsement of advantage-reducing rules on the part of those who assert them. Moral rules are rules, one might say, for not getting ahead. Morality is the system laid down to compensate for the wear and tear that is the unavoidable by-product of our ordinary strivings, through the imposition of certain sacrifices and deprivations.

This might seem puzzling. Though the fiercer and darker aspects of morality were emphasized by anthropologists earlier in the century, what might be termed Freudian pessimism has lost ground to a conception of morality as a source of human flourishing. The motivation behind this equation is understandable; the prohibitory taboos of our ancestors are viewed with scepticism if not dismay, and there can be no doubt that our opportunities and well-being depend on the moral behaviour of others towards us, especially their veracity, impartiality, and benevolence. Yet, the relationship between morality and flourishing is mediate and qualified, not direct and unqualified. Observing the norms of finance, cookery, decorating, and intimate relationships helps us to live good human lives, while meritocratic institutions enable us to parlay our talents and attributes into wealth and influence. Morality, as Kant speculated, is for something other than worldly success, though it is not necessarily for the expression of our rationality or the use of our noumenal wills. Platitudes regarding human

flourishing obscure much of what is interesting and difficult in morality and in moral theory. How many of us can claim that the breaking of an agreement, or some show of partiality, or some occlusion of the truth, has never helped us to carry on with our lives as we wished to, and that moral considerations have never held us up?

Humans are disposed to invent, observe, and enforce advantage-reducing rules of varying degrees of stringency, and they hold high status in the hierarchy of social norms. Yet, as we might expect given their origins, there is considerable disagreement as to how far agents can reasonably be required to restrain and suppress the operation of their natural and acquired powers for their own enjoyment and benefit. In my local culture, for example, we agree that one may not walk into unlocked houses and make off with people's television sets, but we do not agree on whether the manufacturers of television sets may set their wages at whatever level they find to be most profitable. We agree that the well-off have some responsibility for the sick, poorly educated, and demoralized members of the underclass, but we disagree on how far their needs should cut into our enjoyments. We believe that persons should enjoy the attentions of one spouse at a time, no matter how many others they could attract and maintain with money or savoir-faire, but we disagree over their entitlement to non-marital friendship or adventure. Different codes enjoin different degrees of advantage renunciation on members of the communities bound by them or individuals who subscribe to them. Morality is, in this respect, scalar.

First-order moral argument is sometimes aimed at establishing what to do when advantage-reducing rules conflict in a moral emergency. The obligation to do all that one can to save a life may conflict with the duty not to prolong someone's suffering by employing showy medical expertise. But first-order arguments are often addressed simply to the question how moral to be. Moral rules are such that we often feel burdened by them, resist them, and produce what are often plausible justifications for our non-compliance, even when there is no emergency and no conflict between competing obligations. Strict adherence to a principle of veracity can be highly disadvantageous to an agent; loyalty to difficult and demanding friends can prove exhausting; and requests from worthwhile charitable organizations can be irritating. We are faced, in other words, with the problem of exigency. When can aesthetic, prudential, or simple hedonic considerations justify an exemption from an obligation that has been assumed by an agent, or that is held to be generally binding? Are we really required to act as the

famous modern moral theories, such as Kantianism and utilitarianism, say we must?

The argument that the burdens these theories impose—including the burden of submitting all one's proposed courses of action to the test of an impersonal theory—are too great for human beings as they are constituted by nature is frequently cited as a defeater of their seemingly exigent requirements, particularly with regard to issues of social justice. Weaker aspirations with respect to socio-economic and sexual equality have been a striking feature of recent prescriptive moral theory and the reasoning behind this lowering of demand levels has been set out with formidable intelligence in books and articles published over the last two decades and is documented below. No contemporary moral theorist has presented these meta-ethical and substantive issues with greater force and clarity than Bernard Williams, who died as this book was undergoing its last set of revisions.

Williams's meta-ethical scepticism with regard to moral realism and demonstrable obligations is defended here as well founded. To a large extent, it is up to each of us how moral we want to be and what sacrifices we are willing to incur. Moral theorizing is constrained by what we want, now, not what our ideally rational selves ought to want, and by what we find it easy and difficult to do. Nevertheless, it is possible to preserve a good deal more of the revisionary content of the famous modern moral theories than Williams and other critics believed to be possible.

To meet the sceptic's objection to the very idea of an obligation that could be independent of an agent's motivational state, I offer a modal theory of moral judgements that bypasses the question whether moral judgements or prescriptive theories can be true. The assertion that an action in a given context is obligatory has both representational and conative content. The representational content of a moral judgement is given by an idealized moral world. Roughly, to assert that action *ACT* is obligatory in circumstances *c* is to claim that, in a morally good world otherwise like ours, agents all do *ACT* in *c*. A satisfactory theory of morals is a representation of an ideal world that is, all things considered, with respect to its advantage-reducing behaviour, preferable to rival worlds instantiating different behaviour. Though we have no direct access to ideal worlds, only to our own, imperfect one, moral judgements are in principle confirmable. Theorists with different prescriptive commitments disagree on what things are like in a good world. They advance their favoured candidates, projecting paraworlds, fictional worlds for which both verisimilitude and moral goodness are implicitly claimed,

and argue that they are the best. Though the account offered here has significant conceptual connections with both modern contractualism and modern consequentialism, it is formally distinct from them both.

One is obliged to do what a theory says, to the extent that it has been confirmed, but no further. Unconfirmed moral judgements are mere authored norms, with few or many adherents. The confirmation of a moral claim requires only the agreement of reasonable, competent, well-informed judges as to betterness relations between worlds, not agreement as to what the criteria of betterness are. Analogously, confirmation in physics requires agreement by competent judges about a physical phenomenon, not about confirmation theory, a technical branch of philosophy of science or statistics. This simplification of the prescriptive theorist's task ought to be welcome, for it is no easy matter to gain agreement on betterness relations between paraworlds.

Later chapters discuss the problem of exigency in terms of the subjective costs to agents of conforming to particular rules or policies. Heavy subjective costs tend to disqualify policies, but counterweight principles tend to override agent's concerns about costs to themselves. Prescriptive moralists avail themselves of the argument from heavy costs to justify lower demand levels and counterweight principles to justify higher demand levels than an assumed set point. Acceptable moral rules need not be universal and can be relativized to particular reference classes. But prescriptive proposals, even if they arise from within particular cultural settings and reflect the concerns of creatures known to be partial to themselves and to kith and kin, presuppose a detached perspective. There is an anonymity requirement on moral theorizing, a distinct intellectual pursuit with its own methodology that is different from the activity of merely deciding what one is going to do. The requirement implies that the endorsement and propagation of norms that differentially serve the interests of the particular reference class that endorses and propagates the norm qualifies as ideology, not moral theory proper. For, in virtue of knowing that we have powerful interests in how things go for us as individuals, we know about ourselves that we are disposed to look for compromises between moral formulas of obligation and self- or class-interest and that we tend to seek exceptions to prima facie obligations in the form of exemptions and privileges. The anonymity requirement carries no implication to the effect that agents in our world exist in a state of empirical equality. Indeed, the chief reason for adopting it is the observation that they do not.

With this meta-ethical framework in place, I turn to a discussion of social equality. The presupposition in force is that conditions of social dominance in which some members of human societies have worse lives—less access to resources, more anxiety, less leisure, worse health—are rooted in our primate heritage and are exacerbated by technological progress. Human beings are inclined to coerce others and to take advantage of their labour when they are able to do so and both the descriptive and prescriptive sectors of moral theory must build on this assumption. My argument is that morality steps in where nature and the marketplace fail. The existence of moral practices and motivations, in other words, presupposes, not a condition of natural equality, as Hobbes imagined, but a condition of natural and acquired inequality, in which agents possess, temporarily or over the long term, natural or situational advantages, including superior strength, intelligence, knowledge, beauty, alliances, power, or wealth.

To wear down the intuition that moral agents exist in a state of natural equality, I employ two characters, A_1 and A_2, who engage in various transactions. They are equals in their enjoyment of basic human goods and states, but one of them is *primus inter pares*. A_1 and A_2 cooperate for Hobbesian reasons—because conflict is expensive and they want to increase their productive capacity—but their decision to cooperate rather than compete does not make their relationship morally adequate. The initial moment of cooperation announces the beginning of their moral problems, as our interdependency has multiplied ours.

Where social dominance once depended on ferocity, charisma, birth, or alliance, alone or in combination with one another, modern institutions reward competence at specialized tasks with power. Presumed competence is associated in modern societies with the differential enjoyment of authority, prestige, and well-being. Some degree of variance in well-being produced by meritocratic sorting is, I try to show, defensible. Worlds that reward meritorious performance are better than similar worlds that allocate surplus resources according to other protocols. Yet existing distributive systems fall well short of what can be considered just. For, in the first place, large sectors of humanity do not participate in these meritocratic systems. Second, while the tendency of modern institutions to understand merit as specialist competence, rather than as ferocity, charisma, birth, or alliance, points to the role of moral influences that moderate crude advantage-taking, meritocratic systems can remain undermoralized. The modern market economy, and the relationships of employer and employee, investor

and worker, husband and wife to be found within it, represent the modification by degrees of the earliest urban societies founded on two principles: the agricultural, building, and craft labour of large numbers of slaves of both sexes, and the domestic labour of nearly all women. The increase in circulating wealth and in the organization of productive power has a powerful, seemingly intrinsic tendency to increase inequality between classes and nations, and between men and women. It is naive to maintain that observed high variance with respect to well-being is the product of a carefully contrived and well-monitored utilitarian plan to improve the status of the worst-off, and that it is simultaneously the by-product of a well-functioning merit-reward system. It is simply the condition we have inherited, modified, and succeeded in partially moralizing.

The last three chapters are concerned with the fair division of the cooperative surplus and focus on the question how much variance in well-being is morally tolerable. They are linked with the descriptive account of the earlier chapters by the premiss that to have a moral concern is to be willing to accept a reduction of advantage to benefit another, and by the premiss that theory choice cannot reflect one's actual situation. A morally good world, it is argued, exhibits variations in well-being at the margins—with respect to access to the doubtful and speculative, but not possession of the known and necessary components of well-being. Statistical equality of outcomes is further defended as the only plausible test of fair procedures. The last chapter returns to the sociobiological themes of the opening to consider male–female relations, including love, as morally relevant phenomena. The strengths and weaknesses of the argument from heavy costs, as it has been advanced in recent years against the demand for greater social equality between men and women, are assessed in a way that I hope will encourage philosophers and social theorists to investigate more thoroughly the relationship between the constraints allegedly imposed by nature in our actual world and our sense of what is morally right.

Acknowledgements

Work on this manuscript was supported by the Canadian Social Sciences and Humanities Research Council. Many colleagues have discussed its contents with me and offered important criticisms, including Sam Black and Virginia Held. Scott Anderson, David Braybrooke, Avi Craimer, Edward Halper, Cynthia Holder, Peter Vranas, and David Zimmerman commented acutely on individual sections, repairing many deficiencies and errors, as did a number of anonymous referees. David Donaldson and Mukesh Eswaran of the Department of Economics at the University of British Columbia, and Sarah Hrdy of the Department of Anthropology at the University of California, Davis have contributed generously of their expertise. I am especially grateful to Husain Sarkar, who read an entire draft, offering detailed suggestions for improvement, and to my students, Johnna Fisher and Tim Christie, for proofreading and pointed queries. Mohan Matthen, always quick to see the shape of a problem, has been a valued interlocutor throughout the writing.

Permission to reprint previously published material is acknowledged with thanks from the following sources: Kluwer Publishing for 'The Role of a Merit Principle in Distributive Justice', *Journal of Ethics, 7* (2003), 1–38 and the University of Calgary Press for 'The Biological Basis and Ideational Superstructure of Morality', in Richmond Campbell and Bruce Hunter (eds.), *Naturalized Moral Epistemology, Canadian Journal of Philosophy suppl. vol.* (2000), 211–44.

Contents

1
Morality as a System of Advantage-Reducing Imperatives

The theory of morals divides into the descriptive theory of moral phenomena and moral judgement and the prescriptive theory of what we ought, morally, to do. Before treating of moral judgements in the abstract and addressing particular questions of right and wrong, it will be useful to give some attention to moral phenomena, descriptively considered.

The concept of morality is related to but not coextensive with the concepts of care and mutual assistance, both of which have their place in the non-human world. Yet more seems to be required for moral observance than the occurrence of actions-that-benefit-another or actions-that-benefit-the-collective. The care of the crow or the wolf for its offspring benefits them, as the warning call of the goose benefits the flock, without being moral. Ants and bees live in family groups whose members must interact with one another to reproduce, to feed, and to defend themselves and their young, but their cooperation is no more moral than is the symbiosis of tree and vine.

Nevertheless, the altruistic and cooperative behaviour exhibited by social animals has a precursor relationship to human morality. The psychological platform that enables an animal to suppress or moderate its impulses—especially its aggressive and proprietary impulses—is a necessary underpinning for morality as we understand it. However sophisticated or complicated by conditions and exceptions our moral beliefs are, whatever rationale in terms of long-term happiness and general flourishing we provide for them, and however great the satisfactions of morally appropriate behaviour may be, moral emotions and practices involve some degree of repression. An appreciation of this fundamental point is important for progress in the

prescriptive sector of the theory of morals as well as in the descriptive sectors.

1.1. A Platform for Human Morality

Consider the behaviour observed in modern social primates such as baboons and chimpanzees.[1] These animals have distinctive personalities and recognize each other as individuals. They know who their children are even after they are grown, and they have friendships and enmities. Their behaviour is characterized by patterns of loyalty, reciprocity, and revenge for injury or betrayal. The animals form coalitions and may come to one another's defence, but they also refuse at times to assist each other when help would be useful. They compete with one another, chasing and biting each other, snatching each other's food, or displacing one another from desirable resting places. They also retaliate against such interference and attack strangers. Both males and females—but principally females—look after the welfare of infants; there is also occasional infanticide by males, as well as loss of infants through bad mothering or carelessness.

The animals take an interest in the condition of their own and each other's skin and hair. They take turns grooming each other and can treat each other's splinters and abscesses with some success.[2] Aggressive interactions between males and males and between males and females are triggered by feeding competition, or represent redirected aggression towards another animal. Sometimes one animal harasses or attacks another for no evident reason.[3]

In these animals, biological flourishing is compatible with and perhaps depends on a combination of benign neglect, help, especially where the effort may be repaid in the future, and harm, especially where successful retaliation is unlikely. They are neither primarily

---

[1] These details are drawn from M. R. A. Chance and Clifford L. Jolly, *Social Groups of Apes, Monkeys and Men*; Barbara Smuts, *Sex and Friendship in Baboons*; and Wolfgang Koehler, *The Mentality of Apes*.

[2] Koehler describes how a chimpanzee removed a splinter from Koehler's own finger 'by two very skillful, but somewhat painful squeezes with his fingernails; he then examined my hand again very closely, and let it fall, satisfied with his work'. *Mentality of Apes*, 321–2. Koehler observes further that '[if] one is on friendly and familiar terms with an ape who has been injured—say by a bite—one can easily induce the creature to extend the injured limb or surface for inspection, by making the expressive sounds which indicate sorrow and regret, both among us and among the chimpanzees'. Ibid.

[3] Barbara Smuts, *Sex and Friendship in Baboons*, 90 ff.

selfish, nor primarily altruistic, neither exclusively partial to kin, nor indifferent to kinship relations. They are all these things, under different conditions, and different individuals possess these traits and dispositions in different measures. They react and respond to opportunities, threats, or changes in circumstances according to their present moods and temperaments, the perceived configuration of the situation, and their past relationships with others. What an animal does may not be the right solution to its immediate problem from the Darwinian point of view. The decision to stay and fight rather than to flee may result in death; the decision to mate now might result in its having no offspring who survive to maturity. Over the long run, however, the combination of personality traits and reactive habits, as these are distributed amongst individuals in an existing species, is adapted to the most frequent and the most critical situations they face.

There is little reason to ascribe moral beliefs or moral agency to animals that behave in this flexible manner. Only to the anthropomorphic eye are there paragons and reprobates amongst them. The animals cooperate—sometimes. Their cooperation is advantageous to them as individuals and to their kin—usually. They are aware of each other's needs, emotions, and intentions—to some extent. And human observers can easily develop affectionate relationships with individual animals. Yet there is no reason to call their animal society a moral one. This is not because the animals do not have language. For even if their behaviour was accompanied by verbalizations describing, sincerely or insincerely, their actions and intentions, this would not indicate that they had placed themselves under the particular restraints of morality. Nor is its absence explained by the animals' inability to ascribe mental states to others.

Missing from their orientation towards the social world is an interest in regulation as such. There is a certain kind of thought about themselves that the animals do not have, the thought that social interactions require the inhibition of spontaneous impulses, whether these impulses involve aggression or assistance. They may seek on occasion to control the social behaviour of others, breaking up fights or engaging in jealous interventions, and they may suppress their own reactions at times, but it cannot be said of them that they regard the whole field of social interactions as susceptible of moulding and

determination by themselves as agents. Analogously, it might be said that chimpanzees do not have aesthetic beliefs or engage in aesthetic practices, even if they draw or paint when given materials and opportunity, or decorate their bodies by draping them with ropes and branches. For they do not see the surfaces of the world—walls, containers, expanses of skin—as objectionably bare and as calling for remedial action.

When Hume[4] traces the origins of morality to a natural disposition to perform just and benevolent actions, to approve just and benevolent actions in others, and to attribute merit to those who perform them, he expresses the view that morality is not exemplified simply in the performance of actions that happen to benefit others, but requires a social system that regards actions as items for judgement and criticism. A Humean might nevertheless protest against the claim that morality presupposes reflective awareness of social interaction as a field requiring control of natural tendencies by arguing as follows: Suppose we were to happen on a group of social creatures somewhat like humans who possessed speech and reason. Relationships between members of the group appeared to be friendly and affectionate, characterized by mutual assistance and devoid of the conflict, physical aggression, and psychological provocation for which primate societies, including human societies, are noted.

Suppose these creatures were articulate and explained to us that their benevolent actions flowed from their sympathetic identification with the needs of others. Would we not recognize this society as a moral one, even if its members were not conscious of any struggle to regulate their behaviour and that of others? The Kantian position is that there is no morality in this culture, in so far as its members act from inclination, not from a sense of duty. Nor would their acting from a sense of duty render them moral, according to Kant, if dutifulness were simply a special moral emotion unrelated to thoughts expressible as universal imperatives. As a culture might lack painting or theatre, and yet be attractive for other reasons—the extensiveness of its mathematical thought or its melodious songs—the one described lacks morality and is appealing for other reasons. Whatever the formal and substantive weaknesses of Kant's moral

---

[4] David Hume, *A Treatise of Human Nature*, II. III. ii. 500.

theory may be—and I defer their consideration for later—his position captures the sense in which morality is an imposition that is not only an outgrowth and an expression of our natural dispositions but exists as a corrective to them.

Humans walk upright, talk, laugh, share food, care for their off-spring for many years, and use their hands for constructive purposes including building, writing, drawing, and calculating Their fondness for normative rules—for doing things in the right way, often in exactly the right way—is manifest in all their activities.[5] Whether we are aware of them and can articulate them or not, our behaviour and our productions are constrained by internalized canons of appropriateness, decency, taste, and civility that forbid us certain actions that we could easily perform and that deem worthless certain products that we could easily fashion and display. Normative statements concerning what is fitting, good, meet, appropriate, and right to do are asserted, inculcated, followed, and enforced, and they are also scorned, ignored, contested, and evaded. Norms may be explicit and general; into this joint category fall the international codes of conduct pertaining to war, the actions by the commanders of ships on the high seas, and the agricultural regulations of large countries. Or they may be tacit and restricted, like the telephone protocols followed by a group of small-town teenagers or the haircut norms of a group of businessmen. They may be explicit and restricted or tacit and general; there are norms establishing what it is fitting to eat at different times of the day and on different holidays, what we talk about and what words we use, how we greet people, and how we manoeuvre our bodies through the world. We scan for infractions of the rules of fittingness and goodness, comment upon them, and punish them, even if the punishment is only adverse criticism and the rule-breaker is unaware that he is a subject of critical gossip.

The distinction between a species-specific behavioural regularity and a widely followed norm is imprecise. The habit of eating within an hour of arising in the morning and eating again at midday is partly a physiological requirement for active diurnal creatures, partly a convention. Exclusive pairings between males and females are natural

---

[5] Allan Gibbard refers in this connection to our 'broad propensities to accept norms, engage in normative discussion, and to act, believe, and feel in ways that are somewhat guided by the norms one has accepted'. *Wise Choices, Apt Feelings*, 27.

for humans, but marriage is a norm that adds extra rigidity to the typical pattern. Deviance from a species-specific behavioural pattern tends, however, to reduce the biological fitness of a creature, through the working of what Bentham termed a natural sanction, while intentional or unintentional deviance from a norm may actually enhance biological fitness but has the potential to call forth a social sanction.[6] Overeating shortens life and reduces reproductive opportunities, but bigamy might well increase both, though in many countries it is punished by law. The rules humans collectively invent and propound, and to which they try to hold others, extend beyond what is necessary either for biological survival or for the persistence and flourishing of communities. If wealthy businesspersons in Canada, unlike Italian aristocrats of a former era, eschew the wearing of ruby pendants, this is not because the practice is biologically dysfunctional or intrinsically disruptive.

The liking for norms and the pleasure taken in moulding thinking and acting so that it operates within constraints is evident in the great human interest in games, in which we take part cheerfully despite what is often a virtual certainty of losing. Economists like to present us as chiefly motivated by the desire to obtain preferred goods through the acquisition of exchangeable currency, but no rational person would accept the offer of a pile of gold on condition that he abstain from all normatively structured activity. Even those who enter lotteries in the vain hope of obtaining a pile of gold seem to take their chief pleasure in picking their numbers according to some system. Cognitively, we are equipped to follow rules, and affectively we are equipped to enjoy following them, and it is not fanciful to think that the ability to master phonological and grammatical systems is somehow connected with a broader facility with rules. Young animals play, and perhaps they use rudimentary rules or could be taught to use them, as some chimpanzees can be taught, with effort, to use sign language. Human children have a broader aptitude for learning new routines and seem to enjoy the constrained behaviour involved in dancing, singing, and drawing, as well as in talking. They grow up into such norm-governed activities as proving theorems, making

---

[6] Jeremy Bentham, *Introduction to the Principles of Morals and Legislation*, 27 ff.

artistic representations, and creating and participating in elaborate bureaucracies and administrative hierarchies.

Rules encompass regulations, norms, idiosyncratic personal rituals, and social conventions. Any rule can be asserted in the imperative voice: 'You! Do (not) x'.[7] The imperative form of any rule is convertible into a declarative form as a value judgement ('It is wrong (unseemly, inappropriate, immoral, indecent, incorrect, illicit . . .) to/not to x'). Not only do humans proclaim and observe rules, they reflect on them and theorize falsely and truly about their rules. They make certain assumptions regarding them—for example, how frequently certain rules are likely to be broken—and decisions about what to do about it when they are. Some rules are known to need strict enforcement, others are not; some rules are believed to apply universally, while others are believed to apply only to members of one community or class.[8] The logic of rules is non-monotonic; rules admit of exceptions, and exceptions to rules admit of exceptions in turn. Nevertheless, almost all cultures believe that there are some rules that admit of no exceptions and that bind categorically.[9] And they may give them supernatural or at least supramundane significance, insisting, for example, that certain rules were issued by a god, or are observed by an immaterial substance resident within us, or that infractions of important rules are automatically lethal for the rule-breaker, or shameful to his dead ancestors.

Formulas of obligation—statements of the form 'I (you, he, she, it, one, we, they) ought to (should, must) do such-and-such', uttered aloud, written down in books, implied or precisely articulated in public discourse—are expressions of social rules and are ubiquitous in both their hypothetical and their so-called categorical forms. Rules stating moral obligations are an interesting and problematic subclass. There is a greater tendency to regard moral norms and requisites as issuing from a transcendental source and as commanding universal human agreement in principle than there is to regard prudential and aesthetic rules as transcendental or universal. It is often said that moral

---

[7] That moral rules are imperatives backed up by reasons was a major theme of R. M. Hare's work; see *The Language of Morals*, ch. 1 and his retrospective *Sorting out Ethics*, 12 ff.

[8] Robert B. Edgerton, *Rules, Exceptions and Social Order*, 221 ff.

[9] Ibid. 254.

rules take precedence over other rules and other considerations. But which rules are moral rules?

1.2. The Demarcation Problem

The theoretical question what makes a given rule a moral rule—in virtue of what perceived properties are those who treat it as a moral rule doing so?—is different from the question whether anyone does or everyone should endorse the rule. We can agree that 'Doctors should not assist their patients to commit suicide' is a moral rule, rather than a rule of etiquette, even if we think it is a bad rule or that it ought to be disregarded under specific conditions. We can agree that 'Protect your eyes when looking directly at the sun' is a prudential, not a moral rule, even if we think that it is a good rule that all sighted creatures ought to obey. It is difficult, however, to specify the *topic* of moral rules, what they seek to regulate, in a way that is non-committal as between moral theories and that does not import prescriptive considerations into a descriptive task. Though we can sort rules into the categories of manners, dress codes, aesthetic guidelines, professional protocols, game-specific rules, practical in-junctions, and moral imperatives, it is surprisingly difficult to articu-late the criteria employed in making such discriminations. The demarcation problem is not solved by appeal to content. Both moral rules and taboos are largely concerned with prohibitions involving sex, killing, and kinship obligations. And certain concep-tions of virtue or upright living are difficult to distinguish from specifications of elite manners.

It is sometimes said that moral rules are concerned with how to behave or how to live, but this specification is vague. To be told that morality contributes to human flourishing, or upright and decent living, is not to be informed. All rules—the rules of chess, the rules of warfare—instruct us about how to behave in various situations, and both aesthetic and prudential rules (Don't mix plaids and stripes! Save your money! Wear a seatbelt!) tell us how to behave and how to live. There is a wealth of information available from decorators, psycholo-gists, nutritionists, and government agencies on how to flourish as a human being. And to be told that morality is concerned with

minimizing suffering is to be misinformed. The injunction against using your hairdryer in the bathtub is not a moral rule, and the acceptance of a moral rule may even imply that more rather than less pain is morally meet or fitting; suicide and indifference can eliminate it. It might be suggested that moral rules in some way prescribe non-interference with others, but this does not differentiate them from certain rules of commerce and sport.

Asked to itemize their moral beliefs—the declaratives correspond- ing to moral imperatives—most respondents will produce a list of actions to be eschewed, including violations of contract, gratuitous cruelty, deception, fraud, injury, and insult. The current moral litera- ture offers many examples of allegedly objective moral truths. Most of these examples concern the wrongness of harming animals or chil- dren, or torturing people, or engaging in genocide. Leaving aside for now the question of the truth status of judgements of wrongness, it is evident that these beliefs concern actions that are forbidden. Rules are plausibly seen, as David Braybrooke suggests, as 'in origin physical blocking operations that prevent people from acting in ways pro- hibited, or, better, systems of blocking operations'.[10] They are the verbal analogues of pinning someone's arms behind his back. Moral rules tend to be formulated as 'Thou shalt nots'. They mandate a sacrifice of opportunities for gratification; they deny a permission to act in a careless or indifferent way in pursuit of one's self-interest. By extension, they may involve a sacrifice of opportunities deemed symbolically representative of gratification or regarded as likely pre- cursors or empirical signs of the enjoyment of such gratification.

The high degree of confidence in the correctness of moral judge- ments relating to harm to children and animals can be explained by the supposition that they correspond to highly presentable samples of moral rules. This suggests the following semi-essentialist hypothesis: *Moral rules are restrictive and prohibitory rules whose social function is to counteract the short- or long-term advantage possessed by a naturally or situationally favoured subject.* A morality, in short, is a system of com- pensatory or advantage-reducing imperatives that correspond to moral judgements. It follows that a social rule that commands the harming of children or animals cannot be a moral rule, and that the

---

[10] David Braybrooke, 'The Representation of Rules in Logic and their Definition', in Braybrooke (ed.), *Social Rules*, 3–20.

corresponding judgement cannot be a moral judgement. The claim 'You should torture children if you gain satisfaction from doing so' is not an example of a moral judgement that happens to be false. Whether the statement is false or lacking in truth value altogether, it is not a moral judgement at all.

Further, moral rules are those concerned with the adjustment of perceived situational balance of power. At the most basic level, they regulate aggression and the appropriation of goods; they protect the physically weaker members of the group against the strong and agile. Moral wrong is liable to occur wherever persons stand in relationships of unequal social power, whether the inequality is temporary or long-term, circumstantial or based in endowments. Without expropriating tangible property or inflicting visible corporeal damage, the powerful can influence our well-being by withholding information or encouraging false beliefs, by removing or failing to provide opportunities, or corrupting our relationships with others.[11] The duties considered to form the core elements of morality, to avoid interfering with people's possessions, to refrain from exercising lethal force, to tell the truth, to keep promises and perform contracts, even when it would be easy and profitable not to, reduce the advantages of those who observe them. Even the duty to assume responsibility for oneself and to refrain from being a burden on others after sizing up their probable willingness to help falls under the proposed characterization.

'Respect your contracts', according to the hypothesis, is a moral rule that aims to prevent the stronger party from walking away from it because a contract no longer suits him. A_1 in observing the rule vis-à-vis A_2 makes things worse for herself by keeping to her side of the bargain. 'Don't steal' prevents light-fingered A_1 from taking advantage of inattentive A_2, though she loses what is perhaps a rare opportunity to gain thereby. 'Eat no meat' prohibits capable hunters or consumers from taking advantage of vulnerable edibles, at their own nutritional expense. 'Take care of your own children' prevents parents from leaving helpless infants to the kindness of strangers, even if the costs to the parents are heavy. 'Share your wealth' prevents tenacious A_1 from holding on to resources for life that needy A_2 does not have, though A_1 is thereby deprived of many pleasures. The

---

[11] See J. Harvey, *Civilized Oppression*, esp. chs. 3, 'Having the Upper Hand', and 4 'On the Receiving End'.

overall function of moral rules in the social economy is to serve as a brake, not just on our emotions or our inclinations, where the latter are viewed as non-rational velleities, but also—to some extent—on our intelligence, competence, and social forcefulness. It is for this reason that their alleged requirements are perceived as difficult and their justification as problematic. Moral rules are concerned with the regulation of actions that can broadly be described as *self-interested*, as aesthetic rules are concerned with the regulation of appearances, and prudential rules are concerned with maintaining health, wealth, and reputation. Moral wishes are just those wishes amongst all the regulatory wishes we have (such as the wish that more or fewer people would wear shorts) that are concerned with limiting the physical and psychological damage individuals can do to one another in pursuit of their own interests or the interests of their party, class, nation, or tribe. Harms resulting from negligence and indifference, as well as harms resulting from the desire to exploit or injure, can be understood as the effects of self-interest in this sense.

The most succinct attempt to characterize morality in the abstract is perhaps John Stuart Mill's discussion in the last chapter of *Utilitarianism*, and it is useful to hold his characterization up to the definition just sketched. Mill defined justice and injustice as notions pertaining to the upholding of legal rights, the award of goods and the imposition of evils according to desert, the maintenance of contracts, the avoidance of partiality, and the furtherance of equality except where expediency required inequality.[12] Contraventions of justice, he thought, involved 'two things—a wrong done, and some assignable person who is wronged'. To what he regarded as the mandatory *duties* of justice, Mill added the optional *virtues* of generosity and benevolence to make up the subject area of morality, succumbing to the temptation to mix descriptive and prescriptive considerations.[13] If the distinction between duties and virtues is set aside, Mill's characterization might be understood as follows: morality prohibits certain wrong actions and prohibits inaction in the face of unfortunate states. The wrong actions concerned are not merely impractical or unaesthetic; they are typically actions performed with the intention of benefiting or maintaining the status of an advantaged party that exact some costs

---

[12] J. S. Mill, *Utilitarianism*, in *Collected Works*, x. 241–4.   [13] Ibid. 247.

from or that fail to improve the status of a disadvantaged party; negligent actions, though not performed with the intention of harming or refusing help, are morally culpable when they betray self-interest.

The claim that moral rules are advantage-limiting or advantage-reducing is 'semi-essentialist': Moral rules occupy a sector of the normative realm, just as sofas and chairs occupy sectors of the category 'furniture'. As there are 'good' and 'less good' exemplars of sofas and chairs, as well as items that are intermediate between 'sofa' and 'chair', so there are good and less good exemplars of moral rules, as well as rules that are intermediate between prudential and moral rules, or rules of decorum and moral rules. It might be urged at this point that preventing wrong being done by an advantaged agent to another is not the unique aim of morality and that Mill's characterization too misses some of its central elements. The maintenance of personal dignity and integrity and the prevention of personal suffering, it might be insisted, are elements of the influential Stoic tradition and have every right to be considered as principal moral objectives. To meet the objection that the characterization offered is unduly narrow, I shall present some historical evidence that the reduction of advantage and the prevention of 'transitive' harms to the weak are ancient and universal features of what are agreed to be moral codes, and that other features are more or less peripheral.

Funerary inscriptions from the Egyptian Old Kingdom of the Third Millennium BCE provide some insight into the value systems of ancient people. One typical inscription praises the deceased for his or her refusal to kill, rob, commit adultery, trespass, execute ritual impurities, blaspheme, slander, cheat, and neglect the gods.[14] Another cites the deceased's veracity, accuracy and fairness in speech, rescue of the weak, feeding and clothing of the hungry and naked, burial of the poor, furnishing of transportation, honouring and pleasing of parents, and assistance to widows, orphans, and lost strangers.[15] Praiseworthy characteristics seem to fall naturally into two categories. Personal righteousness is exemplified in the failure to execute ritual impurities, blaspheme, or neglect the gods, and in the performance of parent-pleasing activities and observance of measured language. By contrast,

---

[14] Scott N. Morschauser, 'The Ideological Basis for Social Justice/Responsibility in Ancient Egypt', in K. D. Irani and Morris Silver (eds.), *Social Justice in the Ancient* World, 106–7.
[15] Ibid. 106.

the deceased's rescue and charity activities, as well as his or her restraint with respect to robbing and killing, seem to belong to another order of goodness that is specifically moral. Several ancient codices prescribe kindness to animals; opposition to circuses was even a feature of Stoicism. Other prescriptive texts from the ancient world describe an ideal condition in which no one stands to gain or to maintain an advantage through the deprivation or suffering of another.[16]

Or consider two familiar sets of norms, the commandments of the Old Testament and those of the New Testament. The Old Testament rules, the prohibitions on murder, swearing, adultery, and false witness, and the command to honour one's parents, appear to have little in common; personal-righteousness rules and power-restraining rules are bundled together. By contrast, many of the commandments of the New Testament offer variations on a single theme, the partial or total renunciation of advantage, or even the inversion of the relative advantage possessed in some situation by A_1 with respect to A_2. The rules that one ought to divide one's cloak in two and give half to the beggar, love one's enemies, and respond to aggression by turning the other cheek, are exemplary moral rules. The New Testament is accordingly a source of excruciatingly, even perversely advantage-reducing imperatives.[17] By contrast, the Old Testament imperatives are a mixed bundle: the prohibitions against murder and false witness are clearly advantage-reducing, but the other commandments appear to be composites in which morality, taboo, and status considerations are mingled in the formulation of the rule.

The hypothesis nevertheless faces several criticisms:

First, it might be objected that many moral rules are not compensatory or advantage-reducing, and many advantage-reducing or compensatory rules are not moral. Under the first category, one might propose such widely accepted norms as 'Debtors should repay their debts' or 'Talent should be recognized and rewarded'. The repayment rule seems to take further from the weaker party and the reward rule to give further to the advantaged party.

One response to this objection is that the cited rules can but do not always function as moral rules. Repayment and reward rules may

[16] K. D. Irani, 'The Idea of Social Justice in the Ancient World', in Irani and Silver (eds.), *Social Justice*, 5.

[17] v. Friedrich Nietzsche, *The Genealogy of Morals*, tr. Walter Kaufmann and R. J. Hollingdale, 34.

function as pragmatic rules that are beneficially observed in societies that attach great importance to converting natural resources into commodities for human use. They may resemble in this regard the rule 'Interest rates ought to be raised to control inflation'. The latter is usually a good rule for keeping economies on track, but it is not a moral rule. Under other interpretations, the repayment rule and the reward rule can be construed as having moral content. The first may be understood as an instance of the 'Keep your contracts' rule that prohibits disaffected contractors from walking out whenever they can do so with impunity. In so far as a given debtor has the funds or a reasonable prospect of acquiring them and can repay the money, he is in the advantaged position and should make restitution. The reward rule may be understood as requiring that sacrifices not be in vain. In so far as a meritorious person has endured hardship, he should be compensated. 'Share your candy with your friends' may function as a moral injunction not to tolerate the relative deprivation of others, or it may be a prudential recommendation for achieving popularity. Nothing precludes a given social rule's having a dual significance.

A second objection to the hypothesis is that there can be no cross-culturally valid characterization of a moral rule. Different cultures, it might be argued, group their rules governing social conduct and personal dignity together in various ways, and the designation of some subset of them as that culture's moral rules must follow the culture's own discursive practices. To designate a rule as moral is to single it out as an especially important personal conduct rule, and it is not up to us to say whether the naming taboos or clothing regulations of another culture are genuinely moral or belong in the same category with prohibitions on theft and murder. A culture might prescribe a set of what its members designate as 'E-rules' that enjoin fidelity to promises and generosity towards friends, and that require revenge for all insults, as well as the adoption of a distinctive mode of a dress associated with special personal dignity and authority such as the wearing of white shifts and the carrying of a small ceremonial knife. There is no fact of the matter, according to the critic, about whether these are all moral rules or not, and the decision whether to translate the foreign term 'E-rule' as 'moral rule' ought not to depend on the similarity or dissimilarity of the E-rules to some prototype in the mind of the translator.

The objector may point out that even in our own culture the term 'moral' is used in a broad sense and suggest that it is unacceptably revisionary to propose that it refers principally or centrally to rules concerned with advantage reduction. Some moral imperatives, she will insist, forbid an agent to debase himself or waste his talents, or bid him refrain from taking into his body or his mind substances, thoughts, or images of an impure or polluting nature. Kant's rules that one should not use other people as playthings even when they are agreeable to it, nor allow oneself to be so used, nor sell parts of one's body such as one's teeth for profit fall into this category. Many people consider recreational drug-taking and bioengineering to pose, each in their own way, serious moral problems. Yet the alleged wrongdoings of the weekend hallucinator or the professional cloner do not lend themselves easily to our analysis of moral rules as advantage-reducing. Revisionary definitions, the objection might continue, may be called for in the exact sciences, but they have no place in philosophical inquiry, which must be concerned with the common understanding of terms. If a significant number of people describe cloning, and other alterations of organic bodies, as moral issues—not merely a set of prudential, aesthetic, etc., issues, or as expressions of a worry about the taboo status of simulacra, impure hybrid 'mixtures', or artificial life and experience—they must really be moral issues.

One way to meet this objection is to insist that those who assert that cloning is immoral are speaking or writing in an unusual dialect. Prohibitions on pornography-consumption, drug-taking, or gene-splicing, it might be further argued, do not constitute moral rules; they are assignable to the neighbouring category of restraining usage taboos applying to objects belonging, or in this case conceived as belonging, to a sovereign entity, oneself, or perhaps God. Another way of meeting the objection is to point out that some notions of duties to oneself, or perhaps even to nature, have the proposed moral marker to some degree.[18] The belief that the consumption of pornography is contrary to morality is doubtless influenced by non-moral ideas about dignity and integrity, some of them superficial, others arguably profound. Yet it may also be rooted in the idea that the

---

[18] Freud describes such taboos in 'Taboo and the Ambivalence of Emotions', in *Basic Writings*, 828 ff. 'To touch is the beginning of every act of possession, of every attempt to make use of a person or thing.' Ibid. 833.

activity involves the exercise or maintenance of situational advantage by one or another party. The sense that the vending of surgically extracted organs is contrary to morality may be based on non-moral ideas regarding the unseemliness of contact between personal and foreign body parts; again these may be foolish worries or not. This impression may also reflect worries about the temptation to victimize helpless or needy persons that the profitable vending of organs would awaken. By contrast, it may be difficult to see the individual addict or the addicted sector of the population as members of an advantaged class; only if such persons are conceived as escaping ordinary demands and responsibilities and as letting others down can any moral significance be attached to their actions.

The intuition that drug-taking and cloning are activities with moral implications has another basis as well. For most moralists who are concerned with them are worried about the effects of these activities on others besides their perpetrators who may be affected by them. They are simultaneously worried about whether they would be, ex officio, harming anyone in arguing for their prohibition, and about the justifiability of interfering forcibly with other people's preferred activities when one is in a position to do so. There is an implicitly dyadic structure in most moral controversies involving what might at first appear to be purely self-regarding activities.

The semi-essentialist need have no objection to including rules mandating, say, women's haircovering, as moral rules, provided they are not taken without further explanation to be examples of central or focal moral rules and provided their advantage-reducing feature can be made apparent. The position that the *best* examples of moral rules we possess are haircovering rules, anti-intoxication rules, and rules proscribing the making of impure mixtures, such as tomatoes with the genes of fish, has little to recommend it.

1.3. Are Advantage-Reducing Imperatives Natural?

Lucretius regarded the first humans as fiercely amoral individualists: 'They could have no thought of the common good, no notion of the mutual restraint of morals and laws. The individual, taught only to live and fend for himself, carried off, on his own account such prey as

fortune brought him.'[19] These creatures mellowed, he thought, into members of a community. '[N]eighbors began to form mutual alliances, wishing neither to do nor to suffer violence among themselves. They appealed on behalf of their children and womanfolk, pointing out with gestures and inarticulate cries that it is right for everyone to pity the weak.'[20] From our current perspective, Aristotle was wrong about the autochthonous status of moral and political institutions, right about the social propensities of human beings. Lucretius, in turn, was wrong about the solitary and amoral nature of the first men, but perhaps right in viewing morality as a form of mollification.

Working in the Lucretian tradition, theorists have produced quasi-anthropological accounts of the origins of morality that describe the passage from advantage-seeking to altruistic behaviour, emphasizing the roles of reason, fear, and pity in the transition. Hobbes's account in Part One of his *Leviathan*[21] is perhaps the most celebrated use of a naturalistic platform, and it furnishes a model for contemporary accounts based on the Lucretian assumption of a pre-existing state of war or mutual indifference. There are several ways to interpret Hobbes's story. Historians read it as a novel defence of absolute monarchy. Game theorists read it as an account of the discovery of the rationality of interpersonal cooperation. Whether or not a special relationship between monarch and subjects is conceived as its necessary condition, the realization that the cessation of mutual hostilities is the better strategy for those who want to maximize their happiness and security announces the initial moment of moral reflection. 'Hobbes's Theorem', as it might be called, is that the addition of moral regulation to a world increases its hedonic content, the amount of pleasure, comfort, and happiness it contains. And although the theorem does not appear to be true for arbitrarily large increments of morality, it is clearly true for increments up to some level.

Hobbes's notion that cooperation reduces deprivations and produces a surplus of human good is mirrored in contemporary accounts that substitute the cunning of nature, or blind natural selection under conditions of environmental scarcity, for strategies consciously chosen in a state of anxious competition. From the perspective of evolutionary theory, the members of a single species are distinct

[19] Lucretius, *On the Nature of Things*, v. 958 ff.   [20] Ibid. 1018 ff.
[21] Thomas Hobbes, *Leviathan*, 104 ff.

individuals engaged in a competition for reproductive success.[22] The persistence of a trait is like the rational solution to a problem posed by the ambient environment, which may include the presence of con-specifics who share the trait, in so far as traits that are not solving the problem tend to be extinguished by variant traits that solve it better. The disposition to behave morally, to be vigilant about moral infractions in others, and to punish them, could then be explained as an evolutionarily stable strategy, an *ESS,* if we suppose that humans lacking these traits fare poorly in the struggle for existence.[23] A trait it would be beneficial to evolve might seem equivalent to a policy it would be rational to choose.

The view that human morality is simply an *ESS* is tempting but clearly inadequate. Hobbes's notion that a mutual non-aggression pact will be rational for all his warriors to agree to rests on his assumption that they are all equal in the degree of force they can individually exercise and desire to exercise.

Nature has made men so equal in the faculties of the body and mind as that, though there be found one man sometimes manifestly stronger in body or of quicker mind than another, yet, when all is reckoned together, the difference between man and man is not so considerable as that one man can thereupon claim to himself any benefit to which another may pretend as well as. For as to the strength of body, the weakest has strength enough to kill the strongest, either by secret machination or by confederacy with others that are in the same danger with himself.[24]

The equality assumption is basic to the ordinary game-theoretic sociobiological framework. Natural selection reduces the frequency of deleterious traits and increases the frequency of advantageous traits. It is a uniformity-inducing process, offset by the tendency to variation.

This is not to say that *ESSs* require homogeneity down to the level of individuals; Maynard Smith has pointed out that they may be instantiated in distributions of traits in polymorphous populations,

---

[22] This is oversimplified, but if an individual organism is considered for the purposes of the discussion as the bearer of a trait, no harm is done.

[23] If I is an *ESS,* then 'if almost all members of a population adopt I, . . . the fitness of these typical members is greater than that of a possible mutant'. John Maynard Smith, *Evolution and the Theory of Games,* 14.

[24] Hobbes, *Leviathan,* 104–5.

and Robert Trivers takes stable strategies to correspond to the frequency with which individual members display certain forms of behaviour. 'Hawkish' and 'dovish' tendencies can be modelled in terms of patterns that are resistant to self-extermination and invasion alike.[25] This point is important, for in any real-world population of social animals, some are cleverer, or stronger, or more ruthless, or more attractive than others; others are correspondingly dimmer, weaker, gentler, less charismatic, and less able to form alliances. The latter are not 'less fit'. Their own hidden-from-view mosaics of physical and psychological traits serve them just as well in the struggle for existence, though not all their genes will appear with the same frequency in later generations. Yet the former can dominate the latter.

Dominance cannot confer a heritable selective advantage on an animal exercising it, for the advantaged trait would spread through the population and there would be no animals to submit.[26] It could be 'accidental': A certain distribution of individual traits within a group may be stable without its being the case that any one of the polymorphisms confers an advantage. Some people have exceptionally long, slender fingers, but, as this trait has not as far as we know increased its frequency, *it* cannot be supposed to confer a special selective advantage, and dominance might be a trait of this sort. More plausibly, dominance and submission correspond to instructions animals heed when responding to other animals that happen to be larger or smaller, fiercer or more pacific than themselves; they may be relational strategies for getting along in such mixed environments.

Assume a population that is linearly ordered with respect to size and ferocity. Then the rule 'Always defer to a larger animal and seize resources from a smaller animal' is an *ESS* that will sort a population into a dominance hierarchy. Provided the animals do not encounter one another so frequently that the smaller fail to survive and reproduce, and provided conditions of great scarcity

---

[25] Maynard Smith, *Evolution and the Theory of Games*, 16–17; Robert Trivers, 'The Evolution of Reciprocal Altruism'.

[26] Dominance is relatively easy to explain on the hypothesis of group selection; Trivers suggests that it prevents mass extermination in times of food shortage. This explanation might be reconciled with classical Darwinism on the assumption that members of strongly hierarchical social groups tend to be closely related to one another.

do not intervene, there is no reason such a population of unequals cannot persist indefinitely. The existence of rigid social hierarchies is consistent with the uniformity-inducing tendencies of natural selection and, accordingly, with the artificial, reason-driven evolution of social norms. According to the hypothesis above, the domination of individuals by other individuals, by coalitions, and by institutions is typically what morality seeks to prevent. Stable situations and procedures that have arisen through the historical interactions of individuals cannot therefore be assumed to meet the tests of moral adequacy that culture has at the same time produced.

The metaphysical postulate of the moral equality of human beings furnishes a striking contrast to the variance observed in the degree of social power they exercise. Natural equality is a reality in the following sense: from the knowledge that an animal is dominant in its social group, or a person in hers, we cannot infer that it or she is more intelligent, healthier, more resistant to disease, a superior parent, or that its or her genes are better. Each of us incorporates a mosaic of traits that the rigours of the environment have failed thus far to eliminate, and it makes no sense to describe one existing person as a better product of evolution than another even though not all of everyone's genes will maintain their current frequency in future populations.

The 'fitness' of the biologist therefore has only the sketchiest relationship to the ordinary-language notion of fitness as strength, good looks, etc.[27] Nevertheless some humans—whose genes may be slated for extinction—are just now a great deal more successful than others when it comes to attracting admiring attention to their persons, displacing others and appropriating their resources, and collecting a disproportionate number of suitors, mates, or followers. Some people give way easily, are content with modest amounts of everything, do not seek to influence the behaviour of others or recruit them as clients, and try to stay out of the limelight. To what extent should this variance be considered 'natural?' We do not know and cannot easily determine what the original social system of humans was where dominance and subordination are concerned. The primate literature emphasizes the variety of social systems that are to be found

---

[27] On vernacular v. predictive fitness, see Mohan Matthen and André Ariew, 'Two Ways of Thinking about Fitness and Natural Selection'.

in the 200 or so species studied.[28] Some species whose habits are believed to be close to those of early man, such as the savannah baboon, are strongly hierarchical, though the closest primate relatives of humans are not agreed to be so.[29]

The problem of dominance behaviour—the disposition to push others around, to appropriate their resources, injure their offspring, and interfere with their lives—is actual and cannot be considered to have been solved by the evolution of cooperation, by pretheoretical agreement amongst persons equally capable of exercising social force. Yet human morality is a system of norms that limit the expression of dominance. It is made possible by the human capacity for generalization and abstraction, and the capacity to conform to rules that subjects can learn, internalize, and teach. But why do we have such a system? Why do we try, in the name of morality, to reduce and compensate for natural inequalities that permit dominant individuals to accumulate advantages at the expense of weaker ones? Evolutionary ethics does not give a satisfactory answer to this question.

Lucretius and Rousseau, it might be noted, deploy a somewhat more complex model than does Hobbes in their accounts of the evolution of morality. They too posit a renunciation of aggression for mutual benefit, but Lucretius is the first to insist on the importance of pity, an emotion felt by the strong towards the weak, as a moral emotion. Perhaps he sees the appearance of pity as symptomatic of the softening of human ferocity that cooperative behaviour and the production of a cooperative surplus bring in their wake. Or perhaps he sees pity as an indispensable motivator for the rational decision to cease hostilities. Even if these two conceptions, the rational and the sentimental, can be grasped as mutually reinforcing, they are separable. Cooperation between two strong animals can increase their joint advantage. To be sure, coalitions of the weak can be dangerous to the strong, and cooperation with the weak can be beneficial to the strong. Nevertheless, when the strong act from fear, or to increase the advantage they obtain from the weak, they act from an altogether different motive than when they act out of a concern for justice or for the welfare of the weak. The appearance of pacific and even benevolent relations may arise in either case, but it

---

[28] Joan B. Silk, 'Primatological Perspectives on Gender Herarchies'.
[29] Peter van Sommers, *The Biology of Behaviour*, 151.

is only the sentimental motive that can be termed moral. The concessions made to an underclass by a set of revolution-fearing oligarchs are not moral concessions.

Moral rules accordingly have two puzzling features. First, they forbid us to use our intelligence to analyse a situation with an eye to determining what could be done for our own advantage, given the weakness or unpreparedness of others, and to muster whatever social power we antecedently possess to serve our self-interest. The formula of obligation 'Other humans ought not be killed' is a blocking rule, a prohibition that instructs A_1 not to kill A_2, even when A_1 is irritated by A_2's presence, when A_1 is stronger or wilier than A_2 and could succeed in doing so with impunity, and when A_1 would have a better life were A_2 out of the picture. Second, they imply the suppression of our well-honed discriminatory abilities. The formula of obligation 'Care for your existing children' impresses on us that we ought not to abandon even one of them, even if, after rationally sizing up matters, we realize that we could raise more children in the long run by leaving one particularly troublesome one exposed to the elements. The formula implies that we should care for our children, whoever they are, and not increase our personal consumption by depriving any of them of necessities, or fob off their care on others in an exploitative manner.

Hans Kummer observes that moral formulas are characterized by their wide scope. 'As regards killing, respect of possession, or false information, they tend to prescribe the same course of conduct in (nearly) all situations and toward (almost) all conspecifics. Advanced codes include nongroup members, alien races, and even all animate beings among the favoured.'[30] As Edward Westermarck pointed out, in tribal societies and in the ancient world, the stranger was regarded as someone to whom the concepts of the sanctity of life and property did not apply, or did not apply as strictly as the prohibitions against harming fellow citizens.[31] The universal or 'overgeneralized' formula rarely makes an appearance outside literate societies in which it is easy to issue broad proclamations.

---

[30] Kummer, 'Analogs of Morality among Nonhuman Primates', 43. As Jack Goody remarks, 'Enshrined in the written word, passed down from century to century, the generalized, decontextualized statement becomes the touchstone of moral rationality. It implies that all men should be treated in the same way, that status, relationship, age, and sex are irrelevant in making judgments about the conduct of mankind.' 'Literacy and Moral Rationality', 161.

[31] Westermarck, *Ethical Relativity*, 199–200.

Consider a staggered set of policies *D*, *H*, *L*, and *Q*. Each corresponds to a set plan of action and reaction that might correspond to the overall policy of a hypothetical organism. *D* below corresponds to a fully rational strategy, one an animal should follow if it is aware of its own attributes and the attributes of its fellows and has no interest in them other than as a means to an end, the end being its own survival and maximal reproduction.

> *D*: Act always to maintain or promote your own interests, e.g., by consuming all health-enhancing resources, harming competitors, and removing obstructions to your reproductive success.

D may very well incorporate some limiting clauses. It does not command an animal to consume all possible resources (it might die of a surfeit), or to eliminate all competitors (this might be self-defeating), or to produce as many offspring as possible (in that case, none might be viable). But programmes such as 'Kill occasionally' or 'Kill very troublesome individuals' or 'Kill if you can do so without detection' can enhance an individual's chances of survival, and may be part of a given species' typical repertoire, expressing themselves in response to certain types of cueing. *D* allows for altruistic actions, so long as there is a net pay-off to the altruistic agent. It tells the animal to consume, harm, and reproduce only to the extent that this is biologically advantageous for it. An animal set to operate according to *D* need not get stuck in a Prisoner's Dilemma: It can simply make a guess, however wild, about what its partner is likely to do and act accordingly.

Policy *H*, however, restricts the creature further:

> *H*: Act always to maintain or promote your own interests, according to formula *D*, except when you cause substantial harm to others.

H leaves it open to what extent the organism may harm others to pursue large or small gains for itself. But, unlike *D,* it is recognizable as a moral norm in restraining the unlimited pursuit of self-interest.

H is not a rational policy for a purely self-interested being to adhere to. For if some prohibition against harming another actually serves my interests, it is already provided for under *D*. How then could even a weakly limiting policy like *H,* one that a purely rational

self-interested being would not accept, take hold in a species like ours? The moral ascent from *D* to *H* is a small step, but one nevertheless difficult to explain. For, since *D* and *H* really enjoin different patterns of behaviour, it would seem that a *D*-following individual can always successfully invade a population of *H*-followers, and that *H*-followers will fare poorly as intruders in a pre-existing society of *D*-followers.

To be sure, behaviour that formerly increased biological fitness in the technical sense—murderous retaliation, infanticide—may no longer be tolerated once *H* has taken hold, and may decrease the individual's chances of survival and reproduction. What was formerly an *H*-policy is now a *D*-policy. But how did *H* take hold in the first place?

Kummer characterizes advantage-reducing rules as a 'reversion to nonopportunism', noting that this reversion seems difficult for a naturalist to explain, since evolution would seem to favour the development and use of our intelligence and behavioural flexibility. Why, he asks, does nature 'allow a superimposed cultural development to undo just that achievement and, as it were, regress to rigid behavioural rules'?[32] Kummer's answer is that the exercise of too much practical intelligence renders social animals too dangerous to one another. It brings about a situation in which, as Hobbes suspected, too many resources are wasted monitoring the behaviour of conspecifics, detecting their stratagems, and trying to defend oneself by planning one's next pre-emptive strike:

Man as a hunter, forager, or toolmaker can hardly be too clever or versatile; he will always benefit from more foresight and a greater arsenal of selfish schemes. But man as a social companion can be too astute even in his own interest. Every being can become more dangerous simply by becoming less predictable, regardless of whether it appears in the role of an enemy, a competitor, or a cooperator. Cooperation requires that each participant be able to predict the other's actions. . . . Thus behaving in a predictable way increases the benefits and alleviates the risks of social life. If we assume that man's preadaptations offered no way to evolve a brain that was shrewd with tools, predators, and prey, but simple and predictable in dealing with his companions, the evolution of moral capacities might have been the adaptive answer: a selective suppression of shrewd flexibility in the social context.[33]

---

[32] Hans Kummer, 'Analogs of Morality', 43–4.   [33] Ibid.

Compensatory mechanisms are a common feature of biological systems; nature likes to build layers of controllers and releasers that regulate the behaviour of a system at a lower level. The original problem still remains, however. If the 'reversion' to non-opportunism is still in accord with policy D, the ascent to H has not been explained. If non-opportunism involves an ascent to H, the invasion problem has not been solved. It is still unclear how a more predictable, less dangerous animal's genes can invade a population of social animals whose behaviour is a function of the four variables discussed above, and essentially improvisatory. Just how can the rigid type drive the more flexible type to extinction?

One possibility is that differing cultures in separated groups can develop by chance and thrive in differing proportions, just as different physical characteristics can arise by chance in non-interbreeding subpopulations of a single species. Group selection could occur without violating basic Darwinian principles if by-chance rigid populations of related animals left more offspring than by-chance flexible populations.[34] Alternatively, rigidity and moderation of advantage-taking dispositions might be an individual defence strategy evolved in response to punishment and reward by other animals. Robert Trivers notes that punishment of 'cheaters' sometimes appears to be out of proportion to their offences, but that 'since even small inequities repeated many times over a lifetime may exact a heavy toll in inclusive fitness, selection may favour a strong show of aggression when the cheating tendency is discovered'.[35] An emotional commitment to justice, rather than maximization of immediate pay-off, may be a good long-term strategy.

It is inconceivable that natural selection alone is responsible for moral phenomena such as the existence in some minds of a belief in universal human rights. There is simply no plausible account on which the existence of such a belief, or its necessary conditions and accompaniments, could have increased the number of offspring its possessor left.[36] Nevertheless, once the process of moral ascent has got off the ground by taking hold in some minds, further elaborations

[34] As envisioned by Elliott Sober and David Sloan Wilson in *Unto Others: The Evolution and Psychology of Unselfish Behavior*, ch. 4, 132 ff.

[35] Robert Trivers, *Social Evolution*, 388.

[36] This is agreed to by Thomas Huxley, Richard Dawkins, and G. C. Williams; citations can be found in Flack and de Waal, 'Any Animal Whatever', 1–2.

through cultural innovation and transmission may come readily. A few steps up from the vague and somewhat weak policy H, we arrive at the quite strenuous and precise Lockean proviso L:

> L: Act always to maintain or promote your own interests, according to formula D, so long as you do not thereby worsen another's situation, except to avoid worsening your own.

According to David Gauthier, the proviso transforms the Hobbesian state of nature into the 'productive natural condition' of Locke.[37] It is rational on his view for all self-interested beings to accept it, whether or not they are moved by sympathy or fellow feeling. This follows, however, only on the Hobbesian assumption of natural equality. Consider a group of rational self-interested beings devoid of other motives who differ in their individual endowments of size and ferocity, and who are aware of their own attributes and the attributes of the others. For the strong, in this case, the weak are among the natural resources available to them; for the weak, the strong are natural predators they must evade. Suppose the group has the opportunity to write down one fundamental rule that will license and constrain their behaviour. It is not rational for anyone in the group to agree to L.

Depending on how L is interpreted, both the strong and weak have reasons for refusing to endorse it. The strong may believe correctly that the weak are unable to make things worse for them. They will complain that the policy benefits only the weak and that it is not in their rational self-interest to subscribe to it. The weak, however, may interpret it as favouring the strong. For suppose their only chance to acquire some essential good is by taking it from the strong. They are prohibited from doing so if this would worsen the condition of the strong, even if the need of the weak for the good is substantial. Suppose that the strong control the land, enjoying more of its resources, and make a small profit from their ownership of a well. The weak cannot ask for more water at a lower price if their condition, already bad, is not worsened if they do not acquire it. The weak have no reason to endorse L if it is their last chance to establish a basic policy.

If there is no policy that both the strong and the weak must agree on when the strong regard the weak as environmental resources for

---

[37] David Gauthier, *Morals by Agreement*, 208. The proviso was discussed earlier by Robert Nozick, *Anarchy State and Utopia*, 175 ff.

their use, then, in so far as morality is concerned with the regulation of harm, morals cannot spring from the foundation of rational self-interest by agreement. This is not to say that L might not be an important policy rule that is widely accepted for the regulation of certain types of behaviour in contexts where there is agreement that failing to better someone's situation is tantamount to worsening it, or where the strong are uncertain of their hold over the weak, or even where predation is considered a salutary process. L might govern commercial transactions, for instance, or relationships that fall within the purview of a law offering equal protection.

Continuing with the process, we can go on to write a series of even more limiting—and ever less rational, or universally appealing—policies, arriving finally at Q:

> Q: Act always to maintain or promote your own interests, according to formula D, unless by your doing so another's condition is rendered worse than it would be by your not so acting, or not improved.

Q forbids me even maintaining my present advantages if I can assist someone else by renouncing them.

The adoption of a Q-policy will likely militate against the practitioner's biological success as well as his enjoyment of consumption opportunities. 'Kill no one', 'Do not eat animals', and 'Never lie' may represent fatal strategies for individuals. By eating nothing that had ever been alive except fruit fallen from the tree, one might compromise one's reproductive health. By refusing to practise infanticide and continuing to feed infants during a short period of harsh conditions, one might exterminate one's whole tribe. However, even profoundly inhibited behaviour is compatible with survival and the most exigent systems can sustain themselves. Q-policies can flourish when they are restricted to a subculture and new recruits can be attracted to them, or when they gain such currency that there are few threats to them from selfish invaders.

1.4. Morality and Hypermorality

Policies D–Q are meta-rules, not rules of morality. They correspond to programmes that might be imagined as governing hypothetical

organisms. Morality intensity increases as we move up the register from D to Q. Morality is importantly scalar, and this feature can be seen from a comparison of the intensity levels of various degrees of prohibition pertaining to certain categories of action.

We might think in this regard of human behaviour as a sphere pierced by numerous axes, each marked by positions located at points some distance out from the centre.[38] At the centre of the sphere, behaviour is plastic and situationally elicited, subject only to a few inhibitions. There is altruistic care as well as harassment, cooperation as well as competition. We cannot write down the specific patterns of behaviour that characterize this centre, because we cannot return to the moment when it began to be replaced or overpainted by post-Darwinian limiting rules and restraints. Nevertheless, we have a general idea what we would write down if we were asked to articulate, as a set of formulas of obligation or, in Braybrooke's terms, 'blocking rules', the rules at the core falling under policy D. We would write down some prohibitions against incest, against eating certain unclean or poisonous foods, and against killing one's own children. Some distance out, where our creatures begin to think and write their own rules, we can see these prohibitions undergoing a process of generalization. A prohibition against killing kin, which is fitness-reducing, may be elaborated into a rule against killing unrelated tribespersons, consistent with policy H. A prohibition against eating rotten food, which is unwholesome, may be extended into a rule against eating totem animals. A prohibition against interfering in established consortships, which is dangerous, may be extended into a rule asserting the sanctity of marriage consistent with policy L. These prohibition extensions need not be functional, as their predecessor prohibitions were. Their arrival on the scene signals that humans now see social behaviour as a field for control and for decorative elaboration. Compensatory rules can be pushed to extremes that can be described as 'hypermoral'.[39]

Warlike communities that keep the peace amongst themselves but fight their close neighbours occupy a position close to the centre on

---

[38] The notion that morality is scalar has been expressed by Michael Slote, though in connection with a version of consequentialism. See his *Common-Sense Morality and Consequentialism*, 80 ff.

[39] The term 'hypermoral' was coined by the German sociologist Arnold Gehlen in *Moral und Hypermoral*, 146 ff. Gehlen held Nietzschean views that are not under consideration here.

the external aggression axis; 'just war' theorists are positioned some-what further away, and pacifists a good deal further away, at what we might call the 'hypermoral edge'. Practitioners of infanticide under conditions of social stress or upheaval are near the centre, those who would never consider undergoing an abortion are further away, and those who abjure contraception on the grounds that it injures life are on the hypermoral edge. Omnivorous humans are close to the centre, tribes that avoid eating their totem animal are some distance out, and those sects whose veneration for life extends so far that they eat only fallen fruits are on the periphery. Political groups that deny the appropriateness of any distribution from families to strangers belong near the centre; communists are at the edge. A hypermoral position is one that implies a profound renunciation of advantage, a refusal to be pragmatic, or to deploy all the resources one has at hand, whether natural or cultural, native or acquired, to come out ahead, or even to equalize an unequal situation. The claims that one should turn the other cheek, that evil should be repaid with good, that it is always better to suffer than to do evil, all represent hypermoral positions. Their proponent flatly rejects the suggestion that he should employ certain of his capabilities to worsen the situation of another. The seeming obtuseness of the pacifist in her indifference to the appeal to be flexible and appreciative of varying circumstance is a token of her hypermoral commitment.

Is there any historical evidence, one might wonder, for the hy-pothesis that the development of moral ideation and its associated discourse is linked with a reduction in the combination of flexibility, pragmatism, and fierceness displayed by our ancestors? Both Plato and Aristotle appear to regard the establishment of appropriate dominance hierarchies as fulfilling the requirements of justice. Nevertheless, they are concerned that the sorting-out of the population be accomplished by some means other than the ascension of the physically stronger or of charismatic 'new men'; the more reasonable, or intelligent, or the well-born, they think, should rule the others, and this notion displays the elements of moral thinking in politics.

Readers of the chronicles of ancient history are struck by the emotional unpredictability of powerful rulers, their devotion to the 'cult of frightfulness' prescribing rape, execution, and the torching of villages and cities. They bring home the point of the philosophers'

critique of untutored power. The old chronicles describe situations in which ambition comes into full play in the absence or impotence of countervailing moral ideation. They show us that the non-lethality contract longed for by Hobbes, and supposed by some evolutionary theorists actually to have come into force, was superseded by the re-emergence of lethal motives when humans abandoned life in small groups of related individuals for life in anonymous cities and city states surrounded by 'enemies'. The behaviour of our ancestors, if Homer and Herodotus are good guides to it, was highly responsive to context, clever, and inventive. If rational self-interest were our only value, it would command our unqualified admiration. But it does not.[40] Politics and some aspects of human relations seem in former times to have been driven by a flexible, situation-responsive opportunism that has become unusual if not unthinkable today.[41]

In private as well as in public life, moral vigilance, overtly peaceable relations, and the enforcement of regularity of conduct have increased.[42] Modern people even seem to have fewer personal enemies than ancient people did, as Kenneth Dover pointed out in his study of Greek popular morality.[43] National leaders still commit atrocities, passively approved by their henchmen, but they no longer commit them as openly, and if the claim that there has been moral progress since ancient times tends to draw sceptical frowns, we should nevertheless acknowledge that the world of Hume's Stuart rulers was already a different world from that of the ancients. We increasingly place a value on protracted intramental deliberation as a precondition of issuing clear signals and on behaving in a consistent manner.[44]

[40] Herodotus gives many examples of creative problem-solving amongst the ancients. He tells the story of the Egyptian king Sesostris, invited with his family to a banquet by his brother. As they were leaving, their host set fire to the path. 'As soon as Sesostris realized what was going on, he turned to his wife because he had brought her along with him too, and asked her advice. She suggested that he have two of his six sons lie down over the flames and act as a bridge across the fire, so that the rest of them could walk on them and escape. Sesostris did this, and although it resulted in two of his sons being burnt to death, this made it possible for their father and the others to escape.' Herodotus, *The Histories*, tr. Robin Waterfield, 135.

[41] Douglas and Isherwood tell us that during the Hundred Years War in Bordeaux in the 13th cent. most of the 'confused crisscross of lords . . . sniffed the wind, weighed the risks of a change of allegiance, and passed from one camp into another, trafficking in loyalty. Raymond IV, Vicomte de Fronsac, owner of a river fortress, changed sides five times from 1336–1349.' Mary Douglas and Baron Isherwood, *The World of Goods*, 34.

[42] As Gehlen argues, morality leads to a 'stabilisation of the inner life' so that it is not ruled by affective impulses or subject to psychologically costly and inefficient reflection. *Moral und Hypermoral*, 97.

[43] Kenneth Dover, *Greek Popular Morality in the Time of Plato and Aristotle*, 181.

[44] Dover reports various ancient sayings to the effect that the wise man readily changes his mind, ibid. 122. Their meaning is that deliberation, not erratic behaviour, is praiseworthy.

While too extreme a reduction in versatility and intelligent concern for one's own advantage is not always advisable, persons of strong moral fibre tend on the whole to rigidity.

To summarize, human interactions rarely concern persons equal with respect to their persuasive powers or the degree of force they are able to exercise. Because the exercise of morality does not tend to the advantage of the strong, it is surprisingly difficult to explain how moral practices, as opposed to prudentially concessionary tactics, can arise. It is not explanatory to say that morality reflects the fact that all humans are equal in their moral personhood, if not in the degree of social dominance they can exert. The emergence of the notion of equal moral personhood in the face of the manifest empirical inequality of human beings with regard to the degree of social force they can exercise and the proportion of the cooperative social product they are able to control is a moral phenomenon needing explanation. While relative social equality prevails in hunting-and-gathering societies, status and prestige are not evenly allocated. When money and technology facilitate the accumulation of advantage, the difference between one person and another with respect to possession of or access to the components of well-being is marked. The weakest lack the strength and resources to oppose the strongest. They may also lack the guile or the affiliative ability that Hobbes was confident would compensate for a lack of physical strength.

The proposal that moral rules are advantage-reducing imperatives confirms the historical link between our current moral practices and the prelinguistic, protomoral, self-suppressing behaviour and the punitive retaliation or immobilization attempts directed towards social 'offenders' by our non-human ancestors. The earliest moral rules, those that prohibited treacherous attack and murderous retaliation, and that structured property relations and marital attachments, were prohibitions and permissions whose truth or falsity never came into question. Though we now worry more than our ancestors did about justification, the modern institution of morality is still a system of prohibition-and-permission rules comprising positive obligations, such as duties of assistance and duties to perform contracts, and prohibitions on negligence and indifference. Our dispositions, both innate and learned, to interfere with others, to control their behaviour, and to suppress antisocial tendencies in ourselves are the source

of moral normativity. Freud, who noted the depth, universality, and suprarationality of mechanisms of suppression, suggested that the restrictive rules observed in non-literate cultures might 'throw light on the dark origin of our own "categorical imperative" '.[45]

The imposition of prohibitions, he maintained, is associated with sanctity and power, and prohibitions that have no obvious function or rationale are found in many ancient traditions. Their variability from epoch to epoch and place to place may contrast markedly with the beliefs of rule followers that absolute right and wrong are at issue, absolute danger and perfect safety. 'Taboos', according to Freud, concern 'actions for which there [exists] a strong desire.... [Those who observe them] assume an *ambivalent attitude* toward their taboo prohibitions; in their unconscious they would like nothing better than to transgress them but they are also afraid to do it'.[46] Freud's suggestion is worth pursuing. Of course the class of taboo rules is much wider than the class of what we are prepared to recognize as moral rules. Many reported taboos seem to concern actions that nobody could experience a powerful temptation to perform and that are hard to see as the objects of deep ambivalences.[47] A given taboo may not even have a distinctive social function. A. R. Radcliffe-Brown pointed out that any system of codes whose observance produces anxiety and relief and requires mastery by members of the society enhances group understanding and solidarity.[48]

We tend to think, when moved more by biological than by anthropological considerations, that moral rules, unlike taboos, must contribute to human flourishing or at least to human survival, but functionalism is an unwarranted conclusion. If at least some moral rules are the residuals of ancient taboos, they may not have either a strict biological or a distinctive social function. The propensity to

---

[45] Freud, 'Taboo', 824. Samuel Scheffler pursues briefly the idea that the impression of inexorability of morality derives from an unconscious fear of punishment, in *Human Morality*, 80 ff.

[46] Freud, 'Taboo', 831.

[47] e.g., the high priest of Jupiter in Rome, according to J. G. Frazer, 'was not allowed to ride, or even to touch a horse, nor to look at an army with arms, nor to wear a ring which was not broken, nor to have a knot on any part of his garments; he might not touch or even mention by name a goat, a dog, raw meat, beans, and ivy; his hair could only be cut by a freeman and with a bronze knife; . . . and his hair and nails when cut had to be buried under a lucky tree.' J. G. Frazer, article 'Taboo', *Encyclopedia Britannica*, vol. T–Z, p. 13.

[48] A. R. Radcliffe-Brown, *Taboo*, 39.

impose harsh and complex requirements on oneself and others indicates that natural selection has not formed us to like only what is good for us as living organisms.[49] Assuredly we enjoy nutritious foods and protected dwelling places, and we dislike poisonous snakes. All the same, a culture may insist that its members undergo certain painful rituals in the name of honour and sanctity. Circumcision, body piercing, and tattooing are biologically bad for us, for they may result in infections, scarring, and permanent impairment. Yet natural selection does not weed out these decorative practices as fitness-reducing. Humans have surplus resources to draw on that enable them to override, and alternative sources of reward that enable them to ignore, considerations of inclusive fitness when inventing and imposing rules. It is possible that all moral rules modern agents regard seriously have been purified of counter-functional elements and that they contribute to human welfare but there is no particular reason to assume that this is so. Hobbes's Theorem, that the hedonic content of a society is a direct function of its moral regulation, holds only for certain values. After a certain point, one cannot make people any happier or more secure by imposing additional regulations on them.

Two important consequences follow from the conceptual gap between the existence of normative institutions and their justification. First, what is regarded as morality in many cultures, including our own, may embody regulations that are trivial or even harmful to human organisms even if they serve to promote group solidarity. This theoretical possibility should encourage us to look at claims for the intrinsic morality or immorality of well-entrenched practices with a critical eye. Second, even acceptable moral regulations may be biologically or socially counter-functional. A rule may be, from the perspective of prescriptive morality, a good rule, even if it does not prolong the life or reproductive capacity of the persons subject to it, and even if the regulation is exigent in a sense still to be explored.

As 'self-enforcing' norms that do not require the application of external sanctions, moral rules are at once natural, non-natural, and counter-natural. They are natural in the sense that human beings

[49] Cf. Michael Ruse's claim that 'natural selection has made us in such a way that we enjoy things which are biologically good for us and dislike things which are biologically bad', in *Taking Darwin Seriously*, 236.

everywhere have a tendency to construct and enforce them, just as they have a tendency to construct languages and to insist on their proper usage. They are non-natural in the sense that their specific forms are local, like languages, and do not correspond to species-specific dispositions. Finally, they are counter-natural in the sense identified by Kant and Freud. They are difficult impositions that may make large demands on our capacity for self-awareness and social monitoring and that call for the suppression of instinctive or spontaneously arising desires at the same time as they focus attention on them.

2

Paraworlds and Confirmation

As R. M. Hare observes, moral decisions involve the application of principles to particular situations.[1] Moral questions of the form 'How should I behave when... in light of...?' or 'How should we all behave when... in light of...?' presuppose that we have an interest in evaluating moral policies and in soliciting agreement and approval. These assorted interests present us with the problem of moral self-positioning, a problem that is constantly solved in practice, even without conscious reflection. We form opinions about what we ought morally to do, about what our acquaintances ought to, and about what perfect strangers such as government officials and film stars ought to do. Some of us attempt to intuit moral reality on a proposition-by-proposition basis. Others guide their conduct according to principles derived from well-reasoned texts. Others go along with what their parents used to say or with what respected or irresistible authorities have laid down as right and good. Most of us draw on all these sources somewhat haphazardly in everyday life.

A given group or a given person may come to situate itself or himself close to the self-interested centre or towards the outer regions of hypermorality on any moral issue. A religious sect requiring hypermoral lifelong monogamy might be opposed to redistributive taxation. Some vegetarians are not monogamous, as surprising as this might seem, and many defenders of abortion rights are vegetarians. There are even just-war-theorist-vegetarians! The better-known moral theories comprise particular formulas of obligation and rules for generating further formulas, together with reasons for preferring them to alternative rules and formulas.[2]

---

[1] Hare, *Language of Morals*, 56.
[2] Gibbard remarks on these norms and their bearing on the search for belief coherence in *Wise Choices, Apt Feelings*, 168.

What are the characteristics of a moral theory and how are its particular propositions evaluated? This chapter advances the view that moral judgements can, in principle, be confirmed with the help of the apparatus of fictional worlds—paraworlds. Few moral judgements are plausibly regarded as already confirmed and most moral claims are addressed to what might be called 'practical indeterminables'. Nevertheless, to just the extent that a proposition of moral theory is confirmable, it is binding on agents generally.

2.1. Moral Belief-Sets and Theory M

The totality of moral permissions, obligations, and restrictions that N accepts or endorses is the basis of the judgements $j_1, j_2, j_3 \ldots$ that N offers or could offer about the rightness or wrongness of actions, policies, or situations. In so far as N never thinks about and is not asked to pronounce on many actions, policies, and situations, though she can do so if prompted, perhaps after a long period of reflection and deliberation, her system contains some moral rules only implicitly. Her beliefs may not be constrained by consistency requirements. The set of formulas of obligation and permission (formulas of obligation for short) that she endorses, together with the judgements she makes or would be disposed to make on the basis of these formulas, constitutes her moral belief-set.

Establishing the contents of this set for anyone, including oneself, is not a simple task, for the notion of 'acceptance' or 'endorsement' covers a range of attitudes and dispositions to act and to judge. Initially presented moral convictions can be thrown into disarray by skilful questioning. Asking a subject whether it was wrong to eat the flesh of mammals, to withhold medical treatment from newborns with such-and-such life-threatening handicaps, to provide narcotics and stimulants to addicts free of charge, or to tell a lie to avoid wounding the *amour-propre* of an author, would likely elicit a number of expressions of uncertainty as well as some confident judgements about right and wrong. Novel moral problems can present themselves suddenly and unexpectedly, and there is no reason to insist that an agent's response to a query belonged to her system antecedently. Moral avowals do not always correspond to the principles that

would be imputed to the subjects who produce them on the basis of observation. The notion of an implicit moral system suffers from a certain vagueness concerning what is to count as an internalized rule. However, anyone who has at least one moral belief has a moral belief-set, and most people have a number of moral beliefs. Any vagueness that attaches to the notion of a moral belief-set must infect the very notion of a moral belief.

Local moralities are sets of formulas of obligation that are employed by a social unit to regulate, or to try to regulate, its own affairs. The included formulas are believed to be right or proper; they may be itemized and recited, or referenced in contexts of explanation and justification. The social unit may consist of a person, a tribe, an occupational group, a subculture, or another entity that can use the terms 'I' or 'we'. A local morality comprises the rules of conduct and deportment that can be articulated by members of the unit in question as obligations, permissions, and prohibitions; it can be construed as analogous to one of the dialects and idiolects that make up human language. A local morality prescribes responses to instances of transgression and to habitual transgressors. Its codes are supported by positive and negative sanctions, including praise and reproach, reward and retaliation, the bestowal of medals and the communication of thanks, by shaming, imprisonment, and ostracism. Local moralities are supplied with incentives and deterrents. Admonitory songs and stories predict the likely outcomes of certain actions, whether heartbreak or bliss, eternal disgrace or posthumous fame.

The notion of a local morality, whether it is considered under the aspect of a set of rules to which individuals strive to conform or a set of beliefs about right and wrong, is necessarily vague. The inherent difficulties of attributing sets of moral beliefs to individuals or determining which rules they are following are compounded by the difficulties of attributing sets of any type of belief or rule to entire groups or to persons who endure over time. The notion of a local morality is not altogether elusive, however, and anthropologists, sociologists, novelists, and feature writers are able to grasp and articulate important elements of local moralities without pretending to be able to deliver them whole.

An intuitive understanding of local morality is a basis for understanding what a critical morality might be. Kant thought of local

morality as a pastiche of religion, prejudice, sentiment, and folklore and he sought to replace community standards of conduct with universal standards to be adopted and observed by all humans. Philosophers are expert in subjecting to critical scrutiny ordinary notions of reasonable and contextually appropriate behaviour, and they frequently find that local systems come up short. There may be much genuine knowledge and useful insight contained in them, but their contents may appear to need both winnowing and supplementation. And just as the beliefs of some communities, such as ancient soothsayers, are not only factually incorrect but also unhelpful in achieving control over future events, some local moralities appear to be subject to both representational and practical failure. The position that a critical morality ought to replace local moralities need not be ethnocentric. Its proponents are likely to maintain that many of the obligations enshrined in the morality of educated Westerners need winnowing too, while many real obligations are yet unrecognized and unacknowledged by us.

Call M the set of formulas of obligation that partially incorporates, but at the same time wholly supersedes, local moralities in being the right set—the set that ought to comprise one's normative beliefs. Moral nihilists believe that M is the empty set; one ought to have no moral beliefs. Sceptics are uncommitted to the emptiness or nonemptiness of M. Everyone who is not a nihilist or a sceptic believes that M contains some formulas of obligation, even if they are not sure what actually belongs in M. But what could make one set of formulas of obligation the right set? Moral realists have what at first appears to be a clear and good answer to this question: M is the set of moral truths and associated imperatives. One should believe what's true and act accordingly. This answer proves to be remarkably unhelpful.

2.2. Authored and Unauthored Norms

It is often urged that nothing short of an acceptance of moral realism-with-bivalence can capture our understanding of ourselves as persons who strive to correct their moral beliefs and who are able to deepen their understanding of morality by experience and reflection and

through critical, belief-altering tests of moral principles. It is frequently suggested that accounts that portray morality as a system of elective and elected social rules imply that tolerance for every kind of barbarism is inevitable or even mandatory. The notion of a moral standard independent of human preferences that demands to be met, is different, it is claimed, from the notion of an action-guiding rule.[3] Just as there are norms of logic that all discoursing creatures are bound by, whether they decide to heed them or not, and norms of prudence that constitute reasons for action for all long-lived creatures, no matter how recklessly they choose to behave, there are allegedly moral norms that constitute constraints on and reasons for action for everyone. To fail to acknowledge that ethical as well as logical norms exist independently of human agents is to reveal oneself as epistemologically deficient, as lacking an understanding of what moral knowledge is. By distinguishing between authored and unauthored norms, however, we can supply the realist with all that she demands without the absurdities of realism-with-bivalence.

According to the realist, when deciding what I may eat, I should decide to draw the line at shrimp rather than at flounder if and only if it is true that one is not permitted to eat shrimp but is permitted to eat flounder; and I should designate abortions after the fourth month of pregnancy as morally wrong if and only if it is false that a person may undergo or perform an abortion after the fourth month of pregnancy. And just as I ought to believe all and only true empirical statements, provided I have the storage capacity to do so, I should adopt all and only true moral beliefs, provided I have the capacity to do so.

Moral realism is consistent with the view that the notion of a prohibitory rule is central in moral theory. Anthropologically established rule-priority as alleged in Chapter 1 is not the basis of the criticisms that follow. For the imperative, optative, and declarative forms of normative statements are related. The issuing of a command to an agent implies a wish that an act be done or not done. The wish that an act be done or not done implies the existence of a thought that

<hr>

[3] v. Stephen Darwall, *Philosophical Ethics*, 64.

the action is good to do or bad to do.[4] The directed-to-someone imperatives:

    (1) Everyone: Don't eat animals!
    (2) Police: Don't torture!

correspond to the generalized optatives:

    (1′) Would that no one ever ate animals!
    (2′) Would that the police refrained from using torture!

and to the moral beliefs:

    (1″) It is morally wrong (for anyone) to eat animals.
    (2″) It is morally wrong (for the police) to use torture.

The question of the truth status of moral judgements, therefore, cannot be dismissed. Nevertheless, whether or not some moral judgements such as 1″ and 2″ are true, the truth of moral realism—understood as the strong claim that every moral judgement is either true or false, that moral statements are subject to the law of bivalence—is neither a necessary nor a sufficient condition for the establishment of a critical morality. Nor is a belief in, or doctrinal commitment to, moral realism either a necessary or a sufficient condition for advancing good moral theories.[5]

One might imagine that a belief in moral realism is a necessary condition of being a morally serious person, just as a belief in God or some equivalent supernatural being, supernatural force, or supernatural status quo is a necessary condition of being a religiously serious person. If so, anyone who wants to be morally serious should form certain meta-ethical commitments whether or not moral realism is philosophically true. However, to be a morally serious person it does not even seem to be necessary to believe in moral realism. One need only believe that there are situations that are (really) morally significant, that some issues are (truly) moral issues. Chapter 1 established that this condition obtains; morality is a genuine category of anthro-

---

    [4] This is not to contradict R. M. Hare's point that imperatives cannot be reduced to indicatives; they cannot be reduced to indicative statements that do not contain or presuppose normative terms. As he observes, value judgements correspond to imperatives of extremely broad and unrestricted application. *Language of Morals*, 5; cf. 178.

    [5] For detailed analyses of the status of moral predicates, and their bearing on the problem of moral truth, see Simon Blackburn, *Spreading the Word*, 181 ff.; John McDowell 'Values and Secondary Qualities'; and David Wiggins, 'A Sensible Subjectivism'. Confidence in the reality of moral properties and the objectivity of (some) judgements ranges from the highs of Nicholas Sturgeon, 'Moral Explanations', to the lows of J. L. Mackie, *Ethics: Inventing Right and Wrong*, 38–42.

pology and acknowledging its importance is all that is required for being a morally serious person.

It is sometimes suggested that a non-realist can have nothing to say against Hitler and is seriously impaired when it comes to choosing a critical morality. However, the presence or absence of a commitment to moral realism has no necessary bearing on agents' judgemental capacities or dispositions. A non-realist is no less likely than a realist to insist that one ought not to deploy lethal power against helpless persons and that anyone who does so is immoral. The non-realist, to be sure, when asked why he *claims* that Hitler's actions were inexcusable will not answer, 'Because it's true!' but this outburst by the realist adds nothing that is not already present in the non-realist's answer, namely, 'Because that's what I think!' Neither answer addresses the question why Hitler's actions *were* inexcusable: here realist and antirealist will give indistinguishable sets of answers.

Finally, one can care about moral policies and moral judgements and their effects on actions and belief without being a realist, just as one can be a dedicated aesthete who adheres to strict standards of taste and who judges others' appearances rigorously without holding a realist theory of aesthetic judgement. I may simply prefer the condition of the world in which others share my codes and agree with my judgements to the condition in which they don't.

A commitment to moral realism is therefore not necessary for caring about morality or being interested in a critical morality: Theory *M*. It is not sufficient either. The realist identifies *M* with the hypothesized set of true moral propositions but realism cannot explain why we ought to try to discover and to believe just those formulas of *M*. There is no general obligation to discover and believe every true proposition. Even if *P* is true, one should not (prima facie) try to find out that *P* if doing so will overtax one's mental capacities, and one should not believe that *P* if one has no justification for *P*. One should not try to find out or believe that *P* if doing so will spoil one's own or someone else's life. If trying to establish the entire set of true propositions of morality would overwhelm our brains, we should not try to do that. If bivalence holds of moral propositions, but we have no justification for believing any one, we should not endeavour to believe even one. Finally, if believing moral truths (or even certain true theorems of physics or mathematics) would spoil

our lives or cause us to spoil others' lives, we should forgo belief in them. Moral realism provides no assurance that system M is within our capacity to understand, cognitively accessible to us, and benign. It leaves open the possibility that the true system of morality could worsen our lives, were we to adopt it.

Moral realism is accordingly neither a necessary nor a sufficient condition of the existence of a critical morality M with normative force. That said, the hypothesis that there exists a determinate truth value for each and every moral judgement apparently does help to answer the following question: Why do we think that our use of special argumentative methods and procedures in moral discourse achieves good results—better results than would be obtained by unimaginatively following old habits and customs or flipping coins and reading tea leaves to decide what positions to adopt and endorse and what policies to approve and act upon?

However, the more compelling answer to this question is that the special procedures of argument and inquiry in the normative disciplines, including aesthetics and informal logic, ensure that the critical norms enunciated are accessible and benign. They also provide us with reasons for adhering to the norms in question, reducing their arbitrariness. This claim needs explanation.

Many, perhaps most, of the useful practical norms that we prescribe and submit to are both *authored* and *targeted*. The declarative statement, *You are not allowed to use your computer after 10 p.m.*, with its imperative and optative relatives, is an authored norm invented by me and directed to my son. The rule really exists—I created it!—but nobody other than my son is obliged to obey it. It is a fact that my son is obliged to turn off his computer by 10 p.m., but it is not the sort of fact a moral realist is likely to be interested in. By contrast, the declarative statement, *One is not permitted to torture animals for stimulation or diversion*, appears to correspond to an authorless norm and to have everyone as its target, and statements like this invariably attract the approving attention of realists.

The difference between authored and targeted, and seemingly unauthored and universally directed norms is not to be found in their logical form or in their ontological commitments. In both cases, the norm is enunciated with the aim of preventing certain happenings. The problem of bothersome, sleep-robbing, late-night computing is

addressed by the norm I invented. The norm implies an answer to the question 'What should be done about late-night computing in this household?' (Answer: It shouldn't take place.) The problem of harm to animals is addressed by the other norm that we invented, though no one claims personal responsibility for it. The norm implies an answer to the question 'What should be done about people anywhere who deliberately try to hurt animals?' (Answer: They should stop/be stopped.) Moral judgements originate as authored norms. Most remain in this relatively subjective condition, even when there is wide consensus concerning them. They represent the elections of a set of morally interested agents.

Nevertheless, a moral judgement can, in principle at least, transcend its humble origins. A moral judgement can be said to be confirmed when it commands agreement by appropriately informed morally intentioned persons. To paraphrase Rawls, a moral theorist is not seeking the agreement of 'rational', i.e. self-interested, competitors to his own proposed course of action, but the approval of 'reasonable' assessors to his scheme for everyone.[6] Confirmed statements can even be regarded (though I will avoid this locution) as 'true'. Therefore, it is possible that there are some true moral judgements, even if bivalence is not a feature of moral judgements in general. Meanwhile, many moral judgements, including, *It is permissible to eat shrimp* and *It is impermissible to have an abortion in the fourth month*, are probably not susceptible of confirmation or disconfirmation and are almost certainly neither true nor false.

But what is the form of a moral theory and how are its propositions confirmed?

2.3. The Form of a Moral Theory

A moral theory is not a mere collection of rules or judgements concerning the distribution of advantage that some writer happens personally to favour. It is a collection of rules and judgements presented in such a way as to work persuasively on the audience for the theory. Whether in the form of Marcus Aurelius' Stoic *Meditations*,

---

[6] John Rawls, *Political Liberalism*, 52 ff. These assessors must have certain 'macroethical' commitments; see below, Ch. 4.

the treatises of Kant and Bentham, or contemporary accounts of social justice, a prescriptive moral theory typically incorporates three components.

First, there is a supraempirical account of human nature, and, typically, an account of the status of humans vis-à-vis animate and inanimate nature. The moralist makes a set of claims, or indirectly establishes a set of assumptions about the degree to which humans are subsumed under or stand outside the rule of physical or psychological laws and are like or unlike other animals. Terms such as motive, incentive, and sanction may signal the adoption of a naturalistic perspective, while terms such as will, choice, and freedom may signal the adoption of a metaphysical perspective. Second, the moralist presents a set of first-order formulas of obligation, together with a second-order rule or set of rules from which he claims they follow. Third, the moralist portrays the consequences of acting in accord with or against his preferred imperatives. He may issue threats or offer inducements. The non-compliant subject may be portrayed as out of harmony with nature, out of reflective equilibrium, out of touch with his feelings, or as superstitious, old-fashioned, irrational, or brutish. The theorist may speak in the request mode, or the wish mode, rather than the command mode or the declarative mode. He need not assert 'This is right!', 'Do this!' He may only be urging, more softly and a bit regretfully, 'Would that the world were such that we all did that!' Stoicism, utilitarianism, and Kantianism each correspond to narratively intelligible views or pictures of the world and of how its inhabitants ought to behave, just as theories of the extinction of the dinosaurs or theories about the interactions of subatomic particles correspond to coherent pictures of the world and how its constituent entities did or do behave.

A moral theory, with its tripartite structure, can have a purely intramental existence, but usually a theory is articulated and propounded to an audience with the aim of influencing their beliefs and attitudes, and, sometimes, their actions. The pragmatics of theoretical moral communication are complex. There are distinctions to be made between (*a*) the readers to whom the work is directed, the target audience; (*b*) the persons whose beliefs, attitudes, and actions the work purports to represent, the implied moral subjects; and (*c*) the creatures and things that would be affected by changes in or

by the stabilization of the beliefs, attitudes, and actions of moral subjects, the moral community. Theorists' beliefs about the constitution of these categories of addressee may be accurate or inaccurate.

(*a*), (*b*), and (*c*) may coincide. Aristotle's *Nicomachaean Ethics* and the third book of Hume's *Treatise* appear to be addressed to an educated and literate subpopulation, instructing them what to believe about, and how to behave with respect to other members of the same subpopulation for the benefit of that subpopulation itself. However, such closure is rare, and the audience that is intended to receive the doctrine and to assess the reasoning behind it may be only a small sector of the implied moral community. Kant's *Foundations of the Metaphysics of Morals* includes the residents of the South Sea Islands as members of the moral community, in so far as they are regarded as objects of moral reproach. They are not, however, members of the audience for the work and would not have been considered by Kant as competent judges of his theory. Many of Bentham's writings have as their intended audience an educated and literate subpopulation, but they are concerned with instructing it what to believe about and how to behave with respect to a subclass of labourers and prisoners. Rawls's conception of the class of implied moral subjects and of the moral community has expanded from book to book, and perhaps the composition of his audience has done so as well.[7]

That the moral community is not a concept with a fixed reference is obscured in discussions that refer to 'us'—to what we think, to what our judgements are, and to what we value without discriminating between groups (*a*), (*b*), and (*c*). The situational examples offered by moral theorists do not ordinarily suggest that 'we' includes the few remaining members of hunting and gathering tribes, illiterate peasant women of the Caucasus, or political prisoners in solitary confinement. The moral community typically comprises a set of agents wider than the author himself and the members of his intended audience but narrower than the class of all humans past and present, or all rational beings.

A moral text is produced with the intention of revising or reinforcing beliefs and attitudes, or at least in imitation of texts that are produced with that intention, and, as an item of reasoned discourse, it

---

[7] Compare Rawls's *A Theory of Justice* (1971) in this respect with *The Law of Peoples* (1999).

does so by advancing arguments, detailing analogies, and citing relevant facts, and by staging thought experiments and asking the audience to decide their outcome by intuition. The text may also scold, cajole, or threaten. An important modus operandi of the moral text that has been little analysed is its evocation of imaginary or fictional worlds. To understand confirmation effort in moral theorizing, it is essential to investigate this aspect of formal moral discourse.

Consider first what might be called 'narrative-explanatory' theories from the natural sciences, such as the theory of chemical bonds, Newtonian mechanics, or the climate-change theory of the extinction of the dinosaurs. Such theories describe the dispositions and tendencies of entities such as electrons, ions, hydroxyl molecules, planets, tiny spheres suspended from chains, meteors, shock waves, clouds, trees, and so on. Each theory is derived from observations of nature constituting its data set, and it generates predictions, not about what human beings are going to think or say, but about what objects will be observed, when, where, and in what configurations. Antecedently to its being confirmed, a narrative-explanatory theory depicts a what-it-would-be-like-if scenario for its audience. A theory about how the dinosaurs came to be extinct presents an account of what an observer who had dwelt among the dinosaurs would have witnessed. It might recount a sequence of events beginning with the impact of an asteroid and the shock waves propagated by the collision, proceeding through changes in weather patterns, temperature, and food supplies, and ending with the gradual or sudden disappearance of the animals. A theory of chemical bonds will convey a sense of what we would witness were atomic particles and their interactions visible to our eyes. To confirm the theory is to find out that things are as the theory represents them as being, even where visualization of the processes in question is impossible.

One might think that a moral theory has little in common with a narrative-explanatory theory of the physical world. Empirical statements divide possible worlds into those in which the statement is true and those in which it is false; moral judgements do not have this feature. There is something it would be like for the fundamental constants of nature to be other than they are, but there is nothing it would be like for it to be morally permissible (as opposed to being believed to be morally permissible) to torture animals for stimulation

or diversion. Hence, there is nothing that it *is* like for this to be morally forbidden. There is a set of phenomena that the facts about force, mass, and acceleration explain. Call these 'the phenomena for Newtonian theory'. And there is a set of 'moral phenomena' in the form of observed behaviour, moral judgements articulated by individuals, and penalties and sanctions applied for moral infractions. Yet the moralist's theory, unlike the scientist's theory, is not explanatory in the sense of making us see why just these phenomena must occur, given the facts about anything.[8]

Kant's ethical theory resembles in some respects a narrative-explanatory theory in the natural sciences. It represents to us a hidden set of entities and interactions. It explains how the good will hearkens to the moral law, ignoring the solicitations of the senses. Yet these entities and their activities are not detected and tracked by experience and observation. No matter how favourably positioned and well equipped we imagine ourselves as being, we cannot imagine ourselves observing the rights and responsibilities that Kantian theory ascribes to us.

These arguments seem telling against the notion that we can confirm moral judgements by sampling the environment and collecting hidden data from our present surroundings. Nevertheless, the analogy between physical and moral inquiry is worth pressing further. To give a prescriptive theory for actual human beings is to give a descriptive theory for ideal agents, a theory of their moral competence. But how can a theory of moral competence amongst ideal agents be confirmed when we do not have access to their judgements but only to our own (non-ideal) judgements and to the natural world?

The answer to this question is that we rationally and irrationally motivate the acceptance of the statements of moral theory by projecting narrative-explanatory accounts of how psychologically real but morally ideal agents behave and by asking for the approval of an audience that is presumed competent to assess the account. 'Ideal agents' are not to be understood in this context as agents who always or consistently perform heroic or supererogatory actions. Rather, they are to be understood as agents who act in ways such that their

---

[8] This is the substance of Gilbert Harman's essential point in *The Nature of Morality*, 7 ff.

world—or the aspect of it under consideration—is better than the available alternatives. An ideal world is one that is preferred to other, relevantly similar worlds.

2.4. Moral Theories and Paraworlds

A paraworld is a fictional world that is, in some respects, like our world—close enough that we would feel at home there. The inhabitants of a paraworld resemble persons in our world, but they act in a patterned way that is usually, though not always, significantly different from the way agents act in our world. In any event, agents in a given moral paraworld behave differently than agents in a rival moral paraworld do. Moral rules are better regarded as the 'laws of nature' of alternative worlds than, as Kant took them to be, a special kind of law embedded, like the laws of Newtonian mechanics, in our world. In evaluating a low-level universally targeted moral judgement such as 'Vegetarianism is required' or 'One must never lie', or a higher-level universally targeted judgement, such as 'One ought never to carry out a plan that will worsen the position of the worst-off person in a situation' or 'One ought always to ensure that new policies are not Pareto-inferior to existing policies', the evaluator has to consider what it would be like for it always to be the case that the norm was realized. The mobilization of the projective imagination is the ordinary response to a controversial moral claim.

A moral text that depicts a paraworld embodies a set of assumptions about what people are like, what they need and want, how similar to one another or different from one another they are, how they make decisions and interact with one another. The moralist may communicate to her audience her views regarding the differences between humans and animals, adults and children, men and women, or the rich and the poor, or she may give out that there is very little difference between them. A moral text may depict paraworlds of quiet deliberation, erotic or artistic adventure, quiet immersion in an intimate circle of family and friends, or ambitious striving in a race for the acquisition of resources. These worlds may be inhabited by humble ascetics, loving caregivers, flexible schemers, by expert

game players and strategists, or even by subrational improvisers who stop short of 'one thought too many'.[9]

In his 'Gauguin' fable, for example, Bernard Williams projects a paraworld in which at least some agents do not put others' emotional interests ahead of their own personal ambitions. The Tahitian idyll furnishes the backdrop of a paraworld in which 'Gauguin' is portrayed as sharing important human traits, talents, and frustrations with members of the target audience and at the same time as able to realize an ideal, the evasion of formulas of obligation propounded in rival moral traditions. It is a paraworld in which, despite its exoticism, the intended audience can recognize some familiar features of its own experience.

Paraworlds vary according to their creators' implicit theories of human nature. A world in which agents are endowed with strong impulses to set fire to animals or to wage genocidal wars seems terrible to contemplate, the projection of a diseased or perverse imagination. A pessimistic depiction like Freud's will be balanced in a moral text by the author's suggestion that moral learning can keep destructive impulses under control. The more sanguine the theorist's view of human nature, the less repression and coercion his ideal world will contain.

A paraworld has the following special characteristics:

The Reality Constraint
The actors in a moral paraworld are meant to resemble the moral subjects of our world. They are endowed with the motives, preferences, levels of rationality, and overall aims and purposes that are taken to characterize moral subjects in the actual world. They face situations and problems that are morally significant. The causal relations obtaining in our world are maintained in the paraworld.

The Idealism Characteristic
The actors in the paraworld behave in an ideal fashion, performing according to those formulas of obligation that their creator endorses, or refusing to perform according to certain non-exemplary formulas of obligation. Or, if the paraworld is presented for our condemnation, they observe the wrong rules, the rules comprised in a rival moral theory.

[9] Like Bernard Williams's wife-saving hero in 'Persons, Character and Morality', in *Moral Luck*, 18.

In Kant's paraworld, the agent is partially exempt from the laws of physical nature. His ordinary human body, plagued by selfish animalistic desires, is accompanied everywhere by an invisible noumenal self, motivated exclusively by reason. The creatures of Bentham's paraworld are ruled by two masters, pleasure and pain, and Bentham's moral agents recognize this and behave accordingly. They are not influenced by religion, sentiment, ascetic impulses, and tradition, unlike their benighted counterparts in our actual world.[10] They aim chiefly to maximize aggregate utility. In some texts, a moral antitype is conjured up by evoking for the reader the ideal behaviour displayed in the paraworld of a rival. A utilitarian antitype in a paraworld invented by a deontologist might remove the organs from one healthy person to save five others. A deontological antitype in a world invented by a utilitarian might make others miserable by upholding the principle of sincerity to the foot of the letter. The paraworld may even portray as ideal agents subjects who behave no differently than it is believed that moral subjects, in particular, members of the intended audience, already do. The intention of the moralist is to convince the audience that behaviour that has been criticized as morally defective by rival theorists is not so. The claim that the actors in a moral paraworld behave in an ideal fashion does not imply that the actors all observe stringent moral rules, or that they all observe the same rules, or that they are calm or conforming. The ideal world of an anarchist might be one in which everybody behaves wildly and differently from everybody else. The ideal world of a libertarian might be one in which everybody behaves just as he or she pleases. It is their job as prescriptive moralists to persuade us that their worlds are realistic as well as good.

The prescriptive formulas comprised within a moral theory, then, constitute the author's instructions to the ideal moral agents of a paraworld concerning how they are to behave. Emotivism is accordingly false. 'Ought statements', whose surface grammar is that of a declarative sentence, are not equivalent to declarative statements about what the assertor likes, admires, or prefers. For statements about what people like, admire, or prefer, unlike moral judgements, have truth-makers in this world. The semantics of ought statements

---

[10] Bentham, *Principles of Morals and Legislation*, ch. 1 'Of Principles adverse to that of Utility', 8–23.

are, by contrast, irreducibly modal. They have representational content, but this content is given by the exemplification in the idealized paraworlds of the 'is statements' to which they correspond.

If N has the thought that it is morally permissible to perform a particular kind of action ACT in a particular kind of situation c, she has the thought that ACT is a self-interested action in c, but that in the preferred moral world some persons do ACT in c^{11}. More generally, where I is the all things considered preferred, or for short 'ideal', world:

> ACT is morally obligatory in c = Everyone in I does ACT in c
> ACT is morally forbidden in c = No one in I does ACT in c
> ACT is morally permissible in c = Some persons in I do ACT in c

Further:

> ACT is supererogatory in c = Relatively few persons in I do (what is as exigent as) ACT in c
> ACT is prima facie obligatory in c = Usually persons in I do ACT in c

These latter definitions might seem tendentious. A supererogatory action is one that is morally praiseworthy but not obligatory; how does the notion of occasional but infrequent performance in an ideal world capture this dual feature? The answer to this question is that the performance of supererogatory actions makes worlds better than they would be in the absence of such actions. We do not prefer a world in which no one assumes the role of Mother Teresa, for example, to a world in which at least one person does. Yet, in so far as we regard her actions as non-obligatory, we express a preference for worlds in which her role is not adopted by everyone who could adopt it. Similarly, if N judges that truth telling is a prima facie, but not an absolute and unqualified obligation, then she regards it as the case that persons in the preferred paraworld usually do not lie but sometimes do. That they do not lie is a valid generalization, analogous to 'Birds fly': it admits of exceptions. To say that honesty is a moral

---

[11] In standard deontic logic, an obligatory action is one performed in *all* worlds, a permissible action in *some* worlds, and a forbidden action in *no* worlds. The present scheme is offered as psychologically closer to the way in which we think about morality, representing to ourselves just one ideal world, even if the agents in it have different maxims.

ideal or a moral virtue is to say that honest practices are well represented in preferred worlds and that honest dispositions are frequent in them. To deny that non-violent conduct is even a prima facie obligation is to indicate that non-violent dispositions and behaviour are represented no more frequently in ideal worlds than violent ones.

It is important to be able to represent prima facie duties, since it is generally conceded that formulas of obligation generate inferences non-monotonically. According to most informants, the conclusion of the Kantian inference:

P$_1$ Everyone ought never to lie
C$_1$ I ought never to lie
C$_2$ I ought not to lie at this moment

can be, in rational and considered judgement, rejected, if we add premisses to the effect that the lie is told to beguile a child, or that failing to tell it will result in grievous, irreparable losses, multiple deaths, etc.[12] The prima facie acceptable principle that it is always permissible to perform an action that will preserve more human life than one that will preserve less should not generate the conclusion that we may divest one well person of his internal organs to save five transplant candidates from death.

Theorists try to replace weak generalizations with formulas of exception, e.g., 'It is always permissible to perform an action that will preserve more human life than one that will preserve less, *except when* doing so requires an agent to kill an innocent person.' They do not, of course, any more than other fiction writers, attempt to imagine everything that occurs in a moral paraworld but only what happens that is of relevance to the persuasive task. Nevertheless, it is difficult to describe precisely the behaviour of agents in environmentally and institutionally complex paraworlds and to specify formulas of obligation that are both simple and exact.

---

[12] Even Kant showed himself surprisingly flexible in dealing with exceptions to his rule that one should never tell a lie or commit suicide: 'To be truthful in all declarations, . . . is a sacred and absolutely commanding decree of reason, limited by no expediency', Kant says in 'On a supposed right to lie from altruistic motives', in *Works*, viii. 427. The *Lectures on Ethics* contain nevertheless discussions of cases in which the telling of an untruth or the performance of misleading actions is permissible. See the *Lectures on Ethics*, tr. and ed. J. W. Ellington, 228. Elsewhere he suggests that 'Want of candour . . . is still very different from that lack of sincerity that consists in dishonesty in the actual expression of our thoughts.' 'Letter to Maria Herbert', in *Kant: Philosophical Correspondence*, ed. Arnulf Zweig, 188. Elsewhere, by differentiating between sacrificing my life, shortening it by intemperance, and suicide proper, Kant also qualifies the severity of his other major prohibition.

The content of Theory M could never be represented in the description of a single world, for how moral offenders ought to be or must not be treated is itself a moral question. If N is concerned with moral norms for the treatment of prisoners, N needs to invoke a paraworld in which at least some persons have transgressed legal norms, and, in realistic paraworlds, some of these persons will have violated moral norms. Theory M could accordingly only be represented by a hierarchically ordered set of paraworlds in which violators of lower level norms are written in as elements of the reality constraint in considering the morality of punishment, retaliation, and revenge. These complications remind us that the formulation of Theory M is, like the articulation of a physical 'theory of everything', a remote ideal without calling into question the confirmation procedures theorists appear to use in trying to certify or discredit individual formulas of obligation.

The audience's robust moral intuitions limit the class of paraworlds whose generative rules are eligible for acceptance and adoption. The notion that the principles of a good theory ought to reflect moral judgements about which there is wide agreement follows from the need to justify a theory to a critical audience. A theory containing a permission rule that allows anyone to perpetrate harm to anyone else whenever it would benefit him at all to do so generates a world that is morally inaccessible to most of us. Not only do we doubt that, if our behaviour were regulated by such a rule, things would go well; we do not think that we are the sorts of creatures who would find it fitting to our natures to observe such a rule. The 'we' who confidently reject the egoistic paraworld is larger than the 'we' who confidently reject a paraworld in which setting fire to military personnel sometimes happens.

A moral theory, then, can be regarded as confirmed if it is accepted by an audience that is competent to assess the degree to which it satisfies the reality constraint and the idealism characteristic. Whether any particular formula of obligation or any collection of such formulas in a system has ever been confirmed depends on whether there exists or has ever existed a competent audience and whether they have ever come to agreement. This question is not easy to decide. The competent audience might be conceived as the set of all reasonable persons, whatever their state of information. They, however,

have yet to agree on anything and this conception of a competent audience places moral theory on an entirely different footing from any empirical theory, since the class of all reasonable persons is not believed to be competent to settle, or even to try to settle controversies in the natural and social sciences. Only the opinion of certified experts is taken to count. At the same time, no merely institutional criteria seem adequate to the definition of a competent set of judges for moral theory. The association between morality and the dictates of conscience on one hand, and our knowledge that moral authorities of the past propagated harmful misconceptions on the other, make us reluctant to recognize a category of 'moral experts'. Idealization is involved in the very notion of a competent assessor of moral theory.

Sceptics deny either that a unique and competent set of judges can be identified, or that competent judges would agree about anything significant. Nevertheless, it is clear what the moral theorist is aiming at when he presents his work for evaluation, what confirmation effort comes to. Moreover, against the sceptic's protests, we can state with some confidence that, although we cannot provide a general definition of a competent assessor, or identify such persons in the population, the proposition that Hitler's actions were morally permissible has been disconfirmed. Persons who regard advantage-reducing rules as important—that is, who are committed to the reality of morality in the anthropological sense—and who are well informed about Hitler's actions overwhelmingly prefer a world in which no one engaged in the behaviour that the historical Hitler did to a world like ours. That numerous people had or still have other preferences does not alter its status as a disconfirmed proposition.

Prescriptive moralists tend to reinforce their audience's robust prescriptive intuitions (as I have just done) and to concentrate on transforming their softer intuitions in a way that gives rise to what might be called standard methodology or the method of cases. Suppose a prescriptive moralist wishes to budge readers from the soft intuition that affirmative-action programmes are unfair or from the soft intuition that they have no duty to assist distant strangers. She might accomplish this by portraying a benign paraworld, in which moral agents act according to a race or stranger-favouring rule without ill effects, and she might appeal to our liking for theoretical unity by showing that a simple set of instructions is adequate to generate that world. She can try to represent a condition in which preferential

treatment coexists with rewards for merit, showing that there is no inconsistency between the two principles, or in which assistance to strangers and assistance to family members are undertaken from the same motive of care.

Alternatively, the theorist may be concerned to preserve certain softer intuitions from challenge in a rival theory. Often this can be accomplished by pointing to certain features of human nature that make revisionary proposals difficult to implement. A meritocrat, for example, might challenge an egalitarian by describing a paraworld in which persons very different in their levels of talent and effort, such as he supposes persons really to be in our world, are rewarded indiscriminately, or according to other criteria such as age or sex, and asking us to appreciate the disharmony of the resulting world and the frustrations experienced by the hard-working and talented.

Even robust intuitions can be modified by an encounter with a moral text. Like a novel that is hard to start but that becomes increasingly compelling, a paraworld that is initially inaccessible to us can become accessible as we become persuaded that the author's efforts to incorporate the reality constraint have been successful, or as we are increasingly moved by his rendering of the idealism characteristic. The conservation of prior robust intuitions does not constitute an absolute constraint on the eligibility for endorsement of a moral theory, any more than it constitutes an absolute constraint on the eligibility for acceptance of a physical theory.

The claim that prescriptive moral discourse functions in this manner might be doubted. A rival tradition holds that credible prescriptive writing is the communication of moral perceptions and moral discoveries, issuing from or made by theorists who have a finely developed moral sense and a feel for logical coherence. On this account, they are able to perceive or intuit the wrongness and rightness of certain actions and situations and to communicate to an audience those veridical perceptions and intuitions, replacing the audience's pre-existing illusions and confusions. The moral theorist helps the audience to see the moral worth of an action or situation in the same way that a good film critic helps an audience to see what makes a film aesthetically flawed or a fine production as the case may be. On this view, the enunciation of normative positions is consequential on the seeing and intuiting of moral properties in actions and situations occurring in our world, not on imaginary goings-on in ideal paraworlds. For, if the explanation

of the meaning and function of ethical discourse demands explication in terms of the behaviour of ideal agents in alternative worlds, why shouldn't this be true of all normative discourse—whether in logic, aesthetics, or medicine?

According to some meta-ethicists, we can see that *It is wrong to lock little children in broom closets when they have misbehaved*, as we can see that *Hitler was an evil person*. Moral goodness and evil are relational properties that human perceivers are equipped—some better than others—to perceive. Alternative worlds are no more involved than they are when we see that a joke is funny, or even that a lime is green.

Despite the popularity of this theory, it is not a serious competitor. The theory of moral direct perception, considered as a phenomenological account of what it feels like to make a moral judgement *in situ*, is entirely compatible with the account offered here. To have the experience of perceiving or intuiting a moral property in an action or a situation is just to have a certain thought about a paraworld in the same way that to see or intuit a potential mate in a current date is to have a thought about a possible world or a future state of the world, even if the man in the street hasn't yet found his way to this analysis. A critic's normative claim that a film is (really) funny is a claim about what idealized people with good senses of humour *would* all experience, were they to watch the film. The claim that a sofa is really oyster, not beige, is a claim about what colour name linguistically and perceptually competent observers say it is in their worlds.

All normative utterances project a world in which persons like us comport themselves differently from the way they do in our world. In an aesthetically ideal world, they create and surround themselves with different objects, and in a logically ideal world they reason differently and draw different inferences than our agents do. To declare that *ad hominem* arguments incorporate fallacies is just to represent ideal epistemic agents as consistently avoiding recourse to *ad hominem* arguments.

2.5. How Remote are Paraworlds from the Real World?

The hypothesis that defending and challenging moral propositions, in contexts in which the establishment of a critical morality is the task at

hand, depends on the imaginative projection of paraworlds explains why moral philosophers so often appeal to literature as a source of examples and illustrations. Novels furnish ready-made paraworlds. Frequently, a novelist is advancing or criticizing a prescriptive thesis and draws his moral paragons and antitypes accordingly. Like narrators of realistic novels, moral philosophers constitute themselves as reliable observers of moral phenomena. However, the author can only theorize the actual as she or he perceives and experiences it, and unnoticed biases or even fantastic beliefs can deform her or his portrayal. The reader of a prescriptive text has to decide whether the moralist's conception of human nature and the demands placed on it are sufficiently accurate to make his recommendations credible and whether the rules of conduct implicitly or explicitly recommended are suitable for creatures such as we are.

The norms observed by the agents of a literary paraworld might seem adapted to them, given the sort of world they are in and the sorts of creatures they are, but it can seem to the reader that it would not be good for her or for us to live under their moral regime. Critics often challenge a moral theory by arguing that our world is fortunately unlike a given philosopher's paraworld. Julia Annas, for example, argues that the fictional world of *Effie Briest* is a Kantian world and an exceedingly unpleasant place to live. Martha Nussbaum suggests that 'Henry James's *The Sacred Fount* is a fascinating account of what the world looks like to a man who . . . [allows] theoretical intellect to determine his relation to all concrete phenomena, refusing himself any other human relation to them, and yet at the same time priding himself on the fineness of his perception'. A more Aristotelian world, she argues, is preferable to this one.[13]

It is often unclear whether a theory has failed properly to characterize the moral community, or whether its idealism characteristic incorporates a strongly revisionary element. Two examples can be cited:

Alasdair MacIntyre describes a 'practice' as 'any coherent and complex form of socially established human activity through which goods internal to that form of activity are realized in the course of trying to achieve those standards of excellence, which are appropriate to and

---

[13] Julia Annas, 'Personal Love and Kantian Ethics in *Effie Briest*', 15; Martha Nussbaum, 'An Aristotelian Conception of Rationality', in *Love's Knowledge*, 81.

partially definitive of, that form of activity'.[14] MacIntyre lists playing football, chess, farming, architecture, physics, chemistry, biology, painting, and the making and sustaining of family life, as practices. Now, few women have historically been involved in football, chess, architecture, physics, chemistry, and biology at a level involving the pursuit of excellence according to externally established standards, even if their current involvement is much greater than it was. Indeed, except for weaving and sewing it is difficult to think of an activity traditionally associated with women and traditionally performed by them in sizeable numbers that has ever been tested by and made subject to objective standards of excellence. MacIntyre cites the making and sustaining of family life as a practice, but women rarely take cleaning, cooking, and home nursing and education to specialist levels of excellence.[15]

On one reading, then, the moral community consists chiefly of men who, ideally, are all engaged in one or more practices. Their world also contains women, as well as trees, houses, animals, and other features of the landscape. One may feel such a world does not satisfy the idealism characteristic. Interpreted in another way, the moral community consists of men and women and, ideally, the women are fully involved in practices, either in football, chess, chemistry, etc., or in some expanded list of activities that count as practices. Under the latter interpretation, MacIntyre's prescriptive ethics is strongly revisionary, since it effectively asserts that, in a morally acceptable world, either women have to be involved in football, etc. to the same extent as men, or more women's activities have to be tested by and made subject to objective standards of excellence. In so far as MacIntyre does appear to be critical of women's wasting their time and their talents on undisciplined activities that are not subject to external assessment, there is good reason to ascribe to him the revisionary interpretation, but it cannot be said that his text addresses the point directly.[16]

---

[14] Alasdair MacIntyre, *After Virtue*, 175.

[15] E. F. Schumacher argues that there can be no expertise in family relations, since they present a set of 'divergent' rather than 'convergent' problems. *Small is Beautiful*, 79–80. It follows that the maintenance of family life can't be a practice in MacIntyre's sense.

[16] MacIntyre is, nevertheless, critical of modes of life that, however elegant, refined, complex, and meaningful, leave or left people without significant work to do. He describes the lives of aristocratic women of the Meiji era as pathetically meaningless. See *After Virtue*, 223.

A second example, from Colin Macleod, presents the reader with a similar interpretive problem:

[W]e can roughly distinguish three kinds of choices which may legitimately ground differences in the holdings of individuals. First there are choices concerning the mixture of work and leisure in one's life. A person may be able to earn more income by working harder or by putting in longer hours. Second, there are what might be called 'production choices.' These are decisions about what sorts of goods and services to produce or provide. The more we make available what is in demand by others, the more resources we may acquire through market transactions ... Third, there are choices concerning the sorts of risks one is prepared to take in leading one's life. While one person may choose to run high risks with a small chance of a huge payoff, another may prefer to minimize risk in order to secure a more modest but more likely payoff.[17]

In its context, the passage describes a paraworld in which holdings cannot be acquired except by work involving effortful application, and in which any subject can make such applications, though many will choose not to. Such acquisitions, and, presumably only (or chiefly) such acquisitions, are legitimate.

Had this passage appeared (with suitable linguistic alterations) in a seventeenth-century political treatise, readers would have been surprised by the novel plan of social organization being proposed. For most of human history, holdings were not a function of the holder's ability and willingness to produce and exchange socially valuable goods and services. They were taken to be legitimate if acquired by conquest, inheritance, or marriage, or as gifts. The modern reader may not share the old conception of legitimacy but he can nevertheless ask how remote the world evoked in the passage is from the real world.

What are the background assumptions in the passage quoted as to how the world works and how much verisimilitude do they possess? The generalization that reward levels depend on an agent's application and the risk level he or she is willing to assume is valid in many contexts. A philosopher can decide to revise his manuscript, or, alternatively, to entertain himself with little trips to the hardware store; to try to publish a paper in a bottom-drawer journal with a

---

[17] Colin Macleod, *Liberalism, Justice and Markets: A Critique of Liberal Equality*, 50.

high acceptance rate, or to aim for a top-drawer journal with a low acceptance rate. These decisions will influence his outcomes. Most persons, however, lack full control over their output and their risk levels.

A mathematician cannot decide to double her output of mathematics papers or to write riskier ones that might bring her a higher pay-off. She will write the number of papers she can, and they will be timid or bold, depending on the quality of her mind. Farmers in rural subsistence economies, parents with young children, unemployed accident victims living on social assistance who cannot lift, type, or use a telephone comfortably—none of these agents can decide to produce more exchangeable goods, or to sacrifice some leisure. Other agents are uninterested in the prospects of a big pay-off. Or the question of the legitimation of their holdings is moot for them, since they don't have any. The holdings of many young mothers do not depend on their ongoing production-and-risk choices, but on a single past decision: whom they decided to marry.

On one reading of the passage, in a morally good world, people who for whatever reason do not choose to produce very much will not have much by way of legitimate holdings; on another reading, in a morally good world, everyone has substantial control over his or her production and risk choices. The portrayal of a moral paraworld different from our world, it might be insisted, is intrinsically critical because of the difference it tries to signal between actual and ideal conduct, or between inappropriately idealized conduct and truer-to-our-natures conduct. The proffered shoe only fits some moralists, however, in some parts of their texts, and not others. The thesis that Aristotle must have meant that women and slaves ought to realize themselves in politics or contemplation though they did not do so in his time is absurd, and the suggestion that Kant was advocating the full participation of women and servants in the intellectual and political life of his society is no more tenable. In their schemes, women and slaves or servants are not good or focal examples of moral subjects, and the discourse is not about them.

In summary, three conditions must be satisfied by the paraworld in which a moral judgement is descriptively realized if the judgement is to be considered as a confirmed element of M, the set of moral principles to which our actions ought to conform. First, the moral

community must be depicted in a manner that is biologically, psy-chologically, sociologically, and anthropologically realistic. Our dis-positions and tendency, the realities of our various situations, whether they are posited as flexible or inflexible, must be portrayed in such a way as to stand up to criticism. Second, the behaviour of the agents in the paraworld that is commended to the audience must seem to be possible for members of the moral community who are constituted as they are. A theory that places overly exigent requirements on us cannot be confirmed. Third, the paraworld corresponding to M must be judged appreciably better than any of the alternatives from amongst the set of eligible paraworlds. The competent audience is not, however, required to agree on or to stipulate the criteria by which 'betterness' is to be judged, only on betterness itself.

This claim might seem outrageous. Surely, a theory of morals ought to tell us what makes one world morally better than another? This objection betrays, however, a confusion of levels. The task of specifying the criteria for paraworld betterness is analogous to the confirmation theorist's task. It is distinct from the scientist's task or the task of the ordinary philosopher seeking to explain scientific inquiry. It is far easier to get the agreement of competent assessors that $E = mc^2$ than to get agreement on the criteria that competent assessors use. A reputable branch of the theory of morals, analogous to confirmation theory in the philosophy of science, might well address the higher-order normative question of paraworld betterness—what makes one paraworld *really* better than another? My concern here is merely to give a non-normative philosophical account of how the notion of paraworld betterness is employed by rival moral theorists.

The agreement of a competent audience on these three features is necessary and sufficient, according to our claim, for normativity, for the existence of obligations binding on everyone, regardless of their personal views. Moral judgements, on this view, represent prefer-ences, as non-cognitivists maintain, or more precisely, elections. At the same time, they are not mere subjective preferences, or emotion-based elections, or elections made regardless of what the judge believes others' elections to be. They have representational, not only conative, content. When we make a moral judgement, we represent certain patterns of action and forbearance as instantiated in a morally good world, without coming to know that they are.

Do *I* have to do what a confirmed statement in moral theory says people should do? Can meta-ethics show that agents are obliged to act in accord with confirmed moral theories? This might be doubted. No one, it seems, can demonstrate to me that I am obliged to follow the rules of logic in having a conversation, display culturally expected table manners, or dress in workplace-appropriate clothing. I am free to ignore all such norms, provided I can tolerate the resulting sanctions. I am equally free to ignore all formulas of moral obligation presented to me, one might argue, no matter what critical procedures they have been subjected to, provided I can accept the consequences.

This position is, however, simplistic. In so far as a moral theory is a theory about what agents ought to do, agents ought to do as the theory says—provided the theory is confirmed and there are no good reasons for disregarding it. One ought generally to believe propositions confirmed by scientific inquiry, provided there are no important countervailing considerations. Further, *to the extent that* a theory has been confirmed, we are obliged—weakly or strongly—to do what it says. If we fail to do so, our fault is that much smaller or greater, depending on how well-confirmed the theory is.

Conversely, suppose we cannot confirm that one must never take another human life. Is murder then morally acceptable? For it might seem that if no one is impersonally obliged to refrain from murder, murder must be morally acceptable. The permissibility of murder does not, however, follow from confirmation failure. The fact that *we* cannot confirm that one must never take another human life does not compel *you* to prefer non-pacifistic paraworlds to paraworlds in which *some* people kill or murder to those in which no one does.

2.6. Relativism

The notion that moral theories project paraworlds that enable us to evaluate their authors' virtual moral systems does not prejudge the case for universalism over relativism. There is no contradiction in the suggestion that, in a morally ideal world, distinct sets of agents organize their lives differently and behave differently. We can

distinguish between 'world-level relativism' and 'theory-level relativism'. World-level relativism is realized if advantage-reducing
practices within a world are different for different groups. It is a
permission rule for groups. World-level relativism is simply a characteristic of some paraworlds and can be expressed as follows:

World-level relativism
In I, at least one group always/sometimes does ACT in c and at
least one other group never does ACT in c. Or, at least one
group never does ACT in c and at least one other group always/
sometimes does ACT in c.

A trivial degree of world-level relativism results from virtually any
circumstance-specification. The claim that persons may lie, but only
to save their own lives is trivially relativistic. Relativistic content can
also be disguised by global formulations. Suppose N believes that
vegetarianism is the correct moral policy for persons in Southern
countries with a developed food industry who have access to a
wide variety of vegetables and starches but is not required for the
fishers and seal-hunters of the North. She can advance action rules
such as, 'Anyone may eat meat in circumstances in which they are
hungry in the North' and 'No one may eat meat in circumstances in
which they are hungry in the South'. Though all persons in her ideal
world confirm to what are nominally the same rules, they are relativistic in content.

Theory-level relativism, by contrast, is a philosophical thesis, not a
characteristic of worlds. It is true if and only if two distinct moral
systems are both confirmable to the same, impressive extent.

Theory-level relativism
The set of formulas of obligation that generate world W_1 are
confirmable and the distinct set of formulas of obligation that
generate world W_2 are confirmable as well.

One may reject theory-level relativism while accepting world-level
relativism or (less intuitively) one may eschew world-level relativism
insisting that all agents regardless of what group they belong to must
behave alike in c, but that two qualitatively different worlds inhabited
by uniform agents are equally ideal.

World-level relativism—moral diversity within a world—might be
favoured on account of the varying circumstances alluded to in the

dietary example above. It might also be favoured on the assumption that humans have a drive to formulate distinctive styles of personal conduct. If this drive can only be repressed by coercion, a paraworld that incorporates the idealism characteristic will not instantiate a uniform code. Universal conformity to a certain pattern of behaviour—reflecting, for example, universal restrictions on meat-eating or numbers of wives—would, on this view, imply morally objectionable social dominance, through which one group succeeds in controlling another.

Theory-level relativism is not a dangerous or threatening doctrine. It is implausible, though not impossible. It is difficult to confirm to an impressive extent even *one* set of formulas of obligation, and the possibility that we confirm *two* incompatible moral systems to an impressive extent seems remote. World-level relativism is a virtually inescapable characteristic of paraworlds and is no more intrinsically dangerous. At the same time, within a given prescriptive theory what at first looks like a tolerant and generous provision for moral diversity can disguise morally objectionable social dominance. The relativistic aspects of a theory can be, in other words, grounds for rejecting it and the 'ideological' appeal to diversity is criticized below in Sections 4.4 and 4.5.

The sheer difficulty of confirming moral propositions, meanwhile, leaves room for individuals to hold and live by different systems without violating objective norms, to practise what might be called 'practical relativism'. For, although we can often be certain that they do not do certain things, we do not know exactly how moral agents in the best world behave.

Practical problems concerning what ought to be done—what it is right, acceptable, forbidden, advisable, rash, or permitted to do sometimes (but only sometimes)—have determinable solutions, making practical relativism an inevitability. To appreciate this underdetermined aspect of all practical decision-making, consider the targeted imperative:

(3) Please (you, let me) shut the window!

which corresponds to the superficially untargeted declarative:

(3') We need to shut the window.

'Please shut the window!' is not susceptible of confirmation, but its *in situ* equivalent, 'We need to shut the window' does appear to be. If it

is 10°C outside, if A_1 and A_2 are flimsily dressed, if the room is underheated, and if A_2 has the power to close the open window, the judgement expressed when $3'$ is uttered by A_1—it might be argued—is simply 'true'. Shutting the window is objectively practically desirable. The judgement that we need to or ought to shut it resembles judgements like, 'Your (buck-toothed) son needs/ought to have braces' 'Your (myopic) daughter needs/ought to have eyeglasses'. That you ought to get her a pair is seemingly an unauthored rather than an authored norm. You can even be said to have discovered *the fact that your daughter needs/ought to have glasses.* And though targeted to a specific individual, the normative statement can be said to imply that, other things being equal, anyone with a similar defect needs and ought to get glasses.

Statements of practical desirability are, however, only determinable under certain circumstances and determination-favouring circumstances often do not obtain when claims of moral desirability are advanced. A statement of practical desirability is determinable when the considerations supplied or taken for granted are easily recognized as reasonable and when no countervailing considerations are presented or discernible. Buck teeth and myopia over -1.50 diopters are aesthetic and practical deficits that are commonly and easily corrected, and, in most circumstances, there is no reason whatsoever not to correct them.

At the same time, a statement like $3'$ is not theoretically determinable in every context in which it could be uttered. Indeed, $3'$ may prove surprisingly contentious. Does the window need to be shut if A_2 has just climbed out of a sauna, if it is only possible to shut the window by climbing up onto a tall, rickety ladder, and if an under-ventilated gas fire is burning in the room? There may be no fact of the matter as to whether the window ought to be or needs to be shut. Agreement may signal nothing more than A_2's reluctant decision to accept considerations proffered by A_1, or the abatement of A_2's motivation further to contest the issue. And just as there may be no fact of the matter about what constitutes a good diet or a sound financial plan, there may be no fact of the matter about how we ought to behave. Some diets are unhealthy and some financial plans are crazy but there are many reasonable, though mutually exclusive, contenders for the role of the best human diet and the soundest

financial plan. Confirmation effort is most effectively dedicated, in health, finances, and morals, to eradicating the worst and most common policies and practices, not to determining the best. The apparatus of idealized judges and ideal worlds is entirely conducive to this aim.

Moral disputes with others arise because of conflicting perceptions, both of what it is for things to go better or worse in a world and of what is possible, broadly speaking, for moral subjects. Moral agreement may not be reached when there is disagreement over how unpleasant some state of affairs is, when some people sincerely wish to have different experiences from others, and when it is unclear how difficult it is to implement some policy and what the long-term consequences will be. Disagreement about whether it is permissible to institute a taxation system that is steeply progressive, or obligatory to terminate life at the request of dying patients may be interminable under analogous conditions. This is not to deny that we are constantly making optimality judgements in the practical realm and adjusting our beliefs on the basis of experience.[18] To the extent that a person is rational, he avoids driving whilst seriously inebriated, endeavours to save for his old age, and limits his use of household pesticides. Most people have the capacity to recognize the reasons for prudential actions, and, even if they do not exercise the capacity or their motivation to perform the actions is weak or non-existent, they are reasons for the agent.[19] Though 'moral reasons' have some analogous features, moral judgements belong to the wider category of optimality statements and these are rarely determinable.

Optimality statements of the form 'p is the best q for r' are not usually asserted on the basis of preferences but of experientially derived knowledge of what r is like, how r works or what processes occur within r, how p will function as a q for r, given the composition and structure of p, where p fits into the larger scheme of things, and what alternatives to p are available. By asking after what moral rules are best for us, we inquirers make plain to ourselves how essential it is to try to learn about our real as opposed to our perceived require-

---

[18] Cf. Peter Railton, who describes his position regarding moral learning in 'Moral Realism', fn. 7 as 'stark, raving realism'. Railton's paper shows how experience can have a salutary effect on theorizing and moral self-positioning, but it is unclear why realism is warranted by this.

[19] Williams, in 'Internal and External Reasons', mounts a sceptical attack, countered by Christine Korsgaard, in 'Skepticism about Practical Reason'.

ments, how our current modes of life address them, and what alternative modes of life might be available to us that regulate the damage humans can do to one another, to other creatures, and to themselves, differently. For most readers, and certainly for the present writer, the moral prohibition against bombing peasants has great lucidity. No situation is even imaginable in which the context would render bombing peasants a preferable policy to not bombing them. Yet, wherever interesting moral problems—problems to do with fair distributions, with justified warfare, with obligations to family members and strangers—face us, we will have difficulty deciding what is to be done. We will not be inclined to appeal to 'the moral fact that ACT in c is forbidden'.

The position that morality presents a problem of optimization has some affinities with consequentialism. The scheme outlined here is not, however, convergent with it.

'Consequentialism' can be understood in two ways. On one interpretation, it is a controversial world-level moral theory—more accurately, a family of related theories. Let's simplify by taking 'strong consequentialism' to be the world-level theory that it is always obligatory to maximize welfare. Strong consequentialism predicts that we consistently prefer paraworlds in which, *whenever* an agent can save two people by killing one, she does so. 'Weak consequentialism', the view that it is always permissible to maximize the general welfare, predicts that we consistently prefer paraworlds in which, *sometimes*, when an agent can save two people by killing one, she does so. Since it is difficult to establish that we do in fact consistently prefer strong or weak consequentialist worlds to worlds in which agents *never* kill one to save two when given the opportunity to do so—or in which they do so only under some more complex set of conditions—both strong and weak consequentialism are poorly confirmed. They represent authored norms.

On another interpretation, 'consequentialism' is the name of a family of theories of confirmation, not the name of a world-level moral theory. On this interpretation, a moral theory is the best if and only if the world it represents contains more welfare than other worlds. A confirmation-consequentialist could thus favour world-level virtue theory, believing that worlds composed of virtuous agents, and not welfare-maximizers, are definitely better because

they contain more welfare. Confirmation consequentialism is not, however, the best theory of confirmation. It is not a foregone conclusion that, in judging the betterness of worlds, we ought to attend only to information about overall welfare. We should also perhaps attend to information about relations between agents, or their autonomy, or the balance achieved between the aggregate of desirable states and experiences and what deprivations others can be made or allowed to endure.

Can we conclude that the greater the quantity of empirical information we can bring to the construction of a moral theory, the more adequate the theory? This hypothesis is suggested by the reality constraint. Competent judges, one might think, need to know their way around human affairs, and not only what usually happens, or has happened in the past, but also, like good lawyers, what can happen when one least expects it. If they are ignorant, their paraworlds will lack verisimilitude and their prescriptions will lack value.

To be sure, the uneducated peasant, as Tolstoy maintained, may have more genuine moral feeling than the corrupt sophisticate who has read a thousand books. However, the thought experiment that compares the virtuous peasant with the corrupt sophisticate does not address the question whether, other things being equal, moral theorizing is better when informed by more knowledge of the world. Take two persons X and Y, both of whom are endowed with an average degree of imagination and empathy. X is poorly informed about how the world works; she has little knowledge of economic and legal systems and their histories, or the variety of customs and institutions that have existed all over the world. She knows little about crowd behaviour, fear, aggression, and desire, how animals see the world, or the history of medical and religious views on euthanasia. Y is passably well informed on all these matters.

Suppose one learns that X and Y prefer different moral systems. According to the Tolstoyan, one has no basis for thinking that knowledgeable Y is more likely to have picked the better system than illusion-ridden or ignorant X; in fact, the presumption must be the opposite. If one has to choose between them sight unseen, one should choose naive X's system. The Tolstoyan recommendation seems, however, unduly risky. The philosopher can easily 'imagine

a case' in which living under the system picked by ignorant X is preferable to that picked by knowledgeable Y. But if I were forced to stake all my future experiences in the social world on it, I would not decide to flip a coin.

Nevertheless, it cannot be the case that an omniscient being would necessarily pick a different—and better—system than an only moderately well-informed being would. We cannot require competent judges of moral theories to have the extraordinary qualifications of ideal observers. Specialist knowledge in a given area, moreover, is not always a stellar qualification for making ethical judgements. Doctors may be poorly equipped to construct a system of ethics dealing with the end of life, although they know more about the physiology of death than other people. International economists may be poorly equipped to construct a system of global justice, although they know more about wealth and poverty than other people do. A specialist focus virtually ensures that doctors and economists know less than other people do about other relevant subjects. All we can say is that, other factors being equal, the ethical judgement of the person with more physiological knowledge, when it comes to matters of life and death, or economic knowledge, when it comes to matters of global responsibility, is likely to be better.

To summarize, the theoretical question what a critical morality M would look like is equivalent to the question, what set of advantage-reducing rules would it be best for humans (or for some subgroup thereof) to adopt? Since we are interested in what is best for us as we are constituted, rather than what is true, we need not fear, as the moral realist must, that the permission and obligation rules we ought to live under are insufficiently benign. At the same time, interesting optimality statements of the form 'p is the best q for r' are usually practically indeterminable. What is the best way to teach an introductory logic course? What is the best place for an unmarried woman to look for a husband? The only reasonable reply to such questions is, It depends. What sort of experience are you looking for? The analogous question sets limits on the content of viable moral theories. The next two chapters explore some limits to the pretensions of moral theories.

3

Limits on Theory I: Costs to Agents

Morality poses a set of problems about the regulation of self-interest in which we try to choose the best rules of conduct or policy using as good information as we can muster. As individuals deliberating over whether to follow a particular rule, or theorists trying to generate a set of acceptable moral formulas from a few principles, we recognize that there are trade-offs between the limitation of damage to others and the personal and group sacrifices of other desired goods and states, notably prudential and aesthetic goods and states, that we must bear if we adopt more stringent moral rules. We have to decide what quantity of non-moral goods we want to pursue in the form of personal ambitions and selfish or socially narrow goals, recognizing, in a way that is sobering, that doing so forces us to incur certain moral costs. A confirmed set of formulas of moral obligation would be one that is agreed by competent judges to have struck the best balance that can be struck and it would be generally binding. However, we usually have to settle for less, namely, for authored norms that have some aspiration to higher status and that are accordingly somewhat binding on all of us.

This chapter explores the problem of exigency. As recent critics have shown, the moral obligations urged on us by deontologists and utilitarians alike often seem excessively stringent, suited to persons more heroic, ascetic, and far-sighted than we consider ourselves to be. What features of persons and their environments favour lower levels of demandingness than those set by the two famous modern moral theories? How are the costs to an agent of acting in conformity with them judged to reduce their prima facie obligations, and what is the significance of costs to agents for prescriptive theorists?

3.1. Exigency in Moral Theory

Moral rules often forbid agents to take something they badly want to have, or do something they badly want to do. No matter how much you want a first edition of Hobbes's *Leviathan*, it is not morally permissible to steal one from your friend, your library, or your bookseller, even if you can do so undetected. No matter how much you like money and dislike your wife, you are not morally permitted to hide assets from your wife in a divorce case, even if her lawyer will never find out. Morally good people, we agree, do not do these things—or do them rarely, and only under truly extraordinary circumstances.

The satisfaction of having done the right thing often compensates for the sacrifice of not having or not doing. However, it would be Panglossian to suppose that the hedonic equation always balances. Hobbes's Theorem, as it was designated in Chapter 1, states that for at least some values, the addition of moral regulation to a world increases its hedonic content, the amount of pleasure, comfort, and happiness it contains, and is generally true. Hobbes's Theorem, though, does not apply in all local subsets of the world, or for any arbitrarily large quantity of moral regulation. One cannot always assure an individual or a group that his or their happiness or flourishing will be increased by the addition of increments of virtue to his or their conduct.

A thoroughgoing hypermoralist—and this is a creature of fantasy—has adopted a set of moral rules that are all subformulas of policy Q. He never promotes his own interests if someone else's interests can be furthered or maintained by his refusal to exercise a natural advantage, such as superior beauty or intelligence, or a social advantage, such as wealth, freedom, or influence. Even if they fall short of thoroughgoing hypermoralism, the beliefs and behaviour of martyrs, hermits, and ascetics, adherents of certain subformulas of Q, appear to most observers to represent either a fine but unattainable ideal or a frightening deviation from normality. The psychological platform it would take to support a motivation to adhere to Q is not easy to describe, for why should an agent who does not appear to value his possession of some good G—as is evident in his willingness

to renounce *G* for another's benefit—regard it as good that another should enjoy the possession of *G*?

Many ordinary pursuits, meanwhile, invite and tempt people to advance their own interests at the expense of others, to set moral considerations aside. While the acquisition of wealth and freedom is not a zero-sum game, since they can be increased in aggregate, one way to acquire more wealth is to dispossess others, and one way to acquire more freedom is to persuade or coerce others into giving up some of theirs. Influence is ordinarily acquired by displacing or silencing other influence-seekers. Wealth, freedom, and influence are self-multiplying in that their possessors are able to employ them to acquire more of those same goods than others have.

Most goods have at least some tendency to permit the accumulation of advantage. The beauty that enables one to become a fashion model is likely to confer additional opportunities and resources for beautification, such as a free wardrobe or charm lessons. The intelligence that brings admission to an institution of higher learning is likely to confer additional opportunities and resources for the perfection of knowledge and its effective presentation. Conversely, the initial possession of fewer natural and social advantages than others have tends to draw out the advantage-taking tendencies of the better-endowed in the absence of moral ideation. It is easier to steal from the poor than from the wealthy, to induce the already unfree to undertake additional labour, and to silence altogether those who do not have much say in things to start.

Prescriptive moral theories set constraints on the pursuit of self-interest and the accumulation of advantage. Credible prescriptive theories vary nevertheless in the number and intensity of demands they place on their subjects. They may be relatively exigent, inclining to the hypermoral renunciation of advantage, or relatively relaxed, loading agents with few or weak prohibitions. It is frequently observed that the famous modern moral theories—Kantianism and utilitarianism—tend in the direction of hypermorality.

Kant's demand level is high. His critical philosophy denied the possibility of getting to know truths about God, the soul, and the origins of the world, but impressed on readers the inevitability of certain beliefs and experiences and the ineluctability of certain duties. We *must* perceive in space and time, and we *must* apprehend causes

and effects. We *must* believe in God, hope for the world to come, and submit proposed courses of action to the universalizability test. According to his anthropology, humans have tendencies both to passivity and to aggressiveness, in so far as they are ruled by an inclination to indolence and by self-interest. Yet because they are endowed with a faculty of reason that enables them to conceive themselves as partially exempt from the laws of nature, they can be roused to an admiration of pure moral agency and respect for the moral law.

Kant was concerned not only to dissociate moral motivation from inclination and the pursuit of happiness, but virtuous practice and its acknowledgement from social display and social reward. 'Through all the ills and torments of life, the path of morality is determined,' Kant intones. 'No matter what torments I have to suffer, I can live morally.'[1] Moral living can even mean not living. While the *Foundations of the Metaphysics of Morals* portray suicide as a kind of self-contradictory action, Kant maintained in his early *Lectures on Ethics* that it is better to choose death than to consent to life as a galley slave.[2]

Both Kantianism and utilitarianism posit an overall obligation to consider the interests of others that is independent of natural sentiment and independent of the rewards altruism may bring. The source of that obligation was held by Kant to be our rationality and his point was revived by Thomas Nagel, who insists that we are susceptible to the claims of others because, as rational creatures, we do not occupy a personal point of view exclusively. Where sympathetic creatures can adopt the perspective of another person and take her interests into account, rational creatures can adopt an impartial perspective and take into account anyone's or everyone's interests. An agent operating from a purely selfish platform is no easier to understand than a hypermoral agent. How can an agent who values G—as evidenced by his willingness to deprive another of G in order to have more for himself—fail to regard it as good that the other should enjoy the possession of G?

Rational creatures are thus responsive to what Nagel terms 'agent-neutral reasons'. As he expresses it, 'From the objective standpoint, the fundamental thing leading to the recognition of agent-neutral

---

[1] Kant, *Lectures on Ethics*, 156.   [2] Ibid. 155.

reasons is a sense that no one is more important than anyone else . . . [T]here is not a significant reason for something to happen corresponding to every reason for someone wanting to do something.'³ At the same time, the claim that we can and sometimes do take agent-neutral reasons into account does not entail either that we ought always to do so, or that we can do so easily, as Nagel went on to argue. The impartial standpoint that recognizes agent-neutral reasons is more sophisticated, learned, and comprehensive than the personal point of view. It is more philosophical. Yet it exists, so to speak, on all fours with our responsiveness to other reasons. Kant thought of the moral motive as a constantly operating noumenal force competing with empirical drives and instincts; or rather, he insisted that we are impersonally required to picture it as such.

Arguably, Kant's scheme was confused in its representation of the moral motive both as a real force and as an entity of reason; as non-contingently present in every human being and as threatened by our animality. Modern Kantians are inclined to see these tensions as productive. Meanwhile, critics of Kantianism, amongst them, internalists influenced by Hume, are dismayed by Kant's apparent scorn for the idea that a substantial investment in non-moral goods could be worthwhile. 'The most thorough and readily available medicine', Kant says, 'for soothing any pain is the thought, which can well be expected of a reasonable man, that life as such, considered in terms of our enjoyment of it, which depends on fortuitous circumstances, has no intrinsic value at all, and that it has value only as regards the use to which we put it, the ends to which we direct it.'⁴ The metaphysical notion of the good will as a protective device that the subject carries about with him everywhere like a talisman seems . . . superstitious.⁵ Ordinary agents cannot help causing some wear and tear, on others as well as on themselves, as they try to live their lives. The thought that

---

³ Thomas Nagel, *The View from Nowhere*, 171–2. Nagel has always defended the importance of 'impersonal moralities with universal pretensions', amongst which he includes utilitarianism and some forms of Kantianism. Ibid. 199. See also *The Possibility of Altruism, passim.* Altruism, on his view, is not a *mere* possibility, but it is not a consistently powerful and actual motive in human affairs either.

⁴ Kant, *Anthropology*, 107.

⁵ 'The Sumatrans', according to the 18th-cent. traveller William Marsden, 'are firmly persuaded that particular persons are, what they term "betuah" (sacred, impassive, invulnerable, not liable to accident); and this quality they sometimes extend to things inanimate; as ships and boats. Such an opinion, which we should suppose every man might have an opportunity of bringing to the test of truth, affords a humiliating proof of the weakness and credulity of human nature.' Marsden, *History of Sumatra*, 293. Kant refers to the history several times.

our enjoyment of life is intrinsically without value probably does not have the medicinal properties Kant claims for it.

Utilitarianism is the second great exigent moral theory. Bentham presents it as based on a simple yet comprehensive account of human motivation, and he displays his main theses—the irrelevance of motives, the supreme importance of outcomes—in a dry and factual manner. His thesis that 'the principle of utility is capable of being consistently pursued' is doubtful. In unreconstructed utilitarianism, I am actually obliged to suffer; for my actions must increase overall utility if they are to be morally correct. I am obliged to submit to and suffer the depredations of others and to perpetrate direct harm to them if, for some reason, doing or suffering evil will increase overall utility. This consequence sits uneasily with the claim that we are entirely governed by pain and pleasure. Bentham, to be sure, assumes that, in order to be eligible for utility-promoting punishment, a person must actually have committed a crime.[6] He does not seem to consider cases in which deliberately inducing some quantity of undeserved suffering relieves a greater quantity of suffering. Nor does he regard everyday actions by individuals that do not increase the general welfare as immoral or proscribe them. Yet classical utilitarianism is an inherently interfering moral system. It evolved hand in hand with a belief in the need for scientific solutions to all manner of social non-performance. It called for expensive public works projects that would intrude into the lives of formerly free-living individuals with the construction of an array of jails, workhouses, and other allegedly beneficent institutions.[7] Bernard Williams wryly refers to utilitarianism as 'Government House Morality' and his criticisms have unmistakable parallels with the postcolonial critique of totalitarian regimes of the left as well as the right. The collective good is understood in postmodern times to be an elusive notion, and the sacrifice of individuals in its name is no longer regarded as politically acceptable.

---

[6] Bentham, *Principles of Morals and Legislation*, ch. 13.

[7] On utilitarian experimentation in India, see Eric Stokes, *The British Utilitarians and India*. 'The idea of some sudden sweeping transformation of Indian society, of an entirely new system of law to be constructed in the space of a few years, of a new judicial and administrative machinery under which India would be propelled at a bound from feudal darkness into the modern world—this sort of attitude would only flourish in an age brought up to believe in sudden conversion.' Ibid. 242.

Contemporary normative theories have dispensed with Bentham's bricks-and-mortar approach to the exact specification of institutions, as well as with the strictness and purity of the principle of utility and with supporting metaphysics of the Kantian variety. It is no longer considered necessary to establish free will or a human exemption from the laws of nature in order to present a theory of obligations, and rights and permissions may be introduced to improve the palatability of utilitarianism. Their internal coherence and level of argumentative precision make the new versions technically superior to their predecessors. Even in their updated versions, however, the famous modern moral theories appear to a sector of their readers to suffer from the same underlying problems as their predecessors. The relationship between natural sentiment and moral obligation is unsatisfactorily developed in Kantianism. It is positively incoherent in unreconstructed utilitarianism, which implies that creatures who naturally hate pain are obliged to undergo undeserved suffering for the greater good. Life, whether in neo-Kantian systems of autonomy and universal pronouncing or neo-Benthamite theories of resource allocation, tends to look constrained and regimented. It is easy to sympathize with Williams's complaint that, with Kant and Bentham, 'One is left, at any level of importance, only with purely moral motivations and no limit to their application', and that 'there is, at the end of that, no life of one's own, except perhaps for some small area, hygienically allotted, of meaningless privacy'.[8]

Williams is not reporting on what Kant and the utilitarians have between them accomplished. His worry is not that, because of the promulgation of Kantian and utilitarian doctrine and the positive reception that they have met with, everyone's life has been diminished. He is committed to the claim that our lives could never be completely occupied by morality, except through the imposition of some unimaginable tyranny. He is addressing the representational content of these theories. We can imagine living as Kantians or utilitarians and, according to Williams, this would be bad for us.

Wherever exigent moral theories have been less than pernicious in their effects, critics claim, they have been useless. The sceptic insists that theories are at best epiphenomena of positive social change, not

---

[8] Williams, 'Moral Luck', 38.

its motor. They may be genuine responses to the perception of moral inadequacy, but they may at the same time subserve it by expressing a complementary utopian vision to which ideational allegiance can be given in the absence of practical undertaking.[9]

The problem of exigency is expressed as a dissatisfaction with both the form and the content of the famous modern moral theories. The elevation of unconfirmed authored norms to authorless imperatives rooted in mind–independent reality is rightly regarded by their critics as mystificatory. At the same time, their prescriptions are seen as too interfering and repressive where individual lives are concerned, and as provoking moral scepticism by setting standards of benevolence and self-sacrifice that normal human beings cannot ordinarily meet. Attention, meanwhile, to the difference between the first-person and the third-person standpoint has provided the philosophical underpinning for lower-demand normative theories.

3.2. The First-Person Standpoint

Certain fixed and irremovable features of our cognitive and emotional make-up, it is sometimes argued, nullify the formulas of obligation that the exigent moralists urge on us. It matters that *I* am the one asked by the utilitarian to relinquish a large sum of money to feed hungry refugees, or to kill one person to save twenty. It matters that *I* am the one allegedly required by the Kantian to forgo the face- and situation-saving lie, or to keep the promise I devoutly wish I had never made. Certain things are unreasonable to ask of me, even if the outcome they happen to produce is judged to be better than the relevant alternative. How can it be morally incumbent on *me* to murder one person to prevent twenty others from being murdered, or even to prevent twenty other murderers from carrying out their plans to murder one person each? And if I am not always required to bring about the best state no matter what moral sacrifices it might entail for me, why am I always required to bring about the best state no matter what non-moral sacrifices it might entail for me? As Williams observes, 'There is no limit to what a given person might

---

[9] For a sceptical view, see Dwight Furrow, *Against Theory*, 116–17. For a more favourable estimate of the role of moral ideation, see David Brion Davis, *The Problem of Slavery in Western Culture*, esp. 292 ff.

be doing to improve the world, except the limits of time and strength.'[10] He accuses utilitarians of aiming to 'increase a sense of indeterminate guilt in their readers', a tactic that, he points out, is 'likely to be counterproductive and to lead to a defensive and resentful contraction of concern'.[11]

Subjective perspectives, it has been argued—what it is like to be x—are not fusible with objective perspectives.[12] As surprising as this might seem in light of his views on the inexorability of the moral law, these claims derive historically from Kant's idea of a gulf between the moving objects of physical nature and human agents, between things and persons, the phenomenal and the noumenal world.

The first-person standpoint has been crafted by several centuries of literary practice in techniques of introspection and autobiographical narrative. It would be rash to conclude that all persons everywhere experience themselves in the same way and assign the same importance to their own projects. The few remaining hunters and gatherers may have fully human lives without experiencing the pull of pecuniary motives or having any interest in what the sociologist Albert Hirschmann designates as obituary-improving activities, such as the collection of citations and prizes. Nevertheless, the environment, as phenomenologists used to emphasize, presents itself for everyone as a field for action, an array of possibilities and obstacles, or even as an array of obstacles presenting possibilities. My appetites and desires contour the world that appears to me, determining what is figure and what is ground. If I try to assume the perspective of a detached observer of the human race, possibility and freedom seem to vanish. When I watch a colony of ants moving about on the forest floor, some seem to be scurrying randomly hither and thither, whilst others are engaged in definite tasks, lifting and dragging objects many times their size. I can see that their success and failure depend on certain physical parameters—an ant's strength, the size and shape of the objects it is trying to budge, how much help it is getting, and its luck. An ant can get stuck, or take on a task that proves to be too

---

[10] Williams, *Ethics and the Limits of Philosophy*, 77.

[11] Ibid. 212 n. 7. The same narrowing of concern was predicted by E. O. Wilson, *On Human Nature*, 195.

[12] 'We will not know how scrambled eggs taste to a cockroach even if we develop a detailed objective phenomenology of the cockroach sense of taste. When it comes to values, goals, and forms of life, the gulf may be even more profound.' Nagel, *View from Nowhere*, 25.

much for it. A detached observer might see human activity in this way, partly as pointless scurrying and partly as involving endeavours whose eventual success or ultimate futility is mostly determined by factors outside the control of the busy agents. However, this is not how we experience life from the inside, and it is difficult to see why the objective standpoint should be regarded as more authoritative. My desires make the world appear to me as it does; my project is something I cannot consistently relativize to the projects of the other, for they are they and I am I: the Other appears as an obstacle or an avenue for me, depending.

As Kant sighed at one point, 'Man is not so delicately made that he can be moved by objective grounds',[13] and as Hume crowed, '[T]here is no such passion in human minds, as the love of mankind, merely as such, independent of personal qualities, of services, or of relation to ourself'.[14] The cost to me of actions that benefit others is often high from my first-person standpoint. The actions that I deem to be good from an objective point of view often require me to inhibit my spontaneous and pleasurable impulses (and spontaneous behaviour just is pleasurable), or to exert myself in ways to which I am not accustomed (and unpractised actions are by and large unpleasurable). Not only is it difficult to act towards them exactly as I wish they would act towards me, or to act in ways that benefit others at my expense, it is difficult to adopt the objective perspective at all, for it is psychologically disquieting.

On simple utilitarian principles, spending money in expensive restaurants and on high-priced entertainment and luxury articles is forbidden. And this is not a peculiar deduction of utilitarianism. A Kantian too would will that it would become a law of nature that, when A_2 could be saved from starvation for a year by A_1's forgoing a dinner, A_1 would forgo the dinner. Yet the gulf between theory and acceptance, and between acceptance and action, can seem enormous. For Nagel, our ability sometimes to assume the objective posture results in a permanent state of tension between the good life and the happy life that usually cannot be erased by deciding to limit one's aspirations to one or the other.[15] I can recognize, adopting the objective point of view, that certain outcomes are morally good

13 Kant, *Lectures on Ethics*, 46.   14 Hume, *Treatise*, III. 11. i. 481.
15 Nagel, *View from Nowhere*, 189–207.

ones, and that they are within the capacity of people like me to advance. Still, my own concerns, my comforts and discomforts, weigh more heavily with me than they do with a randomly selected stranger, and I weigh my own comforts and discomforts more heavily than I weigh those of a randomly selected stranger.

Partiality towards our own causes, like our spontaneous reactions of gratitude and resentment, appears to be resistant not only to extinction but even to modification. It might seem that in a limited range of cases we can extend our concerns in the direction of impartial benevolence, but always for a specific reason and not because the action performed accords with a formula of obligation derivable in a moral theory. Indeed, the influential notion that objective normative assessments are incommensurable with first-person normative assessments entered metaphysics with P. F. Strawson's celebrated discussion of reactive attitudes.

Strawson was concerned about the encroachment of scientific ways of thinking into normative frameworks. Regarding the spadework in separating the human realm from the realm of inert nature as already accomplished by Kant, and as issuing in an ontological distinction between 'persons' and 'things', Strawson insisted that we could never abandon our commonsense view of persons as for the most part responsible agents, no matter how irrefutable philosophical arguments for determinism might appear. Mere arguments, even if we could not answer them by showing how free agency was possible, could make no dent in our normal and culturally universal view of persons as the source of happenings in the world compelling moral evaluation.[16] We could, Strawson conceded, occasionally see persons as 'things', as momentarily exempt from attributions of responsibility or even as exempt in the long term and as candidates for rehabilitation or treatment. Our reactive attitudes might be suppressed by detailed knowledge about some particular case. We could never, though, suppress the automatic habit of reacting to persons with resentment and appreciation for their offences and kindnesses. There are limits, Strawson argued, to the changes in our basic commitments and practices we can make for purely theoretical reasons.[17] Analogously, it might seem that while I might forgo a restaurant meal and send

---

[16] P. F. Strawson, 'Freedom and Resentment', 83.   [17] Ibid. 84, 95–6.

money to a charity because a television appeal or an account I read in a magazine moved me, I will never do so because I have come to believe that utilitarianism is true or irrefutable. At best, I might offer a utilitarian principle *post hoc* by way of explaining or exalting my motives.

The claim that certain dispositions are invulnerable to revision from certain sources corresponds to psychological and social reality at several levels. As living creatures, we are disposed to resist interference with our projects, with our pursuit of desired objects, and with challenges to the veridicality of our own perceptions. We are reluctant to embrace knowledge that would deprive us of the conviction that we perceive the world accurately and understand why things happen in it, that it is just, and that our conduct is innocent. As affluent moderns, we are disposed to resist any forces that would, really or symbolically, take away any of the things we enjoy. Strawson was able to convert what the Stoic moralist considered a lamentable weakness, my inability not to react with irritation when a clumsy person steps on my foot, into a kind of virtue. His text was implicitly prescriptive; it suggested to the reader that his ordinary reactions of resentment—perhaps even his tendency to vindictiveness—were elements of a form of life that did not intersect with the practice of metaphysical inquiry but that had its own importance and dignity. It held out a permission—an exemption—to carry on resenting, praising, and blaming. Analogously, what at first appears to be a psychological defect—my inability to treat my own preferences and desires as on an equal footing with everybody else's—can be converted into a positive attribute. This disability or defect is a sign that I am a real human being with a unique and interesting self, not a robotic saint or a mechanical utility-computer.

Various proposals have been made for reducing the discrepancy between ordinary inclinations and classical utilitarian mandates. Samuel Scheffler proposes that a moral agent be permitted to include in her utility calculations the benefit to herself of performing a given action, and loosens the requirement that she make all her calculations from a third-person standpoint.[18] For example, it is more valuable to

---

[18] '[A] moral point of view gives sufficient weight to . . . [the independence of the personal point of view] only if it reflects it, by freeing people from the demand that their actions and motives always be optimal from the impersonal perspective.' Scheffler, *The Rejection of Consequentialism* (2nd edn.), 20. Cf. Nagel, *View from Nowhere*, 171 ff.

X to save her daughter from drowning than it is to her to save a stranger. The utility to her of saving her daughter, calculated from her perspective, would likely outweigh the utility to her of saving two strangers. Therefore, a modification might relax the prima facie utilitarian requirement on X to maximize happiness by saving one or two strangers rather than saving only her daughter. To be sure, there is a limit to the use of this strategy. If agents' estimations of utility to themselves are allowed by the prescriptive moralist to weaken prima facie obligations as these stand under unreconstructed utilitarianism, to just the degree they like, these alleged moral subjects no longer seem to operate within a normative system at all. In the limiting case, the formulas of obligation to which they respond are identical with the actions that will give them the most personal satisfaction. Any revision to the standard theories must retain a sufficient level of demandingness to avoid this *reductio ad absurdum*.

This goal can be achieved by recognizing only small agent-favouring departures from utility-maximization as legitimate. The needed prescriptivity can also, however, be introduced by raising the normative bar elsewhere in the theory. Standards of non-moral achievement—aesthetic, affiliative, or economic—that are quite demanding may be imposed on agents as their moral requirements are relaxed. Criticisms of Kantianism and utilitarianism often allude to what in earlier times were considered non-moral claims, such as the claims of children, spouses, friends, or one's vocation, for time and attention, treating them as focuses of devoted obligation.

Williams, for example, attempts to show that a person's aesthetic project can have the kind of importance that renders him impervious to certain kinds of criticism. 'Gauguin' arrives at the idea of going to Tahiti to start a new life as a painter of tropical beauty and beauties. He worries about the decision before making it, but he does not, in Williams's story, query his plan to determine whether it satisfies the test proposed by Kant—that he could will it as a universal rule that everyone in his situation should do likewise. He does not make a serious effort to determine whether the benefits he can produce will outweigh the unhappiness his actions will cause. He pursues his project and goes to Tahiti, where things turn out well for him. He becomes a celebrated artist whose work gives pleasure and inspiration to many, so in the end he does produce a good deal of benefit for others as well as himself. Things do not turn out badly for those

affected by his decision. Williams defies the reader to say that 'Gauguin' did something wrong, not just in going to Tahiti but in failing to submit his proposed course of action to theoretical review.[19] It is irrelevant that such a review might have turned out in 'Gauguin's' favour, that it might be easy to defend his decision on simple utilitarian or even Kantian grounds. For Williams, any assessment of 'Gauguin's' situation in terms of moral theory would have been an imposition. What he refers to as 'the morality system', not just some specific duty, is the focus of his scepticism. We cannot, he thinks, assume that there is 'some currency of satisfactions, in terms of which it is possible to compare quite neutrally the value of one set of preferences together with their fulfillments, as against a quite different set of preferences . . . we . . . cannot in principle gain a standpoint from which the alternative fillings of our life-rectangle could be compared without prejudice. . . .The perspective of deliberative choice on one's life is from here.'[20]

Exactly what the presentation of this example is intended to show or does show has been the subject of much discussion. It hints at several specific moral issues, chiefly, financial responsibility for dependent spouses and children and sexual exclusivity, both of which prima facie duties involving self-sacrifice for the benefit of others 'Gauguin' repudiates. On the assumption that the example concerns these putative obligations, does it show that success at some non-moral undertaking compensates for a moral delict? Or that it is tyrannical to require agents to put all their actions to some impersonal test? Or that the future is so unpredictable that the thought experiments and calculations required by moral theorists as a preliminary to action cannot be performed? Does it question the right of anyone besides 'Gauguin' himself to judge his life? Any of these theses might be extracted, but the claim that Williams appears most interested in defending is the claim that if a person were to behave as his fictional Gauguin does, and if the outcome were to be as it was in the case of the real Gauguin, there would be no basis for saying that she acted in a morally irresponsible manner.[21] In accord with the hypothesis that

[19] Williams, 'Moral Luck', 20–39.
[20] Ibid. 35.
[21] The historical Gauguin's departure was far from impulsive or unpremeditated. Though the plan he unveiled in a letter to his wife to 'flee to the woods on a South Sea Island, and there live in ecstasy, in peace and in art . . . with a new family, far from the European struggle for money' is expressed rather

exemptions and permissions relative to background theories of morality tend to be compensated for by increased demandingness elsewhere in the system, Williams places a burden of artistic achievement on his hero, and saddles him with risk; if his project does not succeed, he may be hounded by regret. Because, the implication is, to live a good life one must normally achieve certain goals with respect to self-expression, the forging and maintenance of personal relationships, and the contribution of something valued by others in the world, Gauguin is not exempt from all normative requirements.

The position that while philosophical argument cannot justify selfish pursuits, it can show us that, when properly compensated by non-moral achievement, they do not stand in need of justification has been explored by other writers. Susan Wolf insists that we need to recognize 'the normal person's direct and specific desires for objects, activities and events that conflict with the attainment of moral perfection'.[22] She lists a number of activities that consume time and money, participation in which precludes the exercise of charity, that are worthwhile and appropriate. According to Wolf, no philosophical theory can tell us how important moral goodness is compared with other forms of goodness, or how much money, time, and effort we ought to devote to other-directed moral pursuits as against selfish pleasurable pursuits; consequently 'the posture we take in response to the recognition that our lives are not as morally good as possible need not be defensive'.[23] Wolf does not claim that it is morally permissible for anyone to dine on champagne and caviar when there is famine in Ethiopia. Nevertheless, in the discursive context—in which it is a prima facie assumption that actions ought to be regulated according to utilitarian criteria, with money spent where it will produce the most marginal utility—the illocutionary force of the argument is the offer of a permission or an exemption from a putative obligation.

shamelessly, the historical Gauguin was self-consciously aware of a conflict between personal needs and social demands. In a book composed for his daughter, who was distressed by his departure, he wrote, 'You sacrifice yourself for your child, who in turns becomes an adult and will sacrifice himself. And so on. There will be nothing but sacrificing people. And this will go on for a long time.' David Sweetman, *Paul Gauguin: A Complete Life*, 341.

[22] Susan Wolf, 'Moral Saints', 424.
[23] Ibid. 435–6.

Nagel, finally, displays a certain ambivalence towards his own discovery that selfishness is irrational. 'Suppression of the full force of the impersonal standpoint', he asserts, 'is denial of our full humanity.'[24] Yet he places only limited confidence in the motivating power of agent-neutral considerations. He emphasizes how difficult it is to maintain the impersonal standpoint and consistently to regard our own interests as no more deserving of satisfaction than anyone else's. For the later Nagel, neither the personal nor the impersonal perspective can be considered privileged. We are somewhat susceptible to arguments from the objective standpoint. We are sometimes moved. To deny that the impersonal standpoint has any authority would be to embrace irrationality. But if someone maintains that we ought always to be moved or that the third-person perspective has a built-in authority that the first-person perspective does not, he owes us an account of why this should be so. Such an account cannot be given in non-moral terms. The third-person perspective is essential in moral theory not because it is specially rational, but because to assert an obligation to do what is objectively best, rather than what one can do, given one's particular powers and stituation, is often to renounce advantage.

Many criticisms of deontological and utilitarian frameworks have in common an implicit appeal to the costs that are incurred by agents when they conform to exigent advantage-reducing policies. An increasingly used tool in the prescriptive moralist's kit is the argument from heavy costs, and it is to a discussion of that argument that I now turn.

3.3. The Argument from Heavy Costs

An important principle of descriptive moral psychology is that informants tend to judge that the physical and psychological costs to an agent of carrying out a prima facie obligation reduce the strength of the obligation. According to the principle, a morally good action that is extremely hard to carry out will tend to be perceived as supererogatory and optional for agents. More precisely:

---

[24] Nagel, *Equality and Partiality*, 20.

Heavy Costs Principle

(1) Subjects usually regard the difficulty of fulfilling a formula of obligation prescribing an action *ACT* in context *c* as tending to weaken its authority.

It needs to be emphasized from the outset that the heavy costs principle is a statement belonging to moral psychology, not prescriptive moral theory. It is a claim about how we judge, or perceive the world, or think about our obligations, not about what we are justified in doing. That said, the principle that the costs to the agent of assuming an obligation are perceived to diminish the strength of the obligation evidently applies quite broadly to all manner of social and political obligations. It is a social rule that one ought to reciprocate invitations. The rule is, however, responsive to the assumed capacities of people in specific circumstances to conform to it. One who lives in a grand house with a chef and servants and never reciprocates dinner invitations will be considered miserly and be blamed for it, whereas one who cannot cook and lives in an apartment with only a hot plate will be seen as only weakly obliged to return invitations. A member of the underground resistance who blurts out names under torture, violating the rule to keep the party's secrets, will be judged less harshly than one who sells them for money, even if she needs money quite a bit. 'Ought' thus appears to be a scalar concept: My perceived obligation to perform a given action can be strong or weak, depending on my circumstances.

'Can' is also a scalar concept, as Björn Eriksson points out.[25] I can do some things easily, others only with difficulty, and this applies to the psychological as well as the physical realm. It is easy for me to clean my living room, given a whole day in which to do it. With some effort, I can clean my whole house in one day, but this is not easy for me. It would be impossible, from an organizational and physical point of view, for me to clean the 500-room office building in which I work in one day. Given my psychological dispositions, it would be difficult for me to work in a public relations firm, but it would be utterly impossible for me to work on a catwalk building an eight-storey skyscraper.

[25] Bjorn Eriksson, *Heavy Duty*, 70 ff., 163.

Moral obligations too are perceived as scalar and appear to be diminished when an agent is unable to perform some action or could perform it only with great difficulty. If an agent cannot swim at all, his failure to save a drowning child is seen as tragic but not culpable. If he can swim, but does not save the child because she is very far out on a frigid, storm-tossed ocean, and it would be all but impossible to save her, his not saving her is still regarded as tragic and not culpable. Culpability is not usually assigned by observers until an unperformed good action gets within range of the agent's actual capacities. If the agent can swim fairly well, and if the child is not too far away, but he feels that someone more vigorous ought to take on this rescue opportunity and does nothing, observers will judge him as morally deficient. Being a little tired is not thought of as a defeating condition of a prima facie human rescue obligation. There is a range of degrees of enablement that are related not just to physical capacities, but also to the strength of emotions, and the strength of ingrained habits, that affect my ability to perform any task. In deciding whether to blame or excuse, we consider these capacities.

Two factors appear to influence observers' assessments of the level of obligation in particular contexts. The first, just as utilitarians might hope, is the benefit that an action in conformity with the formula of obligation will bring about, or the harm that it will prevent. The second, however, is the cost or burdensomeness to the agent of conformity with the formula. These factors offset one another. There are many benefits that an agent could bring about with some effort that she is considered only weakly obliged to bring about, and many harms she could prevent with great effort that she will be considered only weakly obliged to prevent. His rich uncle, Eriksson judges, is more obliged than he is to endow a hospital that will save the lives of 500 persons in a poor country because it would be easier for the uncle to do. Eriksson could sell his house and move to a block of flats in order to give away the money, but psychologically this is hard for him even to contemplate.[26] One is likely to judge that someone busy raising a family of five small children is less obliged to spend an evening attending a letter-writing session to free political prisoners than someone who lives alone. Leaving aside Eriksson's

---

[26] Ibid. 161.

prescriptive determinations, it is clear that our spontaneous judgements at least tend in the direction he indicates. Agents are normally considered strongly obliged to bring about a large benefit at low cost to themselves, weakly obliged to prevent small harms at large costs to themselves, and moderately obliged to bring about middle-sized benefits or prevent middle-sized harms if it is somewhat burdensome for them to do so.

Perceived burdens are subject to multiplier effects in accord with the following psychological principles.

(1) *Relative Deprivation Principle*
Burdens that the agent knows are shared by others in the group with which he compares himself are diminished; burdens experienced in isolation are magnified.

If everyone else in one's reference group is obliged by circumstances to eat fish during the month of February, it is less burdensome not to have meat. It is grating, by contrast, not to be able to take a vacation when one's co-workers can, to wear shabbier clothes, and to serve plainer fare at your table than others do.

(2) *Before the Revolution Principle*
Burdens that the agent did not formerly experience are magnified; burdens that the agent thinks she will soon be relieved of are diminished.

It is humiliating to be defrocked, to suffer a cut in salary, to move to inferior accommodations, or suddenly to find oneself in the midst of a legal battle when all was going well. It is less burdensome to be born into a harem than to be captured and put into one. Conversely, if one believes that things will get better soon, that new opportunities beckon, that assistance is on the way, burdens are easier to bear.

(3) *Externally Imposed Hardship Principle*
Burdens that are imposed by someone else are magnified; burdens that are the by-product of the agent's own projects or the result of the agent's deeper instincts are diminished.

It is not hard to accept deficits such as being a junior in a professional hierarchy that are the result of your own choices and fit into your own plans. The trouble involved in taking care of a baby when one

expected or hoped to have a family is usually cheerfully accepted. Babies would by contrast be regarded as an offensive imposition if they were deposited on the doorsteps of some households selected by lottery, legally requiring to be raised to maturity.

Information about burdensomeness to the individual, as well as information about overall utility and disutility, affects our propensity to blame.[27] The rich man who engages in petty deception by hiding his extra bottle of liquor from the customs officer, or the academic who uses departmental postage to mail her credit card payment may be thought reprehensible, even if the offence is small, for it would have been easy to conform to the regulation.

The finding that burdens are judged to offset obligations at the same time as the utility of outcomes is judged to justify the imposition of burdens is explanatory in two respects:

    (*a*) It predicts that high-demand formulas of obligation will often be judged inapplicable to a particular case or generally inappropriate.

    (*b*) It predicts that motivation, self-reproach, and blame will admit of degrees, according to how hard it is thought to be to perform an action and how morally desirable the action is.

Extremely high-demand theoretical statements, such as the claim that it is never under any circumstances permissible either to contribute to or to fail to prevent the occurrence of pain in another human being, except in the service of that person's physical health, are very difficult to confirm, though individuals may be deeply committed to authored norms such as pacifism and global benevolence. This is simply because it is hard for individuals and groups to pursue their aims and get on with their lives without neglecting some human suffering and often without contributing to it. Manufacturing and selling automobiles, for example, causes numerous fatalities and casualties and is not undertaken for altmistic reasons. One may reasonably hold the view that automobile travel is more dangerous than it ought to be and that the greed of manufacturers who will not cut profits to save lives is objectionable. But competent judges will not rule out as morally illegitimate any human activity whose practice has ever been found

---

[27] Bjorn Eriksson, *Heavy Duty*, 182 ff.

to have made a causal contribution to the suffering of a human being. We can also appreciate that, even if a particular formula of obligation can be confirmed by competent judges, agents may not experience the motivation to conform to it. Note that none of the items below 1 entails that *I do ACT in c*.

> I believe doing *ACT* in *c* is morally right
> I believe the morality of doing *ACT* in *c* to be well confirmed
> I believe I ought morally to do *ACT* in *c*
> I believe everyone ought morally to do *ACT* in *c*
> I believe that I ought morally to do *ACT* in *c* if I believe doing *ACT* in *c* to be morally right and doing *ACT* in *c* is morally right
> I believe I will be seriously morally at fault if I fail to do *ACT* in *c*
> I believe I should not commit serious moral faults and that I will commit a serious moral fault if I fail to do *ACT* in *c*
> Etcetera

Normally, the belief that it is right and good to do *ACT* in *c* is paired with a motivating disposition to try to do *ACT* in *c*, for to experience moral motivation is to be aware of the coexistence of just such paired beliefs and actions, and manifestly we are animals who experience moral motivations. In so far as we do experience moral motivations, we cannot seriously entertain the possibility that a set of confirmed formulas of obligation is objectively binding on us, though we have no inclination, or only a weak and consistently ineffective inclination to act in accord with the formulas. Yet belief and motivation can on occasion come uncoupled without my losing my entire moral capacity, only my moral motivation in this case. There is no impossibility in my believing that considerations speak overwhelmingly in favour of doing *ACT* in *c* and yet not wanting to do it.

The argument from heavy costs is employed prescriptively whenever it is claimed that a proposed formula would be so difficult for agents in general to comply with and is so repugnant to their natural sentiments that it cannot possibly constitute a genuine obligation. The suggestion that one ought to give all one's income to charity except what is required for biological survival presumably falls prey to the argument from heavy costs. An argument from heavy costs may

also be employed to excuse a particular agent from compliance with a rule in a single case, even though the obligation is regarded as remaining in force. Some particular failure of veracity or fidelity or loyalty might be excused on the grounds that the special nature of his case made the corresponding duty hopelessly difficult or impossible for a particular agent to fulfil.

Prescriptive employment of the argument from heavy costs is necessary in moral argument but risky. It would be an elementary mistake to infer from the premiss that a given prima facie obligation is judged by someone to be weakened by the costs of performing the action to the conclusion that the obligation is nullified. It would also be a mistake to infer from the premiss that people generally found it hard to live up to some rule or bring about some outcome that it was not morally required. At the same time, it would be an elementary mistake to infer from the existence of a formal distinction between 'is' and 'ought' that information regarding costs is always irrelevant to the determination of obligations.

A rigorist might insist that moral psychology has no bearing on the question of our real obligations and that whether a defensive backlash is generated by the popularization of high-demand theories is not the concern of the moral philosopher. What we are naturally inclined to do and what we are obliged to do are two separate questions. If it has been established that we really ought to wear our old clothes until they fall apart and give up expensive entertainment, sending the money saved to charity, as Peter Singer argued we should in a celebrated article of 1972,[28] then we have to do that regardless of the psychological difficulty.

This position is, however, confused. The rigorist is right to distinguish between appearance and reality. He is right to insist that *if* it can be established that we ought to wear our old clothes, etc., then we really have to do that, even if our motivation is weak. He nevertheless underestimates the difficulty of confirming moral obligations. The exigency of an authored norm is its proponent's personal concern. By contrast, when a policy, for example the policy of sending all one's income except what is required for subsistence to a charitable organization, is presented as objectively binding, i.e. as confirmable, it has

---

[28] Peter Singer, 'Famine, Affluence and Morality'.

to gain the backing of competent judges who assess it in light of the reality constraint and the idealism characteristic. The rigorist is wrong to maintain that exigency cannot be a genuine reason, as opposed to a motive, for rejecting a particular formula of obligation, for one is not always being unreasonable in citing the heavy costs of meeting a putative obligation as reasons for not doing so. Accordingly, costs to agents can really disconfirm certain *ACT* propositions.

But can the argument from heavy costs furnish a reason for rejecting, not simply this or that formula of obligation, but all moral theorizing across the board? Clearly, Kantianism and utilitarianism are vulnerable to it. High-demand moral theories not only impose burdens, they multiply them. For not everyone is threatened with the demands of these modern moral theories, but chiefly a small Euro-American fraction. Their burdens are amplified according to the relative deprivation principle, for most inhabitants of our planet concern themselves very little with the problem of benevolence to strangers, living instead in blissful ignorance and indifference. Further, high-demand moral theories are a new imposition whose subjective costs are increased according to the before-the-revolution principle. Historically, they arose as a response to industrialization, in the wake of the emergence of contract relations between persons who did not know each other well, popular government, and the spread of objective knowledge about others. The appeal of ancient ethics, with its focus on relationships like friendship, into which the problems of mass society do not intrude, is easy to explain. And, finally, high-demand morality is not a by-product of deep instincts and dispositions, and its requirements weigh on us more heavily according to the externally imposed hardship principle. Kant's insistence that morality is a set of laws that rational creatures spontaneously prescribe to themselves is a noteworthy attempt to lighten our perceived burden by depicting high-demand morality as having an internal source. Yet he fails to convince us that his rules are confirmed and thus objectively binding.

The argument from heavy costs is effective against Kantianism and utilitarianism. If the reflection, ratiocination, and self-denial required to act as these theories prescribe strain our ordinary capacities, their prescriptions are inappropriate. For we cannot maintain that the theories are excellent and yet be unwilling to shoulder the burdens

they entail. In summary, prescriptive moral theorists must take into account the relationship between the formulas of obligation they advance and our ordinary or average capacities. A confirmed theory *M* cannot consist of formulas of obligation that are so exigent that only heroes, ascetics, omniscient beings, or persons devoid of worldly ambition, can do what is morally required of them. Nor can it be so obscure and complicated that ordinary human beings cannot understand what the theory says we ought to do. Facts about the first-person standpoint accordingly place limits on the substantive and formal demandingness of morality.

Nevertheless, the argument against exigent systems from the first-person standpoint is not as powerful at it appears at first glance. It slides from the unquestionable premiss that her first-person experiences and concerns are ineffably different for the subject who has them, to the weaker but still indisputable descriptive conclusion that first-person concerns and experiences are highly motivational, to prescriptive conclusions that are questionable. Its costliness to agents in general counts against any formula of obligation, but never decisively. The costliness of a policy *to me* is not relevant to its assessment, except in so far as costs for me would be costs for anybody else like me.

The heavy costs considerations advanced above do not threaten the enterprise of proposing, defending, and criticizing particular moral claims, or the generalizations that permit us to deduce particular formulas. In commending certain ways of life as appropriate for persons with our psychological constitutions and condemning others as inappropriate, critics of Kantianism and utilitarianism are contributing to the same theoretical enterprise as their predecessors. Chapter 4 introduces a more radical strain of antitheory, frequently conjoined with the argument from heavy costs, that does, by contrast, pose a challenge to the very idea of a moral theory. This challenge is argued to be unsuccessful.

A few predictions concerning the relations between meta-ethics and substantive moral theory can be ventured in the meantime. Costs to agents are frequently cited against the claim that a more egalitarian distribution of social goods is morally required. Now, there is no logical inconsistency involved in holding egalitarian or other high-demand moral views while subscribing at the same time to the heavy

costs principle. However, a commitment on the part of well-off people to greater social equality is obviously more expensive to them than a commitment on the part of the badly-off to greater social equality. It is accordingly difficult to instantiate the role of a well-off egalitarian who sets great store by the argument from heavy costs, and much easier to instantiate that of a well-off oligarch. Edmund Burke was perhaps the first great conservative to cite the heavy costs principle when, in his *Reflections on the Revolution in France*, he lamented the loss of 'all the pleasing illusions which made power gentle and obedience liberal' that had been 'dissolved by this new conquering empire of light and reason'.[29] If our prediction is borne out, the heavy costs principle will tend to figure prominently in conservative thought.

Prescriptive egalitarians who, like the present author, accept the heavy costs principle, need a good deal more by way of theoretical apparatus to explain how egalitarianism can be a well-confirmed position. The challenge is addressed in Chapters 5, 6, and 7.

---

[29] 'All the decent drapery of life is to be rudely torn off. . . . On this scheme of things a king is but a man, a queen is but a woman, a woman is but an animal, and an animal not of the highest order.' Edmund Burke, *Reflections on the Revolution in France*, 67.

4

Limitations on Theory II: Immanent Standpoints

Hume argued that virtuous behaviour is a set of performances through which a society maintains goodwill and easy communication amongst its members, fostering trust and reducing envy. Moral actions and responses arouse sentiments of approbation in observers who appreciate their usefulness. Morality comprises a system of encouragements and deterrents, discursive and practical, emerging from a central core of basic but non-theoretical agreement. It could be said to be immanent in human relations; it does not need to be imposed, in Hume's view, by specialized experts.

In his writings on virtue, Hume does not enunciate formulas of obligation, and neither arduous deductive systems nor ascetic exercises of self-denial pertain, in his view, to the establishment or maintenance of morals. 'Grace ... ease ... genteelness ... must be considered as a part of ethics, left by nature to baffle all the pride of philosophy.'[1] He recites a list of character traits, including the dispositions to justice, fidelity, honour, allegiance, benevolence, humanity, clemency, temperance, sobriety, and chastity, explains their utility in enabling men to live together in confined spaces, and urges readers to cultivate them. The virtues are artificial, in that they require practice and polishing, but they are independent of ratiocination, and, once ingrained, they can be exercised without reflection or deliberation.

Because Hume's approach to ethics is so often cited as an alternative to Kantian and utilitarian prescriptivism, it is important to distinguish between the theoretical strain and the antitheoretical strain in Hume's moral discourse. One might suppose that a virtue theory like

---

[1] Hume, *Enquiry Concerning the Principles of Morals*, sect. 8. 14.

Hume's is only nominally a *theory*, that it is fundamentally opposed to an imperative-based theory like utilitarianism or Kantianism, formulated in terms of policies adopted and followed by agents. This impression is, however, misleading; virtue theory is an ordinary moral theory, subject to confirmation in the usual way.

In a Kantian paraworld, agents behave in a manner that we external observers can describe as falling under a universal rule. To stipulate that ideal agents not only behave in this manner but also consciously plan their actions to accord with universal rules is to advance a more complex theory, one even more difficult to confirm than simple Kantianism. In the competing paraworld of a virtue theorist, virtuous agents are ubiquitous. They too, however, act in what from the observer's perspective is a regular and reliable fashion. Faithful agents serve their masters loyally; chaste agents are selective in their *amours*; clement agents do not punish wrongdoers harshly. To possess a virtue is to tend to the production of some stereotypical set of actions. Is the behaviour of ideal virtuous agents, as conceived by virtue theorists, more improvisational, less predictable, than the behaviour of Kantian agents? There is no reason for it to be so. Though the virtue theorist will insist that her agents do not regulate their conduct by reference to rules, she is likely to conceive them as regulating their conduct by reference to character. Thus, Hume's agents are easily imagined as investing a good deal of time in moral introspection and in discussing and criticizing one another's characters. In that case, they worry, fuss, and obsess about being moral as much as cartoon Kantians and utilitarians do, only their concern is not with universalizing their maxims or advancing the general welfare but, according to Hume's somewhat cynical view, with maintaining their reputations.

Virtue theory and its relatives, then, are simply ordinary theoretical moralities; their assertions are confirmed or disconfirmed, to the extent that this is possible, in the same way as other theoretical claims. They do not pose a meta-ethical challenge to the very idea of a moral theory. Yet there is a radical antitheory strain as well in Hume which does pose a challenge to the very idea of a moral theory and which has been influential.

4.1. Immanentism

A radical critic of moral theory might insist that there is no point in moral theorizing by reference to alternative worlds and no possibility of expert confirmation of formulas of obligation. Williams represents this position when he says that 'morality is not an invention of philosophers. It is the outlook, or, incoherently, part of the outlook, of almost all of us.'[2]

According to one conception of moral philosophy, which I shall designate 'immanentism', the moral philosopher's role is to make visible and understandable the moral aspects of particular ways of life. He does not discover moral obligations, and moral progress does not consist in the invention of better moral theories that capture our obligations more accurately. For we cannot possibly confirm new and surprising moral claims by ratiocination and controlled experiment as we can discover new and surprising scientific truths. We must already have constructed as much morality as we need, for we have been living together for a long time. These ideas are memorably expressed in a well-known passage of Hume's, through the image of two rowers who fall into an easy rhythm without a word having passed between them.[3]

Nor is the rule concerning the stability of possession the less derived from human conventions, that it arises gradually, and acquires force by a slow progression, and by our repeated experience of the inconveniences of transgressing it. On the contrary, this experience assures us still more, that the sense of interest has become common to all our fellows, and gives us a confidence of the future regularity of their conduct.[4]

A Humean might remind us that punishment and praise, criticism and appreciation, were directed at us, and at our instructors before us from our earliest years. The habits of sincerity and reciprocity have integrated themselves into our normal routines, so that to find oneself not behaving in a certain way can cause acute discomfort and anxiety.

---

[2] Williams, *Ethics and the Limits of Philosophy*, 174.   [3] Hume, *Treatise*, III. 11. ii. 490.
[4] Ibid.

The rules we have internalized govern in the first instance our relations with familiars, but we also have rules for dealing with strangers, people who move into our orbits for the first time. Social feedback continues as we encounter more complex and delicate situations, and the actions and decision of agents alter normative standards in turn. Adherence to social norms involving sincerity, reciprocity, and respect for property rights is practical in terms of social energetics; transparency of communication and the performance of contracts reduces the amount of time needed to monitor social transactions and enforce agreements and frees time and attention for other tasks. These norms and their associated modes of inculcation and enforcement represent an efficiency that members of a social group can find their way to without external direction.

MacIntyre expresses this sense of pretheoretical rootedness when he insists that 'I inherit from the past of my family, my city, my tribe, my nation, a variety of debts, inheritances, rightful expectations, and obligations. These constitute the given of my life, my moral starting point. This is in part what gives my life its own moral particularity.'[5] We do not, on this view, choose our moral commitments by surveying a vast array of possible moral codes and assessing them in terms of betterness relations. Rather, we inherit a moral code and we make, in light of experience, small, piecemeal modifications to the shapes of our lives and those of our societies.

An immanentist may acknowledge that many of our actions do in fact conform to what utilitarianism or Kantianism prescribes, even while insisting that the moral theory articulated by philosophers is not a significant engine of personal or social moral development. No one seeks to maximize the satisfaction of all her non-moral preferences, even the ones that can be concurrently satisfied. Most people are fairly truthful and benevolent and will go out of their ways to minimize pain and suffering in their immediate environments. The reason for this conformity to advantage-reducing principles, the immanentist insists, is not to be found in exposure to academic moral discourse, but in our upbringing in communities in which moral practices were a subset of cultural practices.

---

[5] Alasdair MacIntyre, *After Virtue*, 220.

In the view of the immanentist, our behaviour exhibits partial but only partial conformity with the requirements posited by the celebrated moral theories. Where we do extend our efforts and concerns outside the usual realm, or sacrifice our projects or submit to frustration of our desires, exhibiting unusual altruism or moral restraint, it is not because we have decided to apply 'theoretical morality in this case'. According to what might be called the non-theoretical reasons principle, departures from our usual preferences and habits or heroic self-suppression can only come about for internal reasons and not because of what an expert has shown it is right, theoretically, to do. This man gives away a fortune; that slave is manumitted; this female is allowed to hold an important political office. These occurrences are never explainable as consequences of a theoretical commitment to social equality; they depend on the perceptions and motives of individual actors.

Berating people for failing to behave as exigent moral theories say they ought to, or for failing to consult such theories before they act, is misguided, according to the immanentist, since these theories have no special authority. To show that agents who disregard the imperatives of impersonal moral theory are culpable or are acting in bad faith, one would have to establish that they ought to care, or have an external reason to care about governing their actions in accord with impersonal theories. Kant tried to show, Williams remarks, 'how the moral law can unconditionally apply to all people, even if they try to live outside it'.[6] Yet Kant's constructions are unconvincing. Though we resent and blame offensive actions, we do not resent and blame any violation of Kantianism, utilitarianism, etc.

The immanentist seems able to account for the phenomena of morality, as most people experience them, without supposing that agents stand in any necessary relationship to moral theory. Framing and evaluating moral rules and distributive schemes appropriate to whole worlds, he insists, is an airy theoretical exercise, a game played with its own rules, that does not touch our moral experience. His position is similar to that of the Pyrrhonist sceptic who maintains that experience commits us to no particular theory of material objects; we can thus speak of 'moral Pyrrhonism'. It is supported by the

---

[6] Williams, *Ethics and the Limits of Philosophy*, 191.

observation that impersonal moral theories have existed for only a fraction of the history of the human race, while actions and reactions we would not hesitate to describe as moral have existed for much longer. All past and present cultures have positive morality, but only a small fraction, have, in addition, contested theories of morals that purport to state, not only the rules themselves, but also the rules for making up or rejecting the rules.

Immanentism is a meta-ethical view that ought to be without prescriptive content. The knowledge that N believes moral theorizing to be useless and mostly uninteresting should carry no information as to where N stands on questions such as whether it is acceptable to eat chickens raised in cages or treat African-American applicants especially favourably in law school admissions. A theory-shy immanentist can be deeply concerned with social injustice—exploitative labour relations, sexual discrimination, and global economic inequality—just as a theorist persuaded by the heavy costs principle can be an egalitarian. Yet we can hazard the following meta-theoretical prediction: we will not observe many instances of immanentism or moral Pyrrhonism paired with revisionary ideas concerning social justice. This is not to say that the rejection of the modern moral theories is motivated by the desire of members of an advantaged class to retain their advantages. This would be an unwarranted assumption and tantamount to an unjustified *ad hominem* accusation. It is up to the sociologist of knowledge, not the philosopher, to determine what motivations or interests lie behind the promulgation of any doctrine.

Before considering the relations between antitheory sentiments and substantive positions further, it will be useful to explore in detail the preference of the conservative for a world conceived as evolving through the accumulation of minute, anonymous adjustments. For we can represent not only institutions and practices in a world, but morally significant changes in institutions and practices in a world. Revisionary theorists envision worlds that are quickly and dramatically improved, through the agency of prophets and the mass conversion of followers, or through enlightened lawgivers and the cooperation of a compliant populace.

Conservatives have a strong preference, not only for the kinds of worlds in which social distinctions are marked, but also for worlds

that take shape in a certain slow, undirected way. Plato is not a conservative theorist on this definition, for his preference for a hierarchically ordered social system without occupational mobility is countered by his understanding of how such a world comes to be, i.e. through the intervention of a *force majeure*. Marx's position is notoriously complex, for his textual presentation of a world slowly evolving towards equality through the unfolding of inner processes of development is widely appreciated as a rhetorical device for encouraging quick and dramatic improvement by prophetic means.

4.2. Fast and Slow Paraworlds

Consider 'Gauguin's' not merely forgivable, according to Williams, but creditable lack of interest in assessing his actions according to the specifications of an impersonal moral theory. How can his actions be read with respect to his broader social milieu? In Williams's paraworld, 'Gauguin' launches himself forward into a wholly new mode of existence, but family life in Copenhagen remains more or less the same. As pretheoretical core morality is supposed to provide a stable background for moral contests slowly and somewhat arbitrarily decided, so a social world symbolically held fixed provides the background for personal adventure.

Reflection on the sorry plight of the real Gauguin-in-Copenhagen might suggest to a reader that marriage is an institution requiring moral review. Perhaps lifelong obligations cannot justly be contracted in the heat of passion, and perhaps relationships requiring cooperative labour on a daily basis interfere with the aim of developing talents to the full. Perhaps marriage is a relic of some ancient institution and no longer has the same purpose, point, or justification in the modern world, and Gauguin was a harbinger.

This, however, is not the pathway Williams is urging us down in 'Moral Luck'. Elsewhere, he professes rather his admiration for Hegel's notion of *Sittlichkeit* over Kant's 'abstract' morality, praising Hegel's notion of 'a concretely determined ethical existence that [is] expressed in the local folkways, a form of life that [makes] particular sense to the people living in it'.[7] Though Hegel was off the mark, he

---

[7] Williams, *Ethics and the Limits of Philosophy*, 104.

thinks, in imagining a secret teleology of history guiding moral evolution, 'the Hegelian problem is the right problem at least to this extent; it asks how a concretely experienced form of life can be extended, rather than considering how a universal program is to be applied'.[8] Williams argues that it is inadvisable to commit whole societies to potentially dangerous and irreversible programmes of reform; the leaps ought not to be too great, too frequent, or too sudden. We should not try to lock in any substantive set of values for future generations, he says, but only the value of free inquiry.[9] Though individuals are exempt from any overarching requirement to remain rooted in a familiar well-tested mode of existence, and to modify it by degrees, larger groups, the implication is, are not. Taking on individual risk can be a good part of human life, and risk-prone individuals should not be held back to the norms of *Sittlichkeit*. Whole societies, by contrast, ought not to lurch into an unknown and unpredictable future. They, it seems, cannot be fenced in by their dominant discourses and practices; they cannot need to break out.

From the Hegelian perspective, actual states of affairs are right so long as they endure. Whatever is now, and especially whatever has been of long standing in human affairs, is exempt from justifications by comparison to what merely could be. The forms of life that we have adopted are, on this view, like Hume's coordinated rowing, the most natural and effective for us, and cannot be called to account. While modern immanentists distance themselves from some extreme forms of effective coordinated social practice to be found under the headings of militarism, imperialism, chattel or wage slavery, charismatic leadership, and sexual subordination, they for the most part do not perceive these patterns of social dominance operating within modern institutions. Where they do, they either deny their moral wrongness, or deny that much can be done to obviate it, unless history on the grand scale happens to be spontaneously tending in that direction. There is a kind of logic in the position that fast individuals need a slow society, even if slow societies can operate without fast individuals. Hegel was fascinated by the remarkable personality. The figural relationship of the Napoleonic individual to the ground of his culture leaves all its subgroups—its merchants, peasants, prisoners,

[8] Williams, *Ethics and the Limits of Philosophy*, 104.   [9] Ibid. 173.

aristocrats, housewives, blurred into the whole, unconscious of their agency or identity. They are part of the stable background; the farmers and fishers continue to farm and fish, while the generals change the boundaries of nations. In Williams's scheme, the wives continue to bring up the children, while the artists change the boundaries of aesthetic experience.

But if a form of life is not generally satisfactory, surely deprived agents will act to alter conditions? If we see two rowers rowing smoothly, are we not entitled to assume that they are both getting where they want to go? Ordinarily we can. Yet we cannot claim to see smooth rowing all around us. The appearance of harmonious coexistence or even harmonious cooperation between two agents or two groups who are in limited or imperfect interaction with one other may disguise accommodation to impermissible advantage-taking. When A_1 presses an advantage against A_2, A_2 may respond in three ways, by ignoring what is happening, by acquiescing, in the recognition that his choices are constrained, or by openly protesting or resisting. Acquiescence, in turn, can take many forms. It can involve motivated ignorance, a decision to leave the terms of the A_1–A_2 interaction unexamined, or the suppression of the impulse to grieve one's condition or to struggle towards the exit.

A third kind of acquiescence does not depend on a wilful refusal to ponder the A_1–A_2 interaction, or the suppression of rebellious motives. It may call upon the active engagement of A_2's intellect and imagination in constructing a rationale that appears to legitimize A_1's advantage-pressing. Such a rationale may even take the form of a first-person narrative in which acquiescent A_2 represents himself as pursuing his own self-interest and as making deliberate self-advantaging choices along the way, choices that lead to the present state of interaction with benefit-appropriating A_1. These narratives and the ceremonies to which they are attached contribute to cultural density in a way that can appear to furnish excusing conditions for prima facie injustice in the same way that glorious weddings may appear to their participants as well as to observers to erase the more repellent features of many arranged marriages.

The claim that social evolution is driven from inside, from collective wants and desires, not—it is implied—the theoretical insights of alienated geniuses, might be taken as an empirical claim

about how, despite a few frightening blips—the Terror, Stalinism—history has unfolded. It may also constitute a statement of reasoned authorial preference for a world that does not change very fast or very fundamentally. This can be seen from a consideration of the disqualification thesis.

4.3. The Disqualification Thesis

Some kinds of prescriptive theorizing are, in the eyes of critics of moral theory, themselves morally inappropriate. No moral theorist, a Pyrrhonist critic might insist, is entitled to dictate, even through the projection of an ideal world in her own imagination, for the entire species. We are not in a position to pronounce on what others may or may not do or have. Even when no morally objectionable attitudes are involved in making judgements about other persons and groups, we are rarely qualified to do so.

Let's term the prescriptive belief that one ought not make certain moral judgements or assert certain moral claims because one is either not entitled or not qualified to do so the 'disqualification thesis'. Sometimes entitlement and qualification considerations are blended, when, for example, it is held that an intelligible moral judgement presupposes an argumentative context in which there is live dispute. While one might suppose that proponents of the disqualification thesis are concerned only with our entitlement and our ability to make moral judgements about persons geographically distant, or at least psychologically remote from us, this turns out not to be the case. Some proponents of the thesis insist that there are certain judgements we cannot make about our own culture. We can accordingly distinguish between the disqualification thesis (external) and the disqualification thesis (internal).

Before going on to criticize some applications of the disqualification thesis, it is important to distinguish between judging and intervening. Making a judgement and expressing it openly can be and often is an act of intervention. In deciding whether to intervene, by making judgements or in other ways, we have to decide how bad some action or practice really is, how difficult it will be to change it, what else of value might be lost, and how much force or persuasion

would have to be used. These considerations enter into any decision to interfere with another person's or group's settled habits and customs; they are as applicable to one's spouse as to distant strangers. The appropriateness of the judgement I make in such a context—and my qualifications or entitlement to make it—can nevertheless be distinguished from the effects of my asserting it to various audiences, including the audience the judgement is about.

It is one thing to insist that one should never interfere with the established customs of strangers, whether through the use of police or military force, or by telling them off or writing editorials against them. It is another to insist that one cannot or should not form any opinions of the morality of the conduct of strangers. In what follows, I shall ignore the question of intervention to focus on the simpler question of the appropriateness of moral judgements of strangers, including persons who are exotic or remote from us, historically or psychologically.

The first thesis to be evaluated is that, under the following conditions, an observer is disqualified from offering a condemnatory moral judgement with respect to a situation S, or with respect to the actions and responses of one or more agents A and patients P, the participants in S, even when S involves a set of interactions between A and P such that, were interactions of that sort to occur between a set of agents and patients in our local culture W, they would be judged morally defective. Gilbert Harman presents an instance of the general thesis when he states that we cannot judge of Hitler that it was wrong of him to have ordered the extermination of the Jews on the grounds that 'Hitler, like the cannibals, is outside our morality'.[10]

Conditions for Disqualification (External)

(1) S is remote, historically or geographically, and/or A and P in S are psychologically remote, from W, the world inhabited by the prospective judges and its actors.

(2) The As do not share the prospective judges' values and standards.

An additional adverse judgement-precluding condition is sometimes added (though not by Harman), namely:

(3) The interactions between As and Ps were or are part of a way of life that is stable. They are woven into the fabric of

---

[10] Harman, *Nature of Morality*, 109.

the culture and find resonance in other practices. They organize the life of the culture as projects organize the lives of individuals.

Harman suggests that an agent who is judged negatively has to be regarded as accepting a certain rule at the same time as he or she is perceived to have violated it. Hitler fails to meet this condition. For, in failing to endorse a prohibition on genocide, he situated himself outside our morality. He was surrounded by like-minded persons, all of them remote from our morality. He is accordingly disqualified as a candidate for judgement and we are disqualified as judges.

Are we disqualified from judging Hitler? Some evidence for the truth of this controversial thesis might be furnished by speakers' usual reactions to questions like 'Do you think that what Hitler did in Germany in the 1930s and 1940s was morally wrong?' or 'Do you believe that genocidal programs like Hitler's are always morally wrong?' If these questions are posed in a breezy, unassuming way, informants may be puzzled and hesitate with their answers. Informants might also judge that sentences like 'The Samurai ought not to have tested their new swords by chopping off the heads of passers-by' or 'It was unethical of the Aztecs to have cut the hearts out of their captives' have no conceivable use or are even meaningless.[11]

These considerations nevertheless fail to show that speakers are not qualified or entitled to make adverse judgements concerning the morality of Hitler, Genghis Khan, the Aztecs, the Samurai, and other bloodthirsty individuals and groups. The hesitation of speakers under the conditions just described has various explanations besides their recognition of their own disqualification. For example, we often understand terms referring to defunct individuals and groups descriptively. Though the description theory of proper names that treats a name as designating the person who best fits a description associated with the name has been officially discredited, it accounts for what it is easy or hard for us to think. All that many people know about the Aztecs is that they were the medieval Central Americans who for a long time practised human sacrifice, and all that many people know about the Samurai is that they were a medieval Japanese warrior caste of great ferocity. Similarly, many people know little

---

[11] See Williams, *Ethics and the Limits of Philosophy*, 160–1.

about Hitler beyond the fact that he was the man who formulated and carried out a genocidal programme in the 1930s and 1940s in Germany. They may find it hard to give much content to the thought that whoever did those things ought not to have.

Yet on reflection, it is clear that the Aztecs, those very people, could have decided to give up the practice of human sacrifice by morally persuading themselves or by being persuaded by their victims to do so, and that Hitler, that very person, might never have formulated his plans or might have been dissuaded from carrying them out. So the alleged incoherence must be pragmatic, or of some other nature, rather than semantic.

Evidently, the irritating character of the question 'Do you think what Hitler did was morally wrong?' and the perceived aberrance of the related judgements depends on the position, expectations, and intentions of the prospective judges, not to the internal economy of the agent being judged, for a German citizen in 1939 could have condemned Hitler and his henchmen on the grounds that certain prohibitions against harm were neither being acknowledged nor respected. Now, when N asserts sincerely that it was wrong of Hitler to have ordered the extermination of the Jews, N represents himself (given the interconvertibility of declaratives and imperatives) as endorsing the moral rule 'Don't order the extermination of the Jews', or some more general rule, such as 'Don't engage in genocidal practices', and he implies that Hitler violated the rule in ordering the extermination of the Jews. If N asserts that it was wrong of the Aztecs to tear the hearts out of their captives in a religious ritual, he represents himself as endorsing a prohibitory rule forbidding such treatment of captives, or indeed of anyone, that he implies their actions violated. Standardly, moral judgements are asserted by a speaker when she perceives there to be a present need—admonitory, expressive, or behaviour-modifying—for the enunciation of the rule. Such conditions will often correspond to what Paul Grice[12] describes as the doubt-or-denial conditions for informative utterance, though the context can make the enunciation of the judgement pertinent for other reasons.

There are, however, a number of arguments that might still be advanced to support the disqualification thesis (external). Perhaps it is

---

[12] H. P. Grice, 'The Causal Theory of Perception'.

arrogant to judge remote others in distant cultures, even if it is technically possible to make interpretable judgemental statements regarding them and even if one has no intention of intervening in their lives.

One such argument is the argument from entrenchment: Suppose a practice or an institution has endured in a remote culture for many years. Supporting symbolic structures, such as religious rituals and ceremonies, have grown up around it. It then earns the right, it might be argued, to be treated, if not with respect and deference, then at least with moral indifference. We need not approve it morally, but we ought not to condemn it either; indeed, we ought to adopt no moral attitude towards it whatsoever. On this view, the Roman Empire has a different moral status from Hitler's planned Thousand Year Reich. The latter was incompatible with human values and could not have been realized. However, the former institution existed for a long time. Describing the Roman Empire as a morally unjustified institution seems otiose. It just . . . was . . . though eventually needs, preferences, and tolerances changed and the Roman Empire collapsed. Slavery—whether ancient slavery or the New World slavery of the eighteenth century—might be regarded in a similar light.

Second, there is the argument from opacity: It is a condition of judgement that we understand the practices we are judging. The application of any value judgement—for example, a judgement concerning the excellence of a wine, or the ineptness of a detective story, or the beauty of a painting—presupposes familiarity with and an understanding of the kind of object that is being judged. Often this familiarity is absent when we try to judge the practices of a distant culture or the actions of persons whose psychological make-up is atypical. Perhaps we have good insight into what was going on in Germany in the 1930s, and can therefore make appropriate judgements. But, according to the argument from opacity, we cannot make confident judgements against a remote culture.

The anthropologist Evans-Pritchard claimed in this connection that while we modern Englishmen might think that a woman who crawls in the presence of her husband is expressing abjection, we don't know enough about other people's customs to say that African women who crawl in the presence of their husbands are expressing

what our women would be expressing by crawling.[13] After all, it might be argued, if we observed dimorphic Martians adopting certain characteristic poses with respect to one another, say, lifting or lowering their antennae when they met, we would have no basis for supposing that one morphological group was showing a morally objectionable subservience to the other, and we may be in the same position in observing S. So we should be cautious in supposing that the behaviour of the Ps in S unambiguously indicates their status as victims; we should even be cautious about ascribing the roles of A and P to the actors in S. For all we know, crawling by African women is an expression of high status and *noblesse oblige*.

Third, there is the argument from pointlessness: We experience less impetus to condemn or celebrate long ago or faraway occurrences that cannot be influenced by our thoughts and expressions than to condemn or celebrate occurrences that can be. (We might term this the 'That-was-in-another-country-besides-the-wench-is-dead' effect.) Moral judgements are the sorts of things that can in principle make a difference, and if a judgement cannot possibly make a difference, it is pointless to propound it.

In response to the argument from entrenchment, it needs to be pointed out that while institutions are 'tested' by time, time does not actually approve or validate structures or organisms. The knowledge that some entity has survived over some interval does not even enable us to determine whether it is strong or the challenges to it have been weak. A bridge that would have collapsed might hold up thanks to a spell of dry weather; an alga species that would have died out might benefit from nutrient-rich run-off spewed out by a new factory; a boring author may turn up year after year on the undergraduate syllabus because curricular changes are hard-fought. And an institution can be stable without being morally unobjectionable. Its longevity may be due to the very features that make it morally objectionable, namely, that the strong have been successful in pressing an advantage over the weak. Conversely, hypermoral institutions, like experimental communities, may be unstable. We can differentiate between the overall moral goodness of an institution and its likelihood of persisting under given conditions. Though a good

---

[13] E. E. Evans-Pritchard, 'Position of Women', 40–1.

institution that is durable is preferable to a good institution that is ephemeral, we can judge these features separately.

The opacity argument is equally unconvincing. It is true that the notion that it is a practical necessity to sacrifice captives to ensure the recurrence of the winter rain, or that it is necessary for the integrity of a warrior band to waste the villages of rivals does not come easily to us. We may not see the point of being in a warrior band. We cannot know what it was like to have been an Aztec priest or a Samurai warrior. Nevertheless, we are not as badly off as we are in trying to imagine how scrambled eggs taste to a cockroach, to borrow an example of Nagel's. We can think our way into the position of the people who believed these things, and there is no reason to be incredulous that they did. Moreover, our difficulty in imagining what it was like to have been an actor in remote situation S is a distraction. The professions of Aztec priest and Samurai warrior doubtless had many secret intricacies that we never will understand, but more relevant to the question of legitimate judgement is our being able to understand what it is like to be a sacrificial victim or a peasant in a burned-down village, one of the patients. There do not seem to be as many intricate mysteries here.

But perhaps there is much that we do not understand about the role of the alleged victim? In response to Evans-Pritchard's version of the argument, it should be pointed out that from the observation that a conventional gesture can be misinterpreted or overinterpreted by an inexperienced person, it does not follow that we are always prone to misunderstanding and misjudgement. Perhaps we underestimate the dignity of the peasants in the villages burned by the Samurai who might have felt themselves to be involved in nationally important or even cosmically significant events, or the sacrificial victims of the Aztecs, who may have thought an honour was being done them and looked forward to evisceration with pride. Their interpretations need not, however, affect our judgement that what the Samurai warriors and the Aztec priests did showed no moral concern for the victims, in so far as they pressed their advantage over these weaker parties to reinforce their own social positions. It is not necessary that the peasants and sacrificial victims should have accepted our analysis for it to be a correct account of what was happening. Even if we cannot interpret the behaviour of e.g. Martians or crawling women, it is

possible that, if we could interpret it, we would judge it morally unacceptable. For the disqualification thesis to be generally credible, we would have to believe that we can rarely or never correctly interpret what the *As* are doing and what is happening to the *Ps* and that our efforts to do so are futile.

Finally, in response to the pointlessness argument, it can be observed that it may do some good to condemn the dead or the remote, even if they are beyond remonstrating with or cannot take part in moral dialogue. Condemning the dead discourages new present-day followers from reviving doubts and denials of a prohibition by promulgating some immoral programme and condemning the remote may have a similar warning function. It may alert us to the presence of similar practices in unsuspected quarters. Williams appears to overstate the case in insisting that legitimate criticism requires the possibility of a real confrontation between the present-day philosopher and the original agent or his current representatives. All that is necessary is that such a confrontation can take place in the mind of the subject entertaining the proposition.

All three arguments for the disqualification thesis (external) may be turned to domestic use. A representative of the disqualification thesis (internal), Hilary Putnam, finds that some practices that are inside our morality are immune from critical judgement. Certain kinds of radical scepticism about our institutions are incoherent or, as he puts it, 'silly'.[14] It must be impossible for our local culture, the implication is, to get things fundamentally wrong in matters such as the organization of work or the constitution of family life, even if they appear to be so to an observer who is psychologically alienated or reluctant to participate in its central institutions. A critic who is unmoved by the allure of what Thorstein Veblen called pecuniary society, or who, like Simone de Beauvoir, fails to appreciate the charms of the nuclear family, or who, like Freud, concludes that civilization is a source of anguish that is barely supportable without the use of Schedule I narcotics, might be considered by a Putnamian as too distant or too alienated from our institutions to be in a position to offer meaningful

---

[14] According to Hilary Putnam, ' "Is our own way of life right or wrong?" is a silly question, although it isn't silly to ask if this or that particular feature of our way of life is right or wrong, and "Is our view of the world right or wrong?" is a silly question, although it isn't silly to ask if this or that particular belief is right or wrong. As Dewey and Peirce taught us, real questions require a context and a point.' 'Objectivity and the Science-Ethics Distinction', 154–5.

criticism of the economy, or the family, or civilization. Radical criticism, on this view, always presupposes an alienated standpoint that is automatically disqualifying.

Putnam's thesis might be formulated as follows: When the following conditions are satisfied, one is disqualified from offering a condemnatory moral judgement of the situation S or the actions and responses of A and P, the participants in S, even though from some detached or alienated perspective they might appear morally defective.

Conditions for Disqualification (Internal)

(1′) S in our world W, is very different from any situation in W' envisioned as ideal by the prospective judges. The As and Ps in S are psychologically very different from the actors in W'.

(2′) The prospective judges do not share the values and standards of the As and Ps in W.

(3′) The interactions between the As and Ps are part of a way of life that is stable. They are woven into the fabric of the culture and find resonance in other practices. They organize the life of the culture as projects organize the lives of individuals.

The prima facie plausibility of the disqualification thesis (internal) is considerable. Its defender will point out that it is *theoretically* possible that the way we live and what we consider normal and justifiable behaviour is sadly lacking in just the way radical critics tell us. It is *theoretically* possible as well that we have no right to our goods and our houses, that our partialist concern for friends and family is morally unjustified, and that our educational and economic institutions are fundamentally unjust. It is also theoretically possible that I am a brain in a vat or dreaming all the time. We can doubt this or that, he will insist, in particular doubt-inducing circumstances, but we cannot doubt the veracity of all our perceptions, or even our entire body of optical or chemical knowledge. Analogously, we can doubt that some particular law or practice is morally justifiable, but we cannot question the entire economic or domestic basis of our society.

However, the analogy between the theoretical possibility that I am a brain in a vat and the theoretical possibility that I live in a world that is normatively quite a mess, in the ways suggested by Veblen, Beauvoir, or Freud, is poorly motivated, for the suspicion of institutions

and practices need not be hyperbolic. It may be motivated by historical, anthropological, or sociological investigation, none of which can have a bearing on whether I am a brain in a vat. The disqualification thesis (internal) states that the dominant practices of a culture are above suspicion in that culture and qualifies accordingly as ideological. It is true that it is difficult for criticism from detached or alienated perspectives to take hold, and the critic himself may have little reason to wish to influence a society from which he stands radically apart. The stability of S should not, however, be confused with an element of the reality constraint.

The disqualification thesis, in its external and internal forms, is therefore not a theorem of the descriptive theory of morals. It may be regarded prescriptively as an injunction, not merely against interfering with the habits and customs of others, but also against engaging in the symbolically hostile action of passing negative judgement on others. The assumption of a posture of disqualification can have genuine moral significance and we should expect that, like most prohibitory rules, a rule against judging others can be formulated at various levels of demand. The recommended forfeiture of the right to judge might be partial. It might be held that condemnation by outsiders is permitted when and only when there exists the possibility that a condemnatory movement could arise within the culture itself. Or the proponent of disqualification might permit adverse judgement if reasoned persuasion from outside is possible 'in principle'. Each of these positions represents an eligible moral restraining rule. They are in competition with and need to be defended against weaker prohibitory rules that permit judgement in a broader range of cases.

4.4. Opacity and Disqualification

Michael Walzer's discussion of the morality of exchanging women illustrates many of the features of moral discourse identified in the preceding discussion, from the employment of paraworlds in moral argument and world-level relativism, to the deployment of the disqualification thesis (external and internal), supported by considerations of entrenchment, opacity, and pointlessness. It illustrates the striking connection between immanentist hostility to theory

and a disposition to social conservatism reminiscent of Evans–Pritch-ard, at least with respect to certain questions.

Walzer asks us to imagine a society, remote from our own, in which 'women (all women) seem to have been socially constructed as objects of exchange and where rules of exchange follow from the construction. . . . [W]omen are transferred among households, from one patriarchal jurisdiction to another, as if they were objects of exchange.' The women, as they are portrayed, are not interested in remaining in their natal villages, or in making their own decisions where to live, or even in parity with men in these respects. Yet they have not, he stipulates, been brainwashed, physically coerced, or made desperate, and being an exchange object is said to '[bring] some benefits to at least some women (even if the benefits are much greater for men)'. He describes the exchange of women as 'only one part of a larger pattern of relationship, fitted to a system of beliefs, symbolically represented, ritually enacted and confirmed, handed down from mothers to daughters over many generations'.[15]

Walzer asks what we should say about that society and how we should evaluate its institutions. He tries to show that, even if the exchange practice is inconsistent with our local ideas concerning enlightened treatment of women, as long as we cannot find any resistance to it amongst the subjects themselves, we cannot confi-dently describe it as unjust. 'Social construction', he says, 'makes for us a complex and rich world, many features of which will seem so obvious to us that we will not be prompted to ask whether they are, of all possible features of all possible worlds, objectively best. They will have a more immediate objectivity.'[16]

It is important to understand Walzer's genuinely pluralistic com-mitments. He is not prescribing an exchange system for all women, or claiming that men have an intrinsic right to exchange women. In the terms of our analysis, Walzer is merely advancing the claim that a morally acceptable world *might* contain *some* exchanged women—not randomly distributed through the population, but congregating in particular groups. To confirm the proposition that exchanging women is morally acceptable under certain circumstances, one need

---

[15] Michael Walzer, 'Objectivity and Social Meaning', 174.   [16] Ibid. 173–4.

merely gain agreement that the idea of a just world composed, like our world, of non-ideal agents does not exclude the practice.

The audience to whom this prescriptive thesis is addressed can be assumed to occupy the baseline position that the women of their community ought not to be exchanged. Further, they are inclined to think it would be an injustice anywhere, that a world containing any groups of exchanged women is distinctly worse than a similar world with none. The audience might try to explain the nature of the injustice by saying, 'It is wrong to treat women as a commodity' or 'It is wrong to treat any human being as a means rather than as an end.'

The mitigating circumstances that Walzer adduces in order to challenge the higher-demand position that the imaginary community can be judged by our more abstract standards and found wanting include the following:

(1) The system has been in place for a long time and expectations and practices have developed around it.

(2) Though the system benefits men more, it benefits women somewhat.

(3) The women are not coerced and do not object to the system.

Circumstance 1 is relevant because people enjoy their customs and rituals and do not like to change them. Everyone's life planning in the society under consideration depends on the assumption that women of marriageable age are going to be exchanged. Tasks such as the preparation of a trousseau for the exchangeable women, or the selection of a bride by the father of a young man might be welcome interruptions in otherwise wearying routines. Circumstance 2 is relevant, because many practices are justified by the fact that the aggregate benefit furnished is large, even if it is not shared evenly. Consideration 3 is also relevant, for we might think of the women rather as we think of monks who voluntarily enter on a life of service to others and obedience to their superiors. We may not like serving others, and we may not believe that the objects of the monks' or the women's deference are as important as they do, but they might just as well think of our secular, acquisitive mode of life as crass. If the exchanged women are helping men, the situation may be morally in order. Helping is generally morally good, for A_1 in helping sacrifices some opportunity simply in order to improve A_2's state.

Even taken in conjunction, however, these considerations are not particularly convincing. A dense web of enjoyable cultural practices can be expected to grow up around any marriage system; there is no reason to think that the exchange system has a special richness. And since we are considering only judging and not intervening, the costs of changing a set of practices do not need to be considered. Further, though we know that the system benefits the women somewhat, we do not know what benefits are available in differing proportions to men and women living under alternative marriage systems. Implicitly, we are invited to compare the system with one in which women do not benefit at all. Finally, helping, though prima facie morally creditable, is not always a good thing to do. Helping, when it is not reciprocated or otherwise acknowledged, may entail a too-costly sacrifice of the non-moral values of personal dignity and autonomy. When thinking about hypothetical women and giving them certain attributes in our imaginations we can make them seem like monks—ideal monks, not real monks, who may be deluded and exploited. It is impossible, however, to regard exchanged women as individually called to a life of service. Rather, they are born into a condition of future servitude. They are described as acquiescent, but, unlike monks, they cannot opt into or out of the arrangement. Unlike monks, they are not deferential and submissive towards something grand and impersonal; they defer to other human beings whom they perhaps invest with godlike qualities.[17]

Walzer's position wavers between the agnostic view that we ought not to condemn the practice of exchange in a distant culture that we may not understand—a thesis about our right or our ability to judge—and the positive view that there is nothing wrong with exchange in some conceivable cultures—a thesis about the moral acceptability of some policies and practices. The agnostic argument can be conceded immediately. Where we do not understand a culture and have no way to determine what is happening in it, we should not enter a negative judgement against it. If all we could know about a culture was that women were exchanged in it, our judgements of it would always be superficial and worthless. By contrast, the judge-

---

[17] 'The engineer, so precise when laying out his diagrams, behaves at home like a minor god: a word, and behold, and his meal is served, his shirts starched, his children quieted'. Simone de Beauvoir, *Le Deuxième Sexe*, ii. 501–2.

ment that it is exceedingly unlikely that a culture could be organized in such a way that there would be nothing wrong with its exchange system for women is anything but superficial.

The women who are objects of exchange in the example are hypothetical beings, given by the author's description in an imaginary case, not by ostension. The author has not searched through historical or anthropological sources to find a culture where women are exchanged, described its practices in all their depth and richness, and argued that the practice meets the standards of moral acceptability. The exchange of women, we can say, turning to the real world, generally involves an affront to morality. The exchanged woman may play an important role as 'cultural diplomat'. The exchanged woman travels or sends her children back and forth between her new and old villages; indeed, unlike her husband, who remains in his parents' village, she lives in multiple worlds and must adapt to multiple systems of meaning.[18] Nevertheless, becoming an object of exchange exposes women in our world to the dangers of overwork and abuse, for it is the exchanged woman's labour, usefulness as a sexual resource, and her childbearing capacities that are deemed valuable. Women who live with or near their parents and siblings, rather than with or near their husbands, siblings-in-law, and parents-in-law, tend to have a higher status in their households and to have more protection from assault.[19]

Does the reality constraint require the theorist to build the features of overwork, abuse, and excess risk into his model? Not necessarily. It might be argued that the usual by-products of known exchange systems are not intrinsic to the practice. But, in that case, to show that an exchange system can be morally acceptable, the theorist has to provide a credible alternative model. To judge that the situation in Walzer's paraworld was morally in order, we would need to know that the men did not enjoy the advantages at the women's expense that they normally do in exchange systems. Walzer could try to build these compensating and mitigating conditions into the description of his exchanged-women paraworld and then invite us to consider it as

---

[18] Elise Boulding, *The Underside of History*, 46–7.
[19] Women who perform unsatisfactorily in their new households may be sent back to their parents who may be forced to refund their bride prices. Fear of embarrassment, punishment, and disgrace may explain women's seemingly graceful acceptance of the system. Ibid. 45 ff.

just. So various protections and entitlements for the women might be
brought in to offset the disadvantages of having to move to a strange
village away from one's family and accept a stranger for a husband.
Alternatively, he could simply assert that in so far as these further
conditions might obtain, there might be a situation in which women
were exchanged in a morally acceptable way.

The conclusion that a society of exchanged women *might* be just and
that it *might* be wrong for an outsider to condemn it is, in the final
analysis, unsupported by positive argument: no description of a possible society meeting these criteria has in fact been provided. It is clear
at the same time that Walzer intends to comment on practices in our
world, perhaps to criticize preferential systems of marriage, or to
commend women's acquiescence in systems organized principally for
the benefit of men. Under this 'Putnamian' interpretation, the discussion of exotic tribal women as they might be judged by modern liberal
outsiders, functions as a vehicle for a discussion of our local women
aimed at defending certain elements of a status quo against attempts by
radical social critics to reset the level of demandingness.

Walzer does not argue in the article under consideration that the
status of females in our world *W* is beyond such 'internal' criticism.
Elsewhere, he poignantly calls attention to the history of institutions
'that seem designed, above all, to break the spirit of young women'.[20]
Noting that 'freedom in love radically alters the standing of women,
but ... doesn't ... end their oppression',[21] he seeks a third way—community supervision of marriage arrangements—between what he perceives as the evils of overmanaged alliances on one hand and of radical
freedom on the other. Nevertheless, his discussion invites us to pose,
and to answer in a particular way, the following question, which turns
out not to be about exotic marriage customs at all, but about something
we observe all around us. If, in our world, women do what men want
them to and are acquiescent, despite their getting what looks like the
worse half of the bargain, why should we argue with them?

The question reflects a genuine puzzlement that most members of
the audience for the work feel. We are more than a little anxious
about the subject of acquiescent women: our intuitions about this are
conflicted. Had the thought experiment described a situation on Mars

---

[20] Walzer, *Spheres of Justice*, 239.   [21] Ibid.

involving a practice of asymmetrical exchanges between 'pods' of an acquiescent class of differently coloured caterpillar-like creatures whose mode of life was otherwise opaque to us, the disqualification thesis would not have been compelling to debate. An aura of anxiety would not have surrounded it. At the same time, the women in Walzer's paraworld are said to be so unlike our women that we cannot really understand them; they might as well be caterpillars. In the end, we do not know what to say.

In summary, Walzer's thought experiment is provocative. It attaches to an anxiety we experience in our world W and is a stimulus to moral reflection. However, it does not help to establish the disqualification thesis as a defensible theorem of the descriptive theory of morals, and it is too sweeping to constitute a reasonable all-things-considered contribution to prescriptive moral theory. What a prescriptive moral theory requires is a set of criteria for determining when a morally acceptable or unacceptable situation exists; the description of an opaque situation involving inscrutable women cannot point us towards any particular answer regarding the justice of conditions obtaining either in W or W'.

4.5. In Defence of Theory

The Pyrrhonist position in epistemology rests on the confidence that nothing will go seriously wrong if we distance ourselves from a commitment to the existence of material objects distinct from our perceptions. The corresponding position in moral theory—moral Pyrrhonism—is that nothing goes seriously wrong if we do not worry about the relationship between our current practices and unobserved ideal moral system M. The epistemological Pyrrhonist nevertheless fails to recognize that a better knowledge of nature might be acquired were we to attempt to go behind the appearances. For what we produce ourselves and spontaneously approve may be based in illusion or simply incomplete.

Hume was confident that no one would 'tread as willingly on another's gouty toes, whom he has no quarrel with, as on the hard flint and pavement'.[22] As an avid reader of ancient history, Hume

---

[22] Hume, *Enquiry Concerning the Principles of Morals*, sect. 5. 39.

should have grasped the importance of the qualifier 'given that he had no quarrel with him'. 'Everyone' agrees that murder is a terrible crime and all moral codes proscribe it. But they define *it*—the kind of killing that is a terrible crime—differently. The readiness with which sophisticated humans will kill and despoil their close neighbours in warfare for trivial or confabulated reasons should dispel any sunny assumptions about the existence of a uniform and well-internalized moral code we have wordlessly fallen into. 'Don't steal' is ambiguous, and its applications contestable. What about landlords, taxes, and derivatives-traders? North Americans might all be willing to sign their names under the overgeneralized formula 'All persons should be regarded as having an equal claim to life, liberty, and the pursuit of happiness', or to go to war under this slogan, but their day-to-day political conduct will belie this alleged commitment. In short, it is difficult to substantiate the claim that there is a pretheoretical core of moral regulations to which all normal humans subscribe, in the sense that they acknowledge their rightness and strive to conform to them, even if they are from time to time overcome by situational pressures and fail to do so.[23]

The resources of Hume's moral theory in what might be termed the realm of microethics are not negligible. The virtues are moderating influences on the exercise of advantage—which sometimes, though not always, amounts to viciousness—in the one who possesses them. The agent exercising the virtue of fidelity stands with a cause even when his interests are no longer served by it, and the sincere agent conveys the actual state of her mind even when it exposes her to certain losses. A gentle demeanour signals that one will not resort to violence or intimidation to attain desired ends. With some virtues, such as temperance and sobriety, there is no intrinsic advantage-reducing feature, though the intemperate often do place substantial caretaking burdens on others. Adherence to virtuous behaviour in Hume's sense precludes cruelty, betrayal, secret manipulation, and other forms of mistreatment of others to which agents are occasionally tempted.

---

[23] Michael Ruse is confident that 'No one would say that it is morally acceptable for grown men to have sexual intercourse with little girls.' Ruse, *Taking Darwin Seriously*, 212. Of course this is an exaggeration. Ruse means, I think, to advance the view that there is a well-confirmed norm here, regardless of what thousands of people say and do.

The virtues are nevertheless elements of an archaic theory of upright conduct that bundles the observation of moral rules together with other requisites for being an admirable person. The resources of virtue theory for addressing problems of advantage and disadvantage in what might be termed the realm of macroethics are accordingly limited. Hume envisions a society whose members are in constant interaction with one another, confronting one another face to face. The moral community Hume appears to be describing consists of members of a single social class, even if those members differ to some extent in their possession of wealth, wit, beauty, and other social advantages. The virtuous persons of the *Treatise* and the *Enquiry* do not appear in threadbare clothes, they do not have brown or black skins and labour on plantations, nor do they exercise the virtues from or in hospitals and prisons. Further, the virtuous may be presumed to have an interest in avoiding interaction with the pitiful and unfortunate, in so far as such persons are known to arouse the most distasteful sentiments.[24]

We can easily imagine a world of individually virtuous persons, each of whom reliably exhibits each Humean virtue and displays no vice with respect to each person whom he encounters. The world is nevertheless prima facie unjust, since goods are distributed unequally between groups that do not encounter each other—perhaps deliberately. Since not everyone is rowing in the same boat, non-theoretical agreements that fulfil everyone's preferences do not emerge. Game-theory simulations suggest that fair distributions emerge when agents with randomly allocated quantities of resources encounter one another repeatedly and strike bargains. It is reasonable to predict that global fairness will not emerge when agents are antecedently segregated into haves and have-nots and do not encounter one another at random.

The deficiencies of virtue theory can be addressed. A virtue theorist could add 'global benevolence' or 'concern with equality of the sexes' to the list of essential virtues. This move will, however, seem arbitrary, for there is little reason to think that people with these virtues are more admired by their peers and have better reputations than their deficient counterparts, features essential to Hume's account

---

[24] Hume, *Enquiry Concerning the Principles of Morals*, sect. 6. 33.

of why the virtues are good. On the contrary, an avid interest in distributive justice and equality of the sexes can make a person distinctly unpopular amongst his peers. Alternatively, she could follow Hume himself in supplementing the theory of personal virtue with a theory of social justice; in morally ideal worlds, she will say, the inhabitants are both personally virtuous and socially just.

Whether its solution is to be found in a strengthening of Hume's notion of private benevolence or supplementation of virtue theory with a theory of justice, the existence of the problem is undeniable: Virtue theory contains a bias towards moral neglect simply on account of its relatively narrow focus. The world slices, one might say, of the discourse of virtue are small ones, and revisionary aspirations are not at home in a Humean framework.

Why did modern moral theory after Hume evolve an impersonal and universalistic component? This is obviously a complex historical question. A satisfactory answer to it would mention the breakdown of the image of a hierarchically structured cosmos, the sense of global connection despite cultural difference furthered by maritime trade in the late eighteenth century, the beginnings of scientific anthropology and ethnology, and increasingly visibility of slave labour and the emerging underclass in a rapidly industrializing Britain. The immanentist is apt to discount the fact that the famous modern moral theories grew up from inside human life, from the observations and experiences of their founders. They did not come from the Martians or from a star.

Just as natural science can be considered both as an extension of everyday human knowledge based on the operation of our normal sensory faculties and inference mechanisms, and as a corrective to ordinary perception utilizing artificial instruments and schema for perceiving and analysing data, theoretical morality both extends and corrects.[25] We can employ both scientific knowledge and folk wisdom in making practical decisions and we can employ theoretical perspectives as well as community conventions in making moral decisions. The only-because formulation of the non-theoretical reasons principle suggests that there is a sharp distinction between an internal, situational reason for doing something in a particular case

---

[25] As Hume recognized in claiming that it was meaningless to dispute whether justice was 'natural' or not. *Enquiry*, app. III, 173.

and a non-situational, theoretical reason. This conceptual boundary is blurred in experience. Our factual knowledge about the world has a powerful bearing on how we see and react to particular events. So does acquaintance with fiction. Both distant and imaginary places and happenings furnish information or informational content from outside our own lives requiring assimilation, but the knowledge gained is inside us. In acquiring knowledge, our representations of the world and our responses to it are altered by what we are able to absorb. The mere memorization of a theoretical formula or the inscription of one into a personal notebook does not automatically alter anyone's behaviour; I can possess the formula without its making any difference. The sources of the alterations that constitute learning nevertheless extend beyond the personal experiences derived from getting about in one's familiar territory.

Accordingly, no a priori limits can be set to what perspectives one is able to internalize or act upon as a result of engagement with formal moral discourse. Individuals and cultures have been able to give up practices and attitudes of whose rightness they were at one time firmly convinced and upon which a whole range of social and personal expectations depended. It might be argued that moral progress occurred only when individuals made some outcome their concern, or their project, and pursued their goal with the same single-mindedness with which Gauguin pursued his desire to become a skilled and original painter. No empiricist should deny, however, that we are influenced by theoretical discourse, and that our passions and projects would not have the form they do in its absence.

The aristocratic militarism of the Samurai and the priestcraft of the Aztecs were anchored by expectations and obligations inherited from the past and passed down through families. Yet the conduct of these persons vis-à-vis peasants and captives was morally unacceptable. And the 'context and point' demanded by Putnam as a condition of asking about the validity of the ways of life that incorporate those practices can be easily supplied. The subcultures concerned possessed three important characteristics. First, they were founded in social dominance—the dominance of warlords vis-à-vis the populace, priests vis-à-vis captives. Second, they represent recurrent patterns in history; warlords and priests have often assumed privileges of life and death over peasants and captives. Third, they are candidates for moral

criticism, since they are manifestations of advantage-taking behaviour. We can judge the way of life of the people involved we are unable to judge the way of life of Martians, whose odd squeaks and gestures really are unintelligible. The beauty of Japanese armour and the complexity of Aztec art tell us that these practices were embedded into surrounding aesthetic and religious practices of great depth and interest. Nevertheless, these features do not render the agents or patients involved exotically inscrutable, or immune from criticism, or show that they are redeemed by the cultural manifold in which they are situated.

As Strawson, and before him Kant, pointed out, I can never see myself from inside merely as a product of the external play of social forces. The narrative I give about how I arrived here and why I do this or that reflects only the dimmest awareness of the way in which my culture sets the parameters for my agency and my experience. My ability to present to others a personal narrative of deliberative agency, which explains how I came to occupy my role, is determined by my being a member of a species that narrates itself to itself and to others. The cultural and individual narratives and explanations we offer tend to occupy epistemological space so completely that more objective accounts are seen as alien or superfluous. Embedded persons have both advantages and disadvantages when it comes to understanding why things are as they are. They can explain things that seem illogical or unfair to the outsider, but it is another question whether their explanations are, objectively speaking, any good.[26]

To summarize, the embeddedness of a theorist—who is at the same time a moral agent—in a particular culture with its own history and traditions can limit her ability to understand and assess other cultures. She should be modest in advancing formulas of obligation pertaining to persons very unlike the ones she knows. At the same time, she is not a wholly disqualified observer of others' practices, especially if she takes the trouble to learn about them, and she should resist the ideological deployment of the disqualification thesis. Chapter 5 will show that moral theorizing is constrained by an anonymity requirement. The anonymity requirement provides the precise condition

---

[26] As Dwight Furrow comments, 'A kind of moral blindness seems to be built into the structure of narrative histories because the sort of moral obligations they generate are tied to partial, contingent perspectives', *Against Theory*, 65.

that distinguishes a viable moral theory—whether formulated as a virtue theory, or in deontological or consequentialist terms—from an ideology, the latter understood narrowly as the promulgation of a doctrine by a privileged group that is, in the classic formulation of Karl Mannheim, 'unable to see certain facts which would undermine their sense of [rightful] domination' and that consciously or unconsciously 'obscures the real condition of society both to itself and to others and thereby stabilizes it'.[27]

As was suggested earlier, confirmation is a matter of degree. To the extent that a rule or policy is confirmed—and this can only be done through controlled discursive practices—one ought to act in accord with it and is blameworthy for not doing so. But isn't the claim *One ought to act in accord with well-confirmed moral norms* itself a theoretical statement of prescriptive morality? Why must I conform to it?

The answer to this provocative question is that *if* you regard conformity to well-confirmed moral norms as optional, you thereby hold a certain prescriptive thesis. You believe that, in the best world, people do not by and large act in accord with well-confirmed moral norms. As such, your thesis can be assessed for its theoretical cogency and criticized as falling short of ideal levels of demandingness. Your thesis is not irrational, but it is insufficiently moral, for the claim that conformity to well-confirmed norms would be optional clearly favours the better-off. They have reason to exercise the option rather than conforming to the norm and sacrificing an advantage they could otherwise retain. The conservative bias in antitheoretical moral discourse is not accidental.

---

[27] Karl Mannheim, *Ideology and Utopia*, 36.

5

The Anonymity Requirement and Counterweight Principles

Virtue theories like Aristotle's and Hume's do not privilege *me* over the other persons with whom I normally interact. The same obligations of justice, fidelity, honour, allegiance, benevolence, humanity, clemency, temperance, and sobriety are required of each of us to the same degree. They do, however, appear to award a privilege to *us*— to groups. The privilege takes the form of an implicit permission to ignore social injustice that does not concern property relations, narrowly defined. A world of virtuous Aristotelian or Humean agents can contain slaves or exploited labourers, women without rights and privileges, and other deprived and neglected persons; Hume's personal understanding of the world was that it not only could, but did contain such persons, and that their existence did not diminish the quantity of virtue. This is not to say that Kant's personal understanding was very different. His applied moral theory awarded distinct social privileges to members of particular groups: to men v. women, employers v. labourers, and invaders v. indigenous persons. A revisionary radical in his pure moral theory, Kant retreated to a more comfortable status-based theory when he came to discuss law and politics.

This chapter argues that if we care about the distinction between theory and ideology we must observe a strong constraint on moral theorizing, the anonymity requirement. Together with certain counterweight principles that diminish the force of the argument from heavy costs, this resulting package contains what is needed to defend egalitarian proposals against the challenges to them mounted on the basis of the first-person standpoint, costs to agents, and the weight of custom and convention. Though a consistent and thoroughgoing

antitheorist will reject the package—for if moral theory is useless and uninteresting, constraints on moral theorizing are even more so—he forfeits at the same time his claim to be advancing prescriptive claims that are more than authored norms.

5.1. The Anonymity Requirement

The perspective of an agent on the world is a situated one. It is not only personal or subjective but also marked by the agent's identity as a member of this or that group with this or that history.

The significance of group membership for moral theory resides in the fact that policies influencing our levels of well-being are normally formulated with reference to groups. Tax schemes specify how income earners at various levels are treated. Draft regulations separate women from men. University admissions policies divide high-achievers from low-. Individuals may or may not be subject to psychological chauvinism—dislike of or contempt for members of other races, ethnic groups, nationalities, sexes, income-tiers, intelli-gence-levels, etc., and a desire that one's own group be perceived as superior in some domain. Nevertheless, in so far as we are concerned with our own welfare, it matters to us how other groups fare. In some cases, one can expect to be made personally better off by policies favouring another group. Putting swimming pools and other recre-ational facilities in the inner city rather than in the suburbs can make life safer and more enjoyable for suburb dwellers who are less likely to be mugged when they come to the city. In other cases, group-favouring policies such as affirmative action can diminish an individ-ual's chances for success.

Purely selfish agents would choose their social policies according to how much they expected, personally, to benefit from the policies. They would support politicians who promised tax benefits to persons at their income level, whether high or low, assuming they did not think their own security would be thereby threatened. They would favour affirmative action if they were members of under-represented groups and otherwise oppose it. They would fight against public transit systems if they owned cars and vote for them otherwise. If they were residents of Central African nations, they would favour

transfers from wealthy nations to poor ones, but not if they were residents of wealthy nations, unless they expected a greater indirect benefit to flow back to them.

Though most of us are somewhat selfish in our favouring of social policies, we are not entirely so. We are able to some extent to evaluate the impersonal goodness of social arrangements without giving special weight to our own interests. What we normally do to a greater or lesser extent—evaluate policies impersonally—a moral theorist is obliged to do consistently. A theorist acquires credibility by adopting an anonymity requirement as a constraint on theory construction and evaluation. The requirement blocks the formulation of selfish policies and those that inappropriately favour certain groups.

This claim that moral theorizing is constrained by such a requirement calls for further explanation and defence. Consider two conditions, Condition 1, in which persons A, B, C, D, and E each have \$20 and Condition 2, in which person A has \$80 and persons B, C, D, and E each have \$0. According to classical utilitarianism, Condition 1 is preferable to Condition 2. When we take the further step of assigning individuals to identities or 'roles', the assignment of me to the identity of person A, according to utilitarians, cannot influence the evaluation of the two conditions. If Condition 1 is judged superior on the grounds that it contains more total or average utility, it must be so judged wherever I conceive myself as ending up. But what is the force of 'cannot'? I may clearly prefer a state of the world in which I have \$80 and four other people have \$0 to a state of the world in which each of us has \$20. Therefore—it might be argued—the utilitarian assumption that assignments are irrelevant to the choice of systems must be wrong.

Classical utilitarianism is deficient considered either as a descriptive theory about how agents make moral decisions or as a prescriptive theory about how they ought to. However, its deficiencies do not reside in its refusal to consider post-assignment preferences in theoretical contexts. In projecting an ideal paraworld, whether it is with the intention of changing the background beliefs of the audience, or opposing revisionary proposals, the theorist recognizes that the persons in that world can all be assumed to weigh their own pains and pleasures more heavily than those of other people and that some of the parties have an interest in the maintenance or advancement of the

status of their group. A theorist frames rules for various reference groups; people of a given sex, age group, temperament, income level, nationality, occupation, drive level, political persuasion, and so on. She does not evaluate the rules according to how well she or her reference class does in the worlds that realize them.

As a reputable theorist, I cannot write a set of rules that are endorsable only if I am myself in the envisioned paraworld. More precisely:

> *The Anonymity Requirement*
> When acting as a moral theorist, N cannot deem one rule preferable to another because of her identity. If W_1, exemplifying one rule, is deemed better than W_2, exemplifying some alternative, this judgement must be preserved over any possible assignment of N to various roles in W_1 and W_2. Further, the judgement of the audience A charged with confirming the theory as promulgated must be robust over their envisioned assignment to various roles in W_1 and W_2.

It follows from the anonymity requirement that I cannot prefer a set of rules R to a set of rules R' because R contains rules that work to my advantage, or to the advantage of my family, my class, or my country. I am prevented from passing off justifications of my existing privileges as soundly reasoned theory and from awarding myself special exemptions, even on the grounds that they tend to the general good, unless I would be able to appeal to the same grounds from any other subject position. Gyges, if we consider him under the rubric of a moral theorist, violates the requirement. He endorses a rule that reads, 'Only a certain person P may thieve, deceive, and murder undetected'. He prefers that rule to one reading 'No one may thieve, deceive, and murder undetected', but only if P is Gyges.

At the same time, the anonymity requirement does not entail the repugnant conclusions associated with the claim that everyone's interests must be counted equally by everyone. It does not demand that agents weigh costs and benefits to all agents equally, or that any particular value be maximized, regardless of the costs to someone. Worlds in which agents weigh everyone's interests equally do not necessarily satisfy the requirement and their impartial weighing is certainly not sufficient for its satisfaction. For a world *in which* agents

regard themselves consistently from a third-person standpoint—that is to say, considering their own interests as no more important than the interests of some arbitrarily designated person—will clearly be structured quite differently from a world in which agents are subject to some other equally impersonal constraint. It is clear that a paraworld in which agents do, or could come to, regard themselves consistently from a third-person standpoint, does not satisfy the reality characteristic. It is a further question whether a world in which agents were able to weigh costs and benefits perfectly impartially and did so would be preferable to a world in which they were able to but did not.

As a theorist, I can therefore judge that it is sometimes, though not always, impersonally better that agents weigh their own interests more heavily than they weigh the general welfare. This can be seen from a consideration of various versions of the 'trolley problem'. Should I run over one person to prevent my trolley running over five? Should I murder my spouse if it will save twenty? Should I lie to my spouse to prevent five people lying to their spouses? Simple-minded utilitarians may answer yes to all these questions, but it would be difficult to confirm the claim that such things should be done. It would be too much to ask of me that I murder my spouse to save twenty orphans, if a maniac were to offer me the opportunity to do so. It may also be too much to ask of anyone that he shoot down a plane with 300 passengers to prevent it crashing into the White House.

On these questions, intuitions differ so profoundly that, unless theory-level relativism is true, the norms that are enunciated are only authored norms, with no claim to objectivity and so general bindingness. The anonymity requirement does not settle the question what the right thing to do in such dilemmas is. However, it implies that in establishing what the right thing to do is, my judgement must remain consistent whether I suppose myself to be the potential killer, the spouse, an orphan, a passenger, a White House employee, or anyone else who has an interest in the outcome. All things considered, I can prefer a world in which (in some circumstances) I am killed to a world in which some agent (in those circumstances) murders someone else, thereby saving me along with nineteen others. The role of having sacrificed my life to spare another agent from having to do a terrible thing—murder a spouse in order to save nineteen others and me—is not an unacceptable one.

The anonymity requirement is consistent with world-level relativism. It permits a theorist to write different rules for different subclasses on the grounds of varying circumstances (including different preferences) or avoidance of imposition. The obligation to act benevolently, for example, might well be regarded as different for the well-off and the badly-off. Artists might be allowed certain exemptions and permissions that others are not. However, if N writes a rule that exempts artists from certain responsibilities, her endorsement of it as morally preferable to the envisioned alternatives cannot depend on her assumption that she is an artist. If N judges that a world that might contain some exchanged women is at least as good as an otherwise similar world that contains none, his judgement must be robust over his assignment to the role of woman or man, exchanged or not exchanged.

As noted, the promulgation of a permission rule of the Schefflerian variety that states that 'Everyone may assign greater weight to his own interests than to the interests of others' need not violate the anonymity requirement. Yet, certain subformulas of the rule may constitute a violation under specific empirical conditions. Consider the formula of obligation 'Everyone is permitted to devote all his resources to his family and friends and to give none to distant strangers'. One might defend this ACT on the grounds that a world in which both the wealthy and the impoverished devote all their resources to kin and kith is all-things-considered better than other paraworlds in which the wealthy do not do this. Suppose, however, that the poor have few or no resources to circulate amongst their family and friends. In that case, the effect of everyone's conforming to the permission rule will be indistinguishable from the effect of everyone's conforming to a nominally different rule that reads simply, 'Wealthy persons may devote all their resources to friends and family', or from one that reads 'The wealthier a person is, the greater the resources he is permitted to devote to friends and family'.

The situation is similar with respect to a rule R that reads as follows, 'Anyone who has a very great talent that can profitably be exercised is permitted to cease to provide for his children as long as someone else can be found to sustain them'. If the world is divided into two classes, K and $-K$ such that the $-K$s lack talent, the $-K$s' talents are unprofitable or impossible to exercise, or the $-K$s are unable to

find anyone else to sustain their children, the effect of realizing R will then be indistinguishable from the effect of realizing the following rule R': 'Ks who have a very great talent that can profitably be exercised may cease to provide for their children as long as someone else can be found to sustain them'. If the Ks are more likely to possess talents that can profitably be exercised and are empirically more likely to be able to find someone else to sustain their children, the effect of the rule will be indistinguishable from a vaguely stated rule R'' that states that 'More Ks than $-Ks$ are permitted to cease to provide for their children on the grounds of a talent that can be profitably exercised, etc.' To fulfil the anonymity requirement, these equivalent rules should be judged acceptable regardless of the possible roles that could be occupied by the proponent and evaluators of the rule.

The anonymity requirement does not require me to be psychologically indifferent to my potential assignment to various roles in alternative worlds. I might prefer the role of an artist to all other roles in many possible worlds because I like to draw. In that case, I have a non-moral hedonic preference for worlds in which, other conditions remaining the same, I am an artist. Numerous roles in other worlds can be hedonically unacceptable to me without being morally unacceptable to me and so just morally unacceptable. I might prefer non-existence to solitary existence in a world in which I was the last living survivor of a collision between the earth and an asteroid. In such a world, there would no longer be any moral relations between animate creatures, hence, few if any opportunities to engage in morally unacceptable practices. My role might not be morally unacceptable but unacceptable nevertheless on hedonic grounds as being too lonely. By contrast, being the last survivor of a nuclear holocaust might be considered a morally unacceptable role, since my being in that state could have been prevented by human exertion and benevolence. We must distinguish, however, between the judgement that my role in the actual world is morally unacceptable, which is to be understood as the thought that a world with no one like me in it is preferable to worlds with anyone like me in them, from the judgement that I ought to eliminate myself from the actual world. The costs of transition from one state of the actual world to another—in this case, the loss of a human life—may be too high to justify the transition. In general, proposals for changing existing conditions or

redistributing goods have to be evaluated for their morality separately from questions of the goodness of hypothetical conditions or proto-cols for the distribution of goods. Immanentists are properly sensitive to these costs; they need merely to be dissuaded from overestimating them.

There are three main objections to the anonymity requirement, that it is too strong to serve as a basic constraint on moral theoriz-ing, that it is too weak, and that it is pointless. I take these up in turn.

(a) *Objection: The anonymity requirement is too strong*

Why is the requirement good for a theory to satisfy? a sceptic might wonder. Is the anonymity requirement so well confirmed that it could be regarded as an authorless norm with respect to rational rule-projection? Evidently, it is not a condition of rational rule-projection, for Gyges, for one, fails to observe it and, *pace* Nagel, it is not clear that Gyges is irrational as opposed to merely immoral in refusing to renounce the advantages that go along with being invis-ible. Doesn't the anonymity requirement, taken as a prescriptive meta-rule, beg the question against the critics of exigent moralities whose claim it is that agents need not observe the constraints of the third-person perspective in deciding on courses of conduct? The requirement is, the critic might slyly suggest, another authored norm, issued by theorists who have been too heavily influenced by the famous modern moral theories. It is on the same logical footing as the household rule that computers under the direction of subadults have to be turned off by 10 p.m.: just another bossy imposition. Agents have access to information about themselves, it might be argued, that is strongly relevant to what they ought to do: infor-mation about their own needs, desires, abilities, and levels of toler-ance. No matter how well informed a moral theorist is, she does not know what it is like to be me or a member of one of my reference groups. *Her* estimation of what it is like to occupy *my* role is not worth much, theoretically.

In response, it can be conceded that each of us has only vague ideas about what it is like to be some other person or to belong to some other reference class. Nevertheless, arguments in moral theory presuppose that we have enough access to otherness to make

judgements. When Williams invites the audience to agree to the specific exemption from marital duties he requests for 'Gauguin', he presupposes that we can understand 'Gauguin's' situation—perhaps from knowing something about Gauguin—well enough to venture an opinion. Credible oligarchs who favour exemptions for the rich must present themselves as knowing what it is like to be down and out.

The 'Gauguin' of Williams's fable is not a moral theorist. He is not conceived as endorsing a rule that states that husbands should remain at home, except when they are artistically gifted, or that artistically gifted husbands should remain at home, except when 'Gauguin' is one of the reference class. Nor does he endorse a rule that states that persons, with the exception of himself, should submit their proposed courses of action to a Kantian or utilitarian test. His relationship to moral rules in the story is purely negative. He thinks over his problems and his conflicts, but he is portrayed as one of the many persons who adopt a plan of conduct with moral implications without consulting a theory. The disqualification thesis (external) denied, any observer is free to criticize him, approve of him, or refuse to pass judgement on him. Williams, however, in narrating the story of 'Gauguin', is in a different position. He is a theorist, citing the case of a-man-whose-relationship-to-moral-rules-is-purely-negative. He can only be understood as arguing prescriptively—and impersonally—for an exemption from dutiful behaviour for persons with large talents, capacious desires, and relative immunity from retaliation. Williams's claim that there is no legitimate vantage point from which 'Gauguin' might properly be reproached is defended by appealing to the reader for his endorsement of the author's judgement about what ought to happen or need not happen in a particular case.[1]

Any agent knows more about himself than any theorist can know about him. All this means, however, is that agents are in a good position to provide information that can disconfirm theories about what people like themselves ought to do.

---

[1] Williams might be understood as rejecting the Anonymity Requirement. Effectively, he claims that it is acceptable for me to judge the situation in which I kill one person to save twenty to be worse than the situation in which X kills one person to save twenty. As a theorist, however, I have to decide whether a world in which it might happen that I killed one person to save twenty is preferable to worlds in which this could not happen.

(b) *Objection: The anonymity requirement is too weak*

Suppose the world is divided into two classes, the Reds and the Greens. Suppose a Red theorist propounds a set of rules according to which the Reds may live from the labour of the Greens, but not vice versa. Her judgement is robust over her assignment to the role of a Red or the role of a Green; if I *were* a Green, she thinks, though I most certainly am not and can scarcely imagine being one, it would not be a bad thing for the Reds to live from my labour. So the requirement does not exclude exploitative systems or even systems of slave holding.

This suspicion is correct. The theorist has done nothing to violate the canons of proper theory construction. The anonymity requirement contains a bias against exploitative and other unjust worlds since, by and large, theorists and evaluators do not rate highly worlds in which they are exploited or exploit others, but it does not automatically deselect exploitative or unjust worlds. An application of the heavy costs principle could, in theory, override the moral reluctance to be an exploiter. Exploitation can only be excluded by a strong moral preference for non- exploitative worlds, that is, by a substantive commitment, not the use of a formal criterion.

The anonymity requirement is evidently not satisfied by Aristotle's views on natural slavery, for Aristotle would not have considered a state of the world in which the proponent of those views, Aristotle, could have been a natural slave to be a possible state of the world, and therefore could not have considered his position as a natural slave acceptable. Technically, Aristotle does not have a 'theory' of natural slavery—he merely advances some authored and targeted norms in the context of a descriptive theory of different types of human nature. However, one can imagine a theory of natural slavery resembling Aristotle's that is tested by the requirement. Would a competent audience necessarily reject it? According to Rawls, we can show that slavery is unjust by appealing to 'the fact that it allows some persons to own others as their property and thus to control and own the product of their labour'.[2] This seems a rather elliptical proof of the unacceptability of slave-holding worlds; it provides little clue as

---

[2] Rawls, *Political Liberalism*, 122.

to why, all over the world, for much of history, slavery has been considered by reasonable people as a reasonable way to organize labour. How did we get to disconfirm this popular view? For I take it we have disconfirmed it.

The awfulness of an institution need not correspond to the brevity of a proof required to show its wrongness. A more leisured, but ultimately more satisfactory, approach to the question 'Could slavery be just?' requires us to take the theoretical proposal that in some morally acceptable worlds there might be some slaves seriously. This granted, there are three ways in which a theory of slavery might fail a confirmation protocol. First, the claim that some persons are born with the dispositions and preferences of slaves and do not mind being slaves might turn out to violate the reality constraint. Or, even if the theory passed that test, it might fail with respect to the anonymity requirement, in case the competent audience was unwilling to concede that, if they had been born with the dispositions and preferences of slaves, or if they did not mind being one, the role of slave would be acceptable to them. Finally, even if the theory were to pass both tests, it could fail to incorporate the idealism characteristic. It is conceivable that there are natural slaves, that the competent audience would judge that the relevant roles are acceptable, yet still prefer a world in which no slaves were held by anyone to a world in which there were some slaves for the moral reason that slavery involves egregious advantage-taking. But is not slavery simply a violation of human rights? Can't this point be used to exclude a theory as a priori ineligible even before it is put to the test of the reality constraint and all higher tests?

Rights, however, are best viewed as shorthand notations for theory-writers. The right-not-to-be-a-slave eliminates potential theories from further consideration. A right is not a feature of living human beings that prevents us doing certain things to them; for the fact is, human rights can be and often are violated. The ascription of a right nevertheless tells us not to bother debating further the acceptability of permissions, e.g., to enslave our fellows. When we hypostasize rights, we tend to see them as features of the reality constraint, as a kind of aura protecting people from abuse. They are, however, more properly seen as determined by the idealism characteristic.

The tendency to hypostasize rights as possessions of people disguises the fact that one can behave unacceptably to people without

violating what are usually considered their rights. It is not only seriously wrong to chain and flog persons of low motivation to get them to work, it is also somewhat wrong to pursue and harass persons of low motivation to get them to work. The rights theorist cannot account for the latter wrongness in a manner consistent with the former, for being harassed by officials in a welfare office or being the subject of viciously punitive editorials cannot be considered a violation of human rights. Yet if it is thoroughly wrong to control and own their labour by owning persons, then it is somewhat wrong to exercise certain kinds of control over labour by exercising powers that resemble the powers of ownership. The violation of a right should therefore be seen as a kind of limiting case of moral awfulness. One cannot do worse to people than violate their rights.

(c) *Objection: The anonymity requirement is pointless*

Suppose I am a well-off person who judges that all members of my reference class, persons with an income of >$100,000 per annum, ought to reorganize their consumption patterns and send $3,666.66 annually, for reasons to be set out below, to UNICEF. I represent us as all doing so in an ideal world. I am now faced with the prospect of acting on the norm I have judged appropriate, i.e., of having to send $3,666.66 to UNICEF when others in my reference class are not going to do so. *They* are going to spend the money on parties and vacations. While it would be easy for me to send in $3,666.66 if they were going to do so as well, it will now be difficult for me and my obligation is at least prima facie reduced. I should therefore simply have asked how much *I* ought to send to UNICEF, giving no thought to others in my determination. Therefore, the anonymity requirement is pointless. It is an element of the reality constraint, after all, that I have only limited influence on others, and that getting out of step with kith and kin, or merely with my normal group of associates, imposes indirect costs, for example, the costs of being unable to participate in certain social activities or reciprocate the generosity of others, or being thought holier-than-thou.

The appropriate question for me to ask, however, is 'What ought well-off people who will be acting alone in their social groups give to UNICEF?' The amount may well be less than what well-off people

who will be acting in concert with others ought to give, but this should not be too surprising. Obligations can be weakened by context, though they can also be strengthened. On the Erickksonian principles discussed earlier, my fidelity obligations, if I live in a promiscuous society, are somewhat weaker than they are if I live in a chaste society, for a given amount of moral effort can prevent more harm in one case than in the other. If it is the norm in my subculture to give money to UNICEF, rather than taking vacations, I am somewhat more culpable if I take vacations instead, since less moral effort is required in one case than the other to give money to UNICEF. Of course, neither charitable obligations nor fidelity obligations are precise determinables and, to the extent that they are not determinable, I am morally free to exceed or fall short of expectations on either score.

The anonymity requirement functions in a way that is related to, but not equivalent to, Rawls's stipulation that the formulation of a theory of justice is undertaken behind a veil. It disposes of some serious problems with the veil notion. Rawls proposed that an acceptable theory of justice is the theory that would be agreed to as a result of bargaining amongst a set of individuals, not one of whom 'knows his place in society, his class position or social status . . . his fortune in the distribution of natural assets and abilities, his intelligence, strength, and the like. . . . [T]he parties do not know their conceptions of the good or even their special psychological propensities. The principles are chosen behind a veil of ignorance.'[3]

The reason the original position must abstract from and not be affected by the contingencies of the social world is that the conditions for a fair agreement . . . between free and equal persons must eliminate the bargaining advantages that inevitably arise within the background institutions of any society from cumulative social, historical, and natural tendencies.[4]

This explanation of how the veil assures a fair outcome is puzzling, because it is unclear how there could be any bargaining amongst individuals who were essentially identical, in their degree of ignorance and their absence of personal and cultural tastes and preferences. The notion of a contract or a bargain struck amongst some group of persons implies a process of give and take, concessions and com-

---

[3] Rawls, *Theory of Justice* (rev. edn.), 11.   [4] Rawls, *Political Liberalism*, 23.

promises, and the merely formal multiplicity of the discussants provides no basis for such a process. Rawls might as well have said that an acceptable theory of justice is the one that would be preferred by a single individual who did not know his place in society, his intelligence, strength, preferences, and so forth, on the assumption that it would be impossible that two individuals fitting this description should have a rational preference for different theories.[5]

However, the single–chooser formulation does not appear to capture Rawls's intended conception either. The notion that some form of 'bargaining' occurred amongst the contractors in the original position was meant to reflect the idea that different interests were at stake and that those in different roles were in a position to provide information to others concerning their needs and preferences. In short, Rawls's formulation in the passage just quoted is contradictory.

It might seem that to avoid the paradox, we could represent the deliberators as differently motivated, and perhaps even as differently empowered, but as equally reasonable. However, if the deliberators are conceived as equally sympathetic to every possible set of preferences, and as equally well informed about one another and the world, their multiplicity is still only formal. They still constitute in effect a single chooser. Contractualist theories confuse two separate issues, the pragmatic need for agents to tailor their desires, demands, and expectations to one another, to agree on what is going to happen in their world, and the epistemological need for normative theorists to coordinate their information and to agree on what agents are like and what they ought to do. For when Scanlon says that 'when we address our minds to a question of right and wrong, what we are trying to decide is, first and foremost, whether certain principles are ones that no one, if suitably motivated could reasonably reject',[6] he leaves it unclear whether we decide on principles by engaging in a discussion of our individual desires 'on the ground' with our direct competitors for goods, honours, and other resources, or whether we decide on principles by discussing people in general's desires for goods, honours, and other resources with our direct competitors in moral theory. Scanlon refers to 'unity with our fellow creatures' as the desideratum specially

---

[5] As Ted Honderich pointed out in a memorable review essay , 'The Use of the Basic Proposition of a Theory of Justice', 81.

[6] Thomas Scanlon, *What We Owe to Each Other*, 189.

or even uniquely available in contractualism, but the unity of purpose in a well-run institution or the satisfaction citizens from all walks of life might feel in reaching a compromise on taxation policies that everyone can live with is not the same as the intellectual unity with our fellow thinkers that we seek as investigators of the moral sphere.

The claim

(1) A_1 *is morally obliged to do ACT in c with regard to* A_2

is, on our analysis, equivalent to the claim

(2) A_1 *always does (advantage-reducing) ACT in c with regard to* A_2 *in preferred worlds satisfying the reality constraint.*

To confirm 2 is to have confirmed 1; to try to confirm 1 is to try to confirm 2. Now, contractualists appear to take 1 in turn as implying

(3) *If* A_1 *were to propose ACT in c to* A_2*, this would be reasonable; and* A_2*'s agreement to ACT in c would be reasonable; and if* A_2 *were to propose ACT in c to* A_1*, this would be reasonable; and* A_1*'s agreement to ACT in c would be reasonable.*

The 'agreement' might concern anything from the division of labour within a household, to the manner in which a county will deal with resident drug addicts, to the policies of a nation with respect to agricultural subsidies that influence the standard of living elsewhere.

Now, 3 does not of course entail either 2 or 1. It is reasonable for me to invite my daughter to accompany me to the movies on a Sunday afternoon, and her agreement would be reasonable, but going together to the movies is not a feature of overall morally preferred worlds or morally obligatory. Is 3 nevertheless a necessary condition of 1 and 2? The answer to this question depends on how 3 is interpreted. If it is equivalent to 4, the answer is clearly no:

(4) *If* A_1 *were to propose ACT in c to* A_2 *in our world,* A_2*'s agreement would be forthcoming; and if* A_2 *were to propose ACT in c to* A_1 *in our world,* A_1*'s agreement would be forthcoming.*

The contractualist will not take the expectation of actual agreement between existing persons or parties as a necessary condition of obligation, for he is fully aware that not all parties in our world are reasonable and morally motivated. Claim 3 must be understood as referring to idealized agents who are reasonable, very well informed, and moderately benevolent. If A_1 and A_2 are now conceived as just

such impartial theorists who agree on what is to happen to them (as it happens), now that they have shared relevant background information, contractualism simply replicates the theory of confirmation offered earlier. If, by contrast, their agreement is significant because they both get the policies they want, contractualism is first-order moral theory. It carries the implication that

(5) *Worlds in which reasonable, well-informed, morally motivated people obtain the conditions and policies they want are morally preferable to those in which other kinds of people obtain the conditions and policies they want.*

The contractualist idea can be filled in as follows: In the best worlds, agents do not merely happen to act well; they act well as a result of engaging in certain discussions and deliberations that terminate in agreement all around. *No reasonable, well-informed, etc. agent in a contractualist world is ever forced to go along with a moral policy he does not like*, and we might suppose as a corollary that, in contractualist worlds containing the usual proportions of unreasonable and semi-reasonable agents, *the more reasonable a given individual is, the less he finds himself forced to engage in moral performances involving the relinquishment of advantage that he does not wish to relinquish or requesting the relinquishment of advantages that others refuse to give him.*

Though 5 above does not follow logically from the definition of an obligation, its potential for independent confirmation is high; it is difficult to see how one might prefer a world composed of persons like us in which less reasonable individuals were subject to less forcing than more reasonable individuals, and in which reasonable individuals rarely got what they asked for from other reasonable individuals. The contractualist is nevertheless required to substantiate better the intuition that frustrating or disappointing unreasonable people is morally better than frustrating or disappointing reasonable ones. He may be able to firm up this intuition. In any case, it is important to distinguish between an interpretation of contractualism according to which it corresponds to a plausible meta-ethical theory of confirmation and a very different interpretation according to which it corresponds to a mildly arbitrary moral theory.

The response of the contractualist might be that our claim to have explicated the concept of moral obligation is just as unsatisfactory. For

if the reality constraint precludes us representing persons as fully reasonable, how can we convincingly represent such unreasonable beings as conforming to certain moral formulas of obligation that satisfy the idealism characteristic? The response to this probing and appropriate query is simply that *if* a formula of obligation has the true status of an unauthored universal norm, *then* it is ideally acknowledged by everyone, regardless of their degree of reasonableness and their level of moral motivation, and that this interesting feature of obligation (which does not require the existence of any obligations) cannot be expressed in contractualist terms. The topography of contractualism, one might say, is too flat.

5.2. The Partiality Exemption

Consider the claim that a moral system that includes the rule that we ought to transfer some non-trivial portion of our assets to needy strangers is too difficult for us to endorse because natural selection has made us so that we are disposed to care mainly for our kin. We can care a little for our kith too, it might be conceded, but nature has not bestowed on us a disposition to universal benevolence. In so far as a theory represents the bestowal of goods on strangers as obligatory, it imposes an intolerable burden.

This claim can be interpreted narrowly, as pertaining to a prima facie charity obligation to give specific sums to Third World stranger-assisting organizations like UNICEF or Médécins sans Frontières. A wider interpretation is available as well. Nature, though perhaps not natural selection, has made us in such a way that we are disposed to advance the interests of certain groups with which we identify. Our spontaneous inclination to relinquish advantages to members of other groups is weak and our obligation to do so is correspondingly weak.

To evaluate this claim, consider a case in which partiality seems justified. The relations between the Leibniz Society and the Kierkegaard Society are not very close. Each group has certain interests—in fostering the study of Leibniz or Kierkegaard, in expanding its membership or restricting it, in making the work of its members respected and visible, in furthering the researches of younger scholars, and so on. The two groups are indifferent to one another,

though they do not have contempt for one another or think of the other's projects as less than worthwhile. It does not occur to members of the Leibniz Society that they ought to help members of the Kierkegaard Society by, for example, stuffing envelopes for them, or by vacating their meeting room early so that the Kierkegaard Society can have a longer session. Why should they? Group membership normally entails certain group interests and a reluctance to sacrifice advantages.

The anonymity requirement does not directly preclude a policy whereby groups are permitted to ignore or reject the claims and requests of other groups whenever they feel no natural sympathy for them. A policy permitting neglect considerably reduces the complexity of individuals' lives. If the Kierkegaard Society asked us as members of the Leibniz Society to vacate our room a half-hour earlier, we could refuse simply on the grounds that we are not interested in furthering their aims and projects. We are not obliged to debate their request at length or to give reasons for our refusal. Is there a corresponding permission to ignore distant others? We could help people in Central Africa, but do we have to?

A permission to ignore of this type would free individuals from the need to consider the justice and reasonableness of multiple claims for recognition and assistance by Third World strangers and persons with disabling medical conditions. We Northerners could just decide to ignore Central Africans on the grounds that, while there is nothing wrong with them and nothing unworthy about their projects, we are not especially interested in their getting on with their lives. We are not obliged, we might maintain, to debate their requests for help at length or to give reasons for our refusal to help.

There are nevertheless moral reasons not to write too many policies that permit groups to ignore and reject the claims and requests of other groups on the grounds of natural sympathy and partiality. While anyone can benefit on occasion from ignoring another person's grievances, ignoring and rejecting are the prerogatives of the advantaged party in any situation and the policy favours them. The Leibniz Society and the Kierkegaard Society confront each other as equals and for relatively small stakes. A policy of neglect and indifference will be acceptable to me no matter which group I imagine myself assigned to. This is not true of Northerners vis-à-vis the Central Africans.

To what extent are we justified in ignoring complaints and grievances we judge to be bothersome and how far must we expend time
and effort in hearing them out despite their bothersome nature?
Rarely, if ever, is the quantity of advantage we should relinquish to
another group whose personnel may seem strange to us and whose
interests are not our interests a practical determinable. There is a
gradient of possible answers to these questions. A possible world in
which powerful groups consistently ignore the claims of less powerful
groups in whom they are not interested in order to save time and
stress is not, however, minimally morally acceptable and is even
inaccessible to most of us.

The descriptive theory of morals tells us that people in different
societies, and different people within a single society, can be expected
to have various accounts of their obligations to close relatives and to
distant ones, to acquaintances and strangers. The prescriptive moralist
is faced with the task of selecting amongst the multiplicity of possible
formulas of obligation that concern the needs of persons of various
degrees of relatedness and closeness. The claim that partiality is
justified can be interpreted as the claim that, in an ideal world
otherwise resembling ours, the needs and wants of kin and kith are
routinely satisfied before the needs of strangers.[7] If the claim is
sustainable, such a world is preferable to an otherwise similar world
in which people usually or always satisfy the needs of strangers before
turning to their family and friends, as well as one in which they satisfy
the needs of strangers before addressing the wants of kith and kin.
What reason is there to believe that the first distribution protocol is
ideal?

Let there be two worlds, each divided into two equally endowed
populations of haves and have-nots. In W_1, the resources of the haves
circulate entirely within families, who purchase for their children
goods and experiences such as computers, bicycles, and ballet lessons.
In W_2, some resources are transferred to the have-nots, alleviating
their most urgent needs. It is hard to appreciate that W_1 contains
more human flourishing. From the perspective of a situated 'have',
there is more human flourishing apparent in the shining eyes and

---

[7] For a spirited defence of partiality, see John Cottingham's 'Partiality, Favoritism and Morality'.
Cottingham argues that, except under special circumstances in which there is a duty of impartiality, 'It is
morally correct to favour one's own'. Ibid. 358.

happy cries of his child on getting the $700 bicycle instead of the $200 bicycle and in his not having to endure any disappointed looks and reproaches, than in his getting a 'Dear Contributor' letter from UNICEF thanking him for sending $500. Yet his experience does little to confirm the theoretical judgement that worlds in which resources are kept circulating locally are better. Human flourishing appears to require some expropriation of resources from well-off families. The question is not whether, but 'how much?'

It is burdensome to meet the needs of strangers when kith and kin are vociferously representing their wants. The utilitarian thesis that one should adopt the policy that maximizes aggregate well-being impersonally calculated is exigent. An agent could continue to move deprived persons from a condition of neutrality—the state in which existence is not distinctly preferable to non-existence—up to a positive condition of well-being by dispensing his assets bit by bit until he was on the point of falling below neutrality himself. Such a policy is too costly. The agent's desire to consume, to learn, and to express herself will be frustrated if she adopts it. Not only will she have to give up a few luxuries, such as shade-grown organic coffee, imported ham, and Perry Ellis sportswear, she will have to cancel magazine subscriptions and stop buying books and seeing movies. Normal relationships with kith and kin will be distorted by the refusal to maintain an accepted level of expenditure on them. As Mary Douglas has pointed out, material goods 'are needed for making visible and stable the categories of culture'.[8] They support what she terms 'rituals of consumption', including dining out, entertaining, decorating, and dressing, that offer opportunities for the exchange of information and the cementation of personal and familial ties.[9] To make matters worse, the hypermoral agent will be forced into rela- tionships with distant strangers with whom she has nothing in common beyond membership in a common species with the same basic needs. To determine where her newly freed-up resources can do the most good, she will have to give a lot of thought to matters to which she doesn't normally give much thought, such as sub-Saharan politics. These considerations seem to militate against the adoption of exigent rules.

---

[8] Mary Douglas and Baron Isherwood, *The World of Goods*, 59. [9] Ibid. 81.

The question how far we are obliged to depart from the norms of the culture and from settled consumption habits has no objective answer. 'Around here', we outfit our children with good bicycles, and they feel aggrieved if we do not. Nevertheless, local norms still leave a great deal of scope for self-positioning. What kind of bicycle do I buy? How often do I replace children's bicycles? New or used? How much of a concession should be made to the child's desire for reputation and status? The role of the prescriptive moralist is to advance a position on wealth retention and wealth distribution that is a moral position—i.e., that requires some renunciation of advantage—and to make the paraworld in which the corresponding obligations are realized appear to be accessible from here. In doing so, she must take into account the costs levied on agents by the obligation and the multipliers and reducers that influence the estimation of their weightiness.

Though the question how much income a given agent ought to divert to strangers is not a practical determinable, 'Fermi methods'[10] of estimation can nevertheless prove useful. Even when one's access to information is limited, one can make headway with a few rough and ready figures. According to Partha Dasgupta, 'The financial requirements for a broadly-based human resource development strategy designed to meet basic needs would total approximately 5.5% of GNP.'[11] Suppose that global GNP is thirty trillion US dollars. Then approximately 1.8 trillion dollars is needed to meet basic needs universally. There are various ways to calculate what ought to be sent each year.

I can assume, for example, that...

(1) Each person in a world of six billion will contribute equally to the subsistence of the rest. Someone like me should send in $300.

(2) Only the better-off half will contribute to meeting the needs of the worst-off half, and the better-off half do not need any more resources than they already possess and can do with less. Someone like me should send in $600.

---

[10] The physicist Enrico Fermi showed how it is possible to make useful determinations of such seeming unknowables as the number of pianos in Chicago. The figures arrived at are inaccurate, but not by orders of magnitude.

[11] Partha Dasgupta, 'National Performance Gaps', quoted by David Braybrooke, 'The Concept of Needs', 62.

(3) The top 5 per cent of world income earners should meet all the needs of the worst-off. Because three hundred million persons will be providing the total, someone like me should send in $6,000.

I could send in the excess over what I require to meet my own basic needs, approximately $75,000, and if I am a saintly person I will do so. However, it would be hard to confirm the theoretical claim that I am impersonally obliged to do this. Conversely, it is difficult to see why options 1 and 2 should fall victim to the argument from heavy costs since their impact on my life is trifling. Both are consistent with Liam Murphy's plausible suggestion that I cannot be impersonally obliged to impose greater deprivations on myself than those that would be imposed on all of us, were all of us (in the reference group deemed most relevant) to do what we ought to.[12] A world in which some people do impose extra deprivations on themselves is nevertheless morally preferable to a world in which no one does, and of course any sum that I fix on is morally creditable, though, other things being equal, the larger sums are morally more creditable than the smaller, lying higher on the exigency gradient.

5.3. From Theory to Practice

The following general prescriptive principles seem to be tenable in light of the argument from heavy costs. The first limits the scope of the idealism characteristic of a theory. The second informs us that even agents in ideal paraworlds do not perform with perfect regularity.

(1) A moral theorist should recommend some set of advantage-reducing rules that benefit others at some cost to agents, but these rules should not require actions beyond their ability to perform or whose performance would usually seriously overtax them.

(2) A moral agent who has acknowledged a set of advantage-reducing rules as prima facie obligations need not follow

[12] Murphy's 'collective principle of beneficence'; see Liam Murphy, *Moral Demands in Nonideal Theory*, 84 ff.

them to the foot of the letter in case unforeseen or special circumstances would render compliance in a particular case extraordinarily difficult.

To deny 1, one would have to be persuaded that agents can be obliged to perform actions that they cannot in fact perform, and that they can be required, not just seriously to overtax themselves on some occasions, but also to adopt a set of principles that have the usual and customary effect of seriously overtaxing them. To deny 2 one would have to be persuaded that some obligations are so rigidly fixed that no conceivable circumstance could justify or excuse non-performance.

Some theorists have held that there are duties that absolutely must be performed. Kant appeals in his *Lectures on Ethics* to the ancient notion of a fate worse than death. 'If . . . a woman cannot preserve her life any longer except by surrendering her person to the will of another, she is bound to give up her life rather than dishonour humanity in her own person.' Strangely, he does not suggest that, if I discover myself to be a sex maniac, I ought to kill myself to avoid dishonouring humanity by raping people. The notion that, if one cannot fulfil some obligation, even a non-moral purity obligation, one ought to choose death, is problematic in any case. It presupposes that the morally-worse-than-death roles can be identified and opens the door to the inference that I can be obliged to kill someone else to prevent that person occupying a role that is morally worse than death.

It might be suggested that 2 is false because the obligations to refrain from genocide, torture, enslavement of others, etc. are absolute in a way that the obligation to refrain from non-performance of contract or lying is not. This substantive view is compatible with the principle. We can reject as ineligible for further consideration all paraworlds with any genocide, torture, or enslavement, no matter how well off on average their inhabitants are. To insist that some obligations are absolute is to express confidence that there are no unforeseen or special circumstances that could justify an exemption for an agent on an occasion.

Accepting 1 and 2 as general prescriptive principles then does not determine their application. Thesis 1 leaves it open what the criteria of serious overtaxation might be and leaves a theorist free to insist on a demanding set of obligations on the grounds that they do not

exceed human capacities. Thesis 2 leaves open how we are to identify special or unforeseen circumstances and how hard an agent should try to fulfil an obligation under adverse circumstances. How frequently can agents fail to perform a given action without its being the case that a certain moral rule is not embedded in their paraworld? A high-demand theorist will recognize few or no conditions as exempting agents from compliance with a given formula; a low-demand theorist will be more forgiving.

These results suggest that the reported philosophical tension be-tween objectivity and selfishness—construed either as self-interest or as group interest—is a conflation of several different problems:

(1) A theorist can have trouble deciding in a given context what kinds of sacrifices of advantage one ought to be required to make for moral reasons. And, an agent can have trouble simply deciding what to do when an important principle is at stake.

(2) Varying circumstances, or previously unnoticed elements of the reality constraint, such as a disposition to partiality, once pointed out, can create difficulties for a rule a theorist has attempted to formulate. Difficulties can also surface when an agent is faced with unforeseen circumstances or acquires some new information.

For example, N acting as a theorist might have trouble deciding whether people can be lied to or killed when there exist strong personal or group, e.g. 'national', interests in their being deceived or dead. This difficulty affects her ability to envision a morally acceptable paraworld. N acting as an agent might have difficulty deciding whether to tell a lie or to sign up with the Selective Service Administration.

Or suppose N acting as theorist has adopted the pacifist principle that in a minimally morally acceptable world composed of people like us, no human ever kills any other human for any reason. Yet she has somehow failed to anticipate the question: 'If X's grandmother is being raped by Y and X has a gun, is X is permitted to kill Y?' and is thrown into confusion. Pacifist N acting as agent might find herself in the position of having a gun when her grandmother is being raped and be faced with the choice of sticking to or shrinking from her assumed obligation to refrain from killing under all circumstances.

A tension between subjective and objective perspectives can be said to exist when N as a theorist is trying to determine whether a principle whose imposition would provide large benefits, impersonally calculated, is too costly for agents. What might be called the Williams-Scheffler dilemma—should agents save one child of their own or many strangers whenever they are faced with the opportunity to do one but not both?—illustrates that tension. The same tension can be said to exist when N as an agent is trying to determine whether to perform an *ACT* such as letting two strangers drown and saving her own child. The tension between subjective and objective perspectives is wrongly construed as a conflict between situated living agents on one hand and detached theorists on the other.

The emotions of anguish, regret, and remorse are associated with the existential tensions of agents trying to decide what to do. These emotions do not normally affect theorists, who experience purely intellectual difficulties in reconciling values, even if there is room for a kind of intellectual worry. Yet the theorist's worry may be prompted by thoughts about what it would be like to be an agent in the circumstances she is considering, and tragic existential dilemmas involving a conflict between a principle judged to be right and a feeling are important even if infrequent in the lives of individuals. I judge that it is right to kill one to save twenty . . . but I cannot pull the trigger myself. I believe in euthanasia in hopeless cases . . . but I cannot endure my own sick child's being given a lethal injection. I am committed to marital fidelity and the principle of veracity . . . but I'm madly in love with someone else. I think people should give a reasonable amount to assuage global hunger . . . but I adore fine footwear and smart accessories. As a theorist, and as an agent, I have three choices:

(*a*) As a theorist, I can insist that the principle is unimpeachable and that the obligation requires the suppression of certain preferences; as an agent, I can suppress them.

(*b*) As a theorist, I can reformulate the rule in light of my new knowledge of the world, knowledge that at least one person (and probably more than one) has emotional dispositions, inhibitions, and preferences whose existence or strength

were not known to me before; as an agent, I can decide to act in accord with a less exigent rule.

(c) As a theorist, I can ignore the problem, and as an agent I can act in accord with my feelings or out of a blind sense of duty without making any effort to reformulate the rule.

Williams suggests that there is nothing in virtue of which a choice of (c) versus (a) or (b) can be shown to be impossible for a rational person engaged in prescriptive theorizing, or to involve the violation of objective norms. This claim is correct in several respects. The author-less norms of rationality do not make policy (c) irrational and most moral principles we accept have not been confirmed and are not objectively binding. Yet in another respect, the claim that option (c) is always open to us is misleading. My choice of (c) exposes me to first-order moral criticism if ignoring a moral rule involves me in advantage-taking as an agent. It can leave me open to second-order criticism as a theorist if refusing to revise or endorse the rule can be construed as an advantage-maintaining evasion. For while my recognition that one ought to do ACT in c is not always sufficient on every occasion to motivate me to do ACT in c, the following propositions are fundamental elements of the theory of morals.

My recognition that performing ACT in c is obligatory can decisively motivate me to perform it.

I am morally at fault if it has been well confirmed that performing ACT in c is obligatory and I do not.

My moral standing, as well as my motivation, can be affected or determined by what is extramentally the case.

5.4. Counterweights to the Argument from Heavy Costs

Within the constraints imposed by the anonymity requirement, how do prescriptive moral theorists try to secure agreement on the preferability of their paraworlds and thereby confirm their prescriptions, elevating them as far as possible to the status of authorless norms? Chapter 2 suggested that they tend to advance simple rules for reasons of elegance and economy and Chapter 3 suggested that overly exigent

rules are avoided since it is more difficult to convince judges of their obligatoriness. The propensity to advance simple and elegant rules naturally conflicts with the desire to advance fully credible ones, applicable in any situation. Simplicity and elegance may carry the day: Kant's elementary rules—his stipulation of the duties to veracity, benevolence, self-development, and the preservation of one's own life—are greatly admired partly on account of the generality with which they are stated, though the first two duties at least are exigent and admit of exceptions or weakened interpretations.

However, it is not the case that less exigent rules are routinely preferred to rules that are more exigent. Prescriptive theorists can depend on certain intuitions that tend to reduce the force of the argument from heavy costs wherever it furnishes a prima facie reason for weakening an obligation. The costs of telling the truth or refusing to give way to suicidal despair may be heavy; nevertheless, we expect agents to undergo some degree of suffering to uphold the duties of veracity and perseverance. Informants typically regard some classes of difficulty of fulfilling a proposed formula of obligation as not significantly weakening its demand to be complied with.

Consider, for example, a typical 'duty of presence': the prima facie obligation to visit a sick relative in the hospital or to attend a dinner party to which one has agreed to come. The benefit actually conferred or the pain alleviated or spared might be minimal in either case, and this might be easily foreseen. The sick relative might even be in a coma or sound asleep and my contribution to the evening might be small. Getting to the scene might be expensive and time-consuming. Yet it is not considered right to let offset calculations determine policy where many duties of presence are concerned. Most of us have the motivating feeling that we are supposed to visit sick relatives and that we should go to parties once we accept the invitation. Existentialists might shake their heads over this admission of automatism with respect to certain classes of duty, but an observer who is simply reporting on moral phenomena has to acknowledge the existence of the feeling of being obligated to be somewhere and its role in governing our actions.

Agents, then, may be expected to and expect themselves to undergo some measure of trouble and to expend effort to fulfil even

burdensome and/or low-benefit obligations. This expectation holds outside the moral sphere—for not all duties of presence are moral duties—as well as within it. Personal grooming rituals, for example, may be exigent. Costly products may be purchased and applied in a time-consuming way, or trips to the hairdresser may be required at close intervals for little visible benefit. Yet the rituals may be significant elements of a person's everyday activity plan. They can increase his self-perceived aesthetic stature just as the fulfilment of certain presence duties increases self-perceived moral stature, and others, too, may be impressed by the performance of demanding routines that, as Freud speculated, signal reserves of psychic energy as well as of time and money.

The belief that there are duties that must be performed no matter how difficult the conditions, might be thought barely rational. People who take out a second mortgage to fly to a wedding are judged impulsive. Yet whether or not the circumstances ever warrant such actions, duties of presence and related conceptions of right conduct are related to natural principles of justice that are ubiquitous and that are not considered irrational or impulsive. Internalized, certain beliefs about appropriate distributions of advantage—the ill-gotten gains principle, the contract principle, and the culpable ignorance principle—reduce the weight of concerns about difficulty and burdensomeness in the minds of typical human beings. When cited by a prescriptive moralist, their effect, other things being equal, is to move demand levels higher, even when the simultaneous tendency of the argument from heavy costs is to move demand levels lower. That we have these normative beliefs, as well as a susceptibility to the multiplication of our burdens, can be considered an element of the reality constraint. Accordingly, the counterweight principle is as much an element of the descriptive theory of morals as the heavy costs principle:

> *Counterweight Principle*
> Subjects typically regard some classes of difficulty of fulfilling a proposed formula of obligation *ACT* for circumstances *c* as not significantly weakening its authority.

There are three principal types of situation in which a diminished sense of obligation and consequential non-performance brought on

by heavy costs tends to be regarded as moral failure or moral deficiency on the part of the agent who experiences it. In such cases, the
agent is expected to assume a heavy burden for moral reasons and
the costs of performing the action are not regarded as weakening the
obligation.

(1) *Ill-Gotten Gains Principle:* If the costs to the agent, though
substantial, are perceived as resulting from the loss of advantages that were unfairly obtained in the first place, his
obligation will be regarded as less reduced than it might
have been were the advantages obtained fairly.

(2) *Contract Principle:* If the agent is believed to have committed
himself previously to a joint project with others who were
counting on his cooperation, the costs to him of fulfilling
the obligation, though substantial, will not be weighted as
heavily as they would be had he not entered into the
agreement.

(3) *Culpable Ignorance Principle:* If the costs to the agent, though
substantial, are perceived as deriving from correctable mis-
perceptions or false representations, whether or not these are
unique to him, his obligation will be regarded as less reduced than it would be if the costs were based in veridical
perceptions and true beliefs

According to 1, notions of fairness, or correctly distributed advantage, interact with agents' welfare-centred considerations. According
to 2, notions of prior mutual agreement do so as well. Principle 3
suggests that an objective representation of the world interacts with
these considerations. The presence of such counterweights is not
decisive since the logic of rules is non-monotonic: The renunciation
of an unfairly won privilege or continued participation in a joint
project might be so excruciatingly painful to an agent that it is judged
to weaken what would otherwise be a strong obligation on her part.

Because they are proposed as principles of moral psychology, not as
prescriptions about how we ought to think and judge, the above
principles can be tested by intuitive methods, thought experiments of
the familiar type. Readers who judge these cases differently are
sources of important data for the theory of morals, as are readers
who confirm the judgements given.

(1) *Ill-Gotten Gains Principle*

A connoisseur knowingly acquires a set of ancient statuettes from a smuggler who has stolen them from a museum in a foreign country. She delights in the statuettes and devotes her life to studying them, publishing a number of articles on their aesthetic qualities and their cultural significance. The theft is discovered some years later, her ownership is revealed, and the foreign government demands that she return them before her work is finished. The blow is heavy. It would be some consolation and perhaps allow her to continue to work if she could keep just one or two of the statuettes, sending the foreign government a few fakes. Is her obligation to return all the original statuettes overruled by the hardships and frustration of her life project that she will experience?

Most informants judge that it is not, on the grounds that the project itself should not have been undertaken with stolen statuettes, even unknowingly stolen statuettes. When an advantage or a resource should not have been possessed in the first place, most people believe that it ought to be surrendered as soon as this becomes known even if it is troublesome and distressing for the agent surrendering it.

(2) *Contract Principle*

X co-signs a loan for Y, who is about to take up a well-paying job and who needs to raise a certain sum for a down payment. Immediately thereafter Y suffers an unfortunate road accident and lies in a coma for six months waking up immobilized but lucid and able to talk. Meanwhile, the loan comes due. Y cannot pay and X defaults, forfeiting the asset. Y is upset. X insists that he was trying to be helpful in getting Y's loan approved and never anticipated having to pay. Y points out that X should have considered this eventuality before signing and had some back-up plan in place. X retorts that Y should have considered the possibility that he would go into a coma and had some back-up plan in place. Who is right?

Most informants side with Y. If one signs a contract, makes a promise, or knowingly volunteers for a dangerous or risky assignment, they think, one incurs an obligation that is not reduced by the eventual

costs to the agent, even should matters go other than precisely as anticipated. Some informants are inclined to read the 'Gauguin' case as analogous to this one. They see 'Gauguin' as involved in a joint project—family life—in which others are counting on his cooperation. People, they insist, have a duty to be aware of the possible costs to themselves before impulsively entering into joint projects, whether they do so out of generosity and goodwill or in the expectation of a reciprocal benefit. Even if they are not aware, they are still responsible for holding to the original terms.

(3) *Culpable Ignorance Principle*

X is a well-off person who pays high income taxes. The administration of her country is corrupt. A large proportion of her taxes goes into over-billed public works projects, re-election campaigns, and bad loans to students attending phoney educational institutions. *Y* is a well-off person who pays high taxes and believes falsely that he lives under a regime like *X*'s. Both *X* and *Y* feel equally burdened by the restrictions on their consumption by the taxation system obtaining in their separate countries. Who has done worse in maintaining an illegal offshore account that does not require him to divulge his taxpayer identification number?

Most informants judge that *Y*'s obligation to cooperate with the tax system is higher than *X*'s on the grounds that false beliefs that are corrigible in principle do not provide excusing conditions and that *Y*'s belief is merely self-serving. Yet acquiring a correct representation can be very burdensome to agents. A demoralized taxpayer could be in a situation in which no good information about the actual operations of his economic and political system is available, or in which it is extremely difficult to get this information. The obligation to be properly informed may be judged to be weakened by the difficulty of becoming informed. As the present argument is not normative—I am interested for the moment in what judgements members of moral communities spontaneously make—I am prepared to concede all these observations. When it is burdensome to get information, the obligation to get it tends to be perceived as reduced, and, when it is impossible to get a piece of information, subjectively felt costs based on false beliefs may be judged to nullify obligations. Nevertheless,

burdens generated by ignorance when better information is available are not ordinarily judged to reduce the strength of obligations.

The principal conclusion suggested by these thought experiments is that an observer's estimate of the degree of obligation a moral agent stands under varies with the information given. Information about the costs to the agent induces a fall in the estimate of degree of obligation; other information cancels out the fall that would otherwise be perceived. Costs to agents make no determinate contribution to our judgements about what ought to be done. It is sometimes reasonable and relevant to cite them in prescriptive argument and it is sometimes reasonable to insist that they are not relevant.

The thought experiments above were not intended to show, and certainly do not reveal, that specialist endeavours are not worthwhile, that contracts between consenting parties are unbreakable, and that wealth preservation is an ignoble goal. Yet many informants have little sympathy with the inhabitants of these briefly exposed world slices, though these creatures are manifestly trying to get on with their own projects, expressing their own choices and values. Imaginary cases may be described in the moral literature in such a way that the urgency of an attachment or a goal is foregrounded against some pallid restraining rules. Here I have simply experimented with the construction of three situations, employing the reverse technique of making subjective burdens appear somewhat flimsy against a more solid-looking background of obligation.

High-demand prescriptive moralists confronted with the argument from heavy costs are accordingly not helpless. One concerned with the problem of aid to distant strangers should face squarely the fact that much of his audience will perceive it as quite burdensome to send even $100 to UNICEF and will judge, of themselves and of others, that their obligation to do so is low. The moralist need not deny that subjects' perceptions of their burdens are morally relevant; they are ordinarily judged to be so, and there is no higher court of appeal that can declare them irrelevant. At the same time, he can supply evidence that the good achieved is substantial and the burdens less than imagined. While conceding that the benefit provided by a charitable person is perhaps small in relation to aggregate need, he can show that it will be large from the perspective of the beneficiary. He can provide information to the effect that donations reach their

destination, that the conditions to which they are addressed are remediable, and that the specific amounts asked for are reasonable and helpful. He can point out that a year in which $100 was sent to some organization that helps to get people on their feet is likely to be indistinguishable, in terms of the donor's satisfaction of his needs and desires, from one in which no money at all was sent. Indeed a year in which $1,000 was sent might not be markedly different in retrospect from a year in which no money was sent.

Further, the prescriptive moralist might focus on reducing the effect of burden multipliers. He can propose strategies for keeping feelings of relative deprivation in check by giving a social context to charitable donations.[13] He can propose new technologies of generosity such as small automatic withdrawals to mitigate agents' feelings of sudden dispossession and lost opportunities. He can try to supply information about the world economy that demonstrates that the experienced burdens are attributable to ill-gotten gains. Alternatively, he can strive to bring to light some implicit contract, against which the current feelings of resisting agents have no purchase. This advice to the prescriptive moralist should not be understood as cynical or manipulative. Rational argument in prescriptive moral philosophy cannot be understood otherwise than as the advancing of reasons and considerations that influence the setting of demand levels and the adopting of particular formulas of obligation.

As Peter Unger observes, most people throw away solicitations from UNICEF and similar organizations, without thinking they have done anything very wrong. Unger argued that the offence is grave, comparing it to driving past a bleeding stranger on the highway.[14] The reaction of many members of their audiences to the challenges of Singer and Unger was that while their utilitarian arguments against selfish consumption were admittedly forceful and their concerns exemplary, they were not very persuasive. In ignoring what people are known to care about—the protection of their children and themselves from the more brutal aspects of existence, the cultivation of their talents and interests, and the beautification of themselves and

---

[13] Beneficence doesn't have to be all or naught: reduce oneself to penury or do nothing. Compare Nagel on the difficulty of the 'leap' to another kind of life. *View from Nowhere*, 206.

[14] Peter Unger, *Living High and Letting Die: Our Illusion of Innocence*, 9. See also Singer, 'Famine, Affluence, and Morality'.

their houses—they violated, it might be said, the reality constraint. That observation is correct. Nevertheless, Singer and Unger are advocates of massive advantage-reduction on part of the well-off and their critics are not. The critics react to the presentation of a paraworld in which well-off persons perform radical acts of renunciation with distaste. They do not find this paraworld appealing or think those agents are much like them. The critics cannot be proved wrong, but they can be asked to defend their claim that a prima facie obligation to provide a large benefit to those who are very badly off is defeated by the prospect of burdens that may not be very heavy, and that the sceptic suspects are the product of ignorance and ill-gotten gains.

Consider, finally, the claim that moral considerations do not have automatic priority over other considerations. This appears to contradict the claim that moral considerations are overriding. However, both claims are true. The claim that moral considerations are overriding can be taken to mean that we humans attach a surprising or impressive, and at times truly astonishing, degree of importance to reducing our advantages in favour of others and that this is a good feature of our world. The claim that moral considerations do not have automatic priority does not contradict this claim, for it can be taken to mean that we humans sometimes disregard moral considerations or refuse to take them into account and that this is also a good feature of our world. A promise to help someone move furniture can be broken in favour of a once-in-a-lifetime chance for box seats at the opera; established habits of service and sacrifice can be abandoned in order to have an emotionally meaningful life. Worlds in which everyone cares more about morality than anything else are unfit for our habitation.

What Williams refers to as 'the morality system' is experienced from time to time as burdensome. As he points out, its exigency instils in most of the audience for moral theory a diminished sense of responsibility. This diminished sense is, however, offset by our suspicion that the burdens of morality would appear to be less if we recognized the extent to which our advantages are the consequence of ill-gotten gains, or the violation of implicit contracts, or based in culpable ignorance. It is, however, effortful and psychologically costly to seek out and digest information about our privileges and

exemptions. Hence our ambivalence. Any honest person must rec-ognize the existence of conflicts in him- or herself between impartial ideals of justice and the love of ease and luxury, between the desire for purity and integrity and the desire for experience and multiplicity. The world as I found it—as I stumbled into it—and its particular arrangements are not my fault. Nagel observes that the lack of a washing machine by the family next door is not his responsibility, even if he could have bought them one.[15] And indeed, although anyone may intone a list of duties to us in the most solemn of accents, it is still up to us to reply that we do not care, or that we care about something else more. In a striking passage, Williams remarks that 'We are not primarily janitors of any system of values, even our own: very often we just act, as a possible confused result of the situation in which we are engaged. That, I suspect, is very often an exceedingly good thing.'[16]

The claim that we are not the janitors of any system of values can be taken as a denial of the prima facie obligation to do whatever will maximize any particular value. Consider the following scenarios:

> If *X* kills *Y*, it will prevent five other persons from killing five others.
>
> If *X* tells a vicious lie to *Y*, it will prevent five other persons viciously lying to someone.
>
> If *X* makes a slave of *Y*, it will prevent five other enslavements.

Unreconstructed consequentialists maintain that *X* is required to kill, lie, or enslave. It is better to do whatever results in the death of one than the death of five. Unreconstructed deontologists maintain that these actions are forbidden, since the prohibition on these actions cannot be lifted for the sake of any outcome. Williams's remark suggests that these actions are neither obligatory nor forbidden. Someone faced with the opportunity to prevent four deaths *netto* may perform an action unthinkable under other circumstances. Or not. We moral theorists cannot dictate to *X*.

Again, however, the meta-ethical posture of disqualification dis-guises ordinary world-level moral theorizing. If it is neither obliga-tory nor forbidden for *X* either to perform or not to perform the above actions, it is permissible to do *ACT*. This is interpreted in

[15] Nagel, *Equality and Partiality*, 84.   [16] Williams, 'Critique of Utilitarianism', 118.

our scheme to mean that, in morally good worlds, some agents perform *ACT* in *c* and some do not. Williams's remark suggests that this could be somewhat 'random'. Rather than arguing, as a world-level relativist might, that e.g., the police may kill one to save five but ordinary citizens may not, Williams indicates that agents could just decide what to do 'as a possible confused result' of the situations in which they found themselves engaged, some doing one thing, others another.

Williams presents himself at the same time as a theory-level relativist. In effect, we cannot, on his view, decide who is 'right'—the strict consequentialist who maintains that the cited actions are *always* performed in good worlds, the weak consequentialist or weak deontologist who maintains or concedes that they *sometimes* are, or the strict deontologist who denies that they *ever* are. Thus Williams subscribes to the world-level theory that confused and random action is often acceptable, as well as holding the entirely distinct meta-theoretical view that no general theory of agency can be formulated to deal satisfactorily with the dilemmas.

Williams's meta-ethical position is easily defended. The above statements and their variants, e.g. *It is permissible for X to kill Y if it will prevent five other persons from killing five others*, appear to be untargeted but nonetheless authored norms. It is implausible to suggest that this statement can some day, when we know more, and have thought more deeply into the matter, be confirmed or disconfirmed. The corresponding theories—weak consequentialism and its competitors—can each be expected to attract followers and defenders, as well as critics, but none can be confirmed. But what should we say to Williams's world-level claim?

It is unquestionable that we often act in a confused and improvisational manner. Agents stand under time and information constraints that virtually ensure that they will often act either in an intuitive and inconsistent way, or in a manner rigidly dictated by authority and convention, or sometimes in one way and sometimes the other. This can be considered a good thing in so far as it disburdens agents from time wasted on calculation or groping for principles and produces only slight moral harm. It is not clear, however, that this latter condition is mostly satisfied. We can therefore concede the meta-ethical point while continuing to press certain world-level points.

Moral theorists are, in some respects, like janitors—humble toilers whose work is never done. Someone has to do it, though. The burdens of world maintenance and world repair fall upon all our shoulders and dishevelled theories need attention too. We can all appeal for exemptions from the tasks to which we are least well suited, as from the obligation to furnish washing machines for all, but not from all maintenance tasks.

From the standpoint of the individual agent, there is only so much moral good any one of us can or wants to produce. Neither private citizens nor prescriptive moralists acting in the world establish the distribution of the global GNP; for the most part, they do not determine employment patterns or the availability of goods. And our internalized theory of responsibility takes us to be autonomous subjects and takes our actions to count more than failures to act. We all feel this: I am necessarily myself and only contingently a member of some group or other. What I do, I can be held responsible for but not the infinity of things I do not do. Argument and analysis can weaken these intuitions and show us that the situation with respect to agency is not so clear-cut. It can show us that we are not only individually self-interested creatures on the lookout for opportunities, but members of groups that wield collective social power in ways of which they may not be fully aware. In both capacities, we are able to formulate policies for ourselves to address those situations in which we hold anything from a momentary chance advantage over another to durable dynastic, political and economic power, and to think out policies for the collective, even if it does not always respond to expressions of authored imperatives and optatives. The cognitive illusions of non-categorical selfhood, impeccability, and limited agency are powerful, and, like our intuitive theory of physical objects and properties, they are serviceable and resistant to re-education.

The moral theorist has an important part to play; he is not hampered by social powerlessness, as the agent is. In his prescriptive text, he can do what the ordinary agent cannot: control the distribution of the GNP and determine employment patterns and the availability of goods, so long as he respects the reality constraint and as long as his version of the idealism characteristic meets with agreement amongst a competent set of critics.

The following three chapters complete the shift from the descriptive to the prescriptive mode. The argument, it is hoped, will prove strong enough to elevate the qualified egalitarianism defended there from the status of a mere authored norm to somewhat greater objectivity. The argument that the sacrifices they require are too great for human beings as they are constituted by nature is frequently cited as a defeater of exigent moralities. It has produced a surprisingly resigned attitude towards socio-economic and sexual inequality in contemporary moral theory. Empirically minded persons may gloomily conclude that we are not the sorts of animals that are outfitted by nature to construct and inhabit egalitarian societies. Yet where moral theory is concerned, the post-utilitarian discovery of the significance of their personal well-being to agents themselves that centrally informs Williams's moral philosophy need not underwrite an ideological theory of exemptions and permissions. It is true that, as Williams maintains, utilitarians need to 'acknowledge the evident fact that among the things that make people happy is not only making other people happy, but being taken up or involved in any of a vast range of projects'.[17] The immanentist defence of privilege embodied in the reference to the janitorial conception of duty should be rejected as incidental to the discovery in question.

---

[17] Williams, 'Critique of Utilitarianism', 112.

6

The Division of the Cooperative Surplus

Societies in which it is possible to accumulate and store a surplus of goods tend towards a condition of social stratification and towards biases in the distribution of resources and the scope for agency that individuals within them enjoy. The provision of more goods and services in absolute terms to more people creates differently endowed and enabled economic classes. Despite the invention of efficacious techniques for growing crops, for converting raw materials into useful items of manufacture, and for economic forecasting and planning, the variance in levels of well-being across and within countries has increased and continues to increase.[1] Many human beings suffer from chronic parasitic and malnutrition-related diseases; others are well fed and remain healthy and vigorous into old age. Some live in cockroach-infested inner-city apartments with backed-up plumbing, others in luxury penthouses with soft towels and fragrant vases of flowers. Some have political and cultural influence and authority; others do not participate in public life at all. Security of person against crime and the brutality of soldiers and police, and freedom from surveillance and confinement are differentially experienced.

These qualitative differences supervene on basic economic facts. For the most part, countries and subcultures within countries in which incomes are low by surrounding standards are low on objective measures of well-being. Rich persons and rich nations are less vulnerable to luck than poor ones. The former enjoy 'budget redundancies' that enable them to weather the effects of poor production

---

[1] Variance is understood here as a measure of deviation from the mean that is not reduced or increased by changes of scale.

choices, natural disasters, and bets that fail to pay-off.[2] In short, ours is a high-variance world where the three basic goods of liberty, security, and happiness are concerned. The conditions of a life worth living are not met for many people who have not committed any criminal act, as well as for many people who have. In this respect, our distribution protocols fail to discriminate between persons convicted of the most squalid crimes and persons who have done nothing legally forbidden.

A curious visitor to our planet who considered the distribution of the components of well-being amongst all who cooperate to locate the materials for and produce these components might well write down the following questions in its notebook:

(1) Does the liberation of human productive energies through technologies of material transformation and administrative organization require, entail, or cause a high level of objective deprivation amongst human beings?

(2) Does the cultivation of human artistic and intellectual ability through the construction and operation of meritocratic institutions require, entail, or cause the subordination of women to men?

These questions are well worth pondering. 'Perhaps the most significant contrast', Margaret Ehrenberg remarks, 'between forager societies and almost all others in the modern world is the equality between individuals found there, which contrasts with the very marked variations in status found in most other societies, particularly between women and men.'[3] No one imagines that the deprivation of many is a sufficient condition of a high degree of well-being for a few or that the subordination of women is sufficient for the flowering of human creative abilities. It is easy to imagine a world in which deprivation and subordination occur without material progress. At the same time, it is clear that the deprivation and subordination of others contribute to the developmental goals many human beings, corporations, and national governments have historically set for themselves. Is this necessarily a moral problem? If so, what would an economically well-developed and complex world that was nevertheless just look like?

[2] See Douglas and Isherwood, *World of Goods*, 93. The notion of 'budget redundancy' is the economist Aaron Wildavsky's.
[3] Margaret Ehrenberg, *Women in Prehistory*, 52.

This chapter compares procedural approaches to understanding distributive justice—those focusing on how resources are acquired—with outcome-based approaches—those focusing on the resulting patterns of distribution. Both procedures and outcomes are shown to be regulated in just worlds. Contrary to the sceptical views of immanentists, we can make headway in stating the conditions governing a fair division of the cooperative surplus and in showing what greater social equality would actually come to. We can also appreciate why procedural fairness might have a positive relation to equality of outcomes without guaranteeing them, and why the theory of social justice is not, despite the fictional-worlds apparatus needed to articulate it, utopian.

Before taking up these topics, it will be useful to give some further backing to the claim that the notion of distributive justice is a centrally moral notion, i.e. one concerned with the relinquishment of advantage. This will help to lend support to the claim defended in the course of the chapter that the consent of the well-off to redistributive measures that worsen their condition is not a necessary condition of their legitimacy.

6.1. Is Variance a Moral Concern?

From the moral point of view, there is a prima facie obligation not to worsen the status of others to improve mine and indeed to improve the status of those who are worse-off by renouncing advantages I hold. These prima facie obligations are offset by obligation-weakening considerations, such as inefficiency and burdensomeness, which in turn are subject to override. Various formulas of obligation, of various degrees of exigency, are eligible for adoption as rules governing the distribution of valued goods and experiences. Some of the most stringent will quickly fall victim to the argument from heavy costs. Impersonally considered, they are too difficult for me or anyone else to comply with. The ideal of equality may be one such victim. Nagel, for example, argues that even economic equality, only one component of social equality, is too expensive for us, given our selfish interests and our competing values. The motive to acquiring more than others have is so powerful, he claims, that maintenance of

economic equality 'seems to require pervasive governmental control of individual life, serious denials of liberty, strict enforcement of general ignorance, and the absence of democracy'.[4]

Other philosophers go much further, suggesting not only that equality is an inappropriate goal but also that great disparities in outcomes are not necessarily morally objectionable. David Gauthier's description of the market as a 'morally-free zone' is shorthand for the widely shared view that, in certain departments of life, market-based notions of fairness can and should supplant the altruistic framework of morality in discussions of social justice.[5] If the distribution of the components of well-being is justly regulated by markets, and if markets produce a condition of high variance, that condition is just and, a fortiori, morally acceptable. For it would be curious to maintain that a set of distribution rules generated results that were entirely just but morally unacceptable; such a notion of justice would be philosophically uninteresting. Gauthier's underlying position is best interpreted as the position that fair markets are sufficiently moral to ensure that they are interestingly just. Theories of just distribution, even if they are formulated without direct reference to moral considerations, proscribe theft, deceit, manipulation, economic blackmail, coercion, and other forms of advantage-taking. The issue, then, is not whether justice is a concept independent of morality because it plainly is not, but whether particular hypotheses concerning just distributions can be confirmed.

From the first-person standpoint, the mere fact that human beings experience different levels of well-being and deprivation appears to raise no questions about my personal moral status. A familiar observation is this: I can look on others' deprivations from an impersonal perspective, as would a visitor from another planet, and I can appreciate that human effort might be able to reduce a good deal of this misery if people were to do the right things. But the fact is, I don't hover over the world and I have little power to make anyone do the right things. I live in the world as a member of a number of advantaged reference-classes, as a citizen of a G7 nation, well educated, well paid, and in excellent health. Economic security, opportunities for meaningful work, for pleasurable consumption and self-expression,

---

[4] Nagel, *Equality and Partiality*, 29.   [5] David Gauthier, *Morals by Agreement*, 84.

companionship, and so on are all top notch. Preserving them matters to me—a lot.

From a metaphysical point of view, this good fortune is a lucky accident. The logicians tell us I could have occupied any other existing position in the world. That I am where I am, though not who I am, is a matter of luck. I did not choose to be born as a particular person. I competed fairly for the prizes offered without grabbing or elbowing others out of my way. Is the claim of the complement classes against me unlimited? Do not my interests, and my class interests, with which they may be bound up, my desire, above all, to get on with my life amongst my own people, generate their own claims, their own defences and exemptions? As Nagel observes, when we take up an exalted and purely contemplative standpoint, we can appreciate that no human is worth more or deserves more than any other human does.[6] If a God were distributing the components of well-being, there would be no reason to prefer one human being to another, or to favour one country's inhabitants over another. However, no one is handing out goods from above. Their actual distribution depends on the summation of competitive and cooperative activities of individuals and nations, each of whom has a powerful interest in how things go for her, him, and it. The detached perspective, it seems, cannot be assumed as we go about our daily affairs. Whatever is displeasing to reason about a high-variance world viewed *sub specie aeternitatis* disappears when the world is viewed from here, from any subject position, not just the subject position of a privileged person. Williams's implicit assertion—for his parable has no force if not interpreted after this fashion—that moral criticism of 'Gauguin,' who represents the privilege of aspiration over the dreary ubiquity of need, is banal reinforces this point.

The psychological truth that we are self-centred and find it difficult to judge states of affairs impersonally is an important datum for moral theory. Yet we can give sufficient weight to the first-person standpoint in taking a high degree of self-centredness—perhaps even a greater degree of self-centredness on the part of the well-off than the badly-off—as a feature of the reality constraint when framing distribution rules for an ideal world. The fact that worlds with significant

---

[6] Nagel, *View from Nowhere*, 190 ff.

levels of deprivation or subordination may be preferred to worlds with less deprivation by persons who imagine themselves to occupy the same favourable position in them has no theoretical significance at all.

Proper observation of the anonymity requirement in moral theorizing does not, however, necessarily favour the low-variance worlds produced by egalitarian distribution rules. As noted in Chapter 1, a world, or a world slice, consisting of ten happy people eating ice-cream cones is not morally better than a world of ten disgruntled people waiting for a bus. The former world has more hedonic content, but moral excellence and hedonic content are different notions. There may be nothing morally wrong in the world slice in which ten disgruntled people are waiting for a late bus; it need be no one's moral fault that the bus is late. By extension, there may be nothing morally wrong in a world in which millions of people have too little to eat or suffer painful and incurable eye infections; this too may be no one's moral fault.

One can easily imagine a world consisting of both deprived and well-off people that is morally equivalent to a world of only well-off people. If the well-off in the mixed world have not extracted their advantages from the deprived, and if they are not guilty of culpable letting-happen in refusing to ameliorate the condition of the deprived, the two worlds are morally equivalent. While I might on hedonic grounds prefer non-existence to the occupation of some roles in the mixed world, I need not deem it morally unacceptable.

Many deprivations, it will be observed, are unpreventable and irremediable by everyone, no matter how self-sacrificingly anyone wishes to act. An earthquake in a region where houses have been built cheaply to poor standards by incompetent workers might trap thousands of villagers, including the workers themselves, under piles of rubble where they die of thirst. They are much worse off than anyone not trapped; yet there might be no way to save them even with ample goodwill and exertion on the part of their neighbours. The disaster is partly a result of differential competencies, for the earthquake victims might be unskilled at building and too poor to seek the advice of engineers. An earthquake is not, however, a moral disaster unless someone stood to benefit from shoddy building practices, or some persons were able to help the victims, but had self-interested reasons for not doing so.

The emergence of the modern system of production, exchange, and compensation might be viewed as an episode in the history of the species that, like earthquakes, has been bad for some people without its being anyone's fault. It might be the case that there is nothing anyone in our mixed world is doing by way of promoting or maintaining his or her own interests that renders worse or fails to improve the condition of others. Indeed, a possible world can be imagined in which everything a person does to increase his own advantage benefits others ten times over. A high-variance world might have the interesting property that reducing variance by certain transfers from the well-off to badly-off improved their condition in the short run, but ultimately worsened it. Nothing anyone could do in this world would substantially improve the condition of anyone else.

We know nevertheless that behind the scenes of many natural disasters that were not brought about by advantage-takers—floods, epidemics, famines—as well as behind many non-natural disasters such as currency crashes, there is a clever or conniving human being or two, operating at the expense of a weaker party. And the differences in quality of life between individuals, subclasses, and whole countries that are barely hanging on and those that enjoy a surplus could be prevented by the renunciation of some advantage, an advantage in prices demanded or payments offered, for example. Our world does not seem to be one in which no moral action that reduces variance is possible because any limitation on the actions of the well-off and every transfer from well-off to badly-off is futile or self-defeating. If it were, there would be fewer anti-corruption laws, no progressive income taxes, no charities, public institutions or services, or rescue missions. Where action-hemming and redistributive proposals are concerned, political theorists position themselves at various points along the spectrum between the advantage-maintaining or -increasing centre and fringe hypermorality. Low-demand positions that take the advantages acquired by personal dominance—that is by the expression of aggression, charisma, beauty, intelligence, and familial prestige—to be inalienable are understood by their proponents to require careful defence. This suggests that questions of just distribution are tacitly understood as moral questions, and that advantages acquired by classes and nations require the same defence, if serious inequality is to be considered morally acceptable.

There are at least two further reasons beyond the allegedly accidental nature of deprivations and the alleged absence of direct harm or culpable letting-happen why one might conceive distributive justice and morality as unrelated topics. First, it might be argued that the theory of distributive justice is predicated on the assumption that individuals are struggling to increase or maintain their individual advantages with as little cost and trouble to themselves as possible. Questions of social justice concern the division of the cooperative surplus, the social product over and above that which could be produced by each of us working independently for our own sustenance. The question what regimen will come closest to giving us what we all want can be settled without reference to morality. To introduce a contrary action-governing principle, advantage reduction, is to miss the point of the exercise. Second, it might be argued that, while an ideal system of morality might permit individuals and groups to observe different moral rules, practising vegetarianism or eschewing it, or shunning marriage or institutionalizing it, a system of justice must impose the same rules on all participants who interact in a system of production and distribution. Its hallmark will therefore be that it represents a compromise between competing interests. Morality leaves open the possibility of moral choice in so far as few moral rules can be confirmed as right. Justice does not leave us any choices.

Regardless of the appeal of these arguments, a moral theory conceived as a set of principles for projecting a moral world will necessarily contain the elements of a theory of justice. Further, nations and legal units have inevitably to choose an imperfectly-confirmed theory of justice in the same way that individuals set their own levels for honesty, fidelity, or cruelty to animals, recognizing that these levels are open to criticism. Where moral rules typically represent reasonable compromises between the stringency of hypermorality and the non-moral interests of individuals, the rules of justice represent reasonable compromises between action-hemming restrictions believed to be necessary and appropriate and individual demands. Criminal justice, for example, restrains the criminal, but not for every moral failing, and not without a hearing, and the rules of retributive justice both moderate vengeful impulses and overcome the natural timidity that might otherwise be felt in the presence of powerful rule-breakers.

The rules of distributive justice seek to come to terms with the appropriative powers and desires of the able and vigorous.

Rawls's introduction of the difference principle is perhaps the most celebrated example of the employment of an advantage-reducing rule as a central element in a theory of justice. In Rawls's scheme, 'All social values—liberty and opportunity, income and wealth, and the social bases of self-respect—are to be distributed equally unless an unequal distribution of any, or all, of these values is to everyone's advantage.' Effectively, then, individuals are permitted to extract as much of the cooperative surplus as they are able, subject to various safeguards, provided they improve the position of the worst-off.[7] Their freedom of action is thus limited by a prohibition that is surprisingly exigent, for many desirable goods and states—not only income and wealth, but opportunity and respect—are manifestly pursued in our world in ways that do not improve the condition of the worst-off, never mind everyone, and in fact exacerbate it.

Rawls justified the introduction of the difference principle by claiming that, while other conceptions of justice have prevailed in human societies, his does not conflict with the traditional notion he finds, e.g., in Aristotle, and is supported by reflection and by comparison of his with rival distribution protocols.[8] Nor is Rawls's citation of an advantage-limiting rule an oddity. Both Gauthier and Robert Nozick, who make no presumption in favour of equality of outcomes, acknowledge limits to advantage-taking by deeming theft, violence, and parasitism illegitimate means of acquiring goods. They present ideal distribution schemes that might seem either utopian in their faith in natural equality, or else relatively low-demand, but they are not amoral. Gauthier's characterization of the perfectly functioning market as a morally free zone does not signify that ruthless advantage-taking is permitted in the ideal market, but expresses his optimistic idea that in an ideal market from which free-riders and parasites are excluded, additional moral rules regulating the distribution of advantage are unnecessary.

Rawls's principle can be criticized as unwarranted. Amongst the array of advantage-reducing rules governing various contexts that we could write and observe, why should we accept the difference

---

[7] Rawls, *A Theory of Justice* (rev. edn.), 54.   [8] Ibid. 6 ff.

principle and not a weaker or a stronger rule? It illustrates nevertheless the theoretical place in a theory of justice for an advantage-
limiting rule. And if the principle is taken to apply not simply to
the global problem—How is the social product to be distributed
among the national (or world) population?—but to every local subgroup of the population, in every situation, it is a powerful—perhaps
too powerful—advantage-reducing principle. On a local interpretation, in any practice, transaction, or mode of life in which *A*, *B*, and
C participate, the only possible justification for a departure from
equality of well-being as amongst *A*, *B*, and *C* will be that the
worst-off member of the subgroup is benefited. Presumably, Rawls
did not believe the population to have this interesting property of
compactness under his theory of justice, though he evidently did
believe that the difference principle ought to be applied globally, as
well as nationally.

Theories of distributive justice are moral theories, in so far as they
constitute hypotheses concerning permissible and impermissible
forms of taking or maintaining advantage, and obligatory forms of
distributing or redistributing the elements of well-being or their
assumed preconditions, such as money, health care, liberty, or education. A non-moralized socio-economic system is one in which acquisition is wholly unregulated by moral ideation, whatever role is
played by natural submissiveness or native partiality to kith and kin.
A hypermoral social system is one in which the distribution is entirely
regulated by compensatory principles. While all existing human
societies are semi-moralized, a society of rival robber barons who
live by plundering their neighbours approximates to the first ideal
type, while a self-sufficient socialist welfare state that permits no one
any luxuries approximates to the second.

We no longer imagine ourselves as living in a society of rival
robber barons, though, only a few hundred years ago, many of our
ancestors did. The consensus is that we rejected it after the Middle
Ages for Hobbesian reasons. It was stressful and wasteful of human
and natural resources. At the same time, the consensus is that we have
also rejected the extreme levelling of the socialist welfare state for the
reasons crisply summarized above by Nagel. This latter rejection
raises the question whether normative political theory needs to be
and ought to be concerned with outcomes at all. It suggests that

justice requires only the control of procedures—the suppression of robber-baron behaviour—and not any particular distributive outcome.

A procedural theory of justice considers only the mechanisms according to which the components of well-being are acquired and transferred by individuals, not the overall patterns those mechanisms produce. It regards any patterns produced by good procedures as just. To see why, despite their initial promise, procedural approaches fail to capture the betterness of just worlds and require supplementation by consideration of outcomes, it will be helpful to consider a basic prototype model of a procedural theory in some detail. Outcome theories of justice, by contrast, evaluate mechanisms according to the desirability of the pattern—typically, equality, or at least improvement in the condition of the worst-off—they produce. Though both approaches capture fundamental intuitions about justice, neither is self-sufficient.

6.2. Procedural Theories of Justice

Modern procedural conceptions of justice trace their origins to Locke. 'Every man has a property in his own person...', Locke writes. 'The labour of his body and the work of his hands we may say are properly his.'[9] Locke intended to show how the acquisitions of an individual—in his presentation, a tiller of the soil—are legitimate, inalienable, and entirely his to dispose of, if he has mixed his labour with resources available to all. Locke's successors have adapted his acquisition model, according to which the well-being of the tiller depends on just two factors: his skill at tilling and the number of hours worked.

An extended model takes into account what the tiller can gain by exchange of the fruits of his labour. Suppose the tiller is able to reproduce by mitosis. After twenty years, he divides into two tillers, and each new tiller is able to split again after twenty years. The tiller-descendants, carrying their accumulated sacks of grain, spread out to find new land to till and the intrinsic quality of their plots of

---

[9] Locke, *Of Civil Government: Second Treatise*, ch. 5 'Of Property', sect. 27.

land is somewhat variable. The tillers themselves vary somewhat in their abilities, motivations, and personalities. Their holdings begin to vary as a result. Institutions such as banking and a property and grain market spring up over time, as well as new consumption opportunities, some of them prudent, some wasteful. Some personality characteristics and knowledge are transmitted from generation to generation of tiller, along with accumulated material resources; others are not.

Soon, there are thousands of tillers engaged in producing, exchanging, saving, and wasting, all of whom trace their ancestry back to Locke's original groundbreaker. The holdings of each of the original tiller's descendants depend on their skill at tilling and the number of hours they work, but also on their skill and the number of hours they work at buying and selling tillable land and managing their assets prudently, and even the skills and the number of hours their ancestors employed in educating their descendants in tilling, buying, selling, managing, and educating. Whether or not there are significant differences in the holdings of the tillers after many generations, one might suppose that each is entitled to whatever his labour and that of his ancestors has brought him.

Building on this idea, Robert Nozick originally maintained that outcomes involving large end-state differentials were acceptable so long as they represented a series of departures from an initially just condition effected by any number of intervening decisions and transactions that were themselves just.[10] In terms of our model, provided there is no forcible seizure of tillable land and entitlements are respected, and provided buying, selling, managing, and educating skills are deployed without force or stealth (a moralizing condition, it might be noted), the distributions obtained will be just. Since everyone is subject to good and bad luck, lucky and unlucky events, even if they influence transactions, do not generate legitimate claims for redistribution.

On this view, the incidental benefits that accrue to Tiller Y from living in the same society as Tiller X if, for example, Tiller X has produced a technological innovation such as a wheeled cart that

---

[10] 'The general outlines of the theory of justice in holdings are that the holdings of a person are just if he is entitled to them by the principles of justice in acquisition and transfer.' Robert Nozick, *Anarchy, State and Utopia*, 153.

others are able to replicate, is properly regarded as a matter of luck that neither increases nor decreases Tiller Y's entitlement. There-being-wheeled-carts in Tiller Y's habitat can be regarded either as a favourable background condition equivalent to a good climate and fertile soil, or as a heritable benefit that has been bequeathed to her compatriots.

But why should we accept the claim that the world will be just whatever the pattern of holdings turns out to be? An important objection to the procedural theory just sketched is that historical processes of accumulated loss and gain undermine the connection between virtue and flourishing on which the intuition of justice originally rested; the theory is arbitrary, when taken diachronically. Suppose that A_1 and A_2 share a set of founder ancestors, but that, after 100 generations, the fortunes of various branches of the family have diverged and A_1 is well off while A_2 lives in poverty. Imagine that all holdings have been acquired and transmitted in a manner that is procedurally just. Further, no political and environmental events have interrupted or disturbed the acquisition and transfer of assets. No wars or conquests have interfered with the skill and effort of the ancestors, no rapacious leaders have differentially stolen from them, no benevolent ones have differentially endowed them with resources or powers, no plagues or spells of good weather have facilitated or ruined the efforts of some. All transactions involving the buying and selling of land and stock have been unforced and just. It is still the case that A_1's present outcome depends on the competencies, hours worked, and decisions made by ancestors she has never met who happen to share some quantity of DNA code with her and it is unclear why her holdings are said to be just because they are a function of theirs.

The justice of their respective situations will be equally contentious whether the assets of A_1 and A_2 are acquired by mitotic division, or marital recombination, or are acquired through participation in a set of cultural practices that is handed down from generation to generation. Suppose again a common pair of founder ancestors and the subsequent isolation of two branches of the original family into two distinct clans. Each generation either contributes to the wealth-getting capabilities of its clan (e.g., by inventing machinery for extracting resources from the earth) or reduces its capabilities (e.g., by instituting

a badly thought-out taxation system). As is the case with the direct transmissions of assets, subsequent generations may undo the work of their forebears, or they may accumulate the advantage or disadvantage conferred on them. Wheel technology might be lost if several generations of fanatics decide that the wheel is contrary to the will of God. A_2's present outcome still depends on the capability-reducing actions of other people, making her an unfortunate victim. If A_1 is lucky enough to have been born into a culture with democratic institutions, a low index of corruption, and excellent food-production technology, it is unclear why he deserves the benefits he enjoys relative to A_2 and why a theory of justice must confirm his possession of them.

Although it is sometimes assumed that Nozick must have intended to show that the enormous holdings of some persons in our world are just regardless of the deprivations endured elsewhere, this implication does not follow from his theory and did not represent his all-things-considered position.[11] Procedural theories based on acquisition and transmission are virtually worthless as practical tools for assessing existing high-variance societies. For to know that an existing distribution is just, on a procedural theory, we have to know that all transactions leading up to it were just. Though our suspicions may point one way or the other, it is impossible to infer anything about the justice of these transactions from an inspection of their results.

What are the probabilities, in case A_1 and A_2 are observed to differ greatly in their respective levels of well-being, that their current holdings are the result of just procedures for the acquisition and transmission of heritable wealth as sketched above? Three answers seem possible:

(1) We can infer that the procedures have probably been just, since it is reasonable to expect that, after many rounds of legitimate accumulation and transfer, A_1 and A_2 will be much further apart than their ancestors were.

(2) We can infer that the procedures have probably been unjust, since it is reasonable to expect that, after many rounds of accumulation and transfer, A_1 and A_2 will each possess close to the mean value of their combined holdings.

[11] 'Although to introduce socialism as punishment for our sins would be to go too far, past injustices might be so great as to make necessary in the short run a more extensive state in order to rectify them.' Robert Nozick, *Anarchy, State and Utopia*, 231.

(3) We can infer nothing about the procedures.

A priori, 1 and 2 seem equiprobable. On one hand, leveraging and compounding enable individuals to turn initially small advantages into larger advantages and to transmit them to the next generation. Polarization may at first strike us as likely in a fair acquisition and transmission game extending over many generations. On the other hand, we know from experience that it is difficult for human families to preserve and increase their capital over a number of generations. Usually bad luck, politics, many children, or an irresponsible generation dissipate the family fortune. In a fair acquisition and transmission game, we might suppose, there must be regression to the mean.

A second reason for suspecting that a polarized outcome implies unfair procedures is that we assume that transactions that are disadvantageous to one of the transacting parties will not be entered into by rational agents who choose voluntarily under conditions of adequate information. On the assumption that human agents are rational and that they are ordinarily well informed, it is difficult for a procedural theory to explain how significant variance can actually arise as a result of trade and exchange except by opportunism: the exploitation of others' bargaining weaknesses. On the realistic assumption that human agents are not fully rational, that they possess limited information, make decisions based on many factors other than self-interest, and that their choices are normally constrained, it can be inferred that they often enter into contracts that are disadvantageous to one party. On this assumption, however, most holdings in our world have been improperly acquired; and the observed distribution is unjust.

In short, we can infer nothing with confidence about the procedural justice of a society from the observed variance in well-being of its inhabitants. We cannot predict that fair procedures will tend to lead to strongly unequal distributions. Procedural theories of justice that focus exclusively on the share of the resources in the environment individuals can acquire by their own efforts and on their hereditary— i.e., familial and cultural—transmission accordingly afford either too much or too little critical leverage. Either the observed distributions lead us to the conclusion that the procedures that produced them must have been radically unjust, or the question of justice of existing

arrangements turns out to depend on information shrouded in the mists of time. Yet it is worth trying to strengthen the procedural approach before tackling the question whether outcomes matter. This can be accomplished by focusing on the problem of a real-time division of a jointly created social product.

6.3. Basic and Symmetrical Cooperation

Productive activity is often depicted in social-scientific as well as in moral texts as solitary labour dedicated to finding, growing, or manufacturing objects useful to oneself and others. Though it would be more realistic to do so, economists do not begin their reflections with a tribe of humans or proto-humans composed of dominant and submissive individuals, and with differently specialized males and females, or with two tribes, one of which conquers the other and makes agricultural slaves of its members, or even with a village or urban society divided into working families.

Locke's introduction of his servant and his horse into the acquisition scenario suggests that he understood what he did not choose to explore and explain, namely, that the effective use of other living beings, not solitary labour, is the key determinant in the acquisition of wealth. For all elementary productive activities—gathering, farming, grinding, hunting, and building, as well as the most complex activities—were originally carried out by humans in groups, sometimes willingly and of necessity, but often under conditions of enslavement and principally for the benefit of others, and this has been well understood since the beginnings of scientific anthropology in the late nineteenth century. How an individual fares in the world depends less on her interactions with the non-human environment than on her interactions with other persons in cooperative ventures. A bank-teller does not perform the equivalent of digging turf for eight hours each day, extracting, as it were, his pay cheque from the available global resources. He is a participant in a cooperative venture aimed at generating and dividing profit. The apparent rationale for isolating the individual labourer in treatments of distributive justice is that it is a form of idealization that renders certain features perspicuous. Yet all such idealizations obscure the fact that nearly all

human labour is cooperative, and every neo-Lockean deserves to be queried as to the peculiarity of his starting point. If it is necessary to simplify why not begin with a stripped-down, idealized notion of cooperative labour?

Cooperative behaviour is sometimes identified with reciprocally altruistic behaviour, but not all reciprocally altruistic behaviour is cooperative, and not all cooperative behaviour actually benefits both parties. Some altruistic actions are non-reciprocal, like the care of mothers for children, and some non-reciprocal actions are co-operative. Cooperation does not require foresight, planning, or even communication regarding the cooperative activity. Mating, hunting, nest building, care of the young, and like activities are typical co-operative activities in the animal world. At the same time, cooperation is not any kind of autonomous activity on the part of two individuals that happens to mesh. The participants are aware of one another and adapt their actions to each other. Though the level of awareness and adaptation may be minimal in the case of two avian parents feeding nestlings, they do not try to push food down the throat of the same youngster at the same time.

In the human world, cooperation goes beyond a fixed repertoire, and it is appropriate to speak of cooperative activities as generating a surplus even in non-accumulating societies, for cooperation can reduce the amount of individual effort needed to survive or make survival more enjoyable than it would otherwise be. To be sure, cooperation does not always introduce efficiencies, or add utility, or even increase leisure. Generally speaking, however, a creature has no reason to cooperate if it is spared no effort and derives no benefit from doing so.

In any culture, humans need each other to survive. At a pinch, a Crusoe-like individual could build a hut, trap an animal, decorate a wall, nurse a child, and tend a garden, if she had already learned how to do so from watching others. In no culture, however, can people accomplish even these elementary tasks without being shown how to do so, and, in many cases, being helped to do so. The invention of tools, instruments, and institutional contexts for their deployment affords new and often unanticipated opportunities for cooperation. Large-scale building, farming, the practice of the arts and crafts, and trade require individuals to work together, and the escalation of

cooperation permits massive architecture, the production of organized bodies of knowledge and institutions of knowledge seeking, industrial manufacturing, and so on.

Cooperative relationships are rarely symmetrical with respect to the degree of autonomy of the cooperators, the eligibility of their roles, or the fraction of the cooperative product from 0 to 100 per cent that each cooperator receives. For it is frequently tempting to accept divisions that improve one's immediate prospects, even if one would do better in the long run to refuse to join into a project without a more equitable division of the product. The ease with which participation can be induced on terms unfavourable to one of the parties, and the room that the advantaged party has to make those terms less unfavourable, render these relationships open to moral criticism. Suppose 'basic cooperation' is defined as follows:

> *Basic Cooperation*
> Basic cooperation occurs whenever two or more individuals engage in concerted or coordinated actions that enable them to accomplish work that none of them could accomplish alone or could accomplish as easily, and when the cooperative product is apportioned between them.

Galley slaves and their overseer form a basic cooperative group, since concerted manpower performing coordinated rowing movements directed by the overseer enables a large warship to move across the sea, and no individual could make this happen by him- or herself. Getting the warship across the sea is nevertheless someone else's project, not the galley slaves'. The benefits of the cooperative product are partitioned, but most if not all the benefit goes to the shipowner. The subtask performed by the rowers is less eligible than the supervisory task performed by the overseer, for, given the chance, the supervisors would by and large not exchange places with rowers, while the rowers would exchange places with the supervisors.

Basic cooperation, with conditions added, attains the status of symmetrical cooperation:

Symmetrical Cooperation
Symmetrical cooperation occurs when basic cooperation occurs, and, in addition:

(a) The work accomplished is equally important to both parties.
(b) The material or psychological proceeds of the work, or the remuneration indirectly obtained for it, is divided between the parties according to the skill and effort manifest in the product, the performer of the task requiring greater skill and effort being better rewarded.
(c) The material or psychological proceeds of the work are divided according to the eligibility of the subtasks they perform, the less desirable task being better rewarded.
(d) Any indefinitely deferred benefits are equally shared in prospect and associated with real and timely efforts at realization.

The model represents the more diligent and more able worker as deserving a greater share of the product. It also represents the worker who is saddled with or elects the more disagreeable task as deserving a greater share. (These criteria are often in conflict.) It permits uncertain, symbolic, or emotional rewards to count towards satisfying the cooperators' claims, but it prevents delusory promises of reward from balancing tangible benefits. If a couple living in distant cities arrange their schedules and purchase plane tickets to maintain their relationship, the sustenance of their hopes for a joint future is a large part of the cooperative product, even if these hopes come to nothing. If A_1 enjoys free housecleaning, it is not balanced by A_2's acquiring a happy but delusory expectation of marriage. The situation is similar if A_1 and A_2 cooperate to develop an online retail outlet and A_1 pays himself a handsome salary while A_2 acquires only stock options that prove worthless.

Most cooperative enterprises are asymmetrical. For, first, the success of most such ventures—achieving the intended output—is more important to one of the parties than to the other. (To keep matters simple, I shall treat multi-party cooperative relationships as though they were dyadic.) In the majority of cases, one party has more interest in the work being accomplished, and one or the other party may also enjoy the more eligible role, and may make off with the larger or more tangible fraction of the product. Any instance of cooperation by two or more persons affords opportunities for one to take advantage of the other while the activity is being carried out. Even where the benefits to A_1 and A_2 are immediate and real rather

than deferred and/or imaginary, the joint activity may saddle A_2 with the less eligible task, although the cooperative surplus is evenly distributed, or it may result in an unbalanced apportioning of benefits, although the effort invested is the same. Consider the following activities that can be carried out by two people:

(1) A_1 and A_2 use a two-man saw to cut down a large tree.
(2) A_1 and A_2 carry a heavy chest of drawers up a flight of stairs.
(3) A_2 beats the egg whites and A_1 pours on hot syrup in a steady stream.
(4) A_1 works in the stockroom and A_2 minds the till.
(5) A_1 goes to the office and A_2 looks after the baby and cleans the house.

Assume that in each case both parties are aiming at a certain outcome, that they can effectively accomplish the intended tasks together but not alone, and that each receives some benefit from their cooperation. Nevertheless, even in cases in which the tasks performed are apparently mirror images of one another, one party may find it easy to exploit the other. In 1 A_1 can use light saw strokes on the return while A_2 uses heavy strokes, so that A_2 does most of the work of getting the tree cut down. In 2 A_1 can arrange matters so that she is at the top of the stairs and A_2 at the bottom so that A_2 does most of the work of getting the chest of drawers raised. As the separate roles of A_1 and A_2 become more differentiated, opportunities for asymmetrical participation or asymmetrical divisions of the joint product increase, and comparisons between the two roles become more difficult. In 3, A_1 can manoeuvre herself into a position where she performs the less tiring or more interesting subtask, such as pouring on the syrup; and in 4 and 5 A_1 can again fix the situation so that she performs the less tiring, more prestigious part of the joint work. The grander and more productive a cooperative venture becomes, the more likely it is to involve imperfect cooperation and the more imperfect the cooperation is likely to be. Building a pyramid—or a church—or staffing a textile factory are more likely to be basically cooperative activities than symetrically cooperative.

The decision to cease competing as individuals and to begin to cooperate is often regarded as signalling the introduction of moral relations. In light of the forgoing, however, the introduction of some

level of basic cooperation has no unambiguous moral significance. It may mark the end of hostilities—or the beginning of organized warfare. The decision to join forces usually adds utility, but it rarely confers an equal benefit on both parties to the transaction, and it does not imply that both parties are equally motivated to accomplish the task they cooperate on, or that they work equally hard at it. Rousseau saw the loss of primitive autonomy as entailing the corruption of human society, and while his exaltation of solitude is difficult to take seriously, he was right to see interdependency as morally hazardous.

This point was anticipated earlier in the discussion of the evolution of cooperation in Chapter 1. If natural selection produces basic cooperation that is advantageous to a breeding group but not cooperation that satisfies some set of further conditions, it does not produce moral behaviour. Nor does it produce behaviour that resides in a morally free zone in the sense of being exempt from moral criticism. A_1, in the examples above, is able to engage in basically cooperative activities while nevertheless gaining at A_2's expense. While cutting down the tree, A_1 conserves her resources, forcing A_2 to expend more and, while minding the till, A_1 might acquire extra prestige at the same time as A_2 is deprived of social contact and is exposed to the risk of physical injury produced by lifting heavy boxes. Such situations are neither predicted nor accounted for by theories about the emergence of cooperation that regard individuals as equally powerful contractors, or that suppose that discrepancies in power cannot be maintained over the long run.

In the examples above, A_1 dominates A_2, and A_2 submits to A_1 by engaging in basic cooperative behaviour with A_1. Nearly all cooperative arrangements present tempting opportunities for one party to exploit the other by enlisting the other somewhat against his will, or without his being equally committed to the project, by assuming the more eligible task, or taking more of the cooperative surplus generated by joint effort than the exploiter's contribution to the project warrants, or by persuading the other to accept deferred or imaginary assignments of the surplus. But why does A_2 enter into a cooperative alliance with A_1 that favours A_1?

A_1's social dominance may be either natural or acquired. She may have been born tall, with a loud voice, and an authoritative manner that makes others reluctant to question or challenge her. Or, though

born timid and retiring, A_1 may have set out to acquire a commanding manner and succeeded. The acquisition of wealth or titles may give her personality extra force. Or, she may have worked her way up into a position of leadership by completing a lengthy series of skill-testing exercises. If A_1 has been to cooking school and holds a diploma and A_2 has not, it will be seen as natural and just that A_1 should perform the more eligible tasks in the kitchen. It will be difficult in practice to decide whether any given manifestation of dominance behaviour is traceable to conventional or real, acquired or native attributes. Superiority can follow from the possession of purely symbolic indicators of excellence, or the possession of qualities deemed meritorious, or from sheer force of personality.

As Skyrms has recently pointed out, it is not always rational for self-interested A_1 to offer an unjust division of the social product to A_2, and it is not always rational for A_2 to accept bad bargains even when his short-term situation is improved over what it would be were he to reject the offer.[12] Forbearing from domination and refusing to submit to attempted domination can be good *ESSs*; that is, strategies that do well when they meet themselves. But, where individuals are already sorted into the naturally or situationally dominance-prone and submission-prone, when they bear marks or carry flags to indicate the category to which they belong, and when the dominant can control the frequency and type of their own encounters, offering and accepting unjust bargains can become stable practices. (The dominant can, for example, agree to allocate subordinates, meeting and bargaining exclusively with them and not with each other: or they may bargain with each other on different terms.) The motives lurking in and pay-off to A_1 for offering the bad bargain are clear, but A_2's motivations for accepting it need explanation. A_2 may have non-rational motives for cooperation, such as a love of service, or enhanced feelings of self-worth, or he may succumb irrationally to A_1's social charisma. Otherwise, A_2 must believe either that the cooperative surplus will be fairly partitioned, or must believe that he will do better than by refusing to accept a subordinate position. Frequently, both types of motive operate. To explain why a free-living agent takes a position on the shop floor in a highly profitable company at a

---

[12] Brian Skyrms, *The Evolution of the Social Contract*, ch. 2.

very low wage, we might appeal to the agent's belief that (*a*) employment is more dignified than unemployment; or (*b*) the compensation is fair; or (*c*) although the compensation is unfair, there are no good alternatives.

That most cooperative enterprises are imperfect in the ways indicated does not imply that they are morally unacceptable. A_2 might decide to help A_1, furthering a project that is mostly A_1's or even A_1's alone but that takes two persons to accomplish for minimal or no personal reward. If I answer your phone while you get a manicure, we together ensure that you get a manicure and that your phone is answered, but the first outcome may be a matter of perfect indifference to me and the second may not be very important. I might expect or hope for reciprocity in the future, but there is no reason to deny that there can be purely altruistic acts. But what is the difference between A_2's helping A_1 and A_1's exploiting A_2? Do secretaries help their bosses? Do auto workers help the manufacturer? If they participate in asymmetrical cooperation, are not helpers and are exploited, is exploitation always morally unacceptable?[13] How to differentiate between helping and being exploited is a question that occurs to most of us episodically, for example, when we take on some undesirable committee assignment or household responsibility, but it is a question that can be asked in connection with most cooperative enterprises.

To address these questions, we can take either of two routes: (1) We can try to supply a neutral definition of each term and then decide whether 'helping' is always morally creditable and 'exploitation' always morally wrong; (2) We can define 'helping' as 'morally creditable asymmetrical cooperation' and 'exploitation' as 'morally discreditable asymmetrical cooperation.' Neither route, however, terminates at a good answer to all questions. Attempts to provide a neutral definition of either 'helping' or 'exploitation' seem to fail. Building the normative implication into the definition makes it harder to agree on criteria for evaluating actual cases.

By way of trying to create a neutral definition, we might begin by taking 'helping' to be A_2's assumption of a disadvantage to create a benefit for A_1 and 'exploitation' as A_1's putting A_2 at some disadvan-

---

[13] See Alan Wood's useful paper 'Exploitation', in Kai Nielsen and Robert Ware (eds.), *Exploitation*, 2–26.

tage to create a benefit for herself. This procedure fails, though, to reveal a clear-cut difference. Or we might insist that 'helping' is the informed and voluntary award by A_2 of a benefit to A_1 and that 'exploitation' is the involuntary or uninformed award by A_2 of a benefit to A_1. Unfortunately, this proposal does not provide a necessary condition for either helping or exploiting. Perhaps I have to force you or somehow induce you to help me wash the dishes, but your unwillingness does not always mean that I am exploiting you. Some jobs are exploitative although they are accepted voluntarily by informed persons. In any case, mentalistic criteria are notoriously difficult to apply. It might be suggested that an altruistic motive is present in cases of helping but not of exploitation. I might nevertheless be made to help without ever developing the motive, and the cultivation of love for and loyalty to her employer on the part of the employee does not ensure against her exploitation. Nor does the absence of a helping motive in an employee necessarily render her situation exploitative.

We can conclude that the role of the less-advantaged agent in a case of asymmetrical cooperation is often perceived to need a special explanation, since she has entered into a productive relationship with another in which her real share of the cooperative surplus is not proportional to her contribution, and agents who are both rational and reasonable are predicted not to do this. The explanation may be that she is gulled. However, she may also enter into such a relationship when she is as well informed as her counterpart. Two divergent patterns of explanation are then available and we employ the one that appears best to fit the situation: 'Model helping' is voluntary, cheerful, accompanied by an altruistic motive, and appears morally praiseworthy in the flow of advantage from the one with a surplus of resources to the needier party. 'Model exploitation' involves reluctant performance, constrained choice and resentment, and appears morally discreditable in the extraction of a benefit from a weaker party and its award to an advantaged one. These typical markers do not always cluster together. A secretary is likely to be cheerful and to have genuinely altruistic motives; she would not last long in the job if she did not have these attributes. At the same time, she is likely to be at least occasionally resentful of her place in the world and to feel her choices to be highly constrained.

According to the view under consideration, the goodness of a world with respect to its distribution protocols is a function of the degree to which its transactions occur at the symmetrical, as opposed to the basic, ends of the cooperation continuum. But it is not obvious that this is so:

Consider a world of perfectly symmetrical cooperators. They have our ordinary endowments—that is to say, as individuals, they would often prefer to be basic cooperators when it would be advantageous to them to do so. Yet, this being a *moral* paraworld, they control their impulses—or have created institutions that ensure that these impulses are controlled—in ways we suppose it possible for human beings to control theirs or to create institutions. They do not offer exploitative contracts, though they occasionally offer others help. We have reason to think that the world their actions produce will not have the extremes of well-being and deprivation we observe in our world. Accumulated advantage and disadvantage are virtually ruled out by the absence of privilege, for in this world, the better rewards offered to skilled and effortful productions are offset by the lower rewards offered for the performance of desirable tasks. Exploitation is minimized since workers cannot be paid off in emotional terms, with the promise of going to heaven, for example, and since the work must be important to both parties. The world under this description appears to be reasonably just.

Now suppose that this world is constrained by having no more resources than ours does and that its inhabitants have the psychological profiles of our existing persons. Many familiar tasks are not done in this world. These are tasks that are easy to arrange for someone to do under conditions of basic cooperation but difficult to organize under conditions of symmetrical cooperation. Large-scale agriculture may not have a place. Coal mining and factory production probably will not. Palaces, cathedrals, and monumental tombs are less likely to be built. Reflecting on conditions in such a world, a hard-headed realist might insist that we do not have an overall moral preference for the fair division of the cooperative surplus.

A decisive shift away from basic cooperation in the direction of symmetrical cooperation in many industries, the realist might venture, would fundamentally alter the material conditions of life for all of us. Indeed, he might add, it is the worst-off who benefit most from

the ubiquity of basic cooperation. Cheap food, cheap energy, clean washrooms in public buildings, affordable television sets and sports-wear, are all by-products of exploitative labour relations and at the same time apparently vital to the well-being of those who cannot afford to pay a premium for these basic goods.

We cannot, however, take the argument that the reality constraint precludes more symmetrical arrangements very seriously. Confirm-ation from disinterested parties of the provocative thesis that our preference for a procedurally just world is constrained by our desire to see everyone well looked after, with sufficient food and respectable clothing, has not been forthcoming. Yet the objector is right to signal the importance of considering overall outcomes in assessing the justice of a world, not only procedures. It will be useful accordingly to give some attention to outcome theories of justice, specifically, to egalitarianism and the notion of equality that egalitarians consider definitive of a just world. The Rawlsian principle just invoked to the effect that one ought never to alter the procedures of a society in such a way as to worsen the position of the worst-off needs evaluation against procedural and outcome-based theories of justice.

6.4. Equality

If a willingness—in some cases an eagerness—to enter into basically cooperative relationships is not only a result of, but also maintains and generates, significant social inequality, it seems that by making a society more symmetrically cooperative we might be making it more egalitarian. Equality need not be considered, in this case, as a distinct component of justice. We could simply regard it as a by-product of a well-ordered society. And since equality of outcomes is easier to assess than the symmetry of cooperative endeavours, we could take equality as a good approximation for justice.

Egalitarians will insist, however, that more is required. Monitoring spontaneously arising cooperative transactions, they might insist, is not enough to ensure justice. Often, the reason A_2 is worse off than A_1 is simply that A_2 is unable to take part in certain kinds of coopera-tive enterprise open to A_1. Moreover, when deprivations are acute and easily relieved by transfers from well-off to worse-off, then, no

matter how they are generated, there is moral fault in neglecting them.

These points can be conceded. Egalitarianism is nevertheless a problematic position. Why is equality good per se? What should be equalized? Resources? Satisfaction of basic needs? All desires, wishes, and velleities, as far as possible? Every day? As Walzer argues, if an equal distribution of goods amongst the population of the world were effected at 9 a.m., by noon the distribution would have become unbalanced. Some would have frittered portions of their endowments away, others would have mislaid them, and others still would have gambled on them and multiplied their holdings a thousand times, or compounded them by arbitrage, or have employed their wiles and talents to collect portions of others' endowments. Further, while reducing the variance in incomes has a powerful tendency to reduce the variance in well-being with respect to certain forms of consumption and participation, it is insufficient to reduce the social variance between healthy and sick, female and male, vital and depressed, and even between dark and fair. If God awoke one day and decided to make everyone equal, he would quickly realize that he had no clear idea where to begin and what to do.

Egalitarians need not be fazed by such arguments. They may insist that we have a good idea what an omniscient and omnipotent being might do to realize not only economic but broader social equality. After ensuring that everyone had enough food in the refrigerator, well-baby care, and education to the level provided by a good private high school, God could add additional janitorial staff and tennis courts to every public housing complex. He could landscape highways, get rid of pole lights and billboards, and redecorate grocery shops, airports, and bus terminals where most people spend a lot of time. God could build more branch libraries, bring down the price of theatre tickets and canoe rentals, and put more books on tape for the blind. He could improve the taste of ordinary tap water and introduce universal daycare and community policing. He could package potato chips and doughnuts in tiny, beribboned boxes and price them at $10 the ounce, thereby helping to equalize the health status of rich and poor. God could place mothers of schoolchildren on every National Security Council; for that matter, he could place schoolchildren on every National Security Council. In each case, God would be

repairing deficiencies and trimming excesses that result from the differential possession of expert knowledge, social power, and authority by individuals and groups with respect to one another. He would be working on making an egalitarian world.

But what are God's rules of thumb in the above scenario? How does he know what changes to introduce?, the sceptic will persist in asking. Will he also introduce free hard-core pornography for all, and addictive drugs? Intuitively, an egalitarian world is one in which everyone's proper interests, i.e. those interests of his that are neither perverse, arising out of a pathological state or process, nor based in delusion, are satisfied to the same extent. Yet many sceptics doubt that any such set of proper interests can be identified without prejudice. Immanentists may go so far as to deny that there can be meaningful interpersonal comparisons of well-being. Walzer insists in a Pyrrhonist spirit that 'There is no set of primary or basic goods conceivable across all moral and material worlds—or, any such set would have to be conceived in terms so abstract that they would be of little use in thinking about particular distributions.'[14]

The theory of proper interests, immanentists charge, presupposes an inappropriately zoological perspective on human life. The good life for parakeets and poodles, though it extends beyond what is required for biological subsistence, does not vary much from place to place. In the human world, by contrast, the region between the requisites for biological subsistence and culturally mediated desires and aspirations is not occupied by a set of needs that could be written down in a manual. People and communities, immanentists will insist, should be left alone to order their own priorities by experiencing the effects of their own choices and preserving or modifying their orderings in response. Apart from trying out various preference orderings, personally and communally, and experiencing their effects, there is no method that will reveal which orderings are best.

In defence of the egalitarian, it can be shown that proper interests are not as variable and mysterious as they are made out to be. The starting point in this case will be a priori reflection on the notion of a decent life that acknowledges at the same time the empirical

---

[14] Walzer, *Spheres of Justice*, 8.

plenitude of actual or possible needs, desires, and preferences.[15] To that end, it is profitable to distinguish between three categories of the components of well-being: the known, the presumptive, and the speculative and doubtful.

The known components of well-being are the biological requirements of survival. There are certain prerequisites of life and reproduction, including breathable air, potable water, and a certain number of calories. Doing without them is impossible, and anyone who does not have access to them is objectively deprived. While the lack of shelter, clothing, security of person, and assistance when ill may be compatible with survival given a favourable environment and plenty of good luck, they are usually necessary.[16] These needs are often designated as fundamental, or basic, or urgent in Scanlon's[17] sense and their remedies count amongst the first-tier goods. Their provision is, however, insufficient to ensure a decent human life. As Partha Dasgupta remarks, 'The meeting of these needs is a prerequisite for the continuation of one's life. Their fulfillment makes living possible. [But] for life to acquire worth, for it to be enjoyable, other sorts of goods are required. . . . This suggests that, roughly speaking, there are two tiers of goods and services.'[18]

While there is some dispute about the precise composition of a list of second-tier goods, there is general consensus that the following belong on it: opportunities for affiliation, for raising children; mobility; the right to refuse a proposed marriage partner or escape from an actual one without excessive social and economic penalty; freedom from harassment and derogation; some variety and pleasure in food, drink, furnishings, and ornaments; and the opportunity to engage in meaningful work, to advance one's knowledge and understanding, and to participate in decisions regarding the state or other civic unit in which one lives. The needs for these goods can be

---

[15] The problem of objective deprivation and its grades was introduced into the philosophical literature by T. M. Scanlon, in 'Preference and Urgency'. Later contributions to its solution on which I draw below include Amartya Sen, 'Equality of What?'; James Griffin (ed.), *Well-Being: Its Meaning, Measurement and Importance*; Martha Nussbaum, 'Human Functioning and Social Justice: In Defense of Aristotelian Essentialism'.

[16] An overview of the literature on primary goods can be found in Partha Dasgupta, *An Inquiry into Well-Being and Destitution*, 36 ff. See also Braybrooke, *Meeting Needs*, and his follow-up article, 'The Concept of Needs, with a Heartwarming Offer to Utilitarianism'.

[17] Scanlon, 'Preference and Urgency'.

[18] Dasgupta, *Inquiry*, 40.

termed 'presumptive' in the recognition that, while individuals can have decent lives without them, by and large, they are necessary.[19] Presumptive needs are interpersonally and, to a large extent, inter-generationally presentable. They correspond to the grievances that appear repeatedly in letters home, songs of labour, loss, and depriv-ation, fairy tales and tragic novels; and these go well beyond material deprivations.

There is also a 'third tier' of goods, the speculative and doubtful components of well-being.[20] These are objects and states that are aspired to but that have a partial and tenuous connection with well-being; their pursuit is risky in a way that the pursuit of the presump-tive components of well-being need not be. Third-tier goods may be keenly desired, but, obtaining them, the individual frequently feels no better off than he or she did before, once the initial moment of triumph and elation has passed. It is usual to think in this connection of luxurious or frivolous consumer goods and services such as high-performance cars, real and costume jewellery, plastic surgery, hand-tooled leather accessories, and so on, but there are other consumption states whose relation to well-being is equally speculative and doubt-ful. Being in a position to pursue scientific research in a well-outfitted laboratory, having an art collection or a spectacular portfolio of stocks to leave to one's children, possessing the leisure to write a novel or the money to design and build a house are consumption states that strike us as highly desirable, though we know at the same time that they may bring either ample, rich, and deep satisfaction or little more than trouble, anxiety, and disappointment. Most needs allegedly satisfied by exotic sexual experience or mind-altering drugs are of this nature, but so are many intellectual, financial, and artistic pursuits. The elation felt on attaining the desired state is often evanescent, and disappointment at falling short of expectations or ideals may be enduring. Unanticipated side effects are intensified when persons venture outside the realm of the presumptive compon-ents of well-being. The destructive potential of fame and achieve-ment in a meritocratic society is intense, as our glances at the tabloids and our perusal of the biographies of the clever and powerful

[19] For a fuller treatment along recognizably Benthamite principles, see Braybrooke, *Meeting Needs*.
[20] Richard J. Arneson discussed similar non-basic pursuits in a number of articles, including 'Perfec-tionism and Politics'.

remind us. The pursuit of third-tier goods can lead to isolation and loneliness.[21]

The good life is one in which the known and presumptive components of well-being are present, one that is not marked by unusually many or unusually heavy deprivations induced by restrictions on consumption, expression, affiliation, activity, and participation, or by insult and derogation that reduce social honour. Deprivations experienced within these categories appear to represent the main categories of diagnosable and presentable grievances, grievances individuals feel justified in expressing to other persons whom they know, and which they expect to be acknowledged and respected as legitimate. Agents will also tend to grieve the lack of third-tier goods when they possess all the known and presumptive components of well-being and are aware of the availability of these other more speculative and doubtful goods. Prescriptive egalitarianism rests on the highly plausible assumption that unless there is a specific reason—such as punishment or education—to deprive a particular human being of something he needs or wants, one should not do so, and unless there is a specific reason—such as punishment or pedagogy—not to furnish a person with what he wants and needs, one should do so. In good worlds, according to the egalitarian, people are never arbitrarily deprived and successful efforts are made to supply their needs and wants.

Now, a world of symmetrical cooperators is not necessarily an egalitarian world, even if we should expect to find a much greater degree of compression in it. The differential skill and effort of some individuals and their willingness to apply themselves to tasks considered less desirable should result in their receiving quite a bit more than average of the cooperative surplus. Hard-working and capable undertakers, for example, might do very well in such a world, while aspiring artists, musicians, and actors, who insisted on the more eligible subtasks, would fare poorly. Persons who engaged in solitary, hedonistic activities—lotus-eaters—would receive no portion of the cooperative surplus and would have to subsist as best they could. For a strict egalitarian, the resulting variance is an unacceptable outcome. On her view, human beings should not differ in their possession of any of the components of well-being, regardless of their contribu-

[21] Robert J. Lane, '"The Road Not Taken": Friendship, Consumption, and Happiness'.

tions to the social product, unless they are being justifiably punished or appropriately educated, in which case the deprivation is usually temporary and for their own good. Appropriate distributive and redistributive protocols are needed to ensure that the resources needed to acquire the components of well-being flood the population to the same level. In practical terms, this implies a series of transfers from persons possessed of skill, cunning, and accumulated advantage to less favoured ones.

Strict egalitarianism, then, as a prescriptive position, can be defined as follows. All components of well-being should be distributed as evenly as possible, regardless of what individuals contribute to the cooperative ventures in which they take part. Strict egalitarianism is in some ways a morally appealing position, but, for reasons that will be explored more fully in Chapter 7, it is not an entirely tenable position. Though it captures our sense that outcomes matter and are never guaranteed by procedures, it fails, as one might predict, to satisfy our basic intuitions about the existence of a procedural component to justice.

6.5. Justification and Consent

Theories of justice ought, one might suppose, to be formulated in accord with the anonymity requirement. Yet some versions of contractualism seek to do away with this idealizing apparatus, substituting agreement 'on the ground' as a condition of real obligation. Nagel insists in this connection that while 'differences in bargaining power carry no moral weight in themselves . . . they can be given authority to determine results within a system that is legitimate by a standard of acceptability that is not the result of bargaining power'.[22] Accordingly,

Justification in political theory must address itself to people twice: first as occupants of the impersonal standpoint and second as occupants of particular roles within an impersonally acceptable system. This is not capitulation to human badness or weakness, but a necessary acknowledgment of human complexity. To ignore the second task is to risk utopianism in the bad sense . . . The requirement of dual justification is a moral requirement.[23]

---

[22] Nagel, *Equality and Partiality*, 39.   [23] Ibid. 30.

For simplicity, let's concentrate on the implied claim that *if* one proposes to worsen the condition of the well-off by introducing new regulations or distributive protocols, it is necessary and *morally required* (not merely prudent, or politically expedient) to secure *their* consent as potential occupants of certain roles.

This claim appears to be different from Scanlon's claim, discussed in Section 5.1, that a policy acquires legitimacy by being acceptable to all parties who would be affected by it, assuming those parties to be not merely rational and self-interested, but also reasonable. Rather than appealing to Scanlonian idealization, to what reasonable people could not in good conscience reject, Nagel seems to be advancing the intuition that there is no perspective from which one can legitimately demand transition to a non-Pareto-superior condition. The intuition is that if at least one person is worse off in Condition B than in Condition A, then, regardless of how many persons are better off in Condition B, it is better to remain in Condition A. As Aristotle[24] pointed out, it is the weak who favour equality—and, he might have said—who specially object to being parties to basic cooperative enterprises. Numerous well-off persons and nations do not favour greater interpersonal or international equality or controls on the kinds of cooperative arrangements they may enter into. Is their reluctance to relinquish privilege and social dominance indefensible? Why should I, as a well-off person with many desires and interests, support redistributive policies that would reduce my opportunity to consume new and valuable goods and experiences? Nagel, though his views are less cautious, seems here to express Aristotelian doubt that the interests of the weak ought to carry the day regardless of what anyone else wants.

Yet the rationale for claiming that transitions to worse-for-someone conditions are morally illegitimate is hard to understand. If a given distribution scheme satisfying the anonymity requirement has been confirmed, what further justification from situated perspectives is now required? Nagel is right to insist that there is an intrinsic conflict between objective and subjective perspectives and that solutions to social problems must be satisficing and not perfectionist. However, a theoretical justification for dispossession that they are willing to accept is not owed to all existing persons, including the most

---

[24] Aristotle, *Politics*, 1318b.

grasping, socially insulated, and ignorant; this would be supererogatory. The consent of the existing class of well-off persons to it cannot
be a necessary condition of the intrinsic justice of a system.

At the same time, it is right to say that a theory of justice must take
the existence of the well-off and their interests into account. To
rescue Nagel's notion of a dual justification, distinctions need to be
made, first, between a distribution protocol and a redistribution
protocol, and second, between the role of the theorist and the role
of situated agents in a political context. A distribution protocol is a
rule or set of rules for dividing the cooperative surplus in an ideal
world in which no prior institutional structure is envisioned as having
given rise to certain memories and expectations. A redistribution
protocol is a rule or set of rules for reapportioning the cooperative
surplus in a world in which it is already being allocated in certain
historically determined ways, giving rise to memories and expectations that have psychological force. Transition costs now need to be
taken into account.

When a theorist projects a distribution protocol, the interests of the
existing well-off and the existing badly-off do not influence the
choice of a theory. For the distribution protocol is simply the set of
practices observed in the envisioned paraworld and no one there is
antecedently better off or worse off. The existence of some wealthy
and powerful persons is arguably desirable from an impersonal standpoint. As Bentham observed, persons who are much wealthier than
others contribute to the aggregate utility. They make possible libraries
and ballet troupes, Christian Lacroix ball gowns, and other culturally
and aesthetically valuable objects and they furnish gainful employment by investing in wage-paying resource-extraction sites and factories. On the other hand, the wealthy and powerful produce these
fine things by organizing basic cooperative enterprises and by
resisting calls for greater equality.[25] Morally ideal worlds, we should
conclude, can have very wealthy persons and nations in them, but
only if they refrain from certain activities.

---

[25] Walzer's notion of 'complex equality' is a *prescriptive* theory that asserts that social dominance in the
possession of one social good *ought* to be balanced by relative deprivation in another good so that such
hegemony is not possible, not a descriptive theory of 'how the world works'. His *descriptive* claim that 'no
social good ever entirely dominates the range of goods; no social monopoly is ever perfect' is true but
ignores important effects of aggregation. *Spheres of Justice*, 11.

Designing a redistribution protocol is a different task altogether. How do ideal agents behave when they go about redesigning their tax system; or reforming their welfare, insurance, or pension plans; or offering subsidies; or imposing new tariffs? Assuredly, they observe moral constraints on the use of force, even to secure moral ends. They take into account the psychological costs of dispossession in avoiding too aggressive or too suddenly implemented policies. A good redistribution protocol will minimize disappointments and violate existing expectations as little as it can.

The politician's or voter's role, meanwhile, is different from the role of the theorist. To the extent that a theory of just distributions or just redistributions has been confirmed, those who are able to put it into practice ought to do so; a strongly confirmed theory deserves more effort than a weakly confirmed one. How much effort does an unpopular theory, or one disliked by the powerful and influential, deserve?

Suppose, for example, that the redistributive theory that there ought to be a tax on excess consumption (income less subsistence-plus-savings) of 90 per cent turns out to be reasonably well confirmed. Still, nothing will happen unless a politician advances a bill and voters support her. Since the theory has been reasonably well confirmed, I ought to vote for a politician who will advance the bill and she ought to advance it. The obligation to do either of these things is diminished prima facie by the difficulty of doing so. It might be very hard for me to vote for a high consumption tax if I am a rich person with expensive tastes and hard for a politician to advance the policy if there are many powerful others like me. Yet the diminished obligation is offset by ill-gotten gains, the contract principle, and even culpable ignorance. All things considered, the politician should strive to win my support for the policy and I should support it.

If I do give way and support a policy that is not in my interest, my consent does not contribute to the philosophical legitimation of the policy, though it is needed to make the policy actual. The philosophical legitimacy of the proposal depends on its being confirmed, not on its popularity, even if there is reason to think that confirmed proposals tend to collect followers. Justification is not, therefore, dual, though Nagel is correct to suggest that there are two processes: first, determining the goodness of the policy, assuming everyone complies with

it, and second, determining the acceptability of getting everyone to comply with it. The notion that a tax bill would not be legitimate if all actual well-off persons, or even all actual well-off persons deemed to be psychiatrically *compos mentis*, did not agree to it is plainly untenable. The policy would be politically legitimate if voted in the right way, and the policy would be philosophically confirmed if competent judges (idealized reasonable persons) endorsed it.

The claim that one can worsen people's conditions without gaining their consent for an overall benefit need not, as is often feared, open the door to the utilitarian abuse of individuals. We are not licensed to make slaves of other people for the overall benefit of the collective. The reason is not that they will not consent to this—for they might. Rather, it is that after long debate and much experience, we seem to have confirmed the proposition that worlds with slaves are impersonally worse than worlds without them. That those who are now slaves do not mind being slaves does not make a proposal to free the slaves illegitimate on the grounds that their consent and so universal agreement cannot be secured. If *I* would not consider my role as a well-adapted, consenting slave acceptable, I have reason to insist that no world in which slaves exist is even minimally morally acceptable. Nevertheless, it can be just to impose unwilled deprivations.

According to the externally imposed hardship and relative deprivation principles, burdens that shift a subject downward out of his normal reference class are typically experienced as heavier than freely chosen or naturally happened-upon burdens that are shared with others. While it might be a terrible thing for an eminent university professor were he forced to become a worker in a day-care centre, it is not necessarily bad to decide to be a worker in a day-care centre or to find oneself in that role by chance. A redistribution protocol should be misery-sparing and not driven by vengeance, but a distribution protocol that assigns someone to the role of childcare worker is not unjust.

However, the fact that a university professor would regard this as a terrible fate gives us some information about the nature of the work and its ordinary compensation. Service jobs, including nursing, rubbish collection, janitorial labour, childminding, and housecleaning have historically been poorly compensated. These

jobs are not held in low esteem because they are low skill, for they may require considerably more knowledge and expertise than clerical work or retail sales, but because they involve contact with taboo materials, such as blood and excrement, the products of putrefaction, and dirt. It is human nature to avoid contact with these materials, though individuals obviously differ in their levels of fastidiousness. These tasks are at the same time of profound importance to the collective, and where motives such as love and altruism do not suffice, economic coercion ensures that service work is done. When their importance is not recognized and appropriately compensated, it is bad for anyone to be a service worker.

Paradoxically, demoralization and resentment over perceived social inequalities are most profoundly experienced by persons who compare themselves with others whose income and mode of life is only marginally different from their own. They are rarely felt by persons one might otherwise consider to be objectively deprived. People's estimates of their own and others' conditions, their explanations of why they occupy the roles they do, and their estimates of the reliability of their own social judgements tend to be erroneous. W. G. Runciman found that groups that have clear relative deficits of income, status, and social power typically do not perceive themselves as unfavourably positioned. 'People's attitudes to social inequalities seldom correlate strictly with the facts of their own position.... Dissatisfaction with the system of privileges and rewards in a society is never felt in an even proportion to the degree of inequality to which its various members are subject.'[26]

Two opposing conclusions can be drawn from Runciman's finding that objectively deprived persons are unable to perceive their deprivations and are disinclined to consider the reward system of their societies unfair. First, it can be inferred that the moralist ought to care only about subjective happiness or unhappiness, not about objective deprivation or statistical equality in the possession of third-tier goods. It is conceivable that the most stratified society with the fewest opportunities for social advancement will be the one in which people are subjectively the happiest. Attempts to reduce

---

[26] W. G. Runciman, *Relative Deprivation and Social Justice*, 3.

stratification require aggressive 'consciousness-raising' and may burden subjects with knowledge that subtracts from the happiness otherwise to be found in their lives. Alternatively, it can be inferred that distortions in the perception of their own state tend to affect the badly-off. This observation in no way entails that it is not better for people when their objective deprivations are reduced, or when their access to the doubtful and speculative components of well-being is not enhanced.[27]

Robert Axelrod and his co-respondents have shown that two players in a game of Prisoner's Dilemma who act according to the simple programme known as TIT for TAT, in which cooperative actions are reciprocated and defections are punished, experience more total reward than players who adopt other strategies. 'Once cooperation based upon reciprocity gets established in a population, it cannot be overcome even by a cluster of individuals who try to exploit the others... The establishment of stable cooperation can take a long time if it is based upon blind forces of evolution, or it can happen rather quickly if its operation can be appreciated by intelligent players.'[28] Axelrod warns further that envy in games that are not zero-sum is counterproductive:

People tend to resort to the standard of comparison that they have available—and this standard is often the success of the other player relative to their own success. This standard leads to envy. And envy leads to attempts to rectify any advantage the other player has attained. In this form of Prisoner's Dilemma, rectification of the other's advantage can only be done by defection. But defection leads to more defection and to mutual punishment. So envy is self-destructive...

A better standard of comparison is how well you are doing relative to how well someone else could be doing in your shoes. Given the strategy of the other player, are you doing as well as possible...?[29]

---

[27] Runciman studied English manual labourers, whose access to consumer goods such as central heating, telephone service, private schools, fur coats, and foreign vacations was, as one might expect, more limited than that of white-collar workers. Runciman, *Relative Deprivation*, 93. The subjective feeling of being well off can even increase, he found, with objective losses. Ibid. 23.

[28] Robert Axelrod, *The Evolution of Cooperation*, 189.

[29] Ibid. 111. Nozick takes a similarly dim view of envy in *Anarchy, State and Utopia*, 239 ff. Rawls 'assume[s] an absence of envy' on the idealizing grounds that 'it is generally regarded as something to be avoided and feared'. *Theory of Justice* (rev. edn.), 465, though cf. 470. For a different perspective on envy and 'levelling down', see J. Harvey, 'Justice Theory and Oppression', 176 ff.

One might be tempted to infer that exploitative strategies must have been eliminated long ago and that the envious are likely to drive down their own holdings. This inference would be a mistake, however. Perhaps we are moving towards better cooperation, but only slowly, under what amount to the blind forces of social evolution. Perhaps we do not act very rationally with respect to cooperation, because we are still more moved by emotion than by intelligence. Another possibility is that exploitation works as a strategy in our world, and can resist invasion by symmetrical cooperators for a long time. It does not work as a strategy in the games Axelrod describes, because the echo effect, by which defection is punished and punishment is retaliated against, produces a downward spiral in total return. But exploitation does work for one player when the other player is unaware of the defection, or cannot punish it, or is subject to retaliation involving multiples of his own punishing force.

Envy is not always rational, but it is arbitrary in an unfair division of the cooperative surplus to blame the envious rather than the greedy for bringing about the spiralling deterioration of relations. Like other irrational emotions, envy can send a signal that provokes a better response and thereby shortens the duration of an unintelligent exploitative episode.

6.6. Immanentism and the Argument from Inevitability

Both procedural theories and outcome-based theories of justice have a representational aspect. Their articulation and use presupposes that we can compare existing conditions with ideal distribution procedures or end-states. This assumption is taken by some critics to be misguided; it is considered an example of the confusion inherent in the very notion of a moral theory. According to immanentists, the patterns of deprivation and sufficiency that we observe globally are the product of historical processes within which individuals have shaped meaningful lives for themselves as best they could. There is no suprahistorical, non-local standard by which we could judge the absolute justice of any existing distribution, and no standard by which to judge whether a given scheme for the division of any quantity of

the social product is fair. Even the term 'distributive justice', an immanentist might insist, is misleading, for it calls to mind the image of a divine distributor or philosopher king who could get the distribution of goods and experiences right. But there is no such thing as getting it right. We have no idea what 'getting it right' could possibly mean. Immanentism is well expressed by Roger Scruton, who offers a version of the disqualification thesis (internal): 'Goods do not come into the world unowned, and rights are the work of a complex history of human interaction. Free ourselves from that history and from the long experience of conflict and cooperation that is resumed in it, and we simply have no conception of our rights, and no ability to assign them.'[30] Scruton's position is not that our actual, inherited arrangements and whatever system of compensation for our labours has emerged must be optimal. He does not claim, as invisible-hand theorists did, that the best outcome is secured by the free play of particular selfish interests. Rather, he thinks that we have no timeless conception of the right and the just that would enable us to judge existing institutions and the holdings of persons within them objectively. If we are disqualified from speaking of the whole, we are not in a position to think about reconstructing it according to formally elegant criteria. Alterations in the social fabric must be motivated by needs, initially perhaps somewhat inchoate, that surface in the immanent situation. The state to be aimed at is, he says, agreement between negotiating parties, each viewed as rational by the other, not rectification of a situation historically delivered and now imagined from a detached vantage point to be problematic.[31]

This combination of scepticism and commitment to procedure is somewhat unstable. A consistent Pyrrhonist would suspend the evaluative impulse fully, avoiding all endorsements, rather than ac-commodating a few elements of Kantianism in the appeal to the rationality of the participants or of social contract theory in the appeal to consent. In Scruton's account of the capitalist ownership of the means of production, as in Walzer's account of exchanged women, there is an invitation to the reader to agree that a situation is just

[30] Roger Scruton, 'Contract, Consent and Exploitation: Kantian Themes', 215. There is something 'oppressive and irrational', he says, 'in the attempt to state a complete vision of society'. Nozick made essentially the same claim earlier in *Anarchy, State and Utopia*, 160.
[31] Scruton, 'Contract', 226.

because of the patient's aware and consenting role in it, even while the history of institutions in all their entrenchment and opacity carries most of the weight of their justification. However, the immanentist need not retreat from his basic claim that we are unable to judge the justice of practices in which we ourselves are entrenched or in which others are as entrenched as we are in ours.

The immanentist reminds us that existing employer–employee relations which govern distribution in local contexts are not the result of a well-reasoned adoption of a contract by beings who might just as well have been set down on earth five minutes ago. He might well have added that the manufacturing or service employee is not a new kind of human—a rational contractor—who appeared on the world's surface at the dawn of the industrial revolution, just when the 'natural slaves' whose farming and quarrying originally brought wealth into the world had disappeared.[32] He is the descendant of that creature and retains some of his characteristics. At the same time, the wage labourer is delivered from the condition of being a serf in modern dress by the very fact that he does negotiate. Something radically new has, after all, come into the world in the form of the labour contract, whose evolution, as Henry Maine argued, required the dismantling of durable Roman structures.[33]

Because the labourer is not a serf, the question of fair compensation arises as a concrete problem, and with it the need for the philosophers' unhistoricized terminology reflecting the most adequate conception she is capable, in her own moment, of offering. In that case, either current practices are the summation of a set of individual negotiations which appropriately benefited both of the parties consenting to the contract, or they are not. If the former is true, coercion has never played a role in shaping the contours of modern employer–employee relations; it has been fair negotiation all the way. Alternatively, current practices are merely those we happen to have ended up with. In that case, it would be miraculous if our present institutions were just.

Observing agricultural labourers or textile workers on and off the job on their compounds, few of us could distinguish free and slave varieties by observing what they did and how they talked, and the

---

[32] Kenneth Lux discusses the transition and the origins of the idea that laziness is an inherent trait of the labouring classes in *Adam Smith's Mistake*, 174–5.

[33] Henry Summer Maine, *Ancient Law*, p. lxix.

same goes for a variety of occupations. Slavery involves the perform-ance of work that is repetitious and uninteresting to most human beings. So does most specialized wage labour. The labourer improves his condition relative to what it would have been had he refused to enter into a cooperative contract, just as the slave does. To be sure, the wage labourer has exit options. No one will chase him and return him to the workplace in manacles if he turns in his resignation. He can go on strike. Nevertheless, his bargaining position retains traces of his old subservience. The employer has both sticks and carrots. He has something to offer—higher wages, better working conditions, more benefits—and he can make himself an object of trust and loyalty, as well as an object of fear. He also has reserves, and, fre-quently, options, notably the option to invest elsewhere, that im-prove his bargaining position. The labourer can threaten the employer; but he normally cannot offer him more than he already has if the workplace is efficient. Outside the negotiating situation, the economic underclass can threaten the rich both in their enjoyment of life and in their pocketbooks. They can enact criminality and sabotage, and present expensive health problems; at the same time, the underclass cannot easily offer to improve the situation of the rich man, rendering its negotiating power relatively weak.

Wage labour can be considered a partially moralized version of ancient slave labour. Certain advantages have been transferred to the originally less-advantaged party. The wage labourer in a modern society has the freedom to move even if he does not exercise it, and some freedom to change occupations. The advantages the employer is in a position to extract have been reduced, for the employer is required to pay a bankable wage, not only to serve self-interest by providing for the worker's subsistence. In some cases, legal rights and educational opportunities acknowledge no difference between the employer and her children and the labourer and her children, in according with the difference-erasing, generalizing tendencies of moral progress. These transfers have always been hard fought. Pro-gressive legislation was historically resisted by the well-off, even when it was evident that liberal policies did not lift all boats and pushed some beneath the waves.[34] A fundamental question of

---

[34] See Lux, *Adam Smith's Mistake*, 177.

distributive justice is whether given instances of wage labour are sufficiently moralized to be deemed just. Have they been purified of their objectionable elements or do they still retain the mark of their origins? Given that the modern inheritors of the old privileged classes continue to extract labour from others for their own benefit, to what extent is the prima facie moral requirement not to exploit others weakened by overriding considerations?

Immanentists warn that conscious planning is often dangerous or at least utopian in the pejorative sense.[35] Nagel writes: 'Attempts to create a classless society have spectacularly failed the test of moral transformation so far.... It is no use to assert that we all ought to be working for the common good and that this requires the abolition of private property in the means of production. If the personal element of most people's motivation cannot be shrunk enough or the impersonal element expanded enough, a system of comprehensive private ownership seems doomed to degenerate under a combination of stagnation, nepotism, etc.'[36] Some twenty-five years ago, the sociobiologist E. O. Wilson expressed himself in a forthright manner, citing antitheory considerations and the heavy costs argument against greater social equality. 'We believe that cultures can be rationally designed. We can teach and reward and coerce. But in doing so, we must also consider the price of each culture, measured in the time and energy required for training and enforcement and in the less tangible occurrence of human happiness that must be spent to circumvent our innate predispositions.'[37] Both the philosopher and the biologist appear to be writing from an empirical perspective, signalled by such neutral terms as 'motivation', 'test', 'measure', 'innate', and so on.[38] This can produce the misleading impression that it has been scientifically proved that a condition of radical inequality is not only natural, but also of great antiquity, and not only of great antiquity, but also good for us.

[35] 'A theory', according to Nagel 'is utopian in the pejorative sense if it describes a form of collective life that humans, or most humans, could not lead and could not come to be able to lead through any feasible process of social and mental development.' *Equality and Partiality*, 6.

[36] Ibid. 27. The illocutionary intention behind Nagel's book is not to provide a philosophical defence of inequality but to make plain the psychological obstacles in the way of its reduction.

[37] E. O. Wilson, *On Human Nature*, 148.

[38] 'Societies are constantly trying to beat people into shape because they stubbornly fail to conform to some preconceived pattern of human possibility... Political theory is... an empirical discipline whose hypotheses give hostages to the future, and whose experiments can be very costly.' Nagel, *Equality and Partiality*, 29.

As noted earlier, even beneficent policies may have unwanted side effects that make direct attempts at amelioration through social engineering risky. Perhaps God can raise the minimum wage without raising unemployment or inducing inflation, or provide more janitors to housing complexes without raising property taxes, but humans cannot. Alleviating a deprivation here causes another one there. Raise the price of T-shirts and fresh produce and global variance will be reduced but the domestic poor injured. Lower the costs of prescription drugs for some elderly women, and the pension funds of other elderly women will collapse. Provide an elite education to ghetto dwellers, and they will abandon their communities. Build more libraries and gardens with tax money, and the nurses will respond by going on strike. Critics impressed by these difficulties may perceive the prima facie obligation to reduce deprivation as weak.

The observed level of social stratification must represent a set of stable strategies, immanentists allege. If it did not, other systems would have invaded and replaced them, but experiments in the regulated distribution of the social product have turned out badly and have either disappeared or are on the verge of doing so. The historian can point to a series of revolutions and reforms and counter-revolutions and counter-reforms as indicating that real differences in people's abilities and characters will consistently work to undermine anyone's airy preference for symmetry over asymmetry.

People differ greatly, immanentists allege, where ability, ambition, and effort are concerned. Some command and take, others obey and give. These patterns replicate themselves at many locations in the social world, the implication is, because we, like other social species, function well and feel well within stratified systems. The presence of others below us makes us feel proud and secure, while the presence of others above us raises our level of aspiration. Fear of falling into a lower socio-economic class or hope of ascending into a higher one provide the essential motivation needed to accomplish the world's work. Moral Pyrrhonists do not usually object, though they may, to such unnatural impositions as the extension of the franchise to all adults, the taxation of incomes, the provision of social security for the old and ill, or antidiscrimination laws. They worry nevertheless about three egalitarian experiments: steeply progressive taxation, the

strengthening of trade unions, and affirmative action. These experiments were aimed at and in some cases succeeded in equalizing the distribution of resources, reducing disparities in the power of workers vis-à-vis owners, and distributing members of ethnic groups and men and women into professions and occupations in proportions corresponding better to the proportion they compose of the existing population. There is a widespread perception that the experiments were well conducted, that they have run long enough, and that their outcomes refute the hypothesis that greater equality is possible as well as desirable. They are perceived as having failed to reduce socioeconomic inequality, as having worsened human relationships, and as consuming time, effort, and money that would have been better spent elsewhere.

The philosopher seeking to falsify the thesis that stratification and high variance are at once natural, inevitable, preferred by us, and impersonally preferable is not, however, at a loss. He can point out that, wherever slave or semi-slave economies and status-based legal systems are replaced by presumptions of equal entitlement and more symmetrical contract relations, real deprivations have been reduced. He can collect evidence to show how social evolution may nevertheless be resisted and undermined by those who fear that they have something to lose. He will not dispute that there are powerful inequality-producing tendencies resident in humans or that the most respected minds in every generation from Plato and Aristotle onwards are likely to regard variance in outcomes as both inevitable and just. At the same time, folk history, with its litany of grievances against the powerful expressed in songs, fables, and novels, and political history, with its periodic uprisings, does not lend support to the view that inequality is everyone's underlying preference. Reputable economists increasingly point to the collective advantages, impersonally measured, of constraining income disparities.

Critics of high-variance outcomes perceive social institutions as working to maximize differences in income and influence by forcing intrinsically quite similar people through an obstacle course in which the loss or gain of a few points at each level can have dramatic consequences. They acknowledge variations in ability, ambition, and effort, but insist that they are too small to account for observed

outcomes and irrelevant to the human entitlement to most goods. They regard experiments in social engineering intended to counteract the ordinary workings of old institutions and historical drift as largely successful. The problem, they allege, is that they are not seen to be successful. The futility-of-redistribution argument is taken to be persuasive, and the successes of public policy advantage-redistribution measures are rarely trumpeted. More newsworthy are labour disputes, preventable deaths under national health programmes, and the rejection of meritorious job applicants for reasons extraneous to their qualifications. We do not often read about the superior productivity of the unionized trades and the greater self-respect of their members, or the substantial difference that state-financed medicine makes to the health of the poor and even the middle-class citizens of a country, or the personal satisfactions and opportunities to contribute to knowledge that affirmative action programmes have brought to thousands of people. It is helpful in making their case if egalitarians can show that the benefits of low variance have been underestimated and the costs overestimated, that current economic privilege reflects the ill-gotten gains of the past, is based in culpable ignorance, or involves the violation of an implicit social contract.

It is salutary meanwhile to realize that, even if opportunism and self-interest are frequently theorized as the source of all dynamism in life, morality in the sense of advantage reduction is ubiquitous in our competitive world. The existence of teachers, doctors, nurses, firefighters, and public transport workers has moral significance, even if the persons occupying these social roles are not conscious of the moral dimension of their work and think of it in terms of professional status, personal satisfaction, or pecuniary rewards. The provision of opportunities for individual ambition need not conflict with the existence of institutions whose *raison d'être* is the compensation of inequalities and power imbalances. Thus, one popular objection towards social levelling—that it is necessarily destructive of autonomy and hostile to talent—is removed.

To summarize, A_1 and A_2 cooperate for Hobbesian reasons—because conflict is expensive and they want to increase their productive capacity—but their decision to cooperate rather than compete does not make their relationship morally adequate. The initial moment of cooperation may announce the beginning of their moral

problems and our global interdependency has multiplied ours. The human willingness to engage in basically cooperative relationships results in a condition of high variance in well-being and objective deprivations for many. A reasonable theory of distributive justice must therefore incorporate some features of procedural approaches. Just worlds regulate and police their cooperative arrangements to dissuade agents from making and accepting the bad bargains they otherwise would.

We can predict that worlds whose cooperative enterprises are largely symmetrical as defined above do not contain strongly polarized populations of very well-off and very badly-off persons. Just as one hundred tillers on one hundred identical plots of land who consume all that they sow and reap are not likely to vary enormously in their levels of well-being before they begin to exchange, bank, educate, and plan, one hundred pairs of symmetrical cooperators helping each other sow and reap may not vary much in their individual levels of well-being either. However, if we complicate our model by supposing that persons do not merely lend their skill and effort to cooperative tasks of a given degree of eligibility and claim rewards accordingly, but also bring accumulated resources—tools, capital, allies and acquaintances, prestige—that bring entitlements of their own, even a well-regulated world will begin to take on the familiar aspect of high variance. These resources increase the productivity of the cooperative unit. At the same time, they enhance the effects of innate skill and effort. If A_1 and A_2 have exactly the same cognitive abilities and are both willing to work ten hours per day, but A_1 can bring a factory or a fine old name into the cooperative enterprise and claim a much greater share of the joint product on that account, A_1 and his like may project themselves onto a different plane of well-being from A_2 and his like. Outcome approaches to social justice become more, not less relevant, as the procedural aspects of cooperation become more complicated.

But is equality in the possession of some or all of the components of well-being a feature of all just worlds? Strict egalitarianism conflicts with the intuition that worlds that do not discriminate at all with respect to the performance of individuals within them are worse than worlds that do discriminate. The strict egalitarian is committed to the position that persons who are wasteful, destructive, and corrupt, even

while remaining within the letter of the law, ought to have exactly as good lives as persons who add increments of beauty, truth, and justice to their environments.

Chapter 7 argues that just worlds are regulated with respect to outcomes as well as with respect to procedures. They are egalitarian, except at the margin. The distribution of the doubtful and speculative components of well-being is not uniform in just worlds exhibiting mild scarcity, though it does not favour some groups over others. This position is, it should be understood, considerably more stringent than the prevailing immanentist interpretation of the role played by considerations of meritorious performance in distributive justice.

7
The Role of a Merit Principle in Distributive Justice

Suppose there is a given quantity of desirable goods and states, the components of well-being, to be distributed according to some set of rules. Define U as a condition of the world in which needs are universally met. Define M as a condition of the world in which the components of well-being can properly be said to be a function of merit; i.e., the more meritorious are better off than the less meritorious, in proportion to their merit. Suppose we have the opportunity to write down a distributive protocol that will determine the allocation of the components of well-being to everyone. Which protocol should we choose if scarcity obtains to the extent that the complete satisfaction of all their wants cannot be experienced by all? Two very different, though not logically inconsistent, general answers suggest themselves:

(1) *Merit priority*: We ought to choose one amongst the various protocols that realize M even if need-satisfaction U does not result.

(2) *Need priority*: We ought to choose one amongst the various protocols that realize U even if reward-for-merit M does not result.

Of course, we might prefer a protocol that realized neither M nor U, and libertarians like F. A. Hayek have insisted that we should be uninterested in realizing either.[1] Credible libertarians do, however, seem to subscribe to some form of merit priority, as will be shown below; and it is unclear why we would not be attracted by the

---

[1] According to Hayek, 'The values [men's] services will have to their fellows will often have no relations to their merits or needs.' *Law, Legislation and Liberty*, ii. 72.

possibility of realizing at least one and possibly both of *U* and *M*. This chapter will argue that need priority is obviously true and merit priority obviously false. However, this does not settle the case for egalitarianism. Justice does not require that no one's life be better in any respect than anyone else's, only that no one's life be better than anyone else's in some respects. Meritorious performance can confer extra entitlements at the margin of well-being, provided suitable limitations are recognized.

The original dilemma—merit v. need—is soluble. It is the setting of an appropriate threshold for 'needs' that is controversial and there are reasons for thinking that the threshold should be set fairly high. Further, outcomes resulting from the deployment of a merit principle must be unpatterned with respect to various social classes if the conditions of a just world are to be met. In summary, semi-meritocracies are defensible institutions, but only under conditions that are not met in our world.

7.1. Two Distributive Norms

Merit priority and need priority reflect the manner in which two distinct distributive norms appear to govern all human economies. One is the norm of granting resources in one's possession, or under one's direct or indirect control, to those who need them, regardless of whether they have done anything to earn them. The other is the norm of distributing resources according to merit, regardless of need. The non-meritorious deserve deprivation, it is thought, just as the wicked deserve punishment, while the meritorious and virtuous correspondingly deserve fulfilment and reward. These norms may be termed the 'need principle' and the 'merit principle'. Merit is understood for present purposes to include the passive possession of qualities deemed admirable, such as physical beauty or insight into the structure of elementary particles; the active performance of tasks that require strength and effort, such as drilling or digging; and the exercise of coordinated specialist knowledge and effort, such as athletic, musical, or organizational ability that normally goes by the name of talent. I make no apologies for the whiff of theological rectitude and officers' deportment clinging to the term, for my

intention is to question the role of merit in a normative political theory that is consistent with our current empirical knowledge and democratic leanings.

The dual norms are expressed in institutions that are distinct but that coexist in the wider society. Meritocratic institutions distribute money, authority, and prestige on the basis of accomplishments and the outcome of selective and competitive encounters. Simultaneously, compensatory organizations including taxation bureaux, charities, and welfare programmes distribute the components of well-being on the basis of perceived need. The appearance of the two norms is not a special feature of modern market economies that have a monetary surplus available for distribution. Even if the extra privileges accorded to merit are minimal in subsistence cultures, the need principle never enjoys absolute hegemony. Honour and regard can be considered as elements of well-being that are somewhat scarce and that are differentially awarded in response to perceived merit.

The question whether both principles are ethical ones is controversial. A need principle might be introduced on non-moral pragmatic grounds, for example, as a condition of maintaining a workforce fit for exploitation. Additionally, many particular instances of alleged merit-based desert have no moral significance.[2] Ordinarily, however, the supplying of benefits to others at some cost to oneself and the appropriate distribution of rewards and punishments are seen as ethical performances.[3] Yet the merit principle and the need principle are frequently in conflict. Many of the unmistakably neediest—the handicapped, the elderly, the impoverished inhabitants of badly ordered regimes, criminals, addicts, slum-dwellers, and the mentally ill—appear to those who enjoy some degree of control over resources to be deficient in valued attributes such as consideration for others, beauty, sound judgement, and industriousness. To award them resources is to violate the merit principle. Conversely, many persons held to be meritorious—film actors, athletes, CEOs of corporations—are not needy, and to reward them is to violate the need principle.

Interest in the two principles and recognition of their potential for conflict is a feature of modern political discourse. Rawls famously

---

[2] Though cf. George Sher, *Desert*, 7, *et passim*.
[3] By e.g. J. S. Mill in *Utilitarianism*, in *Collected Works*, x. 241 ff.

argued that persons do not deserve their native endowments and therefore do not deserve the benefits that flow from them, including the opportunities further to accumulate advantages.[4] Rewards for merit can at most have an instrumental role in his scheme: 'All social values—liberty and opportunity, income and wealth, and the social bases of self-respect—are to be distributed equally unless an unequal distribution of any, or all, of these values is to everyone's advantage.'[5] Yet earlier scepticism over the merit principle articulated as well by Nagel[6] has been countered by the rearticulation of meritocratic theories of desert. Liberalism, in its classic formulation, is a theory according to which individuals are permitted to accumulate as much by way of resources as their ability and effort allow, subject to certain background constraints. Rawls's claim that 'the democratic interpretation of [the principle of equality of opportunity and the difference principle] will not lead to a meritocratic society',[7] has been deemed surprising, and he has been sternly rebuked as having abandoned the basic commitment that makes liberalism credible.[8] At the same time, the need principle has remained at the centre of welfarism and is focal in capability theories.

Imagine a highly talented, hard-working pianist A_1 and a not-as-talented, less hard-working pianist A_2. A_1 practises hard and productively for four hours every day; A_2 rarely practises. A_1 and A_2 complete for a full scholarship to a prestigious school of music. A_1 and A_2 exist in each of W_1, W_2, and W_3. In W_1, a perfectly meritocratic world, A_1 receives the scholarship and the subsequent benefits of the training he undergoes. In W_2, an imperfectly meritocratic world, less meritorious A_2 wins the scholarship because of his good looks, or a mistake in the computer-generated list of finalists caused by a stray cosmic ray, though in W_2 such outcomes are somewhat unusual. In W_3, an antimeritocratic world, A_2 wins the scholarship and has the better outcome for the same reasons and such outcomes are the rule because

[4] Rawls, *Theory of Justice*, 89.

[5] Ibid. 54.

[6] Nagel took a stance similar to Rawls in 1973, arguing that 'differential abilities are not usually among the characteristics that determine whether people *deserve* economic and social benefits'. 'Equal Treatment and Compensatory Discrimination', 354. More recently he has emphasized the instrumental reasons for rewarding merit in *Equality and Partiality*, 102–3.

[7] Rawls, *Theory of Justice*, 91.

[8] See esp. Samuel Scheffler, 'Reactive Attitudes and Liberalism', in *Boundaries and Allegiances*, 82–3 f.; see also Sher 'Effort, Ability, and Personal Desert'; as well as *Desert*, 109 ff.

the more meritorious candidate is never preferred in W_3. The merit-desert intuition is that W_1 is the just world, and that W_2 and W_3 are normatively inferior worlds, W_3 being even worse than W_2.

The intuition that an injustice is done whenever the more meritorious are not favoured by a reward system can be expressed as follows:

> *The Merit-Desert Principle*
> If A_1 works harder than A_2 and/or has more talent enabling her to produce more goods and services of higher quality, A_1 deserves to enjoy a higher level of well-being than A_2. It would be unjust if A_2 were to obtain as much as or more than A_1. Merit does not merely have a tendency to attract reward in our world, but deserves it.

Belief in the corresponding principle as an axiom of distributive justice is fostered by reflection on examples of its contravention. In justice-conscious democracies, patronage systems that award the most lucrative and visible positions to cronies are regarded as grossly unfair and inefficient. Individuals are often outraged when they are passed over for a raise, a promotion, or a social honour in favour of colleagues they perceive as less industrious and accomplished, or whose natural assets and talents, considerable though they may be, seem irrelevant to the performance of the job in question. People's sense of fairness is such that they may prefer lower aggregates of utility to certain discrepancies, and this preference has always been considered a legitimate point against utilitarianism. Not only is envy a natural reactive emotion, it seems reasonable to distinguish between 'justified' and 'unjustified' resentment in situations of differential reward.

The merit-desert principle seems to operate ubiquitously and effectively and to correspond to a deeply held, non-revisable intuition about justice. We are constituted to expect that the exercise of our capacities will bring us gratification, and the habit of attending to the relationship between exertion and reward is useful to creatures who need to learn from their own mistakes. The belief that those who do not forgo short-term opportunities and resist temptations deserve to reap what they sow reflects the view that knowledge of what Bentham termed 'natural sanctions' is an important element of education. As Melvin J. Lerner remarks in his study of ordinary

people's beliefs about justice, 'In order to plan, work for, and obtain things they want, and avoid those which are frightening or painful, people must assume that there are manageable procedures which are effective in producing the desired end states.'[9]

The merit-desert intuition is so widely shared, the defender of merit priority might argue, that the principle of equitable but unequal distribution it generates is one on which everyone can agree. While I am not a talented piano player or an inventor of great proofs, and while I freely acknowledge that my chances of being one in any world in which my position was randomly assigned are no greater than the actual frequency of such persons in our world, my attachment to the intuition and to its particular applications may be just as great as that of the meritorious agent whom the realization of the corresponding distribution rule would benefit. A person of little merit might prefer to live in a W_2 or a W_3 world, it might be argued, but this could only be for selfish reasons, and could not constitute an all-things-considered rational preference.

It is the apparently non-discardable nature of the intuition to which Samuel Scheffler refers when he remarks of the Rawlsian position on merit and desert, that the view that 'the assignment of benefits and burdens in accordance with a conception of merit or desert.... [requires] justification by reference to something putatively more fundamental: either to the utility of such assignments or to their placement within a larger institutional framework [may be] insufficiently sensitive to the role of...relevant practices in giving expression to our reactive attitudes'. Scheffler regards this discordance as potentially capable of relegating Rawlsian liberalism to a marginal position in political philosophy; it is too much at odds, he intimates, with our normal ways of acting and thinking about ourselves and others.[10] A related argument is that to fail to reward merit is to refuse to participate in an appropriate, characteristically human mode of valuing. Offering financial rewards to the meritorious is, on this view, an extension of the natural human tendency to show appreciation and admiration for outstanding and even for creditable performances. That these rewards can be used to purchase the components of

---

[9] Melvin J. Lerner, *The Belief in a Just World: A Fundamental Delusion*, 9.
[10] Scheffler, 'Reactive Attitudes and Liberalism', 23–4.

well-being is precisely what makes them appropriate tokens of valuation.[11]

For a defender of merit priority, the relationship between the intuition and the principle is as follows: *Because* reasonable persons mostly share the merit-desert intuition, the principle *ought* to regulate the distribution of the components of well-being. Some meta-ethical account of this inference is obviously called for. Normative intuitionists amongst its defenders will accept the inference on the grounds that it is a product of our direct epistemological access to moral reality. A more cautious meta-ethicist will base her acceptance of the inference on the grounds that the intuition is an expression of what psychologists term 'consensus reality', the set of beliefs, descriptive and prescriptive, that humans by and large agree on and believe one another to agree on, adding the further premises that our theories of distributive justice ought to be descriptive of consensus reality, not revisionary where it is concerned. In our own terms, the intuition incorporates, confusedly, a belief about psychological reality and a hypothesis regarding an ideal rule.

Though defenders of ideal markets as paradigmatically just systems officially reject the notion that levels of well-being ought to have any predetermined relationship whatsoever to specific qualities of individuals,[12] their commitment to the value independence of a market is clearly only partial. According to the founder-author of this tradition, Hayek, remuneration is tied to the perceived value of services provided.[13] And, while there is no necessary connection between remuneration and guarantees of well-being, it is empirically observable that the probability that an individual's well-being is above threshold levels increases steeply with initial increments of income above $0 before levelling off. Market systems that are operating properly tend to ensure good outcomes for persons who produce goods and services deemed valuable, and while in theory these persons could be anyone producing anything to any standard at any speed, in practice these

---

[11] As Young remarks (without endorsing the view), 'Many supporters of desert have argued that to fail to accord people their deserts is to fail to treat them as autonomous beings, as people who can actively and purposefully intervene in the world.' 'Egalitarianism and Desert', 335. Cf. Malthus, *An Essay on the Principles of Population*, 95. Abolishing relief, Malthus says, will restore 'liberty and freedom of action' to the peasantry of England.

[12] Hayek, *Law, Legislation and Liberty*, ii. 72.

[13] Ibid.

rewardees are individuals perceived as producing well-made and useful or valuable items in sufficient quantity. Liberty, in other words, does not only disrupt some patterning with respect to outcomes; it produces predictable patterning of its own. Perhaps because they recognize this peculiarity of the founder doctrine, subsequent market theorists have been more frankly meritocratic in their appeal to Lockean models of entitlement generated by virtuous individual productivity. Nozick's celebrated discussion of the former professional basketball-player Wilt Chamberlain's ability to extract resources from his fans by exercising talent and effort overtime is an imaginative extension of the idea of an entitlement that flows from ability and effort that are widely acknowledged and admired.[14]

Developing the Lockean idea of a natural entitlement to that which flows from one's endowments, David Gauthier introduces a thought experiment involving sixteen islands, on which there are sixteen different Robinson Crusoes.[15] Each possesses one or the other of two polar traits: clever/stupid, strong/weak, and energetic/lazy. Eight islands have abundant resources, eight have scarce resources. All possible combinations of Crusoes and islands are realized. Each Crusoe employs her native endowments to exploit the resources of the island. No Crusoe has grounds for complaint, according to Gauthier; each does as well as she can given her ability, levels of effort, and the environment at hand. The level of well-being that each enjoys is not open to criticism.

Gauthier asks us now to imagine that the Crusoes acquire mobility and can leave their islands but can travel only in one direction, making certain kinds of trade impossible. Each Crusoe can now visit or try to settle on the next island downstream, or move further along. Gauthier asks whether it could be wrong for each Crusoe to use his own resources and those of any island he can reach for his own benefit. He concludes that this cannot be unjust, unless a Crusoe violates the proviso that one may not seize the products of another's labour without providing compensation. An invading $Crusoe_1$ is not permitted to make things worse for the resident $Crusoe_2$ than they would have been had he not turned up, but commits no injustice by not making things better. If clever, industrious $Crusoe_1$ arrives on an

[14] Nozick, *Anarchy, State and Utopia*, 159 ff.   [15] Gauthier, *Morals by Agreement*, 219 ff.

island where lazy, incompetent Crusoe$_2$ is failing to eke out a living despite an abundance of resources, there is nothing to criticize if Crusoe$_1$ does not share and waxes fat in the new territory.

Though according to merit priority, few if any of the products of the cooperative surplus require distribution on the basis of need in order for justice to be done, this is not to say that its defenders deny the moral relevance of the concept of need. Hayek acknowledges the need for a guaranteed minimum income for the non-able-bodied. Nozick describes as 'reasonable and intelligible' patterns of transfer including gifts, bequests to children, and charitable donations.[16] It is safe to say that no one—not even the most Malthusian of living theorists of distributive justice—disavows the need principle entirely. (Malthus retracted his claim that the poor had no inherent right to survival.) Accordingly, the reader should not be distracted by verbal issues. To the objection that Crusoe$_1$'s failure to help needy Crusoe$_2$ is wrong, a defender of merit priority might respond that it may be morally wrong without being unjust. Gauthier notes that some categories of needy person are 'not party to the moral relationships grounded by a contractarian theory',[17] but this leaves open the possibility that they are party to some other set of moral relationships. Nozick's expectation that private charity would continue to operate to supply needs unmet by the merit principle reflects another view of the relationship of the two principles. All in all, while the denomination of rules as 'justice-related' or 'contract-based' v. 'moral' or 'non-contract-based' may be important in some argumentative contexts, this partitioning issue has no role to play in the present discussion. The relevant question is whether *some* kind of wrong is done when the need principle or another merit-disregarding principle fails to operate or is overridden in a particular context. When considering the distribution protocols of an ideal world administered by a perfectly just philosopher king, we are trying to compare the outcomes for different categories of person according to different norms, and the names by which the norms are denominated are not germane.

Though the first-person experience of the merit-desert intuition and its violation may be attended by sharp visceral feelings of justice

[16] Nozick, *Anarchy, State and Utopia*, 160 ff.   [17] Gauthier, *Morals by Agreement*, 18.

and injustice, comparable to those associated with retributive satis-faction or frustrated vengefulness, the intuition is not at all precise, and neither is the form of the principle to which it allegedly gives rise. The following considerations put its depth and universality into question:

(1) Other principles besides merit are available for distributing not only basic goods such as food, water, and shelter, but also non-basic goods such as companionship and attention to persons whom we know. It is unclear why these principles are not available for distributing goods of all sorts to persons we do not know.

(2) The merit-desert intuition dissipates when it is considered in isolation, purified of certain assumptions regarding overall sharable benefits. Its alleged status as a widely shared intu-ition of reasonable people or as a fundamental normative principle is accordingly dubious.

(1) It is a well-confirmed moral proposition that babies and elderly parents should have not only their needs for food, water, and shelter met, but should also be provided with the conditions of a decent life, even if they do not yet or no longer exercise their talents in an effortful way or display competence. We not only feed our pets but also try to ensure that they have pleasurable experiences, even though they do not apply their talents consistently to anything. Even prison-ers guilty of heinous crimes who are held to lack merit altogether are given more than what they need to sustain life; they are allowed to watch television, for example, and this is not considered wrong. Homemakers, still a common occupational group in many parts of the world, fit the Lockean paradigm poorly, since their labour is not evaluated and compensated on meritocratic principles and they are often economically dependent on others. Defenders of merit priority are not inclined to deprive them of all the constituents of well-being; though they may well maintain that women's lesser status is appro-priate in virtue of their lesser tendency to engage in competitive exercises. The burden of proof can be shifted to the defender of the merit principle who is required to explain why it should determine the allocation of resources outside, say, the family. The answer to this question should be non-circular, i.e., it cannot consist

in the re-presentation of the merit-desert intuition as uniquely suited to the public realm.

The defender of merit priority can readily concede that it is right to ignore the merit principle when one stands in a particular relationship of friendship or kinship to a needy person. According to the terms of the two-Crusoes story, a just state of affairs *may* obtain when an able and industrious individual who is able to extract resources from the environment (and being able to negotiate a particular wage settlement on the basis of one's merits can be considered as a kind of resource extraction, as we have learned from Nozick) refuses to accept a decline in his level of well-being to assist a non-meritorious individual in need. Gauthier certainly does not insist that an unjust state of affairs obtains whenever a meritorious individual *does* accept a decline in his standard of living to assist another. Nor does he deny that it would be morally wrong to fail to assist an elderly parent, one's own baby, etc. His account accordingly leaves open the question why, if it would be morally wrong (though not unjust) to fail to meet the needs of family members by forgoing the personal consumption of some reward for merit, it is not morally wrong (though not unjust) to fail to meet the needs of others by forgoing either the personal consumption permitted by a merit reward or simply the reward itself.

Several responses are available to the defender of merit priority. One is that there is no *natural motivation* to meet the needs of persons outside the nuclear family or outside some other special related group of kith, kin, and familiar animals and that the wrongness of failing to provide for intimates is related to its abnormality for most humans. The motivation to assist needy strangers is, however, susceptible to cultural, ideological, and ethical influences; what we take to be natural v. abnormal behaviour in this regard is not fixed. Another possible response is that the provision of the components of well-being to these 'exceptional' non-meritorious persons and animals is not inconsistent with the priority of the merit principle and is actually an instance of just reward. Babies and children will someday belong to the economic system as producers, the elderly once played their role, and homemakers and caretakers make the present productivity of the mature and the future productivity of young possible. And if criminals are fed, warmed, clothed, and afforded education and

entertainment at public expense, the defender of merit priority might insist, it is only because we can reasonably expect that some proportion of them—we do not know which individuals—will one day become deserving members of society. Certain social services, such as assistance to the blind and handicapped, might be deemed appropriate because they help them to function as consumers and producers in the marketplace.

Characteristically, however, defenders of merit priority worry about 'utility sinks'—those persons whose irremediable past and present non-meritorious conduct, combined with an institutional readiness to transfer benefits to them, is believed to threaten the entitlements of the meritorious.[18] A defender of merit priority will not avail himself of the observation that the non-meritorious are human beings who are in all relevant respects *the same as* the meritorious or that these persons *might have been* meritorious had they had different life histories since such generous allowances produce a *reductio ad absurdum* of the merit principle. Yet it is unclear why the principle should not be subject to such a *reductio*.

The defender of merit priority who concedes that it is not unjust and is indeed morally required to use funds one could have spent on oneself to feed one's own non-meritorious baby is therefore obliged to explain why it would not be wrong to fail to meet the needs of non-meritorious strangers and would be permissible not to meet them. Suppose that Crusoe$_2$ is failing to sustain herself on her resource-rich island before Crusoe$_1$ turns up, and that she is gradually expiring. There might be various reasons for her poor performance. She might have numerous small children. She might be lame, or prone to dizzy spells and blackouts. Or she might be a hedonistic lotus-eater who lacks motivation. Whatever the reason, suppose she is economically incompetent. She lacks industry, ambition, and skill at finding and using the abundant resources of her island. Gauthier's position is that there is no affront to justice if Crusoe$_1$ lands on her beach, meets her, and does not help her, so long as he does nothing to worsen her condition. He can gather up the fruits of the island for sale on the next one, while Crusoe$_2$, with her flawed body or bad character, heads towards her inevitable demise.

---

[18] Gauthier, *Morals by Agreement*, 18.

Now one can agree with Gauthier that as long as Crusoe$_1$ and Crusoe$_2$ are alone on their respective islands, no questions as to their respective entitlements can arise. Nevertheless, it is unclear how the observation that an individual's level of well-being will be observed to vary with his labour on a desert island and that there is nothing wrong with *that* can be transformed without a great deal of argument into a fundamental thesis of social justice. As two members of a social species whose members are interdependent, Crusoe$_1$ and Crusoe$_2$ form a society even without formal agreement, and new considerations enter the picture. The existence of Crusoe$_2$ is prejudicially construed as merely another environmental condition experienced by Crusoe$_1$ on the new island, and the existence of Crusoe$_1$ as merely another environmental condition experienced by Crusoe$_2$. Even on a low-demand normative theory, it is wrong for Crusoe$_1$ not to feed and clothe Crusoe$_2$, particularly as it is not at all difficult for him to do so, given his cleverness and resourcefulness.

The difference between A_1's culpably *doing something bad* to A_2, and A_1's innocently *doing nothing to stop something bad happening* to A_2 is mediated by a third concept: that of A_1's culpably *letting something bad happen* to A_2. The mediating concept is applicable because A_1 and A_2 can observe each other's actions and are aware of each other's existence and condition, and because direct or indirect means of affecting each others' condition exist and are known to them. Disregard for the needs of strangers, when one is aware of them and has direct or indirect means of supplying them, is unjust, as defenders of need priority have traditionally maintained.

(2) Even if consideration is restricted to able-bodied productive labourers, the merit-desert intuition is less robust than it might seem. It does not easily survive transportation outside the familiar scripts and scenarios of meritocratic competition such as contests, tournaments, raises and promotions, and political power struggles, in which more than simple desert may be at stake. Imagine a village in which the components of well-being are awarded to villagers in proportion to the quality and quantity of the products they manufacture, by which their merit is assessed. The products themselves may be returned as components of well-being to the producers, but the circulation of goods is not a necessary feature of the model. Suppose that the quantity of resources is also fixed: when the stock runs out, no

more will be distributed. For simplicity, we can begin with a village in an array of worlds W_1, W_2, and W_3. Rather than digging resources from the ground and consuming them, the inhabitants manufacture small clay figurines, which they smash on an altar, and they receive the components of well-being in return from the gods. (The model captures better certain features of modernity.) The needs of the villagers are equal, indeed identical. All goods received can only be personally consumed and are not sharable. In a W_1 world, those who can produce the most and best figurines receive more by way of water, food, clothing, shelter, amusements, educational opportun-ities, trusty friends, and so on, and those who perform poorly receive fewer of the components of well-being or goods of inferior quality. In W_2, the merit principle is partially followed, so that well-being is positively correlated with the feature of being a good sculptor, but certain disruptive factors such as luck, class, and sexual discrimination make the correlation imperfect. In W_3, well-being is negatively correlated or uncorrelated with the ability to produce well-made figurines quickly.

It is not obvious that in this set of worlds, in which a unique skill is valued, the W_1 world is normatively superior to the others. Why should a person whose talent for producing figurines is limited and who does not work as fast have a smaller supply of drinking water, less wholesome food, and so on? Nor is it clear why it is preferable to suffer deficiencies because of lack of merit than to suffer deficiencies because of sexual discrimination. Because the stock of goods will eventually run out, being assumed to be fixed, neither meritorious A_1 nor incompetent A_2 will enjoy immortality. But if meritorious A_1 has accumulated reserves, he or she will experience a longer life than A_2, as well as a happier one. And because the components of well-being are stipulated to be personal and cannot be shared, the argument that A_1 deserves a reward for acquiring additional resources that can increase the welfare of her society is not available.

It might be agreed by the defender of merit priority, following Hayek with slight revision, that, under the circumstances, A_1 has no surplus of entitlement over A_2. This is so, he might maintain, because A_1 does not deserve any reward at all. For A_1's productions are of no use to others in her society either directly or indirectly; they are simply requisitions of the gods and, contrary to the hypothesis, they

cannot plausibly be considered to be meritorious. Alternatively, following Dworkin,[19] he might argue that the society of villagers is unjust because it has failed to equalize opportunities by allowing its inhabitants to display merit of various sorts depending on the skills they natively possess, or by providing basic training in the manufacture of figurines. These admissions, though, amount to substantial concessions on the part of a defender of merit priority. The requirements that only genuinely useful products of some durability are eligible to be considered as expressions of merit, and that either special training must be given to those who have no intrinsic gift when it comes to producing such items, or that there must be sufficiently many products that are regarded as valuable to ensure that everyone has sufficient talent and effort to produce at least one type of valued product, are quite stringent. Moreover, their introduction appears to be ad hoc and undermining of merit priority. For the problem the imposition of the extra requirements is designed to address is the problem of the needy; how to arrange matters so that they will have sufficient resources.

It might be argued that A_1 sacrifices leisure and endures boredom and physical discomfort to achieve her level of productivity, and therefore deserves compensation and extra rewards. Suffering through hard labour, it might be maintained, is itself meritorious. This claim is somewhat doubtful. As Nagel suggests, the possession and exercise of a talent may be intrinsically rewarding and external rewards will only further enhance A_1's well-being.[20] Even if A_1 gets tired and bored making figurines expertly, she does not endure tiredness and boredom to help others. Her suffering seems devoid of moral significance.

To experience the uneasy feeling that equal awards of the components of well-being to A_1 and A_2 would be unjust, we have to build up a representation of A_2 as a shirker failing to pull his weight. This involves our conceiving resources as devolving upon A_1 and A_2 jointly, and conceiving both parties as able to determine the quality and quantity of their output. Incompetence will appear under these

---

[19] Dworkin argues that individuals should be insured against the initial risk of being born without talents; all such deficiencies ought to be compensated at the starting gate. 'What is Equality?', pts. I and II. The merit principle nevertheless plays an important role in his framework, in so far as a non-basic level of well-being is not assured as an outcome.

[20] See Nagel, 'Equal Treatment and Compensatory Discrimination', 357.

conditions as a wilful vice that deserves punishment and competence as deserving of reward. The position that *effort* is the only component of merit intrinsically deserving of reward, in so far as innate talent, though not its development, lies outside our control, has several defenders.[21] Such a position flows naturally from consideration of the Lockean digging scenario,[22] in which a person's nutritional status, shorthand for his overall well-being, is entirely contingent on the effort he puts into digging his fields, digging being considered paradigmatic unskilled labour that cannot be evaluated for expertise, grace, style, creativity, etc.

The chief objection to this limiting case version of merit priority is that the notion of effort required is an elusive one, located between a pure metaphysical will whose operations are empirically undetectable and empirically detectable striving that is a function of accidental cerebral organization and environmental influences. A secondary objection is that the intuition that effort deserves reward seems to fail in worlds in which the pure trying activity rarely or never produces results. (There could be a world in which those who do not try very hard produce the best quality and quantity of items and vice versa.) Ultimately, effort seems to be intrinsically deserving of reward only to the extent that we believe that as good, or nearly as good, sharable products can be produced by perspiration as by inspiration. The connection between the sheer goodness of a non-sharable product and the entitlement to the necessities of life is already weak and the intrinsic connection between either hopeless or successful effort to produce a non-sharable product and entitlement cannot be any stronger than it is. However, we cannot rule out the possibility that it is the effort component of merit and not the talent component that ought to count in any defensible application of a merit principle, whether instrumental or non-instrumental.

Summarizing, the merit-desert intuition is best regarded as an intuition concerning appropriate distributions of the components of well-being in well-defined situations in which the products of the meritorious are socially useful and can be bestowed upon others, or where the resources received for the products are at least sharable,

---

[21] For Nagel, effort 'being a manifestation of the will, is the most personal or internal factor, and uniquely suitable to be regarded as the individual's personal responsibility'. *Equality and Partiality*, 106.

[22] Locke, *Of Civil Government: The Second Treatise*, ch 5. 'Of Property', sect 27.

where the expression of merit is costly to individuals and entails sacrifices on their part, effectively *for* the good of others, and where we have a clear notion of what it is to pull one's weight and not to burden others. All these conditions are lacking in the figurine scenario. Further, the intuition is apt to operate more powerfully with respect to a condition in which the quantity of resources available for distribution is not fixed and is influenced by the reward scheme chosen. This condition was also left out of the model. The conclusion that seems warranted is that any obviousness resident in the merit-desert intuition is a function of certain additional assumptions, assumptions that are not clearly independent of the need principle.

7.2. Instrumental Considerations regarding Merit

The intuition that merit ought to determine the level of well-being is likely to materialize, then, when A_1's talent and industry are conceived as influencing the amount of resources available to A_1 and A_2 jointly, and when A_1 is viewed as able to share or bestow them or even as required to do so. The use of a *reward* for capable A_1's making resources available to less competent A_2, or an *incentive* to encourage A_1 to bring down from heaven more of a sharable resource, now seems appropriate, providing respectively a non-instrumental and an instrumental justification for the use of a merit principle. Yet neither type of newly available justification supports the thesis of merit priority. For the intuition behind the appropriateness of rewards and incentives is that a world in which the needs of both the meritorious and the non-meritorious are met is better than a world in which the needs of only one or the other are met. And that is simply the thesis of need priority. For merit priority to be true, W_1 worlds have to be preferable to equally resource-rich W_2 and W_3 worlds in which resources are sharable but incentives are not needed to induce the talented to draw them down, or dig them up, as the case may be.

As noted earlier, some adherents of the merit principle take it as standing in no need of independent justification. It is this class of adherents who privilege reactive attitudes as genuine reasons for doing something whose political influence Scheffler worries

about.[23] The need principle, however, does not seem to stand in need of independent justification either; both are on an equal footing as basic commitments. The most compelling defence of merit priority is not posed by its proponents who maintain that the merit-desert principle is a fundamental and unrevisable prescriptive intuition but by those who maintain that history has shown that the deployment of the merit principle, ignoring needs, barring some few exceptions, is the most effective way to promote universal well-being and to minimize deprivation. This position is subtle, in so far as its defender implicitly concedes need priority but maintains that the universal satisfaction of needs cannot be aimed at directly but only achieved as a by-product. On this view, merit priority provides the proper operating principle, even if the satisfaction of needs universally is the goal.

Many reasons commonly advanced for the ubiquitous employment of a merit principle are instrumental in just this respect. It is better to have more competent pilots, bureaucrats, builders, and police officers than incompetent ones, and if rewarding persons in these categories according to their merit encourages competence, that is a purely instrumental reason to do it. A new good— competent piloting—is thereby brought into the world merely by organizing, or rearranging the reward structure, if not 'for free' then at least (it is hoped) for less than any utility subtracted from others. Disproportionately high rewards, such as CEOs' salaries, create focuses of responsibility and accountability, preventing their organizational diffusion and this is seen as a general benefit. Similarly, one may overreward to encourage literary competency and productivity by giving large prizes on the basis of small and subjective differences in the quality of a product, for example, a novel. More good literature is made available to all through this kind of stimulation, thereby addressing the population's need for good literature.

Yet these examples fall short of showing that a systematic commitment to merit priority maximizes the good that is available to all. It is impossible to make a retrospective study to decide whether 'history' really confirms the hypothesis of merit priority. The claim

---

[23] Scheffler, 'Reactive Attitudes and Liberalism', 31.

to obviousness of the historical thesis can nevertheless be tested in a simplified model.

Consider a mining operation in which there is a fixed amount of gold known to be underground and labourers are set to work to dig it out (the Lockean digging scenario). In each work cycle, the amount dug up is distributed according to protocol. Suppose the labourers are linearly ranked according to their merit; in this case, the ability to dig gold. The hypothesis is that the most gold will be brought out of the mine over some specified interval if the labourers are rewarded in a series of repeated cycles in decreasing order of merit. Since there is no unique way to fix the scale, and since a highly compressed distribution will be virtually identical to an equal one, the hypothesis should perhaps incorporate the specification that differences in payment between individuals or classes of the population are either (depending on exactly which version of the hypothesis is being tested) large by some objective measure or distinctly noticeable to the recipients— quite small objective differences might be strongly registered by them. A sub-hypothesis is that the reward scheme maximizes output through the production of positive and negative incentives. After receiving the first round of rewards, each labourer is influenced to increase or decrease his digging, or to keep production at the same level, and, according to the hypothesis, even if some labourers are induced to decrease their digging, their decrease is more than compensated for by increased productivity in others, which now merits a larger reward.

Stated in this form, the hypothesis is hardly uncontroversial. The assumption that low-merit labourers are by and large stimulated to produce more by receiving small rewards and do not defect to even lower levels of productivity, while high-merit labourers are by and large stimulated to produce even more by receiving high rewards and will otherwise defect to lower levels of production is gratuitous. How much an individual currently on Tier n of the payment hierarchy will be induced to increase or decrease his or her production by the addition or subtraction of $\$x$ of reward is an unknown. If the labourers are ascribed both biological limitations that fix their maximum digging abilities and their minimum nutritional needs and further psychological complexities, designing a schedule that produces maximum total output becomes a complicated task. When they

are able to observe each other's compensation levels and assess each other's merit independently of the 'objective' assessment, numerous motivational factors will be brought into play—including feelings of envy and feelings of solidarity—that will influence how they react to incentives. And rewarding the meritorious who do not need the incentive is inefficient, as is failing to reward those of the non-meritorious who are highly sensitive to incentives.

In short, if the aim is simply to maximize the quantity of gold taken from the mine by playing on the assorted psychological propensities and biological capacities of the labourers, there is no reason to think that a decompressed merit-based scheme must perform better than any of the multitude of schemes that depart from strict observance of the rule that the more gold one dug in the last cycle, the more one is to receive in the next cycle. The hypothesis that the system that maximizes the gold output of the mine will be one that compensates according to merit in this manner *might* be true, but if we ask why anyone is inclined to believe that it is true in the absence of proof, the answer is likely to be the following: The protocol is simple and is judged to give better results than other simple schemes, e.g. equal division. However, if a merit protocol is to be regarded as just on the grounds that it does the *best* job of meeting needs, its simplicity is irrelevant. If more complex schemes that work better are available, the rationale for the simple one collapses. Turning back to the real world, it should be apparent that if the quantity we are aiming to maximize through incentives and disincentives is aggregate well-being, not simply output or throughput of raw materials, the task becomes even more complex. (Increasing output can, for ecological as well as psychological reasons, reduce well-being.) The belief that a linear reward scheme will maximize that quantity is probably false.

In some domains, for example, in the civil service, introducing meritocratic competition and selection procedures in the place of patronage has opened up a livelihood to the middle and lower classes, and enhanced public service, since more competent persons now fill these roles. In other domains, the use of competitions and the introduction of differential rewards for merit has no significant beneficial effects. The efficacy of incentives varies with institutionally created expectations, and they may be ineffective where individuals'

productivity is relatively inelastic, or where they are not motivated by money. 'Performance-based pay', as Nancy Folbre points out, 'may actually lower quality.'[24] When a formerly uncontrolled vocation, such as medicine or teaching, becomes organized under meritocratic principles, self-selection becomes less important in determining the composition of the profession. As a result, the values of the profession can change. This may, but need not, increase the total amount of good available for distribution. Voters would be reluctant to see high political offices filled through objective tests of knowledge of history, political theory, urbanology, finance, and so on that one would normally consider as qualifications for those jobs, and rewarded with salaries commensurate with the power and responsibility they entail. The assumption in force is that formal meritocratic selection procedures and top-notch compensation would not increase the collective good. This assumption may be and probably is seriously wrong. The point, however, is that people are evidently prepared to be accepting of self-selected leaders; those who desperately *want* the office. We infer from their desire a strong motivation to perform the duties of the office assiduously.

Though we might prefer politics to be more meritocratic than it is, these examples show that we cannot assume that the introduction of a meritocratic reward system always increases the total amount of good available in a given domain. There are other ways to increase the total amount of good available. Compensation that follows historical patterns, even where it does not reflect merit, enables people and organizations to plan efficiently, and giving disproportionate rewards to the noisy and overlooking the complacent creates the background conditions for signalling genuinely unjust states of affairs, even if the noisy ones are no more meritorious than their quiet counterparts. And persons whose qualifications render them scarce in our world are awarded a substantial premium for their participation in cooperative enterprises regardless of the merit they are held to possess. This efficiency saves us time we would otherwise have to expend worrying about the definition of merit. The cleaner's success in purging the ward from staphylococcus bacteria with a mop and bucket might make more difference to patient mortality than the surgeon's super-

---

[24] Nancy Folbre, 'Roemer's Market Socialism: A Feminist Critique', 67.

skilled laser ablations. Yet we do not even attempt to reward the cleaner appropriately for her life-saving activities. For cleaners (and teachers of introductory logic courses) are plentiful, and surgeons (and philosophers of quantum mechanics) are not.[25] The incentive is not an incentive to perform better, but simply an incentive to choose one profession rather than another.

For structural reasons, then, it is all-things-considered good policy to award benefits that are not precisely keyed to merit and to tolerate their being awarded to others.[26] As Cohen argues, individuals who are correctly informed as to the large-scale consequences of their individual decisions to reward those whom they admire may change their values or reallocate their funds.[27] Increasingly sober views of executive compensation provide a recent illustration of the influence of information on values and preferences in this respect. In some cases, the total good available for distribution appears to be increased by the introduction of meritocratic incentives, but without being widely or evenly distributed. An increase in the total amount of good available may not mitigate widespread deprivations. Undoubtedly, extra competence is produced by a highly competitive medical system under which doctors compete to be top-rated highly paid specialists in prestige areas such as cardiology. Yet its benefits are consumed by relatively few persons. 'Community based' health care is offered by more numerous, lower-paid, and self-selected rather than specially enticed and competitively selected persons and arguably does a good job. Finally, there are good instrumental reasons to under-reward the meritorious by diverting the components of well-being to those identified as non-meritorious. The State recognizes that the industrial or post-industrial economy, which its laws and courts legitimate, is cyclical in its employment patterns. The least competent workers must be maintained during downturns so that

---

[25] Cohen presents some new arguments against the provision of incentives in Rawlsian fashion. *If You're an Egalitarian . . . ?*, pp.124 ff.

[26] Consider the following list of real, 'institutional' determinants of compensation: Formal qualifications earned, e.g. test scores, degrees, publications; natural advantages, e.g., beauty, height; seniority; prestige of work role, e.g., manual, white-collar; historical patterns of reward in the work location; scarcity/plenitude of role-fillers; degree of moral/legal responsibility for outcomes; history of labour disputes; return to investors; employer's overhead; funds lost, wasted, or diverted to corrupt purposes; state's overhead; state's provision for present and future non-earners. Their positive relationship to merit is either partial or non-existent.

[27] G. A. Cohen, 'Robert Nozick and Wilt Chamberlain: How Patterns Preserve Liberty'.

they are available as a reserve. And in a world in which either real merit is properly rewarded but very unevenly distributed, or evenly distributed but improperly rewarded, the frequency of violent revolution, terrorist acts, criminality, sabotage, slummification, and the risk of disease will be much lower when low- and non-earners are sustained and supported.

It might be suggested that, in a paraworld in which prudential motives operate powerfully, fewer transfers of goods from the well-off to the badly-off are required to assure that needs are met. And a world in which people are motivated to support themselves and do so is morally better, it might be urged, than a world in which they are the passive recipients of the bounty of others. Accordingly, transfers are not the only way to reduce variance. If we could induce people to overcome their bad habits, indolence, and demoralization, educate themselves, choose better leaders, and plan and save in ways that are more rational, we would not have to make transfers. If we apply the right kinds of pressures, it might be argued, incomes and holdings will come to exhibit less variance without the need for heavy-handed redistributive impositions.

In a zero-sum economic game, however, the end result will be the same, and there are not always clear advantages to reducing inequality by moral suasion v. direct transfer. Inculcating prudential behaviour in a resistant subpopulation may be coercive and costly. While exhortation and encouragement are free, or nearly so, and relatively non-invasive, they may have little effect on that subpopulation. Truly efficacious measures may turn out to be more expensive and psychologically distressing than providing the intransigently imprudent with the components of well-being directly. Further, redistribution often does foster prudential behaviour in the non-resistant. The possession of some of the components of well-being such as education, housing, and childcare with more in prospect tends to increase the motivation to defer gratification and assume responsibility.

In summary, it has never been shown that there is a strict and positive correlation between the depth and scope of a society's commitment to meritocratic principles and its ability to meet the needs of all its members. Rawls has been criticized for maintaining that 'the democratic interpretation of [the principle of equality of

opportunity and the difference principle] will not lead to a meritocratic society'.[28] Criticism of his opposition to the merit principle has,
however, been based chiefly on the affirmation of the principle, not
on a posteriori comparisons. A meaningful comparison might consider two populations in which the variance in merit (however it was
established) was the same, one of which was wage-compressed and
the other not, controlling for variables unrelated to compression per
se such as military expenditure and corruption. The aim would be to
determine whether the 'historical' hypothesis that meritocracies have
less objective deprivation was true.

   Instrumental arguments presupposing need priority for the deployment of merit principles, then, are no more powerful considered in
isolation than arguments from pure entitlement or desert that ignore
need. Given that the amount of resources available for distribution
can be viewed as a dependent variable rather than a fixed quantity, the
distribution system selected is not the only factor that determines it.
The quantity R of the components or preconditions of well-being
that can be made available in a given world is a function of many
interacting variables, including its temperature and vegetation, the
food preferences of its inhabitants, their muscular strength and motivational levels. A given reward structure may be one of these
interacting variables, enabling us to speculate that:

$$Wa\, f(x_1,\ y_1,\ z_1 \dots) \ = \ 1R$$

$$Wb\, f(x_2,\ y_2,\ z_2 \dots) \ = \ 2R$$

where Wa and Wb are distinct worlds and the x and y variables
represent different conditions that influence the availability of the
equal 'underground' or potential resources of a world. Wb in the
example has twice as many resources available for distribution as Wa.
For some pair of worlds taking the values $1R$ and $2R$, the *only*
difference between them might consist in the presence and absence
respectively of a given merit principle. But we cannot give a *general*
answer to the question: 'How much does the employment of a merit
principle—e.g., one that rewards exactly proportionately to merit—
contribute to the size of R?' It depends on the world. In a world in
which there is no variance in merit, it will contribute nothing; in a

[28] Rawls, *Theory of Justice*, 91.

236 MERIT PRINCIPLES IN DISTRIBUTIVE JUSTICE

world in which there is considerable variance but the population is
not moved by monetary incentives, it will also contribute nothing.[29]
In a world in which ripe fruit is easy to pluck from the tree and desires
are few, it may contribute nothing as well.

Whether, given the conditions of *our* world, we should prefer to
see more or fewer meritocratic policies in operation depends on the
potential resources it contains and how long they will last, how long
we want them to last, the distribution of merit in the population
under consideration, on the motivation and emotional tendencies
of its members, and on their signalling and signal-reading abilities.
The level of variance in well-being in the three types of worlds is
independent of their meritocratic or antimeritocratic character type.
A meritocratic W_1 world in which everyone's degree of merit
happened to be the same would have low variance of outcomes,
but so would some W_2 and W_3 worlds. And a state of high variance in
well-being may obtain in worlds of any type. While a W_1 world in
which merit is distributed equally and signalled reliably would distribute the components of well-being equally and would give no one
cause for complaint, a W_1 world in which there are significant
numbers of persons who possess less merit than others, or in which
merit is signalled very unreliably and is difficult to detect, has disadvantages for both the meritorious and the non-meritorious.

7.3. Detecting and Assessing Merit

Although Hayek's version of the just protocol requires individuals to
produce goods and services that appear valuable to gain rewards, he
presumably does not regard it as just to reward individuals who only
appear to be producing valuable goods and services. Only some
purveyors of illusion are considered to be justly rewarded even
under the most libertarian of regimes. An evening at the theatre is
good, but not an Initial Public Offering for a fake technology.

---

[29] If the value of R supervenes on assignments to the variables, there has to be some additional
qualitative difference between the two worlds if $f(x, y, z \ldots) = 2R$ in both cases but the worlds have
different reward schemes. The difference might simply correspond to the inhabitants' views of
what constitutes acceptable body size, or their adaptation to a coarser diet, or their ethical beliefs.
I take this to be, generally, Cohen's point against Rawls's instrumental defense of incentives in *If You're
an Egalitarian . . .*, n. 28.

The contrary claim that the merit–desert intuition is indifferent as between real and apparent merit can be tested by rewriting the principle as follows:

> As long as A_1 is *believed* to work harder than A_2 and/or is *perceived* as having more talent enabling her to produce more goods and services of perceived higher quality, whether or not she actually does, A_1 deserves to enjoy a higher level of well-being than A_2. It would be unjust if A_2 were to obtain as much as or more than A_1.

Written in this form, the claim is clearly unacceptable. A wine producer who accumulates a fortune before it is discovered that his synthetic product is fake and fraudulently labelled is viewed as deserving of going to jail. It is considered irrelevant that consumers previously estimated his talents as a vintner to be considerable, were willing to purchase the product, and initially deemed it of high quality. It would be implausible to insist that, while the consumers' preferences changed after they acquired new information about the wine and they no longer desired it, the producer is entitled to the proceeds from what he was able to market before they acquired their new preferences.

Accordingly, if the error rate in detecting actual merit (in the simplest case, ranking two candidates in order) is, say, 50 per cent, it may be *true* that the more meritorious deserve more of the components of well-being than the less meritorious, but the corresponding distributive *principle* will nevertheless be unusable. For, if the error rate is this high, then, no matter what anyone's intentions and efforts are, we cannot ensure that merit *is* rewarded or make our world a W_1 world. In this case, the insistence that the principle is fundamental serves only to promote a false sense of rectitude.

But surely we take great care to ensure that our selection procedures are just and that the tests and competitions we use to assess relative merit really do so? While we might sometimes fail to get the ranking right, it seems incoherent to suppose that our merit-assaying methods are irremediably no better than chance. One might be sceptical that the winner of a tennis tournament on some given occasion is really the best player, but the sceptical statement that, generally speaking, tennis tournaments fail to result in rankings of tennis-playing excellence that are better than chance seems not just

false, but impossible. One can reject facile statements such as 'Tennis-playing excellence is whatever tennis tournaments discriminate' while still insisting that the sceptical statement could not be true under any conditions. To vary a familiar line of argument, if a sequence of presented actions and evaluation decisions in some possible world does not do a reliable job of ranking tennis players, it is not a 'tennis tournament'. This confidence is however unjusti-fied. There are at least four difficulties with the deployment of a merit principle in real-world contexts:

   (*a*) Sweep limitations
   (*b*) Misattribution
   (*c*) Custom and convention
   (*d*) Mimicry

   (a) *Sweep limitations*

To qualify as a bona fide tennis tournament, a sorting procedure need only do a reliable job of ranking the tennis players who entered the competition. So it is easy to imagine, not only a world in which tennis tournaments fail to result in rankings of tennis players that are better than chance, but also a world in which the rankings are considerably worse than chance. All that is required for the condition to be realized is that the vast majority of excellent players do not take part in the tournaments. This can happen for various reasons: they do not know that a tournament is occurring, they do not have the wherewithal to get to the tournament, or they lack information about their own level of ability. It might be objected that showing up for the tournament is a component of tennis-playing merit; the lazy player who stays in bed or misses the bus to the match is less good as a tennis player, but this claim has little credibility outside some very specific circumstances.

   In any selection procedure, we do not want to know who is the best in the world for the position being filled. We want to know who can be plausibly designated as the best, given our unwillingness to spend more than a certain amount of time and trouble collecting and evaluating candidates. There are potentially more of the meritorious in many categories than there are slots to fit them into. Every high

school has persons just as good at what they do as Bob Dylan and Anaïs Nin, but, unfortunately for them, the need for persons in these roles is somewhat limited.

(b) *Misattribution*

Merit is customarily ascribed to individuals in a way at odds with the real determinants of success. The nomination and cultivation of talent and the incitement to effort are optional cultural work in which the subject, his helpers, and his competitors all participate. Her mother loves music or hates it, and the prodigy's talent waxes or wanes accordingly, though not necessarily just in the way one might expect. Talent and effort attract notice only when they are coordinated, and their coordination depends on external opportunities; the talent has usually to be noticed by someone other than the talent-possessor in order for the possessor to receive instruction and the means to develop it. So, although we tend to regard the thanks given by the successful to parents, spouses, managers, editors, etc. as pro forma and conventional, in fact a given display of coordinated talent and effort is attributable only by convention to the one deemed deserving of the reward. When merit is not displayed, it is likely that circumstances and other persons did not cooperate. Thus, the same 'intrinsic' quantity of coordinated talent and effort will lead to different outcomes depending on circumstances, and if the rewarders do not adjust their judgements accordingly, their rewards are, by the merit-desert principle, unjust.

Further, as social scientists have shown repeatedly, humans consistently overestimate their ability to judge performance and promise objectively.[30] In attempting to determine who contributed most to a joint task (and, correspondingly, who failed to pull their weight) and should be rewarded for it, observers are biased in favour of the contributor they most like and admire for extraneous reasons and biased against the contributor they least like and admire for extraneous reasons.[31] Beliefs regarding performance are adjusted in order to

---

[30] On evaluation biases, see Richard Nisbett and Lee Ross, *Human Inference: Strategies and Shortcoming of Social Judgement* and Virginia Valian, *Why So Slow?*, 125–44.

[31] Lerner, *Belief in a Just World*, 34.

satisfy the preference that good things happen to people judged to be good overall.

(c) *Custom and convention*

It seems obvious to us that some people are better than others at some things because they have an aptitude for them and apply themselves to them, and also obvious that it is better in our world to have an aptitude for some things (e.g., plasma physics) than others (e.g., weaving lanyards). The more meritorious are those who are better at the things it is better to be better at. Yet we recognize that there is a strong element of conventionality or historicity in the determination of what is a valuable production. It would be unsatisfactory to define a talent as any competency that can generate substantial monetary rewards since the sense of 'can' is unclear. Any well-honed practice could, in some possible world, generate rewards, but some talents, such as skill at direction-finding in the desert, or knowing the names of thousands of plants and animals, are such that, in our world, they cannot attract large monetary rewards. And contra Hayek, meritorious performances, according to consensus notions of reality, are not concerned with the provision of the most utilitarian necessities; the butcher and baker do not enjoy the most lucrative positions in our society. Those who gratify our non-utilitarian tastes are best rewarded, notably athletes, entertainers, popular authors, and theorists of the arcane and other-worldly. The meritorious name of God is more frequently mentioned in connection with astrophysics than in connection with plumbing or needlework.

(d) *Mimicry*

In our world, rewards are given on the basis of the principle of comparative advantage, applied by a judge who has some discretion over the size of the reward. Consider a simple employer–employee relationship. The employee's earnings reflect what the employer believes or perceives the worker's marginal contribution to the enterprise to be. We might suppose that comparative advantage at least approximates real merit, and that employers are reliable judges of comparative advantage. The selection procedures of the reward-

givers are aimed at producing reality-reflecting rankings. Problems requiring insight are asked on standardized tests and interviews probe for weaknesses and deficiencies in a candidate's knowledge. The objects being judged in such situations are not inert, however, like tomatoes being evaluated at an agricultural fair. The potential employee is a strategizing human being, whose aim it is to achieve the rewards of being perceived as meritorious whether or not he is so. The candidates in a meritocracy are each participants in an arms race against their reward-givers. The competence to *mimic* merit—to display the surface features of merit that will facilitate one's selection—may be obtainable more cheaply and quickly than actual merit, frustrating the judge's best efforts and forcing them to devise newer and more subtle tests.[32] In such strategic situations, there is no reason to believe a priori that reward-givers have a faculty for detecting mimicry that is superior to the candidates' (and their allies') faculty for mimicking, just as there is no reason to suppose a priori that the predator's ability to detect tasty butterflies that merely look poisonous should outstrip the prey's ability to engage in successful deception. Successful mimicry—the ability falsely to appear more competent, experienced, creative, and promising—than the competition must be pervasive in meritocracies, for the greater the rewards offered for merit, the greater the incentive to deception. To make the distribution of the components of well-being highly dependent on attributes that not only can be simulated but that we have excellent reason to believe are often simulated is a policy that cannot be supposed to ensure just outcomes.

As Hume remarked, 'So great is the uncertainty of merit, both from its natural obscurity, and from the self-conceit of each individual, that no determinate rule of conduct could ever follow from it.'[33] Nevertheless, it is just as much a distortion to maintain that no activities and products are really meritorious as it is to maintain that whatever is deemed so or is socially rewarded is so. Rawls asserts that 'there is no set of agreed ends by reference to which the potential social contributions of an individual could be assessed'.[34] This seems

---

[32] Examples of simulation include 'indicator chasing' and the results of 'professionalism seminars' and 'grooming'.

[33] Quoted by Hayek, *Law, Legislation and Liberty*, 62.

[34] Rawls, *Political Liberalism*, 276.

correct, but the observation that we do not have perfect unanimity and that we do have substantial disagreement does not exclude overlapping consensus on one hand and the meritocratic pursuit of discrete sets of values on the other. *Sub specie aeternitatis*, merit appears to be painted or projected onto persons and things in a way that is intrinsically relational and underdetermined by their intrinsic properties. The same can be said, though, of all valuation terms; the atomic constitution of two pictures does not determine which is beautiful. A reasonable person will accept that there are more and less meritorious enterprises and productions, recognizing simply that our ability to make reliable judgements—judgements we would continue to endorse even after severe critical analysis of our methods and assumptions—is much worse than we normally assume it to be and that we are subject to both random and systematic error.

7.4. Objective Deprivation and Thresholds

According to the results of the last three sections, merit exists, though our capacity to detect it reliably is defective. Further, we have some reasons, both instrumental and non-instrumental, to endorse some version of a merit principle, as well as some instrumental and non-instrumental reasons to ignore merit in making distributions. It is now time to return to the original dilemma.

As noted in Section 7.1, merit priority is universally agreed to be false under some interpretations of the term 'need.' Despite occasional claims to the effect that it is illogical or irrational not to schedule rewards on the basis of merit,[35] no credible political theorist subscribes to merit priority under every possible construal of need. Political theorists agree that basic needs, the requisites for biological survival such as fresh drinking water, medical care, shelter, and adequate caloric intake ought to be met universally, whatever else is done with the world's resources. The need principle is not, in fact, deployed even under this basic interpretation, since funds that could, in principle, be used to meet needs are used instead to reward merit.

---

[35] Nozick appears to find a logical connection between merit and reward, assuming the premiss (which he takes as self-evident) that 'people are entitled to their natural assets'. See *Anarchy, State and Utopia*, 225–6.

Yet commitment to the principle is not lacking in the sense that no credible theorist has posited that there is no prima facie right to survival on the part of an already-born person, or any duty to assist, and that the world as we observe it to be is just. This is tantamount to agreeing that we ought to follow a protocol of need priority at least with respect to basic needs. Consequently, even if the use of some form of merit principle is acknowledged to be just—and it has not yet been established that this is so—only a combined protocol such as the following with need priority at its foundation can be considered just.[36]

> *Combined Proposal*
> In any condition R of the world that generates a surplus, re-sources will be directed first to the meeting of needs instantiating U. The surplus, above and beyond what is required to do so, is to be distributed according to perceived merit that is determined in competitions that are as controlled, and free of bias as it is possible at any time to make them, thereby instantiating M. If no surplus is available, U should be instantiated.

The interesting controversy, accordingly, concerns the proper inter-pretation of the concept of 'need' as it appears in the statements of merit priority and need priority. For we do face a choice (or, more strictly, an array of choices) between adopting a minimal and adopting a maximal conception of well-being. For any given level of resources R, which protocol is preferable?

(a) Define the concept of 'need' strictly. Satisfy needs univer-sally and then distribute the relatively large amount that may be left on the basis of merit, with some fine-tuning to reduce undesirable incentive effects.

(b) Define the concept of 'need' generously. Satisfy needs uni-versally and then distribute the relatively small amount that may be left on the basis of merit, with some fine-tuning to increase desirable incentive effects.

---

[36] As is stated e.g. by Roemer, 'None shall consume luxuries while deprivation for others continues to exist', *Theories of Distributive Justice*, 202; and in David Braybrooke's Principle of Precedence, which states that some persons can be required to give up goods they do not need, though not goods they do need, to satisfy others' needs, 'Concept of Needs', 61. The question what to do when radical scarcity does not obtain is not, however, addressed by them.

The strict conception of need refers to the biological requirements of survival—or what are sometimes termed 'first-tier' goods—calories, water, clothes, shelter, and treatment for acute infections and chronic debilitating conditions. It is unclear, however, why one would recognize a natural entitlement to first-tier, but only to first-tier, goods, unless one believed that so long as people are provided with first-tier goods they are almost always able to construct a decent life for themselves. Assurance on this score is lacking: many humans endure just such a marginal state of existence, scarcely preferable to not being alive at all. As observed in Chapter 6, a decent human life requires a 'second tier' of goods: some variety and pleasure in food, drink, furnishings or ornaments, the opportunity to engage in meaningful work and to advance one's knowledge and understanding, along with opportunities for affiliation, mobility, some choice of mates, and freedom from harassment and derogation. The generous conception of need, then, incorporates second-tier as well as first-tier goods.

A fundamentally unjust world is one in which it is the case both that objective deprivation—the failure to possess the known and presumptive requisites of a decent human life—is widespread and that successful merit-mimics, or only a small subgroup of the truly meritorious, enjoy access to the doubtful and speculative components of well-being. The image of the morally corrupt state embodies both features. And this suggests an approach to the solution of the original choice problem.

Having already accepted need priority on the basis of the obvious unacceptability of merit priority, we should choose the generous conception of need for two reasons. First, the strict conception, according to which only basic biological needs have an automatic right to satisfaction, is arbitrary since it is too weak to support the notion of a decent human life. Second, our ability to detect real as opposed to apparent merit and to reward the entire human population for merit is so constrained that it is appropriate to limit the amount available for merit awards.

Accordingly, in a just world containing more than adequate resources to meet them, the satisfaction of known and presumptive needs will be independent from meritorious performance. Merit may nevertheless permissibly entail the award of additional goods and states that persons believe will benefit them, whether or not the

possession of these things will necessarily render them objectively better off, effectively matching the dubious aspects of merit determination with the dubious aspects of the pursuit of the good life. Perceived merit can entitle us to rewards in the form of access to the speculative and doubtful, though not the known and presumptive components of well-being. For if we can know that it is just for differential perceived merit to entail *some* differential access to the components of well-being, and if there is no rationale for allowing it to entail differential access to the known or presumptive components of well-being, the only remaining possibility is that it is just for it to entail differential access to some other category of the components of well-being, namely the doubtful and speculative.

The argument for rewarding merit cannot rest on either intrinsic or instrumental defences of merit principles; these have been shown to be too weak to support even a combined protocol. It can only rest on a preference, based on the recognition that there is some degree of virtue in those inconclusive defences, for merit principles over rival distribution principles. For, in a condition in which we have more than is required to meet first- and second-tier needs universally, the five alternatives available are the following:

(1) Distribute the surplus at random.
(2) Distribute the surplus to historically privileged groups and individuals.
(3) Distribute the surplus equally.
(4) Distribute the surplus according to a Rawlsian ranking in which the relatively worst-off are first, and the relatively best-off are last.
(5) Distribute the surplus in whatever way maximizes future surpluses.

The use of a merit principle seems preferable to each of 1–5, once needs have been met. It is preferable to the other proposals since it makes some concession, rather than none, to the force of the merit-desert intuition and to the observation that the introduction of meritocratic principles can sometimes improve overall well-being.

Egalitarians who favour protocol 3 maintain that the whole remainder of R ought to be divided equally, once needs are satisfied. But it is unclear why, if the satisfaction of a need can be set at a generous level,

the purely formal preference for equality ought entirely to override a merit principle. While the Rawlsian protocol in 4 is appealing in a condition of scarcity, it is unclear why, once needs are universally met, the relatively worst-off, who are no longer in a condition of objective deprivation, should continue to be favoured. The protocol would permit a small number of the least hard-working and competent to enjoy the most subtle and complex pleasures of civilization if it turned out that the relatively worst-off person (who might already have an entirely decent life) was thereby made better off.

Protocols 1 and 2 might be permitted to operate in a marginal way in a just world to gratify needs other than the need for social justice—lotteries for the sake of entertainment, tax exemptions for the monarch for the sake of feudal deference—but they cannot be considered as principles *of* social justice. And the protocol in 5 merely postpones and so evades the question.

Once needs are generously met, departures from equality require no special triggering condition. Provided the known and presumptive components of well-being are provided to all, there can be no objection in the name of justice to allowing those deemed meritorious (a few misidentified and mimics among them) their racehorses, diamond tiaras, fancy chronometers, 200-foot yachts, and other such items, as well as opportunities to use expensive cyclotrons, collect rare books, or construct artificial paradises of their own making, provided we are doing as well as we can with respect to correcting the known deficiencies of our assay methods. The merit-desert principle can be sustained with this amendment.

Several objections can still be made to the combined proposal as interpreted and justified above:

(1) The protocol is exigent. It requires that, in a general 'levelling down', the meritorious accept significant reductions to meet the overwhelming needs of the non-meritorious. There will be little or no surplus to distribute on the basis of merit if needs, generously defined, are met.

(2) The protocol is self-defeating. Only by refusing to meet the known and presumptive needs of the comparatively non-meritorious and by withholding from them the requisites of a decent life, can we stimulate them to develop meritorious

behaviour that will allow them possession of the known and presumptive components of well-being by increasing the total good available.

(3) The proposal is inconsistent. Access to the doubtful and speculative components of well-being consistent with that of one's social reference group is one of the known and necessary components of well-being.

Objection 1 is commonly heard, but not very compelling. Suppose that the level at which it is possible to enjoy a good human life, is set, generously, at 10 per cent of the world's combined GNPs. My rough-and-ready calculations in Chapter 5 suggested that thirty million top income earners (who are not of course the most meritorious persons) could bring about this result by redistributing less than 10 per cent of their salaries. This is hardly 'levelling down'. It reflects a curious conception of the distribution of merit; namely, the idea that there is a tiny meritorious elite suspended above a huge utility sink of persons who are a net drain on the productive capacities of society.

Objection 2 is relevant in a condition in which potential resources are enough to meet needs but in which the condition of the world is such that they are very hard to get 'out of the ground' and the motivation to work is low. The hypothesis advanced is that, in all worlds in which non-adjustable social, psychological, and material conditions are similar to ours, a world whose regime withholds first- and second-tier goods in order to reward those at the top of the perceived merit scale better with third-tier goods will contain *fewer* persons whose first- and second-tier needs are not met. There might be unknown 'laws of nature' in virtue of which this hypothesis turned out to be true, but it cannot be seen to be true on mere inspection. It is rendered doubtful by data indicating that societies with large income variance also have a good deal of objective deprivation.[37] If, contrary to expectations, the hypothesis

---

[37] There is historical and current evidence that rapid growth that increases the Gini coefficient of inequality induces not only relative but, for the worst-off sectors, absolute deprivation. 'Growing numbers of people after 1780 could not afford food', according to Timothy M. Smeeding and Peter Gottschalk, 'Cross-National Income Inequality: How Great Is It and What Can We Learn from It?', 5. The USA has the largest per capita income in the world; inhabitants in the lowest 10th decile of income distribution are nevertheless 'at severe risk of poor health, subsequent poor education performance and diminished achievement'. Ibid. 18. The USA also has the greatest real income inequality amongst the seventeen OECD countries studied.

were true, it would be more reasonable to take it as implying that the realization of a just world is hampered by an adverse environmental condition, than to take it as implying that justice requires punishing the deprived.

Objection 3 confuses the task of designing a distribution protocol with the more complex task of designing a redistribution protocol for a world in which persons have pasts and memories and expectations based in their pasts. Consideration here is restricted to a set of individuals who are not yet fixed in social circles and classes and who have no memories or expectations. No one can suffer a psychologically distressing 'fall' out of her former socio-economic class or claim to be made objectively badly off by suffering depression or demoralization on that account. The design of a just redistribution protocol is an important but distinct task that has to be guided by a decision as to which distribution protocol is most just.

7.5. Statistical Equality of Outcomes Required

A further objection to the combined protocol is that it is too permissive of invidious discrimination. Under the combined protocol, everyone undergoes risk, the risk of being born with too little by way of native endowments to have access to the speculative and doubtful components of well-being. Individuals undergo further risk on account of the gap between real and perceived merit, for their merits may not be appreciated. Now, life is risky in many ways and a just world does not need to exclude all forms of risk, but only unjust risk. So we might wonder what is required for the risk of diminished access to the speculative and doubtful to be fairly distributed.

Recall that our ordinary conception of merit floats between a conception of merit as a special expertise that happens, contingently, to command respect and to attract rewards, and as an objectively valuable attribute. It is clear that some groups—characterized by language, nationality, gender, 'race', or other features—possess more of the special expertise that commands respect and attracts rewards: there are more Japanese physicists than Congolese. But is it conceivable that some groups have more merit, considered now

as an objectively valuable attribute, than others? Suppose persons possessing a certain rare blood type have discovered a set of obscure tasks at which they excel and which others with more common blood types can barely perform. Under what conditions can the rare blood group claim to possess more by way of humanly valuable qualities than other people? Unless the majority values equally performance on those tasks they cannot for some reason do, it is difficult to see why the members of the rare blood group should be considered object- ively meritorious. Of course we can attempt to fix the reference in this world of 'objectively meritorious attributes' and then project a world in which the majority, for some reason, lacks them and does not care about them and a small elite cares about them and possesses them, but this does not undermine the point. Though not everyone is personally musical, musicality can be regarded as an objectively meritorious attribute only to the extent that competence with respect to and interest in music is well distributed through all human popu- lations. It follows that a quality like 'intelligence' can only be con- sidered objectively valuable if intelligence is well distributed and consistently prized throughout human populations. If this is not the case, greater intelligence does not entitle anyone to a better life; if, however, intelligence is distributed and valued across human popula- tions, Nagel's suggestion that a country that rewards the intelligent better than the unintelligent is more unjust than a country that practises sexual or racial discrimination seems unconvincing.[38] On this view, valuing white skin over dark or masculinity over femininity is no worse than valuing intelligence over dull-wittedness.

Suppose, in a world rich in resources, the combined protocol is the basis of distributions. We can envision a condition of the world—call it non-correlation—where membership in a particular group— ethnic, linguistic, age-bracketed, etc.—carries no predictive power with respect to outcomes where the possession of all three tiers of goods is concerned. Under non-correlation, some persons of true worthiness will be edged out by those simulating merit, some will receive referred credit for the competency and effort exercised by others, some will benefit from historically conditioned definitions of merit that have little rational basis, and others will just fail to be in the

---

[38] Nagel, *Mortal Questions*, 99. Nagel denies that statistical equality as between racial groups and genders with respect to outcomes is a requirement of justice, *Equality and Partiality*, 89–90.

right place at the right time, missing the whole competition. At the same time, membership in any group will not increase or reduce the risk of failing to obtain possession of the components of well-being. This world can be considered just, with the error rate of its meritocratic procedures approximately matching the error rate of individuals' judgements of what actually improves their lives.

We can also envision a condition of the world in which degree of risk is strongly correlated with properties such as ethnicity, gender, parental income, place of residence, and so on. This world is inevitably unjust. For, if we are considering merit as an objective property, statistical inequalities of outcome among different groups can only arise through discrimination, i.e., failure of merit assays or equal social investment to develop talent, with respect to particular groups. If, on the other hand, we are considering merit as special expertise contingently possessed by some groups of humans, inequality of outcomes does not imply discrimination, but it does imply an arbitrary conception of human excellence that ought to confer no particular entitlements. This is not to say that every instance of statistical inequality of outcomes in worlds like ours is morally intolerable. It is not morally intolerable that African-American basketball players are more respected and rewarded than Japanese basketball players. In a just world, however, statistical inequalities ought to balance out from group to group.

To be sure, any individual's membership in a reference group can be construed as a matter of luck. It might be argued that the distinction between the correlated world and the non-correlated world is accordingly illusory. Both are equally just, for the risk that any individual assumes, prior to his chance assignment to one or another category of person, is equal. Those who take merit priority seriously are perhaps disposed to regard luck as a force that can be ignored on the grounds that it does not discriminate. On this view, while the world would be in some sense better if luck were incapable of rendering the fates of two persons of equal merit different, the existence of good and bad fortune does not affect the choice of a distribution scheme, since everyone is equally subject to luck and since we cannot by definition control it. Even when luck makes the outcomes of two persons different by casting them into two different reference classes, we can and must ignore it. And it might be argued

further that, just as no individual can be made objectively badly off by suffering a decline in the availability of one of the speculative and doubtful components of well-being relative to others, provided he continues to enjoy the known and necessary components of well-being, no group can be made so. But the recognition that luck is ineradicable and that some percentage of both good and bad fortune is undeserved is itself a reason for insisting on some degree of compression in outcomes.[39] It does not follow from the truism that no one is invulnerable to luck that everyone is equally vulnerable to chance events; the well-off are often insulated by their reserves. If it is right to compensate for undeserved misfortune, it may also be right to subtract from undeserved reward. And this point applies not only to the luck of events but, as Rawls argued, to the luck of situation and endowment. Justice does not consist merely in the assumption of equal risk in an unassigned position, and the argument that what is not necessarily wrong for an individual cannot be wrong for a group fails for related reasons.

Consider a group of free-living Greens in a condition in which known and presumptive needs are universally satisfied. The Greens pursue the speculative and doubtful components of well-being in competitive encounters, along with a group of Reds, with equal, though limited, success for members of both groups. Some environmental change occurs, inducing mild scarcity, and the speculative and doubtful components of well-being as well as the known and presumptive components grow less accessible. Under a new regime, the Greens are persuaded, or persuade one another, or are recruited to farm the land for the Reds so that the known and presumptive components can be supplied to all. The Greens cease to take part in meritocratic competitions, or their competencies come to be viewed, conventionally, as non-meritorious, or they lose the ability to signal merit when faced with competition from merit simulators. Consequently, the Greens renounce, or are required to give up, or simply lose the inclination for the further pursuit of the speculative and doubtful components of well-being, though all their lower-tier

---

[39] The view that radical contingency ought to lead to compression in *judgements*, i.e. to non-judgementalism, was advanced (though not defended) by Nagel in 'Moral Luck', in *Mortal Questions*, 24–38. This is obviously a different conception of moral luck from Williams's; one would not for example expect Williams to favour compression of outcomes.

needs continue to be met, and this to the same high standard as before.

Here, the mere fact of a discrepancy between the condition of the Greens and that of the Reds seems to render the situation unjust, not just in view of the losses of the Greens of their former status, of which they may retain some memory. The burden of meeting known and presumptive needs ought, it seems, to require equal relinquishment of the pursuit of the speculative and doubtful components of well-being by the Greens and the Reds.

Such a scenario would actually be realized in a society that denied access to the speculative and doubtful components of well-being to members of certain identifiable categories by running tournaments to which they were unable to come, by misattributing their successes to others, by deeming their productions non-meritorious, and by accepting fewer mimics from their category than from its complement through the exercise of greater vigilance. For such a society might do a better job of meeting known and presumptive needs universally than a rival system by selectively diverting labour towards agricultural production, childcare, and domestic maintenance. This society would be unjust, not because some persons would enjoy third-tier goods that others did not—for this result is tolerable when it happens 'by chance'—but because some groups would enjoy an advantage in their pursuit.

Even in the event that the known and necessary components of well-being, generously conceived, can all be furnished for less than the cost equivalent to entire social product, the proposal that merit can justly influence distributions of the remainder is still flawed. For a merit principle to have a valid role in distributive justice, even as a complementary principle, human capacities to define, attribute, discriminate, and determine merit must be rendered sufficiently reliable that the threat of the exercise of privilege by some groups and the assumption of excessive risk by others is less than it is under alternative systems in which the realization of M is not an explicit aim.

Consider the position of the Count Raymond de la Cisternas in Matthew Lewis's novel *The Monk*. The young Raymond is setting off in disguise as a 'private gentleman' and receives some words of advice from his father:

Tis true that as the Conde de las Cisternas you would have been received with open arms: and your youthful vanity might have felt gratified by the attentions showered on you from all sides. At present much will depend upon yourself.... You must lay yourself out to please. You must labour to gain the approbation of those, to whom you are presented: They who would have courted the friendship of the Conde de las Cisternas, will have no interest in finding out the merits, or bearing patiently with the faults of Alphonso d'Alvarada.[40]

A person seeking to make his way in the world is judged by others—by members of the public, by authorities, and by official assessors of merit. Dark-skinned people, small or short people, those with certain foreign accents, strange mannerisms, or high voices, are, like the disguised Raymond, dressed as beings of lesser capability in our world, and they must endeavour, despite their unprepossessing garments, to win the approbation of those in a position to help them advance in life. Few persons vote against, fail to select, dismiss, or ignore someone because he or she is a member of a group they do not, for irrational reasons, like. It happens nevertheless that when merit is assessed, some categories of persons do not fare well. It is not necessary for them to fail that someone in a position of authority is against them; it is sufficient that there are excellent reasons for the selector to be in favour of someone else. The noblemen Raymond meets need not discriminate against him if they fail to assist him on his way. But they may have no interest, as his father warns him, in determining his merits and no reason to overlook his faults. If he tries to impress his capabilities on them, he may, in his humble clothing, appear merely froward, and if he gives way to frustration or loses his temper when his underlying noble qualities pass unnoticed, he may be judged even more unsuitable.

It is easy to say 'Not once have I harmed someone because I thought their race, or sex or nationality inferior, and if others of my sort have done so in the past it is not for me to pay their debts.' But one might interrogate oneself as follows: Amongst those on behalf of whom I exerted myself, how many were not of the dominant classes? Amongst those whose faults I bore with patiently and whose merits I troubled to find out, how many of them were?

[40] Matthew Lewis, *The Monk*, 95–6.

8

Moral Equality and 'Natural' Subordination

'When [a man] is in a cooperative and benevolent relation with a woman, his theme is the principle of abstract equality; the concrete inequality to which he can otherwise attest is not posited.'[1] Simone de Beauvoir's remark has not lost its pertinence with regard to modern moral discourse. General moral theory discusses the obligations and entitlements of persons without regard to sex or gender. This discursive posture may express the presumption that between the ordinary run of philosophers and women there exists a cooperative and benevolent relationship. Or it can be interpreted as evasion.

Aristotle, Rousseau, and Kant, amongst others, took note of the division of labour and modes of life between the sexes. They considered the status of men and women relative to one another to pose interesting questions and believed themselves responsible for explaining the special obligations of women and the special privileges of men. Where the old philosophers explained women's subordination as best they could—and it would not have occurred to them to do so by reference to women's preferences or choices, as opposed to nature's plan for them—modern theorists of distributive justice are disinclined to take either an analytical or an evaluative position on the character of women's lives.[2] Whether it is motivated by unease, uncertainty, or indifference, or entirely innocent, this is an oversight. The old philosophers were right to appreciate that men and women stood in a curious relationship to one another where the distribution of the components of well-being was concerned. We should aim to

---

[1] Simone de Beauvoir, *Le Deuxième Sexe*, i. 27–8.
[2] See the criticisms of Susan Moller Okin, *Justice, Gender, and the Family*, 9, also Richard Rorty's remarks in his review of Annette Baier's *Moral Prejudice*, 'Why can't a man be more like a woman?', 3.

recover their interest in explaining and evaluating this noteworthy feature of our world and its relationship to our underlying natures. We need not reproduce their descriptive errors or their unacceptable prescriptions.

8.1. Male–Female Relations in Moral Philosophy

It might seem that the reassignment of the topic of women's social inequality to sociology and gender studies has a benign explanation. Moral and political theory are concerned with relations between rational, reflective agents, not between persons occupying certain social roles. Women, one might think, are included as moral subjects in all reasonings concerning justice and goodness and have precisely the same obligations and entitlements as men.

Yet the claim that gender relations are not a subtopic of distributive justice because women are full moral and political agents is unsatisfactory. The fact that women are rational and reflective and are now widely recognized as such (assuming this was ever seriously doubted) does not entail that existing relations are just, or lie outside the purview of philosophy proper. We do not regard the rich or the poor, the gifted or the ordinary, as irrational and unreflective. We are certain that they have the same rights and obligations as 'ourselves'. Yet we are willing to speak of their interests as a class, and to ask specific questions of the form: What should the wealthy relinquish to ensure a given level of well-being in the poor? What limits to their aspirations must the less talented accept in a spirit of realism?

It might be ventured that, while we know that the interests of the rich and the poor are in conflict, we know the interests of men and women to be in harmony. But empiricists will be curious as to how this harmony of interests has been established. Are not males and females genotypically and phenotypically distinct subclasses that constitute necessary and exploitable resources for one another, which they cannot ignore? The existence of another sex that it can recognize by means of sensory cues is a feature of every dimorphic animal's environment, a potential resource that its genes are disposed to employ to further their own advantage. Literature and the media of popular culture bring into relief the combination of fascination and

indifference, dependency and antagonism that characterizes social relations between the sexes. Few of us enjoy, in this realm, the substantial psychological reserves that make an easy Humean grace a component of our demeanour at all times.

Where subhumans are concerned, we cannot make too much of how the two sexes treat each other, however solicitous of the welfare of individual animals we might be. Each will hold its own, and if one sex has a shorter lifespan, or eats less or receives more wounds than the other, this is not a matter of moral concern anymore than it is if female praying mantises eat male praying mantises. It might seem that we should take the same hard-headed attitude towards the statistical inequalities of modern societies. If an inequality is not caused in large measure by the actions of, and produces no advantages for, a favoured class that they ought to forgo, it isn't a subject for the theory of justice. Being born without an arm is usually, though not always, an unfortunate condition. Yet others do not benefit from the condition and one cannot claim that it is unjust.

Being born a female might be considered just such a natural misfortune. Though it is not as grievous as being born without an arm, being born in this condition reduces one's chances of becoming a significant and personally recognized contributor to civilized endeavours. At the same time, it exposes one to excess risk of beatings, insolvency, and social disgrace. This can be considered mere bad moral luck. Everyone, a philosopher might muse, undergoes the same risk of being born male or female. There is no reason to think that men in enlightened countries take deliberate steps to worsen the condition of women relative to what it would be otherwise in order to benefit themselves or that they tolerate culpable letting-happen knowing that it makes their lives more pleasant than they would otherwise be.

It is nevertheless far from clear that men as a group do not benefit unintentionally from actions and policies that reduce opportunities for female participation and that render women's lives more dangerous in some respects than men's are. While the effects of natural disasters, like the downstream effects of transactions not under the control of single agents, do not incriminate those who ignore them of profiteering, they can incriminate these persons of moral neglect. If gender inequality involves real deprivations, then, whether or not it

is, in some respects, the result of a natural misfortune, we have some obligation to remedy the deprivations at some cost to ourselves, provided the sacrifices are not, impersonally considered, overwhelming and considerable good is to be obtained.

This chapter is dedicated to the following three questions. First, what reason is there to think that statistical inequality between men and women is associated with the kind of inequality that is morally worrisome; namely, the kind that involves remediable objective deprivations? Second, what kind of misfortune is gender inequality? Is it best viewed as the result of a natural disaster, or as the unfortunate summary result of a series of individually unproblematic negotiations? Or, contrary to what was suggested above, does it involve advantage-taking on the part of a privileged class? Third, what are the costs of greater equality and should we be prepared to pay them?

8.2. Are Women Objectively Deprived?

The belief that the division of the cooperative surplus between men and women of the same social class, if not between nations or classes, is more or less just, and that women's lives are overall exactly as good as men's, is held in large measure by both sexes. As Beauvoir notes, in face-to-face encounters, the impression that moral equality prevails may be irresistible.[3] In modern families, questions such as the division of labour, the relative importance of one spouse's career compared with the other's, the investment of resources in further education, and other issues that have a bearing on individuals' social standing and their prospects are discussed openly and often reasonably, allowing for their emotional character, and agreement is ordinarily secured. Legal rights with respect to ownership, liability, and testimony are symmetrical between men and women in most developed countries.

At the same time, objective evidence for women's enjoyment of lower levels of well-being relative to men of their own reference group is not hard to come by. According to most anthropologists, women in nearly all existing and past cultures of record have lower status than men do in two respects: They are excluded by custom and tradition

---

[3] Simone de Beauvoir, *Le Deuxième Sexe*, i. 27.

from prestigious occupations, employments, and activities; and they perform most basic maintenance activities such as feeding, nursing, and cleaning. Men, whether they are unemployed, employed in unskilled positions, or occupy lucrative and visible ones, tend to assume a partial or full exemption from maintenance. E. O. Wilson notes that 'History records not a single culture in which women have controlled the political and economic lives of men. . . . Men have traditionally assumed the positions of chieftains, shamans, judges and warriors. Their modern technocratic counterparts rule the industrial states and head the corporations and churches.'[4] These conditions justify us in referring to women as existing in a condition of subordination.

Educational and employment prospects, legal protection, and access to credit have improved for women in many parts of the world, but women's lower standing is pronounced even in the wealthiest and most rights-conscious nations. The following observations pertain to Western liberal democracies c.2000 CE.

(1) Executive positions such as judge, professor, general, director, president, minister, doctor, mayor, and board member are overwhelmingly held by men.

(2) Men initiate and carry through most significant financial transactions involving the investment and expenditure of public and corporate funds. They own approximately 90 per cent of the world's wealth.

(3) Men constitute the greater portion of the clientele in fine restaurants, first-class sections of airplanes, and luxury hotels.

(4) Men win more prizes, are awarded more badges and medals, and have more buildings, bridges, and roads named after them than women.

(5) Men appear more frequently in non-entertainment magazines, and as subjects of news programmes. They are photographed more often performing tasks requiring specialized training and expertise.

(6) Men come and go from the household with greater freedom than women. Recurrent or permanent defections from the household and the family by men are judged less severely than similar defections by women.

---

[4] E. O. Wilson, *On Human Nature*, 128.

(7) Men, with the exception of professional porters and caddies, carry fewer bags and sacks than women do, and push fewer prams, pushchairs, and shopping trolleys than women do.

(8) Men come into contact with kitchen detritus, vomit, excrement, soiled clothing, and other taboo objects and substances less than women do.

Women are not numerous on the editorial boards of newspapers and magazines that collect and shape public opinion, or on the governing boards of research centres, universities, and regulatory agencies. Women, for the most part, do not decide where national boundaries are to be drawn, how cities are to be laid out, which drugs and surgical procedures to promote, how many airports or railways to build, what rights are to be enshrined in a constitution, and how many bombs and missiles of what kinds a country is to have and when it is to deploy them.

Women's lesser authority and status is not a function of their cognitive abilities. According to the textbook of Maccoby and Jacklin, '[B]eginning in early infancy, the two sexes show a remarkable degree of similarity in the basic intellectual processes of perception, learning, and memory.'[5] There are subtle differences in colour vision, in the ability to recognize and remember faces and to ascertain the emotional states of others (female favouring), and in the ability to solve word problems and rotate imaginary figures (male favouring). Overall, however, women and men are not very different with respect to traits such as spatial ability, reasoning, divergent thinking, creativity, moral judgement, achievement striving, and task persistence.[6] Though the feats of calculation, memory, and representation of the savant syndrome are more commonly exhibited by men by a factor of six to one, both sexes are liable to it. Only 5 per cent of the measurable variance in cognitive ability is attributable to sex, and women's lower maths scores are insufficient to explain their limited participation in science, mathematics, and engineering.[7] The variance in other capabilities, such as eye–hand-coordination may be real and significant, but such differences can hardly explain women's lesser participation in politics, journalism, and the arts.

[5] Eleanor Maccoby and Carol Jacklin, *The Psychology of Sex Differences*, 61.   [6] Ibid. 75 ff.
[7] Stephen Brush, 'Women in Science and Engineering', 412.

Nor is women's lower status explained by the debilitating effects of pregnancy and lactation. Some women seek to improve their personal socio-economic outcomes by making the difficult choice to delay or avoid childbearing. Not only is the decision medically questionable and a complication with respect to marriage, but childless women do not on the whole fare any better in professional hierarchies than women with children.[8] Women perform more physical labour than men in many cultures, and their capacity for industry is taken for granted cross-culturally.[9] Women with and without young children usually perform the agricultural work, exclusive of ploughing with draft animals, in traditional societies. Water carrying is almost universally a female activity, even though women's upper-body strength is 30 per cent less than men's. In industrial economies, women are well represented but poorly paid in factory work requiring manual dexterity, and in post-industrial economies, they are low-wage 'pink collar' clerks and secretaries. Women are compressed towards the low to middle end of the occupational spectrum: few are in jail, and few are at the tops of hierarchies.[10]

Women experience deficits with respect to each of the known and necessary components of well-being—consumption,[11] expression, affiliation, activity, participation, and respectful depiction. They are under-represented in the 'active world' of the collective imagination. A careful tally of listings in the local entertainment guide should convince any reader that modern cinema is overwhelmingly concerned with men, their thoughts and ideas, their conflicts and struggles. Even television and the comics, with their more domestic focus,

[8] According to Virginia Valian, although academic women are less productive than academic men, women with children are no less productive and may even be more productive than women without. *Why So Slow?*, 269–70.

[9] According to Esther Boesrup, in a Central African republic typical of many rural agrarian societies, 'women generally do the most exhausting and boring tasks, while the performance of the men is sometimes limited simply to being present in the fields to supervise the work of the women'. Anne Oakley, *Housewife*, 173 (cited from Boesrup, *Women's Role in Economic Development*). In Burundi, men and women both agreed that women were better suited for work than men. 'Everyone knows', a group of informants told Ethel Albert, 'that men are not suited *by nature* to heavy work.... Men drink too much and do not eat enough to keep up their strength; they are more tense and travel about too much to develop the habits or the muscles needed for sustained work on farms.' Oakley, *Housewife* 174 (cited from Albert, 'The Roles of Women').

[10] Heather Joshi and Pieralla Paci, *Unequal Pay for Women and Men*, 18–19.

[11] Men spend more than women on personal items and intoxicants, particularly in poorer countries. See Dasgupta, 'Food, Care and Work: The Household as an Allocation Mechanism', ch. 11 of *An Inquiry into Well-Being and Deprivation*. Women shop more than men but make chiefly altruistic purchases.

represent the world as approximately two-thirds male and one-third female. Women are more frequently photographed in a state of undress. They are rarely depicted as absorbed in a task, oblivious to the gaze. These representational trends are more evident in the modern world under liberal democratic regimes than they were at earlier times when the power and charisma of hereditary aristocracies elevated some women to positions of prestige and even influence in the absence of meritocratic competition and social mobility. Finally, women are more liable to depression than men and lack social resiliency. Their personal reputations are more vulnerable; their position and status always more precariously maintained. It is estimated that eight times as many women as men are abandoned by their spouses when they develop a serious illness, and widowers are far more likely to remarry than widows are; the ends of women's longer lives are often spent in a state of physical frailty and loneliness. The financial consequences of the death or defection of a partner are more serious for women than for men.

In short, women are less likely at any stage of life to be found amongst the beneficiaries of the ancient system of exemption and privilege, enjoying the kind of life Aristotle understood as a good life for members of the moral community. Walzer, whose apparent tolerance for voluntary female subordination sits uneasily with it, observes that 'The real domination of women has less to do with their familial place than with their exclusion from all other places. They have been denied the freedom of the city, cut off from distributive processes and social goods outside the sphere of kinship and love.'[12] Whether or not Walzer overestimates women's access to the goods of kinship and love, he is certainly correct in his observation that they do not receive their fair share of social goods.

For the most part, women are the patient and willing workers of the world. They engage in activities that make lower cognitive, emotional, and aesthetic demands than specialized work, performing a diverse range of activities to an adequate standard without concentrating on one or two that bring social recognition and reward. While individual women may enter the specialized occupations and enjoy

---

[12] Walzer, *Spheres of Justice*, 240.

privileges and exemptions from ordinary work, they did not in ancient and do not in modern times, make up the proportion of governors and legislators, athletes, or investigators of other worlds— metaphysicians, priests, scientists, and explorers—that their numer- ousness and abilities would seem to predict. This is not to say that the lives of the best-off women are significantly worse than the lives of the best-off men, or that the lives of the worst-off women are significantly worse than the lives of the worst-off men. Nothing precludes the possibility of high degrees of well-being for women or utter misery for men. The initial generalization nevertheless holds despite the existence of numerous exceptions. The depriv- ations implied by women's lesser control over resources, political authority, and enjoyment of specialization opportunities in developed countries are trivial in comparison with the deprivations endured by women in countries in which they are denied basic legal rights and protection from physical abuse. However, in setting the anchor for the status of women at abjection, not at the other end of the spectrum of well-being, we unconsciously represent women as deserving less.

Faced with evidence that millions of interactions between individ- ual parties, each of which may be in order from the microethical perspective, reliably sum to a situation of reduced female liberty, happiness, and authority, women and men have an array of conflict- resolving devices at their disposal to show why, despite the uncontro- versial truth of the observations just cited, women are no worse off overall than men are. They may retail anecdotes of notable excep- tions, as though these refuted the statistical evidence, stress the voluntary nature of the division of labour in male–female partnerships and the importance of personal choice, or draw attention to the personal satisfactions afforded human females by their service roles. They may present the merit-desert intuition, or advance the Aristo- telian observation that what would be a deprivation for a man is not a deprivation for a woman. Statistical social equality, it might be said, is rapidly becoming a reality. Finally, it might be urged that, while women lack social status, they do not lack moral dignity, and only the latter is truly important. For, at least since Kant, most philosophers have insisted on a distinction between social prestige and intrinsic worth as a human being. Human dignity is not read off from a list of

public accomplishments. It is, as Kant maintained, posited, and it is assuredly posited in women as well as in men.

The suggestion that, as long as women have inner human dignity, their lacking wealth or direct legislative power, or even their liability to poverty and depression, is irrelevant to morality is unacceptable. The fact that it is possible for a morally dignified subject to live well in conditions of social deprivation cannot be the foundation of a theory of social justice. I can imagine a cow with the head of a goat. If I now go further and infer that there is no essential connection between being a cow and having a cow's head, I am on the wrong track. The ancient philosophers posited an intrinsic connection between living in a certain way, being regarded as excellent for living in that way, and being an excellent human being. Kant was offended by these elisions, which he sought to correct. The message he and subsequent Kantians have given out concerning the relationship between moral dignity and social dignity has been unclear as a consequence. And indeed it has to be. For the boundary between low socio-economic status and lesser moral dignity is not well defined. This is not to say that being-of-the-gender-that-rarely-has-bridges-named-after-one-of-them entails that you have less human dignity than being-of-the-gender-that-almost-always-has-bridges-named-after-one-of-them does, or that your dignity is injured or violated because there are few bridges named after persons of your sex. At the same time, if you are a member of a group, all of whose members it would be unthinkable or barely thinkable to name a bridge after, it is possible that others consider you as having less importance as persons. If you are a member of the sex that is more frequently aborted, or that dies more frequently of malnutrition, you are in a position to argue that your dignity has been injured—that something has been taken away—or that others are failing to acknowledge something in you. Between trivial and mostly unnoticed injuries to vanity and the serious violation of human rights we can interpolate cases indefinitely.

One who insists that statistical equality is on the way might well be asked for what future year his bets would reflect indifference to gender. Clearly we should prefer the bet that a randomly selected member of the category of, e.g., 'persons having signing authority in the year 2010 over sums of more than one million dollars', or 'persons

observed in the first-class section of an airplane in the year 2010' is a woman to the bet that a randomly selected member of the category 'persons having signing authority in the year 1980 over sums of more than one million dollars', or 'persons observed in the first-class section of an airplane in the year 1980', is a woman. No reasonable person, though, would be indifferent to the bet that a randomly selected member of the 2010 categories—and perhaps the 2050 categories— will be a man v. a women. Although the proportion of the wage gap in the full-time earnings of British men and women born in 1958 and later that can be explained by differences in experience and qualifications has diminished in past decades, the proportion attributable to discrimination has at least remained constant and may have risen.[13]

Perhaps the emotional rewards of femininity (of simply belonging to the childbearing sex) exactly balance the deprivations? On this view, there must be constituents of well-being with respect to which men are deprived to which women have access that even the score, leaving neither sex absolutely worse off. The deprivations allegedly endured by men that might be claimed to even the balance are several. Most men lack the opportunity to form a close bond with an infant and have relatively little control over household arrangements, and it is sometimes said that men are deprived of opportunities for forming intimate ties with same-sex age-mates. Yet history does not record any protests by literary and philosophical men with respect to their exclusion from places, activities, and experiences available to women. Literature and poetry are silent on the subject. Unless it can be shown that there are institutional obstacles that selectively restrict men's, but not women's, full employment of their intellectual, economic, and artistic abilities, the argument from compensating gratifications and frustrations fails.

Being born female is therefore a condition carrying excess risk with respect to the attainment of many of the components of well-being. In this respect it is like being born without an arm or being born into a poor family of goat-herders. These conditions do not preclude happiness and those who have the deficits may never really understand what they are missing. Being saddled with them is compatible

---

[13] Joshi and Paci, *Unequal Pay*, 63–4.

with one's relatives and neighbours suffering their own set of unrelated deficits. Nevertheless, they impact on one's life chances.

Is this a moral problem? Everyone undergoes an equal risk of being born a woman, after all, and the role of a woman is far from being unacceptable. No reasonable person—unless conditions are worse than we think—would prefer non-existence to the role of a randomly chosen human female. It is not unjust, one might argue, but merely unfortunate, that, in a world in which A_1 and A_2 share all their independent properties except that A_2 is a paraplegic, outcomes are worse for A_2. Nor is it unjust that in a world in which A_1 and A_2 share all their independent properties except that A_2 is a childbearer, outcomes are worse for A_2.

This argument is unconvincing. First, it is impossible to view the childbearing characteristic as a disability whose sequelae are unfortunate but not unjust. The able-bodied do not significantly profit from the disabled and may even lose on their account, but non-childbearers do profit from reductions in well-being of the childbearers. Men have benefited and continue to benefit from the reduction in competition afforded by women's non-participation and from the surplus of leisure they obtain by their partial or even total exemption from responsibility for maintenance activities. If there were large numbers of congenital paraplegics in our world, if having a congenital paraplegic in one's household brought a generous subvention, and if congenital paraplegia were a treatable condition, it would be self-interested and unjust for the able-bodied to refuse to treat them on the grounds that their condition was brought on by bad luck.

Imagine an alternative world W' enduring over some ten thousand years, in which each past and present individual is a counterpart of some past or present individual in our world, with precisely his or her capabilities and predispositions—intelligence, speed at calculation, emotional warmth or coldness, love of money, indifference to political power, the tendency to wander, height, and even possession of secondary sexual characteristics, with the following difference: In W'—and this feature differentiates it radically from our world—none of the variance in childbearing ability and responsiveness to children is accounted for by sex. Half of the men and half of the women in W' are subject to pregnancy and experience the same caregiving drives.

If, in W', the distribution of the components of well-being tracked gender, we would consider W' unjust. Why should the women of W' participate as little and have as little influence as they do in our world, and the men of W' enjoy exemptions from back-up and maintenance activities to the degree we observe here? But if W' is unjust, what makes our world just? It cannot merely be the fact that the percentage of women who bear children is greater than 50 per cent and the percentage of men who bear children is nil. For the women and men are assumed to be equivalent with respect to their competence and interests.

An apologist for the status quo who agrees that W' would be an unjust world might dismiss the thought experiment as irrelevant. Women and men in our world are not, he might insist, equivalent with respect to their competence and interests. The childbearing characteristic is not a feature that can be envisioned as snapped onto or off a human person, leaving all other characteristics unaffected. The presence or absence of the childbearing characteristic pervades the characters and determines the behaviour of women and men in a way 'left by nature', as Hume would say, 'to baffle all the pride of philosophy'. It is to this immanentist position, in its latest fashionable garb, that I now turn.

8.3. Some Favoured Explanations for Female Subordination

Sociobiology—or, as it is now termed, 'evolutionary psychology'—offers the latest and most credible approach to the question why women's status is lower than men's in most human societies. The general form of the answer is that women's and men's reproductive strategies not only are different but are especially conducive to social systems involving female subordination.

These strategies, it is alleged, have evolved through competition between members of the same sex to survive and reproduce. The winning strategies manifest themselves through emotions, aptitudes, and dispositions that are underpinned by differences in cerebral organization, in levels of circulating hormones, and in the presence or absence of receptors for these hormones throughout the body.

While each individual is physiologically unique, differences whose workings are perceptible in ordinary life emerge at the statistical level. According to the hypothesis of evolutionary psychology, women typically possess certain attributes incompatible with high social status and/or lack other attributes conducive to status. As a result, women have little motivation to strive to better their own status, and both men and women have little motivation to help them. The possession and lack of these attributes can be explained by conditions in the early adaptive environment and its pressure on the evolution of human physical and psychological traits.

Sociobiological explanations for the subordination of women, even considered as partial explanations, have not captured the interest of female theorists of sexual inequality for several reasons. First, in scientific discourse, women are often considered and spoken of as objects of knowledge in a manner experienced as insulting. Even in recent books on evolutionary psychology, there is likely to be an index entry for 'Women' but not one for 'Men', affording another example of the presumption that the active world of knowledge-seekers is composed of men who transcend the empirical limitations and determinations to which the more inert sex is subject. Second, the Theory of Women delivered by the tradition is famously unreliable. With regard to the nineteenth-century discourse on human sexuality, Michel Foucault remarks: 'When we compare these discourses . . . with what was known at the time about the physiology of plant and animal reproduction, we are struck by the incongruity. Their feeble content from the standpoint of elementary rationality, not to mention scientificity, earns them a place apart in the history of knowledge. They form a strangely muddled zone.'[14] The texts of the medical moralists, he comments, exemplify at once the 'stubborn will to knowledge that has sustained scientific discourse in the West . . . [and the] stubborn will to nonknowledge. . . . It is as if a fundamental resistance blocked the development of a rationally formed discourse.'[15] Much evolutionary psychology seems to its female readers to exhibit the same combination of weak methodology and projective fantasy.

---

[14] Michel Foucault, *A History of Sexuality*, i. 54.   [15] Ibid. 54–5.

Yet the virtual neglect of this literature is not adequately explained by worries about objectification or the scientific status of socio-biology. It is better explained by the images of reality that are reflected in it and their fit or lack of fit with readers' self-images. Male readers are happy enough to learn from this literature that they are by nature status-conscious and promiscuous, and that they control the distribution of resources to women. Females are puzzled to learn that they are by nature indifferent to rank, naturally monogamous, and have evolved to be nourished by men. Often evolutionary psychologists convey the impression that the variance in outcomes between the sexes is difficult, impossible, or dangerous to tamper with, in view of the great antiquity and serviceability of specialized sexual strategies. Historically, moralists who tolerated or favoured the subordination of women did so on the basis of differences they supposed to be given by nature. Those who argued against subordination did so on the basis of samenesses they supposed to have been overlooked and suppressed. In view of those samenesses, it was urged, the subordination of women was illogical or inconsistent.

Regardless of the historical precedents, the refusal to take seriously sociobiological explanations for female subordination is misguided. For evolutionary psychology has the virtue of shifting the discussion away from the (in theory) long-settled issue of female intellectual and artistic competence to consider other traits with respect to which differences between the sexes may actually be pronounced. The hypothesis that it is precisely those traits that hold the key to the explanation of subordination can explain very well the neglect of sameness, and the further neglect of the intellectual and practical inconsistency arising from this neglect. The accusation that the status of women reflects inconsistent beliefs or an inconsistency between belief and practice might have seemed, for a time, quite telling. Even for philosophers, though, this state of affairs does not constitute a crisis. People hold many conflicting views they do not strive to reconcile. In social and political theory, so long as there is agreement about what is interesting and important, the invitation to account for imputed inconsistencies can be put off indefinitely.

The biological disposition theory of modern sociobiology is not, in the hands of its most careful developers, either deterministic or objectionably essentialist where gender is concerned. It is not incon-

sistent with the observations that each person is a unique mosaic of traits, that individuals facilitate their own sorting by conforming to gender stereotypes and by encouraging or forcing one another to conform to these stereotypes, and that some individuals cannot be sorted easily into the category of male or female. The knowledge that someone belongs in the class of males or females does not enable us to make highly reliable predictions about that person's possession of most traits or capacities. Still, nearly 100 per cent of the variance in childbearing capacities is explained by sex, and this fact may be important. Further, there is reason to believe, not only that there is substantial variation with respect to an interest in and responsiveness to young children by adults, but also that some proportion of that variance can be accounted for by sex as well.[16] It is reasonable to believe that some percentage of the variance, however small, observed in other morphological characteristics, competencies, deficits, and emotional responses can likely be explained by specialization for childbearing and childcare.

According to evolutionary psychologists, the different behavioural and emotional profiles of men and women influence the likelihood of various possible social patternings. Some logically possible patterns will never be manifested at all; others will occur frequently. Social systems in which females have lower status and are more burdened are, on this view, predictably common and assume numerous specific forms. These patterns are not plausibly explained as the results of conscious conspiracies, but they cannot be relegated to the category of mere historical accidents either; they represent various courses of least resistance for dimorphic organisms with certain endowments. On this view, just as our cognitive structures divide the class of logically possible experiences from the class of possible-for-us experiences, and just as the size of our teeth and nails, the structure of our digestive systems, and our metabolisms make some forms of nutrition, such as a diet of cellulose, virtually impossible for us and others possible but problematic, our behavioural and emotional tendencies make some possible institutions more difficult to instantiate than others, and render others impossible or virtually impossible. Evolutionary psychology has, however, no normative implications, since

[16] Hrdy, *Mother Nature*, 212. Women hear infant cries more easily and are more moved to respond to them.

normative statements can only be understood as reality-constrained projections of ideal worlds. Persons whose initial moral commitment to gender equality is on the high-demand side should be able to agree on many facts with persons whose initial moral commitment is on the low-demand side.

With these caveats out of the way, it will be useful to consider the three most prominent explanations for female subordination in the literature. The first focuses on male aggression and competition, the second on the physical encumbrances of maternity, and the third on female vulnerability and altruism.

(a) *Aggression and competition*

Life is not easy for primate females. According to Wrangham and Peterson, writing in 1996:

Among [*pan troglodytes*] chimpanzees every adult male is dominant to every adult female, and he enjoys his dominance. She must move out of the way, acknowledge him with the appropriate call or gestures, bend to his whim— or risk punishment. The punishment by a bad tempered male can vary from a hit to a chase through trees and along the ground, until the female is caught and pulled and kicked and hit and dragged, screaming until her throat cramps, reminded to respect him the next time.[17]

Wrangham and Petersen infer that 'Patriarchy is worldwide and history-wide, and its origins are detectable in the social lives of chimpanzees.' The impression that male primates are hard on their own females is backed up by observation of other species. Barbara Smuts found that each female in a baboon troop was attacked by a male slightly more than once a week, and that, on average, each female could expect to receive a serious wound, one taking two or three months to heal, from a male once a year.[18]

The human platform is different from that of *troglodytes* and baboons. Not only is sexual dimorphism reduced in humans, indicating selection pressures against large and threatening males, the human brain is further specialized for the inhibition of impulses and for moral ideation. Yet it is undeniable that men's differential ability to injure

---

[17] Richard Wrangham and Dale Peterson, *Demonic Males: Apes and the Origin of Human Violence*, 205.
[18] Smuts, *Sex and Friendship in Baboons*, 88.

and kill women and women's awareness of their relative physical weakness facilitates control by men of women's behaviour and movements. It creates the expectation in men that women will do what they want them to do, and resigns women to the idea that they ought to behave as men want them to behave.

A related notion is that men's intrinsically higher levels of energy, sexual curiosity, and tolerance for pain translate into accomplishments women cannot expect to match. Competition between men for 'access' to women who select them for their ability to provide 'resources' is seen as a motivating force that spurs the male sex to ever more daring, worthwhile, and lucrative achievements in science, literature, the arts, politics, drama, and sports. Women, with their 'larger gametes', are held to constitute a scarce resource, from which their non-competitive propensities follow.

(b) *Encumbrances of maternity*

In nature, female primates are often accompanied by their young, sometimes an infant and a juvenile, sometimes two infants. Males in many species play with, protect, and take care of juveniles, but the mother–infant bond is intense and universal, and primate mothers may take an interest in their offspring and vice versa for their entire lives. The newly parturient female is hormonally a distinctive creature, and the inclination to respond to a baby's cries, to carry it around, keep track of it, and to feed it seems to depend on the conjunction of the mother's temperament and hard-wiring, social learning by observation of others, and on the behaviour of the child.

Much excited writing pro and con has focused on the question whether maternal care in humans is innate or 'conditioned'. 'There is no such thing as the maternal instinct,' Anne Oakley stated confidently in *Housewife* in 1974. 'There is no biologically based drive which propels women into childbearing or forces them to become childrearers once the children are there.'[19] But one might wonder exactly what is being disputed. Some women do not like children and are annoyed by their dependency; some are careless or vicious and manage to kill or hurt or malnourish them; some are overprotective

[19] Oakley, *Housewife*, 199.

and inadvertently harm their children, but most women desire and welcome the arrival of offspring and are capable parents. Involuntary childlessness is perhaps the greatest source of anguish in women's lives. It is an eminently presentable deprivation.[20]

Maternity seems to explain a good deal where women's subordination is concerned. Women can work, but maternity means that the work must be such that it is easily interrupted. Women's work must not be dangerous or too absorbing, since becoming motherless, or merely suffering maternal neglect, is a worse fate than becoming fatherless or suffering paternal neglect. It should not involve long journeys since young children have to be carried and cannot move at a comfortable adult speed on their own. All this results, according to the hypothesis, in specialization for detail work in or near the home on the part of women and in specialization for work involving travel, risk, and imagination to men.

Social inequality, on this view, follows from the fact that human males are not as interested in and committed to young children as human females are. While individual men may show high levels of interest and commitment and individual women low levels, the average differences between the sexes with respect to parental investment are thought to predict female social inferiority. By allocating more time to caring for and teaching children, women must invariably allocate less time to the production of other objects and states of affairs deemed valuable in a culture. Since childbearing is a salient feature of women, the disqualification of maternity attaches to the sex as a whole.

(c) *Vulnerability and altruism*

The characteristics that specialize women for childbearing and childcare, even if they do not bear on intellectual, artistic, and practical competence, seem to put them at a disadvantage in modern competitive institutions. According to an argument that is rarely propounded aloud, quite apart from the physical encumbrances of maternity, women's greater sensitivity to physical and emotional pain, greater altruism, and overall lack of toughness lead them down different life pathways.

---

[20] Rachel, in the Old Testament.

Women, it seems, do not attach the same importance to defeating and humiliating rivals as men do. It is known that drive levels tested in isolation are the same in males and females. Women have the same underlying desire to master tasks and to perform well as men do.[21] Yet when they are placed in competitive situations, the drive to defeat rivals appears to diminish. Boys appear to respond to competition with greater output, girls with less.[22] In comparison with men, women are observed to express more misgivings about their own abilities, to have lower expectations for themselves, and to be more tolerant of others' failures. They tend to refer their successes to extraneous factors.[23] To the frustration of their teachers, they often appear to be easily discouraged, and seem to require more coaching and personal attention to perform to a given level in professional life. According to Helen Fisher, females do not establish status ladders: 'They form cliques instead—laterally connected subgroups of individuals who care for one another's infants and protect and nurture each other in times of social chaos. Females are less aggressive, less dominance oriented, and this network can remain stable—and relatively egalitarian for years.'[24]

The explanation for this diffidence is thought to be as follows: Women depend on the help of other women to raise their children. This leads them to treat female friends and relatives in kind and conciliatory ways. At the same time, they compete with one another for male attention, but not by signalling their cognitive superiority, fierceness, or athleticism. Rather, a shapely figure, maidenly demeanour, and maternal inclinations are believed to impress men. It might be predicted by evolutionary psychologists that, while male–male competitions for prestige will be eagerly studied by males and females alike, female–female skill competitions (unlike beauty pageants) will be thought relatively uninteresting. Cross-sex competition will be avoided by humans or considered not to matter.

Traits such as smaller size and lesser strength, childbearing, receptivity to infants, and greater patience, as well as a lower level of interest in status as opposed to the goods of affiliation are thus, for the evolutionary psychologist, the causes of women's subordination.

---

[21] Maccoby and Jacklin, *Psychology of Sex Differences*, 134 ff.   [22] Ibid. 149–50.
[23] Ibid. 154 ff.   [24] Helen Fisher, *The Anatomy of Love*, 222.

No malevolent intention on anyone's part need be hypothesized; hence no one can be blamed for women's social deficits.

Even if we accept the evolutionary psychologist's account of our underlying dispositions they do not predict and do not justify the current state of the world. A Martian ethologist given information concerning initial conditions in the early adaptative environment, and information about the competencies, drives, and tendencies of men and women would be unlikely to predict the present condition of the world, including male control of politics, economics, architecture, and culture, or the excess female risk of poverty and abandonment. The ethologist would assuredly not predict that men are more qualified as present-day politicians and artists. Nevertheless, *if* the Martian knew that one sex was going to gain supremacy in these areas, then, knowing *only* that men and women have the preferences and motivations just cited, it might well predict that the winning sex would be the male sex. If the Martian also knew that men are not more qualified than women to decide how things should go and that women do not prefer their condition of enhanced vulnerability, it could predict that Earth would become an unjust place.

The evolutionary psychologist may concede that our institutions have exaggerated the effects of our biology, but he is professionally unequipped to recognize the manner in which the history of our species has created a moral problem that was not present in the early adaptative environment of 75,000–300,000 years ago. Wilson refers to the accumulation of advantage in describing how 'a small evolutionary change in the behaviour patterns of individuals can be amplified into a major social effect by the expanding upward distribution of the effect into multiple facets of social life'.[25] This process of leveraging explains observed historical patterns in the relationship between men and women better than the supposition that they are a direct product of biological endowments that would have manifested themselves in any possible world.

Among the few remaining modern hunters and gatherers and nomadic herders whose lives are considered to resemble most closely those of our distant ancestors, female subordination is minimal, for the confinement and management of women is incompatible with

---

[25] E. O. Wilson, *On Human Nature*, 11.

survival. The emergence of permanent settlements and agriculture in the Neolithic altered the balance. Settlement created the need for intensive domestic work to keep dwelling places habitable, and women's larger caloric requirements in pregnancy and lactation and their lesser musculature encouraged sedentary habits that made them natural candidates for this job. Women became the chief tenders of gardens and fields, as they still are in small villages without draft animals or machinery, and the chief processors of grains and seeds. Arranged marriage and the ownership of women, perhaps suggested to the human mind by the ownership and controlled breeding of livestock, diverted men's energies from courtship and food-getting to cultural productions, displays, and politics.

With the advent of metalworking, the physically stronger males gained control of the manufacture and use of iron weapons and of plough agriculture, with its use of large draft animals, then cart transportation, then trade, and so money, writing, and administration.[26] Women remained generalists; men specialized. The work they perform varies from culture to culture, but in all human societies, women perform a greater number of separate tasks than men do.[27] The urbanization movements of 2000 BCE marked the beginning of women's claustration, exaggerating, to the point of extreme distortion, the female features of modesty and the tendency to energy conservation.

With women's tasks increasingly sequestered and unseen by men, militaristic societies worried about the contagiousness and debilitating influence of femininity. Young men were removed as early as possible from the company of their mothers and sisters, reducing their mutual understanding and their companionship value for one another. The route to high political office proceeded through a military or, by the Middle Ages, a church career, and the development of large administrative structures and political organizations that operated in secrecy tended to women's exclusion.[28] Many unisexual institutions—boarding schools, monasteries, and formerly universities—replicate some features of military discipline and camaraderie. It is easy to state conditions under which a system of sex and gender hierarchy is well entrenched and self-perpetuating. The pathways for men leading to positions of power and influence must be clearly

[26] As suggested by Marvin Harris, 'The Evolution of Gender Hierarchies: A Trial Formulation'.
[27] Boulding, *Underside of History*, 122.   [28] Ibid.

marked and well paved. The most prestigious educational institutions, with the best endowments and the finest facilities, and those requiring the highest parental investments, must be governed and staffed by males and restricted to them. Under such conditions, the actual competencies, dispositions, and preferences of women, though they cannot be entirely submerged, are thwarted.

Human institutions can be considered, like the nest of the bird, as entirely natural productions, springing from the needs and capacities of a species able, like nearly every species, to modify its own ambient environment. In this respect, we can agree that it is natural to create environments in which women occupy the crowded lower tiers of employment hierarchies and do not enjoy certain privileges. Nothing is added, in one sense, to the critique of institutions by insisting that exploitation and deprivation are merely cultural, for the admission that they are natural carries no implication as to the ease or difficulty of remedies. The cultural disability of lacking a high-school diploma is harder to compensate for than the natural disability of happening to lack a front tooth.

In another sense, however, the subordination of women is not natural, for it depends on contingencies that have nothing to do with sexual strategies of the early adaptative environment. If metal were not malleable at temperatures achievable with charcoal fires; if no wild animals had proved themselves amenable to domestication; if grain could not be stored for more than a week; and if no piles of stones over five feet high could stand, women would not be subordinated. This point is eloquently expressed by Sarah Hrdy:

Incontestably, weaker individuals are often victimized by stronger ones. This can certainly be documented throughout the primates, but never on the scale in which it occurs among people, and never exclusively against a particular sex. . . . Only in human societies are females as a class subject to the sort of treatment that among other species would be rather randomly accorded the more defenseless members of the group–the very young, the disabled, or the very old–regardless of sex . . . Human ingenuity, and with it the ability to build walls, to count, and tell tales, to transport food and store it, and particularly to allocate labour (to control not just the reproductive but the productive capacities of other individuals), all of these eroded age-old female advantages.[29]

---

[29] Hrdy, *The Woman that Never Evolved*, 185–7.

The same conditions, as observed earlier, that permit the most varied and spectacular expressions of human artistry and invention, permit at the same time the most varied and spectacular expressions of the will to dominate and control others.

8.4. The Argument from Heavy Costs

Women's past and present deprivations incriminate few identifiable individuals. History reveals for the most part a panorama of microethically unobjectionable choices and transactions, punctuated here and there by a noteworthy act of exceptional antifeminism. Nevertheless, the status of women presents us with a clear example of a moral dilemma. How much ought a well-off group to sacrifice in order to improve conditions for a less well-off group? To what extent does the vigorous and healthy self-interest of the former group, the fact that there is something that it is like to be a member of that group, and that the experiences of individuals within the group are profoundly influenced by membership in the group set limits on what can be asked of them? Moral concern mandates some transfer of advantage from better-off to worse-off, only the questions how much and how soon have no determinate answers. One can only defend the reasonableness of one's proposals in light of the reality constraint and the idealism characteristic.

Greater social equality for women implies some costs for men. Even if we can anticipate benefits to the collective from a reversal of women's fortunes, some individuals will be worse off, for social status and financial reward are limited resources and their allocation is virtually a zero-sum game. The familiar multipliers of costs are likely to weigh in at this stage of reflection. The prospect of greater social equality in Western countries rouses sentiments of relative deprivation; our women seem to lack the biddable qualities they had only a generation or two ago and still have in many places. Affirmative action is seen as externally imposed and the sacrifices implied by greater equality will not be temporary.

In a world in which women are rarely judges or professors, and rarely receive incomes of over $100,000, my chances of enjoying these benefits are greatly increased if I am a man of the class that normally has access to these positions. In a society in which women

are always domestic cleaners and preparers of food, my chances of having to take on these burdensome tasks are virtually nil if I am a man of any class whatsoever. Self-interested men, therefore, have overwhelming reasons to favour a division of labour along customary lines. Moral philosophers do not share these reasons, for they are technically precluded from theorizing as self-interested men. Though the propensity to treat statistical inequality between the sexes as though it does not matter or to deem it other than a proper subtopic of general moral and political theory need not imply a disregard for the professional role, it can betray a certain forgetfulness.

Conversely, moral theorists who are female are obliged to evaluate betterness relations from an impersonal perspective, not with respect to the outcome they happen to prefer for their own sex. They cannot ignore the fact that greater social equality may impose heavy costs on some groups and persons, reducing, prima facie, the prima facie obligation to strive for it. Suppose, for example, that by sacrificing one randomly chosen person by lethal injection, statistical equality between the sexes could be assured. Would it be right to do this? Clearly not. However, the utilitarian sacrificing action is not forbidden because it is always forbidden to worsen the condition of even one agent in ways he could not agree to, no matter what benefit follows. It is simply the case that I judge a world in which gender equality has been produced by an execution to be worse, all things considered, than our existing unfair world and I expect competent judges to support me in this claim.

It would take a brilliant imagination to work out a convincing scenario in which the sacrifice of a single human being would produce statistical equality between the sexes. Even an ordinary imagination, though, can work out convincing scenarios in which some sacrifices by human beings contribute to greater equality. What level of equality can we reasonably aim for? How much would it cost us?

A number of respected philosophers appear to be pessimistic on this score. They advance versions of the familiar argument from heavy costs:

> *The Argument from Heavy Costs against Sexual Equality*
> The condition of women presents a moral problem that prima facie, we are obliged to solve, in so far as it contravenes not only Q but even the weaker moral proviso L that forbids agents to advance

their own interests when the costs to others are substantial. Although many women are accomplished and favourably treated, women have less of most human goods. But the status of women is nevertheless justifiable all-things-considered on the grounds that the difficulty of reducing the variance in the social status of the sexes reduces the obligation to strive for this goal. We would have to sacrifice many other human goods, in addition to the excess portion of male authority and enjoyment, to eliminate relative deprivation, and it is not worth it.

The pessimist's estimation of the reality constraint motivates his adherence to a low-demand position. He may acknowledge that, in fact, men's relationship to women, individually and in aggregate, often involves culpable letting-happen, as a by-product of self- or class-interest, not just the innocuous failure to prevent harm. For men and women know of one another's existence and know something of the conditions under which the other sex lives; the channels of communication are at least partially open. But, on his considered view, strenuous exertions to reduce the variances in agency and influence, and so to reduce advantage-taking between the sexes, are not all-things-considered morally required. The imposition of policies and procedures that transferred a large proportion of the holdings, liberties, and cultural and intellectual authority of men over to women would be disruptive of reasonably comfortable and efficient modes of life and traumatic for both sexes.

This version of the argument from heavy costs is commonly encountered both in the writings of reflective sociobiologists and in general moral philosophy when theorists have swept their gaze momentarily over the question of sexual equality. E. O. Wilson acknowledges that the aggressive use of quotas and remedial education would enable us to manipulate our society to bring about equality in the professions and cultural activities. 'Yet,' he says, 'the amount of regulation required would certainly place some personal freedoms in jeopardy, and at least a few individuals would not be allowed to reach their full potential.'[30] Williams, citing Nagel, presents the

[30] Unlike the majority of political philosophers, E. O. Wilson recognizes and states that 'equal opportunity' as currently understood is likely to leave men's higher socio-economic status intact. His preference appears to be for a society that 'condition[s] its members to exaggerate sexual differences in behaviour'. *On Human Nature*, 132–3. This is puzzling since the main thrust of the book is that counter-natural social engineering tends to be problematic.

argument with unusual frankness. 'It might just be', he ventures, 'that [equality] is too hard and will not work:'

That is, there is a *Spielraum* for human beings, an area in which it is possible for human beings individually—or even for a time societally—to do things of a certain kind, but it is so against the grain that some things are just, to use the phrase used by Tom Nagel, too much to ask. Someone will come along and say, 'Look it is possible to treat women just like men, at least almost just like men. But if we try to adopt this equality of treatment everywhere, there will be anxiety, disaster, collapse,—results which everybody knows are unacceptable to human society.' This is certainly a respectable form of claim.[31]

Nagel agrees that it would be a mistake to try to extend juridical equality so far that it produces statistical equality.[32] The state, he theorizes, exists in order to prevent serious and remediable harms to persons and can guarantee their juridical status—and it has done so, ending racial and sexual discrimination—but it is not responsible for supervising social outcomes. Further, 'The impersonal desire for equality meets severe obstacles from individual motivation at every step; in regard to the basic institutions to which individuals are willing to give their allegiance, in the process of democratic politics, and in the operation of the economy.'[33]

Williams's belief that it could be dangerous to throw open the doors for women by treating them equally everywhere reflects his conception of the social world as governed by *Sittlichkeit* even while the individual is ignobly fettered by ethical theory. His mood of gloomy foreboding might be supposed to arise from contemplation of the difficulties that would be involved in overcoming the disqualifications of maternity and in making women and institutions better adapted to each other than they currently are. Nevertheless, it seems to hint at something darker. Why does Williams think it is 'certainly a respectable form of claim' that a world in which women were treated just like men would spell disaster for human society? We need to

---

[31] '[T]he strongest kind of sociobiological "cannot" would mean that the question never came up at all. As soon as [the sociobiologist] permits "can," then the philosopher says "is does not imply ought" and we have room for free choice. What the sociobiologists say here is, "Look, when we say 'can't' we do not mean 'absolutely can't.' What we mean is 'can't without terrific costs that any group of human beings will count as costs.'"' Williams 'Conclusions', in Stent (ed.), *Morality as a Biological Phenomenon*, 142.

[32] Nagel, *Equality and Partiality*, 89–90.

[33] Ibid. 95.

know what forms of anxiety, disaster, and collapse are more likely to occur, given women's actual propensities and dispositions, when they are treated more equally. Only then can we decide whether the costs associated with a more moral world are really much heavier than we are willing to bear.

One way to interpret this foreboding is as follows: Since Rousseau first expressed it, there has been a presumption in force that women's greater compassion and lesser interest in personal acquisition would enable men to operate as they pleased without the world becoming uninhabitable. Women's altruism, their willingness to 'labour for love', would maintain the collective. Only half of mankind would be fuelled by *amour-propre* to engage in competitive displays and struggles, converting raw materials as fast as possible into artefacts and inventing new intellectual products. The other half would deal with the stresses and strains that are the inevitable by-product of such striving.

Imagine a world in which women are not only treated like men but behave like caricatures of men. A number of women become belligerent dictators, threatening other states. En masse, women adopt the specialist's mode of life, either displacing men or simply adding their labours and effort to double the amount of existing bridge-building, theorem-proving, and merging and acquiring. Further, women develop new predatory habits with respect to young men, and construct a commercial demi-monde parallel to the one we already have to relieve their newly manifest sexual boredom. They stop looking after men and attending to their needs. Social equality has been produced, but at the price of increased aggression and a faster rate of economic throughput, less devotion to the preservation of life. The world is now more dangerous, politically and psychologically, and less attractive than it used to be.

Another source of foreboding is the suspicion that a redistribution of social advantage from men to women might violate Rawlsian principles of distributive justice in worsening the position of the worst-off men. This might in turn have grave consequences for everyone. As a result of increased competition, men who were formerly able to find a social niche might be driven below the threshold of integration and esteem required to sustain productivity and goodwill. They might defect to a resentful and dangerous

underclass. On this view, larger personal incomes, disproportionate respect, and social liberties are preferentially awarded to men in recognition of the fact that the worst-off men are an exceptionally disadvantaged class whose defection can also be dangerous to the collective. Preferential treatment for the gender helps to boost morale in this vulnerable subpopulation.

A third source of foreboding is this: The full participation of young mothers in the important institutions of the modern world seems to require state-funded, board-certified, round-the clock daycare to enable them to meet the work, travel, and entertainment requirements of the modern corporation. This suggests that in any world in which women participate on an equal basis with men in all facets of culture and politics, the comforts of home will be diminished, the intimacies of marriage destroyed by exhaustion, and the acculturation of the young neglected. Overall good worlds, according to the argument from heavy costs, require socio-economic inequality between men and women. Greater equality is a moral luxury that is too expensive for us, not only in terms of money but in terms of our other values, including domestic comfort, responsibility to future generations, and freedom.

Should we be persuaded by these forecastings of doom? In considering this question, it is essential to keep in mind that it is unreasonable to reject all worse-for-someone states when some are morally better. It is often just, as well as relatively inexpensive, to worsen the condition of some people to improve that of others. The knowledge that humans are generally more averse to moving to lower levels of power and wealth than they are eager to advance to higher levels provides only one factual consideration relevant to the assessment of the overall costs of policy change.

The argument from heavy costs for a light, or hands–off, approach to sexual inequality cannot be dismissed out of hand. Its conclusion does not, however, approach the status of a confirmed theorem of the theory of distributive justice. The argument that the removal of the maternity disqualification and the adaptation of women to institutions and institutions to women will be so expensive and burdensome that it ought not be attempted is undermined by three considerations that are commonly recognized as defeaters of the argument from heavy costs. Male advantage reflects the enjoyment of ill-gotten

gains; implies the violation of an implicit contract to cooperate for mutual benefit; and is the product of increasingly culpable ignorance.

Men and women face one another as competitors for the same scarce resources—material goods, autonomy, and respect. At the same time, they are cooperators, dedicated to tasks of interest to both sexes. Women's cooperative role cannot reduce their entitlement to the same level of well-being as men enjoy, nor has nature failed to endow them with the cognitive and emotional resources and dispositions they need to earn their half-share of the cooperative surplus. As competitors, women are nevertheless handicapped by their specialization for one of their cooperative roles—childbearing and the nurture of the young. As cooperators, women are easily exploited in virtue of their seemingly deficient performance as competitors.

The two sexes did not stand in morally precarious relations in the early adaptative environment before the accumulation of male advantage. The suggestion that, by getting in touch with their evolutionary roots, women will come to appreciate the appropriateness of their status is thought-provoking but ultimately unconvincing. The task of the prescriptive moralist is to envision distributive and redistributive protocols that compensate for handicaps and that limit the facility with which women can be exploited to perform the least desirable tasks of the community.

8.5. Recursive Effects of Social Judgement

The extent to which existing meritocratic structures continue to filter men, to develop their talents, to demand that they meet certain performance standards, and to reward them for doing so, is still debated.[34] Many formal barriers have been removed, and it is unusual for any authority to express an intention to exclude, ignore, or decline to invest as heavily in women. But in careers in which learning is continuous, discrimination can produce non-measurable educational deficits that are then taken to justify lower rewards. If

[34] The Scholastic Aptitude Test, performance in which strongly influences college admissions in the United States, was revamped in the early 1970s in ways that reduced the advantage women had previously enjoyed on the verbal section; see Brush, 'Women in Science and Engineering', 408–9.

habits and customs furthering the transmission of helpful inside information, beneficial criticism, and the provision of opportunities in which to learn favour men, they can surpass women whose initial endowments were equivalent. Women's access to the doubtful and speculative components of well-being is thereby limited.

To understand why women's actual level of effort may have little effect on how they are evaluated, and why their incentives to defect to lower levels of striving and to represent defection as autonomous choice are powerful, it is necessary to look briefly at the theory of social judgement.

Men and women hold numerous beliefs about themselves and each other as members of their respective genders, including beliefs they rarely admit to and may not realize they hold. These beliefs offer a proximal explanation for why women's lesser status seems normal and unproblematic to many people, while facts about the hypothesized reproductive strategies of the sex with the larger and less numerous gametes offer a relatively distal explanation. Men, by contrast with women, tend to overestimate their own abilities and to be more optimistic about what their abilities will bring them. Further, they often fail to perceive how much of their success depends on circumstances and on the actions of others.[35] We mostly believe that it is somewhat normal for men to try to annoy, tease, harass, and discipline women, that, unlike a few celebrity exhibitionists on TV, the women one ordinarily meets are retiring by nature and do not seek the limelight, and that women are absorbed in and dedicated to the task of caring for young children, often to the exclusion of other goals and ambitions.

One might suppose accordingly that women's worse outcomes reflect improper stereotyping, but this claim is in many respects superficial.

First, stereotyping is a feature of our normal cognitive apparatus. It enables us to make decisions and predictions in conditions of incomplete information or under time constraints. While it is good advice in some contexts to try to think beyond stereotypes, it is counterproductive to insist that we should stop thinking with them. Second, if women who depart from the typical biological patterns for their sex

---

[35] Valian, *Why so Slow?* 154 ff.

receive favourable treatment while the rest do not, women's overall condition will be little improved. Third, we should be less concerned with representations of groups that smooth out individual differences and more concerned with the accuracy of those representations.

Beliefs about women's dislike of social competition, absorption in child-rearing, potential victim status with respect to men, and lack of competence in public affairs are all *somewhat* true. A sociologically minded visitor from Mars who read the newspapers, walked around in a large city, and watched television would form these beliefs about our women in a matter of days or weeks. And if the Martian were then to read a textbook of sociobiology, it might well go away feeling that it had achieved a deep understanding of the human social world. The Martian would not see much point in striving to better women's status. It will be hard, it would think, and it probably will not work.

Yet many beliefs about women are untrue. It is difficult to over-estimate the disadvantage that accrues to women in situations in which they are in competition with men because they are smaller and lighter than men are and because their voices are higher and more childlike. People perceive women as smaller than they really are because they are smaller than men are.[36] And people perceive women as less competent in public affairs than they really are because they display less competence in public affairs than men do. Both men and women represent women to themselves as smaller and less capable than they really are because they are less of all these things in our world than men are. Misperception can reach startling levels. Married men, for example, believe not only that they are better financial providers and better informed, but that they are more intelligent and physically attractive than their wives are.[37] Because we know that male and female intelligence are equal, we can conclude that a significant number of men are unable to assess the intelligence, relative to their own, of women with whom they interact on a daily basis. It is unlikely that they do better when required to assess the intelligence of women whom they encounter on an occasional basis or in the course of a one-hour interview. Evaluators, it has been shown,

[36] Valian, *Why so Slow?*, 6. Height is a great advantage. Boulding reports research showing that bishops are taller than clergymen; university presidents than college presidents. *Underside*, 35.

[37] Louise H. Kidder, Michele A. Fagan, and Ellen S. Cohn, 'Giving and Receiving Social Justice in Close Relationships', 245.

persistently discount evidence regarding women's achievements. The same objective qualifications–the same degrees, publications, years of experience, and attainment of skill levels–redound to the credit of a woman who is being evaluated less than they do to the credit of a man.[38]

Contrary to Fisher's confident assertion that women prefer conditions of equality, there has been little controlled observation to support the claim of female indifference to rank.[39] Yet women's behaviour in meritocratic institutions is often puzzling to managers. Adult women often seem less motivated than men to maintain party discipline, to accept the authority of others, to help other women, particularly those younger than themselves, and to expect help from older ones. Women do not, in this case, lack ambition; on the contrary, they tend to insist too much, by male standards, on preserving their independence.[40] They may fail to perceive the connection between ambitious striving and social rewards, either because rewards are withheld, or because they come unpredictably, or because they are observed to devolve upon the obviously wrong persons of their sex. To a female observer, the stable and relatively egalitarian system of 'laterally connected subgroups' is more visible amongst male professionals than amongst their female counterparts.

Automatic habits of appraisal and even of self-appraisal are nevertheless responsive to information and criticism. Levels of confidence, expectations, and self-attributions of merit are plausibly seen as reactive states of mind that are developed through social experience, that have a powerful causal effect on how things go, and that are easily influenced and changed by altering the customary habits of response. Affirmative action has effectively made available the reserve of previously unsuspected female competence by forcing those who control and distribute power to depart from their customary modes of directing their attention, reading signals, and awarding resources under their control. It is worth pointing out in this connection that investment in female talent before the introduction of affirmative action did not bring with it a reasonable pay-off for the investor. It

---

[38] Valian, *Why So Slow?*, 167 ff.

[39] Female–female competition and hierarchy-establishing behaviour is the basis of social organization in some primates. See Hrdy, *Woman that Never Evolved*, 128.

[40] Shepher and Tiger, 'Female Hierarchies in a Kibbutz Community', 232.

was once the case that only the most impartial and dedicated persons allocated their time and effort equally between the sexes. Affirmative action brings down the price of what was once an expensive moral luxury. Treating his or her students with equal consideration and attention is now within reach of the average professor.

Culpable ignorance in the Theory of Women is clearly on the wane. Yet not so long ago, many people seemed genuinely uncertain that females had the same cognitive abilities as males. Male savantism has made an overwhelming impression, registering with us as clear proof of overall male capability and female disqualification. Not so many years ago, a certain cultural anxiety hung in the air about whether women could perform complex tasks. Could they really deal with large numbers and make responsible decisions? Could they comprehend tangled legal cases, or would they become confused? Could they propound hypotheses as boldly and structure scholarly articles as elaborately as men? Looking around at the population of women, the intuitive statistician saw little evidence of an ability to do any of these things. He worked out the correlation coefficients in his head and concluded that there must be causal laws at work. There is no lack of objective evidence that women can do things they, for the most part, still do not do, as should be expected from the absence of significant differences in male and female perceptual and cognitive abilities and motivational structures. It is encouraging that hard-won genuine knowledge of women's underlying capabilities is gradually replacing the intuitive sociologist's deductions from experience. A letter of reference received recently for a female candidate reads as follows:

Beyond understanding causal inference models, this work requires familiarity with projections in Hilbert spaces, semiparametric efficiency theory involving tangent space calculations for infinite dimensional parameters, estimating function theory for the purpose of construction of locally efficient estimators. In addition, it involves understanding how to simulate data from a marginal structural model. Jennifer has also implemented a simulation study for the proposed estimators which has as its goal to determine the practical performance and practical challenge of estimation of causal parameters in longitudinal studies in which treatment at a given time is assigned as a function of the observed past.[41]

---

[41] My thanks to the author of this letter, who shall remain nameless, for permission to reproduce this paragraph.

Evidently, Jennifer can access savant capabilities most women—and most men—cannot. Yet, for the letter-writer, she is an ordinary brilliant student, of the sort that appears now and then. Journalists nevertheless hint darkly that women's difficulties with spatial rotation and abstract thought reflect their non-adaptation to big-game hunting and explain why they do most of the housework.

Modern humans attach an importance to achieving and employing correct and effective representations. We believe that it is important to learn how to read competency signals correctly, not only to substantiate the claim that the professions are organized on merito-cratic principles, but also to weed out the inefficiencies that result from preferring the less able. The costs of revising our ordinary beliefs about the nature of physical objects and their motions and discarding our intuitive cosmology, physics, and matter theory have been very high. Intellectual struggles by individuals, and substantial public and private funding, were required to get the reasonably accurate picture we think we possess. Yet no sociobiologists and few moral philoso-phers have expressed anxiety and pessimism about the diversion of resources needed to teach physics and chemistry, or the regimenta-tion the learner must undergo, or the socially disruptive effects of new knowledge in those fields. It has never been considered an argument against teaching physics that the amount of regulation required places some personal freedoms in jeopardy, though millions of high school students can testify that it does so. It will be protested that the theory of gender similarities and differences and the theory of social judgement are far less certain than physics and chemistry, that much that currently passes under those headings is almost certainly wrong, and that to teach what might turn out to be mistaken is far more consequential in social theory than in chemistry. Very well, but all knowledge emerges from error and confusion and in the meantime there are disappointments, wasted efforts, and occasional unintended explosions.

8.6. Policies for Equality

The idealism characteristic of a theory of gender relations is still largely unformulated, perhaps because the reality constraint has

proved so problematic. Certainly, the paraworlds of the sociobiological literature do not encourage readers to see male–female relationships as potentially perfectly cooperative, in so far as they portray the sexes as exploitable resources for one another, which, from a scientific perspective, they are. The cooperative relationship of the modern household is built upon the pre-moral platform and the partners to it are likely to remain residuary opportunists, just as modern employers remain residuary slave-holders. Yet the superposition of moral ideation alters the terms of these primitive forms of getting along. Human ingenuity makes possible both intense exploitation and compensatory moral advantage-reduction.

Whenever a man or a woman joins an architectural firm, or goes to work for a hospital or educational institution, or in a law office, whether as a director or as a cleaner, he or she is entering into a cooperative relationship with members of the opposite sex for a broader purpose. For trust and non-exploitative cooperative behaviour to develop, individuals have to know each other well. Modes of existence in which the contributions of the two parties are distinctly visible to one another, even when they perform separate tasks, appear to be conducive to mutual respect and appreciation.[42]

The possibility of a normalization of the workplace, such that the standards of reciprocity and mutual assistance, as well as friendly rivalry, are maintained in cross-gender interactions, is one of the most appealing aspects of the potential breakup of sex and gender hierarchies. The companionship value of men and women for one another is substantial wherever resentment has not taken hold. When one is given the opportunity to observe men, women, and children in informal surroundings—at picnics and festivals, for example, or while waiting around for something to happen, wherever men's attention is not distracted by competition with other men or attempts to appease them—their easy sociability with children and their friendliness towards women, by contrast with the tension observed under other circumstances, is impressive.

Men stand under a moral obligation to divert some proportion of their energies from productive and directive activities to maintenance and uncompensated amateur activities. This general obligation is

<hr/>

[42] Boulding, *Underside*, 10 ff., 35 ff., 292.

impersonal and objective. It derives not only from the distinct moral preferability of a world in which maintenance is not downloaded onto the sex whose lesser earning capacities are unrelated to the competence and interests of its members, but also from the practical failure of the division of labour with respect to sustainability. The traditional division into homemakers and resource extractors-and-converters has failed to project into a global system in which the maintenance of the habitat proceeds in parallel with and compensates for wealth production. The natural environment was for a long time seen as no one's responsibility, male or female, to look after, and the world is rapidly filling up with manufactured objects that no one knows how to clean, from bathroom taps and home juicers to burnt-out transformers and atomic power plants. It is further reasonable to divert some proportion of funds that would otherwise be spent on roadworks, street light upgrades, and subsidized development projects to childcare provisions for mothers in the active world. All such projects represent investments in infrastructure in which the public has an interest.

A glance at the magazine section of the airport news-stand with its neat division of the separate life-worlds of the two sexes—money, electronics, and muscle building for men; medical and diet news, home decor, and psychological manipulation for women—suggests that the calculated strengthening of gender identity is highly profitable. It is easy to induce people to forgo other consumption opportunities in order to purchase sex-specific esoteric knowledge, though the low news-stand price assures us that the information is neither very secret nor very useful. Yet Wilson's suggestion that 'In theory, at least, a carefully designed society with strong sexual divisions could be richer in spirit, more diversified, and even more productive than a unisex society'[43] seems correct in one respect. In order for women to gain in social dignity, liberty, and enjoyment, it ought not to be necessary for them to adopt the habits, postures, and interests of men. Beyond the permission to strive for sexual distinction with special gender-specific clothes, adornments, and mannerisms, accommodation to different genuine preferences with respect to childcare is reasonable. Insisting on a fifty-fifty division of babyminding might be

---

[43] E. O. Wilson, *On Human Nature*, 132–3.

unacceptably burdensome for most men and unacceptably anxiety-provoking in most women.[44] Any system that demands that women sacrifice virtually all contact with children as a condition of their enjoying substantial participation and political influence and the use of their analytical and creative faculties is exceedingly costly in human terms.

At the same time, we know that many children see too much of their mothers and too little of their fathers. Exposure to the skills, interests, and energy levels of adult men is bracing and salutary for the young of both sexes, and exposure to the weaknesses and dependencies of the young is in turn beneficial for adult men. There are further reasons to be wary of the proposal that a society that strives to enhance rather than to efface sexual division will not only be more productive and diversified but also actually better than one that does not. Michael Chance surmises that the agonistic mode corresponds to a 'residual psychophysiological element' built into the constitution of men, and that social circumstances can elicit and strengthen hyper-vigilant behaviour. Early experience and training directed to what he terms an essentially rank-ordered adult life may strengthen the effects of hormonal biases 'that may, in later life, be at variance with a civilized life, create unsuspected biases of behaviour and perception, and thus lead men and women to become so divergent as not to get on with one another'.[45]

According to legend, male cultural accomplishments are not a function of their exemption from domestic responsibilities and the social expectation that they will employ the resulting leisure profitably. Rather, men's intrinsically greater ambition produces the accomplishment that justifies the exemption and explains the expectation. There is no reason, however, to suppose that sexual curiosity, risk-friendliness, and impatience, to name the qualities most commonly supposed to distinguish the male sex, however well documented, and however hormonally mediated and thus resistant to acceptable tampering they may be, are the precursors of initiative, persistence, creativity, concentration, critical ability, and the ability to withstand criticism. There is no reason in other words

---

[44] For a contrary view, see Virginia Held, *Rights and Goods*, 205 as well as Okin, *Justice, Gender and Equality*, 175.
[45] Chance, 'Sex Differences in the Structure of Attention', 159.

to suppose a pre-institutional connection between competitive and dominance-seeking behaviour and cultural achievement and, indeed, there is good reason not to.

In his study of the focuses of attention in various primate species, Chance contrasts the 'hedonic' behaviour of the chimpanzees he observed with the 'agonistic' behaviour of baboons and macaques, arguing that the preoccupation of the latter with rank order 'has, in their evolutionary past, led to a limited expressive repertoire . . . ; it has imposed upon them a form of social attention that precludes the visual awareness essential for the development of tool use'.[46] To the extent that male chimpanzees experience a greater flexibility in their control of their attention and their emotional arousal, they are free to engage in playful and experimental activities. The ability to ignore status-establishing and maintaining activities and to refocus on other tasks is thought to be conspicuous in females, and it is perhaps not accidental that the Ancients ascribed the majority of human inventions—amongst them, writing, weaving, and numbers—to women.

As noted earlier, male humans are far more likely to exhibit savant syndrome, now considered to stem from damage to the left hemisphere and to higher-level memory circuitry that is compensated by the development of additional habit-memory and right-brain capacity.[47] Though psychologists consider savantism a dysfunction on account of the notable deficits in affect and conversational ability it entails, savant talents such as lightning calculation, mechanical ability, drawing, music, and map-memorizing are highly prized in normal people. It would not be surprising if normal men were slightly more able, or more likely to be able to access some savant capacities, though this is likely to occur—according to the hypothesis—at the expense of their ability to experience the depth and complexity of affect and to produce elaborate and meaningful verbal representations. Yet the differences between the sexes cannot be pronounced in this respect, for we have no doubt that men overall meet the human standard for feeling and language well enough to perform important social roles. To complement our Jennifer X, we have our occasional William S. and Leo T., manifesting a verbal fluency and mastery of emotional nuance remarkable in their sex.

[46] Chance, 'Sex Differences in the Structure of Attention', 144.
[47] Darold Treffert, 'The Idiot Savant: A Review of the Syndrome'.

If girls' presumed greater distractibility, sensitivity to social cues, and integrative abilities are not countered by an education that emphasizes concentration and abstraction, they may not develop valued savant capacities. If boys are not guided to the study of poetry and literature and if adult men do not continue to cultivate the arts of language and the shadings of affect in later life, Chance's vision of a depressingly polarized society in which the sexes do not understand each other and cannot get on well is likely to be realized. Traditional education was compensatory in forcing girls to do word problems and trigonometry and boys to ponder romantic novels; traditional notions of culture presupposed a common ground. The assumption was that some degree of repression could be justified as a necessary condition of the liberation of potentials and the enhancement of opportunities in later life. Though the educational process was effortful and not entirely successful, the thinking behind it was sound.

8.7. Love as a Morally Relevant Phenomenon

Nowhere is the discrepancy between first-person and third-person viewpoints as evident as in the experience of romantic love, which might be defined as the conjunction of delight in the speech and company of another, solicitude, and desire, together with a second-order demand for exclusivity or at least considerable privilege with respect to companionship and disclosure.

Love is at once an important subject of imperatives and a claimant on exemptions. It is characterized by, to paraphrase Plato, the involuntary assumption of a position of disadvantage, as well as self-serving resourcefulness. Myths and stories link love with sacrifice and labour, more often labour for than labour alongside, and wherever the labour is for another's benefit and involves self-sacrifice, it introduces moral significance into the relationship. Love is a great shredder of contracts, the severer as well as the forger of human bonds, stating its own demand for exemptions. Duties of presence are forgotten and their associated automatisms interrupted. Further, the vulnerabilities of the pair offer outlets for the controlling and even persecutory impulses of the socially dominant. Williams's 'Moral Luck' is perhaps really a *plaidoyer* for the privilege demanded by love, represented in the story

less by exotic Tahitian women than by 'Gauguin's' painting, to which he stands in a genuinely intimate relation, with which a powerful authority—what Williams terms 'the morality system'—threatens to interfere.

Sociobiologists may think they know what love is for, what its function or functions might be. But the notion that it produces the motives to parental care is not credible. Why should attachment to an unrelated man be a condition for a woman's caring for her own baby? The function of love may be simply to ensure conception with a preferred consort in a low-fertility species. Or its purpose may be to maintain fluidity in social systems, preventing them being dominated by autocratic individuals. A creature that is highly motivated to evade social control and select its own mates may have an advantage over a less emotional one. Deepening the mystery is the fact that homosexual pairs experience the same romantic emotions. In what follows I shall speak of men and women as offering the more visible and frequent examples of the phenomenon, but I do not mean to underestimate the intensity or worth of same-sex pairings.

Human ideation, in any case, makes all functional accounts inadequate. As E. O. Wilson remarks, the initial experience 'permanently alters the adolescent mind'.[48] It is a fountain of creativity that kicks away writer's block, sweeps out accumulated emotional debris, and dictates their own poetry to clods and pedants. The predisposition to the emotion is so great that it is capable of creating its own object. People fall in love with faces glimpsed in a window, film stars and characters in books, and with persons they have merely heard about. Even defeated love takes its time departing; our mental universes are populated by not only our relatives, living and departed, and assorted authority figures who have to be reckoned with, but the wronged or wronging ghosts of the past. Love did not need invention and both sexes are assuredly subject to it, but in periods of rough manners, it goes into cultural decline and needs periodic reinvention.

Where personal relations between the sexes are concerned, humans appear to operate with three principal systems, related in different ways to the phenomenon under discussion, the romantic or courtly, the labour-dominant, and the vice-driven. Individuals take

---

[48] E. O. Wilson, *On Human Nature*, 60.

part in—and also refuse to take part in—some or all of these systems simultaneously, in the courtly, because its modes of address and receptivity come naturally, wherever education or law has not suppressed them, in the labour-dominant, as creatures partaking in the struggle for existence. Vice—occasional relations that exclude mutual love and responsibility—is an accessory system. Moral problems arise from the intersection and interaction of the three systems, confusion or disagreement amongst participants as to which system of relationship is in play, and from the perils inherent in each.

Courtly relationships are based in elective affinity, in a preference for one person's company over the company of others. Their emotional temperature ranges from, at the low end, the weak but pleasing dependencies of acquaintances and colleagues who are less than perfectly indifferent to one another, to, at the high end, romantic obsession. They are characterized by mutual deference and attention. Their terms are not enforceable, they require trust between individuals that is not backed up by the approval of others or legal sanctions, and they may or may not be durable. Lacking external validation, romantic friendships, as Kant pointed out, tend to destroy themselves in quarrels and misunderstandings.

Any society that attaches importance to the emotions of individuals recognizes these preferential bondings and allows them some role in the organization of that society, through the permission rules governing the initial choice of a mate, the rights of divorce and remarriage, or socially tolerated infidelity by one or both sexes. Courtly relations may be precursors to fixed, labour-dominant relations, or noticed and fostered by third parties in order to found them. Or they may coexist as separate, paramarital systems. Such systems may be developed and formalized by non-labouring social elites—the society described by Lady Murasaki in fourteenth-century Japan, in which the lovers pass their days composing and hand-lettering poems for one another, or the historians of the *amours* of princes and princesses in eighteenth-century France. Even in small villages in which surveillance and gossip assist religious authorities in enforcing strict norms, loving attachments arise between men and women of the same age. The idiocy of rural life, as Marx saw it—or the idiocy of the life of the aristocratic Genji, as MacIntyre sees it—is perhaps mitigated by the way in which people tend to find particular

others interesting. They brave disgrace and even—in the case of women—execution or jealous murder, for reasons of preferential attachment.

Wilson describes the pair-bond as natural for humans and the intensity of these relations and their ubiquity in every period of history leave no doubt that such inventions as group marriage or Plato's community of wives can never be more than thought experiments or the shortest-lived of social experiments. But Wilson does not quite succeed in explaining which form of pair-bond should be considered natural.[49] In any case, what is natural is only one consideration, though an important one, with respect to the constitution of social rules. Courtly modes of interaction between men and women, together with the vicious ones, can either stabilize or destabilize labour-dominant marriage, and films and stories, as well as workplace guidelines, correspond to different modalities in which societies discuss the threat of destabilization with themselves, and through which resolution of the conflict is hopefully, but inadequately, sought. Many novels affirm on their surface the precedence of *plein air* contract over the darker affinities, and the right of its upholders to apply force, while lodging a protest underneath. Institutional codes of conduct seek to prevent the confluence of political and emotional ends, as well as the appropriation of young love by aged vice, recognizing how tempting and at the same time how dangerous to the participants and to others such hybrid relationships can be. We are forced, in these matters as elsewhere, to elect positions that reflect our best estimations of reality, causal relations, and optimality, but no one can claim that their judgements in these matters are true or even well confirmed.

In the labour-dominant system, long-term partners select one another or are selected for one another—often, but not always through love and preceding courtly relations—to serve as helpmeets and companions in the service of economic production and biological reproduction. This may involve joint labour in maintaining a household and raising children but also cooperative production, as occurs in peasant societies or family-run commercial enterprises. Importance is laid on the durability of these pair-bonds, and natural

---

[49] E. O. Wilson, *On Human Nature*, 139 ff.

sentiment, inner resolve, and external pressure contribute to their maintenance in varying proportions. They are the subject of contract and publicly witnessed, and there is legal recourse in the case of abandonment. Only a very high degree of mutual or one-sided disaffection, traceable to causes that can be enumerated and object-ively verified, is regarded as justifying the violation of the agreement to work together, especially when children enter the picture.

Long-term monogamy is the least discriminatory of possible mar-riage systems in the following sense: It tends to even out the chances of reproductive success, at least amongst men and probably amongst women as well, by reducing the role of favour and preference in the distribution of resources. It furnishes the benefits of companionship and cooperation to more persons than other systems, including a system of transitory, hence highly competitive, bonding. In this respect, it offers prima facie moral advantages, preventing those with unusual allure from collecting too many mates and helpers and those with relatively little from being left out. It diminishes anxiety over the possible loss of a pleasing companion, gives rise to the satisfactions of narrative continuity and shared history, offers the opportunity to enjoy the company of one's own children and to influence their development, and provides assistance in daily living for the old. It is conducive to the preservation of wealth. Monogamy frees up energies for pursuits other than courtship in the young, and reduces ambient levels of jealousy. At the same time, long-term monogamy's moral and non-moral disadvantages—overfamiliarity, excessive dynastic-patterning, hidden violence, appropriation of labour, and marital condescension—have to be factored into the balance. To embark on it in a serious way is to renounce an advantage over and against a deceivable or dependent intimate. The exclusivity demanded is experienced as hard—a little hard for most people, very difficult for others, impossible for some. Where emotional security is concerned, marriage is thought to confer overwhelming benefits, yet abandonment has especially grave consequences in a culture that is socially and economically organized for formal monogamy. The anguish of the repudiated partner is perhaps no less in more fluid systems, or in unsanctioned unions. But to the insult—even if it leads hyperbolically to exile, the convent, or the grave—is not added the injury of financial shock and chaos in the domicile.

In vice-driven relationships, sensation, power, and revelatory knowledge are sought and are either acquired by misrepresentation of the quality and magnitude of the cooperative surplus in prospect, or simply paid for. Preference is one-sided or feigned for advantage. The term love may figure, as euphemism, or as a vehicle of deceit. For the sake of their own well-being, individuals are often called on to determine whether they are inadvertent participants. The boundary between courtly relations and vice is not always clear, for a single night can be the beginning of a great romance or mere exploitation. The boundary between labour-dominant marriage and vice is equally fuzzy; exactly what the trophy wife does for her maintenance may decide it.

The regulation of vice is the concern of public officials who deal with imagery and behaviour, and with their by-products, but vice impinges on private life as well, in so far as individuals must decide whether to participate in it or tolerate the participation of their intimates. Friedrich Engels's view that vice is the natural accompaniment of economic coercion and that it poisons and subverts all preference-based male–female relationships,[50] is shared by many persons whose repulsion from commercial sex is considered rather inarticulate and negligible, in so far as they often cannot name any specific harms that arise necessarily from the renting out of one's person to strangers or for the production of simulacra. The associated evils—disease, stress, drug-addiction, brutality, and the habit of mendacity—are held by libertarians to be contingent and unrelated to the essential character of the system, products of its partial repression, or inconsequential in the face of the rights to commercial and personal freedom. Were prostitutes to view their work and to have it viewed in the same light as, say, appliance repairmen or hairdressers, its sequelae, they think, would trouble us no more. Second-tier goods, one might suppose—and access to the opposite sex is a known and necessary component of well-being—should be supplied to all, regardless of the merit of the needy person. The devotion or good manners normally required to attract the favourable attention of women should not be preconditions of men's obtaining it. Vice, some believe, reduces the frequency of rape.

---

[50] Friedrich Engels, *The Origin of the Family, Private Property and the State*, 138.

It is not clear, however, that a world with a free market in women would have less brutality, stress, addiction, and disease than one without. On the grounds advanced by Williams, it would be unjustifiable to require *me* to become a prostitute to reduce the overall frequency of rape or grievous frustration in the population, is it right to assign some more tractable person this duty in a better world? Further, there are serious externalities to both prostitution and pornography. Disrespect transfers to all members of the-sex-that-lets-itself-be-prostituted, just as the maternal disqualification transfers to all members of the-sex-that-has-the-babies. Both prostitution and the easy availability of pornography reduce the leverage of wives and lovers by breaking their monopoly on the provision of gratifying experiences. One might feel that that particular monopoly ought to be broken, but female refusal provides needed balance in a world in which women are disadvantaged by their lesser earning power and have few means at their disposal to induce men to upgrade their behaviour. Access to the other sex is best considered a second-tier good, like parenthood or friendship. These affiliative goods are adequately supplied in more attractive worlds, but personal effort, not merely the exercise of purchasing power, is needed to obtain them.

Labour-dominant relations, meanwhile, are potentially as genuinely cooperative as any other relations. Two or more individuals engage in concerted or coordinated actions that enable them to accomplish work that neither could accomplish alone or accomplish as easily. The questions that can normally be asked about cooperative relationships can be asked about domestic partnerships, as well as all other mixed-sex partnerships. Is the work accomplished of importance to both parties? Is the cooperative surplus real, or deferred, or even imaginary? Is the cooperative surplus appropriately shared? Does it reflect the eligibility of the subtasks performed? Does it overcompensate for scarcity and accumulated advantage?

The formalities of marriage emphasize its cooperative aspects. At the same time, the romantic love that normally precedes and ushers in the prospect of labour-dominant relations often seems to make such questions irrelevant, or reduces the motivation to bargain, leaving many actual relationships at the basic end of the cooperative spectrum. Though game theorists emphasize that it is better to decline

exploitative offers than to improve one's condition relative to its present state, this policy is rational only under the assumption that the bargaining game with the same player will have further rounds. Many significant decisions are one-off; the same game will never be played again opposite the same partner. And relevant information regarding the propensities and dispositions, hence the likely future actions, of the other bargainer may be unavailable, or available but psychologically difficult to grasp. Rational, self-interested persons invited to play a single-transaction game—to decide to accept or issue an offer of marriage or not—often make a decision that improves their condition relative to what it would otherwise have been while creating a standing situation of injustice.

Societies that value the nuclear family and that consider the presence of affective ties between mothers and fathers of signal importance act semi-rationally from the economic point of view in making the institution of marriage easy to enter into and difficult to escape. Such incentives and restrictions are conducive to the fair distribution of the cooperative surplus, in so far as single parenthood is a liability for a woman in a wage-based economic system. Yet the incentives and restrictions do not always work as intended and contingency plans for their failure are lacking in our overconfident society. Nor is the emphasis on stability conducive in every way to human well-being. Again, the litany of universal human grievances bears witness. We know that people are made miserable, desperate, and even suicidal by laws, authorities, and relatives that stipulate or interfere with their companionship preferences. Individual happiness is fostered by greater trust of the pair-bonding instinct and of individual preferences, by deference towards these preferences from third parties, by easier exit in case of unilateral or bilateral disaffection, and, finally, by minimization of the unfortunate consequences of abandonment for adults and children, in short, by concessions to the biological platform that moderate exigent moralities. At the same time, we know that inaccessibility promotes ideation, that ideation can give rise to idealization, and that idealization produces what we think of as the greatest achievements in art, literature, and culture. Mild repression is consistent with the generally benign nature of a good moral system.

Human animals like to hang themselves with the weights of grave responsibility. Koehler's chimpanzees behaved in a way he at first found puzzling:

Almost daily, the animals can be seen walking about with a rope, a bit of rag, a blade of grass or a twig on their shoulders. If Tschego was given a metal chain, she would put it around her neck immediately... Tercera also has strings running down the back of her head and over her ears, so that they dangle down both sides of her face. . . . Chica, the sturdy, at one time took a fancy to carrying heavy stones about on her back; she began with four full pounds and soon reached a powerful block of lava weighing nine pounds.

These observations led Koehler to believe that the pleasure of adornment lies in 'the extraordinary heightened bodily consciousness of the animal. It is a feeling of stateliness and pride, indeed, which occurs in human beings when they decorate themselves with sashes or long tassels knocking against their legs . . . : when anything moves with our bodies we feel richer and more stately.'[51] *Pace* Williams, the enhancement effect of the burdens and encumbrances of the morality system and its often heavily born responsibilities is not to be underestimated. Williams encodes happiness as flight and evasion. Though, from the objective standpoint, romance is a significant element in most human lives, this encoding cannot be taken as the fundamental insight of a theory of male–female relations, or of a morality for a social world.

[51] Koehler, *Mentality of Apes*, 95.

Bibliography

Abramovitch, Rona, and Strayer, Fred, 'Pre-school Social Organization', in Lester Kames, Patricia Pliner and Thomas Alloway (eds.), *Aggression, Dominance and Individual Spacing* (New York and London: Plenum, 1978), 107–28.

Alexander, Richard D., *The Biology of Moral Systems* (Hawthorne, NY: de Gruyter, 1987).

Annas, Julia, 'Personal Love and Kantian Ethics in *Effie Briest*', *Philosophy and Literature*, 8 (1984), 5–31.

Aristotle, *Nicomachean Ethics*, tr. W. D. Ross, in *Basic Works*, ed. Richard McKeon (New York: Random House, 1941).

Arneson, Richard J., 'Perfectionism and Politics', *Ethics*, 111 (2000), 37–63.

Axelrod, Robert, *The Evolution of Cooperation* (New York: Basic Books, 1984).

Baier, Annette, *Moral Prejudice: Essays on Ethics* (Cambridge, Mass.: Harvard University Press, 1994).

Beauvoir, Simone de, *Le Deuxième Sexe*, 2 vols. (Paris: Gallimard, 1949).

Bentham, Jeremy, *Introduction to the Principles of Morals and Legislation* (Buffalo: Prometheus, 1988).

Blackburn, Simon, *Spreading the Word* (Oxford: Clarendon, 1984).

—— *Ruling Passions* (London: Oxford University Press, 1998).

Boulding, Elise, *The Underside of History* (Newbury Park: Sage, 1992).

Braybrooke, David, 'The Concept of Needs, with a Heartwarming Offer to Utilitarianism,' in Brock (ed.), *Necessary Goods*, 57–72.

—— *Meeting Needs* (Princeton: Princeton University Press, 1987).

—— *Natural Law Modernized* (Toronto: University of Toronto Press, 2001).

——, 'The Representation of Rules in Logic and their Definition', in Braybrooke (ed.), *Social Rules* (Boulder: Westview, 1996), 3–20.

Brock, Gillian (ed.), *Necessary Goods* (Lanham, Md.: University Press of America, 1998).

Brush, Stephen, 'Women in Science and Engineering', *American Scientist*, 79 (1991), 404–19.

Burke, Edmund, *Reflection on the Revolution in France*, ed. J. G. A. Pocock (Indianapolis: Hackett, 1987).

Chance, Michael R. A., 'Sex Differences in the Structure of Attention', in Tiger and Fowler (eds.), *Female Hierarchies*, 135–62.

—— and Jolly, Clifford J., *Social Groups of Apes, Monkeys and Men* (London: Cape, 1970).

Clutton-Brock, T. L., and Harvey, Paul, 'Evolutionary Rules and Primate Societies', in Clutton-Brock and Harvey (eds.), *Readings in Sociobiology* (San Francisco: Freeman, 1978), 300–3.

Cohen, Gerald, *If You're an Egalitarian, How Come You're so Rich?* (Cambridge, Mass.: Harvard University Press, 2000).

—— 'Robert Nozick and Wilt Chamberlain: How Patterns Preserve Liberty', *Erkenntnis*, 11 (1977), 5–23.

Copp, David, 'Moral Realism: Facts and Norms' (Review of David O. Brink, *Moral Realism*), *Ethics*, 101 (1991), 610–24.

Cottingham, John, 'The Ethical Credentials of Partiality', *Proceedings of the Aristotelian Society*, 98 (1998), 1–21.

—— 'Partiality, Favoritism, and Morality', *Philosophical Quarterly*, 36 (1986), 357–73.

Daniels, Norman, 'Wide Reflective Equilibrium and Theory Acceptance in Ethics', *Journal of Philosophy*, 76 (1979), 256–82.

Darwall, Stephen, *Philosophical Ethics* (Boulder: Westview, 1998).

Dasgupta, Partha, *An Inquiry into Well-Being and Destitution* (Oxford: Clarendon, 1993).

Davidowicz, Lucy, *The War Against the Jews* (New York: Holt Rhinehart and Winston, 1975).

Davis, David Brion, *The Problem of Slavery in Western Culture* (Ithaca, NY: Cornell University Press, 1966).

DePaul, Michael R., 'Two Conceptions of Coherence Methods in Ethics', *Mind*, 96 (1987), 463–81.

Diana, Lewis, *The Prostitute and her Client* (Springfield: Charles C. Thomas, 1985).

Douglas, Mary, *Purity and Danger* (London: Routledge and Kegan Paul, 1969).

—— and Isherwood, Baron, *The World of Goods* (London: Allen Lane, 1978).

Dover, Kenneth J., *Greek Popular Morality in the Time of Plato and Aristotle* (Oxford: Blackwell, 1974).

Dworkin, Ronald, 'What is Equality: Part I: Equality of Welfare'; 'Part II: Equality of Resources', *Philosophy and Public Affairs*, 10 (1981), 185–246; 283–345.

Edgerton, Robert B., *Rules, Exceptions and Social Order* (Berkeley and Los Angeles: University of California Press, 1985).

Ehrenberg, Margaret, *Women in Prehistory* (London: British Museum Press, 1989).

Eisenman, Stephen, *Gauguin's Skirt* (New York: Thames and Hudson, 1997).

Engels, Friedrich, *The Origins of the Family, Private Property and the State*, tr. Alec West (New York: International Publishers, 1975).

Eriksson, Björn, *Heavy Duty* (Stockholm: Almquist and Wickell, 1994).

Evans-Pritchard, E. E., 'The Position of Women in Primitive Societies and in our Own', in *The Position of Women in Primitive Societies* (London: Faber and Faber, 1965), 37–58.

Fisher, Helen, *The Anatomy of Love: The Natural History of Monogamy, Adultery and Divorce* (London and New York: Simon and Schuster, 1992).

Flack, Jessica, and de Waal, Franz B. M., 'Any Animal Whatever: Darwinian Building Blocks of Morality', in Leonard D. Katz (ed.), *Evolutionary Origins of Morality: Cross-Disciplinary Perspectives* (Bowling Green: Imprint Academic, 2000), 67–78.

Folbre, Nancy, 'Roemer's Market Socialism: A Feminist Critique', in Erik Olin Wright (ed.), *Equal Shares: Making Market Socialism Work* (London and New York: Verso, 1996), 57–70.

Foucault, Michel, *A History of Sexuality*, vol. i, tr. Robert Hurley (New York: Vintage, 1988).

Frazer, J. G., article 'Taboo', *Encyclopedia Britannica*, 9th edn. (New York: H. G. Allen, 1888), vol. T–P, p. 13.

Freud, Sigmund, 'Taboo and the Ambivalence of Emotions', in *Basic Writings*, tr. and ed. A. A. Brill (New York: Modern Library, 1938), 821–64.

Furrow, Dwight, *Against Theory* (New York: Routledge, 1995).

Gauthier, David, *Morals by Agreement* (Oxford: Clarendon, 1986).

Geach, Peter, 'Ascriptivism', *Philosophical Review*, 69 (1960), 221–5.

—— 'Assertion', *Philosophical Review*, 74 (1965), 449–65.

Gehlen, Arnold, *Moral und Hypermoral*, 2nd edn. (Frankfurt and Bonn: Athenaum, 1970).

Gibbard, Allan, *Wise Choices, Apt Feelings: A Theory of Normative Judgment* (Cambridge, Mass.: Harvard University Press, 1990).

Gilligan, Carol, *In a Different Voice* (Cambridge, Mass.: Harvard University Press, 1982).

Goodin, Robert, *Protecting the Vulnerable: A Reanalysis of our Social Responsibilities* (Chicago: University of Chicago Press, 1985).

—— 'Vulnerabilities and Responsibilities: An Ethical Defense of the Welfare State', in Brock (ed.), *Necessary Goods*, 73–94.

Goody, Jack, 'Literacy and Moral Rationality', in Stent (ed.), *Morality as a Biological Phenomenon*, 153–66.

Grice, H. P., 'The Causal Theory of Perception', *Proceedings of the Aristotelian Society*, suppl. vol. 35 (1961), 121–52.

Griffin, James, *Well-Being: Its Meaning, Measurement and Importance* (Oxford: Clarendon, 1986).

Hare, R. M., *The Language of Morals* (New York: Oxford University Press, 1964).

—— *Sorting out Ethics* (Oxford: Clarendon, 1997).

Harman, Gilbert, *The Nature of Morality* (Oxford: Oxford University Press, 1977).

Harris, Marvin, 'The Evolution of Gender Hierarchies: A Trial Formulation', in Miller (ed.), *Sex and Gender Hierarchies*, 57–80.

Harvey, J., *Civilized Oppression* (Totowa: Rowman and Littlefield, 1999).

—— 'Justice Theory and Oppression', in Catherine Wilson (ed.), *Civilization and Oppression, Canadian Journal of Philosophy*, suppl. vol. 25 (Calgary: University of Calgary Press, 1999), 171–90.

Hayek, Friedrich, *Law, Legislation and Liberty*, 2 vols. (London: Routledge and Kegan Paul, 1976).

——, *The Mirage of Social Justice* (London: Routledge and Kegan Paul, 1976).

—— *The Road to Serfdom* (Chicago: University of Chicago, 1994).

Held, Virginia, *Rights and Goods* (New York: Macmillan, 1984).

Herodotus, *The Histories*, tr. Robin Waterfield (Oxford: Oxford University Press, 1998).

Hobbes, Thomas, *Leviathan*, vols. 1 and 2 (Indianapolis: Library of Liberal Arts, 1958).

Honderich, Ted, 'The Use of the Basic Proposition of a Theory of Justice', *Mind*, 84 (1975), 63–78.

Hrdy, Sarah Blaffer, *Mother Nature: Maternal Instincts and How They Shape the Human Species* (New York: Ballantine, 1999).

—— *The Woman that Never Evolved* (Cambridge, Mass.: Harvard University Press, 1981).

—— *An Enquiry Concerning the Principles of Morals*, ed. Tom Beauchamp (Oxford: Oxford University Press, 1998).

Hume, David, *A Treatise of Human Nature*, ed. L. A. Selby-Bigge, 2nd edn. (Oxford: Clarendon, 1978).

Irani, K. D., 'The Idea of Social Justice in the Ancient World', in Irani and Silver (eds.), *Social Justice*, 3–80.

Irani, K. D., and Silver, Morris, *Social Justice in the Ancient World* (Westport and London: Greenwood Press, 1995).

Joshi, Heather, and Paci, Pierella, *Unequal Pay for Women and Men: Evidence from the British Cohort Study* (Cambridge, Mass.: MIT, 1998).

Kagan, Shelly, *The Limits of Morality* (Oxford: Oxford University Press, 1989).

—— *Lectures on Ethics*, tr. Louis Infield (Indianapolis: Hackett, 1963).

Kant, Immanuel, *Anthropology from a Pragmatic Point of View*, tr. Mary J. Gregor (The Hague: Nijhoff, 1974).

—— *Foundations of the Metaphysics of Morals*, in *Ethical Philosophy*, tr. J. W. Ellington (Indianapolis and Cambridge: Hackett, 1983).

—— 'On a Supposed Right to Lie from Altruistic Motives', in Lewis White Beck (tr. and ed.), *Critique of Practical Reason and Other Writings in Moral Philosophy* (Chicago: University of Chicago Press, 1949), 346–51.

Kidder, Louise H., Fagan, Michele A., and Cohn, Ellen S., 'Giving and Receiving Social Justice in Close Relationships', in Melvin J. Lerner and Sally C. Lerner (eds.), *The Justice Motive in Social Behaviour: Adapting to Times of Scarcity and Change* (New York and London: Plenum, 1981), 235–59.

Koehler, Wolfgang, *The Mentality of Apes*, tr. Ella Winter (New York: Harcourt Brace, 1925).

Korsgaard, Christine, 'Skepticism about Practical Reason', *Journal of Philosophy*, 83 (1986), 5–25.

—— *The Sources of Normativity* (Salt Lake: University of Utah Press, 1994).

Kummer, Hans, 'Analogs of Morality among Nonhuman Primates', in Stent (ed.), *Morality as a Biological Phenomenon*, 31–47.

Lane, Robert J. '"The Road Not Taken," Friendship, Consumption, and Happiness', in David A. Crocker and Toby Linden (ed.), *The Ethics of Consumption* (Lanham, Md.: Rowman and Littlefield, 1998), 218–48.

Lerner, Melvin J., *The Belief in a Just World: A Fundamental Delusion* (New York and London: Plenum, 1980).

Lewis, Matthew, *The Monk*, ed. Howard Anderson (Oxford: Oxford University Press, 1995).

Locke, John, *Of Civil Government: Second Treatise* (Chicago, Henry Regnery, 1955).

Lucretius, Titus Carus, *On the Nature of Things*, tr. W. H. D. Rouse, rev. Martin Ferguson Smith (Cambridge, Mass.: Harvard University Press, 1975).

Lux, Kenneth, *Adam Smith's Mistake* (Boston and London: Shambhala 1990).

Maccoby, Eleanor, and Jacklin, Carol, *The Psychology of Sex Differences* (London: Oxford University Press, 1975).

McDowell, John, 'Values and Secondary Qualities', in Ted Honderich (ed.), *Morality and Objectivity: A Tribute to J. L. Mackie* (London: Routledge and Kegan Paul, 1985), 110–29.

MacIntyre, Alasdair, *After Virtue* (Notre Dame: Notre Dame University Press, 1984).

Mackie, J. L., *Ethics: Inventing Right and Wrong* (Harmondsworth: Penguin, 1977).

Macleod, Colin, *Liberalism, Justice and Markets: A Critique of Liberal Equality* (Oxford: Clarendon, 1998).

Maine, Henry Sumner, *Ancient Law* (Tucson: University of Arizona, 1986).

Malthus, *An Essay on the Principles of Population* (1798; Amherst, NY: Promethueus, 1998).

Mannheim, Karl, *Ideology and Utopia*, tr. L. Worth and E. Shils (New York: Harcourt Brace, 1936).

Marsden, William, *The History of Sumatra*, 3rd edn. (1783, Kuala Lumpur: Oxford University Press, 1966).

Matthen, Mohan, and Ariew, André, 'Two Ways of Thinking about Fitness and Natural Selection', *Journal of Philosophy*, 99 (2002), 55–83.

Maynard Smith, John, *Evolution and the Theory of Games* (Cambridge: Cambridge University Press, 1982).

Merton, Robert K., 'The Matthew Effect in Science', *Science*, 159 (1968), 56–63.

Mill, John Stuart, *The Collected Works of John Stuart Mill*, ed. John M. Robinson, 33 vols. (Toronto: University of Toronto, 1962–91).

Miller, Barbara Diane (ed.), *Sex and Gender Hierarchies* (Cambridge: Cambridge University Press, 1993).

Morschauser, Scott N., 'The Ideological Basis for Social Justice/Responsibility in Ancient Egypt', in Irani and Silver (eds.), *Social Justice*, 101–14.

Murphy, Liam, *Moral Demands in Nonideal Theory* (New York: Oxford University Press, 2000).

Nagel, Thomas, 'Critical Notice of Rawls's A Theory of Justice', *Philosophical Review*, 82 (1973), 220–34.

—— 'Equal Treatment and Compensatory Discrimination', *Philosophy and Public Affairs*, 2 (1973), 348–63.

—— *Equality and Partiality* (New York: Oxford University Press, 1991).

—— 'Libertarianism without Foundations', in J. Paul (ed.), *Reading Nozick* (Totowa: Rowman and Littlefield, 1981).

—— *Mortal Questions* (Cambridge: Cambridge University Press, 1979).

—— *The Possibility of Altruism* (New York: Oxford University Press, 1970).

Nagel, Thomas, *The View from Nowhere* (New York: Oxford University Press, 1986).

Nielsen, Kai, and Ware, Robert (eds.), *Exploitation* (Atlantic Highlands: Humanities Press, 1997).

Nietzsche, Friedrich, *The Genealogy of Morals*, tr. Walter Kaufmann and R. J. Hollingdale (New York: Random House, 1969).

Nisbett, Richard, and Ross, Lee, *Human Inference: Strategies and Shortcoming of Social Judgement* (Englewood Cliffs: Prentice-Hall, 1980).

Nozick, Robert, *Anarchy, State and Utopia* (New York: Basic Books, 1974).

Nussbaum, Martha, 'Human Functioning and Social Justice: In Defense of Aristotelian Essentialism', *Political Theory*, 20 (1992), 202–46.

—— *Love's Knowledge* (London: Oxford University Press, 1990).

—— and Sen, Amartya (eds.), *The Quality of Life* (London: Oxford University Press, 1993).

Oakley, Anne, *Housewife* (London: Allen Lane, 1974).

Okin, Susan Moller, *Justice, Gender and the Family* (HarperCollins: Basic Books, 1989).

Omarck, Donald R., Strayer, F. F., and Freeman, David G. (eds.), *Dominance Relations: An Ethological View of Human Conflict and Social Interaction* (Hamden: Garland, 1980).

O'Neill, Onora, 'Justice, Gender and International Boundaries', in Nussbaum and Sen (eds.), *Quality of Life*, 303–23.

Pietroski, Paul M., 'Prima Facie Obligations, Ceteris Paribus Laws in Moral Theory', *Ethics*, 103 (1993), 489–515.

Putnam, Hilary, 'Objectivity and the Science-Ethics Distinction', in Nussbaum and Sen (eds.), *Quality of Life*, 143–57.

Radcliffe-Brown, A. R., *Taboo* (Cambridge: Cambridge University Press, 1939).

Radin, Paul, *Primitive Man as Philosopher* (New York: Appleton, 1927).

Railton, Peter, 'Moral Realism', *Philosophical Review*, 95 (1986), 163–207.

Rawls, John, *The Law of Peoples* (Cambridge, Mass.: Harvard University Press, 1999).

—— *Political Liberalism* (New York: Columbia University Press, 1993).

—— *A Theory of Justice* (rev. edn., Cambridge, Mass.: Harvard University Press, 1971).

Rheingold, H. L., and Hay, D. F., 'Prosocial Behaviour of the Very Young', in Stent (ed.), *Morality as a Biological Phenomenon*, 93–108.

Richards, Robert, 'A Defense of Evolutionary Ethics', *Biology and Philosophy*, 1 (1986), 265–93.

Roemer, John, *Egalitarian Perspectives* (Cambridge: Cambridge University Press, 1994).

—— *Theories of Distributive Justice* (Cambridge, Mass.: Harvard University Press, 1996).

Rorty, Richard, 'Why Can't a Man Be More Like a Woman? and Other Problems in Moral Philosophy' (Review of Annette Baier, *Moral Prejudice*), *London Review of Books*, 24 Feb. 1994, 3–6.

Ross, W. D., *The Right and the Good* (Oxford: Clarendon, 1930).

Runciman, W. G., *Relative Deprivation and Social Justice: A Study of Attitudes to Social Inequality in Twentieth Century England* (Berkeley and Los Angeles: University of California Press, 1966).

Ruse, Michael, 'Evolutionary Ethics: Healthy Prospect or Last Infirmity?', in Mohan Matthen and Bernard Linsky (eds.), *Philosophy and Biology, Canadian Journal of Philosophy*, suppl. vol. 19 (Calgary: University of Calgary Press, 1988), 27–74.

—— *Taking Darwin Seriously*, 2nd edn. (Amherst, NY: Prometheus, 1998).

Santangelo, Antonio, *The Beginning and Meaning of Culture: The Cerebral Activity Underlying It* (Milan: La Pietra, 1993).

Scanlon, T. M., 'Preference and Urgency', *Journal of Philosophy*, 72 (1975), 655–69.

—— *What We Owe to Each Other* (Cambridge, Mass.: Harvard University Press, 1998).

Scheffler, Samuel, *Boundaries and Allegiances: Problems of Justice and Responsibility in Liberal Thought* (Oxford: Oxford University Press, 2001).

—— *Human Morality* (New York: Oxford University Press, 1992).

—— *The Rejection of Consequentialism*, 2nd edn. (Oxford: Oxford University Press, 1994).

Schein, Martin (ed.), *Social Hierarchy and Dominance* (Stroudsburg: Dowden, Hutchinson and Ross, 1975).

Schumacher, E. F., *Small is Beautiful* (London: Abacus, 1974).

Scott, John, *Poverty and Wealth: Citizenship, Deprivation and Privilege* (London and New York: Longman, 1994).

Scruton, Roger, 'Contract, Consent and Exploitation: Kantian Themes', in Howard Williams (ed.), *Essays on Kant's Political Philosophy* (Cardiff: University of Wales Press, 1992), 213–27.

Sen, Amartya, 'Equality of What?', in *Inequality Reexamined* (Cambridge, Mass.: Harvard University Press, 1992), 12–30.

Sen, Amartya, and Williams, Bernard (eds.), *Utilitarianism and Beyond* (Cambridge: Cambridge University Press, 1982).

Shepher, Joseph, and Tiger, Lionel, 'Female Hierarchies in a Kibbutz Community', in Tiger and Fowler, (eds.), *Female Hierarchies*, 225–47.

Sher, George, *Desert* (Princeton: Princeton University Press, 1987).

—— 'Effort, Ability, and Personal Desert', *Philosophy and Public Affairs*, 8 (1979), 361–76.

Silk, Joan B., 'Primatological Perspectives on Gender Hierarchies', in Barbara Diane Miller (ed.), *Sex and Gender Hierarchies*, 212–35.

Singer, Peter, 'Famine, Affluence, and Morality', *Philosophy and Public Affairs*, 1 (1972), 229–43.

Skyrms, Brian, *The Evolution of the Social Contract* (Cambridge: Cambridge University Press, 1996).

Slote, Michael, *Common-Sense Morality and Consequentialism* (London: Routledge and Kegan Paul, 1985).

Small, Meredith, *Female Choices* (Ithaca, NY: Cornell University Press, 1993).

Smart, J. J. C., and Williams, Bernard (eds.), *Utilitarianism: For and Against* (Cambridge: Cambridge University Press, 1973).

Smeeding, Timothy M, and Gottschalk, Peter, 'Cross-National Income Inequality: How Great Is It and What Can We Learn from It?', *Focus*, 19 (1998), 15–19.

Smuts, Barbara, *Sex and Friendship in Baboons* (New York: Aldine, 1985).

Sober, Elliott, and Wilson, David Sloan, *Unto Others: The Evolution and Psychology of Unselfish Behavior* (Cambridge, Mass.: Harvard University Press, 1998).

Stent, Gunther (ed.), *Morality as a Biological Phenomenon* (Berkeley and Los Angeles: University of California Press, 1980).

Stokes, Eric, *The British Utilitarians and India* (Delhi: Oxford University Press, 1982).

Strawson, P. F., 'Freedom and Resentment', in *Studies in the Philosophy of Thought and Action* (London: Oxford University Press, 1968), 71–96.

—— *Individuals* (London: Methuen, 1959).

Sturgeon, Nicholas, 'Moral Explanations', in David Copp and David Zimmerman (eds.), *Morality, Reason and Truth* (Totowa: Rowman and Allanheld, 1984), 49–78.

Sweetman, David, *Paul Gauguin: A Complete Life* (London: Hodder and Stoughton, 1995).

Tiger, Lionel, and Fowler, Heather T. (eds.), *Female Hierarchies* (Chicago: Beresford Books Service, 1978).

Treffert, Darold, 'The Idiot Savant: A Review of the Syndrome', *American Journal of Psychiatry*, 145 (1988), 563–72.

Trivers, Robert, 'The Evolution of Reciprocal Altruism', *Quarterly Review of Biology*, 46 (1971), 35–57.

—— *Social Evolution* (Menlo Park: Benjamin Cummings, 1985).

Unger, Peter *Living High and Letting Die: Our Illusion of Innocence* (Oxford: Oxford University Press, 1996).

Valian, Virginia, *Why So Slow?* (Cambridge, Mass.: MIT Press, 1999).

van Sommers, Peter, *The Biology of Behaviour* (Sydney, NY: Wiley, 1972).

Walton, Kendall, 'How Remote are Fictional Worlds from the Real World?', *Journal of Aesthetics and Art Criticism*, 37 (1978), 11–23.

Walzer, Michael, 'Objectivity and Social Meaning', in Nussbaum and Sen (eds.), *Quality of Life*, 165–77.

—— *Spheres of Justice* (New York: Basic Books, 1983).

Westermarck, Edward, *Ethical Relativity* (London: Kegan Paul, Trench and Trubner, 1932).

Wiggins, David, 'A Sensible Subjectivism', in *Needs, Values, Truth*, 3rd edn. (Oxford: Clarendon Press, 1998).

Williams, Bernard, 'A Critique of Utilitarianism', in Smart and Williams (eds.), *Utilitarianism*, 77–150.

—— *Ethics and the Limits of Philosophy* (London: Fontana, 1985).

—— 'Internal and External Reasons', in *Moral Luck*, 101–13.

Wilson, Catherine, 'Natural Dominance: A Reply to Michael Levin', *Philosophy*, 73 (1998), 572–92.

—— *Moral Luck: Philosophical Papers 1973–1980* (Cambridge: Cambridge University Press, 1981).

—— *Problems of the Self: Collected Papers 1956–1971* (Cambridge: Cambridge University Press, 1973).

—— 'On Some Alleged Limitations to Moral Endeavor', *Journal of Philosophy*, 90 (1993), 275–89.

—— 'Prospects for Noncognitivism', *Inquiry*, 44 (2001), 1–24.

Wilson, E. O., *On Human Nature* (Cambridge, Mass.: Harvard University Press, 1978).

Wolf, Susan, 'Moral Saints', *Journal of Philosophy*, 79 (1982), 419–39.

Wood, Allen W., 'Exploitation', in Nielsen and Ware (eds.), *Exploitation*, 2–26.

Wrangham, Richard, and Peterson, Dale, *Demonic Males: Apes and the Origins of Human Violence* (London: Bloomsbury, 1996).

Wright, Patricia Chapple, 'Variations in Male–Female Dominance and Offspring Care in Non-human Primates', in Miller (ed.), *Sex and Gender Hierarchies*, 127–45.

Young, Robert, 'Egalitarianism and Personal Desert', *Ethics*, 102 (1992), 319–41.

Zweig, Arnulf (ed.), *Kant: Philosophical Correspondence 1759–1799* (Chicago: University of Chicago Press, 1967).

Index

Relative Deprivation Principle, 88, 92, 137, 158, 199, 277

relativism, x, 131, 161; theory-level *v.* world-level, 62–4

rights, 136–7, 257, 262, 298

risk, 59–60, 102, 117, 164–5, 168, 175–6, 193, 248, 250–2, 256, 264

Radcliffe-Brown, A. R., 32

Rousseau, Jean-Jacques, 21, 184–5, 254

rules, 6–10, 13–14, 16, 21–2, 31–3, 35, 37, 71, 96

Runciman, W. D., 200

Scanlon, Thomas, 139–40, 192, 196

Scheffler, Samuel, 81, 131, 217, 228–9

Scruton, Roger, 203–4

Singer, Peter, 91, 158–9

Sittlichkeit, 101–2, 280

Skyrms, Brian, 185

slavery, 135–6, 108, 179, 199, 204–5, 208

sociobiology, *see* evolution, evolutionary psychology

Strawson, P. F, 80–1, 124

subordination of women, xii, 58, 60, 113–19, 165, 254–61, 266–77

suicide, 132, 148, 152

taboo, vii, 8, 13, 15, 32, 124; substances, 200, 259

theory, moral 36–8, 43–6, 52–6, 93, 96, 119, 123, 126–7; and practice,

147–51; as burdensome, viii–ix, 76–7, 92–4, 96–7, 159–60, 162; as intrusive, 104–5, 113, 133–4; as useless, 76–7, 98–100, 112, 137, 202; information and, 68–9, 139, 159–60, 162; local *v.* critical, 37–8; *v.* scientific theory, 44–8, 61, 122–3. *See also* confirmation, ideology

Trivers, Robert, 19, 25.

Unger, Peter, 158–9

universalism, 22, 62. *See also* relativism

utilitarianism, ix, 44, 75, 78, 80–1, 92, 128, 163, 199, 278. *See also* consequentialism

vice, 227, 294–5, 298–9.

virtue, virtue theory, 12–13, 95–6, 120–2, 126

Walzer, Michael, 113–19, 203, 261

well-being, xi, 154, 191–4, 201, 224, 243–6, 252, 254, 257, 260, 298. *See also* deprivation

Westermarck, Edward, 22

Williams, Bernard, ix, 75–7, 82–4, 97, 101–2, 111, 134, 151, 159, 160–1, 163, 279–80, 293–4, 301

Wilson, E. O., 206, 258, 274, 279, 290, 294, 296

Wolf, Susan, 84

The Great Gypsy Moth War

The Great Gypsy Moth War

The History of the First Campaign
in Massachusetts to Eradicate the
Gypsy Moth, 1890–1901

ROBERT J. SPEAR

University of Massachusetts Press
AMHERST AND BOSTON

LC 2004030724

ISBN 1-55849-479-0

Designed by Steve Dyer
Set in Sabon by Binghamton Valley Composition
Printed and bound by
The Maple-Vail Book Manufacturing Group

Library of Congress Cataloging-in-Publication Data

Spear, Robert J., 1942–
The great gypsy moth war : the history of the first campaign in Massachusetts
to eradicate the gypsy moth, 1890–1901 / Robert J. Spear.
p. cm.
Includes bibliographical references and index.
ISBN 1-55849-479-0 (cloth : alk. paper)
1. Gypsy moth—Control—Massachusetts—History.   I. Title.
SB945.G9S64 2005
632'.78—dc22
2004030724

British Library Cataloguing in Publication data are available.

To Deena

O wad some Pow'r the giftie gie us
To see oursels as others see us
It wad frae monie a blunder free us
An' foolish notion
What airs in dress an' gait wad lea'e us
An' ev'n Devotion

—ROBERT BURNS, *"To a Louse*
   on seeing one on a lady's hat at
   Church"

Contents

Illustrations

Preface

WORK ON THIS BOOK began in 1994 at my home, then located in Accokeek, Maryland. The impetus for my efforts was the constant spraying for the gypsy moth that drove my chemically sensitive wife and me out of our home every year around Mother's Day. I began to distribute a newsletter called *Gypsy Myths* to my community, and my research for this publication subsequently served as the basis for the additional research that is presented in this book.

I was fortunate to find a few surviving documents that were a researcher's dream come true: eyewitness accounts of events that often allowed me to let the story be told by the people who lived it. I have left these recountings largely as I found them—grammatical errors, colloquial expressions, and all. Where I felt the need for clarification, I have enclosed it in square brackets to distinguish it from any parenthetical passages in the original. Most of the photos and other graphic material come from *The Gypsy Moth*, the epic monograph by Edward Forbush and Charles Fernald. The originals from which the plates were derived are long gone.

With regard to citations for personal correspondence and unpublished material, I have tried to be specific about where these are located, including library call numbers and the box and folder numbers of archived collections, in the hope that this information might be of some use to other researchers. This detail is sometimes absent from the Boston Society of Natural History Archives at the Lyman Library because Lyman's holdings had not been catalogued at the time I did my research there.

I recall with fond memories all those whose help and assistance were freely given to me during the years this book was in preparation and express my gratitude to them here both collectively and individually. The libraries of some of our great educational and governmental institutions have been a source of much of the basic factual data incorporated in this book, and among the treasures found in these places are the librarians and archivists themselves—the people who so faithfully maintain the great repositories of our history and

make them available in good order to the researcher. I think it would be hard to find a more sincere, supportive, and helpful group anywhere, and every one of them without exception went well beyond the call in helping me with my explorations.

My off-line research began at the Comstock Memorial Entomology Library at Cornell University in my beloved home city of Ithaca, New York, where chief librarian Marty Schlabach and his assistant, Benjamin W. Fierce, welcomed me to the world of highly obscure publications of considerable age in stacks that rolled on wheels. I also was courteously received at Cornell's Mann Library, Olin Library, and the Cornell University Library Annex (yes, next time I will bring my own M&Ms).

Thanks also to Michael Milewski, senior archivist of the Special Collections and Archives Section, and Leonard Adams of the Government Documents Department, W. E. B. Du Bois Library at the University of Massachusetts Amherst. Their work behind the scenes made every hour I spent in Amherst unusually productive. I also thank Mike's wife, Heidi, whose wickedly good Polish galumpkis and New England hospitality were a welcome respite from five nights of thin cheeseburgers.

My thanks also to Elizabeth Marzuoli, reference archivist at the Massachusetts State Archives, Dorchester, for bringing out mountains of heavy book boxes for me to peruse and remaining cheerful even when I asked for the wrong ones. Sean Fisher, archivist and historian for the Metropolitan District Commission (successor to the Metropolitan Park Commission mentioned in this book), provided many relevant materials even before I knew to ask for them, earning both my gratitude and my admiration.

Mark C. Scott, reference librarian at the Massachusetts State House Library in Boston, astutely guided me through arcane indexing systems to the treasures they reference. Special thanks as well to Betsy Lowenstein, chief, and Christine Gebhard, preservation assistant, of the Special Collections Department there, whose kindness to a stranger included some much-needed extra time in the reading room and repairs on the fly to fragile old documents so they could be copied before I left.

I have been cordially received at a number of local public libraries and historical societies. The assistance and contributions of Richard A. Duffy and Bill Mahoney, trustees of the Arlington Historical Society in Arlington, Massachusetts, greatly aided my initial research. Particular thanks go to the reference librarians at the public library in Medford, Massachusetts, the entomological ground zero of this book, who prefer to be recognized as a group.

Philip J. Pauly of Rutgers University, professor of history and a man of considerable patience, was steadfast in his encouragement of my project, directed me toward a number of rewarding sources, and left me a much better

historical sleuth than I had been before we met. Special thanks also to Edward H. Smith, professor emeritus of entomology at Cornell, for his important observations, suggestions, and continued support. Also among those who helped me through the research doldrums were Mary P. Winsor of the Institutes for the History and Philosophy of Science at the University of Toronto, and Pamela Henson, historian at the Smithsonian Institution.

Considerable assistance through long-distance research was given by archivist Robert Young at the Museum of Comparative Zoology, Harvard; Robert Cox, American Philosophical Society, Philadelphia; William Cox, associate archivist, the Smithsonian Institution, Washington, D.C.; Carolyn Kirdahy, curator of objects, Museum of Science in Boston (successor to the Boston Society of Natural History); Ellen Mann, special collections, National Agricultural Library, Beltsville, Maryland; and Nick Natanson, National Archives and Records Administrations, Washington, D.C.

My sincere thanks to those I conscripted to read my manuscript to eliminate factual errors, make comments, and help me clarify areas that needed it (and there were many), among them, Philip Pauly for general historical accuracy; Edward Smith for entomological accuracy and sections on C. V. Riley; Sean Fisher, archivist and historian of the Metropolitan District Commission for sections on the Park Commisioner; Alexander F. Thornhill, whose only failing was to be my loyal friend, for typographical errors caught; and Deena Spear, my patient and long-suffering spouse, for her loving encouragement even though there must have been times when she questioned my sanity.

I conclude by expressing my appreciation and regard for Bruce Wilcox, director of the University of Massachusetts Press, for his confidence in my book and helping me to get the work published during extremely difficult financial times; Carol Betsch, managing editor, for her endless patience, inexhaustible good will, and gentle hand; and copy editor Patricia Sterling, who possibly understands the manuscript even better than I do!

The Great Gypsy Moth War

Introduction

O N JANUARY 1, 1896, a committee on gypsy moths of the Massachusetts State Board of Agriculture published its monographic report, *The Gypsy Moth, Porthetria dispar (Linn.): A Report of the Work of Destroying the Insect in the Commonwealth of Massachusetts, Together With an Account of Its History and Habits Both in Massachusetts and Europe*. Today this volume of nearly six hundred pages, with its thick appendixes, numerous plates, and drawings is referred to simply as *The Gypsy Moth*. Edward H. Forbush, director of fieldwork against the moth, and economic entomologist Charles H. Fernald, a professor of zoology at the Massachusetts Agricultural College and adviser to the committee in charge, each wrote about half of the report, with help from Fernald's assistant, Archie H. Kirkland, and entomologist Samuel Henshaw of the Agassiz Museum at Harvard.

The Gypsy Moth, a history of the first half of the first campaign to exterminate the insect, is a tale told the way Forbush and Fernald wanted to tell it. The text celebrates the belief of economic entomology in itself and its champions, who waged the war under damaging handicaps, although many of their wounds turned out to be self-inflicted. The tone of the volume is so unremittingly assured that even a hundred years later one writer referred to it as "a hymn to the belief that knowledge is ammunition," characterized its authors as scientific zealots, and described its philosophical underpinnings as a "testament of obsession."[1]

It is from this work alone that almost all of what is now believed about the campaign to exterminate the gypsy moth has been drawn, which may prove the thesis that history is not always what happened. Economic entomologists and their historians generally have tended to advance the idea that the insect was nearly wiped out and victory within reach, and that the campaign failed because of an irrational act of the Massachusetts legislature in discontinuing annual appropriations. New research shows that this was not quite the case.

During the latter half of the nineteenth century, the time in which this story took place, great changes were sweeping the country. Colleges and universities were converting from religion-based institutions of rote learning into modern

secular schools of scientific training and practical application. The promise of technology beckoned, but the hold of theological assumptions was still strong. In the field of natural sciences, the ideas of Darwin, Huxley, and Spencer emerged to dominate, though not replace, the older ideas of divine or "special" creation. Scientific men of the time wavered between these two mighty and often conflicting forces. Strange juxtapositions temporarily existed; amid transitions and tensions, the journey into the new century did not proceed smoothly.

The decade of the 1890s was marked by social, political, and economic turmoil on a scale some historians believe was not matched even by the turbulent decade of the 1960s. The events described in this book occurred at a time when the assets of both men and nature were being plundered in a way and at a pace that had never been seen before, when the very resources of the earth first revealed their limits, and when many species of animals began to live on the edge of extinction. Also rising in this time were the ideas and philosophies of conservation, ecology, replenishment, and protection of a finite biosphere, all contending strongly for acceptance.

Entomology, a young field that was also in transition during the late nineteenth century, was still dominated by amateurs and men who were either self-taught or whose college degrees were in other subjects. The study of insects was roughly divided between two groups: the taxonomists (also called systematists), who discovered insects, named them, described their features, put them in order, and catalogued them; and the agriculturalists, who studied the life cycles of damaging insects, especially in the larval stage, and made recommendations to farmers on how best to protect their crops. Entomologists found employment wherever they could, for their opportunities were not extensive at the time. Although all practitioners took nets into the field, in the 1890s taxonomists and systematists worked primarily in museums and educational institutions, whereas agriculturalists spent most of their time at a few colleges or in government offices.

Agricultural entomology was redefined by the formal emergence of a new applied branch called economic entomology, which occurred, by a fateful coincidence, during the summer of 1889—the same summer in which great swarms of gypsy moths first began to plague eastern Massachusetts—following the establishment the year before of agricultural experiment stations. The rapid change in this science from a classical to a practical orientation proceeded with great difficulties and some monumental missteps, and the first of these was the war against the gypsy moth.

The accidental release of the European gypsy moth (*Bombyx dispar*) in Medford, Massachusetts, on a windy spring day in 1869 was, of course, an entomological event, but it was also a historical event, although mention of

the campaign against the insect will not be found in any general history book. The story of this particular war is relegated to scraps of information scattered in local historical societies, newspaper archives, and university libraries, and to a few rather obscure documents from government agencies such as the old Massachusetts State Board of Agriculture or the bureau of entomology of the U.S. Department of Agriculture (USDA) in its earliest years. Because the facts of this war remain sprinkled here and there in bits and pieces and are strikingly absent from most of the history of economic entomology, their importance has been diminished, and the lessons to be learned from them have been obscured.

What these lessons were (or should have been) will likely remain a subject of debate. In the broadest sense, the history of the gypsy moth campaign serves to remind us that we have not yet found a good response to invasive insects and continue to resist the notion that there may not be one. It also questions the supposition of expertness freely granted those who claim to have the knowledge to guide us through extermination campaigns, even though their voices may be used to mask other elements and interests.

Although this book will not entirely resolve differences of opinion on these points, it presents additional information that will perhaps enable the reader to draw new conclusions. It examines the gypsy moth war from a historical as well as an entomological viewpoint. The manner of the moth's introduction, the course of the war against it, and the reasons for the war's failure have become a matter of lore and misconception. Lacking an understanding of the conditions and underlying causes of the moth's success, campaigns against the insect ever since have largely followed the flawed Massachusetts model. Indeed, practically all insect eradication campaigns have their roots in this epic.

The gypsy moth war is distinguished from any war this nation has fought against human adversaries because the hostilities have never ceased, and the insidious consequences of more than a century of unremitting warfare—and its continued heavy impact on both the environment and the daily lives of every American—have gone unrealized. In our time we have come to think of battles against insects as a long and ancient part of our history, but few realize how modern the practice is as presently carried on, and even fewer have understood how dangerous it has become.

The decision to treat the discovery of concentrated colonies of gypsy moths as a grave danger to Massachusetts in particular and the country in general was based in part on the need felt by economic entomologists of the time to prove the worth of their new discipline, and in part on the twist of fate that caused the insect to appear in Massachusetts, then the only state in the nation that would make large appropriations to exscind the invader within its boundaries.

Anthropologist Margaret Mead's famous saying that a small group of dedicated individuals is the only thing that has ever changed the world was never truer than during this tumultuous period when just six unlikely men, for varying reasons that are set forth in the text, devised, executed, and lost the first war against the gypsy moth. These were Nathaniel Southgate Shaler, a Harvard professor and dean of the Lawrence Scientific School; Charles Valentine Riley, chief in entomology at the U.S. Department of Agriculture; Leland Ossian Howard, Riley's assistant and successor; Charles Henry Fernald, entomologist and professor of zoology at the Massachusetts Agricultural College; Edward Howe Forbush, an ornithologist who became the state superintendent of fieldwork against the moth; and William Robert Sessions, a former politician and secretary of the Massachusetts State Board of Agriculture. These men would be considered historical small fry, forgotten bit players in the theater of American life, had their actions not profoundly changed the course of history.

The entire field of science changed in the nineteenth century as the age of the generalist ended and the age of the specialist began. British author Doron Swade has commented that the first half of the nineteenth century was the last period in history when it was possible for one man to know all there was to know about every science, when securing an all-encompassing knowledge was "an aspiration and not an affectation."[2] Many of the principals of this book were born in the first half of that century, and a few still pursued the idea of acquiring an encompassing knowledge. Men such as Shaler and Fernald possessed formidable intellectual capacities that they applied to an extraordinarily broad range of interests, although Forbush, Sessions, Riley, and others had only secondary school educations. Fernald and Riley were self-trained in entomology; Shaler was principally a geologist; Forbush dropped out of school to become a taxidermist and a mechanic; Sessions was a farmer turned politician; and Howard was a federal bureaucrat who had hoped for a career in medicine. Others on the state's gypsy moth committee were businessmen and merchants with no agricultural or entomological credentials at all. No committeeman was expected to devote more than one or two evenings a month to this task, even though it was a task that no other state agency in America had ever attempted.

Riley was removed from influence by the vagaries of federal politics and an untimely accident, and Shaler removed himself for personal reasons, both men departing midway through the campaign, leaving Fernald, the most respected agricultural entomologist in Massachusetts, to gain unprecedented power in planning the battle. Forbush prosecuted his wishes with unyielding determination. Sessions, a canny veteran of Massachusetts political life, pushed the complementary goals of economic entomologists and the Board of Agriculture through the state legislature, using his great skill in political manipulation.

Members of the committee seem to have simply followed everything their entomologist told them to do. The concerns of other scientists over the scope of the campaign, the concerns of legislators over its cost, and the concerns of the public over its dangers were all swept aside.

All of these men were manipulating various niches and conditions in the rapidly changing world of the 1890s for reasons that were not alone concerned with the destruction of a formidable insect invader. Their success in promoting themselves occurred in part because all elected officials in Massachusetts then served one-year terms, and all were constantly running for re-election.[3] Turnover was markedly high, and the level of experience in state government was correspondingly low. The administrative duties of the state were commonly delegated to unpaid volunteer boards or low-paid, part-time commissions of citizens who, like the legislators, were inexperienced and constrained to rely on the advice of experts of questionable competence, merely rubber-stamping what was given to them.

Even the structure of government was not comprehensive enough for the task. Since the state had no foresters or forestry bureau (the office of state forester would not be created until early in the next century), the care of forests was placed under the Board of Agriculture, whose members regarded timberlands as a sow-and-reap system and who were concerned not with the ecology of wooded land but with its economy. Under these conditions, power fell into the hands of an immature bureaucracy, and a small group of economic entomologists and their supporters suddenly found themselves wielding a great deal of authority to undertake a task for which they were almost completely unprepared—the first attempt anywhere to field a publicly funded army of men and equipment to assault a foreign insect and destroy it completely within three years.

New England forests at the time this narrative begins included second-growth hardwood stands that had replaced a forest with a large component of softwood. From antiquity, the great mixed woodland of the region had contained vast tracts of white pine in the southern and central sections mixed with spruce and fir in the north. After the arrival of Europeans, these stands had been heavily logged for commercial purposes, and much acreage in Massachusetts was cleared entirely of both hardwoods and softwoods to make it suitable for farming; by 1880, more than 80 percent of the state's forests had been cleared. But with the population in a steep decline as farmers gave up on the region's thin, rocky soil, abandoned their farmsteads, and moved to the more fertile lands of the Midwest, trees immediately sprang up on the deserted farmland.[4]

The new forest seems to have been different from the old and was dominated by opportunistic species such as oak. Fire burned through substantial

portions of Massachusetts and neighboring Rhode Island several times during the eighteenth and nineteenth centuries, and since the oaks were more resistant, owing to their thicker bark, they remained the dominant tree in many regions.[5] Oaks reclaimed burned or logged-over areas faster because they grew well in poor soils, tolerated shading better, and sprouted off the stump, whereas softwood species required richer soil, grew poorly in the absence of sunlight, and renewed only from seed. The introduction of the gypsy moth and the massive human interference that accompanied colonial expansion proved to be an unfortunate coincidence. The forests of Massachusetts always would have been vulnerable to the gypsy moth, but the insects escaped into an environment that had only recently come to contain a high percentage of the very hardwood tree that was most attractive to them.

All of what has been described above was a powerful undercurrent rushing beneath a calmer surface that might seem unremarkable to the modern eye. The last decade of the nineteenth century was probably the first decade in the history of America when a visitor from the present time might feel in familiar surroundings. Houses in populated areas had begun to have central heating, sanitary plumbing, and electricity, and telephones were coming into general use. Steel-hulled steamships plied the oceans, and fast trains crossed the countryside. The automobile was about ready to take to the road, and the airplane would soon rise above the horizon. People in the suburbs were taking jobs in the cities and commuting to work.

The first two chapters of this book cover the arrival in Cambridge, Massachusetts, of E. Leopold Trouvelot and illuminate his efforts to establish himself as a breeder of an improved silkworm, which led to the importation and release of the gypsy moth in America. Trouvelot's story is not well understood, and his role deserves reappraisal. The next three chapters deal with the overpopulation of gypsy moths and to what might be termed "false starts" in managing the resulting real and imagined problems.

The remainder of the book follows the efforts made to control, contain, and kill the invaders, whose ability to survive caused proponents of the war against them to cross the line in an effort to achieve their aims. By the middle of the war, almost all economic entomologists knew that eradication could not be attained, yet they continued to urge the Commonwealth of Massachusetts to pour increasing amounts of money into the conflict on the basis of their statements as scientific men that the goal was within reach. Not above manipulating the state legislature to attain their ends, in effect they perpetrated a fraud on the Commonwealth. Or perhaps they were not conspirators in the usual sense but just overly zealous in their desperate fight to retain their jobs and protect their credibility and reputation. Readers will have to decide for themselves.

Years in the Shadow of Science

T HE GREAT GYPSY MOTH WAR began in 1890, but the story starts thirty years earlier, when Etienne Leopold Trouvelot left Europe for Boston, Massachusetts. Trouvelot was born on December 26, 1827, in Guyencourt, Department of Aisne, France. His education and upbringing remain a mystery, but many traits he manifested later in life suggest that he must have been an intelligent and talented student. He was a gifted artist, illustrator, lithographer, and engraver, and the levels to which his skills were developed imply that he had been provided with the best professional instruction. Among the benefits of a nineteenth-century training in art would have been the honing of his powers of observation, necessary for the accurate rendering of subjects in nature.

Little is known about the man, his private life, or his family. Were it not for the astronomer Edward S. Holden, who began a personal photographic collection of his colleagues and other scientific men in the 1890s, posterity would not have even a single photograph of Trouvelot. Though Holden's picture reveals the lines of age setting in around his eyes and shows the first streaks of gray in his hair and beard, his face retains an appealing, boyish quality. Many others have tried to draw his personality from this picture and have concluded that he was a dreamy, wistful romantic or in some other way disconnected from the practical concerns of average mortals.

No one who worked in the natural sciences, however, as Trouvelot did, could be so detached from the world around him. He had a quick and inventive mind, and his friend Nathaniel Southgate Shaler noted that he was "extremely experimental."[1] One suspects he was a gentle and kindhearted human being who thought of insects in a way that was almost romantic. He saw organization and admirable industry in the societies of ants and intelligence in the activities of a tiger swallowtail larva when he watched it roll up the leaf on which it was feeding to keep from being washed off by a heavy rain.[2] He worried that experiments in which an insect was mutilated would cause it pain or prevent it from finding food, and it saddened him to observe an insect

E. Leopold Trouvelot.
Photo courtesy of the Mary Lea Shane
Archives of the Lick Observatory,
University of California, Santa Cruz.

deprived of the company of its own kind. He wrote of one case where he had
removed the antennae of a male *Promethia* moth and placed the handicapped
creature next to a female: "The male Promethia had his sight; he could see
near him another insect like himself, but his eyes alone could not tell him
whether the insect was of the same species and of another sex, so he died near
the object he would have desired if [his sense organs] had not been removed."[3]

The consensus is that Trouvelot came to America at the age of thirty, although it is not clear whether his decision was caused by unfavorable conditions in France or by opportunities in the United States. A few authors have
suggested that he was a liberal republican and anti-Royalist who fled the
Second Empire when the succession of the Napoleonic line was established in
1856 by the birth of Napoleon IV.[4] Others have speculated that he was forced
into exile. There are, unfortunately, no surviving records from Trouvelot himself that would settle the matter.

Trouvelot seems to have been living in Paris at the time of his decision to
depart.[5] He may have been there for employment or to study art, and he was
possibly influenced by the great French naturalist and entomologist Felix-
Edouard Guerin-Meneville, (1799–1874), who acted as a confidant or mentor
of some sort; Trouvelot is known to have corresponded with him from the
United States, and Guerin-Meneville also supplied Trouvelot with specimens
of insects and the eggs of exotic silk moths. Guerin-Meneville was a naturalist
in the old style with a broad range of interests, and he was the author and

publisher of journals and such illustrated and hand-colored works as his *Dictionnaire pittoresque d'histoire naturelle*, published in Paris between 1836 and 1839. He catalogued and named many creatures from all over the world, especially Crustacea (aquatic arthropods), Coleoptera (beetles) and Lepidoptera (moths and butterflies). Perhaps it was the influence of Guerin-Meneville and the artists who created the beautiful illustrations in his books that inspired a talented young man about to embark for the New World to combine natural history, entomology, and art as his life's work.

Trouvelot's obituary in *Nature* states that after the coup d'etat in 1852 he went directly to Cambridge, Massachusetts.[6] There seems to be no record of Trouvelot's whereabouts between 1852 and 1856, however, and there is no listing for him in either the *Cambridge City Directory* or the *Boston City Directory* during those years. His arrival in America, then, probably occurred at the end of 1856 or the beginning of 1857, given the birth records of his children: a son, George, was born about the time Trouvelot apparently reached Massachusetts; and on June 5, 1858, a daughter, Diana, was born.[7] Diana's birth record shows that Trouvelot's wife, Adelaide, called Adele, was born in France.

The record also lists Trouvelot's occupation as "lithographer," which indicates how he was earning an income in the United States, and for many years afterward he said that his pencil was his "only resource to support his family."[8] His skills were immediately appreciated, and he had "always a great deal to do in lithography, of very easy work."[9] Within a decade he commanded a fee of ten dollars a day at a time when an average factory worker was making less than twenty-five cents an hour. Trouvelot remained a man of modest financial means but independent enough to send his son to be educated at the Boston Latin School.[10]

Medford, Massachusetts

In 1857, Trouvelot took up residence in the small town of Medford, which is near to Cambridge and easily accessible from Boston. Founded in 1630 and located on the Mystic River in Middlesex County about five miles north and a little west of Boston, Medford is the fourth oldest English settlement in America. Its population was approaching five thousand at the time Trouvelot arrived.[11] He bought a new residence at 27 Myrtle Street directly from the builder,[12] and in the federal census for 1860 he gave the value of this property as $1,100. Trouvelot's dwelling was on the then-remote fringes of Medford's Glenwood district—an unofficial and unincorporated name that some documents refer to as "Middlesex"—which later writers characterized as "wild and wooded."[13]

Trouvelot House, 27 Myrtle Street, Medford, Mass., circa 1895. From *The Gypsy Moth.*

Myrtle Street was nevertheless in a neat, working-class neighborhood where most of the residents owned their houses. E. W. Wood described it as being "occupied by mechanics" and said the wood-framed structures were built on small plots averaging about 12,000 square feet each. Most residents had food gardens, and many also had fruit trees.[14] The U.S. census for 1860 lists Leopold Trouvelot, age thirty-two, and his wife, Adelaide, age twenty-six, living on Myrtle Street in Medford with their two children, a boy age three and a daughter age two (though the children are incorrectly identified as "Stephen" and "Adelaide"). Trouvelot again gave his profession as "lithographer."[15]

The 1870 census shows L. Trouvelot residing in Medford with Adele, George, and Diana Trouvelot.[16] Adelaide's age is given as thirty-four; Trouvelot's is incorrectly listed as thirty-two. George and Diana are shown as fourteen and twelve years of age, respectively. Their father informed the enumerator that both his children were born in Massachusetts, making them U.S. citizens. He again gave his occupation as "lithographer," while his spouse was "keeping house," and both children were "at school."

Behind Trouvelot's new house was a south-facing lot variously given as five to eight acres in size. Edward Samuels recorded that Trouvelot's land was "surrounded with scrub oak and huckleberry bushes . . . loaded with fruit."[17] Just south and a little west was the intersection of Riverside and Spring Streets, and south of that the Mystic River, flowing from its source in the Mystic Lakes west of Medford, twisted its way through a salt marsh eastward toward the ocean. Trouvelot's house, one of the last on the block and one of the farthest

east of the town, was situated at a point where Myrtle Street angled away from the railroad tracks and entered about twenty undeveloped acres of scrub oak.[18]

Trouvelot and the Rise of Natural Science

It would be easy to assume that Trouvelot came to America to undertake silkworm research, since he was engaged in it almost immediately upon his arrival, and that he chose Boston because Massachusetts had a reputation as a state that actively fostered all aspects of the silk trade, following the efforts of sericulturalist Jonathan Holmes Cobb in the 1830s and 1840s. This scenario is not entirely satisfying, given Trouvelot's wide range of interests. These included astronomy, a field of study that overlapped his interest in entomology, and Harvard College in Cambridge was one of only a few American institutions that could boast its own astronomy facility. Between 1847 and 1867 its fifteen-inch Boyden refractor was the largest astronomical telescope in the United States. Leland Ossian Howard reported that by 1869 Trouvelot was connected with the Harvard Observatory and held the title of "professor."[19] Other evidence suggests that this date is ten years too early: Jan Herman and Brenda Corbin relate that Trouvelot did not begin an official association with the observatory until 1872, when his drawings of celestial events came to the attention of Joseph Winlock, the observatory's director.[20]

In any case, between 1850 and 1880, Massachusetts was the undisputed center of science in America, and Harvard College was the center of science in Massachusetts. The cause of Harvard's preeminence was the presence of the Swiss-born naturalist Louis Agassiz, who made Cambridge a beacon for those seeking knowledge.[21] When Trouvelot walked down the gangplank in 1856 or 1857, he found himself at the center of the greatest craze for the natural sciences in the century. Agassiz had proposed to write a natural history of the United States and everything in it and was turning everyone from farmers to fishermen from East coast to West into collectors of specimens. He was also selling advance subscriptions to his projected ten-volume work, *Contributions to the Natural History of the United States*. So intensive was the effort that as author Edward Lurie has put it, "If any literate individual in America or Europe failed to hear of Agassiz and the *Contributions* from 1855 to 1857, it was surely an accident."[22]

Concentrated at Harvard was a growing number of French-speaking Swiss who were engaged in this important work with Agassiz. In 1859, Agassiz and Asa Gray founded the Museum of Comparative Zoology (MCZ) at Harvard, an institution that was inundated from the start with more specimens than it had men qualified to describe and catalogue. To help in the work, Agassiz at

first employed a number of his American students and later some European professionals. Trouvelot ingratiated himself with this group, for the chance to be among those who spoke his native language and the opportunity to gain knowledge and experience would have drawn him as a lamp draws a moth.

Trouvelot even gathered specimens for the museum's collection, probably at the request of Agassiz or one of his assistants. In the annual report of the MCZ for 1863, museum assistant Addison E. Verrill recorded Trouvelot's donations of "six bird's nests and eggs, dry," and Frederic Ward Putnam acknowledged Trouvelot's contribution of five specimens and four species to the museum's reptile collection.[23] The annual report of the museum for 1864 records Trouvelot's second contribution of birds, eggs, and reptiles.[24]

Trouvelot would have become acquainted with people of influence at Harvard because he was there when many of them arrived. He met geologist Nathaniel Southgate Shaler, future dean of the Lawrence Scientific School, when Shaler was still a student, and he was there in 1867 when the German entomologist Hermann August Hagen first arrived in America. Trouvelot knew Samuel Henshaw, who was active in the Boston Society of Natural History and a cofounder of the Cambridge Entomological Society; he also knew the great fossil entomologist Samuel Hubbard Scudder, who was then Agassiz's graduate student; he likely met most of the talented young students who studied under Louis Agassiz or Herman Hagen, such as John Henry Comstock, Albert John Cook, Henry Guernsey Hubbard, Alpheus Hyatt, Edward S. Morse, Alpheus Spring Packard, Frederic Ward Putnam, Philip Reese Uhler, and Burt Green Wilder. Some of these men corresponded with him later on; some visited his outdoor insectary in Medford in the 1860s; and some asked him to write accounts of his work for popular publication.

If Trouvelot did not meet all these men at the MCZ, he mingled with many of them when he joined the Boston Society of Natural History, an organization whose membership included many distinguished New England naturalists. In 1867, Trouvelot read a paper titled "On Monstrosities observed in the wings of Lepidopterous Insects, and on the method of producing them artificially."[25] Notice of this presentation was published in the premier issue of the *American Naturalist* magazine. Another paper, published about ten years later, was titled "The Use of Antennae in Insects."

The picture that emerges of Trouvelot between 1857 and 1866 is similar to that of other autodidacts of his time who became versed in a wide variety of subjects in order to maximize their opportunities to advance their prestige and make themselves employable. The rise of the scientific disciplines in America had briefly opened a window of opportunity and placed almost all interested individuals on a near-equal footing, regardless of their training. Nowhere was this truer than in entomology, long considered a fringe discipline at best, in

which nearly everyone at the time was self-taught and even an amateur could make significant contributions.

Experiments with Silk Moths

Trouvelot seized upon silk moths as his potential pathway to scientific respect and financial reward. Howard states that Trouvelot "for his pleasure and interest was engaged in the study of wild silkworms with the idea that a species of commercial value might be found, and that perhaps something might be done in the way of cross breeding allied species, thus producing not perhaps a better quality of silk than that of the silkworm of commerce, but a hardier insect, which would require less artificial attention and at the same time would be more resistant to disease."[26]

Trouvelot was occupied with silkworm research for much of the time between 1859 and 1870, and possibly earlier, and he was interested particularly in the American Luna, Prometheus, and eye-spotted Cecropia moths. All of them were classified at the time as silkworms in the family Bombycidae, which leaves little doubt about where he was applying his efforts. In a series of articles he wrote for the *American Naturalist* magazine beginning in March 1867, Trouvelot stated that he had been studying American silk moths "for over six years."[27] Around 1860 he had begun concentrating his attention on what he called the "American silkworm," *Telea polyphemus*.

Once the Civil War began in 1861, the supply of cotton from southern fields was disrupted, and the textile mills of New England lay idle while the northern states looked elsewhere for raw fiber; thus a window of opportunity opened for those hunting fortune and new sources of silk. But Trouvelot's experiments with *Telea polyphemus* were undergoing a rather laborious beginning. He searched diligently for caterpillars in the spring of 1860 and found only two males. The next year he found twelve caterpillars and from their cocoons reared a single mated pair that produced three hundred fertile eggs. Of this number at the end of the third year just twelve insects survived to pupate, but by then Trouvelot had gained enough experience to ensure their survival, and the moths increased in number rapidly thereafter.

Trouvelot's experiments with silkworms were known to the scientific community in Cambridge, and over the years a small number of scientific men made the trip to Medford to see firsthand the work that he was doing. One of these was entomologist Alpheus Spring Packard, then just twenty-three years of age. Packard was preparing a synopsis of the American silk moths, which he published in 1865, and he later became a noted member of Charles Valentine Riley's Rocky Mountain Locust Commission. Packard believed Trouvelot began working with the gypsy moth five years earlier than had been thought:

"About 1862 I went out to Medford and saw Mr. Trouvelot; went over to his farm about the same time when this moth had unfortunately been brought to this country, although I did not know it at the time, as he did not mention the fact to me."[28]

According to Trouvelot's own account, he ultimately had no fewer than a million caterpillars, all of which were descended from the original surviving *T. polyphemus* pair of 1861, feeding behind his house on Myrtle Street. To contain his hordes of larvae he constructed a stupendous barricade to encircle his grounds—a wooden fence eight feet high that encompassed his full five acres of shrubs and small trees.[29] Netting was stretched from the perimeter of the fences across the trees, and was supported in the middle on posts, making it possible for Trouvelot to walk upright through his specialized insectary. Despite all his precautions, though, birds took a heavy toll on his investment; the mesh was too coarse and not in good repair, which allowed birds to get underneath. In 1866 he constructed a shed behind his house and transferred some of his moth-breeding attempts inside it, feeding the larvae by hand, though older caterpillars still had to be placed in the open under the netting. Sometime in 1865 or 1866, Edward A. Samuels, researching his book on the birds of New England, visited Trouvelot's silkworm farm: "Mr. Trouvelot, of Medford, Mass . . . has a tract of about seven or eight acres enclosed, and mostly covered with netting. He is obliged, in self defence, to kill the birds which penetrate into the enclosure and destroy the worms. . . . He says [the robins] came from all quarters to destroy his silkworms, and gave him more trouble than all the other birds together."[30] Samuels's intriguing comments raise the question of whether or not the insects he saw in Trouvelot's back yard were gypsy moths. Samuels said they "resembled, when small, the young caterpillar of apple-tree moth."[31] There is no longer a way to determine Samuels's expertise in identifying larvae, but it is perhaps an odd coincidence that in 1865 he mentioned the gypsy moth in a paper he read before the Massachusetts State Board of Agriculture: "During the year 1848 an enormous quantity of the *Bombyx (Ocneria) dispar*, a well known enemy of [German] gardens and forests, had devoured the foliage of the trees, which in some localities were quite bare. In the autumn, millions of their eggs were discovered, enveloped in a silky sort of covering, and attached to the trunks and branches. Many were removed; but the hand of man was powerless to work off the affliction, and the owners of the trees resigned themselves to their loss."[32]

The puzzling question of why Samuels would have spoken to an agricultural organization on the topic of a foreign insect that at the time was not known in North America can be answered once the original text is in hand: Samuels was not talking about insects per se but about the power of birds as natural controls to offset the awesome multiplication of most insect species. It

is an indication of things to come that economic entomologist Archie Howard Kirkland later used this passage to show how dangerous the moths were. Unfortunately, however, to strengthen his case he left out the last sentence: "But on the approach of winter the titmice and wrens paid daily visits to the affected trees, and before spring had arrived the eggs of the insect were entirely destroyed."[33]

By the time of Samuels's visit to Medford the Civil War was over, and with it ended that era's best opportunity for riches in the silk trade. Trouvelot's experiments had gone well enough, but he could not rush nature, and it had taken him until 1865 to gain sufficient experience to contemplate raising silk-worms on a commercial scale. His silk moth experiments had been hard work with little reward for Trouvelot, who put in long days overcoming the problems of cultivating *T. polyphemus* and who is generally credited with discovering the best way to unreel its cocoon.

In the course of his work, Trouvelot made himself into a respectable entomologist. He studied assiduously to improve his knowledge, and he once wrote to Samuel Scudder, a prominent Boston entomologist, that during the winter of 1868–69 he had "hardly gone to Boston more than twice, having worked to my favorite studies all winter."[34] He had begun a collection of insects, mostly lepidoptera in the family then named Bombycidae, and his writings for the *American Naturalist* refer several times to his "cabinet" of specimens. He told Scudder that he was acquainted with almost all of the one hundred species of New England butterflies then known to entomologists.[35] Trouvelot understood the population dynamics of moths and butterflies in a way that most other entomologists of his time would not realize for another thirty years. He mentioned that if even one of every hundred larvae survived and reproduced, populations would not decline from year to year and might even increase.

Trouvelot was also aware that Lepidoptera received the world mainly through their antennae, although he had not worked along these lines far enough to discover the phenomenon of pheromones or understand their chemical basis. He noted the important contributions of small mammals in reducing moth populations and the similar suppressing effect of toads and snakes at a time when little was known about them in this respect and almost no other naturalists were working along these lines.

Trouvelot also had an interest in parasites that was remarkable for the times. He observed caterpillar parasites such as the Ichneumon fly and was the first to describe the methods it used to parasitize its host. At this time, little was known about many insects and almost nothing was understood about parasitic insects except that they existed. Until 1868 no one in America except Trouvelot is known to have seen an Ichneumon fly in the act of depositing her

eggs on a caterpillar. Trouvelot had written to Dr. Wilder at Cornell that he had witnessed such events, and that the fly alighted not on the caterpillar's back but along its side.[36] At one point he sent Scudder drawings of an entozoan (parasite) of rabbits with an explanation of its habits, and included drawings of a large dipterous larva he found on the rabbit's neck.[37]

Dividing his time between his canvas and his caterpillars would have allowed Trouvelot to work at home when the insects were in their larval state. During the caterpillar season the silkworm experiment demanded ceaseless attention: the insects required continuous feeding; the breeding platforms had to be swept clean three times a day; the netting required constant repair; and in the time left free, Trouvelot assumed the Sisyphcan task of keeping the birds from devouring his insects.

In the fall of 1866, Trouvelot's practical experiments with *T. polyphemus* seem to have reached their peak. At this time he was trying to raise two "broods" annually, or at least to stagger the breeding times under controlled conditions so that the hatch of caterpillars would be spread throughout the spring and summer. Although Trouvelot was satisfied that he had solved the difficult problems of breeding this insect in captivity, the silk it produced, although useful, was considered coarse and inferior to the fine silk of *Bombyx mori.*

About this time, Charles Valentine Riley, in his post as state entomologist of Missouri, was writing on the American silk moths in his *Reports on the Noxious, Beneficial, and Other Insects of the State of Missouri.* Trouvelot and Riley exchanged correspondence on Cecropia and *T. polyphemus* moths, and it seems that Riley, then young and not fully experienced, respected Trouvelot's work. Trouvelot had succeeded with *T. polyphemus* to a point beyond that attained by all other researchers and was accepted as an expert on the species. He had discovered that the emerging moth produced a "dissolvent acid" that allowed it to leave its rigid cocoon without breaking a single fiber. He described it so well that in his annual report Riley quoted Trouvelot's description verbatim.[38]

The Insect Invasion

America was being infiltrated by a host of foreign insects that arrived on purpose or by accident, but because of the disorganized state of entomology, men of science were slow to understand the adverse consequences, and government authorities were ambivalent about regulating the practice. Entrepreneurs did not think twice about bringing a new species of silkworm or a new variety of Italian honeybee into the country, because these insects were considered legitimate items of commerce. There were no legal, moral, or ethical

restraints against the practice of transporting alien insects anywhere. The Japanese oak silk moth (*Antheraea yamamai* [Guerin-Meneville]), called colloquially *tensan* in Japan, was brought to Austria around 1860, and by 1868 the Baron de Bretton was able to reel 16,000 cocoons per year.[39] The Japanese had been raising *tensan* commercially for more than a thousand years because its silk was so prized that it commanded a premium price. Yet for some reason the interest of the Austrians in *tensan* silk waned; the project was abandoned, and the insects were released. The species is still found today in parts of southern Austria in the area once known as Tyrolea and also in northern France, where its defoliation of trees has become a problem.

In 1865, Townend Glover, the first federal entomologist, had an epiphany on this matter while attending the Paris Exhibition. He realized that one day the continued arrivals of new insect pests in North America could prove to be a disaster. In his section of the 1865 *Report of the Commissioner of Agriculture*, he issued a prophetic warning that described the future history of the gypsy moth in North America: "As European insects are at any time liable to be introduced into this country . . . their nature and habits cannot be too well understood here. . . . One pair of new noxious insects will do more harm than hundreds of the well-known varieties, as the progeny might commit their ravages unsuspected till they multiplied past the possibility of extermination."[40]

The Gypsy Moth Comes to America

O N NOVEMBER 2, 1866, Trouvelot sailed for Europe, where he could obtain the eggs of continental silk moths as well as some recently introduced exotic specimens.[1] It is likely that he stopped in Paris to see Guerin-Meneville, a man who would have been most aware of the latest introductions and their availability. Trouvelot might have had the idea that a few imported varieties would do well in North America or that he could find some that would interbreed with the New World's silk moths. On the basis of his experiences with Cecropia and Polyphemus, he would have insects that could tolerate handling, relocation, and disruptions well, would thrive on a varied or changing diet, and would not be aggressively sought by natural predators—in short, moths with traits that would lend themselves to commercial production practice. He also knew that a replacement silkworm should be highly resistant to disease. In many of these respects, the gypsy moth would have seemed an ideal candidate.

As a practical matter, raising millions of caterpillars in captivity required enormous amounts of vegetation, and for most caterpillars the leaves had to be fresh and of a certain variety or they would refuse to eat. One solution to this problem would be a caterpillar that would eat whatever was locally available. Trouvelot must have looked around him and, seeing almost nothing but oaks, determined to find an insect for which oaks were the preferred species. Some years later, Nathaniel Shaler recalled that a preference for oaks was one of the traits Trouvelot had looked for when selecting silk moths for his experiments.[2]

There were some drawbacks to using the gypsy moth as a silkworm. The cocoon spun by the gypsy caterpillar is a slap-dash affair of thinly crisscrossed strands barely adequate to support the pupa; unreeling it would be not only impossible but pointless; and the silk spun by the larva, being coarse, ragged, and mildly toxic to some, would have had no commercial value at all.

So one can only speculate that the attraction lay entirely in its extraordinary vitality.

Trouvelot was back in Medford by March, when he wrote to Scudder that he had been "absent from home" and was replying to letters he found waiting for him on his return.[3] He could have resumed his experiments with *T. polyphemus*, because he was on the verge of a great success in farming them, but he seemed intent on trying some European and exotic Asian species. Most entomologists and others who have studied this period believe that Trouvelot brought gypsy moth egg masses with him when he came back, although any evidence that he did so has long since vanished.

Trouvelot wrote a lengthy article in three parts about his silkworm project for the then new magazine called the *American Naturalist*. The idea for the magazine came from Frederic W. Putnam, curator of the Essex Institute, and the editors were Alpheus Hyatt, Edward Morse, and Alpheus Packard. The common link of these four young men was that they had all been students of Agassiz at the Museum of Comparative Zoology, and all had varying degrees of acquaintance with Trouvelot as a result of his presence there and in the Boston Society of Natural History. Packard had visited Trouvelot a few years earlier and already knew about what otherwise would have been an obscure experiment taking place in an isolated woodlot behind a nondescript house in Medford. Although the content of the *American Naturalist* was not rigorously professional, Trouvelot's writings, appearing in the magazine's first year of publication, conferred on him a certain importance and strengthened his link with the rise of science in America during the 1860s.

Trouvelot most likely went to France for his specimens, but Warren W. Rawson, chairman of the first Massachusetts gypsy moth commission, said that the eggs themselves came from Germany.[4] So did Muriel L. Guberlet when she wrote about Trevor Kincaid's part in searching for gypsy moth parasites early in the twentieth century.[5] Howard later wrote that other European silk moths held Trouvelot's attention but was unable to specify the types of insects or give the dates they were imported.[6] Trouvelot may have brought back nothing pertaining to sericulture but only placed orders for merchandise to be sent to him later.

In a letter written from Paris to Archie Kirkland in Boston, G. Haushalter, a former neighbor of Trouvelot's on Myrtle Street, mentioned that one of the shipments Trouvelot received from his sources in France had contained an unexpected addition: "Mr. Trouvelot, Jr., told me that the eggs of the insect were sent to Mr. Trouvelot by accident by M. Gerard Mennevel of Paris in 1868, and almost at the same time eggs came from Japan which contained the microbes of the [caterpillar] cholera. The eggs of the gypsy moth developed and the insect escaped, but I don't believe the family of Mr. Trouvelot have a

precise knowledge of how or in what stage of development."⁷ Walter C. Wright of Medford also believed that the introduction of the eggs was accidental: "I was acquainted with Prof. Trouvelot, and also well acquainted with Lewis Prang, a warm friend of his; and Lewis Prang's statement to me was that the importation was entirely accidental, that the gypsy moth bunch of eggs came on a package of other eggs . . . and they hatched out and [Trouvelot] discovered them."⁸

In a letter written in 1870 in his small, fine hand, Trouvelot told geologist William Healy Dall in Washington, D.C., that the moth he was trying to import was *Bombyx [Antheraea] yamamai,* a large and beautiful oak-eating Japanese silk moth that was a relatively recent introduction in Europe. Guerin-Meneville had classified this insect as a silk moth, *Bombyx yama-mai*, known as *tensan* in Japan—the same insect that Baron de Bretton in Austria tried to raise five or six years earlier. Even though the European experiment with *B. yama-mai* had failed, Trouvelot still felt that the insect was valuable and the only one whose introduction he would recommend.⁹

Haushalter's letter and Wright's testimony increase the possibility that the gypsy moth eggs arrived accidentally and that Trouvelot began his work thinking he was raising some other exotic species of silk moth. All entomological historians have been somewhat skeptical of this scenario because it sounds self-serving, it was put forth long after the gypsy moths escaped, and that someone as knowledgeable as Guerin-Meneville would not have noticed something wrong with the items he packed for Trouvelot seems unlikely. But this, too, is simply speculation.

Michael Gerardi and James Grimm state that the original number of gypsy moths was very small.¹⁰ Trouvelot himself indicated at one point that his initial stock of *Bombyx dispar* larvae was so meager that it could be netted entirely on a single bush in his back yard. Through the spring of 1868 he continued his experiments with his new exotics, raising them alongside his considerable inventory of *T. polyphemus*. At some point of uncertain date and by unknown means, Trouvelot discovered what his new species actually was, possibly by showing the larvae or egg masses to Hagen, who was the only entomologist in the state who would have recognized them on sight. Trouvelot then made the fateful decision to work further with this fortuitous acquisition to see if anything useful could be done with them.

The gypsy moth was then classified as *Bombyx dispar*, which incorrectly placed it in the same genus as the silkworm *Bombyx mori*, but Trouvelot seems to have accepted this designation without question. The taxonomic confusion contributed in no small way to the mischief that followed. During Trouvelot's lifetime the insect was known variously as *Phalaena dispar*,

Liparis dispar, Porthetria dispar, Psilura dispar, and *Laria dispar.* Within the years covered by this volume it also would be called *Ocneria dispar, Hypogymna dispar,* and the name by which it is known today, *Lymantria dispar.* Scientific books of Trouvelot's time commonly used *Bombyx dispar,* a name that did not die out until nearly the end of the nineteenth century.

The success that had rewarded Trouvelot's experiments with *T. polyphemus* was not repeated in his work with *B. dispar,* and the expertise he had acquired earlier turned out to be of little use to him. At first he tried raising the larvae in his breeding shed and then placing them outside to feed on the net-covered trees behind his house. The period of time he experimented with them was relatively short, and the number of gypsy moth larvae never reached anywhere near the million mark he had claimed for his *T. polyphemus.*

Driven by powerful instincts, the newly hatched gypsy moth larvae seek food high in the leafy canopy, ascending the trunks of trees early in the day and spinning scanty little webs of silk on the undersides of leaves, where they rest during the night. Although Trouvelot took steps to protect his caterpillars and confine them to his yard, he might not have understood how extraordinary the precautions for the gypsy moth needed to be. Each day some small number of insects certainly escaped. Trouvelot was fully aware that the larvae of other moths, such as *T. polyphemus,* all had prodigious appetites: "One who has had no experience in the matter could hardly believe what an amount of food is devoured by these little creatures. . . . What a destruction of leaves this single species of insect could make if only a one-hundredth part of the eggs laid came to maturity!"[11]

Although robins and other birds ate the plump and smooth-skinned *T. polyphemus* in great numbers, far fewer birds preferred hairy caterpillars such as *B. dispar,* and some would eat them only to fend off starvation. Over forty species of birds are now known to prey on the gypsy moth, but only about fourteen have an impact on a gypsy moth population explosion—blackbird, bluejay, catbird, black-capped chickadee, crow, grackle, nuthatch, oriole, chipping sparrow, robin, tanager, vireo, red-winged blackbird, and woodpecker[12]—plus two champion gypsy moth destroyers, the red-billed and black-billed cuckoos. These large, foot-long birds often appear in great number in areas infested with gypsy moths, cicadas, armyworms, and other insects that undergo population outbreaks; they eat spiny, hairy, and poisonous caterpillars. But Trouvelot does not mention the appearance of cuckoos. It seems he had ominously fewer problems with birds while breeding gypsy moths than he had while breeding *T. polyphemus.*

After the Civil War ended and the southern cotton plantations recovered, interest in finding alternative silkworms waned and the silk industries in the

Northeast collapsed. Pasteur had shown that removing adult individuals from the breeding stock whenever microscopic examination revealed they were infected could prevent silkworm disease from spreading. So as Trouvelot's incentives for success became less compelling, he may have concluded that he had done enough work with *Bombyx dispar* to know that the insect held little potential as a silkworm.

The years from 1866 to 1870 seem to have been Trouvelot's last and busiest in entomology. His silk moth experiments reached their peak, and so did his output of writing. He gave a short talk on the intervals of egg hatching and molting of the Phasmidae at the Boston Society of Natural History in November 1866.[13] An illness hc suffered in the spring of 1867 delayed the drawings he was finishing for Packard's book on moths, and at the time he was also negotiating to do the drawings for Scudder's book on eastern American butterflies.[14] Two papers he wrote for the Boston Society of Natural History and his work for the *American Naturalist* appeared in 1867, and a third paper unrelated to entomology was published by the Boston society in 1870.

Of the two 1867 papers, one in particular, "On a Method of Stimulating Union between Insects of Different Species," reveals unambiguously that Trouvelot believed he had worked out a system for inducing different species to mate, and that he thought it might be possible to obtain viable hybrids from "closely allied species" as others had already done: "I have in my cabinet a specimen given to me by Mr. Guerin Meneville, which is a hybrid from the ailanthus silk worm (B. cynthia) and the castor oil silk worm (Bombyx arrindia). This hybrid is said to be from the twentieth generation. I have often obtained union between insects of different genera; of course there was too great a separation between these types to obtain impregnated eggs."[15]

The idea was clever and simple: three adult moths of the same species would be required, two males and a female. A fourth moth that was a female of a related species would be placed in a cage with the first female, and when mating time arrived for the first female, both males would be released into the cage. One male would find and mate with the female of his own kind, but the second would unite with the other, apparently unaware that his union was with a female of a different species. Trouvelot told a meeting of the entomology section of the Boston Natural History Society that his experiments had revealed the method, and that it had always worked successfully.[16] From the information available to him and as a result of his own research, Trouvelot must have believed there was a small but real chance of breeding a hybrid that could propagate its type through following generations, and it seems reasonable to conclude that many of the exotic moths he had imported were intended for this type of experiment. For Trouvelot, this work simply

represented the same things he always had always done, though with a different kind of moth.

Then, disaster struck: the gypsy moths got away from him.

The Mysterious Escape

In gathering the facts about the gypsy moth's escape, chroniclers of the past did not fare much better than researchers of the present, and the true story had been lost before the turn of the nineteenth century. Alice Bailey Ward, writing in 1893, said, "A cluster of tiny eggs had been blown out of Mr. Trouvelot's window and, like the dust on the palm of Moses, lifted and whirled, had brought forth a plague."[17] In 1897, Fletcher Osgood, who wrote with the advantage of knowing those who had known Trouvelot, could come up only with the following:

> This menacing forager of the Eastern Hemisphere was brought over twenty-six years ago by a French savant, in considerable numbers, to Medford, a suburb of Boston, Massachusetts. The object is said to have been to cross the creature with the delicate silkworm, and so originate a robust, silk-producing hybrid for America; but the statement has been gravely questioned. The scheme, whatever it was, came to nothing, and the gypsy caterpillars, liberated from their netted enclosure by a gale, spread slowly over Medford.[18]

In statements prepared for the Massachusetts gypsy moth committee in 1893 and 1894, a few of Trouvelot's neighbors from 1869 recalled the sight of him searching for the eggs in his yard and stated that "he was much disturbed on being unable to find them."[19] Stories persisted that an agonized Trouvelot tried to warn certain entomologists and possibly officials in local or state government of what had happened, but the course of events shows that any warnings he gave were not taken seriously. Charles H. Fernald, in his 1889 *Bulletin of the Hatch Experiment Station*, related that two of Trouvelot's contemporaries, both experienced entomologists, knew the particulars of the moth's escape, but Fernald himself neglected to tell the story: "Mr. Samuel Henshaw and Dr. Hagen of Cambridge have both informed me that the entomologist who introduced this insect was Mr. L. Trouvelot. . . . Dr. Hagen told me that he distinctly remembered hearing Mr. Trouvelot tell how they escaped from him after he had imported them."[20]

Hagen told Henshaw that Trouvelot spoke on the subject before the entomological section of the Boston Society of Natural History. Hagen also

claimed to have written a record of the gypsy moth affair for the *Entomolo-gische Zeitung Stetten*, a German-language entomology journal, but he could not remember which volume.[21] Henshaw was unable to locate the document, and it appears that if Hagen did write such a paper, it was never published. Haushalter said that Trouvelot had written "a concise resume of the whole affair for a certain American entomologist whose name escapes me."[22] Charles Riley and Samuel Scudder seem the most likely recipients, since Trouvelot was corresponding with both men around this time, but there is no record of any entomologist claiming to have received Trouvelot's recounting.

Charles Riley, entomologist of Missouri from 1868 to 1877 and author of nine famous reports on the insects of that state, did write in his second report: "Only a year ago the larva of a certain owlet moth (Hypogymna dispar), which is a great pest in Europe both to fruit trees and forest trees, was acciden-tally introduced by a Massachusetts entomologist into New England, where it is spreading with great rapidity."[23] That report appeared in 1870, and notice of the gypsy moth introduction was published in *American Entomologist* and *Insect Life* the same year.[24] Riley's statement that the moths escaped "only a year ago" fixes the date as 1869, which suggests that the insects got away from Trouvelot almost at once. The moth's release was widely known in a short time in places as distant as Missouri. News of the escape was promptly distributed both locally and regionally; entomologists were aware of the threat it posed; and the spread of the moths had been observed. Outside of the small circle of agricultural entomologists, however, the escape of the gypsy moth attracted almost no attention at all.

Geologist Nathaniel Shaler was aware of the gypsy moth experiment even before the escape took place. He had engaged Trouvelot to draw the maps for the *Kentucky Geological Survey*, a compilation that Shaler, who was born in Kentucky, had created from various surveys of his home state.[25] Trouvelot must have mentioned his attempt to breed gypsy moths, and a nervous Shaler urged Trouvelot to destroy his imports: "About thirty years ago I had in my employment a Frenchman, a remarkable man, who was exceedingly experi-mental. . . . He had the idea of bringing, and had already brought from Eu-rope, specimens of the gypsy moth, with a view of crossing them with some American moths, in order that he might get a hybrid silkworm that would feed on oak leaves. Learning of it I spoke to him about it and told him of the risk which he was running, the risk of settling a pest with us. . . . I begged him to destroy the creatures, which he told me he would."[26]

Shaler knew not only about the gypsy moths' escape but also about their importation, and in 1895 he related the details to Forbush. In *The Gypsy Moth*, the monograph published in 1896, Forbush mentioned hearing the story from Shaler but omitted it from the book, and Shaler's own recounting

has since disappeared. In 1890 and 1891, commissions appointed by the state of Massachusetts to exterminate the gypsy moth attempted without success to correspond with Trouvelot, who was by then living at Meudon near Paris. Fernald, addressing a meeting of economic entomologists in 1895, said that he also had written to Trouvelot and had not received an answer. The information he finally acquired came secondhand: "I was informed a short time ago that a gentleman was with Mr. Trouvelot in Paris not long before his death, and Mr. Trouvelot told him that he brought the eggs over from France, and when they hatched he put them on a shrub near his house and covered them with a mosquito net, and that a storm came up in the night and tore the net to such an extent that the insects escaped. I suppose that this is the way that the insect escaped, although we have another story."[27]

Entomologist Archie H. Kirkland, writing in 1905, filled in a few details that Fernald left out. He shed no light on what the "other story" might have been but said that the "gentleman" in question was "the late Alvan Clarke, the well-known lens maker of Cambridge."[28] This must have been Alvan Clarke's son, Alvan Graham Clarke, since the elder Clarke had died in August 1887. Trouvelot's story of the gale and the shredded netting conflict with his comments that his nets already had holes in them big enough to admit a robin and the eyewitness accounts of his Medford neighbors who swore they saw him looking for eggs in the grass outside his house. Despite romanticized embellishments of the great getaway, one of which depicts a frantic and exhausted Trouvelot digging in vain through the Medford dump for his discarded egg masses, the truth of the story is likely mundane: Trouvelot had treated the gypsy moths no differently from the others he raised, which allowed the insect to escape. The tiny caterpillars simply crawled away or were wafted by the breezes into areas nearby.

Trouvelot after the Gypsy Moth

Most entomological historians consider that Trouvelot abandoned his insect work at this point, but tracking Trouvelot is like following footprints across a river. For a few years after the gypsy moth escaped, he continued his silkworm research, but then disaster struck again. As he mentioned in his letter to Dall, the shipment from Guerin-Meneville had been infected, and by 1870, disease had swept through his insectary and destroyed most of his caterpillars.[29] In addition, he no longer had enough time to spend attending silkworms because he was occupied with other obligations.[30] Some of these were likely in the field of astronomy, in which Trouvelot, now entering his forties, began to pursue the successes that had eluded him in entomology.

Trouvelot always retained an interest in entomology, though, and confided

to Scudder that he enjoyed drawing insects.[31] He kept up his correspondence with Riley into 1870, and in 1877 he wrote an article on insects' use of antennae for the *American Naturalist*. Samuels, writing for *Scribner's* in 1879, still considered Trouvelot to be America's most knowledgeable silk moth researcher.[32] In 1880, Trouvelot engraved the woodcuts for Packard's bulletin on the Hessian fly, published by the U.S. Entomological Commission.[33] Trouvelot's contribution to Scudder's book on the butterflies of the eastern United States was substantial as well.[34] Although he ceased working for Scudder after 1882, and the butterfly book was not published for another six years, Trouvelot lent or donated captured specimens for study, and Scudder's records credit him with coloring 112 illustrations.[35]

If Trouvelot continued to work with caterpillars after the escape of the gypsy moths, anything on a large scale must have concluded by mid-1872, because at this time he moved with his family from Medford to 99 Garden Street in Cambridge. There he began a productive association with Professor Joseph Winlock, director of the astronomical observatory at Harvard College, and the *Cambridge City Directory* for 1873 gives his occupation as "assistant at the observatory."[36] Winlock engaged Trouvelot to work as an artist in the preparation of a volume of drawings to be published by the observatory, underwritten by a $2,500 grant from the Bache Fund. Trouvelot made the original sketches and the finished drawings for thirty-five lithographic plates, beginning his work on July 11, 1872, when the project started.[37] The book was published to great acclaim in 1875, and Trouvelot's drawings were admired for their "great fidelity and artistic beauty."[38]

The *Annals of the Astronomical Observatory at Harvard College* for 1876 lists "Mr. Trouvelot," as an observer and reports that he was not associated with the observatory after his work as an artist was completed in 1874. In 1875, Trouvelot was at work for Shaler on the maps for the *Kentucky Geological Survey*, published in 1876, and for the *Cambridge City Directory* that year he gave his occupation as "draughtsman."

Trouvelot quickly gained a reputation for his astronomical illustrations. In 1876 he exhibited many of his exquisite pastels in the Art Gallery and the Naval Observatory exhibitions of the Centennial Exposition in Philadelphia. After 1876 he was again associated with the Harvard observatory and in 1878 entranced the public with 24-by-36-inch drawings of sunspots and the Andromeda nebula. Scribner's publishing house listed Trouvelot's *Astronomical Drawings* as one of its most successful books of the period, which is all the more remarkable, since the volume contained just fifteen chromolithographs yet sold for the prohibitive price of $125.[39]

In 1881, Trouvelot, still residing at 99 Garden Street with his son, George,

listed his occupation in the *Cambridge City Directory* as "astronomer." In this year he attained his highest honor when he was elected to the American Academy of Arts and Sciences.[40] He also received an offer from the French government to take a well-paying position assisting solar astronomer Jules Janssen at a new observatory housed in the reconstructed Meudon castle just outside Paris. Opportunities for advancement in scientific fields were few and far between at this time, and when one appeared it was never taken lightly. Trouvelot accepted the offer—though only after difficult consideration—and the *Cambridge City Directory* for 1882 holds the last listing for him in the United States.

Although some evidence suggests that the moth's escape had been completely forgotten by the few people who knew about it, Haushalter cited as one of Trouvelot's reasons for leaving America that reporters seeking information about the gypsy moth were beginning to harry him. In any case, Trouvelot set foot on his native soil again in 1882, the same year that his former neighbors on Myrtle Street first began to notice that their fruit and ornamental trees were being attacked in the spring by a strange, hairy, black caterpillar with crimson and blue dots on its back.

The Gypsy Moth after Trouvelot

For the first few years after the escape, gypsy moth activity in the vicinity of Myrtle Street and the nearby Glenwood Station was too slight to attract attention. The area into which the moth had gone consisted of small trees and dense underbrush. The Medford fire chief often complained about the frequency of blazes in this area and the difficulties of extinguishing them, and it is likely that the recurrent conflagrations helped at first to keep the gypsy moth population down. Still, the moths were spread throughout an area that was extremely favorable to their survival, and although fires were an important factor, perhaps their failure to increase their numbers swiftly was caused by the disease that had come unnoticed on Guerin-Meneville's shipment from Paris.[41]

Trouvelot, normally communicative on the subject of caterpillars when writing for magazines or rubbing shoulders with well-known naturalists and entomologists, fell silent when it came to exchanging a few words with his neighbors about the portent of recent events. Only he could have identified gypsy moth larvae on sight, and Forbush states that Trouvelot is known to have seen them in the woods near his house during the years immediately following their escape.[42] As far as can be discovered, though, Trouvelot remained mute about his observations, attempting no further warnings to his

neighbors except for one instance noted by Haushalter: "I personally remember him destroying egg clusters and asking myself and companion to do likewise and telling us at the same time of the development from the eggs to the full grown insect. . . . Mr. Trouvelot . . . was worried greatly by reporters and having informed very fully some American gentlemen, he decided to say nothing more."[43]

At the time, only Trouvelot might have spoken with enough authority to spur his neighbors to action. Yet when the residents of Myrtle Street and surrounding neighborhoods made statements to the gypsy moth committee two decades later, they could not understand how the presence of such a voracious insect had escaped notice for twenty years and were uniform in their recollection that neither they nor anyone else knew what the caterpillars were. Riley and Howard were also puzzled about the insect's invisibility: "It is, indeed, a curious fact that during these twenty years the insect has not become a pest, and still more curious that the moth does not seem to have found its way into the collections and is not mentioned in the check-lists."[44]

Trouvelot: Pioneer Researcher or Entrepreneur?

In the last analysis, was Trouvelot a scientist or a businessman? In an era when the distinction between scientific and commercial endeavor was beginning to narrow, it might not be unfair to say that he was both and neither. He had concerned himself with broad areas of experimentation during his years of fascination with insects: the breeding of better silkworms, the mechanics of raising them, and the process of transforming their raw silk into a commercially useful form. Trouvelot's attempts to secure them were more entrepreneurial in concept than scientific; the nets he placed were intended not to protect the North American forests from the gypsy moth but to protect the gypsy moth from the birds. Trouvelot was also a prospector of sorts. He had wrapped his enterprise in a scientific mantle, yet he was not only studying but mining the insects of North America. His underlying hope was to get rich, and he referred to his silkworm farm not as a scientific or field laboratory but as his "infant industry."[45]

As a part-time scientific researcher, Trouvelot's few experiments seem rather shallow and insubstantial, and his reports reveal more about his powers of observation than about his scientific acumen. Nevertheless, his method of work and his perspective on research were much different from those of other entomologists of his day. His areas of interest—parasites; the function of antennae in moths and butterflies; the effects of mammals, birds, and reptiles on insect populations—would have made him a worker far ahead of his time had he concentrated on entomology.

Female gypsy moth.
From *The Gypsy Moth.*

Male gypsy moth.
From *The Gypsy Moth.*

One might expect that a scientific researcher who worked for ten years on a project of great magnitude would have published his findings in a scientific journal and used his skill as an illustrator to record the insect in detail, as was the practice of all naturalists of the day. Yet as Trouvelot mentioned to Dall, the popular articles that appeared in the *American Naturalist* were the only things he ever wrote about his silkworm experiments.[46] Trouvelot drew professionally and had little time to draw for pleasure. As he told Scudder, "I have not in my possession over a dozen drawings of larvae and pupae of New England butterflies."[47]

Trouvelot's idea of crossbreeding insects must be regarded with some amazement. Although interbreeding individuals of the same species for the selection of desirable traits had been practiced for generations in everything from livestock to silkworms, the kind of hybridization that Trouvelot considered was an unknown art in the scientific world of the mid-nineteenth century. He had devised a clever way to trick dissimilar moth species into mating, but the hope of creating a fertile hybrid was too far ahead of its day. Gregor Mendel's seminal work with peas in Europe was proceeding in obscurity at this time, and the famous fruit fly experiments in the United States, which were the first attempts to understand genetic manipulation of insects, were still fifty years in the future.

The most that can be deduced about Trouvelot's scientific or entrepreneurial goals was that he cast his net as widely as he could and tried a number of different schemes without having had previous experience in any of them. Like many others of his time in similar circumstances, if success had come in great measure with one of his projects, he likely would have abandoned the others— as he seems to have dropped his work with insects when his astronomical drawings brought him recognition and prestige.

Reviewing his decade of effort with silk moths, which must have been on

Gypsy moth egg mass.
From *The Gypsy Moth.*

Female gypsy moth larva.
From *The Gypsy Moth.*

his mind when he wrote to Dall, Trouvelot reflected on the ephemeral promise of this kind of work with substitute insects such as Cynthia and Ailanthus: "I have seen this worm and know its products. I am decidedly adverse to its introduction as I know positively that the culturist could not realize in the end of the season the money he would have spent for buying the eggs. . . . All of us are inclined to look too often through the colored glasses which are the same color as our favorite ideas."[48]

The Caterpillars Are Coming!

E ACH SPRING DURING THE 1880s, hundreds of caterpillars crawled over the shed behind William Taylor's rented house at 27 Myrtle Street. Taylor knew that the former occupant, Leopold Trouvelot, had experimented with sericulture but was unaware that the insects he saw were not silkworms. Taylor had no use for the annoying caterpillars and sold the shed to W. B. Harmon on nearby Spring Street. It was this act, Taylor later told the gypsy moth commission, that caused the appearance of the insect in another location and explained how its numbers came to be so great.[1]

The Harmon house was located at the end of a sparsely built-up street and adjoined a wooded lot even larger than the one behind Trouvelot's old house, but the gypsy moth activities there at first attracted no attention. The vague warnings published by Riley had been met with indifference, and interest within the entomological community had been brief. In short, as Trouvelot's little blunder was soon forgotten, the gypsy moth became widely though thinly dispersed. Its greatest concentrations occurred along transportation routes, as these offered the best means for distribution: egg masses or larvae were transported on wagons, either attached to some inconspicuous spot or as part of the load. Egg masses were later found in piles of bricks on their way to job sites or on the bark of firewood distributed to homes throughout the city.

Trouble began occurring as early as 1882. Mr. and Mrs. J. W. Flinn, who lived near Trouvelot's house until 1886, noted that the insect was becoming destructive, defoliating apple and pear and maple trees in their yard, eating the peas and beans and corn in their garden, and entering their house, where the couple "would even find them upon the clothes hanging in the closets."[2] The moths overspread the wooded areas south of Myrtle Street and crossed the railroad tracks, but did not advance very much to the north. William Taylor's problems with caterpillars had not ceased with the sale of Trouvelot's shed, and his experiences gave warning that there was something nasty about these little creatures: "I fought the caterpillars of the gypsy moth for ten years

before the State did anything. In their season I used to gather them literally by the quart before going to work. It is a fact that I have been made so sick while doing this that I vomited up my breakfast."[3]

By 1883, reports of defoliation in Medford were increasing but were still paid little attention. Mary and William Belcher of 29 Myrtle Street had been bothered by caterpillars for six or eight years, but Mary Belcher later told the gypsy moth commission that the problems they caused were so slight that nobody bothered to ask what the caterpillars were. This situation soon changed. By the spring of 1886, trees on the Fenton estate at 10 Myrtle Street were so full of caterpillars that shaking the branches brought a shower of larvae down on one's head. Thomas and Lina Mayo of 25 Myrtle Street awoke one morning in the spring of 1887 and were startled to see what appeared to be the results of a fire in the verdant woods behind their house. The puzzled couple investigated and discovered that the charred appearance was caused by thousands of black gypsy moth caterpillars clustered under the branches.

By 1888, moth populations in Medford had risen, and pronounced defoliation was occurring in the neighborhood. D. W. Daly of 5 Myrtle Street watched as his fruit trees were stripped bare. In the mornings he spent an hour sweeping dustpans full of larvae off the side of his house. Lina Mayo's fruit trees had been defoliated for several years in a row, and nine had died as a result.[4] She had spent most of her time during the summers of 1887 and 1888 trying to rid her premises of the larvae: "The caterpillars [covered] the basement and clapboards of the house as high as the window sill. They lay in a solid black mass. I would scrape them off into an old dish pan holding about ten quarts. When it was two-thirds full I poured kerosene over the mass of worms and set them on fire. I used to do this a number of times a day. It was sickening work. I have used, in burning caterpillars, five gallons of kerosene in three days."[5]

The Swarms of Medford

The mild winter of 1888–89 produced so little snow that the mortality of the gypsy moths' overwintering eggs was negligible. Unimpeded by natural restraints and presented with abundant sources of food, moth populations exploded. Similar outbreaks were reported two miles away at West Medford and at Edgeworth, about a mile to the east. In Glenwood the depleted food source triggered a mass migration of larvae across Myrtle Street, turning its surface black with the bodies of fast-moving caterpillars.

Citizens could only stare in disbelief as the dirt streets became carpeted with millions of larvae that seemed to have materialized out of the earth. People cried out, "The caterpillars are coming!" as a vast, black, living wave

of insect life undulated and writhed down the street. Witnesses recalled that it was impossible to count the caterpillars because of their great numbers and fast movement. The insect armies moved from one source of food to another, and none of the hastily mounted defenses could stop them. Great, pulsating masses of larvae stripped any plant along their path in minutes. Many residents later mentioned how the caterpillars moved from "yard to yard, house to house, and street to street" with almost supernatural precision.[6] J. S. Cotton of Medford said they were "the most ravenous worms I ever saw. They would eat almost everything."[7] Mary Belcher spent hours sweeping caterpillars into a pan or scalding them with boiling water, after which she dug a hole and buried them "so as to prevent a stench."[8]

The streets of older cities such as Medford and Malden were lined with majestic elm trees, and after defoliating all the fruit trees, the caterpillars thronged toward these towering giants from all sides as if drawn by a beacon. One resident said their black bodies looked like a living carpet unrolled across the ground and up the trees. The larvae ascended the trunks in massive swarms, turning them black with caterpillar life, and defoliated the elms within two days. Residents walked down the middle of the streets to avoid the thousands of caterpillars spinning down from the trees. The larvae so thickly covered the sidewalks that one could not walk anywhere without crushing them. The ruptured caterpillars exuded slimy ooze that made footing uncertain; people hurrying home often slipped and fell into the gore. Myrtle Street was so bad that people detoured around it rather than face the swarms. Kerosene became in short supply, as many residents used ten or fifteen gallons each week to fuel caterpillar crematoriums in ditches, pails, and storm drains.

The oaks surrounding McGowan's tannery were swiftly denuded. F. T. Spinney's wife grabbed a torch and burned the caterpillars off tree trunks in her yard on Cross Street, while her husband scalded the larvae on their fence with boiling water. J. C. Miller of Lauriat Place had some printer's ink and banded his fruit trees with it, which saved them. He had to work fast because the caterpillars occupied themselves in the Spinney's yard only a few hours before swarming again. Miller said he destroyed thousands with rags soaked in kerosene.[9] Crushing and burning the caterpillars, and the smoke and stench of their funeral pyres, made some people sick. Others proved sensitive to the irritating hairs of the larvae; the caterpillars that fell on William Belcher's unprotected neck and wriggled under his collar caused a painful rash and raised blisters on his skin.

Not knowing what else to do with the mounds of dead caterpillars, some people swept heaps into the gutters and left them there; some incinerated them; others buried the insects in backyard pits. A few fed the living insects to their hens. Still more attempted to save their trees by tarring them or wrapping

their trunks with sticky bands of cloth, but the caterpillars came in such un-thinkable numbers that they bridged these barriers before the bands could be changed. One resident said so many were vying for space that they jostled each other off the trees in bunches; another commented that the insects were so tightly packed there was not enough space between them to place a pin. D. M. Richardson reported that the caterpillar columns left a visibly trampled path in the dirt behind them where they crossed the road.[10] One resident watched in amazement as a surging wave of starving larvae passed through her strawberry beds without eating a leaf; another stared in terrified fascina-tion as all arboreal foliage disappeared before her eyes. Oddly, the pear trees on Myrtle Street remained almost untouched, although the pears on other streets were stripped almost completely. Curiosity seekers were drawn to see the effects of the defoliating insects for themselves, and many returned home with unnoticed living mementos of their visit.

Commuters, rushing to catch their trains wore coats and hats in the mild spring weather as they ran through the maze of suspended larvae, arrived at their destinations covered with caterpillars. Sylvester Lacy of 9 Daisy Street dreaded going to the railroad station, which he likened to running a gauntlet.[11] Many gypsies rode the train to Boston concealed in the cuff of a gentleman's trousers, nestled in the pocket of an overcoat, hidden behind an upturned collar, or perched on the brim of a lady's hat. Caterpillars swarmed across the rails, which were stained green by their crushed bodies after the train had passed.

Life began to revolve around the caterpillar swarms as people sought ways avoid them, but there was no escape. Mrs. I. W. Hamlin, who lived at the corner of Spring and Myrtle Streets, wrote: "Time and time again I have stayed out in the yard for two hours at a time catching caterpillars. But in half an hour afterwards they seemed to be just as thick again. It was a common remark in our house, 'Well, it is time to go out and make our rounds again,' and then we would sally out with our pans."[12]

Homes did not provide a refuge. Doors could hardly be used, and the caterpillars poured through basement vents and screenless windows; large numbers came into houses by crawling down the chimneys. The hungry in-sects foraged through the dwellings, eating potted plants and any vegetable matter they could find in the kitchen. People retiring for the evening would find caterpillars beneath their pillows and turn down their blankets to find caterpillars between their sheets. The sound of millions of caterpillars chewing was clearly audible. Even the noise of the caterpillar droppings was loud enough to keep many awake, and a disgusting stench hung heavily over the town. J. O. Goodwin of Hall Park, Medford, wrote that the swarms made the ground look like a Persian rug, and the black insect masses covered houses up

to the eaves. Goodwin hated the caterpillars and fought them relentlessly: "When they speak of a hundred tons [of larvae] being destroyed, I am quite sure that I have destroyed more than two tons myself."[13]

Selectman W. C. Craig of Medford was riding home on the afternoon train from Boston one day when he saw a small orchard that was barren of leaves. He remarked to the lady next to him that he was not aware of a fire occurring in this particular orchard. The woman replied that there had been no fire but that the armyworm had stripped the trees. Most people believed the insects were armyworms, since the *Boston Herald* had reported a serious outbreak of that insect in nearby Maine toward the end of May.[14] Craig went to the town building in Medford and, in the company of several others, set out to investigate. They found, as he later recalled, an insect that no one had ever seen before.[15]

Craig did not have to look long for more caterpillars; in the days that followed, the caterpillars found him. Swarms of them nearly engulfed his house on Woburn Street, and he and his family exhausted many long afternoons scraping the messy creatures from their trees with wooden shingles. Craig could not walk out his front door and reach the sidewalk without crushing hundreds of them into a slimy green mass. When the worms were not in his shade trees, they were in his fruit trees; when they were not in his fruit trees, they were in his flowers and gardens. He would not have any spinach, dandelions, or tomatoes that year. Whatever kind of worm had visited Medford seemed to eat just about anything. W. B. Harmon's orchard on Spring Street was completely defoliated. Stupendous numbers of caterpillars had swarmed toward Crockford's greenhouses. Encountering 27,000 carnation pinks, they ate them down to the ground and, once inside the glass structures, denuded every single rosebush there.[16]

Craig made an inspection with a friend, the civil engineer and surveyor J. O. Goodwin. At the end, he was sure these caterpillars were not armyworms, and he decided to inform his colleagues on the board of selectmen. Craig also met with influential citizens and state officials to warn them of the danger of leaving the insects unchallenged. Former Senator Boynton, the former Medford mayor, General Samuel Crocker Lawrence, and Representative J. Henry Norcross, among others, personally guaranteed funds to fight the insect through the Medford road commission until a town meeting could be called.[17] Craig recounted: "I conferred with other members of the board, but we had nothing to do with the trees on the streets or in the orchards of town. Mr. Goodwin and myself waited on the road commissioners and asked them to spend some money stopping the ravages."[18]

The road commission met on July 1, 1889 but the commissioners did not have any idea what to do about the problem. Earlier that year, many trees in

Medford had been wrapped with fabric bands soaked in sticky printer's ink to protect them from the canker worm, and the commissioners, believing that technique might be effective against the new caterpillars as well, decided to refresh the ink, a task that was begun the next morning. Early the next evening the low angle of the setting sun cast the shadows of coming events over the citizens of Medford: when the fabric bands were lifted, thousands of fat, hairy, black caterpillars were discovered hiding beneath them.[19] At a July 15 Medford town meeting, $300 was voted to the roads commission for protecting the trees from the caterpillars, augmenting an earlier appropriation of $500 for the usual care of shade trees.

John Stetson, who lived about a mile west of the old Trouvelot house and saw that the defoliation of his trees and shrubs was unusually severe, later said, "I discovered [the caterpillars] in 1888 on a quince bush. I noticed one day that the leaves were all off from this bush. I examined it, and found there were worms clustered on the limbs."[20] When the same kind of defoliation happened the following year, he took some larvae to Boston and showed them to William Sessions, secretary of the Massachusetts State Board of Agriculture.

William Robert Sessions (1835–1914) was a tough and pugnacious self-schooled farm boy who had survived a crippling accident as a youth. He had held the offices of moderator and selectman in the Town of Wilbraham and later the Town of Hampden. He had served in the Massachusetts legislature, both house and senate, where he gained a great deal of experience in the brawling, bare-knuckled style of politics practiced in the public arena of his day. In 1887 he was appointed state agriculture secretary.[21]

While pondering what to do with Stetson's samples, Sessions made a crucial decision that irreversibly altered the course of subsequent events. He could have availed himself of the expertise concentrated in Boston, where an inquiry to the Natural History Society might have secured the services of an entomologist such as Samuel Henshaw or Samuel Hubbard Scudder, the latter considered the greatest American expert on moths and butterflies. Or Sessions could have tapped into the unparalleled resources at Harvard College, which was then America's premier institution for entomological instruction, thanks to the presence of Hermann August Hagen, a man whose opinion was so highly regarded that Leland Howard called it "the last word" in entomology.[22] Instead, Sessions told Stetson to send his specimens halfway across the state to be examined by a self-trained entomologist, Charles Henry Fernald, a professor of zoology at the Massachusetts Agricultural College in Amherst, of which Sessions was a trustee ex officio. That Sessions preferred to take the matter to Fernald was likely due to his belief that the services of an agricultural entomologist would be more advantageous than those of any other kind of entomologist; without a doubt he viewed the problem as an agricultural one. With

this decision, the die was cast; the new insect henceforth would be viewed as an agricultural pest, and the agricultural philosophy in approaching the problem would attain a tenacious stranglehold for the next ten years.

Charles Henry Fernald

Charles Henry Fernald was born on March 16, 1838, at Mount Desert Island off the Maine coast in the house that his great-grandfather had built and in which three subsequent generations of Fernald men had been born.[23] He came into the world at a time when formal educational opportunities were scarce. As a young boy he tutored himself in the many natural subjects that interested him. At the age of fifteen he went to sea during the summer and was both a student and a teacher in the local public school during the winter. He taught himself to draw because he remembered things better once he had illustrated them.

He studied music with Maria Elizabeth Smith, whom he married in 1862. The new Mrs. Fernald also developed into a capable entomologist and collector, becoming one of just a handful of women who were making their way in a field that would remain almost exclusively male for nearly a century more.[24] According to Arnold Mallis, the couple began studying entomology at the same time, and Maria eventually became an expert in many of the same insects that interested her husband, including the Tortricidae, Coccidae, and the Tinead moths.[25] Charles once said that his wife could reach out a window, take a moth on the wing, and deposit it in a cage without disturbing so much as a single scale.[26]

When the Civil War broke out, Fernald was enrolled in the Maine Wesleyan Seminary and Female School, then the largest college preparatory school in the state. He volunteered for the navy, and during his shipboard years he studied to enter Bowdoin College, from which he subsequently received his bachelor's degree and an honorary master of arts degree. After teaching at Houlton Academy, he became the chairman of natural history at Maine State College (now the University of Maine) in 1871, and over the next fifteen years he taught botany, physical geography, human anatomy, human physiology, comparative anatomy, and veterinary science.[27] Fernald's areas of expertise included entomology, botany, geology, mineralogy, and zoology—all of which he taught himself—in addition to algebra and trigonometry. He claimed no linguistic skill but mentioned in a letter that he had a working knowledge of French and German. Howard said no entomologist in America knew more about moths,[28] Charles Adams Peters marveled that one man could know so much about so many things.[29] And Mallis referred to Fernald as a "one-man university."[30]

In 1886, Fernald accepted an appointment as professor of zoology at the Massachusetts Agricultural College in Amherst, a land-grant institution that later became the University of Massachusetts. Before he departed from Maine, the state college there awarded him an honorary Ph.D., although he always preferred the title of "professor." At Amherst, Fernald was also placed in charge of entomological research at the Massachusetts Agricultural Experiment Station, founded in 1882 and later renamed the Hatch Station, a position in which he initially served without pay. He soon revived a course in entomology that had languished for ten years after the death of H. J. Clark, and one that had lost almost its entire collection of insects to fire in 1884.[31] He was appointed as entomologist of the station in 1887.[32] The same year he wrote a paper on beetles and, a year later, another on the Orthoptera of New England, publications that initiated a flow of entomological writings from the college.[33]

Charles Adams Peters, later a professor of chemistry at the agricultural college, had been enrolled in Fernald's courses as a young scholar and recalled him as a kindly and soft-spoken man whose students sometimes referred to him as a "fussy old fool" but who was fondly remembered by many who had received their education under his tutelage.[34] If one substituted a cap, turtle-neck sweater, and a peacoat for the dress jacket and bow tie shown in the photo, Fernald could be taken for the sea captain he once wanted to be. Fernald described himself as short and stout and, at 185 pounds, too heavy for his height. He is remembered as a genial and affable man, but he possessed a sarcastic streak, and Peters said that when things were not going well, Fernald could become very difficult to deal with. He led a quiet and self-restricted life, immersed in his work; he did not like or attend athletic games at the college, did not smoke, and used alcohol, he said, only to preserve his specimens.[35]

On May 27, 1889, when Stetson's samples were sent to the experiment station, Fernald had departed for a summer of study in Europe a few days earlier. Maria Fernald had taken over entomological work at the station, and her adult son, entomologist Henry Torsey Fernald, was living in Amherst at the time.[36] The caterpillars puzzled the Fernalds, and by a process of elimination they concluded that the larvae might not be a native species. Maria and Henry pored over the station's library, but most books of the day illustrated insects only in their adult form. On June 1, Maria Fernald wrote to Stetson: "Your letter and the box of larvae were received this morning, and I am very sorry that I am not able to give you the information you desire. [The caterpillars] are new to me and also to the station. . . . I think it cannot be an insect which has been abundant enough in past years to cause much damage or it would have been known by some of us."[37]

Charles Henry Fernald in middle age.
Photo courtesy of Special Collections
and Archives, W.E.B. Du Bois Library,
University of Massachusetts Amherst.

The Fernalds decided to raise the insects until the larvae transformed, and they set up a small insectary in an old barn near the experiment station. The first fact that mother and son noticed about these caterpillars was an ominous one: unlike the caterpillars of other species that died when raised in captivity, these particular insects fed voraciously and thrived. As Henry Fernald recalled later: "The rearing was successful, and when the moths emerged it was evident that they were unlike anything known in this country, so a search through European books available was in order. Finally, in Wood's 'Index Entomologicus' illustrations of them were found and the insect was recognized as the gypsy moth, a well known and serious pest in Europe."[38]

The discovery of the gypsy moth was made known to the local press in Massachusetts, and others as far south as Washington, D.C., learned of the invasion in the July 13, 1889, issue of the *New England Farmer*.[39] Mrs. N. W. C. Holt of Winchester, Massachusetts, sent some living samples on mulberry and apple branches to Charles Riley, then serving as chief federal entomologist in Washington, and Riley said there could be no doubt what the insects were if Mrs. Fernald had identified them.[40] Word was sent to Professor Fernald by mail, and the letter reached him in London.[41] He had been in Berlin just the summer before where he had observed the conclusion of a large gypsy moth outbreak.[42] As he continued his travels during the summer, the professor consulted with colleagues in England, France, Austria, and Germany about the gypsy moth.[43] Kirby at the British Museum warned him: "You should

spend any amount of money to exterminate [the gypsy moth] because it will spread over your entire country. [Yours] is a country admirably favorable to the spread of this insect and it will do a great deal of damage."[44]

Back in Medford, once the last of the large caterpillars pupated, surely a palpable sense of relief swept over the beleaguered citizens. The trees were devoid of foliage, and there was hardly anything green to be found anywhere except the leaves of strawberries and the tops of some onion plants. Mrs. S. J. Follansbee of 35 Myrtle Street said that the cocoons stuck to the sides of the trees as thickly as the egg masses had, and in some places "hung from the trees in bunches as big as a pint dipper."[45] The eaves and gutters of houses were stained black where the caterpillars had clustered, and pieces of steps, railings, and piazzas that had been torn up in the search for them lay scattered about. Picket fences were destroyed or devoid of paint, and there were scorched areas in many yards marking the caterpillars' crematories. On almost every street a number of trees had been cut down to deprive the insects of food and nesting places, leaving fresh, oozing stumps in many front yards.

Next, residents throughout the infested region saw gypsy moths fluttering in uncountable thousands, and soon some trees bore so many egg clusters that their trunks looked as if they had been wrapped in coarse yellow felt. Pearl Martin, a Medford road commissioner, employed some men to scrape egg masses from the trees and burn them in kerosene. Once the workers became practiced at spotting these clusters, they were astonished by the great numbers of spongy masses apparent everywhere. After just a couple of days it became obvious to all that the problem was too great to confront with a small group.

Organizing Entomologists

While the stunned and bewildered townsmen of Medford, Malden, and surrounding Massachusetts communities were catching their breaths, at the end of August leading entomologists were gathering in Toronto for the forty-second annual meeting of the American Association for the Advancement of Science (AAAS). Riley believed that those working in agricultural entomology should create their own specialized organization and that the AAAS meeting would be the place to split off from the society's entomological club and form the American Association of Official Economic Entomologists, later shortened to Association of Economic Entomologists.[46] The small group elected the absent Riley as president, Stephen A. Forbes as vice president, and John B. Smith as secretary. Membership was limited to those who were working in the field of agricultural entomology, with expedient exceptions made for serious college students and others deemed worthy. The new association was quite small

and so eager for applicants that it nearly included among its charter members one E. P. Thompson, a mathematician who had fallen in with the group by accident.[47]

In economic entomology it was thought more important to learn the best points to attack a single pest insect than it was to describe a hundred innocuous new species. The economic entomologist believed that arthropods were either pests and therefore of economic importance or not pests and thus economically unimportant. Most already believed, as did Fernald, that in the entire insect kingdom with its uncounted thousands of species probably no more than five were directly beneficial to man: the honeybee (*Apis*), the silkworm (*Bombyx mori*), the cochineal insect from which red dye was made (*Dactylopius coccus*), the insect from which shellac was made (*Lacifer lacca*), and the lady beetle (*Vedalia [Rodolia] cardinalis*), which consumed harmful scale insects.[48] Even spiders, mantids, and other insect-eaters were not important if the insects they ate were of no interest economically, and innocuous insects were simply ignored.

By adopting such a rigidly circumscribed field of endeavor, the economic entomologists decisively distanced themselves from other groups of entomologists. Amateurs were regarded as "enthusiasts," a derogatory term of the time, who would not be able to understand the work of economic entomology. Systematists and collectors were faulted for concerning themselves only with adult insects that were generally less harmful than the larvae, which caused most agricultural damage. Taxonomists were viewed with some aversion for their practice of fine-splitting insect genera to the point where one variety could hardly be told from another and then claiming credit for their "discoveries" of new species. Economic entomologists found this proclivity so annoying that at their first annual meeting they voted unanimously to approve a resolution by Albert Cook, based on a strongly worded letter from Fernald, that "bulletins of the experiment stations and agricultural colleges should not contain descriptions of new species."[49]

The curious coincidences in the natural world that exacerbated the impact of the gypsy moth in its new North American home were not the only chance influences to affect events in Massachusetts. Just two years before, in 1887, the U.S. Congress had passed the Hatch Act, which created the agricultural experiment station system in all states in the spring of 1888. Until that time few states had experiment stations, and there were only three state entomologists. The Hatch Act greatly increased the need for entomologists to fill positions that were opening in agricultural colleges, experiment stations, geological surveys, and the many natural history museums that were springing up, particularly in the East.[50] But the initial effects of the act proved contrary to

intentions: the lack of entomologists was so acute sometimes that, as Leland Howard said, "it became necessary for men to undertake the work who had no training in entomology at all."[51]

The restricted focus of their work notwithstanding, economic entomologists thought of themselves as thoroughly modern scientists whose views were actually broader than those of their contemporaries. Economic entomologists were among the first in America to accept Charles Darwin's theories of evolution and the contemporaneous thoughts of T. H. Huxley and Herbert Spencer. Riley said that persons in his profession were generally not wedded to theological assumptions and that he himself kept all of Darwin's works "at my elbows."[52] Economic entomologists entered the gypsy moth years influenced to greater or lesser extent by such ideas as survival of the fittest, natural selection, and the balance of nature, although it became clear that they did not completely comprehend the ramifications of these ideas.

Within a few years the life-history studies of economic entomology would go well beyond anything that had been done before and would require practitioners of the discipline to understand the insect and its relationship to nature in its entirety. This prompted Stephen Forbes to declare that economic entomology was "a special division of ecology" and that economic entomologists were in the vanguard of scientists developing a field that would succeed the older study of natural history.[53] (In modern times, when the terms "ecologist" and "environmentalist" are used almost interchangeably, the image of these entomologists literally and figuratively entering their field of work to restore the balance of nature with kegs of arsenic seems incomprehensible.)

The theory of Thomas Malthus (1766–1834) that man's expanding population would outstrip his ability to grow crops was still given great emphasis, and the feared competition between man and insects for food raised the specter of famine. The trend in agriculture was toward monoculture—growing a single crop on the largest possible field. Almost all entomologists of the time understood that insect problems were greatly exacerbated by this practice and that planting a wide variety of crops on smaller farms would largely prevent the danger. Unfortunately, decisions in agriculture were being made not on scientific considerations but on economic ones.

Malthus was barely in his grave when the mechanization of farm equipment resulted in an oversupply of food, and many of the mouths to be fed in America's burgeoning cities were those of people no longer needed to work on the farm. Wheat prices fell so low that many growers were compelled to raise other crops. In Georgia, cotton grown at a cost of seven cents per bushel sold for only five cents per bushel. Farmers in Kansas could not get ten cents a bushel for corn and burned their crops for heat during the winter rather than sell at a loss.[54]

Economic entomologists, however, remained convinced that crop losses inflicted annually by insects would continue to rise and that these losses were an unacceptable waste even in times of abundance. They began preparing for the conflict they were sure was coming. The Hatch Act, which had brought about a sweeping change in the relationship of agriculture and entomology, also gave entomologists a cohesive center of operations in which the substance of their work was largely economic.[55] They had donned the uniform of crop protector and adopted the appealing stance of science in service to agriculture.[56] The labors of earlier naturalist-entomologists such as Thomas Say, John E. LeConte, Thaddeus W. Harris, William D. Peck, and Asa Fitch had taken the avocational and recreational nature of insect study and turned it into a science. Now Riley and his small camp would take the science of entomology and turn it into a profession.

The Consequences of Medford

Fernald returned from Europe in early September 1889 and went immediately to Medford, where he spent an entire day inspecting the infested territory. He could not spare enough time to visit the regions outside of Medford, but he saw convincing proof that the outbreak could not be confined to just one town.[57] The situation left him deeply concerned: "There was a region of perhaps a square mile in which the trees, trunks and branches, were literally covered with clusters of eggs, so that they were yellow. After what I had been told by the entomologists in Europe, I felt quite alarmed about the matter. I thought we had an invasion that demanded careful attention."[58]

Fernald conferred with Sessions, and the two rushed to make another inspection of Medford. A sense of foreboding came over both men when they observed gypsy moth egg masses beyond counting everywhere they looked. They urged Chairman Wadleigh of the Medford selectmen to petition the state legislature to order extermination of the insect by the Board of Agriculture. Wadleigh asked Fernald how extermination should be carried out, and Fernald replied that the foliage should be sprayed with Paris green, a common arsenical insecticide. The selectmen approved a petition at their meeting of October 25, but the legislature was not scheduled to convene again until early January.

The crucial point of the petition was Fernald's recommendation that the insect be *exterminated* rather than suppressed or controlled. Between his first inspection of Medford in September and the middle of November, he researched the European gypsy moth in his library and by correspondence with European colleagues. He knew the problem was not the moths but the larvae, or "worms" as some called them, which fed on any of several hundred

different kinds of foliage. Their preference for oak presented Fernald with a grave scenario, since the forests of Massachusetts had become dominated by various species of oak. The insects were also said to devour orchard fruits and field crops, another unsettling characteristic, because agriculture in eastern Massachusetts was moving toward orchards of increasing size and decreasing variety, and the principal agricultural activity in the Boston region was market gardening, in which acreage was farmed intensively.

By this time the name of Leopold Trouvelot as an entrepreneur and re-searcher in the natural sciences had slipped into obscurity, and his part in the importation and escape of the gypsy moth had been all but forgotten. Fernald knew the man who had liberated the gypsy moth only as "the entomologist" and had no other knowledge of the moth's American history. He wrote letters to Samuel Scudder, Samuel Henshaw, and Herman A. Hagen for assistance and asked if the insects had increased in number since their escape.[59] Henshaw responded: "I have your favor of the 12th and it happened that I saw Dr. Hagen the same day that I received it and he wished me to include his answer to your letter with mine. The entomologist referred to is Mr. L. Trouvelot and the locality was West Medford. That is all I can give you as positive."[60]

Fernald was surprised that an insect of such conspicuous habits had been on the loose for twenty years and apparently remained invisible the entire time. He told Henshaw that he "could not find a word on it from anyone."[61] He had gathered sufficient information by November, however, to compose an illustrated bulletin titled "A Dangerous Insect Pest in Medford" in which he advocated the use of Paris green to kill the insect. He suggested spraying the poison at the rate of one pound to 150 gallons of water soon after eggs hatched in the spring and predicted that within two or three years the moth would be completely destroyed. Riley, crediting Fernald with the choice of extermination and the use of Paris green, made a premature prediction of success: "If Professor Fernald's recommendations are carried out at all strictly we have little fear of the spread of this pest, and agree with him that it can be entirely killed out with the expenditure of a little time and money."[62]

Riley's optimism was echoed by others in the state, including the editors of *Garden and Forest* magazine. They wrote that it would not be a difficult matter to exterminate the gypsy moth if Fernald's directions were followed and that a successful conclusion would benefit the state by resulting in general legislation to exterminate all pest insects in the Commonwealth.[63]

A letter of opposition, unsigned but apparently written by someone knowl-edgeable in entomology, appeared in the November edition of the same mag-azine. The writer had learned of plans for a state appropriation through a newspaper article in the *Boston Evening Transcript,* and his comments set the tone for many events yet to come: "The outcome of these efforts will be very

interesting. It is, at least, very improbable that every specimen in such a considerable area (about one and a half square miles, according to the article quoted) can be destroyed. The insect has probably come to stay, and, ultimately, the best way to keep it in check, outside of the artificial remedies, may be the importation of the parasites and natural enemies to which it is liable in Europe."[64]

The state Board of Agriculture paid for 45,000 copies of Fernald's bulletin and distributed them throughout Medford and surroundings. On December 6, 1889, the bulletin was published in the *Medford Mercury*. Fernald said, in part: "In this country [the gypsy moth] occurs only in Medford, Mass., and so far as I could learn at the time of my first visit to that place, it occupied an area in the form of an ellipse, about a mile and a half long by half a mile wide. This represents the territory where the outbreak occurred and where the insects were very abundant; but without a doubt they are distributed in smaller quantities outside this ellipse, but how far it is now impossible to tell."[65] Fernald did not consider himself linked to Medford's problems and regarded his part in events as incidental. As far as he was concerned, publishing the danger bulletin ended any association he may have had with whatever plans were being considered for dealing with the gypsy moth: "I simply performed a duty laid upon me when I accepted the position of entomologist at the Station here. I finished all the law requires of me when the Bulletin was distributed in that I gave the best methods possible for individuals to clear their trees and shrubs from the pest. By now the citizens of Medford petition the legislature for aid in destroying the insect, or to introduce parasites from Europe; it is no affair of mine."[66]

Still, Fernald clearly had a sense of foreboding about his role in the events that were now compounding, and on November 26 he wrote to Samuel Henshaw to inform him of the Medford selectmen's appeal to the state legislature: "If they do this, and the legislature grants their requests, it is possible that I may be consulted in the matter; and if it seems desirable to attempt to destroy these larvae with poisonous insecticides, I surely think some competent person should be in charge of the work which will probably occur in the months of April and May. . . . [I]f your other duties will permit of your undertaking the job, I will recommend you."[67] Henshaw responded on November 28 that he would undertake the work, and Fernald reminded him on November 30 that there was not yet any work to undertake.

He also revealed to Henshaw that the radical approach to the problem he had proposed contemplated not only the eradication of the entire species by spraying with poison but the suspension of some civil rights, and he was already making plans to thwart the opposition that he was certain would come:

> I did not advise going to the legislature for an appropriation in my
> Bulletin because that might have drawn opposition too soon, but I
> did advise the town officers of Medford to do it, as they are the
> interested parties, and I further urged them to get an act passed au-
> thorizing whoever does the work to go onto any man's land and
> shower the trees, for without a doubt there are cranks in Medford
> as elsewhere who might obstruct the work and forbid one from go-
> ing on to their land unless the state legislature passed an act author-
> izing it.[68]

Fernald had become grouchy about his position and complained to Henshaw
that for his work at the experiment station he was paid the "paltry sum of
$500 a year" and might well to give it all up "at any time." He did not give
"two shucks" about the gypsy moth affair but asked Henshaw to collaborate
with him in stopping "the opposition of the Boston and Cambridge
entomologists."[69]

On December 10, 1889, Dr. Martin appeared before the Medford selectmen on behalf of the road commissioners to ask that they request state aid in
destroying the gypsy moth. The selectmen instructed their clerk to ask William
R. Sessions what measures to take to bring the matter before the next meeting
of the Massachusetts General Court, as the state legislature was called. Shortly
thereafter, Dr. Martin discharged the workers who had been destroying egg
masses because his small budget had been exhausted.

Fernald had returned to Amherst with the intention of continuing the preparation of a monograph on the North American Pyralidae, a work he had
begun the year before, yet his role in the gypsy moth story continued to be a
prominent one. The Medford selectmen repeatedly asked for his counsel on
how to deal with the insects, and he always tried to accommodate them. On
December 17 he wrote from the Hatch Experiment Station and formally advised the selectmen to request financial assistance from the state for this
undertaking.

In private, Fernald could not have been as confident about his advice to
exterminate the insect as he maintained in public. Neither he nor any other
entomologist of his time could say with certainty that spraying alone would
kill 100 percent of a given species, and nobody knew whether the moth's
probable North American predators would prove effective. The only alternative plan on which he could fall back was one he had not recommended—to
transplant the moth's natural enemies from Europe—though he had given
some thought to the possibility and had mentioned eleven known parasites in
his special illustrated bulletin published just a month earlier.

As the year drew to a close, Fernald wrote to Dr. Hagen—a man Herbert

Osborn called "the most learned entomologist in America"[70]—asking for information about the gypsy moth and about the possibility of importing predatory insects from Europe. Fernald posted the letter and went off to enjoy Christmas festivities with his family at their home on Hallock Street in Amherst. It was the holiday season, and the Fernald residence was a hub for social functions as well as a center for off-campus educational activities in entomology, since all the Fernalds were entomologists. The merriment this year would not be much different from that of years past, but life for the Fernalds and most of the people in eastern Massachusetts would no longer be the same. Fernald would never again set foot on a ship for Europe, although he did not know that at the time, and his work on the *Pyralidae* would not be started for another thirteen years.

No Holiday Affair

WITH THE NEW YEAR celebration behind him, Fernald returned to his duties at Amherst to await word from Hagen. In his reply to Fernald on January 15, 1890, written in his awkward English, Hagen gave some bad advice at a bad time: "I myself have seen O. dispar many times in large numbers on property belonging to my father. I have helped kill them, for the next year, very few were left or found. Mr. C. F. Freyer, one of the most prominent lepidopterist in 1879 tells a similar story. A species as nearly related as O. moracha, is of course very dangerous, but a species attacking so many things is not dangerous. To import for O. dispar enemies from Europe, would make Massachusetts a laughing stock in the opinion of all scientific men in Europe."[1]

Upset with Fernald's danger bulletin, Hagen thought it was hastily prepared and sensational, and he did not like Fernald's plan to have the state "sprinkle [the gypsy moth] with Paris Green."[2] Fernald had fired off a letter to Hagen with the surprising demand to know where this statement had appeared in anything he had published.[3] A puzzled Hagen replied that it was on page five of the bulletin.[4]

Hagen's advice was based on his experience with the gypsy moth while he was a young man in Europe, and he did not grasp the probable course of events in America. His reputation gave much weight to his assurances that the gypsy moth might prove to be less terrifying than some had feared. Perhaps Fernald relaxed somewhat with the thought that the problem might not become too serious after all, and Hagen's words may have allowed him to feel more comfortable about the consequences of a failed attempt at chemical eradication. In any case, if importing natural predators would bring unfavorable review to the state and the new branch of economic entomology, then importation was even further out of the question.

The Calosoma Beetle

News of the gypsy moth outbreak was the subject of much discussion in the Department of Agriculture in Washington. Coleopterist Eugene A. Schwarz, a man Leland Howard considered the best entomologist in the office, and Bernard E. Fernow, chief of the forestry division, pointed out that an important adversary of the gypsy moth in Europe was the predacious beetle *Calosoma sycophanta*. European beetles of this genus had evolved a small leg spur that allowed them to climb trees with rough bark, and it was their habit to scale oaks in search of gypsy moth larvae. American Calosoma species also attacked gypsy moth larvae but did not have a similar spur and were thus unable to climb. Nothing came of these discussions because Charles Riley, chief of the bureau, was in poor health and absent from his desk for long periods, leaving the federal office of entomology without effective leadership.[5]

Fernald already knew about the beetle; it had been the insect foremost in his mind whenever he wrote to his European counterparts for information. Although the life history of the large and colorful Calosoma was not fully known during the 1890s, it was believed to live four years and prey almost entirely on the gypsy moth. It spent most of its life hibernating underground, emerging to become active during the larval stages of its prey and afterward returning to the ground. A Calosoma larva consumed about 41 gypsy moth caterpillars each year, a young adult beetle approximately 240 and a mature adult 270.

Through one of those unexplained adaptations of nature, Calosoma also attacked the pupae, though with a preference for cocoons containing females, which they devoured at a rate three times greater than those of males.[6] Since for every female moth destroyed, the next year's population dropped by about five hundred, just two beetles in a season's work might reduce the number of larvae by more than 125,000 the following year. That a relatively small number of beetles could have so dramatic an impact on the dynamics of population balance showed the appeal of natural controls.

Given the recent success with the lady beetle in California, the thoughts of many turned toward parasites. In January 1890, Riley and Howard published an article in *Insect Life* in which they listed twenty-four hymenopterous gypsy moth parasites of European origin. Soon after the article appeared in print, Riley received a letter from the Reverend Henry A. Loomis, then living in Yokohama. Loomis had read about the Massachusetts gypsy moth swarms and wanted to inform the entomologists of a parasite that kept the insect under control on the Japanese islands. He packed some of these insects in a small box and sent them to Washington. Although the parasites were dead when they arrived, Howard was able to identify them as *Apanteles fulvipus*, a

species of small wasp. Loomis made several more attempts to send living parasites to America, but all were unsuccessful.

The Act of 1890

The Medford petition for state financial aid was ready on January 15, 1890 (though the Massachusetts General Court had not yet convened), and was followed by applications from other moth-infested communities around Medford—Arlington, Everett, Winchester, Stoneham, Wakefield—and the cities of Malden and Somerville. Support for the petition also came from agricultural interests, including the Massachusetts Agricultural College, the Essex County Agricultural Society, and the Massachusetts Horticultural Society, groups that had been unnerved by reports that the new insect enemy devoured row crops. That fear persuaded Governor John Quincy Adams Brackett to bring the matter to the attention of the state legislature in his annual message of January 1890: "A new enemy is at present threatening the agriculture, not only of our state but of the whole country. I refer to the Gypsy Moth (Ocneria dispar), a European insect which has recently appeared in the state. They are said to attack almost every variety of tree as well as the farm and garden crops. . . . If their eradication is to be attempted, immediate measures are of the utmost importance."[7]

Members of the legislature's joint standing committee on agriculture visited the infested region early in 1890 and were shocked by what they saw in Medford. The walls of buildings, trunks of trees, posts and rails of fences, and even stones lying upon the ground were almost entirely covered with egg masses. (The famously fecund female moth's egg-stuffed abdomen is so big in proportion to the rest of her body that a later entomologist referred to her as little more than a sack full of eggs. One observer reported a case where a single female laid 1,400 eggs over a period of ten days.)[8] In addition to the uncounted numbers of egg masses the visiting committee observed, there were at least twice as many they could not see, for the female gypsy moth has a propensity for crawling into deep crevasses, squeezing beneath overhanging rocks, hiding under branches, disappearing beneath porch steps, or retreating into the openings between stacked firewood to lay her eggs; in short, she often deposits them where discovery would be unlikely.

On Monday afternoon, February 17, 1890, the committee on agriculture began hearings in the Green Room of the State House in Boston with the intent to secure what one local newspaper called "the extermination of the deadly gypsy moth."[9] Among those testifying were Nathaniel Shaler of Cambridge and Warren W. Rawson (the younger) of Arlington. Representative J. Henry Norcross of Medford subsequently introduced legislation for an

appropriation of $25,000 to exterminate the moth, supported by the amazing testimony given before the committee about conditions in the region. Board of Agriculture member J. W. Stockwell, who was in the hearing room when Medford citizens described events in their town, recalled that the testimony about conditions would be impossible for the average person to conceive: "If I could remember and bring it to you as it was given before that committee you would hardly believe it possible."[10] Leland Howard later reminisced that reading the testimony of the townspeople had reminded him of "the plagues of Egypt as described in the Bible."[11]

The legislative vote of approval was taken on March 14, 1890, under great pressure to expedite the process. The *Boston Evening Transcript* noted that the bill was rammed through "at express speed."[12] The full title of the legislation was "An Act to Provide against Depredations by the Insect Known as the Ocneria Dispar or Gypsy Moth." If one were constrained to fathom the thrust of the act from its language, rather than its history, one would conclude that the Massachusetts legislators did not understand the nature of the problem or the purpose of the act, for most sections were worded as if the menace at hand were a civil insurrection. One contemporary writer commented that the legislation "read like war documents."[13]

The act established and funded a commission to fight the moth, and one paragraph gave commission agents almost martial authority, allowing them to enter upon the premises of any person at any time, without a warrant, for purposes of insect extermination. Another paragraph removed the rights of citizens to refuse the commission and fined anyone who did. Property owners could sue for damages, but any award would be offset by the amount of any "benefit." The experts who defined benefits would have been the same ones who authorized the act, making it unlikely that any citizen would prevail in litigation or that any award would be very large. Another section provided heavy fines for citizens who knowingly transported the gypsy moth in any stage of its life cycle from an infested area into an uninfested one—punishment less severe but similar in concept to the penalty reserved for providing aid to an enemy in time of war.

A Campaign of Many Agendas

The small fraternity of economic entomologists did not need long to realize that the coincidental organization of their association, the appearance of the gypsy moth, and the formation of a state extermination commission presented them with a breathtaking opportunity for self-promotion. The best possible coincidence was that the infestation had occurred in Massachusetts, a small state of waning national influence and long past its prime as an agricultural

power. Still, the Commonwealth maintained a reputation as progressive in science and education and could now claim enough vision to recognize the need to deal with an insect problem and make an appropriation for that purpose. Fernald later wrote to Herbert Osborn that legislation against the gypsy moth would never have happened in any other state.[14]

Although the rush by economic entomologists to monopolize the situation was due to a fortuitous coincidence, most of this group knew from the first that there would be more to the undertaking than just killing gypsy moths. The passage of time revealed their three-part agenda: first, eradicating the moth; second, trying out ideas toward this end at the expense of the state; third, the advancement of economic entomology. Elated entomologists from the start referred to the proposed gypsy moth project as "the experiment" and saw it as a way to bring entomological work into both federal and state governments.

Despite the recommendation of Fernald, Shaler, and Sessions that the work be superintended by the Board of Agriculture, the legislature specified a commission that would report directly to the governor. Less than a week after the legislation was passed, Governor Brackett appointed a salaried commission of three men: Warren W. Rawson of Arlington, Pearl Martin of Medford, and J. Howard Bradley of Malden. Only Dr. Martin had even the slightest knowledge of fighting the insect. Rawson's appointment might have come about because Brackett was from Arlington and knew him personally. Rawson (1847–1908), known as "the younger" to avoid confusing him with his father, was a scion of one of New England's famous market-gardening families. He owned a successful seed store, was active in agricultural affairs, and held membership on the state's Board of Agriculture.[15] He was known for his contributions to greenhouse design and improvements in open-field irrigation systems. Rawson was the first to use heated greenhouses for commercial fruit and vegetable growing and among the first to use electric lights in his operations. His book, *Success in Market Gardening and Vegetable Grower's Manual*, self-published in 1887, reached seven editions and was republished well into the twentieth century.

Fernald was astonished by the appointments; he had simply taken it for granted that someone knowledgeable would be in charge, as he wrote to Henshaw: "I had supposed without any doubt that either our Director or Mr. Sessions would have been appointed on the commission, and in that case, it was my intention to invite you to take the entire charge and responsibility of the work and to pay you a liberal salary . . . but:—'the best laid plans of mice and men,' etc."[16]

News that the state commission would be composed of laymen dismayed the economic entomologists. Joseph Albert Lintner, state entomologist of New

Warren W. Rawson, the younger, in an undated photograph.
From *Biographical Review*.

York, felt that events in Massachusetts presented an opportunity that must not be lost. He wrote to Fernald that the idea of a lay commission operating without an entomological adviser was preposterous, and he wondered why Fernald had not been appointed chairman: "I supposed that, of course, you would have been chairman of the commission, and its controlling head, as you should have been. . . . I feel a deep interest in the matter, for the appropriation offered an excellent opportunity to test and show the value of economic entomology. If the experiment fails, it will stand in the way of obtaining state aid in other cases where it may be needed. It promises now to be a failure."[17]

On March 18 the first meeting of the new gypsy moth commission took place in Medford, a town that initially served as its base of operations.[18] Daily meetings were held until August 1, after which the commissioners met at least once a week for many months. As Rawson later said, "It required a great deal more work than we expected."[19] The commissioners decided to inspect the region and mark infested trees with pieces of red flannel. The original extent of the area thought to be harboring insects was a rather modest three-quarters of a square mile, a zone about half a mile wide by a mile and a half long, but the more the commissioners looked for signs of the moth's presence, the more they found.

They began their campaign on March 23 with a hastily assembled force of twenty men who claimed they could recognize gypsy moth egg clusters on sight. In three days they marked every infested tree they found in Medford,

Malden, and Somerville but burned egg clusters for only one day before being stopped by two days of heavy rain. The number of men was quickly increased to sixty, all of whom were issued kerosene torches. Rawson believed that if the weather held, his men could take care of the entire infested area in a week. But hatching time was approaching, and the commissioners knew nothing about poisons and spraying apparatus. Rawson often turned to Charles Fernald and Nathaniel Shaler for advice. Shaler favored a strategy of containment, whereas Fernald recommended that in addition to spraying larvae, egg masses should be scraped or cut from the trees and burned in kerosene.

The new commissioners were slow to realize the magnitude of the task that lay before them, but they were optimistic that even multiple infestations would not be hard to clear out. Rawson thought the moths would be under control the first year and mopped up the next year: "We have 60 men using torches and we can go over a large territory in a day when there are but few nests in each tree. And when there are large quantities of them [eggs] we shall burn the trees and all the territory near them. By doing so before they hatch out we will have the greater part of them burned up. Then when they hatch out we shall be ready for them."[20] The untrained men under Rawson's charge focused on little more than incinerating egg masses and applied themselves so assiduously that they burned one hundred barrels of kerosene in just a few weeks. The hot flames of the kerosene torches frightfully damaged many heavily infested trees. When not used on standing trees, the torches were turned on the ground to set fires that consumed the underbrush. Thickets were raked clean and burned, and acres of healthy trees were felled and set ablaze simply because they were covered with too many egg masses to remove. The worst news of the summer was that the insect had been found in the woodlands of the nearby Middlesex Fells, gravitating toward its natural forest habitat.[21]

Lintner wrote to Fernald again on April 7, urging him to find a way to take control of the events unfolding in Massachusetts. Rawson's commission was considering hiring as advisers entomologists in whom Lintner had no confidence, and he hoped that Fernald could still be appointed: "I wrote to [Chairman Rawson] . . . and further stated that it was quite discernible that persons acquainted with insects should be employed in the attempted extermination. I also expressed my regret that the commissioners had not seen fit to engage you to take charge of the work, as you were especially fitted to supervise it."[22] Lintner told Rawson that the work as than arranged could only result in failure, and later, complaining that Rawson had not replied, Lintner again reminded Fernald, "A failure in this experiment would militate against the cause of economic entomology."[23]

Fernald either did not realize that he was becoming hopelessly entangled with the pending gypsy moth campaign, or he lacked the will to state plainly

that he wanted no long-term entanglement with it. In his exchange of letters with Lintner he did not mention his reluctance to serve in any capacity. As entomologist of the Hatch Station, he felt unable to refuse the requests of the commissioners for his advice, and he likely thought that by supporting a solid candidate for advising entomologist, he could relieve himself of both problems with a single stroke. Fernald recommended Samuel Henshaw as the best choice, and in April the commissioners did interview Henshaw for the advisory position. Afterward, a dazed Henshaw wrote to Fernald:

> I went to Medford with [Rawson] and met the other members of the [commission]. . . . Mr. Rawson favored having [an adviser] and Mr. Martin did not see very much need of having one as he knew the gypsy moth as well as any entomologist, though he concluded that perhaps it would be "just as well to have one even if they did not follow his advice." It would have amused you quite a little to hear him say that the larva of the gypsy moth were not like that of the *caterpillar* and to ask what stage came after the caterpillar and if all insects came from eggs, etc.[24]

The meeting went well enough for Henshaw to suppose that he was hired, although the parsimonious commissioners did not broach the matter of payment for his services and could not agree as to whether or not they could afford an adviser. They invited Henshaw to discuss matters with them again at their next meeting, but Henshaw declined to attend, writing Fernald that he thought the three commissioners would be too much for him, and in any case he had no idea what his services were worth.[25]

Fernald doubtless saw the situation with the commission for what it was and—though with some apprehension at the thought of becoming further enmeshed with the gypsy moth commissioners—urged Rawson to visit Amherst and study the spraying apparatus kept there. The meeting was not reassuring. Fernald wrote to Henshaw that Rawson had stayed "about three minutes," and then left "probably [thinking] he has got all the information I could give him!"[26]

Nathaniel Shaler recommended a thorough inspection to determine the extent of the moth's expansion and advocated paying schoolboys a bounty for bringing in egg masses and caterpillars. The problem with this suggestion was that schoolboys would have to be trained to recognize egg masses and larvae. The commissioners feared that citizens, either in their zeal or out of ignorance, might spread the moths by improperly handling the eggs. Dependable help from the general public was doubtful, leading to the possibility that sufficient manpower would not be available when it was needed most.

The commissioners decided to proceed along the lines they had already laid out, inspecting areas where the moth was reported and marking infested trees with red cloth tags. As soon as the appropriation was released, employees hired by the commission were sent out to begin removing egg masses. It was a learning experience for all. The men developed effective techniques as they went and created specialized tools from experience and from the scant information Fernald could give them about the methods used in Europe.

The commissioners adapted Joseph Burrelle's recommendation from the 1840s on how to deal with the coddling moth in apple orchards: that is, banding tree trunks with cloth under which the larvae would be trapped, then handpicking the larvae and destroying them in an oven.[27] Later, workers hit upon the technique of scraping the trunk bark smooth in order to encourage the larvae into hay rope bands, and later still they discovered that raking and burning the ground clear of weeds and debris also improved control.

Workmen were issued large metal pails that each held about a peck, which they filled two or three times a day with egg clusters scraped from trees and walls. In places that were difficult to reach, such as crevices in walls and the undersides of fence railings, egg masses were burned with a large kerosene torch. A team of men entered Wellington Willows, an area not far from Trouvelot's old house, and found the willows covered with egg masses from the ground up; one resident described them as being "as thick as spawn in a fish."[28] The task of removing all the masses by hand was too laborious and expensive to attempt in the time available with the number of men employed, so the commissioners hit upon the idea of destroying the egg masses collectively. The field workers were supplied with axes, and all the beautiful old trees were cut down and burned.

These actions were taken in part out of desperation and in part because the commission was split on the subject of spraying; those opposed thought it was too costly and not effective. The editors of the *New England Homestead* faulted the commission for failing to secure competent advice and for wasting their energies scraping trees. They said that spraying with poison was the only "proper remedy, and must be employed notwithstanding the work already done," and that "the commission deserves public censure for adopting its own 'practical' plans to the exclusion of the known and simpler remedies approved by science and experience."[29] Fernald was delighted by this stance, which he called a "sharp rap on the knuckles," and he tweaked the commissioners by informing them that henceforth they must submit specimens of larvae for identification "to their own entomologist, Mr. Henshaw."[30]

The State of the Art

The commissioners subsequently bought fifteen new spraying machines for $75 apiece.[31] But the equipment with which Massachusetts went to war against the gypsy moth was primitive and unreliable, for most of the pumps for spraying trees had not existed long enough to prove themselves under conditions of actual use. The first of these "garden engines" to be designed for small trees was the "Florida" pump, manufactured in 1880 by the C. J. Rumsey Company of Seneca Falls, New York, and it was not until 1889 that the Nixon Nozzle and Machine Company introduced its classic "Little Giant" and "Little Climax" pumps.[32] The only suitable spraying nozzle available at this point was the eddy chamber or "cyclone" nozzle, a misting device invented by William S. Barnard. Often called the "Riley" nozzle because Barnard was working under Charles Riley when he designed it, this spray head first appeared in 1880. It had been more or less perfected by 1885 and was then considered the best nozzle for tree work, even though it clogged frequently. About 1890 the French-made Vermorel nozzle was introduced. It was considered superior because blockages could be quickly cleared by means of an integrated pushpin.

Even the term "spraying" was so new that it was not in common use. The term "syringing" was applied to greenhouse work; "sprinkling" described applying liquid to low-growing row crops; and "showering" was used in reference to larger plants and trees. Although most of the pumps were not very powerful, a few of the larger ones could attain pressures of 160 pounds per square inch (psi). Once these were introduced for practical use, there was an immediate cry for pumps that operated at even higher pressures. The pump manufacturers were mystified by this turn of events. One said that of course his company could produce a machine capable of attaining 200 psi, but he could not understand why anyone would want to spray at that pressure, since all it would do was burst the hose.

The insecticides were no more reliable than the equipment that dispensed them, and at this time there were few to choose from. Paris green, made from arsenic mixed with the smokestack residues of copper smelters, often burned the leaves of plants. Its nearest and cheaper rival, London purple, burned the foliage even worse, and the efficacy of both these insoluble arsenical poisons varied widely and unpredictably. Contact insecticides consisted mainly of whale oil and soap emulsions, sometimes mixed with kerosene. Pyrethrum, an old standby made from chrysanthemum flowers, was too expensive to use except in greenhouses. Economic entomologists had so few options that Leland Howard of the federal bureau of entomology often bantered with Beverly

T. Galloway and others in the bureau of phytopathology about which of them had fewer remedies to suggest to their correspondents.[33]

Spraying began on May 12 under the supervision of C. A. Longley. Following Fernald's recommendation, the men used Paris green, some wearing backpack sprayers and the rest operating a new lightweight, horse-drawn apparatus intended for spraying orchards. The majority of the spraying was done in the Glenwood and Wellington sections of Medford, and Edgeworth in Malden, where—to paraphrase the commissioners—on Monday they would spray, Tuesday it would rain and wash the arsenic off the leaves, so Wednesday they would spray again, and Thursday it would rain, and so on. The constant spraying annoyed residents of the towns and became the biggest budget drain on the commission. The spraying was ineffective: one apple tree was sprayed fifteen times with Paris green in an effort to rid it of caterpillars.[34] But the commissioners later reported that the tree was not permanently injured by either the insects or the arsenic.

Owing to the limited period during which the insects were in larval form, spraying was completed by July 23.[35] Meanwhile citizens fought the surging masses of insect life as they had for the previous several years, with fire, water, and coal oil. Caterpillars were so crowded in some places that no part of the pavement could be seen between them, and they fell from the trees in such numbers that residents carried umbrellas on sunny days. On the roofs of many houses the presence of uncounted thousands of caterpillars resulted in so much excrement that it overflowed the rain gutters and plugged up the downspouts. In the densely infested Glenwood brickyard the workmen needed shovels to fill pails with larvae and the remains of pupae.

One Medford resident, Winslow W. Fifield, told of an old pump on his premises from which hung a bucket he used to water his horse. After moths fell in the water and drowned, Fifield said he could not rinse the bucket well enough so that his horse would drink from it. During the caterpillar season, the supply of foliage was sometimes so swiftly reduced that the caterpillars swarmed toward new food sources while they were still the size of ants. Fifield spent ninety minutes in the morning clearing his property, only to have to repeat the process at noon and again in the evening. He estimated that in four and a half hours of work each day he had destroyed millions of insects, "more moths than any man living," without causing an appreciable reduction in their numbers.[36]

Fifield's statement might have been disputed by J. O. Goodwin, who wrote of the problems faced by average citizens trying to protect a few trees on their small lots: "During the past week or ten days I have personally attended to the matter and have killed millions of Gypsy Worms which have congregated below the paper [bands] on my trees. . . . The number of worms cultivated on

three or four worthless trees on the premises next to my own is astonishing; numbers fail to convey an adequate idea. . . . [F]ifteen minutes after killing every worm to be seen on the trunk of the tree below the tarred paper, hundreds can be seen making their way up."[37]

Some men of the gypsy moth force carried only a hand whisk and a large metal pail. The larvae were so multitudinous that it was possible to sweep them into a pail up to the brim before any could crawl out. Kerosene was then poured into the pail and the contents set ablaze—whereupon the workman busied himself with other tasks because of the unbearable smoke and stink of cremation. Some of the infested towns were barren of green foliage by the end of the caterpillar season. J. W. Harlow had no raspberries or blackberries because the larvae had eaten most of the berry bushes.[38] Other neighbors had no fruit, as their apple and cherry tree foliage was consumed, and gardens were once again reduced to nothing but ravaged stems. It was a bad year to be a vegetarian in Medford.

On May 9, 1890, the commissioners reported to Governor Brackett that the infested area was "some sixteen times as large as at first represented," or about fifty square miles, and would require an appropriation at least twice as large as the original.[39] Brackett wrote to the General Court in support of the request on May 15, noting that the additional funds, if made available quickly, would save the state a great deal of money later on.[40] A supplemental appropriation of $25,000 was made by the state legislature on June 3, allowing the employment of enough extra workers to bring the field force to over one hundred men.[41] The inexperienced hires were employed for only thirteen days between June 16 and June 28, 1890, and thereafter most of the remaining men worked only until August 1. Workers entered the property behind Trouvelot's house, cut down every tree on it, and set one hundred acres of nearby brush afire. Later in the season the men returned to burn the brush a second time. Similar work took place in Arlington, Chelsea, and Everett.

Not realizing the threat of dispersion by wind, the commissioners feared only distribution of the insect by vehicle. Knowing that disturbed larvae would spin down from the treetops, they thought the caterpillars would crawl up the wheels of wagons from below and hide under the floor planks, but they soon discovered that most fell into the cargo from above when the passing wagons severed their threads. As patterns of infestation quickly appeared along heavily traveled routes of commerce, the commissioners took steps to prevent it. One hundred men were hired and designated as special police to guard the roads leading from Medford and Malden. For twelve hours each day these men, divided into squads of five, halted and inspected all outgoing wagons and destroyed any gypsy moth larvae they found.[42] The tool used for sweeping larvae off the tops of wagons and carriages was an ordinary house-

hold feather duster. The sight of officers crawling over the tops of vehicles and attacking little gypsy moth caterpillars with feather dusters was more than the average Massachusetts teamster could silently stand, but at a public meeting in December, Rawson gracefully defended the practice:

> We have had considerable fun made of us for keeping men upon the road with feather dusters to brush off the tops of wagons and carriages. That was an idea of mine. The commissioners found that certain teams were constantly going through this infested territory and stopping at a certain place, and there [we] found the gypsy moth. . . . All through the summer we made the owner of every brick team and every manure team provide a canvas cover for his wagon, so that it could be brushed off after passing through the infested district. In that way we have stopped the spread of the moths, and it was the only way we could do it.[43]

W. B. Harmon, the suffering soul who had gained himself a monumental headache when he bought Trouvelot's old shed and had it moved to his property at 55 Spring Street, endured the worst of the 1890 infestation. The moths had spread into the wooded areas north of his residence, and he could only watch as hundreds of thousands of caterpillars swarmed from this redoubt into his orchard and devoured every leaf of every tree in it, ruined all his fruit, and then destroyed his garden. Larvae crawled up the side of his house and clustered so thickly that no one dared open the windows or doors: "We could not step out of doors either on the grass or the walk without crushing the caterpillars under foot. Over our front door the house was black with them. . . . It is no exaggeration to say that there were pecks of the caterpillars under the door steps and on the fence. We had both the steps and the fence split up and burned to deprive the pest of its harboring places."[44] Several residents who lived through the infestation later recalled seeing Harmon's residence and that of his neighbor, a Mr. Plunkett, black with caterpillars and Postmaster Spinney's house on nearby Cross Street so thickly covered that "one could not have told what color it was painted."[45]

Medford and environs must have been quite a sight as the employees of the commission went about their business of "sprinkling" and burning, while homeowners did what they could. Many residents kept large metal cans, pails, or coal scuttles in their yards to receive the thousands of caterpillars they swept off their houses, brushed from trees, or picked each evening from porches, railings, and board walks. Scores of citizens brought pots of boiling water from their houses to scald the hairy crawlers on their fences, and soon the paint was blistered off most of the pickets in Medford. Others either

doused the insects with kerosene and set them ablaze or dug pits, raked the larvae in, and buried them alive.

In the dark of night the caterpillars could be heard eating leaves, and the sound of their excrement striking the ground sounded to some like the splatter of heavy rain. In a statement prepared later for the Massachusetts gypsy moth committee that replaced the original commission, Mrs. Thomas F. Mayo, who lived at 25 Myrtle Street next door to the old Trouvelot house, said: "In the night-time the noise of the worms eating the trees sounded like two sticks grating against each other. In the months of July and August I have gone out in the morning and raked up from under the elms a pile of leaves three or four feet high. These leaves had been cut off by the caterpillars, and usually there was a worm on the underside of every leaf. I would pour kerosene over the mass and set it on fire, and the squirming of the caterpillars would cause it to rise up as if it had a life of its own."[46]

The eerie flickering of gypsy moth funeral pyres in almost every yard illuminated sections of the streets at night, and an unpleasant, smoky stench floated constantly over the towns. Some residents talked of selling their homes and moving away, but no one who had been reading the papers would buy a house in Medford. By the end of July, after the spraying stopped, the force of workers had dwindled to about forty men still occupied with scraping egg masses from trees in the infested region. A few others filled cavities in trees that were observed to have harbored egg masses, and the remainder made a final, cursory inspection of the places known to have been infested.

In Washington, Charles Riley learned that the infested area was much larger than first thought and that no one knew for certain whether the moths had yet been contained. Riley was a practical man. Despite his inclination to poison these unwanted insects by the millions if he could, he understood that everything had changed and resigned himself to the idea that the great eradication campaign was over. As he wrote in *Insect Life* that September, "The territory occupied by the pest is much greater than was at first supposed, and extermination appears almost impossible."[47]

In Amherst, Fernald and his assistants were busy moving into a new experiment station on the campus of the Massachusetts Agricultural College. The building included a photographic studio, an attached shed, a glass house, and a large greenhouse in the Victorian style.[48] Fernald loved the facilities of the new building and thought there were none finer anywhere: "[My lab is] the most complete and fully equipped of any I have ever seen. [It] contains every good idea that I have ever seen in other laboratories and nothing has been spoiled by the fancy of the architect. In equipment we have everything needed or useful."[49]

On December 6, 1890, the last gypsy moth employee was discharged, and

the thrifty commission ended its work for the year with nearly half its $50,000 appropriation unspent. The commissioners now believed that the moth occupied territory twelve miles long and four miles wide. The fringe areas were scouted, and in only one place were moths found outside those limits. During the year, two tons of Paris green had been sprayed on approximately 70,000 trees. The first commission had done what it could, but the boundaries of the infested area were too great and the insects too numerous to be successfully countered by a small, inexperienced commission and a relative handful of unskilled workers.

A Secret Second Effort

As the season's work progressed, Shaler had become disillusioned with the Rawson commission and exasperated by its conduct. He thought the group did not give their duties serious attention, and the commissioners individually and collectively appeared not to comprehend the gravity of the task before them. Shaler no longer trusted their judgments when they believed the moth occupied just three towns, he said he knew it had spread into Somerville, Cambridge, Lexington, and at least nine other towns. Rawson, Martin, and Bradley's lack of vision had been incomprehensible to him, as had been their failure to notice the presence of the insects where the caterpillars were so obvious that, as he later said, "You could find [them] on almost any wagon."[50]

Shaler, unnerved by the appearance of the gypsy moth in his adopted state, was distraught over his inability to convey the urgency of the situation to Rawson's group. He saw a divided and rancorous bunch that lacked leadership and would not listen to advice. He had recommended a thorough inspection, but none had been made; he had pleaded for containment of the moths by cordoning off the infested areas and then driving the invaders inward, but the commissioners had done just the opposite. Commission employees were hired without screening and sent into the field with few tools and no training. The proficiency of the men with arsenical poisons was notable by its absence.

Shaler told Fernald that he "had the ear" of the governor-elect, William Russell, and would present the matter to him privately, causing Fernald to hope for a quick reorganization of the commission.[51] Fernald had recommended hiring an adviser, but the commissioners dawdled for so long that the one individual who was interested changed his mind. Riley, in his presidential address to the second annual meeting of the Association of Economic Entomologists in November 1890, said that the extermination effort in Massachusetts "threatened to become farcical," and it was only through good fortune that the work proved as successful as it had.[52] The scientific community was

incredulous and the average citizen distressed by the commission's doings. Riley observed that the commission was unpopular and its work "severely criticized."[53] Sessions, convinced that the insect was nearly invincible, believed that the war to stop its spread should be one without quarter:

> This creature feeds upon the foliage of almost all our deciduous trees and shrubs, as well as upon the crops of the farm. Its power of multiplication seems almost without limit. If it cannot be entirely stamped out, it will be forever a menace not only to the crops and trees of our state, but to those of the whole continent. I desire to again record my sense of the importance of earnest work by those in charge of the matter. Scientists all agree in believing that, if it is possible to extirpate the pest, it should be done, let the expense be what it may.[54]

At a public meeting held in Worcester on December 2, 1890, Commissioner Rawson, attending as a member of the Board of Agriculture, was asked, "What is the prospect for success in the campaign against the gypsy moth?" From Rawson's answer, one can see that the gypsy moth commissioners considered the matter well in hand and the worst of it over. They were proud of their parsimonious handling of the state funds entrusted to them: "We took as the basis of our experiments [in killing moths] the experience of the Agricultural Experiment Station at Amherst, or the professors there, in spraying the trees with Paris green. We asked and secured, as many of you know, an appropriation of $50,000. We shall have expended at the end of the year about $30,000 of that appropriation. I do not think we shall require so large an appropriation another season."[55]

Many citizens at the meeting, however, regarded spraying as ineffective, since they had seen that Paris green was useless against late instar larvae. There were complaints from the public, anger over the spraying of private property, and ridicule of other efforts to exterminate the moth. There were also serious complaints about the competency of the fieldworkers and the commissioners, and rumors had begun to fly that the commission had mismanaged the effort and misappropriated state funds.

The gathering was rather lively, and one gets the sense that the average farmer and estate holder in Massachusetts did not view the potential severity of the infestation with the same dread as did the Board of Agriculture and the economic entomologists. Their attitude was a slap in the face to Sessions and showed him that in addition to fighting the moths, the board would also have to fight the public's apathy and bestir the farmers and landowners to action. The thought of such indifference made him angry, and he used the meeting as an opportunity to underscore his point:

I hope the sentiment of the [agricultural] community will be made manifest to the Legislature, that we want the campaign continued and we want it continued in the best possible manner. This is a big fight; this is no holiday affair. If this moth gets away from us, the whole country must suffer. . . . [The commission] will not limit their efforts to the use of paris green, but they will resort to any other method which seems likely to produce the desired results in the destruction of these pests. They adopt the motto of an Irishman in a fight, "Wherever you see a head, hit it."[56]

[CHAPTER 5]

Preparations for War

Nᴀᴛʜᴀɴɪᴇʟ Sʜᴀʟᴇʀ, now committed to injecting himself forcefully into the gypsy moth campaign, had one last obstacle to overcome: the support Rawson enjoyed because of his friendship with the Republican governor, J. Q. A. Brackett. Shaler's opening came when Brackett left office after serving a single year and was succeeded by William Eustis Russell, a thirty-four-year-old, reform-minded Democrat and Harvard graduate. Shaler knew Russell personally and after attending his inauguration in early January 1891, he met the new governor on the street in front of the State House. He expressed his concerns that the gypsy moth commission was a divided, rancorous, and inexpert group under suspicion of corruption and mismanagement. Russell said he had already decided to appoint a replacement group with Shaler as chairman. Startled, Shaler replied that he would not accept the responsibility unless the legislature put the work under the Board of Agriculture.[1]

At its annual winter meeting in Boston on February 3, 1891, the Board of Agriculture "voted on a motion of Nathaniel Shaler that a committee of three be appointed by the Chair to represent the board in matters of legislation and agitation concerning the destruction of the gypsy moth."[2] The motion passed, and Shaler, representing Martha's Vineyard, was appointed to this lobbying committee along with Francis Henry Appleton of Peabody and S. B. Bird of Framingham. The purpose of this committee was to wrest control of the gypsy moth campaign from Rawson, Martin, and Bradley by convincing the governor that establishing a new commission under the Board of Agriculture would be the best course of action for the state. Shaler's group contended that Rawson's commissioners had conducted themselves improperly, were incapable of handling the task entrusted to them, evidenced conflicts of interest, and displayed other faults serious enough to warrant their removal. They argued that the proposed replacement group would be superior even if it consisted of men as inexperienced as Rawson's who would be advised by the same entomologist Rawson had used.

Shaler, Appleton, and Bird submitted a report assuring Russell that in

Nathaniel Southgate Shaler.
Photo courtesy Ernst Mayr Library of
the Museum of Comparative Zoology,
Harvard University.

proper hands the problem with the gypsy moths would disappear. They argued that an unpaid committee would save the state $4,000 each year and
that the "evil" insect was an agricultural pest that should be dealt with by
people familiar with agriculture. Shaler stated to the governor in his special
communication that a committee appointed by the Board of Agriculture and
aided by "proper experts" could quickly and efficiently deal with the danger.[3]
Russell may not have been as knowledgeable about the state of affairs as some
thought, and he perhaps received a one-sided perspective from Shaler. His
response shows that he did not even know the correct name of the insect,
which he called the "Egyptian moth."[4]

Charles Fernald's part in all remained advisory in nature, although it would
be to his advantage if the commissioners were ousted and the work placed
under the Board of Agriculture. The community of economic entomologists
had been encouraging him to take control of the campaign, since Rawson's
commission had not employed an entomological adviser. The replacement of
the original commission was a second chance that had fallen into their laps,
one that would serve to advance their agenda and allow one of their own to
be in a position of authority.

Russell had written to Rawson on January 23 asking him to explain what
had been going on and noting, "The Commission is one placed by statute
under the control of the Governor, and therefore one for whose work he is

directly responsible."[5] In response, Rawson prepared a special report detailing the year of work and sent it directly to the governor without showing it to anyone else. Unlike all the accounts that followed, it was never published, and it has not survived.[6] Its contents must have confirmed the governor's suspicions, however, for on February 20 he sent a notice to Rawson alleging six counts of improper conduct: first, that disharmony had obstructed and delayed the work and that plans had been put into effect and contracts entered into without consideration by the full commission; second, that commissioners had sold goods to the commission at fixed prices and also fixed the contract price for teaming and livery; third, that blank payroll forms had been signed and filled in later; fourth, that commissioners had knowingly overpaid for horse teams; fifth, that a commissioner had used men employed by the state to circulate brochures for his private business; and sixth, that spraying had gone on all season despite its cost and even though the commissioners had no idea whether the procedure was proving useful and, in fact, were bitterly divided on the issue. Governor Russell wanted answers to all these allegations, and he wanted them in less than four days.[7]

While the commissioners prepared their response, the state auditor reviewed their books and found that acts of financial misconduct had indeed occurred. From powerful agents of the executive branch and respected members of their communities, Rawson, Martin, and Bradley had become lawbreakers who faced the prospect of a thousand-dollar fine and a year in jail. They responded to the governor by the appointed hour on February 24, however, and suffered only embarrassment for their misdeeds. The next day Russell dismissed them all, abolished their commission, and ordered them to turn over their papers and property to William Sessions.[8] The same day, Russell sent a four-page letter to the executive council of the General Court in which he outlined his reasons for creating a new commission and revealed the admissions of the original commissioners. In addition, he sent a special message to the legislature nominating Sessions, Shaler, and Appleton as commissioners locum tenens, noting that these nominees wished to serve without compensation.[9]

Sessions, Shaler, and Appleton, who had agreed to serve for six weeks until a new commission was created, were dumfounded when Russell said he expected them to constitute the permanent committee, but it should not have surprised them that Russell would proceed along this line since the Board of Agriculture had insisted from the start on having the work under its control. Sessions later testified he had protested strongly against having the board do the work, and that the governor had removed the first commission for reasons known only to him.[10] His recollections contradict Russell's statement that the

conditions of the appointment were made in accordance with the wishes of the appointees and are contrary to Shaler's statements that he and Sessions had lobbied personally for the change.

Shaler later said he would not have accepted his commission had it been a permanent one, but that he was proud of his part in removing Rawson's board and believed it was a feather in his cap to have helped abolish at least one commission in Massachusetts.[11] Many others also were relieved by the removal of the Rawson Commission, and J. G. Jack of the Arnold Arboretum summed up their reasons:

> The results arrived at in reducing the pest last season were better than many people anticipated and as good as was to be expected from inexperienced and more or less careless management. Land-owners naturally made much complaint and opposition to the invasion of their grounds by employees of the Commission for the purpose of searching for the cocoons of the Gypsy Moth, or more particularly for the application of insecticides (chiefly arsenical) to trees, shrubs and other vegetation. The act establishing the Commission gave it power to invade any private place in furthering its object, and the ignorant workmen employed were in many cases apparently very careless in the use of the Paris Green and indifferent as to the thoroughness of their work.[12]

The act of March 14, 1890, was superseded by the act of 1891, chapter 210, which increased the authority of the commission. The new commissioners had received their charge of duties on March 4, 1891, at a conference set up for that day at the Board of Agriculture offices in Boston. Four distinguished entomologists, Charles Valentine Riley, Charles Henry Fernald, Samuel Hubbard Scudder, and Samuel Henshaw, had been invited to appear and make recommendations to the commissioners, although Henshaw was unable to attend. Prominent citizens and elected officials of all infested communities had also been invited, and many were present, including Mayor Wiggin of Malden, Selectman L. S. Gould of Melrose, Selectman W. C. Craig of Medford, and Warren A. Peirce, a civic leader and coal merchant of Arlington. Present in addition to Shaler, Appleton, and Sessions was Edward Howe Forbush, awaiting his official appointment as director of fieldwork. Conspicuous by their absence were the original commissioners, Martin, Bradley, and Rawson. The incoming commissioners had not spoken with the outgoing commissioners before the meeting, so no one in the room had a clear idea of the details surrounding the task ahead of them.

Shaler, about fifty years old and at the height of his intellectual powers, is

Charles Valentine Riley, circa 1886.
Special Media Services Division,
National Archives & Records
Administration.

known to history as an eminent geologist, zoologist, and prolific writer on a
wide range of subjects. He had been Leopold Trouvelot's colleague and friend
and was familiar with the gypsy moth infestations occurring nearby. Shaler
was a tall, athletic, and sinewy man with steel-gray hair and beard.[13] Author
David Livingstone described him as a man with "feverish vitality"[14]—perhaps
a symptom of the emotional instability that had occurred a number of times
during his life. He had suffered collapses from an unnamed mental condition
in 1866 and again in 1872, and recovery from each had required more than
two years. Recuperating from one such bout in Europe during the summers of
1866, 1867, and 1868, Shaler had encountered examples of gypsy moth defoliation, and the recollection of those sights haunted him.[15]

The star entomological adviser to the new commission was Charles Valentine Riley, forty-seven, chief in entomology at the U.S. Department of Agriculture. Riley was a man of medium height and build, whose longish, wavy hair,
handlebar mustache, and mode of dress were in keeping with his reputation
as a flamboyant and volatile artist.[16] Although he was self-trained, Riley was
a respected but highly controversial entomologist who was nearing the end of
his luminous career and was in poor physical and emotional health. He was
often absent from his desk in Washington and spent months at a time in
Europe, ostensibly on entomological matters. He was plagued with frequent
headaches, was unable to concentrate, and suffered from periods of debilitating chronic insomnia. He had wide mood swings and could easily be either

confrontational and argumentative or convivial and charming. One modern chronicler believes that if Riley had lived at the end of the twentieth century, he would have been diagnosed with bipolar disorder.[17] Howard wrote of Riley's condition at the time: "He could sleep on a long railway journey, . . . [or] in a barber's chair [better] than he could sleep in his own bed at home. It seems not to have occurred to him to install a barber's chair in his house, but after a sleepless night he would often go to the barber and pay by the hour for a chance to make up lost sleep. All this must have affected his disposition seriously."[18]

Another adviser was Samuel Hubbard Scudder, fifty-two, a fossil entomologist and an eminent authority on Orthoptera and Lepidoptera. Like Shaler, he had been a student of Agassiz, and he is still known today for his extensive and sometimes controversial contributions to insect classification. He is remembered as a man who was perpetually behind schedule because of his penchant for overextending himself even more than Shaler, who was famous for it. Scudder is also remembered for a memorable account, written in 1874, of three days spent studying a pickled fish under the tutelage of Professor Agassiz.[19] Howard called him "a delightful, scholarly man, and a charming writer" and one of the most distinguished entomologists of his generation.[20]

Charles Henry Fernald was also present at the meeting. Approaching his fifty-third birthday, he was then in good health but had suffered from lifelong asthma and was susceptible to severe and prolonged illness from colds. Many letters written to him during the 1890s include wishes for his speedy recovery from influenza and similar ailments, and the slightly shaky hand noted in his replies was a sign of incipient rheumatism.

Civil Warriors

Many of the participants in the room were middle-aged veterans of the Civil War. Fernald had served as first mate on the steamer *Housatanic* and later as ensign on the ironclad monitor-class ship *Patapsco*; Appleton was a brevet general; Riley had been a private in the 134th Illinois Volunteers; Shaler, a Unionist, had been captain of the Fifth Kentucky Battery; and Sessions had attained the rank of sergeant in the Forty-sixth Massachusetts Infantry. Others in the room who were not mentioned by name in the stenographic transcript had likely served the Union cause as well.

The influence of the war on these men and on the subsequent course of events cannot be ignored. The entomologist Stephen Forbes probably described the feelings of all Civil War veterans when he wrote that the young soldiers had been molded like "lumps of hot iron between jaws of cold steel."[21] Livingstone notes that the war's events had "a deep effect" on Shaler and left

him with a "predilection for military history."[22] Service in the War between the States taught men lessons they drew on all their lives. Among these was an acceptance of the need to do terrible things in pursuit of triumph; victory in war was the single greatest example of an end that justified the means.

The participants with agricultural backgrounds would not have thought much differently in this situation than did the war veterans; they also understood that a stark threat required a stark response. Many surely remembered the episodes of the devastating livestock disease pleuropneumonia that had occurred in Boston and vicinity in the 1870s, and that the method used to eliminate it was slaughter. The same tendencies to think of the proposed campaign as a military one was unmistakably exhibited by members of the General Court when they drafted the legislation against the moth. Insect problems were nothing new to farmers of the region, who had been dealing with the Hessian fly, the chinch bug, the Colorado potato beetle, and the plum curculio. Yet the argument persisted that there was something different about the gypsy moth, and the response to this invasive insect was unprecedented. For the first time in the nation's history, a well-funded and well-organized program, initiated and controlled by the state, would send an army against a nonhuman foe. It was nothing less than total war against an insect on a scale never before seen or contemplated, and one for which military experience would be an asset.

A modern military truism is that in times of crisis men do not rise to their occasion but fall to their level of training. With no precedents to guide them, the old soldiers in the room could not help but think of the coming engagement in the same terms as a military one against a human adversary, and they began to plan for a contest in which there was territory to be regained, fronts to establish, counterattacks to mount, and an enemy to besiege. The fog of war was already closing in. Little was known about the insect's habits, and to worsen an already bad situation, the information available indicated that the moth in America was exhibiting behavior unknown to European entomologists. The existing situation was unclear, the boundaries of the infested region were uncertain, and there were disturbing reports that the invader had already reached western Massachusetts and southern Maine.

One does not have to imagine what was on Shaler's mind as the participants gathered in the room. A complex and multifaceted man, he was pulling together some widely separated facts and reaching some disturbing conclusions. He understood that the frontier era of American history had come to a close. The westward expansion that had been occurring throughout his lifetime had ended. There were no more virgin fields to plow and no more pristine forests to log. Shaler believed that the conservation and protection of natural resources would become increasingly necessary, and he saw this need arising

first in the nation's woodlands. Gifford Pinchot, a man sparing in his praise of others, later said that no one spoke about the forest with greater authority than Shaler.[24]

In his book *The Forests of North America*, published in 1887, Shaler had expressed the view that the sheltering and providing forest was the cradle of Western civilization. He now contended that the moth's destructiveness, if left unchecked, could destroy all the forests on the continent and even bring down civilization, and his reputation was so impeccable that not a single man in the scientific community challenged this conclusion. Shaler believed that the power of the gypsy moth to cause damage in America exceeded that of all other insects combined. He believed that locusts had reduced North Africa, once called the granary of Rome, to a barren country, causing enough damage to alter the course of history, and he saw a parallel with the gypsy moth: "The startling change which has occurred along the whole southern coast of the Mediterranean within 2000 years, which occurred shortly after the Christian era, the pauperizing of that country, was accomplished by an insect. Seeing what I saw about Medford when the [gypsy moth] went unhindered, I came to the conclusion that if it made ravages of that nature, that scope, over this country, it might break down our civilization."[25]

As chairman, Shaler opened the meeting with remarks in which the normally genteel Kentuckian faulted the previous commission for allowing the moths to expand their range: "I begged [the commissioners] to bend their energies to bringing in the boundaries [of the infested area] as far as possible, to pay the market price for eggs and grubs, and to put their inspection work in progress; but they went into a miscellaneous sprinkling and burning over the whole territory. The result now is that, as nearly as I can ascertain, it would take a line thirty miles long to enclose the area the insects occupy."[26] As far as Shaler could surmise, the insect was abundant in an area of ten square miles and was scattered within an area of about fifty square miles. Since its females could not fly, its main forces moved outward at a slow rate. Its egg clusters were largely laid in the open and were vulnerable eight months of the year. The city of Boston and the Charles and Mystic Rivers prevented the enemy from deploying farther south, and the ocean blocked its eastward retreat. With the insect concentrated along roads where the nozzles of heavy spray equipment could be brought to bear against it, the odds of a successful extermination seemed high.

Fernald also held to the idea that the insects had not spread into the forests and would be within easy reach along the roadsides: "As the moth is distributed in great measure by vehicles, it makes its first appearance where the teams stop, and begins its work of destruction in the door-yard, orchard and garden.

Thus the danger to the forest, in case the moth were allowed to propagate unchecked, would be comparatively remote."[27]

The conviction with which Shaler and Fernald made their pronouncements had a pivotal influence on Riley, and it was Riley who gradually commanded the greatest attention during the conference. His reputation was due in part to his position with the Department of Agriculture but even more to his record of practical experience. Fernald may have known more about moths, and Shaler's expertise about forests may have been greater, but no one had more experience than Riley when it came to handling big problems in the field. But he was ambivalent at first; as he responded to a question from Appleton: "Is it practicable to exterminate it or not? . . . I have serious doubts, because if it may be said to occur in an area of say fifty square miles, if it is found even in a number of central points of distribution in that area, there is great danger. . . . [M]y own fears would be that it has got into the woods and on trees that are not so easily treated."[28]

Riley asked several times if anyone knew whether the moths were in the woods or not, and Shaler reassured him that they were "still confined to the artificial grounds," meaning trees and crops under cultivation and domestic plantings and gardens around residences.[29] The position taken by Shaler and Fernald was astonishing because it was totally speculative. There was a good reason why nobody knew if the moths were in the woods or not—nobody had looked! Fernald had limited his inspection to a single day in the populated parts of Medford, and the only other survey had been a haphazard affair attempted the year before by a small number of men under Rawson's commission, who scouted areas along the streets and central sections of towns already known to be infested.

Riley, asked to give dispassionate advice, briefly touched on many important points including quarantines, parasites, spraying, and destroying egg clusters. He doubted that exterminating the insect was possible, given the size of the infestation, but nevertheless covered his bases thoroughly. In contrast, Fernald remained singular in his support of extermination. He kept pushing the idea, saying it would be "highly desirable" to stamp out the insect. That such an attempt might not succeed did not seem to trouble him, and at one point he stated that if extermination failed, other methods could be used to contain the moths. Even Riley soon warmed to the idea of eliminating the invading insects. As the meeting progressed, he became less a detached adviser and more a passionate advocate for war, falling in with Fernald's idea of extermination. He understood that an opportunity for the new scientific branch had presented itself, one that, if skillfully handled, would provide the lasting glory snatched away despite two earlier successes: the results of the

U.S. Entomological Commission's study of the Rocky Mountain locust in the 1870s, and the use of natural controls to clear the California citrus groves of the cottony-cushion scale insect (*Icerya purchasi*) in the late 1880s.

During the worst of the citrus scale infestation, Riley had learned of a parasitic fly in Australia that attacked the scale. Prevented by congressional action from going himself, Riley sent Albert Koebele to Australia instead. Koebele stumbled upon the Vedalia beetle (*Rodalia cardinalis*) while looking for the fly and realized the importance of his discovery; within a year the beetles brought the scale under complete control. But the California success was in many ways more serendipitous than scientific. Still, Riley had been at the center of this highly visible triumph and was so proud of his part in it that he named his first child Cathryn Vedalia Riley.

The earlier work on the Rocky Mountain locust had been a first-rate piece of scientific investigation. The commissioners had discovered the breeding grounds of the locust, identified the insect as a separate species, determined the conditions causing outbreak years, and predicted how long the swarms would last. Before any of the findings could be put to practical use, however, the insect became extinct. Still, in the minds of many the elimination of this fearsome scourge could be attributed to the work of the commission.

As a result of such events, economic entomologists found themselves arguing against their greatest successes. The conditions surrounding both endeavors had been so singular that no eastern entomologists believed they were likely to happen again, but the public remained unconvinced. The idea that problems with insects on a grand scale could be solved quickly had resulted from the Rocky Mountain work, and the value of natural controls had been strongly impressed on all those who knew about the California success. A test for economic entomology that was free of capricious factors was needed, and in this respect no insect could have served better than the gypsy moth.

Legions of *Hypogymna dispar* rampaging through Massachusetts presented staggering implications. Everyone in the room already had seen that the insects would swarm through fields and orchards, devouring foliage to the last stem and twig, and Shaler had voiced his fears that when the larvae had done their worst in the orchards, the great eastern forests would fall next. The insect was known to attack row crops in Europe; thus a consuming march of caterpillars threatened the vulnerable American midwestern plains—a lush agricultural prize. The presence of the gypsy moth justified the existence of economic entomology and fulfilled the prophecy that a great war with insects was looming. All that stood between mankind and the alien hordes were a few brave economic entomologists. If they could stem the tide, no one could doubt their value, and the science of economic entomology would no longer be regarded as a backwater discipline for second-rate scholars.

Riley, like many of his colleagues, believed that with the establishment of the experiment stations in July 1888, a "new era" had begun in economic entomology.[30] One suspects that he intended to take part in another great success story but had not yet made up his mind between natural control and chemical eradication. The California episode had split economic entomology and resulted in a near-brawl over who deserved the most credit, a problem that Riley was not going to let happen again. He attached so much importance to the meeting that he hired a stenographer at his own expense to make a record of everyone's comments for publication and posterity.[31]

Assuming that gypsy caterpillars would succumb to spraying as easily as tent caterpillars and canker worms, Riley based his plans on Shaler and Fernald's questionable hypothesis that there were no caterpillars in the woods. Given an appropriation of $100,000, he saw no reason why the insect could not be exterminated with a single spraying campaign that would last no more than four weeks. Riley had much faith in the effectiveness of spraying arsenical pesticides such as Paris green, and argued that if only roadside trees needed spraying, a spectacular kill could be achieved. Such a triumph would be a showy debut for chemical entomology in New England, especially if done right before the eyes of the citizens, so Riley argued not only for a course he thought would be the most effective, but also for one that would be the most conspicuous:

> Individually I have always felt, and so expressed myself, and still feel, that the proper way would be to use whatever funds the state will give you during a limited time, and concentrate all effort and all expenditure in the month of June on the destruction of the caterpillars, and not to bother about the destruction of the eggs or the prevention of the spread of the insect . . . Therefore, as a single spraying will kill five thousand caterpillars just as well as one, there is nothing to be gained by the work of destroying the eggs.[32]

Although spraying devices were becoming available through commercial channels at this time, there was no corresponding apparatus for attacking moths in their egg, pupa, or imago stages, thus limiting all options for mechanized attack to the larvae. Work against the insect in any of its other three life stages would have to be done by hand. None of this mattered to Charles Fernald, who thought the moths could be eradicated wherever they were found. As far as he was concerned the effort would be made for extermination only, and it would be done with chemicals. He knew that in order to ensure a continuing stream of appropriations, the campaign would have to be carried out in a certain way, and the history of the campaign reveals what he had in

mind. His rationale was that a complex condition represented only an accumulation of simple conditions; thus, if it was possible to destroy insects on one tree, it was possible to destroy them on all trees. "Defoliation," "extermination," and "eradication" would become terms with indistinct and flexible meanings. Ridding the Commonwealth of the gypsy moth would be presented not as an uncertain task but as a simple matter of time and money. In keeping with the approach of economic entomology, the practical work would be accomplished through a marriage of business, science, and the state.

All parties would emerge from the battle with something they wanted. The state would be rid of the moth and admired by other states for its progressive leadership stance. The Board of Agriculture, which had long been little more than a record-gathering organization constituted with volunteers, would take a large step toward becoming a powerful administrative and regulatory body. Practical entomology would triumph over not only the insects but also the impractical branches of entomology. Other states would follow suit against their insect enemies, creating many new jobs for economic entomologists. Science and technology would defeat the enemy, and chemicals delivered by human hands would prevail over the unreliable and capricious techniques of natural controls. Sprayers would work where prayers had not: poisons would replace predators.

One can imagine Fernald in the conference room as he introduced his theories of extermination, speaking in a voice so soft and silky that Peters said it came very close to sounding feminine: "Suppose we have a tree like the elm I see yonder, and suppose we know it to be the only tree in America that is infested. I think you will all agree with me that for a small sum of money all moths on it could be destroyed. Suppose there were two,—suppose all the trees on the Common were infested. If they could be destroyed on all those trees, it is only a question of time and money to eradicate them from a much larger territory."[33] While Fernald outlined the approach of economic entomology and expressed the challenge it must meet, he still considered himself as a participant only to the extent required by his duties as entomologist of the Hatch Station. He served notice that he did not want to participate in the process over the long term and suggested that the commissioners hire someone else as their entomological adviser. He agreed with Riley that the size of the territory to be treated was "stupendous" and treating it an unprecedented experiment, but he put his reputation on the line by stating his belief that the insects could all be destroyed.[34]

Samuel Scudder, who had not embraced economic entomology, entered the meeting room late. His intellect and personality were markedly different from those of the others in attendance. Clinging somewhat to the old school, he had been among the last of the era's great entomologists to accept Darwin's

theories of evolution. Now, although he had not heard the remarks made earlier by Riley and Fernald, he had already given some thought to the gypsy moth problem. When Shaler asked him whether it would be better to collect egg masses or spray larvae, his response came out in a rush:

> The caterpillar is a very liberal feeder, so, of course, it is very much more difficult to reach by spraying, because the spraying is not to be confined to a few kinds of trees, but to a very large number, so that one would say you would have to spray almost everything you came across. So with the eggs, which are laid not always on trees, but on almost anything else. . . . [I]t seems to me that nature has indicated the easiest means of attack. The eggs are laid in batches, and are exposed for eight months of the year. Therefore it seems to me that the egg is the place to attack.[35]

Riley, becoming increasingly excited about the thought of a grand confrontation, strongly disagreed with Scudder. He urged that the state of Massachusetts "make the experiment" of eradication. He believed that if spraying could not kill the caterpillars, the only recourse left would be clear-cutting the entire Middlesex Fells. "It pays better," he said prophetically, "to make one grand effort than to fritter your energies away over a number of years, and then fail."[36]

Riley may have abandoned natural controls as the primary means of subduing the gypsy moth because there were at least two obstacles across that path. The first was the language of the state legislation, which called specifically for extermination. The second was the practical matter of finding natural predators of a foreign insect. In 1886 the U.S. Congress had restricted the search for biological insect controls to the United States and in 1888 attached a rider to the Agriculture Department appropriations bill prohibiting federally funded foreign travel for department employees. This proviso had been aimed at Riley in retaliation for his long visits abroad each year on the taxpayer's dollar while ostensibly in search of entomological information. Restricting the search to the United States would make the chances of finding predators or parasites of the European gypsy moth a frustrating, probably futile, exercise.

Alternatively, a hunt for foreign predators could be paid for by the state of Massachusetts. Such a search might become a costly proposition, but Riley understood that if the eradication program fell short, the state would eventually be forced to approach the federal government for aid much as the California Board of Horticulture had done in its struggle against the cottony-cushion scale. If Massachusetts had to battle the gypsy moth alone, Riley thought the easiest way to win that battle would be with chemical insecticides, not with

other insects. He warned the commissioners to make their first effort their best. A failure would make it difficult to get another appropriation from the state, in which case help from the federal government could not be expected. As he had told the Californians two years earlier: "I would not hesitate, as United States Entomologist, to send someone [to a foreign country to search for predatory insects] with the consent of the Commissioner of Agriculture, were the means for the purpose at my command. But, unfortunately, the mere suggestion that I wanted $1500 or $2000 for such a purpose would be more apt to cause laughter and ridicule on the part of the average committee in Congress."[37]

The resistance met by Riley was more than just the reaction of a spiteful congress to a flamboyant entomologist. The passage of the Hatch Act, creating state agricultural experiment stations, was seen as the capstone of a process that had begun in the 1860s with federal help in establishing the land grant colleges. Many legislators believed the act satisfied any responsibilities the national government may have had to individual states in matters of agriculture. The prevalent theory of the time was that of laissez-faire, and the distance between the federal and state administrations was kept wide to prevent development of a paternalistic central government with dependent states. The tone of the times was typified by President Grover Cleveland's famous refusal in 1887 to sign a bill that would have provided federal money to help drought-stricken Texas farmers buy seeds; the reasons he gave could easily have applied to insect problems:

> I can find no warrant for such an appropriation in the Constitution, and I do not believe that the power and duty of the General Government ought to be extended to the relief of individual suffering which is in no manner properly related to the public service or benefit. A prevalent tendency to disregard the limited mission of this power should, I think, be steadfastly resisted, to the end that the lesson should be constantly enforced that though the people support the Government the Government should not support the people.[38]

Citizens at the meeting who were not swept away by the idea of bug slaughter took exception to Riley's proposed approach. One of the original commissioners had written that the spraying his commission had done was "worse than ineffective, to the great expense of the state."[39] Mayors and selectmen had seen trees sprayed so many times that the caterpillars were glistening with arsenic without being affected in the least. But Riley refused to believe that spraying didn't work; he argued that failed sprayings were due to impure arsenic, disproportioned mixtures, or inexpert application. The citizens

present contended that combatting the moth by hand and destroying the eggs or capturing larvae under burlap bands had proved to be both highly effective and safe, but Riley was dismissive: "I remember distinctly a little cedar tree not more than six feet high in my own grounds that was attacked by the bagworm. I thought I would see whether I could not clear them off. I worked for two consecutive months picking off from the tree the issue of not more than two females. . . . Yet in the Smithsonian grounds I have absolutely stopped similar injury on larger trees in a few minutes by spraying."[40]

No one knows why Fernald, did not express any reservations about the failure of spraying and yielded the stage to Riley while the laymen in the room expressed their misgivings. Had Fernald confirmed that the spraying of gypsy moths had indeed been ineffective, Riley might have reconsidered. But Fernald placed absolute reliance on scientific experimentation—especially his own work at Amherst where he felt he had the finest laboratory in the country— and until controlled experiments proved that the gypsy moth could *not* be dealt with using arsenical spray, he would pay no attention to the anecdotal reports of common men.

Scudder alone among entomologists in the room remained unconvinced that the moth could be exterminated. He cautioned the group that if the insect could not be destroyed, it would have to be held in check indefinitely. And he was beginning to see the unfolding plan to concentrate on spraying for what it was—a high-profile campaign to demonstrate the killing power of economic entomology: "I don't understand the force of the arguments used by my neighbors on either side [Riley and Fernald] of delaying the work by not taking the eggs at present. Why do they want all the caterpillars out that they can get, in order to exterminate them?"[41]

When Riley began to explain arsenical pesticides and spray nozzles, Scudder excused himself from the meeting. The relationship between the two had cooled considerably during the 1870s when Scudder, a taxonomic "splitter," had proposed a great revision of the Lepidoptera, and Riley had been in the forefront of vociferous opposition. At about the same time, Riley was trying to regain the job of chief federal entomologist, but Scudder had taken a prominent role in supporting the incumbent, J. H. Comstock. Scudder was also instrumental in blocking Riley's membership in the National Academy of Science, which Riley never forgot.[42] Scudder was put off by Riley's "high and mighty" tone.[43] And he made no secret of believing Comstock to be a more effective chief entomologist.[44] The notion that all was not well between the two is reinforced by the dismissive comments Riley made after Scudder left the room: "I am so impatient of any efforts to simply check it. I have nothing to say about checking it; I speak for stamping it out. Mr. Scudder simply says he doesn't think it will be exterminated."[45]

   Riley could not conceive that a spraying program would fail. He repeatedly urged the group to "show what you can do," and to "make the attempt" at extermination in order to avoid the disgrace of standing idle while a pest took over the country: "All other means are puerile as compared with destruction by the arsenicals. All other means are now abandoned in fighting the canker-worm, the coddling moth and some other insects, and intelligent spraying at the proper time has come to be looked upon as the most efficient means of protection against these insects."[46]

   The meeting came to an end at six o'clock, by which time the small room, with its windows closed against the chilly March winds, was likely filled with smoke from all the oration and the liberal use of tobacco (a habit that seemed endemic to all Civil War veterans). The course of the war had been decided, but the solution to the problem had not. The opinions of citizens had been totally dismissed. Shaler and Sessions were unsure of their chances to eradicate the moth, but they had just taken decisive action at the highest levels of state power to bring gypsy moth work under the Board of Agriculture, and they could not very well go on record now as recommending that it was best to do nothing. Fernald had proposed extermination; the act passed by the state legislature mandated extermination; and the law limited the commissioners to extermination.

The Moth Slayers

P RESENT AT THE MEETING of March 4 was Edward Howe Forbush of Worcester, director-designate of fieldwork at a salary of $50 per week. Forbush was born in 1858 in Quincy, Massachusetts, to Leander Pomeroy Forbush and Ruth H. Carr. A man of medium height and lithe, athletic build, he had prominent ears and nose, and a high forehead surmounting a face that reminds one of a scholarly owl, an impression reinforced by the large, round eyeglasses he wore later in life. It is an indication of the times that Forbush was largely self-educated, but unlike others of the era, he made a conscious decision to reject the educational opportunities available to him: "I determined to forgo a college training, to earn my own living, to be independent of all assistance, and to train myself by experience, observation and reading. So at the age of fifteen years I gave up school. My vocations for the next seven years were those of farmer, laborer, and mechanic; my avocation, the study of nature. Thus I grew up independent, self-supporting, developing body and mind, preparing myself for the work that I seemed best fitted to do."[1]

At the age of sixteen he was appointed curator at the Natural Museum of Ornithology in Worcester, Massachusetts, and later became president of the Worcester Summer School of Natural History. He taught himself to draw birds and illustrated his own books on ornithology. Forbush loved to hunt, and soon after dropping out of school he taught himself taxidermy; for some years he supported himself by operating a hunting and taxidermy business called the "Naturalists' Exchange" at 424 Main Street in Worcester. He advertised himself as a maker of "instruments and supplies for taxidermists, entomologists, oologists, botanists, and mineralogists, and a dealer in birds, mammals, skins, mounted specimens, bird's eggs, insects, shells, fossils and minerals."[2] On June 28, 1882, he married Etta L. Hill, and sometime afterward he sold his share of his taxidermy business—in which he had become partners with William S. Perry—to the naturalist and ornithologist Charles K. Reed and his son. When Forbush assumed his position as field director for

Edward Howe Forbush in midlife.
Special Media Services Division,
National Archives & Records
Administration.

gypsy moth work he was thirty-three years old with the first two of four young children to feed.

History does not tell much about Forbush in his earlier years. His intentions must be deduced from his actions, but in one matter there is no mystery: what he really wanted most of all was to be the state ornithologist of Massachusetts. Like most men in the natural sciences of his time, Forbush saw the direction being taken by state governments in making such areas "official" within their bureaucratic structure. Forbush was a dedicated, persistent—some might say stubborn and obsessive—man, and a good organizer. Henshaw remarked on Forbush's "tireless energy."[3] Something about him impressed the new gypsy moth commissioners, who wrote of their choice: "Mr. E. H. Forbush of Worcester was appointed director of the field work on March 12, 1891. . . . The commission was obliged to secure his release from an engagement for scientific work in order to obtain his services."[4]

Finding a qualified man to assume the duties of field director was not easy. There were no precedents for the work, so there was no pool of experienced applicants. According to some estimates, there were approximately eight hundred individuals in the United States engaged in some form of entomological work at the time.[5] But those who subscribed to the tenets of economic entomology numbered no more than two dozen, and none of them was available.

Fernald had again recommended Samuel Henshaw instead of Forbush for

director of fieldwork under the new commission, no doubt hoping, as he had hoped before, that having a qualified entomologist in charge would allow him to slip back into his professorial duties at Amherst. Henshaw, thirty-seven, was already known for his *List of the Coleoptera of America North of Mexico*, published in 1885. He was considered an economic entomologist because of his multipart work, *Bibliography of the More Important Contributions to American Economic Entomology*, the first three volumes of which were published by the U.S. Government Printing Office in April 1890.

Henshaw was a short, strong man whose reclusive nature has presented difficulties for historians. R. T. Jackson wrote that Henshaw's principal characteristics were his "sensitiveness, sense of fun, his personal integrity and his devotion to his work and friends."[6] Mary P. Winsor, on the other hand, has described him as a man who was "rigid, humorless, lacking in ideas, and antisocial."[7] Henshaw may have been obsessed with detail and blunt in speaking the truth, but his correspondence with Scudder, Fernald, Howard, and Riley show that he was both respected and highly trusted by his colleagues.

Commissioners Sessions, Appleton, and Shaler held two meetings with Henshaw, but their offer came at an awkward time because Henshaw had just accepted a promising position at the MCZ, assisting H. A. Hagen. He did seriously consider accepting the post of field director and even obtained a leave of absence for this purpose from his duties at the Boston Natural History Society.[8] But even though the wages offered by the commission tempted Henshaw, he was wary of promises that sounded too good to be true. Once he had seen what the job would entail and the pressures he would be under while directing this sort of work, he rejected the offer: "I looked over the matter and talked it over with [the commissioners] at two meetings, and then decided I would not have anything to do with it on the general ground . . . that it would be absolutely impossible to exterminate an insect of these habits, unless you are willing to go to the extent of making the region which it infests an absolute desert."[9]

The problems of finding an entomologist were so great that the commission had to consider those at work elsewhere in the field of natural sciences. Forbush's selection could not have been based on his credentials, because he had none. He was an adventuresome high school dropout who had been a taxidermist until a few years earlier and then a self-made naturalist in the business of getting himself sent on expeditions. He knew nothing about the gypsy moth, lacked formal training in the sciences, and had never been responsible for a large payroll or run a big organization with many employees.

The commissioners were in haste to find a field director, however, and could not be choosy. With less than three weeks from their inception on February 15 to the advisory meeting on March 4, they were anxious to make their

selection. The caterpillar hatch was only seven weeks off, and the commissioners wanted to have an administration organized by then that could place a force of men in the field. William Brewster, assistant in ornithology and mammalogy at the Museum of Comparative Zoology, knew Forbush as a skilled taxidermist who frequently prepared or mounted specimens for the museum, and it may have been through him that Forbush's name came to the attention of others. Forbush maintained that the offer of field director surprised him, that he had neither solicited the position nor even desired it.[10] He later testified:

> I received a communication from a friend in Cambridge early in 1891, saying that Frank Bolles, [Governor Russell's] brother-in-law, I think, who was then secretary of Harvard College, had recommended me for a place on this Gypsy Moth Commission. . . . The next time I came down [to Boston] I went into the State House and saw the Governor. . . . I told Gov. Russell then and there that I did not want my name mentioned in the matter in any way, I did not want to be considered and I should not take the place if it was offered to me. I supposed that settled it.[11]

Forbush had not yet experienced the persuasive skills of Nathaniel Shaler, whom he did not know, and he was surprised to receive a telegram from Shaler asking him to come at once to the board's rooms in Boston. Forbush, preparing to leave on an expedition, had just learned that he would be delayed for weeks by ice that blocked his route in the northern latitudes. With time on his hands and little money in his pockets, he decided that meeting with Shaler could do no harm.

History shows that Shaler not only feared the moth but was a compelling speaker, so doubtless he presented a moving argument why Forbush should help fend off the grave danger facing the Commonwealth. Forbush never had a chance; his self-educated mind and naturally formed independence were no match for Shaler's erudite supplications, and his horizons surely expanded during his talks with the dignified professor from Harvard. Before the two parted, Forbush agreed to help organize the field force for a period of six weeks while the northern ice melted and the commissioners searched for a permanent director. Had it only been so, he never would have lamented later: "I began to organize the force. I left my family. I never went home. I stayed right there, never saw home for a week, and got right in the field and organized a force. Then they sent off and got my contract annulled . . . and I have been here ever since."[12]

The day after his appointment, Forbush took a train for the three-hour trip

to Amherst. He went to the agricultural college and engaged nine students to use as his core of inspectors. Then he spent a few days discussing the gypsy moth with Fernald, who, averse to the idea of further entanglement with the work, likely saw in Forbush a bright and capable man whose lack of experience with insects was an asset. The new field director presented a clean slate on which the ideas of economic entomology could be written, and the work Fernald feared would fall on him could now be delegated to Forbush. He suggested to Forbush that entomology students from the agricultural college train the field force to watch for evidence of parasites throughout the long season of work and advised Forbush to experiment with native parasites to see if they could be used effectively against the gypsy moth. He did not want the state to incur the expense of importing European parasites if native parasites "might be able to render all the assistance that could be expected."[13]

The spraying devices being researched at Amherst—some were kept in storage there—were of great interest to Forbush, since most entomologists believed that intelligent and concentrated use of spraying devices would bring a quick end to the invaders. Before the two men parted, an informal relationship had worked itself out. Fernald would be the architect of the thrust against the insects, and Forbush would be the sword in his hand: "From that time Professor Fernald's advice and assistance were always freely sought by the committee and director [of fieldwork], and as freely given. All plans made were submitted to him for approval and were only perfected after a careful consideration of his recommendations."[14]

The outcome of the meeting surely pleased Fernald. The generous appropriation expected from the legislature, the capable men appointed to the new board of commissioners, and the application of scientific insect extermination principles reassured him that this time the job would be done right. Either the worst would be over in a few years, or Forbush would gain enough experience to carry matters forward on his own and let Fernald's life get back to normal. Forbush was still thinking of his "elaborate expedition" into the Newfoundland interior, an adventure now delayed so he could prepare an inept and ragtag army to fight an invading insect about which he still knew little.[15] The expedition was the "scientific engagement" from which the committee had secured his release. Forbush had been unsure about assuming the obligation, and some years later remarked to his friend and colleague, John B. May, that he had accepted only out of a "sense of civic duty."[16]

Forbush felt that his time with Fernald had been well spent, and the unlimited access he had been given to Fernald's tremendous store of knowledge was reassuring. He would have no time in the next six weeks to study the history of the gypsy moth in North America and its method of distribution. The administrative and physical details of forming an army would require enor-

mous amounts of his time, and he still saw his term of service extending only six weeks. Thanks to Fernald he would enjoy the services of knowledgeable young assistants while the commissioners planned the best course of action against the invaders, leaving him free to apply his efforts where they were needed most.

Groundwork

The new commissioners met with some of the former commissioners on March 12 at the agriculture offices in Boston and were given a map showing the expansion of the moth during the previous three years. This was the first time the new commissioners learned the probable extent of the moth's dispersal. Prior to 1888, the insect was thought to be concentrated only in the Glenwood section of Medford. In January 1890 the moth had been discovered in parts of four towns and the city of Malden; by January 1891 it could be found in varying densities in thirty communities, including the northern periphery of Boston. The commissioners accepted the map as reliable and called the line drawn around the infested area "the boundary of 1891." The boundary remained the farthest extent of the extermination effort that followed in succeeding years, and the area it enclosed was the focus of almost all the work during the life of the state commissions.

The Board of Agriculture held a meeting on Tuesday morning, April 28, at eleven o'clock in Boston's Commonwealth Building to discuss the gypsy moth and develop a program to carry out the mandates of the legislative act. The entomologists did not wait long to cash in on the state's largesse; there was an item on the agenda asking the legislature for even more money.[17] Thirty-two board members were present, as well as Charles Fernald and Edward Forbush. The act was read by Secretary Sessions; Shaler described the situation; and Fernald answered entomological questions. Forbush spoke about the costs of the proposed campaign, estimating that the following year at least $50,000 would be required. The commissioners held out hope that the moth had not made such a great expansion in such a short time but that the apparent increases discovered were the result of better reporting.

Operations of the interim commission were put into effect quickly. It reopened the office facilities and warehouse used by the first commission and took stock of the contents. It published a set of eleven rules and regulations

Map of 1891 showing the spread of the gypsy moth
from its original point of infestation.
From *The Gypsy Moth.*

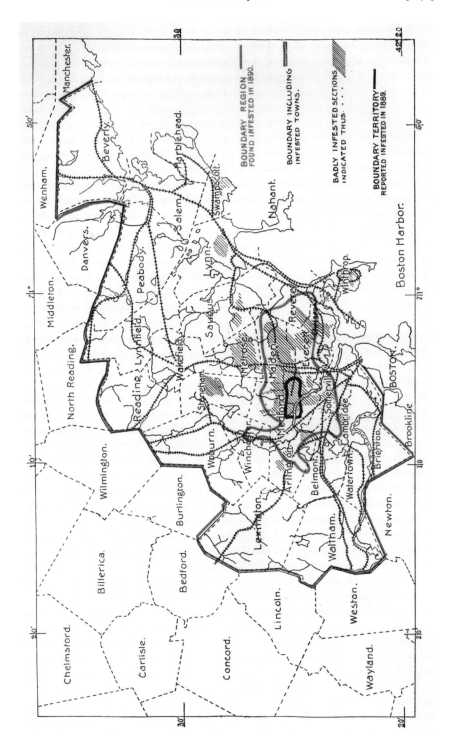

for the general public and had them widely distributed. Citizens were forbidden to move any life form of the gypsy moth from one place to another. Residents and businessmen of Medford, Everett, Chelsea, Malden, Melrose, and Arlington were prohibited from driving wagons with hay, manure, wood, bark, trees, rags, lumber, or shrubbery without a written permit from the board and without covering their wagons with canvas tarpaulins. Teamsters were told to expect delays at checkpoints while their vehicles and cargoes were inspected.

Forbush was certainly mindful of the conditions that had doomed the first commission, for he took extraordinary steps to ensure that all actions of his administration would withstand any audit. Meticulous record keeping was instituted for everything done, from hours at work to numbers of individual insects destroyed. Items of equipment, such as axes, were obtained by purchase order. Each axe was stamped with a serial number before being issued, and each man was to use and be responsible for only the axe he was issued. A journal of the axe was kept and its condition noted each time it came in for a new handle or sharpening. No axe could be discarded until a committee member or his designee had examined it and signed a written document condemning it. Lists of condemned property were kept indefinitely. Records were kept in this manner for every piece of equipment in the committee's inventory from two-ton spraying wagons to pocket-sized inspection mirrors.

Forbush's Army I

Forbush complained for the duration of the campaign that he could never find enough qualified men to fill the positions available, even though the great waves of immigration that Massachusetts was still experiencing during the 1890s included a large percentage of able-bodied men between the ages of fifteen and forty-five.[18] But Forbush required that any man hired be able to speak and read English, which most of the immigrants could not, and every man was compelled to make a written application, tell about himself, give as many references as he could, and swear that he did not have a police record. There were tough vision standards, as well. Lists of acceptable applicants were kept, and men were hired in the order they applied. There was no age restriction, but any boy hired was expected to do a man's work. No inquiries were made into the applicant's religion, politics, or associations outside of work.

At the lowest level of Forbush's hierarchy were the laborers who did most of the actual work of scraping trees, collecting egg masses, killing larvae, and operating spray apparatus. Although the wages of a gypsy moth fieldworker

were considered good, his life was not pleasant, since it required subservience to quasi-military authorities of questionable competence, subjection to the harshest weather, and submission to long, grinding hours of service. There were no benefits. Incapacitated workers were dismissed and replaced by others, although if a man had training, experience, and a good record, he would likely be hired back once he regained his health. One visitor noted "the pains taken in examining the men for field work and the almost military exactness required of them in their labor."[19]

A training course of a few weeks was mandatory for all employees. Workers tolerated their schooling with varying amounts of grace but among themselves referred to Forbush's educational efforts as "caterpillar kindergarten." A workman's wages started at $1.50 per day, and after three weeks of satisfactory service basic pay was increased by fifty cents. Discipline was as strict as the men would tolerate. No smoking, drinking, or profane language was allowed while on duty. Five minutes' loafing on the job was punished by forfeit of an hour's wages. Fieldworkers were issued police-style caps and numbered blue badges; failure to wear the cap and badge while on duty caused immediate dismissal, and a lost badge cost a full week's pay. Each day's work began and ended with a military-style formation and calling of the roll. The men addressed their superiors as "sir."[20]

No laborer was assigned to work in the town where he lived, so all workmen had to incur additional time and expense for commuting. Regardless of the distance they traveled, inspectors called the roll at seven o'clock each morning. The length of the workday was nine hours at the designated location, not including the time taken for morning and evening roll calls, equipment maintenance, meals, and other duties and obligations. These requirements made the actual workday twelve or more hours for some men, in particular the "special police" assigned to inspect wagons leaving the infested district. Sixty-hour weeks were not only common but expected. The *Rules and Regulations for Agents and Employees of the Commonwealth* listed the roll call time at the conclusion of work not as a specific hour but as "night."[21] Despite the long hours of summer daylight, men reported leaving for work and returning home in the dark.

Above the "privates" in this army were the inspectors, who wore red badges and whose jackets and pants were a light blue similar to the uniforms of postal workers. An inspector was responsible for a squad of four to six men, commonly called a "gang." Inspectors were required to carry "section books" of one hundred pages in which they kept meticulous records of the fieldwork: the number of trees, buildings, fences, walls, hedges, and other objects inspected daily; the number of each on which a moth was found; the

number of each form of the moth found and destroyed by hand on each estate; the number of trees cut or treated by banding, burlapping, cementing, or scraping; and the number of acres of brush or woodland burned over.[22]

Inspectors warned passersby of spraying, ensured that windows of nearby houses were closed, prevented spraying crews from getting drift on themselves, and ascertained that only marked trees were treated. The inspectors were also charged with reporting any damages caused by the workers, the particulars of accidents on the job, and "the language and means used by persons obstructing their work."[23] They also kept time records of their men and did their best to sort out the "new and contradictory orders [that were] issued every other day or so."[24] Only inspectors were allowed to mix batches of poison in the field or to draw water for the tanks from standpipes.

Next higher in rank were the special inspectors, garbed in dark police blue topped with a white cap. Later, six superintendents were added to ease the demand for Forbush's personal supervision of large areas, and later still the superintendents were provided with assistants. (The "supers" were kidded that the dainty white fringes on their badges were appropriate for men who did not have to get dirty doing real work.) At the top of the army was Field Director Forbush, who wore civilian clothes and visited the combat zones in a private carriage pulled by a fast horse. An ever increasing staff at the office and the storehouse supported fieldworkers, sometimes numbering as high as thirty employees. These included Forbush's personal secretary, clerks, typists, stenographers, cartographers, janitors, quartermaster, machinists, mechanics, and a chemist.

Also included in the army was a small, clandestine group of men called "spotters," who were paid to spy on the others, moving constantly from place to place, observing from secret locations, and reporting any rule violations back to Forbush; they traveled by horse and bicycle, and were despised by the regulars. Further, at Fernald's request and in keeping with the notion that the gypsy moth campaign would be a test bed for economic entomology, a small "experimental force" was created (later renamed the "scientific corps"), which consisted mostly of college men whose work in the field would be along different lines than that of the average laborer. As the field force became known as the "gypsy moth army," one of the original members of the experimental force wrote to his college newspaper: "The word 'army' was applied first, I think, by the newspaper men, and as if to further carry out the ideas the writer at one time received an order from the Director to allow Mr. ——— to report to the office at noon 'as he had been detailed for duty in the experimental squad.' Quite military, was it not?"[25]

First Forays

By March 19 the nucleus of the field force for the summer of 1891 began to form when nine students from the agricultural college were released from their classes and reported to the agriculture offices in Boston. There they received instructions and were dispatched to Malden. They were joined the next day by fewer than a dozen men who had worked under Rawson. Forbush had culled most of Rawson's roster by laying out stringent standards, hiring only those he felt were fitted by both nature and training for the work that lay ahead. The experienced men had done little more than burn egg masses off the trees, while Forbush and the college boys had no experience at all. They would have to learn how to recognize the eggs of the gypsy moth and distinguish them from the eggs of native moths, how to recognize larvae and pupae, and then how to teach all of what they had learned to new employees. So little was known about the moth or its habits that any man with experience in the natural sciences was delegated to observe the habits of the enemy and report back to headquarters all he had learned.

The force numbered sixteen men when work began on March 20. Forbush took them all to the Gilman Osgood farm in Belmont to make their first attempt at eradicating the gypsy moth; he selected the Osgood farm because the infestation there was reported to be small and isolated. It was perhaps predictive that an unpleasant surprise awaited them: the colony turned out to be neither as small nor as isolated as they thought. The recruits destroyed egg masses during the morning but stopped later in the day to make their initial attempt at scouting, which provided another vexing discovery: even their inexpert inspection revealed many other colonies thriving in the area.

The college men went on to work in the experimental corps, while most of the men who had worked under the first commission were given the rank of inspector and sent to scout the extent of the infested region.[26] Scouting continued in a cursory fashion during the spring with the idea of finding all existing gypsy moth footholds in the territory and making maps that would enable the field superintendents to demarcate their areas of responsibility. J. O. Goodwin of Medford, a civil engineer, did the mapping. While this task was in progress, Forbush continued increasing the field force whenever he could find the right men to hire. As new squads of men were formed, they were assigned to an inspector and sent into the worst areas of Medford and Malden to pick egg clusters and discover how the clusters were hidden.

More scouting was undertaken, beginning in Medford and working through forty-two cities and towns. The colonies and locations of the moth increased on a weekly basis, and the number of men hired soon rose to over one hundred. By the end of May the tally of infested towns had reached fifteen.

Substantial new colonies were found in Lexington and Melrose. Thirty town-
ships were infested, including Revere, Saugus, Wakefield, and Winchester.
Forbush pulled his recruits out of Medford and Malden and sent them to the
infested regions of the outlying towns. The only good news was that for the
moment, colonies in the woodlands were few in number, small in size, and
widely scattered.[27]

The Dexter Elm and Other Revelations

The commissioners visited the infested communities to talk with citizens and
found them nearly unanimous in their opposition to Riley's all-out spraying
assault. Most believed that spraying gypsy moth larvae would not work and
that destroying egg masses was the quickest, safest, and most effective way to
combat the insect.[28] The towering elm trees lining many of the streets, however, posed a severe test for either spraying or handpicking. The greatest of
these was the two-hundred-year-old elm on the Dexter estate in Malden, a
magnificent specimen 110 feet tall with a circumference of 29 feet at the base
and a leafy crown 104 feet in diameter. During the previous outbreak unchecked numbers of swarming gypsy moth larvae had completely defoliated
trees of nearly this size in less than three days.

The workers were daunted by the request that Forbush made of them.
Forbush said later that he had also harbored doubts about clearing such a
large tree but did not let on to his men. The plan elicited much laughter from
the citizens, who told Forbush he would need a balloon to get his men to the
top of the tree.[29] Forbush selected four of his most experienced workers and
sent them into the elm to rid it of egg masses. They used a sixty-five-foot
fireman's extension ladder as a means of gaining access to the mighty elm, a
ladder so heavy it required six men with block and tackle to deploy it.

Working without safety nets, the men scraped egg masses from the trunk to
the very top of the tree, risking their lives by inching out as far as they dared
on the slender young branches in the crown. In the most famous photo taken
during the gypsy moth campaign, the daredevils in the tallest branches seem
to disappear into the massiveness of the tree. The first crew removed
thousands of egg clusters over a period of four days before announcing that
the tree had been cleared. The following morning Forbush sent a second group
of workers into the same tree, and before they were through they found another six hundred egg masses. Forbush learned that the eggs were not easy
to find despite being hidden in plain view, that even experienced men working close to known egg mass concentrations could overlook them by the
hundreds, and that there was value in using fresh crews to examine areas

The Dexter Elm on the Dexter estate in Malden.
Posed photo probably taken in 1894 or 1895.
From *The Gypsy Moth.*

previously worked over. A final lesson was learned when egg clusters that both crews had missed hatched at the start of the caterpillar season.

Pondering Parasites, Probating Pesticides

Fernald continued to vacillate on the subject of parasites and predators, his instincts as a scientist conflicting with the demands of economic entomology. He had not rejected the systematic approach to investigating insects and believed that he should be free to work in whichever mode seemed to him appropriate for the situation. These opposing pressures led him to investigate parasitic insects and establish insectaries at Amherst and Malden while maintaining an official stance in opposition to the idea. The gypsy moth commission held meetings on the subject and, urged on by Nathaniel Shaler, began to push Fernald to explore the possibility of importing parasites and other natural enemies of the gypsy moth. The commissioners' recommendations were sent up to Secretary Sessions, who then passed them on to Fernald, as in this example written on March 17: "What Prof. Shaler suggests is that you open a correspondence with men you knew in Europe in regard to the importation of parasites of the G. M. . . . Shaler thinks they could be procured by you through your professional connections. . . . I understand the idea to be to open a correspondence as preliminary to sending the parasites when we want them if we want them."[30] Fernald had already been through the drill often enough to know the Europeans were likely to lack enthusiasm for the idea. Moreover, but the project bogged down when Shaler received notice that his mother was dying and departed Cambridge for his family home in Kentucky.

In April the commission's headquarters was moved from Medford to Malden, where better facilities were available and rail links were more numerous. The Malden building on Commercial Street was an old livery stable built on piles six feet above swampland on every side except the street, and everyone who worked in it disliked the structure. Fernald and his assistants prepared a room in which they began experiments with arsenical insecticides. So many subject and control caterpillars died that the professor could not tell if the deaths were due to the insecticides or to the unhealthful surroundings. The test results were thus thrown into question. The testing indicated, however, that Paris green was still the insecticide of choice, though at that time there were not many others to try. Paris green was a formula of 40 percent copper and 60 percent arsenic that burned foliage at strengths as low as four ounces in fifty gallons of water. London purple, an alternative arsenical, burned the foliage even worse, and contact insecticides such as whale oil and kerosene-emulsion types were unsuited for general-purpose spraying. Given the results

of these experiments, then, the committee ordered more than a ton of Paris green for use during the summer.

On April 28 the Board of Agriculture met and officially chose Sessions, Shaler, and Appleton as "a committee with full powers to exercise all the duties and powers conferred by . . . House Bill No. 228."[31] The interim commission was dissolved and replaced by a committee consisting of the same three men. Sessions was appointed both secretary and chairman. Between the funds remaining from the previous commission and an appropriation of $50,000 on June 3, 1891, the committee had roughly $74,000 available for fieldwork.

Discouraging Citizens

Fifty thousand copies of the law of 1891 were printed and distributed wherever the moth was found. A bulletin of information and a colored plate of the moth were created, and thousands of copies were distributed throughout the state. One hundred and fifty specimen cases containing mountings of the moth in various stages of its life cycle were prepared and set up for exhibition in post offices and other public places within the infested territory.

Citizens were instructed not to remove or alter special marks placed on trees, fences, or buildings by fieldworkers. They were also told not to scrape or remove egg masses unless supervised by a fieldworker but were encouraged to burn all scraps and rubbish on their property. Destructive searches that resulted in damage to walls, fences, and other property would be repaired, or the owner could make the repair himself and request reimbursement. Residents were encouraged to screen their windows and to call in their dogs when state agents entered their premises.

The purpose of the rules was to eliminate the public from any but the most trivial aspects of the work. In this regard the gypsy moth leaders were of one mind. Remembering the events of the previous year, they considered that citizen apathy and opposition had been more detrimental to the work than the bungling efforts of an inexperienced commission. They thought the idea that citizens could provide any effective pressure against such a widely distributed insect was absurd. The economic entomologists wished to eliminate all disruptive influences on their experiment and viewed the citizens of the Commonwealth as incapable of doing such work themselves or understanding the work when others did it. The committee and its field director did not even take into account the fiercely independent streak of farmers and fruit growers in the Bay State who were opposed not so much to controlling the moth as to letting the state's minions trespass on their land.

The reasons against enlisting schoolboys to collect eggs, as expressed by some of the most intelligent men of the time, present a glimpse into the mind-set of the era. The committee members were convinced that young boys would regard the undertaking from an economic viewpoint and set up seasonal businesses collecting eggs for profit. They would thus defeat the process by not reporting every location or not collecting all the egg masses they found but leaving large areas of infestation unmolested in order to guarantee a bountiful supply of egg masses the following year. When this contention was first expressed at the meeting of March 4, 1891, everyone in the room found the argument so convincing that not a single person spoke out against it.

[CHAPTER 7]

Summer 1891

WHEN J. O. GOODWIN's mapping was finished, the infested region was divided into sections, and each was assigned to a foreman or an inspector. Additional men were hired and trained, a process that continued all summer until the field force numbered 242. The committee inspected residential areas treated by the first commission to determine whether earlier work had been effective. Workmen dismantled fences, pulled up wooden boardwalks, tore apart the steps of houses, and entered buildings, actions that at first astonished the public. Although few egg masses were found on trees, some cellars were badly infested, and quarts of eggs were removed. Ripping apart steps and piazzas yielded bumper crops of egg masses while creating a reservoir of ill will among the populace.

Section eight of Medford, which included the house at 27 Myrtle Street where Trouvelot had pursued his will-o'-the-wisp thirty years earlier, now contained houses, shops, and factories. In 1886 the Andersen Pressed Brick Company constructed a facility on land that included a portion of Trouvelot's back yard. The streets leading into the city center featured gardens and orchards on both sides, and three thousand heavily wooded acres in the Middlesex Fells lay just a quarter-mile away. As the committee glumly noted, "Here we have all the requisites for the sustenance of the insect and all facilities for its transport in all directions."[1]

The first commission had treated section eight extensively, but agents who entered the district in March 1891 were alarmed by the conditions they found. The brush and woodland contained so many egg masses that they could not have been destroyed by hand even if all the men available had been put to work. Female moths had been present in such great numbers at egg laying that thousands had deposited their eggs on the ground in plain sight. Others had crawled into an old stone wall and covered it with egg clusters. Workers tore down the wall and inspected every rock. The number of larvae calculated to hatch from just this one wall ran into the millions, which Forbush said would have "let loose a destroying host upon the entire neighborhood."[2]

Cleaning the yard of the Andersen Pressed Brick Company disheartened the workers, for the entire premises were infested. The men inspected 232,195 individual bricks (some of which were completely covered with egg masses), scraped them clean, and burned the eggs on the spot. Workers ripped up floorboards of sheds in the yard to get at the egg masses underneath, repeated the procedure on the wallboards, then tore out everything under the roof. The destructive search for egg masses weakened some sheds to the point of collapse; these structures were pushed over and burned. A guard was posted at the gate, and every brick shipped out was inspected. Workers sent to clear the Muller Brothers Tannery in North Cambridge burned 30,000 egg clusters, but in most other places egg clusters were so numerous that no attempt was made to count them.

The egg masses destroyed in the first six weeks of work filled eight horse-drawn carts and prevented the hatch of 400 million caterpillars. This number included only clusters destroyed by hand; no records were kept for those destroyed by other means. Field equipment was expanded to include small, specially made oil stoves in which eggs were burned. In an effort to destroy egg masses on the ground, the leaves and underbrush were saturated with crude petroleum oil and set ablaze. This process was not effective because much of the oil soaked into the ground before it could be ignited, and the blaze was too weak to consume the eggs. In experiments with the air-pumped naphtha burners used by painters and plumbers to produce a hot flame, egg masses on trees and rocks could be incinerated, causing the eggs inside to burst like corn in a popper.

Meanwhile, the ice melted in the northern latitudes, but the Newfoundland trekkers departed without Forbush. The never-would-be leader of that expedition found himself in command of a much more imposing organization and in possession of far more power and authority than he had ever experienced before. Hundreds of men awaited his orders, and he insisted that they do a thorough job, adhere to the high standards he set, and work over the same ground again and again until it was swept clean of the insect.

Joined in Battle

By the middle of April the gypsy larvae began hatching and feeding. This was the moment the economic entomologists had been waiting for: the mighty blow that would knock the invaders down by the millions and clear the infested area within a single season was about to be struck. There was no lack of opportunity for engagement. Near McGowan's Tannery in Medford, larvae gushed from between the walls of the tannery building and were collected by the pailful.[3] One resident of Medford estimated that he saw a million

A typical "heavyweight" sprayer in the field, circa 1891.
From *The Gypsy Moth.*

caterpillars just at the intersection of Fountain and Salem Streets. Because Forbush had abandoned work in the center districts, the hatch in Medford and Malden was unhindered, and larvae were exceptionally numerous there. Saugus too experienced heavy infestations, with residents reporting that they could hardly go out the doors of their houses.[4]

Misfortune and confusion occurred at once. The abnormal and extended hatch of the larvae that began in mid-April did not conclude until June 17. By July 10 the moth could be found everywhere in all its forms; scouts even reported the presence of newly laid egg clusters.[5] Since Forbush barely had plans in place for fighting the moth in its successive individual stages, neither he nor the committee knew what to do when confronted by all the stages at once, and Fernald, too, was confounded. With the state's foot soldiers engaged completely, Forbush ordered his mechanized units into the field. More than thirty teams and some 230 men were employed to carry the spraying forward: "When the caterpillars appeared, spraying was commenced with a large force of men and teams equipped with hogsheads of paris green and water, pumps, hose, ladders, oil suits, etc.—an extensive and expensive outfit."[6]

Twenty heavyweight rigs were sent into Medford, and the rest were deployed on the periphery of the infested area. The driver and a helper alternated

stints at the pump while standing on a plank that was supported at one end by the top of the pesticide tank and at the other by a special brace raised on poles above the teamster's seat. The pump required a strong and continuous effort to maintain pressure. The discomfort of the workers was increased by the requirement that they work in the warm days of late spring wearing their uniform jackets.

The spray crews were instructed to work toward the center of the infested region, slaughtering the gypsy armies as they went. The rigs were designed for use on smaller trees in orchard rows, consequently they were fitted with short hoses and lacked throw. If the trees to be sprayed were tall, the spray men mounted stepladders to gain a few extra feet of height. For very tall trees the nozzle man was instructed to climb the tree, followed by helpers bearing the heavy hoses, and to spray from below as they ascended. All the spraying crews were subjected to large amounts of drifting and dripping pesticides.

Wagon checks were tried again after the larvae emerged. Shaler, Forbush, and several inspectors supervised the work of the police personally, but the examination of individual carts and wagons was abandoned after two weeks by vote of the committee when it became obvious that the manpower, time, and energy could be better utilized elsewhere. Forbush regarded wagon checks as so ineffective that he once said he believed "if a man had an edict published against carrying yellow dogs out of the infested regions they might be carried out in a carriage and be missed by such an inspection."[7]

A small number of men sent to check reports of moth activity found road-side infestations in six more towns, areas which, added to those already known, proved too large for the force. Once again Forbush abandoned work in Malden and Medford and sent detachments to the outlying areas. As state crews abandoned the center, local governments were forced to take over the work there, tending and replenishing the tarred paper strips put on their trees for cankerworms and gypsy moths the year before. Disgusted residents ignored the committee's edict not to work and resumed battling the hordes of larvae. The hatch was largest in Medford and Malden, and local crews visited the trees repeatedly to refresh the sticky barriers, using their heavy brushes to apply new printer's ink and crush the caterpillars under the bands. Forbush, impressed by how much protection the bands provided, admitted that the banding work alone averted the much-feared total defoliation of all the trees in these two communities.

To the consternation and dismay of all, however, it became evident that Paris green did not work well on gypsy caterpillars. The crews spraying on the periphery suffered failures and, after advancing inward for several days without effect, retreated to the periphery for second and third sweeps. As a consequence of spraying these infested areas more than once, half of the

communities scheduled for spraying were not reached during the summer. If Fernald and the economic entomologists were surprised by these events, the populace was not. Citizens had warned the committee not to expect good results from spraying, and the summer's events proved them right. The remarks of citizens also had their effect on the moth gangs and even on some of the young entomologists, such as Dexter M. Rogers, working in the field for the first time. Rogers was not impressed with modern technology and chemicals: "During 1891 we sprayed almost continuously while the larvae were in existence. I made up my mind that spraying was useless with extermination in view. . . . The only way—and I have advocated it to our director and to the employees—is to get down and dig for them. Those we cut in two we know have been killed. When we treat an egg cluster we know it is killed. Science is a nice thing, but thorough work is better. Eternal vigilance is the only thing that will get the last one."[8]

Work was further slowed by unreliable equipment, and frequent breakdowns required that the apparatus be disassembled and cleaned barehanded by workers in the field. Cracks appeared so frequently in metal pump flanges and fittings that Forbush ordered the storehouse to be kept fully stocked with complete sets of replacement parts. The insecticides corroded the hoses within a few days, requiring maintenance that took the sprayers out of service. Pumps with leather valves were especially trouble-prone, and the metallic filters on the suction line corroded after just a few days' use. Forbush stipulated that each nozzle on each wagon be flushed twice a day by turning it toward the bottom of the tank and pumping at maximum pressure for five full minutes.[9] Piston pumps had no sealing rings, and messy packing made of hemp or cotton wicking saturated with oil, tallow, and black graphite had to be manually wound around the piston and secured with a packing nut before the pump would work.

The state recalled its thirty rigs and upgraded them to double their spraying capacity. They were sent back into the field, only to become stuck in rough woodland terrain again. The heavy wagons were once more withdrawn from the brush and set to work on the streets. Crews were ordered to spray all living vegetation within two hundred feet of any plant on which a caterpillar was found. Since nearly all vegetation hosted larvae, this order resulted in the spraying of just about everything, as Scudder had predicted. Citizens were alarmed to see their homes, yards, and gardens drenched with arsenic when there was no sign of caterpillars.

Twelve lightweight spraying units utilizing fifteen-gallon tanks were dispatched to outlying areas. These tanks could be removed from their horse carts and carried across rough terrain by a crew of two. The units were filled from hydrants where available, or their tanks replenished with water pumped

from wells or streams. Medium sprayers equipped with tanks of 100 gallons or less required a crew of three; the heavyweight sprayers with 160-gallon tanks were assigned a crew of five: two men were needed to operate the pump, two to spray, and an inspector to direct the operation. The teamster became the sixth crewman when spraying. His job was to agitate the insoluble arsenic mixture by means of a special paddle built into the tank.

Inspectors ensured that the men wore their badges at all times while spraying and enforced the no-smoking rule during working hours. They also tried to prevent the hose from kinking and the spray from dripping on the workmen's clothing—the latter an impossible task. A fifty-foot section of heavy rubber hose was the most that one man could carry. Each wagon was equipped with eight lengths, but two lines of two hundred feet were employed for most operations. A toolbox containing wrenches, packing materials, and other tools needed to disassemble a pump was sent into the field with every wagon. Forbush prized men who could strip a pump and repair it, and it irked him no end when tardy budget appropriations cost him the services of his skilled mechanics. Without field repair, a sprayer had to be sent to the shop for work that could keep it there for several days of an already short spraying season.

Operating the pump exhausted the men. In the hot days leading into summer, fatigue became a constant factor, and one of the main complaints about the double-acting pumps was that the men often had to stop and rest. E. G. Lodeman called the labor of maintaining line pressure with a hand-operated pump "severe."[10] One student from the Massachusetts Agricultural College wrote for his college magazine:

> The work we are at now is spraying trees with paris green. Each inspector has a barrel mounted on a one-horse cart of some kind. To the barrel which holds about one hundred gallons of water is attached a pump and four hundred feet of hose in two lines of varying lengths. To work this we have four men and the driver. Carrying the hose up the trees is the hardest part of the men's work in spraying. But working the pump is no snap . . . (the job) takes all our time, leaving us so tired at night that we cannot study or do much of anything else.[11]

Popular opposition to spraying led to mass meetings in Medford, although little of consequence resulted. Citizens who wanted no arsenic on their property often turned their garden hoses on freshly sprayed fruit and ornamental trees. Some landowners were arrested for preventing moth exterminators from entering their lands, and one citizen who tried to cut a hose on a spraying tank was hauled before a magistrate. Henshaw noted that the fumbling attempts of

the field force "increased an already existing strong feeling against the use of Paris green, and many landowners did all in their power to annul or neutralize the work."[12] This aspect troubled the college men, who noted that "although we have many amusing experiences with people, it is not exactly a pleasure to invade a man's premises against his will, and know that he would kick you out if he was able."[13]

The citizens did support banding and burlapping trees, or picking larvae and scraping egg masses by hand. But they would endure the caterpillar swarms, tolerate the disgusting odors, and suffer the consequences to their trees and gardens rather than have arsenic sprayed in their yards, on their houses, and over their vegetables and fruits, and they did not believe the entomologists such as "Professor" Riley who tried to convince them the practice was safe.[14]

Riley's Return

During the spray effort, Riley returned to Massachusetts and went into the field with Henshaw to advise the crews, but the techniques of spraying were immaterial because the pesticides didn't work. Riley, who could not believe that arsenical poisons were not effective, fell back on the usual arguments about incompetent applications and applicators. He remained convinced that any delinquencies were the fault of the people rather than of the plan. Disturbed by the complete failure of his single-spraying strategy, he could not understand the refusal of the gypsy moth larvae to die when poisoned with the purest, finest, bolted arsenic applied in the most intelligent fashion.

Riley had chosen wisely when he engaged Henshaw to be his agent in Massachusetts. Both men knew how to cut to the quick, and neither was hesitant to express his views. As if to compensate for his lack of social graces and his short stature, nature had provided Henshaw with remarkable eyes and a mind that was equally sharp in seeing the point in a situation. Riley was especially interested in biological observations of the larvae and charged Henshaw with the task of noting any behavior of the gypsy moth in America that differed from its behavior in Europe.[15] Henshaw was astonished to find that in some places parasitic insects were present in great numbers, and he was appalled when the executors of the war not only failed to use the parasites to their advantage, but also destroyed them: "I saw in Medford a district where a parasitic fly was fairly swarming, and shortly after that the woods and brush were cut down and burned without any intimation of one of the best causes of the extermination of the insect being used."[16]

Nevertheless, the more Riley looked at the operation the more distressed he became and the more he blamed the committee for not devoting enough

time to the undertaking. He claimed that the treatment of trees had been rushed and the spraying had been uneven, and he was appalled to find that wagon crews were using nozzles intended for ordinary garden hose.[17] Although the spraying had nearly eliminated canker worms and tussock moth larvae, it had not delivered much of a blow against the gypsy moth. Riley complained long and loud to anyone who would listen and managed to offend almost everyone on the project:

> The members of the committee having the matter in charge were unable to give much personal attention to the work, and the spraying was being performed in a crude and unsatisfactory manner and without entomological supervision of an advisory character. No well directed and carefully conducted experiments had been made to ascertain what special methods are best for this particular case. . . . [I]n no instance, where trees were examined that had been treated, was it difficult to find living caterpillars on them.[18]

Riley later wrote to Henshaw that he felt "a good deal discouraged and disappointed" in what he had seen but wished to refrain for the time being from further public comment on the "blunders made and the want of intelligent guidance." He complained to Henshaw that so much valuable time had been squandered he could no longer see the value in helping the committee in any official capacity, after which he sent a shipment of a dozen cyclone nozzles to Sessions.[19]

Riley published the stenographic report of the March 4 meeting in *Insect Life*, and the distribution of this transcript annoyed Shaler greatly. He felt that exposing the discussion to the public was a reckless act, even though Riley had first offered the transcript to all present for their comments and revisions. Shaler was further insulted by Riley's assertions that the commissioners were slackers and later said that he had lost all confidence in Riley's judgment. Henshaw's report, delivered to Riley on December 7, 1891, and published by the federal agricultural department early in 1892, supported Riley's contentions. While noting that the committee members had given more time to the work than could have been reasonably expected, Henshaw said that "it was undoubtedly a mistake to appoint men to look after such important work . . . who were already more than occupied with other work. The fact that they were appointed with the distinct understanding that their services should be given gratuitously, while not equivalent to saying that their services would be slight, does indicate that they would be secondary to more important affairs."[20]

Riley did not endear himself to Sessions when he made it plain that the

extermination program was going to collapse unless changes were made at once. Sessions did not want to hear even a whisper that he should reorganize a committee that had just been reorganized two months before. Riley pressured Sessions to appoint Fernald as advising entomologist even though Fernald, who still had no official relationship to the board, had already begun the experiments Riley claimed were lacking, and Forbush had gone to great lengths to assign only his best men to the spray wagons.[21] Riley did not understand that the gypsy moths' ability to tolerate arsenic bordered on the supernatural. The pesticides had failed so utterly that workers were compelled to switch to crude contact insecticides after the fourth molt (when the insect sheds its skin). These formulations were a mixture of fish oil or whale oil soap diluted in boiling water and were used only when caterpillars could be drenched in large numbers.

After failing to persuade anyone in authority, Riley concluded that extermination would have to be abandoned. He continued to urge the Massachusetts men to reconsider their approach but found that he was largely disputing himself. His original arguments against anything except extermination by spraying had cost many valuable months, and it was likely now too late to make up lost time. Shaler, Sessions, and some other members of the committee had come to consider Riley a liability. Where they had once eagerly solicited his opinions, they now felt constrained to keep him at arm's length. For his part, Riley was "quite surprised that the committee is so unwilling to take my advice, although they are quite willing to express their thanks."[22] Later, he said that the condition of the campaign had been so disturbing to him that he was unable to discuss it without finding fault.[23] Returning to Washington, he recorded his visit to Massachusetts in the next issue of *Insect Life*, admitting that "as the possibility of extermination becomes doubtful, all effort looking to the control of the species as one to be continually dealt with grows in importance, and it is strongly recommended that an effort be made to introduce some of the natural enemies of the species which are known to occur in Europe."[24]

Thereafter, spray wagons surrendered their place of prominence to hundreds of foot soldiers bearing rolls of burlap. The simple technique of wrapping tree trunks with bands of cloth impressed everyone with its effectiveness and became the main method by which the larvae were combatted for the remainder of that season. Over 68,000 burlap bands were deployed during the summer, trapping millions of caterpillars. Forbush noted in his report for 1891 that one gang of three men who did nothing but visit burlap bands killed almost 120,000 caterpillars and pupae in just two days.[25]

Fernald had resisted pressure to formalize his relationship with the gypsy moth committee, and at the height of the summer's battles he made one more

attempt to have Henshaw take over as adviser. But Henshaw was becoming less enamored of insect extermination and had cooled to the idea of entanglement with the work as he became more involved in his duties at Cambridge. On June 18, 1891, Fernald was conscripted to act as the committee's adviser, making official the relationship that had existed unofficially since before the first commission was formed. Fernald accepted this obligation with reluctance and only after considerable persuasion by committee members, notably Nathaniel Shaler, who could twist an arm like few others. As Fernald said some years later: "I was invited down to meet [the committee] and they asked me to act as their entomologist, and I consented to do so after considerable urging on their part. I knew very well that it . . . was not to my advantage. It was a care and labor which I dreaded, but I entered into it in good faith and I have given this insect the best study of my life."[26] Fernald became very active in this capacity, visiting the field on many occasions and making suggestions and recommendations. This burden became so great that he had to be assisted by one of his most talented students, Ephraim Porter Felt, who later served as the state entomologist of New York. Fernald also had to engage a man to take his place in Amherst whenever he was in Boston, and for the duration of the campaign he paid for his substitute out of his own pocket.[27]

In Washington, Riley pondered what to do once officials in Massachusetts had accepted the failure of chemical extermination. He had corresponded with the Reverend Henry Loomis in Yokohama, and during a visit to Washington, Loomis delivered some cocoons of the Apanteles parasite. Riley sent these to the gypsy moth committee, although no living insects emerged. During the summer Loomis also shipped Apanteles pupae to the Board of Agriculture in Massachusetts, but Sessions and Fernald made no mention of receiving them.[28] Loomis sent Riley some Japanese gypsy moth larvae as well, which arrived after Riley returned from Medford. None of the larvae was parasitized, but Riley believed that although they were of a different species—*Ocneria japonica*, larger than the European variety—the two species were related so closely that whatever insect parasitized one would also attack the other.

Travels Not Taken

The weakness of the chemical extermination strategy placed Fernald in a heightened state of apprehension. After receiving Sessions's letter of March 17 and continuing until the end of July, he tried without enthusiasm to arrange for shipments of parasites from other countries. Riley, Henshaw, and he held a series of discussions about who should travel to Europe. Fernald, who had the advantage of the long summer recesses observed by the colleges of his

time, could travel abroad between semesters and was no stranger to European entomologists. But he wondered how he could spend time overseas during the heaviest gypsy moth work and concluded that travel might not be possible for him. Henshaw did not want to go but said that Riley would make the trip instead. When Riley learned that Fernald had deferred to him, he wrote the professor to express mixed feelings about taking such an important role: "It is hardly accurate to say that I wanted to go. I urged that the effort not be postponed and also urged you as the best man available for the mission. I expressed my willingness to go on certain conditions, as, while the trip would be pleasant I should have to make many sacrifices in other directions."[29] Riley went on to express his belief that the matter should not be delayed, and that so much time had already passed it was not his willingness but his ability to make the trip that was the stumbling block. He reiterated his feeling that Fernald should go or, if that were not possible, send a trusted agent. He concluded by stating his wishes for Fernald's success, and added, "If I can be of any service in one way or another, command me."[30]

Fernald, unable to delegate anyone to go to Europe and arrange for parasite shipments, quickly lost what little interest he had in the idea. European entomologists considered the usefulness of imported parasites against the gypsy moth to be practically nil, and Americans regarded the idea of going abroad for this purpose as either a waste of time or an opportunity for a leisure voyage at somebody else's expense. The problem, as Fernald remarked a few years later, was that he could not get any qualified entomologists to take the idea seriously: "During the course of the work on this insect several very competent men offered to go abroad to bring over parasites. . . . When these cases were carefully examined it was found they wanted to take a pleasure trip to Europe at public expense. Prof. Riley wrote me frankly that he was getting tired and needed a few months rest and if he could get a matter of $15 a day he should like to go."[31] But Fernald clung to the idea that native parasites should be given a chance to prove their effectiveness and that otherwise the work against the gypsy moth, if not going very well, was at least going well enough. Riley was bewildered by Fernald's logic, as he mentioned to his staunch friend Henshaw: "I am utterly amazed at Prof. Fernald's published statement, which does not at all agree with what I saw myself and what you saw with me. . . . [I]f Professor Fernald considers that a Tachinid, which is in all probability a general parasite, will be of greater value than any foreign species could be, and if it is for this reasoning that he bases the action of the committee in deciding not to introduce any European parasites this year, all I can say is that his position is very weak indeed."[32]

Rising Birds

At about this time, workers noticed birds appearing wherever larvae were concentrated, and within the year more species were seen to feed upon the caterpillars in Massachusetts than in Europe. Forbush wrote: "Unfortunately, there were at that time only eleven observers on the force who could accurately identify birds in the field. . . . The notes made by them indicated that thirteen species of birds were feeding upon the moth in one or more of its forms."[33] Forbush required that any species of bird seen taking the larvae, pupae, or imagoes be reported to him at once. News from the field confirmed that cuckoos relished the larvae, eating up to twenty an hour and bringing numerous catches to their young. In fact, the cuckoos ate so many gypsy caterpillars that their stomachs were lined with the larvae's body hair. The gypsy moth workers loved the cuckoos, and as Forbush later wrote, "a gathering of cuckoos anywhere was looked upon as a sign of a caterpillar outbreak."[34]

Investigations soon revealed other birds too were taking hairy gypsy caterpillars. Baltimore orioles were adept at plucking larvae from their hiding places beneath the burlaps; bluejays were prized because they searched bark crevasses, cracks, and holes in trees for hidden larvae; and crows enjoyed snatching larvae that were hiding under branches. Catbirds flocked to infested areas and plunged without hesitation into the densest thickets and heaviest underbrush to pluck out both caterpillars and pupae from otherwise inaccessible concealment. Chickadees fed on the pupae and were seen taking female imagoes. Redstarts, kingbirds, and flycatchers took male moths on the wing. Red-eyed and yellow-throated vireos, always known to feed upon the hairy tent caterpillar, also found the gypsy caterpillar to their liking, and in voraciousness they were second only to cuckoos. Scarlet tanagers proved to be insatiable: Forbush recorded a single male tanager that ate thirty small gypsy moth caterpillars in five minutes and continued eating at that rate for eighteen minutes more.

Hot Spots

Despite the activities of birds and the labors of men, hot spots kept popping up all over the region that required teams of men deployed in one place to give up their work and rush to another. One such hot spot was in Arlington, about two miles due west of Medford, where a contingent of caterpillars was found attacking a grove of trees. The trees were sprayed, but spraying failed to kill the larvae, which then consumed the grass as they dispersed into the nearby woods. As the battle continued, sprays and fire killed uncounted thousands of

larvae, but thousands more survived to pupate in mid-July. The area was stony, and large numbers of caterpillars crawled beneath the rocks to pupate. Workers rolled field stones over and collected the pupae underneath at the rate of about one every three seconds, averaging eleven hundred per hour per man.

Another hot spot occurred in Swampscott, a seacoast community between Lynn and Marblehead, where a gang sprayed so extensively that the larvae became soaked with Paris green. When this failed to kill many, the entire location was drenched again. The battle continued until the larvae had stripped all the leaves over an area of three or four acres; the caterpillars appeared in such massive swarms that spraying with contact insecticides killed two bushels of them on just a few apple trees. Finally, six gangs of men with oil sprayers arrived to burn the larvae, all the underbrush, and anything else on which the insect might feed. At the H. W. Spurr estate in Arlington, field workers carried out pupae by the basketful and destroyed them by fire.

While these nasty little fights were taking place, the larvae were successfully pupating in the areas the men had abandoned.

The last female moths laid their eggs during the second week of July, and the major battles of 1891 ceased. About sixty-five men were dismissed and sent home. The remaining hundred or so men began to kill egg masses and clear brush, their numbers dwindling as summer turned into fall. Henshaw observed the search for egg masses as part of the report he was preparing for Riley: "The probability of the detection of every egg mass scattered over an area of fifty square miles seems very small, especially when it is remembered that they are placed in almost every conceivable situation upon the trunks, branches, and even the leaves of trees and shrubs, upon fences, the sides of houses, under stone walls, piazzas, board walks, etc. So far as my observations go the search for the eggs has been carefully done, though I have found masses of the eggs after the inspection of the locality had been completed."[35]

After the larvae pupated, the intensity of the conflict temporarily died away, but the attacks against the gypsy moth had left their mark on an outraged and horrified public. In comparison with this most recent work, the doings of Rawson's commission seemed benign and innocuous. Poison had flowed in copious amounts from the nozzles of the spray wagons as the chemical was sprayed repeatedly in a vain effort to kill the larvae. The spraying of ornamental and fruit trees in private yards had left houses and fences with grayish-white streaks of arsenic. Many cases were reported of residents and workmen sickened by accidental contact with the spray, but these instances were downplayed as much as possible because arsenic was believed to be the only useful chemical available. At least three cases of poisoning could not be easily dismissed, however: these occurred to several women who had arsenic

blown in their faces by capricious shifts in the spring breezes during spraying. The skin on the faces of two of the women had erupted into terrible blisters; the third, an older woman, was so severely affected that she almost died.[36]

The public was beginning to demand work in natural controls, but Sessions called upon Fernald to submit a report that would justify continued spraying. Fernald sent the report to Boston in early August, and Sessions replied: "Your report received just now. Thanks for the same. As Shaler says, if we have your approval we are willing to face the whole crowd of objectors including H. S. Official Entomologists. It will give us standing with the legislature next winter and with the people of the state who must pay the bills."[37]

In September, while Shaler was in Washington, he called on Riley at the Department of Agriculture. The meeting did not go well; Shaler again complained about the publication of the stenographic transcript in *Insect Life*, and Riley wrote to Henshaw shortly afterward that there was no reasoning with Shaler, whom he found opinionated beyond any rational justification and who had forgotten Riley's offer to submit the transcript to all concerned parties for verification. Riley told Henshaw, "I know that it is a truthful report as far as it goes, and if it had been a complete report of all that was said, I think Prof. Shaler would have had more reason to be offended."[38]

From November 20 through the end of December, about forty of the most experienced workers were deployed to make an inspection and were instructed to move outward from each infested town until they reached a town that was not infested. The moth was found in three additional cities, four additional towns, and two wards of Boston. Consequently the area occupied by the gypsy invaders was redrawn to include about two hundred square miles. The inspectors worked in haste to have their results tallied by January 1, 1892, so that the legislators would have their report by the fourth Wednesday in January; hence, many infested places were overlooked, and the report served to approximate the size of the infested region without accurately describing its condition. The constraints placed on Forbush caused him to ignore the wooded sections thought to harbor moths. This final inspection as well as all those made under his direction during the year had been limited to "the neighborhood of traveled highways."[39] It was also learned later that even Forbush's most experienced men were not as qualified as had been thought, and colonies sometimes escaped detection for several years.[40]

All those involved in the campaign at the highest level simply ignored everything that had gone wrong and claimed that the year's work had been a great success. The committee was not embroiled in any major scandal, and the gypsy moth was believed to be less invincible than had been thought. Forbush wrote that the limbs of trees in infested orchards that had given no harvest the previous year had actually broken down under the weight of all their fruit.

The moths had been so decimated by the fieldwork that examples of their destructiveness could be found only in Arlington and Swampscott. Sessions was sure the remaining pockets of infestation were very small, and he hinted that the remainder would be exterminated the following spring.[41] He boasted later that if all the eggs destroyed in 1891 had hatched and the caterpillars had survived to full growth, their aggregate weight would have been one hundred tons.[42]

[CHAPTER 8]

The Cyclone Burner (1892)

T HE MEMBERS of the gypsy moth committee were encouraged by their
apparent successes in 1891, but there were aspects of the situation that
continued to trouble them. Although they had begun their tenure with disdain
of the first commission's methods, within the year they were doing much the
same things themselves—spraying everywhere, felling trees, and setting the
scrub woods on fire. They had to admit that they found conditions greatly
improved wherever the first commission had worked, but there was ample
evidence that the scientific guidance that had failed Rawson had failed them
as well. Every passing day seemed to reveal some discouraging news. Eggs
hatched in fields that had been burned over twice the previous year, and the
fecundity of the moth never ceased to dismay them. The spraying on which
they relied once again proved ineffective. Gypsy larvae ate great quantities of
the poison without succumbing to its effects even though smaller doses killed
canker worms, tent caterpillars, and tussock moth larvae. The mobile spraying
squads were kept off balance the entire summer, dashing from one spot to
another, spraying with little effect and without ever finishing their task.

Riley had been in the state late in January to give a talk before the Massachusetts Horticultural Society in which he expressed his fear that the gypsy
moth was now "beyond control," and absent a massive and well-funded effort
he could see no reason for further attempts to exterminate it.[1] He also complained to Henshaw that he had noted "a concerted effort to misrepresent and
pitch into me" by members of the gypsy moth committee. The positions taken
by Fernald and the apparent lack of knowledge he saw in Forbush represented
a growing concern for him. He noted that an interview Forbush had given the
New England Farmer contained "a long list of mis-statements" to which he
felt obliged to reply, and he urged Henshaw to do the same.[2]

After 1891 the use of Paris green as a gypsy moth insecticide was for
the most part abandoned. This was a heavy blow for the committee to bear,
since Paris green was the best pesticide available, and there was nothing to
replace it except London purple, a concoction with even worse phytotoxic

characteristics. An apologetic Forbush wrote in his annual report for 1892 that the committee had sprayed only because it was "the method that had been most strongly recommended by the best authorities."[3] This was doubtless a sensitive issue all around, since the "authorities" were Fernald and Riley, two of the best entomologists in the country. The state of affairs unsettled Fernald, and after 1891 he began to have anguished doubts about the prospects for victory. The course of events had left him without alternatives, and he wrung his hands in frustration: "I tried [more experiments] myself and did not believe my own eyes, and tried it a second year, till I was convinced we had an insect that could eliminate more poison from its system than any insect I had ever before dealt with. Then the question arose, what could we do? What could we do if Paris green, the best insecticide known to us, would not destroy this insect? How could we deal with it?"[4]

The duties thrust upon him by the gypsy moth committee burdened Fernald, who was having difficulty finding enough time to meet his educational demands. He was going through an unhappy period at Amherst and had decided to leave that institution. He thought that a closer association with state work might solve his problems, although the question of his compensation had not been resolved to his satisfaction. On January 25 he wrote to Sessions about working out some arrangement to free him of his college duties while the campaign against the moth was in progress. Sessions begged off by saying he would have to discuss it with Shaler, who was out of town:

> I fear the trustees, president and faculty would be down on the committee if we arranged such a bargain. The people of the state would not relish your absence from the Hatch Station. Nothing I am sure would please the committee on gypsy moths more than to have your constant participation in their work. It would give us greater strength and prestige with the Legislature and the public. But the committee on agriculture have not yet acted on our appropriation and until we know what funds we are to have at our disposal we cannot "talk business."[5]

It was dawning on Forbush and Fernald that successfully concluding the war might take much longer than they had considered. To get the job done would require meticulous attention to matters of the finest detail, and forces under the committee needed to be increased in number and given much additional training. Men would have to be hired permanently to keep from losing them. Appropriations would have to be large enough to cover the payroll for twelve months and work enough found to keep men busy all year.

Efforts in the field had proved time-consuming. It took four men a full hour

to spray a single tree to Forbush's demanding standard. Not spraying correctly was worse than not spraying at all, since the tree would have to be sprayed again. Clearing a large roadside tree of egg masses also could take up to an hour if the tree had to be climbed, and a heavily infested tree took even more time and required an extra man. An experienced worker needed twenty minutes to clear egg clusters from an average fruit tree. If he worked nine hours without stopping, he might clear twenty-seven trees a day, a level of performance that was seldom approached in actual practice. Moreover, after the first man was done, a second of greater experience would have to examine every tree cleared and, if this second inspector found egg masses, he would have to clear the tree again, after which a third senior employee would perform another inspection. And there were millions of trees that needed attention.

Throughout the winter, the committee, its field director, and its entomologist devised their strategy for the year. The last scouting had been tabulated, and for the first time since the war against the moths began, the committee believed it finally knew the area occupied by the insects.[6] The field force would be used in the inhabited areas to hold the insects in check where they were most numerous. This would buy time for the field director to recruit and train a permanent force of men and for Fernald's staff at the research station to develop new approaches to extermination. The committee did not seem concerned if all the work could not be done at once, claiming that "Experience [has] shown that the moth can be eradicated, that it has been destroyed in many limited fields."[7]

The weather turned against the exterminators during the winter, often forcing a halt to egg destruction and further inspections. When possible, masses on trees along the roads were destroyed in order to lessen the chance of larvae spinning down onto passing wagons during the spring hatch. This emphasis on roadside work was done to compensate for the discontinued roadblocks. Before the hatch the trees were wrapped with sticky bands, which the committee hoped would provide a seasonal barricade that would not need to be checked every day. Through the winter of 1891–92, Forbush kept fifty men at work in Medford and Malden, believing that the concentrated efforts of even a small force could make a great difference. Although he was bound to Fernald's scientific point of view, Forbush had been impressed by the simplicity and effectiveness of burlaps and soon became a convert to the effectiveness of killing egg masses. The techniques were neither technological nor scientific, but they always worked. He noted in his annual report that if he had been able to send one hundred men to attend burlaps in Medford and Malden in the fall of 1891, the moths there could have been exterminated by that work alone.[8]

The committee and its leadership believed they had given a beating to the gypsy moth the previous year, even if it had been the result of archaic tactics. Had they been more experienced, they would have known that after a few years of massive outbreaks, moth populations generally declined for the next few years or even a decade, and during these periods the moth presented itself in a very innocuous way. Thus, the committee, perhaps lulled into a false sense of security, requested only $75,000 for the new year's work. The members thought more funding was not needed because of Forbush's difficulties in filling the ranks of his field force, and they were concerned that the state legislature, which was hoping for quicker and more favorable results, was becoming anxious about the amount of money required to destroy the moth. Although aware that the requested amount was too small, the committee later publicly blamed many of the year's disappointments on the lack of an adequate appropriation. This began a long-running and damaging confrontation with the legislature over the amount and timeliness of moth funds.

Shaler, who lived within the infested district, gave more time to his duties than most committeemen and claimed he had spent hundreds of hours examining the work in progress. The Board of Agriculture had been stung by the criticisms expressed in Henshaw's report to Riley, and every man on the committee regretted his decision to work without a salary. Each one felt he had put in too many hours, and one testified before a legislative hearing that the committeemen now believed they should be paid for their work.

The committee had managed to conserve a little over $5,000 from the appropriation of 1891, which it used to retain about forty-five experienced men at an average pay rate of $2.25 per day. These men did what they could, but heavy snows late in the season hampered their mobility. The committee presented its request for an appropriation as soon as the legislature convened in the early days of January 1892. But the $75,000 asked for was not granted in full until the first of March—a date the committee considered late, but it proved to be one of the earliest release dates and allowed work to start sooner than was possible in subsequent years.

The speed of legislative action was not nearly fast enough for Forbush, who had dismissed his best forty men at the end of January when his funds ran out. He complained that he was "obliged to discharge many faithful, efficient and experienced men, for want of money to pay their wages."[9] Most of these men found work elsewhere before money became available on March 1, so Forbush had to seek new men and train them. The rigorous screening of potential candidates, including new character references that he had set in place that year, further slowed the process of rebuilding. Most of the men were rejected for poor eyesight; a large percentage was eliminated for causes that were not made public. Forbush hoped that these new hires would be employed by the

state for the duration of the campaign. He wanted a dependable, stable group that would allow him to reduce the considerable amount of time that the experienced men were taken from the field to train the recruits. He considered the force hired and trained for 1892 to be one of the best ever to take the field, although its small number and lack of experience hampered it: "The inspection was not in all cases thorough, as a large proportion of the force engaged in it was necessarily composed of inexperienced persons, and there were not enough expert men to reinspect their work. Thus we were unable in the spring of 1892 to do thoroughly the work which might have been done in the fall of 1891 had sufficient money remained. We were also unable to secure and train men enough, in the short time at our disposal in the spring, to cover the entire field."[10]

Students from the agricultural college were still used to augment the field force during the summer, and each one was brought in at the rank of inspector and given charge of a section one mile square. This caused some resentment among the older men who did not like being directed by "boys," but the result seems only to have been a lot of grumbling. The young inspectors and their gangs had authority to "enter any place and do whatever we think necessary to destroy the eggs."[11] One young student wrote a brief account of some of his experiences for his college magazine, *Aggie Life*: "One or two have threatened to shoot the inspector if he came into his yard. Many inquire about the work and wish us success. . . . [W]e are obliged to go under all piazzas, to take the base boards off from picket fences, or sometimes to take a fence down entirely. In these cases the owners often object, sometimes with quite strong language, but when they see we pay no attention to them they give us no trouble."[12]

One inspector, S. R. Huston, said so many men had been hired to kill egg masses that the payroll quickly depleted the budget, causing a large percentage of the men to be laid off, and leaving too few to attend the burlaps. Huston did not believe that extermination was possible and said hardly anyone else believed it, either. Citizens freely expressed these opinions, but the workers did not. Employees did what was asked of them and gave the state a good day's work. The uncertain status of their jobs dampened their enthusiasm, however, and the constant layoffs made a career with the gypsy moth committee undesirable: "They hire three hundred men in June; discharge two hundred of them in August. . . . Two men dismissed claim to be equally as efficient as [one] retained. So the men in the summer know the place is only temporary and they do not care much. . . . [T]he majority of people were indifferent in regard to the matter and do not believe in it. They do not have any objections to the commission. They say, 'well, it gives employment to men so it does some good, but I don't believe they will exterminate the moth.' "[13]

The failure of pesticides caused renewed interest in natural predators and parasites, although such work was incidental because of the mandate for extermination. Five species of beetles and a number of spiders were seen eating caterpillars, but their effect was deemed slight. Fernald instructed workers to begin sending egg masses to field headquarters, where they could be inspected. He and his assistants examined twenty thousand eggs individually, found only one that was parasitized, and discontinued the effort.[14] Several parasites that attacked the gypsy moth pupa were discovered. Afterward, all dead pupae found in the trees of the outlying districts were presumed to have been killed by parasites and were left untouched so that the parasites could escape; all other dead pupae were collected and examined in the lab for signs of parasite attack. Fernald consulted some American specialists, Dr. W. G. Farlow and Dr. Roland Smith, about the use of "vegetable parasites" (molds and funguses) to control the gypsy moth and was told it would be a waste of time.[15]

His query about vegetable parasites reveals an intriguing side of Fernald: he investigated the subject of natural controls throughout the campaign without allowing any work along these lines to be implemented. In his capacity as entomologist of the Hatch Experiment Station he was free to pursue such work but not with funds appropriated by the General Court for extermination. He looked for the presence of disease as well, both as a hopeful matter for control of the gypsy moth and as an unwanted agent that might destroy predatory insects, but apparently never found anything conclusive. As he wrote to R. W. Glaser some years later: "I went down there every week and was around with the men in the field in every part of the infested region, and if they or the field director had noticed anything of the kind [disease] they would surely have told me, for they all knew that we were hunting for and breeding all the parasites we could find."[16]

Through *Insect Life*, Fernald kept abreast of the correspondence between C. V. Riley and Henry A. Loomis in Japan and of their attempt to bring Japanese parasites to America. On September 1, 1892, Loomis wrote to Riley: "I still believe the Ichneumon fly found here will destroy the Ocneria dispar. It will require demonstration to prove the contrary, as their food and habits are identical as far as I can learn. It is the destructive power of this microgaster that prevents the moth from being a formidable scourge in Japan. It is really wonderful how effectively it works."[18]

The committee asked Fernald to make a "close and critical" inspection and submit another report on the subject of importing parasites. He did so but consistently continued to recommend against importation. His opposition puzzled the committee and a number of scientists who asked what the compelling drawbacks were. Fernald presented the weak explanation that he wanted first to see whether native parasites would increase in number: "After

A cyclone burner in use against egg clusters in a rock wall, circa 1892.
From *The Gypsy Moth.*

making a close study and finding that our native parasites were at work on the insect it seemed to me that it would be wise to wait a little before attempting to import others, as there seemed to be a danger that secondary parasites might be imported with the primary ones and thus undo all that we attempted. My advice was taken in that case, whether rightly or wrongly remains to be seen."[17]

The Cyclone Burner

The committee had a deadly surprise called the cyclone burner waiting for the enemy this spring. The new device consisted of a small-aperture cyclone nozzle at the end of a twelve-foot iron pipe that was connected to a wooden vat by a short length of rubber hose. The vat was fitted with a hand pump and held fifteen gallons of paraffin oil. The apparatus was light enough to be moved into the field by two men, one who operated the pump and one who held the metal wand wrapped in an insulating wooden handle. A match ignited the vaporized oil spray, and the flame produced was so searing that not even a gypsy moth egg mass could withstand it.

Although the device was imperfect—the oil quickly corroded the rubber hose and clogged the nozzle—the burner was celebrated as a potent new weapon. It all but replaced the naphtha burner as a mass destroyer of egg

clusters. The flame would be swept along the ground, a technique called "blazing" by the men, incinerating whatever it touched and killing every living thing in its path. Only eggs deposited under rocks might escape, although the hellish fire often shattered the rocks. Intended as a device to incinerate egg clusters in leaf litter, the burner also proved effective where swarms of live caterpillars occurred on the ground. Osgood called the flame of this device "fearful."[19] And when Fernald witnessed the first demonstration of the cyclone burner, he could not believe his eyes. He later remarked to his colleagues: "We have a method of burning which I can not describe. It approaches as near the Tophet as anything I can think of. It is the most terrific blaze I have ever seen."[20]

The apparatus weighed 150 pounds when loaded and used fuel at a prodigious rate: to burn over an average pasture required filling the tank fifty times and consumed 750 gallons of oil.[21] The fine paraffin had an unpleasant odor, and it soaked into the clothing of workers, who were obliged to dress in heavy rubber coveralls or full body "oil suits" and boots to keep themselves from igniting. Working in smothering garments next to the searing heat of the cyclone burner during the long, hot days of summer taxed the endurance of the men greatly. The burner was an awkward size, and the pump operator had to work bent over in an uncomfortable position with one foot on the lid of the keg to keep it from lifting during the upstroke. When blazing the walls surrounding farms or gardens, they had to carry a large metal sheet into the field to set behind the rocks being flamed so that crops would not be damaged. Most workers did not view being on a cyclone burner crew as an enjoyable way to spend their summer.

When not needed for its flame, the cyclone burner could be converted into a lightweight sprayer. Crews liked the twelve-foot pipes because many trees could be sprayed to their tops without climbing. (Even spray crewmen chosen for their lightness and agility still damaged the limbs of many smaller trees, such as those growing in orchards, when the tree had to be ascended, and the climbing irons they wore made holes in the bark that provided entry for other insects and disease.) The burner pole could be fitted either with the specially made four-headed cyclone nozzle or, when a vaporous spray was desired, a modified Vermorel or Riley nozzle. The fine mist discharged by these nozzles blew away easily in the wind, however, so spraying from the downwind side was a tricky proposition.

The state equipped its forces with special mirrors to aid in the inspection of inaccessible places, and with pocket tins that contained a pair of metal tubes with brushes attached to their caps. One tube held creosote for poisoning eggs and the other held white paint with which workers painted a ring around treated egg masses. About 100,000 fertile egg clusters were destroyed, considerably fewer than the year before. This reduction may have been due to the

effects of the previous year's work, a natural decline in gypsy moth numbers, or the use of the new cyclone burners, since incinerated masses could not be counted.

The caterpillars swarmed again during the late spring and summer, but their activity seemed more localized than in past years. Winchester was experiencing heavy infestations, and thousands of insects completely engulfed the spruce trees in front of Louis Goddu's house.[22] Swampscott was becoming a perennial hatchery for the insect because the terrain there made cleansing work very difficult. As A. R. Bunting, chairman of the Swampscott Board of Selectmen, stated: "The gypsy moth caterpillars were very thick in the spring of 1892 at the Marshall place on Humphrey Street. The trees for two or three acres were stripped of their leaves. It looked as if a fire had been run through them. There was no more sign of a leaf in May or June than there would be in February."[23]

After the spring hatch, there was no intense spraying with Paris green as had been done earlier. Only two sprayers were in use—equipped with the latest nozzles, replacing the garden hose nozzles used the year before—and then only where infestations were heavy or concentrations of larvae warranted the use of contact insecticides. Most of the state's spraying apparatus remained in storage at field headquarters at Malden while the forces wrapped 150,000 yards of burlap bands around thousands of trees: "The habits of the caterpillar are such that the method of banding the trees with burlap appears the most effective one yet devised to dispose of this form of the moth. . . . [B]urlapping and hand-killing disposed of nine-tenths of the gypsy moths in the infested region during the summer, and in many localities they were exterminated by this work alone," the Board of Agriculture reported.[24]

During the summer, chemist F. C. Moulton began experiments with substances that might be effective at destroying egg clusters. He tested some fairly ghastly chemicals—benzene, bromine, chlorine, carbon disulphide, hydrocyanic acid, hydrogen arsenide, hydrogen sulfide, potassic cyanide, and hydrochloric acid—most in both liquid and gaseous forms. Harry B. Ramsey recalled that Moulton's experiments were sometimes spectacularly unsuccessful: "Mr. Moulton was a very quiet, modest person who evidently was bound up in his profession and did not mingle with the men in the field. He had a small room partitioned off in the storehouse, which was an old livery stable on Commercial Street, Malden, Mass. Several times during these experiments there were explosions heard from his room, and men working on tools would have to go outdoors until the gasses evaporated."[25]

Nathaniel Shaler discovered that inexpensive creosote oil, manufactured by the Carolina Oil and Creosote Company in Wilmington, North Carolina, worked best at soaking into the egg mass and killing all the eggs. Thinning the

oil with carbolic acid and turpentine allowed the mixture to be used effectively even during the coldest months. The formula later included 10 percent coal tar, which darkened the masses and allowed workmen to see which ones had been treated. The poisoned egg masses could then be left in place, saving time and allowing the fieldworkers to unburden themselves of the clumsy egg-burning ovens they had previously used. Leaving the egg masses also allowed workers to compare the number of new ones with the old to determine whether moth populations were increasing.

The late summer inspection cost a considerable amount of money, and as a result most of the workers were let go at the beginning of September. The forty to fifty men remaining gave as much time and attention as possible to expanding this inspection, and the spotty review did produce some good news: the boundary of 1891 had held, and all new infestations were still contained inside it. Although 1892 was a light year for gypsy moths, the committee took credit for a 90 percent reduction in the moth's numbers. The efficacy of the cyclone burner and of applications of burlap and sticky tar, the reduction in larvae, and the containment of the insect's outward spread greatly heartened the committee. In June 1892, Fernald made a personal inspection of Medford and was elated by what he saw. The town for all practical purposes had been wiped clean of gypsy moths. "I scarcely found an insect," he said happily.[26]

The sagacity of the economic entomologists seemed to have been confirmed at last. Some residents of the central infested towns were finally experiencing relief from the caterpillar swarms and were grateful to the state for taking on the work. Rose A. McCarty of 26 Myrtle Street wrote to the committee that in the fall of 1892 she and her family had harvested their first crop of apples in seven years.[27] M. M. Ransom of 18 Lawrence Street in Medford wrote that although the work of the gypsy moth commission had killed two of his trees, "I do not consider that I lost the two trees, but rather gained the rest, which would have been lost save for the work of the [gypsy moth] department."[28] Others said that if gypsy moth gangs had not worked on their properties, they would have been forced to sell their houses at a great loss and move away.

Forbush's small budget altered his plans to create a standing army. A force of 235 men had been put to work that spring banding trees, after which many were dismissed only to be called up again to tend the burlaps. The force was reduced after the caterpillars pupated and then increased once more in September to conduct inspections that had not been done the previous winter. Workers left the force the moment they could find stable employment elsewhere, and the task of training new hires became one that continued through the years. Forbush complained that it made no sense to discharge the best men at the end of the year, and that if the force had to be rebuilt anew each spring, weeks of valuable time would be wasted training the recruits.[29]

The gypsy moth committee still considered the outcome of 1892 to be in its favor and expressed optimism that eradication remained a viable course. That fall, Fernald, Forbush, and four men spent three days in Medford looking for egg masses and were able to find only two. Fernald, who had been the first to call for extermination and later changed his mind, changed his mind again: "While I have for some time had grave doubts of the possibility of complete extermination, I am now led to believe that such a thing is really possible, provided the work be continued for several years with sufficient appropriations to keep the entire territory under careful supervision."[30]

Forbush took pains to note that in the entire infested region, thanks to the work of the field force, these formidable insects had perceptibly injured fewer than twenty trees.[31] He thought that infested towns on the perimeter should be cleared of moths by the end of 1893, and that the moth ought to be rare everywhere in another year. He claimed that 99 percent of the egg clusters had been destroyed and that colonies in more than three hundred locations had been exterminated. He boasted that wherever the caterpillars swarmed in greatest densities, "it was comparatively easy to reduce their numbers."[32] Given what he termed a trained and efficient force, total extermination would occur over the next several years: "[The committee] believed that they had now learned by experience how to eradicate the moth. A large number of colonies had already been exterminated, and it had been proved that the moth could be exterminated wherever it was found."[33] In his portion of the annual report for that year, Forbush expressed his belief that few people outside the Board of Agriculture appreciated the magnitude of the work and mentioned that if the committeemen had known the moth's full distribution at the start, not one would have had the courage to attempt extermination.[34]

The Metropolitan Park Commission I

Looming ominously ahead of the committee, however, were large, wooded areas that lay within the infested region. The most prominent of these was the Middlesex Fells, a rugged, rocky tract of 3,200 acres bordered by the five most infested communities in the Commonwealth: Malden, Medford, Melrose, Stoneham, and Winchester. It lay in the hills that surrounded Boston on three sides, and its scenic features, rivers, lakes, and magnificent trees made the area desirable as parkland and a watershed for the growing city. The Fells constituted the second largest of the wooded parkland "reservations," exceeded only by the 4,190-acre Blue Hills. But other large tracts such as the 2,000-acre Lynn Woods were also inside the 1891 boundary.

The citizens of the area loved the Middlesex Fells as one of the few remaining, large, open spaces convenient to Boston. Special laws had protected the

Fells since the middle of the seventeenth century, and the woodlands had been held in common for the first 150 years of European colonization. Hog and cattle reeves were mandated to keep livestock out of the woods, and the opportunistic cutting of trees or kindling of fires was punishable by fines. Forbush said the Fells enclosed some of the finest trees in the eastern part of the state, and that their loss "would be considered a calamity by the citizens"[35]— without noting whether any such losses would come as the result of the gypsy moth or of his chopper gangs.

There was dismay, then, though little surprise, that the gypsy moth was in the Fells, since the southern boundary of the woods was less than half a mile from Trouvelot's former residence on Myrtle Street. The committee did not want to combat insects in wooded lands, but the Fells provided the gypsy moths with a stronghold from which they could swarm every year, not to mention the possibility of high tree mortality within the reservation itself. By this time the committee's favorite method of attack in any infested woodland place consisted of clear-cutting the trees after egg-laying time, followed by a complete burning of the land in winter and a second burning in the spring— in effect, saving the forest by cutting down the trees. The committee proposed to take this course of action in the Middlesex Fells during the winter, a task it told the legislature could be done for a an estimated cost of $400,000.

When word of this plan got out, however, there was uproar from the public and from those in charge of the reservations.

At this time, stewardship of the Middlesex Fells was passing from various individual owners into the hands of the newly created Metropolitan Park Commission (MPC).[36] The Massachusetts legislature had set up a temporary commission in 1892, with influential *Boston Herald* journalist Sylvester Baxter serving as secretary; he became chairman on June 3, 1893, when the MPC became a permanent commission. The mandate of the park commission was to acquire and develop a series of large spaces around Boston for public use, and it had just made its first three major land acquisitions for this purpose: Beaver Brook, Blue Hills, and the Middlesex Fells. Commissioners Baxter, Charles Francis Adams, Philip A. Chase, William B. de las Casas, and landscape architect Charles Eliot were not about to allow parkland trees to be felled wholesale.[37]

The creation of the long-awaited parks commission thus presented unexpected and unwanted complications for the gypsy moth committee. The MPC commissioners and their supporters were drawn from the highest social and political levels of the state, and they and their parkland acquisition program generally enjoyed strong legislative, public, and private backing. The members of the gypsy moth committee and the State Board of Agriculture were mostly small businessmen and farmers whose program of moth extermination was

not generally understood or appreciated, who drew little public support, and who were increasingly at odds with the legislature.

The appearance of the gypsy moth in the Fells caused the mandates and methods of the two boards to come into conflict. Clearly, imposing the moth committee's methods of work on the parklands would have come at great financial and political cost. At some point it became obvious to the committee not only that the MPC would have the last word in this matter but that the state legislature would not give serious consideration to such a large additional monetary request. The plan to log and burn the Fells was quietly shelved.

[CHAPTER 9]

Lead, Arsenic, Burlap, and Fire (1893)

THROUGH SESSIONS AND SHALER'S skillful maneuvering and considerable influence, the gypsy moth committee continued to enjoy the support of the state's highest elected official. Speaking before the combined house and senate on January 2, 1893, Governor Frederic T. Greenhalge encouraged the legislators to support the extermination campaign, noting that the situation could not be resolved by partial measures:

> The ravages of this insect have undoubtedly been restricted and minimized, but no precautions have been sufficient to prevent its doing considerable injury. The area of its depredations has not been extended, which is the main feature of encouragement. Upon the whole the weight of scientific testimony, and the best practical judgment seem to favor the continuance of our labors in the direction already taken. To what extent, in what manner, and at what cost this perplexing task is to be prosecuted must be determined by your wisdom, care and experience.[1]

At the annual meeting of the Board of Agriculture in Boston on February 2, the gypsy moth committee was increased in size by two, with E. W. Wood of West Newton and William H. Bowker of Boston joining Sessions, Shaler, and Appleton. During the winter, Fernald continued to test Paris green at Amherst, at last resigning himself to the reality that his best insecticide was largely useless against the gypsy moth: "Experiments with Paris green, repeated each year since the work began, have shown that this substance, in any proportion that will not greatly injure the foliage, will not destroy all the caterpillars when small and only a small proportion of them when more than half grown."[2]

More legislative hearings were held in February, and the gypsy moth

committee collected statements from citizens who believed that the state's efforts against a formidable insect had staved off a catastrophe. Hearings were held every year because the state legislature did not consider gypsy moth extermination to be an ongoing program and treated each year's appropriation as a new matter. The hearings sometimes took just a week, while in other years they lasted as long as a month. From the few surviving reports one can tell that the tone of all the hearings was similar: that is, rancorous, divisive, and unpleasant.

In 1889, Fernald had indicated that the complete destruction of the moths would take about three years, with financial needs diminishing from one year to the next. The three years and more were now completed, and the moth had not been exterminated. In addition, the continued effort was requiring more money, not less, and the General Court was becoming less amenable to the matter, not more. The committee raised its appropriation request from $75,000 to $160,000 and requested that an independent committee be formed by the legislature to report on gypsy moth extermination, no doubt hoping that the results of the moth work would be favorably reported to the General Court. After the hearings for 1893 had ended, the finance committee reduced the moth appropriation to $100,000—an action the gypsy moth committee felt was caused by public opposition to the thought of burning the Middlesex Fells—and did not vote that appropriation until April 12. No independent committee was appointed.

During the hearings, Andrew H. Ward suggested an insecticide made from arsenate of soda, but it burned foliage even worse than Paris green.[3] Fernald delegated F. C. Moulton, a field inspector and graduate chemist, to find a way of precipitating arsenate of soda in water, and after some trials Moulton settled on acetate of lead. This resulted in a fine suspension of lead arsenate that did not quickly settle to the bottom of the tank, as did the coarse arsenic suspension of Paris green. On March 23, Moulton sprayed the formula on a plant in the office, marking the first time it had been tried on living vegetation and beginning a long period of experiments with the new poison.[4]

Lead arsenate was expensive to manufacture, and it worked slowly. Like other arsenicals, the new pesticide was fatal to honey bees, so orchards could not be sprayed while the trees were in bloom. Fernald found that a mixture of one pound to 150 gallons of water killed potato beetles and tent caterpillars in the lab, but it took three times that amount to kill a laboratory-raised gypsy caterpillar. The fine suspension of lead arsenate permitted the use of a tight mesh filter on the suction line, reducing greatly the previous tendency of the nozzles to foul. Forbush gave the order to modify the state's thirty heavyweight spraying rigs, which had lain idle for two years, and make them ready for use.

To the surprise of the leadership, Moulton applied for a patent on his discovery, although the effort ultimately proved unsuccessful. Fernald told his colleagues in economic entomology: "The Commonwealth of Massachusetts has entered a protest. . . . Whether the chemist will succeed in getting the patent I do not know, but I hope not. I wish him no harm, but I want this Commonwealth and other States to have the advantage of any discoveries we may make."[5]

In 1893, the legislature of Massachusetts passed a "resolve" to petition the U.S. Congress for financial help, but it died in Washington, putting Massachusetts on notice that it would have to continue the struggle alone.[6] As Riley had foreseen, the federal government could not be counted on for assistance. Petitions from the General Court of the Commonwealth to the federal government were made every year until the end of the decade, but Congress did not act favorably on any of them.

During the wait for the state legislature to act, expert men were lost to other employers, fieldwork was suspended, and fieldworkers were dismissed for lack of funds. The release of money allowed the number of fieldworkers to be increased again, but valuable time was lost while the newest employees were trained. The force of 1893 reached only 150 men at its largest, almost 100 fewer than the force of 1892. The manpower reduction allowed the committee to hoard money to buy the most accurate scouting possible of large areas just outside the boundary that had never been inspected, and it permitted them to keep the moth program going until the next appropriation was secured the following spring.

The decision of the committee to decrease their force by nearly 40 percent had also been influenced by the financial panic of May 1893 when the U.S. Treasury became technically bankrupt. Railroads, businesses, and banks failed, and legal tender for payrolls was in short supply. Under the circumstances, operating with reduced manpower and funds, the committee made a tactical decision to concentrate its forces in the outlying towns on the theory that should the moths gain in strength anywhere, it would be better if they did so in the central zones where they were surrounded. Work in Medford, Malden, and neighboring communities was abandoned except for a small number of men detailed to each place "to do all that could be done to advantage."[7] Forbush sent his men into the field as soon as they could locate egg masses in most of the common locations, relying on his core of experienced men in the second wave to pick up whatever might have been missed.

Experiments with light creosote oil the previous year had been successful enough that the fieldworkers were instructed not to scrape egg masses into cans of kerosene any longer or to burn them on the trees, rather they were to soak the masses with the killing oil, which imparted a dark, unnatural color

that alerted other workers not to treat them again. Dilute nitric and carbolic acid also were used to destroy the eggs, but creosote proved to be the most effective, safest, and the easiest to use.

The principal work of the season was placing cloth bands on the trees. Fieldworkers entered the woods carrying rolls of burlap and balls of twine suspended from a shoulder rope. Extra burlap was piled in large-wheeled handcarts that could be easily pulled across rough terrain. Burlap was wrapped around each tree at a height of four or five feet. A few inches of overlap were allowed, after which a quick slash of the knife cut the burlap to length. A piece of twine was passed around the center of the band, cut, and tied off; the top half of the fabric was then folded over the lower half.

The men became very proficient at this task and could wrap trees with surprising speed, banding almost 420,000 trees before the larvae emerged. But the small force was at a disadvantage once the larvae ascended the trees. The success of banding depended on daily visits to remove the larvae, and with only 150 men available to tend 420,000 trees, many areas received little attention. Gypsy moth gangs made specified rounds so that no tree would go more than a few days without having its bands cleared, but in the central zones some trees were checked only once a week. During the months of May, June, July, and sometimes August of every year, almost all the men spent almost all their time killing the larvae found under the burlaps in the outer zones.

Some of the remaining men were diverted to brush *raupenleim* (literally, "caterpillar glue") on the trees, further reducing visits to the burlap bands. This imported German formula, a sticky goop that clung to the tree trunk and barred the paths of ascending larvae, had proved itself so effective the previous year that the committee had imported several additional tons of it for use in the current summer. For unexplained reasons, the *raupenleim* did not work as well again. When it was troweled into the hollows of infested trees, however, it made an excellent filler that saved much time over the old ways of nailing a tin patch over the cavity or mixing mortar plugs.

A bad infestation occurred at the Harmony Grove Cemetery in Salem, where Superintendent George W. Creesy and his men had considered the gypsy moth campaign a kind of social program to give unemployed men some work. But as the moths covered cemetery buildings, fences, and tombstones with yellow nests, the astonished Creesy became "a sudden and earnest believer in the gypsy moth department."[8]

The committee elected to do little spraying in 1893 other than the field tests of lead arsenate. It took ten times the amount of poison to produce the same results in the field as were obtained under controlled conditions, and pesticide mixtures as high as thirty pounds of lead arsenate to 150 gallons of water were needed to kill gypsy caterpillars in the wild. Forbush turned the cyclone

Workers wrapping trees with burlap bands, circa 1893.
From *The Gypsy Moth.*

burners loose in great number during the summer, utilizing a method of extermination he said guaranteed "certain destruction."[9] When there were lulls in
the fighting, fieldworkers took on the disagreeable task of inspecting neighborhoods for eggs and pupae amid the piles of rubbish commonly found
behind houses, a task that Forbush intensely disliked: "Not only are all sorts
of waste material from all parts of the house from cellar to garret thrown into
the back yard, but refuse from the kitchen is also frequently deposited there,
together with a collection of empty but unclean cans. . . . Old shoes, broken
bottles and earthen ware, cast-off articles of apparel, corn husks and the withered tops of vegetables in all stages of decay, bones, fish heads, lobster and
oyster shells are also common constituents. . . . Amid such associations the
gypsy moth loves to dwell."[10]

Forbush therefore thought one way to eliminate the gypsy moth was to

eliminate garbage. Rubbish was hauled off, buried, or burned. Forbush felt such work was ennobling, saying, "Cremation is a cleansing process; bonfires mark the progress of civilization."[11] Fernald, who was less emotionally entangled in the matter, found a better use for the empty cans, placing them along infested fences, walls or hedgerows. The caterpillars then crawled inside the cans to pupate, and female moths laid their eggs in the cans. Afterward, the workmen picked them up and disposed of everything together.

The year 1893 was quiet on most fronts, although the committee remained uncertain about the condition of the woodlands and wondered if the boundary of 1891 still delineated the range of the moth. No traces of the insect could be found in ten previously infested towns, and Forbush claimed that over eight hundred moth colonies had been destroyed since the war started. He was rather casual in his definition of a colony, saying that although some were of substantial size, such as ten acres, others were "not more than a few square rods," and many consisted of no more than "one or two trees."[12] It would have been easy and tempting to inflate the count of destroyed colonies since laymen would assume that a colony consisted of substantial numbers of insects over a significant amount of territory, and all subsequent tabulations of destroyed colonies must be regarded with this in mind.

During the year the gypsy moths occupied Cambridge, and Riley wrote that the insect was spreading despite the committee's claims to the contrary.[13] Riley was still trying to obtain gypsy moth parasites from Loomis in Yokohama, but the effort was not going any better than it had before. In November he received a small box of cocoons containing parasites of the old genus Microgaster, but Loomis's attempt had failed again, for many of the cocoons were empty, and in many others the parasite had succumbed to the attack of a hyperparasite.[14]

In the fall, rail lines and rights of way radiating from the central zones were inspected beyond the state lines of New Hampshire and Maine. Men went through the towns just outside the infested outer towns, and places where light infestations had been reported were inspected again. This was a risky practice, since much of the effort did not reveal the presence of gypsy moths, did nothing to reduce the number of insects in the places where they were found, and yet consumed $13,000 dollars of a very small budget.[15] Field inspector S. R. Huston described the activities of his crew of eight men during a typical inspection: "We went to Danvers, Wenham, Hamilton through to Manchester and back to South Lynnfield and worked up through there, and finally we struck in around the northern part of Lake Suntaug and found [one] dry pupa on a pine tree. We continued our search about a week longer and found a colony of about eight or ten nests. We continued until December and

found nothing more. This was the results of three months' search."[16] Bartholomew Hennelly told about working on a crew that had been sent to inspect
the infestations reported in Woburn. The woods were thick with underbrush
that grew to the height of a man's head, and it had rained hard the night
before:

> We must have gone, I suppose, over perhaps 40 or 50 acres of wood
> land to inspect it. Of course, we had not gone in there fifteen feet
> before we were soaking wet, and there was not a tree looked at the
> whole time we was in there. . . . [Special Inspector Hubbard] ordered
> us to separate out 100 feet apart and push right along. It was a walk-
> ing match to see how fast you could walk through the woods, look at
> a tree here and there. Those trees there might as well never have been
> reported as being inspected at all, because they don't know today
> whether the gypsy moth is up there or not.[17]

Shaler had been tabulating the movement of swill wagons, manure haulers,
and others for the years 1889 through 1893 and had sent two men to examine
every place the drivers stopped to rest or unload their cargoes. This investigation revealed an old and established colony of gypsy moths in Boston's Franklin Park. New colonies were discovered near Lexington, Woburn, and Dan-
vers, but Forbush was quick to assure residents that every remnant of the
moth in those places would be destroyed by the end of the year. His answer
was the inferno. He loved the cyclone burner and its capabilities, and after the
eggs had been searched for with all possible thoroughness, the burlaps were
all wrapped, and the spraying had done all that it could, the time was right to
apply the cleansing power of the deadly petroleum blast. He wrote, "Fire can
be used either to destroy the eggs of the moth, to kill the caterpillars or to
starve them by burning all nearby vegetation on which they feed."[18]

The gypsy moth committee, however, becoming desperate for larger appropriations, in its annual report did not hesitate to paint a gloomy and frightening picture of what might happen should future appropriations decline or be
eliminated. It predicted the "defoliation of all trees, shrubs and bushes, the
destruction of fruit trees, and the despoliation of gardens." Hosts of caterpillars would bring their disgusting swarms into houses and buildings, and the
stench of the dead would be nauseating.[19] The committee was feeling the close
scrutiny of the General Court on the costs of scouting, the sums that were
being diverted to fund Fernald's work on parasites, and the money spent on
the development of unsuccessful new pesticides and apparatus. The committee
kept hundreds of pages of meticulous records of all this activity and asked for

an additional $2,000 to be used in part to print the documents and in part to resume the experiments that had been discontinued because they were not in line with extermination.

The infested territory and surrounding belt of uninfested towns that had just been inspected—over four hundred square miles of land—would have to be inspected again within eight or ten months down to every last tree, shrub, fence, and stone. The examination would have to be even more painstaking than the one before so that not a single egg cluster escaped detection. The central parklands, comprising of twelve thousand acres in which grew more than five million trees and probably three times as many shrubs and bushes, had never been scouted, for the mere mention of putting even the most tangled parkland thickets to the torch had drawn a storm of opposition from the public. It would take the patience of Job, the wisdom of Solomon, and the strength of Hercules to labor through the problem of the central woodlands.

In spite of the many remaining troublesome concerns, the successes of 1891 and 1892 had continued, and the sustained kill rate of 90 percent caused optimism. There was more good news from the inspectors: the Dexter elm was found to be free of all gypsy moth activity. Forbush wrote that the moths had been almost eradicated from the outer towns, and that even in areas where burlaps were attended only once a week, the moths had been "considerably reduced in number."[20] Fernald, whose mind had yet to settle on one side of the extermination question or the other, was satisfied on the whole with the work: "It has been a greater surprise to me than to anyone else, perhaps, to see what has been accomplished from the first; for few persons, if any, have followed and watched the work more closely than I have been able to do from the time the presence of the insects was reported. Only those who have carefully and frequently inspected the work can fully realize how much has been accomplished."[21]

The caterpillar swarms were still impressive, but many citizens noticed that the outbreaks seemed less severe. The year's work had produced an excellent overall showing for the forces of Massachusetts, and the gains for the gypsy moth seemed small compared to its losses. This was not an outbreak year, moth populations were holding steady or diminishing, and the committee was relieved to find that even in the towns and woodlands where little work had been done, conditions seemed to be better than they were the year before.

The respect the economic entomologists desired also seemed to be close at hand as a result of the eradication campaign. Mrs. Alice Ward Bailey, writing under the name A. B. Ward, was a frequent contributor to period magazines such as *Scribner's*, *Harper's*, and the *Atlantic Monthly*. After interviewing Fernald at the experiment station at Amherst and listening to his glowing review of the year's campaign, Ward enthused in print that the gypsy moths

had been dealt a resounding defeat: "What could have been a national disaster has in all probability been averted. The gypsies will soon be forgotten."[22] Further, the Commonwealth, planning for the World's Columbian Exposition to be held in Chicago during 1893, was seeking exhibits of agricultural work that would "reflect the most credit upon the State." Through the efforts of Francis Appleton, the gypsy moth committee prepared a special display case for shipment to Chicago. The Massachusetts Board of World's Fair Managers called the gypsy moth work "important" and had no doubt that the lessons taught by the display would be valuable to scientists elsewhere.[23]

As the summer turned into fall, the committee felt more relaxed than it had in some time, so its members were unprepared when Fernald's letter of resignation, dated October 19, arrived at the Board of Agriculture office in Boston. Fernald remained disgruntled with his circumstances in Amherst and was still hoping to fill the vacancy at Harvard caused by Hagen's death. Sessions was in Chicago at the time, and it was not until October 27 that Fernald's letter came to his attention. Sessions wrote to Fernald promising to bring the matter before the committee when it next met, on October 31.[24] At the meeting, a motion was made by Shaler and approved "that the Committee ask Prof. Fernald to reconsider his resignation."[25] Shaler himself wrote to Fernald the next day, adding his personal request for Fernald's continued help and offering a bit of friendly advice: "Permit me to suggest that my own experience shows that a head-worker often becomes discouraged and is apt to take an over-gloomy view of the situation. Every now and then I come to the conclusion that the world is intolerable, but after a week or two the sun gets up again, and I breathe more easily. I am always threatening to resign, but while the process has gone on for thirty years, the deed becomes year by year more unlikely."[26]

On November 13, Fernald wrote Shaler that he was now disposed to go cautiously in regard to abandoning his association with the gypsy moth work and asked Shaler to support his application to Harvard. Shaler revealed that Hagen's situation in Cambridge had never been what it seemed—his meager salary was maintained by gifts from his friends—but promised to support Fernald: "It would be a capital arrangement to have you here, for we should obtain some good teaching and bring you directly into the gypsy moth work, where you would always be on hand for effective control. I shall present these points to Mr. [Alexander] Agassiz in a vigorous way."[27]

Forbush's Army II

The policies of Massachusetts with respect to state employees were changed in 1893 to prohibit the hiring of anyone who was not a citizen of the United

States and a legal resident of the Commonwealth. After the financial collapse of 1893, the economic status of New England was so severely depressed that from 20 to 30 percent of the labor force was looking for work. This pool of potential applicants was English-speaking, so Forbush's supposed difficulties of increasing his field force are puzzling, especially since the state was paying even the newest workers excellent wages for unskilled labor. Forbush thought of his army as being divided into two unequal parts. The larger part comprised new hires and men with the least experience; the smaller part, old hands with the most experience. The committee had kept the force small during the year so it could save a substantial portion of the appropriation of 1893 to keep the most experienced men employed as scouts through the winter.

The trend toward the military model for field personnel was reflected in the adjustments Forbush made to his army this year. Members of the force were required to provide themselves with a uniform of light colored jacket and pants. The application of spray disturbed the larvae, which dropped from the leaves and could fall unnoticed on the workers' clothing, hitch a ride, and drop off at a distance to form new colonies; the light-colored cloth made the dark-colored larvae easier for other workers to see.

Visiting Entomologists I

On May 31, 1893, the gypsy moth committee had authorized Fernald to invite "not more than six entomologists from neighboring states to come and inspect the work."[28] Fernald proceeded in haste, and the visitors were on the scene within two weeks. Fernald carried out the wishes of the committee with one slight exception—instead of inviting entomologists, he invited economic entomologists, almost none of whom could be called unbiased or objective. Among the five who accepted the invitation was Dr. Joseph Albert Lintner, state entomologist of New York, a forceful advocate of chemical insect slaughter; he had once written: "Continue then to pray with fervor, as often as you join in the Church's solemn litany, 'We beseech thee, good Lord, to give and preserve to our use the kindly fruits of the earth, that in due time we may enjoy them,' but do not fail to supplement your prayer with the force pump and London purple."[29] The other four were Clarence M. Weed of the New Hampshire State Agricultural College at Durham and a founding member of the American Association of Economic Entomologists; John B. Smith of New Jersey, who taught economic entomology at Rutgers, a well-known advocate of insect extermination; Fernald's son, Henry Torsey Fernald; and Alpheus Spring Packard, presumed to be an economic entomologist because of his critical work on Riley's Rocky Mountain Locust Commission. Most of these

men were unprepared for what they saw and could make few suggestions because the scope of the endeavor was unprecedented in entomological history. They were impressed with Edward Forbush and amazed at the storehouse, with its complement of spraying apparatus. One called the building an "arsenal," and Fernald later remarked with pride that "the whole work was a revelation to them."[30]

Given the efforts of the workers and a decline in the moth population for 1893, the results for the season were impressive, convincing many of the supposedly doubtful entomologists such as Joseph Lintner that the great experiment could be a success. As he wrote to Fernald: "It was a surprise to me that in the brief space of three years the fearful ravages of the insect as described to me and as pictured in photographs could have been reduced to such comparative harmlessness . . . and that in the ride of an entire day through several of the infested towns, including a visit to localities which had been frightfully scourged, not a single example of the caterpillar was found by me, although a diligent search for it was made."[31] Since Lintner was the entomologist outside Massachusetts most familiar with the work, however (he had been a recipient of all the annual reports),[32] his professed surprise must be taken with a grain of salt. In fact, Lintner never saw the ravages of the moth personally but admittedly based his conclusions on what he had been told by others and on photographs he had been shown.

The New Jersey state entomologist, Professor J. B. Smith of Rutgers, was also convinced that extermination lay within reach: "I was, I think I can truly say, free from actual prejudice, yet with a disposition to believe . . . that actual extermination was impossible, an impression to which I had given public expression. I am pleased to say that I have seen ample evidence to induce a change of opinion, and my belief is now that if the committee is as well supported as it deserves to be it will accomplish the end for which it was created."[33] Likewise, Fernald's son, H. T. Fernald of Pennsylvania State College, was not unexpectedly impressed by the results of his father's work: "I felt some doubt as to whether it was possible to exterminate the gypsy moth, as I had some previous knowledge of it and of its ravages in Massachusetts. . . . Since my visit a careful consideration of the methods used and of the results already obtained has convinced me that extermination is not only probable, but certain, if the work can be prosecuted for a sufficient length of time."[34]

The inclusion among the visitors of Alpheus Spring Packard, then living and working in Providence, Rhode Island, is a bit surprising because in later years he became an influential opponent of insect extermination. Nor was he impressed by what he saw in eastern Massachusetts but seemed to believe that if he had nothing good to say, his report should at least give no offense: "In

the short time I spent I saw nothing to find fault with, but much to commend. I say this without wishing to merely say something pleasant, but because I mean it."[35]

Fernald and the leadership of the gypsy moth work would not give the time of day to any man who expressed a negative opinion about the work without having seen the killing fields in person. They had an unshakable belief that scientists and thinkers of their day would be impressed by looking at bushels of severed caterpillars, grassy fields remarkable only for their lack of diverse life, or gangs of exhausted men chopping down the forest. They seemed oblivious to the notion that there was nothing scientific about their undertaking. The matter of successful fieldwork was one of good organization, the maintenance of schedule and discipline, fair weather, and good luck.

At about this time, Sessions received a letter from Ellwood Cooper of Santa Barbara, California, who had written to encourage the use of parasites. Cooper, who eventually became the California state commissioner of horticulture, mentioned a European parasite he thought would be useful in both California and Massachusetts and inquired whether the committee would share expenses to import the insect in quantity. Fernald rejected the idea out of hand. Sessions was not much taken with the plan, either, as he wrote to Fernald: "I am of course aware that nothing of the kind can be undertaken at present. Our appropriation is for extermination as well as for preventing the spread of the [gypsy moth]. This gentleman speaks as 'from the book' saying 'no insect pest can be totally destroyed.' We are trying to prove the contrary."[36]

The year ended with the Board of Agriculture forming a subcommittee under F. H. Appleton to appeal for help from the federal government and the U.S. Department of Agriculture. The chances of success were very slim, since Agriculture Secretary Julius S. Morton held on principle that there should be no federal interference in matters concerning individual states. Riley, with evident pleasure, noted:

> The thing that strikes me as curious, however, is that, according to the report by Professors Smith, Lintner, etc., who were invited by the Gypsy Moth committee to inspect the work last summer, the work has been very satisfactory. I cannot reconcile this with the appeal now made for federal aid. It looks to me very much as if my advice and the position I took on the question are being thoroughly justified and vindicated and that the committee will come to regret that it did not follow my advice.[37]

Rebounds and Resignations (1894)

FORBUSH WAS DETERMINED not to let the moth escape the boundary of 1891. He knew it was easy to overlook the insect and feared that moth colonies established outside the boundary would reinfest areas that had been cleared. The committee had hoarded nearly $30,000 into the new year, and eighty-three men worked through the early months of 1894 making another inspection of the region. Three previously unknown colonies discovered outside the boundary of 1891 and a colony in Boston's Franklin Park proved to be at least four or five years old while places like the Middlesex Fells showed increased moth populations. Forbush sent inspectors great distances, even to towns and villages in neighboring states. He ordered several inspections made following his practice of repeating passes through suspect regions.

Forbush considered these inspections so crucial that he took men from work even during the swarms and sent them out to scout, weakening his effort and draining the financial resources of the committee. This practice was a source of intense dissatisfaction in the central districts, whose residents could not understand why men were taken from places where the caterpillars were abundant and sent to work in places where they were scarce. Egg masses that engulfed the trees in the central districts were left untouched while skilled men searched for one or two in places where they could hardly be found, leaving the abandoned communities to form and pay for their own gypsy moth gangs.

Some, such as the perennially pro-extermination J. O. Goodwin, accepted the responsibility as a personal one. Goodwin banded his trees and hired men to work for several weeks at the height of infestations. At times the caterpillars came in such overwhelming numbers that Goodwin could not keep up with them. His men were using a large stove containing a hot fire to incinerate the larvae, but they heaped in so many insects that the fire would be extinguished before the day was half over.[1]

In February 1894 the Board of Agriculture reorganized the committee, gave

it new responsibilities, changed its name to "the committee on gypsy moths, insects and birds," and increased its size from five to six members. The sixth member was the board's secretary, a member ex officio of all committees. The gypsy moth committee became one of eight standing committees, and its members included Chairman E. W. Wood, Francis H. Appleton, William H. Bowker, Augustus Pratt, and F. W. Sargent. Revised bylaws required the board to hire six specialists, including an entomologist and an ornithologist, as advisers. The specialists were required to attend the board's annual meetings at their own expense.[2]

Restive members of the state legislature demanded to know what the outcome of the extermination effort was likely to be and how much more money it would cost over a period of ten years should extermination fail. At legislative hearings in February 1894, the committee promised that within a few years at least twenty-four of the thirty-three infested communities would be free of the moth, though admitting that eight thousand "estates" probably would remain infested. The costs of extermination on these estates could run as high as $328,000, in addition to the $100,000 it would take each year to prevent reinfestation of cleared areas.

Residents of the infested areas testified to the destructiveness of the insect, many of them a little too obviously at the behest of the Board of Agriculture, telling the legislators that combatting the pests individually did not work. Former senator Low described seeing the walls of houses and nearly all the trees covered with egg nests. J. O. Goodwin was by now so paranoid about the moth that he claimed they would "kill every living thing on the face of the earth if they are not destroyed."[3] The finance committee, however, announced that it would reduce the appropriation request by 40 percent, and the moth committee once more blamed the influence of misguided public opposition for the reduction.

Francis H. Appleton resigned in protest, stating that without sufficient funds it would be impossible to accomplish the task the committee had been charged to do. He was likely uneasy with the path of events because the committeemen seldom visited the field and relied too heavily for advice on Forbush, Fernald, and their associates. Appleton, who lived in the heart of the infested district, observed, "The general public by and large was not interested in the work."[4] Nathaniel Shaler also resigned his position early in 1894, claiming ill health and the press of other obligations. Charles Fernald requested that he, too, be relieved of his duties, citing the negative effects on his academic obligations and research work of the gypsy moth committee's demands—although he later said he had become discouraged over the lack of progress in the field and the constant reductions in appropriations.[5] There is evidence that

Edward Forbush tried to relinquish his work at this time as well but that the beleaguered committee refused to consider his request. Forbush's departure would have been serious enough at any time, but losing him along with Fernald would have been a catastrophe. The pool of potential replacements was painfully small, and by the time other men could be found, the entire field force might have collapsed from lack of leadership.

The executive committee of the Board of Agriculture implored all these men to reconsider. The work of the gypsy moth committee had quickly made it the most important standing committee, but there were no other board members available to fill their positions.[6] Appleton was insistent, however, and at the meeting of July 26, 1894, the board relented. John B. May wrote that Forbush tried to resign twice but that the committee would not accept his resignation.[7] Although the exact date Forbush tendered his resignation is not known, the situation at this juncture and the actions of other members of the gypsy moth leadership group strongly suggest that Forbush's attempt to dissociate himself from gypsy moth work occurred at this time.

The resignation of four key members of the gypsy moth campaign had no effect on the legislature at all. Fernald and Forbush were coaxed back into their critical roles. Although Appleton and Shaler went on to other things, neither would be free of the gypsy moth for many years. The gypsy moth committee immediately petitioned for an additional appropriation of $65,000 and again asked that an independent panel review their work. Neither request was granted.

The Aliens Advance

The committee's funds were expended by May 1, and fieldwork ceased until May 23 when the legislature voted an appropriation of $100,000. The hatch occurred during this hiatus, and a frustrated Forbush could only watch as the trees pullulated with larvae beyond counting. The workforce was reassembled as quickly as possible and the new men sent into the field as fast as they could be trained. The reports they sent back to headquarters were completely unexpected, darkly foreboding, and deeply troubling: the gypsy moths were everywhere, swarming by the tens of millions and overwhelming the fieldworkers with their vast numbers.

The effect of this news was devastating. The most careful and costly inspection of the campaign, just completed, had indicated a war going so well that Forbush had reduced the size of his army. Yet somehow, either vast numbers of egg masses had been overlooked or the fecundity of the moths had increased beyond even the wildest expectations. Since Fernald and Forbush had not

anticipated a large population rebound, no strategies for this contingency were in place; there were too few men available to respond, and there was not enough money to hire enough additional employees.

Over 624,000 trees were banded, and an undersize army of 250 men was sent to attend them. A desperate effort was begun to cut as many trees as possible in areas where the caterpillars swarmed most densely. Implementing this practice required an immediate infusion of new employees, but it also allowed Forbush to relax his employment standards. Men did not need much training to chop down a tree, and tying burlaps required only diligence rather than expertise.[8] Spraying rose to the highest levels since the campaign began; nearly 15,000 individual trees were treated, almost three times the number treated the previous year. But records of larvae killed by spraying were impossible to compile. Although millions were poisoned, the slaughter barely made a difference. The tally at season's end showed that 1,153,560 caterpillars were killed by hand, all taken under burlaps.

Fernald and his assistants devised a plan in which laboratory-raised females were placed in cages surrounded by sticky paper to which the luckless males adhered when they sought the females. Thousands of moths were thus destroyed, the idea being that if enough males could be removed from an area the females would lay sterile eggs. The experiment was abandoned when even the females in the traps were fertilized, and many of the surviving males were seen to mate with at least four wild females.[9] After the female moths had laid their eggs, the committee's employees trimmed more than eight thousand trees, cut down some six thousand more, and burned ten thousand acres of brush and woodland.

Forbush began discharging men early in August and continued through the fall until only 133 were left, even though he was desperate to undertake another complete scouting to discover why the increase of larvae had occurred. He also needed to investigate the next belt of towns surrounding the boundary of 1891 to see whether the gypsy moths had broken through the lines, but the area was so large that the commanders once again decided to abandon all efforts in the central infested towns and concentrate on places that had never been inspected. It was crucial that the moths remain contained. If they slipped past the boundaries, and if the hatch next spring were as large as the one that had just taken place, the war would be decisively lost.

The residents of the central districts again watched in dismay as the forces of the state left them to their own devices. Walter Wright complained that scouting was a waste of time and money, saying that only a little inspection would suffice to show the presence of the insect and give an idea of its numbers. Wright told Forbush that the work as presently done was like a fire department that responded to a single call by soaking the entire community.[10]

Oliver J. McCarthy, a six-year veteran who had participated in a number of "scouts," considered scouting to be worthless:

> [We sprayed] on the outside of the Lexington Valley colony in 1894, where there were no moths, leaving the center of the colony untouched, where there were lots of them. [We scouted] the road sides in Lexington in 1893 and 1894 and leaving the woodland go where there were large colonies of the moth. Why, we have been up there and banged around the road sides in Lexington and had a good time with different inspectors, drank hard cider, etc., never got a bug. Half a mile beyond there was millions of them.[11]

In the fall, destruction of egg masses resumed. Leland Howard observed the egg hunters at work and was impressed by their skill: "The eggs must be searched for in inconceivable crevices, trees must be climbed, and egg clusters, which cannot be reached by hand, must still be painted by means of brushes attached to the extremities of long poles. The process, however, is carried on very effectively and much more rapidly than would be supposed."[12]

Inspections showed that the moth was continuing its spread into the Boston districts of Roxbury and Dorchester, and colonies were found within the city itself. The area infested by the moth thus increased to 220 square miles, although the committee felt that for the most part the boundary of 1891 remained intact. While the situation in some of the treated towns improved, the number of colonies in the Lynnfield woods and similar places was rising. The practice of concentrating on the outer towns left at least sixteen separate interior wooded areas as sanctuaries for the moths. Forbush noted that scattered colonies existed in woodlands from Lexington to the sea and from East Lexington to Salem in a belt a mile wide. The insects were entrenched in a fifty-square-mile block in the heart of the boundary where the committee estimated that 12,000 acres were infested, and attending to these areas would require work on no less than five million trees. To ensure that the moth had not infiltrated farther inland, much of the winter inspection work again was done in towns and villages outside the boundary, an area much larger than the containment zone, and searches were made at a great cost in time and money. In some years these inspections constituted the committee's single largest expenditure and became a source of contention with the legislature, which felt that appropriations for moth extermination should be spent on exterminating moths, not on traipsing through the woods in the middle of the state with pads and pencils.

The mood of the gypsy moth fighters was much different at the end of 1894 than it had been the year before, when victory seemed within easy reach. It

was becoming a tricky matter to claim on the one hand that the infested territory had been reduced by half while reporting on the other that new colonies were being found outside the boundary with every inspection. The moths expanded their range southward into Boston and reappeared in places from which the committee thought they had been cleared. The experiments with lead arsenate had showed that even its greater potency could not exterminate the moths. It was increasingly difficult to recruit and retain competent fieldworkers. Public opinion about the gypsy moth work remained unfavorable; there was a strong likelihood that the General Court was going to reduce appropriations to the point of uselessness; and the support of fellow entomologists seemed to be wavering.

Fernald, in two states of mind about the work and his part in it, wrote in his report for 1894 that he had visited the infested regions often and inspected the work carefully. In a guarded way, he said that everything had been done that could be done with the money available, and that the fieldwork had been thorough and carried out along approved lines.[13] If the extermination program showed any sign of failing, it was due to the stinginess of the last two legislatures, and the blame must be put where it belonged. The General Court, by chapter 71, Resolves of 1894, authorized the gypsy moth committee to prepare the most detailed and comprehensive account yet issued of the progress in the war against the gypsy moth and its likely outcome, and to elaborate on "the scientific facts ascertained." The committee was directed to present the report to the next legislature at the beginning of January 1896.

Visiting Entomologists II

The gypsy moth committee was heartened by the response of the entomologists who had visited the work zone in 1893, and the committeemen began to see that the value of these visits was more than just scientific. As Sessions noted in a letter to Fernald, they could also favorably influence public opinion.[14] Fernald again solicited comments from the few men who, he believed, represented the best that economic entomology had to offer. Leland Howard said that in 1894 there were probably, by this standard of judgment, fewer than thirty qualified entomologists in the entire United States.[15]

Most of the men who accepted the invitation, and on whose opinion so much emphasis was placed, had never seen living gypsy moths, let alone swarming colonies defoliating trees, which most of them still had not seen when they left. They were shown instead areas that the field force claimed to have cleared in previous years, and they viewed unremarkable land or grassy meadows that had once contained young forests. Many of the visitors spent

just a single day making cursory inspections. Two did not arrive until mid-July, when the insects were pupating. Vermont entomologist George H. Perkins remarked that some of the worst defoliation he saw was caused by canker worms.[16] The entomologists' visits were arranged to make the best possible impression on them. Workers were notified in advance to be busy when the distinguished guests were driven by. Private I. J. Colbert recalled that nobody of importance was ever brought into the field that the workers did not know about in advance, and the workers were told to be laboring assiduously when the guests appeared. Colbert said this was standard policy; that visitors always saw the work under the most favorable conditions, he thought, "account[ed] largely for the favorable opinions that we hear from time to time."[17]

Among some of the more far-seeing practitioners, the question was not whether the insect could be exterminated but whether it *should* be. They asked whether the present undertaking required so much effort and money that it could not be sustained, and whether it would be better to follow the European practice of controlling the insect only where it became a nuisance. John Henry Comstock of Cornell University, former chief in entomology at the U.S. Department of Agriculture, sounded a call for reassessment: "I have come to have grave doubts as to the advisability of attempting to exterminate this pest. I am not prepared to say that I consider extermination impossible, but it seems to me that the attainment of this desired end is highly improbable."[18] Comstock was doing his best to support a fellow entomologist in a difficult situation, but he knew it was not just that the possibility of extermination was questionable, but also the idea that the state would continue to provide funding for any extended period: "[If] the Legislature appropriates less than two-thirds of the sum [deemed necessary], it is hardly probable that succeeding Legislatures would furnish the means necessary to carry this work to its conclusion. . . . I respectfully suggest that you consider the advisability of adopting a different method of combatting the pest."[19] In short, Comstock's report made several almost heretical recommendations: first, that the scope of the effort was too narrow and should be broadened; second that the use of natural adversaries and parasites would eventually bring the moths under control; and third, that the rejected approach of the California Board of Horticulture should serve as a model for the campaign.

Professor F. L. Harvey of Maine State College at Orono, though impressed by the work in progress and the triumph that seemed to lie so near, saw the Achilles heel of the undertaking: "The present number of men employed seems to me to be inadequate, as large areas of the infested district have to be neglected while inspection is going on in others. Unless a large force can be kept constantly employed for some years, the idea of extermination will have to be

abandoned."[20] Harvey thought the idea of holding back such a powerful natural force by handpicking, poisoning, and burning larvae was problematic at
best. He let slip the third agenda of the campaign when he noted his hope that
the gypsy moth committee would settle the issue not for the good of the
Commonwealth but "for the good of economic entomology," and that every
state would have an entomological commission "with duties as broad as the
requirements of economic entomology."[21]

Harvey also told Fernald that he had learned of some naturalists who were
breeding gypsy moths outside of Massachusetts.[22] Harvey did not mention
any names, but J. A. Lintner, state entomologist of New York, had obtained
egg clusters shortly after the publication of Fernald's first danger bulletin and,
as he later claimed, before the laws of Massachusetts prohibited distribution
of the insect. Wanting some specimens for his personal collection, he had taken
the eggs to his office on the top floor of the capitol building in Albany, New
York, where he raised the larvae to maturity. The caterpillars pupated and
were about to emerge at the time Lintner was leaving for his vacation in Keene
Valley, New York, so he took the pupae with him because he did not trust his
assistant to keep the moths from escaping. As the moths emerged, Lintner
killed them one by one and mounted them, labeling the location as "Keene
Valley, New York."[23]

A few years later, when an inspector from Forbush's office was in Lynn,
Massachusetts, at the house of an amateur entomologist, he spotted one of
the labeled specimens with alarm. The rumor that gypsy moths were in New
York sent Fernald running for the train to Albany for a conference with Lintner, but upon his arrival he received a confession instead. Fernald could
scarcely upbraid his reckless friend, because he himself had taken gypsy moths
to Amherst, far west of the infested zone, so that he could experiment on them
conveniently in his own laboratory. Lintner was a staunch ally and a respected
official entomologist who took a splendid view of the work in the Bay State;
he wrote that he considered "this effort being made now in Massachusetts as
one of the greatest undertakings in modern science."[24] He was also an unmit-
igated hawk on the issue of destroying the insects: "It is a wise saying, if
construed aright, that 'Providence is ever on the side of the heaviest artillery.'
Fight the insect as you never have before, and do not sound an inglorious
retreat or yield a pitiable surrender, just as the instruments of warfare and the
insecticidal ammunition with which you may wage effectual fight, have been
placed within your reach."[25]

Leland Howard, the newly appointed successor to C. V. Riley as chief in
entomology at the U.S. Department of Agriculture, believed, to the contrary,
that the war was meaningless and proposed the almost unthinkable course of
taking no further action at all:

If the appropriation were taken away the insect will not only speedily reach its former destructive height, but will spread far and wide over the country. It may be urged that it will only be a few years before the insect will take its place as a naturalized member of our fauna, and will become subject to the same variations of increase and decrease as our native species, and that it will, in fact, become little more to be feared than species already existing with us, particularly if its natural European enemies are introduced.[26]

Howard had the curious ability to belong firmly to one camp or the other or, often, to both at once. The gypsy moth might be exterminated, it might be suppressed, or a running fight with it over the entire East Coast might go on for a hundred years; it didn't really matter to him as long as economic entomologists were in control. Howard knew that the Massachusetts experiment was in deep trouble, but his typical response was to present an unfailingly cheerful outlook, no matter what the reality of the situation might be: "The work upon the gypsy moth . . . is one of the most remarkable pieces of work, judging from the results, which has yet been done in economic entomology. . . . The infested territory has been reduced by one-half, and within the districts within which the gypsy moth at present exists it is, practically speaking, a comparatively rare insect."[27]

The visiting entomologists were often amazed not just that the work was taking place but that the Massachusetts legislature continued to vote relatively large appropriations. Fernald recalled that some could hardly believe the work was still going on:

> Dr. Howard and Professor Comstock of Cornell University were here with me at one time and we went over the territory, and we would go back to the hotel and sit down in the evening in my room and talk it over. . . . Professor Comstock said, "New York would never have appropriated so much money as would be necessary to exterminate [the gypsy moth]." Dr. Howard said, "I don't know of a state in the Union that would appropriate so much money as this." They knew that I was from Maine formerly and they said, "Would Maine do it?" I said, "No."[28]

Without adequate funds the entire initiative would collapse, and this point was impressed on the visiting experts. The question of allocations was not one that could be determined from inspecting the field, so no doubt it was discreetly suggested to the visitors that their observations include the need for continued funding. Almost all their reports did so—a uniformity that strikes

one as less than coincidental. The future of economic entomology would be decided in the next few years, and it would likely have no future if there were no jobs for the men that were coming from schools like Fernald's. Fernald made all his students take the examination for the field force, and Forbush was always happy to hire those who passed. A number of young, college-trained entomologists started their careers by working for the gypsy moth committee at the rank of inspector or as a member of the experimental squad, their salaries paid by the Commonwealth of Massachusetts.

The Metropolitan Park Commission II

The Board of Agriculture and its gypsy moth committee had to deal with the single-minded board of the Metropolitan Park Commission to work out an arrangement for insect control in the Middlesex Fells and other reservations. Both boards were driven by the particular urgencies of their situation and mandate, and both considered their work to be of commanding importance. The entomologists and agriculturists thought of the extermination attempt as representing the greatest experiment of its type in the history of science. Everyone in the MPC felt the same about park work, as typified by the comments of the commission's senior landscape architect, Frederick Law Olmsted: "Nothing compares in importance to us with the Boston work, meaning the Metropolitan quite equally with the city work. The two together will be the most important work in our profession now in hand anywhere in the world."[29]

Any association of these two strong-willed and zealous boards was bound to be an uneasy one at best. The committeemen and the commissioners had held a series of meetings beginning on March 6, 1894, and it is evident from the few surviving letters that the gypsy moth committee emerged somewhat hobbled by the park commissioners, who would allow only work not in "conflict with the plans of the park commission."[30] Forbush became subservient to the various superintendents of parks in which he wanted to work. His men were to wear a badge while in the parks; trees could not be cut down until they had been inspected and tagged; and infested trees were to be burned only with the consent of the park superintendent.[31]

The MPC was engrossed in the early stages of its task, and gypsy moths were not high on its list of priorities because the park commissioners believed that none of the reservations was seriously infested. Their landscape architects were more aware of the insect's potential for destroying thousands of dollars' worth of new plantings as well as ancient and irreplaceable trees. They mentioned in their 1894 report that, "this voracious creature . . . must be fought as zealously as fire if the trees are to be saved alive."[32]

The park commissioners at first were relatively amenable to the gypsy moth committee because moth work was advantageous to both parties. The removal of dead and dying trees served the purposes of the gypsy moth committee by reducing the number of breeding places that would otherwise require treatment on an annual basis; the park commissioners saw it as a way to improve the chances of struggling young seedlings and to reduce the threat of fire. Thereafter, however, the interests of the two groups diverged: the park commissioners wanted the clearing done once, whereas the gypsy moth committee argued that the grounds would have to be cleaned and burned twice each year until the gypsy moth was gone.

The differences between the two groups were widened by the state's Boulevard Act of 1894, Chapter 228, which authorized the MPC to create thoroughfares in district reservations and connect them with streets and electric rail lines from the cities of Boston, Malden, and others. Legislation to link the parks and reservations had been strongly pushed by the MPC. The act was signed into law by Governor Russell partly to further the work of the metropolitan parks and partly because the state was in recession after the financial collapse of 1893, and road building created jobs for the unemployed.[33] The last thing the gypsy moth committee wanted through the wooded regions was a network of roads that would provide unparalleled opportunities for the dispersal of the gypsy moth during its larval stage, and nothing within reason could prevent it.

Intelligent Spraying

Riley always contended that spraying had to be done intelligently to be successful; the ultimate achievement mostly depended on the skill and experience of the man at the end of the hose. The goal of the nozzle man was to float a fog of insecticide on the foliage, watching as the liquid built up. At the moment when the leaves became wet, the suspension became visible as a white coating, at which point the spraying had to cease or the water would run off the leaves, taking the arsenic with it. If all were done well, an even coating of poison would remain on the leaves after the water evaporated.

After a tree or a small cluster of trees had been sprayed, the entire apparatus had to be moved. Fragile, fabric-wrapped rubber hoses had to be rolled up and returned to the wagons. The tanks required frequent refilling, which meant driving to the nearest source of water (although sometimes a water wagon stood by). At a hydrant, the tank could be filled easily, but water from streams or wells had to be pumped by hand. Once the tank was refilled, a new batch of poisons had to be mixed, allowed to precipitate out, and then be agitated, after which the wagon had to be driven back to the work area

and its hoses and nozzles recoupled for use. A typical wagon was spraying only half of the time it was in the field, and that much only if nothing malfunctioned.

Lead arsenate did not kill as fast as the older varieties of poison, and some time passed before Forbush and Fernald realized that the proportion of 5 pounds to 150 gallons of water was too low. The concentration was doubled to 10 pounds per 150 gallons, and subsequently tripled to 15 pounds before even a modest effect was noticed. Moreover, lead arsenate was most effective when used early in the season, but the committee could not count on spring spraying because of frequent budget delays and rainy weather. One crew mixed 40 pounds to 150 gallons of water and reported that after spraying, the caterpillars vanished, but Forbush realized that the continued use of heavy concentrations was out of the question: "Although [lead arsenate] is the most effective poison yet used on the gypsy moth caterpillars, doubtless it would have failed, like Paris green, to check their ravages when they were in full force. After four years of experimenting I am constrained to believe that no form of arsenic, unless used in unsafe quantities, can be relied on to hold the gypsy moth in check, much less to exterminate it."[34]

For several years no one in authority seemed to know what to do with this dangerous substance. The committee used the material sparingly because it was expensive, unreliable, and highly toxic to honey bees. It was effective against a wide range of other insects, however, and once word of its efficacy got out, the committee's reluctance to apply the chemical was not shared by others. In less than ten years the use of this poison swept across the country from East Coast to West. Fernald encouraged the widespread use of lead arsenate because he felt it showed the value of economic entomology and reflected well on his profession and the progressive nature of the Commonwealth. Economic entomologists, farmers, and fruit growers hailed the discovery as a boon to agriculture, and the gypsy moth committee and the Massachusetts Board of Agriculture claimed it as their great gift to humanity. By the end of the first campaign this chemical was being produced by many New England companies, including Bowker Chemical in Boston, Swift & Co. in Boston, and Merrimack Chemical in North Woburn. The toxic wastes produced by unrestricted production still pollute part of the greater Boston water supply.

To Kill a Gypsy Moth

Forbush and Fernald were gripped by a compelling need to discover why it took so much arsenic to kill a gypsy moth caterpillar and how many gypsy moths would have to be killed each season to keep their populations from

increasing. During the summer of 1894, gypsy moth larvae were fed controlled amounts of arsenic and then dissected by A. H. Kirkland at the Hatch Experiment Station in Amherst, after which F. C. Moulton analyzed their organs and tissues in the Harvard chemistry lab. The insect had a remarkable capacity for excreting most of the arsenic it ingested and tolerating whatever was left; it could withstand more than twelve times the fatal proportional dose for an adult human being. Living insects were found to contain large amounts of the poison, which did them no harm and remained with them through their pupal stage. Measurable quantities of arsenic could also be found in the imago, though the vitality of the insect and its reproductive functions were hardly affected. Fernald put it succinctly when he said that after the larvae were more than a few weeks old, they were able to eat Paris green and "grow fat."[35] He told his colleagues: "I took some of the insects home and fed a large number of them, and I could not believe my own results and had my assistants try it again. I had tried it in the field, and I tried it three years in succession myself, and I am obliged to say that you can not kill this insect with Paris green unless you use more than it is possible to put on the trees without destroying the foliage."[36]

During a series of experiments with other poisons, Moulton fed a strychnine-covered piece of lettuce to a caterpillar. After about an hour the caterpillar stopped moving and appeared to be dead. When Moulton looked an hour later he saw the caterpillar was alive and had resumed eating the poisoned leaf. After the second feeding, the stunned caterpillar rolled over on its back and apparently died again. When Moulton visited the cage after several hours it was his turn to be stunned—the caterpillar had revived once more and appeared to be normal.[37] Although the gypsy moth did not have the nine lives of a cat, it demonstrably had at least three.

Both Forbush and Fernald originally miscalculated the potential for the moth's annual increase and were unprepared for large hatches of larvae. They could not understand how population explosions occurred after exhaustive scouting indicated a great decline in the moth's numbers. Although the scouts could not count single caterpillars, it was possible to count individual egg clusters, a method adopted after it became the practice to destroy egg masses with creosote and leave them in place. By counting the fresh egg clusters within the known limits of a colony, and comparing that number with the egg clusters of the same colony from the previous year, a determination of increasing populations could be made: "The ratio of the average annual increase of ten such colonies was found to be 6.42—that is, six or seven egg clusters on an average may be found in the second season to one in the first season."[38]

A surviving caterpillar reproduces, and the capability of the moth in this respect was unbelievable. If only one male and one female from the same

cluster survived, they could produce enough larvae to ensure that the population remained the same the following year; moth populations retained their
density after suffering losses of 99.6 percent. A survival rate that produced
even one more female allowed the moth population to double, and if just four
gravid females survived, the total hatch of larvae the following spring could
be four times the number of insects produced the year before.

Observation and work in the laboratory during the early outbreaks showed
that most egg masses contained up to 600 eggs, but Fernald estimated the
average at a very conservative 500 eggs per cluster, and by the end of work
for 1891, Forbush was using 468 as the average number.[39] Fernald concluded
that destroying six of every seven egg clusters each season would eliminate 85
percent of the insects before they hatched, and given another seven or eight
percent reduction based on the destruction of the insect during other stages of
its life, he believed that population increases would be checked. Ten colonies
were selected and their egg masses counted. The data extrapolated from these
few colonies then served as a model for almost the entire duration of the
campaign. Massive outbreaks occurred because the scouts were unable to
make an accurate count of the number of fresh egg clusters, because the assumed number of eggs in each cluster was off the mark, and because the
directors had underestimated the percentage of eggs that would have to be
destroyed in order to cancel the moth's gains.

Fernald believed the magic number needed to hold the gypsy moth population steady was 90 percent elimination. The terms "90 percent," "nine out
of ten," "nine-tenths," or their inverse—"10 percent," or "one in ten"—
appeared often in the annual reports of the committee. For example, at the
close of fieldwork for 1891, Forbush reported that a 90 percent reduction was
sufficient to hold the moth populations steady: "The spraying and other treatment of the trees redoubled the fruit crop of the district. The measures used
disposed of the annual increase of the moth, and *reduced the numbers originally found by about ninety percent*" (emphasis added). Forbush repeated this
percentage in his annual report for 1892 and reaffirmed his belief that the
committee's work had kept the moth populations from increasing: "Nine
tenths of the moths in the region found infested had been destroyed, and there
was no immediate danger from them *as long as they were kept under control*"
(emphasis added).[40]

[CHAPTER 11]

Unusual Business (1895)

T HE STATE LEGISLATURE asked Massachusetts senators and representatives in the U.S. Congress to request $100,000 to assist in the fight against the gypsy moth. In early January 1895, Francis Appleton, once again drawn into the war, joined William Sessions, William Bowker, and Edward Forbush before House and Senate committees in Washington to support legislation introduced by Massachusetts Senator William Cogswell.[1] Since Massachusetts would not allow gypsy moth appropriations to be spent outside the state, the delegation traveled at its own expense, with some help from Cogswell's office.

The visit by the Massachusetts delegation, which included a meeting at the Department of Agriculture, had been planned for late 1893 or early 1894 but had been postponed—possibly on Riley's advice that chances for success were slight, given Agriculture Secretary Morton's opposition to "federal interference in state matters"—and possibly because of the disintegrating situation in the office of entomology at the USDA.[2] The tempest concluded in 1894 when Riley, embittered by his failure to be appointed professor of entomology at Oxford and passed over for the post of assistant secretary of agriculture, resigned, much to everyone's relief.[3] His successor, much to everyone's surprise, was his former assistant, Leland Howard, a far more complaisant man.

Cogswell introduced the Massachusetts delegation to Secretary Morton, who gave them a cordial but cautious hearing, fearful that opening the federal purse to assist in the fight against the gypsy moth would flood him with similar requests from every state in the union. The delegation reported that Morton seemed disturbed by the photographs Sessions had brought but would not give them assistance because they had "not followed the advice of Prof. Riley."[4] With Riley now out of the way, it was possible to recast his role in the gypsy moth campaign from that of a strong advocate of spraying to a champion of natural controls.

The problem for the delegation was not that they hadn't listened to Riley but that they had. They tried to explain to Morton the reasons why they had not been able to change course, but Morton was not convinced and indicated

that if the matter came before Congress, he could not support it but would offer no opposition. When Fernald learned of the events in Washington, he wrote to Herbert Osborn that he had little faith in obtaining a congressional appropriation, saying, "I am absolutely certain that we cannot get aid from Congress without [Morton's] sanction, and I do not believe we could if he should favor it."[5]

The U.S. Senate hearing on the resolve occurred on Friday, January 4, and the Massachusetts delegation also appeared the next day at a special Saturday hearing of the House Committee on Agriculture. Senator Henry Cabot Lodge, a Bostonian, amended the bill and brought it before the Senate, which resolved to appropriate $40,000 for use against the gypsy moth, but the bill died in conference. This was a double setback, because it would have been much easier to get a state appropriation if the federal government had shouldered part of the burden.

Upon the empty-handed return of the delegation, the Massachusetts Board of Agriculture requested an appropriation of $200,000 from the state for 1895, but the General Court balked. On February 11 a divided legislative committee on agriculture held public hearings that were attended by hundreds of citizens and subsequently recommended an appropriation of $150,000. The legislature was convinced that the board had asked for a large amount knowing that the request would be cut back, and the attitude of the General Court was typified by the comments of Senator Alfred E. Barker: "If I go to a man and ask him for ten dollars a few times and I get five dollars each time, I know his policy, and if, sir, I don't ask him for twenty dollars when I want ten dollars, then, sir, I am not a real smart fellow. Now, if this gypsy moth committee came up here for five years and asked for a certain amount of money, and failed to get it each time by about 50,000 dollars . . . and then did not come up and ask for more than they wanted, they are not smart enough to wipe out the gypsy moth in Massachusetts."[6]

Large numbers of furloughed gypsy moth workers attended the legislative hearings in Boston, packing the galleries and irritating the legislators, who thought the men had been sent by the gypsy moth committee to intimidate the opposition and influence the appropriation. The legislators wanted the workers removed, but Sessions argued that these men at the moment were private citizens who were not employed by the state and had the right to observe the hearings.

The committee carried over 133 men into 1895, but the large payroll soon exhausted its funds, and on February 6 the entire force was dismissed. The committee waited through February for its appropriation, and then through March, and finally through April while the state legislature attended to other

matters. During this time the committee could do nothing but make preparations and attempt what it could with a small number of volunteers.

Continued Experiments

Among other things, Fernald and his assistants at the experiment station tested
the effects of temperature extremes on moth eggs. They found that the eggs
could withstand temperatures of 130 degrees Fahrenheit and still hatch. Egg
masses at eighty degrees were plunged into a mixture of calcium chloride and
snow at twenty below zero, dropping their temperature one hundred degrees
in fifteen minutes; within three weeks all the eggs hatched. Early instar larvae
tolerated cold better than heat; late instar larvae tolerated heat better than
cold, each case corresponding to the probable climatic condition at that phase
of their lives.

   Fernald also tested food preferences and identified about three hundred
plants on which the caterpillars would feed; moreover, he verified that whatever a gypsy moth larva would eat, it would eat in great quantities; one female
consumed a stupendous 212 square feet of leaves during her life.[7] A starving
gypsy moth caterpillar will devour almost anything, including field crops,
garden plants, and even turf grass. Fernald noted that some of the plants he
tested came from regions hundreds of miles away from Massachusetts: "Some
cotton plants were brought from the South, and we find that it is a very
excellent food plant for them. They revel in it; in fact, they ate the whole thing
up. If they should ever get into the South I think they would be capable of
committing sad havoc there."[8]

More Moths Than Ever

It is the nature of Nature to favor first one side and then the other, but conditions in 1895 remained ideal for gypsy moths. In the warm and early spring,
uncounted legions of caterpillars hatched, once more taking everybody by
surprise. Forbush was desperate to start work and furious with the legislature
for delaying the appropriation again. Three months of the best working
weather had been lost, during which the eggs could have been destroyed with
ease. He would be forced to exterminate the larvae after the hatch by spraying,
which would be less effective, cost him ten times as much money, and reduce
the amount of work that could be paid for later. Forbush was not going to be
caught unprepared again or the gypsy moths would run riot. He recalled his
best men on the first of the month and put to work those who agreed to wait
for remuneration. He exceeded his authority and further strained relations

with the legislature by hiring staff for his office, purchasing supplies on unofficial credit, and interviewing candidates for positions at a time when there was no money to pay them.[9]

By the time the legislature passed an appropriation on May 17, the caterpillars had undergone their third and fourth molts. With his veteran force of 1894 scattered, Forbush scrambled to organize a response. Most of the new workers had to be trained; consequently, they were used at the tasks of lowest skill. Since it was too late to destroy eggs, the new recruits banded trees with burlap, and they cut and burned brush. The caterpillars clustered so thickly on the trees that men had to sweep them off the trunks before they could tie on the burlaps. To compensate for the ground lost during the egg season, Forbush instituted twice-daily inspections, and in some places the bands were visited even more often. The numbers of caterpillars increased, and Forbush kept hiring more men, but all the new workers had to squeeze through the administrative bottlenecks he had set in place: every man was trained to a minimum standard, and groups were formed and assigned to competent superintendents; supplies and equipment were bought and units organized. No matter how urgent the situation, Forbush would rarely let any group of men take the field until he believed they were ready.

Forbush had discovered that young Kirkland, just one year out of college, harbored a drinking problem that suddenly burst into the open. This put Forbush in an awkward position because Kirkland and Albert F. Burgess were two of Fernald's most beloved students. Matters came to a head in June when Kirkland and some other members of the force were caught in an embarrassing situation, but Forbush elected to take the high road in his letter to Fernald: "Jones was discharged for neglect of duty and confirmed habits of intoxication. I have no charges to bring against the lady you speak of. Mr. Kirkland says he has stopped drinking entirely. . . . I have promised him to say nothing about his last affair if he will stop it. So hereafter I am dumb."[10]

Although Fernald may have been disappointed in his recent graduate, he likely was not as concerned as Forbush, because he had again decided to resign. But that he had placed Kirkland first on a short list to replace him presented further difficulties for Forbush, who would in that case have to work with Kirkland as an equal—a possibility that did not bode well for either man. As Forbush wrote to Fernald: "I should much prefer not to have any further responsibility concerning [Kirkland] or the insectary, and if you decide to sever your connection with the work I shall ask the committee to relieve me of any further responsibility in that connection. . . . Knowing Kirkland as I now do I prefer to have nothing further to do with him, but if it is for the best interests of the work I am ready to do anything honorable to keep him here."[11]

By mid-July, 360 men were engaged with tremendous numbers of insects

in the biggest battles of the campaign to date. In the town of Dorchester an infestation of caterpillars occurred just fifty feet past the point where snow had stopped inspectors the previous year. In a single area of several acres, eighteen bushels of caterpillars were killed. William Tyner of Sargent Street in Dorchester found gypsy moth larvae clustered so densely on his oaks that they resembled a swarm of bees, and he said they could "strip a large oak tree down to twigs in three day's time."[12] In Boston, dense swarms climbed to the balconies of houses and in such great numbers they could not be knocked off as fast as they came. Mrs. J. T. Lane remarked that the caterpillars under her gutters lay "in one great, long, black, repulsive mass."[13]

The growth rate of the caterpillars was astonishing as well, and it became evident that they would pupate early. Although their doing so would limit the amount of foliage the insects might strip, it also ensured that a remarkable abundance of larvae would transform into moths and that the resulting number of clusters and eggs in each would exceed anything known before. Colossal colonies appeared again in Medford and Saugus, and the southern portion of the Middlesex Fells experienced its first severe defoliation. Workers found areas of dense infestation in the Fells where the caterpillars lay in blankets around trees, branches, and bushes and in thick, carpetlike mats on the ground. The committee was used to the defoliation of individual trees by the block in towns and villages, but this year the moths were in the forest, defoliating trees by the acre. The cyclone burners roared incessantly as workers formed skirmish lines to halt the swarming caterpillars. Ornamental vegetation was sprayed with lead arsenate, but the ratio of 10 pounds to 150 gallons had to be tripled.

As the caterpillars continued to invade the woodlands, the committee was forced to deal with acreage containing mature trees, which they did with the only tools they had—axes and fire. In Woburn, ten acres of mature oaks forty to sixty feet tall were cut, and the land was burned over twice.[14] Although cutting deprived the next hatch of food, the work only partially damaged many of the thickly dispersed egg masses. Tens of thousands of individual eggs were scattered on the ground, and the oil soakings and burnings that followed failed to destroy them all.

Work was most difficult on metropolitan parklands, as park commissioners ruled out the cut-and-burn method favored by the gypsy moth committee. Meetings were held to resolve the problems, and the committee always took great pains to report how harmonious they had been and how much mutual cooperation had been attained. But Leland Howard noted that the commissioners had been "far less complaisant" than individual landowners. And even had the commissioners turned matters over to the gypsy moth committee, it would have become apparent that Forbush did not have enough money or

men available to carry out the work; he would have had to abandon other areas to send men into the woodlands, and the net gain would have been zero. Still, the reluctance of the park commissioners to allow drastic measures in the Middlesex Fells and elsewhere was perhaps the final factor that made winning the gypsy moth war impossible. The committee could only hope that the park commissioners would recognize the consequences of their policies. All that could be done until then was to stabilize the situation, with the centers of moth infestation cordoned off and besieged by the state.

There was something about the view of the common man toward bug slaughter that brought out derisive streaks in Forbush and Fernald. With Forbush it is seen in his condescending condemnation of conditions found behind the dwelling places of common folks, and with Fernald it comes out in his presidential address to the Eighth Annual Meeting of the Association of Economic Entomologists in August 1896: "Last year the chairman of the board of selectmen in a Massachusetts town refused to use any of the public money for the protection of the trees along the streets from the cankerworms, because the idea of fighting insects was 'agin nature.' This year that same man's apple trees are as bare of leaves as though a fire had run through his orchard, and therefore I am of the opinion that it will be 'agin nature' for that man to gather a crop of fruit from his trees this fall."[15]

Fernald was so desperate to vanquish the moth that he championed imposing a "moth tax" on every citizen in the state, and he believed that if the insect escaped the Commonwealth, the tax should be levied on the entire country. He saw nothing wrong with the practice of trespassing on the land or premises of citizens to exterminate gypsy moths. His only reservation about accepting funds from the federal government was one of state's rights: he did not think agents of the federal government should be allowed to enter the lands of private citizens but thought the practice permissible when done by the state. If citizens were unhappy about the invasion of their property, campaign leaders were unsympathetic. Fernald regarded it as necessary to achieve the ends of the campaign and believed that the average Massachusetts citizen should accept trespass by state workers as "the lesser of two evils."[16]

Insect Predators Arise

In the thick of the most discouraging battles of the war came some good news: a rise in insect predators of the gypsy moth in almost all stages of its life. Wasps and hornets were observed chasing male moths and capturing them on the wing; *Vespa maculata* was very active in this respect. During the larval season, *Polistes pallipes*, the common paper wasp, was frequently observed stinging and killing gypsy moth caterpillars, eating part of them and then

flying off with other parts to provision the embryo cells in their nests. The wasps were active for hours every day, taking one gypsy caterpillar after another. Ants were active in attacking female moths at egg-laying, while harvest spiders (*Phalangium dorsatum*) consumed eggs from within the clusters. *Phidippus tripunctatus*, another spider, killed gypsy moth larvae in the field and in the insectary. Native Calosoma, Harpalus, and Carabas beetles fed continually on caterpillars, while some species of Dermestes attacked the pupa and devoured eggs in the clusters. Tiger beetles (Cicindela), assassin bugs (*Sinea diadema*), centipedes (*Lithobius forficatus*), and spiders—the cobweb weaver (*Steododa borealis*), the jumping spider (*Phidippus galathea*), and several others—were also destroying the insect.

Parasitic Diptera were seen laying their eggs on the caterpillars. Predaceous Diptera such as *Dasyllis sacrator* attacked female imagoes at egg-laying, while *Asilus sericeus* was observed to seize flying males. Insects of the Hemiptera and Heteroptera were among the most useful of all predators, especially *Podisus serieventris* and *Podisus cynicus*, the soldier bugs, which were widely distributed throughout the region infested by the gypsy moth. Mites were very effective in destroying egg masses and were considered important predators because of the speed with which they accomplished their aims.

News of rising predation was encouraging to Fernald as he continued correspondence with European colleagues about natural predators. Although the replies he received were helpful, the gypsy moth in the old country could be found over such an extended range that Europeans had never contemplated extermination, preferring to deal with it only at those times when localized population increases made it destructive. Population outbreaks and injury to forests and orchards were much less severe in Western Europe than what Fernald saw in North America, and Fernald's European colleagues were astonished by the reports he sent to them. Experts such as Antonio Montiero of Portugal, Professor Henry of France, Professor N. Nasonov of Russia, and Max Fingerling of Germany, to a man, believed that destruction of egg masses offered the best hope for control. Even the greatest European experts were convinced that importing insects would be a wasted effort. Bernard Altum, a well-respected German entomologist, dissuaded Fernald from making any efforts along those lines: "I have never known of a devastation in Germany equal in severity and extent to that in your country. So far as I know, all of the devastations of dispar in this region have occurred on limited areas, and have always quickly disappeared. An importation of predaceous insects to oppose this destructive dispar, e.g. Calosoma sycophanta, etc., cannot possibly be of any industrial importance."[17]

The failure of pesticides and the rise of natural predators compelled Fernald to continue investigating parasites, and he began to collect native "bugs," as

he called them, that preyed on the gypsy moth. Not trusting himself to identify them, he sent them to P. R. Uhler, a knowledgeable amateur entomologist in Baltimore, to be named.[18]

Small animals were the next group observed attacking the moth. Skunks devoured female moths on the ground and ate pupae as well. Wood frogs consumed female moths, and tree frogs would take small larvae. Common garden toads were almost machinelike in their consumption of gypsy moth larvae and were especially effective in brush land. One dissected toad was found to have eaten sixty-five larvae in a single day. Many of these effective control creatures, however, had been driven off, suppressed, or killed outright by being drenched with arsenical sprays or incinerated alive by the cyclone burners.

Canker worms were numerous during 1894 and 1895, and outbreaks of Tussock moths added to the general misery of the state. For the first time, trees were dying after successive defoliations. It was frustrating for the fieldworkers to fight an infestation of gypsy moth caterpillars defoliating a stand of trees while another kind of larva defoliating a different stand nearby had to be left untouched. Most of the birds that had considerably reduced gypsy moth populations in the past were glutting themselves on the hairless canker worms. Until this point, even Forbush had maintained that predation by birds was not a significant factor in depressing moth populations, but the difference this year was so striking that it could not be ignored.

During the early summer, experiments and research that had been done at Amherst and in the Malden storehouse were consolidated in a new insectary built on leased land at the edge of the Malden woods. This relieved the researchers of working in the swamplike atmosphere of the storehouse on Commercial Street and removed the risk that experiments would cause a secondary gypsy moth outbreak in Amherst, which was outside the boundary of 1891. The one-and-a-half story insectary building was rather small at sixteen by twenty feet but had a six- by eight-foot greenhouse on the south wall and a covered shed seven by eight feet on the north. Squeezed into the small space on the first floor was a main laboratory with closets, a private laboratory, and a chemical room. On the floor above was a single room for employees.

In view of Fernald's continual attempts to resign as entomological adviser, because of his workload, the committee elevated Archie Kirkland to the position of assistant entomologist, and he took over the entomologist's tasks at the insectary, where he had been working since 1892. The young man might have had his faults and temporarily succumbed to the temptations of youth, but Fernald knew him as a skilled and tireless worker and a promising young entomologist who had published twenty-six papers while he was still a college

Archie Howard Kirkland at the time he joined the fieldwork against the gypsy moth.

Photo courtesy of Special Collections and Archives, W.E.B. Du Bois Library, University of Massachusetts Amherst.

student. He was very fond of Kirkland and often referred to him as "my friend and co-worker."

The caterpillar advance during 1895 was furious but short. In the abnormally warm weather the larvae underwent fewer molts, and most of them pupated after six or seven weeks. This prevented the areas of defoliation from being worse than they would have been had the larvae fed longer. In some communities where ornamental shrubs and trees were being stripped, arsenate of lead at the rate of 30 pounds to 150 gallons of water was used to good effect. At the end of the season the workers were exhausted from their efforts, but Forbush reported that the outward thrust of the invaders had been blunted. Over a thousand colonies of the moth had been eradicated. The actions of the year ended in a draw, but in the now-silent woods, inspectors found uncountable numbers of egg clusters. Unless something new could be devised, the following summer would be a nightmare.

The insect kept appearing in localities both outside and inside the boundaries of the infested zone. In Saugus, Woburn, Lexington, Arlington, Medford, and the Middlesex Fells, at least three thousand acres of woodlands had become densely infested. Regardless of everything new the gypsy moth committee could muster, the moths always seemed to be one jump ahead of them. There was a serious new problem to deal with this year when Fernald discovered that the dreaded San Jose scale insect had finally reached Massachusetts and had been discovered in five localities within the western part of the state.

The early pupation of the gypsy moth did allow Forbush to begin a huge scouting project in June instead of September. He proposed to inspect all 12,000 acres of woodlands within the boundary of 1891, something that had never been done before. This project lasted through the year and was still unfinished when the appropriation ran out. Forbush planned to complete the work, weather permitting, as soon as the appropriation for 1896 was in hand.

The benefits were questionable, however: Bartholomew R. Hennelly was sent with a gang of forty men under Special Inspector Nelson and Superintendent Williams to scout portions of the Middlesex Fells near Grosvenor Avenue in Medford. Because Forbush would not allow men to work in areas where they lived, all the men in the party had come from other parts of the state and were not familiar with these woods. A line was formed with the men roughly one hundred feet apart, and the scouting began. After about a mile, the line became hopelessly separated, and Nelson and Williams decided to reverse direction. About ten men had wandered out of earshot, and the thirty men who could be located were sent off at a trot through the woods, attempting to check the trees for moths while keeping each other in sight. Hennelly said that three or four more of the remaining men got lost and straggled out of the forest some time later but that not a single tree in the Fells was scouted.[19]

Riley and Fernald at the Entomologists' Annual Meeting

The seventh annual meeting of the Association of Economic Entomologists was held at the end of August 1895. On the afternoon of August 28, Fernald presented a lengthy account of gypsy moth work in Massachusetts, using specimens and photographs to illustrate his talk. Some aspects of the lecture and the discussions with Riley that followed were remarkable for their candor—as Fernald surely recognized, for he told officers of the association that his comments were not for publication. When C. L. Marlatt asked permission to publish a redacted transcript, however, saying the talk was "the most satisfactory and interesting statement of the work of the commission that has ever been made," Fernald changed his mind.[20] Of his association with the work in Massachusetts since 1891, he related: "I was then asked to act as entomologist [to the committee], and in an unhappy moment, I consented, and, although I have since resigned, the committee has declined to accept my resignation, and I still hold that position. I was at first prone to judge of this foreign insect by the habits of our home insects, and I am not sure but that Professor Riley and I both had the same inclination."[21]

Fernald went on to say that Scudder's advice to destroy the egg masses had been right, and that in the five years he had spent studying the gypsy moth he

continued to find new and startling facts no one had anticipated. He admitted
to a mistake in basing all his advice on his lab studies, since it had become
obvious that the gypsy moth behaved differently in the field. He noted that the
responsibilities of his position weighed heavily on him and accepted the blame
for anything that had gone wrong, saying that he had given the best advice he
knew how to give and that only time would tell whether or not he had been
right. Fernald was not ashamed of what he was doing. His state was making
a magnificent fight, in his opinion, not only for itself but also for the whole
United States.

Riley, recently resigned as chief federal entomologist, was at last unbur-
dened from the need to speak in guarded terms and defend his actions.[22] He
apologized on the record for his harsh criticisms of the earlier gypsy moth
commissions. It was, he said, due to his misunderstanding that the hardiness
of this exceptional insect prevented control by ordinary means, and he now
knew that the failure to eradicate the moth was not due to any ineptness on
the part of those charged with its extermination. Riley also said that perhaps
it would be better not to have the work done by a state commission but to let
individual landowners take responsibility, which was the way problems with
all other insect pests were handled. The events in Massachusetts had shown
him the danger of applying conventional remedies to insects about which little
was known. While he had always favored extermination by spraying and had
thought that destroying egg masses would be a waste of time and money,
Riley admitted to the assembled entomologists that his position on these subjects had been extreme.

Less than three weeks later, on September 14, 1895, Riley lay dying on a
cobblestone street in Washington, D.C. While racing his high-wheel bicycle
with his fourteen-year-old son, he hit a granite paving block that had fallen
from a wagon. He was thrown over the handlebars, hit his head against the
pavement, and fractured his skull. He died that evening, leaving behind a wife
and six children. He was fifty-two years old. In a strange coincidence, just ten
days later, on September 24, the great French scientist Louis Pasteur died in
Paris. It had been Pasteur's discovery of the microscopic origin of silkworm
disease that had saved the silk industry worldwide and was probably a major
cause of entrepreneurs' abandoning their work with American silk moths.
Death had removed another principal figure in the gypsy moth war that year
with the passing of E. Leopold Trouvelot, age sixty-eight, on April 22 at
Meudon, France. Even though Trouvelot's rash actions had caused great troubles and horrific expense to the people of Massachusetts, there is hardly to be
found any record of harsh words spoken against him or condemnation of his
acts.

Business as Usual

In the midst of trying to rid eastern Massachusetts of the gypsy moth, a number of different people came to the same conclusion: there was an opportunity to make money from this insect. The tactics adopted by the leaders of the war to achieve their ends opened wide the door to lucrative speculation and avaricious enterprise, a door through which some of the ingenious people of New England eagerly rushed. With a reluctant or wavering landowner of a large woodlot or woodland acreage, the committee would first attempt a conciliatory approach, explaining the ravages of the moth and offering to reduce the damage the landowner would suffer. The committee gained nothing by understating its case, and fear alone was often enough to persuade the landowner to permit heavy thinning, or sometimes a complete clear-cutting, followed by several burnings of the brush. The landowner was told that he came out ahead because the Board of Agriculture paid the cost of felling his trees. The argument would be made that cutting trees and burning brush improved the woodland and raised its value. But if the landowner remained obstinate, the committee would turn to a group of "complaisant" men who would offer to buy the infested acreage. No records naming these men survive, but they were likely shrewd individuals who used the weight of the committee and the inferior position of the landowner to further their own ends. Land changed hands at distressed prices, the buyers knowing that the committee would fell the timber and clear dense undergrowth. These new owners would sell the best logs for furniture and the remainder for firewood. They sold or rented the acreage for agricultural land if they did not plan to use it themselves, or they subdivided the property and sold it for building lots. The committee later claimed that moth colonies in these woodlands had been wiped out, when in fact it was the woodlands that had been eradicated.

Men who owned large tracts of timber became ardent supporters of gypsy moth work and appeared at hearings year after year to speak in favor of extermination. Some lobbied their state representatives, as Senator L. W. Ross testified at hearings held later in the decade: "One man, who is a very wealthy man and one of our best citizens, said that he had been informed that I was opposed to the gypsy moth appropriation, and he hoped I would see my way clear to change my views, and I asked him why, and he says, 'I will admit that it is a rather personal matter; I own considerable land over there and they have cleaned up my land for me. . . . [T]hey have asked me to come and see you, knowing I am a friend of yours, and see if I could not induce you to vote for this appropriation.' "[23]

Senator James E. Bailey of Arlington contended that among the few people in his district who favored gypsy moth work, most were individuals who had

benefited from the labors of gypsy moth gangs. Certain legislators from Boston known as "machine Democrats" viewed the entire gypsy moth campaign as a kind of make-work program that provided jobs for unemployed men in their districts. Many of these politicians did not believe that the gypsy moth could be exterminated, and Bailey said some of them had told him so personally, but they continued to vote for the appropriation.[24] Bailey told the story of one gypsy moth man who was working on land adjoining his father's property in Arlington: "He had been up a cherry tree and was on the ground, using opera glasses, etc., looking for nests and moths. He was doing his duty; I don't deny that. A little girl of about eight years old stood about and watched him looking for these moths, etc. She said to him, 'What are you looking for?' He said, 'Two dollars a day.' "[25]

Since the first spraying devices at the committee's disposal were crude and unreliable, warranting development of improved apparatus, equipment manufacturers also found opportunities for profit. Some worked to make wagons that could bear the weight of large barrels of pesticides even on rough terrain. Others began to develop lighter and more powerful backpack sprayers, nozzles, and tanks that would allow spraying to greater heights. Nozzles, hoses, pumps, tanks, and couplings all needed to be reinvented. Forbush placed his brother-in-law, E. C. Ware, in charge of employees at the Malden machine shop, and a two-year program to develop, build, and test new spraying equipment began.

Chemical companies and private entrepreneurs submitted dozens of samples of new pesticides that they claimed would kill gypsy moths. These mostly worthless concoctions were given to Fernald and his small staff for testing, straining the resources of the scientific corps, which exhaustively appraised every sample. A. B. Ward noted that Fernald not only tested insecticides from outside sources but also worked on the development of new formulas himself.[26]

The Battle Rages On

The Commonwealth's problems in its attempts to eradicate the gypsy moth, according to an amazing assertion from a European entomological society, occurred because American entomologists did not realize that the female gypsy moth could fly as powerfully as the male; if the Americans would make late night observations, they would confirm this for themselves. This claim baffled and disturbed Fernald just as he was bringing the gypsy moth monograph to completion. Forbush assigned men to work in the forests all night long looking for flying female gypsy moths. Failing that, he built several of what Fernald later described as wooden "Towers of Babel" around some

trees, and field personnel ascended into the leafy canopy to make nocturnal observations of specially painted lady gypsy moths.[27] All this effort went for naught, and afterward Fernald was irritated about being criticized for not reporting what he didn't find.

So much money had been expended in the struggles of the year that Forbush had to release 116 men in September. The remaining 152 men, his most experienced veterans, continued their inspections. Forbush sent them again to the peripheral towns, up and down railroad lines and well-traveled roadways, and sometimes into adjoining states. Before they were through, the men had inspected well over fourteen million trees and found only about 6 percent infested with the gypsy moth—though scouting revealed such astonishing numbers of egg masses in the recently infested woods that the hatch of 1896 promised to be the worst of the entire campaign.

Although Forbush admitted that the contest against the moth had appeared hopeless, by the end of the year he believed the insect had been held in check and that conditions in the infested woodlands were not as severe as he had feared. Three forested regions of about a thousand acres each—the portion of the Middlesex Fells that lay mostly in Medford, the northern Lynn Woods near Saugus, and woods that lay partly within the common borders of Arlington, Lexington, and Malden—would take years to clear, but the situation elsewhere, he claimed, was better than it ever had been before.

The year had been a difficult one for Fernald. He again invited entomologists from nearby states to tour the infested region and make recommendations. The visitors were pleased with what they saw, he said, but he did not publish their comments: "These reports have been simply for the legislature, and how many members of the legislature will read a report of any length when you are asking for money? The more money you ask for, the less they will read your report, and the committee has said these reports must be very short."[28] He was still dissatisfied with his situation at Amherst; he was behind on almost all his work there and could not seem to find a way out of his responsibilities to the gypsy moth committee. Despite his reluctance about being dragged ever deeper into the embrace of economic entomology, he still yearned for success and respect as a systematist, and he stubbornly pursued work on his monograph on the North American Pyralidae. For reasons known only to him, he also undertook the "Herculean task" of working alone on the entire group of Microlepidoptera in North America. He wrote to Scudder of the "intense pressure brought to bear on me from all over the country to work up and describe new species" and of the lack of leisure time that drove him to work as he did "whether I will or no."[29]

Fernald spent a good part of the year writing his half of the gypsy moth monograph, but his heart was not in it. He put off the obligation as long as he

could and tried to persuade Henshaw to write most of it for him.[30] He quarreled with Forbush over which of their names should appear first. In addition, he was so upset with the colored plates drawn by Joseph Bridgham of Providence that he refused to accept them until overruled by the committee, which was determined to have the book ready for the state printer by the first of the year.

The Politics of War (1896)

W HILE CONDITIONS in the field were becoming more fluid, conditions in the legislature were hardening over the question of funding. Rumors flew that opponents of extermination had enough votes either to reduce the moth appropriation to a crippling level or to defeat the bill altogether. The constantly changing nature of events had brought the war in from the fields and forests of eastern Massachusetts to the streets of the capital city, and the next great battle would be waged in the corridors of the State House in Boston.

The committee had carried over nearly $40,000 to pay the wages of 121 men through mid-March 1896. This force spent most of its time creosoting egg clusters, burning brush, and felling trees in preparation for the summer. All involved hoped their appropriation would be approved early, but Forbush heard persistent rumblings from the legislature that obtaining any funds would be no easy task. To ensure the swiftest possible response, Sessions placed the committee's annual report in the hands of the senate clerk on the first day the legislature was in session—ten days ahead of the date required by law.[1]

The committee and its top people by now were spending as much time in back-room maneuvering as they were fighting moths in the field. Hearings were scheduled before the agriculture committee on Tuesday morning, January 28, in the State House. Fernald, Forbush, and Sessions believed they were vulnerable, and there is a surge of correspondence between them concerning tactics, strategy, and the influence of their friends and foes in the legislature. Many letters are couched in guarded terms, and the preparations for the critical hearings are often referred to as "the other matter," or "the matter now before us." On January 22, Sessions wrote asking Fernald to come to Boston the day before the hearings and discuss strategy: "We think we have a good legislative committee and we want to put in our case with shrewdness so as to cover the ground and not tire the [committee]. We want your advice and we also want advance notice what the others will say and arrange to avoid repetition and increase the proper presentation of all points necessary."[2]

The hearings began on January 28, and the transcript reveals that the board's strategy was to deflect all criticisms and smother the opposition with economic entomologists. Without saying whether it was likely, Sessions, Forbush, and Fernald would argue that exterminating the moth was possible, but with the proviso that enough money always be available. Every opportunity would be taken to recount the insect's ravages in Europe and to maximize the tales of caterpillar swarms in the Commonwealth. Fear of the gypsy moth was to be their cudgel, and it was a weapon they wielded with a practiced hand.

Sessions was a savvy political infighter by nature and experience, and he had devised a strategy to take advantage of inexperienced adversaries. He opened with an audacious gambit by reading into testimony portions of a speech that Leland Howard had made in 1894, material so prejudicial to his cause that one might expect his opposition to use it. Sessions intended to show that although the nation's highest economic entomologists appeared not to believe the gypsy moth could be exterminated, those appearances were deceiving. Howard's excerpt stated, in part: "Under the circumstances, therefore, any course other than energetic and well directed effort to keep the insect within its present boundaries will be shortsighted in the extreme, although it is doubtful to my mind whether absolute extermination will or ever can be brought about."[3]

To counter such statements, Sessions dribbled hearsay evidence into the hearings often, including his secondhand opinion that Howard had not meant everything he wrote. He said Howard had admitted privately that his doubts were based on his perception that the state would discontinue appropriations.[4] Sessions made another utterly surprising point by claiming that Howard was prevented by his superiors at the USDA from expressing favorable opinions of moth work. He suggested that these restrictions had caused Howard's personal statements to be taken out of context, that most laymen could not understand what Howard had meant, and that it had become a sore point with Howard to be constantly misquoted.

Fernald confirmed that only he and a small group of his peers could understand insect work. He was proud that the United States was ahead of Europe in economic entomology because the Europeans did not use insecticides: "I was in Berlin in 1889 and the trees all around were filled with [female] gypsy moths. . . . I asked an official of the public garden if they had ever used poisonous insecticides and he had never heard of such a thing. He said they would begin the next day with fire engines and wash the female moths down to the ground and crush them [with rollers]. Just think of that."[5]

Fernald told some horror stories about gypsy moth swarms in Europe. One favorite was about the time police in Penza, Russia, were mobilized to shovel

up mounds of dead caterpillars because the horrible stench of the decaying insects made people sick. His question about who would want to live in such conditions, however, was parried by Warren Frost, one of four brothers, market gardeners, who was unimpressed by such shopworn tales of terror. Frost said any market gardener in Boston would be happy to have so much wonderfully rich decaying matter for fertilizer and called Fernald's bluff by asking to be told where such heaps could be found because he wanted to buy some.[6]

On the second day of testimony, Forbush took the stand to defend his actions. He admitted that the work had gone slowly because of the high standards he set for the workers, but he felt that if a tree died as the result of defoliation or careless work, he personally should be made to pay for it. He explained his strategy of making successive passes to diminish the enemy's numbers and said that his ultimate goal was "to sweep these insects into the sea."[7] Barker asked what he would do if given a million dollars; an amused Forbush responded that he could never find enough men to justify such a big payroll.

Forbush revealed that he and Fernald "had almost come to blows" on the subject of parasites.[8] Forbush and many entomologists believed the state should import parasites, but over the years they had come to agree with Fernald. Fernald affirmed that he refused a request from the gypsy moth committee to go abroad for this purpose, saying he feared that introducing secondary parasites might make matters worse. Using a seafaring term, he told Barker, "There are a great many holes in this skimmer . . . and I do not feel like soldering them all up."[9]

Whenever the brothers Varnum and Warren Frost were in the room, they hurled stinging criticisms at Forbush without mercy. Varnum thought the anxieties about insect dangers were unnecessarily raised, and he questioned the dioramas and other displays that the gypsy moth committee had sent around the region:

> What are all these preserved pictures [and displays] brought here for? It is to strike terror into the souls of the [hearing] committee. What did we have the exhibit at the Mechanic's Fair for? All the birds stuffed on an old dead tree and two old hens at the base of it picking up gypsy moths. . . . It is so that thousands and thousands of people might see that dreaded pest. . . . As far as the Board of Agriculture is concerned, in making their selection for a field director to engineer this big scare, they could not have gotten a better one if they had raked the Commonwealth all over.[10]

After listening to Forbush explain scouting and how his men painted marks on the trees to indicate their condition, the work done, the crew responsible, and the date of completion, Varnum Frost complained that there was a tree in the yard next to his that had "half the alphabet on it."[11] Frost noted it was no secret in Arlington that the properties of certain parties were well cared for, citing one instance in which an estate of thirty acres had received days' worth of treatment, whereas not an hour of work had been done in the adjoining yard. He also disliked what he called "the big scare." He said growers were told that half a billion dollars' worth of crop damage was done annually by insects, yet the market was so glutted that Massachusetts growers had a difficult time selling their produce.[12]

Warren Frost was incensed that gypsy moth gangs were pouring acids into tree hollows and burning out cavities with fire to kill egg clusters or larvae. He said such work drove away insectivorous bluebirds and owls and destroyed their nesting places, which he called "the most terrible practice I ever heard of."[13] Further, he was losing his patience with the exaggerated claims of the board: "I have been acquainted with this board for several years, and the wise ones have all drawn out of it, and I recommend to Brother Sessions and Mr. Forbush not to hang on too long. It's going to burst; the whole thing is going to burst. The sentiment is setting in strong. We are not going to be hoodwinked much longer."[14] The four Frost brothers refused to permit gypsy moth gangs on their farm and removed burlaps that Forbush's men had tied on their trees, saying they would take care of their land themselves. At one point Forbush visited the Frosts personally to order the burlaps replaced under penalty of law, and a tense standoff of several months ensued before Forbush decided to let the brothers have their way.

The records of the 1896 hearings are incomplete between January 31 and February 23, but some information about them is found in letters written to Fernald by Kirkland, Howard, and Forbush. Fernald had fallen ill after the hearings of January 31 and returned to Amherst, leaving an excited Kirkland alone to experience the unfolding drama that would likely decide the fate of the gypsy moth committee. Kirkland attended most of the hearings and wrote often to keep Fernald apprised. By February 1, he thought the matter was well in hand, noting the appearance of only a few opponents, whom he characterized as "feeble" and "mostly dead and wounded."[15] But Fernald reminded him not to count his chickens before they hatched, and Kirkland was forced to agree by February 6, when he learned that the greatest opposition would occur after the hearings, when the appropriations bill went to the floor of the house: "Guess your advice about not counting legislative 'chickens' is good. F. H. Appleton we are told is aiding and abetting a petition to the House

asking that the amount of appropriation be made $50,000. This possibly to please Bailey [the] ex-representative from Arlington and Winchester . . . I'll stop here; think probably you'll need to go out and chase yourself around the house to rest your head after reading this."[16]

Appleton was not some ignorant citizen to be brushed off. He had served on the gypsy moth committee for three years and was a respected member of the Board of Agriculture. In the months since he had traveled to Washington as a member of the Massachusetts gypsy moth delegation, he had concluded that too much money was being spent trying to accomplish the impossible, and his views carried a great deal of weight. Appleton had invited Leland Howard to speak before the Massachusetts Horticultural Society on February 15 while the hearings were still going on, and Howard had accepted. Forbush was convinced that Appleton would use the occasion to let an unwitting Howard make statements that could later be used against the gypsy moth committee. To prepare for what lay ahead, Forbush urged Fernald to meet Howard's train at Springfield and ride with him to Boston.[17]

Fernald wrote to Howard in Washington; Howard told Fernald on February 10 in a letter marked "private" that his talk would be on scale insects, not gypsy moths:

> I feel, however, that I must be posted as to [Appleton's] exact attitude and as to whether he is in any way antagonistic to yourself and the present Gypsy Moth Commission before I express any sentiments on the subject of the Gypsy Moth to him in conversation. I am therefore hurriedly writing to you to see if you will not immediately let me know any facts which I ought to know. . . . [W]rite me immediately on receipt of this letter addressing me at the University Club Boston where I shall arrive on Friday night.[18]

Howard's letter of the tenth and Fernald's of the eighth crossed in the mail, but Howard wrote again on the eleventh asking Fernald to explain briefly his support of extermination so that he (Howard) would be in agreement with the gypsy moth committee should anyone ask. He said he wanted to see the experiment succeed and promised not to interfere—even though he had already concluded that extermination was beyond reach: "To you personally I do not mind expressing my doubts as to ultimate extermination, without an expenditure of a sum of money which will be entirely out of the question. But it is yet an unsettled point with me whether I have any right to advance such an opinion. The conduct of the investigation . . . will be such a magnificent experiment that I am anxious to see it carried out."[19]

Opponents regrouped behind the Massachusetts Society for the Promotion

of Agriculture and presented their case on February 23 through attorney Richard M. Saltonstall. Forbush became nervous again and asked Kirkland to write Fernald and implore him to return to Boston. Kirkland wrote the letter but decided he had heard enough and instead would spend those days with Fernald in Amherst naming insects.[20] The opposition presented their petition without animosity toward the board or the gypsy moth committee. As Saltonstall stated in his opening remarks, those opposed to the extermination effort simply wished to express their view that eradicating the gypsy moth was impossible and that the nature of the work should be changed: the committee should prevent the insect from spreading and restrict exterminative work to places where outbreaks occurred. The petitioners also recommended an appropriation of $5,000 to send Fernald abroad to arrange for shipping back parasites. Twenty prominent people—including Charles Sargent, head of the Arnold Arboretum; Francis H. Appleton, now a former member of the Board of Agriculture; Augustus Hemenway, a metropolitan park commissioner; and J. D. W. French, president of the Bay State Agricultural Society—had signed Saltonstall's petition. Seven other signers of the petition were trustees of the Society for the Promotion of Agriculture.

Saltonstall questioned Forbush about the number of men needed to inspect a million burlaps daily, hoping to show that the effort was impractical. He himself had computed that one man could examine three hundred trees in a ten-hour day, so the task would require well over 3,000 employees, which he called "a small army."[21] Forbush shot back that any man who could not attend five hundred burlaps a day would not be working long for him. Saltonstall recalculated his numbers and said the work would require 2,000 men, which he still thought was a small army.

Sessions hammered away on everybody, including his former colleague Francis Appleton, who had maintained for two years that extermination was impossible and that scientists and entomologists were divided on the point. Sessions tried to portray Appleton as one who would not listen to the advice of experts:

SESSIONS: Did I understand you that your opinion of the possibility of this thing would not be changed by the opinions of economic entomologists on this matter?
APPLETON: I do not think I made that statement. I would not put my opinion against theirs. What I say is that where doctors disagree, I have the right to choose my own doctor.[22]

The protracted hearing of February 25 included the testimony of Samuel Scudder, Alpheus Packard, and Nathaniel Shaler. Scudder was the strongest

witness; there was no doubt in his mind that extermination was impossible regardless of the appropriation: "I was one of those consulted when the committee held a conference in 1891. I stated then that I did not believe in extermination, and I have found nothing since then to change my views. . . . I think the committee would have to expend $100,000 [per year] for a hundred years before they would get anywhere near extermination, and the last would be the worst of all."[23] Packard was a weaker witness but not on the point of extermination. He said it would be best to use fungal diseases to which caterpillars were very susceptible. Kirkland thought both men had sounded ambivalent and could not believe that any entomologist would speak out against the work of his brothers. He wrote to Fernald that Packard and Scudder must have been paid for their testimony and were under pressure to "do justice to those that had hired them."[24] Kirkland noted that Sessions's grilling of Appleton had been "very direct and somewhat severe and left Mr. Appleton in a rather peculiar light."[25]

The dread of the gypsy moth affected many at all levels from professor to private citizen, and fears were expressed in many ways. J. O. Goodwin of Medford, long an advocate of extermination, had become completely paranoid about the matter: "If we cannot exterminate this pest, let the pest override us and we will die . . . It simply comes right down to the survival of the fittest. If that infernal gypsy moth is able to conquer us, then we ought to die."[26]

Nathaniel Shaler testified that even though small and tardy appropriations had lessened the chances of success, the question of extermination was still open, and the state should make certain the insect could *not* be crushed before giving up. He repeated his argument that the gypsy moth could cause the fall of civilization: "Mr. Chairman, it seems to me that I do not exaggerate the importance of this question when I say that upon the extermination of this insect may depend the value of our agriculture in this Commonwealth and perhaps in every Commonwealth. . . . In other words, we are in the face of the greatest danger that this Commonwealth has ever put itself against. I know of no position which has been so serious."[27] When Saltonstall asked Shaler if he knew that Riley had expressed doubts about extermination, Shaler snapped back that he had "no confidence whatever in Mr. Riley's judgment."[28]

Shaler believed that the gypsy moth had been in the country since 1862, brought over in egg form "thousands of times" on the oaken shipping casks of imported wine. Shaler appears to have based his apprehensions on the few areas of defoliation he saw in Europe rather than the many areas where there was no damage. He was no doubt intent on doing as much as possible to get the appropriation, which may have influenced his testimony, or it might have been that he could not take a level view of the problem. He was an influential

man to whom other influential men listened with respect. His views were given the same weight as those of experts, and witnesses who opposed him were chided for their impudence, as Senator James A. Bailey of Arlington discovered:

> [Prof. Shaler] said that our civilization was threatened and might fall if the gypsy moth were not fought along the lines that it has been fought. . . . I was roasted on the floor of the house . . . because Prof. Shaler said that extermination was possible and I, a humble pupil of his, dared to think it was not possible . . . with all respect to Prof. Shaler, whom I love and who is one of the leading professors at Harvard University. . . . Prof. Nathaniel Southgate Shaler is not the professor of entomology there, he is professor of geology and paleontology. . . . [H]is knowledge of entomology I suppose he himself would say was not expert or profound.[29]

Forbush wrote to Fernald on February 26 to inform him the hearings had gone well, and that the opposition had not quoted Howard.[30] The agriculture committee visited the Middlesex Fells with Sessions and gypsy moth committee members Wood, Pratt, and Avery on February 27, and Sessions said the group "saw eggs enough to satisfy them on that point."[31]

Fernald's presence was no longer needed, and he could not have come anyway, because he was bedridden with chills and a fever. With Fernald indisposed, it became Kirkland's lot to rebut Packard and Scudder. Fernald advised Kirkland against tackling either one head on. The mild-mannered Packard was a man of considerable courage. During the Civil War he had received commendations for his bravery under fire and as a youth had undergone unsuccessful surgery to correct a cleft palate without anesthetics or antibiotics. Fernald impressed on young Kirkland the idea that he should speak of both men only in the highest terms and then use their testimony to make it appear that they favored extermination. Kirkland responded that he had "paid tribute to Packard and Scudder" and, as far he knew, had not said anything to embarrass Fernald or the gypsy moth committee.[32]

Sessions saw the opposition petitioners as weak, and his pugnacious style contrasted with Saltonstall's more avuncular and lawyerly approach. Sessions hammered the point that all the opposing experts were unqualified because they were not economic entomologists. He shrewdly worked from published documents and correspondence of economic entomologists without having any testify other than Fernald. The opposition could not compel independent entomologists to be present, so no examination of them was possible. The testimony from those connected with the extermination campaign in response

to direct questioning was remarkable for its nonresponsiveness. The witnesses were so evasive that at one point a frustrated Saltonstall could hardly speak straight.

Testimony heard in response to documents presented by Saltonstall showed that some economic entomologists did in fact think extermination impossible. Sessions and Forbush made the outrageous claim that every one of the entomologists who had voiced doubt about extermination—including Leland Howard, Joseph A. Lintner, J. Henry Comstock, and Charles V. Riley—believed the opposite and had said so in private conversation. The investigative committee was informed that the entomologists' doubts arose only because they thought Massachusetts would not appropriate enough money to do the job. Sessions finished up with some surprises for his frustrated opponents. The night before the hearings concluded, he visited a number of prominent Bostonians and obtained their signatures on a petition supporting extermination. He presented the petition to Chairman Barker the next day, saying that it took little effort to get signatures on a petition, and that the names on his petition carried no less weight than did those on his opponents' petition.

Next, Edward Forbush delivered his rebuttal. Forbush, a natural speaker, always sensed when his words would have their greatest impact. Given his brief but impassioned plea to continue the work, it is not difficult to understand why he always made a strong impression on those who met him:

> I have hunted this moth as a hunter hunts a deer. I have learned its habits and where to find it. I know when it is in a place and when it is gone. I tell you, gentleman, this thing can be done and if you give us the means we will do it. Let these people come in and say it cannot be exterminated. I am glad to have them express their opinion, but if we get the means to exterminate it, in spite of all carping we will go on and exterminate it. We will do it. We can do it. I know it.[33]

In closing, Sessions fired a salvo from Leland Howard in Washington. Since the opposition had presented documents in which Howard expressed doubt about wiping out the gypsy moth, Forbush had written to Howard imploring him to take a stand in favor of the Massachusetts campaign. Howard delivered a resounding vote of approval for his colleagues in Massachusetts without ever stating that extermination was either possible or likely: "I consider Mr. Sessions as a man of excellent common sense and wide agricultural knowledge; I consider you an executive officer beyond compare; I consider Prof. Fernald a man whose ripe entomological judgment cannot be questioned. You have all three given this gypsy moth such study as to make your opinions

worth a hundredfold more than those of any other individual or individuals. I am perfectly happy to abide by your judgment."[34]

The acrimonious tone, nasty tricks, and corybantic maneuverings behind the scene were not unusual for gypsy moth hearings. This one may have been the most contentious, because much was at stake, but there are references in other documents to the acerbic and spiteful relationship that existed between the legislature and the Board of Agriculture. In this case, though, opponents of extermination were not expecting such slashing attacks and had come to the hearings with confidence in Sessions, Fernald, and Forbush; they merely wished to have the moth program proceed along more realistic lines. Sessions took advantage of their conciliatory stance to make his attack most effective, but in doing so he created powerful enemies. There would be more hearings to come. Members of the opposition would not forget how they had been met, and the Board of Agriculture and its gypsy moth committee had not heard the last of Saltonstall and the men he represented.

Packing the Hall

The legislative hearings closed on February 28, but other public meetings occurred afterward. The joint agricultural committee held a hearing in Winchester on the evening of March 6 to take testimony from inhabitants of the infested district. Kirkland wrote to Fernald that the gypsy moth committee had been quick to ensure that friends of the work would be in evidence.[35] Oliver McCarthy, then employed by the gypsy moth committee, said that all the men on his gang were instructed to go to Winchester and pack the hall[36]— a recollection that was confirmed by Bartholomew Hennelly, another employee who showed up that night. A Winchester man said that he looked around the crowded room and had not been able to recognize more than six local residents, and Hennelly commented that outsiders did the greatest amount of talking: "An outside man that spoke there in favor of the bill was Mayor Allen of Woburn, who was invited there by one of the inspectors and made a very powerful plea for continuation of the work. . . . After the hearing was over he came outside and was talking to some of the employees about the hearing, and he told them he was thankful that the committee had not asked him to describe the gypsy moth, because he could not have told it from an elephant."[37]

Forbush and Kirkland had ensured that the Board of Agriculture was well supported, and in addition to invited officials such as Mayor Allen they got a surprising boost from a discharged inspector named Noyes, who claimed that he "came there not because he loved the management of the work but because

he was an honest man." Noyes's convincing speech and Allen's plea were enough to make several legislators reconsider their stance.[38] Kirkland and Forbush were elated by the results. Kirkland told Fernald, "We swept the boards—Nary a peep of opposition."[39] And Forbush exulted, "We have met the enemy and they are ours."[40] By March 9 the battle had swung in favor of moth extermination, but the Winchester gathering represented the last straw for Senator Barker, who had been at first merely dismayed by the political maneuverings of the Board of Agriculture but became deeply disturbed when he discovered that the board had packed the Winchester hall. Barker remained a force to be reckoned with, and the hopes for a quick appropriation were soon dispelled. Kirkland wrote that the "appropriation business is still hanging fire, owing to a split in the committee."[41]

Forbush depleted his budget and began laying off his remaining men. There was not much time left for cyclone burning before the insects emerged and crawled into the trees; the caterpillars had enjoyed two seasons of favorable conditions, and Forbush admitted to "many forebodings" about what the next season would bring. The legislative debate was still raging on April 23, but Appleton's plan for a reduced appropriation of $50,000 had been decisively rejected.[42] The contentious legislative debate seemed to have no end, but friends of agriculture in the General Court did push through a $10,000 emergency appropriation that became available on April 28. Meanwhile, the gypsy moths hatched, and as Forbush had feared, there were so many that his depleted forces could not contain them: "In some of the colonies where the burning was not done the scattered eggs on the ground among the dead leaves produced a sufficient number of caterpillars to strip the foliage entirely from the trees in the center of each colony, so that all the labor of the season of 1895 served only to prevent the increase of the colonies, and failed to contribute to the progress of extermination."[43]

Even when there was money, Forbush was having trouble finding enough men to push the work. The gypsy moth payroll contained over three hundred names, but the number working on any given day averaged fewer than two hundred except for a few months in the summer. To relieve Forbush of his burden and allow him to direct operations from his command center, the gypsy moth committee voted repeatedly to enlarge his office staff and administration. Both Forbush and Fernald had assistants, and superintendents were given deputies. The structure had grown to include agents, general agents, special agents, special inspectors, and acting inspectors. The staff of the office and storehouse fluctuated, but usually included a bookkeeper, stenographer, two clerks, three copyists, quartermaster, storekeeper, teamster, purchasing agent, mechanic, machinist, draftsman, and a custodian. The result, in the parlance of the time, was "a head too big for the body."[44]

Fernald was again wearying of all the contentious aspects of working for the gypsy moth committee. Even the release of the monograph in May did not cheer him. *The Gypsy Moth*, at its final length of almost six hundred pages, was received with great praise in the world of economic entomology and indifference almost everywhere else. That American entomology, in the space of six years, had come to know more about the European gypsy moth than the Europeans did was generally unappreciated by the public at large. Fernald felt only relief that the monograph was now out of the way; it had cost him "a vast amount of time," and "as a work on economic entomology it is as well done as I can do with the time at my disposal."[45] He was eager to hear the opinions of his colleagues, especially those outside the field of economic entomology such as Scudder, and he became "exceedingly annoyed at the negligence of the parties at headquarters in sending out the gypsy moth Reports." He wrote to Scudder, "If we live long enough you will doubtless get a copy," and complained he did not know how to make Forbush's staff work faster.[46]

On May 29 he wrote once more to resign his post as entomological adviser. Sessions replied a few days later: "Yours of May 29 containing resignation as entomologist to the gypsy moth committee . . . received. . . . I know that the committee and Mr. Forbush will be very reluctant to have the official connection between yourself and the committee severed. It will seem like the beginning of the end and the committee will feel weakened and bereft without you. . . . The committee have looked to you as a tower of strength in this work."[47]

The appropriation finally went through the house on May 14 after a bellicose debate. The bill worked its way through the General Court, and the governor signed the resolve on May 21—after Senator Barker managed to reduce the amount to $100,000. Several years later Barker said that his actions had saved the state $50,000 dollars and that of all the deeds he accomplished in the legislature, this one pleased him the most.[48] The appropriation, less the $10,000 emergency fund, became available on June 4, and the long and damaging confrontation temporarily came to an end.

Forbush had used a skeleton force to continue the fieldwork and even now had to carry on with only half of what he needed. He began to band the trees before the larvae pupated, but there was not enough time to complete this task. Colonies had become so large that many more trees needed burlap, but the men had to stop banding new trees in order to check the bands already in place. By June 20 the force abandoned the central districts and spent the rest of the season killing caterpillars in the outer towns. The caterpillars swarmed out of the infested parklands in the central district and once again took possession of the inner towns.

Two new but well-established colonies were discovered in Brookline, and

Forbush diverted what few men he could to reduce the worst of that infestation. Trees in the woodlands had suffered two defoliations in one year, and in several places a number of them were dying. Lead arsenate at the rate of 20 pounds to 150 gallons of water was used in portions of the Middlesex Fells; Forbush believed the kill ratio this year was close to 99 percent. The moths were pupating by June 23, which Kirkland said was the earliest date on record. The colonies in the Lynn woods, Saugus, Medford, and Woburn were very bad. In one hundred-acre area of Lynn, 400,000 egg clusters were removed but at least as many left untouched.[49] Kirkland jotted a quick note to Fernald that "the wooded region round about is pretty thoroughly infested."[50]

With Forbush's needs attended to, the state appropriation in hand, and the fieldwork passing for normal, the gypsy moth committee was able to devote its attention to Fernald's resignation. Fernald claimed that he had scarcely worked a full day on his own research since the gypsy moth committee was formed, and he did not want to delay his projects longer. He had either tendered his resignation or asked to be relieved of his duties every year since his connection with the committee began.[51] These repeated attempts had always hit hard, and the climate surrounding the work was now so unfavorable and the eradication program enjoyed so little support that only Fernald's presence imparted any credible standing with the state's citizens and the scientific community. Consequently, Wood responded to Fernald:

> The committee feel that your withdrawal from connection with the work will largely take away its prestige with scientists throughout the country, and imperil the success of any effort that may be made to induce the federal government to assume the work or assist in its prosecution. . . . The committee will also be shorn of strength which your experienced advice has always given them, and fears that your resignation will be interpreted by the public as an acknowledgement of the hopelessness of a continued contest with the moth.[52]

In August, Massachusetts endured a horrific heat wave of such tenacity that men and women were dying on the street, and the prolonged high temperatures taxed the men at work in the field who were compelled to wear a uniform jacket. Yet Forbush maintained a torrid pace and burned through almost his entire year's appropriation in just ten weeks. Funds ran out in mid-August, and large numbers of employees were furloughed. Kirkland wrote to Fernald that he and Burgess were the only men left in the scientific corps.[53]

The committee continued to insist that the gypsy moth was a danger to agriculture, even though it was ever more manifesting itself as a forest insect. Many economic entomologists perpetuated alarmist arguments, including

John Bernhard Smith of Rutgers, who at this time was president of the Association of Economic Entomologists. Smith called the gypsy moth "the most dangerous pest ever introduced into the United States."[44] His gloomy argument did double damage, since it appeared in his textbook of economic entomology from which future generations would study.

Conditions in the wooded heartlands became worse during 1896, and the forces of the state were stretched too thin to contain the insects. When the towns were cleared, moths from the woods reinfested them; when the woods were cleared, moths from the towns reinfested them. It only took a year or two for the insect to recover from the most punishing losses. Areas frequented by tourists were almost impossible to keep cleared. Insects were found every year in the wooded groves surrounding the graves of the poets Lowell and Longfellow in the Mount Auburn cemetery, and insects constantly reinfested the Bunker Hill monument and the site of the Charlestown carnival. Drill fields, camping grounds, and the land around churches, schools, hotels, and public offices also presented an endless problem. Similar situations began to occur elsewhere in the state, and the committee told the legislature they wanted to make a complete inspection of the entire Commonwealth.

The committee compiled records of commercial trade through Medford and Malden: the kinds of cargo, the frequency of trips, the nature of the business, the destination of the wagons, whether the return trip was made full or empty, and even the places where the drivers stopped to rest (it learned that a surprising amount of manure and swill was in motion on any given day). The heaviest wagon traffic went south into Boston, but the committee was persuaded that the city's lack of trees made it inhospitable for the gypsy moth. Further, the members believed that the areas south of Boston would remain free of the moth and did not pay much attention to them—with the result that commercial vehicles moving out of Boston toward the south were not checked and carried the moth into regions that were thought to be safe.

In the fall the few remaining men creosoted egg clusters, and at year's end they were working their way back toward the central district. Although Forbush believed that the outer woodlands were in good condition, the metropolitan parks concerned him, and he must have wondered at times whose side the park commissioners were on. Once streets, driveways, boulevards, and electric railcar lines had been cut through the woods, creating a network of transportation and recreational driving, Forbush estimated that over a million egg clusters had been laid in the Fells alone—representing a potential hatch of 500 million caterpillars. If the roads were not closed during the caterpillar season the larvae would be dispersed far and wide.

By the end of the year's work, Forbush's records showed that of more than ten million trees inspected, only 5 percent harbored egg masses. Over half a

million trees had received burlaps, and about 132,000 had been cut down. Inspectors had examined 25,000 buildings, 44,000 wooden fences, and some 300,000 linear feet of stone walls. The larvae destroyed by hand numbered nearly two million, and almost 442,000 pupae and over 44,000 imagoes had been destroyed. Forty-three hundred trees had been sprayed with lead arsenate, and 885,000 viable egg masses had been creosoted.[55]

Thousands of old orchard trees were cut down and burned; while others that were old or damaged but still considered productive had cavities filled with cement or sealed up with sheets of tinplate—which deprived the gypsy moth of places to deposit eggs but also eliminated the favored nesting places of bluebirds. The remaining nesting places were possessed and defended first by English sparrows and then by starlings, which drove the remaining bluebirds away. This beautiful songbird was turned into a rare species in eastern New England; the best that could be expected was that once the war against the gypsy moth—grimly lead by the ornithologist Forbush—had ended, the bluebirds would somehow reestablish themselves.

The Association of Economic Entomologists passed another resolve at its August meeting in Buffalo that failure to continue the work in Massachusetts would be "a national misfortune." To Forbush, there was no middle ground: they must either fight until victory had been won or quit the field. He dismissed the option of containment as "nonscientific": "I leave it for those who believe it is the wisest policy for the State to adopt [the course of containment] to estimate what the annual appropriations of $50,000 would amount to from now to the end of time."[56]

By the end of 1896 and for the rest of the decade, the annual reports of the gypsy moth committee took on a predictable pattern: the extermination effort was said to be achieving its aims (a statement supported by tabulations showing ever increasing numbers of insects killed, egg masses destroyed, trees banded, and woodlands cut or burned); extermination was assured within another few years, even though new colonies were being discovered all the time (additions explained away as being caused not by any deficiency of the effort but by inadequate surveying in consequence of a chronic shortage of funds).

By the time the year ended, some of the tumult had died down, and things were returning to normal within the gypsy moth organization. The committee offered to lighten the burden on Fernald by increasing the duties of Archie Kirkland and by having both Kirkland and the committee go to Amherst to consult with Fernald there rather than in Boston. After some delay for reflection and a lot of lubrication from the board, Fernald, with undisguised reluctance, once again withdrew his resignation. His decision greatly relieved the

committee; as Kirkland wrote him late in December, reporting on the last committee meeting of the year:

> Mr. Sessions . . . spoke of the tiresome trips you had to take and of the value of your services and of the necessity of retaining them by making it as easy as possible for you. . . . Mr. Wood spoke of the cost of the Insectary and that it would be a loss [should you resign]. . . . Mr. Pratt said "as long as the professor was good enough to withdraw his resignation last summer we ought to accede to any plan that he thinks will benefit the work or make it easier for him." It would have done you good to have heard some of the things they said about you in the discussion.[57]

Fernald's control over the campaign thus became absolute, for the Board of Agriculture and the gypsy moth committee felt helpless without him, and the thought of losing his services frightened them so deeply that they allowed him to do whatever he wanted: to disregard infectious diseases or imported parasites as possible weapons; not to petition the General Court to revise the extermination law were all policies he advocated. His contentions that extermination was only a matter of time and money, that if small areas could be cleared so could large areas, and that the state's only options were to exterminate or not to exterminate ruled the thinking of the board.

The year marked a turning point for Fernald personally as he realized that removing himself from his duties as adviser was now out of the question. He had made himself the guiding and indispensable force behind a war that could not be won and could not be lost, and the more he tried to escape, the more he was drawn in. The college had appointed R. S. Lull to assist him at the experiment station, eliminating Fernald's argument that he did not have enough time to do all his work. The genie of remorse and doubt that had visited Fernald at the seventh annual entomologists' meeting the year before seems to have been put back in its bottle, and there are no more reports that Fernald sought to resign or in other ways to be relieved of his duties after this time. In his annual report, he noted that everything that could be done with the amount of money available had been done. He called on the General Court, with language that he would use for the rest of the campaign, to make up its mind whether it wanted the committee to exterminate the moth, hold the moth in check, or abandon moth work entirely. Other options were no longer considered.

Fernald also convinced himself that his knowledge of the gypsy moth was encompassing, and he boasted to Scudder, "I think an examination of the

literature gone over [in the monograph] together with the attention I gave the subject the summer I was in Europe will convince one that I have the condition of this moth in Europe pretty well in hand."[58] Fernald was apparently unaware of the work of Austrian entomologist Fritz Wachtl and his colleague Hans Kornauth, published in 1893, which showed how a special growth of hairs on the first instar larvae of the nun moth (*Psilura monacha*) allowed the insects to be borne by the wind over considerable distances.[59] These "aerostatic" hairs, as they were then called, sprouted from hollow, globelike growths called "aerophores" on the larva's back. Wachtl and Kornauth noted that gypsy moth larvae in their first instar grew the same type of hairs and hollow sacs, and concluded that they also would be carried by the wind much farther than had been previously thought. This and the number of eggs in a mass were the two missing pieces of information that would have allowed the gypsy moth committee to understand why moth colonies were constantly found in unexpected places.

Regardless of the celebration following the hearings in February and March, the reduction of their gypsy moth appropriation by half was a warning to the Board of Agriculture that opinion in the General Court was still running strongly against them. During meetings in the fall, Sessions sounded the entire Board of Agriculture members to learn what they thought of the moth work. The feeling of the moth committee was that the General Court was very displeased, that its enemies in the legislature were getting stronger, and that cessation of appropriations was imminent. The committee decided "to strike the legislature as soon as it convenes for an emergency appropriation and test the sentiment."[60] The committee also decided to retain about $9,000 at the end of the year to cover any expenses for closing down the work and to pay off any outstanding debts.

A Moth Too Many (1897)

THE GYPSY MOTH COMMITTEE reported a balance of $8,849.85 at the start of 1897 but expected to use the money to shut down all fieldwork.[1] This was the last year state commissions were permitted to retain funds for more than twelve months. New state laws required the complete expenditure of allocations in the same year they were made, although work could continue for the month of January until legislative action was taken.

The General Court held hearings on the gypsy moth appropriation in mid-January, a month earlier than usual. Unlike the previous year, this time nobody showed up to argue, not even the Frost brothers. The absence of a single adversary disturbed the representatives, several of whom directed the court clerk to ascertain whether notice of the meetings had been published.[2] On January 29 the appropriation was debated in the house, with opponents and proponents divided along geographical and political lines. Whatever their differences, many elected men expressed concern that the federal government had again declined to help in the fight.

Members of the house from the western districts of the Commonwealth opposed the bill, as did a group of representatives who were concerned about the growing debt burden of the state and questioned the ability of the gypsy moth committee to handle large appropriations wisely. Supporters included representatives from badly infested areas and politicians from Boston who liked the jobs the moth program provided their constituents. Representative Sanderson of Lynn recalled seeing egg masses on uncounted hundreds of trees worked on by a handful of men because there was not enough money to hire more, and he scolded his colleagues:

> The general idea among members from the western part of the state is that [the matter] is a sort of a humbug. I wish to say to them that when they have something more to contend with than a canker worm, a tent caterpillar, or a woodchuck coming out and eating up a cabbage, they will give some attention to this question. The gypsy moth

is a reality and if any member does not believe it, he can easily find the workings of it within an hour's ride of this state house.[3]

The Massachusetts Society for the Promotion of Agriculture, a group opposed to the gypsy moth campaign, engaged the services of John B. Smith, the short and portly state entomologist of New Jersey, to refute the possibility of extermination. The society somehow had been duped into believing that Smith could be objective and was likely to support their opposing view.[4] They had even agreed in advance to publish Smith's findings, no matter what they were.

By some odd chance, Fernald was in Boston to inspect the field and consult with the Board of Agriculture when Smith arrived. In another astonishing coincidence, it just so happened that Leland Howard and Charles Marlatt were also in Massachusetts, ostensibly to get an early start on their report for the federal government. The jovial Smith, a phalanx of his colleagues augmented by William Sessions and several members of the moth committee, spent ten happy days in Massachusetts gathering facts. Given Smith's well-known gregarious nature and his "truly Teutonic fondness for beer," one cannot imagine him pining his evenings away in solitude, bereft of the companionship of his fellow entomologists.[5] As was their custom, these brethren of the net likely gathered at the end of the day in the hotel restaurant or one of their rooms to hash over events, practically guaranteeing that Smith's report would stick like glue to the goals of economic entomology. It should have come as no surprise that Smith expressed enthusiasm for the concept of eradication and endorsed it heartily while raising the usual concerns about financial support.

Despite his "great sense of humor," however, Smith was no fool.[6] He had originally followed a career in law but abandoned that pursuit to become another of the era's self-taught entomologists. His legal training had doubtless made him aware of the term "collusion," and the generally supportive tone of his report was tempered by the recommendation that insect enemies of the gypsy moth be imported from Europe. This departure from the standard line can be viewed as a subtle recognition that manmade efforts alone could not accomplish the task of extermination. The gypsy moth committee immediately diminished the force of Smith's argument by opposing the idea as "problematic" but hastened to add they would gladly take up such work if the General Court provided more money.[7] The Society for the Promotion of Agriculture, although completely flimflammed, kept its part of the bargain and published Smith's findings in several local newspapers, an event in which Fernald, Howard, Marlatt, economic entomologists, and the gypsy moth committee took great delight.

Public Relations

Smith's opinions and the glowing reports from the gypsy moth committee could not hide the realities seen by every citizen in the infested region. The efforts of the entomologists to represent themselves as bona fide experts on everything from ornithology to the safety of insecticides to the practices of forestry were unconvincing. The entomologists had no idea how to win over the public, and the more they tried to sell themselves as the great hope of the Commonwealth, the more foolish they looked. Forbush and Fernald seemed baffled that the average citizen was not nearly so enamored of killing insects as they were or had grave reservations about the liberal use of arsenic in residential areas. When pronouncements by men such as "Professor" Riley were made about the safety of arsenical sprays, Forbush and Fernald simply could not understand why no one believed them.

The sensationalist tendencies of the press were being put to good use by the opposition in discrediting the gypsy moth leadership. The management of the campaign loathed the tone of the press, especially when it was turned against them. The idea of brawling with the public through the newspapers was abhorrent to them, but the voices of opposition could not be allowed to go unanswered. After attempting a goodwill campaign of sorts and using the stature of other entomologists to bolster their claims, it finally occurred to the committeemen to fight fire with fire. What they needed was a good public relations specialist to strike a little fear into the hearts of those less knowledgeable.

The work of a local writer, Fletcher Osgood, on the municipal water system of Boston, published in the *New England Magazine* in 1896, attracted their attention, but the committee's mandate left no opening for the employment of propagandists. Osgood was thus hired and trained like any new employee and went on the rolls as a special agent. His occupations included journalist, gypsy moth agent, teacher, and justice of the peace. Although his skill as an insect warrior probably was no worse than that of the others, his skill with words was used to quash the arguments of an ignorant citizenry. He escorted politicians and other notables through the work zones, glibly countering any tendencies on their part to believe that the work of extermination was ineffective. Osgood had bigger plans than just filling out bug reports, however. He quickly ingratiated himself into the upper echelons of the office and by early 1897 had become Forbush's personal secretary.

Osgood's flair for overexcited writing was typical of the times. His first piece on behalf of the committee, "A State in Arms against a Caterpillar," was published in *Harper's Magazine* for August 1897 and began: "The State in

arms is Massachusetts; the caterpillar, a hairy creeper, spinner and cruncher, soot-gray in ground color, dotted with crimson and blue. When full grown he is thick and long as a pill-phial. He is hardy and appallingly prolific, and he is named the gypsy caterpillar, child of the gypsy moth."[8]

Osgood's breathless prose went on in an alarmist vein to restate the familiar theme of the stench given off by decaying caterpillar corpses and warned his readers that if left unchecked, the gypsy moth would devour every living plant in the United States within eight years:

> Let the "gypsy" once get free of the bounds within which, as we shall see, the State of Massachusetts has up to this time confined him; let him then multiply according to his nature, and not only would all our fruit and field crops go down before him (tobacco very doubtfully excepted), but the shade upon which depends our water supply would be more seriously threatened by this creature than it is now by forest fires or the woodsman's axe. The water supply of many districts, too, might well suffer extreme pollution by dying hosts of caterpillars.[9]

The effect of Osgood's efforts was not what the entomologists had hoped. Over time, the committee did better with the large newspapers of Boston by dealing with the most prominent editors. The committee also discovered that newspaper reporters would print almost anything they were given about the gypsy moth campaign, often after only the most cursory field inspections or a meeting in the board's offices. It still galled the committee and the campaign leadership, especially Fernald, when stories with sensational headlines were published, but by the end of the decade all four of Boston's major dailies had given their editorial support to the gypsy moth campaign.

The *American Naturalist* magazine, however, published in Salem, Massachusetts, had for years opposed gypsy moth work in reasoned editorials. The frequency of such writings increased at this time, providing a highly credible opposing view to the claims of economic entomologists. And newspapers and magazines outside the Commonwealth, beyond the reach of the committee's public relations men and not directly affected by the issues of politics and jobs, were more detached in their reports. The *New York Times*, for example, said of the war in Massachusetts that the "remedy [was] worse than [the] disease."[10]

The War Drags On

The General Court remained divided on the subject of extermination, and the appropriation of $150,000 made available on February 26 passed by only

three votes. Although the sum was only 75 percent of the amount requested, it enabled Forbush to make an early start. Men worked from the beginning of the year, and by the first of April tremendous amounts of underbrush and dead wood had been removed. There were 354 men on the rolls, concentrated in the infested sections of the Middlesex Fells in Medford, the massive Saugus Woods colony, and the Mystic Woods. By the end of May the trees in all these infested areas were wrapped with burlap.

Work in the Fells again brought the gypsy moth committee into disagreement with the Metropolitan Park Commission. The park commissioners had second thoughts about their policy of cooperation because gypsy moth gangs tended to commit such blunders as spraying arsenic on patches of edible berries inside the reservations or felling specimen trees. On April 7, Secretary John Woodbury of the MPC sent Forbush a set of seven regulations governing moth work in the reservations. Only dead or decaying wood could be cut and burned at times and places designated by the park superintendent and in his presence. The gypsy moth committee was instructed to pay the park official for his time. Living growth could not be cut except by special permit. Spraying was allowed only if it did not endanger life or foliage. Warning signs had to be posted in advance, and plants bearing edible fruit could not be treated at all. If stone walls were torn down, the committee would pay the cost of restoring them.[11]

Flooding stone walls with crude petroleum oil to kill the egg masses was tried in the park, eliminating the need to tear the walls apart and rebuild them. The raw oil was pumped through the cyclone burner and sprayed on the surface, seeping into and killing the eggs laid there. Burlapping continued in the woodlands, and spraying was done when weather permitted. May and June were abnormally wet, ruining Fernald and Kirkland's plans for large-scale tests using various formulations of waxed Paris green and barium arsenate.[12] The war effort had achieved a precarious balance with the insects, but then an unexpected turn of events changed everything.

A Moth Too Many

On May 8, Joseph B. Pike of Somerville reported an unusual defoliation pattern on his pear trees: caterpillars were consuming the leaves from the top down. Agent Osgood made a cursory investigation and at first reported that the insects were tent caterpillars. He later instructed Pike to collect some specimens and spray his trees with arsenical poisons: "I examined one day a small estate in Somerville, finding no trace of the gypsy moth about it. Members of the family occupying the estate assured me, however, that they had been troubled by a strange caterpillar which had assailed their pear trees and these only.

[Mr. Kirkland], the assistant entomologist of the gypsy moth department was unable on the meager data I could furnish him to identify this caterpillar . . . even when I sent him a bottle of [them]."[13]

A second complaint was received on May 14 from Roland Thaxter of Harvard that his pear trees too were being defoliated from the top down. This roused Kirkland to visit Cambridge and collect specimens. The caterpillars reminded him of a European insect called the brown-tail moth (*Euproctis chrysorrhea*.) In a hastily scrawled letter to Fernald on May 22, Kirkland asked: "Is not this insect Liparis Chrysorhoea [sic], the "brown-tail"? . . . Professor Howard was out with Minott yesterday and was unable to place it. I have compared it with Ochsenheimer and it seems to tally. . . . Osgood is ready to rush into print about it. . . . The people are alarmed and complaints are coming in thick and fast."[14]

Fernald came at once, and he and Kirkland began to investigate where and how the brown-tails arrived. They worked circumspectly, fearing public reaction to another invasion by a foreign insect. Citizens in Somerville told the two sleuths that a caterpillar fond of pear trees had been a nuisance since 1892, but many had already discovered that if the nests were clipped off the branches and burned during the winter, the insect could be controlled with ease. Fernald and Kirkland guessed the brown-tails had been in the state since 1890, and by following the instances of increasing damage to the center of the worst defoliations, they came to a florist's shop in Somerville. They learned that the business had imported roses from France and Holland until 1890, raising them behind their greenhouses before selling them. The brown-tail was common in France and Holland where it was a pest of roses. Roses were shipped in cold weather when the plant and its insect passengers were dormant. When the men walked behind the greenhouses, they saw two blocks filled with pear trees—a perfect habitat for brown-tails. This clinched the case, at least circumstantially, and Kirkland later called the appearance of the brown-tail in the same place as the gypsy moth "a strange fatality."[15]

Although the gypsy moth is not found in European literature until the middle of the eighteenth century, references to the brown-tail occur two hundred years earlier. Linnæus listed it as a silk moth in the genus Bombyx, the same one in which he had placed the gypsy moth.

The brown-tail outbreak was not large, but the damage was considered as bad as anything the gypsy moth had done and left the land looking as if it had been "swept by fire."[16] Residents in Somerville who tried to hand-pick the brown-tail discovered that the larvae packed in their "nettling hairs" a poisonous sting that sent some people to the doctor. One resident remarked that the fence and gateposts of her driveway were so thickly blanketed with larvae that "they looked as though they were covered with fur," but added that no one

dared touch the gates all summer.[17] Mrs. D. C. Chase of Somerville wrote: "While cutting the limbs from the infested trees my husband was badly poisoned, his eyes in particular being affected. In cleaning the window screens in the house I was also badly poisoned; the skin of my body was much inflamed as if a mustard paste had been applied."[18]

The McGarr family of Somerville suffered more than most, at one point being forced to abandon their house. The brown-tail nettles would even attach themselves to washing hung on the line; Mrs. McGarr said that when her husband put on his clean flannels, "they made him almost crazy." Other health problems in the household were even more serious: "The doctor who was called in to attend my mother said [the caterpillars] had poisoned her blood. [My mother] grew worse and finally died of this poison about the middle of August. . . . My son was also taken quite sick, and finally became so ill that he also had to be removed from the house. . . . I have never entirely recovered from the effects of the poison."[19] Fieldworkers too were affected by the poisonous brown-tail, especially when attending burlaps, and a number of casualties occurred.

The eggs of the brown-tail hatch and the larvae commence eating about the time the gypsy moths pupate. After about a quarter of their life has passed, brown-tail larvae spin communal cocoons of several hundred individuals and pass the winter in a suspended state. The larvae emerge in the spring two to four weeks before the gypsy moths do, and eat the tree buds before the leaves open, and following that, the flowers of fruiting trees, and, if available, the fruit itself and the twigs from which it hangs.

War on Two Fronts

While Kirkland and Fernald tracked down the center of the brown-tail invasion, gypsy moth larvae were hatching. Some trees had been banded with "insect-lime," a sticky substance that prevented the caterpillars from crawling up the trunk. To everyone's surprise, the formula used this year was most effective: many larvae starved to death because they could not cross the band, and the remainder were so weakened they were easily destroyed by fire. The early spring was unusually rainy, and the precipitation produced a lush growth of foliage. Burlap bands were not effective since food was abundant, and in the absence of sunlight the gypsy moths did not need to hide. Workers in the forest discovered that jarring smaller trees caused the larvae to fall to the forest floor or spin down on strands of silk. The crews would move on, and the gypsies would attempt to crawl back up the tree trunks and hide beneath the burlaps, where they were squashed by a second wave of crews.

In the Middlesex Fells and other areas of woodlands, the workers en-

countered gypsy moth larvae in great armies that covered hundreds of square feet of the forest floor with a hairy, black blanket. Contact sprays were used, or the ground was swept with fire from the cyclone burners, raising clouds of dark, foul-smelling smoke. Outside the Fells, where the egg masses engulfed the tree trunks, the trees were cut down and burned, eggs and all. Counting the dead was out of the question, and time was of the essence, both with regard to the spread of the insect and the depletion of the budget.

Insects in the woodlands occurred in isolated colonies, but to find them, workers had to inspect all the woodlands several times. The most experienced inspectors were entrusted with this work, which they did by forming men into a line and spacing them about one hundred yards apart. The men would trot through the forest, trying to spot egg clusters or insects. A few egg masses or a dozen feeding larvae were enough to indicate the presence of a colony, and after the location was noted, a second team returned for a more detailed inspection.

On May 25 the gypsy moth committee gave written notice of the brown-tail to Governor Roger Wolcott, and two days later Fernald and Kirkland delivered additional information to Wolcott personally, assisted by Leland Howard, who with Charles Marlatt had been inspecting Massachusetts for the federal government. The deadline for presenting new business had passed, so Wolcott sent a message to the General Court, which referred the matter to its ways and means committee. This committee allocated $10,000 against the brown-tail by deducting the amount from the gypsy moth appropriation. The bill was defeated, however, and a separate request for $6,000 to fight the new pest was adversely reported out of committee on June 8. The legislature at length passed a bill introduced by Albert Clarke of Wellesley requiring local authorities to suppress the brown-tail at their own expense. The legislation was even more draconian than that for the gypsy moth and showed that the General Court had learned nothing about the nature of such problems. Sections 3 and 5 of the act compelled owners of infested premises to put themselves under the direction of state authorities to combat the moth at their own risk and expense and subjected them to fines and incarceration for not complying. Section 4 provided financial penalties for mayors and aldermen of cities and selectmen of towns that refused to obey.

The center of the new infestation occurred along the Fitchburg Railroad tracks at the Somerville depot, and Forbush sent some men to spray the area with contact insecticides. On June 24 the Board of Agriculture ordered the mayors of Cambridge, Everett, Malden, Medford, and Somerville to take measures against the invaders. An inspection discovered more than fifteen infested communities, but there was not enough time or money available to undertake

effective work. The brown-tail moths emerged from their pupae during the first week of July and flew away, and a discouraged Kirkland wrote to Fernald: "Bad news. The brown tail females fly well. Not a strong flight like our butterflies but a slow whirring flight like that of the tent caterpillar moth. . . . Took some females today and by letting them go they flew about the room after the most approved style. The male flight is strong like that of the gypsy."[20]

Both sexes of the brown-tail are nocturnal fliers and soar where prevailing breezes aid their dispersal. Strong southerly winds reaching forty-eight miles per hour occurred in New England on July 14, 15, and 16, and within a few days the brown-tail was blown into New Hampshire. On July 19, Kirkland went to Somerville to spend the night examining streetlights. He found that both males and females were drawn to the glowing lamps: "The Electric Light Company employees tell me that they often find from one to two quarts of moths in the lamps. Another interesting feature is the fact that the toads, which assemble underneath the lamps, devour the wounded and fluttering moths. Thus, between the lamps and the toads, something like a clean sweep is made."[21] Kirkland also reported that flocks of English sparrows followed the fence lines where the imagoes hid during the day and consumed them in great quantities.

Since the General Court had charged the Board of Agriculture to oversee work against the brown-tail without providing financial support, Sessions used money from the incidental fund to notify communities and undertake inspections, which caused criticism of him and the board. Ultimately, the burden fell on municipal authorities, many of whom simply passed the buck to their local police. At the end of July, Forbush fell ill and was moved to the hospital in Worcester. Fernald was vacationing at his ancestral estate at Southwest Harbor, Maine, when Kirkland wrote him with the news: "Sunday of this week Mr. Bailey visited the Worcester City Hospital and saw the Director. . . . I infer that the Director has been in a much worse condition than the doctors report. It seems he has a serious stoppage of the bowels, which complicates his condition."[22]

During the summer the number of gypsy moth fieldworkers approached four hundred, but by August the shrinking budget dictated a reduction of 125 employees. The remaining workers were sent to scout, but about ninety remained in the Middlesex Fells creosoting gypsy moth egg masses. A two-year-old colony was found at Lincoln outside the boundary of 1891, but Forbush insisted it was destroyed by the time his men pulled out. In early September, Forbush, now recovered, ordered a two-week hiatus in the work, recalling his men on September 20 and sending them into the Saugus Woods and Malden.

In the Fells they worked so hastily that the usual records of destruction were not kept. Even the practice of ringing the treated egg masses with paint was discontinued; only a single mark was made on each tree to indicate that it was infested. Forbush wryly noted the savings to the state in time not spent tabulating results and in the cost of white paint.

Killing Chemicals

During the year the state used three tons of lead arsenate, purchasing the chemical components from Wm. H. Swift & Company in Boston. The two principal ingredients were acetate of lead and arsenate of soda. The mixture was prepared in the warehouse to meet the need for fresh batches in the field. Chemist F. J. Smith used calibrated ballast blocks on one end of a balanced beam and hung on the other end a cloth sack that he filled with the chemical until the beam balanced. The sacks were labeled and tied together in pairs, one of each chemical. Two men could prepare half a ton of poison daily in this way. When spray rigs went into service, pairs of sacks were carried along to replenish the tanks.

In the field, the ingredients had to be dissolved separately because moisture in the air caused an unwanted reaction when dry salts were mixed together. Each spray wagon was equipped with two ten-gallon kegs, which were filled from hydrants, wells, or streams. Where possible, the kegs were warmed in the sun, after which a sack of chemical was immersed in the water for fifteen or twenty minutes. After the salts precipitated out, the keg contents were poured into the main tank, and water was added according to a ratio provided by the chemist. Machinist E. C. Ware devised a twenty-five-gallon tank of galvanized metal using a lightweight Johnson pump, and machinist John Hancock developed a three-headed nozzle capable of delivering a cone of poison mist sixteen feet in diameter at a distance of eight feet. Kirkland reported that under the most favorable conditions, lead arsenate killed up to 80 percent of gypsy moth larvae, though normally the percentage was half that or less.[23]

During the campaign there had been public concern about the dangers to animals of arsenical spraying. When the threat to people was debated, it was entomologists and chemical company representatives who contended that the sprays were safe. Claiming that the press frightened the public with sensationalized stories of supposed cases of arsenical poisoning, the committee attempted to prove its point by noting that only one in every ten men on the spraying wagons "suffered more or less from arsenical poisoning."[24] Kirkland had been detailed to investigate this subject, a task that had occupied him for

nearly a year, and during 1896 he had examined some workers who appeared to be poisoned. Most of the spraying crews and nozzlemen refused to provide Kirkland with urine samples, but in June 1897 he collected eight samples and delivered these to Moulton for analysis. Moulton found varying levels of arsenic in six of the eight samples, leading Kirkland to understate that "in some cases men engaged in spraying acquire dangerous amounts of arsenic."[25]

Some of the men who exhibited little or no arsenic in their urine still complained of loss of appetite, biliousness, and digestive tract disturbances, all classic symptoms of arsenical poisoning. Kirkland believed that the odorous acetic acid used in the manufacture of lead acetate often made the men anxious and caused them to become nauseated. He also theorized that much of the problem could be attributed to the "complete indifference" of the men toward the dangers of working with poison. Handling and spraying pesticide had become an ordinary task, leading workers to relax their alertness, and since they had been selected for their physical fitness, they had come to feel impervious to the poison. Kirkland noted one case where a careless worker allowed spray residues to trickle down the pole and along his arms, soaking his entire upper body with arsenic. Such cases were likely the exception, but all men who handled nozzles absorbed arsenic to some degree.

Kirkland found a lame horse going to slaughter and persuaded its owners to feed it arsenic-soaked hay to simulate contaminated grass. After a few weeks, Kirkland reported, he was amazed to find the horse's condition actually improved. No such misconception was present two years later when the committee's chemist, F. J. Smith, was asked to analyze milk and urine samples from a cow that had eaten grass beneath sprayed trees. Smith was horrified to find that the family's children had been given milk from the obviously sick cow, saying that he "should not dare give such milk to young children."[26]

During the period of Kirkland's investigations, the medical community in Boston and knowledgeable men at Harvard were engaged in a bizarre debate as to whether arsenic in low doses was actually beneficial to humans: increasing sexual drive, promoting weight gain, improving complexion, aiding blood circulation. Four Harvard physicians—Frank Winthrop Draper, William Barker Hills, James Jackson Putnam, and Frederick Cheever Shattuck—published papers warning of the danger of prolonged exposure at low levels, and legislation restricting arsenic in the Commonwealth had been attempted without success since 1872.[27] The industrial use of arsenic was widespread, and the poison was also a common pigment for green-colored products of all kinds, including United States paper money! Although the State Board of Agriculture was heavily promoting the use of arsenic in the gypsy moth program, it is one of the odd juxtapositions of those times that certain of its members, led by

Appleton, were active in attempting to ban arsenic in other forms of commerce.

A number of medical practitioners remained convinced that arsenic could not pose any threats to humans unless it was deliberately abused, and many continued to prescribe it for medicinal purposes. These doctors often attributed some of the milder symptoms that Kirkland observed in the gypsy moth men, such as digestive upset or general anxiety, to other causes. Since the early symptoms of arsenical poisoning include a sense of greater energy, the apparent vitality of the spray men may have been a symptom of arsenical poisoning, as likely was the improvement Kirkland noted in the lame horse.

The medical community in general, by its own choice, remained outside the debate over the danger of exposure to arsenical sprays, leaving the field to entomologists, agriculturalists, and business entities that promoted the commercial use of arsenic.[28] Not surprisingly, the opinions of these groups tended to minimize the dangers of chronic arsenical poisoning, and their assessment of the lowest harmful levels of arsenic was anywhere from ten to one hundred times greater than those assumed by concerned physicians.[28]

On August 12 the Association of Economic Entomologists held its ninth annual meeting, at the Central High School in Detroit. Controversy swirled around the young organization, much of it caused by the arsenical spraying programs in Massachusetts. In a rambling address to the membership, President Francis Marion Webster warned that the trend he saw developing disturbed him because it prevented the organization from broadening its research and moved it toward spraying chemicals as the single answer for all problems: "I question the propriety of including the spraying of crops in the domain of economic entomology, as I believe it properly belongs with horticulture and agriculture. In other words, I question the right of an economic entomologist to demand or expect that he shall be allowed to devote the major part of his time in this manner."[29]

Horticulturists and arborists, in a strange parallel to the medical doctors, remained largely on the sidelines during the early days of the war against the gypsy moth. Slow to understand that spraying had an impact on plants as well as insects, these groups deferred to the entomologists. The fallacy in treating forests as another kind of farm had not yet become clear, and there was a lack of countervailing expertise in this area. Massachusetts would not create the office of state forester for another ten years, and during this period the only groups that spoke out against spraying with any force were the market gardeners of the Boston region and the citizens of heavily sprayed communities. Since neither of these bodies was well organized, both were overshadowed by the supposed expertise of the economic entomologists, who largely had the field of pesticide safety to themselves.

Leland Ossian Howard, circa 1886.
Special Media Services Division, National Archives & Records Administration.

The Many Opinions of Leland Howard

In July the U.S. Congress funded an investigation of the situation in Massachusetts, and Leland Howard wasted little time preparing a pamphlet that was published in November. He lifted most of it from the monograph of 1896 and added a few personal observations. He took everything related to him by Forbush and Fernald at face value, put it in the best possible light, and used the publication to commend the progress of economic entomology. He traveled to Massachusetts four times in 1897, making his first trip in May with Marlatt. His September visit was to ascertain the condition of the infested region, and the visits of July and November were used to interview individuals who opposed the eradication program.

Howard's praise for the work of his fellow economic entomologists gushed like water from a ruptured main. He crowed that gypsy moth extermination was approaching, and the few insects remaining in the Lynn Woods should not be feared. He opined that any part of the park could be freed of the moth in a short time, that colonies everywhere within the boundary of 1891 had been reduced to insignificance, and that small errors of the past, such as overlooking a straggling colony, were unlikely to happen again. He exulted that no further work ever would be required in Waltham, and that there would be no difficulty clearing Woburn, with the assurance of someone counting his chickens before they hatched. At times Howard's eagerness was embarrassing.

The organization of the work was "perfect"; the interest of the employees was "vivid": the employees were enthusiastic about their "important" work; they dragged themselves to the job even when they were sick; and so on: "The effort of (Massachusetts) will rank as one of the great experiments in economic entomology in the history of the world. . . . No criticism can be made, even in the light of present experience, since it has been in the hands of the State board of agriculture. . . . [I]t is safe to say that, even at this time, the total outcome of the work has been of great value, not only to the country at large, but to all civilized portions of the globe."[30]

Howard knew that on several occasions the agriculture committee had taken statements of opposition from men of high scientific standing. He professed to be baffled by these contrary opinions, and his report omitted the names of the objectors and failed to mention their objections. He finessed his summation by saying not that he could find no one against the work but that he could not find a single opponent who understood the work.[31]

Declaring Victory

By November 10, most of the remaining men were working in the Medford woods, where, as Kirkland wrote to Fernald, there was plenty for them to do. Money remained for only two more payrolls, and the men were laid off in alternation so that the best could have partial employment for the rest of the year.[32] Most of the men were let go by the last week in November and the rest a week later, and afterward, Forbush stewed in frustration as the most beautiful December in memory passed without any work being done. The release of the field force provided a potential pool of expert men for efforts against the brown-tail, but their services went unused. Several jurisdictions and some private estate owners hired a few men, but most private property owners refused to participate, and local authorities refused to prosecute them.

The gypsy moth committee finished the year by announcing that the outer towns were in good condition, and that if the full request of $200,000 had been appropriated, all the colonies everywhere would have been cleaned up. The committee also stated that extermination of the moth was "certain," pending a timely disbursement of funds. Fernald, in his portion of the annual report, treated the extermination of the gypsy moth as a fait accompli—with the usual proviso: "Since all the experts who have carefully and fully investigated the matter believe extermination to be possible, and, as previously stated, we have already exterminated numerous colonies, many of them in the most unfavorable places and of considerable extent, there can be no question but that what has been done in one place can be done in another, and that the

extermination of this insect is possible, so that the result is dependent entirely upon the action of the legislature."[33]

The General Court did not share this assessment and was preparing to cease appropriations. The legislators were weary of providing large sums of money for moth eradication that was endlessly claimed to be possible and bearing the blame whenever something went wrong. The "imminent" destruction of the moth, as projected by the committee in its 1897 annual report, would take another ten years and cost an additional $1.5 million. Fernald had harped publicly for several years that if the legislature was unwilling to continue investment in the gypsy moth program, it should abandon the work, and the General Court was now inclined to agree.[34] But the gypsy moth committee survived another year because the appearance of the brown-tail moth had added a new uncertainty at a time when the legislature was not in session.

The committee and its field director ended 1897 in a curious mood of self-righteousness, bravado, and lingering doubt. The annual report was a mass of contradictions and conflicting evidence about developments in the field. The committee had been buoyed by what it thought was a great success in the woodlands, the one area it had feared to attack. Forbush believed that the work on the rock-strewn and cluttered forest floor was equal to anything ever done in the towns and cities, and he expected to find few caterpillars there the following year. Fernald believed that if he could not find any egg masses, then none were there to find. A feeling began to emerge within the leadership that the doom of the moth was impending and unstoppable—by anything except the loss of funds.

Forbush put his own reputation on the line by making a long and arduous personal inspection of all infested areas, concluding that more progress toward extermination had occurred in the last ten months than at any time before:

[Extermination] is only a question of time and adequate appropriations. People who hold opposite opinions seem to be impressed by the belief that the gypsy moth is generally distributed over the whole so-called infested territory of more than 200 square miles. This, emphatically, is not the case, nor has it ever been the case. Outside the central towns the moth is found only in isolated swarms or colonies, separated by wide intervals of uninfested grounds. In fact, the greater part of the region called infested has never been invaded by the moth.[35]

Looking toward the coming battles, the committee declared that the Commonwealth now held the moth "in the hollow of her hand."[36] Forbush

announced that the time had arrived for the vaunted moth to get its due. Most of the infestations in the outlying towns had been eliminated, and any scattered survivors would succumb to inevitable death the following season. The danger of expansion past the boundary of 1891 had been removed. There was no longer any need to spread out the men, and in the spring the entire field force could be concentrated in the central towns. The moth would be pursued into every hiding place and ruthlessly expunged. Burning, spraying, burlapping, and crushing with steel brushes would be used without mercy until not a single gypsy moth colony, egg mass, or straggling refugee could be found in the state.

The long-sought victory would have to be bought before it could be won, of course, and the bargain price was $200,000 and not a penny less.

Do or Die (1898)

STATE ENTOMOLOGIST of Maine F. L. Harvey, had been watching the spread of the gypsy moth in Massachusetts with some concern. He knew about the discovery of the brown-tail there, but did not think he would have to deal with the newer insect first. But when Massachusetts inspectors, trying to ascertain the brown-tail spread that had begun in Somerville, called on George E. Osgood, a physician who spent his summers in Maine, they learned that the brown-tail was already out of the state. As Sessions wrote Harvey: "[Dr. Osgood] saw the brown-tail moth in South Berwick, Maine, while on his last summer's vacation, and was sure that it was identical with the Somerville pest. . . . [H]e professionally treated two cases of poisoning by contact with the moth and said that the symptoms of the patients were identical with those of his Somerville patients. . . . The premises in South Berwick are owned by the doctor's father-in-law, Andrew Whitehouse."[1] Early in 1898 Harvey wrote to Whitehouse, who thought the insects had been brought to Maine in winter nests on some roses bought at a Somerville nursery. Because his boy had been badly poisoned by the insects, he had cut down and burned all his infested vegetation.[2] Harvey could only wait and hope that Whitehouse had managed to destroy the colony.

In Massachusetts the San Jose scale was spreading beyond the thirteen communities where it first had been found. The board was focused on moths, but elsewhere the scale insect was the real terror to be faced. Unlike the gypsy moth, which had taken nearly thirty years to occupy an area of several hundred square miles in a single state, the scale became widely distributed in thirty-one states over a period of about ten years. Even entomologist John B. Smith of New Jersey, who proclaimed that the gypsy moth was the ultimate in terrifying insects, wrote in 1898 that research on the San Jose scale now preoccupied entomological work at every agricultural station in the country.[3] This information was no secret to Charles Fernald, who knew the scale had eclipsed both of the foreign moths but publicly maintained otherwise. In a letter to his son Henry, then working in Harrisburg, Pennsylvania, Fernald

advised, "The San Jose scale is the most important insect now in this country, and you should make a critical study of it."[4]

Do or Die

The gypsy moth committee planned to focus its effort for 1898 on the infested woodlands, including the Middlesex Fells, in the heart of the boundary of 1891. It was to be an encompassing effort with nothing held back, a do-or-die attempt to destroy the moths in these strongholds regardless of political and financial cost. The war had reached a decisive point, and it was becoming obvious even to the Metropolitan Park Commission that something would have to be done about the gypsy moth in the reservations. The commissioners had been slow to recognize the threat because the work of Forbush's men had shielded them from the gypsy moths at their worst, and as late as 1897 they still believed fire was the biggest threat to their new woodland parks.

One has only to look at photographs of typical conditions found in the Boston reservations, such as those in the Menotomy Rocks Park in Arlington, to marvel that extermination was even attempted by the means then available. Photos show nothing but crowded young trees as far as the eye can see, most of them no more then ten or twelve feet tall with trunk diameters of less than four inches. It still astonishes the viewer of more than a century later to contemplate that each of these trees would have to be individually inspected, wrapped with burlap, and then tended almost every day for eight or ten weeks. In addition, running among the shrubby growth in the large tracts there were often miles of loosely piled stone walls two or three feet in height. All these walls had to be pulled apart, each rock examined for egg masses or pupae, and then the walls rebuilt.

The year of the great attack began inauspiciously. The committee was disorganized, underfunded, and limping along with about 150 men. In Malden, Kirkland was working up a report on the Podisius predators with substantial help from Philip R. Uhler and Samuel Henshaw. Fernald was ill again in Amherst; Forbush was beginning to lay off his workers; and everybody was unsure about the disposition of the legislature. Rumors were flying that Governor Wolcott had turned against moth work, and the governor's annual message was awaited with apprehension.[5] A company of two hundred men was hired and sent to burn brush, cut trees, and destroy egg clusters wherever they were found in the Medford and Saugus woods. Forbush sent the entire eastern division of his field army, numbering about fifty men, to scout Saugus and vicinity. Special Inspector Taylor C. Lyford was in the company and was disgusted by the events of the day: "We were lined out and started in ten feet apart. When we got to the other end of the line some of the men were a quarter

mile apart, some 100 feet, some four, six, or eight, right into Lynn, a wild goose chase, going at a horse trot rate of speed. . . . I don't think one-tenth the nests in there were found. They could not have been. . . . There was not one tree out of 25 that even had a scout mark on it."[6]

When funds ran out at the end of January, work stopped and the men were dismissed. An emergency appropriation of $20,000 was made in February, and men were recalled to work in Melrose and Everett. The work continued in an atmosphere of odd normality; Forbush was making contingency plans for the spring; Fernald was recuperating; and gypsy moth committee meetings were occupied with routine business. Kirkland was speaking at farmers' meetings about the gypsy moth and taking members of the house agricultural committee on tours of the infested region. As always, he reported his doings to Fernald: "On Friday last I had Mr. Brisebee of the [agricultural committee] at Malden and gave him quite a trip. He talks as if [they] were going to take considerable time to consider the matter; this looks as if it might be June before we get an appropriation."[7]

At the end of the month the money ran out again, and the force was laid off in stages between March 11 and March 18. But contrary to expectations, the General Court did not indulge in long and rancorous hearings, stunning even the most supportive observers by granting the gypsy moth committee the entire amount it had asked for and passing the measure by a comfortable margin. Kirkland attended the final sessions of the legislature and reported to Fernald: "The house passed . . . our bill of $180,000. Two amendments of 150 and 125,000 [dollars] were offered, but the larger sum passed by a vote of 86 to 44. The debate was interesting; was on broad lines so far as friends of the bill were concerned. Opponents made free use of ridicule, slander, and abuse and lost their case."[8]

The full allocation did not become available until the middle of April, but the emergency allocation allowed the fieldwork to be carried out at full strength. It seemed the legislature intended to give the entomologists enough rope to hang themselves or prove they could exterminate the moths, the task the *American Naturalist* called "hopeless."[9] Forbush was less than grateful; the early appropriation still came too late as far as he was concerned: "Many experienced men had removed to considerable distances; some had found better jobs; and it was difficult in fact, impossible, to get them all together again."[10] By April 23, 322 men were prepared to work, but the caterpillars were already swarming. It was too late to burn or spray, so most of the men wrapped trees with burlap.

Meanwhile, the results achieved by individuals and communities fighting the brown-tail were so dismal that the legislature repealed the law of 1897 and placed responsibility for controlling the brown-tail with the Board of

Agriculture. The new law was worded like the gypsy moth act, but the penalties for uncooperative elected officials had been removed and placed instead on the citizens. Yet it mattered not a whit if anyone transported the insect, since it could get anywhere it wanted to go without help, and threats of imprisonment aimed at the ordinary townsman were senseless because even the entomologists did not believe the brown-tail could be eradicated. Obstinate estate owners were liable for fines of $200 or up to sixty days in the house of correction, or both, for failing to do their part. The legislature also voted to make all present and future employees of the moth committee take an oath of allegiance to the state.

Even with a substantial appropriation in hand, the gypsy moth committee made a great effort to economize so that every dollar possible could be spent in the field. The scientific corps borrowed supplies and materials from Fernald whenever they could and made what Kirkland termed "the best trade" for insecticides, which, Kirkland judged, saved the entire cost of arsenic compared with the previous year. Forbush reduced the office stenography pool to one person and embargoed the sole remaining typewriter so that Kirkland was obliged to write his letters to Fernald by hand and apologize, with good reason, for his sloppy penmanship.[11]

In addition to waiting for his annual appropriation from the state, Forbush also had to wait for the MPC to meet and vote on his requests to work in the Fells. In April he received a letter from the commission's secretary, John Woodbury: "At the meeting of the Board held yesterday it was voted to give your committee permission to burn over the ground in a few restricted localities in the Middlesex Fells Reservation under such supervision as is required by the Superintendent of the Reservation, the cost of said supervision to be paid out of the funds at the disposal of your committee. The work is to be stopped immediately if the Superintendent deems it detrimental to the Reservation."[12]

The concerns about fire were rendered moot by a cold and wet spring that spoiled last-ditch efforts to control the insects by spraying arsenicals or blazing the ground. Despite the reservations expressed about using burlap bands in woodlands, this method again proved the most successful, and the committee now planned the way it cleared woodlands so that larger trees were left standing to receive burlaps. It declared that the last two years had shown conclusively why burlapping was the most effective way of destroying gypsy moth caterpillars, and that without these bands the state forces would have been overwhelmed. Economic entomology, crippled by its limited arsenal of chemicals, was glad to have a dependable method to fall back on. It was a favorite technique of the committee because it drew little ire from the public, and it was a favorite of men in the field because it worked. One optimistic field

Burlap rolling machine.
From *The Gypsy Moth.*

assistant assured to Leland Howard that the last gypsy moth larva in the Commonwealth would be caught under a burlap band.[13]

During the battles of 1898 the committee purchased fifty-four bales of burlap and cut each one into 4,363 yards of strips a foot wide. In earlier years, each man had used a knife to cut his own strips in the field, but now a serviceable burlap-cutting machine was developed and constructed by E. C. Ware. A large, serrated knife similar to a hay knife was driven by an elliptical gear to slice the burlap, which was then tightly rolled on another of Ware's inventions, a man-powered burlap-rolling machine. Thus the committee was able to prepare miles of burlap for its own needs, using just a few employees. The compact rolls were loaded in high-wheeled carts and pulled into the woods by hand, ensuring that the men had ample supplies to work efficiently.

Hundreds of millions of larvae hatched that spring, and vast numbers of gypsy moth caterpillars issued from the Middlesex Fells, requiring between fifty and one hundred men to remain in Medford all summer. Another large contingent was tied down in Malden the entire season, doing nothing but

killing immeasurable numbers of caterpillars. Migrating swarms covered one house to its window frames; larger trees required three burlap bands to trap all the larvae; and all foliage was stripped from all shrub land around the city. Forbush ultimately committed two full "divisions" to Malden, nearly two-thirds of his available forces, and he even sent the cartographers, janitors, and mechanics from the field office into the fray. The gypsy moths had outflanked him again, and he mused that the insect seemed to "spring up like a mushroom in the night."[14]

E. C. Ware equipped his one hundred-gallon cyclone burner with a one-man pump that could supply up to six men. Lengths of iron piping and tee fittings were carried into the field, fastened to the tank, and laid on the ground. By connecting flexible hoses to the fittings, the men were then able to spray a considerable area, after which the iron piping was detached, the apparatus moved into a new location, and the process repeated. The new machine enabled crews to form skirmish lines and incinerate vegetation in a swath sixty yards wide. Ware's device, manufactured in the committee's own shop by machinist John Hancock, was not corroded by lead arsenate and needed no packing material because it was machined of brass. The simple and reliable pump fit inside the tank. The device was self-agitating and protected by a relief valve so that the hose would not burst. The key to its success was the availability of quarter-inch spraying lines, but Ware and Hancock had to design and build couplings that did not reduce the inside diameter of the tube. Having developed both a powerful insecticide and a greatly improved machine with which to dispense it, however, the committee was unable to do much spraying because the weather became unfavorably wet in the crucial month of May.

Burning was resumed when the weather permitted, beginning on two hundred acres partly lying in the Middlesex Fells. The super cyclone burners spewed for three months as the men worked back and forth through fields and forests until entire tracts in Medford and Malden had been burned to a crisp. Osgood noted that a thick pall of smoke hung over the region all season as woodlands, brush lands, vacant lots, and rubbish heaps were put to the torch.[15]

Because cutting the trees in the Middlesex Fells and other parklands was forbidden, every tree there had to be inspected every year, banded with burlap, climbed, and cleared by hand. The committee did not have enough manpower to undertake this task, so it hit upon a novel plan: if it could not cut down trees in the reservations, it would cut them down everywhere else, freeing men to work in the parkland. Chopper gangs were organized to cut away brush and fell trees on three thousand non-park acres throughout the infested regions.

Declaring Victory

Charles Fernald served as president of the Association of Economic Entomologists in 1898, and in August the members held their annual meeting in Boston. Speaking before the group, Forbush once again sounded an optimistic note: "In no previous year have we been able to speak so confidently of progress so early in the season. The great wooded tracts, especially in the eastern, western, and northern divisions of the infested territory, are now in excellent condition. More than ever this year I have been impressed with our power to cope with and in due time to utterly extirpate the gypsy moth when we are sufficiently supported by legislative grants."[16] About half a dozen members of the association treated themselves to an inspection trip of the boundary zone and the storehouse at Malden, after which they pronounced themselves entirely satisfied with the work and passed a resolution: "the work of the gypsy moth committee in the State of Massachusetts having been inspected in all its details by a large number of the members of this association, and its methods of operation observed, it is our opinion that too much praise can not be bestowed upon those who are carrying out this important work."[17]

These approbations carried little weight with the Massachusetts General Court, since economic entomologists were fond of passing this sort of resolution, and their objectivity was suspect. Further, the "large number" referred to must have been a relative one, given that the association at this time could not muster more than fifteen members for its annual meetings. Leland Howard was a familiar visitor who remained cheerful about whatever he saw. His name had been dropped so many times that it was somewhat the worse for wear, but it always had some effect because he was still the chief entomologist for the federal government—an institution that had little interest in what was bugging Massachusetts. Howard was in the field between October 7 and 14 and wrote Fernald to express his glowing admiration of the work and to praise the efforts of Superintendents Harris and Bailey in the Lincoln colonies. Howard urged Fernald to produce a monograph on the brown-tail moth, and with regard to the accomplishments of the year he said: "I cannot see how the most critical person could go over the ground now, especially if he had known the conditions of three years ago, without expressing entire satisfaction with the work which has been done and without being thoroughly convinced of the wisdom of the State's policy."[18]

There were other visitors to the infested zones besides economic entomologists. Whenever possible, committee members took influential state legislators on a tour, hoping that the beneficial nature of their work would be so evident that even untutored politicians could recognize it. Not all of these expeditions produced the desired results, according to Fletcher Osgood, who

often guided such less than memorable events: "I vividly remember that when one of Boston's well-known Senators came out of what was then known as the Saugus River gypsy moth colony in Saugus . . . I found upon his coat a sluggish gypsy caterpillar. . . . The season of the gypsy caterpillars had passed, and they had become so rare that the Senator at least seemed to have removed one of the only two caterpillars we had discovered in the colony that day."[19] And Senator Leonard Ross remembered being told " 'We will show you a case of extermination'; they took me to Brookline to Mr. Schlesinger's place. 'Here we have exterminated it; the last bug is gone,' and I said 'yes, but on the other side of the fence while you are hunting here is another colony.' "[20]

Senator Alfred Barker also had little faith in the explanations of entomologists because he saw them all as self-serving:

> They show [a man] around and say, why there were 15 tons of caterpillars here three or four years ago, . . . do you see any bugs? Why, the gentleman walks through there . . . and he does not see any bugs. There may be 10,000 of them in that acre and he does not see them. There may be eggs enough in that acre, gentlemen, to seed the whole Commonwealth, and he will not see one of them. They keep him there a day and a half, possibly two days, and when he has got through he says, "Why, yes, if you have exterminated them from this acre, you can exterminate them from ten acres; if you can exterminate them from ten acres you can from a hundred," and so on. "I guess they can be exterminated," and so they get his opinion [quotation marks added].[21]

The work of the chopper gangs was halted by snow on November 26, and progress was slowed by the bitter cold weather that followed the storm; most of the snow was still on the ground five weeks later. The end of the year came, and the committee ran out of funds before the choppers ran out of trees. On November 29 the entire gypsy moth field force, augmented by a large number of new hires under a different appropriation, was set loose on the brown-tail moth. The force of 524 men worked in the worst infested regions of Somerville, Cambridge, Medford, and Everett. More men worked in December than had been employed all year. Inspections were made, and of the original thirty-three infested communities, only seven were declared free of gypsy moths. Eleven new towns reported gypsy moths for the first time, but inspectors reported they could not find signs of moth activity anywhere except Manchester.

The committee was considering how much it could expect to accomplish against the brown-tail and decided to fob the matter off by asking for $10,000

to suppress the moth or $25,000 to exterminate it. Forbush considered that at least $50,000 would be needed in any case and wrote to Fernald that the committee had made a great mistake by not asking for enough money.[22] The work of the year had been concentrated in the forested portions of the zone, rather than the communities, and the directors of the field force were convinced that they had dealt the gypsy enemy a powerful blow: "Egg clusters are now in most cases rare and hard to find, even in localities where the caterpillars were killed by the millions only so recently as the past summer. In the Saugus woods, where the caterpillars taken in past seasons have been estimated at thousands of bushels, it is difficult to find egg-clusters today. In the woodlands of the Mystic valley, outside of Medford, the same condition prevails, and egg-clusters can now be found there only by long and tedious search."[23]

None of this meant much to Walter Wright, whose estate continued to prove vexatious. Wright promised a young boy five cents for each egg cluster he found. The boy worked all afternoon but had not found many eggs—until he came to a stone wall, separating Wright's land from a neighbor's, which a gypsy moth gang had burned out earlier in the year; in fact the land next to it had been blazed so severely that Wright said it nearly had been reduced to an open field. Yet in that 789-foot-long wall the boy found one hundred egg clusters. When the boy's father came by, he took a turn at the wall himself, found three hundred more egg masses, and scolded his son for not being thorough.[24]

The brown-tail moth was so different in its habits that Fernald, writing in the annual report for 1898, felt it should not be grouped with the gypsy moth and that it was unproductive to wage war on both insects at once. He chided the legislators for being so ponderous in their deliberations that by the time any of them could be convinced the brown-tail was a threat, it would have spread completely throughout the country.[25]

Fernald had vacationed at West Harbor, Maine, during the summer, constantly answering mail from Forbush, Kirkland, Sessions, and others. He was deeply disturbed when the news arrived that his old friend Joseph Lintner had died while vacationing in Italy. He and Lintner were considered the old guard, a group that was increasing in influence even while diminishing in number. Fernald was wearing down; his rheumatism was getting worse and he was increasingly prone to colds and flu. The requirements of his academic work and the continued demands of the gypsy moth committee made it difficult for him to finish anything. In a letter to entomologist Harrison Dyar shortly after he returned from West Harbor, he complained that to discharge his duties to the college, the insectary, and the gypsy moth committee he would need to be three men.[26]

As the trials of the year concluded and the moth committee began preparing its annual report, Forbush was working up a section on the newly developed spraying machines. But Kirkland was concerned that too much of the wrong thing said in the wrong way would hurt their chances for the next appropriation: "I question the wisdom of filling up the annual report to the legislature with technical matters . . . but still if [Forbush's] article is made readable and practical and shows that we are looking after economy in methods it may have a good effect. I hate to urge Forbush to write anything these days because the finished productions contain so much of Osgood's bluff and bluster."[27] Howard disagreed with Kirkland, and in November he reminded Fernald of the campaign's third agenda: to advance the cause of economic entomology through useful work, even if the people and the state seemed unimpressed: "Perhaps some of your committee, as practical men, may not see the importance of so much scientific detail, but you know as well as, or better than I do, how essential to the scientific credit of work is the published record of all its details, and also how often upon apparently insignificant scientific discoveries will depend ultimate practical results of great value."[28]

The park commissioners observed with concern the efforts of the gypsy moth field force in the Fells during the season. It became clear to them that the more work was done, the more work needed to be done, and they likened the drastic methods they witnessed to throwing kerosene on a fire. William de las Casas advocated a new approach:

> There has been an earnest effort, both on the part of the officers of the Board of Agriculture and the employees of the Commission, to avoid any friction in the performance of their duties; but the point of view of the object to be attained is necessarily so different that it seems desirable, if this kind of work must continue from year to year, that some arrangement should be arrived at by which this work should be done by the employees of the [Park] Commission, directed, of course, by competent persons.[29]

The Olmsted Brothers noted that the gypsy moth had been in the Fells since the commission acquired it but had stripped leaves only in a few localities each year, regardless of work done by the gypsy moth committee. The brothers had monitored fieldworkers all year, trying without success to devise a system that would allow both park commission and moth committee to achieve their ends. After observing the dreadful "petroleum blasts" of the cyclone burners and the resulting condition of the forest floor, however, and enduring the entreaties of Forbush to cut all but twenty or so trees per acre, the Olmsteds concluded that the work of the two groups was inimical: "We have assented, with

regret, to the cutting of the larger undergrowth in certain sections, knowing that it will spring up again from the roots; and we have protested, generally with success, against the total cutting, and burning of the smaller ground cover, which gives the forest-floor its charm. Except in some limited areas of severe infection, where everything combustible on the surface of the ground was burned by the petroleum blast (most of which work was not done under our inspection), we have prevented the destruction of any pines or hemlocks.[30]

At a meeting of the Board of Agriculture in Amherst on December 8, Sessions read aloud the committee's annual report and asked the board members to endorse it individually so that it would carry extra weight with the legislature. But although the report was endorsed unanimously, a number of board members were concerned about what was taking place in their name. William Bowker had written to Fernald in October to express his feelings that "if we would live happily and successfully we must put ourselves in harmony with [the laws of nature]."[31] And if the opinion of the legislators can be judged by votes in the General Court, about one in three was outwardly opposed to eradication efforts, and even among those who supported the undertaking there were serious reservations. Some agriculture board members had seen ominous warning signs, as Charles E. Parker of Holden said:

> I do not believe the [gypsy moth] appropriation bill would have gone through our Legislature last year if it had waited until later. I question whether the Legislature will willingly grant [another] appropriation, except the [federal] government takes hold and does its part. It has been said that we are not only working for Massachusetts, but for the United States; then why should Massachusetts pay all the expense? It seems to me that the gentlemen of [this] board are the ones to . . . get the [federal] government to appropriate $100,000, while Massachusetts puts in another $100,000. . . . It seems to me you should do this before our Legislature sits. I bring these thoughts to you because they are my strong convictions, and I believe now is the time to act.[32]

During this meeting, Sessions resigned as secretary of the board, although he retained his place on the gypsy moth committee.

Further scouting at the end of 1898 revealed that the brown-tail had spread to thirty-two additional cities and towns. Kirkland wrote to Fernald that the moth could be found from Manchester to Scituate and as far west as Waltham, and that there was no longer hope that the insect could be exterminated.[33] Fernald had become very sick again and had written to Harrison Dyar that he could continue working only "if my life and health are spared."[34]

Forbush marshaled all the men he could and sent them to cut down brush-

wood and undergrowth to make the areas ready for work the following spring. He was disturbed because work in the woods had not gone as well it needed to. He was disgusted with efforts against the brown-tail because they were a drain on his time, energy, and resources, and he thought even the idea of trying to control this fast-moving insect was absurd. He had come to the odd conclusion that Kirkland was maneuvering against him, and he was angry with Fernald over disagreements in the final report on the brown-tail. Forbush settled matters by washing his hands of the entire affair, as Kirkland added in his second letter to Fernald that day:

> On Wednesday night Mr. [Albert] Burgess met Mr. Forbush at the office, Mr. Forbush having previously arranged for the men who were working on the brown-tail moth to come to the office at that time. When they arrived, Mr. Forbush told them that he should turn over the entire brown-tail work to Mr. Burgess and would have nothing more to do with it. This, of course, was all news to Mr. Burgess, but he handled the matter in very good shape and has been in the field scouting with these men since that time. The work stopping for the year as it does today, I think that the whole matter will now blow over.[35]

Fernald, despite his prestige and the powerful influence he wielded, had become almost superfluous to the project. Control over the conduct of the war had slipped from his hands into those of Forbush, and his presence now merely dignified the process and maintained the facade of scientific credibility. The success of the conflict rode no longer on the discoveries of entomology but on the backs of a few hundred sweating laborers earning two dollars a day. Improvements came not from the laboratories of universities but from the hands of machinists, and the theories of economic entomology yielded to the methodologies of administrative detail.

It was not the gypsy moths that were fighting for their lives, but economic entomology. There was hardly a shred of science being applied in the field; even Kirkland's findings about arsenic additives did not influence the course of the war in the slightest, and Fernald's experiments might as well not have taken place for all the good they did. For a group of scientific men who were going to prove the value of applied work, almost nothing practical had been produced. Science seemed even more exhausted than the men who worked themselves into profound fatigue day after day under the hot summer sun. As technology and state-of-the-art experiments failed, leadership passed from detached intellectuals and scientific academics to men who, as Forbush said,

hunted the moth as a hunter hunts a deer—and whose mood moved closer to Dexter Rogers's view that scientific ideas were nice, but the only way to eliminate the invaders was to cut them in half one by one. The war reverted to a dreary fight in which a few hundred men armed with strips of burlap and small knives were sent into the field to confront billions of gypsy moths.

[CHAPTER 15]

Failure Is Not an Option (1899)

T HE YEAR 1899 began with Kirkland shouldering many of the responsibilities normally handled by Forbush, who was "confined to his house by
an attack of the grip."[1] The gypsy moth committee assembled on January 3
but enacted little business. Work on literature for the brown-tail moth halted
because there was no money left, and problems with the San Jose scale were
demanding more time from Fernald and his assistants at Amherst. Thanks to
late appropriations, legions of caterpillars, and recalcitrant park commissioners, and despite the positive spin put on the events of 1898, the committee's
forces had barely escaped a rout. The field leaders were in a grim mood, and
in their annual report they protested being compelled to undertake a task for
which they were never given sufficient funds.[2] The committee proposed that
one last, unfettered effort be made to crush the enemy in the heart of his
strongest hold:

> Your committee believe that the attempt to exterminate the gypsy
> moth in eastern Massachusetts has been justified by the results al-
> ready obtained, and its practicability demonstrated. They therefore
> plan to continue the work in 1899 on the same lines as in 1898. An
> appropriation of $200,000 is therefore recommended for the work of
> the ensuing year, this sum to be expended in no half-way measures of
> suppression, with the results of continuing the work indefinitely, but
> with the sole view of the extirpation of the gypsy moth from this
> Commonwealth.[3]

Impressive results would be needed to allay mounting fears in the General
Court, but an uninspected belt of towns surrounding the infested area would
need to be examined thoroughly. The committee said the state should expect
at least ten more years of inspections and minor efforts to ensure that the moth
had been truly eradicated. With regard to the sum of nearly a million dollars
already expended to fight the gypsy moth, the committee quoted Howard's

dismissive remark that the amount was but "a drop in the bucket" compared with the potential losses from billions of unchecked larvae; Fernald likewise brushed off the expenditures as "a mere bagatelle" when viewed against the costs of protecting the entire state indefinitely.

The legislators did not think the money spent was inconsequential; to them the outflow of cash represented a financial hemorrhage that had to be staunched. The state was throwing good money after bad, and the vague predictions for the outcome of the effort left politicians suspicious that the campaign would become a perpetual money sink for the taxpayers. Moreover, the war against the gypsy moth had been overshadowed by a real war against Spain, and for the first time in years the governor's inaugural address made no mention of exterminating insects.[4]

Four hundred men were retained to destroy egg masses in the woodlands during January. The committee met on January 18 to reconstitute itself after the death of S. S. Stetson, following which the members voted to suspend all effort within a few weeks. Kirkland wrote, "It hardly seems probable that we shall work the entire month through."[5] Efforts ceased on February 1, and the entire force was dismissed after the legislature failed to vote an appropriation. An emergency allocation of $30,000 dollars became available in mid-February, passing after contentious legislative debate and squeaking through by just a few votes. Work did not resume for a week due to heavy snow accumulations. The bulk of the appropriation was used to pay for the expenses of January, and the remainder lasted until March 9, at which time about three hundred field workers were dismissed.

Meanwhile the yearly hearings and debates on the gypsy moth appropriation had been taking place, and it was common knowledge that the appropriation bill did not have enough votes to pass. Testimony given in 1900 by Senator Ross and others left little doubt that the lobbying effort on behalf of the gypsy moth bill had been intense: "We were hounded almost to death, almost to desperation, [employees of the gypsy moth department] were piling in, and they would come to this man and say to him: if you will vote for this man and so and so, he will vote for your bill. . . . [I]t was common knowledge that many bills were tied up, held back, until certain people were seen."[6] Legislators were promised the opportunity to obtain jobs on the field force for unemployed men in their districts if they voted for the measure. Senator Ross identified Kirkland as one of those who had lobbied him on several occasions about supporting the gypsy moth bill and who had informed him that he might as well vote for the bill and get his share of men employed.

At the same time, legislators who were trying to pass an appropriation to renovate Carney Hospital in Boston similarly did not have enough votes because of prejudice against Carney, which was a Catholic hospital. In a great

example of logrolling, supporters of the gypsy moth appropriation and those in support of Carney Hospital voted for each other's bill. On April 15 the gypsy moth appropriation of $170,000 passed by a small margin, much to the ire of opponents who had once again been outmaneuvered by the surprising political skill of the gypsy moth leadership. The editors of the *American Naturalist* were dismayed by the sums of money given to the Board of Agriculture in the last two years and wrote: "Is it not sometimes the part of wisdom in a prudent business man to let a bad investment go, rather than to lose more money by trying to save what is already lost?"[7] Senator Ross, who voted in favor of the appropriation in 1898 and against it in 1899, recalled: "A member of the House said to me that he would sooner cut off his right hand than vote for the Carney Hospital appropriation, and yet, when the vote was taken, he voted for it, and I asked him why. He says, 'God knows I had to do it to save the gypsy moth appropriation,' and so the methods that were adopted to get this measure through . . . so completely disgusted me that I was forced to think I had done something wrong in my vote the year before."[8]

As soon as the money became available, the force was reassembled and sent into the field. The problems of almost every preceding year were repeated: skilled employees had been lost; new hires could not be used until they had received training; and the lack of experienced workers made each step longer and costlier. Forbush decided that the main effort of the year would be made with burlap because of the need to work in wooded parklands, where the commissioners were very restrictive about allowing fire. By the end of spring his force of 570 men had banded 2,500,000 trees, an undertaking that consumed fifty-three tons of burlap cloth and uncounted miles of twine. To this astonishing number was added one million still useful bands from the previous year. Forbush wrote: "The work of burlapping was pushed with utmost diligence. All other work was given up, and wherever caterpillars were found the burlaps were examined as often as appeared necessary. In those localities where the greater number of larvae were found the bands were visited once a day and even oftener in extreme cases. As a result of this work the larvae were killed off so rapidly that few matured."[9] In addition, the spring of 1899 was a dry one favorable to both caterpillars and spraying. Kirkland reported that the weather made the application of lead arsenate especially effective. Forbush too said that the weather was ideal and that wherever trees were sprayed, the caterpillars were almost entirely destroyed.

Although the moths were present in greater or lesser concentrations throughout the infested district, the worst spots were in Georgetown, Newton, and the Middlesex Fells. The severest infestation occurred in July in the Long Hill colony at Georgetown, which, along with the colonies in Newton and

Manchester, were new infestations that had been discovered during the winter—and all the new ones found this year were outside the boundary of 1891. The colony at Georgetown was particularly distressing to the committee and the field director because it was only eight miles from the New Hampshire border. People living in the Newton region had reported infestations every year since 1897. The street commissioner of Newton testified at the hearings of 1900 that he had discovered the colonies in 1895 and given notice, but nothing had been done. The scouts Forbush sent in 1897 and 1898 reported that they did not see any signs of the gypsy moth. There is no telling why the inspectors could not find any, but by 1899 the colonies were large and well established.

Once again, the committee found it had spoken too soon about the scarcity of egg clusters throughout the region. The spring hatch of caterpillars swarmed in enormous numbers for a third consecutive year, and several acres of trees were defoliated. Although the devastated area was small by modern standards, so many denuded trees in one place presented an alarming sight. Citizens reported that the speed of the caterpillars as they swarmed from defoliated areas was like a fire spreading outward across a dry forest floor.

In Georgetown, thousands of caterpillars crawled over every tree, reminding Kirkland of "the almost incredible tales told of the now historic moth outbreak of a decade ago in Medford."[10] Twenty men with cyclone burners battled the hungry larvae for days. For the first time an attempt was made to confine the insects by cutting an isolating path around the infested area. Stupendous quantities of caterpillars were destroyed, but they could not be killed fast enough, and astonishing numbers of them survived to pupate. As female moths appeared and began to lay their eggs, Forbush called for drastic action as Kirkland described: "Fire and axe were applied. . . . Trees were felled and thrown with their festoons of pupae and clusters of eggs into bonfires; the flame of the cyclone burner was applied to ground, ledges and walls, and all remains of the moth were done away with."[11]

The Newton colony was intractable, and thirty men were sent there to band the trees. It should not have surprised anyone that the more the insects were fought, the wider became the area in which they were found. The tract occupied by this single and supposedly small concentration ultimately was found to encompass four square miles, compelling Forbush to keep his men in Newton for a month setting pastureland afire, felling trees, and putting an old building to the torch. Fletcher Osgood, a participant in the wild struggle, wrote a melodramatic review of his comrades in combat: "Such is the life of the gypsy moth worker—combating the pest with axe and brush hook, chemicals and flame, with knife, spatula and crushing palm, in all weathers and in

all seasons, called it may be to make of his working ground a veritable slaughter pen, wherein the devastating pests are flung by brimming bushels into trenches, like the dead in battle."[12]

The leadership of the campaign took the position that the work through the end of 1897 had been only suppressive in nature because of meager funding. Having stated a number of times that they required $200,000 annually to exterminate the moth, and having at last received it for two years in a row, their need for success now became absolute. The moths could not be allowed to gain more ground. Forbush threw all the force he could muster into the battle, and pushed his men past the limits of their endurance.

J. S. Pray, who worked for the Olmsted Brothers, had visited the infested parts of Georgetown and Newton before any work was done and recalled being impressed with the "immense, sickening masses of larvae and pupae upon the old trees there and upon the old shanties within the infested district."[13] He said of the workers: "They were as hard worked men during the season as can be. They were working much harder than they had any right to from their own personal point of view, and many of them, as you know, knocked themselves out physically by the intense strain, . . . the hard, physical strain of it day after day."[14] Sometimes the men became so fatigued they could hardly stand on their feet, yet as C. W. Brown testified, if they fell out for even fifteen minutes toward the end of a grueling stint, they were docked an hours' pay: "It was not customary to loaf at all. . . . I says [to Inspector Holbrook], 'we will go in and rest, I am tired.' And I says, 'you can put it on to the bottom of your report, and if they wish, they can dock us for the time, as I am completely exhausted.' . . . I have worked for a good many different people, a good many bosses, [in] a good many different parts of the country, but I never in my life worked for a Commission that extracted so much from their men."[15]

So many caterpillars survived to pupate that the committee decided to destroy pupae by burning brush and scrub woods in July and August, despite dangerously dry conditions. As leaders had feared, the moths were now making annual forays from their woodland strongholds into areas previously cleared of their kind. The patient citizens of Medford demanded an explanation; Walter Wright could not understand why the committee clung to the idea of eradication when all evidence seemed to the contrary: "Here [in Medford], nine years later, within half a mile of the origin [of the gypsy moth in America], in a mere village neighborhood, on level grounds, no wood lands, simply apple trees in good preservation, the moth was not exterminated, so that over 50 were taken from one tree at the first search last summer. . . . I should not dare to estimate the number taken under burlaps in Medford last year at less than two million."[16]

Arlington was also heavily infested, but to show that the state was gaining the upper hand, some inspectors began to present inaccurate numbers. General Agent J. A. Farley, a high-ranking member of the director's office, observed as one special inspector and a crew of two men worked through a dense colony on Oakland Avenue one Friday morning. After watching for some time, Farley asked the special inspector for his estimate of egg clusters and was told there were about two hundred. After finishing work, the special inspector reported to his superintendent that only twenty-three egg clusters remained. Incredulous, Farley returned to Oakland Avenue the next day: "My estimation of the nests in that colony, according to my experience, was that there was 6,000 nests. The leaves were literally plastered with nests, so that you could work on a space of a square foot for an hour, treating nests, and then turn [the leaves] over and spend another hour. There were over two acres infested in that way."[17]

Fernald and Forbush were hard put to understand why so many larvae were hatching each spring and remained baffled by the mechanisms of gypsy moth population dynamics. They theorized that population outbreaks were related to favorable weather conditions that allowed insects to pupate faster than predators could depress their numbers, but they refused to consider the possibility of inaccurate reports. They directed the scientific corps to collect more egg clusters and count the individual eggs. The average obtained was not the 450 to 500 eggs per cluster that Forbush and Fernald had been using for most of their campaign calculations but a little over 600 per cluster.

Since much of the work in the last days of the war was being done in the Middlesex Fells, the clusters counted were probably taken from there. The greater number of eggs per cluster indicates that the moths were living under highly favorable conditions and their colonies were robust. In 1895, Forbush had claimed 90 percent destruction but wrote in 1896 that he did not understand what caused massive outbreaks.[18] In the annual report for 1897 he cited 95 percent destruction of the moth in all its forms, showing that he still employed very nearly the same methods and continued to estimate about a six-and-one-half times annual increase of the moth per year.[19]

Much of the effort was concentrated in the woodlands where the insect in all its forms was destroyed by hand. The committee reported that the beautiful Lynn Woods area was thoroughly infested and the magnificent Fells in even worse condition. The committee used what it termed "heroic" efforts in the woodlands outside the reservations, which consisted of burning all brush and cutting all trees labeled as "worthless." The strategy was to drive surviving gypsy larvae to the few remaining large trees, where they could be captured under the burlap bands and killed. This effort became extreme during the last two years of the campaign as the field forces engaged billions of moths in

forested areas that could not be sprayed. Private woodlands were logged extensively and, some felt, excessively in the compulsive effort to deny the larvae
their food. I. J. Colbert, who worked on a chopper gang during the last few
years of the campaign, recounted his experiences on land belonging to a Mr.
Cox in Winchester:

> We cut in the neighborhood of 2700 cords of wood. We went through
> that piece of wood land, which was an unusually fine, straight growth
> of wood, we went through that wood and cut everything about clean,
> probably left one tree every 50 or 60 feet. . . . The wood was split and
> piled, logs were sawed and saved, and everything was done in ship
> shape. The ground was cleaned up, the brush burnt, wood piled in
> cords so that it could be easily measured, and everything was done
> except selling the wood and cutting it up for fire wood. If we had a
> little more time we probably would have done that.[20]

The park commissioners had other ideas. They would not allow even the
youngest saplings to be destroyed, which forced the gypsy moth warriors in
some cases to clear infestations by crawling on their hands and knees to over-
turn rocks and inspect the trunks and lowest branches of the smallest trees.
Tall trees had to be cleared of egg masses one at a time by light and agile men
called "squirrels," who donned metal climbing irons to ascend the trees without ladders. After the female moths had laid their eggs, the workers undertook
the astounding task of removing more than three million burlap bands from
tree trunks distributed throughout a region of more than 220 square miles,
clearing off or creosoting all the egg masses found underneath, and then tying
all the burlaps back on again.

Brown-tail Breakout

Roland Thaxter, with his son Charles Elliot and family, departed Cambridge
in June for their summer place on Cutts Island, Kittery Point, Maine. The
brown-tail moths were making life miserable for everyone each summer, and
the thought of cool Maine nights and pure, refreshing ocean breezes without
any brown-tail hairs in it was very appealing. In 1897, Roland Thaxter had
been among the first to notify the gypsy moth committee about the new caterpillar defoliating his pear trees, and his house was at the center of Cambridge's brown-tail infestation. There were many kinds of moths flapping
about the Maine island at night as well, but this time the Thaxters came across
some that looked too familiar. They netted a couple and realized the insects
were brown-tail moths. On July 14, 1899, young Charles wrote to the Maine

State entomologist, F. L. Harvey: "We have caught two brown tail moths this month, one on the wing July 3d and another at rest July 12. My father thinks the cocoons or caterpillars must have been brought here from Cambridge two summers ago on our household goods, as brown tail moths were plentiful about our house in Cambridge while we were packing. My father feels sure that they were not brought this year and thinks that they are likely to have become established on this island."[21]

Harvey wrote to the Thaxters asking for samples, which they sent. The insect was identified as a brown-tail, making the spread of imported moths a problem that now affected three states. Exterminating the brown-tail in Massachusetts at once became a pointless effort when Harvey announced that the moths were on the Maine border with New Hampshire.[22] Nevertheless, a feeling was starting to come over the field superintendent and others that this insect was not going to become the feared second wave of incessant defoliation. The initial surge of expansion had been a fluke, for the brown-tail was not as rugged as the gypsy moth, and it attacked a far narrower range of hosts. Clipping winter webs and burning them guaranteed that an area would be free of brown-tails the following summer. The night-flying moths were taken in great numbers by bats. The moths flew into arc lights and electrocuted themselves at the rate of more than a hundred per fixture each night. Each lamppost became a moth dispensary for predatory birds. English sparrows made daily visits to the lamps and captured the moths easily. Waiting toads devoured injured moths that fluttered to the ground.

Fernald and Forbush, anxious to get an idea of how potent a suppressing force was exerted on the brown-tail moth by birds and bats, assigned the task of enumerating the brown-tail's losses to Kirkland, who soon found himself in a quandary. If he canvassed the arc lights late in the afternoon, birds would have eaten most of the moths. If he tried again at dawn, the bats would have finished their work, leaving nothing but piles of moth wings on the ground under the globes. The most Kirkland could do was count wings and divide by four. But he also discovered an unsuspected and surprising ally: "Whatever may be the sins of the English sparrow, we must give them credit for destroying large numbers of brown-tail moths. Not only do these birds eat the moths themselves, but they also feed them to their young. I saw the sparrows repeatedly hunting along fences and carrying off the resting moths to their nests in July of the present year. At Somerville last year it was no uncommon sight to see flocks of twenty or more sparrows collecting the moths from a picket fence."[23]

By the middle of summer the gypsy moth campaign was entering its twilight months, placing its leadership in awkward personal and professional positions. Forbush's health was becoming a concern to him, although he did not

generally advertise it to others. He insisted publicly that the forces of Massachusetts were doing the best and most effective work they had ever done, but privately he cautioned chemist F. J. Smith that after this year there probably would be no more work for him. Smith wrote to Fernald on June 13, 1899, to see if this were true and to ask Fernald's help in finding a new job.[24]

Interest in control by parasites continued to wane. C. Kochi, a Japanese student of Fernald's at Amherst who was doing graduate work at Cornell under Comstock and Gage, sent a hymenopterous parasite to Fernald on July 15 with the promise to send another one soon.[25] As with the Japanese parasites sent in earlier years by Loomis and Riley, however, there seems to be no record that Kochi's specimen arrived alive or that any further work was done with it.

Laissez–Faire

During the middle of August, Forbush and Kirkland took a break from the constant demands of their work in Massachusetts and traveled to Columbus, Ohio, with Fernald to attend the eleventh annual meeting of the Association of Economic Entomologists. Kirkland, who was the association's secretary this year, presented a paper on lead arsenate, and Forbush read two papers, one on birds that attacked hairy caterpillars and another on the gypsy moth work in Massachusetts; in the latter he confidently announced to the audience that "Porthetria dispar will be a rare insect in the infested region in the year 1900."[26]

Perhaps the most astonishing moment came during the opening address by President Charles Lester Marlatt, an expert on the San Jose scale. Although he confined his talk to this particular insect, his words were aimed at all insects that entomologists had declared as pests and were attempting to eradicate:

> Has an important insect pest ever been exterminated? Does not the locust still flourish, and is not the cankerworm still a burden? Are not all the insect plagues of our forefathers to the remotest times still with us? . . . [A]re we not merely repeating and putting into effect the boast of the courtiers of King Canute that at his command the tide would roll back; and are we not, like that good old king, though unwittingly, giving a practical demonstration of our own impotence by having the tide of failure roll up around our bodies?[27]

Marlatt went on to propose a laissez-faire approach to what he called the normal progression of nature; he counseled that only small, localized exterminations should be attempted when conditions were dire because it was obvious to him that nature was capable of taking care of herself. Not a person

in the room, he continued, had ever been deprived of the necessities of life because of an insect. Marlatt recalled growing up in the midwestern corn and wheat belt during the worst days of the chinch bug, the Colorado potato beetle, and the Hessian fly, and pointed out that not a farm in his memory had ever been abandoned solely because of insects. It was undesirable to cry out in alarm every time a new insect pest was discovered, he said, and hasty failures at extermination only served to make economic entomologists look foolish.

The effect of Marlatt's speech was to throw the small assembly of economic entomologists into turmoil. Just nine months before, Fernald had released an updated danger bulletin in which he stated unequivocally that the gypsy moth was the greatest insect peril in the country.[28] The document dwelled on such inflammatory points as the insect's ravages in Europe, the extreme devastation of forest trees, the loss of domestic crops, the vastness of regions overrun, and the numbers of people driven from their homes by an insect that was claimed to be far more destructive in North America than it was anywhere else. Marlatt's condemnations went right to the heart of that document, and Forbush responded that exterminating insects had both an optimistic and a pessimistic side. He made the astonishing argument that when a foreign insect was weak (as the gypsy moth was, he thought, because the female could not fly), it was vulnerable, and therefore extermination was a good course—somehow forgetting that after almost ten years of effort and expenditures approaching a million dollars, the Commonwealth had been able neither to eradicate the moth nor to hold it in bounds. He contended that had a laissez-faire policy been followed, "many States would now be suffering from the pest."[29] The discussion that followed was lengthy and intense. Most of those in attendance did not believe Marlatt's observations: some argued against them; others simply rejected them outright. Forbush claimed later that every entomologist at the meeting had opposed Marlatt's conclusions.[30]

Reconsideration

Fletcher Osgood had resigned from state employment and entered private industry in May 1899; he remained interested in the campaign, however, because he was working on an article about the gypsy moth war for publication the following year. Osgood wrote to a state representative, Crosby of Middlesex, and asked to interview him. Crosby had been on vacation in Maine, but upon his return in early September he invited Osgood to visit and learned that Osgood had concluded extermination could not succeed: "In the course of his remarks Mr. Osgood told me that Mr. Forbush himself had told him after the passage of [the gypsy moth bill] that this work was merely a question of patronage. Mr. Forbush has denied it. . . . And Mr. Osgood says to me, 'I

will give Mr. Forbush the credit of sighing when he said it.' . . . I believe in a burst of frankness, in a burst of disgust, if you please, the field director spoke the truth and spoke his true sentiments at that time."[31] Osgood also mentioned that eggs treated in the lab with the same creosote oil that had been used for years were now hatching. When Crosby asked him what that meant, Osgood replied, "You can draw your own inferences."[32]

As the leaves fell from the trees, the remaining members of the field force turned their attention to a halfhearted assault on the brown-tail moth, a task that occupied them for the rest of the season. Workers used pruning shears on long poles to reach into the canopy and snip nests off the branches; then the fallen vegetation and its slumbering insect inhabitants were raked into piles and burned. The workers were unenthusiastic about combatting the brown-tail, and Osgood noted a similar lethargy on the part of the public: "I have seen little orchards of short pear trees loaded with brown-tail webs, as if they bore a heavy crop of withered fruit, which the occupants or owners, at no expense to speak of, could readily have cleared, but which they chose to neglect. . . . Such incidents are typical of a prevailing mood. Allowing for many exceptions, we must, I think, admit that the average owner or occupant of an estate is indisposed to clear it of the brown-tail, even though the law requires that he shall."[33]

Forbush prepared his annual report, complaining as usual that he did not have enough men to prosecute the work, and that he could not find enough men to hire. He also stated again that work in the field would have gone better if he had been given more money in a timely fashion. But in the last two years of the campaign, that argument had lost much of its force: the Board of Agriculture received the full amount it had requested for two years running, and emergency appropriations had been made available to tide the fieldwork over until the full appropriation came to a vote.

In fact, the actual number of men at work against the moth was always larger than Forbush claimed. Little notice was given to the gypsy moth gangs created by infested communities such as Medford, Malden, Newton, and others—municipalities left in the lurch so many times that they had formed their own crews, and some even bought their own spraying apparatus. It is no longer possible to know how many additional men were at work on their own or employed by agencies outside the Board of Agriculture, but in the central cities gangs of fifty men or more were reported, indicating that manpower was not a severe problem.

Samuel Crocker Lawrence, Medford's wealthiest citizen, attended to his four-hundred-acre estate, Seven Hills, located in the heart of the city. Lawrence kept his magnificent parklands open to the public and owned modern sprayers that he used to battle the gypsy moths from the beginning.

Lawrence's men helped citizens who could not afford to take care of their properties themselves, and toward the end of the campaign he often employed more than one hundred workers at a time. Some estimates are that he spent a half-million dollars of his own money on gypsy moth work before the campaign was over.[34] General Lawrence did not reveal the amount he spent fighting insects except to say it was more than he cared to mention. His forces alone boosted the number of men by 25 percent. Municipal gangs raised that figure even higher. Other citizens such as Albert S. Sise, Walter Wright, and the Frost brothers were doing much the same work as Lawrence, although on a smaller scale. Perhaps thousands of individual landowners large and small throughout the infested region were also going after the moths or hiring professional exterminators to do the work.

Since Lawrence's support was critical to the success of the effort, his crews were trained by the state early in the war. Late in the campaign, many citizens felt that Lawrence's crews were more efficient and got better results than the state's forces. Courteous and helpful, they were welcomed wherever they went. State crews needed to press for the maximum amount of work in the shortest possible time, and not being members of the communities in which they worked made them largely indifferent to the citizens. Many residents became restive about the constant intrusion by state employees on their properties, and writers such as Eugene Wambaugh were concerned that the intrusions were becoming excessive.[35]

In October the remaining members of the state's army fell upon the gypsy egg clusters in Georgetown and Newton. Scouts went through the region noting areas that needed attention, followed by chopper gangs that "cleared up" the land and made the remaining trees ready for burlapping. The choppers had a busy year, felling nearly 469,000 trees and trimming almost 100,000 more.

Forbush always allowed for a certain number of bad-weather days when idle men could not draw pay. Stretches of good weather tended to use up his budget faster. When gypsy moth money ran out late in the season, the men would work under the small brown-tail appropriation until it was exhausted. The appropriations for 1899 were expended by the end of November, causing a cessation of the work and the release of all workers except field superintendents and their assistants, who remained employed until the end of December.

Despite the rising numbers of insects killed and the discovery of new colonies in Newton and Georgetown, Fernald, Forbush and the committee became almost delusional about the ultimate effects of their work and publicly stated that extermination was approaching. The committee reported at the end of 1899 that all the large moth colonies had been wiped out and that the remains of the smaller colonies would be gone within a few more years: "It is

unnecessary at this time for the committee to reaffirm its belief that the entire extermination of the moth is a possibility. The results of the past two years' work are sufficient to dispel any doubt on this point, and to make it plain to the most skeptical that if sufficient funds can be provided for a few years longer the accomplishment of the desired end will be an assured fact."[36] The committee also held that after a decade of combat the infestation was still confined within the boundary of 1891. Although the boundary had been enlarged to encompass about 225 square miles, colonies found outside the original limits were considered temporary and thus listed as exterminated within a year or two. In fact, the actual area of infestation had grown to 359 square miles[37]—information commonly known within the circle of economic entomologists in New England and by Leland Howard in Washington but apparently not to the public at large or the General Court of Massachusetts.

The committee, the field director, and the advising entomologist proudly pointed out that in many areas where infestations previously had been severe, one would be hard pressed to find even a single caterpillar during larva season. Moths populating the woods and parklands were now so strongly entrenched, however, that nothing within reason could be done to drive them out, and each spring the larvae would swarm from these places by the hundreds of millions. Later, when gypsy moth colonies in other states were thought to be undergoing extermination, the number of insects killed annually dropped dramatically until larvae, egg masses, and pupae were nearly impossible to find, yet in the Massachusetts campaign the number of insects killed each year rose markedly. Fernald dismissed the increased counts as proof that the state was gaining on the caterpillars. Former committee member John G. Avery too was sanguine about the appearance of massive new colonies: with the committee's experience and the materials available, he asserted, colonies of any size could be exterminated in the first year.[38]

When Forbush took the position as superintendent of fieldwork he had no idea what demands the job would impose on him. The gypsy moth campaign became all-encompassing, but Forbush considered himself equal to the task both mentally and physically. Although he was not an imposing specimen, he took great pride in his mental toughness and physical stamina. He liked to tell how he had cured himself of rheumatic fever after being caught in the open during a three-day rainstorm, a treatment that he later delighted in calling the "water cure."[39] Throughout his life, he had relied on himself at times when his life was at stake, no help was at hand, and failure was not an option. Yet even an individual who enjoyed the robust health that Forbush claimed could not continue such stressful work indefinitely without ill effects. Problems with his health showed up as early as 1897, when Howard observed that he was dragging himself through each day when he should have been in a sickbed.

During 1898, Forbush's health continued to be a source of concern, and during the effort for 1899 he was unable to work for many months, during which other factors too began to influence his position as field director.

Forbush took risks when he felt risks needed to be taken, even to going it alone when his instincts told him he must. He ran the campaign the way he ran his life, pushing himself and his troops as hard as he dared. Most of the men hated the pressure but stayed on because they could not make better money "on the outside."[40] The workers also resented Forbush's practice of "spotting," which subjected them to observation by men hired to see whether they were really working. Spying had been going on since 1892. Nathaniel Shaler had spied personally during his tenure and sometimes hired men at his own expense to spot for him. The workers thought it was crazy to have the director, an eight-dollar-a-day man, and his superintendents "spotting with fast horses."[41]

Forbush finally reached his limits of physical endurance and patience with the General Court; sometime during the second half of the year, he tendered his resignation. The committee, as once before, refused to accept it, instead granting him a three-month leave of absence and afterward stating that the reason for his resignation was poor health. Fernald wrote to to Leland Howard: "I suppose you have heard that Forbush has been given a leave of absence for three months and Kirkland has been put in his place. How did you find the work down there [in the infested region] and how were you impressed with it? Please write me about this matter as you feel and indicate what you are willing for me to make use of in my report."[42] The issue of health may have been a smokescreen, since John May mentions nothing about health problems at this time in his biographical sketch of Forbush but attributes the resignation to diminished appropriations. Forbush was well enough in early 1900 to ready personally his newly purchased retreat at Wareham, Buzzard's Bay, where he immediately began work on his book *Two Years with the Birds on a Farm.*

As acting superintendent, Kirkland wrote the annual report presented to the state by the board at its meeting in January 1900. Kirkland was remembered as a young man who had graduated from college six years before and experienced personal difficulties that tarnished his image. Since then he had pulled himself together, become a good entomologist, married a fine and interesting young woman, and become a Methodist. He slipped into the director's role with ease and displayed great maturity in dealing with a crisis situation. Fernald wrote: "He was my assistant . . . on the gypsy moth work, the last three months Acting Director where he showed himself to be such a man of affairs as to surprise [me] and the Gypsy Moth Committee. He is a man of presence, a good public speaker, and what the western people call

a hustler, one who will work incessantly."[43] Kirkland declared that the end of the gypsy moth was in sight, and the committee considered this statement "indisputable."[44]

On December 8, 1899, a special meeting of the Board of Agriculture was held in the Town Hotel at Amherst. The board wanted to review its powers and positions and hear the comments of Charles Fernald, who also was present. The two-dozen board members in attendance voted to accept Kirkland's report, with thanks to Fernald and Forbush for all their hard work. Board members, as exemplified by Charles E. Parker of Holden, held out hope that a federal appropriation might be made in time to bail out what was starting to feel like a sinking ship. A motion was made that the governor request the state legislature to "memorialize" the United States Congress for help in exterminating the gypsy moth, and after the motion was voted on and passed, the meeting adjourned.[45]

[CHAPTER 16]

The Last Hurrah (1900)

T HE COMMITTEE BEGAN the last year of the nineteenth century operating through January without an appropriation. The board formed committees that formed subcommittees to make one last effort for a federal appropriation, but in the end the matter was referred back to the gypsy moth committee for some unknown heroic solution; E. W. Wood, Francis Appleton, and William Sessions were delegated to draft such resolutions.[1] But events were moving too fast to be changed.

Scouts spent a great deal of time inspecting Boston and its wards of Roxbury and Dorchester. When Roxbury had been scouted in 1897, only one caterpillar had been reported; when it was scouted again in 1899, only three caterpillars were discovered, which led the committee to declare the ward practically free of gypsy moths. Then, in January of 1900, a huge colony was found on West Cottage Street, an infestation so well established and severe that 1,600 egg nests were taken from a single elm tree.[2] Moths were found everywhere except Franklin Park, which the committee pronounced cleared. The picture emerging from 1899 was not good. Despite a year in which the largest field force had operated under the most generous appropriation, the moth had made gains. Everett, Malden, Medford, and Melrose were listed as infested, and all the other inspected towns contained egg masses except Georgetown, where only a single cluster was reported.

Medford was in the worst condition, with egg clusters visible in almost every part of the woods. Although such individuals as Samuel C. Lawrence and Albert S. Sise had expended considerable sums in private engagements with the moths and achieved acceptable results, others had not fared as well. Walter Wright's estate remained infested even though he fought moths all season long with hired help; his employee reported destroying "twenty-eight thousand larvae in a space of thirty square feet."[3] A large percentage of homeowners had given up the fight as unwinnable, leaving the moth with multiple retreats from which it could reinfest the lands of those who had worked to clear their premises.

The committee on gypsy moths, insects, and birds finally got what it had been asking for—an independent panel to investigate the work and report to the General Court. But it soon became clear that the panel's members were no friends of the gypsy moth committee, the Board of Agriculture, or the policy of extermination. On January 16, 1900, a special joint investigating committee of the Massachusetts house and senate was created to determine the question of extermination and report its findings by February 15. Because the Senate did not concur until January 22, the deadline for the report was extended until March 22. The house members of the committee were Charles F. A. Smith of Waltham, James F. Bliss of Boston, Edwin J. Mills of Fall River, Charles A. Carruth of Athol, Charles O'M. Edson of West Brookfield, Temple A. Winsloe of Boston, Frederick O. MacCartney of Rockland, and John L. Donovan of Boston; members from the senate included Loyed E. Chamberlain, Thomas W. Kenefick, and C. W. Hazelton.

On January 26 the investigators hired stenographer Arthur T. Lovell and got to work. They held seventeen public hearings, beginning on January 30 and concluding on February 26, and called 125 individuals to testify (members interviewed citizens who could not attend). Witnesses included present and former senators and representatives, members of the Board of Agriculture, entomologists, town officials, market gardeners, farmers, citizens, and a large number of present and former gypsy moth workers.[4] On three of the days that no hearings were scheduled, committee members visited the infested regions, although in February there was little to see. The format was the same as it had been for all previous hearings with the Board of Agriculture allowed to present its witnesses first, followed by the opposition, and concluding with a rebuttal period during which all witnesses could correct errors or clarify ambiguities.

The annual reports of the gypsy moth committee and the monograph of 1896 were closely scrutinized by Alfred E. Barker, the former senator, who believed his stand against appropriations several years earlier had turned the moth men against him and was responsible for his defeat at the polls. He testified that the moth committee had long misrepresented its progress:

> Their reports here show that they have never given the Commonwealth the true state of affairs, or else they have made those reports for the purpose of getting from this Commonwealth their annual appropriation, and getting it bigger every time. . . . There is only one thing consistent in their reports from beginning to end, and that is: More money, and more money, and give it to us quick; that is all. . . . There is not a point of failure which they point to here; there is not a place where they have made a promise that has not been fulfilled where they have not come back and laid it on the Legislature.[5]

Charles Fernald was among the first to testify and did his best to protect others involved in the work, saying that he was personally responsible for any errors or mistakes and that any missteps by the board occurred because they were "following the advice which I have given them as closely as they could."[6] Fernald received a polite hearing from the investigators, but his disputations had been heard before and were now considered fantasies. No longer able to present any compelling arguments and sensitive to comments made about him by others, he had trouble focusing, sometimes contradicted himself, occasionally asked the investigators to repeat their questions, and digressed into anecdotes about the campaign. At a couple of points, the chairman interrupted Fernald to ask him the purpose of relating these reminiscences. Fernald's luster had dimmed, and Senator Leonard Ross testified that he had endured entomology in general and Fernald in particular longer than he cared to: "I have known of Prof. Fernald, the entomologist in this work,—and I care not whether he is present,—I believe him to be an enthusiastic, capable and efficient entomologist; I believe he is worth more as an entomologist because he is prejudiced . . . I believe that Prof. Fernald would believe that he was doing his duty honestly if he were to see every dollar in the treasury of the Commonwealth spent to exterminate bugs."[7]

The investigators were keen to know why work with parasites had been blocked so often, and again Fernald tried to shoulder the blame. He had never been able to take the decisive step of recommending a legislative petition amending the enabling act so that such explorations could begin. At one point during questioning the following exchange occurred:

> CHAIR: Now you say there has been no effort made by the Legislature to send experts across the water; you say here nobody has ever asked it. That is true, is it not?
>
> FERNALD: . . . I am very sure the Legislature has not been asked.
>
> CHAIR: You asked the Attorney General if it was possible under the present appropriation to do such work, and you found you could not?
>
> FERNALD: We could not do it without a direct act of the Legislature.
>
> CHAIR: Did you ever ask . . . for a direct act of the Legislature?
>
> FERNALD: I never have.
>
> CHAIR: Why has not the Board done it; is it not that important a matter?
>
> FERNALD: I think it is because I have advised them not to.[8]

Barker was incensed over the political incursions and manipulations of the gypsy moth committee and its field organization: "There is no man that knows

better his adversary than the man who meets him in battle, and when a man stands up and says he don't fight and he don't play politics, and I meet him in the arena and get whipped . . . I know he is in politics, and I know whether he is a good fighter or not. And I will say this, and I will say it without any personality at all, that these gentlemen not only know politics, but they are past masters in the art of legislative manipulation."[9]

The investigating committee worked swiftly and thoroughly because the matter was not new to them; many of the most expert men who testified had been advising the legislators since 1896, and others had testified in previous years before the ways and means or joint agricultural committees. In the eyes of the joint committee members, the views of a number of scientific men had "shed much new light on the scientific side of the work."[10]

Forbush returned from his recuperative leave in Florida in time to testify at the hearings and resume his position of field director.[11] Fernald and the gypsy moth committee viewed Forbush's return with relief. Fletcher Osgood was making a strong bid for the director's job and had gained support among civic leaders and legislators such as Wallace Spooner of the twenty-sixth district, Suffolk, who wrote letters to the legislature in Osgood's support.[12] Fernald was unhappy about the prospect of dealing with Osgood officially and wrote to Leland Howard that Osgood's maneuverings would cause them "a lot of trouble."[13]

As the hearings progressed, evidence began to accrue in favor of those opposed to gypsy moth work. In an effort to avert the inevitable, Fernald played his last card by once more soliciting letters from colleagues in other states. The results proved to be too little and too late, but one of the responses reveals how far the economic entomologists were prepared to go to influence public opinion. Ephraim Felt, Lintner's successor as state entomologist of New York, had conspired to have a letter in support of moth work published in the April edition of *Country Gentleman* magazine, commenting on the adverse recommendations of the investigating committee. Felt wrote to Fernald: "This letter is not signed, though written by me, as I thought it might have greater weight if it apparently came from the editors and not from one who could be supposed to be even indirectly interested in the work."[14]

The investigators said they were unable to substantiate claims of permanent injury caused by the gypsy moth and concluded that the reports of damage had been vastly exaggerated. They challenged the economic argument that had been the mainstay of the extermination campaign. The investigators claimed that the gypsy moth committee failed to show where any serious economic harm had been done by the insect over the preceding ten years and then dismissed the claim that the insect was a menace to agriculture:

We find no substantial evidence that gardens, crops or woodlands have suffered serious or lasting injury, or are likely, with that proper precaution and oversight which prudent owners are predisposed to give their own interests, to be subjected to that devastation which one would have a right to anticipate from [the board's] reports. . . . It appears to us that the fears of the farmers throughout the State have been unnecessarily and unwarrantably aroused, evidently for the purpose of securing the effect of those fears upon the matter of annual appropriations.[15]

Put off by the committee's practice of advertising the insect in a way that frightened, rather than informed, the public, the investigators did not "share these exaggerated fears"; they said that "the prophesies of devastation and ruin are unwarranted, and in the most charitable view are but the fancies of honest enthusiasts."[16] The investigators noted that those awaiting the moth always expressed the greatest alarm, whereas the farmers and market gardeners who lived within the infested district remained confident they could handle the problem themselves. Representative Crosby of Middlesex testified: "I believe also that a large part of the pressure that comes in favor of this work . . . has been caused by apprehension, almost hysteric in some cases, caused by the discussion of this question and caused by much of the literature which has been put forth by this commission, not alone by this commission. In other words, I believe that the dread and apprehension from the gypsy moth does not come from the infested district. I know it certainly does not come from my district."[17]

Although the investigators conceded that the board had made "fair" and "reasonably accurate" reports over the years and had praise for Fernald's scientific work, the matter of expenditures had galled them for some time, and they let loose their full displeasure on Forbush and the gypsy moth committee. They were especially upset about the size and structure of the field force and the quality of supervision, and they were particularly displeased by the practice of scouting, which they called "hunting for work." Forbush's practice of retaining his most expensive employees between appropriations was faulted repeatedly, as was his practice of using these "officers" to perform the work of "privates" at no loss of salary. The investigators accumulated much evidence to show that often the ratio of ranked men to privates was 1 to 1, and during April 1899 there had been thirty-one clerks, stenographers, and other office personnel drawing pay while no fieldworkers were on the rolls at all.

Forbush was further rebuked for insisting on obsessive accountings of trees cut down, walls torn out, trees burlapped, acres burned, egg masses destroyed,

caterpillars crushed, and other minute statistics that required a large number of individuals and long hours to collect and compile. The investigators thought the results obtained were worthless and that the money spent would have been put to better use in the field. Endless inspections far from the infested regions were also singled out as undertakings that produced little of value but put a drain on the budget with such costs as equipping the men and paying boarding expenses for them and their horses.

The report noted that the committee's efforts to exterminate the moth were misdirected and that the organization of the work had resulted in an "unwise, unbusinesslike and extravagant expenditure of State funds, in part due to the principal [sic] under which the work is now carried on, and in part due to mismanagement." The investigators believed no private enterprise could sustain its operation burdened with so many mid- and upper-level employees and so little grasp of the fundamental problems, and they cited a mass of evidence "showing instances of misdirected efforts, inefficient management, incompetency, and entire failure properly and wisely to safeguard the State's interest."[18]

The investigators saved some of their best remarks for scouting as it was organized under Forbush, calling it barren of results and a waste of money. They noted the tendency of men in the scouting parties to hunt squirrels or take naps—so much evidence had been brought forward they had no choice but to believe it—and ridiculed those who stayed on the job as well:

> Dozens of men racing through the woods a hundred yards apart, with the avowed object of locating nests and noting evidence of the existence of insects, present a ludicrous and contemptible exhibition of inefficient management somewhere. Sixty scouts solemnly tramping through the streets of Boston last January, at an expense of over $125 per day to the State, looking for the last moth and an opportunity for spending more money in the coming summer, present an element of grim humor too pronounced to be resisted.[19]

The board was also chastised for laying waste great tracts of land to deprive the gypsy moths of food. In one instance, more than twenty-five hundred cords of wood were cut and sold from the lands of H. L. Cox, even though Cox, who lived there, testified that he had no knowledge of gypsy moths being present. The investigating committee pointed out that the state performed the work, the owners reaped a profit, and the employees received their pay, but all this had done nothing toward extermination. Devastating the land to fulfill what the investigators termed the "prophesies" of the board's entomological adviser showed only how desperate the board was to exterminate the gypsy moth.

The average private was a pick-and-shovel man who turned burlaps because it paid well, and it would be easy to believe that these men cared for
nothing more than their paycheck. Yet some of them, such as Joseph F. Toole,
were appalled at the radical work they were asked to do: "In 1896 there was
132,468 trees cut, in 1897 it is 279,101 trees, in 1898 they cut 376,468 trees,
and in 1899 they cut 468,790 trees, making over a million trees they have cut
since the commission started. Now I want to know how long it would take
the gypsy moths to kill a million trees."[20] Inspector Ralph Hoffman said the
work "made a terrible havoc in places that were beautiful, and at the same
time [destroyed] the nesting places for numbers of birds which would keep
down . . . insect pests."[21]

The skills acquired by the gypsy moth committee over the years in manipulating the appropriations process disgusted the legislators. The wheeling,
dealing, logrolling, management of public opinion, advantage taken of inexperienced elected officials, question of patronage, and the political nature of
Forbush's office had become matters of great concern. Many legislators had
come to loathe the annual gypsy moth hearings, which they said were always
announced by the presence of Director Forbush in the lobby, Professor Fernald in the witness chair, the board stenographer in the gallery, moth men
packing the halls, and Mr. Kirkland behind every pillar and column.

Forbush was accused of using his office to help citizens circulate petitions
supporting moth work and in one case initiating such a petition personally.
His practice of having his office stenographer in the gallery recording each
legislator's remarks—"so that the Board might know what was said against
them"[22]—drew a sharp rebuke for not maintaining a respectful distance between the administrative and legislative branches of the government:

> The evidence satisfies us that the activity of employees in interviewing
> local representatives in the Legislature is fostered and encouraged by
> high officials [of the board], and that public sentiment is developed
> and directed for no other purpose than to change the present honest
> and conscientious opposition. No doubt those having the matter in
> charge, in view of the opposition that has arisen each year to the
> appropriation, and the feeling of antagonism that has each year been
> plainly shown, and believing so thoroughly as they have in the neces-
> sity for continuing the work, have felt justified in allowing such things
> to be done.[23]

The investigative committee said the entire ten years of the gypsy moth
campaign had been based on the prophesies of economic entomologists, but
that the state could no longer follow such guidance absent assurances that

could not be given. The attempt to do something unprecedented in the natural world might have possessed some merit as a scientific experiment, but the time was over for trials intended to prove the pet theories of economic entomology at the expense of the state. The question no longer involved the possibility of extermination because, as the investigators put it, "extermination may be possible and yet not practicable."[24] The joint committee concluded that the war had been against nature, and nature, they said, "is quite capable of taking care of herself."[25]

The economic entomologists had taken the position that reliance on natural controls to the abandonment of work in all other areas was unwise, but the investigators wanted to know why the entomologists had insisted on working in all the other areas while abandoning practical work in natural controls:

> Climatic influences, diseases, the preying of the higher upon the lower forms of life, the untranslated but ever-working law of migration and distribution, have one and all sprung into operation. The land still yields her bounty, vegetation still blossoms and is fruitful, the foliage is still green and the temporary annoyances are almost forgotten. It may be true that, until the insect or its parasite is thoroughly acclimated in a new country, the workings of these natural laws may be suspended; but the history of insect life shows that the law is never repealed.[26]

John B. Smith, the New Jersey entomologist who had long supported extermination in Massachusetts, provided the Commonwealth paid for it, was also criticized. Crosby discounted Smith's argument and the entire supposition of expertness on which it rested: "[Smith] says 'the moth may be,' he does not say that it can be. This is his opinion. It 'may be exterminated in America . . . provided money in sufficient amount be always available when needed.' I believe that any man who has been a member of the Legislature for more than one year knows that the Legislature will never, no matter how much they endorse this work, place sufficient funds in the hands of this Commission so it will always be available."[27] Crosby added that the work was not appealing to anyone with common sense, although inexperienced legislators often were persuaded to vote for appropriations after enduring poorly reasoned arguments for months on end. He said that assertions by those believed to be scientific men received a lot more weight than they deserved, that they were "inconclusive statements that scientific men make, which are taken for really more than they are worth."[28]

Marlatt's laissez-faire speech had damaged the notion that economic entomologists did not disagree about extermination. James Fletcher, dominion

entomologist of Canada, wrote to express his regrets to Kirkland (his reference to "wealthy people" was a swipe at Marlatt, who was financially independent): "I am sorry to hear you are having trouble with your appropriation. I am afraid Marlatt's ridiculous nonsense with the swell French name will not help you much. Laissez-Faire may do with wealthy people who do not care whether they succeed or not."[29] Francis M. Webster also wrote to Kirkland expressing his dismay that opponents of the gypsy moth bill were using Marlatt's speech, but added, "I do not think that any of us are much surprised that such is the case."[30] Forbush tried to convince the investigators that Marlatt had not meant what he said, that his talk had been restricted to the scale insect, and that Marlatt had later expressed his admiration for the work being done in Massachusetts.

The hearings of the investigative committee revealed, in addition to Marlatt, the identities of scientific authorities who were against the gypsy moth program. These included William T. Sedgwick of the Massachusetts Institute of Technology, Samuel H. Scudder of Cambridge, John Sterling Kingsley of Tufts College, Samuel Henshaw of the Agassiz Museum, C. S. Minott of the Harvard Medical School, and P. H. Rolf of the South Carolina Agricultural Experiment Station. All these men were of the same mind on the subject of extermination. As Sedgwick said: "I do not pretend to be especially expert in this matter, but it does seem to me as a scientific man and a naturalist, perfectly clear that the trials already made have sufficiently demonstrated the improbability of extermination, and that it is unnecessary and would be improper to continue them longer. I believe, therefore, that experiments aimed at extermination should be abandoned, and that the gypsy moth problem should be attacked in some other way."[31] Minott added: "I am of the opinion that the undertaking of the State of Massachusetts to exterminate the gypsy moth is, from the very conditions of the undertaking, entirely independent of any zeal, capacity or resources of the commission, an undertaking which is necessary to fail. I see no other possible result before it."[32]

Scudder, Henshaw, and Kingsley had been opposed to gypsy moth extermination from the start. Scudder recognized the danger of the insect but thought that to extirpate the invader completely it would be necessary to continue work long after no gypsy moths could be found, and in his opinion "no legislature could be induced to give $200,000 year after year after actual excessive damage had ceased."[33] Henshaw added that extermination was the province of nature and observed that the results of the extermination effort had succeeded only in spreading the moth further. He said that to destroy the moth beyond any doubt would require that the entire infested zone be turned into an "absolute desert."[34] He thought that a small appropriation for some state work should be available, but that property owners should deal with the

problem individually, noting there was "no reason why people should harbor such a dangerous pest on their places any more than they should harbor rattlesnakes or gunpowder."[35] Kingsley had been even more outspoken and earned the derision of many economic entomologists such as Clarence Weed, who wrote in 1894: "I was sorry to see Kingsley's editorial in recent naturalist. These chaps that rely on parasites show such a woeful ignorance of the laws of the subject that I am preparing a general article to enlighten them."[36]

Dozens of men who were or had been employed by the board testified in support of those opposed to extermination. These men told the investigators most emphatically their belief, based on their years of experience working against the moth every day, that extermination was not possible and that it would be better to reduce the moth's numbers only in places where infestations were serious.

Blinded by the Light

At the annual meeting of the Association of Economic Entomologists in 1898, President Herbert Osborn had told the membership that differences among scientists should be handled quietly because open dissent retarded the advance of science and the acceptance of its work. Osborn feared that open dispute would prejudice the public, a group he thought was mostly uninformed, merited little respect, and was slow to "adopt the results of science and inclined to be suspicious of even well-established points."[37] Yet the sword of silence swung both ways, and it undercut the credibility of testimony from economic entomologists, for their unanimous stance in support of extermination had astounded the legislature and, perhaps even more than the actual lack of progress of the effort, caused elected officeholders to seek opposing views. The investigators found a deep reservoir of contrasting perspectives from men who, in their opinion, had more scientific credibility than the whole lot of economic entomologists put together.

The joint committee forced the gypsy moth program under the glare of scientific objectivity, something the moth committee had managed to avoid by allowing only economic entomologists to express opinions. The state's method first puzzled and later angered economic entomologists, many of whom considered that no true men of science would publicly oppose a colleague in another field, right or wrong. The committee and the board were incensed by the testimony of Scudder, Henshaw, and Rolf. They were not as angered by the testimony of former employees since they considered much of it to be spiteful, but the accusations of other entomologists were viewed not as a matter of differing opinions but as acts of betrayal. Fernald was outraged, and Henshaw's appearance especially irritated him, as he wrote to Howard:

I have spent the last two weeks in Boston and leave here tomorrow to
return and the end is not yet in sight. Henshaw appeared before the
committee yesterday morning in opposition to continuation of the
work and was introduced as Professor Henshaw of Harvard University, an expert on such matters. His opinion will be taken by the
Committee in opposition to yours and mine—just think of it: There
has been more lying before that investigating committee during the
past week by opponents of the work than I ever heard in all my life
before. I did at one time incline towards the Universalist doctrine, but
I have now entirely abandoned it and feel that if there is not a hell,
there ought to be.[38]

Fernald remained indignant about "Professor" Henshaw, although when
Forbush was mistakenly addressed as "Professor," Fernald raised no objection. He later wrote to Baron von Osten-Sacken that Scudder and Henshaw
"never even took the time to look into the matter [and] fetched their conclusions from such thoughts as occurred to them in their libraries."[39] Fernald
even became suspicious of Leland Howard, a man who sometimes acted more
like a politician than a brother entomologist. Since Howard made several
comments over the years that showed how quickly he could leap from one
side of the issue to the other, Fernald wrote to him for promises that there
would be no surprises during the hearings.

As the hearings wore on, Kirkland, Fernald, and Forbush endured many
charges and accusations, and they all became edgy and short-tempered. Kirkland often referred to his opponents' tendency to use sarcasm as a tool that
would cost them their cause, yet he fell into the same trap himself, mocking
witnesses who did not base their opinions on the words of economic entomologists: "I should almost think of bringing in Mother Goose's Nursery Book as
an authority on matters of entomology. They say a man is known by the
company he keeps, and perhaps a man is known by the authorities he cites."[40]
A frustrated Fernald complained that the investigators wanted everything
both ways, criticizing Forbush for the practice of counting caterpillars and
then criticizing him for not counting them.[41] Irritated by Kingsley's opinion
that the difference between a systematic and an economic entomologist was a
matter of common sense. Fernald told the investigators: "I am a systematic
entomologist and also an economic entomologist, have been at work for many
years, only I work for a few hours on systematic entomology. I turn, because
my work calls for it, to economic entomology. As I sat there and listened to
[Professor Kingsley] I tried to recall what sort of mental emotion I went
through when I changed from one to the other, when I put off my common
sense and worked as an idiot."[42]

Forbush, doing his best to refute the points made by his opposition, went down his list of detractors, mentioning his regret that Varnum Frost was absent because a "hearing without Varnum Frost [was] like the play of Hamlet with Hamlet left out."[43] Becoming increasingly emotional as the day went on, he appealed to the investigators for understanding, relating how he had worked "day and night" for the last several years, rising from his bed and leaving his house so early on a Monday morning he could not even say good-bye to his sleeping children, and returning so late at the end of the week that if his children were still awake he would have to be reintroduced to them. He said he had done his best under the circumstances and came to understand that suppression was "the utmost nonsense." He stated that those who thought the insect could be restrained with an expenditure of $50,000 annually were wrong. Always a fine public speaker, Forbush told the investigators that the moths were a great natural force as powerful as the ocean: "Take your hand off this thing and it will rise like a rising sea. . . . I believe in extermination, I know it can be accomplished, I know if it can be accomplished in one place it can in another; and I am working in that line and will so long as the money is given and I have anything to do with it. If I am not doing this thing right, if I am a scamp or a scoundrel, turn me out."[44]

The gypsy moth committee members, sensing the probable outcome of the investigation, made one last attempt to sway the legislature of 1900 by sending a written appeal through the investigative committee. In it, they claimed that gypsy moth extermination was "the broadest, most far-reaching, the most momentous question before any state legislature in the country" and warned that once the gypsy moth escaped, no power on earth would be great enough to stop it.[45] The acrimony between the two committees was so strong, however, that the investigators ignored the appeal, so the General Court never heard the board's final plea.

The gypsy moth committee tried to influence the public one last time with the publication of another article by Fletcher Osgood. "The Gypsy Moth in Massachusetts," which appeared in the *New England Magazine*, toned down the rhetoric and was more factual than Osgood's earlier effort in *Harper's*, "A State in Arms against a Caterpillar."[46] By the time the new article appeared in February, however, the investigators had largely made up their minds about funding the gypsy moth war.

On April 5, 1900, the wheel of the gypsy moth campaign came full circle. William Sessions became the last defender of the extermination experiment in testimony he gave alone before a joint session of the ways and means committee and the agriculture committee. Sessions maintained that the actions taken to exterminate the gypsy moth had been in response to public demand; he insisted that the Board of Agriculture had been reluctant to attempt the task,

completely forgetting that he and Nathaniel Shaler had been the driving force behind the effort to bring the state to war against the gypsy moth. He managed to chip away at the conclusions of the investigators but found himself saddled with the hopeless task of defending Fernald's years of inaccurate predictions and Forbush's huge and ineffective bureaucracy. Sessions stated that the committee would gladly relinquish its burden but made a plea to let the work continue: "If you call on us to lay [our duty] down, we shall relinquish it with pleasure; only, as our last word, we pray you, for the good of the State in the future, for the good of coming generations, let the work go on, and history will applaud the broadness of your foresight, the wisdom of your verdict."[47]

Quitting the Field

Upon receipt of the report from the investigative committee, the General Court voted against further appropriations for gypsy moth extermination. The Board of Agriculture's mandate to extirpate the insect was permanently canceled, and the remaining members of the workforce were let go for the last time. F. C. Moulton was hired for the year to collect all the tools and materials left after ten years of combat, make an inventory of them, and consolidate them at the storehouse in Malden. Through the year, Moulton also inspected portions of the infested region, a lonely figure with pad and pencil making his way across the hushed battlefields. The silence was not unsettling to Moulton, for as Osgood had noted in one of his articles, a striking feature of extermination work was the quietness with which it took place. Men swept back and forth through the forest for weeks, and except for calling out their tallies to their foreman every hour, they spent the entire day turning burlaps and killing larvae without speaking a word.

The Committee on Gypsy Moths, Insects, and Birds remained in existence and was required by law to make an annual report for the year. Members noted signs of the moth recovering the territory from which they believed it had been driven and listed areas in which the insect had made "great gains."[48] Malden, Everett, and Medford were generally infested; the moth's advance had been greatest in Melrose; it only lightly occupied Winchester, Arlington, and North Lexington. But in one yard owned by a Burlington market gardener, Moulton found thousands of nests, and elsewhere a total of fifty-one trees had died after being stripped for two consecutive years. The rapid rise in the moth's strength dismayed committee members, all of whom still believed in extermination and saw years of effort—"accomplished in the face of most discouraging difficulties"—slip away.[49]

The state made two final appropriations for gypsy moth work. An amount of $18,000, covering the period from January 1 to the end of April, 1900, was

used to pay the expenses of the committee members, the rents of the office, storehouse, and grounds, and the final wages of the fieldworkers, the adviser to the committee, and the director of fieldwork. At the the end of the year the sum also covered payment for Moulton's services, property rental, supplies, tools, printing, and the teaming, livery, and board of horses. On May 14, 1901, by Chapter 378 of the Acts of 1901, the Massachusetts General Court appropriated $1,000 and directed the Board of Agriculture to sell all its moth war–related property: "[to] dispose of said property on or before the first day of September in the present year, either by transferring the same to some state department or commission that may have use for it, or by sale at public auction."[50] The contents of the storehouse, including all the heavy spraying rigs and other large pieces of equipment, were transferred to the Metropolitan Park Commission (Sessions commented that since the assets of the Board of Agriculture had gone to another administrative arm of the state, the financial loss to the Commonwealth was minimized). In this ironic turn of events, the MPC became heir to the work that it had so diligently restricted. The remaining inventory was sold at auction and the money turned over to the state treasury.

The gypsy moth committee continued for a few more years, but it was a group without a mandate and with nothing to do. Not many of its reports, documents, maps, and other files, which were left with the Board of Agriculture in Boston for safekeeping, have survived. A few typewritten transcripts of the hearings were eventually bound into books and now repose in the special collections section of the Massachusetts State House Library in Boston. The Massachusetts Committee on Gypsy Moths, Insects, and Birds closed its books for 1900 on January 1, 1901, with a balance of $67.16.

Massachusetts had gone to war against the gypsy moths with great optimism, believing the conflict would be brief and the outcome certain. Instead, the fight against the insects lasted for more than ten years and became enormously expensive. The Commonwealth had appropriated $1,155,000 during the campaign, plus another $20,000 for work against the brown-tail moth. Charles L. Marlatt and others estimated that landowners, businesses, and homeowners expended an equal amount during the same period.[51]

The military aspects of the eradication campaign had been obvious, but the force sent against the insects was always too small and too poorly equipped to gain victory. Few realized just how much too small that army was. There were seldom more than five hundred men on the rolls, and the average number in the field at any given time was no more than half that. The Europeans, when dealing with similar pests such as the nun moth, would send three thousand regular army troops into a region of fifteen or twenty square miles,

concentrating more than six times the men in an area less than a tenth the size of the Massachusetts combat zone. The Germans, when confronted with caterpillar swarms in their forests, usually did not even attempt to save individual trees. Instead, they dug miles of trenches, allowed the caterpillars to crawl in, and then either set the insects ablaze with kerosene or simply buried them.

In Massachusetts the strain of combat had taken its toll on many in leadership positions, from Kirkland's period of excessive drinking to Forbush's several breakdowns to the resignations of committeemen Appleton and Shaler for their health and well-being. Fernald was glad the need to make frequent trips to Boston had ended; his rheumatism had become so severe that at times it almost incapacitated him. As he wrote to Leland Howard a few years later, the added duties placed on him during the gypsy moth campaign had nearly caused him to break down.[52]

Fernald, Howard, Sessions, and Kirkland had played their end game skillfully, parading their small contingent of economic entomologists back and forth across the ramparts until they looked like a battalion, but in the end their charade failed. It is perhaps the finest of ironies that the economic entomologists' war against the gypsy moth was lost because it had become uneconomical to continue fighting. The results achieved by economic entomology proved exactly the opposite of what had been hoped for, and the discipline was weakened considerably. Many entomologists had become like the blind men in the fable who discovered an elephant by taking hold of its tail. Most of them knew by the middle of the war that the cause could not be won with the means and technology at their disposal, yet they repeatedly urged the Commonwealth to continue the war on the basis of their opinions as professional scientists that victory was near. When it was no longer possible to ignore the San Jose scale in Massachusetts, Archie Kirkland wrote to Fernald that it would be "very difficult in any way to carry through insect legislation after the experience the legislature has had with the gypsy moth."[53]

The insects earned respect even from those who spent years trying to kill them. Osgood called the moth a "tough and hardy creature."[54] Forbush spoke of its "wonderful reproductive powers and its remarkable tenacity of life."[55] Howard noted that the insect was "wonderfully resistant to the action of ordinary insecticides."[56] And Fernald wrote, "They are very loathe to die, and will hang on to life with wonderful power."[57]

Ignoring the Lessons

The silence that Nathaniel S. Shaler accorded his four years on the committee is resounding. In his autobiography, Shaler, who was a prolific author and

diarist, does not mention Riley, Scudder, Forbush, or Fernald and not even Trouvelot himself, all of whom he knew personally. Neither does he mention the war against the gypsy moth nor the great eradication experiment. His involvement in the work is buried in a single sentence in Sophia Shaler's memoir, written after her husband's death: "The different state boards (the Highway, the Metropolitan Park, and the Gypsy Moth Commissions) upon which he served, and the mining organizations with which he was connected, filled up most of the hours left over from his college duties."[58] There is no record of Shaler having much more to do with the gypsy moth in any official or advisory capacity after his testimony at the hearings of 1900. He died in 1906 as the result of an infection following surgery to remove his appendix.

Leland O. Howard had penned more than his share of lines on the insect when motivated by his zeal to further the ends of economic entomology, but in his autobiography, *Fighting the Insects*, written in 1933 when he was seventy-five years old, he became positively spartan on the results of the great experiment. He frequently mentioned contemporaries such as Fernald and Riley in other contexts, and became loquacious when describing his trips abroad to collect parasites early in the twentieth century. Yet in this summation of his life's work the humiliating collapse of the gypsy moth campaign is accorded only a single passing reference with regard to a general question about the development of spraying machines that could operate on hilly terrain.

Charles Fernald was only too glad to rid himself of anything that combined politics and insects, and once the war was over, he wasted little ink on his experiences. Everything he wrote for public consumption after the turn of the century says the same thing in different ways, but privately Fernald remained disturbed and confounded by the outcome of events. He maintained for the rest of his life that the extermination of the gypsy moth was prevented at the last moment by the actions of the state legislature, although as time passed he did modify somewhat his stance on foreign parasites, writing in 1904:

> We were confronted by the fact that there is no known parasite in the world that confines its attacks to the gypsy moth alone, for if this were the case the prospect would be far different from what it is now. . . . The closing of the work by the legislature and the rapid increase and spread of the moth since that time has in all probability rendered extermination impossible. . . . It seems probable therefore that we would do well in the future to ascertain what advantage may now be obtained from our parasites and to satisfy the "general public" it may well [be time] to try the importation of parasites and predacious insects from Europe.[59]

After the collapse of the extermination campaign, Fernald's friend and former student Archie Kirkland left Boston to work in the pesticide branch of the Bowker Company in New York City, which by most accounts was not a happy time for him. When the Commonwealth of Massachusetts renewed the war on gypsy moths in 1905, Kirkland and the aging Fernald were once again brought together to prosecute the work—but that is a story for another time.

Edward Forbush, unlike most of the others, had worked against the gypsy moth in the field on a daily basis. Although Forbush wrote copiously on the insect in his official capacity as director of fieldwork and left some additional references in a few brief and informal presentations before the Association of Economic Entomologists, almost nothing of a personal nature is to be found after his period of service as field director. The biographical sketch written about him in 1928 by John Bichard May, his associate and successor in the division of ornithology, is the only surviving postwar document that mentions the battle.

This sketch, however, was written in honor of Forbush's seventieth birthday and his mandatory retirement from the Massachusetts Department of Agriculture, so it is a flattering, if somewhat inaccurate, tribute. Its forty pages include such things as a two-page genealogy of Forbush's ancestry and tend to dwell on his adventures as a young "naturalist." To cite one example, a recounting of a few days' experiences during an expedition to Florida spans four pages, while in contrast, the work against the gypsy moth, which occupied nine years of Forbush's life and nearly a quarter of his term of public service, is given just a bit more than a single page. And that small review presents a surprising revision of the campaign's priorities: it emphasizes strategies such as increasing the numbers of beneficial birds, testing native and foreign parasites, and investigating "every other conceivable enemy of the moth." Moreover, it says that the plan of the gypsy moth committee was to clear small "demonstration areas," an idea utterly absent from the surviving written history of the campaign. The topic of spraying commands a single sentence, and blame for the collapse of the effort is assigned to the "shortsighted policy" of the state legislature and to "petty politics."[60]

After the end of the first campaign, Forbush was eventually appointed to the post he had wanted all along—that of state ornithologist of Massachusetts—and the danger to birds from arsenical sprays became a question he had to consider from the opposite viewpoint. Although he tried to walk a path between his friends in entomology and his colleagues in ornithology, he gradually withdrew from the Association of Economic Entomologists, at first downgrading his membership from active to associate and then resigning altogether. Ultimately, he could no longer deny that using poison sprays and baits for insect control sometimes killed birds in numbers, and that the

extreme practices of laying waste entire tracts of forest drove away desirable birds so completely that it often took years for their populations to recover.

The Shadows of Medford

The gypsy moths retreated to their forest strongholds to emerge anew in following years; likewise the economic entomologists withdrew to their redoubts in the agriculture experiment stations to regroup but not to reconsider. With their individual jobs safe and the direction of their profession now established, they were not inclined to question the validity of their insect philosophy. The failure of the campaign was seen as being due to external factors in the legislature and the citizenry, not to anything wrong with their doctrine and fundamental beliefs. Fernald, Howard, Kirkland, and others quickly mended fences with their counterparts in other branches of entomology and for a while turned to more pressing insect problems such as the San Jose scale.

If the economic entomologists had suffered their first defeat, they had also experienced their first taste of real power, which they found addictive. In little more than a single decade since the creation of the agricultural experiment stations, these men had been catapulted from figures of questionable sanity who ran through the fields netting bugs to individuals who had the power to call down chemical drenchings in residential neighborhoods, suspend the rights of citizens, and have their rules and regulations given the power of law. As Herbert Osborn noted in his presidential address to the tenth annual meeting of the Association of Economic Entomologists: "The entomologist of the present bears a very different relation to the public than he did a quarter of a century ago. New knowledge and new responsibilities have come to him; whereas then his opinion was presented and received as a gratuitous matter to be experimented with if convenient, his dictum now carries the force of authority, and often has the support of state and federal law."[61]

When the time of insect danger came again, the economic entomologists would present their reconstituted extermination programs with greater sophistication than before. As Osborn had noted, one of the three great tasks that lay ahead for economic entomology was the "education of the people to appreciate this need."[62] He proposed to present instructions about future insect extermination programs so explicitly that citizens would have to follow them without deviation. He advocated the idea that schoolchildren should be trained to accept the views of economic entomology, views such as Howard's that insects were a danger and that wars against them were endless. Others took up this message and presented it so successfully that by the middle of the new century it might be fair to say that scarcely anyone in the country could remember a time when he or she did not loathe insects.

Epilogue

ALMOST EVERY economic entomologist writing in the years that followed the end of the first campaign claimed that the gypsy moth had been nearly eliminated from eastern Massachusetts as a result of the actions taken against it. In fact, the gypsy moth was nowhere near eradication; these hardy insects were widely dispersed both inside and outside the boundary of 1891. The last words on the contention that the gypsy moth had been reduced to insignificance in Massachusetts go to Charles H. Fernald and his friend and field general, Edward H. Forbush. Speaking at the fifteenth annual meeting of the Association of Economic Entomologists in 1903, Fernald said that conditions after ten years of war were what they had been at the beginning, with gypsy moths occupying the original centers of infestation "in fair abundance."[1] In testimony before the joint investigative committee, Forbush admitted that the moths had actually "spread and increased, especially in the wood lands" constituting "the first points of invasion."[2]

A large gypsy moth colony in Providence, Rhode Island was already well established by 1898. Although it was not discovered until July 13, 1901, the known breeding dynamics of the moth indicate it was at least three years old.[3] The gypsy moth committee received this news with astonishment and disbelief, and for several years afterward the group contended that "the moth was deliberately taken to Providence and purposely scattered by some malicious or irresponsible person."[4] There was also a growing infestation in Newburyport, Massachusetts, which spilled across the New Hampshire border. This colony was also found in 1901, but given the habits of this moth, it had certainly been established before 1900. The sheer numbers of insects occurring just one year after cessation of the work and their distribution in two additional states convincingly rebut the arguments that they had been controlled, contained, and nearly exterminated.

The advance of the gypsy moth in New England during the next several years was slow but steady. In 1905 an infestation was found near a velvet mill in Stonington, Connecticut, although unaccountably not reported until the

*Archie Howard Kirkland,
circa 1905.*

Special Media Services Division,
National Archives & Records
Administration.

following year. Authorities in the four infested states of Massachusetts, New Hampshire, Rhode Island, and Connecticut appealed to the federal government for help, and at the end of 1905 the first federal appropriation was made for work against the gypsy moth. The sum of $82,000 to be disbursed by Leland Howard through the U.S. Department of Agriculture, marked the beginning of a federal involvement in the gypsy moth war that continues into the present. Maine joined the list of infested states in 1906 when state and federal inspectors found gypsy moth egg masses in Kittery, Elliot, York, South Berwick, Wells, Kennebunk, and Kennebunkport, and, most unexpectedly, a single cluster on the grounds of the National Soldiers' Home in Togus, eighty-one miles from all other known locations.

The second campaign against the gypsy moth, begun in 1905, was marked by a hasty alliance of the USDA, which began a program of importing parasites under Leland Howard, and the Commonwealth of Massachusetts, which placed its new moth program under the control of Archie Kirkland. The arguments made for extermination, the confusion and misstatements about the moth, the exaggeration of its danger, and the frightful methods used to prosecute insect warfare were repeated almost without exception everywhere the insect appeared. The fight against the gypsy moth in Massachusetts, which under other circumstances might have remained an obscure piece of local history, now burgeoned into a national misadventure that would span the entire twentieth century.

The USDA's bureau of entomology undertook the importation and release of as many supposed parasites (technically, *parasitoids*) of the gypsy moth as could be found in Europe, Russia, and Japan. A group of federal entomologists located first in North Saugus and later in Melrose Highlands, Massachusetts, imported millions of parasites of more than forty species and released them into the wild without even cursory life-cycle studies. Without secure trials of any kind, some were sent to states far removed from those infested by gypsy moths to be used against other insects, and some were sent to Canadian entomologists for the same kind of experiment with no idea whether the insects would be effective, transmit diseases, or attack nontargeted species. Record-keeping during the importation period was lax and disorganized. William Fuller Fiske, the entomologist in charge of the labs, noted that no one was sure how many parasite species had been received—he thought the number was between forty and fifty—and no one was sure how effective they were. Fiske said that about thirty appeared to attack the moths, and about twenty were thought to be important.[5]

Howard's approach to natural control of the gypsy moth seemed desperate and was arguably reckless and irresponsible. He intended to release into North America every known insect adversary of the gypsy moth without exception, ignoring the potentially massive disturbance of natural balance on an entire continent and risking all consequences for the sake of exterminating one single species of insect.[6] One tachinid (fly) parasitoid he imported, *Compsilura cocinnata*, is a case in point. Howard knew that it hunted a large number of nontarget species in Europe and would likely do the same in the United States.[7] Howard released the insect anyway, arguing that the presence of alternative hosts would ensure the parasite's survival. He considered this an acceptable trade-off, even if the imported predator attacked every one of the "hundreds" of available domestic species.[8] Howard also knew that *C. cocinnata* would compete against native parasites with a high probability of success but took the detached view that the conflict would offer "a most excellent opportunity to answer numerous questions which naturally arise when this subject is considered."[9] Howard did not care if other caterpillars were attacked because he believed, as did almost all economic entomologists of his time, that only a handful of insects were directly useful to man and, except for the silkworm, that there was no such thing as a beneficial caterpillar.

An alignment of New England interests that wanted gypsy moth control with southerners who wanted control of the Texas cattle tick secured an unexpectedly large federal appropriation of $250,000 in the 1907 agriculture appropriations bill.[10] Some of this money was used to fund the parasite importation effort, which had become quite controversial. Prominent citizens of Boston claimed the government was moving too slowly, while an additional

dispute arose between proponents of the California method of natural pest control and the plans of the eastern entomological establishment to import parasites and continue spraying at the same time.

When Ellwood Cooper, who later became the California commissioner of horticulture, told the citizens of Boston he would send them a gypsy moth parasite that would accomplish what they desired if Massachusetts would put $25,000 in escrow to be paid to him only if the gypsy moths were controlled, the eastern entomological establishment was incensed. Leland Howard later called Cooper's claim "preposterous."[11] Kirkland said the proposals were "specious" and labeled the Bostonians who supported the idea as "dilettantes." The Californians, who thought the easterners were too reliant on spraying, responded by saying that any enormously expensive method that had to be repeated and was usually unsuccessful was "idiotic."[12] But the Californians were beaten back when the easterners used Fernald's old scheme of convening a congress of thirty sympathetic economic entomologists to affirm the eastern plan.

The federal approach under Howard emphasized the use of insects to fight insects, but the effort to import and establish foreign parasites was often disrupted by the outbreak of disease among gypsy moth and brown-tail moth populations. Among these was the wilt disease (nucleopolyhedrosis virus, or NPV) of the gypsy moth, which appeared in North America for the first time in 1907. No one knows how or where it was introduced, but it had likely come with the insects themselves. Although this and other naturally occurring and highly selective diseases promised to be outstanding control agents, their presence only frustrated those entomologists who viewed epizootics as major disruptions to their work with imported predator insects. Howard and state officials in Massachusetts created a small group of scientists to explore fungal and viral pathogens, but the effort was assigned a low priority and was not well funded; in fact, trips to Japan to collect samples of fungally infected caterpillars were made possible only upon receipt of anonymous private donations.

The work with fungal diseases, to which caterpillars are highly susceptible, uncovered strains for both the gypsy moth and the brown-tail that had the ability to sweep away entire populations. The problem with these pathogens was that once they were released into the wild, they could no longer be controlled, a condition unacceptable to economic entomologists because it made them superfluous. In the case of the brown-tail, disease would appear spontaneously in populations that had been targeted for artificial inoculation, and no one could tell whether the naturally or the artificially seeded spores caused moth mortality. A promising entomophagous fungal pathogen, deadly to the gypsy moth and highly selective in its action, was released into the wild near

Boston in 1910 and again in 1911, but it was so difficult to work with and the results were so disappointing that the project was abandoned and largely forgotten.

After five years of intensive efforts importing, breeding, and releasing parasites, federal entomologists concluded that they had done all they could. In Howard and Fiske's final report, published in 1911, some important conclusions were expressed or implied.[13] The first was that the plan to stop the spread of the gypsy moth with European and Asian parasites had failed. The second was that the gypsy moth was a forest insect and not an agricultural pest; therefore, the legendary suburban infestations of the 1890s in places such as Medford were unlikely to happen again, since the insects migrated away from populated areas into their preferred woodland habitat.[14] Howard put the matter in plainer terms when he wrote in *National Geographic*: "Neither the gypsy moth nor the brown-tail moth are longer to be feared as shade tree enemies or as enemies of orchards and gardens. Both have become regulated to the class of forest insects, so far as their ravages are concerned."[15]

The public was slow to grasp the consequences of the unfettered importation of alien species. As perpetrators of such acts, the worst offenders by far were not private entrepreneurs such as Leopold Trouvelot but the federal government itself and its ongoing policies of importing and distributing foreign plants and seeds. Agencies such as the U.S. Office of Plant Importation ultimately imported almost 200,000 foreign plants, some along with their own diseases and their insect pests.[16] In fighting the gypsy moth the bureau of entomology under Howard carried out the largest and most purposeful importation of alien insect species in the nation's history. Writers such as William Temple Hornaday, though he called the importation of the gypsy moth a "winged calamity," were beginning to question such practices: "The man who successfully transplants or 'introduces' into a new habitat any persistent species of living thing assumes a very grave responsibility. . . . The enormous losses that have been inflicted upon the world through the perpetuation of follies with wild vertebrates and insects would, if added together, be enough to purchase a principality. The most aggravating feature of these follies in transplantation is that never yet have they been made severely punishable."[17]

The use of arsenical sprays continued to rise despite the parasite program. In 1909 and again in 1910 the federal men in New England used five hundred tons of lead arsenate to combat the gypsy moth. Manpower needs were rising, too. The Massachusetts program under Kirkland employed 1,200 men during peak periods of insect activity in 1906; by 1910 more than 2,700 men were employed in gypsy moth work. Yet many of the scientifically supported assumptions underlying the work done against the gypsy moth in the 1890s had been disproved by the end of 1912. The practice of applying heavy oils and

flammable fuels such as kerosene to combat insects on trees was shown to damage the trees through their bark to a depth below the vital cambium layer. Oil sprayed on the ground to burn brush and leaf litter contaminated the soil and poisoned the plants at their roots. Fires across the brush and scrublands were discovered to harm the shallow-rooted tree varieties. Research showed that all substances previously used for banding trees prior to 1900 were injurious over time. Burning egg masses from tree bark with torches was invariably damaging. And evidence mounted that spraying did poison birds, if not directly, then indirectly.[18]

Nevertheless, mechanization of spray apparatus continued as Frank Rane, the Massachusetts state forester, introduced the first motor-truck-mounted sprayer in 1911, an invention that revolutionized insect spraying programs. The pump ran from a takeoff on the main engine and was powerful enough to throw at least two streams simultaneously to the tops of most trees. The costs of inventing new technology while supporting old technology in the war had risen markedly since the days of the first campaign, when $200,000 per year was considered a fat budget. As costs rose to a million dollars per year to fight the gypsy moth in New England, the end was nowhere in sight.[19]

Aside from importing parasites, the major work done by the state and federal agencies fighting the gypsy moth consisted largely of clearing roadside strips in the most heavily infested districts to prevent the larvae from spinning down and being carried away on vehicles. Despite a strenuous effort over a very wide area, however, pockets of gypsy moths kept appearing at some distance from the infested regions, a circumstance that was at first blamed on the growing number of gasoline-powered "horseless carriages." It was not until 1912 that the importance of wind dispersion was understood. Entomologists had known since the early days of the first campaign that the larvae could be blown by the wind, but the general consensus was that they were not blown far—perhaps no more than one hundred yards.[20] It dawned only slowly on some of the researchers that the prevalent theories about moth spread could not entirely explain all the infestations that were being observed. Under the right conditions the larvae could be blown much farther and in sufficient numbers to start new colonies miles away—which may partially explain how the gypsy moth reached the southeast corner of Vermont in 1912, marking the point in time when portions of all six New England states were infested.

In subsequent years the appearance of gypsy moths in areas where they had not been found before was not always referred to as an advance or a distribution but as "wind spread." The knowledge of wind spread led to a shift in tactics by the federal units in Massachusetts: they moved their bases of operation from the centers of the most heavily infested districts to the leading edge of the advancing moth legions, especially on the western front. A picket line

twenty-five miles wide was established in the middle of the state, and it was repeatedly, thoroughly, and unsuccessfully worked on to eliminate any colonizers that had blown in from the east. In reality, it was Shaler's old strategy of containment on the periphery, now expanded to a size the old scholar could never have anticipated.

On March 1, 1913, the federal gypsy moth work in the northeast was reorganized, and Albert Burgess was placed in charge of the entire New England region.[21] This same year, after passage of the Federal Plant Quarantine Act, the entire infested area was quarantined.[22] In order to move products and materials out of New England, inspectors had to certify that they were free of the gypsy moth in any of its life stages. Localized infestations were discovered in North Castle, New York, in 1914 and in Bratenahl, Ohio (a suburb of Cleveland), the same year, but these colonies apparently died out.[23]

By the start of the First World War, gypsy moths in Massachusetts alone could be found in an area of more than 2,500 square miles, and Kirkland noted that the central towns within the old boundary of 1891 were now completely infested. In other states the gypsy moth concentrations covered anywhere from five hundred square miles in New Hampshire to one square mile in Connecticut. Multiple invasions of Connecticut and New York occurred at the beginning of the 1920s. Nearly half a million dollars in combined state and federal funds were expended at this time to control the gypsy moth in Connecticut alone.[24]

The most worrisome expansion of the moth's territory was discovered on June 30, 1920, when workmen on the Duke estate at Somerville, New Jersey, discovered swarms of caterpillars feeding on evergreen trees. Thomas J. Headlee, the New Jersey state entomologist, noted that from the outset the size of the infestation indicated it was one of long standing. The European moth normally prefers deciduous trees, so the destruction of evergreens was a real scare. Subsequent investigations determined that egg masses of the moth, according to Harry B. Weiss of the New Jersey Department of Agriculture, had "probably" been introduced on European blue spruces imported from Holland in 1911 and that the insects were of the European variety that normally feeds on oak.[25]

Because the large New Jersey infestation was isolated, extermination was the only acceptable plan, and the insect was fought in the same detailed and painstaking ways that had been used in Massachusetts in the 1890s—with arsenical sprays, burlap, creosote, axes, and fire. Even though the infestation in New Jersey had declined by 97 percent on its own in one year, well before any work against the moths was begun, exterminative measures still persisted for ten years afterward at an expense of almost $2 million. Entomologists took credit for what they claimed was the first real elimination of the gypsy

moth but were never able to explain why the methods that had failed in every other place had succeeded in New Jersey. While New Jersey struggled to contain its first infestation, gypsy moth activity in the original bug-ridden areas of New England had finally begun to decline to the approximate levels of infestation noted in 1905.

At the end of the 1920s, functional cohesion of work against the moths had disintegrated, fragmenting into individual and uncoordinated efforts by federal, state, and local authorities as well as private individuals and organizations. Dexter Rogers and Albert Burgess on the federal team in New England noted in one report that any one gypsy moth agency seldom knew what any of the others was doing. In consequence, the number of people working against the gypsy moth at this time cannot be accurately tabulated, but it is likely numbered in five figures. So many men had worked against the gypsy moth over twenty-five years that it was possible to form experienced gangs in most eastern Massachusetts communities simply by calling for volunteers. The brown-tail moth, although still capable of producing large flights along the northeastern seaboard, was struggling against diseases, effective predators, and imported parasites. The Canadians reported serious problems with the brown-tail in the Maritime Provinces, but the moth's range seemed to be receding, and the infestations in New Brunswick and Nova Scotia had practically died out.

With the failure of the importation effort, work reverted to time-tested mechanical methods, and hope for success was transferred to the prospect of good results from silviculture as championed by Frank Rane. Rane's idea was to create "Black Forest" towns all over the Commonwealth where softwood forests would replace stands of susceptible hardwoods. Rane hoped ultimately to replant almost the entire state and create a vast, manmade woodland that would be impervious to the gypsy moth. Consequently, he and his state officers worked on logging off all the oaks in the Commonwealth and implementing a basic reforestation with pines and other resistant species, while Howard's federal men doggedly persisted in importing parasites and other schemes to contain the moth's advance.

Spraying continued to rise to higher levels each year. At one point during the First World War, Rane took delivery of an entire trainload of lead arsenate—twenty-nine boxcars.[26] He considered that this quantity, if carefully rationed, might be enough to supply his sprayers for a single season of eight or ten weeks. At the end of the 1920s, Massachusetts alone had a fleet of three hundred spray trucks. The economies of mechanized work had reduced the costs of spraying from thirty dollars an acre to six dollars an acre in many cases.[27] Once commercially produced truck-mounted sprayers became availa-

ble, the old horse-drawn units were retired and sold to farmers and other individuals for personal use.

As plan after plan failed, the job of the federal group largely became one of reporting the inevitable advance of the gypsy moth and moving the boundary line to a new location. The culmination of this practice came in 1923 with the establishment of the "Thou Shalt Not Pass" zone, at times facetiously called the "Verdun," "Hindenburg," or "Maginot" line. This barrier zone, twenty-five to thirty miles wide, extended for 250 miles along the Hudson River from Long Island, New York, northward to the Canadian border and contained about eight thousand square miles of land. The zone was the idea of Leland Howard, who saw the Hudson River valley in eastern New York as the last and best natural barrier to contain the moths in New England.

Between the Connecticut River valley in central Massachusetts and the Hudson River valley in eastern New York, the Berkshire Mountains constituted the heart of the extermination zone. Those familiar with the Berkshires would be astonished that anyone thought it could be defended against an insect with the habits of the gypsy moth. Its rocky and steep terrain was extremely favorable for the moth, inhospitable to men on foot, and impossible to cover with the mechanized equipment of the day. Yet despite the economic depression of the 1930s, millions of dollars were poured into the extermination effort annually, and in some years more than three thousand men were continuously employed.[28] The roster was filled from welfare rolls with inexperienced workers who were sent into the field after just two weeks of training.[29]

At the time it was defined, the zone was already known to be infested in many places and presumed to be infested in many others, making any claim that it would be an effective barrier somewhat suspect right from the start.[30] During its entire period of existence, the zone was never fully inspected, and Burgess, the federal entomologist in charge, acknowledged that it always harbored hundreds of active colonies. The great New England hurricane of 1938 was blamed for its destruction and the dispersion of the moth beyond it, but this assumption must be seriously questioned. In 1925, G. W. Herrick of Cornell University, in his book *Injurious Insects*, noted that gypsy moths could be found in most of eastern New York, an observation also made by Connecticut entomologist Neely Turner in 1922. Significant moth infestations had been reported in New Jersey and Pennsylvania even before the hurricane, and the moth had already made an end run around the line in Canada. The barrier zone was abandoned a few years after the hurricane, but some entomologists tried for years to have it reestablished, even after the moths had spread westward well beyond the Hudson River valley.[31]

World War II and DDT

The Second World War relegated the gypsy moth war to the back burner, but work against insects in general took on a high military priority, once again stirring up the battlefield mentality of many economic entomologists. In his book *War and Nature*, Edmund Russell showed how the methods used by entomologists to exterminate insects and the development of chemical weapons to exterminate humans through both world wars took on a frightening similarity.[32] Ironically, records kept by the USDA reveal that during the period of the Great Depression and the Second World War, gypsy moth activity declined to very low levels in all the infested states, even though little work against the insect was being done. Some entomologists suggested the barrier zone as a possible reason for this lull.[33]

It was during the Second World War that an astonishing new pesticide called DDT was developed and put to use with spectacular results. DDT killed almost every insect it touched, and when sprayed on surfaces it would persist effectively for months. In the unnatural conditions caused by war, the new insecticide was highly effective at eliminating body lice and the insect vectors of war diseases such as yellow fever, typhus, and malaria. Spraying programs thus saved many lives in areas where the destruction of water supplies, food stores, and hospitals, along with concentrations of weak and undernourished refugees living in unsanitary conditions, had created conditions favorable for the spread of disease. As a result, this caused many Americans to believe that the three greatest things to come out of the war were "the three p's,"—plasma, penicillin, and pesticides.

Discussions about the use of DDT dominated meetings of the Association of Economic Entomologists. Its 1944 meeting in New York was referred to for years afterward as "the DDT meeting" because of the preponderance of papers on the new insecticide. High-level government planners were envisioning a peacetime war against the gypsy moth, a decision not altogether surprising, since a philosophy of unending war against insects had been part of economic entomology's underpinnings from its inception in 1889.

In postwar America, federal programs against insect pests were resumed with a fervor and zeal that went far beyond anything known before. A vigorous chemical industry had emerged from the war with a great production capacity and desire to expand its markets, and a giant federal bureaucracy stood willing to accommodate it. Moreover, war surplus planes that could be easily converted for aerial spraying were numerous and inexpensive, and there was a willing corps of recently discharged pilots ready to fly them. In one hour, one pilot in one spray-equipped C-47 could cover an area that would have taken nine heavyweight hydraulic ground units and their crews all

season. A single planeload of insecticide could treat an area as large as one truck-mounted apparatus could treat in four years and do so at a twenty-fifth of the cost. Leaders who were not afraid to drop the atomic bomb on human adversaries in cities were manifestly undisturbed by using DDT, the atomic bomb of pesticides, against insect adversaries in the nation's eastern forests.[34]

The appearance of DDT and its variants along with the new air war against the gypsy moth ended the lead arsenate era almost overnight. The old-fashioned hydraulic sprayers were retired; cyclone burners disappeared from the scene. The once-ubiquitous burlap bands had been dismissively referred to as "petticoats" for years, even though they had never lost their effectiveness. The caution owed to any new and terrible formulations for use against insects seemed all but gone. The thinking in applied entomology championed the idea that all available technology should be used, no matter how horrible.

For more than a century, the American population had been flowing from rural farm areas into the great cities. After the war the tide reversed, and individuals poured outward from the cities to establish a new lifestyle in the suburbs. The resulting sprawl in the Northeast, creating communities in places where the gypsy moth was either approaching or was already present, once again made what was essentially a forest insect into a pest of town parks, school playgrounds, residential backyards, flower and vegetable gardens, tree-lined boulevards, and specimen plantings. But this time, in the collision of humankind and the insect, pesticides that were not arsenic-based separated citizens of the twentieth century from their counterparts of the previous century.

Arsenic was an old poison, and the average man and woman in nineteenth-century Massachusetts could never be persuaded that it was not dangerous. In comparison, so little was known about DDT that neither entomologists nor chemists of the time understood how it worked. Between an absence of knowledge about modern insecticides, on one hand, and a flood of propaganda that reported only their benefits, on the other, the average citizen lost his fear of the chemical. Reassured at every turn that the modern formulations were deadly to insects but harmless to humankind, a substantial number of individuals began to demand that their homes and surrounding environments be kept free of such insect pests as the gypsy moth.

Between 1946 and 1952, aerial spraying was done everywhere the gypsy moth could be found. Delivery systems were refined to allow planes to remain airborne longer and apply the spray in wider swaths over greater areas. Broadcast sprayings over entire forests took place, including their lakes, rivers, and streams. Multiple sprayings were common, regard for overspray and drift did not exist, and the effects of pesticide residuals and breakdown products were

not even considered. Despite it all, it seemed the gypsy moths would never be dislodged.

Then something almost miraculous took place: traps set in Pennsylvania and New Jersey during the summer of 1952 did not catch a single male moth. Nothing even remotely comparable had occurred in sixty years of combat. Officials credited their eradication programs and declared the two states free of moths. Millions of acres had been suddenly recaptured from a previously invincible enemy. The gypsy armies in those states had not only been driven off; they had been obliterated down to the last individual—convincing proof that the chemical war against them could be won. Optimistic plans were drawn to eradicate the moth from New York and Connecticut. After that, the invaders would be pushed back into Massachusetts.

Not all government entomologists were convinced that such plans were wise when viewed against ominous reports coming from the field. Some, like Frank E. Todd and S. E. McGregor, noted that the ever increasing use of pesticides had driven beekeeping out of many apple-growing areas and had "nearly wiped out the bee industry" in cotton-producing states.[35] Further, so many other insects had become resistant to DDT so quickly that government entomologist W. N. Bruce wrote in 1952, "The usefulness of DDT and other chlorinated compounds is coming to an end."[36] Without yet knowing of the damage done to birds, fish, and the environment, and ten years before Rachel Carson's *Silent Spring* was published, a small but growing group of field entomologists already understood that the low numbers of insects did not signal victory, and that when the inevitable insect advance resumed, it likely would comprise highly resistant individuals against which even the deadliest pesticides would not work.

To ensure total destruction of the enemy, federal entomologists intended to soak the northeastern forests in a rain of pesticides that not even the legendary hardiness of the gypsy moth could withstand. John Corliss, chief of the USDA division of gypsy and brown-tail moth control, believed that planes and sprayers could completely eliminate the moth. He smelled victory in the oily, pesticide-fouled air. "Current objectives are to conduct trapping and scouting surveys in Pennsylvania until extermination there is assured," he wrote confidently in 1952, "eliminate general infestation in New York by 1953 with only mop-up of isolated incipient infestations remaining in succeeding years."[37]

In post–World War II America, few entomologists thought any longer of natural controls for the gypsy moth. Some estimates are that within two decades, more than nine out of ten economic entomologists were working directly or indirectly for chemical pesticide manufacturers, while less than 2 percent of field entomologists were actively researching natural controls for any insect.[38] As one entomologist succinctly put it, "Biological control work

was dropped."[39] The shortage of individuals with experience in natural controls was so acute that in 1966, when the chemically resistant cereal leaf beetle invaded the upper Midwest, a facility created in the southern Michigan city of Niles to research biological control of the beetle had to recruit technicians from among retirees and housewives living in the area.[40]

The heady days of the new gypsy moth campaign did not last long. Under pressure from the intense post-World War II sprayings, the insect expanded its range dramatically, and as repeated drenchings with pesticides indiscriminately killed the predator populations so painstakingly set out thirty years earlier, moth populations rebounded. The imbalance of nature continued with memorable results. In 1950s Europe a gypsy moth outbreak might defoliate five hundred acres; in 1950s America it might defoliate fifty thousand acres.

By 1955, with the war against gypsy moths not going well, spraying increased to a frenzied level that would not be matched again for thirty-five years. Aircraft pilots were paid according to the number of gallons sprayed, and there was little to dissuade these aviators from putting in long days with fully opened valves or from spraying the same areas more than once.[41] In 1957, New York, New Jersey, Michigan, and Pennsylvania, in conjunction with the U.S. Department of Agriculture, aerially sprayed more than three million acres of forest to "eradicate the gypsy moth from the periphery of the infested area and suppress them in the center"[42]—a strategy similar to the one unsuccessfully used in Massachusetts sixty years earlier. Spraying also occurred in other northeastern states, and some prominent state entomologists, including Neely Turner and J. Gordon Horsfall in Connecticut, became so appalled at the rage against the gypsy moth that they refused to endorse the government plan.[43]

Aerial spraying occurred with increasing frequency over heavily inhabited areas of the Northeast. In one case that borders on the surreal, the New York state and federal departments of agriculture, citing an implausible threat from the gypsy moth to New York City and environs, announced plans to spray densely populated Nassau County, Long Island, with DDT in fuel oil.[44] In 1957 a group of thirty residents seeking an injunction had their case heard by Judge Walter Bruchhausen in the U.S. District Court for the eastern district of New York. After Bruchhausen denied a temporary injunction, the spraying took place. The plaintiffs pursued the case to the U.S. Court of Appeals, hoping to obtain a permanent injunction, but the case was dismissed in 1959 because injunctive relief was moot. In 1960 the U.S. Supreme Court declined to hear the case, though Justice William O. Douglas strongly dissented.

Although the plaintiffs lost their case, they won a publicity bonanza that sobered the entomological profession. Others concerned about the dangers of pesticides were encouraged to explore legal remedies, and the number of law-

suits filed began to increase.[45] The compelling testimony given by the plaintiffs' witnesses resulted in a trove of information that attracted a fifty-one-year-old marine biologist named Rachel Carson who was writing a book about the dangers of indiscriminate pesticide use. Russell notes that for her book, Carson "[drew] largely on evidence presented at the trial."[46]

Following the 1957 spray turmoil the USDA, with little explanation, abruptly called a halt to massive forest sprayings for gypsy moths in the northeast and turned its sights on the fire ant in the South. Both the fire ant and gypsy moth programs, however, caused the public to become concerned over aerial spraying, and opposition to insect eradication programs began to manifest in diverse institutions—from the National Audubon Society to the U.S. Congress—while magazines such as *Reader's Digest*, *Life*, *Saturday Evening Post*, and, improbably, *Sports Illustrated*, questioned the practice in print.[47]

Houghton-Mifflin published Rachel Carson's *Silent Spring* in 1962. The book remained on the best-seller list for more than thirty weeks and was continuously in print for more than forty years. Carson's level tone and well-researched warnings resonated across the entire nation and so strongly raised the American consciousness that former vice president Al Gore called it "the beginning of the modern environmental movement."[48] Several important developments occurred largely because of *Silent Spring*. Spraying DDT for gypsy moths was discontinued in 1966, and the Environmental Protection Agency (EPA) was created in 1970. Pesticide approval and regulation was removed from the USDA to the EPA, at last weakening the agricultural philosophy that had gripped the gypsy moth program for more than eighty years. In 1971 the USDA ordered a cessation of all "blanket spraying of huge uninhabited woodlands."[49]

In 1975 the National Academy of Sciences published a series of books on pest control. In the fourth volume, *Forest Pest Control*, a forest study team chaired by Richard S. Miller of Yale University noted that all the state and federal agencies responsible for combatting the gypsy moth had finally conceded that the insect, after one hundred years on the North American continent, had become a naturalized part of the forest fauna. The book also pointed out that the gypsy moth had been found as far west as California.[50]

Sentiment against gypsy moth programs continued to rise and manifest in actions against spraying, as New Jersey entomologist J. D. Kegg wrote in 1978:

> The pesticide controversy has resulted in an anti-spray sector which consists of outspoken individuals, special interest organizations, legislators and administrators, who through their own power or the use of the court system, can severely curtail gypsy moth spray operations.

For example, laws limiting spraying against the gypsy moth have been passed in Connecticut and a new administration in Albany has greatly curtailed spray operations in New York. Even within the federal government we have agencies opposing gypsy moth chemical control in heavily infested forests.[51]

The summer of 1981 was the nadir of the struggle against the gypsy moth, a time when the insect seemed unstoppable and when its voracious habits resulted in the "defoliation" of thirteen million acres[52]—the greatest damage to trees ever caused by a single insect species in the United States.[53] The treatments, the trappings, the pesticide sprayings and everything else humans had tried had failed utterly to control the moth or even appreciably diminish its numbers. Foresters, entomologists, and officials at all levels could only watch helplessly as the ravages of nature seemingly gone berserk unfolded before their eyes. The caterpillars were everywhere in frightful numbers, moving relentlessly through New York, New Jersey, and Pennsylvania toward the great hardwood forests of Appalachia.

Pennsylvania was one of the two states most affected in 1981 (the other was Massachusetts). The first report of the gypsy moth in the Keystone State came in 1932, when the insects were discovered in Luzerne County. They quickly spread into every county, and by 1972 the state's department of environmental resources was spraying heavily to control the invaders. Unlike the early infestations in Massachusetts, where authorities had to contend with areas several hundred acres in size, by the early 1970s estimates were that the moth was active in over two million acres in Pennsylvania and moving generally south. Even those few million acres in Pennsylvania might have been considered a manageable area, but by 1975 the gypsy armies in the United States had extended their range to over 200,000 square miles. The forests of south-central Pennsylvania were heavily defoliated by the gypsy moth again in 1982 and 1986. The chemical weapon most relied on by Pennsylvania authorities was trichlorofon (Dylox), which proved so dangerous that the state ceased using it in 1983 and switched to Dipel, a product based on a naturally occurring moth pathogen, *Bacillus thurengiensis*.

The work of R. W. Campbell in the 1960s and 1970s doubtless underscored the sense of frustration that arose as a result of the astonishing successes of the gypsy moth against all adversaries. Campbell analyzed data available for the years 1911 to 1931 and came to the gloomy conclusion that as gypsy moth populations became denser and more widespread, outbreaks would become more severe and could last for ten years or longer. Campbell pointed out that science and the profession of entomology still had few tools available to deal with the gypsy moth, the only option was either to do nothing

and hope some naturally occurring phenomenon would halt an outbreak, or to continue spraying wherever it was arguably needed in the knowledge that such actions would not solve the problem.

Back to the Future

From this point onward the story of the gypsy moth in America becomes so diffuse that it is difficult to follow. The spread of the insect, however, is well documented. The front wave of the advancing moths passed quietly into Rock Creek Park in Washington, D.C. in the late 1970s, and during the 1980s the insects moved into Maryland, southern Virginia, eastern West Virginia, and northern North Carolina. Gypsy moths are increasingly found in Ohio, Michigan, Wisconsin, and other states of the Midwest. By 1994 they had established footholds in Arkansas, Tennessee, and Georgia. At present the gypsy moth has been reliably reported in almost every state of the union, including western states such as Washington and Oregon, where the Asian variety of the moth has occasionally been found.

The gypsy moth remains the only forest insect regulated by a USDA domestic quarantine. Many entomologists believe that no other forest insect has been studied so thoroughly or subjected to such unremitting eradication efforts.[54] No other forest insect has had so much money spent on it, and there is a good chance that the gypsy moth is the most expensive insect of any kind—with the possible exceptions of the cotton boll weevil and the spruce budworm.

A review of the current condition shows that the nation is still living with the consequences of decisions made almost a century ago with regard to importing predatory insects. This practice continues into the present on a smaller and more opportunistic scale, but the search for gypsy moth parasitoids and predators has been made in practically all parts of the globe where the insect can be found. During the campaign of the 1890s, any work in nonchemical approaches to insect control was dominated by the policies of Charles Fernald, and history seems to have proved him right in his decision not to import foreign parasites. He was concerned about the danger of secondary infestations and possibly feared other unforeseen consequences, as revealed by his comment that the idea was like a skimmer with too many holes in it.

In New England today, only nine of the original forty-seven imported gypsy moth predator species remain active, and only one, *Compsilura cocinnata*, is credited with suppressing the brown-tail moth so heavily that it exists at present only in small enclaves on islands off the coast of Maine.[55] There is a dark side to this phenomenon, however. Some foreign imports turned out to prey on other species whose reproductive capacities had not evolved to balance such great losses. Once loose in the field, the advance of *Compsilura cocinnata*

outpaced that of the gypsy moth because it found many alternate hosts in native North American insect populations. Today, entomologists know that *C. cocinnata* attacks almost one hundred other insect species. At present, the populations of some of North America's largest and showiest moths have been so deeply depressed by this foreign parasite that it has caused alarm in entomological circles.

Still with us in modern times is the concept of the barrier zone, which in its present manifestation is a variant of the 1890s encirclement strategy. The current zone, from North Carolina to the Michigan peninsula, was established as part of the "Slow the Spread" (STS) program begun in 1993. The goal of STS is to decrease the rate at which the gypsy moth moves into new areas. The expectation is likely the same one common to all barrier zones: to buy time until some newer or better method can be devised. But the usefulness of STS is immediately questionable, since the gypsy moth is constantly discovered at varying population levels in locations all across the country.[56]

Although the gypsy moth is a forest insect, almost no state sprays large woodland tracts any longer. Yet the claim that the gypsy moth will defoliate forests and kill all the trees is still heard today in places where the moth is first appearing—as are claims that were made in Medford more than one hundred years ago, that the gypsy moth is an alien species with no natural enemies—for it is in these areas that the bulk of present-day gypsy moth programs take place.[57] Evidence confirming the improbability of massive tree mortality is abundant but ignored, since it tends to reassure the public when those promoting spraying would prefer otherwise. A ten-year study in Connecticut beginning in the 1970s revealed that average tree mortality was less than 4 percent in forest stands that had suffered two successive years of defoliation, leading the researchers to conclude that gypsy moth infestations do not destroy forests.[58]

Even in the worst case, nature provides benefits. In Pennsylvania, which suffered much tree mortality during the 1980s, a thoughtful reassessment made fifteen years later by the U.S. Forest Service and the Pennsylvania Department of Natural Resources concluded that state forest lands in the formerly infested regions had become less susceptible to future destruction by the gypsy moth. Although the percentage of oaks had declined, the composition of the forests had become more diverse, and the order of tree succession observed in these areas provided habitat for wildlife species under stress from the lack of young forest ecosystems.[59]

The story of the gypsy moth in America has been one of nearly unremitting sameness interspersed with surprising and fateful events. One such incident occurred in 1989 when a fungus spontaneously appearing in Connecticut had spectacular results against gypsy moth concentrations. Work by Joseph Elk-

inton of the University of Massachusetts at Amherst and Anne Hajek of the Boyce-Thompson Institute at Cornell University in Ithaca, New York, ultimately proved that this fungus was *Entomophaga maimaiga*, and that it was the same genetic strain that had been seeded near Boston in 1910 and 1911.

What had happened to this fungus over the interim decades will probably never be known. *Entomophaga maimaiga* is distributed by the wind and can spread up to four hundred miles in a single year. It also is unusually hardy, having been known to survive as a resting spore for a decade or more. Yet even this longevity would fall far short of the seventy-seven-years between its original seeding in Boston and its reappearance in Connecticut, which suggests that the fungus may be naturally or otherwise reintroduced from time to time.

It is thus an outstanding natural control that many believe will help reduce the gypsy moth problem in America to a point where it is no greater than it has been in Europe. In places where the fungus has been artificially seeded, results have been exceptional. Bacteria and viruses exert control over the gypsy moth only when certain conditions are present including high population densities, insufficient food, and stressed or weakened colonies. The fungus, however, is effective at all densities and most conditions if sufficient moisture is available, and once released, requires little further attention. It is hard to overlook that the one potential control given the least attention by several earlier generations of entomologists has turned out to be the most important.

With the appearance of the fungus, the vast bureaucracy that has grown up around the gypsy moth is beginning to crumble. The myths of gypsy moth invulnerability and the absence of natural predators have at last been punctured. Priorities at the beginning of the twenty-first century have shifted; political pressure for moth extermination has diminished; scarce financial resources are being allocated to other programs; and many of the individuals who once specialized in the gypsy moth are moving into other areas of study.

There is little doubt that in the future the gypsy moth will appear in numbers from time to time and on occasion may even cause damage to trees. There is no less doubt that the insects will die down or move on again, and the natural cycle will continue as it always has. As horticulturalist Liberty Hyde Bailey said more than one hundred years ago: "After a time, a check will come. The potato beetle has already passed its zenith. The codling moth and the curculio have lost much of their fury in the east. The enemies of insects increase as well as the competitors. Parasites, finding innumerable insects on which to prey, increase with great rapidity, until they devour their own means of support. They, in turn, succumb, and the defeated host rallies; so the alternate warfare goes on forever. Witness how the tent caterpillars come and go."[60]

Notes

Abbreviations

BSNH	Boston Society of Natural History Archives, Lyman Library, Museum of Science, Boston, Massachusetts
CM	Commonwealth of Massachusetts
CM-BA	Commonwealth of Massachusetts, Board of Agriculture
CM-GC	Commonwealth of Massachusetts, General Court
CM-House	Commonwealth of Massachusetts, Legislature, House of Representatives
CM-MPC	Commonwealth of Massachusetts, Metropolitan Park Commission
EML	Ernst Mayr Library, Special Collections, Museum of Comparative Zoology, Harvard University, Cambridge, Massachusetts
MSA	Massachusetts State Archives, Dorchester
MSH	Massachusetts State House Library, Boston
SIA	Smithsonian Institution Archives, Washington, D.C.
UMA	W.E.B. Du Bois Library, Special Collections and Archives, Charles H. Fernald Collection, Record Groups 40, Series 11, University of Massachusetts Amherst
USDA	United States Department of Agriculture

Introduction

1. Kim Todd, *Tinkering with Eden.*
2. Swade, *Difference Engine.*
3. Terms of office did not become two years in length until the 1920s; four-year terms were instituted in the 1960s.
4. Foster and O'Keefe, *New England Forests*, p. 8.
5. Graham, *Dragon Hunters*, p. 66.

1. Years in the Shadow of Science

1. N. S. Shaler testimony, CM-GC, *Hearing before the Joint Special Committee*, pp. 317–18.

2. Trouvelot, quoted in Leighton, "New England Butterflies," pp. 171–72.

3. Trouvelot, "Use of Antenna in Insects," p. 196.

4. Hubbell, *Broadsides from the Other Orders*, p. 175.

5. "Cost of Fighting a Pest," *New York Times*, May 1, 1897.

6. "E. Leopold Trouvelot," *Nature* 52 (1895): 11.

7. CM, Birth Records.

8. Trouvelot to Scudder, September 20, 1869, BSNH.

9. Trouvelot to Scudder, September 26, 1869, BSNH.

10. Lawrence, *Proceedings of the Two Hundred Seventy-fifth Anniversary*, p. 55.

11. Barrett, *Historical Sketches*, p. 31.

12. Liebhold, Mastro, and Schaeffer, "Learning from the Legacy of Leopold Trouvelot," p. 20.

13. Osgood, "Gypsy Moth in Massachusetts," p. 677.

14. Wood testimony, CM-GC, *Hearing before the Joint Special Committee*, p. 84.

15. *Federal Census for Massachusetts*, 1860, microfilm spool 16, p. 631.

16. *Federal Census for Massachusetts*, 1870, microfilm spool 20, p. 401.

17. CM-BA, *Thirteenth Annual Report*, pp. 104–5.

18. Samuels, *Birds of New England,* p. 156.

19. Howard, *Gipsy Moth in America*, p. 7.

20. Herman and Corbin, "Leopold Trouvelot," p. 1.

21. Sorensen, *Brethren of the Net*, p. 5.

22. Lurie, *Louis Agassiz*, p. 197.

23. Museum of Comparative Zoology, [Fifth] *Annual Report* (1863), pp. 24, 28.

24. Museum of Comparative Zoology, [Sixth] *Annual Report* (1864), p. 23.

25. Boston Society of Natural History, *Proceedings* 2, (1866–68): 118–120. See also "Proceedings of Scientific Societies." *American Naturalist* 1, no. 1, p. 56.

26. Howard, *Gipsy Moth In America*, pp. 7–8.

27. Trouvelot, "American Silk Worm," p. 32.

28. Packard testimony, CM-GC, *Hearing before the Joint Standing Committee*, p. 1.

29. Trouvelot, "American Silk Worm," p. 146.

30. Samuels, *Birds of New England*, p. 156.

31. Ibid.

32. CM-BA, *Thirteenth Annual Report*, p. 116.

33. Ibid.

34. Trouvelot to Scudder, March 18, 1869, BSNH.

35. Trouvelot to Scudder, September 26, 1869, BSNH.

36. Wilder, Burt G., "Unwelcome Guests of Insects," p. 471.

37. Trouvelot to Scudder, April 11, 1868, BSNH.

38. Riley, *Fourth Annual Report*.

39. Peigler, "Wild Silks of the World," pp. 154–55.

40. Townend Glover, quoted in Howard, *History of Applied Entomology*, p. 39.

2. The Gypsy Moth Comes to America

1. Trouvelot, "American Silk Worm," p. 149.
2. Shaler, testimony, CM-GC *Hearing before the Joint Special Committee*, pp. 317–18.
3. Trouvelot to Scudder, March 30, 1867, BSNH.
4. CM-BA, *Thirty-eighth Annual Report*, p. 59.
5. Guberlet, *Windows to His World*, p. 166.
6. Howard, *Gipsy Moth in America*.
7. Haushalter to Kirkland, August 4, 1896, Box 2, Folder 72, UMA. "Caterpillar cholera" was a term used at the time to denote the *Wipfelkrankenheit*, or wilt disease, of the gypsy moth. It is likely the *nucleopolyhedrosis* virus. Haushalter probably misunderstood the name of the Parisian supplier, whom Trouvelot said was [Felix Edouard] Guerin-Meneville, the noted naturalist, entomologist, and author.
8. Wright, CM-GC, *Hearing before the Joint Special Committee*, p. 630.
9. Trouvelot to Dall, May 1, 1870, Record Unit 7073, Wm. H. Dall Papers, circa 1839–1858, 1862–1927, Box 16, Folder 39, *SIA*.
10. Gerardi and Grimm, *History, Biology, Damage and Control of the Gypsy Moth*, front flap.
11. Trouvelot, "The American Silkworm," *American Naturalist*, April 1867, p. 85.
12. Gerardi and Grimm, *History, Biology, Damage, and Control of the Gypsy Moth*, p. 136.
13. Boston Society of Natural History, 11 *Proceedings* (1866–1868) p. 89. There is some unresolved confusion about this date: the meeting at which Trouvelot spoke was held on November 28, 1866, but Trouvelot wrote in the *American Naturalist* that he sailed for Europe on November 2, 1866.
14. Trouvelot to Scudder, May 11, 1867, BSNH.
15. Trouvelot, "On a Method of Stimulating Union, pp. 136–37.
16. Ibid., p. 136.
17. Ward, "Agricultural Experiment Station," p. 67.
18. Osgood, F., "State in Arms against a Caterpillar," p. 458.
19. Forbush and Fernald, *Gypsy Moth*, p. 4.
20. Ibid., pp. 3–4.
21. Henshaw, to Fernald, September 17, 1889, Box 8, Folder 209, UMA.
22. Haushalter to Kirkland, August 4, 1896, Box 2, Folder 72, UMA.
23. Riley, *Second Report*, p. 10.
24. *Insect Life* 2, nos. 7 and 8 (1870): 208.
25. Shaler, *Kentucky Geological Survey*, 1875.
26. Shaler, testimony, CM-GC, *Hearing before the Joint Special Committee*, pp. 317–18. See also Forbush and Fernald, *Gypsy Moth*, App. A.
27. Fernald, "Notes on the Gypsy Moth," p. 59.
28. CM, [First] *Annual Report of the Superintendent for Suppressing the Gypsy and Brown-tail Moths* (1905), p. 9.

29. Trouvelot to Dall, May 1, 1870, Box 16, Folder 39, SIA.

30. Ibid.

31. Trouvelot to Scudder, September 26, 1869, BSNH.

32. Samuels, "Summer Entomology," pp. 402–3.

33. Packard, "Hessian Fly: Its Ravages, Habits and Means of Preventing Its Increase," *U.S. Entomological Commission Bulletin* no. 4, (1880), in Pauly, "Fighting the Hessian Fly," p. 381.

34. Scudder, *Butterflies of the Eastern United States.*

35. Scudder, "Notes on Drawings." See also Scudder, *Butterflies of the Eastern United States*, 1: xi.

36. *Cambridge City Directory for 1873*, p. 372.

37. *Annals of the Astronomical Observatory of Harvard College*, 8:3.

38. "Editor's Scientific Record," p. 908.

39. "History of a Publishing House," p. 798.

40. "Trouvelot, E. Leopold," in *Dictionary of Scientific Biography*, 8: 472.

41. Trouvelot, to Dall, May 1, 1870, Box 16, Folder 39, SIA.

42. Forbush and Fernald, *Gypsy Moth*, p. 4.

43. Haushalter to Kirkland, August 4, 1896, Box 2, Folder 72, UMA.

44. Riley and Howard, "Imported Gypsy Moth," pp. 208–9.

45. Samuels, *Birds of New England*, p. 156.

46. Trouvelot to Dall, May 1, 1870, Box 2, Folder 72, UMA.

47. Trouvelot to Scudder, March 18, 1869, BSNH.

48. Trouvelot to Dall, May 1, 1870, Box 2, Folder 72, UMA.

3. The Caterpillars Are Coming!

1. W. R. Taylor, CM, *Statements from Eye-Witnesses.*

2. CM-BA, *Report on the Work of Extermination* (1895), p. 40.

3. W. R. Taylor, CM, *Statements from Eye-Witnesses.*

4. Forbush and Fernald, *Gypsy Moth*, p. 10.

5. CM-BA, *Report on the Work of Extermination* (1895), p. 38.

6. Forbush and Fernald, *Gypsy Moth*, p. 6.

7. J. S. Cotton, CM, *Statements from Eye-Witnesses.*

8. M. Belcher, ibid.

9. CM-BA, *Report on the Work of Extermination* (1895), pp. 40–41.

10. D. M., Richardson, *Statements from Eye-Witnesses.*

11. S. Lacy, ibid.

12. CM-BA, *Report on the Work of Extermination* (1893), p. 16.

13. J. O. Goodwin, testimony, CM-GC, *Hearing before the Joint Standing Committee*, p. 7.

14. "Army of Squirming Worms," *Boston Herald,* May 27, 1889, p. 9.

15. W. C. Craig, testimony, CM-GC, *Hearing before the Joint Standing Committee*, p. 10.

16. CM-BA, *Report on the Work of Extermination* (1895), p. 39.

17. Craig testimony, CM-GC, *Hearing before the Joint Standing Committee*, p. 11.

18. Quoted in Forbush and Fernald, *Gypsy Moth*, p. 33.

19. *Medford Mercury*, July 5, 1889, MED.

20. Hitchcock, "Professor Trouvelot's Mistake," pp. 1988–91.

21. "Portrait of William R. Sessions Given M. A. C.," *Springfield Republican*, May 11, 1921, UMA.

22. Mallis, *American Entomologists*, p. 123.

23. Fernald to Scudder, July 12, 1894, Scudder Correspondence, BSNH.

24. Sawyer, *To Make a Spotless Orange*, p. 137.

25. Mallis, *American Entomologists*, p. 146.

26. Ibid., p. 147.

27. Ibid, p. 142.

28. Howard, *Gipsy Moth in America*, p. 37.

29. Peters to unknown recipient, March 1963, Box 1, Folder 1, UMA.

30. Mallis, *American Entomologists*, p. 142.

31. Fernald to A. Agassiz, November 8, 1886, bBg 320–322, EML.

32. "Entomology and Zoology at the Massachusetts Agricultural College," pp. 5–9.

33. Alyokhin, "Short History of the Department."

34. Peters to unknown recipient, March 1963. Box 1, Folder 1, UMA.

35. Fernald to Haynes, September 17, 1900, Box 6, Folder 1, UMA.

36. Maria Fernald doubtless took her husband's place in his absence, since experiments with living insects could not otherwise have continued, although no records exist showing her in this capacity officially. Charles Fernald was a part-time entomologist of the station; his official position at Amherst was always professor of zoology. He was not able to devote himself principally to entomology until the appointment of R. S. Lull to the department of zoology as an assistant in 1896.

37. Fernald to Stetson, *Medford Mercury*, June 5, 1889, Box 6, Folder 1, UMA.

38. Fernald, Henry T., "Address to the Fernald Club," pp. 9–11.

39. Howard, *Gipsy Moth in North America*, p. 9.

40. Riley, "Importation of Ocneria Dispar," p. 86.

41. Fernald, "Notes on the Gypsy Moth," p. 60.

42. Fernald, "Dangerous Insect Pest in Medford," p. 4.

43. Fernald to Hagen, January 14, 1890, bMu 968.10.1, EML.

44. Fernald testimony, CM-GC, *Hearing before the Joint Standing Committee*, p. 6.

45. CM-BA, *Report on the Work of Extermination* (1893), p. 15.

46. Smith, Edward H., "Entomological Society of America," p. 13.

47. Howard, *History of Applied Entomology*, p. 109.

48. CM-BA, *Thirty-Fifth Annual Report* (1887), p. 78.

49. USDA, Proceedings *First Annual Meeting of the Association of Economic Entomologists*, p. 180.

50. Sorensen, *Brethren of the Net*, p. 86.

51. Howard, *History of Applied Entomology*, p. 106.

52. Riley to Hagen, October 27, 1883, BSNH.

53. Croker, *Stephen Forbes*, p. 119.

54. Burson, "United States 1890s," pp. 1–2.

55. Croker, *Stephen Forbes*, p. 102.

56. Sawyer, *To Make a Spotless Orange*, p. xix.

57. Fernald testimony, CM-GC, *Hearing before the Joint Special Committee*, p. 49.

58. Fernald, "Notes on the Gypsy Moth," p. 60.

59. Fernald to Henshaw, September 12, 1889, bMu 968.10.2, EML.

60. Henshaw to Fernald, September 17, 1889, Box 8, Folder 209, UMA.

61. Fernald to Henshaw, September 20, 1889, bMu 968.10.2, EML.

62. Riley and Howard, "Imported Gypsy Moth," p. 209.

63. "Legislation against the Gypsy Moth," *Insect Life*, p. 150.

64. Letter to the Editor, *Garden and Forest*, November 20, 1889, p. 562.

65. CM, *Special Bulletin of the Hatch Experiment Station*, November 1889.

66. Fernald to Hagen, January 14, 1890, 968.10.1, EML.

67. Fernald to Henshaw, November 26, 1889, 968.10.2, EML.

68. Fernald, to Henshaw, November 30, 1889, 968.10.2, EML.

69. Ibid.

70. Mallis, *American Entomologists*, p. 123.

4. No Holiday Affair

1. Hagen to Fernald, January 15, 1890, EML.

2. Fernald to Hagen, January 14, 1890, bMu 968.10.1, EML.

3. Ibid.

4. Hagen to Fernald, January 15, 1890, EML.

5. Howard, *Fighting the Insects*, p. 47.

6. Ealand, *Insects and Man*.

7. Brackett in Henshaw, "Report upon the Gypsy Moth," p. 75.

8. Forbush and Fernald, *Gypsy Moth*, p. 264.

9. "About Town Matters in Arlington," p. 1.

10. J. W. Stockwell testimony, CM-GC, *Hearing before the Joint Special Committee*, p. 415.

11. Howard, *History of Applied Entomology*, p. 116.

12. *Boston Evening Transcript*, May 15, 1890, p. 3.

13. Ward, "Agricultural Experiment Station," p. 68.

14. Fernald to Osborn, February 9, 1895, Box 8, Folder 213, UMA.

15. R. A. Duffy, personal communication with author, September 16, 2001.

16. Fernald to Henshaw, April 14, 1890, bMu 968.10.2, EML.

17. Lintner to Fernald, March 29, 1890, Box 8, Folder 199, UMA.

18. In Forbush and Fernald, *Gypsy Moth*, Fernald gives the date as March 22.

19. CM-BA, *Thirty-eighth Annual Report* (1890), p. 60.

20. Rawson to Fernald, March 30, 1890, Box 3, Folder 102, UMA.

21. J. G., Jack, Letter to the Editor, *Garden and Forest*, June 4, 1890, p. 277.

22. Lintner to Fernald, April 7, 1890, Box 8, Folder 199, UMA.

23. Ibid.
24. Henshaw to Fernald, April 11, 1890, Box 2, Folder 66, UMA.
25. Ibid.
26. Fernald to Henshaw, April 17, 1890, bMu 968.10.2, EML.
27. Baker and Heinton, "Traps Have Some Value," p. 407.
28. Forbush and Fernald, *Gypsy Moth*, p. 42.
29. Fernald quoted in letter to Henshaw, May 24, 1890, bMu 968.10.2, EML.
30. Ibid.
31. Riley and Howard, "Legislation against the Gipsy Moth," p. 78.
32. Lodeman, *Spraying of Plants*, p. 197.
33. Howard, *History of Applied Entomology*, p. 65.
34. Forbush and Fernald, *Gypsy Moth*, p. 159.
35. Henshaw, "Report upon the Gypsy Moth in Massachusetts," p. 77.
36. W. W. Fifield, testimony, CM-GC, *Hearing before the Joint Special Committee*, pp. 95–96.
37. Riley and Howard, "Experience with the Gipsy Moth," pp. 126–127.
38. CM-BA, *Report of the Board of Agriculture on Destroying the Gypsy Moth* (1893), p. 17.
39. Rogers and Burgess, *Report on the Field Work*, p. 11.
40. Brackett to Massachusetts Senate and House of Representatives, May 15, 1890, Record Series GO, vol. 107, MSA.
41. Fernald and Forbush, *Gypsy Moth*, give the total number as eighty-nine.
42. Riley and Howard, "Legislation against the Gipsy Moth," p. 78.
43. CM-BA, *Thirty-eighth Annual Report*, (1890), p. 62.
44. W. B. Harmon, CM, *Statements from Eye-Witnesses*.
45. Forbush and Fernald, *Gypsy Moth*, pp. 17–18.
46. Ibid., p. 15.
47. Riley and Howard, "Legislation against the Gipsy Moth," p. 79.
48. "Three Architectural Tours," p. 17.
49. Fernald to J. B. Smith, June 14, 1898, Box 3, Folder 117, UMA.
50. Shaler testimony, CM-GC, *Hearing before the Joint Standing Committee*, p. 3.
51. Fernald to Henshaw, December 8, 1890, bMu 968.10.2, EML.
52. Riley, "Outlook For Applied Entomology," p. 200.
53. Riley and Howard, "Efforts to Stamp Out the Gypsy Moth," p. 365.
54. CM-BA, *Thirty-eighth Annual Report* (1890), pp. xxii–xxiii.
55. Ibid., p. 59.
56. Ibid., p. 62.

5. Preparations for War

1. Shaler testimony, CM-GC, *Hearing before the Joint Special Committee*, pp. 318–19.
2. CM-BA *Minutes* (1891).
3. CM-GC, *Acts and Resolves*, 1890–91, p. 1152.

4. Russell to Shaler, February 7, 1891, Agency Code GO 1, Record Group 568X, Letters Official, 1861–1926, MSA.

5. Russell to Rawson, January 23, 1891, Agency Code GO 1, Record Group 568X, Letters Official, 1861–1926, MSA.

6. E. W. Wood testimony, CM-GC, *Hearing before the Joint Standing Committee*, p. 2.

7. Russell to Rawson, February 20, 1891, Agency Code GO 1, Record Group 568X, Letters Official, 1861–1926, MSA.

8. Russell to Executive Council of the Massachusetts State Legislature, February 25, 1891, Agency Code GO 1, Record Group 568X, Letters Official, 1861–1926, MSA.

9. CM-GC, *Acts and Resolves*, 1890–91, pp. 1150–52.

10. Wood testimony, CM-GC, *Hearing before the Joint Standing Committee*, pp. 1–2.

11. Shaler testimony, ibid., p. 12.

12. J. G. Jack, "Can the Gypsy Moth Be Exterminated?" *Garden and Forest*, March 11, 1891.

13. Hobbs, "Nathaniel Southgate Shaler," pp. 924–26.

14. Livingstone, *Nathaniel Southgate Shaler*, p. 47.

15. Shaler testimony, CM-GC, *Hearing before the Joint Special Committee*, p. 325.

16. Howard, *History of Applied Entomology*, esp. p. 92.

17. E. H. Smith, personal exchange with author, 1998.

18. Howard, *History of Applied Entomology*, p. 92.

19. Lane Cooper, *Louis Agassiz as a Teacher.*

20. Howard, *History of Applied Entomology*, pp. 18–19.

21. Croker, *Stephen Forbes*, p. 42.

22. Livingstone, *Nathaniel Southgate Shaler*, p. 29.

23. Ibid., p. 167

24. G. Pinchot, *The Fight for Conservation*, 1906, in Livingstone, *Nathaniel Southgate Shaler*, p. 324.

25. Shaler testimony, CM-GC, *Hearing before the Joint Special Committee*, p. 321.

26. Forbush and Fernald, *Gypsy Moth*, App. A, p. iii. See also "(Stenographic) Report of a Discussion on the Gypsy Moth." *Insect Life* 3, nos. 9 and 10 (1891): 368–81.

27. CM, *Special Bulletin of the Hatch Experiment Station.*

28. Forbush and Fernald, *Gypsy Moth*, App. A, p. iv.

29. Ibid.

30. Riley to Henshaw, October 28, 1889, bMu 2339.10.2, EML.

31. Riley to Henshaw, September 29, 1891, bMu 2339.10.2, EML.

32. Forbush and Fernald, *Gypsy Moth*, App. A, pp. v, xvi.

33. Ibid., pp. vii–viii.

34. Ibid., p. viii.

35. Ibid., p. xii.

36. Ibid., pp. v, xvi.

37. Riley, address to California State Board of Horticulture, Riverside, April 12, 1887, in Graham, *Dragon Hunters*, p. 22.

38. *The Nationalizing of American Life, 1877–1900*, ed. R. Ginger, p. 189.

39. Russell to Executive Council of the Massachusetts State Legislature, February 25, 1891, Agency Code GO 1, Record Group 568X, Letters Official, 1861–1926, MSA.

40. Forbush and Fernald, *Gypsy Moth, App. A*, pp. xv–xvi.

41. Ibid., p. xv.

42. Riley to Hagen, July 15, 1885, bMu 2339.10.1 (26)–(40), EML.

43. Scudder to Packard, June 6, 1881, bMu 2497.10.10–12, EML. See also Riley to Scudder, June 1, 1881, bMu 2339.10.4 (41)–(43)-2339.10.2, EML.

44. Scudder to Packard, May 29, 1881, bMu 2497.10.10–12, EML.

45. Forbush and Fernald, *Gypsy Moth*, App. A, pp. xvii–xviii.

46. Ibid., p. xiv.

6. The Moth Slayers

1. May, "Edward Howe Forbush," p. 40.

2. Letterheads in the Forbush folder, Special Collections, EML.

3. Henshaw, "Report upon the Gypsy Moth," p. 78.

4. CM-BA, [*Special*] *Report* (1891), p. 7.

5. Sorensen, *Brethren of the Net*.

6. R. T. Jackson, "Samuel Henshaw," in Mallis, *American Entomologists*, p. 459.

7. Winsor, *Reading the Shape of Nature*, p. 219.

8. Fernald testimony, CM-GC, *Hearing before the Joint Special Committee*, p. 1107.

9. S. Henshaw, testimony, ibid., pp. 680–81.

10. May, "Edward Howe Forbush," p. 55.

11. E. H. Forbush, testimony, CM-GC, *Hearing before the Joint Special Committee*, p. 1301.

12. Ibid. p. 1302.

13. CM-BA, [*Special*] *Report* (1891), pp. 8–9.

14. Forbush and Fernald, *Gypsy Moth*, p. 46.

15. May, "Edward Howe Forbush," p. 54.

16. Ibid., p. 55.

17. CM-BA, *Minutes* (1891), April 21, 1891.

18. *Nationalizing of American Life*, edited by R. Ginger. pp. 9–10.

19. Harvey to Fernald, *Gypsy Moth*, App. E, p. xlv.

20. Osgood, "State in Arms against a Caterpillar," p. 463.

21. "Rules and Regulations of the State Board of Agriculture," in Forbush and Fernald, *Gypsy Moth*, App. B, p. xxiii.

22. Forbush and Fernald, *Gypsy Moth*, pp. 51–52.

23. "Rules and Regulations of the State Board of Agriculture," in Forbush and Fernald, *Gypsy Moth*, App. B, p. xxiv.

24. "Communications," p. 123.
25. Ibid.
26. Forbush testimony, CM-GC, *Hearing before the Joint Special Committee*, p. 1269.
27. Forbush and Fernald, *Gypsy Moth*, p. 54.
28. Ibid., p. 118.
29. Forbush testimony, CM-GC, *Hearing before the Joint Standing Committee*, p. 5.
30. Sessions to Fernald, March 16, 1891, Box 3, Folder 114, UMA.
31. CM-BA, [*Special*] *Report* (1891), p. 6.

7. Summer 1891

1. Forbush and Fernald, *Gypsy Moth*, App. C, p. xxviii.
2. Ibid., pp. xxviii–xxix.
3. CM-BA, [*Special*] *Report* (1891), p. 7.
4. L. Mansfield, CM, *Statements from Eye-Witnesses*.
5. Henshaw, "Report upon the Gypsy Moth," p. 80.
6. CM-BA, [*Special*] *Report* (1891), p. 7.
7. Forbush testimony, CM-GC, *Hearing before the Joint Special Committee*, p. 315.
8. D. M. Rogers, testimony, CM-GC, *Hearing before the Joint Standing Committee*.
9. "Rules and Regulations of the State Board of Agriculture," in Forbush and Fernald, *Gypsy Moth*, App. B, p. xxv.
10. Lodeman, *Spraying of Plants*, p. 212.
11. "Communications," p. 123.
12. Henshaw, "Report upon the Gypsy Moth," pp. 79–80.
13. "Communications," p. 123.
14. Forbush and Fernald, *Gypsy Moth*, p. 56.
15. Riley to Henshaw, June 20, 1891, bMu 2339.10.2, EML.
16. Henshaw testimony, CM-GC, *Hearing before the Joint Special Committee*, p. 684.
17. Henshaw, "Report upon the Gypsy Moth," p. 79.
18. Riley and Howard, "Extermination of the Gypsy Moth," p. 474.
19. Riley to Henshaw, June 20, 1891, bMu 2339.10.2, EML.
20. Henshaw, "Report upon the Gypsy Moth," p. 81.
21. Riley to Henshaw, June 29, 1891, bMu 2339.10.2, EML.
22. Riley to Henshaw, July 10, 1891, bMu 2339.10.2, EML.
23. Riley, *Address to the Massachusetts Horticultural Society*.
24. Riley and Howard, "Extermination of the Gypsy Moth," p. 474.
25. *Special Report of the State Board of Agriculture* (1891), p. 17.
26. Fernald testimony, CM-GC, *Hearing before the Joint Special Committee*, pp. 50–51.
27. Ibid., p. 82.
28. Riley and Howard, "Japanese Parasite of the Gypsy Moth," p. 227.
29. Riley to Fernald, July 23, 1891, Box 8, Folder 220, UMA.

30. Ibid.

31. Fernald to J. H. Bowditch, February 5, 1904, Box 6, Folder 1, UMA.

32. Riley to Henshaw, July 10, 1891, bMu 2339.10.2, EML.

33. Forbush and Fernald, *Gypsy Moth*, p. 209.

34. Forbush, "Birds Useful to Agriculture," p. 47.

35. Henshaw, "Report upon the Gypsy Moth," p. 79.

36. "The Dangers of Arsenical Poisoning Resulting from Spraying with Insecticides," in Forbush and Fernald, *Gypsy Moth*, App. F, p. lxv.

37. Sessions to Fernald, August 10, 1891, Box 3, Folder 114, UMA. The initials "H. S." almost certainly stand for "History Society," since many of the opposing entomologists were members of the Boston Natural History Society.

38. Riley to Henshaw, September 29, 1891, bMu 2339.10.2, EML.

39. Osgood, "Gypsy Moth in Massachusetts," p. 678.

40. Ibid.

41. CM-BA, [*Special*] *Report* (1891), p. 10.

42. Sessions testimony, CM-GC, *Hearing before the Joint Standing Committee*, p. 4.

8. The Cyclone Burner

1. Riley, *Address to the Massachusetts Horticultural Society*.

2. Riley to Henshaw, February 18, 1892, bMu 2339.10.2, EML.

3. Forbush and Fernald, *Gypsy Moth*, p. 62.

4. Fernald testimony, CM-GC, *Hearing before the Joint Special Committee*, p. 52.

5. Sessions to Fernald, January 26, 1896, Box 3, Folder 114, UMA.

6. CM-BA, *Report on the Work of Extermination* (1892), p. 13.

7. Ibid., p. 9.

8. Ibid., p. 18.

9. CM-BA, *Fortieth Annual Report*, (1892), p. 264.

10. CM-BA, [*Special*] *Report* (1891), p. 15.

11. "Letter," p. 99.

12. Ibid.

13. S. R. Huston testimony, CM-CG, *Hearing before the Joint Standing Committee*, p. 13.

14. Forbush and Fernald, *Gypsy Moth*, p. 63.

15. In the terminology of Fernald's time, molds and fungi were both considered vegetative matter with parasitic effects on their hosts; later they would be called disease pathogens.

16. Glaser, "Wilt of Gypsy Moth Caterpillars," p. 101. Diseases were also considered parasitic at the time.

17. Fernald, "Notes on the Gypsy Moth," p. 61.

18. Riley and Howard, "Further Notes on the Japanese Gypsy Moth and Its Parasites," p. 195.

19. Osgood, "State in Arms against a Caterpillar," p. 460.

20. Fernald, "Notes on the Gypsy Moth," p. 62. "Tophet" is apparently an anglicized

version of a Jewish term for a particularly unpleasant and painful condition or place and derives from the Hebrew word *topet*, a place where children were burned (*American Heritage Dictionary of the English Language*, Third Edition).

21. J. H. Bowditch testimony, CM-GC, *Hearing before the Joint Special Committee,* p. 479.
22. L. Goddu, CM, *Statements from Eye-Witnesses.*
23. A. R. Bunting, ibid.
24. CM-BA, *Fortieth Annual Report* (1892), p. 274.
25. Ramsey, "Notes on the Discovery of Lead Arsenate."
26. Ward, "Agricultural Experiment Station," p. 68.
27. R. A. McCarty, CM, *Statements from Eye-Witnesses.*
28. M. M. Ransom, ibid.
29. CM-BA, *Report on the Work of Extermination* (1892), pp. 6–7.
30. CM-BA, *Fortieth Annual Report* (1892), p. 297.
31. Ibid., p. 276.
32. CM-BA, *Report on the Work of Extermination* (1892), p. 19.
33. Forbush and Fernald, *Gypsy Moth,* p. 65.
34. CM-BA, *Report on the Work of Extermination* (1892), p. 21.
35. Forbush and Fernald, *Gypsy Moth,* p. 101.
36. "Short History of the MDC" (in 1919 the name was changed to the "Metropolitan District Commission").
37. "Members of the First Metropolitan Commission," App. B, p. 32.

9. Lead, Arsenic, Burlap, and Fire

1. CM-GC, *Acts and Resolves 1896,* p. 672.
2. CM-BA, *Report on the Work of Extermination* (1893), p. 35.
3. Caesar, "Fifty Years of Entomological Progress, Part II," p. 12.
4. Moulton to Fernald, undated, Folder 209, UMA.
5. Fernald, "Notes on the Gypsy Moth," p. 61.
6. CM-GC, *Acts and Resolves 1892–93,* pp. 1486–87.
7. CM-BA, *Report on the Work of Extermination* (1893), p. 5.
8. CM-GC, G. W. Creesy, *Statements from Eye-Witnesses.*
9. CM-BA, *Report on the Work of Extermination* (1893), p. 20.
10. Forbush and Fernald, *Gypsy Moth,* p. 193.
11. Ibid.
12. Forbush testimony, CM-GC, *Hearing before the Joint Standing Committee,* p. 7.
13. Riley and Howard, "Gypsy Moth in Cambridge," p. 53.
14. Riley and Howard, "Parasite of the Japanese Gypsy Moth," p. 335.
15. CM-BA, *Report on the Work of Extermination* (1893), p. 5.
16. S. R. Huston testimony, CM-GC, *Hearing before the Joint Standing Committee,* p. 15.

17. B. R. Hennelly testimony, ibid., p. 632.
18. CM-BA, *Report on the Work of Extermination* (1893), pp. 30–31.
19. Ibid., p. 9.
20. Ibid., p. 20.
21. Ibid., p. 34.
22. Ward, A. B., "Agricultural Experiment Station," p. 68.
23. CM, *Report of the Board of World's Fair Managers*, pp. 59–60.
24. Sessions to Fernald, October 27, 1893, Box 8, Folder 223, UMA.
25. Sessions to Fernald, November 1, 1893, Box 8, Folder 223, UMA.
26. Shaler to Fernald, November 1, 1893, Box 109, Folder 221, UMA.
27. Shaler to Fernald, November 15, 1893, Box 109, Folder 221, UMA.
28. Sessions to Fernald, May 31, 1893. Box 3, Folder 114, UMA.
29. Joseph A. Lintner, "Our Insect Enemies and How to Meet Them." address to the New Jersey Board of Agriculture, Trenton, N.J., February 1, 1889.
30. Fernald to Osborn, February 9, 1894, Box 8, Folder 213, UMA.
31. Lintner to Fernald, June 22, 1893, App. D, Forbush and Fernald, *Gypsy Moth*.
32. Lintner to Fernald, June 2, 1893, Box 8, Folder 199, UMA.
33. J. B. Smith to Fernald, June 20, 1893, App. D in Forbush and Fernald, *Gypsy Moth*.
34. Henry T. Fernald to Fernald, June 19, 1893, App. D in ibid.
35. Packard to Fernald, June 19, 1893, App. D in ibid.
36. Sessions to Fernald, June 6, 1893, Box 3, Folder 114, UMA.
37. Riley to Henshaw, November 3, 1893, bMu 2339.10.2, EML.

10. Rebounds and Resignations

1. Goodwin testimony, CM-GC, *Hearing before the Joint Special Committee*, p. 245.
2. CM-BA, *Minutes* (1893).
3. Goodwin testimony, CM-GC, *Hearing before the Joint Standing Committee*, p. 9.
4. F. H. Appleton testimony, ibid., p. 7.
5. Fernald, testimony, CM-GC, *Hearing before the Joint Special Committee*, p. 58.
6. CM-BA, *Minutes* (1894), July 26, 1894.
7. May, "Edward Howe Forbush," p. 55.
8. CM-BA, *Report on the Work of Extermination* (1894), p. 18.
9. Fernald, "Notes on the Gypsy Moth," p. 66.
10. W. C. Wright, CM-GC, *Hearing before the Joint Standing Committee*, p. 3.
11. O. J. McCarthy, testimony, CM-GC, *Hearing before the Joint Special Committee*, p. 515.
12. Howard, *Gipsy Moth in America*, p. 16.
13. CM-BA, *Report on the Work of Extermination* (1894), p. 27.
14. Sessions to Fernald, May 29, 1894, Box 8, Folder 223, UMA.
15. Caesar, "Fifty Years of Progress in Entomology, Part II," p. 16.

16. Perkins to Fernald, July 1894, App. E in Forbush and Fernald, *Gypsy Moth*.
17. I. J. Colbert, testimony, CM-GC, *Hearing before the Joint Special Committee*, p. 596.
18. Comstock to Sessions, July 17, 1894, App. E in Forbush and Fernald, *Gypsy Moth*.
19. Ibid.
20. Harvey to Fernald, July 1894, App. E in ibid.
21. Ibid.
22. Ibid.
23. Fernald testimony, CM-GC, *Hearing before the Joint Special Committee*, p. 73.
24. Lintner, *Report of the New Jersey State Board of Agriculture, 1893–4*, pp. 55–56.
25. Lintner, "Address to the New Jersey Board of Agriculture."
26. Howard, "A Brief Account of the Rise and Present Condition of Official Economic Entomology," p. 59. In *The Gypsy Moth*, Appendix E, p. l.
27. Ibid.
28. Fernald testimony, CM-GC, *Hearing before the Joint Special Committee*, pp. 54–55.
29. Frederick Law Olmsted to his partners, October 28, 1893, in Morgan, "Charles Eliot," p. 13.
30. CM-BA, *Report on the Work of Extermination* (1894), p. 16.
31. Carruth to Forbush, March 29, 1894, Agency Code EN4, MDC, Record Series 1055X, MSA.
32. CM-MPC, *Report* (1894): "Landscape Architects' Report."
33. Haglund, "Emerald Metropolis," p. 10.
34. CM-BA, *Report on the Work of Extermination* (1894), p. 17.
35. Forbush and Fernald, *Gypsy Moth*, App. A, p. viii.
36. Fernald, "Notes on the Gypsy Moth," p. 64.
37. Forbush and Fernald, *Gypsy Moth*, p. 474.
38. Ibid., p. 95.
39. CM-BA, [*Special*] *Report* (1891), p. 21.
40. Forbush and Fernald, *Gypsy Moth*, p. 60, 62.

11. Unusual Business

1. CM-BA, *Minutes* (1894), July 26, 1894.
2. Riley to Henshaw, November 2, 1893, bMu 2339.10.2, EML.
3. Mallis, *American Entomologists*, p. 78.
4. Fernald to Osborn, February 9, 1894, Box 8, Folder 213, UMA.
5. Fernald to Osborn, February 9, dated 1894, Box 8, Folder 213, UMA. Fernald's date on this letter is incorrect, since the events mentioned did not occur until 1895.
6. A. E. Barker testimony, CM-GC, *Hearing before the Joint Special Committee*, p. 793.
7. Fernald, "Notes on the Gypsy Moth," p. 66.
8. Ibid., p. 64.

9. CM-BA, *Report on the Work of Extermination* (1895), p. 1.
10. Forbush to Fernald, June 29, 1895, Box 7, Folder 176, UMA.
11. Ibid.
12. CM-BA, *Report on the Work of Extermination* (1895), p. 42.
13. Ibid.
14. Howard, *Gipsy Moth in America*, p. 21.
15. Fernald, "Evolution of Economic Entomology," p. 10.
16. Forbush testimony, CM-GC, *Hearing before the Joint Special Committee*, p. 1094.
17. Forbush and Fernald, *Gypsy Moth*, pp. 287–88.
18. Fernald to Uhler, November 10, 1894, bMu 968.10.3–968.10.7, EML.
19. Hennelly testimony, CM-GC, *Hearing before the Joint Special Committee*, p. 703.
20. Marlatt to Fernald, September 17, 1895, Box 8, Folder 204, UMA.
21. Fernald, "Notes on the Gypsy Moth," p. 61.
22. Riley to Scudder, May 9, 1894, Scudder Correspondence, Riley folder VI, BSNH.
23. L. W. Ross testimony, CM-GC, *Hearing before the Joint Special Committee*, p. 458.
24. J. A. Bailey Jr., testimony, ibid., pp. 767–69.
25. Ibid., p. 70.
26. Ward, "Agricultural Experiment Station," p. 74.
27. Fernald, "Notes on the Gypsy Moth," p. 63.
28. Ibid.
29. Fernald to Scudder, April 28, 1896, Scudder Correspondence, BSNH.
30. Ibid.

12. The Politics of War

1. CM-BA, *Report on the Work of Extermination* (1896), p. 6.
2. Sessions to Fernald, January 22, 1896, Box 3, Folder 114, UMA.
3. Howard, Presidential Address.
4. Sessions testimony, CM-GC, *Hearing before the Joint Standing Committee*, p. 14.
5. Fernald testimony, ibid., p. 6.
6. W. Frost testimony, ibid., p. 6.
7. Forbush testimony, ibid., pp. 7–8.
8. Ibid., p. 17.
9. Fernald testimony, ibid., p. 18.
10. V. Frost testimony, ibid., p. 17.
11. Ibid.
12. Ibid., p. 19.
13. W. Frost testimony, ibid., p. 24.
14. Ibid.
15. Kirkland to Fernald, February 1, 1896, Box 2, Folder 72, UMA.
16. Kirkland to Fernald, February 6, 1896, Box 2, Folder 72, UMA.
17. Forbush to Fernald, February 5, 1896, Box 1, Folder 47, UMA.

18. Howard to Fernald, February 10, 1896, Box 8, Folder 181, UMA.
19. Howard to Fernald, February 11, 1896, Box 8, Folder 181, UMA.
20. Kirkland to Fernald, February 20, 1896, Box 2, Folder 72, UMA.
21. Forbush testimony, CM-GC, *Hearing before the Joint Standing Committee*, p. 7.
22. Appleton testimony, ibid., p. 7.
23. Scudder testimony, ibid., pp. 2–3.
24. Kirkland to Fernald, February 27, 1896, Box 2, Folder 72, UMA.
25. Ibid.
26. Goodwin testimony, CM-GC, *Hearing before the Joint Standing Committee*, p. 245.
27. Shaler testimony, ibid., p. 2.
28. Ibid.
29. Bailey testimony, *Hearing before the Joint Special Committee*, p. 771.
30. Forbush to Fernald, February 26, 1896, Box 1, Folder 47, UMA.
31. Sessions to Fernald, February 28, 1896, Box 3, Folder 114, UMA.
32. Kirkland to Fernald, February 28, 1896, Box 2, Folder 72, UMA.
33. Forbush testimony, *Hearing before the Joint Standing Committee*, p. 11.
34. Howard to Forbush, in ibid., p. 3.
35. Kirkland to Fernald, March 6, 1896, Box 2, Folder 72, UMA.
36. McCarthy testimony, *Hearing before the Joint Special Committee*, p. 514.
37. Hennelly testimony, ibid., p. 691.
38. Kirkland to Fernald, March 10, 1896, Box 2, Folder 72, UMA.
39. Kirkland to Fernald, March 7, 1896, Box 2, Folder 72, UMA.
40. Fowler to Fernald, February 27, 1896, Box 2, Folder 72, UMA.
41. Kirkland to Fernald, March 21, 1896, Box 2, Folder 72, UMA.
42. Kirkland to Fernald, April 23, 1896, Box 2, Folder 72, UMA.
43. CM-BA, *Report on the Work of Extermination* (1896), p. 18.
44. CM-House, *Report of the Special Committee, House Document No. 1138*, p. 6.
45. Fernald to Uhler, May 25, 1896, bMu 988.10.3–968.10.7, EML.
46. Fernald to Scudder, June 8, 1896, Scudder Correspondence, BSNH.
47. Sessions to Fernald, June 3, 1896, Box 3, Folder 114, UMA.
48. Barker testimony, CM-GC, *Hearing before the Joint Special Committee*, p. 743.
49. CM-House, *Debate*, p. 2.
50. Kirkland to Fernald, June 29, 1896, Box 8, Folder 195, UMA.
51. Sessions testimony, *Hearing before the Joint Standing Committee*, pp. 8–9.
52. Wood to Fernald, September 30, 1896.
53. Kirkland to Fernald, August 12, 1896, Box 2, Folder 72, UMA.
54. John B. Smith, *Economic Entomology*, p. 271.
55. CM-BA, *Report on the Work of Extermination* (1896), p. 38.
56. Ibid., p. 14.
57. Kirkland to Fernald, December 23, 1896, Box 2, Folder 72, UMA.
58. Fernald to Scudder, June 8, 1896, Scudder Correspondence, BSNH.
59. Ealand, *Insects and Man*, p. 68.
60. Kirkland to Fernald, October 19, 1896, Box 2, Folder 72, UMA.

13. A Moth Too Many

1. CM-BA, *Report on the Work of Extermination* (1897), p. 9.
2. CM-House, *Debate*, p. 7.
3. Ibid., p. 1.
4. Fernald to *Boston Advertiser*, February 2, 1899.
5. Mallis, *American Entomologists*, p. 315.
6. Ibid.
7. CM-BA, *Report on the Work of Extermination* (1897), p. 15.
8. Osgood, "State in Arms against a Caterpillar," p. 458.
9. Ibid., p. 459.
10. "Cost of Fighting a Pest."
11. Woodbury to Forbush, April 7, 1897, Agency Code EN4, MDC, Record Series 1055X, Book 7, MSA.
12. Kirkland to Fernald, May 4, 1897, Box 2, Folder 72, UMA.
13. Osgood, "State in Arms against a Caterpillar," p. 682.
14. Kirkland to Fernald, May 22, 1897, Box 2, Folder 72, UMA.
15. Kirkland, "Report to the Massachusetts Horticultural Society," 1902, in Fernald and Kirkland, *Brown-tail Moth*, p. 11.
16. Fernald and Kirkland, *Brown-tail Moth*, p. 17.
17. Ibid., p. 21.
18. Ibid., p. 32.
19. Ibid., pp. 35–36.
20. Kirkland to Fernald, July 6, 1897, Box 2, Folder 72, UMA.
21. Kirkland to Fernald, July 19, 1897, Box 2, Folder 72, UMA.
22. Kirkland to Fernald, August 4, 1897, Box 2, Folder 72, UMA.
23. Kirkland, "On the Preparation of Arsenate of Lead," pp. 46–48.
24. Forbush and Fernald, *Gypsy Moth*, p. 162.
25. Kirkland, "Danger from the Use of Lead Arsenate," p. 91.
26. F. J. Smith to Fernald, June 13, 1899, Box 8, Folder 221, UMA.
27. Whorton, *Before Silent Spring*, p. 41.
28. Ibid. pp. 36–67, 81–82.
29. Webster, "Present and Future of Applied Entomology," p. 9.
30. Howard, *Gipsy Moth in America*, pp. 24, 30, 35, 37.
31. Ibid., pp. 22–24.
32. Kirkland to Fernald, November 10, 1897, Box 2, Folder 72, UMA.
33. CM-BA, *Report on the Work of Extermination* (1897), pp. 13, 18.
34. Ibid., p. 15.
35. Ibid., p. 45.
36. Ibid., p. 50.

14. Do or Die

1. *Sixteenth Annual Report of the Maine Agricultural Experiment Station*, pp. 35–36.

2. Ibid., p. 36.

3. John B. Smith, "Germany's Exclusion of American Fruits," p. 432.

4. Fernald to Henry T. Fernald, April 20, 1898, Box 6, Folder 1, UMA.

5. Kirkland to Fernald, January 3, 1898, Box 2, Folder 72, UMA.

6. T. C. Lyford testimony, CM-GC, *Hearing before the Joint Special Committee*, p. 722.

7. Kirkland to Fernald, February 15, 1898, Box 2, Folder 72, UMA.

8. Kirkland to Fernald, March 17, 1898, Box 2, Folder 72, UMA.

9. "Scientific News," p. 385.

10. CM-BA, *Forty-Sixth Annual Report* (1898), p. 412.

11. Kirkland to Fernald, April 21, 1898, Box 2, Folder 72, UMA.

12. Woodbury to Forbush, April 7, 1898, Agency Code EN4 (MDC), Record Series 1055X, Book 8, MSA.

13. Howard, *Gipsy Moth in America*, p. 18.

14. CM-BA, *Forty-Sixth Annual Report* (1898), p. 463.

15. Osgood, "State in Arms against a Caterpillar," p. 462.

16. Forbush, "Recent Work of the Gypsy Moth Committee," p. 80.

17. CM-BA, *Forty-Sixth Annual Report* (1898), p. 431.

18. Howard to Fernald, November 7, 1898, Box 8, Folder 181, UMA.

19. Osgood, "Gypsy Moth in Massachusetts," p. 681.

20. L. W. Ross testimony, CM-GC, *Hearing before the Joint Special Committee*, p. 454.

21. A. E. Barker testimony, ibid., pp. 804–5.

22. Forbush to Fernald, November 30, 1898, Box 7, Folder 176, UMA.

23. CM-BA, *Forty-Sixth Annual Report* (1898), p. 416.

24. W. C. Wright testimony, CM-GC, *Hearing before the Joint Special Committee*, p. 634.

25. CM-BA, *Forty-Sixth Annual Report* (1898), p. 433.

26. Fernald to Dyar, September 15, 1898, Box 6, Folder 1, UMA.

27. Kirkland to Fernald, September 25, 1898, Box 2, Folder 72, UMA.

28. Howard to Fernald, November 7, 1898, Box 8, Folder 181, UMA.

29. CM-MPC, [Seventh] *Annual Report* (1898), pp. 33–34.

30. Ibid., pp. 51–52.

31. Bowker to Fernald, October 21, 1898, Box 1, Folder 9, UMA.

32. CM-BA, *Forty-Sixth Annual Report* (1898), p. 8.

33. Kirkland to Fernald, December 31, 1898 (1), Box 8, Folder 195, UMA.

34. Fernald to Dyar, December 19, 1898, Box 6, Folder 1, UMA.

35. Kirkland to Fernald, December 31, 1898 (2), Box 8, Folder 195, UMA.

15. Failure Is Not an Option

1. Kirkland to Fernald, January 4, 1899, Box 8, Folder 195, UMA.
2. CM-BA, *Forty-Sixth Annual Report* (1898), pp. 416, 422.
3. Ibid.
4. Roger Wolcott, "Governor's Inaugural Address," January 5, 1899, in CM-GC, *Acts and Resolves*, 1899.
5. Kirkland to Fernald, January 18, 1899, Box 8, Folder 195, UMA.
6. Ross testimony, *Hearing before the Joint Special Committee*, p. 460.
7. "Editorial Comment," p. 389.
8. Ross testimony, *Hearing before the Joint Special Committee*, p. 453.
9. USDA, *Proceedings of the Eleventh Annual Meeting of the Association of Economic Entomologists*, p. 105.
10. CM-BA, *Forty-Seventh Annual Report* (1899), p. 366.
11. Ibid., p. 367.
12. Osgood, "Gypsy Moth in Massachusetts," p. 688.
13. J. S. Pray testimony, CM-GC, *Hearing before the Joint Special Committee*, p. 273.
14. Ibid., p. 274.
15. C. W. Brown testimony, ibid., p. 1202.
16. Wright testimony, ibid., p. 632.
17. J. A. Farley testimony, ibid., p. 585.
18. Forbush and Fernald, *Gypsy Moth*, p. 96.
19. CM-BA, *Report on the Work of Extermination* (1897), p. 26.
20. I. J. Colbert testimony, CM-GC, *Hearing before the Joint Special Committee*, p. 590.
21. *Sixteenth Annual Report of the Maine Agricultural Experiment Station*, p. 37.
22. Fernald and Kirkland, *Brown-tail Moth*, p. 49.
23. Kirkland to Fernald, in Fernald, "Brown-tail Moth," p. 29.
24. F. J. Smith to Fernald, June 13, 1899, Box 8, Folder 221, UMA.
25. Kochi to Fernald, July 15, 1899, Box 8, Folder 192, UMA.
26. USDA, *Proceedings of the Eleventh Annual Meeting of the Association of Economic Entomologists*, p. 107.
27. Ibid., p. 6.
28. CM, *Special Bulletin of the Hatch Agricultural Experiment Station* (1899).
29. USDA, *Proceedings of the Eleventh Annual Meeting of the Association of Economic Entomologists*, p. 21.
30. Forbush testimony, CM-GC, *Hearing before the Joint Special Committee*, p. 408.
31. Crosby testimony, ibid., p. 914.
32. Ibid.
33. Osgood, "Gypsy Moth in Massachusetts," p. 684.
34. Seaburg and Seaburg, *Medford on the Mystic*, p. 53.
35. Wambaugh, "Present Scope of Government," p. 121.
36. CM-BA, *Forty-Seventh Annual Report* (1899), p. 349.

37. Howard and Fiske, *The Importation into the U. S. of the Parasites of the Gipsy Moth and the Brown-tail Moth*, p. 49.
38. J. G. Avery testimony, CM-GC, *Hearing before the Joint Special Committee*, p. 291.
39. May, "Edward Howe Forbush," p. 46.
40. McCarthy testimony, CM-GC, *Hearing before the Joint Special Committee*, p. 519.
41. Ibid., p. 514.
42. Fernald to Howard, October 21, 1899, Box 6, Folder 1, UMA.
43. Fernald to W.A.H., March 7, 1900, Box 6, Folder 1, UMA.
44. CM-BA, *Forty-Seventh Annual Report* (1889).
45. CM-BA, *Minutes* (1899), December 8, 1899.

16. The Last Hurrah

1. CM-BA, *Minutes* (1900).
2. R. W. Marshall testimony, CM-GC, *Hearing before the Joint Special Committee*, p. 490.
3. CM-BA, *Forty-Eighth Annual Report* (1900), p. 357.
4. CM-House, *Report of the Special Committee*, House Document No. 1138, p. 2.
5. Barker testimony, CM-GC *Hearing before the Joint Special Committee*, pp. 804–5.
6. Fernald testimony, ibid., p. 51.
7. Ross testimony, ibid., p. 452.
8. Fernald testimony, ibid., p. 1103.
9. Barker testimony, ibid., p. 805.
10. CM-House, *Report of the Special Committee*, House Document No. 1138, p. 4.
11. Forbush to Fernald, March 5, 1900, Box 8, Folder 195, UMA. This letter on the board's letterhead states that scouting parties had not found any brown-tail moths in New Hampshire.
12. Spooner to Massachusetts agriculture secretary, December 19, 1899, Box 8, Folder 195, UMA.
13. Fernald to Howard, January 8, 1900, Box 8, Folder 181, UMA.
14. Felt to Fernald, March 31, 1900, Box 7, Folder 173, UMA.
15. CM-House, *Report of the Special Committee*, House Document No. 1138, pp. 4–5.
16. Ibid., p. 5.
17. Crosby testimony, CM-GC, *Hearing before the Joint Special Committee*, p. 899.
18. CM-House, *Report of the Special Committee*, House Document No. 1138, p. 10.
19. Ibid., pp. 8–9.
20. J. F. Toole testimony, CM-GC, *Hearing before the Joint Special Committee*, p. 737.
21. R. Hoffman testimony, ibid., p. 1428.

22. CM-House, *Report of the Special Committee, House Document No. 1138*, p. 11.
23. Ibid., p. 12.
24. Ibid., pp. 12–13.
25. Ibid., p. 24.
26. Ibid.
27. Crosby testimony, CM-GC, *Hearing before the Joint Special Committee*, p. 902.
28. Ibid.
29. Kirkland testimony, ibid., p. 1414.
30. Ibid.
31. W. T. Sedgwick testimony, ibid., p. 1068.
32. CM-House, *Report of the Special Committee, House Document No. 1138*, p. 16.
33. Ibid.
34. Ibid.
35. Henshaw testimony, CM-GC, *Hearing before the Joint Special Committee*, p. 682.
36. Weed to Fernald, January 24, 1894, Box 8, Folder 234, UMA.
37. Osborn, H., "Presidential Address to the Tenth Annual Meeting of the Association of Economic Entomologists," pp. 9–10.
38. Fernald to Howard, February 10, 1900, Box 6, Folder 1, UMA.
39. Fernald to C. R. Osten-Sacken, June 24, 1902, Box 6, Folder 1, UMA.
40. Kirkland testimony, CM-GC, *Hearing before the Joint Special Committee*, p. 1416.
41. Fernald testimony, ibid., p. 1072.
42. Ibid., p. 1083.
43. Forbush testimony, ibid., p. 1268.
44. Ibid., pp. 1303–5.
45. CM-BA, *Forty-Eighth Annual Report* (1900), pp. 366–67.
46. Osgood, "Gypsy Moth in Massachusetts," p. 677.
47. CM-BA, *Forty-Eighth Annual Report* (1900), p. 367–68.
48. CM-BA, *Forty-Ninth Annual Report* (1901), p. 4.
49. Ibid., p. 6.
50. CM-GC, *Acts and Resolves* 1901, p. 295.
51. Marlatt, "Fifty Years of Entomological Progress, Part I," p. 13.
52. Fernald to Howard, April 13, 1903, Box 6, Folder 1, UMA.
53. Kirkland to Fernald, January 20, 1899, Box 8, Folder 195, UMA.
54. Osgood, "Gypsy Moth in Massachusetts," p. 688.
55. Forbush and Fernald, *Gypsy Moth*, p. 215.
56. Howard, Presidential Address, p. 59.
57. Fernald testimony, CM-GC, *Hearing before the Joint Standing Committee*, n.p.
58. Shaler, *Autobiography*, pp. 396–97. There is no surviving record of Shaler as a park commissioner, and archived documents of the Metropolitan District Commission confirm that he never served on the MDC board.
59. Fernald to Bowditch, February 5, 1904, Box 6, Folder 1, UMA.

60. May, "Edward Howe Forbush," p. 55.
61. Osborn, "Duty of Economic Entomology," p. 7.
62. Ibid.

Epilogue

1. USDA, *Proceedings of the Fifteenth Annual Meeting of the Association of Economic Entomologists*, p. 56.
2. Forbush testimony, CM-GC, *Hearing before the Joint Special Committee*, p. 1303.
3. CM-BA, *Report of the Board of Agriculture on Extermination of the Gypsy Moth* (1901), p. 6.
4. Ibid., p. 7.
5. Fiske, *Parasites of the Gypsy and Brown-Tail Moths*, p. 12.
6. Howard and Fiske, *The Importation into the U.S. of the Parasites of the Gipsy Moth and the Brown-tail Moth*, p. 14.
7. Ibid., p. 221.
8. Ibid., p. 225.
9. Ibid., p. 221.
10. "Appropriation to Fight the Moth," p. 12.
11. "The Parasite Element of Natural Control," p. 411.
12. "The Present Status of Biological Control Work in California," p. 294.
13. Howard and Fiske, *The Importation into the U.S. of the Parasites of the Gipsy Moth and the Brown-tail Moth*, p. 5.
14. Ibid.
15. Howard, "Explorers of a New Kind," pp. 38–67.
16. Carson, *Silent Spring*, p. 11.
17. Hornaday, *Our Vanishing Wildlife*, p. 330.
18. *Twenty-Fifth Annual Report of the Massachusetts Agricultural Experiment Station*, pp. 81–84.
19. Sanderson, *Insect Pests of Farm, Garden, and Orchard*, pp. 5–6.
20. Forbush testimony, *Hearing before the Joint Standing Committee*, p. 7.
21. Burgess, "Report on the Gipsy Moth Work in New England."
22. Burgess, "Value to Uninfested States of Gypsy Moth Control," p. 559.
23. Ibid.
24. Turner, "Entomology in Connecticut," p. 35.
25. Weiss, H. B., *New Jersey Department of Agriculture*, p. 168.
26. *Fourteenth Annual Report of the Massachusetts State Forester*, p. 11.
27. CM-BA, *Fifty-Ninth Annual Report*, p. 291.
28. Burgess, "Recent Work in Control of Gypsy Moth and Brown-tail Moth," p. 774.
29. Burgess, "Gipsy Moth Work West of the Connecticut River," p. 585.
30. "Gipsy Moth Barrier Zone Maintenance Problem," p. 721.
31. Large portions of the same general area were redesignated as a "suppression zone" after World War II and finally abandoned in the 1960s.

32. Russell, *War and Nature*.

33. Weseloh, "People and the Gypsy Moth," p. 183.

34. Messenger and Popham, "From 0 to 5,000 in 34 Years," p. 251.

35. Todd and McGregor, "Insecticides and Bees," p. 131.

36. Bruce, "Insecticides and Flies," p. 326.

37. Corliss, "Gypsy Moth," p. 698.

38. Carson, *Silent Spring*, p. 258.

39. Weseloh, "People and the Gypsy Moth," p. 183.

40. Graham, *Dragon Hunters*, pp. 103–5.

41. Carson, *Silent Spring*, p. 161.

42. Russell, *War and Nature*, p. 214.

43. Waggoner, Paul E., "James Gordon Horsfall," p. 204. See also http://www.books
.nap.edu/books/; and "Neely Turner 1901–1989," *American Entomologist*,
p. 170.

44. Carson, *Silent Spring*, p. 158.

45. Ibid., p. 160.

46. Russell, *War and Nature*, p. 221.

47. Ibid., pp. 216–18.

48. Gore, introduction to 1994 printing of *Silent Spring*, p. xix.

49. Kegg, "Realities of the Gypsy Moth Problem," p. 154.

50. *Forest Pest Control*, pp. 114–15.

51. Ibid., p. 155.

52. The definition of "defoliation" is rather loose. It implies total leaf loss, but more
likely refers to lesser degrees of damage. Tree "defoliation" does not necessarily
equate with tree mortality.

53. Hajek, "Entomophaga maimaiga," p. 1. See also http://www.nysaes.cornell.edu/
ent/bcconf/talks/hajek.html.

54. Fosbroke and Hicks, *Coping with the Gypsy Moth*, p. 2.

55. Imported predator insects are also thought to have completely dominated the satin
moth (*Stilnoptia salcis*), a foreign insect, closely related to the gypsy and brown-
tail moths, that was brought into Massachusetts around the turn of the nineteenth
century.

56. Hajek, "Entomophaga maimaiga," p. 2.

57. Author's personal observations from gypsy moth informational meetings held in
Maryland during the early 1990s.

58. *Eradication of Exotic Pests*, p. 230.

59. Gansner et al., "Tracking Changes in the Susceptibility of Forest Land Infested
with Gypsy Moth."

60. Bailey, "Natural Checks," p. 191.

Bibliography

"About Town Matters in Arlington." *Arlington Advocate*. February 14, 1890.

Alyohkin, Andrea. "A Short History of the [Entomology] Department." http://www .umass.edu/ent/about/history (accessed September 1999).

Annals of the Astronomical Observatory of Harvard College. Vol. 8. Cambridge: Press of John Wilson & Son, 1876.

"Appropriation to Fight the Moth." *College Sentinel*, October 2, 1907. Amherst: Massachusetts Agricultural College.

"Army of Squirming Worms," *Boston Herald*. May 27, 1889.

Bailey, Liberty Hyde. "Natural Checks." In *Survival of the Unlike: A Collection of Essays Suggested by the Study of Domestic Plants*. New York: Macmillan, 1896.

Baker, K., and T. E. Heinton. "Traps Have Some Value." In *Insects; Yearbook of Agriculture*. U. S. Department of Agriculture. Washington, D.C.: GPO, 1952.

Barnes, Jeffery K. *Asa Fitch and the Emergence of American Entomology*. New York State Museum Bulletin, no. 461. Albany: University of the State of New York, 1988.

Barrett, Edward W. *Historical Sketches: Schools of Medford and Other Topics*. Medford, Mass., 1936.

Berenbaum, May R. *Bugs in the System; Insects and Their Impact on Human Affairs*. Reading Pa.: Perseus Books, 1995.

Biographical Review. Vol. 27, *Containing Life Sketches of Leading Citizens of Middlesex County, Massachusetts*. Boston: Biographical Review Publishing Company, 1898.

Boston Society of Natural History. *Proceedings of the Boston Society of Natural History* vol. 11, *1866–1868*. Lyman Library Archives. Museum of Science, Boston.

Bronson, T. E., and Earl D. Anderson. "Choosing and Using Hand Equipment." In *Insects: Yearbook of Agriculture*. U.S. Department of Agriculture. Washington, D.C.: GPO, 1952.

Bruce, W. N. "Insecticides and Flies." In *Insects: Yearbook of Agriculture*. U.S. Department of Agriculture. Washington, D.C.: GPO, 1952.

Burgess, Albert Franklin. "Report on the Gipsy Moth Work in New England." *Bulletin of the U.S. Department of Agriculture, Bureau of Entomology*, no. 304. Washington, D.C.: GPO, May 21, 1915.

———. "Gipsy Moth Work West of the Connecticut River and in Pennsylvania and New Jersey in 1933." *Journal of Economic Entomology* 27 (June 1934).

————. "Recent Work in Control of Gypsy Moth and Brown-Tail Moth." *Journal of Economic Entomology* 29, no. 4 (August 1936).

————. "The Value to Uninfested States of Gypsy Moth Control and Extermination." *Journal of Economic Entomology* 33, no. 3 (June 1940).

Burson, George. "United States 1890s: Populism." In *U.S. History Curriculum*. Aspen, Colo.: Aspen School District, 2001.

Caesar, L. "Fifty Years of Entomological Progress, Part II, 1899 to 1909." *Journal of Economic Entomology* 33, no. 1 (February 1940).

Cambridge City Directory for 1873, Cambridge, Mass: Greenhouse, Jones, 1873.

Carson, Rachel. *Silent Spring*. New York: Houghton Mifflin, 1962.

"Cecropia Moth." *American Entomologist* 2, no. 4 (February 1870).

Church, John A., "Scientific Miscellany." *Galaxy* 23, no. 5 (May 1877).

Commonwealth of Massachusetts. [First] *Annual Report of the Superintendent for Supjpressing the Gypsy and Brown-Tail Moths* (1905). Boston: Wright & Potter, 1906.

————. [Second] *Annual Report of the Superintendent for Suppressing the Gypsy and Brown-Tail Moths* (1906). Boston: Wright & Potter, 1907.

————. *Birth Records*. Microfilm spool 19, vol. 115, record No. 185. Massachusetts State Archives, Dorchester.

————. *Report of the Board of World's Fair Managers*. Boston: Wright & Potter, 1894.

————. *Special Bulletin of the Hatch Experiment Station of the Massachusetts Agricultural College*. Amherst: Massachusetts Agricultural College, 1889.

————. *Statements from Eye-Witnesses of the Ravages of the Gypsy Moth* (ca. 1894). Call no. 632.34M3.S795, Massachusetts State House Library, Boston.

————, Board of Agriculture. *Thirteenth Annual Report of the Secretary* (1865). Boston: Wright & Potter, 1866.

————, Board of Agriculture. *Thirty-fifth Annual Report of the Secretary* (1887). Boston: Wright & Potter, 1888.

————, Board of Agriculture. *Thirty-eighth Annual Report of the Secretary* (1890). Boston: Wright & Potter, 1891.

————, Board of Agriculture. *Fortieth Annual Report of the Secretary* (1892). Boston: Wright & Potter, 1893.

————, Board of Agriculture. *Forty-sixth Annual Report of the Secretary* (1898). Boston: Wright & Potter, 1899.

————, Board of Agriculture. *Forty-seventh Annual Report of the Secretary* (1899). Boston: Wright & Potter, 1900.

————, Board of Agriculture. *Forty-eighth Annual Report of the Secretary* (1900). Boston: Wright & Potter, 1901.

————, Board of Agriculture. *Forty-ninth Annual Report of the Secretary* (1901). Boston: Wright & Potter, 1902.

————, Board of Agriculture. *Bulletin on the Gypsy Moth Danger and Protection From It*. Boston: Wright & Potter, 1898.

————, Board of Agriculture. *Minutes* (1891, 1893, 1894, 1895, 1899, 1900).

————, Board of Agriculture. [*Special*] *Report on the Work of Extermination of the Ocneria Dispar, or Gypsy Moth* (1891). Boston: Wright & Potter, 1892.

————, Board of Agriculture. *Report on the Work of Extermination of the Gypsy Moth* (1892). Boston: Wright & Potter, 1893.

————, Board of Agriculture. *Report on the Work of Extermination of the Gypsy Moth* (1893). Boston: Wright & Potter, 1894.

————, Board of Agriculture. *Report on the Work of Extermination of the Gypsy Moth* (1894). Boston: Wright & Potter, 1895.

————, Board of Agriculture. *Report on the Work of the Extermination of the Gypsy Moth* (1895). Boston: Wright & Potter, 1896.

————, Board of Agriculture. *Report on the Work of the Extermination of the Gypsy Moth* (1896). Boston: Wright & Potter, 1897.

————, Board of Agriculture. *Report on the Work of the Extermination of the Gypsy Moth* (1897). Boston: Wright & Potter, 1898.

————, General Court. *Acts and Resolves Passed in the Years 1890–91.* Boston: Wright & Potter, 1891.

————, General Court. *Acts and Resolves Passed in the Years 1892–93.* Boston: Wright & Potter, 1893.

————, General Court. *Acts and Resolves Passed in the Year 1896.* Boston: Wright & Potter, 1896.

————, General Court. *Acts and Resolves Passed in the Year 1901.* Boston: Wright & Potter, 1901.

————, General Court. *Report of a Hearing Before the Joint Standing Committee on Agriculture upon the Extermination of the Gypsy Moth, January 28–February 28, 1896.* Call no. 632.34M3.G32h. Special Collections and Archives. State House Library, Boston.

————, General Court. *Report of a Hearing Before the Joint Special Committee appointed to Inquire into the present state of the work of Exterminating the Gypsy Moth, January 30–February 26, 1900, Vol. 1 and 2.* Call no. 632.34M3.G32he. Special Collections and Archives. State House Library, Boston.

————, House. *Debate in the House on a Bill making an appropriation for continuing the work of exterminating the Gypsy Moth, second Reading. January 29, 1897.* Call no. PAM 632.34M3 G32d. Special Collections and Archives. State House Library, Boston.

————, House. *Report of the Special Committee, House Document No. 1138.* Boston: Wright & Potter, 1900.

————, Metropolitan Park Commission. [Third] *Annual Report of the Metropolitan Park Commissioners* (1894). Boston: Wright & Potter, 1895.

————, Metropolitan Park Commission. [Seventh] *Annual Report of the Metropolitan Park Commissioners* (1898). Boston: Wright & Potter, 1899.

"Communications." *Aggie Life* 1, no. 99. (1891) Amherst: Massachusetts Agricultural College.

Comstock, Anna Botsford. *The Comstocks of Cornell*, edited by Glenn W. Herrick and Ruby Green Smith. Ithaca, N.Y.: Cornell University Press, 1953.

Cooper, Lane. *Louis Agassiz as a Teacher.* Ithaca, 1945.

Cooper, Thomas C. "It's a Bug-Eat-Bug World." *Atlantic Monthly* 287, no. 2 (February 2001).

Corliss, John. "The Gypsy Moth." In *Insects; Yearbook of Agriculture.* U. S. Department of Agriculture. Washington, D.C.: GPO, 1952.

"Cost of Fighting a Pest." *New York Times.* May 1, 1897.

Croker, Robert A. *Steven Forbes and the Rise of American Ecology.* Washington, D.C.: Smithsonian Institution Press, 2001.

Fernald, Charles H. "The Evolution of Economic Entomology." In *Proceedings of the Eighth Annual Meeting of the Association of Economic Entomologists*, U.S. Department of Agriculture, Division of Entomology, bulletin no. 6, n.s. Washington, D.C.: GPO, 1896.

———. "Notes on the Gypsy Moth in Massachusetts." In *Proceedings of the Seventh Annual Meeting of the Association of Economic Entomologists.* U.S. Department of Agriculture, Division of Entomology, bulletin no. 2, n.s. Washington, D.C.: GPO, 1895.

Fernald, Charles H., and Archie H. Kirkland. "A New Insect Pest in Massachusetts: The Brown-Tail Moth." Amherst, Mass.: Hatch Experiment Station, 1897.

———. *Brown-tail Moth.* Massachusetts State Board of Agriculture. Boston: Wright & Potter, 1903.

Fernald, Henry Torsey. "Address to the Fernald Club." In *Fernald Club Yearbook.* Amherst: University of Massachusetts. January 1939.

Fiske, William Fuller. *Parasites of the Gypsy and Brown-Tail Moths Introduced into Massachusetts—A General Survey of the Work.* Boston: Wright & Potter, 1910.

Forbush, Edward Howe. "Birds Useful to Agriculture." In *Forty-eighth Annual Report of the Massachusetts State Board of Agriculture.* Boston: Wright & Potter, 1901.

———. "Recent Work of the Gypsy Moth Committee." In *Proceedings of the Tenth Annual Meeting of the Association of Economic Entomologists*, U.S. Department of Agriculture, Division of Entomology, bulletin no. 17, n.s. Washington, D.C.: GPO, 1898.

Forbush, Edward H., and Charles Henry Fernald. *The Gypsy Moth, Porthetria dispar (Linn.); A Report of the Work of Destroying the Insect in the Commonwealth of Massachusetts, Together With an Account of its History and Habits Both in Massachusetts and Europe.* Massachusetts State Board of Agriculture. Boston: Wright & Potter, 1896.

Fosbroke, Sandra, and Ray H. Hicks, Jr. *Coping With the Gypsy Moth in the New Frontier.* Morgantown: West Virginia University Books, 1987.

Foster, David R., and John F. O'Keefe. *New England Forests Through Time.* Cambridge: Harvard University Press, 2000.

Gansner, David A., and John W. Quimby, Susan L. King, Stanford L. Arner, David A. Drake. "Tracking Changes in the Susceptibility of Forest Land Infested with Gypsy Moth." *Gypsy Moth News*, edited by Daniel B. Twardus (electronic publication).

Morgantown, W. Va.: U.S. Forest Service, http://www.fs.fed.us/ne/morgantown/4557/gmoth/gmnews.html. (connection refused since September 2003).

Gaul, Albro F. *The Wonderful World of Insects.* New York: Rinehart & Company, 1953.

Gerardi, Michael H., and James K. Grimm. *The History, Biology, Damage and Control of the Gypsy Moth.* Cranbury, N. J.: Associated University Presses, 1979.

Ginger, Ray, ed. *The Nationalizing of American Life, 1870–1900.* New York: Free Press, 1965.

Glaser, R. W. "Wilt of Gypsy Moth Caterpillars." *Journal of Agricultural Research* 4, no. 2 (May 15, 1915).

Gore, Albert. Introduction to *Silent Spring.* New York: Houghton-Mifflin, 1994.

Graham, Frank Jr. *The Dragon Hunters.* New York: E. P. Dutton, 1984.

Guberlet, Muriel L. *The Windows to His World: The Story of Trevor Kincaid.* Palo Alto, Calif.: Pacific Books, 1975.

Haglund, Karl. "Emerald Metropolis," In *Arnoldia* 53, no. 4 (1993).

Hajek, Ann E. "Entomophaga maimaiga: A Fungal Pathogen of the Gypsy Moth in the Limelight." Paper presented to Cornell Community Conference on Biological Control, Ithaca, N.Y., April 11–13, 1996.

Henshaw, Samuel. "Report Upon the Gypsy Moth in Massachusetts." *Reports of Observations and Experiments in the Practical Work of the Division* [of Entomology]. U.S. Department of Agriculture, bulletin no. 26, Washington, D.C.: GPO, 1892.

Herman, Jan K., and Brenda G. Corbin. "Leopold Trouvelot: From Moths to Mars." *Heavens Above; Art & Actuality.* Exhibition at Science, Industry and Business Branch. New York Public Library, Spring 2001.

"History of a Publishing House." *Scribner's Magazine* 16, no. 6 (December 1894).

Hitchcock, Stephen W. "Professor Trouvelot's Mistake" *Yankee Magazine.* June 1971.

Hobbs, William Herbert, "Nathaniel Southgate Shaler" [obituary]. In *Wisconsin Academy of Science, Arts, and Letters*, undated detachment ca. 1906, Ernst Mayr Library, Special Collections, call no. bMu 7518.80.1, Harvard University Archives, Cambridge.

Hornaday, William Temple. *Our Vanishing Wildlife; its extermination and preservation.* New York: New York Zoological Society, 1913.

Howard, Leland Ossian. "Presidential Address." In *Proceedings of the Sixth Annual Meeting of the Association of Economic Entomologists.* US Department of Agriculture, Division of Entomology, bulletin no. 2, n.s. Washington, D.C.: GPO, 1894.

———. "Brief Account of the Rise and Present Condition of Official Economic Entomology." Extract from the President's Address before the Sixth Annual Meeting of the Association of Economic Entomologists. In Forbush and Fernald, *The Gypsy Moth.*

———. "Explorers of a New Kind." *National Geographic* Vol. 26, no. 1 (July 1914).

———. *The Gypsy Moth in America.* U.S. Department of Agriculture, Division of Entomology. Washington, D.C.: GPO, n.d.

————. *Fighting the Insects*. Reprint. New York: Arno Press, 1980.

————. *A History of Applied Entomology*. Washington, D.C.: Smithsonian Institution, Lord Baltimore Press, 1930.

————. *The Insect Menace*. New York: Century, 1931.

————. "Parasite Element of Natural Control of Injurious Insects and Its Control By Man." *Annual Report of the Smithsonian*. Washington, D.C.: GPO, 1927.

Howard, Leland Ossian, and William Fuller Fiske. *Importation into the U.S. of the Parasites of the Gypsy Moth and the Brown-tail Moth*. U.S. Department of Agriculture, Bureau of Entomology, bulletin no. 91. Washington, D.C.: GPO, 1911.

Hubbell, Sue. *Broadsides from the Other Orders*. New York: Random House, 1993.

Jack, J. G. "Can the Gypsy Moth be Exterminated?" *Garden and Forest*, March 11, 1891.

Kegg, John D. "The Realities of the Gypsy Moth Problem in the Northeast." *Bulletin of the Entomological Society of America* 24, no. 2 (1978).

Kirkland, Archie Howard. "Danger from the Use of Lead Arsenate." In *Report of the State Board of Agriculture* [1897]. Boston: Wright & Potter, 1898.

————. "On the Preparation of Arsenate of Lead." In *Proceedings of the Ninth Annual Meeting of the Association of Economic Entomologists*. U.S. Department of Agriculture, Division of Entomology, bulletin no. 9. Washington, D.C.: GPO, 1897.

Landsburg, Alan. *The Insects Are Coming*. New York: Warner Books, 1978.

Lauck, Joanne Elizabeth. *The Voice of the Infinite in the Small: Revisioning the Insect-Human Connection*. Mill Spring, N. Carolina: Blue Water Publishing, 1999.

Lawrence, William B. *Proceedings of the Two Hundred Seventy-fifth Anniversary of the Settlement of Medford, Massachusetts*. Medford: Executive Committee, 1905.

Leighton, Margaret Wentworth. "New England Butterflies." *New England Magazine* 18 no. 2 (April 1895).

"Letter," *Aggie Life* 1, no. 99. Amherst: Massachusetts Agricultural College, n.d.

Liebhold, Andrew M. "Etienne Leopold Trouvelot; Perpetrator of Our Problem" *Gypsy Moth News* 20 (electronic publication). Morgantown, W. Va.: U. S. Forest Service. http://www.fs.fed.us/ne/morgantown/4557/gmoth/gmnews.html. (connection refused since September 2003).

Liebhold, Andrew M., Victor Mastro, and Paul W. Schaeffer. "Learning from the Legacy of Leopold Trouvelot." *Bulletin of the Entomological Society of America* 35 (Summer 1989).

Lintner, James Albert. "Our Insect Enemies and how to Meet Them." *Eighth Report of the Injurious and Other Insects of the State of New York*. Albany: University of the State of New York, 1893.

Livingstone, David N. *Nathaniel Southgate Shaler and the Culture of American Science*. Tuscaloosa: University of Alabama Press, 1987.

Lodeman, E. G. *The Spraying of Plants*. New York: Macmillan, 1908.

Lurie, Edward. *Louis Agassiz: A Life in Science*. Baltimore: Johns Hopkins University Press, 1988.

Mallis, Arnold. *American Entomologists*. New Brunswick, N.J.: Rutgers University Press, 1971.

Marlatt, Charles Lester. "Fifty Years of entomological Progress, Part I, 1889 to 1899." In *Journal of Economic Entomology* 33, no. 1. (February 1940).

Maine Agricultural Experiment Station. [Sixteenth] *Annual Report*. Maine: 1898.

May, John Bichard. "Edward Howe Forbush: A Biographical Sketch." In *Proceedings of the Boston Society of Natural History* 39, no. 2. (April 1938).

"Members of the First Metropolitan Commission." In *History and Description of the Boston Metropolitan Parks*. Boston: Wright & Potter, 1900.

Messenger, Kenneth, and W. L. Popham. "From 0 to 5,000 in 34 Years." In *Insects: Yearbook of Agriculture*. U. S. Department of Agriculture. Washington, D.C.: GPO, 1952.

Miller, Gary L., "Historical and Natural History: Insects and the Civil War." *American Entomologist*, 43: 227–45.

Miller, Richard S., ed. *Forest Pest Control*. Vol. 4. Washington, D.C.: National Academy of Sciences, 1975.

Morgan, Keith N. "Charles Eliot, Landscape Architect: An Introduction to His Life and Work." *Arnoldia* 59, no. 2. (1999). Reprinted from Charles W. Eliot, *Charles Eliot, Landscape Architect* (rept. of 1902 ed., Amherst: University of Massachusetts Press / Library of American Landscape History, 1999).

Museum of Comparative Zoology. [Fifth] *Annual Report of the Trustees* (1864). Boston: Wright & Potter, 1864.

———. [Sixth] *Annual Report of the Trustees* (1864). Boston: Wright & Potter, 1865.

New Hampshire. *Twentieth Annual report of the Trustees of the College of Agriculture*. Concord: Ira C. Evans, Public Printer, 1900.

Olmsted, Frederick Law, Sr. and Frederick Law (John) Olmsted Jr. "Landscape Architects' Report." In *Report of the Metropolitan Park Commissioners* (1894). Boston: Wright & Potter, 1895. Agency code EN4.10, record series 1318S (MDC) Metropolitan Park Commission Annual Reports. Massachusetts State Archives, Dorchester.

Osborn, Herbert. "The Duty of Economic Entomology." In *Proceedings of the Tenth Annual Meeting of the Association of Economic Entomologists*. U.S. Department of Agriculture, bulletin no. 17, n.s. Washington, D.C.: GPO, 1898.

Osgood, Fletcher. "A State in Arms against a Caterpillar." *Harper's New Monthly Magazine* 95, no. 565 (June 1897).

———. "The Gypsy Moth in Massachusetts." *New England Magazine* 21, no. 6, n.s. (February 1900).

Pauly, Philip J. "Beauty and Menace of the Japanese Cherry Trees." *Isis* 87 (1996).

———. *Biologists and the Promise of American Life*. Princeton: Princeton University Press, 2000.

———. "Fighting the Hessian Fly: American and British Responses to Insect Invasions, 1776–1789," *Environmental History*. July 2002.

Peigler, Richard S. "Wild Silks of the World." *American Entomologist* 39, no. 3 (Fall 1993).

Pier, Arthur Stanwood. *The Story of Harvard*. Boston: Little, Brown, 1913.

"Portrait of William R. Sessions Given M.A.C." In *Springfield Republican*, May 11, 1921. Presidents and Trustees Collection, Record Group 2, Series 3, Special Collections and Archives, W.E.B. Du Bois Library, University of Massachusetts Amherst.

Ramsey, Harry B. "Notes on the Discovery of Lead Arsenate." *Fernald Club Yearbook, 1940*. Record Group 40, Series E4/00, W.E.B. Du Bois Library, Special Collections and Archives, University of Massachusetts Amherst.

Riley, Charles V. *Second Report on the Noxious, Beneficial, and Other Insects of Missouri*. Jefferson City, Mo.: Horace Wilcox, Public Printer, 1870.

———. *Fourth Annual Report on the Noxious, Beneficial, and Other Insects of the State of Missouri*. Jefferson City, Mo.: Rogan and Carter, 1872.

———. "Importation of Ocneria Dispar." *Insect Life* 2, no. 3. January/February 1889).

———. "Japanese Parasite of the Gypsy Moth." *Insect Life* 4, nos. 5–6 (December 1891).

———. "Outlook for Applied Entomology." *Insect Life* 3, no. 5 (January 1891).

———. "Report of a Discussion of the Gypsy Moth." *Insect Life* 3, nos. 9–10 (June 1891).

Riley, Charles V., and Leland O. Howard. "Experience with the Gypsy Moth." *Insect Life* 3, no. 3 (November 1890).

———. "Extermination of the Gypsy Moth." *Insect Life* 3, nos. 9–10 (June 1891).

———. "Further Notes on the Japanese Gypsy Moth and its Parasites." *Insect Life* 5, no. 3 (January 1893).

———. "Gypsy Moth in Cambridge." *Insect Life* 6, no. 4. (May 1894).

———. "Imported Gypsy Moth." *Insect Life* 2, nos. 7–8 (January/February 1890).

———. "Legislation against the Gypsy Moth," *Insect Life* 3, no. 2 (September 1890).

———. "Parasite of the Japanese Gypsy Moth." *Insect Life* 6, no. 1 (November 1893).

Rogers, Dexter M., and Albert Franklin Burgess. *Report on the Field Work Against the Gipsy Moth and the Brown-Tail Moth*. U.S. Bureau of Entomology, bulletin no. 87. Washington, D.C.: GPO, 1910.

Russell, Edmund. *War and Nature*. Cambridge: Cambridge University Press, 2001.

Samuels, Edward A. *The Birds of New England*. Boston: Noyes, Holmes and Company, 1870.

———. "Summer Entomology." *Scribner's Monthly Magazine* 18, no. 3 (July 1879).

Sanderson, E. Dwight. *Insect Pests of Farm, Garden, and Orchard*. New York: John Wiley & Sons, 1912.

Sawyer, Richard C. *To Make a Spotless Orange*. Ames, Iowa: State University Press, 1996.

Scherbakov, T. C. "Observations on the Gipsy Moth." *Works of the Natural History Museum of the Tauric Government Semstvo, 1914* 3. Simpherpol, Russia: Tauric Government Semstvo Press, 1914. (Typescript extraction, Comstock Entomological Library, Cornell University, Ithaca).

"Scientific News." *American Naturalist* 32, no. 377. (May 1898).

Scudder, Samuel Hubbard. *Butterflies of the Eastern United States and Canada, with special reference to New England.* Vols. 1–3. Cambridge, Mass: By the author, 1888–89.

———. "Notes on Drawings." Handwritten MS. In Scudder Collection, Box 6, Lyman Library Archives, Museum of Science, Boston.

Seaburg, Carl, and Alan Seaburg. *Medford on the Mystic.* Medford: Carl and Alan Seaburg, 1980.

Shaler, Nathaniel Southgate. *Kentucky Geological Survey.* Boston: J. Mayer & Co., 1875.

———. *Autobiography of Nathaniel Southgate Shaler, with a Supplementary Memoir by His Wife.* Boston: Houghton Mifflin, 1909.

"Short History of the MPC." http://www.magnet.state.ma.us/mdc/history.html (accessed September 1999).

Smith, Edward H. "Entomological Society of America: The First Hundred Years, 1889–1989." *Bulletin of the Entomological Society of America,* Fall 1989.

Smith, Harry S. "Present Status of Biological Control Work in California." *Journal of Economic Entomology* 19, no. 2 (April 1926).

Smith, John Bernhard. *Economic Entomology for the Farmer and Fruit Grower.* Philadelphia: J. B. Lippincot, 1896.

———. "Germany's Exclusion of American Fruits." *North American Review* 166, no. 497 (April 1898).

Sorensen, W. Conner. *Brethren of the Net: American Entomology, 1840–1880.* Tuscaloosa: University of Alabama Press, 1995.

"Successful Career Ended" [obituary of Warren W. Rawson]. *Arlington Advocate,* August 15, 1908.

Swade, Doron. *The Difference Engine: Charles Babbage and the Quest to Build the First Computer.* London: Viking Press, 2000.

Thornton, Tamara Plakins. *Cultivating Gentlemen: The Meaning of Country Life among the Boston Elite, 1750–1860.* New Haven: Yale University Press, 1989.

"Three Architectural Tours." Campus Beautification Committee, UMass Arts Council, and the University Gallery. Amherst: University of Massachusetts, 2000.

Todd, Frank E., and S. E. McGregor. "Insecticides and Bees." In *Insects: Yearbook of Agriculture.* U.S. Department of Agriculture. Washington, D.C.: GPO, 1952.

Todd, Kim. *Tinkering With Eden: A Natural History of Exotics in America.* New York: W. W. Norton, 2001.

"Trouvelot, E. Leopold." In *Dictionary of Scientific Biography* vol. 8. Edited by Charles Coulston Gillespie. New York: Charles Scribner's Sons, 1978.

Trouvelot, E. Leopold. "American Silkworm." *American Naturalist* 1–12. Edited by Alpheus Spring Packard, Edward S. Morse, Alpheus Hyatt, and W. F. Putnam. Salem: The Essex Institute, 1868.

———. "On a Method of Stimulating Union Between Insects of Different Species." *Proceedings of the Boston Society of Natural History* 11 (1867).

———. "Monstrosities Observed in Wings of Lepidopterous Insects and How They May Be Produced." *Proceedings of the Boston Society of Natural History* 11 (1867).

———. "Observations on the Phasmidae." *Proceedings of the Boston Society of Natural History* 11 (1868).

———. "Tendencies of Trees to Bend Toward the East." In *Proceedings of the Boston Society of Natural History* 13 (1870).

———. "The Use of Antennae in Insects." *American Naturalist* 11, no. 4 (April 1877).

Turner, Neely. "Entomology in Connecticut." *Twenty-fifth Anniversary Book.*

U.S. Department of Agriculture, Division of Entomology. [Proceedings] *First Annual Meeting of the Association of Economic Entomologists.* Periodical bulletin. Washington, D.C.: GPO, December 1889.

———. *Proceedings of the Sixth Annual Meeting of the Association of Economic Entomologists,* Washington, D.C.: GPO, 1894.

———. *Proceedings of the Seventh Annual Meeting of the Association of Economic Entomologists,* Bulletin no. 2, n.s. Washington, D.C.: GPO, 1895.

———. *Proceedings of the Eighth Annual Meeting of the Association of Economic Entomologists,* Bulletin no. 6, n.s. Washington, D.C.: GPO, 1896.

———. *Proceedings of the Ninth Annual Meeting of the Association of Economic Entomologists,* Bulletin No. 9, n.s. Washington, D.C.: GPO, 1897.

———. *Proceedings of the Tenth Annual Meeting of the Association of Economic Entomologists,* Bulletin no. 17, n.s. Washington, D.C.: GPO, 1898.

———. *Proceedings of the Eleventh Annual Meeting of the Association of Economic Entomologists,* Bulletin No. 20, n.s. Washington, D.C.: GPO, 1899.

———. *Proceedings of the Fifteenth Annual Meeting of the Association of Economic Entomologists,* Bulletin no. 40, n.s. Washington, D.C.: GPO, 1903.

Waggoner, Paul E. "James Gordon Horsfall, January 9, 1905–March 22, 1995." National Academy of Sciences. *Biographical Memoirs,* vol. 72. Washington, D.C.: National Academy Press, 1997.

Wambaugh, Eugene. "The Present Scope of Government." *Atlantic Monthly* 15, no. 483 (January 1898).

Ward, Alice Bailey. "An Agricultural Experiment Station." *New England Magazine* 15, no. 1 (September 1893).

Webster, Francis Marion. "The Present and Future of Applied Entomology in America." In *Proceedings of the Ninth Annual Meeting of the Association of Economic Entomologists,* U.S. Department of Agriculture, Division of Entomology, bulletin no. 9. Washington, D.C.: GPO, 1897.

Weiss, Harry Bartholomew. *The New Jersey Department of Agriculture, 1916–1949.* Trenton: New Jersey Agricultural Society, 1950.

Weseloh, Ronald M. "People and the Gypsy Moth: A Story of Human Interactions with an Invasive Species." *American Entomologist* 49, no. 3 (Fall 2003).

Whorton, James C. *Before Silent Spring: Pesticides and Public Health in Pre-DDT America.* Princeton: Princeton University Press, 1974.

Wilder, Burt G. "The Unwelcome Guests of Insects." *Harper's New Monthly Magazine* 37, no. 220 (September 1868).

Wilder, Marshall P. *History and Progress of the Massachusetts State Board of Agriculture for the First Quarter of a Century.* Boston: Rand, Abery & Company, 1878).

Winsor, Mary P. *Reading the Shape of Nature: Comparative Zoology at the Agassiz Museum.* Chicago: University of Chicago Press, 1991.

Wolcott, Roger. "Governor's Inaugural Address." January 5, 1899. In Commonwealth of Massachusetts, General Court, *Acts and Resolves Passed in the Year 1899.*

Worthley, Leon Howard. "Spraying of Woodland and Shade Trees." In *Journal of Economic Entomology* 4, no. 2 (April 1911).

Index

ROBERT SPEAR was born in New York City. He received bachelor of music and master of science degrees from Ithaca College. A man of varied and eclectic interests, Spear has taught in the public schools of New York and currently is self-employed as a violin maker. He has written on a variety of subjects including violin acoustics, loud-speaker design, and, most recently, gypsy moths. He is married to Deena Zalkind, with whom he shares a self-designed Prairie Style house in Ithaca, New York, and the affection of two embarrassingly friendly dogs, Yuppee Dupp and Pocca.